Noam Chomsky
LANGUAGE AND POLITICS

EDITED BY C. P. OTERO | EXPANDED SECOND EDITION

PRESS

EDINBURGH · LONDON · OAKLAND

Language and Politics
by Noam Chomsky
Edited, with an Introduction and Notes, by Carlos-Peregrín Otero
Second edition, revised and expanded

ISBN 1-902593-82-0

AK Press	AK Press U.K.
674-A 23rd Street	PO Box 12766
Oakland, CA 94612-1163	Edinburgh, EH8 9YE
USA	Scotland
(510) 208-1700	(0131) 555-5165
www.akpress.org	www.akuk.com
akpress@akpress.org	ak@akedin.demon.uk

The addresses above would be delighted to provide you with the latest complete AK catalog, featuring several thousand books, pamphlets, zines, audio products, video products and stylish apparel published and distributed by AK Press. Alternatively, visit our websites for the complete catalog, latest news and updates, events and secure ordering.

Library of Congress Control Number: 2003113035

Printed in Canada on recycled paper

Cover photo by Matthew Septimus
Copyediting by Elizabeth Wollman
Indexing by Chris Carlsson

Editor's Acknowledgement
We are greatly indebted to the interviewers, and to the publications and Web sites (referenced in the Editor's Notes) where the interviews first appeared.

Table of Contents

List of Abbreviations:

The abbreviations listed below for the titles of Chomsky's books are those used in the Introduction and the Notes. The books are given in chronological order of composition. Where there is no explicit mention, it should be understood that the place of publication is New York and that the publisher is Pantheon.

1949

MMH — *Morphophonemics of Modern Hebrew.* Undergraduate thesis (1949) developed into a master's thesis, University of Pennsylvania, 1951. Revised later that year. First published in 1979, in a series entitled "Outstanding Dissertations" (Garland Publications).

1955

LSLT — *Logical Structure of Linguistic Theory.* MIT, 1955–1956 typescript and microfilm. First published by Plenum, 1975. (Paper, University of Chicago, 1982, with an Index.)

1957

SS — *Syntactic Structures.* The Hague: Mouton, 1957.

1966

CL — *Cartesian Linguistics: A Chapter in the History of Nationalist Thought.* Harper & Row, 1966.

1968

L&M — *Language and Mind.* New York: Harcourt, Brace & World, Inc., 1968. (Expanded edition, 1972.)

1969

APNM — *American Power and the New Mandarins.* 1969. (Reprint, New York: The New Press, 2002, with a Foreword by Howard Zinn.)

1970

AWA — *At War with Asia.* 1970. (Reprint, AK Press, 2004, with a Foreword by Christian Parenti.)

1971

PKF — *Problems of Knowledge and Freedom: The Russell lectures.* 1971.

1973

FRS — *For Reasons of State.* 1973. (Reprint, New York: The New Press, 2003, with a Foreword by Arundhati Roy.)

1974

PME — *Peace in the Middle East? Reflections on Justice and Nationhood.* 1974. (Included in **MEI**. See 2003 below.)

1975

RL — *Reflections on Language*. 1975.

1977

L&R — *Language and Responsibility*. Based on conversations with Mitsou Ronat (1976), published in French in 1977. Translated from the French translation by John Viertel. 1979

EFI — *Essays on Form and Interpretation*. North Holland, 1977.

1978

HR — *"Human Rights" and American Foreign Policy*. Nottingham, England: Spokesman Books (Bertrand Russell House), 1978.

IS — *Intellectuals and the State*. Johan Huizinga-lezing 1977. Baarn, The Netherlands: Het Wereldvenster, 1978. (Included in **TCW**.)

1979

PEHR — (with Edward S. Herman) *The Political Economy of Human Rights*. Boston: South End Pres, 1979. (2 volumes.)

1980

R&R — *Rules and Representations*. Columbia University Press, 1980.

GE — *The Generative Enterprise*. A discussion with Riny Huybregts & Henk van Riemsdijk [1979–1980]. Dordrecht: Foris, 1982.

MASM — *Modular Approaches to the Study of the Mind*. California State University Press, 1984. (Distinguished Graduate Research Lecture Series 1 [Nov 1980].)

1981

LGB — *Lectures on Government and Binding: The Pisa Lectures*. Dordrecht: Foris, 1981. (Corrected edition, 1982.)

RP — *Radical Priorities*. Edited, with an Introduction and Notes, by C.P. Otero. Montréal: Black Rose Books, 1981; expanded second edition, 1984; revised and expanded third edition, AK Press, 2003.

1982

TNCW — *Towards a New Cold War. Essays on the Current Crisis and How We Got There*. 1982. (It includes **IS** and the chapter of **HR** not included in **RP**.) (Reprint: The New Press, 2003, with a forward by John Pilger.)

1983

FT — *The Fateful Triangle: The United States, Israel and the Palestinians*. Boston: South End Press, 1983; Montréal: Black Rose Books, 1984. (Updated ed., 1999.)

1984

EP — *Ecrits Politiques 1977–1983*. Peyrehorade (France): Acratie, 1984 (March).

RI — *Réponses Inédites à Mes Détracteurs Parisiens.* Paris: Spartacus, 1984 (April).
KL — *Knowledge of Language: Its Nature, Origin and Use.* New York: Praeger, 1986.

1985

TT — *Turning the Tide: U.S. Intervention in Central America and the Struggle for Peace.* Boston: South End Press, 1985. Expanded second edition: *Turning the Tide: The U.S. and Latin America.* Montréal: Black Rose Books, 1987 (with a 1986 postscript—the nucleus of **CT**).

1986

P&E — *Pirates and Emperors: International Terrorism and the Real World.* New York: Claremont Research and Publications, 1986; Montréal: Black Rose Books, 1987. (Reprints: Brattleboro, VT: Amana Books, 1986, and (with a fourth chapter) Montréal: Black Rose Books, 1987.) (See 2002 below.)

1987

P&I — *On Power and Ideology: The Managua Lectures.* Delivered at the Universidad Centroamericana, Managua, in March 1986. Boston: South End Press, 1987; Montréal: Black Rose Books, 1987.
LPK — *Language and Problems of Knowledge: The Managua Lectures.* Cambridge, MA: The M.I.T. Press, 1988 (actually, summer of 1987).
ChR — *The Chomsky Reader.* Edited by James Peck. 1987.
LPS — *Language in a Psychological Setting.* Tokyo: Sophia University, 1987. (Sophia Linguistica Special Issues 22.)
GG — *Generative Grammar: Its Basis, Development and Prospects.* Kyoto University of Foreign Studies, 1987. (Studies in English Linguistics and Literature, Special Issue.)

1988

CT — *The Culture of Terrorism.* Boston: South End Press, 1988; Montréal: Black Rose Books, 1988.
MC — (with Edward S. Herman) *Manufacturing Consent: The Political Economy of the Mass Media.* 1988.

1989

NI — *Necessary Illusions: Thought Control in Democratic Societies.* Boston: South End Press, 1989.

1991

DD — *Deterring Democracy.* London: Verso, 1991. (Reprint, "with a new afterword," New York: Hill and Wang, 1992.)

1993

Y501 — *Year 501: The Conquest Continues.* Boston: South End Press, 1993.
RC — *Rethinking Camelot: JFK, the Vietnam War, and the U.S. Political Culture.* Boston: South End Press, 1993.

1994

WOON — *World Orders Old and New*. Columbia University Press, 1994. (Rev. ed., "with an update on the Palestinian predicament," 1996.)

1996

P&P — *Powers and Prospects: Reflections on Human Nature and the Social Order*. Boston: South End Press, 1996.

1999

POP — *Profits over People: Neoliberalism and Global Order*. New York: Seven Stories Press, 1999.
FT — *The Fateful Triangle: The United States, Israel and the Palestinians*. Updated ed., Cambridge: South End Press, 1999.
NMH — *The New Military Humanism: Lessons from Kosovo*. Monroe, Maine: Common Courage Press, 1999.

2000

NGDL — *A New Generation Draws the Line: Kosovo, East Timor and the Standards of the West*. London/New York: Verso, 2000.
RS — *Rogue States: the Rule of Force in World Affairs*. Cambridge: South End Press, 2000.
NHLM — *New Horizons in the Study of Language and Mind*. Cambridge: Cambridge University Press, 2000.

2001

9-11 — *9-11*. New York: Seven Stories Press, 2001. (Expanded edition, 2002, including "Reflections on 9-11," first published in Sweden in August 2002.)

2002

N&L — *On Nature and Language*. Cambridge: Cambridge University Press, 2002.
P&E — *Pirates and Emperors, Old and New: International Terrorism in the Real World*. Cambridge: South End Press, 2002. (New edition, expanded from 3 to 7 chapters plus an Introduction. See 1986 above.)

2003

MEI — *Middle East Illusions: Peace, Security, and Terror*, Lanham, MD: Rowman and Littlefield Publishers Group, 2003. (See 1974 above.)
P&T — *Power and Terror: Post 9/11 Talks and Interviews*. New York: Seven Stories Press; Tokyo: Little More, 2003.
RP — *Radical Priorities*. Revised and expanded third edition. AK Press, 2003. (See 1981 above.)
CD&E — *Chomsky on Democracy and Education*. New York and London: Routledge Falmer, 2003.
Hegenomy or Survival. New York: Metropolitan Books, 2003.

Book-length Chomsky Bibliographies:

Sgroi — *Noam Chomsky: Bibliografia 1949–1981.* A cura di Salvatore Claudio Sgroi. Padova (Italy): CLESP editrice, 1983. 361 pp.

Ramaiah & Chandra — *Noam Chomsky: A Bibliography.* Compiled by L.S. Ramaiah & T.V. Prafulla Chandra. Gurgaon, Haryana (India): Indian Documentation Service, 1984. 92 pp.

Koerner & Tajima — *Noam Chomsky: A Personal Bibliography, 1951–1986.* Compiled by E. F. Konrad Koerner & Matsuji Tajima with the collaboration of C. P. Otero. Amsterdam/Philadelphia: John Benjamins, 1986. 217 pp.

Editor's Preliminary Note to the Second Edition

As indicated in the "Bibliographical Note" at the end of the volume, where more recent collections are listed, before 1992 *Language and Politics* was the only book-length collection of Chomsky interviews, and until 2002 it was the only one in which Chomsky answers different interviewers (in a few cases, multiple questioners from the audience). When it first appeared it was fairly comprehensive up to 1988—and even more if we were to add two interviews included earlier, as chs. 20 and 21, in *Radical Priorities* (revised and enlarged third edition, AK Press, 2003) and one included, as ch. 24, in his recent collection of writings, *Chomsky on Democracy and Education.* It continues to be an irreplaceable source for some of the views of the interviewee on a broad range of subjects about the natural world and the human world—and about himself as a person (truly exceptional in more than one way, but still human), something rarely found in his writings.

This revised and expanded second edition includes one more of the earliest interviews (#5 in the new numbering), still little known, which was unavailable to the editor when the book was first sent to the printer. This addition stands out in several respects, one of them being that it clearly attests to Chomsky's concern for ecology from early on.

Of the very many interviews done after 1988, this new edition includes a very small, but highly representative, sample, and of unusual significance. Three of the newly added interviews were done in the 1990s: one in November 1990 (as the United States government was gearing up for the Gulf War) and one in November 1991 (soon after the collapse of Bolshevism in the Soviet Union), both of which are still completely unknown outside Finland. The third one was first published in May 1995 in a not widely read journal. The other four were all conducted between Feb. 11 and Aug. 29, 2002. As is to be expected, they elaborate or expand on the themes of *9-11* (2001), Chomsky's first 21st century bestseller and the first of his books to appear almost simultaneously in 26 countries. As in the first edition, the subheadings of these additional interviews are supplied, within the context of the collection, and so are their titles.

Another important novelty of this edition, apart from its high standard of professionalism (a far from negligible difference) is a much needed index, which will hopefully make it possible for the interested reader to get much more out of a book that has much to offer to those ready to look for it. It is not without interest that Chomsky's analyses of over a decade and a half ago are directly applicable to the post 9-11 world—and potentially even more enlightening for many than they could be in 1988. Those inclined to do so will be able to find an updated and far more comprehensive discussion of a range of themes touched on here, and today in everybody's mind, in several of his most recent books, including *The Fateful Triangle: The United States, Israel and the Palestinians* (updated ed.,

1

1999), *Rogue States: the Rule of Force in World Affairs* (2000), *9-11* (2001, 2002), *Pirates and Emperors, Old and New: International Terrorism in the Real World* (2002), *Middle East Illusions: Peace, Security, and Terror* (2003), *Power and Terror: Post 9/11 Talks and Interviews* (2003), and especially in his most recent book, *Hegemony or Survival: America's Quest for Full Spectrum Dominance* (2003).

An added bonus of this edition is that now the interviews appear in strict chronological order, which makes it much easier for the reader to see some of the themes and arguments unfold in successive takes. The only exception is the last interview, a particularly lucid exposition of his encouraging views on the prospects of human endeavor, given the range of social organizations humans appear to be able to create (from this perspective, it can be seen as a sort of supplement to "Two Conceptions of Social Organization" (1970), ch. 7 of *Chomsky on Democracy and Education*), which, arguably, deserves special treatment, since it seems particularly apt to close the collection.

A point of departure and a perspective likely to be helpful is suggested by this quote from the Introduction:

> "He was always on the side of the losers—the Spanish anarchists, for example. The first article he wrote was a political editorial in the school paper on the fall of Barcelona (signalling the defeat of the Spanish Republic by the rebellious fascist army) in late March 1939, a few weeks after his tenth birthday. When, after a brief interlude, the war engaged the great powers directly, he was rather skeptical about much of the patriotic interpretation of the conflict, and did not know anybody—literally not a single person—who shared his skepticism. He had a dream, remote from the conscience of his teenage peers, that he would bring about a (libertarian) socialist future."

Carlos-Peregrín Otero
May 5, 2003

Editor's Preliminary Note

On June 24, 1988, the Inamori Foundation announced the recipients of this year's Kyoto Prizes, sometimes characterized as Japan's version of the Nobel Prize, one difference with the latter being that the Kyoto Prizes encompass only three categories: basic sciences, advanced technology, and creative arts and moral sciences. This year, the fourth they have been awarded, the 45 million yen (some $350,000) prize in basic sciences was won by Noam Chomsky.

This award can only reinforce the widespread belief that if there were a Nobel Prize for linguistics or a more inclusive field, it would have been awarded long ago to Chomsky. It is no less reasonable to expect that if in the years ahead the recipient of the Nobel Prize for Peace is chosen from among those who have contributed the most and continued to be most committed to bringing about a more peaceful and better world, Chomsky's name will be high on the short list.

Chomsky's epoch-making contributions to linguistics, and to the cognitive sciences more generally, which have strongly influenced psychology, philosophy, and some of the best work in artificial intelligence, are likely to have an impact on many other fields, among them the brain sciences, ethics, aesthetics, anthropology, sociology, history, education and language teaching, and their implications for our general culture are far reaching (see Editor's Notes to I2—I1, I2,... is to be understood as "(see) interview 1, 2, ... "). If the usual standards had been applied to him (and presumably they would have been, had he not challenged official doctrines), he would have been seen for many years now as a towering figure in the history of civilization. It is not hard to see that some of the greatest minds had failed where finally Chomsky succeeded.

To begin to gauge the significance of his revolutionary ideas we have to consider that our language is central to everything we do. More than any other human attribute, language distinguishes us from all other animals; without language there would be no possibility of culture and cultural development. This pervasiveness goes well beyond what the naked eye can see. Almost two hundred years ago, a brilliant art theorist (A. W. von Schlegel) argued that, because it is built on language, literature underlies all the other arts, thus being the fundamental art form.

Since language is the most central human attribute, discoveries that result in deeper understanding of language can profoundly affect what we think of ourselves and of our place in the course of biological evolution and cultural development—particularly our place in the present and future social world. Psychologists of every school agree that only through a successful analysis of language can we hope to come to terms with our thought and action. A deep understanding of language is thus a prerequisite to a deeper understanding of our humanity. Furthermore, the progress made in the psychology of language furnishes suggestive models for other aspects of cognitive psychology.

Language is also the great equalizer. Every normal human being, short of pathology, can, in principle, become a native speaker of any language. In terms of our present understanding there are no differences in language capacity among individuals. Every normal human can make creative use of language. What is not the same across individuals is the ability to creatively use language as an art medium (Shakespeare's ability as a literary artist stands out above most others).

In addition to his contributions to the study of language and mind, Chomsky has also made outstanding contributions to our understanding of the political world we live in, the ideologies that disguise it and their roots in the history of ideas. The fact that he was the only activist and critic of United States domestic and foreign policy to make Nixon's "enemy list" (I43) and to be directly attacked by high state officials is a tribute to his persistence and effectiveness. It would make little sense to pretend that the author of the non-scientific studies is not the scientist (I41). The approach and the style of argumentation is the same in both cases—and without parallel among students of society and ideology, to the best of my knowledge.

Another thing to note about Chomsky is that he appears to be among those that have both good fortune and good sense, who, as Livy remarked, are not very many. To appreciate this it might be helpful to remember that even Bertrand Russell, to whom Chomsky has sometimes been compared, does not have a perfect record on this score. Chomsky seems to have an uncanny sense of how things can be expected to turn out, and routinely anticipates what often takes others by surprise. His earliest understanding of the world and the people around him already showed a wisdom far beyond his years. His first known writings and statements clearly reflect his mature thought. One gets the impression that his deep understanding of things, particularly along the political dimension, has been with him from his earliest teens. His initial insights on the workings of power appeared to be more sophisticated than those of most people at any age. A chance meeting is often enough for him to have a pretty reliable intuition of what can and cannot be expected of someone—a gift that seems to have been manifest from the very beginning.

It is the luckiest of all accidents that those deeply committed to bringing about a better world—in particular, those who hope to change the character and course of American society—have such a compañero among their midst. It would be hard to imagine a more inspiring source of information and analysis for those who genuinely love their country—which is to say, those who love its children and refuse to deprive them of the best of their alternative futures—or even to imagine a more valuable and more effective resource for the success of a cultural revolution of the broadest range.

The present collection of interviews, prepared to commemorate Chomsky's sixtieth birthday, is offered as a much needed road map. It aims at contributing to the discussion of the crucial issues of the day, not only among people already committed, but also, most importantly, to the discussion between the committed and the still uncommitted who are simply uninformed or misinformed, or in need of deeper understanding.

I believe the dialogue form offers a number of advantages. It allows treating topics of some intricacy or even of a highly technical and substantial nature in an easily readable form. The interviewer stands there for us, in a way. If there are points in the answer that are not readily understandable, he or she can ask for amplifications and explanations, which can be checked and analyzed further. Informal conversations also have the advantage of allowing people to delve into current and sometimes controversial topics, and make it more natural to express opinions that, for a number of reasons (they are not considered to be very original, or timely, or whatever) are not addressed in the articles and books of the interviewee. It also allows for some interaction of views: an answer can suggest a new or different question.

This is particularly true in the case of Chomsky's interviews. Many who read him or attend his talks are often surprised to discover that he can be at his best in his extemporaneous answers—typically informative, balanced, and employing striking examples—to questions people happen to have on their minds. The representative sample offered here should be of great interest to those people and to many others who have not had similar opportunities. In some cases (selections 5, 16, 17, 24, 33, 37) it is even possible to compare his answers with those of several other people—and to draw some inferences. Most, if not all, of the interviews collected in this volume are little known. A few have not been published in English or have not been published at all. The earliest of them (April 11,1968) appeared first in Dutch, and then in English in a Dutch journal few know of; the most recent ones, for the most part still unpublished, are a few months old. Significantly, most encounters took place after the late 1970s, and their frequency seems to increase as time goes on—evidence that he is more and more in demand (I18, I46).

The range of topics is very broad, including questions of great importance and urgency, some of them rarely addressed with both honesty and insight. They cover questions of both science and ideology, showing, incidentally, how difficult it is to demarcate the spheres of "Chomsky's two worlds." A topic that comes up again and again (many times in this book—see the Editor's Notes to I48) is the relationship between his discoveries about language and his libertarian social theory, with revealing differences in treatment (compare the answer given to an insidious inquisitor in I18 with, e.g., those elicited in I13, I25, I26, I41); a related topic is the study of language as a model for the study of other cognitive structures, including perhaps a sort of "universal grammar" of possible forms of social structure and social interaction (I11, I27, I34). Chronologically, the coverage extends from Chomsky's personal background and intellectual development to the latest political events. Some of the ideas discussed in this book are not found elsewhere, on occasion the published information is elaborated or updated in his answers, and some defining themes (including major ones) first appear in one of these interviews.

No attempt has been made to eliminate redundancy and repetition, and this for a number of reasons. An important one is that the somewhat varying formulations of essential points may prove helpful, particularly to those unfamiliar with Chomsky's work; even the simplest and most basic points discussed in these interviews have been widely misunderstood. It is also helpful, and sometimes revealing, to relate an answer to its context, and the contexts are different in the different interviews. More generally, it is often the case that we have to be told something 10 times before we begin to really listen. The texts have been edited as lightly as possible, often not at all (in those cases in which the questions were submitted and answered in writing, what was actually written has faithfully been reproduced), though some punctuation and paragraphing has been silently supplied when it seemed that it would help the reader. All the subheadings in the table of contents (regularly boldfaced, to the closest approximation, in the text), except for those in I6 and I34, have been supplied, as have the titles when a specific title was lacking (in a few cases, a non-generic title was modified or replaced, as indicated). The material in the Editor's Notes should help the reader to continue the dialogue. The Introduction attempts to provide a unifying perspective on Chomsky's thought and action, and their historical and practical significance for the transition through "the third emancipatory phase in history."

I am greatly indebted to Noam Chomsky for all I have learned from him and for the example, encouragement and help he has provided over the years. I am sure I am not alone in recognizing that he has directly or indirectly inspired some of the best thought and action of the second half of this century, and no doubt will continue to be a major source of inspiration in years to come, extending well after his sixtieth birthday.

I am very thankful to David Barsamian, a less old but much appreciated friend, for his very special contribution and help, to which he added the responsibility of transcription, a difficult and demanding job carried out with professional skill and unusual dedication and care by Sandy Adler. I am also very grateful to Hannu Reime for his outstanding contribution and for his transcriptions (and to Jan Koster, who twice led me to him). Robert Freidin went well beyond the call of duty when prompt help was needed to complete a text or to check one difficult to read, to provide me instantly with materials that were hard to find or obtain (including I34, of which I was not aware) and with information not readily accessible, and, in particular, to send a wealth of comments on the first draft of the Introduction virtually by return mail. Donald Kalish's contribution is harder to comprehend but not hard to value. Thanks are also due to Jamie Young and Nancy Peters, always prompt in answering my queries and sending needed materials, including in this case two interviews I did not know of; to Alan Strozer, who diligently provided immediate help when it was most needed, and to Leslie Atik, who unknowingly contributed to this work by having contributed with unusual competence and dedication to two other projects still in progress; to Esther Torrego, for a copy of an interview I had not seen and other welcomed materials; to Tim Stowell, for bringing immediately to my attention a unique item; and to Yona Sabar, for his helpful tips about Semitic languages and their study. The unflagging support of Judith Strozer and Daniel Otero's strong backing of the project, together with that of David Otero, has made all the difference.

Carlos-Peregrín Otero

Los Angeles, August 1988.

Introduction: The Third Emancipatory Phase of History, by C. P. Otero

He always felt completely out of tune with almost everything around him. Until quite recently, he was always either alone or part of a tiny minority, ever since he had any political awareness—and he was politically aware since his childhood.[1]

As a boy of nine, in 1938, he used to sit in the front row of the Hebrew class at Mikveh Israel, in Philadelphia, paying little attention to the teacher. He was not being disrespectful; he happened to have covered the ground long before, at home, with his parents[2]—who sent him to an experimental progressive school (essentially a Deweyite school) from infancy, before he was 2, until he was about 12 years old. When he was 11 or 12, he read proofs of his father's edition of an outstanding medieval grammar of Hebrew, and he already fixed his attention on and retained something that eight years later was to guide him in the creation of the theory for which he is known and admired around the world.

He was always on the side of the losers—the Spanish anarchists, for example. The first article he wrote was a political editorial in the school paper on the fall of Barcelona (signalling the defeat of the Spanish Republic by the rebellious fascist army) in late March 1939, a few weeks after his tenth birthday. When, after a brief interlude, the war engaged the great powers directly, he was rather skeptical about much of the patriotic interpretation of the conflict, and did not know anybody—literally not a single person—who shared his skepticism. He had a dream, remote from the conscience of his teenage peers, that he would bring about a (libertarian) socialist future.

When on Aug. 15, 1945, he was shocked by the news of the Hiroshima bombing ("surely among the most unspeakable crimes in history," he was to write twenty years later—a war crime that dwarfs Guernica), he literally could not talk to anybody at his summer camp and never understood anyone's reaction. He just walked off by himself into the woods and stayed alone for a couple of hours. He felt completely isolated.[3]

Understandably enough, he was deeply interested in Zionism as it was then understood, and was involved in the Zionist movement directly, but the position he held, while it did have some standing and support, nevertheless was very far from the mainstream. He was interested in socialist-bi-nationalist approaches, and already in 1946 and 1947 was planning to go to what was then Palestine, live on a *kibbutz* (as he did in 1953) and work for Arab-Jewish cooperation—the main reason why he had learned Arabic.

He was, of course, emotionally drawn to such groups as Hashomer Hatzair, which in those days professed a commitment to socialist bi-nationalism in Palestine and *kibbutz* values, as well as the Hebraic culture which he was very much part of. If he could never bring himself to join it was because he was radically opposed to its various Stalinist and Trotskyist tendencies. Although his interest in radical politics with an anarchist or left-wing (anti-Leninist) Marxist flavor could not have been greater, he had always been strongly anti-Bolshevik. His position was already crucially distinct from those of any of the existing movements on the left.

What could a young man such as he do under the circumstances? One thing that was not in his power was to turn himself into somebody else. A seeming alternative was to find a refuge far away, but that was a mirage which the Vietnam War quickly dispelled.

The fact of the matter was that for a Noam Chomsky there was only one real option available: to try to change the world around him—to endeavor to bring about a cultural revolution which set the long overdue new standards in the course of civilization that he envisioned. Was that a feasible enterprise for just one individual? Could it at least be attempted? Not immediately or directly, in any case. For one thing, he still lacked an appropriate fulcrum. What he already had firmly in place—perhaps the single most important thing he had going for him at the time—was a solid moral foundation of venerable roots.

1. Justice versus Power

A uniqueness so out of the ordinary as Chomsky's at 18 could not be due just to a rare biological endowment, which, it appears, became legendary and began to inspire general awe from his early teens. A high level of moral and intellectual development cannot be biologically inherited. What is innate is the genetic constitution, including the basic structure of the mind and the principles that determine its properties and development. But the fact that the course of development is largely internally determined "does not mean that it will proceed without care, stimulation, and opportunity." All human development, including the development of moral judgment, "is heavily determined by the nature of the environment, and may be severely limited unless the environment is appropriate":

> A stimulating environment is required to enable natural curiosity, intelligence and creativity to develop, and to enable our biological capacities to unfold.

Not surprisingly, "if a child is placed in an impoverished environment, innate abilities simply will not develop, mature and flourish."[4]

It is then a lucky accident for a child to be born in the right place and at the right time. Some would argue that Chomsky's first stroke of luck was to have been born in "Quaker, egalitarian Philadelphia" rather than, say, in "Puritan, hierarchical Boston."[5] It is far more obvious that things may have been otherwise had he been the child of a different family. Fortunately for him, it appears ("though of course others reacted to the same conditions quite differently"), he grew up "in an alien culture, in the Jewish-Zionist cultural tradition, in an immigrant community in a sense." His parents, who greatly influenced him (I3), were "very much involved with Jewish affairs, deeply Zionist and interested in Jewish culture, the revival of Hebrew, and generally the cultural Zionism that had its origins in the ideas of people like Ahad Ha'am, but increasingly, in mainstream Zionism,"[6] and he was deeply immersed in the Jewish cultural tradition. He probably did more reading in that area than any other until he was maybe 15 or 16, and the reading certainly had a strong influence on him.

The next range of family (uncles and cousins) was in part Jewish working class. Some of his mother's relatives in particular were "dirt-poor." But they were intellectually rich ("far richer than any university I know"). Several of his relatives, some of whom worked in sweatshops,[7] were very much involved in the politics of the Depression period ("politics were alive then"); a few of them were, or had been, on the fringes of the Communist Party. In particular, one uncle on his mother's side (her sister's husband) who had a newsstand in New York which became a sort of radical center, "had been through a lot of the Marxist sectarian politics—Stalinist, Trotskyite, non-Leninist sects of one sort or another," and with his help and advice Chomsky managed to learn by his earliest teens all there is to know about the topic (in sharp contrast with some of his contemporaries, both senior and junior).[8]

Chomsky's radical uncle, who died some fifteen years ago (I9), was a very interesting person who had a lot of influence on his nephew in the late 30s and following years. Under his influence Chomsky had assimilated what is enduring in Freud's work before he was 18 (although his uncle had not gone beyond the 4th grade in school, he knew Freud's work so well that people started sending patients to him and he became a lay analyst). About the time of Pearl Harbor, that is, when Chomsky was 13 or 14, he would catch the train up to New York and he would "hang out" all night and participate in lively discussions and arguments, at his uncle's kiosk or in his apartment nearby ("the great moments of my life in those years were when I could work at the newsstand at night and listen to all this"). Sometimes he would go out from Penn Station into the Fourth Avenue bookstores "reading what I could."

That, of course, was not all. As a child of the Depression, he learned a great deal from what he saw around him. Some of his most vivid, earliest memories are of people selling rags at his door, of violent police strike-breaking, and other equally illuminating scenes. As a child of practically the only Jewish family in a bitterly anti-Semitic Irish and German Catholic neighborhood, with open support for the Nazis until the United States entered the war, he was deeply impressed by the rise of Nazism and other horrors of the 1930s, which affected him very much, particularly the Spanish Civil War.

As he remembers it, the Jewish working-class culture in New York, "the most influential intellectual culture" during his early teens, was very unusual (and was not there to stay—a few years later it had died out):

It was highly intellectual, very poor; a lot of people had no jobs at all and others lived in slums and so on. But it was a rich and lively intellectual culture: Freud, Marx, the Budapest String Quartet, literature, and so forth.

At this point it is almost unavoidable to ask whether the radicalism of these immigrants was related to the highest values of Jewish culture, and if so to what extent. The question has been raised many times before. More than half a century ago Albert Einstein observed that "it is no mere chance that the demands of Socialism were for the most part first raised by Jews." And although on another occasion he wrote that the Jewish tradition of "love of justice and reason" had produced Spinoza and Karl Marx (as well as Rosa Luxemburg, he might have added), he probably had in mind more people than the famous few.[9]

This view of the best in the Jewish tradition is not without interest. In a recent study of the American Jewish immigrant radicals from 1880 to 1920 (the period in which Chomsky's relatives came to this country), it is argued that the Jewish cultural (including ethical) values of their upbringing made American Jewish immigrants work at educating and mobilizing the best in people and sustaining loyalty to the highest ideals of social justice. Socialism for them was more than a social doctrine; it was an ethical system which, when taken seriously, as many libertarians do, leads to building a thoroughly new society. The study tries to show that the exploration of its topic provides evidence that Jewish cultural values were critical in the formation of the radical consciousness of the Jewish immigrants.[10]

This, however, is not specific enough for our purposes. To identify the strand that is closest to Chomsky's libertarian vision of a just and decent society we have to distinguish the "prophetic" approach to revolutionary change from the "apocalyptic" (or priestly) one. The terms "prophetic" and "apocalyptic" are used here roughly in the senses given to them by Martin Buber, sometimes referred to as the chief disciple of Ahad Ha'Am—though Buber tainted with religiosity the secularist cultural Judaism of his inspirer.[11] What is particularly important in this context is that in the prophetic tradition the goal of cultural change in the broadest sense (including revolutionary social change) is the pursuit of justice, not the conquest of power.

Oversimplifying considerably, we could say that the best of the libertarianism of the 18th century represents an original development of the prophetic tradition as understood here, whereas the Jacobinism of the 19th century (continued, not without enhancements, in the 20th) was fed by the apocalyptic one.[12] An almost perfect example of 20th-century apocalypticism is Trotsky's conception of the revolution (which often leads to mass murder, as in Kronstadt). It contrasts sharply with the prophetic conception of his contemporary Emma Goldman ("one of the great people of the world," "a mountain of integrity," "a proven genius for honesty and courage"):

What if she had not been a Jewess? asked the *London Times* To ask the question, as they say, is almost to answer it. Her life would have been very different.

The truth is, she was born on the fringe of two cultures, the Jewish and the Russian ... By 1869 the walls between the two were crumbling. She was made irresistibly aware that the cramped ghetto was not the only world. Living fully in neither world, she was forced to make her way through two antagonistic cultures. This experience in itself encouraged a wider look and the habit of digging for the roots of the questions—one definition, incidentally, of radical.

On this interpretation, it was by virtue of her birth and cultural background that "Emma Goldman became one of the heirs of a great ethical tradition which persistently stressed the rights of man and social justice":

As Ahad Ha'am once wrote, prophetic Judaism emphasized absolute justice and evidenced sharp intolerance of evil in any form. While prophetic Judaism was eclipsed by priestly Judaism, the former continued to provide an element of tension. Thus, while Emma had a generous contempt for rabbis as pathetic symbols of Russian authority, she still was one of the "people of the Book": the prophetic tradition and the folk literature of the Bible, its gorgeous imagery and thunderous accounts of renunciation and bravery, had an inevitable impact on the sensitive and intelligent ghetto girl. She dreamed of becoming an avenger like Judith: she would cut off the head of evil and run with it through the streets so that all could see and feel relieved. Who could doubt that the prophets whispered a captivating message down through the centuries to Emma?[13]

Although the aspiration towards a just society appears to have been alive since at least biblical times, it was only in the 18th century that it emerged as a realistic possibility. Perhaps the most lucid of the 18th-century social critics that understood not only that society was changeable but that major changes were long overdue was Rousseau. If we restrict our attention to the libertarian Rousseau of the *Discourse on Inequality* and see this work as an original development of Cartesian ideas (ignoring a crucial departure from them in his speculations on the origin of language), Chomsky can be seen, and has in fact been seen, as "a new Rousseau" or the Rousseau of our age. It is in any case clear that the roots of Chomsky's social thought are to be found in the Enlightenment, as he emphasizes at the end of I46.

In part inspired and propelled by some of the ideas Rousseau expressed perhaps better than anybody else, the 18th century succeeded in going beyond what has been called the first emancipatory phase of history, the one which had made serfs out of slaves, to the phase which made wage earners out of serfs. But since at least 1767 insightful revolutionaries have been aware that a wage earner is still a serf, and a serf is still a slave. For Chomsky, in particular, cultural development and committed action in support of social change should contribute to bringing about the conditions for "the fullest, richest, and most harmonious development of the potentialities of the individual, the community and the human race," as Wilhelm von Humboldt wrote towards the end of the 18th century (in 1792, to be exact) in his classic book on the limits of state action. For this to be possible we must go well beyond the political revolution the libertarians of the Enlightenment strived for, to the economic revolution—the third emancipatory phase of history, which is to make unoppressed creative agents out of wage earners, "a final act of liberation that places control over the economy in the hands of free and voluntary associations of producers."[14]

Well-informed libertarian socialists have always argued that this major transformation cannot be brought about by the conquest and use of power, but only by the general enlightenment and personal commitment of a large number of people willing to struggle for a more just organization of society.[15]

2. Enlightenment versus Inquisitionalism

Enlightenment covers two related but very different dimensions: the intellectual and the ethical. An intellectual giant is usually referred to as a genius; one sense of "prophet" is that of moral giant. In the ancient world, excellence along the first dimension is most striking among the Greeks, who produced several outstanding geniuses in just a few centuries; excellent along the second dimension is often associated with the Jewish prophets. There is fairly general agreement that the synthesis of the essential cultural contributions of these two exceptionally endowed peoples is at the root of our civilization.[16]

This is only one reason why the Jewish experience is of great interest to the student of cultural development. A student of culture and cultural change who pays special attention to Jewish history and has important things to say about the Jewish prophetic tradition is precisely Ahad Ha'am, the author read by Chomsky's father with great interest and admiration long before anyone could have surmised that some central ideas of cultural Zionism (adopted also by Einstein, it appears)[17] could, in part, open the way to a higher intellectual and moral level, which the thought and action of his son would contribute to make possible just a few years later.[18]

Ahad Ha'am's perhaps "most famous single essay," one he frequently recurred to later, is the one titled "Priest and Prophet." For him, prophecy "is, as it were, the hallmark of the Hebrew national spirit":

> It is pre-eminently among the ancient Hebrews that prophecy is found, not as an accidental or temporary phenomenon, but continuously through many generations.

As he understands them, "the fundamental idea of the Hebrew prophets was the universal dominion of absolute justice," and he was convinced, as Chomsky is, that the "moral law" is an objective standard of value. He argued that the Jewish concept of justice and righteousness ("truth in action"), in contrast with the Christian emphasis on mercy, demands that each individual be treated as fully equal. The prophet, he wrote (and it is hard not to think of Chomsky),

> can only see the world through the mirror of his idea; he desires nothing, strives for nothing, except to make every phase of the life around him an embodiment of that ideal with all his strength; for its sake he lays waste his powers, unsparing for himself, regardless of the conditions of life and the demands of the general harmony. His gaze is fixed always on what ought to be in accordance with his own convictions; never on what can be consistently with the general condition of things outside himself. The prophet is thus a primal force.

In contrast, the priest, far from being a primal force, is just "an accidental complex of various forces, among which there is no essential connection."[19]

To better understand this view, one should keep in mind that the notion of "prophet" we are considering must be sharply distinguished from the notion of shaman or seer, common to many cultures, including the Jewish culture, where it appeared apparently before the more characteristically Jewish notion of prophet (or social prophet, a term sometimes used), closely associated with one of the central elements in our "Judeo-Christian heritage," which is so much a part of "Western civilization." The prophets in this sense generally stood in defiant opposition to the corruption of the rulers and their pliant tools, and to the priests (*cohanim*, singular *cohen*) as apologists of the powerful and privileged. As Martin Buber writes (*nabi* is the Hebrew term for prophet):

> The connection of the *nabi* with the future is not that of one who predicts. To be a *nabi* means to set the audience, to whom the words are addressed, before the choice and decision, directly or indirectly. The future is not something already fixed in the present hour, it is dependent upon the real decision, that is, the decision in which man takes part in this hour.[20]

Also interesting in this context is Ahad Ha'am's view of mainstream Judaism. As a child of the Enlightenment, he saw it as completely anachronistic. Jews had, for centuries, been the victims of rigorous self-segregation behind a wall of rituals and irrational beliefs rather than free and independent minds.[21] An independent mind could not be forced to accept doctrines not of his own choosing. He stood for a Judaism which had as a focal point "the ideal of our nation's unity, its renaissance, and its free development through the expression of universal human values in terms of its own distinctive spirit," thus winning its rightful place as one of the great culture-bearers of world civilization.[22] Breathing new life into Hebrew culture should therefore be the main goal of Zionism. The people, not the faith, and the school, not the synagogue, were to be taken as the central core. Before a radical Zionist solution of the problem of the Jews could be attempted, the morale and the organization of the people were to be fortified.

It has been argued that this cultural conception of Zionism was heavily influenced by Russian populism—as was Bakunin's conception of anarchism—in particular in its distrust of state power: it is not the state but the national culture, a vital spiritual force, that is the source of community life.[23] Given this background, it comes as no surprise that Ahad Ha'am, "one of the people," was, from the very beginning, a sharp critic and the foremost opponent of Theodor Herzl's political Zionism, which derived from the Prussian or Prussian-like tradition that subordinated the German nation and culture to the state.[24]

In his insightful article "The Jewish state and the Jewish problem," Ahad Ha'am correctly predicted that if political Zionism came to be successful, the new state would be dominated by assimilated Western Jews, which in general were more conservative than the Eastern Jews, and more practiced in the intrigues and manipulations of backroom maneuvering. The alternative he saw was to construct a native Jewish community in Palestine and from 1920 on he advocated a binational Jewish-Arab confederation (recall that in his student days and for many years Chomsky not only advocated a similar proposal—within a libertarian socialist framework—but was ready to put his efforts into it).[25] As can be imagined, he was strongly against Herzl's technocratic vision of a Palestine turned overnight into a state, let alone a Spartan one.

Anyone who advocates these and related ideas, has exacting standards of personal integrity, and is always willing to offer a principled defense of his commitments is likely to be denounced for his "lack of pragmatism" and similar crimes, and Ahad Ha'am did not fail to be. At one point, this distinguished and widely admired proponent of cultural Zionism was accused of being a threat to the "fragile alliance" between Eastern and Western Jewry and even the "worst enemy of Zionism," another way in which he seems to prefigure Chomsky.

Reading Ahad Ha'am and about him, one easily gets the impression that he would not have been too surprised by the evolution of Zionism after the Holocaust or by the contemporary forms of extreme chauvinism associated today with the Sparta of the Middle East (perhaps the closest thing to a Rambo among the states—I36). The Israeli politician who paid the most attention to his views was Chaim Weizmann, who, with Buber, had defended him when he was the object of vicious attacks by his fellow Jews. How much attention? A sample illustration will suffice. Whereas Ahad Ha'am was unsparing in his criticism of what he considered to be unfair and contemptuous treatment of the Arabs by Jewish settlers, his "disciple" has statements like the following to his credit:

> With regard to the Arab question, the British told us that there are several hundred thousand negroes there, but this is a matter of no consequence.[26]

This tribalistic form of racism is not unexpected if there is any truth to Moshe Dayan's principle that "whoever approaches the Zionist problem from a moral aspect is not a Zionist," which he attributed to Ben-Gurion.

From this perspective the fact that some of the most unethical among the influential "American intellectual elite" who have used the most devious tactics against Chomsky are Jewish is particularly striking, and perhaps revealing—if Einstein is right:

> The pursuit of knowledge for its own sake, an almost fanatical love of justice and the desire for personal independence—these are the features of the Jewish tradition which make me thank my stars that I belong to it.
>
> Those who are raging today against the ideals of reason and individual liberty and are trying to establish a spiritless state-slavery by brute force rightly see in us their irreconcilable foes. History has given us a difficult row to hoe; but so long as we remain devoted servants of truth, justice, and liberty, we shall continue not merely to survive as the oldest of living peoples, but by creative work to bring forth fruits which contribute to the ennoblement of the human race, as heretofore.

There is little reason to think that Einstein meant to suggest that the Jewish people is different from all other peoples in that all individuals who comprise it are true to their higher selves, and that rascals, not to say criminals and even genocidal maniacs, are not found in their midst.[27] Ariel Sharons (or Joshuas, for that matter) are, and were, found all over the world, let alone debased scoundrels; in fact, the events chronicled in the Bible which make it "one of the most genocidal texts in our literature" (134) are not few or far between.

It is therefore not surprising that there are people who fall somewhat short of Einstein's model Jew. What is surprising, to the point of defying credibility, is to discover that a significant part of the Jewish component of the American intellectual elite is also so ignorant of the best of their tradition that not only do they fail to strive towards its higher values in their personal lives, but they cannot even recognize them realized in those who have inherited more than a touch of the prophetic urge of their Jewish ancestors—pariahs themselves in their own society, and often victims of their fellow Jews' irrational outbursts, no doubt.[28] Understandably, those devoid of even a shadow of the prophetic urge are not willing to risk much less than Chomsky has risked and continues to risk (or even risk something quite meager, as the case might be), but that should make it easier, not more difficult, for them to admire rather than vituperate and subject those capable of taking a steeper path to updated versions of the infamous *auto-da-fé*.

Much of the surprise vanishes, however, when one realizes that before an advanced level of civilization is reached the emergence of prophets among the people of a society will naturally give rise to a proliferation of blind defenders of the shattered faith. This suggests that a people of prophets is likely to be a people of inquisitors. The Jewish people appears to be a case in point, perhaps since long before 1967. There is evidence, for example, that the Jews of Castile established a country-wide inquisition in the 14th century—more than one hundred years before the establishment of the better known "Holy Inquisition" by the Catholics. But the roots of the phenomenon are even older. Since at least the 11th century those identified as Karaites, perhaps the only dissenting ("heretical") group within Judaism that has survived to our own times, were often flogged to death if "unrepentant." The power of the Jewish inquisitors even over non-heretics had no clear limits (recall the quote about Emma Goldman). Here is an illustration:

> Jewish women who cohabited with gentiles had their noses cut off by rabbis who explained that 'in this way she will lose her beauty and her non-Jewish lover will come to hate her' ... Adulterers were imprisoned, after being made to run the gauntlet through the Jewish quarter. In religious disputes, those thought to be heretics had their tongues cut out.[29]

The preceding remarks barely scratch the surface of the topic, but may nevertheless shed some helpful light on the contrasting backgrounds of Chomsky's position and moral caliber and the position and moral caliber of some of his detractors.

Before leaving this topic it should perhaps be added that a more immediate source of Chomsky's view than Ahad Ha'am's is the work of Rudolf Rocker, particularly his major study *Nationalism and Culture*, "an outline of the most important causes of the decline of our civilization" (written by 1933, half a century before the invasion of Lebanon, and first published in 1936–1937 in Barcelona, in a Spanish translation by the distinguished anarchist theoretician and activist Diego A. de Santillán). In his 1936 preface to the English edition, published in 1937, the last of the original social thinkers (I32) before Chomsky has this to say about the reaction of some of his contemporaries "against all the social and intellectual achievements of the past two hundred years," the "relapse into a new barbarism …whose representatives do reverence to the fanatical belief that all decisions in national and international life are to be reached only by means of the sword." The new "political religion"

> values human personality only as it may be of use to the apparatus of political power. The consequence of this absurd idea is the mechanizing of the general social life. The individual becomes merely a wheel or a cog in an all-leveling state machine which has become an end in itself and whose directors tolerate no private right nor any opinion which is not an unconditional agreement with the principles of the state. The concept of heresy, a concept derived from the darkest periods of human history, is today carried over into the political realm and finds expression in the fanatical persecution of everyone who is unwilling to surrender to the new political religion and has not lost respect for human dignity and freedom of thought and action.

(Rocker did not live long enough to see that the new conception of heresy is far more retrograde than the medieval one—see I41.)

In the 1946 epilogue to the second English edition he goes on to say that "no power can maintain itself by sheer force alone; it is always compelled to justify its ambitions by a certain ideology to disguise its real character":

> Thus nationalism was evolved into a political religion, for the purpose of replacing individual conceptions of right and wrong by the notion about right as preached by the national state, such as expressed in the sentence: 'my country, right or wrong.'[30]

As Chomsky has observed, if the commitment to the universalist ideals of the Enlightenment and the principle of national self-identification so dear to enlightened Romantics, which are not in conflict from a logical point of view, have been in conflict in practice, to the point that the tension has proven virtually irresoluble, it is because "the system of modern nation-states escapes the dilemma by rejecting the principles of solidarity, human equality, and universal justice." It is in this system that "the most vicious and self-destructive of human impulses have received the fullest expression" (see the last two sections of I45):

> Exponents of national movements, Zionism among them, often disparage the 'Enlightenment ideal of the unity of man,' exalting rather purity of race and self-interest of the nation. At least this is true of the more reactionary elements that inevitably gain ascendancy as the national state is established.[31]

(Recall Ahad Ha'am's prediction.)

3. Responsibility versus Respectability

A key element in the prophetic tradition of the Enlightenment is the notion of individual responsibility, prominent already in Chomsky's very first "non-professional" article (Spring 1966), "The Responsibility of Intellectuals," which gained him, virtually overnight, respect and admiration all over the world immediately after it appeared, expanded, in the *New York Review of Books* (Feb. 23, 1967)[32]. Later in the year, his jail cell mate for one night, Norman Mailer, who had heard that Chomsky, "although barely thirty, was considered a genius at MIT for his new contributions to linguistics," would insightfully portray him as "a slim sharp-featured man with an ascetic expression, and an air of gentle but absolute moral integrity" in *The Armies of the Night*, which captures "with marvelous accuracy and perception" the spirit and character of the demonstrations that took place at the Justice Department and the Pentagon on the weekend of Oct. 19–21, 1967.[33]

"It is the responsibility of intellectuals to speak the truth and to expose lies," Chomsky writes at the beginning of his very first political essay:

> Intellectuals are in a position to expose the lies of governments, to analyze actions according to their causes and motives and often hidden intentions. In the Western world at least, they have the power that comes from political liberty, from access to information and freedom of expression. For a privileged minority, Western democracy provides the leisure, the facilities and the training to seek the truth lying hidden behind the veil of distortion and misrepresentation, ideology, and class interest through which the events of current history are presented to us.

A few pages later he already makes the obvious point (which he has made again and again since then, but is still rarely made by others) that "American aggressiveness, however it may be masked in pious rhetoric, is a dominant force in world affairs and must be analyzed in terms of its causes and motives." He continues with another basic observation which is still far from generally assimilated:

> There is no body of theory or significant body of relevant information, beyond the comprehension of the layman, which makes policy immune from criticism. To the extent that 'expert knowledge' is applied to world affairs, it is surely appropriate—for a person of any integrity, quite necessary—to question its quality and the goals that it serves. These facts seem too obvious to require extended discussion.

If it was not already clear to the readers of Chomsky's first essay where the roots of his thought and action are to be found, by early 1971 it was even less difficult to discover. Just the fact that Chomsky was selected by Trinity College, Cambridge, to give the first memorial Bertrand Russell lectures is highly significant, as will be seen directly, and was rightly taken at the time to be "an indication of the esteem in which he is held throughout the world, both as a philosopher and as a political and moral spokesman."

Russell had been a major representative of the prophetic tradition immediately before Chomsky, who considers him "one of the select few among the true bearers of consciousness" and "an inspiring figure...to several generations, mine among others."[34] Similarities between the two are not hard to find. Crucially, much of what Erich Fromm writes in his memorable homage to the "philosopher of the century" would apply no less well to Chomsky. For example, when Fromm emphasizes that prophets "did not seek power, but avoided it":

They were not impressed by might, and they spoke the truth even if this led them to imprisonment, ostracism or death. They were not men who set themselves apart and waited to see what would happen. They responded to their fellow men because they were responsible. What happened to others happened to them. Humanity was not outside, but within them. Precisely because they saw the truth, they felt the responsibility to tell it; they did not threaten, but they showed the alternatives with which man was confronted.

(Recall the quote from Buber about the *nabi*.)

In contrast, Fromm argues, the priests use disinformation and indoctrination to control and subjugate their fellow humans and, "when they have anaesthetized man enough, they declare that man is not capable of being awake and of directing his own life, and that they, the priests, act out of duty, or even compassion, when they fulfill the function of directing men who, if left to themselves, are afraid of freedom." (Chomsky makes essentially this same point again and again—see the next section.) In particular, the secular priests of our time "have administered the idea of freedom to protect the economic interests of their social class."

In Fromm's view, the right and duty to disobedience is perhaps the first one to be mentioned "among the ideas which Bertrand Russell embodies in his life." Since Prometheus is for Marx the patron saint of philosophers because he "would rather be chained to the rock than to be the obedient servant of the gods," Russell, a philosopher himself, could be seen as "renewing this Promethean function in his life"—in sharp contrast with most philosophers, who "were not disobedient to the authorities of their time"[35]:

In most social systems obedience is the supreme virtue, disobedience the supreme sin. In fact, in our culture most people, when they feel 'guilty,' actually are feeling afraid because they have been disobedient. They are not really troubled by a moral issue, as they think they are, but by the fact of having disobeyed a command.[36]

These remarks shed some light on the moral stature of those who choose a far more demanding alternative. In a virtually unknown four-page article written on February 26, 1984, in support of Yesh Gevul (I49), precisely under the title "The Duty of Disobedience," Chomsky notes that "in a society founded on the use of violence against its own citizens, one can hardly expect individuals to follow the dictates of conscience—and, in fact, of law—and to refuse to participate in wars of aggression, or even to condemn them publicly":

The personal costs may simply be too high. The duty of disobedience can be undertaken by ordinary people, those who are not saints or martyrs, to the extent that a society is truly free and the violence of the state is curbed ... Even in the most humane and democratic society it requires considerable courage to refuse to take part in crimes against peace and other war crimes. During the American war in Indochina, many thousands of young men took this step, and many suffered severely for it. Speaking personally, I was proud to be associated with them, to support their actions, and to take part in resistance to this war of aggression. The participants in Yesh Gevul, and their supporters, are following in the honorable tradition of those who refused to serve in Indochina, and like them, are a credit to the society in which they live.

Thus it is understandable that Chomsky was not very eager to become politically engaged when the shocking escalation of the Vietnam War in the early 1960s made it difficult for him not to. Although as a student he had had no real conscious commitment to teaching at a university and expected his life to be politics, the course of his existence had taken a quite different turn. In 1955, after four years as a Junior Fellow of the Society of Fellows at Harvard at the end of which he received a PhD. in linguistics from the University of Pennsylvania, he had joined the MIT faculty and after less than six years, when he was only 32, had been appointed full professor in the Department of Modern Languages and Linguistics (now the Department of Linguistics and Philosophy). What is more important, by then he had singlehandedly created the first cognitive science and a new sub branch of mathematics (an extension of abstract algebra) closely related to computer science (I1), and was beginning to be extremely successful as a teacher.[37] The publication in 1957 of his very first book, *Syntactic Structures*, based on some of his class notes (and quite limited with respect to his first, monumental work, *The Logical Structure of Linguistic Theory*, which he had written in a few months as a graduate student—I3), had launched what is sometimes called Chomsky's revolution in linguistics, the main development in the emergence of the cognitive sciences.[38] His dilemma is clearly expressed in what he told an interviewer for a local paper in early 1980 (I41):

> I was very reluctant to do it, to be quite honest, because I knew perfectly well that it was the kind of thing that could only escalate. I really had a pleasant life. I liked my work, I had success, everything was set up the way I wanted it to be, and I knew that this was going to be a lot more pleasant than what I was getting into. It didn't turn out as badly as I had thought—I expected that the likely consequence would be a prison sentence for a long period, and other kinds of unpleasantness. I've never particularly enjoyed demonstrations, or being maced or teargassed. I never thought that was great fun.[39]

But whatever qualms he may have had about risking his and his family's admittedly "privileged" existence, he quickly took the plunge and has never pulled back from his activism once he decided to make the commitment. Since then he has given countless speeches, taken part in numerous symposia and public forums, travelled extensively and written prolifically (he has published more pages in the last two or three years than most creative people in a lifetime, and their number is not the most remarkable thing about them). He has also attempted to do more than expose and explain the facts and help us to understand their significance.

Some might be inclined to argue that by taking upon himself responsibilities that most people would be able to carry out if they put their will and mind to it, he has ignored a heavier responsibility he does not appear to be aware of, namely, the responsibility of not unnecessarily risking his life, and with it many fruitful years of irreplaceable creative achievement. It is, at any rate, particularly striking, and only superficially paradoxical, that if he had wrapped himself early on in the mantle of the extraordinarily successful great achiever that he soon proved to be, he would have spared himself a great deal of trouble. It is unimaginable that, for example, someone with the track record of a hack would dare to doctor Einstein's letters to the editor, address him as someone of less worth than the editor himself (a near impossibility in some cases), or libel him the way Chomsky has been libeled.[40]

There is no need to review here the harassment, the ridicule and abuse that Chomsky has endured in the course of his efforts, "the shameful suppression and distortion, the revilement by apologists for the criminal violence of the state." We can only hope that "this was more than compensated by the deep respect of decent people throughout the world."[41] All of those who value reason, liberty and justice, who are captivated by his vision of a better society, who find him to be one of the most inspiring figures of our time, cannot help being thankful for his humanity and his extraordinary gifts.

Many others fear him instead, and are not prepared to confront him in the open. As we can now read in the final paragraph of a recent thesis on his political writings by a British author,

> the United States does not lack for opportunities to debate positions such as Chomsky's, but it is tempting to conclude that such effort is not made because his [antagonists] fear that they could lose the argument… An attempted rebuttal of Chomsky could be launched; that it is not is surely an indictment of American intellectual life. If the political health of the American republic depends … on being constantly agitated, then Noam Chomsky's exclusion damages that health. It is the commentators who decline to debate who abrogate their intellectual responsibility and injure the health of their society much more than Chomsky.[42]

In this context it might be instructive to examine a recent attempt to come to terms with Chomsky's work which departs from the usual standards of mainstream intellectuals. The author is honest and straightforward enough to recognize some obvious, but often denied or ignored truths, including the following:

1. If only for the role he played during the Vietnam War, Noam Chomsky should be honored as a national hero.

2. Americans are no longer convinced that our government has the right to destroy any country it wants to. And to the extent that this is true, Chomsky, along with others like him , deserves much of the credit. He did his job well.

3. [*The Chomsky Reader*] vividly illustrates the remarkable moral and intellectual consistency that he's maintained for more than twenty years.

4. From his earliest political writings, Chomsky has been against both sides of the Cold War. He views the Cold War as an arrangement from which both superpowers benefit. The United States and the Soviet Union, he believes, are united in suppressing any striving toward independence in less powerful nations.

5. He's been strongly influenced by anarchist thought, and accordingly maintains a healthy disrespect for all nation-states.
6. Chomsky is immensely productive: I'm reviewing two of his books because he came out with a second one before I could finish writing about the first. I can think of 15 books he's published on political subjects, and I'm probably forgetting a few.
7. No one who has attacked Chomsky on the Faurisson issue has ever tried to support the case with evidence from his other writings. There's good reason for that—the evidence all goes the other way ... Chomsky can be justly proud of his support for free expression ... Anyone who looks at David Caute's new book on 1968, *The Year of the Barricades*, will see that Chomsky consistently defended the rights of men he must have hated ... To harp on Faurisson is nothing but a way of avoiding real argument ... If some people cling to a distorted interpretation of the Faurisson affair, this may be because it helps them shrug off Chomsky's views about the Middle East.
8. Those who have read Chomsky's books on the Middle East and who thought them too critical of Israel might be surprised if they took another look at them now—now that the Palestinian uprising and the policy of "force, might, beatings" have made the ugliness of the occupation impossible to ignore. What struck some readers as inflamed hyperbole a few years ago seems common sense today ... Chomsky's great crime was to look at the realities of the occupation when most Americans preferred not to.
9. His early work in general seems the work of a man deeply patient, deeply reasonable, deeply humane. It's suffused with a luminous moral intelligence.
10. [In *The Fateful Triangle*] he tells an important part of the story—the part that's traditionally been neglected or suppressed.
11. I think he's the most valuable critic of American power that we have ... From his earliest writings to his latest, Chomsky has looked with astonishment at what the powerful do to the powerless. He has never let his sense of outrage become dulled.
12. No one has given himself more deeply to the struggle against the horrors of our time.[43]

The recognition of these truths is, however, of no help to the reviewer when he tries to explain why Chomsky "elicits such violent reactions." His problem appears to be the following:

In the 1960s, Chomsky was widely respected. His articles on the war appeared in the *New York Review of Books* ... Around the mid-1970s this changed ... Chomsky is now treated with a weird mixture of neglect and abuse. His books are seldom even reviewed—he's not important for that, you see—the *New York Review* quietly dropped him; other liberal magazines followed suit ... It's strange, isn't it that he's never invited to write for the *New York Times* op-ed page or its Book Review, or for *Harper's*, or the *Atlantic*, or the *Village Voice*. Why is he so isolated?

Why indeed. One reason could be the sharp turn to the right of elite intellectuals—in contrast with the general population (see I42)—perhaps easiest to detect in the *New York Review of Books*. Significantly, Chomsky was not the only contributor dropped by 1972–73. The *NYRB* dropped all dissidents: Florence Howe, Paul Lauter, Peter Dale Scott, etc.—even investigative reporters like Seymour Hersh. It is therefore not particularly surprising, contrary to what is often suggested, that the *NYRB* (not very) "quietly dropped him" by 1972–73 (along with a host of others).[44]

What about the "other liberal magazines"? The trouble is, there were no other liberal magazines. The assumptions of the last two sentences of the quote are all false. In fact, the journals are more open now (I41) than in the 60s.[45]

At this point we may ask why the *NYRB* dropped the dissidents, including Chomsky. Could it, by any chance, be due to a combination of truth number 11 and a generalized form of truth number 10 (supplemented with a modicum of truth number 8)? The missing premise appears to be "anyone who aspires to respectability among the 'American intellectual elite' must suppress or distort facts that pass beyond acceptable limits." Truth number 10 in generalized form is that Chomsky regularly tells the "important part of the story—the part that's traditionally been neglected or suppressed." Ergo, Chomsky is not respectable for the "American intellectual elite."

We still need the not unreasonable premise "the elite in control of liberal magazines are in the business of suppressing or distorting the important part of the story" (not in the business of informing the population of the naked truth) to straightforwardly conclude that the *NYRB* has no use for critics of Chomsky's honesty, caliber and distinction (now, at any rate). What is really needed instead by "those preparing to 'face the responsibilities of power,' or in plain English, to set forth on a life of crime, to 'play hardball' in their efforts to 'maintain [the present] position of disparity' between our overwhelming wealth and the poverty of others" is the "soothing doctrines" of "one of the saints of modern American liberalism."[46]

Particularly revealing in the unusually fair piece under consideration is the distorted picture of the world it betrays. Its author is impressed with what he sees as Chomsky's "isolation"—with respect to a handful of members of the intellectual elite. "When his name comes up," he writes, "sophisticated people smile. Chomsky … we all know where he ended up, don't we?" Let's put aside the fact that Chomsky has written in recent years a second monumental work which represents not only a great improvement over the first but also a new and far more original milestone in the history of ideas[47], since the type of "sophisticated people" referred to are usually too ignorant to take note of such things. Still, it is somewhat shocking (or it would be in a different time and place) that the fact that masses of people continue to fill, if anything in greater numbers, every large auditorium in which he speaks, and the fact that they listen to him with the greatest interest and respect and admiration—week after week, month after month, year after year—should count for nothing for those who value "popularity."

Consider a not untypical case. In the last week of January 1988 he gave at least one lecture a day in Los Angeles on topics ranging from linguistics, philosophy and psychology to the media, the Middle East and Central America.[48]On Jan. 27 he spoke to a full house in the largest UCLA auditorium (it seats close to 2000) and similarly on Jan. 29 on the Santa Barbara campus of the University of California. The UCLA event—organized, with quite limited means, by essentially three students and two faculty—is of particular interest in this context. A large crowd representing a gamut of ages and backgrounds stood for a considerable length of time in line to be able to get in (it was necessary to distribute tickets to control the situation), and many of them stayed until they heard, late in the evening, the answer to the very last of a number of questions that followed his talk and a panel discussion with political science students and faculty. The turnout is even more impressive when one considers that one of the better known members of the Israeli Cabinet, Shimon Peres, had spoken on the same topic (in a manner of speaking) in the very same auditorium (Royce Hall) a couple of months earlier with far from comparable success in spite of the efforts of several organizations with considerable means at their disposal. Is Chomsky more "isolated" from the people that matter than Shimon Peres? Is the reception he gets from people of all walks of life everywhere a sign that "he's been forced to the margins"? Only if the margins of the elite are understood to be the center, as one can foolishly assume—or if one indulges in wishful thinking.

The piece also suggests that "Chomsky's political writings thus far can be divided into two periods, or two manners, with the break occurring in the late 1970s … in Chomsky's later work we hear less of a humane, less of a human voice." The author also gets the impression that Chomsky "continues to expose the reigning lies only because it's the moral thing to do, not because he expects to accomplish anything … his style exudes despair."

The correctness of the last observation is easily put to the test. Here is a somewhat truncated sample from the closing chapter (a magnificent one) of *Turning the Tide*, published in 1985:

> It is possible even for those who are not saints or heroes to come to understand the world in which we live, and to act to stop the terror and violence for which we share responsibility by turning the other way.
>
> It can be done. Our own recent history shows that, and we need not pretend to ourselves that we do not know the way. The mass popular movement against the war in Indochina undoubtedly had significant effects. It raised the costs to the war criminals who conducted it. It prevented the state from declaring a true national mobilization …

(The reader who so wishes can turn to the book for more.)

As for the idea of the two periods, it faces some obvious difficulties. Do we "hear less of a humane, less of a human voice" in, say, *Language and Problems of*

Knowledge, written in 1986, than in *American Power,* written by 1968? It is not immediately obvious that we do. Granting that Chomsky is "indignant because the values he cherishes are being strangled," is it true that "increasingly, the reasons for his indignation—the values he cherishes—are hard to see in his work?" For example, are the values he cherishes more difficult to see in the Managua lectures (1986) or in *The Culture of Terrorism* (1988) than in, say, *For Reasons of State* (1973)? Hardly. Is there any reason to doubt that the quote from *Turning the Tide* I left unfinished implies "a world of human agency, a world in which people can sometimes be persuaded by reasonable argument"? Of course not. The conclusion is inescapable: the qualification "early" in truth number 9 is out of place.

This is not to deny that Chomsky believes there are people who might never be persuaded by reasonable argument. He is not a fool. Is there any evidence that the typical commissar (whatever the stripe) is more open to reason than the typical gangster? Are the people who control the American media and other institutions open to reason? If one is to plausibly argue that Chomsky speaks now "in a different voice" (perhaps more in the voice of the prophet), it is necessary to specify in reference to whom. To the suffering people of Nicaragua or the Palestinians of the uprising? The answer is clearly no. To those who attend his talks? The answer is clearly no. More generally, to those who do not shrink from their responsibility? The answer is again no. To whom, then? No one minimally acquainted with his writings would find it difficult to answer. Reading him one easily gets the impression that now he has an even lower opinion of intellectuals than he once had and that he does not harbor very many illusions about them (compare the first quote in this section or the end of I1). What could be the explanation for a change of this nature?

A possibility that comes readily to mind is that, uncharacteristically, he might have underestimated (up to a point) what can be expected from the intelligentsia—his deep distrust of them, derived from his almost instinctive and unusually keen sense of how things can be expected to operate, notwithstanding. Perhaps some of the extremes of the 1970s took him by surprise. First came the reaction to the October 1973 tragedy ("a very close call for the State of Israel"), for which those who "quite successfully suppressed any discussion of the dangers and alternatives bear a measure of responsibility."[49] Next the project of shifting the onus for the Vietnam War to the Vietnamese, so that the United States is the injured party—a project which continues to be amazingly successful. Then the contrasting reactions to the simultaneous massacres of Cambodia and East Timor in the late 70s, which, together with the project just mentioned, provided a more accurate calibrator of the moral level of the "secular priesthood" than anything that had gone on before. And to top it all off, the Stalinist (more precisely, Zhdanovist) attempt to misrepresent the so-called Faurisson affair—aided and abetted by the lack of reaction of those in a position to know the truth, including people one would have thought close to the unsurpassed linguist and certainly aware of his intellectual and moral caliber, who could not claim they were as ignorant and uninformed as some of his vilifiers are (see I16).

Is it possible that even Chomsky, with all his insight, could not have anticipated the degree of cowardice and moral depravity secular priests are capable of? Could it be that he still had something to learn in the 1970s?

4. Innatism versus Environmentalism

In the fierce reaction of the intelligentsia against Chomsky's work there is more than meets the eye. It is, of course, the reaction of the priests against the prophets. But what is at its root? The answer is plain: the very conception of "just what it means to be human" (I3), hence of a meaningful "democratic society." This is exactly what is at stake. Like their earlier counterparts, today's secular priests are apocalyptically Hobbesian worshippers of the beastly Leviathan, otherwise known as state power; whereas Chomsky, who is prophetically Cartesian, places the freedom and dignity of a human being above everything else. The consequences of adopting an apocalyptic rather than a prophetic approach to people and social organization are not hard to see. A quick look at the record of one of the superpowers, or of any state for that matter, more than suffices.

It is not very difficult to understand why the debates about innatism and environmentalism ("nature or nurture") tend to be debates between different value systems. If it were true that our minds are at the mercy of the environment, there would be no argument against control of behavior either by force or by other means, in particular through educational practice oriented toward strict guidance and direction, or even effective techniques of conditioning and "scheduling of reinforcement." Under environmentalist assumptions, elitism and its sequels, racism and intolerance (including loyalty oaths and other devices for "externalizing" minds), would be much easier to formulate and defend.[50] In other words, environmentalism is useful to those who seek, or wish to retain, power, and are understandably wary about being undermined by "heresy" or "conspiracy," which is why it is just as attractive in Washington and New York as it is in Moscow and Leningrad.

It has been pointed out that some of Lenin's writings suggest that he conceived of the masses as a tabula rasa upon which the intelligentsia must imprint the particular choice of consciousness that foresighted leaders choose as the right one—after all, the vanguard party is by definition the repository of all truth, the best interpreter of the interest of the masses. It is essentially no different in the West, as Chomsky stressed in the first chapter of his first non-technical book, in the second of his Russell lectures and many times since 1971. As he was to put it a few years later,

> this set of beliefs corresponds very well to the demands of the technocratic intelligentsia: it offers them a very important social role. And in order to justify such practices, it is very useful to believe that human beings are empty organisms, malleable, controllable, easy to govern, and so on, with no essential need to struggle to find their own way and to determine their own fate ... It is plausible that statist ideo-

logues and administrators are attracted by this doctrine because it is so convenient for them, in eliminating any moral barrier to manipulation and control.[51]

With this in mind it is easier to understand Chomsky's intensely negative reaction to the intellectual milieu of Cambridge and the surrounding Boston area when he arrived there in 1951, which brings to mind the contrast between Philadelphia and Boston some people speak of. It was a reaction that seems to have had something in common with his feeling the day the Hiroshima bomb was dropped:

> Computers, electronics, acoustics, mathematical theory of communication, cybernetics, all the technological approaches to human behavior enjoyed an extraordinary vogue. The human sciences were being reconstructed on the basis of these concepts. It was all connected … Some people, myself included, were rather concerned about these developments, in part for political reasons, at least as far as my motivations were concerned … because this whole complex of ideas seemed linked to potentially quite dangerous political currents: manipulative, and connected with behaviorist concepts of human nature. [52]

Here is the root of Chomsky's irreconcilable opposition, since his early childhood, to much of what he found around him in the world in which he was born. He was against virtually the whole cultural context in its most sophisticated version. For him, fighting against what he saw as dangerous intellectual developments was part of fighting against the Cold War and the general climate of jingoism that was prevalent in "the decade of indifference."

The first step towards bringing down the house of cards that was preventing a higher degree of cultural development from emerging was for him to show that the postwar reconstruction of the human studies, re-christened "behavioral sciences," lacked any solid foundation. And that is exactly what he succeeded in doing. His achievement is considered to be a major strand in the so-called 'cognitive revolution' (the second cognitive revolution, in his view—I48, I49), which he has since spearheaded. But this is only part (obviously a crucial part) of what we might understand by the Chomskyan revolution, a cultural phenomenon of far broader range, as we will see in the next section.[53]

To begin to appreciate Chomsky's insight and originality one would have to place oneself in the cultural context of Cambridge when he appeared on the scene. A telling sign of the dominant mood was that everyone at MIT at the time was convinced that finite automata would solve everything, and in particular that language could be accommodated within a type of abstract automata known as a Markov source—everyone except Chomsky. He, on the contrary, succeeded in demonstrating that a generalized form of Markov process that he had developed for the purpose was much too narrow to account for human language.

The day he delivered his epoch-making paper presenting his demonstration at a symposium on information theory held at MIT—Sept. 11, 1956—has recently been taken to be the "consensual birthdate" of the cognitive sciences. Presumably an important reason for the choice is the novelty and implications of Chomsky's new approach, which "excited all of us," in the words of the psychologist George Miller, author of one of the three papers discussed in the symposium.[54] That early paper (Chomsky was 27 at the time) was already an attempt to characterize language capacity on a computational model, that is, a model involving rules and representations which is capable of specifying an infinite range of sentences, the necessary but not sufficient support for "the creative aspect of language use" (we will return to this notion) that every normal speaker exemplifies daily. But he still had to fight a big and long-lasting battle at MIT; it took time before his revolutionary new ideas began to sink in. Some would say that the battle is still raging, at least in some provinces.

These new ideas constituted the first major step towards a scientific theory of the mind/brain—the mind being just an aspect of the brain, in this view. In a similar way, Mendelian genetics can be taken to be the first, crucial step towards molecular biology (cf. 112), which is part of physics (in a broad sense). A still closer analogy perhaps is 19th-century chemistry, which developed abstract representations of complex molecules long before the physicists were able to show, in the early part of the 20th-century, that there really are things that have the properties attributed by chemists to molecules—a discovery that did not diminish at all the validity and utility of the chemical level of analysis, something we should not lose track of, as some people tend to do. We could say that cognitive linguistics as understood here is to the future brain sciences as chemistry is to quantum physics. Without information about valence, molecule and so on, the physicist would not have known what to look for; without information about the linguistic representations and computations, the brain scientist would not know what to look for.[55] Furthermore, Chomskyan linguistics represents a really new breakthrough for the natural sciences since Galileo and Newton: before Chomsky no one had even come close to extending the application of the natural science approach to the study of the mind/brain.

Perhaps the most widely known attempt is that of Freud, a thinker to whom Chomsky has sometimes been compared—quite misleadingly, it would appear. One of the earliest comparisons that comes to mind is the one provided by the *London Times Literary Supplement* of Nov. 16, 1967, where Chomsky (still in his 30s) was seen as "something of a Freud: creative, stimulating, the founder of a devoted school, the author of techniques and ideas which are likely to be of lasting value." A few years later his work was described as "one of the most remarkable intellectual achievements of the present era, comparable in scope and coherence to the work of … Freud" in John Searle's "Chomsky's Revolution in Linguistics" (1972). For Yale psychiatrist Marshall Edelson, who is impressed by what he sees as "the congruence of the theories of Freud and Chomsky," "Chomsky like Freud is one of the great ones; he has changed entirely the study of mind."[56]

What is missing in every one of these views is that Chomsky succeeded in his attempt to construct a partial theory of mind, while Freud did not.[57] In fact, Freud himself leaves no doubt that the very possibility of incorporating the study of the mind/brain into the natural sciences never entered his mind.

It is true that Freud believed that "the contribution of psycho-analysis to science consists precisely in having extended research to the region of the mind" and that "without such a psychology, science would be very incomplete." But he makes clear what his real goal was when he writes that "strictly speaking, indeed, there are only two sciences—psychology, pure and applied, and natural science."[58] This remark leaves little doubt that he, not unlike those of his contemporaries concerned with the topic, saw a basic bifurcation between the natural sciences and what we might call the "nonnatural sciences," as people who have not assimilated Chomsky's work still do.[59] In other words, Freud's view is consistent with Vico's wrong-headed criticism of Cartesian epistemology and of the Cartesian attempt to extend the natural science approach to the study of humans and society. This is not to say that Vico was entirely wrong. Chomsky would be the first to recognize that it is not unlikely that literature "will forever give far deeper insight into what is sometimes called 'the full human person' than any mode of scientific inquiry can hope to do."[60]

It is also clear that what Chomsky calls "Plato's problem" (the problem of explaining how we know so much given that we have such limited evidence), the central epistemological problem, was not Freud's concern. In his celebrated study of dreams Freud did not go beyond the conclusions outlined in chapter VI of *The Interpretation of Dreams*, titled "The Dream-Work," where he deals with "a new problem, an entirely novel task—that of examining and tracing the relations between the latent dream-thoughts and the manifest dream content, and the processes by which the latter has grown out of the former":

> one can never be really sure that one has interpreted a dream completely; even if the solution seems satisfying and flawless, it is always possible that yet another meaning has been manifested by the same dream. Thus the degree of condensation is—strictly speaking—indeterminable.

Such observations immediately bring to mind Chomsky's distinction between a deep structure and the corresponding surface structure and logical form (grammatical meaning), and the rules and principles of grammar which relate various levels of representation. This suggests the possibility of a research program not unlike that of generative grammar (just as we study the range of humanly attainable languages extending the natural science approach to an aspect of the humanities, we might also try to study in an analogous way the forms of dream expression), but such a program has never been initiated or even proposed, let alone carried out. We are therefore still far from having a theory of dreams which is comparable in precision, richness and explanatory power to Chomsky's theory of language (language posing a special, and central, case of "Plato's problem"):

> After more than fifty years of Freudian psychology, most psychologists are quite skeptical about the reality of the underlying, unconscious [read: subconscious—CPO] structures that Freud wrote about, ... there does not seem to be any way of determining whether these unconscious [read: subconscious] structures are just the

invention of Freudian psychologists or whether they have some further 'underlying reality."[61]

It might be mentioned here that a successful research program on the forms of dream expression modeled on the theory of language developed by Chomsky and other linguists in his wake would perhaps make it possible to move on to an investigation of the relationship between the forms of dream expression and the syntactic forms of language. And although, in Chomsky's view, one would not expect to find the same representations and the same principles in such different mental activities as dreams and language, he does not think that it is at all unreasonable "to search for a more abstract relation between the two systems."[62]

In this light it is perhaps easier to begin to understand the immense importance of Chomsky's achievement in the history of civilization. The fact that there is still not much awareness of it tells us something about the prevailing intellectual and moral culture. Yet it is something that should not be ignored by those that are committed to bringing about a better world and who have every intention of using the main resources that can help to reach that goal.

It has been repeatedly pointed out that, to have a real chance of success, not only the moral but also the intellectual level of a radical movement would have to be far higher than in the past. Activists, like other people who are involved in education and social analysis, have much to gain if they keep an eye on what is happening in the sciences, particularly the most relevant sciences, and the most relevant to the work of an activist are the cognitive sciences. Anyone trying to educate himself and help educate others would be well advised to be acquainted with at least some of the most basic knowledge about human nature available today. When it comes to working for progressive social change, ignorance is certainly no more helpful than it has always been.

The 1960s were barely over when the leading behaviorist concluded that humans are "beyond dignity and freedom." It is important to understand why there is no reason to think that such a conclusion is correct.[63] A related behaviorist idea is that organisms have certain intellectual capacities, such as the capacity to carry out inductive reasoning (from the particular to the general), and that humans differ from other animals in that they can apply these capacities, these "general learning mechanisms," more extensively (to language learning, games, science, problem solving, and so on). According to this view, which is not unrelated to the Marxist doctrine that there is no immutable human nature, human cognitive systems (language being the most central one) arise in accordance with general principles of induction, analogy, association, habit formation, and so on.

As Chomsky has made clear, this approach to the study of humans, which is full of implications, assumes a kind of epistemological dualism that is particularly striking among people who see themselves as natural scientists. It amounts to studying everything in the physical world, including humans below the neck, in one way (the natural science approach), and humans above the neck in another way (the behaviorist approach). Yet the human brain differs from the spirit of the angels in that it is part of the physical world. Hence, a cognitive system such as the language system is very much part of the brain; it is what Chomsky calls a "mental organ." Why shouldn't we use the canons of the natural sciences when we study humans above the neck?

The parallel between sexual maturation and linguistic maturation might make it easier to see how reasonable Chomsky's view is. Both sexual maturation and linguistic maturation are alike in that they take place late in life (the former later than the latter in fact). The organism that will eventually undergo those processes begins as an embryo with some kind of structure, the environment provides it nutrition, things happen along the way, and at the end the organism reaches a mature state (first linguistically and then sexually).

However, the two processes were never viewed as parallel before Chomsky brought the parallelism to our attention, and they are still not usually viewed as parallel, even by non-behaviorists. No behaviorist, no matter how radical, has been known to argue that sexual maturation is due to learning (e.g., one sees other people undergoing it and tries to imitate them, perhaps because of peer pressure). It is generally assumed that what happens is that the organism proceeds in an internally directed course, shaped and modified by the environment (inadequacy of nutrition, for example, may prolong the process, but it will still be the same internally directed process).

In contrast, when it comes to linguistic maturation, everyone, before Chomsky, and many people even today (35 [now over 50] years after his initial major discoveries) assume that children literally "learn" their native language or languages, as if the principles of language could be learned the way one learns the telephone numbers of one's friends. Could it be that we have more evidence against "learning" in the case of sexual maturation than in the case of linguistic maturation? Just the opposite is true. In the case of the study of sexual maturation nobody knows what is going on physically (embryological development, one of the most intriguing phenomena in the whole of biology, continues to elude genetic and biochemical analysis), whereas there is very strong evidence that at least some crucial parts of language are not learned.

An extremely simple example might be sufficient to suggest why this is so. Consider the two seemingly simple English sentences "John believes he is intelligent" and "John believes him to be intelligent." Any speaker of English knows that the pronoun "he" in the first sentence can refer either to the person named John or to someone else, whereas "him" in the second sentence cannot refer to John—it can refer only to someone else (see I28).[64] Since English speakers are not taught this peculiarity about English pronouns in the different structures in which it is manifested when they are children, or trained to make the difference, or provided with the relevant experience to discover it themselves and apply it to other cases, the conclusion is inescapable that, miracles aside, what is not found in the linguistic environment is a contribution of the genetic endowment of the human brain (the higher apes are incapable of a similar feat).

This is only a tiny sample of the kind of evidence that supports Chomsky's notion of the "language organ," a language-specific biological system, not unlike the circulatory or respiratory system, which "interacts with early experience and matures into the grammar of the language that the child speaks." In Chomsky's view there is no more reason to believe that the basic properties of language are learned than there is to believe that the sun sets. What he calls "mental growth" is just "physical growth." The "growth of language," just like the growth of any other physical system, is determined by some fixed properties (modified to some extent by the environment), which is why everybody achieves the same very rich complex states of knowledge in spite of the meagerness of the evidence and the diversity of individual experience, although there are of courses considerable differences from individual to individual in the facility to put them to use.

If that is the case for language, the same should be true for other "mental organs" as well (the null hypothesis), in which case the behaviorist theory of "general learning mechanisms" such as induction is more than open to question, and might not be more promising than the geocentric theory of the sunset. As Chomsky has written,

> It would be surprising indeed if we were to find that the principles governing [language] are operative in other cognitive systems, although there may be certain loose analogies, perhaps in terms of figure and ground, or properties of memory, as we see when the relevant principles are made explicit.[65]

But since our understanding of ourselves has more direct implications for our social organization and the design of our institutions than the earth's rotation, these revolutionary new ideas can make a much greater contribution than those of the Copernican and Galilean revolution to free us from the domination of false beliefs inherited from the past—as well as to free us from ourselves.

The anachronistic character of some aspects of this domination can be most readily seen by comparing the differing shadows that Charles Darwin and his slightly younger (nine years) contemporary, Karl Marx, have cast over us. From the vantage point of molecular biology, Darwin's ideas—and this is no disparagement of Darwin's genius— are only the germ of what is known today about the selective theory of natural evolution. He could not in his day have had the slightest inkling of the chemical mechanisms of reproductive invariance or of the nature of the mutational perturbations these mechanisms undergo.[66]

When we move from the field of modern biology to the study of human nature and human society, the picture is very different. It is often the case that Marx is less at odds with what is known today than some 20th-century Marxists are—beginning with the very question of human nature itself.[67] The "cognitive revolution," initiated, like the revolution in biology, in the early 1950s, has made little difference so far in the study of human nature and its cultural products, in particular in the study of culture and cultural evolution.[68] It could be said that when it comes to the study of physical mechanisms only with respect to the theory of vision have some far-reaching results been attained and that the cognitive sciences have a long way to go before brain scientists can seriously begin to search for the physical mechanisms that underlie knowledge of language. But no reasonable person would say that Mendelian genetics did not represent an important advance with respect to Darwin's understanding, or that chemistry was not a necessary and important step towards quantum physics, and it can be argued, as suggested above, that Chomskyan cognitive linguistics is to the molecular biology or physics (neurology) of language as chemistry is to the physics of quanta.

An important difference between the significance of chemistry and the significance of the cognitive sciences is that the latter contributes to our knowledge of ourselves, and to our understanding of culture and cultural development, including revolutionary social change, in ways that chemistry does not. This is the main topic of the next section.

5. Anarchism versus Elitism

The fact that it has been shown that there is no basis to the assumptions of the behaviorists and other environmentalists about the nature of the mind/brain, and that Chomsky and other researchers following in his footsteps have since provided a great deal of evidence in support of rich intrinsic mental structures that underlie the development of cognitive structures (in particular, language), is not without consequences for social thought and action.

If our minds are richly structured biological organisms and furthermore there is no evidence (or only conflicting evidence) that we are biologically programmed to obey our superiors in a hierarchy which is genetically determined—this has been argued to be the case with baboons, for example—then it is a rational conclusion that no one has the right to control someone else's life and character and mode of thought, or to "externalize" anyone's mind, or to impose external constraints on anyone's freedom of thought and expression. This hypothesis—abstain from interfering, since there is no known reason that justifies interference—is the null hypothesis, hence a legitimate hypothesis even in the absence of positive evidence.

Fortunately, we can already do a little better than the null hypothesis, mostly because of Chomsky's discoveries and the research they have stimulated. To Chomsky, as to the Cartesians, the only sure sign that another organism has a human mind "is its use of language in the normal, creative human fashion, free from control by identifiable stimuli, novel and innovative, appropriate to situations, coherent, and engendering in our minds new thoughts and ideas." This set of properties is sometimes referred to as "the creative aspect of language use," a creativity which reflects the freedom of thought and conception, and also the consciousness of this freedom. A human being is therefore essentially different from a chimp.[69] Following this Cartesian model, Rousseau constructed an argument against the legitimacy of established authority, whether that of political power or of wealth (since power and wealth deny to humans their essential attribute of freedom, in varying degree). Combining these speculations, Chomsky relates language and freedom in the following way:

Language, in its essential properties and the manner of its use, provides the basic criterion for determining that another organism is a being with a human mind and the human capacity for free thought and self-expression, and with the essential human need for freedom from the external constraints of repressive authority. Furthermore, we might try to proceed from the detailed investigation of language and its use to a deeper and more specific understanding of the human mind. Proceeding on this model, we might further attempt to study other aspects of that human nature which, as Rousseau rightly observes, must be correctly conceived if we are to be able to develop, in theory, the foundations for a rational social order.[70]

There is no scientific evidence to support each of these ideas, but whatever evidence there is that bears on the matter suggests that it is highly plausible that they are correct. If they are, then central to the very specific intrinsic nature of a human being is a creative impulse. As Chomsky has pointed out, "our own experience and the insights that arise from it—which are not to be discounted in areas where scientific evidence is so sparse—lend a certain credibility to this view." In addition,

at an experimental level there is some evidence that voluntary, self-willed action plays a very significant role in learning and acquiring knowledge. This work supports the observations and guesses concerning the intrinsic, self-willed character of anything of real significance that is acquired by a child in the course of learning—or an adult as well, for that matter.[71]

From this point of view, then, the purpose of social organization cannot be control, with or without maximization of profit, but rather maximization of freedom, as libertarian socialists and anarchists have always argued. In particular, the goal of education should be to provide the conditions of freedom necessary for the growth of the creative impulse of the child. This includes, in Chomsky's view, a complex and challenging environment that children can imaginatively explore and, in this way, quicken their intrinsic creative impulse and so enrich their life in ways that may be quite varied and unique.

It is not hard to see why ruling elites find this family of ideas quite threatening. If the approach is on the right track, as it appears to be, the institutions that make ruling elites possible are nothing but a residue from earlier stages in cultural development—no less of an anachronism than slavery, to be consigned to the dustbin of history. Under the assumptions of the preceding section, our moral and ethical system owes much to some innate human faculty, but, as in the case of language (or vision and so on), the environment is relevant, as the existence of cultural (and individual) divergence and of stages in the course of civilization shows.

One generation after Rousseau, Thomas Jefferson, generally considered one of the most politically advanced minds of his society ("that government is best that governs least"), could still both own slaves (including some of his own children) and eloquently extol self-evident truths about equality and inalienable rights without eliciting sharp criticism from his contemporaries. In fact, his fellow slave-owners did not regard what they were doing as wrong and even argued that what they were doing had a high moral value because if you own something you are likely to treat it with more care than if you rent it, as in the wage system of industrial capitalism. The argument is not absurd, yet today it is generally considered repugnant in most places. As civilization progressed, we came to understand that slavery is an infringement on essential human rights, and an intolerable affront to human dignity. This is not only a change of moral consciousness but "an advance toward understanding of our own nature and the moral and ethical principles that derive from it."

In Chomsky's view, there may be no end to such discoveries if civilization survives, because truly decent and honest people

> will always seek to discover forms of oppression, hierarchy, domination and authority that infringe fundamental human rights. As some are overcome, others will be revealed that previously were not part of our conscious awareness. We thus come to a better understanding of who and what we are in our inner nature, and who and what we should be in our actual lives.[72]

But since cultural development is not linear, cumulative and irreversible, there is always the possibility of regression, as some contemporary phenomena show. They represent steps backwards with respect to earlier historical experiences and cultural advances.

A particularly enlightening experience is provided by the colonization of the "New World." A review of *The Chomsky Reader* in a major newspaper takes the author to task for describing the slaughter of the American Indians as "one of the greatest exercises in genocide in human history ... which we celebrate each October when we honor Columbus—a notable mass murderer himself." This judgment, the reviewer suggests, shows "blistering and humorless rage."[73]

Consider then the attitude towards the actions of his own state and the unwavering determination to change them of Bartolomé de las Casas, a Spaniard just a year younger than Copernicus, which makes him close to half a millennium older than the reviewer. When he arrived in Hispaniola, in the West Indies, in 1502, no one would suspect that he was to become the very first European to have a deep perception of the injustice of the Spanish colonial system, to expose the war against the Indians and the oppression they were victims of, and to call for the abolition of Indian slavery. For more than ten years he was a willing participant in the conquest of the Caribbean and took part in a number of expeditions, for which he was rewarded with a royal land grant and an allotment of Indians. As late as 1513, probably the year in which he received holy orders, he was one of those who carried out the bloody "pacification" of Cuba (war was peace long before Orwell).[74]

But he was not able to remain indifferent to the fate of the American Indians for too long. On Aug. 15, 1514, four centuries before World War I, he announced in a now famous sermon that he was giving up his Indian slaves. From then on he appears to have been tireless in his efforts to secure a better treatment of the indigenous population. He never ceased in his activities and he wrote many books and petitions and innumerable letters in which he drew from an ever-increasing reservoir of facts and made a few simple points over and over again (he completed his last two works at the age of 90, just two years before his death) both in America, where he spent most of his life, and at the court, making special trips to Spain when necessary. One of his major points was that those calling themselves Christians were wiping out the Indian "nations" in two ways: as a result of an "unjust, cruel, bloody and tyrannical" war and of "the hardest, harshest and most horrible oppression ever suffered by humans or beasts." Like many other members of his order (Dominican), he was against the use of any force whatsoever. As he states in his work on "the only way" to attract all peoples to civilization, "understanding must prevail and the will has to be kindly moved and exhorted."

His testimony leaves no doubt that he witnessed what can be legitimately described as "one of the greatest exercises in genocide in human history" (for some figures, see 143, 146). To select just one quote: in the very first section of his much discussed *Very Brief Account of the Destruction of the Indies,* a province-by-province description of the bloody deeds of the Spaniards during the conquest (originally drawn up in 1542, published in 1552 and soon translated into many languages), he states, without worrying too much about the bounds of decorum, that "the reason why [those calling themselves Christians] have killed and destroyed such an infinite number of souls is that they have been moved by their wish for gold and their desire to enrich themselves in a very short time."[75] This sort of straightforwardness has of course made him a controversial figure throughout the centuries and a favorite target of unremitting and often virulent attacks, perhaps because "in a certain subtle way, Las Casas brings out in many of us our deep-seated feelings on life and the meaning of history."[76]

When in 1550 he was given a chance to take part in what in retrospect appears to be "one of the most curious episodes in the intellectual history of the Western world," Las Casas, who had left Spain without a university education, seized the opportunity and confronted directly the most respectable apologist of state power at the moment, reputed to be one of Spain's most learned scholars, at a council presided over by the foremost Spanish theologians. As a distinguished American student of his ideas and actions has written,

> then for the first, and doubtless for the last, time a colonizing nation organized a formal enquiry into the justice of the methods used to extend its empire. For the first time, too, in the modern world we see an attempt to stigmatize a whole race as inferior, as born slaves according to the theory elaborated centuries before by Aristotle.[77]

The main question under debate was whether the war against the Indians could be justified as a "just war" (see editor's note to 124). Las Casas, who had first seen the light one day while he was reading the Bible and appears to have drawn his inspiration quite directly from the prophetic tradition,[78] was firmly convinced, as prophets are, of the unity of the human race (every human being is created in God's image, and being all children of one and the same father, they all belong to the great family of humankind) and had no doubts about the full intellectual and moral capacity of the Indians, who for him were normal human beings, "not demented or mistakes of nature, nor lacking in sufficient reason to govern themselves." On the basis of his convictions he argued that there was no justification for the use of force against the Indians or for making them slaves. As already mentioned, he advocated friendly persuasion.

In contrast, his opponent, who had never set foot in America and might never have seen an American Indian in the flesh, concluded that

> the Indians are obliged by the natural law to obey those who are outstanding in virtue and character in the same way that matter yields to form, body to soul, sense to reason, animals to human being, women to men, children to adults and, finally, the imperfect to the more perfect, the cheaper to the more precious and excellent, to the advantage of both. This is the natural order, which the eternal and divine law commands to be observed ... Therefore, if the Indians, once warned, refuse to obey, they can be forced to do so for their own welfare by recourse to the terrors of war.[79]

He cites numerous examples of Spanish superiority (he boasts that a few Spaniards were able to rout thousands upon thousands of Indians "who fled like women"), among them the humanitarian sentiments of the Spanish soldiers during the sack of Rome in 1527, of which he had been a witness (at least he was in Rome at the time).[80] He justified the ensuing "pacification" by the "good" brought about by the Spaniards, which, he claimed, heavily outweighed the bad—agreeing with St. Augustine that it is a greater ill that one single soul should perish without baptism than that innumerable innocent quasi-human creatures be decapitated in a "just" war (here he draws on Thomas Aquinas). It is at this point that he elaborates on the benefits bestowed by Spain on America, the main one being of course the Christian religion.[81]

It may appear far-fetched to compare Las Casas with Chomsky. No one has argued that he was a major intellectual genius, and having died when Galileo was two years old, he could scarcely have been a major natural scientist well-versed in modern logic and in the art of sophisticated argumentation. Some of his assumptions are surely not acceptable to Chomsky. Still, it is tempting to see a certain parallelism between the two from a moral perspective. Las Casas seems to have been, with respect to the first modern nation-state which became a global empire, and more importantly, with respect to its widespread victims, what Chomsky is with respect to the U.S. empire (which in fact is built in part on land of the Spanish empire, taken over directly) and to its Third World victims. He also seems to have been possessed by an unusually strong and persistent prophetic urge, displaying seemingly boundless energy throughout a long and agitated life. He could always take another initiative, review the facts once more for anyone who cared to listen, write one more letter denouncing the latest evil, or a whole, and often lengthy, book (even though some of his writings have been lost, his works written in Spanish add up to five large volumes, and some of his books he wrote in Latin).

If there is some semblance of parallelism between the two, it might be a useful exercise to compare the respective reactions they elicited from the powerful of the time and their mandarins, and count the number of intellectuals who rallied behind each of them—even though the world in which Las Casas lived was mild in comparison to ours.

In 1516, when he first brought the problems that concerned him throughout his life to the attention of the court, he was appointed to a commission to investigate the status of the Indians. His arguments before the Spanish parliament in Barcelona in 1519 led the emperor, who was in attendance, to accept Las Casas' proposal for Indian-Spanish cooperation. In part under the influence of his *Very Brief Account of the Destruction of the Indies*, which he wrote in Spain while he was awaiting an audience with the emperor, Charles V signed the so-called New Laws of 1542 and 1543 (to be revoked in 1545 under the pressures of various lobbyists), which established (on paper at least) that the owners had to set the Indians free after the span of one generation. Would anyone expect today's emperor to know about the existence of our Las Casas and about his ideas, let alone to listen to him and to sign his recommendations into law?

Mainly to ensure the enforcement of the new legislation, Las Casas was named bishop of Chiapas, in Guatemala. That made it possible for him to provide much needed additional regulations, which he strictly enforced. Although his strictness led to general opposition on the part of many Spaniards, and he resigned his bishopric after a brief tenure, his influence at the court and at the Council of the Indies continued to increase. During his final years, the most defiant and persistent prophet that the Spanish empire gave rise to came to be the indispensable adviser to both the Council of the Indies and the crown on many of the problems relating to the Indians. A knowledgeable student of the field writes that "neither the assaults of his contemporaries nor the outbursts against him in the latter part of the sixteenth century seem to have shaken the confidence of the crown of Spain in Las Casas." Moreover, his *Very Brief Account* and the other eight "inflammatory" treatises that he had printed in Seville in 1552, "after almost 40 years of privately admonishing the crown," apparently were printed "without any previous royal scrutiny and not one of them carried any indication that it had been approved for publication by the Council of the Indies."[82] Mainly due to his unflagging efforts, the Aristotelian doctrines of his strongest opponent never gained official sanction. In view of this, can we say, four centuries later, that we are living in a culturally developed world?

Las Casas, who has had a considerable international influence since the 16th century, particularly in 18th-century France and during the Spanish American movements of independence (1810–1826), and continues to be a popular hero in the New World, is of course not among those to be blamed for the fact that his opponent's ideology was the one that was actually operative for the privileged—or the related fact that there has been no dearth of scholars who sought and continue to seek to destroy the "black legend" about Spanish colonization. Nor is he to be blamed for the fact that there have continued to be vigorous defenders of his opponent down to our own day in both Spanish-speaking and English-speaking lands, some of whom claim that his opponent's position has been misunderstood—as the much-admired Spanish Aristotelian had often done. It is no secret that "the idea that someone else should do the hard manual work of the world appealed strongly to 16th-century Spaniards" (even in the 20th-century it is pleasant for the rich for the dispossessed to do the hard work), "and when to this doctrine was linked the concept that the inferior beings were also being benefited through the labor they were performing for their superiors, the proposition became invincibly attractive to the governing class."[83]

To appreciate all this we must recall what Jefferson's ideas and actions were like two and a half centuries later—and he was perhaps one of the most progressive minds of his society.[84] In contrast, Las Casas, who early in his life had proposed the introduction of black slaves to the Caribbean islands in order to spare Indians the heavy labor which was destroying them, later repented and opposed black slavery as well as Indian slavery, "and for the same reasons."[85]

But Las Casas was an almost unique exception. Intellectuals are not generally attracted by prophetic (i.e. non-elitist) views of human nature and human organization. The real attraction for them is power and privilege, for reasons that Chomsky has made familiar. That is why they are usually prone to rationalize the behavior of their tribe, their ethnic group, their nation-state, or their empire, as the case may be. The epigraph to *Political Economy of Human Rights*, taken from Orwell's "Notes on Nationalism," comes readily to mind: "The nationalist not only does not disapprove of atrocities committed by his own side, but he has a remarkable capacity for not even hearing about them." (Compare 118 and 145.) This brings us to the other problem concerning human knowledge that has intrigued Chomsky for many years. Recall that the first was the problem of explaining how we can know so much, given that we have such limited evidence (Plato's problem, which is at the core of the cognitive sciences). He is also intrigued by the problem of explaining how we can know so little about the structure and functioning of our society, given that we have so much evidence. He calls it "Orwell's problem," because Orwell was as impressed as anyone who lived through the Stalinist period (in a narrow sense) with "the ability of totalitarian systems to instill beliefs that are firmly held and widely accepted although they are completely without foundation and often plainly at variance with obvious facts about the world around us" (preface to *Knowledge of Language*).

A crucial difference between these two epistemological problems is that the first one involves unconscious knowledge, which is essentially a matter of genetic endowment (nature), whereas the second one involves conscious scientific knowledge, which requires cultural development (nurture), the hallmark of humankind. No other animal is capable of conscious knowledge. It is our conscious knowledge and the related evolution of culture and society, which language makes possible, that sets us apart from all other species, as Rousseau appears to have understood before anyone on record. Only through cultural transmission can the human species become less imperfect, an option not open to the chimps, perhaps our closest relatives, which continue to live as they did thousands of years ago, when they shared the earth with the earliest humans.

Orwell's problem is then crucial in the study of cultural anthropology and cultural change. Not that there is or will be a "doctrine of social change fixed for the present and the future, nor even, necessarily, a specific and unchanging concept of the goals towards which social change should tend," but it can be reasonably argued that "at every stage of history our concern must be to dismantle those forms of authority and oppression that survive from an era when they might have been justified in terms of the need for security or survival or economic development, but that now contribute to—rather than alleviate—material and cultural deficit."

If this is essentially correct, neither Bolshevism (a term translated into Newspeak as "communism") nor "free enterprise" (Newspeak for "capitalism"—see I9, I35) are fit systems for the year 2000. In particular, predatory capitalism "is incapable of meeting human needs that can be expressed only in collective terms" and its concept of a competitive being "who seeks only to maximize wealth and power, who subjects himself to market relationships, to exploitation and external authority, is anti-human and intolerable in the deepest sense":

> The only justification for repressive institutions is material and cultural deficit. But such institutions, at certain stages of history, perpetuate and produce such a deficit, and even threaten human survival.[86]

The anachronistic survival of repressive institutions puts to the test the instinct for freedom that Chomsky assumes to be deeply rooted in human nature (I13, I25, I45). It makes one wonder why the revolutionary mass movement which the present stage of history loudly demands has not yet arisen. An obvious place to look for the answer is in the present level of our cultural development. There is little reason to doubt that Chomsky is right to stress that a necessary precondition for a constructive mass movement is a sufficient general understanding of social reality (including an understanding of ourselves) on the part of a large number of people, if not a majority.

There appear to be three main barriers to such an understanding. In our historical context the most evident barrier is the massive propaganda system, which does its best to mystify everything. One of its major successes is the still persistent Cold War paranoia (I16). Mystification is of course the province of the intelligentsia, the subservient "experts in legitimation" (Gramsci), who in the process obligingly contribute the Orwellian rhetoric (I35). We are, however, a stage beyond what Orwell imagined; that is, a stage beyond what Soviet totalitarianism has achieved (I36). There is an obvious safe way of escaping the awesome misinformation machine: To not expose oneself to the media or to the writings of the state ideologues. It is a well-documented fact that "lower-status groups" tend to be less willing than the well-read to support the criminal actions of the state. A growing part of the electorate, approximately half in 1984, eloquently expresses its views about the pseudo-choice offered them by not voting at all, and there appears to be widespread awareness of the way the political system actually functions (I44).

A second avenue of escape from the propaganda system is to give most of one's time and effort to extracting the facts that are scattered in the flood of untruths with the help of sources that become available to those who know about them, in particular declassified documents. Few of course can do that. Chomsky is the greatest exception.

The second barrier that an independent mind must overcome is the difficulty of developing an insightful understanding of the facts and of discovering important truths about the real workings of power. This requires the application of the principles of rational inquiry, much as researchers do in the natural sciences. To make some sense out of what lies behind a confusing range of events, decisions, and pronouncements one has to begin by trying to isolate some highly representative cases that can serve to organize and facilitate our understanding of less clear-cut phenomena, facing from the start the question of how private economic power functions in our society. Only in this way is it possible to succeed both in identifying the basic elements (social and economic) that play a crucial role in policy formation and in isolating some principles that have explanatory force over a significant range. This is out of reach for anyone bent on skirting the forbidden questions, scrupulously avoided by the "respectable" critics and other gifted "experts":

Who sets foreign policy?

What interests do these people represent?

What is the source of their power?[87]

Few have been accomplished masters in this art since the Enlightenment, and no one has, arguably, ever done it better than Chomsky. His contribution to our understanding of Orwell's problem and his social and political analyses of current issues are very much part of his revolutionary thought, comparable to the Freudian revolution. Because of this second component, Chomsky's revolution goes well beyond the revolution he spearheaded in linguistics and the cognitive sciences. It gives us no other choice than to squarely face the main issue to be resolved in the third emancipatory phase of history which is to place us on the outset of a new age.

There is still a third barrier that has to be overcome—perhaps the most insidious one: the difficulty one finds in identifying and exploring one's submerged fears, desires, motivations and self-serving beliefs. Here there is an obvious point of contact between the Freudian revolution and Chomsky's revolution in the broad sense. In fact, Orwell's problem is just an analogue in the domain of social and political life of what might be called "Freud's problem." Freud left no doubt that the temptation to avert painful ideas, impulses and feelings is buried deep within each of us. Chomsky takes this insight a step further:

> To ask serious questions about the nature and behavior of one's own society is often difficult and unpleasant: difficult because the answers are generally concealed, and unpleasant because the answers are often not only ugly—in foreign affairs, roughly in proportion to the power of the state—but also painful. To understand the truth about these matters is to be led to actions that may not be easy to undertake and that

may even carry a significant personal cost. In contrast, the easy way is to succumb to the demands of the powerful, to avoid searching questions, and to accept the doctrine that is hammered home incessantly by the propaganda system. This is, no doubt, the main reason for the easy victory of dominant ideologies, for the general tendency to remain silent or to keep fairly close to official doctrine with regard to the behavior of one's own state and its allies and dependencies, while lining up to condemn the real or alleged crimes of its enemies.[88]

To this general human predicament we now have to add the very special burdens of our troubled times. In particular, the drift towards mutual annihilation, which has a seemingly inexorable quality (137). As Chomsky has remarked, "the factors that impel it forward appear to be out of control, beyond our ability to influence or constrain them." One can only hope that this perception is false. As he writes, "whether the tide can be turned in this case is not clear, though it is plain enough that it will not long flow in its present course." What is especially relevant in this context is the nature of a very treacherous trap:

> One effect of the development of nuclear weapons has been to induce a feeling of powerlessness on the part of much of the population, and at the same time to reinforce the doctrine that the state must be free to conduct its affairs without popular interference or even scrutiny, given the awesome forces that it and its enemies command ... Another effect of these developments has been a tendency to stare at apocalyptic visions, dismissing political analysis and past approaches to action as now irrelevant in the face of imminent total destruction.

While understandable, he goes on to say, this is a most serious error. "The paralysis that results from contemplation of awesome visions of destruction" is not what is needed; what is needed is "clear-headed analysis and action over a broad range, often with quite specific and limited goals."[89]

The second emancipatory phase of history of the 1700s, which culminated in the conversion of dark-age serfs into wage slaves, was immediately preceded by a broad cultural revolution. The revolutionary new ideas of the Enlightenment put forth by the first generation of modern libertarians, spearheaded by Rousseau, brought about in a few years a general cultural transformation of a large number of people, who quickly became capable of seeing themselves and seeing the world around them in a light which had never shined before in the history of humankind. This cultural transformation in turn led directly to a popular revolution that brought the question of true political democracy to the fore not less than two hundred years ago.

Social organization is now far more complex than it has ever been and the preparatory revolutionary new ideas that the next major cultural transformation requires have to be correspondingly more advanced and sophisticated. It is our good fortune that the required new concepts have become available on time. They make it easier to understand why it is simply wishful thinking to expect that true economic democracy, an overdue fundamental emancipatory aspiration, can be attained without a change of moral consciousness that results in a much needed advance toward a better understanding of our own nature and the moral and ethical principles and moral values deeply rooted in our very being. Wage slavery and the need to rent oneself to survive, which goes hand in hand with a system of ruling-elite decision and public ratification, would otherwise be harder to see for what it is, as chattle slavery was not long ago. Under the new light we can begin to see that wage slavery is not essentially different from debt slavery or forced labor, exemplified in a particularly striking form in the slave laborers (*Sklavenarbeiter*) of Nazi Germany, who, unlike most slaves, were often not even cared for as valued capital. This is why the concept "wage slave" was used not only by Marxists but also by American slaveholders in the antebellum South to refer to laborers under capitalism. We can also come to understand that contemporary science and technology can relieve humans not only of most, if not all of the types of tasks assigned to chattel slaves, but also, more generally, of the over specialized, stultifying labor carried out by many wage slaves. If we are not capable of understanding this, we can be sure that we have not been touched by the Chomskyan revolution (in either the broad or the narrower sense).

The needed basis for a general spiritual transformation and much clear-headed analysis has been available since Chomsky's critique of behaviorism and his first books on more current issues have appeared in print. What is still to come is action over a broad range, which is no less needed to really bring about the epoch-making transformation. The conviction that we have the power and the responsibility to bring about a better world is slow to spread, but it cannot be otherwise if it is to be the result of people persuading themselves (146). Many still do not know that the most committed and certainly the most knowledge-able and passionate skeptic we have among us has persuaded himself that it can be done, and has offered some argument and evidence in support of his estima-tion. If more and more people come to know about this it can be decisive, and the stakes are far too high. It is important for concerned people to think the mat-ter through for themselves, and to come to understand the extent to which they can influence state policy.

As to how it can be done, the closing words of *Turning the Tide* remind us of a truism too easy to forget:

> There are no magic answers, no miraculous methods to overcome the problems we face, just the familiar ones: honest search for understanding, education, organization, action that raises the cost of state violence for its perpetrators or that lays the basis for institutional change—and the kind of commitment that will persist despite the temptations of disillusionment, despite many failures and only limited successes, inspired by the hope of a brighter future.

6. Coda

Innumerable humans can do things that Noam Chomsky cannot do: he could never run a 4-minute mile, play the violin like Jascha Heifetz, write a Shakespearian play or a Beethoven quartet, and so on. Humans who have excelled are usually super gifted in only one way. The exceptions to this general rule are very rare. When seen as part of the "gene flow," these rare exceptions represent compounded statistical errors in the roulette of chance and necessity played by nature.

I submit that Chomsky is a good candidate for this class. Being a revolutionary scientist, he is certainly a statistical error, and so are those in the tiny class to which Galileo and Newton belong (truly revolutionary new ideas appear infrequently, as up-to-date students of intellectual history know). Galileo and Newton launched the first non-cognitive natural science (reconstructed by Einstein and his epigones at the beginning of the 20th century), and Chomsky, singlehandedly, more than launched the first cognitive natural science.[90] This is not to claim that he has also launched what we might call the "volitive natural science" which would truly unify his linguistics and his politics, if his view of human nature and his vision of a future society are on the right track. But then chances are that such a science will not emerge for a long time to come, if ever. Performance or human action involves not only cognition but also will and choice, which so far at least have been out of reach for our science-forming capacity—though not for the artist's intuition.

Most revolutionary scientists and thinkers, however, have excelled only along the intellectual dimension—they do not appear to have been super gifted along the moral dimension. Some were clearly not (Frege, for example, to whom Chomsky has sometimes been compared, not without reason, since Frege and Russell are to contemporary logic what Chomsky is to contemporary linguistics). In other words, the revolutionary thinkers of the past were not also "prophets" in the sense of Ahad Ha'am, Martin Buber and Erich Fromm; they were not fed on, and did not feed, the hope rooted in the belief that the contribution of a single, uniquely lucid individual can make a very big difference in the history of civilization (to update a profound ancient insight). Nor were any of the known prophets major intellectual figures. Chomsky appears to be a unique, or almost unique, exception to the rule. The only other plausible candidate that comes readily to mind is Bertrand Russell. There might have been other cases in the secular history of humankind, but it may be safe to guess that the number is not very large.

Given his exceptionality along both the intellectual and the moral dimension, it is not very surprising that he is a really committed anarchist intellectual. Had he not been morally gifted, he would again have to be considered a statistical error among the class of intellectuals, which is not known to harbor an abundance of anarchists. This is of course not a new phenomenon—nor very hard to explain. How many intellectuals have been drawn towards libertarian socialism or anarchism in the course of history? How many of those intellectuals were or are deeply committed to bringing about a better (more culturally developed, hence more just) society? In fact, committed anarchists who are not intellectuals are not very common either in the population at large.

It would be hard to deny that the most extraordinary accident in Chomsky's case is that someone with his brain appeared on the surface of the earth precisely in 1928. The gene lottery did not have to come up with such a prize in 1928 rather than, say, 1988 or 2198, if ever (much earlier than 1928 might not have helped at all, for the reasons mentioned in I4).

But the accident of his genetic endowment is not the only unlikely lucky accident. His early years constitute an almost unbelievable series of unlikely lucky accidents. The second one, it would appear, is that he was born at the right time in the right Philadelphia home, was from the beginning immersed in a very rich culture, and soon found himself in the midst of a very advanced segment of the "prophetic minority" (in the precise sense suggested in section one).

The third lucky accident is that he was fortunate to attend a libertarian school from 2 to 12 (his own children, who grew up in the Boston area, were not equally lucky), and did not really attend college in the normal manner.

The fourth lucky accident was that his father was an accomplished student of historical linguistics (one of the outstanding Hebrew scholars of his time). It was his father's work that suggested to him his view of linguistics as an explanatory science (I3) and provided the historical analogy which was to be the source of epoch-making work in generative grammar.[91]

The fifth lucky accident was that the very acute left libertarian thinker the young radical student met through his unusual political contacts, and was immediately impressed with, happened to be a distinguished linguist (Zellig Harris), perhaps the best linguist alive at the time, certainly the best prepared to initiate someone with Noam Chomsky's mind and inclinations in the field of linguistics and to interest him in the study of philosophy, logic and mathematics, fields which were to change the course of his life and to open for him the wide avenue to major discoveries.[92] That rare combination of up-to-date technical training and familiarity with the traditional study of language and literature made all the difference (I3 and I4). Recall A. N. Whitehead's observation in his discussion of Kepler (applicable also to Darwin, in his view) that "novel ideas are more apt to spring from an unusual assortment of knowledge—not necessarily from vast knowledge, but from a thorough conception of the methods and ideas of distinct lines of thought," of two different subjects—at least, as they are thought at the time.[93]

The sixth lucky accident is that, seemingly at exactly the right time, he met a fellow student (Morris Halle) whose ideas converged with his and who was to get him into MIT (through the back door, so to speak), perhaps the only institution of higher learning in the country capable of providing him with some much needed breathing space, given the limited number of potential antagonists in the "humanities" in a university that focuses on advanced technical knowledge. He was thus able to become a full professor in a very distinguished institution at 32, to receive an endowed chair at 37, and to be appointed Institute Professor (a rank reserved for scholars of special distinction, mostly Nobel Prize winners) at 47.

Had he been a teacher in a lesser institution, let alone in an unknown high school or small college (as the great mathematician Alfred Tarski had to be for years), he would no doubt have been far less tolerated than he has been, and much less free to carry out his work as an activist (a conclusion which may come as a great surprise to some who are aware of the degree and extent of toleration accorded to him). He would also have had less credibility as a sharp critic of "respectable" and powerful new mandarins and their associates. If even his association with MIT, and the fact that he has been teaching a course on intellectuals and social change there (in different guises) for some twenty years, is not enough to secure for him the right to speak about domestic and foreign policy in some places, one can imagine the reaction if he had been part of a less distinguished faculty.[94]

There is more. Some people with super gifted minds are not unusually articulate. Chomsky is not one of them. In addition to being highly articulate, he is an extremely quick and formidable debater who can instantly see the flaws in an argument. Since he is also a voracious reader with a prodigious memory who is thoroughly familiar with fields as different as metamathematics and political "science" (I45), he cannot have even the opportunity granted to Las Casas of debating the strongest of his opponents before a council of the foremost "theologians" of the day. No one seems to feel ready to debate him on a public platform on a topic he masters (this proposition was last put to the test last Fall at UCLA and a few months earlier at the University of Colorado).[95] Under the pressure of the activism of the 60s, he was once invited to debate the Vietnam War in a regular television program (no expert dared to debate him on the topic), but understandably was never invited again. Many a national and international reputation would dissolve in no time were the "expert" to debate Chomsky on national television for more than a few minutes.

The point of all this is not to praise a particular individual but rather to describe a natural phenomenon which happens to be a potentially close to inexhaustible resource, so far only very partially put to good use, in the struggle for the alleviation of suffering and the general improvement of the world in which we live. It is a great responsibility if what can be done is not done. There are many things that even an intellectual and moral giant would not be able to do without the help of a large number of people, but there are also many people who can do something, and do it much more effectively, if they use the most valuable resources available to them. As of today it is hard to imagine a better Trojan horse than Chomsky to penetrate the walls which hide the elite from scrutiny and accountability. Confusions and misunderstandings about "hero worship" are not very helpful when it comes to attaining a challenging goal. In a discussion of non-human nature on this earth it would be rather unreasonable to pretend that the highest mountain is not higher than a nearby hill—that there is no such thing as Mt. Whitney or Mt. Everest. Similarly, it is an obvious fact that human genius is not scattered (I1). Not everyone can understand or do what especially gifted people can understand or do (run a 4-minute mile, play the violin like Heifetz, compose a Beethoven sonata), and nothing is to be gained from denying or even ignoring obvious facts.

In contrast, the population of the West Bank and Gaza, Central America, East Los Angeles, Watts, Harlem and the rest of the world stands to gain a great deal in a relatively short time if concerned people, and in particular the authentic Left (under the assumptions of this introduction, "non-libertarian left" is an oxymoron), do not take too much longer to become more generally aware of our well-timed stroke of luck.[96]

Notes

1. "I haven't really changed my political views much since I was 12 years old," he is quoted as saying in a review of **PEHR** (1979)—see List of Abbreviations above—in the *Valley Advocate* (Northampton, MA), Feb. 13, 1980; similarly, in Paul Barker's "Noam Chomsky's Two Worlds," *New Society*, April 2, 1981, pp. 7–10, where he adds: "What's right is right." Additional information from these two sources is used below.

2. His mother was the teacher in the Hebrew class, and his father was the school's principal. See Israel Shenker (who was "a backward classmate, aged thirteen"), *Horizon* 13:2 (Spring 1971), pp. 104–9 (or in his book, *Words and Their Masters*. Photographs by Jill Krementz. Garden City, NY: Doubleday, 1974—a reprinting brought to my attention by Morris Halle) From about age two, a strong influence on Chomsky in his formative years was John Dewey. See **CD&E** (2003), in particular the Prologue, p. 25; also, the editor's introduction, in particular Sect. 1.

3. Interview in **ChR** (1987), one of the best points of entry into Chomsky's work and its background (excerpted in Jim Peck, "Noam Chomsky: An American Dissident," *The Progressive*, July 1987, pp. 22–25). See also James Peck's admirable introduction.

4. I42 See also **LPK** (1987), pp. 171–6 & last page.

5. See E. Digby Baltzell, *Puritan Boston and Quaker Philadelphia: Two Protestant Ethics and the Spirit of Class Authority and Leadership*. New York: Free Press, 1979 (a reference I owe to a Philadelphian colleague, Paul Smith) and *Jewish Life in Philadelphia 1830–1940*, edited by Murray Friedman. Philadelphia: Institute for the Study of Human Issues, 1983, 290ff. Friedman writes in his Introduction that the Philadelphia community "has produced or directly influenced some of American Jewry's most interesting and significant leaders," of which he mentions eight ("just a few"). "A number of important writers, scholars and artists," he continues, "including Clifford Odets, Samuel Grafton, Marc Blitzstein, David Riesman, I.F. Stone, and Noam Chomsky grew up and honed their early talents, often in rebellion against the second-generation world they found here."

6. See William Chomsky [1897–1976], *Hebrew: The Eternal Language*. Philadelphia: The Jewish Publication Society of America, 1957 (8th printing, 1986), especially p. 183 and 275ff. Cf. now *At the Crossroads: Essays on Ahad Ha'am*, edited by Jacques Kornberg. State University of New York, 1983, not a very sympathetic collection, as is perhaps to be expected in today's moral and intellectual climate. Ahad Ha'am, the pen name of Asher Ginsburg (1856–1927), means "one of the people" in Hebrew.

7. See Murray Friedman (ed.), ch. 4.

8. Recall Susan Sontag's 1982 discovery that there were "many lessons to be learned" from the Polish events (the *Soho News*, Feb. 16, 1982), perhaps helped in part by the short-lived French "new philosophy," a media favorite for several years (cf. **PEHR**, 1979, II, p. 297, and I16); compare Chomsky's comment (the *Soho News*, March 2, 1982, pp. 10–11). See also the "excellent detailed analyses of Leninist and Stalinist institutionalized terror going back to the Revolution" (I35) given in Gregory P. Maximoff, *The Guillotine at Work: Twenty Years of Terror in Russia.* (Data and documents.) Chicago: Alexander Berkman Fund, 1940. 2 vol. (the first volume has been reprinted by Cienfuegos Press, Orkney, Great Britain, in 1979), and also Bertrand Russell's *The Practice and Theory of Bolshevism* (written in 1920), the contemporary report by the Spanish anarchist Angel Pestaña (1886–1937), *Setenta Días en Rusia: Lo que Yo Vi* (1921; 2a ed. Barcelona: Tipografía Cosmos, 1924[?], 226 p.), Emma Goldman's *My Disillusionment in Russia* (1923), and the books by Boris Souvarine (*Stalin: A Critical Survey of Bolshevism*, Alliance Book Corporation, 1939—first published in French in 1935) and F. Beck [pseud.] & W. Golin [pseud.] (*Russian Purge and the Extraction of Confession*. London: Hurst & Blackett, 1951—also Viking, 1951,

minus the "publisher's note" of the British edition), all of which were either unknown to or ignored by both the pro-Communist intellectuals and the anti-Communist intellectuals of the "nouveaux philosophes" variety.

9. *Ideas and Opinions*, Laurel Edition, pp. 185, 174. See also his "Why Socialism? (1949)—the opening article of the *Monthly Review*—which is instructive to compare with the last two chapters of **FRS** (1973). Cf. Uriel Tal, "Jewish and Universal Social Ethics in the Life and Thought of Albert Einstein," in *Albert Einstein: Historical and Cultural Perspectives*. The Centennial Symposium in Jerusalem [March 14–23 1979]. Edited by Gerald Holton & Yehuda Elkana. Princeton UP, 1982.

10. Gerald Sorin, *The Prophetic Minority*. Indiana University Press, 1985. In a recent poll, 50% of Jewish Americans identified a "commitment to social equality" as the most important Jewish quality; however, only 29% (against 50% in the general population according to this particular poll—other polls give up to two thirds) support the establishment of a Palestinian homeland in the occupied territories (reported by Robert Scheer, *Los Angeles Times*, April 12–13 1988). It is not without interest that Jack Newfield (a co-signer with Chomsky, Spock and others of "A Call to Resist Illegitimate Authority," which was at the origin of *RESIST*—see editor's notes to I19 and I21), "prepared" by his mother's "Old Testament morality ... to empathize with the humanist values of the New Radicals" of the 1960s, chose an almost identical title (*A Prophetic Minority*) for his book on the "New Radicalism," which seemed to him, "at bottom, an ethical revolt against the visible devils of racism, poverty, and war, as well as the less tangible devils of centralized decision-making, manipulative, impersonal bureaucracies, and the hypocrisy that divides America's ideals from its actions from Watts to Saigon" (New York: The New American Library, 1966, pp. 22, 24).

11. See M. Buber, *Paths in Utopia*, New York: Macmillan, 1950 (Beacon paperback 1958), first published in Hebrew in 1946, ch. 2. Cf. Israel Shahak, "The Jewish Religion and Its Attitude to Non-Jews," Khamsin 8 & 9 (1891), pp. 27–61 & 3–49, respectively, especially 8, pp. 39–40.

12. Cf. W. J. Fishman, *The Insurrectionists*. London: Methuen, 1970.

13. Richard Drinnon, *Rebel in Paradise: A Biography of Emma Goldman*. The University of Chicago Press, 1961. (Phoenix edition, 1982.) A note at the end of the sentence about Ahad Ha'am refers to the version of his "Priest and Prophet" I quote in the next section. Drinnon continues: "This, of course, is not the first time that it has been suggested that modern radicals owe a great deal to the prophets. While Ernest Renan may have been guilty of oversimplification when he found the forerunners of Saint Simon and other radicals in the prophets, he had his eyes on a valid insight." He also points out that Goldman and the Russian radicals "were drawing on the same tradition."
    The quotes within parentheses are from Rebecca West's Introduction to Emma Goldman, *My Disillusionment in Russia*. Doubleday, 1923. (Apollo edition, 1970). The study on the Jewish religion by Shahak cited above, in particular the fact that "observance of the religious laws of Judaism, as well as their inculcation through education, were enforced on Jews by physical coercion," sheds some light on the origin of Goldman's "generous contempt for rabbis."

14. FRS (1973), p. 378.

15. A very illuminating discussion of this topic, which brings out the decisive contrast between Chomsky's position and a position quite common among Marxists, is found at the end of the "debate" between Chomsky and Foucault on Dutch television in 1971 as transcribed in *Reflexive Water: The Basic Concerns of Mankind*, ed. with a preface by Fons Elders. London: Souvenir Press, 1974, pp. 134–97. See C.P. Otero, "Chomsky vs Foucault: Pursue Justice or Grab Power?" (UCLA ms., 1999), to be included in *Chomsky, The Masters of Mankind*, ed. by Mark Pavlick. Monroe, Maine: Common Courage Press (forthcoming).

16. Cf. J.D. Bernal, *Science in History*, The M.I.T. Press, 1971, 157ff.

17. See Isaiah Berlin, "Einstein and Israel," in his *Personal Impressions* (Penguin, 1982), p. 148, which tacitly provides one more example of the contrast between the prophet and the secular priest (see RP, p. 24). Incidentally, Berlin's observation about Einstein's position appears to raise some questions about his essay on Chaim Weizmann in the same volume, from which the name of Ahad Ha'am is conspicuously absent.

18. Thorstein Veblen, Ahad Ha'am coeval and one of Einstein's favorite authors, shows no awareness of the position of the cultural Zionists in his noted essay, "The Intellectual Pre-Eminence of Jews in Modern Europe," *Political Science Quarterly* 34 (1919), pp. 33–42, reprinted in *The Portable Veblen*.

19. "Priest and prophet," *Contemporary Jewish Record* 8 (1945), pp. 233–40; the translation from the Hebrew is by Leon Simon. Not surprisingly, there is an expression in Hebrew that "connotes the idea of self-sacrifice and readiness to devote one's life to an ideal," namely *mesirut nefesh*, as one would expect, the English equivalents of this and others Hebrew expressions and terms (*nefesh* is generally rendered by 'soul', but it is the property of all living beings) "fail completely to convey even the shade of the meaning of these repositories of Jewish experiences." Neither *nefesh* nor *ruah* (generally rendered as 'spirit')

"have the implications of disembodiment, such as are indicated by their English equivalents"; *ruah* "in the Greek translation connoted the un-Jewish concept of spirit-versus-body" (William Chomsky, pp. 4ff.). Perhaps Cartesian metaphysical dualism makes no sense to a speaker of Hebrew. Cf. **R&R** (1980), ch. 1.

20. Introduction to his *The Prophetic Faith* (New York: Macmillan, 1949 (paper, 1985)).

21. There is some evidence in support of this view. See Shahak's article on the Jewish religion.

22. Quoted in Robert M. Seltzer, *Jewish People, Jewish Thought: The Jewish Experience in History.* New York: Macmillan, 1980, p. 697; see also the following pages, from which I draw in this section. I also draw from several of the essays edited by Kornberg, in particular from his contribution to the volume.

23. Cf. Kornberg (ed.), introductory essay and pp. 128, 194–5.

24. Cf. Niels Bohr's 1922 view of the contrast between the values of the Teutonic knight (and its Prussian incarnation) and those of the most representative heroes in the Scandinavian sagas, as reported in Werner Heisenberg's *Physics and Beyond: Encounters and Conversations,* New York: Harper & Row, 1971, ch. 4 (see also ch. 18). A classic study of the general topic is Rudolf Rocker's *Nationalism and Culture,* from which I quote below.

25. Recall that since 1946 he was planing to go to what was then Palestine, live in a *kibbutz* and work for Arab-Jewish cooperation. He did not do it until the summer of 1953, and then only for a few weeks. Since he was completely unskilled, he did only unskilled agricultural work, which he enjoyed very much. He liked the (very poor) *kibbutz* a great deal in many ways and felt that, abstracting it from context, it was "a functioning and very successful libertarian society" (**ChR** (1987), p. 8). His latest visit to Israel and the occupied territories was in the Spring of 1988, on the occasion of an international conference on his work ("The Chomskyan Turn") at Tel Aviv University (36; cf. his "Scenes from the Uprising," *Z* magazine 1:7–8 (1988), pp. 9–20).

   For "a voluminous record of attempts to lay the basis for Arab-Jewish cooperation in Palestine" (**PME**, 1974, p. 41; cf. p. 88), see Aharon Cohen, *Israel and the Arab World.* New York: Funk & Wagnalls, 1970 (abridged ed., Boston: Beacon Press, 1976), first published in Hebrew in 1964. Born in Russia in 1910, Cohen emigrated to Palestine in 1929. An expert in Arab affairs, he was a member of the Arab Department of the Histadrut and served as secretary of the League for Arab-Jewish Rapprochement and Cooperation between 1941 and 1948. He died in 1980. (*Dissenter in Zion: From the Writings of Judah L. Magnes,* ed. by Arthur A. Goren, Harvard UP, 1982, p. 401).

26. Quoted by Chomsky, from a Hebrew source (see his note 28), in the edited text of a talk he gave at Tel Aviv University, April 13, 1988, titled "The U.S. and the Middle East: Israel's Role in U.S. policy," which is to appear in Israel in Hebrew translation. The reference for the quotation I give next is given in his note 27.

27. See, for example, Israel Shahak, "The 'Historical Right' and the Other Holocaust," *Journal of Palestine Studies* 10:3 (1981), pp. 27–34, and his article on the Jewish religion cited earlier (n. 11).

28. Cf. Harry M. Bracken, "Culture and Jewish Culture," *Canadian Jewish Quarterly* 3:4 (1968), pp. 42–48.

29. See Shahak's article on the Jewish religion, *Khamsin* 9, p. 12.

30. 1978 edition (Michael E. Coughlin, Publisher, 1985 Selby Av, St. Paul, MN 55104), pp. viii, pp. 537, 551. It is a reprint of the second, expanded edition (Los Angeles, 1947), with an important Epilogue by Rocker. The publisher contributed a preface and an additional bibliography. As the translator, Ray E. Chase, points out in his preface (dated March 1937 in Los Angeles), when he went to London, Rocker, who was not Jewish, became interested in the Jews of the East Side (a working class neighborhood), went to live among them, learned their language, participated in their struggles, and from 1898 until the outbreak of the World War he was the editor of the Yiddish *Workers' Friend* and of the monthly journal of social theory and criticism, *Germinal*—as any other distinguished intellectual would do under similar circumstances. See William J. Fishman's *East End Jewish Radicals, 1875–1914.* London: Duckworth, 1975.

31. "Introduction" (written in the Fall of 1974) to *Dissent and Ideology in Israel.* Edited by Morris Blatt, Uri Davis & Paul Kleinbaum. London: Ithaca Press, 1975.

32. The original, 1966 version has been reprinted in *Classics of International Relations,* ed. by J. Vasquez. Prentice-Hall, 1986, pp. 67–76. The definitive version has been reprinted separately and in several collections, and translated to several languages, sometimes more than once (there are at least four Spanish translations).

33. See **AP** (1969), 367ff. A well-known picture in which both Chomsky and Mailer can be seen at the Pentagon Peace March accompanies George Steiner's review of **PKF** in the *New York Times Book Review,* Jan. 9, 1972, p. 23, and Daniel Yergin's "The Chomskyan Revolution," the *New York Times Book Review,* Dec. 3, 1972; a picture by Minoru Aoki, with the caption "Confrontation with the War Makers, Washington, D.C., October 27 [presumably for Oct 21], 1967," appears opposite to the inside title page

in *The Power of the People*, ed. by Robert Cooney & Helen Michaloswki, "cooperatively published" by Peace Press in Culver City, CA, 1977 (reprinted in 1987 by New Society Publishers, Philadelphia).

34. **PKF** (1971), pp. x & 92.

35. See Bertrand Russell, "The Duty of a Philosopher in this Age" (dated August, 1964), in *The Abdication of Philosophy: Philosophy and the Public Good*. Edited by Eugene Freeman. La Salle, Illinois: Open Court, 1976.

36. Eric Fromm, "Prophets and Priests," in *Bertrand Russell: Philosopher of the Century. Essays in His Honor* edited by Ralph Schoenman. London: George Allen & Unwin, 1967.

37. See the Appendix (1986) to Koerner & Tajima. In contrast, "Einstein did not give rise to what you might call a school; he was not the one to generate disciples" (Peter G. Bergmann in *Holton & Elkana*, p. 399).

38. See Robert Sklar, "Chomsky's Revolution in Linguistics," the *Nation*, Sept. 9, 1968, pp. 213–17.

39. First reference of note 1. (The verb "to mace," first used in 1968 (not exactly by sheer chance), means 'to attack with the liquid Mace (a trademark)', "a temporarily disabling liquid that when sprayed in the face of a person ... causes tears, dizziness, immobilization, and sometimes nausea" (*Webster's Collegiate Dictionary*).)

40. Cf. Christopher Hitchens, "The Chorus and Cassandra: What Everyone Knows about Noam Chomsky," *Grand Street* 5:1 (Autumn 1985), pp. 106–31. Included in *Noam Chomsky: Critical Assessments*, ed. by C. P. Otero, London: Routledge, 1964, vol. III, pp. 401–421.

41. **PLF** (1971), p. ix.

42. Shaun Harbord, *A Historian's Appraisal of the Political Writings of Noam Chomsky*. Master of Arts in History thesis, Department of Humanities, University of Kent at Canterbury, November 1987, pp. 130–1.

43. Brian Morton, "Chomsky Then and Now," the *Nation* 246:18 (May 7, 1988), pp. 646–52. Cf. George Scialabba's reply to Michael Albert and Lydia Sargent and their counter reply in *Zeta* magazine 1:7–8 (Jul–Aug 1988), pp. 5–8.

44. Those who can use some comic relief at this point might appreciate the following recent story. A novelist who writes regularly for the *New York Times* and the *Washington Post* was greatly surprised by the reactions his idea of sending them a profile on Chomsky elicited from his usual contacts in those papers. This experience, unimaginable for him before he went through it, apparently stimulated his interest in finding out why The *New York Review* had stopped publishing Chomsky and tried to get the account of the editors. Robert Silvers refused even to answer the phone. Out of curiosity, he phoned Gore Vidal in Italy, asking him to intercede. He did, and Silvers was willing to take his call, but told him he'd have to check with his lawyers before answering. When he called back, Silvers told him that their lawyers had advised them not to say anything. Vidal checked later with Barbara Epstein, who told him that Silvers is constantly bombarded on this topic and is entirely paranoid about it.

45. His article "The Iranian-American Conflict" (Nov. 16, 1979) was commissioned by the *Los Angeles Times* (see **RP** (1981/1984/2003), ch. 5), and so was the article on the PLO that they published on July 25, 1982—this was not the last time he was asked to contribute; only the last time he found the time to do it. It could be argued that the Los Angeles daily is not a national newspaper, and that in the 60s, or when the 60s were barely over, he once shared a page of the *New York Times* ("The crisis managers," June 25, 1971, p. 35) with Barry Goldwater, but no one would claim that this exceptionally broad spectrum was typical of the *Times* even in the 60s.

46. See Chomsky's review-article on the work and "fortune" of Reinhold Niebuhr ("the official establishment theologian" from World War II through the Kennedy years) in *Grand Street* 6:2 (Winter 1987), pp. 197–212; see also his most recent book, *Necessary illusions*.

47. *Lectures on Government and Binding* (1981), soon to be supplemented by *Concepts and Consequences of the Theory of Government and Binding* (1982), followed by *Knowledge of Language: Its Nature, Origin and Use* (1984, published in 1986) and *Barriers* (1986), any of which would be enough to secure a different author a distinct place in the history of linguistics, as would his more recent technical studies of human language as a mental organ, in particular *The Minimalist Program*, Cambridge MIT Press, 1995, and subsequent technical papers.

48. See Kathleen Hendrix, "The Unbridled Linguist: Political Activist Professor Noam Chomsky Never Claimed to be a Diplomat," *Los Angeles Times*, Feb. 1, 1988, Part V (View), pp. 1 & 2, a searching article-interview, illustrated by a large picture, which includes information about several events of the week, in particular the reaction of some rich liberals from the local elite to his remarks in a gathering originally scheduled to raise funds for Central American activism. At one point the namesake of a Los Angeles company yelled out that he'd bet $100 that one of Chomsky's claims would turn out to be "a lie," and immediately actor Ed Asner called out that he would take that bet. But interestingly, after Chomsky sent him, at his request, photocopies of the 85 articles at issue, he did not bother to review the material ("Not

being a historian, I am bored by re-reading old op-ed pieces," he wrote). As one of the host's daughters, "a supporter of the Task Force and a grass-roots organizer on peace and justice issues," is quoted as having said to Hendrix, "it was as if they had been told there was no Santa Claus." A reader from Woodland Hills (Bill Becker) who commented on Hendrix's "fine article … on Noam Chomsky and the intellectual and moral integrity he brings to the discussion of U.S. policy," had a similar intuition (*Times*, March 2, 1988): "We need more people like Chomsky who are not afraid to learn about the wider world and do not hide from the unpleasant truths about the United States that they find there." (In the interview Chomsky was quoted as saying that some people in the gathering were "naive, with no concept of what goes on in the world and their role in it" and "very insulated from reality": "Talk to a group of welfare mothers and they know much more about the world than someone living in a stockade in Beverly Hills.")

49. **PME**, 1974, pp. 25 & 178.

50. See **RL**, 1975, p. 126ff.; for more extended discussion, see Harry Bracken, *Mind and Language: Essays on Descartes and Chomsky*. Dordrecht: Foris, 1983.

51. **L&R** (1979), p. 90.

52. See "Creativeness vs Receptiveness" in my introduction to **RP** (1981/1984/2003); cf. the opening pages of *Language and Mind*, first presented as a Beckman lecture at the University of California at Berkeley in January 1967, and the introduction (completed in 1973) to the published version of his *Logical Structure of Linguistic Theory*, pp. 39–40.

53. For two early, non-technical presentations, see John Searle, "Chomsky's Revolution in Linguistics," the *New York Review of Books* 18:12 (June 29, 1972), pp. 16–24 (reprinted in *On Noam Chomsky: Critical Essays*, edited by Gilbert Harman, New York: Doubleday, 1974—part of the series Modern Studies in Philosophy—published in 1982, with a new introduction by Harman, by The University of Massachusetts Press), and Daniel Yergin, "The Chomskyan Revolution," the *New York Times Magazine*, Dec. 3, 1972, pp. 42–3 & 112,…,127.

54. Howard Gardner, *The Mind's New Science: A History of the Cognitive Revolution*. With a new Epilogue by the author: "Cognitive Science after 1984." New York: Basic Books, 1987 (first published in 1985), p. 28. The correct title of Chomsky's paper is "Three Models for the Description of Language."

55. **LPK** (1987), pp. 185–6.

56. *Language and Interpretation in Psychoanalysis*. Yale UP, 1975, 2ff. In contrast, Lacan does not remind him at all in style or method of Freud: "Lacan's philosophizing and his linguistics are probably wrong for psychoanalysis," Edelson goes on to say. "The titles themselves, contrasted with some of Chomsky's, hint at the difference between these two"; cf. notes to I18. Needless to say, observations of this character do not have much appeal for readers of trendy "critical theory." Three recent exceptions are *Critical Theory Since 1965*, edited by Hazard Adams & Leroy Searle (University Presses of Florida, 1986), which includes a selection from Chomsky's *Aspects of the Theory of Syntax* and some discussion of its ideas; Jim Merod's *The Political Responsibility of the Critic* (Cornell UP, 1987), where other ideas of Chomsky are given some of the attention they deserve; and *The Linguistics of Writing: Arguments Between Language and Literature*, edited by Nigel Fabb, Derek Attridge, Alan Durant & Colin MacCabe (Methuen, 1988), where Chomsky is (in a way) present from page 1. Cf. notes to I4.

57. This is not to deny that it makes sense to speak of the Freudian revolution referring to his investigation of self-serving beliefs that made humans all over the world more aware of some aspects of their behavior and the behaviors of others, which Chomsky had assimilated by the time he was 18, as mentioned above, and which are easily detectable in his writings (from the first pages of *American Power and the New Mandarins* to some the interviews in this collection, e.g. I46.)

58. *New Introductory Lectures on Psycho-Analysis* (1932), lecture 35. He goes on to say that "Sociology, which deals with the behavior of man in society, can be nothing other than applied psychology." In Chomskyan terms cultural anthropology (including social anthropology and sociology) deals, or should deal, with the study of the use of human cognition (the use of human cognitive structures, e.g. the use of the language faculty in its mature state, as when humans use language). I return to the topic in last section.

59. The term "nonnatural sciences" is meant to include both Heinrich Rickert's "cultural sciences" (Kulturwissenschaften), a conception which greatly influenced Max Weber, Carl Jung and Ernst Cassirer, and Wilhelm Dilthey's "sciences of the spirit" (Geisteswissenschaften), since both notions assumed the bifurcation natural/nonnatural science. Cf. R&R (1980), pp. 16ff.

60. See **R&R** (1980), p. 242, and also chapter 1. In two letters of early 1984, he wrote: "If I am interested in learning about people, I'll read novels rather than psychology" (Jan. 4); "I think the Victorian novel tells us more about people than science ever will" (April 8)—see Marcus G. Raskin & H.J. Bernstein, *New Ways of Knowing*. Lanham, MD: Rowman & Littlefield, 1987, pp. 130 & 150, respectively. In the Managua lectures (**LPK** (1987), p. 159) he writes that it is overwhelmingly probable that "we will always learn more about human life and human personality from novels than from scientific psychology." He

himself seems to have learned a great deal reading novels, in particular those of Mendele Mocher Sfarim (ChR (1987), p. 12).

61. Justin Leiber, *Noam Chomsky: A Philosophical Overview*. New York: St. Martin's Press, 1975, p. 23; cf. F. Cioffi, "Freud and the Idea of a Pseudo-Science," in R. Borger & F. Cioffi (eds.), *Explanation in the Behavioural Sciences*. Cambridge UP, 1970, and John C. Marshall, "Freud's Psychology of Language," in R. Wollheim (ed.), *Freud: A Collection of Critical Essays*, New York, Anchor Books, 1974, pp. 348–365. For Leiber, it is not Freud's work but rather Einstein's scientific revolution that is to be compared with Chomsky's, and he discusses seven points about Einstein's work that he considers relevant for the comparison. Cf. R.I.V. Hodge, "Freud, Chomsky and Depth Analysis," *UEA Papers in Linguistics* 1 (1976), pp. 46–64.

62. "Language and Unconscious Knowledge" (1976), reprinted in **R&R** (1980), where the quote is on p. 253. (Cf. "We ask whether the two theories are too-concrete realizations of the same system of principles that should be formulated at this more abstract level—more or less in the way that rotations of a plane figure and addition of integers are two realizations of the principles of group theory." KL (1984), 4.2, p. 255.) It might also be possible that work in several domains, some of it consciously related to ideas on the structure of human language (an outstanding example is Fred Lerdahl & Ray Jackendoff's *A General Theory of Tonal Music*, MIT Press, 1983) might fall within a general theory of symbolic function, a discipline which, Chomsky believes, "may not lie very far beyond the horizons of current inquiry."

63. See Chomsky's "Psychology and Ideology," reprinted in **FRS** (1973) as chapter 7, which includes his second major critique of Skinner's hypotheses. The first one appeared in *Language*, the journal of the Linguistic Society of America, in 1959, shortly after Chomsky's 30th birthday, contributing to spread his growing reputation well beyond the fields of linguistics and psychology. It has been reprinted as a separate item as well as in several collections, once with an interesting introductory note by Chomsky (in *Readings in the Psychology of Language*, ed. by Leon A. Jakobovits & Murray Miron, Prentice-Hall, 1967). See the second section of my introduction to *Chomsky On Democracy and Education*, esp. n. 7.

64. The example, due to Chomsky, is given in I26 and also found in the last chapter of "Nature and Nurture," part IV of Phil Donahue's *The Human Animal: Who Are We? How Do We Behave the Way We Do? Can We Change?* New York: Simon and Schuster, 1985, p. 319. The quote I give next appears on page 320.

65. R&R (1980), I, p. 44. "Similarly," he goes on to say (n. 62), there may be some principles of growth and development that are common across a considerable range, perhaps for reasons that lie ultimately in physics. The classic work of D'Arcy Thompson comes to mind." This is why it is wrong to suggest, as he does in I34 (see also I11), that "the only level at which such principles can be formulated is cellular biology, where it all falls together. But the organs become what they do become because of genetic instructions that give them particular directions and because of the way in which that intrinsic structure relates to the environmental context."
For an informative overview of some of the relevant research both in biology and in the cognitive sciences, and arguments in support of the conclusion that "contrary to received wisdom, there is no known process, either in biology or in cognition, that literally amounts to learning" (contrary to environmentalist assumptions), see Massimo Piattelli-Palmarini's "Evolution, Selection and Cognition: From 'Learning' to Parameter-Fixation in Biology and in the Study of Mind," MIT, Center for Cognitive Science, 1987, Occasional Paper #35. (A shortened version appeared in *Cognition* 31 (1989), pp. 1–44.)

66. The point is made by Jacques Monod on page 24 of his book *Chance and Necessity: An essay on the Natural Philosophy of Modern Biology* (New York: Alfred A. Knopf, 1971), which grew out of a series of lectures he gave in February of 1969 in California (at Pomona College).

67. See my contribution (originally titled "Human Nature: From Medieval Scholasticism to Chomskyan Rationalism") to the "round table" "The Concept of Human Nature in Chomsky," *Quaderni di Semantica* 2 (1981), pp. 235–80. Reprinted in part in *Noam Chomsky: Critical Assessments*, ed. by C.P. Otero. London: Routledge, 1994, vol. 3, pp. 283–90; see also pp. 294–307.

68. There is no space here to develop the topic and give a critical appraisal of recent books such as Charles Woolfson, *The Labour Theory of Culture: A Re-Examination of Engels's Theory of Human Origins*. London: Routledge & Kegan Paul, 1982, which takes as its "base-line" the "brief, unfinished essay by Engels" on "the transition from ape to man" which was found among his papers after his death, and goes on to argue that the qualitative difference that separates the highest ape from the (creative) human animal was brought about by the introduction of social labor. Woolfson is of the opinion that "little sustained attention has been paid by Western Marxists to evolutionary theory," and he attempts to redress the balance by looking for an answer in "recent findings in archaeology, linguistics and paleontology" that "have raised important questions about the role of labour in human cultural development." Compare Chomsky's view, as expressed in the fall of 1977: "At a certain level of complexity many of the human brain's most striking capacities may have to do with the laws of physics. They may relate to the density

and packing of neurons in the brain, for example. Perhaps there is only one way of physically solving such a packaging problem, and that in turn may lead to certain consequences like speech or the ability to deal with numbers" (quoted on page 326 of Richard M. Restak's *The Brain: The Last Frontier. An Exploration of the Human Brain and Our Future.* Garden City, NY: Doubleday, 1979); see now **LPK** (1987), pp. 166–70 & pp. 183–5 (cf. **FRS**, 1973, p. 396, or **ChR** (1987), p. 147, from "Language and freedom," written in 1970).

Another interesting example is *Cultural Materialism: The Struggle for a Science of Culture* (New York: Vintage, 1979) by Marvin Harris, who suggests that Chomsky's influential critique of B. F. Skinner's *Verbal Behavior* "was instrumental in encouraging cultural idealists to get inside people's heads as a respectable form of scientific activity" (p. 282—see also p. 15), an insight which can be used as a yardstick to measure the level of Harris's "cultural materialism."

Also interesting (multiply so in fact) is *Cultural Analysis: The Work of Peter L. Berger, Mary Douglas, Michel Foucault and Jürgen Habermas*, edited by Robert Wuthnow, J. D. Hunter, A. Bergesen & E. Kurzweil. Boston, London, Melbourne and Henley: Routledge & Kegan Paul, 1984 (reprinted in 1985).

69. On the basis of anatomical evidence, chimps and gorillas would seem to be each other's closest relatives, but a study of their genes (in particular, the nucleotide sequence of the same stretch of DNA from an individual of each of the three species) suggests that chimps are actually closer to human beings than they are to gorillas, so chimps and human beings may be indeed each other's nearest living relatives. It also seems clear that the common chimp-human stem existed only briefly—perhaps from half a million to a million years between 5 and 10 million years ago. One of the implications of these findings is that the early human ancestors may have been knucklewalkers, as the gorilla and the chimp still are. This conclusion raises questions about evolutionary studies based on anatomical form since little in modern human anatomy or in the hominid fossil record suggests knucklewalking (*Scientific American*, March 1988, p. 18).

70. **FRS** (1973), p. 394; **ChR** (1987), p. 145.

71. "Toward a Humanistic Conception of Education" (*Work, Technology, and Education: Dissenting Essays in the Intellectual Foundations of American Education.* Edited by Walter Feinberg & Henry Rosemont, Jr. University of Illinois Press, 1976), based on a talk he gave at the University of Illinois on April 1, 1971. Reprinted in **CD&E** as ch. 9.

72. **LPK** (1987), pp. 153–4.

73. Steve Wasserman, *Los Angeles Times* (The Book Review), Aug. 30, 1987. The phrases quoted by Wasserman appear on pp. 121–2 of **ChR** (1987).

74. I may perhaps be forgiven for being somewhat anachronistic. The law which abolished the use of the word "conquest" and substituted "pacification" was not promulgated until 1573.

75. *Tratados de Fray Bartolomé de las Casas.* México: Fondo de Cultura Económica, 1965 (actually, 1966), p. 21. A recent English translation is *Bartolomé de las Casas, The Devastation of the Indies; A Brief Account.* Translated from the Spanish by Herma Briffault. Introd. by Hans Magnus Enzensberger, with a dossier by Michel van Nieuwstadt. New York, Seabury Press, 1974. Cf. T. Todorov, *The Conquest of America*, New York: Harper & Row, 1983), esp. pp. 5 and 150.

76. Lewis Hanke, *All Mankind is One: A Study of the Disputation between Bartolomé de Las Casas and Juan Ginés de Sepúlveda in 1550 on the Intellectual and Religious Capacity of the American Indians*, Northern Illinois UP, 1974 (completed on the eve of the 500th anniversary of the birth of Las Casas), p. xiii. On the "echoes of the controversy," see pp. 113ff.; "one of the most virulent attacks" was delivered in 1963 by the oldest and most distinguished Hispanist of his time," who called Las Casas, in addition to "paranoic," "a medieval canonist," "backward," "backward Dominican," "feeble intelligence," "childishly vainglorious," "as blind to reality as a delirious person obsessed with chimerical projects," "a sower of confusions," given to "excessive moral tone," "pathological tendency," "pathological certainty," "feverish delirium," "delirium of grandeur," "insatiable egotism," "infantile blustering," "hot-headed inflexibility," "impulsive misrepresentation of the facts," "mania for argumentation," and so on and on (see pp. 140–1 for a fuller list, and pp. 150–1 for the Spanish terms).

77. Lewis Hanke, *Aristotle and the American Indians: A Study in Race Prejudice in the Modern World.* London: Hollis & Carter, 1959, introduction (written in Austin, Texas, in November 1957). A very close variation on the theme appears on p. xi of the author's "last publication" on the topic referred to in the previous note, p. xi.

78. A very knowledgeable student of his life and work, Manuel Giménez Fernández, wondered whether his father, Pedro de Las Casas, was related to Jewish families in the area with the name Las Casas.

79. Las Casas, *In Defense of the Indians … Against the Persecutors and Slanderers of the Peoples of the New World Discovered across the Seas.* Translated, edited and annotated by Stafford Poole, C.M. Northern Illinois UP, 1974, pp. 11–12. The quotes are from the "summary of [Juan Ginés de] Sepúlveda's position."

80. This is not his most convincing evidence. According to one eyewitness account of the revolting actions of the soldiers during the infamous assault, the Spaniards "even surpassed the Germans" "in cruelty and perfidy." The reference is given in Hanke 1959, p. 137, n. 5.

81. Hanke 1959, pp. 17, 44ff., 52, 59.

82. Hanke, "The Significance of Bartolomé de las Casas Today" (dated May 27, 1965), one of the introductions to the 4th centennial edition of the *Tratados* quoted above (n. 75).

83. Hanke, p. 13. The parenthetical remark is essentially taken from one of Chomsky's most important technical papers, "Conditions on Transformations" (1970), a milestone in the recent history of linguistics (see **EFI** (1976), p. 126).

84. A dozen years after Jefferson's death (22 years before the outbreak of the Civil War) Frances Anne Kemble, the famous English actress, born in 1809 (the same year Darwin and Lincoln were born), could still paint "a picture so brutal in its realism that was unacceptable to Victorian society" (*Journal of a Residence on a Georgian Plantation in 1838–1839*. Edited, with an Introduction, by John A. Scott. New American Library, 1961). The quote is from Scott's introduction, who points out that Kemble's account of life among the slaves and slaveholders "stands in sharp contrast to the contemporary work of Harriet Beecher Stowe," *Uncle Tom's Cabin*, which has never, since its first publication in 1852, "been out of print nor lost its hold upon the public's attention." (I am indebted to Kathleen Hendrix for bringing Kemble's book to my attention.)

85. Hanke 1959, p. 9; see in particular the reference he gives in his note 32. Sadly to say, not even Las Casas fought as hard or as steadily against black slavery as he did against the oppression of the Indians.

86. **FRS** (1973), p. 371; pp. 403–4 (**ChR** (1987), pp. 153–4).

87. **TNCW** (1982), p. 93.

88. **TNCW**, p. 9. Cf., e.g., **AP** (1969), p. 17; **PKF** (1971), p. 101; **TT** (1985), p. 1. These and other passages bring to mind the impact of his radical uncle (section one).

89. **TT** (1985), p. 249.

90. For a brief outline, with some testimonies by his students, see the appendix to Koerner & Tajima's bibliography. A major collection of articles on his work, including some outstanding ones, is *Noam Chomsky: Consensus and Controversy*. Edited by Sohan Modgil & Celia Modgil. New York: The Falmer Press, 1987. A more comprehensive one is *Noam Chomsky: Critical Assessments*, edited by C. P. Otero, London: Routledge, 1994 (8 tomes).

91. See **LSLT** (1955/1957), p. 51 n. 46 of printed version. The core of his father's work was an edition of David Kimhi's Hebrew grammar (see reference below), a sort of summation that marks the closing period of the "Golden Age of Hebrew grammar," a basic strand of the so-called Golden Age of Jewish cultural creativity, which lasted about three centuries (10th to 13th—Kimhi lived about 1160–1235), during the Spanish period (see W. Chomsky 1957/1986, 113f., 172ff.; cf. Shahak, 9, p. 10), when "Hebrew grammar seems to have been the pivotal and all-absorbing scholarly interest among Jewish intellectuals of all walks of life." Then came "the wane of grammatical research and of any studies outside of the Talmud" and most of the Jewish scholars of the subsequent generations "regarded the study of grammar as a waste of time, and some even considered such study heresy." Interestingly, the rise of the Karaite sect, toward the end of the 8th century—see the second section of my Introduction—which "rejected rabbinic tradition as expressed in the Talmud and emphasized the diligent scrutiny of the Bible as the basis for its tradition," had been "a significant factor in focusing the attention of the Hebrew scholars on a more searching study of the language of the Bible":

> The knowledge of Hebrew grammar, consequently, became a vital need at that time. Grammatical accuracy served as a criterion for the recognition of the merits of literary and religious compositions, and grammatical knowledge constituted the measure of Jewish learning and scholarship. Interest in Hebrew grammar was, therefore, not confined to professional grammarians, but gained vogue among statesmen, poets and philosophers. Samuel ha-Nagid, Juda ha-Levi, Ibn Gabirol and others, all concerned themselves with Hebrew grammatical problems to a greater or lesser degree and wrote about them more or less extensively.

> See "Introduction: David Kimhi and the Age of Hebrew Grammar" (especially pp. viii & xiv) in *David Kimhi's Hebrew Grammar* (Mikhlol), systematically presented and critically annotated by William Chomsky, M.A., Ph.D. Published for the Dropsie College for Hebrew and Cognate Learning by Bloch Publishing Co, New York, 1952–5713 (long in preparation—the original Dropsie College Ph.D. thesis was completed in 1933).

92. "Harris was also a very acute left libertarian thinker. Though he wrote nothing, his thinking in these areas had a great impact on many young people, me among them" (Chomsky, p. c., August 1988). This is a recurrent theme: "I intended to drop out of college and to pursue these interests. The vague ideas I had at the time were to go to Palestine, perhaps to a *kibbutz*, to try to become involved in efforts at Arab-

Jewish cooperation within the socialist framework, opposed to the deeply anti-democratic concept of a Jewish state (a position that was considered well within the mainstream of Zionism). Through these interests, I happened to meet Zellig Harris, a really extraordinary person who had a great influence on many young people in those days. He had a coherent understanding of this whole range of issues, which I lacked, and I was immensely attracted by it, and by him personally as well, also by others who I met through him. He happened to be one of the leading figures in modern linguistics, teaching at the University of Pennsylvania. His interests were very broad, linguistics being only a small corner of them, and he was a person of unusual brilliance and originality. I began to take his graduate courses ..." (**ChR** (1987), p. 7); "I met Harris and found that his political insights and understanding were extremely impressive and broad-ranging, very much in the range which I was trying to explore myself. That was the initial contact, and through that contact, I began taking some of his courses. The first thing I did, before I had taken any linguistics at all, was to proofread his book *Methods in Structural Linguistics*, which must have appeared in 1950." (*The Pennsylvania Gazette* 79:1 (Oct 1980), p. 24—see Bibliographical Note). The last line of the Preface (dated Jan 1947) to the first edition (1951) of *Structural Linguistics* (the title was later shortened under the impact of Chomsky's work) reads: "N. Chomsky has given much-needed assistance with the manuscript." In an article published in *Language* in 1957, Harris refers to what he owes to his many conversations with Chomsky, "in addition to being a great pleasure in themselves."

93. *An Introduction to Mathematics*, Oxford UP, 1948 (first published in 1911), p. 101.

94. As late as August 1984, that is, almost a year after the publication of *The Fateful Triangle*, the Center for Near Eastern and North African Studies at the University of Michigan in Ann Arbor revoked its offer to sponsor a lecture by Chomsky on U.S. policy in the Middle East, and the departments of history and political science declined to sponsor Chomsky's lecture (in contrast with the Department of Ethics and Religion, and the Program in American Culture, which was the event's primary sponsor). The reason given by the director of the Center was the concern about "Chomsky's credentials in the Middle Eastern field" (*Michigan Daily*, Oct. 20,1984, p. 1). As is often the case, the person "who worked hard to make Chomsky's visit possible" and thus contribute to the education of "a capacity crowd of over 1000 students" (he regularly attracts large crowds, some much larger than this), was not a professor of political science or history, but rather a professor of English, Alan Wald.

95. In one of these cases there is some written testimony—a letter addressed to Michael C. Ehelers, Cultural Events Bd., University of Colorado Student Union, dated in Washington, June 12, 1987:

Dear Mr. Ehlers:

Thank you for your invitation and your kind words. Unfortunately, however, I must decline.

It is a little early to be scheduling appearances for January, and, in any case, while I enjoy debating serious opponents, I do not regard Noam Chomsky as an authority in the field of Latin American affairs. Given the variety of capable and respected critics of U.S. policy in Central America available for debates like this, I really think it is unnecessary for students to be pandered to with someone like Chomsky.

I hope you will forgive my unsolicited advice, and, once again, thank you for your invitation.

Sincerely, /s/ Elliot Abrams

The letterhead reads: United States Department of State, Assistant Secretary of State for Inter-American Affairs. Cf. the letter Abrams wrote to the Director of *Index on Censorship* on July 29, 1986, reprinted in *Middle East Report* 143 (Nov–Dec 1986), p. 27, and the note by the Editors; see Chomsky's comments in "The US and the Middle East," *Journal of Palestinian Studies* 16:3 (Spring 1987), pp. 25–42—based on his AAUG convention Keynote Address of Nov. 15, 1986.

96. The point of departure for this introduction is a brief article, "Chomsky y la Lucha por la Justicia," which appeared in a monographic issue on Chomsky of the Basque weekly *Punto y Hora*, December 1987. (I am grateful to Eva Forest for her suggestion, her interest and her contagious optimism of the will.) That article in turn derives in part from a newspaper article I wrote at the request of the Madrid daily *El País*, where it appeared on April 29, 1986, on the occasion of the first Madrid symposium on Chomsky's work (it is reprinted almost in full in the same monographic issue of the weekly). I have also drawn freely from other work of mine, in particular *La Revolución de Chomsky: Ciencia y Sociedad*. Madrid: Tecnos, 1984; "Nature Humaine et Organisation Sociale: De Humboldt à Chomsky," *L'Arc* pp. 91–92 (1984), pp. 21–30; and *Chomsky's Revolution: Cognitivism and Anarchism*. Oxford: Basil Blackwell (to appear).

Editor's Notes to Interview 1

Delta ["A review of arts life and thought in the Netherlands" published in Amsterdam] 11:3 (Fall 1968), pp. 5–23; it had first appeared in Dutch translation ("On Gesprek met Chomsky," De Gids 131 (1968), pp. 6–18). The interviewer is J. F. Staal, a well-known Dutch philosopher, logician, linguist, and Sanskrit scholar who is two years younger than Chomsky. During the 1967–68 academic year he worked with Chomsky at MIT (the interview took place on April 11, 1968); soon afterwards, he joined the faculty of the University of California (Berkeley campus). Staal made no attempt "to convert the style of the spoken word into that of written language." He appended the following note to the word "commitment" referred to in the answer to the last question: "See on this point Huibert Drion's article 'Intellectuals and Democracy' in the Summer 1968 issue of *Delta*."

The term "prophet" is obviously not being used in the sense of the Introduction (see in particular the quote from Martin Buber given there).

On the actual "negotiated settlement," almost five years later, see chapter 3 of **TNCW**, based on a talk delivered on January 25, 1973, the day in which the text of the January 24 treaty and the White House interpretation of it appeared in the press. For more on the NLF (National Liberation Front), see **TNCW**, pp. 28–9, and references cited there. The careful reader will not fail to see that Chomsky's view of the Indochina war differs from the views of other critics (in particular, from the view presented in Gabriel Kolko's massive *Anatomy of a War: Vietnam, the United States, and the Modern Historical Experience*, Pantheon, 1985) in fundamental respects—as it does in depth of explanation.

On formalization and on the relationship between formal logic and the logic of natural languages, see Chomsky, "On Certain Formal Properties of Grammar," *Information and Control* 2 (June 1959): pp. 137–67 (reprinted in *Readings in Mathematical Psychology* 2, edited by Luce, Bush, Galanter. New York, Wiley and Sons, 1965, pp. 125–55) and "Formal Properties of Grammars," *Handbook of Mathematical Psychology* 2, edited by Luce, Bush, Galanter, pp. 323–418. New York: Wiley and Sons, 1963.; "The Formal Nature of Language," in *Biological Foundations of Language*, edited by E.H. Lenneberg. New York: Wiley and Sons, 1967, pp. 397–442 (German version, "Die formale Natur der Sprache," in *Psychobiologie*, edited by K. Scherer, S. Stahnke, and P. Winkler. Munich: Deutscher Taschenbuch Verlag, 1987, pp. 345–56); **LGB**, p. 335ff.; and "On Formalization and Formal Linguistics," *Natural Language and Linguistics Theory* 8 (February 1990): pp. 143–47. See also C. P. Otero, "Language, Meaning and Interpretation: Chomsky Against the Philosophers," in *Semantics: Critical Concepts*, ed. by J. G. Rexach. London: Routledge, 2003.

On the form of society, see also I19; on philosophy, I44 and I45.

1. The Intellectual as Prophet (11 April 1968)

I should like to ask you some general questions, starting in the realm of politics and moving on into problems of scientific or scholarly interest. I am not going to ask you much about Vietnam. But I am going to ask you to play the prophet. What do you think might happen after Vietnam? Is the United States going to enter into similar adventures? What will be its future role in the world?

It is still very premature to think in **post-Vietnam** terms because I suspect we still have a substantial way to go before that problem is out of the way. I think what happens next depends very heavily on how the Vietnam situation is resolved. My guess is that the only resolution of the problem of Vietnam will be something which will certainly be a defeat for the policy that has been followed in the United States for the last, well almost 20 years now, and I don't think it will be possible to disguise the defeat. That is, what I presume will happen—unless we move into a Third World War or something of that sort—is that the United States will simply have to withdraw all of its troops and all of its bases and permit a solution based on domestic political forces, which would mean no doubt that the National Liberation Front would take over and that reunification may very well follow fairly shortly.

But how is one going to do that without losing face and in a graceful way?

I think it will be disguised as a negotiated settlement or it may even be disguised as a victory or carried out under international auspices; but I think the substance will nevertheless be something like what I just described and I imagine that that fact will have enormous domestic repercussions. When the realization dawns, there is going to be a real conflict between the chauvinist repressive reaction and the newly organized and still rather weak semi-radical groupings. I think that there will be a wave of repression, and it will be extremely important to see how people can respond to it and react to it and whether they can overcome it. If they can't, then I imagine we'll move into a form of society that may be called "liberal" but will, in reality, be very restrictive and extremely repressive and will continue with the kinds of international policies that led to Vietnam and that are almost certain to lead us into similar situations elsewhere—one doesn't know where—maybe Greece, maybe somewhere in Latin America, maybe Thailand or the Philippines. And I don't think that the American people are ready to face another Vietnam without something like a national mobilization, which would mean probably a sharp restriction on freedom. It's hard to know how it will be presented.

So you don't foresee that as a reaction to this, some kind of isolationism might develop?

There might be a short-range tendency to keep from intervening with military force but I don't believe it can last very long because the fundamental assumptions of policy that led to Vietnam still remain, and if there is a serious revolutionary outbreak in one or another place—let's say in Greece or somewhere in Latin America, perhaps Guatemala, or in a place like Thailand—I think the United States would be drawn in, following the same assumptions, if a similar situation arose. After all we have already something like forty thousand troops in Thailand; apparently the American Air Force is involved directly in bombing raids in Guatemala, not to speak of American advisers and so on. And in the case of Greece I should suspect something similar would happen.

And that those assumptions would change you consider unlikely?

It is not out of the question. I think the prospects might be even slightly hopeful; but it could only follow a very serious internal conflict in the United States. Maybe it will just be a conflict of ideas—I hope so. Maybe more than that will be necessary before we begin to adopt a very different attitude towards international affairs. As long as the premises are that we have to contain revolution, maintain the status quo, maintain stability in every country where we have the military force to do so—as long as that assumption dominates policy, then it seems to me we are bound to get into similar situations elsewhere. Now the fact of the matter is that so far, at least, in the political arena there is nobody who challenges this premise in any serious way.

There is something you didn't mention while talking about external "stability": Internal stability is decreasing very rapidly —how will that interfere with things?

That's what I had in mind when I said there would be some kind of internal conflict in the United States. Partly it will be based on the race and poverty issue and partly it may be based on the pretty strong anti-imperialist tendencies on the part of students, especially at the better universities. And maybe these two forces will combine. It is hard to know. Now I don't know what the outcome of that might be. If the forces that have dominated American society since the Second World War succeed in maintaining the same framework of thinking and of action, if the Cold War liberal ideology, in other words, continues to dominate, as it now does in the political areas, I think there will be some form of repression. I think it's not out of the question that we may find lots of students in jail; we may find that the centers of the cities are turned into black ghettos which are blocked off by force, really, by troops, and that urban civilization, such as it is, will exist in a periphery around the cities. We may find that the businesses and restaurants and theaters and shopping centers and so on move out to the periphery of the city, while the center slowly becomes poor and black. I think that is one possible direction and I assume that any such restructuring of urban society would be accompanied by maybe some subtle forms of repression among the socioeconomic elite, students and so on. I wouldn't say this is necessary or even likely, but it seems to be at least possible.

You mention poor and black several times together. Is one of those the basic factor? I have a feeling as a foreign observer that the racial problem is the basic problem, not the poverty problem.

The poverty problem in the urban East at least largely involves the Negro community. In certain other parts of the country that is less true. Appalachia has a terrific problem, the Mexicans have a very serious problem in the Southwest and of course there is the possibility that unskilled labor in general hasn't got a very bright future in a technological society. And that means that parts of the population that are prevented from entering the educated segment of society may find themselves displaced really, having no function. Of course one of the most unfortunate things that is happening in the country is that there is enormous tension between the white working classes and the black community. In fact, probably the unions are as racist as any group in the society, which is quite understandable, because they are the ones whose place in the society is directly threatened by an influx of unskilled labor in a new immigration, which is really what the black community amounts to—a kind of an internal immigration. As you can see in places like Milwaukee, for example, the hostility to open housing seems to be very largely based in working-class communities, many of them immigrant communities. Whether that can be broken down and these forces can work together is another question. There doesn't seem to be much sign of it today.

Will American intellectuals leave the country? You mentioned this possibility. In the past you have almost advocated it. What do you feel about it now?

The only group that is likely to leave in detectable numbers is students subject to the draft. It is conceivable that there might be thousands of students who don't want to fight in Vietnam or a similar war. But unless there is a very serious domestic repression of a sort that doesn't seem to be imminent, I would doubt that there would be an emigration of intellectuals except to avoid the very pressing problem of military service. At least there are no signs of it. I am not sure; I would imagine that many of these students who do get involved in resistance would choose jail rather than exile. It depends to what extent they can keep their own resistance communities together. If they know that there is a community that they can move back into and a political function they can fulfill when they get out of jail, then there is an incentive to remain in the country, and, perhaps, become a full-time radical activist. A lot of kids are thinking in these terms. But whether it is realistic or not is very hard to judge.

There seem to be various reasons for resistance. So if Vietnam would hopefully be brought to some kind of solution, the unity of the resistance might also be affected?

Yes, I think the resistance will be very isolated and also its strength will be diminished enormously if the particular problem of Vietnam is solved, or at least becomes quiescent. However, as I said, I think that the general international situation is so unstable that I can't imagine this period of quiescence remaining for very long. What happened in Vietnam is that we weren't able to keep the lid on rebellion. Now there is incipient rebellion in many other countries, and it is very likely that we won't be able to keep the lid on at least somewhere. On the other hand, if we do manage to control the Latin American situation, where small applications of military force have been sufficient to maintain the American-oriented elite in power—if that continues to be the case, then it's possible that the general population will sink back into its former apathy.

Is there any chance that what is now called resistance might concentrate mainly on the racial problem?

It's very hard. The people who are involved in resistance are trying to relate their efforts to black liberation, as it is called, but it is not an easy thing to do. For one thing contacts between the white and black communities are very restricted. The resistance work would have to be mostly internal to white society and there is only a limited number of concrete modes of action that can be carried out in white society on the issue of racism. For example, it is possible to try to put pressure on the government and on the various institutions to allocate resources to the black community. It is possible to put pressure on the city administration to keep the police out of the black communities. And maybe there'll come a time when people will actually try physically to prevent police or troops from entering. But these are not day-to-day, ongoing activities.

What about, for instance, talking to Southern whites?

The real problem by now is Northern cities. I am no great expert on this, but as everybody knows a substantial part of the Negro population in the South is essentially being driven off the land with mechanized agriculture and is falling into the classical pattern of dispossessed agricultural workers moving into the urban centers. Very largely that means immigration to the North. And that's where the real heart of the problem is probably going to remain.

We have been talking about the future of the United States in the world and a rather grim picture has emerged from that. What do you think the future role of the United States in the world ought to be?

I think that first of all we should immediately remove any military force from every country. I don't think we should be giving much in the way of military assistance to other countries. What I think that we ought to be doing basically is giving substantial capital grants to countries which are well-enough organized so that they can make some use of them. Countries like China and Cuba, for example, whatever one may think about their social organization, though I happen to think there are many good things there. It seems to me that these are countries that are going through a period of primitive accumulation of capital. Now in the past every historical instance of early capital accumulation has been accompanied by a good deal of terror and authoritarianism. It is true of England; it is true of the United States; it has been true everywhere. And I assume that one should take for granted, I think, that under any social system, capital accumulation will be combined with authoritarian practice. People have to be made to give up some substantial part of what they are creating so that capital investment can take place. Now I think we can alleviate that process by assisting the countries which put capital to productive use by helping them get past this early stage and then it is up to them to see where they can go from there.

You mentioned as possible recipients for grants of that type countries which are well organized, and I wondered when you said that, who is to determine that? Then you mentioned China and Cuba. Now this made me think of something else in connection with resistance. The attacks on the American government have been rather extreme, and that may be justified or not—I cannot really say—but in connection with that the idealization of the other party is a thing which did strike me. Now I would personally fully agree with you that the United States should get out of Vietnam—the sooner the better. On the other hand, to say that the NLF or some other group is a much more representative group than the puppet government which is now in South Vietnam, I think that we are not really in a position to judge. And I would not be too much convinced that that would be a good alternative for Vietnam. The question really is, does the United States have anything to do there? Now in connection with mentioning China and Cuba, I could for instance think of India as a country about which there is much more reliable information and where we know that the organization is not too good. But at least we know it for certain.

I am not proposing that we should assist the NLF in their effort to organize South Vietnam, but rather that we should stop interfering in the internal affairs of Vietnam. We have no right to impose conditions on the social or political structure of Vietnam, though we have a responsibility to use our resources to aid Vietnam and other countries to carry out modernization and industrialization on their terms. As to your second point, which is well taken, I would certainly be strongly in favor of real capital assistance to India. I think one of the great tragedies of the last couple of years is the way in which India has been forced to readjust its internal economic structure, under American coercion, to permit, for example, ultimate American domination of the fertilizer industry. I think this is a great tragedy. In fact what we should have done is to enable India to manage its own agriculture and its own agriculture-related industry. We should be building steel plants and so on and so forth. So I don't mean to exclude India as a recipient. However, I think that India has not yet solved some of the problems preliminary to economic growth that China has apparently solved—the solution to problems of land utilization and distribution of goods and so on has progressed farther, along with much more political authoritarianism, in China than in India. And I think one simply has to evaluate what the impact of a steel plant is in India as compared with a steel plant in China. Now I understand that a number of leading Indian economists have argued that steel plants in India are not a very good idea, that what they need is "middle-level technology," and not the kind of technology which will try to make them compete in a market where they can't compete. So that's what I meant by talking about well-enough organized societies. I think it is up to India to try to determine in as decent and equitable a way as they can what kinds of economic development make sense for them, and those are the kinds that we have to give them the facilities to carry out. Undoubtedly they will make innumerable mistakes in doing so, as will Cuba and China and any other country, but still I think it has to be a matter of free capital grant, rather than the kind of foreign aid that we give, which as everyone knows is very closely tied to purchase of American products and often is associated with forcing on the recipient country the condition that they open their economy to American investment and to American managerial control, and soon. The story of the fertilizer industry in India in the past few years is a clear example of this.

The change of mind needed for that is very considerable. How likely is it that it will come about?

I don't think it will come about in the near future. And I am not certain that it can come about without a really substantial change in American society; but it is at least possible and I think one should work for this in the expectation that it would come about without a fundamental change of American institutions.

Would it come from the universities, would it come from the churches? Where would it come from?

The most likely source is the universities. The university is a rather parasitic institution. Nevertheless it has a certain social function in a complex, highly industrialized society like this, which gives it a certain amount of leverage. And the elite that's trained in the universities, if they manage to develop a political perspective and, in fact, moral consciousness, could affect policy rather substantially, I think. That is at least a possibility. That is the only thing that, realistically, one can work for in the short range, it seems to me. The possibility could be enormously enhanced if students become directly involved in potential mass movements for social reform here—community-organizing efforts, for example.

How will American universities develop and how will research develop within a society which you have earlier depicted as becoming decreasingly liberal—though you said it might call itself liberal?

My own feeling is that in a society like this, science will very much develop along lines which are set by internal dynamics, by concentration on problems that are of interest and on the border of research. The impact of government on science is generally to distort it towards purposes which are usually, in essence, coercive in nature. But I think that in a rich country like this that effect will always be—at least we can hope will be—rather slight.

Technology on the other hand is heavily influenced by demand, and a powerful government controlling enormous resources and very closely linked to the corporate structure of the society will very heavily determine the nature of the technology that's developed, I think in a very negative way. For example, just consider the extent to which technology is being used for either destruction or else for largely wasteful activities such as space, as compared with the utilization of technological resources and intelligence for things like, say, improvement of agriculture—you know, farming the seas or the kind of low-level or middle-level technology that is probably the most useful to the underdeveloped world and so on. Or for such problems as urban development, which we desperately need. So I think the future for science is reasonably bright and the future for technology is less promising.

And as far as the social sciences are concerned, increasingly these have become over the last couple of years a kind of technology of manipulation and control, and I would imagine that that would continue. The social sciences offer a double service to the coercive institutions in the society. For one thing they do to some extent provide them with better techniques of control. But to an even greater extent they provide them with an ideological cover for the coercion that they carry out. They do it in the name of science, in other words, and in the name of decent ideals and so on. I think that the danger that the social sciences will provide the basis for coercive ideology is a very great danger.

As to the other parts of the universities, for instance, the humanities, I suspect that they are going to be centers of rebellion and opposition, and it is very hard to know if they can maintain themselves since they are in a sense more peripheral to the ongoing functioning of the society. I suspect that the opposition and rebellion that we see developing within some of the fields of the humanities might find an association with the people involved in the natural sciences. I think, incidentally, that this is a fairly safe projection; we can see it happening now and, in fact, we can also see it happening in the Soviet Union. That is, I suspect that this remark is not only characteristic of the United States but of highly organized industrial societies like the United States and the Soviet Union, maybe even Western Europe in the future.

You mentioned control in the social sciences in connection with technology. Would you say that technology is the cause for such things as behaviorism, or is it the other way around?

I think there are really two major reasons for the enormous prestige of behaviorism. One is its utility in providing a kind of ideology for coercive institutions, but I really think that is a minor reason. The main reason for the development of behaviorism is that is seems to me that almost every field develops towards the area where a few simple ideas provide a lot of things to do. There are many areas where without thinking too hard you can do lots of work, carry out variations on other things that people have done and so on. Behaviorism developed out of a few experimental ideas which can be applied in almost infinite variation for PhD dissertations and small papers, which enable one to move up the academic hierarchy and to add small footnotes to some future field of psychology. That is the way fields develop, I think.

So you explain behaviorism rather by some kind of intellectual laziness—not the laziness of doing the jobs because the jobs are infinitely many and varied. On the other hand, one may as well invoke the principle of simplicity and say, well there are so few postulates that are necessary, why should we go in for more and more complicated ones?

I am not sure that is different. Perhaps "intellectual laziness" is a fair term, but it is not as if lack of laziness would have led to something else. I think that if people didn't take the easy way out, probably they couldn't think of anything to do at all. It is not as if there are obvious alternatives to variants on, say, operant conditioning. Other things to do are pretty hard to discover.

It rather reflects on the people, then.

In the sense that people are not geniuses, by and large. But after all the mass of science is done by pretty ordinary people who are reasonably clever, and who understand and can carry out other people's ideas, maybe with innovations and maybe working very hard at it. I don't think "laziness" is really a fair word. I think if a person were to push his intellect to its limits he would, with extremely rare exceptions, find himself working within a framework that is already pretty well fixed. And he would be tending automatically towards certain kinds of research or experiments or dissertations, for instance the conventional studies of minor poets. It's not only psychology that operates within a framework that is reasonably well understood—you can lay out the problem, you know how to go about it, then you work on it. I think that is the way all fields develop.

Now some fields like, say, physics and mathematics, have been fortunate in that when people worked in this way—and they very often did—they did manage to get to deeper and deeper and more and more crucial issues. Other fields, such as, say, literary scholarship and psychology, have not been so fortunate. That may be something intrinsic. It may be that the really interesting problems in—

just to mention those two—literary scholarship and psychology are just too deep for the ordinary mortal, whereas there are plenty of problems in physics and mathematics which an intelligent person who has mastered a certain technique can work on and solve and which lead to further progress.

*I thought such **differences between fields** might rather be related to certain historical and cultural backgrounds.*

Well, it is conceivable. It is very hard to say because there just hasn't been, outside of physics and mathematics and now maybe biology and a few things in other fields, there really hasn't been any work that one could call intellectually deep. We don't know whether that is because of, as you suggest, historical conditions or because of something intrinsic about the relation between the problems and the nature of the human mind. Maybe we can understand just that kind of problem and not some other kind of problem. I wouldn't want to propose that really. It is a counsel of defeat, and much too premature, but still it could be true.

Plato would say something like that, that we can understand ideas but we can't understand matter. And Bergson would say the opposite, that we can understand the material world. You yourself have sometimes predicted a merger of linguistics, psychology, and philosophy. Now behaviorism is applied both to the social sciences and to the humanities. You have taken examples from both. Where do you place linguistics, psychology, and philosophy?

I think linguistics, psychology, and philosophy in certain areas might be able to break out of this narrowness and to deal creatively with moderately deep problems. It seems to me that there are concepts in these fields that permit exploration and study, and that do have a moderate degree of depth. I think that is why these fields are interesting and that is what is drawing people into them.

There is stubborn resistance in all the three of them. Where is it most manageable?

Since we are talking about resistance … Well, I think in all three fields. First of all philosophy is very loose, there are lots of things going on. There are moods which prevail for periods and then they pass, and other moods come and so on. Psychology and linguistics are easier to talk about. I think very roughly there is a generation gap and I presume that the problems that now exist in those disciplines will simply resolve themselves over the next ten years or so, by the replacement of older people by younger people. Which is what ought to happen in any field. I think it has happened in fields like physics at various points in their development. Max Planck is supposed to have said that he didn't intend to convince his colleagues, but only their graduate students, and that the future of the field would be determined by that. Whether he actually said it or not, the remark is probably appropriate to many fields.

So for psychology and linguistics the passage of time will do, and in philosophy what is to be done is capture the fashion?

That's right—a very healthy thing for philosophy would be to rethink its own historical origins. I think it has been much too unhistorical and has lost a lot of the insights of the past. Fruitful lines of thinking and development have been abandoned partly because of fashion and partly because of what I mentioned earlier, the availability of certain simple, reasonably well-understood problems where you can do technical work that will succeed and will even be rather classy in a way, and elegant. In a way I think philosophy always has to keep going back to its own sources and try to return to the central problems that every generation somehow rethought and reformulated.

If you are playing the prophet anyway, what about the role of logic?

Logic has in the last 10 or 15 years become a very substantial subject on its own. I suppose that its relation to philosophy will decrease and decline simply because it's too hard to do serious work in logic without really concentrating on it, approaching it from the point of view of rather solid mathematical understanding.

And what about the relation of logic to linguistics?

Well, the relation to linguistics might be in one of two domains. One is in the area of semantics where a lot of linguistic work is beginning to recapitulate some of the thinking in logic and logical philosophy of the last 50 years. Out of that might grow something rather healthy perhaps—reinterpretation of this tradition in logic and philosophical logic from a point of view more connected to real natural languages. I think that could be very useful. But that has very little to do with contemporary logic. In that respect I think contemporary logic has little to contribute, except perhaps in the development of modal logics, which might open up some new ideas.

Now as far as more technical mathematical logic is concerned, it seems to me that whether there will be contact or not depends on how mathematical linguistics develops. That is the other domain where there might be a point of connection. Now mathematical linguistics I think came to a rather critical point in its extremely brief career about two or three years ago, when some simple ideas were basically exhausted. That is, mathematically, linguistics can develop insofar as empirical linguistics exhibits certain formal structures which are simple enough so that they can be studies in a perfectly abstract way, but complex enough so that they will retain empirical interest. Now those two conditions are hard to satisfy simultaneously. The early work in mathematical linguistics was concerned with ideas which are simple enough to study from a mathematical point of view, but which are not complex enough to have very much to do with real language structure. The whole theory of phrase structure grammar, I think, was kind of interesting and I spent a lot of time on it myself. But I think it got about as far as it could from the point of view of any impact on linguistics. I think it made some contribution to our understanding of natural languages, it sharpened up some issues, provided some models against which the empirically oriented work could be compared and that's very useful. It gives intellectual reference points and it suggests the kind of problems that one could look at—say certain problems of complexity and ambiguity and so on and so forth. Some empirical work was perhaps even spurred by these formal insights. On the other hand, what happened a few years ago is that the additional problems that existed internal to the theory of phrase-structure grammar were perhaps somewhat interesting from a mathematical point of view, but don't seem to have any empirical significance as far as anybody knows. So the field developed then into an obscure branch of mathematics which will be as interesting as its practitioners will make it. Frankly, I lost interest in it personally at that point, just because of my own interests; other people may feel differently. So in a way mathematical linguistics is in a plateau, I think, and will remain so, I would guess, until further empirical work on language structure manages once again to formulate concepts which are amenable to mathematical study, more intricate and complex concepts that are more well-motivated empirically.

I think maybe that out of a lot of the very interesting work now going on in transformational grammar there may come a sharpening and clarification of notions which would make it possible to undertake a new mathematical study, and maybe a lot of the questions that were asked about phrase-structure grammars could now be re-asked and many new questions could be asked about these new, richer systems. At that point one would hope that there would develop a new upsurge of mathematical linguistics and at that point I think current contemporary mathematical logic might very well be relevant. Ideas from recursive function theory and model theory and the theory of more elaborate logics seem at least to be in the same neighborhood as the kind of formal questions suggested by language study and it might turn out that a new field would develop out of this convergence. But I think that is still in the future somewhat.

One could state rather bluntly what you said about mathematical linguistics—put it in the icebox until we need it. This seems to be a more strongly empiricist bias than you generally exhibit. If you look at the development of physics and mathematics, very often mathematics develops some abstruse theory, goes deeper and deeper into it, and there comes physics where it can all be applied. It might be well if all parties remained active.

Yes, I agree with you basically and, for example, if somebody asked me how to run a linguistics department—which few people fortunately do—I would suggest that they keep teaching courses in mathematical linguistics and encourage students to get enough mathematical background to work on it if they want or at least to follow what people do in it, and furthermore that they should try to retain contact with those people who are now more towards pure mathematics, who really do push the field forward. And they should constantly be on the lookout for ideas in the formal sciences that might suggest new lines of approach. But what I was saying was really based on a very personal guess, that I would never try to convince anybody of, as to where the likely progress might be in the near future. That's the kind of thing that a person really has to guess for himself and obviously I wouldn't put much credence in what anybody else said about that. I hope nobody else puts much credence in what I say about that.

I should like to comment on some aspects of your work in their historical setting and I should like to have your reactions. You have often stressed the superficiality, literal as well as otherwise, of certain behavioristic, taxonomic, positivistic approaches in linguistics, philosophy, and psychology. While in America this emphasis is timely, in Europe, especially on the Continent, some people are likely to say that they have always made such claims. But this may merely indicate that they continue to be unaffected by the neo-positivist criticism of about half a century ago. I would like you to say more clearly something which may be obvious to you and in the United States, but not elsewhere. When you advocate ideas which happen to have a long traditional history, you continue to strive for explicitness, formalized expression, and also refutable statements—in short, the scientific approach which was in some branches of science only attained during the interregnum of behaviorism, taxonomy, and positivism. Some clarification of this point may be useful too when you move further into philosophy.

I'm glad that you raise this point, because I suspect that I have not been too clear about my own opinions in this regard. First let me say that to my knowledge, there has been no more concern on the European continent than in the United States for those elements in the historical tradition that I, at least, find illuminating and suggestive. I am surprised, frankly, at the reaction on the Continent that you cite, and that I have noticed, that the critique of, say, taxonomic tendencies in linguistics is only appropriate to American work. In my own attempts at critical analysis (for example, in *Current Issues in Linguistic Theory*) I was not aware of making a distinction at the English Channel, and I spent a good deal of space on what seemed to me to be serious defects in the approach of Troubetzkoy and, farther back, Saussure. Of course my own attention has been focused on work of the 1940s and 1950s, and this was largely American work, because of the war.

However, this is not the main point. What I would like to make clear is that in criticizing behaviorist and taxonomic approaches I am not suggesting that we should simply return to the "pre-positivistic" era. Not at all. The contributions of the recent period are extensive, fundamental to future progress, I think. But it seems to me that these ideas have been essentially exhausted and that a new approach is necessary, one that represents a kind of synthesis of some classical ideas and some of the modern insights. I have tried to say this in various places, but the point has perhaps been hidden in the criticism of prevailing views—which I think one should try not to eliminate, but to transcend, a very different thing.

Let me be concrete. Consider the matter of discovery procedures in what I have called "taxonomic linguistics." In my opinion, one of the fundamental contributions of taxonomic linguistics was to have posed the problem of formulating a discovery procedure, an essentially mechanical technique for arriving at a grammar from data. I do not think that the suggested solution to this problem was correct, and I have tried to show serious and deep-seated inadequacies in it. However, we know that in some sense there must be such a procedure; children, after all, learn their language. And I think that there is some hope of formulating an empirically adequate "theory of language acquisition"—idealized in important respects, to be sure—along the lines that are now being explored: the study of properties of universal grammar, evaluation procedures, and so on. If we were able to formulate a narrow, restrictive schematism for universal grammar and a proper evaluation procedure, we might be able to suggest an explanation, in these terms, for the ability to acquire knowledge of a language, on the assumption that this structure is available to the language learner as an innate property of mind. In my opinion, this approach is quite reasonable, and it represents a fusing of traditional concepts with the advances of the "positivistic" period.

I have asked you a lot of things, you have covered a wide ground and I have taken a lot of time. Is there anything else you would like to say?

I guess I would say something rather personal. For an American intellectual now it seems to be that there are some rather difficult choices, given the present state of affairs. One choice is to become an almost full-time political activist. Now the present state of the world and America's role in the world would certainly justify such commitment. On the other hand, there are plenty of people, including myself, who don't find that prospect in the least appealing, because there are other things we would like to do. The second possibility would be to drop the whole business and make use of the very rich resources that this country provides and the very high status and pleasant life it affords to anyone who becomes fully professional. That's very tempting and that's the second possibility. Now those choices may be difficult and may have their own problems, but when you have made either of these two decisions your way is pretty clear from then on.

On the other hand there is a middle ground which I would like to occupy, and I think people are going to have to find ways to occupy: namely, to try to keep up a serious commitment to the intellectual values and intellectual and scientific problems that really concern you and yet at the same time make a serious and one hopes useful contribution to the enormous extra-scientific questions. Commitment to work on the problems of racism, oppression, imperialism, and so on, is in the United States an absolute necessity. Now exactly how one can maintain that sort of schizophrenic existence I am not sure; it is very difficult. It's not only a matter of too much demand on one's time, but also a high degree of ongoing personal conflict about where your next outburst of energy should go.

And unless people somehow resolve that problem, I think the future is rather dim. If they do resolve it, I think it might be rather hopeful.

Editor's Notes to Interview 2

"Noam Chomsky's View of Language: Noam Chomsky. and Stuart Hampshire Discuss the Study of Language," *The Listener* (London) 79:2044 (30 May 1968), pp. 686–91, edited and introduced by Alasdair MacIntyre. Reprinted in *Readings in Transformational Grammar*. Edited by Mark Lester. New York: Holt, 1970, pp. 100–13, with a brief editorial note which points out that the subject matter of the interview—"perhaps the most important" of the selections in the *Readings*—is "a topic fundamental to all teaching." However, it was excluded from the second (1973) edition of the book, together with two other contributions by Chomsky (out of the four of the first edition).

The interview was done in England. The introduction by Alasdair MacIntyre which preceded the published transcription begins as follows: "At a purely technical level, the work of Chomsky could only be assessed by an expert in linguistics. But Chomsky's achievement is in part to have made linguistics more important for workers in many disciplines. Even metaphysical questions have been revivified by what he has done. Can we understand man simply as a product of his environment? Is there something distinctive about human nature—apart from its complexity—which sets men apart from the rest of nature?" Then, after reviewing the 17th- and 18th-century philosophical debate on these questions, "partly centered on the relationship between the human mind and sense-experience," MacIntyre makes "three points one ought to make about Chomsky's achievement": the first is that Chomsky not merely pointed out that there must be deep grammatical structures and rules of a certain type, but he actually mapped them; the second is that his work has not only had "important effects in linguistics," but it also raises questions "about the structure of the brain, about the analogies between the output of certain types of computer and language, about the nature of the algebra which we need to map deep grammatical structures and about the relationship of linguistics to philosophy" ("it is in fact a paradigmatic example of the type of work which breaks down conventional boundaries between disciplines"); and the third is that his work is concerned with sentences, and the same sentence can be used to say quite different things. This "is not at all a matter of ambiguity" (e.g., the sentence "all men are mortal" is quite unambiguous, and yet it may be used not only to assert that all men are mortal but also, among other things, to answer the request "Give me an example of a major premise in a syllogism"), something not fully explained by a theory of syntax, and we still lack a theory that completes the explanation. "Nonetheless," MacIntyre goes on to conclude, "we can be sure that in this, as in several other fields, it is not only the case that Chomsky has helped to provide some new answers to some very old questions: he has also made it possible to ask questions which no one has ever asked before." See the Editor's Notes to I1.

A report on the Harvard experiment then in progress is found in "Project Grammarama," chapter 7 of George A. Miller's *The Psychology of Communication*. Seven essays. New York, Basic Books, 1967 (Penguin, 1968).

2. A Cartesian View of Language Structure (May 1968)

Am I right in thinking that your studies of language have led you to the conclusion that there are certain underlying structures common to all languages, which constitute something like a universal grammar?

It seems to me that the evidence available to us suggests that there must be some very deep inborn principles, probably of a highly restrictive nature, that determine how knowledge of language emerges in the individual, given the scattered and degenerate data available to him.

Your evidence is derived from the study of the learning of language?

If one wants to study learning in a serious way, what one really has to do is to study a **kind of input-output situation**. We have an organism of which we know nothing. We know, or can discover, what kind of data is available to it, and the first question we must try to answer is: What kind of a mental structure does the organism develop when that evidence is presented to it? And after we have answered that question, that is, when we have some conception of what is the knowledge that results, we can ask the question about the processes that intervened, that led from the data available to the knowledge that resulted. We study the input data available to the child, or in principle we might study that, but the more intensive study is directed to the "output" knowledge that is possessed by the person who has mastered a language. The input-output situation is this: a child who initially does not have knowledge of a language constructs for himself knowledge of a language on the basis of a certain amount of data; the input is the data, the output—which of course is internally represented—is the knowledge of a language. It's this relationship between the data available, and the knowledge of the language which results from the child's mental activities, which constitutes the data for the study of learning—of how the transition takes place from the input data to the resulting knowledge.

I understand that your evidence is sufficient to establish that this learning isn't the kind that can be explained on the stimulus-response model.

When we analyze carefully the nature of the knowledge of language that a person has, once he has mastered his language, we discover that it simply does not have the properties which are implied by the stimulus-response concept of how learning takes place. The stimulus-response theory can only lead to a system of habits—a network of associations, or some structure of that sort. And it is quite impossible to formulate as a system of habits or as a network of associations the processes which will account for the sound-meaning relation that all of us know intuitively when we've mastered English. Take a sentence such as "John kept the car in the garage." If one thinks for a minute, it becomes clear that the sentence is ambiguous: it can mean either that John kept the car that happened to be in the garage and sold the other one, or that the place where John kept the car was in the garage.

On the other hand, if I form a question from that sentence, if I say, "What garage did John keep the car in?" it's unambiguous. It can't be referring any more to the car that was in the garage, and in fact from the sentence "John kept the car that was in the garage," I can't form that sort of question at all. You can't say in English: "What garage did John keep the car that was in?" This kind of evidence relates to well-formedness of sentences, to the association of sound and meaning. Some sentences are ambiguous, some are unambiguous. Some are connected with one another as paraphrases or by implicational relations and so on. When one organizes all of this information and tries to formulate the principles that underlie it, what I would call a grammar—a theory of the sound-meaning relations in language—then this grammar has properties that are quite inconsistent with the notion of associative net or of habit structure.

The striking properties of the grammars that we are led to by this study are two in this connection. The first is that they have what one might call a creative aspect to them, that is that they, in the technical sense, generate—they specify or characterize—an indefinitely large number of sentences, each with its associated interpretation. And of course it's a crucial fact about language that a person is quite capable of using and understanding sentences that have no physical similarity—no point-by-point relationship—to any that he's come across in his linguistic experience or has produced earlier.

This creative aspect of language is quite incompatible with the idea that language is a habit-structure. Whatever a habit-structure is, it's clear that you can't innovate by habit, and the characteristic use of language, both by a speaker and by a hearer, is innovation. You're constantly producing new sentences in your lifetime—that's the normal use of language. When you read the newspapers or walk down the street you are constantly coming across new linguistic structures which you immediately understand, which have no feeling of lack of familiarity, but which are nevertheless not in any definable way similar to others that you've experienced before. So much for the notion of habit-structure. Of course there are elements of skill involved.

But doesn't this only show so far that we are predisposed to make some associations of meaning and sound? Would this give us any grounds for saying that the predisposition was in its content something general?

No, it doesn't as yet. I think in order to reach that further conclusion, one would want to turn to another very characteristic aspect of the grammars that we are led to when we study such sound-meaning connections as I illustrated in the example I gave. In order to account for such facts, we are led to postulate **highly abstract structures**—structures which have no direct connection with the physical facts, which are related to the physical facts only by a long chain of operations of a very specific and unique and highly abstract character. This is the second aspect of grammar I mentioned, in addition to what I called "the creative aspect": the abstract character of the structures that we must postulate in order to account for such phenomena as the ones I mentioned. This abstractness is of a sort which cannot be represented as an associative net. It's a technical matter to show that, but I don't think it's very difficult.

Furthermore, when we look at these abstract structures and the intricate set of processes that relate them to the physical event, we discover that the structures and the processes meet highly restrictive conditions. One can think of many possible formal operations which are not permitted in a natural language, even though they're very simple, and one has to ask the question why this is so. I mentioned a moment ago the process of forming a question. We have a sentence such as "John kept the car in the garage," and we can form a question by transposing "the garage" to the front of the sentence and replacing it by "what," so we get "What did John keep the car in?" On the other hand, we can't apply that process to the sentence: "John kept the car that was in the garage." Now it's a very general property of English—and of all language, I suppose—that there are certain complex noun phrases, such as "the car that was in the garage," from which a noun phrase cannot be extracted by an operation of question formation or anything else. That is apparently a linguistic universal. And it's not only universal but also unlearnable. As language learners, we had very little evidence, in fact I think no evidence, to show us that you cannot form the question: "What did John keep the car that was in?" Of course we've never heard such a sentence, but for that matter we've never heard most sentences that we come across, so the fact that we know you can't do that must be because of some intrinsic limitation on the operations that we are permitted to construct.

So the evidence comes from observation of the actual learning process and also has a comparative linguistic side. It's important to you to find that there are in fact no languages which don't exhibit exactly these transformations?

There is a comparative linguistic side to it very definitely, but I really think that at the present stage of the subject, though this may seem paradoxical, the best evidence as to what is a universal property of language comes from study of a single language. The reason is this: that if one thinks again of the process—suppose you think of yourself as a scientist who's trying to study a black box which has certain data as input and a grammar as output—well, any property of the output which goes beyond the organization in the input must, vaguely speaking, be attributed to the character of the device. We have to ask what in the device led the output to have this specific property. Anything that must be attributed to the device, by virtue of the study of this input-output relation, must be a universal of language—that is, if we assume that people are not genetically endowed in such a way that they can learn one rather than another language. And by posing the problem in that manner we can really get a great deal of very strong evidence about what must be a linguistic universal from the deep study of a single language.

Of course we have to test that against comparative evidence. Such a hypothesis must stand the test that it is not refuted by some other language. In this sense comparative evidence is relevant but it is actually less illuminating, at the moment at least, than deep study of a single language.

I ask this question principally because I am thinking of the classical theories of philosophers who have believed in doctrines of innate ideas, of innate predispositions to form certain ideas, or who have held that there are certain categories of thought which will be reflected in any language which is successfully used in communication. They have wished to speak of the human species as a whole, with no suspicion that they're merely saying there must be some such predispositions in any successful language use. I just wondered whether, when you speak of linguistic universals, you are really saying what they said—namely, not only that there must be some predispositions, but that they must be universal ones?

Making the assumption (which is an empirical assumption, but I think no doubt it's correct) that there is no racial differentiation detectable as far as ability to acquire a language is concerned, if we assume that much uniformity in the human species, then we must assume that what we demonstrate about the person who has learned English, about the intrinsic capacities that made it possible to learn English, will also be true of the intrinsic capacities that made it possible to learn Japanese or Russian or some African language.

Now I think that the logic of the argument that I was sketching a moment ago is rather similar to that of the people you mentioned (for example, Descartes) who did really try to discover the principles that determined how our knowledge is formed by looking at **the disparity between data and knowledge**. Descartes asks: How is it that when we see a sort of irregular figure drawn in front of us we see it as a triangle? He observes, quite correctly, that there's a disparity between the data presented to us and the percept that we construct, and the knowledge of the properties of triangles that we automatically use in dealing with this data. And he argues, I think quite plausibly, that we see the figure as a triangle because there's something about the nature of our minds which makes the image of a triangle easily constructible by the mind: it's a kind of schema that automatically one imposes on data instead of some irregular figure which logically speaking could have just as well been the basis for our interpretation of experience. Quite similarly, here we have a human being—a child, let's say—who has certain data before him. He constructs on the basis of this data a certain grammar the detailed characteristics of which must reflect properties of his mind, since on the basis of the data that was presented many alternative grammars could have been constructed. Yet he picks a particular one. And that must be because of certain mental properties that restrict his interpretation of this data. Other people pick the same one, which simply shows that they are like him in their innate mental properties.

I think a certain amount hinges, if one is to speak of innate ideas, on how abstract the transformations are. Are they so abstract that you couldn't properly speak of them as a specific grammar, in the sense in which one speaks of a grammar of a particular language? The notion of a universal grammar has always been open to the charge that, insofar as it's universal, it'll be so abstract as scarcely to amount to a grammar.

I think again this is an empirical issue, and my feeling is that universal grammar, that set of properties which is common to any natural language **by biological necessity**, is really a very rich and highly articulated structure, with very explicit restrictions on the kinds of operations that can occur, restrictions which we can easily imagine violating. If a mathematician were asked to design operations on sentences, he would think automatically of certain very elementary operations—such as reading the sentences back to front or permuting the third word with the tenth word—and he might study such simple operations. However, such operations simply do not exist in natural language. For example, there's no natural language which forms questions by reading declarative sentences backwards. It's not so obvious why that should be so, because that's a very simple operation. It's a much simpler operation to state than the operation by which we formulate questions in English, let's say.

Nevertheless, the principles that determine what operations may apply in a natural language preclude such simple operations as reading the sentence backwards or permuting the third and the tenth words. And all these operations meet very interesting formal properties which are by no means obvious: they are what you might call structure-dependent operations, operations which apply to a sequence of words, not by virtue of the internal content of that sequence, but by virtue of an abstract structure associated with them—its structure as a set of phrases and so on. And it's by no means a trivial property of natural language that all of the operations that apply to sentences are structure-dependent operations in this sense. That's an example of a simple linguistic universal that you can't explain on the grounds of communicative efficiency or simplicity or anything of that sort: it must apply to a biological property of the human mind.

I was just going to ask that. Do you begin to have the possibility of functional explanations of just these structures being chosen from the indefinite variety of structures that might have been? Because, after all, philosophers have continuously argued that there are certain necessities of human thought in communication—that, for example, noun phrases must function in a certain way, that statement-making itself requires this. This was all, in their case, a priori and uncontrolled by detailed observations, and the argument was essentially, so to speak, a functional one: what is required for human beings, who are medium-sized objects, to make references and statements.

What is interesting are the kinds of principles which meet two conditions: First, they are universal but not merely by accident, not merely because no language violates them, but rather because no language could violate them; Second, they do not have the property that you have just mentioned—namely, that they're somehow necessary for organisms of approximately our size and role in the world. I think the interesting universals are the ones which are not necessary in this sense and there are many such. I've just mentioned two actually. One, the principle that makes it impossible to form a question such as "What garage did John keep the car that was in?" That's an impossible question, on the basis of some universal principle. Second, the principle that makes it impossible to form a question, let's say, by reading a sentence back to front. Neither of these principles has any connection whatsoever with our function in a world of a certain sort. These are formal principles. One can easily imagine a language which violated these principles, a language which did not have only structure-dependent operations, and such a language would be just as usable as our own. You could say the same things in it that we can say. Instead of having our complicated rule for formation of questions, this language would have a very simple rule, so that the question associated with "John saw Bill yesterday" would be "Yesterday Bill saw John."

From my position I would certainly have to predict that if an artificial language were constructed which violated some of these general principles, then it would not be learned at all, or at least not learned with the ease and efficiency with which a normal child will learn human language. For example, I would have to predict that if someone were to construct a language which was like English, except that it had structure-independent operations in it, a child presented with the data from this language would have a very hard time learning and using it.

And that's not only because it had two principles of organization within it but because one of the principles of organization was an unlearnable one?

One which is not adapted to his language faculty. He might be able to learn in some other way, like solving a puzzle. For example, we could certainly, as intelligent human beings, break a code that used structure-independent operations. If I were presented with a kind of Martian system which formed questions by reading declaratives back to front, probably I'd be able to figure it out, but not by means of those properties of mind which the child applies to the data presented to him to discover a grammar.

I think that we could show this empirically: we should be able to show that there would be a qualitative difference in the way I would interpret and master this material as compared with the way I would master and interpret the material from a normal human language. Preliminary experiments of this sort have been carried out by a group around George Miller, the Harvard psychologist. He has a project in which he's tried to construct what are from a mathematical point of view extremely simple languages: these are languages described by finite-state automata. And what he's trying to discover is whether humans will find it harder to learn the organizing principles for such languages than they would to discover the organizing principles of natural languages. My guess is that he'll get a positive answer in this experiment. It's a very hard experiment to do, because he has to have a long exposure period and it's not of the order of the usual psychological experiment.

Does this hypothesis have definite implications for the teaching of language?

I think it has some implications, perhaps of a rather negative sort. A good deal of the foreign-language instruction that's going on now, particularly in the United States, is based on a concept of language diametrically opposed to this. It's based on the assumption that language really is a habit structure, that language is a system of skills and ought to be taught by a drill and by the formation of stimulus-response associations. I think the evidence is very convincing that that view of language structure is entirely erroneous, and that it's a very bad way—certainly an unprincipled way—to teach language. If it happens to work, it would be an accident for some other reason. Certainly it is not a method that is based on any understanding of the nature of language. As I mentioned earlier, our understanding of the nature of language seems to me to show quite convincingly that language is not a habit structure, but that it has a kind of creative property and is based on abstract formal principles and operations of a complex kind. My own feeling is that from our knowledge of the organization of language and of the principles that determine language structure, one cannot immediately construct a teaching program. All we can suggest is that a teaching program be designed in such a way as to give free play to those creative principles that humans bring to the process of language-learning, and I presume to the learning of anything else. I think we should probably try to create a rich linguistic environment for the intuitive heuristics that the normal human automatically possesses.

As in classical literary education?

As in the classical literary education, which I think was on the right track. It certainly fits much more closely to my feeling about the knowledge of language than does the modern linguistic approach, with its emphasis on habit and skill and pronunciation ability.

What is peculiar about this is that here we have a traditional philosophical claim— the claim of empiricist philosophy at all periods, or at any rate from the 18th century onwards—that language is learned by association of ideas and by reinforcing responses, that concepts are formed in this way by abstraction, and that our grammar is a cultural phenomenon which varies with different cultures, with no common underlying structure and no necessity to prefer one structure to another; and then one has a contrary philosophical tradition, that there are predispositions to form certain ideas and to organize concepts in a certain order, and even more strongly, that these ideas can be stated in a propositional form. The suggestion now is that a set of exper-

iments, together with adequate statistical theory, show that one of these philosophical traditions was misguided and that the other—although we don't know yet how specific these abstract transformational principles are and whether they be anything like the traditional innate ideas—was correct. Is the conclusion you have reached one which is subject to controversy among others working in the field?

It's highly controversial, though much of the controversy is somewhat beside the point and I'm sure things will become sorted out over the years. A good deal of the controversy does not have to do with the conclusions but with the nature of the goals. This approach to the study of language and the study of mental processes in general does, as you say, run counter to a long-standing tradition, and I think one of the major problems that make it difficult for people even to investigate the correctness of what is being proposed here is that they first have to see that there is nothing necessary in the tradition that it opposes. The empiricist view is so deep-seated in our way of looking at the human mind that it almost has the character of a superstition.

But supposing we take other features of human behavior which have nothing like the same function or the same complexity, but which bear a certain analogy to what might metaphorically be called the language of gesture. One might find that there was a predisposition in children to acquire gestures, expressions, which they couldn't have seen or learned in the classical empirical way, that the output bore very little relation to the input. This would lead one to say that somehow in the physiological structure there was a predisposition to behave in this sort of area in a certain way.

For example, smiling rather than crying when you're happy.

One would accept in general about human behavior that it must be a genetic inheritance with a cultural layer on top, and similarly for ritual behaviors of various kinds. No doubt if one carried out the same analysis of the games that children play and saw the alternatives and the speed with which they learned them, one would be deeply impressed by this.

I'm sure they would not be able to learn other sorts of games which are from an abstract point of view equally simple, because they are not well adapted to their particular mental structures.

So one ought not to be surprised by this in respect to language. On the other hand, there is a peculiar factor that enters with language, which relates it to the philosophical tradition we were speaking of, the empiricist tradition, which has always denied that there was anything that could be called innate ideas, meaning by this substantial propositions, beliefs as opposed to predispositions to behave in certain ways. Supposing one found that there were preferences for certain sound orders or word orders that really were very general, this might seem a feature of human behavior which in no way upsets the empiricist's picture—any more than it would if there was a predisposition to represent a scene on a piece of paper, given a pen, in a certain way.

Well, I don't quite agree with that, you see. It seems to me that empiricists have been a bit fuzzy on this. If you look at the actual mechanisms of learning proposed by classical empiricism—by Hume, for example—or at such modern variants of empiricism as so-called learning theory in psychology, than these mechanisms really do not leave any room for such things as the principles of the sort that you mentioned. Particular principles of representation have no place within Humian learning theory. Humian learning theory says, after all, that there are impressions presumably determined by the nature of the sense organs and that these impressions are associated by certain specified mechanisms—contiguity, similarity and so forth. Modern psychology adds very little, frankly, to this picture. One can add certain assumptions about stimulus sampling or about techniques of building up hierarchies, but the additions that have been made in modern learning theory don't seem to me to go beyond this sort of domain or process in any fundamental fashion; this domain simply does not incorporate general principles about how knowledge is organized of the sort I mentioned in connection with language, of the sort that you're describing in connection with techniques of representation or of the organization of games.

I suppose that the contrast here, which empiricists would insist on, would be between knowledge in the sense of propositional knowledge, which is said to be innate, and features of behavior, such as the tendency to represent on paper a solid body in a certain way, which may greatly vary culturally. Nonetheless, given all the possibilities there are of representation as something built-in, I don't see why empiricists should be upset by this feature of behavior, though they should be distressed if these predispositions amounted to something that could be called propositional knowledge or even to restricted categories of thought.

At this point we are running into a difficulty with the concept of knowledge as it is customarily used in the modern philosophical tradition, which is very different from the way in which it was used in classical rationalist philosophy. And this makes it very hard to come to grips with the issue that divides the classical rationalists and the empiricists. I would want to use "knowledge" in the sense in which Leibniz uses it: as referring to **unconscious knowledge**, principles which form the sinews and connections of thought but which may not be conscious principles, which we know must be functioning although we may not be able to introspect into them. The classical rationalist's view is that there are many principles which determine the organization of knowledge which we may not be conscious of. You can think of these principles as propositional in form, but in any event they're not expressible. You can't get a person to tell you what these principles are.

Incidentally, I think that the rationalist didn't go at all far enough: in fact the one fundamental mistake that I think is made by the Leibnizian theory of mind is its assumption that one could dredge out these principles, that if you really worked hard at it and introspected, you could bring to consciousness the contents of the mind. I don't see any reason to believe that the sinews and connections of thought, in Leibniz's sense, are even in principle available to intro-spection. They may interrelate in some complicated way with certain principles that are available to introspection, but there's no more reason to suppose these principles to be available to introspection than there is to suppose that the prin-ciples that determine visual perception should be accessible to introspection—the principles, as in the case of Descartes' example, that make us see a certain irregular figure as a distorted triangle.

Ultimately I think that there will definitely some day be a physiological explanation for the mental processes that we are now discovering, but I think this will be proved true for a not very interesting reason. It seems to me that the whole issue of whether there's a physical basis for mental structures is a rather empty issue, for the simple reason that if you look over the course of the history of modern science, what you discover is that the concept "physical" has been extended step by step to cover anything that we understand. For a Cartesian physicist, the idea of attraction at a distance was not a physical process, and in fact for Newton himself it was an occult quality of objects. Well, when this became absorbed into our understanding, then of course it became a physical process, because the notion "physical" was extended. Similarly, electromagnetic phenomena that would not be physical processes in the sense of Descartes, which didn't involve pushing and pulling, became physical processes when we began to understand them. When we ultimately begin to understand the properties of mind, we shall simply, I'm sure, extend the notion "physical" to cover these processes as well. What is at issue is only whether the physiological processes and physical processes that we now understand are already rich enough in princi-ple—and maybe in fact—to cover the mental phenomena which are beginning to emerge. That's an empirical question. I don't know what the answer to it is, but I have no doubt that if they are not rich enough, we shall add new principles and call them physical principles.

Yes. But one is thinking now of those principles which you have to acknowledge in trying to write an accurate grammar—which is what it amounts to—these in-built predispositions. One thinks of facing a certain restriction on human thought as if we were wearing spectacles—if we took them off, we couldn't see at all. Does the discov-ery of these predispositions and principles—in their most specific form, assuming that they can be discovered—offer the possibility of bursting out of the restriction?

It seems to me that the right approach to this problem is to go back to another long-discarded idea which I think is nevertheless quite appropriate: the idea that there are **faculties of the mind**. If we want to develop an understand-ing of the structure of something as complex as the human mind, we shall be forced to recognize many sorts of components which could be called faculties, and which differ from one another in their properties and interrelate in complex ways. One of the faculties of the mind, I suppose, is the language faculty, which has certain restrictive principles such as those that I've mentioned. But there are many other components to the mind aside from the language faculty. That's why

I said earlier that we might very well be able to break a code that violates some of the principles of language that are incorporated in the language faculty.

You think of logical and mathematical powers as really distinct?

They might be quite distinct from our particular language faculty. I think that the language faculty is that property of the mind which, when applied to the normal linguistic data of everyday life, develops this very highly articulated, very abstract structure of human grammar which determines knowledge of language. However, we have many **other mental faculties** apart from this. Ability to acquire a language is not our only mental faculty and I have no doubt that these other mental faculties also have their limitations. That there are such limitations would seem to me to follow from the fact that we are a biological organism. We can tell what a frog's limitations are, and some more complicated organism than us might be able to tell what our limitations are. I don't see that there's any contradiction in the idea that we could discover what our own limitations are in some fashion, but at the moment of course we can't get anywhere near that, except possibly in the case of certain artificially isolated components of the mind like the language faculty.

Yes, but you're therefore making rather strong contrasts between the faculty that is exercised, say, in pure mathematics and the faculty that's exercised in recognizing and constructing new sentences. From the historical point of view, there's a certain paradox here if these two are separated too absolutely, because one would suppose that the logical structure and the linguistic argumentative structure have to be kept somehow under a single faculty.

I think it would be dogmatic at the moment to take any position on this issue. All we can say is that we have evidence that the language faculty has such-and-such properties. We know for a fact that those properties are not a general limitation of human intelligence. We know perfectly well that we would be able to figure out a language that had structure-independent operations of certain sorts. All right, so that just tells us that there are faculties beyond the language faculty. What the nature of those faculties are, how they are interrelated to the language faculty—these are questions that have yet to be discovered by the study of other cognitive systems, by a study which may be analogous to the study of language.

One of the reasons why I think the present-day study of language is most interesting is that it suggests a way in which other cognitive systems could be studied. There are many other things that we know besides language, and I think it would be very reasonable to look into some other system of knowledge that we have, rather as the rationalist philosopher suggested that we look into our belief system about the external world to see if we can construct something analogous to a grammar of this belief system, and then ask how that "grammar" was developed on the basis of the data available to us and what this input-output relation shows us about the intrinsic nature of the mind that mediated this connection.

Do you think that when one thinks of these principles of order and transformation and preferred structures in language as restrictions, they set a restriction on scientific thought?

I suspect that the properties of the language faculty are probably closely associated to the faculties that lead us to what we call common sense—our common-sense knowledge of the world, that is. At the level of maturity at which a child is acquiring competence in language, he's also acquiring a vast amount of highly structured knowledge of the physical world and of human action and motivation. We don't know too much about the nature of that knowledge but there's no question that it's intricate, complex, highly organized and so on.

This whole mass of knowledge falls into what we roughly call common sense and we know from the history of science that **common sense knowledge** has had its limitations, that it's necessary to try to make this incredibly difficult leap beyond common sense to some sort of abstract picture of the nature of experience, of the nature of the physical world. Making this leap is a uniquely human ability, and it involves properties of the mind that we do not yet even begin to understand. I would suppose that there are restrictions on these further faculties. And a very fascinating question would be to try to think of a way of discovering these restrictions. If we could discover some of them, we could begin to say something about the possible bounds of human knowledge.

Editor's Notes to Interview 3

This unique and little-known interview appeared in a collection edited by Stanley Rosner & Lawrence E. Abt (*The Creative Experience.* New York: Grossman Publishers, 1970, pp. 71–87). It was conducted in Chomsky's study in his home in Lexington, Massachusetts, no later than Winter of 1969 (the proofs referred to are those of *American Power and the New Mandarins,* which was first reviewed in March 1969) and perhaps as early as spring of 1968 (the earliest dated interview in the volume was conducted on March 2, 1968, and at least four others were done in 1968).

Of special interest in this context is the Paul David Saltman interview, which took place in August 1968. Saltman, a professor of biochemistry who pioneered research on iron chemistry and other subfields, is the only other interviewee of Chomsky's generation included in the book (the oldest one is the astronomer Harlow Shapley, born in 1885). Like Chomsky, Saltman was born in 1928 and was a full professor by 1961. Other similarities are even more surprising—and bring out Chomsky's singularity in a particularly clear way. Saltman's father was an immigrant from Russia who came over at the age of 16 (Chomsky's father, born in 1897, emigrated from Russia in 1913 to avoid being drafted in the Czarist army). He was "very political, very much involved with the left-wing movement at that time." The earliest exposures Saltman remembers "were lessons at the dinner table about the Abyssinian War" (cf. **AP**, p. 324). Fundraisers in his father's home were very much a part of their lives and there was "constant exposure to all kinds of intellectual stimuli." He majored in chemistry, and found himself "bored and totally disenchanted with science" by the time he was a senior. And his "Zellig Harris" came to the rescue just in time (cf. **ChR**, p. 7): "Then I got a very exciting professor in my senior year, James Bonner, and I was really captured by the man and the way he presented his subject. I went abroad to study for a year in Paris, really captured a whole new approach to science. I really was bludgeoned to death by science at Cal Tech ... There really was no love in science there. Plenty of hard work. If it weren't for the fact that I played basketball and wrote for the paper and participated in politics, I could have gone crazy. I would have left that joint ... I didn't see this creative experience in science literally until I went abroad for a year and worked as a researcher. I had never really done research and understood the process of research as a creative and as a fun experience. Science was never fun. I didn't ever feel I was in the game for four years" (Rosner & Abt, pp. 124–5).

It should perhaps be added that at least 10, possibly as many as 16 or more of the 23 interviewed for the book (9 scientists and 14 artists) are Jewish. Also noteworthy is that in the interviews "there was a general underemphasis, and with some a refutation, of the significance of the dream life to creativity" (p. 391)—with the exception of one scientist and one artist: Chomsky and the Nobel laureate novelist Isaac Bashevis Singer. Chomsky's remarks bring to mind those by Henri Poincaré, the distinguished mathematician, on unconscious creativity (see *The Creative Process*, edited by B. Ghiselin, University of California Press, 1952, 37 ff.)

Chomsky's very first linguistic work is *Morphophonemics of Modern Hebrew*, his first attempt to construct a generative grammar. It began as an undergraduate thesis (1949), later developed into a master's thesis, University of Pennsylvania, 1951, which he revised later that year. It was first published in 1979, in a series entitled "Outstanding Dissertations" (Garland Publications).

The work done with George Miller includes "Pattern Conception" (1957); "Finite State Languages" (1958), reprinted in *Readings in Mathematical Psychology*, Wiley, 1965; "Finitary Models of Language Users," and "Introduction to the Formal Analysis of Languages," which appeared in *Handbook of Mathematical Psychology*, Wiley, 1963. See Sgroi and/or Koerner & Tajima for additional information.

This interview seems to be the only testimony in print in which Chomsky talks freely about his creative powers—in fact, he appears to be still somewhat awed by them. The reference to the "generative principles of language" he was led to some 15 years earlier (more than 35 years ago) by his innovative and far-reaching analysis of the verbal complex and the formation of questions with modals is particularly timely at the current stage of theoretical development. In essence, Chomsky's early insight into what is sometimes called "Affix movement" and Joseph Emonds' 10-year-old insight into what is now called "Verb movement" (*Linguistic Inquiry 9*, 1978, pp. 151–75) converged a few months ago in a very stimulating paper by the French linguist Jean-Ives Pollock, an important contribution to recent—and for some, spectacular—advances which shed new light on some basic underlying similarities and differences between languages, in particular between English and French (and other Romance languages). These advances, made possible by the brilliant analysis Chomsky worked out in his graduate student days, were re-elaborated and extended by him in an extraordinary lecture he gave on Jan. 29, 1988 at UCLA (the basis for his paper "Some Notes on Economy of Derivation and Representation," written 7 months later), an important step towards the "minimalist program" of the 1990s (see his book *The Minimalist Program*, Cambridge" MIT Press, 1995, and subsequent technical papers). Nothing could symbolize better the fantastic progress of the field in the last 30 years.

3. The Creative Experience (Winter 1969)

Can you tell us something about your technique? Is it a matter of plugging away at a problem?

No, I'm usually working on quite a number of different things at the same time, and I guess that during most of my adult life I've been spending quite a lot of time reading in areas where I'm not working at all. I seem to be able, without too much trouble, to work pretty intensively at my own scientific work at scattered intervals. Most of the reasonably defined problems have grown out of something accomplished or failed at in an early stage.

How does a new problem arise for you?

My work is pretty much an attempt to explain a variety of phenomena in which there is an enormous amount of data. In studying how one understands sentences, you can pile up data as high as the sky without any difficulty. But the data are pretty much uninterpreted, and the approach I've tried to take is to construct abstract theories that characterize the data in some well-defined fashion so that it is possible to see quite clearly where the theory you're constructing fails to account for the data or actually accounts for them.

In looking at my theories, I can see places where ad hoc elements have simply been put in to accommodate data or to make it aesthetically satisfying. While I'm reading about politics or anything else, some examples come to my mind that relate to the problems that I've been working on in linguistics, and I go and work on my problems in the latter area. Everything is going on at once in my mind, and I'm unaware of anything except the sudden appearance of possibly interesting ideas at some odd moment or the emergence of something that is relevant.

Would it be fair to say, then, that you have the problems you're working on in the back of your mind all the time?

All the time, yes, I dream about them. But I wouldn't call dreaming very different from really working.

Do you literally mean dreaming?

Yes, I mean it literally. Examples and problems are sort of floating through my mind very often at night. Sometimes, when I am sleeping fitfully, the problems that I've been working on are often passing through my mind.

Do they pass through your mind in a dream in the same form in which you were working on them?

Well, as far as I know, in exactly the same form. The dream life doesn't seem to have a different framework or to involve a different approach. So it's just a sort of slightly less concentrated and conscious version of the same thing as during the day.

How did you ever become interested in linguistics as a scientific field?

I think that my interest actually comes from **two sources**. In the first place, I sort of grew up with the study of language. As a child, I became interested because my father was working on a medieval Hebrew grammar, and I used to read his proofs when I was 12 or 13 or so. So I knew something about historical linguistics from informal background, but I wasn't professionally interested in it at all. And then, when I got to college, I was much more interested in radical politics than anything else. I became involved with Zellig Harris in connection with left-wing Zionism (more accurately, radical alternatives to Zionism). He was the professor of linguistics at the University of Pennsylvania, and I had a lot of personal contact with him. I was really a kind of college dropout, having no interest in college at all because my interest in a particular subject was generally killed as soon as I took a course in it. And that includes psychology, incidentally.

I went to college with great enthusiasm, and I was interested in everything. But as soon as I took a course in some subject, that took care of that area. By the time I was a junior, I was perfectly willing to quit college and go to a *kibbutz* or something of that sort. Then I ran into Harris. He was the first person I'd met in college who was in any sense intellectually challenging, and we became very good friends afterward. He was perhaps twenty years older than I, and since I liked him and liked the things he was interested in, I took his courses, just to have something to do, and I got interested in the field and sort of put it into the center of my concerns. In retrospect, although it was really an independent influence upon me, it did tie in some way with my childhood.

What sort of work did your father do?

My father was a Hebrew teacher, and he did scholarly work on medieval Hebrew grammar, as I have said. He did a book on David Kimhi, a 13th-century Hebrew grammarian, and this was something I grew up with. At the time, it didn't seem to have any real contact with linguistics, but I now know that it really did in the sense that some of my own work later on was modeled on it, and quite consciously, on things that I had picked up totally informally from an acquaintance with general ideas in the history of linguistics.

Some of the reasons why some of my work was successful, I know, is because it grew out of a framework different from the accepted structural linguistics at the time. It was borrowed from some of the much older sources which at the time I didn't understand very well.

Did the sources you speak of grow out of, in part, the work of your father?

In part, definitely yes. The structural linguistics that I was studying grew out of the work of Leonard Bloomfield and others. It developed in part in parallel with radical behaviorism in psychology and was very similar to it, and in some ways equally trivial and beside the point, I think. That is, I think that the assumptions were just as debilitating, and the framework just as pointless. One of its characteristics is a sort of infantile obsession to worry about explanations. This is a point of view that was expressed quite explicitly by Martin Joos, for example. The work in structural linguistics, as I knew it, was concerned with collection and careful organization of data. This can be really deadening stuff, but it was really the tone of much of the field when I got into it. I was saved from this approach to some extent by the fact that I was acquainted with a different and more informal tradition which was concerned with explaining why a form has such-and-such a property and offering an historical explanation for it.

From the very beginning of my work I have tried to explain the characteristics of a given stage of the language by trying to understand what a person knows about his language, not by means of historical explanation, which would be irrelevant, but rather by trying to attribute to him certain mental characteristics from which one could derive the facts—just as an historical linguist would seek to explain things by looking at the historical stages of its development. I was very early conscious of this different approach.

We assume that you mean that, in studying Hebrew, one would not be interested in studying a particular work and its various forms in terms of what a rabbi might say about it but rather a particular form is used because its author has certain psychological needs to express himself in a particular way.

Let me give you a more technical example which is closer to what I have in mind. If you take the Hebrew word malchay, it seems to violate regular rules in that one would expect to have kay rather than chay after a closed syllable, as in the form malkee. So why do we have malchay and not malkay, let's say? An historical linguist might argue, and I was aware of this when I was ten or twelve years old, that the underlying form at one stage of the language was malachim—malakeem rather—and the k became ch after a vowel. At a later stage, the vowel was dropped so that you have a post-vocalic form appearing after a consonant, and that is why there is a violation of the apparent regularity that you don't have a ch after a consonant.

This is an historical explanation?

Yes, that's an historical explanation, but you know it's the kind of explanation that one can give for many phenomena. In the historical tradition in linguistics that I was loosely familiar with, this was typically the form of explanation offered. I have tried to ask comparable questions about how the speaker of the language organizes his knowledge so that the form is such-and-such or that the syntactical structure is such-and-such, and I think that this is the only innovation I've introduced into the field of linguistics.

Of course, most speakers of a language know nothing of what its history has been, but each, as a child, was faced with a mass of data that he has to make up some coherent theory about, and the theory has to be rich enough to enable him to carry out his normal creative use of language. It turns out, if the theories I have worked on are correct, that the theory of language the child develops has interesting formal similarities to some of the language's historical development. That is, they contain within them a kind of residue of historical evolution. What this really means, I think, is that at every stage of the language there's a very abstract theory that people who speak the language have that characterizes, through some process, the phonetic forms. What changes in historical evolution is sort of the tail end of this process, by and large. The common core of the language very rarely changes. After a long process of development, then, the language still may preserve more archaic features in its more abstract structure.

If you want a loose analogy, I ask you to think of Haeckel's theory of biological recapitulation. Suppose that it's true, for example, that in the ontogenetic development of an organism an early mutation will probably be lethal, whereas a mutation that affects a later stage of development may very well be viable. This is similar to phenomena that we encounter in the development of language. Of course you can't take the analogy literally. There are all sorts of reasons why it doesn't provide a perfect account of what occurs in language.

Has this approach led to an interest in why a particular individual, in the light of his particular history, speaks or uses a certain language?

That's an interesting question, but it's beyond the bounds of this kind of study. This is really an attempt to move into individual differences, and we don't have the tools, as yet, for this kind of inquiry. Perhaps this will some day change, but this is the present state of the field, I believe.

You mentioned earlier in our discussion that, in trying to construct a theory of something, you used abstraction and placed some reliance on intuition.

Yes, I always thought, from the beginning, that the whole scientific aura of linguistics and psychology was in part something of a fraud. And part of my belief came from the fact that under Harris' influence I became interested in school again and saw that things could be interesting. I started taking graduate courses in technical philosophy and mathematics and modern logic and began really studying some serious stuff. When you approach the behavioral sciences with this kind of background, you see right off that you've been totally missing the point. I mean it's a sort of mockery of science to use the framework of behaviorism with its narrow concept of theory and experimental design because nothing of this sort really goes on in serious science.

The work in linguistics was very similar. I mean that there was a lot of talk in the field about how scientific we were and how we were just like the physicists, and of course all that was missing was the intellectual content of what we were doing.

Is there some aspect of psychology that has been influential?

Yes. I've been very close, over the years, to people like George Miller who, I think, is moving in the right direction toward some conception of the cognitive processes that is far more abstract and deeply rooted than the behaviorist framework will tolerate, a conception that may offer some insight into some of these processes. Miller was one of the very few psychologists that I've had any acquaintance with, at least in this specific area, who was really able to see what is wrong with the behaviorist tradition and is really able to go on to the next stage.

I've found it very easy to work with him, and I've learned a lot from him, and I think he's learned a lot from me. We were able to work together very effectively. You are aware that there have been lots of changes in psycholinguistics in the past few years.

What about your book, Language and Mind?

This is based on a series of lectures that I gave at the University of California at Berkeley. They were addressed to a university-wide audience, and they were relatively non-technical. There was an attempt to draw together, in the first of three lectures, some historical developments in the study of language and mind. I really tried to show that there is a classical tradition that grows up in rationalist philosophy and psychology in the 17th century and continues with very interesting work to the mid-19th century, when it is virtually replaced by a later "scientific" tradition. I put "scientific" in quotes because it was in another sense less scientific although it had more trappings of science than the earlier work in these fields. Of course, the newer research techniques increased enormously the available data as well as the reliability of data, but it seems to me that they entirely missed the point of, let's say, physics. That is, one should be interested in an intellectually satisfying deep explanatory theory, and this is more important than getting data accurate down to the tenth decimal place.

I tried to suggest that, by synthesizing these two traditions, one of which aimed at a basic understanding, and the other that is concerned with making sure that your data are reasonably correct and constitute a good sample, one can make scientific progress. One can begin to ask some of the old questions when using the refined methodology that did come out of this modern tradition, and you get some interesting answers. Well, you see, I'm convinced that language is species-specific as a biological attribute and that some of its deepest properties are really genetically determined. It's quite pointless to expect animals to speak or anything of that sort: it's just like expecting humans to fly. There is a sort of dogma to the effect that the human mentality is perfectly plastic and that humans can learn anything. I don't think this is true at all. I think human mentality is very narrowly constrained, and it can develop in certain directions and not in others; and one can see this, for example, by doing a careful analysis of cognitive processes, such as linguistic processes. That's roughly what my book's about.

So this approach has had quite an impact on the field generally?

That's not the question you should ask me, but my perception is that almost all of the young bright people in linguistics are vaguely acquainted with this area. There is plenty of conflict in this area, and my students think that I'm an old fuddy-duddy who doesn't understand a thing. I suspect that anyone going on, whether you like it or not, is within this framework. In psychology, psycholinguistics still has a very heavy residue of the old verbal behavior formulation. Take a look at a journal, say the *Journal of Verbal Learning and Verbal Behavior*. About 90 percent of it is association studies: you know, the effect on changing the list position of items, and so on.

Are the findings of psychoanalysis relevant to your field?

Well, that's an interesting question. I've been searching to find some point of contact because I'm very much concerned with unconscious cognitive processes. It seems to me that the work we've done shows as conclusively as one can show with this kind of material that in these areas most of the processing of experience, at least with respect to language, is not only unconscious but is beyond the range of conscious processes. I mean that one cannot introspect into the way in which he interprets a sentence any more than he can introspect into the way he perceives physical objects or digests his food. As far as I have been able to determine, however, I'm not able to see anything in **the Freudian tradition** that tries to develop a notion of unconscious processes in the area of cognitive thinking. This seems to me a real gap.

But Freud does make a great deal out of the use of language, doesn't he?

Well, you see, it's a very different kind of use. He's not talking about the unconscious cognitive processes, he's not talking about the thinking processes; that is, how one makes an inference or how you understand what somebody says when he fashions a sentence, or how we perceive objects in the three-dimensional world. This is a whole domain of questions that involve biological processes that are to an important extent species-specific. We want to know how these things are organized.

You'd be getting closer now to the questions Gestalt psychologists ask, wouldn't you?

In many ways. Except that I think the Gestalt psychologists are too peripheralistic in their concepts. **Köhler**, for example, tried to relate these considerations to field properties of the brain. I think that's too superficial: I mean that there's a much more abstract processing that goes on that probably has nothing to do with closure or any of these grossly physical properties of things. I've learned a lot from Gestalt psychology in this sense that it searches for integrative processes that aren't immediately evident in behavior. And also from other psychologists, like **Lashley**. Or, I should have learned from them. In fact, after I had learned independently just about everything Lashley had said, I discovered that he had done some very interesting work along just the lines that concerned me. Lashley was a professor at Harvard when I got there, and he had important things to say about language. I came as a graduate student and met all kinds of people, but I never even heard Lashly's name! About 10 years later, Meyer Schapiro, the art historian at Columbia who knows everything about everything, told me that he couldn't understand why I didn't refer to Lashley because he had been saying many of the same things.

I discovered that Lashley had given a very sharp critique of what was going on at the time and had very interesting suggestions about the necessity for deeper integrative mechanisms not only for language but for coordinated motion and so on. There's been something of a Lashley revolution in the last few years. His papers have been reprinted and have influenced many in the field.

What we're interested in getting through to you is the birth of ideas. Is there some way we can separate this on-going line of work you're involved in, or is it a kind of continuing process?

I just don't know. I know that the major work I've been doing for the past twenty years simply seems to be the obvious thing to do. For a long time I worked on it in near-total isolation. Most of my work is published, but in fact I have a long, almost 1,000-page book, which I wrote when I was a graduate student at Harvard, that still isn't published.

In your present area?

Yes, and it has almost everything in it, in a general way, including the basic ideas. Lots of it is wrong. Nobody would read it at the time. A part of it was my doctoral dissertation which almost no one looked at at the time, that is the mid-50s. I had been working along structural linguistic lines, following ideas of Harris, which were in some ways related to radical behaviorism. His idea was that there is no mental reality at all. The only thing you can do is develop analytic procedures which can be applied in a mechanical way, in principle programmed for a computer. You take a body of data, apply these analytic techniques, and the result is the grammar. This struck me initially as rather persuasive, and I worked for a long time trying to fill in the holes in the procedures that he had suggested, where they didn't work properly. For at least five years I worked very hard, and this was conventional linguistics. I knew more mathematics and logic than most people in the field at that time, and I was able to try more sophisticated techniques. But in spite of this it was a total fiasco, and gradually I began to work on this other approach. Because it didn't have any connection with the more conventional work, it aroused little interest. There were some exceptions. Particularly, I got a lot of encouragement and help from Morris Halle, who has been a close friend and colleague since we were graduate students.

However, I felt I was getting some place in explaining strange things about language and in finding regularities and principles that really worked. But this was totally out of the structure of the field at that time. Public lectures and articles that I submitted for publication met with the reaction that this work was not in linguistics. When my book went to a publisher in 1955, it got the same reaction. In 1953 I took a trip to Europe. I remember on the ship thinking about what I had been doing the previous five years and recognizing very clearly that one line of approach that I thoroughly believed in was an obvious failure. Another approach, which I was following because it intuitively seemed sort of right, though I didn't really believe in it, was working out. I then decided to abandon the first and commit myself entirely to the second.

Can you tell us what made the new approach seem "natural"?

When I first got into the field, I was really doing two things: I was learning the techniques and I was asking about the kinds of questions one might deal with using these techniques. The attempt to develop and apply these techniques led in a direction that grew quite fruitless. The other approach involved asking the most naive question about what happens when you as a person who speaks a language come across a sentence you've never heard before. It doesn't take a mathematician to know that the number of sentences that you come across and try to understand is astronomical. Obviously one must have in mind, somehow, a set of principles that are sufficiently rich to assign an interpretation to an arbitrary sentence that you've never encountered before. What would this principle be? Well you go ahead to search for it. For some reason it never occurred to me that this insight refuted all the work I had been doing. It was only after three or four years that it became obvious that I was really getting somewhere.

What do you mean that you were getting somewhere?

I was able to explain things about the language. For example, if you look at English, there are some funny curiosities. Take the formation of questions. When you form a question from "John will come tomorrow," the corresponding question is, "Will John come tomorrow?" On the other hand, when you form a question from "John reads a book" it is "Does John read a book?", not "Reads John a book." On the other hand, you say, "Is John here?" not "Does John be here?" which would look like the analogue of "Does John read the book?" Now you can look at this as some crazy fact, but I was able to show that if you formulate certain fairly general principles, generative principles of language, then it had to be that way and exactly that way. In many areas it has been possible to show that we just know intuitively, as speakers of the language, the curious forms that sentences have because of some very general principles we have internalized and use quite unconsciously. This kind of example struck me as very exciting because it is more along the lines of what we know of science in general. We are interested not only in organizing data, and we get excited when we find an intuitively satisfying **explanation**.

What you have just said leads naturally, we think, into the question of the roles of mood and the emotions in your work, which has been so largely abstract. Are you aware of the roles of your emotions and moods?

I know that some things get me very excited and other things are just dull. The exciting things are what one wants to follow. I can't describe them very well.

Do your ideas emerge when you are happy or unhappy?

I think it's probably the other way around. I'm so aware of the fact of having hit upon a train of thinking that seems to be getting somewhere that I get excited and so on, but I'm not aware of the opposite. I'm thinking of periods of my life when I've ranged very widely in mood but have not been different in productivity.

Does it ever happen that you find yourself up a blind alley?

Not too often. I've been kind of lucky in the sense that there have always been plenty of alleys that were open.

What do you do when you can't figure something out?

I turn to something else.

You don't bang your head against the wall?

Rarely, no.

You just stop for a while?

Yes, and I come back at a later time. There are still lots of things that I can't see any way to handle. Of course, you know that once I got graduate students we have a very lively department with very bright kids — they provide all sorts of other ideas about the work. And also more blind alleys, too. There's a very real interplay here that I find very exciting.

Is Dr. Harris at MIT?

No, he's at the University of Pennsylvania. In fact, we really lost intellectual contact in linguistics within a few years of our acquaintance, although we have stayed very close friends.

What about the place of visual images in your work. Are you dealing only with words, with images, or with auditory stimuli?

One part of what I was interested in for a number of years was really a kind of mathematics. It was the study of the formal properties of certain systems and rules, what kind of structures could be generated. The systems were suggested by language, but they were really considered in terms of themselves, and they were really part of the theory of abstract algebra or something of the sort. Working on these problems, I certainly used concrete models that involved visual imagery. I was interested in the formal properties of graphs and that sort of thing.

Your work appears very highly cerebral, and yet aren't you searching for meanings behind your thoughts?

As far as I am aware, it is "highly cerebral." Something that makes sense may be a very abstract principle that doesn't seem to have any direct connection with the data, and I have arrived at it through a complex series of processes. If it's surprising, it's exciting.

Something surprising is exciting?

If the principles themselves are implausible ones, in the sense that there is no a priori reason for language to be based on these principles rather than others, and if certain phenomena can be explained from the interplay of many such principles, it's exciting. There is a very intellectual relationship among the principles that one seeks.

What about the role of surprise in your work?

By searching the consequences of certain assumptions through a long process of inference, one is able to predict certain empirical results. If these results turn out to be correct, and if they do not directly reflect the assumptions upon which they are based, we have something that is surprising and exciting.

Surprising because it's not logical?

It's logical in the sense that there's a logical connection. It's very far from being self-evident. In fact, if you make slight modifications in the principles you thereby get overwhelming differences in the predictions which hopefully are false. In these cases you will discover things which yield satisfaction and really give the field life, as far as I'm concerned. If you didn't have such things, I wouldn't be interested in the field at this time.

Then your discovery of the relationships between your data and the generalizations of your principles is what's really creative for you?

Yes, that's right. That is the creative experience.

Are there aesthetic and affective reactions, too?

Yes, that's the whole business! It's the kind of experience I had when I was studying mathematics and logic really seriously and finally got to understand something—the same kind of excitement. Of course, I didn't discover it in that case, but in a sense you rediscover it when you finally grasp it, and it's that kind of experience that occasionally comes also from literature or music or something of the sort.

When you come upon a discovery like this, what about your techniques? Do you pursue it, do you get involved in it, is there a quality of urgency to get it down on paper, or do you just let it simmer?

This varies. For example, when I was a graduate student, I really worked out most of this stuff, although I wasn't communicating it to anyone, and I worked with a really incredible intensity. In looking back, I don't see how it was possible. In just a few months I wrote my book of close to 1,000 pages, and it had in it just about everything that I've done since, at least in a rough form.

There are some proofs over there. Do you just sit down at this typewriter, and the material all of a sudden comes out?

Yes, that's a different field, politics, and this is a 300-page book which is also the work of only a year or so really. But it's stuff that I've been thinking about for years. Ever since I was a child I've been thinking about the material in that book. For example, when I was a ten-year-old kid, I was very much interested in the Spanish Civil War, and I got to know about it through reading and friends. I remember writing an article for the school newspaper on the fall of Barcelona, for example. Since then I've been interested in the anarchist movement in Spain and other things, but I never dreamed of writing anything about it, but this book has a good bit of material on the anarchist revolution in Spain. It's a sort of distillation of things that I'd had on my mind for years and years, but had never bothered writing about.

Well, it sounds as if the pot has been boiling a long time and the soup's just getting ready to be served.

I guess so. Well, the linguistics thing was kind of like that, too, but it was over a shorter period. When I finally decided to write it down, it came very fast and freely. Most of the time I work directly at the typewriter. You know, I don't work it out and then write it up, but I sort of work in into the first draft. Even in my technical work I do that.

We have just one final question, we think. You spoke of the role of your father as a source of interest and stimulation. What about the role of your mother?

That would be more in the area of general **concern about social issues**, I suppose. As a matter of fact, one major part of my intellectual life has been politics. During my childhood, there was always plenty of discussion in my home about really interesting and important issues. I mean that my own linguistic work has always been a small part of my intellectual life. I have also been very much interested in philosophy and have read in it fairly extensively. For example, I have been quite interested recently in 17th- and 18th-century rationalist philosophy, in connection with issues that I've been thinking about in a vague way for along time.

Have you published this?

Yes, in 1966, a book called *Cartesian Linguistics*. It was a quite different departure.

What has your specific interest in philosophy been?

Well, it sort of converged upon a critique of empiricism.

Logical empiricism?

No, all empiricism. I got started with a critique of logical empiricism, but I really think that the whole empiricist tradition has some very fundamental flaws and these are responsible for the fact that it has had so little impact on the actual work in fields that have real intellectual content, as compared with its impact on weaker fields like psychology and linguistics or the social sciences. It seems to me that the empiricist framework has been debilitating in these fields because it tends to restrict theoretical and intellectual content, if taken very literally. That is a problem that interests me in intellectual history. That's why I'm so interested in the rationalist philosophy and its implications for biology and the human sciences.

Your interest, then, is in the conditions of thinking?

Yes, and just what it means to be human. This involves some special kind of mind, a special type of biological development, special ways of dealing with interpersonal relations and intellectual structures, and so forth. I think the study of language fits here.

There is one final question. You got into linguistics, and you weren't happy the way the field was at the time.

That is a little misleading. I wasn't aware of this until afterward. It took me several years to come to this realization.

There's something a little deceiving about this that we ought to go into. What is the place in your life of the need to prove something, to be competitive, which appears sort of hidden in what you've said.

It's not hidden at all! Well, for example, when I had come to believe that structural linguistics was on the wrong track, I began to work very hard in an attempt to provide a definitive disproof of the claims of people working in the field. My competitiveness was perfectly obvious and, although perhaps I should-n't admit this, there was a sort of aggressive element in it that I am perfectly aware of.

Editor's Notes to Interview 4

New Left Review 57 (Sep–Oct 1969), pp. 21–34. The interviewers were R.B. [Robin Blackburn], G.S.J. [Gareth Stedman Jones], L.R. [Lucien Rey], but the questions are not identified by interviewer. It took place in England, presumably at the time Chomsky delivered the Locke lectures. It has been translated into Italian, Spanish, German (see Koerner & Tajima, p. 166).

This interview is the best source, if not the only one, for the illuminating suggestion that the "ideal situation" for the discovery of generative grammar "would have been to have someone in 1940 who was steeped in rationalist and romantic literary theory and also happened to know modern mathematics." As mentioned in the Introduction, the thought lends some support to A. N. Whitehead's suggestion that "novel ideas," such as those of Kepler (or Darwin), "are more apt to spring from an unusual assortment of knowledge—not necessarily from vast knowledge, but from a thorough conception of the methods and ideas of distinct lines of thought," of two different subjects—at least, as they are thought at the time (*An Introduction to Mathematics*, Oxford UP, 1948, p. 101—first published in 1911). On "the character, sources, and general development of romantic aesthetic theory," see **CL** (1966), 16ff., where the reader is referred (note 35) to M. H. Abrams, *The Mirror and the Lamp: Romantic Theory and the Critical Tradition*. Oxford UP, 1953 (Norton paperback, 1958) for further discussion; see now also *The Literary Absolute: The Theory of Literature in German Romanticism*, by Philippe Lacoue-Labarthe & Jean-Luc Nancy. Translated with an introduction and additional notes by Philip Barnard & Cheryl Lester. State University of New York Press, 1988 (first published in Paris by Seuil in 1978). Compare the quote by Chomsky about structuralism, Lacan and Derrida in the notes to I18.

4. Linguistics and Politics (Spring 1969)

It is clear from your writings that you were thinking deeply about politics long before the Vietnam War became a dominant issue in America. Could you tell us something about the background to your present political stand?

I have been involved in politics, intellectually if not always actively, since early childhood. I grew up among the radical Jewish community in New York. This was during the Depression and many of my immediate relatives were active in various left-wing and working-class movements. The first "political" article I remember writing was in a school newspaper, an article about the fall of Barcelona. The Spanish Civil War, of course, was a major experience from childhood which stuck.

I was connected loosely with various types of groups, searching for something that was within the Marxist or at least revolutionary tradition, but which did not have the elitist aspects which seemed to me then and seem to me today to be disfiguring and destructive. In the forties, when I was a teenager, I would hang around left-wing book shops and the offices of offbeat groups and periodicals, talking to people—often very perceptive and interesting people who were thinking hard about the problems of social change—and seeing what I could pick up. Then I was much interested in a Jewish organization which was opposed to the Jewish state in Palestine and worked for Arab-Jewish co-operation on a socialist basis. Out of all this, from my relatives and friends, I learned a great deal informally and acquired a certain framework within which my own way of thinking developed.

In fact, I more or less got into linguistics this way, through my connections with these political groups. I was very impressed by Zellig Harris, who was the head of the Linguistics Department at the University of Pennsylvania, and I found I had political interests in common with him. He had a kind of semi-anarchist strain to his thought. Then I withdrew during the fifties from political involvements, though of course I retained my intellectual interest. I signed petitions, over the Rosenberg case, for instance, and went on occasional demonstrations but it did not amount to much. Then, in the sixties, I began to become more active again. Like most people, I had something to do with the civil rights movement. But in retrospect I think I was very slow in getting involved. It was only when the Vietnam War began escalating that I began to take any really active political role. Much too late, I am afraid.

How effective do you think the anti-war movement in America has been? How effective do you think it can be in the future?

I think if the movement was able to consolidate and act it could probably end the war. I think it is a great tragedy that it has more or less collapsed in the last few months. In the past I think it had had a marginal effect. The major factor has been the National Liberation Front and the struggle in Vietnam itself. But I think there is some evidence that political action in America has limited and retarded American aggression. I think the will to prosecute the war has been weakened by the turmoil and dissidence in American society itself. The domestic cost began to become too high. Of course, without the Tet offensive, this would not have weighed so greatly but I think it has been an important factor nonetheless. Pressure for ending the war became really quite substantial. The *Wall Street Journal* opposed the war, for instance. I think that if, after Nixon was elected, there had been sufficient disruption and turmoil and demonstrations, then it might have hastened the end of the war considerably. But, for various reasons, this did not take place.

Do you think that the chain of insurrections on the campuses is a form of solidarity with the Vietnamese, apart from the anti-war movement as such?

I am of two minds about that. These insurrections are not specifically directed against the war so it is not so obvious that they are part of the cost of the war. There was a shift in student politics between the Pentagon demonstration in October 1967 and the Columbia action in spring 1968. My own feeling is that this shift did not do much to help the Vietnamese. If the student movement had focussed its energy and its activism more directly against the war, it would have been a much more powerful force in cutting down the American military effort. Obviously, anyone rational has to recognize that student insurrections are part of the fall-out from the war in Vietnam. But it is not so clear that they would stop if the war stopped. So in this sense they are less effective tactically than unambiguous **anti-war actions**.

But it is hard to see how the student movement could avoid campus issues. There are real contradictions on the campus which affect the students and which the student movement could not ignore. A number of the insurrections seem to have arisen spontaneously out of the campus situation.

I am not so convinced that people active in the student movement should simply find the most lively issue and work on that. That is a bit unprincipled. They ought to be finding the issues which are the most important and trying to make those issues important to the people whom they are trying to reach. That is different from finding issues which seem to have some life and selecting them because they may be useful issues for building a movement. Now I do not think that is necessarily wrong; building a movement concerned with social change, perhaps **revolutionary change**, is important. But I think one has to be careful to avoid opportunism and to try always to find principled issues rather than issues which happen to be convenient at the moment. The necessity to end the Vietnam War seems to me so urgent that I would be perfectly willing to be enormously involved in a movement that would end when the Vietnam War ended, if that movement helped to end the war. I feel that ending the Vietnam War is the highest priority for any radical or revolutionary movement in America.

What do you think are the most effective forms of action the anti-war movement might take in the future?

Draft resistance has been effective and could be even more effective if it were to become a well-organized and cohesive movement. I also think that sabotage is perfectly justified against the war and should be publicly supported. In Milwaukee, for instance, there were 14 people who simply went in and took the draft files out and burned them all with napalm. That was an important act and it could have been even more important had it been the signal for large demonstrations and actions in support of what they did.

It is not simply a question of action limited to universities. For instance, in California there have been actions involving both students and workers. Don't you think this is an important step forward, given that the American working class have not yet played any significant part in the anti-war movement?

If the Vietnamese have to wait until we build a serious political movement against all forms of capitalist repression in the United States, then they are all going to be dead. It is true that active opposition to the war has been middle class or even upper-middle class, but that is a politically very important part of the population. It is difficult to repress, in the sense that there is a high political cost to the repression of these classes and that gives a lever for protest against the war which should be exploited. I have nothing against using the inegalitarian aspects of American society as a weapon against its foreign policy. In any case, we cannot delay on the Vietnam issue in order to build a movement on more long-term issues. Even if these two goals were in conflict, I think we should give priority to the goal of ending the war. But I do not think they are in conflict. Principled opposition to the war will lead directly to principled opposition to imperialism and to the causes of imperialism and hence to the formation of a principled anti-capitalist movement.

You have made many very persuasive and moving indictments of American imperialism in Vietnam. Could you spell out the reasons why the United States went into Vietnam?

I think the United States went in for a lot of reasons and I think they have changed through time. At the moment, I think we are staying in largely because there is a big investment in error and it is very hard for people who have invested an enormous amount of prestige in their commitment to a policy simply to admit defeat. So they are looking for what they choose to call an honorable peace, which does not exist, in their sense. But if we look back further we find a different set of reasons. If you read the State Department's propaganda of 1950/1951, you will find that their intention then was to give sufficient support to the French to enable them to re-constitute French colonial rule and to eradicate Communism there.

When the French proved incapable of carrying this out, then the United States simply took over. Dean Acheson made it clear that when China was "lost," the United States would not tolerate any further disturbance to the integrated world system it was attempting to construct and revolution in Vietnam was seen as an erosion of that system. Now it is perfectly true, as many people point out, that the United States can survive without Vietnam as a colony, that the United States does not need Vietnamese rubber or anything like that. But I think the very fact that Vietnam is so unimportant in this respect shows how desperately necessary it is felt to be to maintain an integrated world system. They are willing to make this great commitment even to hold a marginal, peripheral piece of their empire.

If one looks into it even more deeply then one discerns other things going on. For example, the United States fought the Second World War, in the Pacific theater, primarily in order to prevent Japan from constructing its own independent, integrated imperial system which would be closed to America. That was the basic issue which lay behind the Japanese-American war. Well, the United States won. The result is that now it must develop a system in which Japan can function effectively as a junior partner. That means the United States has to grant Japan what it needs as a partner, namely markets and access to raw materials, which for Japan, unlike the United States, are desperate necessities. Now the United States can very well survive without Southeast Asia. But Japan cannot. So if the United States wants to keep Japan securely embedded within the American system, then it has to preserve Southeast Asia for Japan. Otherwise Japan has other alternatives. It would turn to China or to Siberia, but that would mean the United States had lost the Second World War, in its Pacific phase. Once again a substantial industrial power would be carving itself out an independent space which, taken to its logical conclusion, would be separate and partially scaled off from the American world system.

I think the United States recognized this danger immediately after the Second World War and accordingly began to reconstitute the imperial relations between Japan and its former colonies. People in the Philippines were upset and taken aback by this. They thought they had helped the United States win the war and they were puzzled to find the United States building up Japan as an industrial power again and ignoring the Philippines. But the reason for that is plain. Japan could not be ignored and the United States wanted it to play its allotted role in the American system, similar to that played by Britain in the Atlantic. The consequence of that is that sources of raw materials and a market for Japanese goods must be maintained in Southeast Asia. The United States does not have to sell motorcycles there for itself but Japan does have to and the United States has to ensure that it can, if the American system there is to remain stable.

Another factor that was very important and is extremely suggestive for the future is that the Vietnam War became an ideological instrument for the strategic theory of the Cold War intelligentsia that moved into power with Kennedy. This was to be the testing ground where they could show how by properly designed counter-insurgency programs they could control potential revolutionary movements anywhere on the globe. They put an enormous commitment into this. When the technical intelligentsia becomes involved in the design of policy, this is a very different matter from when a corporate elite or an aristocracy becomes involved in policy-making. To put it in a nutshell, when someone like Averell Harriman happens to make a mistake, it does not seem to him he has lost his right to be running the world. His right to be running the world is based on the fact that his grandfather built railroads. But if Walt Rostow or McGeorge Bundy happen to make a mistake, when it turns out they got everything wrong, then they have lost their only claim to be at the center of power, which was that they had superior knowledge to other people. The consequence of this is that policies designed by this technical intelligentsia have a peculiar persistence. Other people's claim to power need not be diminished by failure in the same way, so they can be somewhat more pragmatic and opportunistic.

You do not think that power has been transferred in any substantial way from large capital to the intelligentsia? Would you agree that power still remains where it has always been, with large capital, and that the new prominence of the intelligentsia does not mean there is some new mode of production or some new, qualitatively different stage of capitalism in the United States?

The idea that power has shifted from capital to knowledge is pretty much a fantasy. But the technical intelligentsia is providing great service to the corporate elite that has been running America throughout this century and I think they do make their own contribution, a very dangerous contribution. The intellectual community used to be a kind of critical voice. That was its main function. Now it is losing that function and accepting the notion that its role is to carry out piecemeal social technology.

Don't you think American imperialism is right, within its own terms, to fear popular uprisings and revolutions wherever they occur, in however small or distant a country, simply because there is always the threat of contagion?

That is true. There is such a threat, and it is a serious one. The goal of designing an integrated world economy to be dominated by American capital is the highest priority for the corporate elite that manages the United States. This is not just a matter of having safe areas for American investment and markets and control of raw materials though, of course, these are important. There is also the need to maintain a high level of defense spending, war spending basically. This has been the main "Keynesian" mechanism for maintaining what they call the health of the economy. The United States was still in the Depression in 1939. There were nine million unemployed. The war ended that. American industrial production quadrupled during the Second World War. It was done by running a tightly managed economy with government intervention, largely in arms, but multiplying out to the rest of the economy.

Now this lesson in economics was taught to precisely the people who could benefit from it, namely the corporate managers who came to Washington to manage the war-time economy. Arms production is ideal from their point of view. It keeps the economy running and it does not conflict with private interests. But of course the taxpayer has to be willing to foot the bill. Hence the Cold War paranoia which goes with this enormous arms production. Without this great fear of the Communists or the Third World or China, there is no particular reason why 50 percent of a tax dollar should be spent on a public subsidy to war-based industry. These things all tie in together.

Could you say something about the campaign you have been involved in against MIT participation in the United States military program?

I have simply been following the lead of the students who have done a very good job on this. MIT manages two laboratories financed largely by the Pentagon and NASA to the tune of something like $125 million a year. About 4,000 people are employed there largely on war-related projects. They are involved in designing the guidance system for the Poseidon MIRV system and in research on ABM systems and very many things of that kind. They are involved in counterinsurgency too, techniques for detecting tunnels and detecting people hidden in dense foliage, everything. Now there are a number of alternatives open to us in a campaign against participation in "defense" programs of this kind. We could try to sever the connection between the university and the laboratories where this work is done. This happened recently at Stanford. But the students have opposed this. They have insisted from the beginning that this would not be an acceptable way out. In effect, it would mean only a kind of terminological shift. The work would go on, but under a different name. The same university people would be involved in it, but as consultants maybe instead of as staff.

There is no particular point in trying to develop pure universities in a criminal society. I would rather have the laboratories right in the middle of the campus, where their presence could be used to politicize future engineers, for instance, rather than having them hidden away somewhere while the campus is perfectly clean and cloistered. I feel this way about chemical and bacteriological warfare too. I would prefer to have a building in the middle of the campus, called Department of Bacteriological Warfare, rather than have it right off the map at Fort Detrick or some place nobody knows of. It could be actually retrograde, in this sense, to try to cut all connections between the university and the Department of Defense.

So this means taking a second alternative. We aim to try to keep control over the laboratories but to try to control also what kind of research is done in them. Of course, this is difficult, because there are limited funds for anything except military research. It brings the problem of establishing a student/worker alliance to the forefront too. As things stand now, the workers in the laboratories—scientists, technicians, unskilled workers—are terrified of the idea that war research might stop. In fact, when we started picketing, the union there, whose members are mostly machinists and so forth, entered a suit to prevent MIT from dropping war research. You can see the logic behind their action. They do not see any alternatives to war research and development within the New England economy.

We have somehow to get people to see that there are other things technology could be used for, that there is no good reason why the public subsidy they are living on should be used simply for purposes of destruction. We have to keep the issue alive and open. We have to try to reconvert the laboratories. We have to try to build up social and political pressures for a socially useful technology. It means making ideas that sound utopian at first seem real and possible. It is a big order and we do not expect to do it in a short time.

You seem to reject the liberal idea that there can be limited reforms in American society but, at the same time, you do not seem to see much immediate future for revolutionary action.

We should set up the germs of new institutions where we can. We should try to make people realize what is wrong with this society and give them a conscious vision of the new society. Then we can go on to a program of action for great masses of people. A democratic revolution would take place when it is supported by the great mass of the people, when they know what they are doing and they know why they are doing it and they know what they want to see come into existence. Maybe not in detail, but at least in some manner. A revolution is something that great masses of people have to understand and be personally committed to.

In order to broaden the social base of the student movement, do you see good prospects for work in high schools?

The potential there is very great. According to recent reports, about 60 percent of the high schools in America have had fairly significant student protest, usually over a political issue. This offers the same sort of potential as common action with the Richmond Oil workers in California: there is a radicalization, a politicization of a part of the population hitherto uninvolved in politics. We can envisage a loose set of connections ranging throughout high schools and colleges which could serve as the base for a really substantial political movement.

If there is going to be severe repression of the student movement, as seems more than likely, this brings out the need for better organization and for more intellectual coherence. Do you think the time for relying on ad hoc modes of action and ad hoc slogans is past?

Without a revolutionary theory or a revolutionary consciousness there is not going to be a revolutionary movement. There is not going to be a serious movement without a clear analysis and a theoretical point of view. Naturally the student movement has to be able to defend itself against repression. This has to be broadened out beyond the student movement. The Black Panthers are subjected to intensive repression and we should not allow this to be forgotten.

What do you envisage by revolutionary theory?

There are certain crises of capitalism that cannot be overcome internally. They can be overcome only by the total reconstruction of social relations. All economic and political institutions should be placed under democratic control through direct participation by workers and by those involved because they live in a particular geographical area, for instance, or on the basis of other forms of free association. To take an example, there is at the moment a serious crisis of capitalism with respect to the problem of how to use technological resources to serve human needs rather than the need to maintain a senseless, irrational and predatory economy. This problem cannot be solved within the framework of capitalist ideology or the capitalist system of production. Certain human needs can only be expressed collectively and that requires an entirely different system. I think issues like the extension of democracy, the satisfaction of human needs, the preservation of the environment, are of the first importance. A revolutionary theory ought to be concerned with developing points of this sort and translating them into something that is immediately meaningful.

Do you not accept Leninism as the basis of the revolutionary theory you would like to see develop? Are you anti-Leninist as well as anti-Stalinist?

It would be a grotesque error to say that Stalin was simply the realization of Leninist principles or anything like that. Lenin himself insisted, quite correctly, that in a backward country like Russia the revolution could not succeed unless there was an international revolution. There are different strands in Lenin's theories. On the one hand, there is *State and Revolution*, which is basically fine, and on the other hand, there is the effective dismantling of the Soviets, there is Kronstadt and the suppression of the Workers' Opposition, which was under Lenin's aegis at least. We could go into the history of all this and we could criticize one thing and laud another. But I think there are really two competing tendencies. There is a model which stresses the leadership role of the vanguard party of committed intellectuals, which controls and determines the course of the movement. That is an aspect of the Leninist tradition which laid the groundwork for Stalin. Then, contrasted to this, there is a model which sees the revolutionary movement as based on voluntary mass associations which have control themselves and which are encouraged to exercise it, politicizing themselves in the process. This is a tendency associated more with Rosa Luxemburg and her criticisms of Lenin's concept of the party, though, of course, we should not forget there is also the Lenin of the *April Theses* and of *State and Revolution*.

Do you not think that the Leninist tradition should be held responsible for the Chinese and Vietnamese revolutions if it is going to be held responsible for Stalinism?

Frankly I think the Chinese overestimate their dependence on the Bolshevik model and they underestimate the populist element that exists in Maoism. Without this they might not have had the success they did in involving masses of people in a way which was not characteristic of the Russian Revolution.

Lenin stressed the need to involve the masses.

Yes, that is the side of Lenin which shows up in the *April Theses* and *State and Revolution*. But after the Bolsheviks took power, they followed a very different course.

What kind of explanation would you give for the Cold War? Do you accept some version of the convergence theory?

I think there is a kind of convergence in the sphere of the involvement of the technical intelligentsia at the center of power. There is an old anarchist critique of the role of the intelligentsia in bureaucracies which rings very true. There is also convergence in the evolution of large centralized economic units. But, of course, the Cold War took place without respect to any convergence of this kind. I think the main reason for the Cold War was that the Soviet Union constructed a closed order in Eastern Europe. One can see this by reading statements of the American ruling elite, like the study entitled "The Political Economy of American Foreign Policy" published in the mid-50s which identifies the primary threat of Communism as the refusal to continue to complement the industrial economics of the West. Any society which is closed is a threat to the United States. This applies both to the Soviet Union and to pre-war Japan. Of course, the Soviet threat involved socialized production and the Japanese threat did not. But basically they were threats of a very similar sort. They closed off significant areas of the world and made them inaccessible to American capital. The United States had to combat this threat. In one case, by the Pacific phase of the Second World War and, in the other case, by the Cold War.

You do not think it was also because the Soviet Union offered an alternative model of society?

An alternative model of development. If you compare the areas of the Soviet Union which are directly north of Turkey and Iran with the areas directly south of the border, there is a very striking difference in development. But the same was true of pre-war Japan and its New Order. I think the threat of independent development is probably more important than the threat of socialized production. It is a threat to the aim of constructing an international system, dominated by the United States, in which there will be a free flow of capital and goods and raw materials.

But although the American economic penetration of the Soviet Union is still relatively small, there has been a very marked shift in attitude towards a detente. Why is China seen as so much more of a threat than the Soviet Union?

The Soviet Union has already been given up. And it has been a long-standing element of American belief that the China trade is going to be of very great significance for the economic development of the United States. That goes back to the 1780s, back to the time when the west coast of America was settled by merchants interested in the China trade. One of the main reasons why the United States took the Philippines in the late 19th century was as a coaling station for the China trade. Of course, there is an element of mythology in this, but in the formation of policy, it is what people believe that counts, not what is true.

All the same, that seems a very economistic line of argument. Surely both the Bolshevik and Chinese revolutions were a threat because of force of example, because of the political ideological repercussions? Japan is a quite different case. The Japanese, like the United States, tried to crush the revolution in China. That is not really true of the Soviet Union.

The Japanese did not set out to crush the Chinese revolution. For example there was no Chinese revolution in Manchuria in 1931 or North China in 1937. They set out to dominate China, and crushing the Chinese revolution was a by-product. I think if China happened at that moment to be fascist rather than communist, but also excluded from the present American world system, then it would be perceived as a threat to the United States. But perhaps I have been underestimating the ideological threat. It is true to say that the success of a popular mass revolution, as in China, does give people elsewhere ideas. It teaches people that property is not holy and that we can make a revolution too. If China were fascist, it would not have this ideological impact on other parts of the world, but it would still be perceived as a danger if it were separated from the American world system and engaged on an independent path of development.

We would like to ask you something about your work in linguistics. Do you think there is any connection between your specialized work there and your political views, which you have been talking about?

Scientific ideas and political ideas can converge and, if they converge independently because they have each developed in the same direction, that is fine. But they should not be made to converge at the cost of distortion and suppression, or anything like that.

For instance, in your work in linguistics, you use concepts like "freedom," "spontaneity," "creativity," "innovation" and so on. Is that connected in any way with your political views? Or is it just accidental?

A little of each. It is accidental in that the way these concepts arise in the study of **language** and the theses they sustain are appropriate or inappropriate, true or false, quite independently of politics. In that sense, it is independent. And similarly, in my opinion, a **Marxist-anarchist perspective** is justified quite apart from anything that may happen in linguistics. So that in that sense they are logically independent. But I still feel myself that there is a kind of tenuous connection. I would not want to overstate it but I think it means something to me at least. I think that anyone's political ideas or their ideas of social organization must be rooted ultimately in some concept of human nature and human needs. Now my own feeling is that the fundamental human capacity is the capacity and the need for creative self-expression, for free control of all aspects of one's life and thought. One particularly crucial realization of this capacity is the creative use of language as a free instrument of thought and expression. Now having this view of human nature and human needs, one tries to think about the modes of social organization that would permit the freest and fullest development of the individual, of each individual's potentialities in whatever direction they might take, that would permit him to be fully human in the sense of having the greatest possible scope for his freedom and initiative.

Moving along in this direction, one might actually develop a social science in which a concept of social organization is related to a concept of human nature which is empirically well-founded and which in some fashion leads even to value judgments about what form society should take, how it should change and how it should be reconstructed. I want to emphasize again that fundamentally the two are logically independent, but one can draw a sort of loose connection. This connection has been made occasionally. Von Humboldt, for example, who interests me particularly, combined a deep interest in human creativity and the creative aspect of language with what were, in the context of his time, libertarian politics.

Another concept which is crucial to your work in linguistics is that of "rules." How does that fit in with the stress on freedom?

I think that true creativity means free action within the framework of a system of rules. In art, for instance, if a person just throws cans of paint randomly at a wall, with no rules at all, no structure, that is not artistic creativity, whatever else it may be. It is a commonplace of aesthetic theory that creativity involves action that takes place within a framework of rules, but is not narrowly determined either by the rules or by external stimuli. It is only when you have the combination of freedom and constraint that the question of creativity arises.

I would like to assume on the basis of fact and hope on the basis of confidence in the human species that there are innate structures of mind. If there are not, if humans are just plastic and random organisms, then they are fit subjects for the shaping of behavior. If humans only become as they are by random changes, then why not control that randomness by the state authority or the behaviorist technologist or anything else? Naturally I hope that it will turn out that there are intrinsic structures determining human need and fulfillment of human need.

What is the role of human history? Surely human needs and their fulfillment are historically determined. What kind of scope do you give to historical determinations?

I think we have to be very cautious about this until we have a much broader understanding of the range and extent of possible variations in human behavior. Things that seem to us great variations in language, for instance, would seem to some super-intelligence as minor modifications. As human beings, as living human beings, we are primarily interested in the differences among ourselves and that is perfectly proper. As a human being, living in the contemporary world, I am very much interested in the difference between English and Japanese because I cannot understand Japanese and it would be useful to be able to. But as a linguist I am interested in the fact that English and Japanese are rather minor modifications of a basic pattern and that other linguistic systems could be imagined which violate that basic pattern, but that they do not in fact anywhere exist. Now it is possible to carry out this study as a linguist because we can move up to a level of abstractness from which we can survey a vast class of possible systems and ask how the existing human linguistic systems fit into this class. And I think we will discover that they fit into a very narrow part of it.

A serious study of morals or of social systems would attempt the same thing. It would ask itself what kinds of social systems are conceivable. Then it would ask itself what kinds have actually been realized in history and it would ask how these came into existence, given the range of possibilities that exist at some moment of economic and cultural development. Then, having reached that point, the next question is whether the range of social systems that human beings have constructed is broad or narrow, what is its scope, what are its potentialities, are there kinds of social systems human beings could not possibly construct and so on. We have not really begun this kind of investigation. Hence it is only a guess when I say that the range of possible social systems may turn out to be very narrow. Of course, there is an enormous human significance in living in one social system rather than another, in capitalism rather than feudalism, for example. Whereas there is no human significance, other than accidental, in speaking one language rather than another. But that is a different question from asking which kinds of system of social organization are possible for human beings and which kinds are not.

You have spoken about a possible convergence of your work in linguistics with your political ideas. Did your political ideas have any influence in the work you have done in linguistics up till now? Did they suggest hypotheses, for instance?

I do not think so. I worked for quite a few years trying to carry out a behaviorist program. As a student, I was very much convinced that it would be possible to construct simple inductive principles that would explain how language is acquired. I thought that there should be simple inductive principles which would lead directly from a corpus of data to the organization of that data and that such an organization is what language would, in fact, consist of. But at the same time I was also, on the side, trying to write generative grammars. I assumed that generative grammars were just for fun and my own private hobby. I thought the attempt to build up analytic procedures was the real stuff. It was only much later, a long time later, maybe four years of really hard work, that I finally managed to convince myself that the attempt to build up analytic procedures was nonsense and that generative grammar was the real thing.

How did you get interested in generative grammar?

It had been around a long time. As I understand Humboldt, for instance, he had a concept similar to generative grammar. In any event, whether Humboldt did or did not, one thing at least is clear: if he did have a concept of generative grammar he could not do anything with it, because he did not have the techniques for using it. There was no way to take his insights and turn them into a rich, explanatory theory. That required new notions which eventually grew out of work on the foundations of mathematics. The notion of recursive systems of rules, for example. This work only came to fruition in the 1930s. But by then most people had completely forgotten about Humboldt and his kind of insights. I happened to be very lucky since I began to study the foundations of mathematics, not thinking it had any bearing on linguistics. Of course, it turned out to be just what was needed.

I think the ideal situation would have been to have someone in 1940 who was steeped in **rationalist and romantic literary and aesthetic theory** and also happened to know **modern mathematics**. Such a person would have seen very quickly what to do. As far as I was concerned, it was pure accident. It just happened I grew up having some knowledge of historical linguistics largely because my father, who was a Hebrew scholar, was working on medieval grammatical texts and the history of the language. In historical linguistics it is taken for granted that there are underlying processes and that you can explain things by looking at how these processes interrelate. Of course, this is usually done in a very atomistic fashion and there is not much theory or system to it, but at least the concept of explanation is there. And then, as I said, I had also done some work in modern mathematics and logic, so I was able to combine these two interests. At first, I thought it was just a hobby. It took years and years before any of it was published. Even after I was convinced myself, I still could not get it published. Very few people saw any value in this work.

Do you now think that your work on generative grammar looks forward to further scientific advances?

I think that among the biological characteristics that determine the nature of the human organism there are some that relate to intellectual development, some that relate to moral development, some that relate to development as a member of human society, some that relate to aesthetic development. I suspect that they are restrictive and that we shall find that all of these constraints can be said to constitute human nature. To a large extent, they are immutable. That is

to say, they are just part of being human the same way as having legs and arms
is part of being human.

Are you saying you think there is a generative grammar for social relations?

Not necessarily. That is, I do not think our capacities for having decent
social relations, relations that would lead to some new form of society, would
necessarily have the same structure as a generative grammar. I simply think that
they must be constrained by some set of principles. But, of course, I cannot specify the principles.

*Do you think there is some intrinsic disposition towards order in human beings which
would spontaneously emerge if it was not repressed in some way?*

I presume so. The only justification for any repressive institution is economic or cultural backwardness. In time, we should move to the gradual elimination of all repressive institutions without limit, as far as I can see. Just looking
at the epoch that we are in now, it seems to me that our present level of technology permits enormous possibilities for eliminating repressive institutions.
Automation makes it unnecessary for people to carry out the kind of imbecile
labor that may have been necessary in the past. It is often said that advanced
technology makes it imperative to vest control of institutions in the hands of a
small managerial group. That is perfect nonsense. What automation can do first
of all is to relieve people of an enormous amount of stupid labor, thus freeing
them for other things. Computers also make possible a very rapid information
flow. Everybody could be put in possession of vastly more information and more
relevant information than they have now. Democratic decisions could be made
immediately by everybody concerned. Computers also make simulation possible,
you can run simulation experiments, so that you can test decisions without bearing the cost of failure.

Of course, that is not how this technology is actually used. It is used for
destructive purposes. You get a situation where, even if the Vietnam War was
ended, resources would simply be redistributed to something like ABM systems.
The electronics industry has not got a decent cut out of the budget since the
Vietnam War got going. So they want an ABM system. The percentage of government expenditure on advanced technology has been reduced since the
Vietnam War escalated, for the simple reason that you have to supply all the soldiers with uniforms and bullets and shoes and so on. But the end of the war
would not divert any money to meeting collective needs on extending democratic practice. It would to back into aerospace and telecommunications, for the
Defense Department or the Space Agency. Within a capitalist framework it could
hardly be otherwise.

Editor's Notes to Interview 5

This little known interview, which shows that, contrary to what some people believe, Chomsky's concern with ecological issues was present from early on (not without some intimation that he is a *rara avis* even at MIT), was first published in a collection of "conversations" completed by Christmas 1972: *On Growth*, ed. by Willem L. Oltmans. New York: Capricorn Books; G.P. Putnam's Sons, 1974, pp. 284–291. A brief note on Chomsky lists eight of his "best known books" (though, surprisingly, not *Syntactic Structures*, the first and most celebrated one), in addition to his doctoral dissertation. There is also a reference to "Chomsky's Sharp Criticism of Skinner's *Beyond Freedom and Dignity*, 'The Case Against B. F. Skinner,' the *New York Review of Books*, Dec. 30, 1971," parts (in a slightly different form) of what was to become "Psychology and Ideology," ch. 7 of *For Reasons of State* (1973).

The British historian Arnold Toynbee (1889–1975), the Harvard psychologist B. F. Skinner (1904–1990), MIT economists Paul Samuelson (b. 1915)—the first Nobel laureate for economics (1970)—referred to in I16 (and in **TNCW** (1982), p. 380 n. 59), and Carl Kaysen, and Harvard sociologist Daniel Bell, all referred to in this "conversation," are the interviewees in conversations 5, 7, 8, 9 and 66, respectively. It is interesting to compare their answers (and those of many others) with Chomsky's (or Linus Pauling's). John Kenneth Galbraith (identified by Oltmans as a Harvard economist) was not among those interviewed. Oltmans also provides the following identifications:

"Mikhail A. Bakunin (1814–1876), Russian anarchist and writer.

Herbert G. Wells (1866–1946), British novelist and writer on social and political problems.

Bertrand Russell (1872–1970), British philosopher, mathematician and writer."

On what the then president of the National Academy of Science described as "the gap in the use of language," see **RP** (1981/1984/2003), ch. 26, and **KL** (1984), ch. 5, keeping in mind that Chomsky shares only in part the widespread belief that misuse or control of language is a central feature of what he calls "Orwell's problem" (see the last section of the Introduction and the Editor's Notes to I35). For some general background on the topic, see C.P. Otero, "Chomsky's View of Semantics and Orwell's Problem," in *Aspects of Language: Studies in Honour of Mario Alinei*, vol. II (Theoretical and Applied Semantics),ed. by N. van der Sijs et al., Amsterdam, Rodopi, 1987, pp. 357–371.

On *The Political Economy of American Foreign Policy* (Holt, 1955), the study of the Woodrow Wilson Foundation referred to, see **RP**, ch. 19 n. 8, or **CD&E** (2003), ch. 8 n. 8.

On "the game of comparative advantage," see **RP** (2003), ch. 28.

The background of *On Growth*, not generally known, is not without interest.

It was a colleague of Chomsky's at MIT, Professor Jay W. Forrester, the prime mover of an MIT group of people that had been developing "system dynamics" since 1956 (p. 217), who told Oltmans (a journalist who had covered foreign affairs and international relations for twenty years, shortly before for NOS National Dutch Television in the United States) about the Club of Rome—which had just "made a start by looking into the question of how to manage the globe" (p. 306)—and "its assignment to Forrester's system engineers at MIT to study computer models on the limits of the planet as a whole" (p. v). The team leader for the MIT report (*The Limits to Growth; A Report for the Club of Rome's Project on the Predicament of Mankind*, [by] Donella H. Meadows [and others]. New York, Universe Books [1972]) was Professor Dennis L. Meadows, who was to leave MIT in the fall of 1972 to take charge of a new faculty of system analysis at Dartmouth College and set up "an entire new department with a staff of 15 instructors and professors" (p. 18).

Early in 1971 Oltmans had begun producing a documentary film for NOS on the information he obtained in Washington. This film, which was shown on Sunday, Sept. 26, 1971, in prime time, "caused a major sensation in the Netherlands," a Club of Rome sponsored exhibition being organized in Rotterdam which drew "tens of thousands of visitors" (v–vi).

The MIT report *Limits to Growth* was presented to the American public and press at the Smithsonian Institution in Washington, D.C., on March 2, 1972 (the Dutch edition sold a quarter of a million copies in less than a year). News about the plans for a U.S.-USSR combined think tank reached the front page of the *New York Times* on Oct. 14, 1971, just "a few weeks after the subject had been shown on National Dutch Television," and on Oct. 4, 1972, 12 nations (in addition to the U.S. and the USSR, Canada, England, France, Italy, West and East Germany, Czechoslovakia, Poland, Bulgaria, and Japan) "signed an agreement in London to set up an Institute of Applied Systems Analysis" (p. vi).

On July 6, 1972, during a conversation with the founder and chairman of the Club of Rome, Dr. Aurelio Peccei (also chairman of Italy's foremost think tank, vice-president of Olivetti and member of the board of Fiat), Oltmans decided to collect and publish opinions about *Limits to Growth*. Initially, he "intended to gather some 30 interviews," but soon he decided no to limit himself "to comments by economists, systems engineers, biologists or ecologists, but to look for reactions from a wider range of disciplines" and "the series grew to seventy conversations" (p. vi). Actually, later he was to bring together 49 more conversations, this time not "from the Western sphere of culture (with the exception of U Thant)," but from people from "the developing nations, or so-called Third World, the socialist countries, and Japan" (with two exceptions), although, for reasons apparently out of his control, "a heavy accent in this conversations has fallen on the USSR and Japan" (*On Growth* II, ed. by Willem L. Oltmans. New York: Capricorn Books; G.P. Putnam's Sons, 1975, p. vii).

See also interviews 26 and 45. Cf. **N&L** (2002), 4.iv.

5. The Major Problem of the Limits to Growth (Fall 1972)

MIT computers have produced Limits to Growth *as a first step to study the way to global equilibrium. How useful do you think that kind of approach is to the world's problems?*

Without commenting on the empirical adequacy of the Forrester study and related studies I don't think that there's any doubt whatsoever that their general point is qualitatively correct, i.e., there are limits to growth, set by natural, by physical and chemical, law. It would be inanely optimistic to simply assume that technology will somehow develop and overcome any problem posed by the finite limits of resources and the finite capacity of the ecological system to tolerate pollution and destruction. Of course, that's not the case. There is no doubt that irrational economic growth will press the limits of natural law at some stage, probably not a very distant stage. This is a prospect which has enormous social consequences.

A Major Technique for Social Control

The crucial point—which, as far as I see it, is not brought up by the Forrester study but is quite central, nevertheless—is that as the prospects for limitless growth fade, a major technique for social control will be lost. The idea that economic growth will continue without limit has been a very effective device for controlling and limiting demands for redistribution of wealth, for example. And this is quite explicitly understood. Walter Heller, chairman of the Council of Economic Advisers under President John F. Kennedy, made it very explicit that the notion of limitless growth could be employed to bring about consensus instead of conflict by overcoming the demands for redistribution of wealth, which would certainly be heard if one could not look forward to gaining more of life's benefits by some other method.

Of course, the privileged are willing to tolerate talk about redistribution only as long as it is rhetoric. They are never willing to see talk translated into action, which means that as soon as the limits of growth are seriously faced, a violent class war might erupt in which the tremendous resources of destruction that are available to the privileged will be used to destroy anyone who challenges privilege—whether it's a Third World country trying to separate itself from the Western-controlled global economy or whether it's disaffected groups in the industrial societies themselves.

119

Bertrand Russell once said that there would never be real freedom in democracy until those who do the work control the management. That's the kind of class war you just referred to?

That is right. It's conceivable that owners of capital will tolerate workers taking control of their own insurance programs. They might call it "co-determination," as they do in Germany. But when it comes beyond that to an actual share of management and profit and determining the direction of an enterprise and the character of the work that is done, of course that will not be accepted. At that point serious struggle will arise, the kind of struggle which has been suppressed by the prospects of unending growth.

Would that explain the barrage of protests to Limits to Growth *by economists like Samuelson or Kaysen?*

It is very striking that the liberal and progressive economists have on the whole been quite negative towards this thesis that growth will reach certain limits. I think the reason is exactly the one expressed by Walter Heller, which I quoted. He pointed out quite correctly that when, in his phrase, you don't have to rob Peter to pay Paul, when anyone can gain, then consensus replaces conflict. That is perfectly true. It's perfectly true that if you can promise to everyone that his lot will be better tomorrow, then even the underprivileged and the dispossessed have reason to accept a society which is strongly prejudiced against them. But those reasons disappear, as Heller and other liberal economists quite understand, as soon as these prospects no longer exist.

Do you feel H. G. Wells' dream of elegant engineers ruling with perfect benevolence (instead of our new mandarins) will come through some day?

Subservience of the Intelligentsia

I tend more to accept, with some qualifications, a much earlier prophecy than H. G. Wells', namely, that of Bakunin and other left-wing social critics since. Bakunin saw the scientific intelligentsia as a new class. It would be the most despotic, the most authoritarian, the most ruthless class that would ever rule in human society, and would control the resources of wealth and knowledge, and force the uneducated masses to live and work and march to the beat of the drum, or words approximately to that effect.

However, I think there's one qualification necessary in Bakunin's original forecast of the rise of the new class, which as far as I know was the first such prophecy. Also in the many later variants on this theme, I mean recently by people like [Harvard economist] John Kenneth Galbraith or [Harvard sociologist] Daniel Bell, who claim to see a transfer of power into the hands of the technical intelligentsia. In my opinion they are wrong in seeing a real transfer of power into the hands of a scientific intelligentsia. Rather what we are seeing, in this stage of industrial society, is that the technical and scientific intelligentsia

[Galbraith's educational and scientific estate] are able to perform very significant services for those who really do own and manage the central institutions of society. In fact, they are able to provide them with the results of science and technology and scientific management and so on. Far more significant is that they are able to legitimize authoritarian control of wealth and institutions by masking this control in the aura of science. Everyone knows that science is good and noble and worthy, and everyone is deeply in awe of technical expertise. If the intelligentsia can make it appear that authoritarian control by the privileged and allegedly the talented is a necessary condition of modern life, then they will have succeeded in legitimating precisely that kind of privilege. I believe that probably is the major contribution of the intelligentsia in the service of power and privilege.

How to influence the complex, biologically given system of the human mind, globally? Where to start to influence man's mind?

The Best Way to Influence the Human Mind

Fox News

I think the best way to influence the human mind is by presenting "evidence" and "argument", by persuasion and by explanation. These are by far the most effective techniques for influencing the human mind. It is perfectly true that one could invent the kind of behavioral technology that would make you stop smoking, if you smoke. But it's also equally true that with a rational explanation as to why you should stop doing it, you might very well come to the same conclusion. Now, the proper way to influence the human mind is by the art of explanation. There's nothing much deeper that can be said than that. Any other techniques of influencing the human mind are simply another form of service to those who want to wield coercive power. Ultimately I think one should look forward to a society in which choice and decision reside in the hands of freely associated individuals. One precisely does not want to employ the controls of the behavioral technologists or, for that matter, the techniques of the military interrogator or prison guard. It is important not to be caught up in the fraud and pretense of scientists who claim otherwise.

Wouldn't you agree with Skinner that survival is the planet's foremost value right now?

He actually says that survival of a culture is the highest value of that culture. With that view of course I do not agree. I think that there should be very significant changes and alterations of cultural and social institutions. Changes that one might call its replacement rather than its survival. But survival of the species of course remains a value.

Toynbee has warned of the <u>Germanization of America.</u> The U.S. is the second largest state management in the world right now. How do you see its future develop?

Only One Technique for Government Intervention in the Economy

There is not going to be any simple reform or in fact any complicated reforms that will change the present situation. There's the matter of outright aggression, as in the case of Vietnam, which is in fact a traditional colonial war in which the United States is trying to destroy a radical nationalist movement struggling for independence and to extricate its society from the global economy dominated by the United States. In the traditional manner, the United States is unwilling to tolerate this, and it uses the vast resources at its command to destroy the indigenous nationalist movement. Nothing particularly new about that. It's the scale that is new. But the phenomenon is familiar from history.

But is there a visible trend towards a Germanization of America?

Not because they are Nazis. It's because there's nothing else available. There is no other technique for government intervention in the economy, other than the production of waste. This has to do with the fact that the government cannot act in such a way as to conflict with the needs of the real rulers of the society. The government, for example, is not going to pour money into a mass-transportation system when most of the top corporations get their profits from irrational use of the automobile. Nor is the government going to produce anything useful because, if it does, it will compete with the private empires that control the economy. Furthermore, government intervention in the economy has to be tolerated by the taxpayer who pays the bill.

Incidentally, the same liberal economists introduced one of the most regressive tax proposals of modern times in the United States. The taxpayer can be whipped into line when he believes that his life is threatened, so he'll be willing to pay for military expenses. The state religion is powerful enough so that when national prestige is on the line, as in the space race, then the citizen can be beaten into submission and will tolerate spending for it, for a time. But these various conditions on governmental intervention in the economy—namely, that it not conflict with the interests of ruling groups but rather enhance those interests, that it be tolerable to the citizen who has to pay for it—if you look into these conditions, they virtually determine that government intervention in the economy will be the production of military waste, of military goods which will sometimes be used, as in Indochina.

Philip Handler, the president of the National Academy of Science, explained to me how the participating scientists in the National Academy often are not even aware of the gap in the use of language. "They would not be able," he said, "to put down on paper what divides them." In your field of cognitive psychology and linguistics, would it be possible to bridge these still-prevailing gaps between politicians, diplomats and scientists?

I would not like you to think, because it is not true, that linguistics and cognitive psychology have contributions to make in this domain. It is an interesting and important field. I happen to devote my intellectual energies to it. But we are not going to solve the problems you raise. It's misleading—and it's in fact part of that subversion of science that I mentioned earlier—to believe that this is a matter for scientific and technical expertise to solve.

The answer to this problem is in the hands of every single human being. It requires no profound insight into the mysteries of science to see it. People are under ideological controls which are determined very specifically by the structure of privilege and power in their societies. In the United States there is an official state ideology which is propagated daily and drilled into everyone from childhood onwards. Quite naturally people who are incapable of extricating themselves from that ideology will have a very distorted and perverted view of things that happen, of the affairs of everyday life and things that happen in the world or what they see in front of them. I think this is true of every other society as well.

The answer is to try to gain understanding of social and political processes, to see how power is being exercised. There is no contribution of science that is going to make any significant contribution. Data are available to people. People have to decide to use their intelligence, to free themselves from ideological constraints, to penetrate the duplicity and the distortion that is an intrinsic component of any system of power, ours or any others. People must try to investigate for themselves what no scientist could tell them, namely, what are the conditions for decent human existence and how to achieve them.

But with one-third of the world illiterate and another third of the world having no schools whatsoever and with the population increasing to seven billion by the year 2000, how to do it if we are to live?

Responsibility of the Citizen of an Advanced Industrial Society

The major problem of *Limits to Growth* is not posed by the underdeveloped world. It's posed by the advanced industrial societies, where people are literate, where people are committing their vast resources, material and intellectual, to destruction, to waste and so on. It is here that people have to extricate themselves from the ideological controls that distort the thinking about these matters. One cannot pass the responsibility over to scientists, and one cannot pass the responsibility over to the illiterate peasants of the Third World. The responsibility lies right in the hands of every citizen of an advanced industrial society.

How then do you view the period immediately ahead?

If in fact the limits of growth, which certainly exist, become apparent in this period, then I believe there will be a very significant social upheaval in the industrial societies, as the great mass of people who are underprivileged, dispossessed, oppressed in many ways, recognize that they no longer have any reason to accept a system of inequality and injustice which is prejudiced against them. Not having such a reason, they will begin soon to explore the ideological assumptions, to challenge them and to challenge institutional structures that are oppressive and unequal. As soon as they begin to do this, they will be met with force, because those who have power and privilege will never tolerate any serious challenge to that privilege.

I cannot predict the outcome of that kind of struggle. Clearly it will depend on the state of consciousness and organization achieved at the point when massive force is used to crush efforts to attain equality and justice.

Incidentally, I think that something of the same sort can perhaps be expected on an international scale. Just as the privileged and the affluent in a particular society will use force and terror and violence to protect their privilege if ideological controls no longer work, the same is true of the relationship between advanced industrial societies and the so-called developing and very often not-developing world. If some—say, some Third World society, so-called—decides to extricate itself from the global system which is prejudiced against it and decides to use its limited material and human resources for its own benefit, then one can predict with a high degree of probability that the privileged of the world will not tolerate that behavior and will attempt to crush it by force, as, for example, they have been attempting in Vietnam for the last twenty-five years.

I recall there was a study, in fact, one of the very few studies of the political economy of American foreign policy (by a conservative group, incidentally). They pointed out, absolutely accurately, that the primary threat of communism is the unwillingness or the inability of the communist powers to complement the industrial societies of the West, i.e., their unwillingness to play their role in the game of comparative advantage, their backward and subservient role. That is the primary threat of communism, and it is in fact true. What we call communistic societies are societies trying to undertake a kind of do-it-yourself program of development with mobilization of the population and generally some kind of authoritarian control over it. What we really objected to was that they no longer complement the industrial societies of the West.

If that tendency develops elsewhere in the world, of course, the threat will be resisted by force if necessary, by the use of all the resources of technology and science which are available. I think these are plausible speculations for the next half-century [1972–2022].

Editor's Notes to Interview 6

"Noam Chomsky: Universal Principles of Language Structure," *Indian and Foreign Review* 10:5 (Dec. 15, 1972), pp. 20–22. The interview was probably held the day Chomsky delivered his Jawaharlal Nehru memorial lecture on "Science and Ideology" at New Delhi, that is, on Nov.13, 1972, or shortly before or after. The interviewer, Shyam Ratna Gupta, chief editor of the *Review*, opens his presentation pointing out that Chomsky is often described as the "Einstein of linguistics" and closes it by giving the gist of his "famous" Nehru memorial lecture:

"Professor Chomsky has brought his profound learning to bear on such a vital issue of our time as the direction the advancement of science and technology should take—or should be given—so that it subserves the needs of mankind as a whole, lessens inequality as between nations and among people, and guides us towards a world society, free from crippling poverty and disease. The tools of science and technology should not, he implies, support political or economic aggrandizement at the behest of the leading coterie of the superpowers."

It is interesting to compare this interview, and more generally the intellectual and moral level of the "Third World" biweekly in which it appeared more than 15 years ago, with recent issues of leading magazines of the "First World."

"New economics" refers to the tools derived from Keynes, and to "military Keynesianism." For more on this important topic, see the special issue (4:4, August 1972) of *The Review of Radical Economics* "On the New Economic Policy: The New Economics and the Contradictions of Keynesianism," in particular the article by Richard B. Du Boff & Edward S. Herman, "The New Economics: Handmaiden of Inspired Truth" (pp. 54–84), a subtitle derived from the title of a chapter in which Robert A. Brady describes the accommodation of German scientists to the social philosophy of Nazi state power ("Science, Handmaiden of Inspired Truth," chapter II of *The Spirit and Structure of German Fascism*, New York, 1937). Brady is also the author of the important study *Business as a System of Power*, Columbia UP, 1943, referred to in **TNCW** (p. 380) after quoting Paul A. Samuelson's (see the Editor's Notes to I5) and Herman's grim economic predictions. See **RP**, editor's notes to ch. 19.

6. Language Structure and Behaviorist Psychology (November 1972)

A linguist or a philologist will readily recall the biblical story of the unfinished tower of Babel at Babylon and the underlying allegorical significance that language has more often proved to be a source of tension and misunderstanding than of unity and universal love. As an erudite linguistic scholar, can you enlighten us why language should cause friction and divisiveness?

I would like to qualify this question. Language differentiation is also a source of cultural variety and the excitement that results from it. I suppose that the divisiveness caused by multiplicity of languages is merely a special case of the conflict caused by chauvinism, group identification or cultural differentiation and so on, under conditions of restricted opportunity and limited resources for development. It is natural, though perhaps unfortunate, that people should band together on some occasions to try to obtain more for themselves than they would attain in a system of equitable distribution.

Variety: Source of Happiness

I think that the answer to the problem of divisiveness, caused by a variety of languages, is not to promote cultural uniformity or anything of that kind but rather to eliminate the reasons such as impoverishment which make human beings band together to oppress and dominate their fellows. It would seem to me that the variety of languages and cultures is—and should be—a source of human happiness and enrichment.

Are there any linguistic principles which underline universality of all languages of the world?

My own work leads me to the conclusion that there are far-reaching, deep-seated universal principles of language structure. I think we tend to be unaware of them and pay attention only to differentiation of languages because of a very natural response to variety as distinct from the essential shared properties of mankind. A fish, for example, may be unaware of the fact that it lives in the water. Similarly, as human beings we pay little attention to the fact that we speak a language of a specific and restricted type. That is only natural. On the other hand, we pay attention to minor, marginal variations which distinguish one language from another. But if we can establish a kind of psychic distance from the object and try to see how similar normal common characteristics really are, against the background of a possible variety that can be imagined, I think we will discover that language structures really are uniform. This uniformity results from the existence of fixed, immutable, biologically determined principles, which provide the schematism which makes a child capable of organizing and coming to terms with his rather restricted experiences of everyday life and creating complex intellectual structures on that basis.

Uniformity in Language Structures

Thus, the same principles that restrain and limit the possible variety of language also provide for the scope of human intelligence, enabling us to make incredible, inductive leaps from the phenomena of life to the amazing intricate and complicated intellectual systems that the mind creates.

In other words, there is basic unity in diversity. But could you perhaps indicate what this uniformity actually consists of in terms of either the language structures or forms?

It is difficult to be concrete without becoming rather technical. But I think in a general way we can say that a person's knowledge of his language is based on a system of rules and principles. If you look carefully at these rules, you will discover that the rules themselves are of a narrow range. There are certain kinds of rules that are permissible; there are other kinds of rules that are not permissible. There are also strict conditions on their application.

Questions in English

Let me take the simplest kind of example. Consider the process by which one forms questions in English. Consider the sentence, "The man is tall," and the associated question, "Is the man tall?" Observing many such examples, a linguist might postulate, tentatively, that the operation of forming questions is the following: search the sentence from left to right until you find the first occurrence of the word "is," and then place it at the beginning of the sentence. Applying this operation to the sentence "The man is tall," we form "Is the man tall?" correctly. Actually, this operation works very well for the vast majority of cases.

But we know, as speakers of English, that the postulated operation is incorrect. Consider the sentence: "The man who is tall is angry." Applying the postulated operation, we form "Is the man who tall is angry?," which is gibberish. The correct form should be: "Is the man who is tall angry?" The correct operation selects not the left-most occurrence of "is," but rather the occurrence of "is" that follows the subject of the sentence, which in this case is the phrase: "the man who is tall."

The correct operation is structure-dependent, in the sense that it applies to a sentence by virtue of the structure of the sentence, by virtue of the analysis of the sentence into phrases such as its subject, its predicate, and so on. The incorrect operation postulated earlier is structure-independent, in that it applies to a sentence independently of any structure, merely by virtue of the physical forms that constitute it. But the structure that is relevant happens to be quite abstract. It is not physically marked in any way in the linguistic signal. Rather, it is imposed by some mental operation as we hear or read the sentence. It would thus be quite difficult to program a computer to apply the correct, structure-dependent operation, though it would be a trivial matter to program a computer to apply the incorrect, structure-independent operation.

So far as is known, all operations in all languages are structure-dependent in this sense. Furthermore, this is not something that people have to learn, but rather something that they know without learning. Thus, suppose an English-speaking child has heard only sentences such as, "The man is tall." When he wants to form, for the first time, the question corresponding to "The man who is tall is angry," he will not make the mistake of applying the structure-independent operation to form: "Is the man who tall is angry?" Children make many sorts of errors, but never errors of this sort. In other words, children reject the structure-independent operation and apply the structure-dependent operation even though their experience is quite consistent with either.

Structure-Dependent Operations

This is a fact that requires explanation. As I mentioned earlier, one cannot argue that the structure-dependent operation is somehow simpler. On the contrary, since it involves an abstract structure, not physically marked in the linguistic signal itself, an outside observer knowing nothing of human language might conclude that it is more complex and less natural. Yet all human languages are based on the principle that operations are structure-dependent, that operations apply to abstract structures imposed on a linguistic signal by the mind and not marked in the signal itself. That is the way the human mind operates.

To humans, all of this seems obvious, because we take our normal capacities for granted. But if we establish the proper psychic distance from the phenomena, we see that this property of the mind is by no means an obvious or necessary one. As we investigate language—and I believe other products of human intelligence—we discover many principles of this sort. These principles constitute the intrinsic, innate structure of the human mind. They provide the basis for organizing experience and developing intellectual structures, such as language, on the basis of this experience.

One of the great reformists of the English language was G.B. Shaw. He remarked that language was invented by man to communicate his feelings, emotions and thoughts but was often used to conceal them. On another plane, Matthew Arnold, I think, suggested that great writers buried knowledge under a load of abstruse or obscure words so that only the select few who worked assiduously should discover and profit by it. May I invite your comments on these views?

Well, in the case of Shaw I assume that there was a touch of irony. He may very well be referring to the academic profession. I do not believe that a great writer is one who conceals his thoughts in obscurity. Nevertheless, it may be that a great writer uses such economy of means in his expression that the reader will be forced to determine his meaning for himself on the basis of his own intellectual ability. I think one of the major techniques of writers who may seem abstruse or obscure is to force the reader to become a kind of creator.

Synthesis of Languages

What solutions would you suggest for promotion of a better and speedier synthesis of languages?

I should begin by saying that by no means am I an expert in the practical problems, but my view is there is very little that can be done to language, except possibly to change the vocabulary to some extent. I think there is fair evidence that a child can develop native command of several languages with no difficulty if he is presented with each language in a particular situation. It seems the real answer to language problems is to make use of whatever opportunities there are to enable young children to use their intuitive capacity to acquire many languages so that ultimately there may not be any obstacles to communication between most people.

Do your viewpoints on "transformational analysis" of languages or on syntactic structures help towards lessening of language chauvinism and tensions?

No. They do not. But I think they might if they are understood. The real source of these tensions is much deeper than the choice of a mode of group identification—problems exist, group identification and conflict will take place. I think this kind of work, if understood, might contribute to the realization that there are overwhelming similarities that unite the human race as a species, and that the varieties exist within minor variations, the depth and specific character of which it is possible for us to understand.

"New Economics": What It Means

In your stimulating Nehru memorial lecture you commented on the tendency of social scientists and behaviorists to base themselves almost wholly on concepts of materialism. You have also referred to theories of "new economics" which, I presume, point to the quality of life, not to acquisition indiscriminately of worldly goods or multiplication of material requirements. What pattern of growth, or rather of development of human society, would you recommend?

Well, I think this question has to be answered differently for different societies. For India, I think the major thing that has to happen is for the great mass of population to reach, through its own efforts, a way to participate meaningfully in the democratic processes and in economic development, with participation in a decent existence, physical and moral.

This is not the main kind of problem of growth and development which exists in the United States. The problem there is to overcome domination and hierarchy, the system of private ownership of resources and means of production. Most of the problems of the American society can ultimately be traced in some fashion to the fundamental injustice of private or state capitalism, a form of industrial civilization which has no answer for the problems of the 20th-century. This system of social and economic organization now stands in the way of progress towards solution of the serious problems of injustice, exploitation, waste and irrationality of industrial society.

Behaviorist Psychology

What correct view would you suggest for a balanced development of social and behaviorist sciences?

The first thing that has to be done is for the social and behaviorist scientists to recognize honestly the extent to which their ideological constructions merely reflect the pattern of distribution of power. On the other hand, there are also intellectual limitations which are not ideological in their origin. For behaviorist science, psychology and related fields are opposed to the fundamental nature of science, which is perhaps somewhat ironic since behaviorism developed as an attempt to create a scientific approach to human behavior and society. Behaviorist psychology is constructed more or less on the model of Babylonian astronomy. The major thinkers and scientists within behaviorist psychology have been explicitly opposed to mentalism, which generally means the development of abstract theories that deal with behavioral evidence but are not efforts merely to organize and arrange the evidence, but rather to explain it on the basis of deeper properties. Whatever justification there might have been in earlier stages, say fifty or sixty years ago, for development of behaviorism, by now it is primarily a system of arbitrary and dogmatic constraints on theory construction. Now, physics would never tolerate such dogmatic constraints. Psychology and the social sciences must abandon such arbitrary constraints and try to develop explanatory theories in the manner of the natural sciences. My position is that behaviorist science has to become mentalistic in order to become scientific.

International Authority

You have referred to science and technology turning out monsters enslaving mankind. Would you recommend an international agency which should keep a vigil on scientific and technological advances so that they do not lead us towards man's destruction?

I would not be opposed to the development of an international authority but would also not personally spend much time on it. The fact is that international agencies are useful, and one is happy that they exist. But their ability to function is enormously limited. Everyone realizes that the United Nations can operate insofar as the great powers are in agreement on some course of operation, which means that the United Nations as an international authority is a debating society, or an agency of the great powers or for their aims. It can hardly serve as a kind of international agency, useful authority or watchdog. It may help organize opinion, lead to some interaction among people who may be isolated, maybe serve as a source of communication. But the great powers and ruling groups within them are certainly not going to pay attention to any international authority.

Scientists and technologists have a conscience and to the extent that they could probably be brought together under an international authority, they should probably exercise what might be called a kind of self-control or self-restraint in the development of those weapons which are absolutely destructive and have no other but negative value for human beings. What are your views on this?

I do not agree with the premise of this question. I don't think that scientists and technologists have a conscience in their capacity as scientists and technologists. They may function as human beings as many other human beings do. But in so far as they function politically as scientists and technologists, and identify themselves in that category and function within it, I suspect they will tend towards something quite different, namely central management and bureaucratic control in which scientists and technologists achieve some degree of power and try to dominate others. They would thus simply function within the framework of a system of power and authority. It seems to me that the control over the destructive character of science and technology has got to come through the mobilization of masses of the population who are affected by it. I do not want to see the tyranny of the majority destroying intellectual freedom; still I think of a kind of complicated interplay between social consensus expressed by democratic forms of popular organization along with preservation, as much as possible, of freedom of operation by anyone in the society. Somehow there should be constant adjustment between sometimes opposing tendencies. The problem can receive no general solution.

Opposition to Leadership

What new value sets would you propound to assure a better, more enlightened leadership for nations of the world?

The value sets I would suggest are in opposition to the principle of leadership. Hierarchy and domination are necessary under conditions of social deprivation and economic deficit. In a war one has got to have leadership. It is probably true that in the early stages of industrial development hierarchy and domination were necessary. But as material deficit and external conflict diminish, the necessity for economic and political leadership also lessens. The task for a modern industrial society is to achieve what is now technically realizable, namely, a society which is really based on free voluntary participation of people who produce and create, live their lives freely within institutions they control, and with limited hierarchical structures, possibly none at all. It remains to be seen how far we can proceed towards this goal.

Editor's Notes to Interview 7

This interview appeared as "One Man's View: Noam Chomsky. Are Universities Too Conservative? Do They Collude with Corporations to Obscure the Way Power Works in Our Society? Noam Chomsky Thinks So and Explains Why," *Business Today*, May 1973, pp. 13–15.

7. The Universities and the Corporations (May 1973)

Do you think that within our society as it is now composed there should be a direct relationship or any direct ties or responsibilities between the university and the corporation?

Under the present conditions, if there is no relationship between wealth, however expressed, and the universities, the universities will collapse. This is obvious, because the universities exist on the basis of the supply of funds that come from the government, and basically from the wealthy. So in that sense there has to be a relationship. I think that's unfortunate, myself, but that's the fact of social organization.

By their very nature, it often seems that the faculty assume a liberal or radical or critical view of the society.

I don't agree. I think the faculty is a very conservative group. That is, it is considered liberal within the spectrum of American opinion, but American opinion on the whole has shifted so far to the right as compared with, say, Western Europe, that by the general standards of the Western European democracies, the faculties in American universities are really quite conservative.

Then, do you think faculty are failing in a role that they might play of supplying a liberal thrust in society—one of positive criticism?

Well, I don't care what kind of opinions people have. I think the university should tolerate a large diversity of opinion, which it does not. I think there is a severe failure—the failure is one of honesty, in my opinion. That is, I don't believe that scholarship within the university attempts to come to grips with the real structure of the society. I think it is under such narrow ideological controls that it avoids any concern or investigation of central issues in our society. And this is not merely a matter of opinion; I think this is easily demonstrable.

Is it possible within the society as it is now constructed to let the faculty have a more free role?

I don't think that anyone is stopping the faculty from doing it. Because of their profound conservatism, the faculty in the ideological subjects such as history, political science and so on, find ways to avoid studying basic issues about the nature and exercise of power in our society. Or if they do study them, they

135

do it in a perverse and confusing fashion. In fact, the very nature of academic specialization contributes to that. For example, consider the study of political economy—there's a specialization of fields which makes it very difficult to investigate the central topics in the structure of American society within some academic department.

I think the most striking example of this that I know of is the study of foreign policy. There was a recent survey that appeared in the *Annals of the American Academy of Political and Social Sciences*. The author investigated two hundred major works in what he called the respectable literature on international affairs and foreign relations, and he discovered that more than 95 percent of them make no mention whatsoever of the relationship between corporations and foreign policy, and that less than 5 percent give the subject passing mention. Now of course it's obvious to any 10th grader that that's a central issue. And the fact that academic scholarship so systematically avoids what is a central issue is just a very dramatic indication of the ideological controls under which it operates.

From what I've read myself, that article itself seems pretty conservative in its considerations.

You see, what's striking to me is two things: First of all, the fact that he was able to unearth it; namely, that within the mainstream, everybody avoids this topic like poison; and secondly, his own attitude toward that fact. That is, having noticed that there's a mass of literature that avoids the central issue (I think there's a periphery that touches the real issue), it never occurred to him that maybe it's the periphery that's the respectable literature, and the mass—that's the literature of advocacy. He himself is so caught up in the ideological structure of the society that he can't see what his own data suggests to him.

Considering the whole nature of society, as you see it, is there a way that faculty members and corporations can try and solve some of these problems?

We're looking at it rather differently. I think faculty and corporations are communicating beautifully. The corporations plainly want academic scholarship to create a web of mystification that will avoid any public awareness of the way in which power actually functions in the society, and the faculty has caught the message and they do it magnificently. They spin confusions and mystifications beautifully, and they do things like refusing to study the questions of corporations and foreign policy. I think the communication is working excellently. Of course, never good enough. For example, Agnew is not satisfied that only 92 percent of the press supports Nixon—it's got to be 100 percent. In this respect, too, I'm sure that corporations aren't satisfied that only more than 95 percent of the major foreign policy works failed to mention this issue; they'd rather have no one mention it. But the communication is going pretty well.

What about in the political sphere? It seems to me that faculties were solidly for McGovern, at least at Princeton and the Ivy League schools. Now I don't know if this is pervasive in the country, but it seems to me that on the political front, these faculty are not going along with your analysis. I don't think the comparison between the faculty and the press is really valid here.

I think it's a good comparison. I don't know the actual statistics, but I suspect that if you took the newspapers read by Princeton professors, you'd also find that they are atypical in the country as a whole. But if you take the faculty at large I think you would discover that rather like the press it's a conservative institution—very tightly tied to the ideological controls of modern society. I should mention that supporting McGovern really doesn't prove very much; McGovern is also a conservative.

What do you think the general trend in the university community is? Is it to continue this conservative trend, or do you think that the periphery is becoming more vocal?

I think there was a brief period in the 1960s when largely as a result of disillusionment with the Vietnam War a student movement developed and there was something like a mass movement of dissent. In the wake of that, there were some efforts at opening up the universities slightly to permit a wider expression of opinion than the conservatism that dominated the ideological subjects had allowed. But I think these controls are being reasonably effectively reestablished. I don't think that it's likely that the major universities at least will tolerate much diversity of opinion. For example, take a case in point. Harvard has just fired four of its major radical economists—refused to grant them tenure, that is. Of course, a couple of them did get jobs elsewhere, University of Massachusetts and so on. But I think that's what I'd expect.

This hiring policy has come up quite a bit. Conservatives often accuse universities of having hiring policies against conservative professors. Do you think this might be true?

I suspect that's true as well. I think the universities tend to be what is called liberal. It's a pretty narrow orthodoxy; how you place it in the spectrum of opinion depends on which spectrum you're using. If you use the spectrum, let's say, of a Western European democracy, it seems to me our faculty is quite conservative. If you use American opinion, it's more or less on the left. But it's still pretty narrow; it doesn't tolerate much dissent. It's not merely political constraints that are imposed; as I mentioned before, academic specialization itself, and the particular manner in which it works, functions in such a way as to eliminate great areas of research that would tend to give us some sort of integrated view of the way society functions.

About ethical investing by the university, do you think this practice will have any effect within the corporation? Will it play any role in reform or cause any sort of change?

It is very minor, although it might affect something. Right now in England, for example, there's a great turmoil over practices that have recently been exposed of British investing in South Africa, and it's possible that that will raise the level of wages slightly of black workers in South Africa—probably only temporarily, though, until people forget about it. But these are not things which can have much impact. Power and wealth is too centralized to affect. It has to respond marginally to turmoil of the periphery.

What then do you really think the goals of society must be?

Personally I'm in favor of democracy, which means that the central institutions in the society have to be under popular control. Now, under capitalism we can't have democracy by definition. Capitalism is a system in which the central institutions of society are in principle under autocratic control. Thus, a corporation or an industry is, if we were to think of it in political terms, fascist; that is, it has tight control at the top and strict obedience has to be established at every level—there's little bargaining, a little give and take, but the line of authority is perfectly straightforward. Just as I'm opposed to political fascism, I'm opposed to economic fascism. I think that until major institutions of society are under the popular control of participants and communities, it's pointless to talk about democracy.

In this sense, I would describe myself as a libertarian socialist—I'd love to see centralized power eliminated, whether it's the state or the economy, and have it diffused and ultimately under direct control of the participants. Moreover, I think that's entirely realistic. Every bit of evidence that exists (there isn't much) seems to show, for example, that workers' control increases efficiency. Nevertheless, capitalists don't want it, naturally; what they're worried about is control, not the loss of productivity or efficiency.

Turning to the British attempt within the system to socialize: Is that still touching on the periphery or has it been effective?

The British approach was to take over marginal and defunct industries that were no longer profitable and make the public bear the cost of them. That's called socialism. It has no bearing on anything; as far as I know, the concentration of capital and the degree of control by private capital over the economy and the distribution of goods haven't changed significantly; there's merely been a little softening of the structures.

How do you view the possible transition of the economic system to libertarian socialism?

One can imagine it happening by a series of very radical reforms, imagining it happening by social revolution, but it would be a fundamental change in the nature of social organization however it happens. I don't think it's very likely to happen unless there's at the very least considerable awareness of the possibility of another kind of organization and a real commitment to achieve on the part of a large mass of the population—of course, that's nothing like the case here. And the universities and other ideological institutions are working very hard to prevent it from being the case. This is the respect in which they are very loyal servants of the corporate state. For example, the questions that I've just been discussing aren't dealt with in the university curriculum. To my knowledge, up to until about two or three years ago, I know of one book on workers' control in the United States, a very hostile one. In the last two or three years, again as a result of the activity of the 60s, there has been a little discussion that will subside if the ferment subsides.

All the communist revolutions have been in basically non-capitalist societies.

I don't think they're communist revolutions. I think what are called communist revolutions are authoritarian—are revolutions of development that introduce structures which are politically authoritarian and socially egalitarian, and basically they take a do-it-yourself kind of approach to development. That's what we call communist. It has nothing to do with what we call communist in the tradition of Western European socialism, so I don't think there are any communist revolutions, at least in the traditional sense.

Do you think that strict Marxist development is still viable in the way capitalism has developed since the mid-19th century?

Well, I think it would be very surprising if the analysis given by Marx a century ago would be directly relevant to problems of capitalism today; I think it is only marginally relevant. In some general way, though, I think his point of view is useful to our present consideration.

Is there any up-to-date analysis in any country which deals with this? Does Lenin come much closer?

No, Lenin is much farther away. Lenin was merely a kind of authoritarian, although one can say that what he said was of some validity for developing societies. But it has no bearing on the advanced industrial societies, and if anything it would be a step backwards for those advanced countries.

Is there any appropriate analysis?

I think there is a very significant, if undeveloped, tradition that grew out of Marxism and anarchism. It presents a range of opinion which is important but hasn't been developed, since it's been carefully excluded. Anyone's chances of airing this viewpoint in the universities or elsewhere are pretty slight, so there's been very little advance.

What possibilities do you see for the future?

Well, for example, I think one can imagine perfectly well a movement developing for combined worker and community control of industry. I think it makes a great deal of sense. Why should workers agree to be slaves in a basically authoritarian structure? They should have control over it themselves. Why shouldn't the communities have a dominant voice in running the institutions that affect their lives? If such a movement develops, it could take a variety of forms: a parliamentary system, with a new party developing that would be outside the structure of the Republican and Democratic consensus; or it could take direct action forms, like simply taking over economic institutions.

So you feel it's possible to work within the parliamentary system?

Yes, theoretically. My guess is that the possibility would not be realized. Those who really have power in this society tolerate democracy only so long as it doesn't infringe on their power. If, through the parliamentary system, we ever began to expropriate industry, then the people who have wealth and power would destroy the parliamentary system. In this respect there probably wouldn't be any way within the system. But any revolutionary I've ever heard of must prefer peaceful non-violent means if these are possible. But it's rarely been possible because of the resistance by those who want to preserve their privileges.

Editor's Notes to Interview 8

"An interview with Chomsky," *Black Rose* 1 (1974), pp. 63–92. It took place in January, in Cambridge, Massachusetts. The interviewers were David Dobereiner, John Hess, and Doug Richardson; a third party to the discussion was Tom Woodhull, "who was connected with the West Coast situationist group, Negations." The questions asked by the situationist are identified. The transcription was edited by Richardson and Hess.

Published by the Black Rose Collective, a group of anarchists from the Boston area, *Black Rose* was originally "intended primarily as a creative theoretical contribution to left anarchist and libertarian thought and praxis." The leading article of this first issue is "On Hierarchy and Domination," by Murray Bookchin.

Koerner & Tajima (p. 169) give the reference of a German translation by Dieter Stafski, which I have not seen ("Interview mit Chomsky," *Marxismus und Anarchismus* by H. Koechlin, N. Chomsky & M. Rubel, vol. III: Unsere Wünsche sind Erinnerungen an die Zukunft, Berlin: Karin Kramer, 1976, pp. 37–88). There is a recent German version by Peter Peterson ("Klassenbewusstein und Ideologie der Macht," in *N. Chomsky, Arbeit, Sprache, Freiheit: Essay & Interviews* zur libertären Transformation der Gesellschaft. Mülheim an der Ruhr: Trafik, 1987, pp. 30–46). I retain Peterson's title.

From more on Chomsky's view of Bolshevism ("socialism"), see the Editor's Notes to 140.

8. Class Consciousness and the Ideology of Power (January 1974)

It is not common for linguistics professors, or any professors in America for that matter, to become radicals. How did it happen? What was it that led you to develop and accept a radical critique of American society?

Well, as far as I personally was concerned, it was the other way around actually. I got into linguistics actually more or less by accident through contact with radical friends, one of whom happened to be a professor of linguistics. And at a time when I was more or less thinking of dropping out of college, through political contact with him I got interested by accident in work that he was doing and got back into the field. So the problem in my case was not how the linguist became a radical, but rather the opposite. It was the radical student becoming the linguist sort of by accident.

How did you become a radical student? Were your folks radicals?

Oh, I kind of grew up in that background. Not my immediate family, but all my aunts and uncles were part of this kind of Jewish radical intelligentsia in New York and I just sort of grew up in that environment. Most were CP [members of the Communist Party], but by the time I was 12 or 13 I had worked out of that phase and ... One uncle who just died recently was active in the anti-Bolshevik left. That is, there were small splinter groups at that time which were critical of Bolshevism from the left and they were really sort of Marxists criticizing the Bolsheviks as a right-wing deviation from traditional Marxism ... sort of correct. There was some personal contact that I had with some of that literature and some of the ideas and I just got interested in it.

What about anarchism?

Well, at that time in the early 40s I was a high school student. I had already been interested in the Spanish Civil War, just reading the newspapers and so on, and I followed it up some. And I used to spend some time hanging around the Fourth Avenue second-hand bookstores in New York where there were some anarchist offices. I met some of the people. There was an office of Freie Arbeiter Stimme at that time and I got some news from those people. I lived in Philadelphia so whenever I had some free time I took the train to New York and poked around there.

In your article, "Notes on Anarchism," you were pretty sympathetic to anarchism. You talk about the "process of rehabilitation" of Daniel Guérin, reintegrating anarchism into the twentieth century. Do you see anarchism as being really that relevant to social problems in the advanced capitalist countries?

Well, as you know very well, anarchism covers a broad spectrum. That particular strain that Guérin isolated and studied I think is a valuable one. It's one that converges pretty much with libertarian Marxism, I think. Marxism also covers a pretty broad spectrum and there is a point at which some varieties of anarchism and some varieties of Marxism come very close together, as for example, people like Karl Korsch, who was very sympathetic to the Spanish anarchist movement, though he himself was sort of an orthodox Marxist. And out of that complex of ideas, anarcho-syndicalist ideas and libertarian socialist ideas, it seems to me that there is a very applicable … In fact, I think those are exactly the appropriate ideas for an advanced industrial society, one which … It seems to me that anarchism in that sense suggests certain principles of organization which are extremely realistic. Sort of a natural evolution with a high enough level of technology and communication and elimination of onerous, but necessary, labor. Under those conditions it seems to me entirely possible, in fact essential, to move toward these social forms so very much appropriate to advanced industrial society.

In that context (a) what do you think of Marx's class analysis and (b) what social economic group in this country do you think is the most relevant to radical transformation?

Well, I think the general idea of **class analysis** is indispensable. Whether Marx's particular formulations were either historically accurate or applicable today can be questioned. I would tend to agree with Bakunin's criticism of Marx that the notion of "the dictatorship of the proletariat" in a partially agrarian society would be a very repressive and destructive system, as in fact … I'm not implying the Bolsheviks introduced the dictatorship of the proletariat, they did not, but the particular perversion of it they introduced gives some justification to that analysis and I think one could make other comments of that sort. But the insight that class analysis is indispensable to understanding of social processes, I don't have any doubt that that's true.

Which Bakunin agreed with.

Right. There are questions of interpretation and so on, but I don't see how any socialist could fail to agree with that, or any social scientist for that matter. As far as contemporary society is concerned, it seems to me that you can identify roughly a class of productive workers which now includes a pretty diffuse spectrum going all the way from manual laborers to technicians to scientists to creators of intellectual culture.

You mean productive in the sense of material goods?

No, not necessarily. I mean, artists are productive in this sense, creating parts of our material and intellectual culture.

Professors ...

Some of them. Occasionally. They could be, in principle. Like in any other field. Artists, for example, could be drawing posters for the state or something. But this seems to me a very diffuse sort of class, but it's a class of productive people, and I think that class should play the role that Marx's proletariat played. That is, it should include everyone. It should have control directly of its own productive work, both the conditions of it, the distribution of it, and so on.

So the proletariat as defined by Marx, the industrial worker, is not as important because it is a minority.

Well, if you really think of the proletariat as being blue-collar laborers, of course that's a diminishing part of the working class in this broader sense. I doubt that Marx would have disagreed with this, frankly. As I read Marx, what he regarded as crucial to the notion of proletarian was that of productive work, and in different societies different people have to deal in productive work.

I think Sweezy makes the point that certain sectors of the working class have more power because what they produce seems more essential.

Well, that's kind of a technical issue almost. You have to look and see what is more important in a particular factory, the engineer who decides what machines will be there and what they'll do, or the guy who stands on the assembly line and turns screws. I have no objections about that. I'm sure it varies. I don't think you can make a generalization at that technical level. It would depend on the industry. Let's take a laboratory, certainly part of the productive apparatus of society. And there the technicians are certainly essential as regards ideas. I don't see fundamentally any difference between them as far as contribution to production is concerned. Neither can get along without the others.

Do you sort of see this wider proletarian class being radicalized by material privation or much more psychological aspects of alienation? One could scarcely argue that most professors at MIT are materially deprived, yet many of them suffer tremendous psychological alienation or displacement.

No, in fact professors at MIT and so on belong to the very top few percent of income. But it's always been true ... You couldn't say that Engels was materially deprived either. I don't see anything peculiar about that. I think a lot of people happen to be concerned about others or something. It may vary. But as a class, I wouldn't expect professors at MIT to be spearheading the revolution.

No, but you mentioned technicians and others. The experience in Chile and other areas seems to prove that they are essential. The question then is radicalizing them. Does that come out of . . .

material deprivation or some psychological understanding?

Yeah.

Well, I think it's very demeaning ... There's a kind of strain in the radical tradition which sort of runs like this caricature. It says: "Look, I understand about the problems of oppression, lack of democracy, and so on. But those guys over there, all they understand is that they're not getting enough to eat. So therefore I have to put it all in their terms. I have to sort of put it in terms of material deprivation and so on, because that's the only way they'll connect with me." And that's considered very radical by a lot of people, but I don't see any reason particularly to believe that sort of nonsense. There's no special reason why wealthy or educated people should have more concern over oppression, let's say... If you look at some of the actual documentary material that's come out of real revolutionary struggles—for example, some of the Spanish collective stuff— what is very striking about it is that at the very poorest, most oppressed level of the population you see a tremendous concern for justice, not for material goods.

But that's not the case, for example, with Marxist parties.

Okay, but they don't grow out of revolutionary struggle. These really were groups of intellectuals.

But what we're trying to get at would be, here you have a difficulty where there's a fuel crisis and people are talking of another collapse of capital like the Depression, and the revolutionary movements tend to see things in apocalyptic terms, mainly that we try to build our organization and when capital collapses we move right in.

I don't see or believe in that, though there is a kernel of truth to it. The kernel of truth is that affluence and, even more than affluence, the prospect of endless growth, has been a very effective technique of social control. The logic is sort of this: the prevailing ideology asserts in effect that each individual is purely a consumer, a person who tries to maximize consumption, and in that act life is given ... life is exhausted or something. Now, if you accept that ideology, and furthermore you can believe that material production will increase without limit, then you can conclude that it's sort of rational not to be opposed to the inegalitarian society even though you may suffer from it, even though that society is biased against you. If you are an "economic man" in this sense that you can hope that more commodities will be produced or something or other, it's sort of rational to accept the society biased against you in the hope that in the future you'll be able to consume more than you consume today. Now, there are all sorts of things wrong with this ideology, but the point is that if the factual assumptions ... The effectiveness rests in part on the ability to get people to adopt the ideology that they are nothing but atoms of production and maximizers of consumption. But the other part of it is that it rests on the fact, or the former fact, that you could rely on prospects of endless growth. In this perspective I think that material deprivation can have an important effect in challenging the whole ideological system, which does lead to the conclusion that you ought to be subservient and obedient. It's in this respect that I think there's a kernel of truth to the idea that material deficit or the fuel crisis or whatever can contribute to some sort of new consciousness.

[Situationist:] I'd like to get the meaning of "psychological alienation" more precise. I'll set up two poles and you can play with them as point of definition. One pole is the moralist pole, whose essence is appealing to the emotions of guilt, duty, and sacrifice, which heavily affected the New Left. The other pole sees subjectivity as basically pleasure seeking, appealing to emotions of desire and the imagination. Those are the two poles and I'd want to know how you see that kind of psychology operating.

Well, I don't think you have to make a choice. I think both poles are quite valid. That is, I think there's a very good reason for feeling guilt, let's say, over, frequently, our treatment of poor people or the Vietnamese. I do feel responsible because I contribute to the functioning of this society, by passivity for example. I allow it to go on. In all these respects, in any respect in which you don't act in an extreme way to put an end to these things, you contribute to it, through passivity, through obedience or whatever. I don't see any reason not to feel guilt about that nor do I see any reason not to appeal to the guilt that I think ought to be shared by other people like me, students or faculty or any other people I'm talking to. I think that's quite valid. I don't see any reason to reject what is a proper, I think, and accurate response to these conditions of inequality and oppression.

At the same time I don't see any point in getting a kind of guilt hang-up over it, and sort of deploring my own guilt or anything of that sort. The thing to do is use that perfectly valid emotional response as a basis for changing your pattern of action with respect to those things. So at one pole I see a lot of validity to what you're deprecating. At the other pole it seems to me entirely true that if a revolutionary movement is to have any validity for the great mass of the population, it has to open up new options to them and the option of being able to live in a society in which you are not an oppressor can be, could be, very liberating. Should be. And it seems to me, for example, to get back to what we were talking about before, the possibility of living in a society where the human essence is not defined by the assumption that you have to be a kind of economic man that maximizes production and who produces on demand, these are very liberating possibilities, just as much for the wealthy as for the poor, for the privileged as for the underprivileged. And here too at the opposite pole again, it seems to me there's a good deal of validity to what you say. But it seems to me true that it's an objective fact about our society that people like me, let's say, contribute in many ways to the perpetuation of oppressive and destructive institutions and I don't see any reason to be blind to that fact. I don't therefore take a vow of poverty because I don't think that would help in the least. Nevertheless, I am aware of it, and I respond to that awareness and I think it's perfectly appropriate that one part of the awareness should be a kind of feeling of guilt.

Isn't the point that the Left in this country particularly never got past that?

What I disliked more about the New Left, I guess, response was not the guilt trip, which I thought was legitimate and proper, but rather the other thing I mentioned before, the business about trying to pretend to be a member of the working class and talk in terms of the values which it was assumed must be their values—material deficit rather than the need for freedom or something along those lines. And I thought that was completely phony.

It seems to me that operating from principles and such things is not totally the same as operating from psychological sacrificial guilt tripping. In most of your writings you stress moral principles and you affirm action based on these principles. How do you think principles and moral sensibilities can be restored to a cynical, mass-indoctrinated, consumption-oriented society like ours?

Well, I think the principles of this society, namely consumption-oriented, etc., just have to be confronted with better principles which will be more appealing to people. Plainly people have other needs … People in their daily lives do not really live as maximizers of consumption. I mean, it's not true, let's say, in a family that everyone tries to get as much food as he can away from other members of the family. The official values of society are very remote, I think, from most of our actual life with other people. And that conflict ought to be made perfectly clear. Then I think there's a necessity to attack, to criticize, actively the official values, in part by a demonstration of how far they really are from the way you really act as a human being, and want to act. Now that's of course only one part of the story.

Is that demonstration possible through logical argument or do you think that possibly the way those other values are instilled makes it almost impossible to change?

There is obviously a disparity between the values that people really live by when they can exercise a choice and the values that they are taught they live by. And I think it's important that that be brought out any way you can. But the idea of maximizing consumption is only one aspect of that. Other aspects which also have to be integrated into that are the idea of being subservient as a producer, which is probably more important. Now the idea that production, in the broad sense, has to be organized in a hierarchic and autocratic system, that too is an essential part of the governing ideology and here the critique of that ideology goes well beyond logical argument.

It's precisely at this point that radicals want to build alternatives. And in fact at every level. I think you could say the same things about consumer cooperatives or other efforts to build solidarity among people by whatever means. All of these things, which are not really alternatives to a logical argument. They are complementary to it. First of all, they illustrate by action and organization the ways in which theological arguments are correct and how the gaps between official values and human values can be overcome. So these go hand in hand. On the other hand, it's going to be true, I think at least, that if we ever get anything like a kind of just society, things like my standard of living may very well not exist. In that sense there will be, I think, material deprivation in some manner for a large part of the population. And I think there ought to be. I don't think we should overlook that fact and just pretend that everyone will have more.

You see economic democracy as basic to that because in your article on anarchism you sort of merged anarchism with anarcho-syndicalism. You didn't talk about, for example, anarcho-communism. Lately we've been doing work on Reich and it doesn't seem to us that merely economic democracy is sufficient. Although it's a necessary condition, it's not sufficient. Reich claimed that people internalize in their character structure a great deal of the authoritarian, autocratic society and it's very difficult to exorcise that. How does that sort of fit in to what we should do, if you want to give advice or whatever, in our "propaganda," and how does that fit into the question of merely workers' councils or perhaps something much wider?

Well, first of all, I'm not very good at advice. I mean, if I could give you advice, I'd be doing it myself. So I don't know what to do. But I think your general point is quite well taken. I wouldn't want to suggest that propaganda or attempts towards workers' councils are the end-all of socialist agitation. But I do think that it's crucial for people to be able to … I think that a central aspect of the authoritarianism you mentioned is internalized, a very central aspect of this is the authoritarianism of work. It's in this respect that I think I have a personal privilege. The fact of the matter is that people like myself do have workers' control. We do control our own labor enormously. There's very little constraint on it. We can decide when we work, why we work, how we work, what we do. To the extent that there are responsibilities, they are self-imposed. They may be very extensive, but they are self-imposed. And, if somebody wanted to fink out, he could do it. Nothing would ever occur.

Like yourself? You mean everyone in the knowledge factory?

Not everyone. This is an elite institution. I mean professors who have sort of made it at MIT. I don't think that kind of privilege has to be reduced, rather that kind of privilege I think has to be generalized. But it may very well be that some of the material things that go along with that would have to be reduced in a very just society.

But you're not talking of a return to scarcity?

I don't think there's any return to scarcity. I think that people of my standard of living are just tremendously wasteful probably, from the point of view of what potential exists. Now maybe that's wrong. Maybe there are productive resources that haven't been used and that will be shown under some other society. I don't know. I'm skeptical myself. Incidentally, I think that I and others would benefit by that reduction in many ways. Take the obvious thing. It is almost physically impossible for me to get to work without a car. It would take me around two hours to get to work without a car because of where I feel like living. Now there's no necessity for that. Very trivial, rational alternatives can be devised. For example, there is a railroad line which goes within a mile of my house and they could put railroad trains on it. So there would be a trivial way in which my material standard would be reduced by an economist's measure if I were to go to town by railroad, but my personal comfort would be increased enormously. So in this respect I'm not meaning to suggest that reduction of material level necessarily means even less physical comfort—quite apart from any ideological or psychological factors, it may mean more physical comfort.

I think what you're saying reflects back on the polarity that's been made earlier between the sort of masochistic character and the pleasure-oriented person. I think the real issue behind that is not that they're both valid, and we should assume both, but that the character structure gets fixated in one pole or the other. In other words, Reich makes the point that the masochistic character will put all its energy into that side and will express that in political work. Whereas someone who is oriented toward life and the development of his own sexuality, his own powers, will be oriented the other way, but will still have a moral sense. The New Left did seem to have this very masochistic attitude. It expressed itself in trashing and a predilection toward authoritarian organization.

You call that masochistic? You mean the Weatherman sort of thing?

Well, Weatherman, clearly.

I didn't get that sense. I mean I wasn't really close to it and I disagreed with it, but the people I knew at least seemed to me to have a very different rationale, one which I thought was wrong but different. It seemed to me what they were saying was the way you can reach the working classes is by approaching them on their level, namely violence and destruction. I even remember being told by academic intellectuals, people kind of like myself, that if you really want to be serious about opposing the war what you have to do is go down to a bar on Third Avenue and pick a fight with a guy sitting next to you over any issue. And after you beat each other up for a while, then he takes you seriously, and you start talking about the war. I mean I was told that in those words and I think that that was sort of the core of the Weatherman ideology, at least as I understood it, and that's extremely ...

[Situationist:] But that's the problem with the New Left, always working to be like someone else, to bring some group into the mainstream of American life. This Christian service ethic.

From what I could see of the early 60s civil rights activity, it was trying to help with self-organization of poor and oppressed people and I'm all in favor of that.

[Situationist:] But to what end?

Well, to ends that they will choose when they get into the position to choose. You know, the activist who's coming in from the outside may well have his own ideas, but his main idea ought to be that they're going to make the choice. And to compare …

But they're going to be entirely Christian …

Well, why? Once they've decided to set up rural cooperatives or that they can organize their own unions and fight for their rights and so on, why should they make Christian choices? If they do, well, that's the state of their cultural and other commitments and fine, I'm not going to force them to do something else. But the point is, the outside activist, like the civil rights worker, was doing just the right thing when he tried to integrate himself as much as possible into those struggles, suffer with the people, work with them, help as much as he could, bring his talents where they were valuable, but not try to dictate any solutions.

One of the attractive things about the early New Left was the earmark of joy, with a lot of interesting and fun-like activity.

[Situationist:] Oh yeah? Well, I went to meeting after meeting without joy.

That sounds more like late-60s to me. Around '67 or '68 that became true and then everybody had to be more of an orthodox Marxist-Leninist than the guy sitting next to him and all sorts of strange things happened then.

It's exactly when very fine ideological distinctions began being made that that sort of behavior, that sort of attitude emerged. When people began being very self-righteous and becoming the two percent of the group that was correct that I experienced those attitudes coming into the New Left.

See, I think this is connected with the kind of point you were making. That is, there were certain almost built-in limits to what could be achieved by the earlier movement. And those were given by very powerful institutional facts about this society that just couldn't be transcended by that kind of movement. And it seems to me that when the New Left ran up against them, when it ran up against the realization that all we're doing, with all that, we're not going to accomplish more than getting some people organized in a better union than they might have been in otherwise or that they can vote where they couldn't vote before, so they could vote for Humphrey or some damn thing. When those realizations began to sink in, then I think the New Left disintegrated into this, it tried to find a messianic solution in Marxist-Leninism for the most part. So I kind of agree with part of what you're saying about the institutional structures that were just too rigid, too firmly embedded, for any of the earlier activities to shake them much and understandably this did lead to … well …

The late George Lichtheim once said: "The history of Marxism is too important to be left to the post-Leninist sects, those tiny ferocious creatures devouring each other in a drop of water." And this seems to be particularly true of the Left in America. But at the same time it seems that Leninism is a sort of consistent extension of certain aspects of Marx's writings, at least his public writings, and it's always described as "Marxism in practice." So how do you see Marxism as different from Leninism and where did Lenin deviate?

Well, first of all there are, I think, very different strains of **Leninism**. I mean there's the Lenin of 1917, the Lenin of the *April Theses* and *State and Revolution*. That's one Lenin. And then there's the Lenin who took power and acted in ways that are unrecognizable as far as I can see when compared with, say, the doctrines of *State and Revolution*. For a Marxist, maybe for Lenin himself had he looked back, this would not be very hard to explain. There's a big difference between the libertarian doctrines of a person who is trying to associate himself with a mass popular movement to acquire power and the authoritarian power of somebody who's taken power and is trying to consolidate it. So I don't think that transition is maybe very difficult to explain. So, in talking about Lenin, I'd ask which Lenin you are talking about. And of course that is true of Marx also. There are competing strains in Marx. But I think it's characteristic and unfortunate that the lesson that was drawn from Marx and Lenin for the later period was the authoritarian lesson. That is, it's the authoritarian Lenin who persisted, the one who concentrated on conquest of state power by the vanguard party and destruction of all popular forums in the interests of the masses. That's the Lenin who became known to later generations. Again, not very surprisingly, because that's what Leninism really was in practice. And I think it's a tremendous tragedy for the socialist movement as a whole that the Russian Revolution was identified as socialist.

See, here Lenin himself was ambivalent. He never identified it as socialist. He said some kind of state capitalism and probably you can't have socialism in a country like Russia and so forth. He varied, but basically that is what he was saying and that's sort of accurate. But then, of course, the kind of party ideologues and their various slaves in the so-called socialist movements, for their own purposes, had to identify what they were associating themselves with as something a little better than just state capitalism, though that's in fact what it was. And so they then incorporated the whole socialist tradition within this extremely reactionary structure and thereby virtually destroyed it.

In terms of building a movement in this country, around concepts that are embodied in libertarian socialism, do you think that it's useful to continue to use the word anarchism? Do you think that it has an historical value, or do you think we should be more specific and talk about council communism or libertarian socialism?

Well, I think it has value. I think it's a very significant part of the whole broad anarchist movement. I mean the various socialist variants of it, whether communism-anarchism or anarcho-syndicalism, which were concerned with organization in complex society based on equality and solidarity. Now there is another strain of anarchism which is concerned only with, which really gives no weight to notions like equality, solidarity and so on. That's the right-wing anarchism and that's an extreme form of authoritarianism as far as I can see. It's perfectly obvious that under the formulations of someone like, say, Murray Rothbard, you will get such inequalities of power that it would be like living under Genghis Khan or something like that. Even though everyone will be technically free, they'll be free to make contracts with the person who has all the power, who owns the police and so on, or they'll be free not to. That kind of thing, in my opinion, just has to be discounted. But I don't see any reason to abandon the notion of anarchism because it has some strange periphery that also uses it.

Just as you wouldn't abandon Marxism.

Yes, like I wouldn't abandon **Marxism**. After all, we're not interested in making heroes and identifying ourselves with them, but of finding what's valid in various ideas and concepts and actions of the past that have some use for us.

To get back to Leninism, what about the question of, for example, Vietnam or China or the "Third World" movements in general? There is a real disagreement among anarchists on the question of the NLF [National Liberation Front] and the worth of these movements in general.

[Situationist:] May I rephrase that a bit? Would you apply the same paradigm to, say, the response of the Western European and to some extent the American Communist Party and the way they sort of idolized the Bolshevik revolution as their model or as the proof of what they said? Do you think you could apply the same thing to the Third World currents in the New Left?

I think it's similar except less pernicious because … It's less pernicious only for accidental reasons, namely because the impact on western socialist ideology is much slighter, partly because it doesn't exist any more, and it did exist then, more. In that respect it's less pernicious. But basically it's the same error. A very similar error, let's say. I wouldn't regard the Third World revolutionary movements as socialist in any sense. I still do think that they can be treated with sympathy and call for support, but that's a different issue. I did follow Solidarity's position on the NLF, and that's the one thing I really disagreed with, very seriously. In fact, virtually everything else I agree with on down the line. They were perfectly correct, and perfectly irrelevant, in pointing out that North Vietnam is not a libertarian socialist society. I mean, they don't claim it, it's not true, it couldn't be true. And I think they are also perfectly correct in saying we ought to criticize that society. However, not while the bombs are falling, in my opinion. There were a lot of things wrong, let's say, with England in 1943. But I don't think that was the time or the place to point them out, particularly if you happened to be living in Nazi Germany. And that's the situation here. The West is really trying to crush these movements and I think that everyone here and in England is responsible for that. London Solidarity, you see, by not preventing the British government from assisting in the crushing of Vietnamese independence, were in a certain sense contributing to it. And therefore I think that they are in a very weak position to be criticizing North Vietnam as non-socialist, though that criticism is nevertheless correct.

[Situationist:] Okay. I agree with that. For the most part. Except it seems that the way the Left in general, the anti-war movement, presented or managed to sell the NLF and the North Vietnamese was very much that they were creating a revolution, a socialist revolution. Thus they were bringing about a situation like that after the Bolshevik revolution, leading to the support of socialism in one country, etc.

See, I think the right attitude to take toward the Bolshevik revolution was the kind that Bertrand Russell took. He said, look, you know, this is pretty rotten. But he also said that for the people of the West to talk about the oppressiveness of the Russian Revolution while they're contributing to it by supporting the counter-revolution, this is grotesque.

[Situationist:] In the sense that … if you're being moralistic it seems like it is really hard to keep more than one idea in your head at one time … if you're going to whip people into a frenzy to do something it has to be directed toward that one thing; it has a tendency toward Manichaeanism basically, right?

But I think this is all quite apart from being opposed to the American war. I think that is just off in a different dimension. You see, it seems to me that it was always a mistake for the anti-war movement here to take the position of being for the NLF, or for North Vietnam or anything. What we should always have been for is getting the bloody hands of Western imperialism out of there. After that, it is their problem.

Incidentally, I think it is a complicated issue. If we really look at North Vietnam, or say the Pathet Lao in Laos, which I did try to learn something about, I mean, first of all it is an egalitarian society that they're building; it's a society that has a lot of commitment to social welfare. It has some version of local democracy. It's very hard to know what version, something though. There is some kind of participation at the level of planning and so on at a local level. But all of this is embedded within a fantastically authoritarian structure. You know, with total control from the top, with very little leeway for free access to information, or I suspect, though I couldn't say for sure. And what elements of democracy or popular control there are, probably are what function through the Communist Party apparatus. Now that's a tricky thing itself. You see, the Communist Party structure extends from the central committee down through the cells and factories, and from the little I could make out, I think that there probably is some sort of flow of control, and so on, through that structure, but of course that is very far from workers' control. And, you know, I think the thing to do is to understand what those societies are about, sympathize with what's good, criticize what is bad, offer alternatives, etc. In fact, I was interested to see that they're kind of open to this. For example, I had an interview with Pham Van Dong who had read *American Power and the New Mandarins* in the French translation, and his first remark about it was that it was too anarchist ... We had some discussion about that, you know ... I'm sure I didn't convince him, he didn't convince me. Though he perceived at once that this was a kind of anarchist critique of Communism, among other things, and you know, I think, if you have any respect for those people at all, you would be quite plain and clear about your critique of them, try to enter into a discussion with them if you can.

[Situationist:] I think that you may have inadvertently played against yourself, though, because, you know, both the capitalists and the state capitalists, in their global chess game, have tried to represent the world where there's only two options; there's no third force. They did this in the Spanish Civil War. They did it very much in Hungary. I mean, it was incredible the similarity the way the Americans presented it as "these people want capitalism," and the way Russia presented it as "these people want fascist counter-revolution." Neither one of them would let any voice emerge and say, "No, they don't want either, they want something that is neither capitalism as we know it" nor, (quote) "socialism as we know it." In other words, it ruled out the possibility of a third force. The failure of the American New Left to identify itself as, "No, we don't want what they have in Russia," every time someone said, "Well, why don't you move to Russia," is, I think, one of the most damaging things you could have done. That is a lot of the reason we didn't reach more ordinary Americans who have these heavy anti-Communist fears. It's because we didn't identify ourselves as clearly, not that (and a whole lot of people, my parents among them, really thought that we were either knowingly, or inadvertently) because we were naive, playing into the hands of the second force.

Well, I get letters about this all the time. I've got one right here, let's see if I can find it ... here, read this, that's a typical response of that kind. It says, "Are you a card-carrying Communist, or just a sympathizer," or something like that ... or "how could you say all these bad things about President Nixon if you weren't ... " But, the point is, though I think your point is correct, I think that as a criticism, it is not valid. Because a lot of people, me included, made a big effort to do this. It is just very hard to break through the given ideological assumption that, you know, you're either for us or for the Russians. No matter how you say it, no matter how much you do about it, it is just very hard for a lot

of people to see that there is another possibility, even when you keep saying that
there is and why there is, and so on. Maybe more could have been done in that
direction, but …

[Situationist:] Did you ever precisely, ah, mention the councils?
Of course, in "Notes on Anarchism."

Sure, and in *American Power and the New Mandarins*, one of the big discussions was about Spanish anarchism, and in fact, one of the main points I was
trying to make there was that Bolshevism and American liberalism are basically
manifestations of the same thing. Now, that was kind of abstract and I don't
think that many people knew what I was talking about, really, and I probably
didn't do it right and so on, and I'd agree with all that, but, you know, I was by
no means alone in this. A lot of people were trying to do that kind of thing. But
it is very hard to break through when the prevailing assumption is you're either
a Communist, meaning Russian apologist, or you support American imperialism. You see, I think a more valid criticism would be that the New Left did kind
of idealize Cuba and China and Vietnam in particular, which was really quite
silly. You know, I've seen people come back from Vietnam talking about how the
Vietnamese were all into love and, you know, this sort of thing, which is ridiculous. Whatever they're doing may be valid or not valid, but it's surely not that.

You have always argued, even in your latest book, that the NLF was independent,
not a puppet of China or USSR or anyone. Last year you argued that the agreement
that Kissinger signed was essentially the program of "the enemy." In view of Kissinger's
globetrotting, and what everybody is saying about an engineered solution by the
superpowers, with China and Russia putting pressure on the DRV [Democratic
Republic of Vietnam] to thwart any offensive by the NLF, is it still possible after Tet
to say that the NLF is an independent force and that the DRV is independent of
either China or the Soviet Union?

See, I don't think that Kissinger's globetrotting or his global plans had any
effect, really, on what happened in Vietnam. I think he tried to make them have
an effect. But I don't think they did. For several reasons, for one thing because
neither the Russians nor the Chinese ever were very enthusiastic about
Vietnamese Communism, and they didn't need Kissinger to make them less
enthusiastic than they were likely to be in the first place.

Why do you think that was?

Well, in the case of China, in part, because I think China does not want to
see independent and strong societies on its borders. And a Vietnamese-dominat-
ed Indochina under the Communists, well, that would be a strong and a very
independent force which would have no use for China, and would go its own
way. And the Chinese have no interest in that. It's kind of the same reason why
Stalin was opposed to the Greek communists—he didn't want to see a Balkan

communist federation. It's really great-power politics, basically; it didn't matter whether they were communist, fascist, or anything else, they would be strong, independent, have popular support, and so on.

As far as the Russians are concerned, I think they are terrified in part by precisely the libertarian elements in Indochinese communism, which are there, alongside the authoritarianism. I mean, it is just that kind of thing that is very frightening to the Russians, just as those elements in Chinese communism are frightening to the Russians, and for obvious reasons. But, quite apart from that, the Russians are very racist, and I think there is probably just a lot of race hatred involved, and that kind of thing. But the main point, really, as far as the Russians are concerned, is that their international policy has always been to try to achieve what they call "detente," and that means subordination to the United States. What they want to be, as far as I can see, is to be accepted within the American system as a sort of union partner, where they do their job, we don't bother them, etc. For this, support of Vietnamese nationalism is kind of inconsistent. They couldn't refuse to do it because then they would have lost whatever credibility they had, internationally, or in the Third World, or whatever, and that is important to them too, as leverage, and for power purposes. But nevertheless, I think that's a fundamental aspect of their policy, and it didn't take much convincing to get them to go along. But I don't think they had anything more than marginal effect on affairs in Indochina, simply because they don't have that much leverage.

Now, however, I do think that there is a very good sense in which you are right when you ask whether the NLF has ceased to be an independent around the time of Tet, or something like that. But I don't think that had anything to do with China or Russia. I think that just had to do with the success of the American offensive. See, I think that the United States did really succeed to a large extent in grinding them down. The American war really was against South Vietnam, the other stuff was a side-show. And the war against South Vietnam was, in a sense, successful. That is, it pretty much destroyed that society, and since the NLF was a social force rooted in that society, by destroying that society I think the U.S. undermined the movement. And I think that was part of the purpose of the war, was to force the NLF into dependence on the outside, so it could be an authentic South Vietnamese movement. Just the same reason the United States tried to drive China into the hands of Russia.

How do you see a decision like that being made?

By the United States, you mean?

Yes, in terms of strategy: "What we want to do is force the NLF into a close association with the North, in order to discredit them."

Yea, that's hard to say. I guess the more sophisticated people were probably aware of it, and what they were doing. The ordinary hack probably just did that work in a sort of reflex fashion. He probably believed his own propaganda. I mean, the propaganda from the beginning was: these are agents of the North. And, you know, the Bundy-types probably believed it and went ahead and acted on it. But, some people in there must have known what was going on, better than what comes out on the surface. Take somebody like Robert Perlman, the guy who ran the pacification programs, who is a real technocrat, I mean a real brutal technocrat, but, you know, he said it very openly, "Look, none of our programs are very effective, but we've just got to grind them down by sheer weight and mass," or something like that … And that's about it.

How much influence did people like Pool, who argued similar things like that—the destruction of the countryside, saturation bombing, the concentration compounds—have on policy?

That's really hard to know. I suspect that all these people like Pool, Huntington and the rest, were really just peripheral ideologists; people who sort of viewed what happened and tried to sugar-coat it a bit.

For example, the role of a research institute like the Center for International Studies, are they mainly sugar-coating ideologists, or do they in fact really have an influence on policy?

Well, again, it's hard to judge, but I just can't believe that those people ever really had much to do with anything. They wanted to, I think, but I doubt if they succeeded. See, Huntington I don't think understands even to this day why people are so outraged by the stuff he wrote. I, for example, probably his main critic, I never even criticized him. I just said look what the guy is saying, you know, and quoted long passages. And he doesn't understand, he says, "Well, so what, I mean, what's the fuss about, what's wrong with that."

There has been such a tie between the university and the military. Kissinger was plucked from Harvard, and there was this thing, the Foreign Affairs Association, that a lot of university people belonged to, that apparently did have some real inputs into the government. Does Nixon act independently of the liberal intelligentsia of the Northeast, does he just throw them out?

No, I think that there's a sort of filtering system, though a very substantial part of the liberal intelligentsia does aspire to government service; they really are the Bolsheviks, basically. But, of course, only those get in who have the proper commitments and ideologies. When Kennedy is looking for an historian to adorn his administration, you know, he'll pick Arthur Schlesinger and not Barrington Moore. That is because he says the right things, he believes the right things, you know, that kind of business. The same thing here; if a guy like Kissinger wants to gain power, he'll propose the kind of international policies that are acceptable to the people who run the society, then they'll make it look as if he is determining things. You can find out exactly how much Kissinger is determining policy by asking yourself what would happen if Kissinger made a proposal that went counter to the interests of the American ruling class. Well, he'd be teaching history at Georgia Tech, or something.

He seems like a clever technocrat, a yes-man, sort of thing.

He manages to articulate and formulate policies that are very much in the interests of ruling class groups, so they make him their manipulator.

Then the question becomes how policy is made. Because Vietnam and Watergate have brought out a lot, and there's all this cowboy-Yankee stuff, and all the rest. How do you think the decisions are made? I mean, they are clearly made to strengthen the capitalist system, but there also seems to be competition, and I can't seem to accept the mechanical Leninist view that the state is merely the executive committee of the capitalist class.

Well, there is something to that, I think.

Yes, there is some truth there, but yet there is such conflict.

Yes, because the ruling class itself has internal conflicts, and, I think, there is a kind of dynamic involved that goes on everywhere. It's the kind of dynamic that led to the Interstate Commerce Commission being taken over by the railroads. Those elements of the ruling class that have a particular interest in one or another sphere of governmental activity will probably tend to dominate them. What they do may be in conflict with class interests of others, but the others do not care that much; it's not a major thing with them, so they let it go.

And I think pretty much the same is true of foreign policy. There are some elements of the ruling class, I mean, the corporate lawyers who deal with multinational corporations and therefore represent a kind of general interest in a free, international, global economy and such things. Those are the people who will try to take over, and succeed in taking over, decision-making positions in the foreign policy system, exactly the way the railroads will try to take over the ICC, or any other utility will try to take over the government structure that regulates it. Of course that means that often they will be doing things that are harmful to other elements of the **corporate system** that may not care that much about it, and suffer marginally. And sometimes this can break out into real conflicts—serious conflicts. But still, with all those qualifications, it seems to be not unfair to speak of the **state executive** as simply a branch of the ruling class which is governing this particular centralized structure.

I thought that was important because if you see the state merely as a class organ, then the dictatorship of the proletariat as a class organ becomes feasible, but if you can see that the state, particularly in modern society, where the government is 30 percent of the economy, the largest employer and corporation, etc., the something is different there, and the state is much more than just the executive committee of the ruling class. In fact, it has its own interests.

It does have its own independent interests, and I think you see that, for example, to some extent in some of the particular directions that state capitalism takes. Part of the impetus towards militarization of state capitalism has to do with special interests that have developed within that sector itself, and have just achieved a lot of decision-making power. Here, I think, someone like Seymour Melman is on to something important, though I don't accept his analysis completely. It seems to me that he is on to something when he says that there is a partially independent managerial system in the whole pentagon structure, which simply has tremendous assets at its disposal. And though of course it could be liquidated by the real ruling class at any moment by simply withdrawing its resources, nevertheless, that's not what happens because of its interpenetration with them and so on.

There is a lot of talk around about military coup, fascism, etc. It seems that, while the military has tremendous tie-ins with the defense industry, etc., that it may in fact have interests of its own, an ideological interest or whatever, that may coincide with certain segments of the ruling class, but one suspects that, from seeing fascism in operation, that there are independent elements within it that can dominate the activities, that aren't in fact, necessarily business elements.

They can, but I think the record pretty well supports that view that fascism is a last resort on the part of the ruling class that simply can't hold on to its privilege any other way. And that's why I wouldn't expect this happening in the United States, in a short time at least.

[Situationist:] Do you see the dangers of narrowly seeing fascism in those terms, I mean, the whole of Reich's Mass Psychology *was an attempt to point out to the Leninoids running around at that time, that to cast fascism in those terms was far too facile. That it has also to do with character structure, authoritarian character structure, people raised in father-dominated families from early in life, the church, you know, the whole complex of institutions that predate adult life.*

Also, this thing of people's conscious, calculating motives, economic man, and the subconscious of people, I mean, if fascism were just in the most narrow, reductionist sense, economic, then where did the role of the marching bands and the whole macho appeal that had people having collective orgasms at the Nuremburg rallies, where did that come in? It obviously went to something much deeper in people's psyche.

Yes, I don't disagree with that, but those same factors of personality structure, family structure, and so on, are just as true in pre-fascist periods. And I think it is correct to say that those are factors which can be easily exploited by a fascist organization, or by a so-called communist organization, or by any effort to carry out mass mobilization. In fact, to some extent, the whole Kennedy mystique here, at a lower level, appealed to that kind of thing, and there are elements of that in the New Deal, and so on.

But the question is, when will the ruling classes resort to such methods, when will they try to make such an appeal to these strains of authoritarianism in family and personality? Well, I think, by and large it is true to say that they will do so when it's the last resort for the preservation of their privilege. And I think there is a really good reason for that, and that has to do with the nature of capitalism as such. I mean, true, we don't really have capitalism, we have some variant of it. But if you think about the ideal form, which we approximate to some extent, I mean, capitalism is basically a system where everything is for sale, and the more money you have, the more you can get. And, in particular, that's true of freedom. Freedom is one of the commodities that is for sale, and if you are affluent, you can have a lot of it. It shows up in all sorts of ways. It shows up if you get in trouble with the law, let's say, or in any aspect of life it shows up. And for that reason it makes a lot of sense, if you accept the capitalist system, to try to accumulate property, not just because you want material welfare, but because that guarantees your freedom. It makes it possible for you to amass that commodity.

So, this means, that quite apart from just material welfare, even the need for freedom, and so on, these needs are to some extent met, if you have enough wealth and power to purchase them on the sort of free market. And that means, I think, that what you're going to find is that the defense of free institutions will largely be in the hands of those who benefit from them, namely the wealthy, and the powerful. They can purchase that commodity, and therefore they want those institutions to exist, like free press, and all that. However, this is only true up to a point. If those free institutions ever turn out to be striking at their privilege, of course, the rules of the game are changed, like, say, Chile as a case in point. I would expect the capitalist class to defend the freedom of the press, so-called, and the freedom of the legal system, because they're the beneficiaries of it, but only up to the point where there really is some kind of an effort to redistribute privilege.

I think this raises the issue of what the anarchist attitude to transitional form should be, and how deeply we should get involved in politics, because it is very tricky in this country to distinguish between genuine decentralizations of power, which presumably we would support, and decentralizations of power which simply make the whole structure more powerful and efficient in its repression.

Yes, that's a very serious issue and I think you have to face it concretely at every instance. Take the impeachment issue right now, that's a case in point.

Right.

I'm very skeptical about the radical involvement in any of these impeachment things. It seems to me that they tend to contribute to the mystification of the presidency. While I think you may make a point that Nixon is a crook and a bastard and all this sort of thing, and let's get him out, but for the Left to contribute to the belief that that's going to introduce any serious changes is simply to add to the belief that the president is some kind of god or king, and that what we have to do is get the right god in there, and then the whole story.

Some of the things that have come out are really bad. For example, I got this thing from the emergency Civil Liberties Committee, who are really a good bunch of people, the people who take all the hard cases that the ACLU [American Civil Liberties Union] won't touch, etc. But they had this petition, and, I mean, I usually sign everything that comes around, but this was so bad that I just couldn't sign it. It was saying we have to impeach the president because this is the only way to restore the dignity of the presidency and to build our national honor, and it was just contributing to the worst sort of beliefs, you know, exactly the reasons why the intelligent corporate elite wants to get rid of Nixon in the first place—because he's diminished all of these. It's hard to revere the president when he's busy robbing everybody to build something in San Clemente. They want this guy out of there, he's striking right at the heart of the ideology.

How do you view the process of decentralization, then? Do you have a scenario of that, is it apocalyptic, or gradual, does it happen in phases?

Well, I don't have much of a sense of apocalypse. In principle, I think it's right that you have to build the organization of the future in the present society somehow. People have to have a picture of how they would run their community, or industry, or whatever it is, and they have to fight to do that to whatever extent they can. At the same time, I suppose that at some point, the ruling class will simply strike back by force, and there was to be defense against that force, and that probably means violent revolution. And I wouldn't be surprised if that is inevitable at some stage, simply in order to resist the force that remains in the hands of the privileged, who as in Chile or anyplace, will try to strike at any kind of free institution if it begins to take away their privilege.

You included a chapter "On the Limits of Civil Disobedience" in your last book, For Reasons of State. *Then you think that we definitely will have to go beyond that sort of thing?*

Oh yeah, that was about the Berrigans really, and I think that what they are doing is really important and I have a lot of respect for them, and so on, but that has a very narrow social significance. It's precisely useful in a case like the Vietnam War, when there is a kind of a marginal class interest of the ruling class which will be conducted if the costs aren't too high at home, and where a large part of the population sees that it is sort of wrong. Now under that combination of circumstances, civil disobedience can be effective. It can be a way of mobilizing this large part of the population that sees that it's wrong to raise the cost to the point where people who run the society will decide that it's not worth it. And that is useful and important and you know, a courageous thing to do, and I'm all for it, but it has virtually nothing to do with social change as far as I can see.

Do you want to make any suggestions as to some kind of organizational form, or comment on what kinds of strategies could effectively resist the modern technological police state, which seems so far to have resisted all attacks?

That is going to be very important. The techniques of surveillance and control, and all that stuff that's developing is a very serious thing. And, well, I think we just have to try to organize people in communities to tear down television cameras and organize the technicians to try to disrupt this. It's very serious. Somebody told me about an article in the *National Review* recently, I don't know whether or not you read it, I don't; but someone told me about this article by a guy named Miles Copeland who was, maybe still is, in the CIA. The article was about domestic surveillance and how great it's getting along. Apparently James Buckley introduced some kind of a bill saying that there should be a special category of people who are permitted to get all the intelligence information from all sources, and since they are very respectable we can be certain that they won't do anything wrong with it, and so on.

It's amazing how very little popular resistance there has been to this.

There's not very much awareness of it. In fact, the kind of awareness that's coming is coming from funny places. A lot of the left-wing journals now have letters from prisoners, really interesting letters about stuff going on in prisons. Well, you know, that's where you'd expect it first, in the total-control institutions like prisons and schools. That's where you first see the behavior modification...the drugs ...

The electrodes in the brain ...

The psychosurgery... Incidentally, we're going to have a big meeting here Friday to try to at least get some information out about this sort of thing, and see if there isn't something that kind of technically-oriented people can do, simply as a service, as a defense to communities, against this kind of intrusion and operation. Well, here's a concrete step where I think you can see the beginnings of a way of relating an immediate community interest to an immediate interest of MIT technicians; of a lot of things like that, here is one.

I hear that MIT is wiring one of the housing projects in this area with cable TV, free of charge. I can't imagine why they would go through such lengths of generosity.

There was a story around about cable TV having a two-way capability.

It has control possibilities beyond surveillance. It allows for much more selective programming in propaganda terms. You can devise one set of programming for housing projects, another for suburban neighborhoods, thus specializing and refining propaganda input.

I know a lot of people on the Left interested in media thought that there were a lot of opportunities in this cable TV thing, but it would be so voracious.

I think that what's developing out of that whole situation is that this so-called free-access, or open-access, is being recognized as an illusory public-relations gimmick, used by cable corporations to obtain franchises in towns and communities. Since the community groups don't actually own or operate the TV systems, as soon as something controversial gets on, it gets put off.

Who runs the whole thing? Is it a corporate thing?

The FCC [Federal Communications Commission] has designed certain free-access rules, but they're very vague, and right now, in New York City, they're in the process of being defined, and they're being defined mostly in restrictive terms. As far as ownership and ultimate control, and probably control of the FCC, are concerned, these are basically the same people who own everything else: Sylvania, Hughes Aircraft, and AT&T are all big in the cable industry.

I think that a lot of the radical groups that tried to snatch cable-TV up when it first came out had a very manipulative sense toward it, viewing it in traditional power-structure terms, as an opportunity to be slick and "trick" people into the revolution, or to advertise their organization, something like that.

Could I ask a philosophical question? I wondered why you are much more sympathetic to Marx's economic determinism, than, say, Skinner's behaviorist theory, which is another form of determinism.

Well, first of all, again, I don't read **Marx** as an economic determinist. I mean, I think he was talking about how patterns of choice are influenced by material interests and other interests that are defined in class terms, and he was talking about the significance of relations to production in defining classes, and what they will be, and all of that is correct. I think he was identifying crucial factors that play a role in social action in a class society. That need not be deterministic.

Now as far as the **Skinner** thing is concerned, my feelings are really rather different. I just think it's a fraud, there's nothing there. I mean, it is empty. It's an interesting fraud. See, I think there are two levels of discussion here. One is purely intellectual: What does it amount to? And the answer is zero, zilch … I mean, there are no principles there that are non-trivial, that even exist.

Skinner, not Marx.

Yes, Skinner. Now the other question is, why so much interest in it? And here I think the answer is obvious. I mean, the methodology that they are suggesting is known to every good prison guard, or police interrogator. But, they make it look benign and scientific, and so on; they give a kind of coating to it, and for that reason it's very valuable to them. I think both these things have to be pointed out. First you ask, is this science? No, it's fraud. And then say, OK, then why the interest in it? Answer: Because it tells any concentration camp guard that he can do what his instincts tell him to do, but pretend to be a scientist at the same time. So that makes it good, because science is good, or neutral, and so on.

What it does is give a kind of cloak of neutrality to the techniques of oppression and control; and in that respect, it's the same kind of thing that the liberal intelligentsia gave to imperial domination. They tried to make it look kind of like an exercise in pragmatism, in problem solving, which is perfectly neutral. In fact, it's interesting ... I've quoted dozens of times remarks by some of these counterinsurgency specialists, who try to say, "Look, it's just like physics, certain inputs, certain outputs, you know, totally neutral ethically. Just a matter of solving certain problems. Only some kind of crazy moralist would be concerned about it." Well, that is the behaviorists' contribution: to take the standard techniques of control and oppression and coercion, and try to make them disappear, to insulate them from criticism or understanding by assimilating them into science. And that has nothing to do with Marx.

I still feel that there is perhaps an analogy between saying, you know, that a class of people will do certain things under certain economic conditions, like if the ruling class is really threatened, they will use violence to defend themselves, and Skinner's assertion that if you use certain behavior reinforcing devices, an individual is bound to ...

Well, it's the "is bound to" part that's significant. If you say, "he tends to" then of course it's true. I mean you can make very good generalizations about what people tend to do under certain circumstances. You know, you tend to go to the beach when the temperature is high, not when it's low.

But it's not law?

Right, first of all, it's not a law, you have individual control. And the principles of tendency themselves are kind of trivial. You don't have to go to scientists to find out anything about them.

But by the same token, could you say that in certain situations the ruling class could, for moral reasons, say, voluntarily give up their privileges?

Sure, it's conceivable, I just don't think there's any reason to believe it's going to happen. And, you know, Marx himself speculated that it might happen in England. And it could be; I could imagine that in a country like Sweden, say, which is a funny sort of mixture of things (and I don't know that much about Sweden), but it seems conceivable, that if it were not for external pressures, the deterioration in control and self-confidence and so on, on the part of the ruling class might reach a point where they simply would have no effective defense, either physical or moral. They've got to have a moral defense as well. That is, they have to convince themselves that what they're doing is right. Very few people can act if they don't convince themselves of that. Of course it wouldn't happen in Sweden because it would be conquered or something if that took place. But apart from that, that describes the kind of an evolution of both the sort of moral deterioration and the deterioration of power on the part of the ruling class groups that might make them maybe defect, or refuse to fight for their privilege, or something of that sort.

You have written a great deal about the technocratic mentality of the planners of Vietnam, etc., who are always working within a certain framework, which they never question. How would that fit in with the trend in Western, or at least Anglo-American society towards positivism? I mean, I can see where, for example, the Soviets and the Germans could use Hegelianism. But it seems in the West there is this positivistic tendency that tends to exclude all morality as pure subjectivity. How would this fit in with that mentality?

Well, positivism has nothing to do with science or anything like that; it has to do with capitalism. It has to do with solving technical problems in the interests of whoever sets those problems and determines what are the right solutions. And there's nothing wrong with that. If, suppose let's say, we had a community that was controlling its own local organization or industries or whatever, and they wanted a certain type of problem solved—well, you'd solve it in any way which best met those conditions.

The ideological utility of this kind of pragmatism is that it contributed to the belief that there is nothing ideological about this, that it's simply neutral, that it is scientific, that it does not reflect privilege of power, which is of course garbage. In order to establish that, it was elevated to a universal ideology centuries ago. The whole end of ideology debate is very amusing in that respect, because what many of the exponents were correctly criticizing in earlier ideologies, pointing out that they did in fact universalize particular interests; but then they went on to say, you know, we just solve problems, technically, and we have no ideology at all. Which, once again, is carrying out exactly the same activity that they themselves had accurately criticized in an earlier generation. The belief that they're just neutrally solving problems is of course nonsense, when you realize who places the conditions on an acceptable solution, who defines the problems, who is going to be able to make use of the solutions you will come up with, who will reject the ones he doesn't like, and so on.

This is a problem that always fascinated me. You know, philosophy can define a great deal, and limit a lot of choices. I'm not sure if there is a revolutionary philosophy, but I can't ever see anything progressive, any sort of libertarian thing, coming out of positivism. It just seems to exclude it completely. The whole thing that moral choices are purely subjective.

Well, I'm not sure about that.

A lot of the mentality of "the backroom boys," etc., seemed to reflect that.

I don't think it's fair to put the guilt for that kind of thing on the positivists, who were mostly sort of liberals and socialists, and that sort of thing, you know, who felt that it was possible by application of reason to achieve goals that are humanly desirable. Take someone like, say, Bertrand Russell. He's a person who always agreed, basically, with Hume, that reason is the slave of passion; I mean, you just have to decide what kind of things you want for whatever reason, and you use intelligence to try to achieve them. And someone like say, Rudolf Carnap, who was a positivist par excellence, who was nevertheless a very strong civil libertarian and a courageous liberal and one of the earliest people to oppose the Vietnam War, and all that. And that's perfectly consistent with his believing that you can't give a scientific justification for value judgments, which may very well be true.

The fact that guys like the Bundy-types, later made use of this terminology and framework, and distorted into an instrument of class-rule, that's something else.

I didn't mean the people, but rather that tendency of thought.

Well, insofar as it tends to put to the side value judgments, or questions of choices and where they come from and so on, of course, it can have a very reactionary effect. But that is not inherent to the point of view, it is inherent to the distortion of it.

Anarchism is often criticized for being utopian and unable to deal with complicated practical situations. One of the most complex situations around now is in the Middle East.

Yes, I think it's a perfect example of the utility of anarchism, really. What you have in the Middle East is an almost classic example of the total absurdity of people organizing themselves into state systems. I mean, what do the Jews of Israel gain, as human beings, by identifying themselves as the ruling group in a Jewish state? The only effect of that decision is destructive to them themselves. Take the rise of the whole theocratic control in Israel. That has nothing to do with roots in Judaism at all, it never existed. It's a reflection of the establishment of the state system. And to the people of the country that is terribly oppressive. Most of them aren't religious; they don't want any of that nonsense. But they are wedded to it once they insist that there by a state system which somehow distinguishes them from everyone else.

Well, how does it distinguish them? By some kind of ideology that has to be created. Obviously it's going to be theocratic. And that means all kinds of interference in everyone's daily life, like, they're not going to let you get married when you feel like it, and every other kind of thing. So, aside from the fact that it breaks up obvious common interests among, say, Palestinian and Jewish workers, or intellectuals, or anyone, apart from the fact that it leads to endless wars and will probably end up destroying both sides, apart from all that, just in their daily lives it turns out to be oppressive and destructive, for those who win as much as for those who lose. I mean, there couldn't be a more dramatic example of the absurdity of people organizing themselves into state systems for the purposes of mutual destruction. And until that is overcome, there is just no hope there.

Do you have a scenario for a libertarian solution there?

Yes, I think the only solution there, ever, and I've always believed this, has been to develop a common interest on the part of Jews and Arabs, which would transcend the national conflict. And there is such a common interest, namely, building a libertarian socialist society. If they want to identify themselves nationally in that society, OK. I don't see much interest in it, but if that is what people want, fine, that's their choice. There's no reason why you can't have national institutions even existing side by side, you know, and people choosing to identify themselves one way or another, if that's the way people want it. And also it ought to leave an option for people who don't want it, who don't want to be a part of one or the other of those systems. And that's perfectly feasible, you know, it could be done. I mean, it seems to me the only hope there really, for the people of that region, is to be able to build on that kind of joint socialist commitment. Incidentally, you know there was an early strain of the Zionist movement that insisted on this. And they were right, all along. They were right in opposing the Jewish state, and they're right today.

Would you also say that the world fuel crisis points to the absurdity of national control of international resources?

But here I think one has to be pretty cautious, because you see the line of thinking is arising in the United States which says: Why should those crazy sheiks have all this resource to themselves?

The next thing is to invade.

Yes, they don't say, Why should we have General Motors all to ourselves, or why should we have grain to ourselves, or something like that.

The [Boston] Globe just had an editorial that said if we don't solve the problem soon, we'll all be at the mercy of a troupe of "sheiks in bed sheets," which in view of their recent comments on racism seems …

Oh, I'm sure we are going to hear a lot of that stuff pretty soon.

Do you think we'll also see a corresponding rise in anti-semitism?

Yes, if you look at the election we had out in Lexington, the local newspaper had the first anti-semitic letters that I ever encountered, the last week or two.

Around the campaign?

Actually, what it was is,they have a thing at Lexington Green, at Christmas, with a display of Christ, and so on. And a lot of people objected to it on the grounds of separation of church and state, etc. And there's always a fight about it, every Christmas. So this year, the letters in defense of it have a distinctly anti-semitic tone to them, a couple of them; saying well, you know, you're criticizing our putting the display on the green, but we have got to freeze because of you, and that sort of thing.

But you know, I think both things can go side-by-side, that is, anti-semitism can develop alongside of racist anti-Arab feeling. And I think that is just what is going to happen this winter.

Both sides are being set-up to be sacrificed.

I think that's just what's happening. You know, they have worked themselves into a system where they are both pawns of the superpowers. Purely on the basis of a commitment to a state system. That's the whole trouble right there. There couldn't be a better argument for anarchism.

In view of what we were talking about earlier, and just what you were saying, what hope do you see for the future? I mean, many people in the movement are depressed of late, a lot has collapsed, and there seems to be a retrenching backwards. We've been trying to come to some grips with this. What do you see for the future?

Well, it seems to me as hopeful as it did a couple years ago. I mean, the movement of the last ten years was very reactive. It was reacting to particular atrocities. It was never sort of structural, it was never really dealing with the society—why it should change, how it should change. Not much, at least, there were parts that were. Well, you know, it seems to me that now is the time to try to rebuild real popular structures, that aren't based on peripheral, marginal groups like students, but that really grow out of living communities that will continue and that have a very great need to overcome repressive structures.

Editor's Notes to Interview 9

This illuminating interview has never been published. The text reproduced here interweaves the typewritten answers dated March 28, 1977 with a translation of the questions submitted in French by the late Mitsou Ronat for publication in the Paris weekly: *Nouvel Observateur*.

The book *Dialogues avec Mitsou Ronat* (1977) which she refers to, an extensive (several session) interview with Chomsky at MIT in early January 1976, has been translated back into English by John Viertel as *Language and Responsibility* (1979).

Bains de Sang (1974) is the French translation of a book by Chomsky and Edward Herman which was suppressed by its American publisher (*Counter-Revolutionary Evidence: Bloodbaths in Fact and Propaganda*. Preface by Richard A. Falk. Andover, MA: Warner Modular Publications, 1973); see **PE** (1979), I, pp. xiv-xvii). It was also translated into Italian (1975), German (1975) and Spanish (1976); see Sgroi, pp. 228–30, for further details.

Langue: Théorie Générative E'tendue (Paris:Hermann, 1977; Spanish translation, 1979) is a collection of articles by Chomsky, Ronat and other linguists. In her point about some Spanish examples in this collection, Ronat seems to have in mind grammatical devices for suppressing the agent in which the resulting expressions appear to suggest something akin to a natural process (compare "the ice melted and the money disappeared" with "John melted the ice and took the money").

On the document he refused to sign and its implications, see **RP** (1981/84/2003), ch 2.

9. Materialism in Linguistics and the Morality Criterion
(28 March 1977)

A report published by the Nouvel Observateur *on the repression that the military junta is unleashing in Argentina points out, while describing the massacres, this curious fact: Chomskyan linguistics, said to be "materialist," and liable to prison. How do you perceive the interesting fact that you are placed side by side Marx and Freud, and the physicists that investigate "matter"?*

The reported decision of the Argentine Junta to ban "Chomskyan linguistics" as "materialist" is of course of importance only as an indication of their continuing effort to crush freedom and culture in Argentina, in their criminal assault on the people of that unhappy land. Needless to say, one does not discuss the issue itself with fascist murderers.

Extricating the issue from this grotesque context, there are some interesting questions. In discussion of the mind-body problem, or of materialism, it is generally assumed that we understand what is meant by "body." That is, we come to the problem with a basic understanding of the material world and its principles, and we ask whether the principles and entities postulated in some domain (in this case, the domain of mental representations and processes) can be "reduced" to a material basis, presumed to be understood, or whether even the richest concept of "matter" will not accommodate this domain.

But a little thought about the history of science suffices to show that the initial assumption is highly questionable. Surely our ideas about the material world have changed radically in the past several centuries. To the Cartesians, action-at-a-distance was incomprehensible, and it seems that Newton too considered it an "occult quality." The success of Newtonian physics led to the incorporation of this mysterious property of matter within the common sense of the next generation. As physics extended its scope to incorporate electromagnetic forces, massless particles, and other novel ideas, it was the basic concept of "body" that changed. There is little reason to suppose that the fundamental history of science has come to an end. Thus it is certainly imaginable that our present concept of "body" (our basic picture of the "material world") will be shown to be fundamentally inadequate, as has so often been the case in the past. If so, then the question of "reducing" the theory of mind to a materialistic basis cannot be posed in any clear terms.

Roughly speaking, it seems reasonable to say that our concept of "matter" will be extended to include any domain that can be shown to be in some sense "continuous" with physics. If this new domain requires new physical assumptions that can be integrated with the rest of natural science, then our concept of the material world will have changed, and the new domain will have become part of physics in an expanded sense of "physics." The question whether linguistics "qualifies as materialist" then can be rephrased. A positive answer might arise in one of two ways: (1) by showing that the theory of language can be "reduced" to physics as now understood, as many biologists now believe that problems of life have in effect been "reduced" to biochemistry, ultimately physics; or (2) by showing that physics can be extended, if need be, to include the principles of this new domain, as it has been extended in the past to include many phenomena and principles that were entirely beyond the scope of the "material world" as previously conceived.

About the future of science, we can only speculate. But some speculations seem not unreasonable. There seems no reason to doubt that at least some of the questions that are central to linguistic research may some day be answered in such a way that reduction to the physical sciences as presently understood should be possible. Thus, consider the nature of "linguistic competence," that is, the problem of determining what constitutes knowledge of language. It seems that such knowledge can be represented by a system of rules and principles of mental computation, and it does not seem difficult to imagine a material basis for such systems, though it remains to discover the actual physical mechanisms involved, and this may prove a very difficult task. Or consider the question of "universal grammar"—those aspects of our knowledge of language that are derived from our biological endowment, common to the species, and are presumably genetically programmed. Again, we know of no reason to doubt that the mechanisms that determine this endowment and thus fix the general nature of language can in principle be discovered without fundamental modification of our notions concerning the material world.

When we turn to other questions, however, the matter is much less clear. Consider what is sometimes called "the creative aspect of language use," that is, our ability to use language freely to express our thoughts, independently of the control of identifiable stimuli. It is this ability to which Descartes appealed as a kind of criterion for the existence of "other minds." Honesty requires us to concede that we have no insight into any possible physical basis for this normal human ability. Whether this remarkable and apparently unique human ability can be reduced to physics as now understood, or whether physics can be extended in some natural way to accommodate it, remains an entirely open question, **a perplexing mystery.**

From the very first pages of your Introduction to the collection of papers Langue: Théorie Generative E´tendue, *you appeal to the concept of acceptability of sentences, a notion related to what you call "performance," but based on the grammar—the grammar of what you call "competence," that is, knowledge of language. On the other hand, in* Bains de Sang Constructive: Violence Contre-Révolutionaire, *you refer to the acceptability of the rhetoric of imperialism and militarism in the context of the Vietnam War, Southeast Asia and Latin America. Could we say that there is an underlying "grammar" or "model" of the rhetoric of war? Could it be studied independently? Isn't that what you implicitly tried to do in* Bains de Sang?

There is an analogy, though I am not personally inclined to press it very far. In any state, there is a framework of belief and principles that is constructed to provide a justification for the violence of the state, undertaken on behalf of those who control it. The task of the intellectuals is to ensure that this system of ideology is not seriously questioned. Of course, not all agree to serve as a "secular priesthood" in this manner. Thus, in the report of the Trilateral Commission on the crisis of democracy, they distinguish between the "technocratic and policy-oriented intellectuals" (the "good guys," who merely serve external power) and the "value-oriented intellectuals" (the "bad guys," who engage in critical analysis and "delegitimation"). Americans (and others in the trilateral world) are supposed to admire the former and have contempt for the latter. The ideological institutions (the press, journals of opinion, schools and universities) are generally committed to ensuring that "value-oriented intellectuals" are disregarded, condemned and dismissed. In the case of our enemies, on the other hand, we are supposed to despise the "technocratic and policy-oriented intellectuals," who we call "apparatchiks" or "commissars." And we are to praise the "value-oriented intellectuals" as courageous dissidents. All of this is natural enough. What is remarkable is only the willingness of American intellectuals to act out this farce.

The American apparatchiks who control the ideological institutions must ensure the sanctity of a certain system of belief. Among its sacred tenets are the following: the United States is traditionally committed to freedom, national self-determination, human welfare, and all good things; but it occasionally errs, in an excess of benevolence, as, for example, when it came to the aid of the people of South Vietnam, defending them from Communist aggression, or when it tried to save freedom in Chile from the totalitarianism of Allende. Some more perceptive analysts concede that quite generally the United States seems to act in contradiction to the principles to which it is committed. This is regarded as "ironic" or perhaps "tragic," but of course it cannot lead a responsible person to question the commitment of the American government to the principles that it consistently violates.

Here, incidentally, we see very clearly the distinction between, on the one hand, the natural sciences and other domains that are expected to meet serious intellectual standards, and on the other hand, **the ideological fields**, such as much of the social and behavioral sciences or contemporary history. Thus imagine a physicist who produces a theory, subjects it to empirical test, discovers that it regularly fails, and then concludes that all of this is "ironic"—but the theory stands. In such fields as modern history this behavior is considered quite respectable. For example, no one thinks it unusual that Arthur Schlesinger should write without qualification that "human rights is replacing self-determination as the guiding value in American foreign policy." That "self-determination" was our guiding value—despite Guatemala and Chile, the Dominican Republic and Vietnam, and so on—is a dogma that needs no defense. Examples can be accumulated without end.

The success of the current "human rights" campaign is a case in point. That states are committed to violence in the interest of ruling groups is hardly news. If we consider modern history since World War II, what state wins the prize, when we count up the number of people murdered, villages and cities destroyed, farmland devastated, attempts to escape from grinding poverty and oppression crushed? The competition is not even close. Yet few eyebrows are raised when the United States launches an international crusade for the defense of human rights.

But let us even put that aside. To determine **the sincerity of a moralist** who never tires of telling us of his concern for human rights, we ask how he responds to violations that he has supported and for which he shares responsibility. Thus, if Germany in 1946 had launched a human rights campaign, we would ask what its leaders have to say, for example, about death camps. In the case of President Carter and his admiring acolytes, we ask, correspondingly, what they have to say about Vietnam or Chile, for example. They leave us in no uncertainty on this score. In Vietnam, President Carter explains, "the destruction was mutual": we bombed their villages and they shot down our pilots. Since "we went there to defend the freedom of the South Vietnamese," with no desire "to impose American will on other people," there is no reason for us "to apologize or to castigate ourselves or to assume the status of culpability." Nor do we "owe a debt" in any manner, the president explains, in the midst of one of his sermons on human rights (press conference, March 24; text in the *New York Times*, March 25 [1977]). It is predictable that the hypocrites who write editorials for the *New York Times* will have nothing to say about this interesting interpretation of history, and expression of Christian morality. And when a minor functionary offered an apology for American behavior in Chile, he was quickly reprimanded and called home to learn some lessons in the doctrine of "human rights."

We thus see quite clearly the significance of the current pontification about human rights: it is simply a crusade on the part of the administration and the secular priesthood of intellectuals, with the purpose of restoring the system of beliefs that was eroded by the Vietnam War. To paraphrase Arthur Schlesinger, human rights will be as much a "guiding value" for the future as self-determination has been in the past.

The intellectuals play other games as well. One useful device is to pretend that questions of policy—say, counter-insurgency—are purely technical, with no moral component. Or to be more precise, that is true of policies undertaken by the United States, though obviously not others. This is a perfectly reasonable position, on the assumption that the United States and its leaders are uniquely benevolent and well-intentioned, in contrast to those awful people elsewhere in this iniquitous world. One recalls Heidegger's explanation, in 1935, that Germany must preserve the cultural heritage of Western civilization from the onslaughts of the barbarians outside. Once the principle is established that American policy is free from any value-laden critique, then it is easy to dismiss critics as "irresponsible" or "emotional," and naturally to deny them a voice in the media or a place in the universities, which are, after all, committed to dispassionate inquiry and not mere emotional outbursts, such as, for example, an analysis of U.S. policy in terms of the interests of the corporate elite that controls the state executive.

Perhaps one might go on to describe the underlying system of dogma defended by the "responsible intellectuals" as an underlying "grammar" that specifies legitimate discourse. How useful the analysis is, I am not sure. But there is no doubt that it is very important to try to expose the miserable antics of the "technocratic and policy-oriented intellectuals," particularly outside of the United States, since there are, by now, only limited opportunities to do so within.

Let's take an example, the term "pacification," used by the American propaganda machine during the Vietnam War as well as by the supporters of a French Algiers during the Algerian war. It's the example underlined in Langue *by Carlos Otero as a typical case of manipulation of the vocabulary. Do you think that there can be a political manipulation, conscious or not conscious, of syntax? Do you know of an example at the level of syntax? (Carlos Otero describes the shift, in Spanish, from "el dictador ha promulgado esas leyes" ['the dictator has promulgated those laws'] to "se ha promulgado esas leyes" ['one has promulgated those laws', where the suppressed agent hides behind the indefinite sense of "one"]. Isn't there likely to be similar shifts in the use of language of the people in power?*

I agree that analysis of the sort mentioned can be quite illuminating, and Otero's discussion, which you cite, is a case in point. Another familiar example, from a different domain, is the use of the term **"free enterprise"** to designate a system of autocratic governance of the economy in which neither the community nor the work force has any role (a system that we would call "fascist" if translated to the political sphere). Much of this manipulation is surely conscious, as can sometimes be documented. Beyond the level of vocabulary, one finds such manipulation not in the syntax of the language, I believe, but in the system of ideas and beliefs imposed on the populations subject to indoctrination by those who control the economy, the state, and the ideological institutions.

You just refused to sign a text denouncing the present situation in Vietnam. The reason you have given is that the "denunciation" comes from those who considered the Vietnam War and its enormous massacres perfectly "acceptable." Isn't that in line with the reasons you presented in your Dialogues avec Mitsou Ronat *regarding an editorial of the* Washington Post *entitled "Deliverance," in which the liberal rhetoric tries to reconstitute the legitimacy of the American intervention in Vietnam by conjuring up the "good impulses" at the root of its origin?*

The matter is more complex. It is not correct to say that the text in question originated with supporters of the war. On the contrary, its initiators and signers included many people who had courageously opposed the war. My own decision not to sign was based on two factors: (1) reservations about the text itself; and (2) assessment of the protest as a political act. Let us put aside (1), for brevity; in fact, had the text been acceptable as a document I still would not have signed, because of the nature and context of this political act. One must bear in mind that public protest is a political act, to be judged in terms of its likely human consequences. Those who reject the criterion are either very thoughtless or deeply immoral.

There never was much doubt that the protest would reach the public through the American mass media, which would distort and exploit it for their propagandistic purposes. That proved to be the case. The protest was released at a press conference called by the International League for Human Rights. Predictably, the press exploited the occasion, in prominent news reports and editorials, to advance its current effort to reconstruct recent history so as to place American actions in Vietnam in a more favorable light. This is a very important matter. Unless the insights into the nature of state policy achieved during the 1960s are obscured, it will be difficult to rally public support for further interventions in the interest of those who control the state and its ideological institutions.

The press and academic scholarship are constructing a **version of history** that is just along the lines of the *Washington Post* editorial to which you refer. According to this version, there was a war between South Vietnam and North Vietnam originating with the "aggression from the North" that the Kennedy intellectuals sought to foist upon the public at the time of their ascendancy. The U.S. government, in accordance with its longstanding commitment to self-determination, moved to defend the South. The peace movement, in contrast, supported the Communist aggressors. Thus there is a symmetry between the commitment of the government, defending the South Vietnamese, and that of the peace movement, supporting Hanoi. But the liberal intellectuals took a more serious and honorable position. Unlike the peace movement, they did not defend Communist aggression. Unlike the government, they recognized that the original American exercise in benevolence was unwise—the South Vietnamese leadership did not deserve our aid—and our efforts in their behalf became too costly and too cruel, as the government was drawn into the quagmire. Therefore, the liberal intellectuals influenced the government to withdraw from this unwise and finally cruel exercise of our traditional benevolence. They were hampered in this noble effort by the peace movement, with its irrationality, hysteria, and commitment to Communist aggression.

This is a tissue of lies from beginning to end, but there is little doubt that it will become the official history, solemnly presented in textbooks, academic studies, and the press, as we now in fact already see.

Given the actual historical context, what were the predictable consequences of the protest, as actually conducted? Predictably, it was exploited by the propaganda system for its ends. The press reports and editorial comment observed soberly that at least some segments of the peace movement now see their error in "supporting Hanoi" and "celebrating" Communist aggression (the remainder are incorrigible Stalinists). These elements are "sadder but wiser now," as the press put it. The liberals, who supported the war until it became clear that it was too costly and always concealed its true nature and origins, are vindicated. We can now return to the glorious days of Camelot, having dismissed the challenge of the 1960s to free exercise of state violence and force. These were the predictable consequences of the protest, given the circumstances, and its actual consequences as well, as should now be evident to everyone.

To place all of this in what seems to me the proper light, consider the following **analogy**. Suppose that World War II had ended in a stalemate in late 1944, with Germany remaining a world-dominant power, internally unchanged. By that time, of course, there was a "pragmatic opposition" to the war within Germany, not unlike the liberal opposition to the Vietnam War in the United States. Anyone who was not a total idiot could see that German policy was unsuccessful, and there is evidence that even Himmler was considering a separate peace that might involve getting rid of Hitler. Suppose that under these circumstances, some honest anti-Nazi resisters had called a press conference in Berlin, presenting to the Nazi press a protest against the atrocities against collaborators committed by the French resistance—which, I emphasize, vastly exceeded anything credibly charged to the Vietnamese. Or suppose that they chose to protest, in this fashion, against misdeeds committed by Jews who were liberated from concentration camps. How would we evaluate such an act, even if the contents of the protest were accurate? The situation is not fundamentally different in the present case.

It is interesting, if depressing, to see how the protesters are themselves contributing to the machinations of the propaganda system. Thus they insist that people who resisted the American war have a "special responsibility" to protest against alleged human rights violations in Vietnam. But why do they have a "special responsibility" in this regard? Surely it cannot be argued that these people have a "special responsibility" to initiate public protest against every evil; a person who undertook this responsibility would quickly go mad. Ergo, there must be something special about Vietnam. What is that? There is no answer, apart from the assumptions of the American propaganda system. On these assumptions, there is indeed a "special responsibility," in this case. Since allegedly the protesters were supporting Hanoi, just as the U.S. government was supporting the independence of South Vietnam (unwisely, as it turned out), the protesters now have a special responsibility to confess their errors and condemn the North Vietnamese. Of course, if—as was in fact the case—opponents of the war were protesting American aggression, first in South Vietnam and then in the rest of Indochina, then they have no "special responsibility" with regard to alleged human rights violations in Vietnam. Similarly, honest anti-Nazi resisters would have had no "special responsibility" to condemn misdeeds of the French resistance or the Jews, and they certainly should not have done so through the medium of the Nazi press. By accepting this "special responsibility" the protesters thus reveal a tacit acceptance of the basic principles of the state propaganda system.

Sometimes, honest protesters claim that they must "bear witness" and show the world that they respect a "single standard." Superficially, these motives seem reasonable. On closer analysis, the first is revealed to be absurd and the second profoundly immoral. Thus is it true that we must always publicly protest against any evil? Surely not. To speak only from personal experience, I have occasionally—and correctly—refrained from public protest against crimes committed against dissidents in Eastern Europe, because I had good reason to believe that such protest, in particular cases, would harm the individuals concerned, perhaps by associating them with me. One should engage in such public protest when the individuals in question so desire; otherwise, it would by scandalous to "bear witness." Again, public protest is a political act, undertaken (or not) in terms of an assessment of its human consequences.

What of the principle that we must "clear ourselves" before the bar of public opinion and show the world that we do not have a "double standard"? Observe that protest undertaken on these grounds is entirely self-serving. Its moral level is not different from protest undertaken to ensure that we get to heaven, or simply because someone is paying us to protest. Once again, **the moral level of an action** is evaluated in terms of its predictable human consequences, in particular, with regard to those who are suffering or will suffer from oppression. If it is undertaken simply for personal gain, it is without moral value; indeed, it is despicable.

Do these considerations imply that an honest anti-Nazi never protested, under the circumstances imagined, against atrocities committed by the French resistance or Jews released from concentration camps? Or that American resisters should never protest human rights violations or other indefensible acts committed by the victims of American violence? Surely not. But the manner and character of such protest requires careful consideration, in both cases. And such protest can only be evaluated in terms of its likely consequences, at least if we are concerned with questions of morality rather than just saving our souls or our "image." In the present case, the effect, predictably, has been to support the American propaganda system. The victims of the next episode of imperial violence, tolerated or supported by an obedient population, will not thank people who have chosen to protest in this manner. These are considerations that others too might well bear in mind, for example, when they write for American journals, specifically, journals of American liberalism, even those few that emerged from the catastrophes of the recent past with at least a shred of decency.

I might add one further point. The protesters in question, and the press which so severely distorted and misused their protest, agree that the bloodbath in Vietnam, confidently predicted by apologists for the violence of the American state, did not occur. (Knowing their past practices, we need hardly speculate about the consequences, had the agents of American imperialism emerged victorious.) But **the American bloodbath** still continues. As Jean Lacouture observed, on returning from a visit from Vietnam, "En fait la guerre contre les deux empires d'Occident est gagnée, mais elle ne pas finie. Elle n'en finit pas de finir." Its victims still suffer and still die. Vietnamese sources report that in the single province of Quang Tri, 750 people were killed last year by unexploded ordnance. We may bear this in mind when President Carter hopes for normalization of relations with Vietnam, with the following comment: "We have come through the Vietnam War years with a lot of scars, psychological and others, which need to be healed. There remains now, I think, no hatred in the American people." Or when the mass murderer William Colby, now a respected public lecturer, writes in the *Washington Post* that we should all "turn away from the past, from recrimination over broken promises and antagonistic policies, toward a future of mutual respect and repair of the damages of the war." Perhaps it is not quite that simple.

I am sure that the International League of Human Rights would agree that protests against the French or against Jews through the Nazi propaganda media would have been wrong, indeed obscene. Similarly, they would understand that it would be ugly and improper were Russian dissidents to protest in *Pravda* against some atrocity committed by Czech resisters, or if South African liberals were to protest against black violence in the apartheid press. But they cannot draw similar conclusions with regard to the United States. The reason, one must assume, is that they are so committed to the standard illusions concerning the U.S. government, the press, and the American intellectual community, that they simply cannot comprehend that similar principles apply. In this case, then, a failure to consider the human consequences of a public act is compounded with naive submissiveness to the state propaganda system.

The term "extended theory" in generative grammar brings to mind the term "extended reproduction" in Marx's economic analysis ("erweiterte Reproduction" in the German original). Is the kinship of the two terminologies more than sheer chance? Is it a reminiscence of or a reference to the tradition of scientific philosophy?

The similarities in terminology are merely fortuitous, and on my part at least, unintended.

The analysis of language plays a revolutionary role in the current development of the human sciences. Isn't it "a great leap forward" that an ideology of behavior and cybernetic automata is replaced by an exploration of the creative aspect of language use—a creativity subject to rule, but a creativity that changes the rules?

I would like to refer here to the discussion of the first question. Several issues must be distinguished: (1) What constitutes our knowledge of our language? (2) What is the basis for the acquisition of this knowledge? (3) How is this knowledge put to use? As remarked earlier, there seems to be no reason to doubt that in principle we might find the actual mechanisms involved in the mental representation of the grammar we have constructed when we know a language, or the innate schematism that makes this achievement possible, that by restricting severely the form of possible grammars, permits us to acquire rich and extensive knowledge of language in a uniform way with limited and varied experience. So far, there is no conflict with cybernetic models, though as far as I can see, little to be learned from them.

When we turn to the third question, however, the situation appears different. The theory of language use falls naturally into two parts: (1) the theory of perception and understanding, and (2) the theory of production. As for the former, it seems possible in principle, within the framework of current understanding, to construct a theory that will deal with the "processing" of sentences, roughly, the assignment of structure and meaning to presented sound. As for question (2), we do not know how to formulate a reasonable inquiry. How do people proceed, in their normal lives, to produce new utterances as an expression of their thought or for other ends? **Questions of will** inevitably intrude, and here contemporary science fails us entirely. It is possible that in this connection we face absolute limits to human scientific understanding. Contrary to Cartesian doctrine, there is no basis for the assumption that human reason is a universal instrument, available for all contingencies. Rather, it is a biological system, with its inherent scope and limits. There is no reason to presume that its scope includes the theory of human behavior and human freedom. The evidence of intellectual history, at least, suggests that it may not. Our understanding of these questions has not progressed significantly beyond classical antiquity. Nor does anyone, to my knowledge, have a reasonable suggestion as to how to proceed to accommodate the creative aspect of language use or other exercises of human will within the framework of the natural sciences—which are, after all, a production of the human mind, with its contingent power and limits—even in principle. The problem simply mounts when we consider true creativity—the kinds of creative acts to which we attribute aesthetic value, for example—and beyond, to the kinds of creativity that involve modification of some system of rules, as in the creation of new literary genres or musical idioms or systems of scientific thought.

You define the role of the intelligentsia as the "manipulation of social control." Do linguists run the risk of participating in such manipulation and, if so, how? If not, why not?

It is a constant risk, for anyone. **Intellectuals** are a special social formation in modern industrial society. They have developed characteristic ideologies of social control, consistent with their place in society, actual or anticipated. In the Marxist-Leninist tradition, these take the form of the principle of the "vanguard party," which reconstructs society, allegedly in the interests of the proletariat—though why any Marxist should expect the "vanguard party" to serve any interests other than its own remains a mystery. Under state capitalism, the intelligentsia have developed the theory that power should shift—or, some claim, is shifting—to those who have the talent of special training to organize and control social and economic processes, the scientific intelligentsia. Bakunin predicted a century ago that under state socialism, the "Red bureaucracy," a "new class," would create the most despotic and savage authoritarianism that the world had ever seem; while under state capitalism, the intelligentsia would "beat the people with the people's stick," in his trenchant phrase. He was, I believe, right on both counts.

The technical intelligentsia are highly privileged in modern industrial society. They are linked in style of life and class consciousness to those who have effective power, and the inducements to serve those who have effective control over society are very great. I have already mentioned some of the ways in which this can be done. Linguists are prey to these tendencies and options no less than others, though their work is rather marginal, as far as social control and manipulation are concerned. One simply has to make a choice as to where one's commitments are, and where one's energies will be directed.

Could you explain why the reduction of the definition of language to its aspect of communication seems to you negative and even dangerous?

One must first answer the question: What do we mean by "communication"? If we mean "transmission of information," conveying beliefs, initiating requests for action, and the like, then it seems quite obvious that although language is used for "communication," it serves other ends as well. Perhaps the statistically most common use of language is simply to construct and strengthen social relations among individuals. Casual conversation, for example, is probably motivated, for the most part, by the need to create social bonds or to place oneself within a comfortable social matrix. In much, perhaps most conversation, one has no "instrumental ends." Or language can be used, and commonly is used, simply for self-expression or for clarifying one's thought, or in myriad other ways. If we broaden the concept of "communication" to include such uses of language, then we can say that the purpose of language is "communication," but only because the latter concept has been deprived of any significance.

What is "dangerous" about the effort to "reduce" the use of language to communication? Two things, I believe. On the one hand, it reinforces the tendency to pursue analogies, which are quite fruitless as far as we know, to "communication systems" of other animals. In my view, this may be regarded as an instant of what literary critics sometimes call **"the pathetic fallacy,"** the attempt to invest some part of nature with human qualities. A more serious danger is that this view, as usually developed, tends to reinforce the belief that what humans do, they do for "instrumental ends": to gain something for themselves, advance their position, increase their power, and so on—and, furthermore, that there is some a priori necessity for this to be so. This is not only a vulgar and demeaning view, but it is also—thankfully—quite false, I believe.

Is there a general question which no one asks you and which nevertheless seems to you more important than all the questions you are asked?

Important questions can be elaborated without end, and I would not presume to imply that I know which ones are crucial or essential. The questions that have been posed touch on many points of great interest, and, naturally, omit many others. I do not feel that I can designate some specific area that stands out among others as deserving special comment.

Editor's Notes to Interview 10

Interview conducted by Roger Hurwitz, David Woolf and Sherman Teichman in March 1977; "also included are excerpts from written material by Professor Chomsky" (see **TNCW**, ch. 11, first published in *Seven Days*, April 11, 1977, and in French translation in *Le Monde Diplomatique*, April 1977). It was published in *Leviathan* 1:1–3 (Spring 1977), pp. 6–9 & 86—a Boston University "Tri-Quarterly Journal of Middle East Politics and Culture," which must be added to the long list of new periodicals that have featured Chomsky in the first issue. See also I30.

On "national interest," see **CD&E** (2003), appendix to ch. 7.

The "special relationship" is a major theme of **FT** (1983), where the figures relative to U.S. aid to Israel are updated (p. 10):

"It is possible that recent aid amounts to something like $1000 per year for each citizen of Israel when all factors are taken into account. Even the public figures are astounding. For fiscal years 1978 through 1982, Israel received 48 percent of all U.S. military aid and 35 percent of U.S. economic aid, worldwide. For FY 1983, the Reagan administration requested almost $2.5 billion for Israel, out of a total aid budget of $8.1 billion, including $500 million in outright grants and $1.2 billion in low interest loans. In addition, there is a regular pattern of forgiving loans, offering weapons at special discount prices, and a variety of other devices, not to mention the tax-deductible "charitable" contributions (in effect, an imposed tax), used in ways to which we return …"

For more recent developments suggesting the possibility of a two-state settlement, see Editor's Notes to I50. It of course continues to be true that "The U.S. doesn't care about … whether Israel exists or fails to exist. What they care about is that the U.S. dominate the region as long as it's an important region in world affairs."

For a post-Iran Contra hearings view of some of the topics considered here, see **CT** (1988), in particular ch. 8.

10. Oil Imperialism and the U.S.-Israel Relationship (March 1977)

Given the fact that now you have a government dominated by people like Carter and Brzezinski who were deeply involved in the Trilateral Commission, which emphasized maintaining a strong relationship with both Western Europe and Japan, will there be a new emphasis on new policy?

First of all, I don't think there is any significant difference between the Trilateral view and the Kissinger view. The difference is more in style than in content. Many people in power regarded Kissinger as a kind of nut. He understood the basic ideas but he was playing the game like a clown, with the show for the media and the personal nonsense. That's not the way you conduct serious affairs. I think the Trilateral Commission is, in effect, taking the basic thrust of Kissinger's policies and is trying to implement them with a rational plan, without the dangerous clowning. When things become personalized and an erratic, irrational person takes over, you never know what's going to happen. The Commission would rather have done it in a sensible coordinated way.

But Trilateralism still means that Europe and Japan ought to be subordinated to overall American interests. There's no deviation from that policy. Trilateralism is **a shift from the policy of, say, 30 years ago,** when it was assumed that the U.S. would unilaterally organize most of the world. Now everyone has to recognize that there are other sources of power within the so-called First World, the world of industrial capitalism, but those are supposed to be regional powers.

It's almost a capitalist version of polycentrism.

Yes, with exactly the same tacit conditions that are already assumed in polycentrism, that there's one power that's the first power. Kissinger made the policy very explicit—one of Kissinger's problems from the point of view of the ruling class is that he's much too explicit.

Is there a U.S. foreign policy in the Middle East?

Yes. There's been a very consistent U.S. foreign policy in the Middle East at least since the Second World War whose primary concern has been to ensure that the energy reserves of the Middle East remain firmly under American control. The State Department noted in 1945 that these reserves constitute "a stupendous source of strategic power, and one of the greatest material prizes in world history."[1]

Basically it is a policy meant to keep Saudi Arabia, which has by far the largest known stores of petroleum, under American control. This has been quite explicit since World War II. In fact, during the war the government acted to expel Britain, and later France, from the region. There were forms of chicanery used to achieve that end, which was achieved, certainly, by the formation of ARAMCO [Arabian American Oil Company] in 1947.

Given U.S. control over Western Hemisphere resources, the United States thus effectively controlled the major energy reserves of the noncommunist world, with all that implied with regard to the organization of international society.[2]

A number of years later, the American position in the Middle East was extended. Following the CIA-backed coup in Iran in 1953, American oil companies controlled 40 percent of Iranian oil. By the mid-50s, American dominance of the region and total dominance of Saudi Arabia was virtually complete.

American penetration of the Saudi economy and military has been extensive. There are now about 30,000 Americans in Saudi Arabia, mostly ARAMCO employers. U.S. exports to Saudi Arabia and Iran amounted to $2.8 billion each in 1976, with sales to Saudi Arabia projected to reach $4.8 billion in 1977.

How deeply are we involved?

A Senate Foreign Relations Committee report estimated that by 1980, there may be 50,000-60,000 Americans in Iran, many engaged in military training.

Furthermore, OPEC [Organization of Petroleum Exporting Countries] investments in the West, with the U.S. share doubling to 44 percent in early 1970, have relieved balance-of-payments problems and "help explain the dollar's strength" and "the recovery of the American stock market earlier this year."[3] Saudi Arabian investment in U.S. Treasury bonds is unofficially estimated at $5 to $10 billion, though it is a closely guarded secret.[4]

Could you comment on the approach that says that U.S. foreign policy in the Middle East isn't credible unless we have an independent energy policy?

That's based on a complete misunderstanding. Suppose the U.S. had 100 percent of its own energy right here. That wouldn't affect in the least American desire to control the Middle East because we want to make sure that nobody else has access to those cheap resources of energy. One of the ways the U.S. keeps control over Europe and Japan is by having a stranglehold on their energy supply. Therefore, if there was a solar energy or shale breakthrough, giving the U.S. its own energy supply completely independent of Middle East oil, we still would want to ensure control over that region as long as Middle East oil remained cheap and accessible.

Back in 1945, the Western Hemisphere was, by a large margin, the largest producer of oil, with most of it coming from the U.S. or the Caribbean.

Nevertheless, the U.S. was absolutely insistent on kicking the French out of that tiny share they had of Saudi Arabian oil. In fact, the U.S. pressed to get Europe and Japan to shift to an oil-based economy after the Second World War, in part as a way of ensuring American control over them. Europe and Japan both have coal, but it is better for the U.S. if they are dependent on a foreign, American-controlled source of energy. In a sense, the major potential enemies of the U.S. are Europe and Japan. Russia is another world. They control their own empire and we can't do much about it at this point. But Europe and Japan are potential threats. They are the areas where most of the American investment is, so they have to be controlled by the American government.

The real fear of the U.S., which is occasionally voiced quite explicitly (for example in Kissinger's "Year of Europe" speech in April 1973), is that Europe could become a system comparable to the U.S. in strength and that it would then set up the kind of bilateral arrangements with the Middle East and North Africa that we regard as an American prerogative. If this ever happened, the U.S. would in fact be a second-class power in the world.

After the energy crisis erupted, Kissinger again (in January, 1974) warned against the development of bilateral arrangements with the oil producers, although the United States did not refrain from extending its own bilateral arrangements. The Washington Conference of February 1974 brought the EEC [European Economic Community] powers into line on this issue.

In a recent study for the Harvard University Center for International Affairs, Robert Lieber reviews the failure of France's attempt to organize an independent European policy in the face of German-American agreement "on the need for an agreed code of conduct limiting bilateral deals." The problem facing the EEC powers was that "to follow the French position meant a serious breach with the United States, which the Germans and then the British found intolerable. In the end, given America's energy resources, its economic strength (particularly its limited vulnerability to international resource and financial problems), and its superpower military political standing, the Atlantic approach seemed to offer payoffs in dealing with tangible problems which the French-led policy simply could not deliver."

Simply put, American pressures to conform to U.S. "global interests and responsibilities," strongly backed by Germany, could not be resisted. Lieber further notes that "it was widely observed that the U.S. had benefited from the crisis both economically (through her multinational oil companies and the weakening of rival economies) and politically (by the reassertion of her leadership) ... the crisis left the U.S. more dominant and the community weakened in its influence on issues of security, finance, and economics because of its lack of a single voice."[5]

How do you understand the oil-rate hikes?

I think part of the apparent American effort to maintain and raise oil prices can only be understood as an attempt (successful in this case) to punish and control our competitors, namely Europe and Japan. The rise in oil prices often attributed in the popular press to "Arab sheik's," in fact has only a marginal relation to the Arab-Israeli conflict. As noted in the Senate report cited above, "The leadership within OPEC in rising prices has come from Iran and Venezuela, countries which have a minimal interest in the Arab-Israeli dispute." Some commentators go so far as to claim that "Since 1971, the United States has encouraged Middle East oil-producing states to raise the price of oil and keep it up,"[6] although by now the rise in price may be harming the American economy as well. This buttresses the basic American concern to control the energy resources and to use those resources as an implement to dominate the world of industrial capitalism.

One result of the oil embargo, in which the American oil companies were the cutting edge, was the wiping out of Japan's dollar reserves. Although by 1976 Japan recovered somewhat, primarily because of her winning construction contracts with Arab countries, the embargo created a $2.5 billion trade deficit for Japan with Middle Eastern countries from 1973 to 1975. It is not simply a coincidence that the United States, Germany and Japan are competitors and "leaders in the race to supply the oil-production nations with consumer goods and equip them for rapid industrialization;"[7] and that these countries are also the leaders in the recovery from world recession.

How did the embargo affect other areas of the international economy?

The rice in oil prices was accompanied by a comparable increase in the price of coal and uranium, and in fact other commodities as well. To cite only one case, "by the end of 1973, U.S. wheat exports cost three times as much per ton as they had little more than a year before."[8]

As for the prospects that prices may drop, the analysis in the current London *Economist* annual review seems plausible enough; the consumer countries cannot organize to this end, for one reason, because "two of the most powerful of the so-called consumer countries, the United States and Britain, are now producers of high-cost oil themselves (in Alaska and the North Sea) and they would stand to lose enormous investments if the price of oil dropped substantially" (not to speak of the value of other energy resources). Furthermore, there is "widespread acceptance among energy experts of the fairness of today's oil prices" which "are merely what had long be expected by the end of the 1970s anyway ..."[9] One person's "fairness," of course, is another's "cruel exploitation," but those with the power are generally in the former camp, not only in this regard.

Would you comment on the relation between the U.S. government's policy and the interests of the American oil companies?

The oil companies are the major international corporations. Since oil has become important, they have virtually owned the State Department. They are the corporations within the American imperialist system that have the greatest concern for American foreign policy. Because they have the largest overseas investments, their influence over foreign policy has always been extremely strong.

But it would be a mistake to say that the government is controlled by the oil companies. The government policy reflects the overall interests of American capitalism. So, on occasion, the particular interests of the oil companies may seem rather parochial and short-sighted from the point of view of the larger interests of American capitalism.

We can see how this worked in Iran. In the wake of the CIA coup there, the U.S. government wanted American oil companies to take over a substantial part of Iranian oil. A government directive was issued to the oil companies explaining that it was "in the security interests of the United States" for them to help "provide to the friendly government of Iran substantial revenues on terms which will protect the interests of the Western World in the petroleum resources of the Middle East."[10]

For reasons having to do with rather myopic and narrow business concerns, the oil companies weren't particularly interested in the plan. They simply had too much oil. They wanted to ensure their position in Saudi Arabia, and realized that joining the consortium would reduce their liftings form Saudi Arabia. In accord with the long-run interests of American capitalism, the government simply stepped in and ordered them to join.

A position paper put out at the time by the Department of State, Defense and Interior to the National Security Council simply described the oil companies as instruments of U.S. foreign policy and concluded that they should be treated as such. In return and on grounds of "national security," Truman called for termination of anti-trust actions against the companies in January 1953.

American scholars typically take such incidents as support for the general doctrine to which they are committed, namely, that the government simply serves some abstract "national interest" and that policy is at best marginally influenced by the concern of major corporations. Myra Wilkins, for example, notes that "The Truman Doctrine, for instance, committed the United States to defend Greece and Turkey against Communism, and in the process created security for corporate Middle Eastern oil investments; yet, Texaco's chairman of the board testified that the promulgation of the doctrine caught him by surprise,"[11] referring to Senate testimony.

How literally should one take such testimony?

It is an open question, but it may well be accurate. If so, the case simply illustrates a natural principle, quite well-supported by such evidence as is available: corporate executives are concerned with specific problems of maximizing profit, extending market control, and the like, while the state executive, largely staffed by their representatives, is concerned with long-term, enduring and general interests of American capitalism.

The case for the standard doctrine would be stronger if foreign policy were not so systematically directed to "creating security for corporate Middle Eastern oil investments" and the like. As long as the state uses its power to enhance "profits beyond the dreams of avarice,"[12] as in the case of the oil companies, and to secure the conditions for their enhancement, it is hardly necessary for those concerned directly with business operations to attempt to intervene in affairs of state.

Could you speak in more detail about the oil companies owning the State Department and the way that is manifested in terms of policy?

Well, if you look at the staffing of the top positions in the State Department, it has been pretty much an oil company preserve. Most of the top people in the Department come from either energy corporations, from the Rockefeller Foundation or from law firms that are very closely linked to oil corporations. The mechanism is very obvious. Say you have a regulatory commission that regulates the railroads. The railroads are going to try to get control over it. Foreign policy is analogous to regulation of affairs affecting international corporations, and therefore they're going to try to gain control over it, which they've largely done.

Will U.S. foreign policy in the Middle East shift if they find larger oil reserves elsewhere? It has been projected that China, by the year 1990, will be producing 8 million barrels of oil a day.

I know of no evidence for that at all. China has larger oil reserves than anybody thought, but it doesn't begin to compare with the Middle East as far as anybody knows. There have been reports coming from Japan that China has refused to supply them with oil except through American oil companies. I suspect that when the history of this period becomes known, we'll discover that one of the reasons for the sudden American interest in China is to ensure that China doesn't form a kind of close trading bloc with Japan, instead of working for American interests for control of Japan. The evidence is much too sparse, but I suspect that something of the sort is going on. So even though China's oil resources are much less than those of the Middle East, the U.S. is very concerned that China not supply our industrial rivals independently.

Does the Soviet Union have a foreign policy in the Middle East?

Yes. It would like to have as much influence as possible in the region, but the Soviet Union understands very well that that's an area of primary American concern. Just as the Soviet Union will brook no American interference in Eastern Europe, which is of primary concern to them, they known that the U.S. will brook no interference in the Middle East, which is of primary concern to the U.S.

Russian policy has been fairly constant since World War II. It has been what they call "detente," which is to say, there are two big superpowers and each controls an empire and they leave each other alone. Basically the U.S. doesn't intervene in Eastern Europe and Russia doesn't intervene in the American empire. That is why Stalin tried to call off the Greek guerrillas. (Incidentally, Greece was considered part of the Middle East at the time; in fact, Greece was in the Middle East section of the State Department.) Stalin succeeded in getting the French communists to cooperate with the restoration of capitalism with American dominance and he expected in return that the U.S. would allow him to control everything in Eastern Europe that he wanted. And that's more or less the way it has worked out, rhetoric aside.

Russia will try to maintain what influence it can in the Middle East, but there's no evidence that it's willing to risk a nuclear war, which is probably what would happen if it ever made any serious moves in the region. At the end of the October [1973] war, the Russians asked the U.S. to have a joint peacekeeping force in the Sinai to impose the cease-fire. The U.S. refused. We weren't going to allow any Russian troops in the region. The Russians then made some veiled threats to do it themselves, at which point the U.S. called a worldwide nuclear alert, and we came unpleasantly close to a nuclear confrontation, over virtually nothing. I don't think anyone is going to seriously threaten American dominance over the region. It would very likely lead to war.

At the moment, the parochial interests of the oil companies appear to involve a commitment to political accommodation in the Middle East.

Yes, that's true. They are pressing very hard—privately, publicly, any way they can—to persuade the U.S. government to take an "even-handed stand," a code word for **support of a two-state solution on the '67 borders**. For years the oil companies have been pressing for this solution, on their own and through the Saudi Arabian government, but the U.S. government has ignored the pressure.

My speculation is that the U.S. regards the current situation as extremely favorable to their long-term interests. The tension, the high level of armaments, the military confrontation, are favorable, and the strength of Israel and Iran poses a strong military threat to independent action on the part of the oil-producing powers. It's an extremely dangerous policy, but that's the way it is.

That's one view, which has been held by virtually everyone. It seems to have been Kissinger's view, for example.

Were there different views?

There were sharp differences in outlook between individuals. Many are hard to identify because they don't speak out much, but we can compare, for example, the views of Secretaries of State William Rogers and Kissinger. Rogers' view was that there should be a political settlement, meaning something like returning to the June '67 borders, with a Palestinian state on the West Bank and in the

Gaza Strip, and various other conditions of demilitarization and national guarantees. Let's call that a "two-state settlement."

When Kissinger took control of Middle East policy in the fall of 1970 (according to his testimony), there was an abrupt switch in official American policy, from Rogers plan rhetoric to Kissinger rhetoric.

Under Kissinger's initiative, the United States by late 1970 abandoned even a rhetorical commitment to a political settlement and was clearly supporting a very different program, namely, the Israeli program of developing and ultimately annexing substantial parts of the occupied territories, a policy that led directly to the October 1973 war.

Israel's development policies as well as numerous official and semi-official pronouncements make it clear that the goal is to realize the so-called "Allon Plan," which would integrate into Israel the Golan Heights, the Gaza Strip, parts of Northeastern Sinai with a strip of the Sinai extending to Sharm El-Sheikh (Israeli Ophira), the Jordan valley, a large area around Jerusalem, and substantial other parts of the West Bank, excluding areas of Arab population concentration. The latter areas would be left under local or Jordanian civil administration and Israeli military control, thus alleviating what is referred to in Israel as "the demographic problem," namely, the problem of incorporating a large Arab population into a Jewish state, while still facilitating the flow of organized Arab workers into Israel as a cheap labor force.

The real choices are between political accommodation and military confrontation. The American government is split over the question. Consider someone like Edward Sheehan. My suspicion is that Edward Sheehan speaks for the CIA. I'm told he was the political officer in the Egyptian embassy in the 1950s, which is usually a CIA post, and I suspect that he speaks from a point of view that exists in the "intelligence community," favoring political accommodation. A political settlement is a perfectly satisfactory fall-back position for American imperialism. It would probably cut down the conflict in the region, at least the Arab-Israeli conflict.

So here are two easily crystallized positions, both of them being realistic options for the region. The U.S. government has consistently supported the first, Israeli occupation, which is essentially a drift toward the Allon Plan. That would leave Israel, from a superficial point of view, in a very powerful position. In fact, I think it would leave Israel in a very precarious position because the military confrontations are very dangerous and very damaging internally.

But if you add up the guns, Israel is in a very strong short-term position, and could be instrumental in U.S. domination of the Middle East. The U.S. government doesn't care about the long-term consequences—whether Israel exists or fails to exist. What they care about is that the U.S. dominate the region as long as it's an important region in world affairs.

Anyone who didn't hold that position simply couldn't get near the center of government because it's just too crucial for American capitalism. The Middle East oil reserves are, by a very large margin, the largest and the cheapest energy resources in the world, and whoever has control over them runs a good part of the world.

How much autonomy over foreign policy does the U.S. allow the area?

I wouldn't think that the oil-producing countries could ever stray very far from the American fold, at least Saudi Arabia couldn't. The U.S. controls the region through a kind of tripartite alliance of Israel, Iran and Saudi Arabia. The alliances with Israel and Iran are completely overt. The relation to Saudi Arabia is much more complex. On the one hand, the Saudis have an interest in restoring Arab control over Jerusalem; in fact, they would like to control the entire area. On the other hand, they also have a stake in Israeli power, deriving from the desire of their ruling elite to see the maturity of American hegemony over the region, which would serve their interests very efficiently. They want to be merged into the American system; they want to ensure that there's no Russian influence there; they want to make sure that any radical or nationalist currents within the Arab world are crushed or contained. For all three purposes, American hegemony over the region is useful. Israeli power, like Iranian power, serves that interest, so their position is somewhat ambiguous and very crucial. What Saudi Arabia decides to do will very strikingly affect the future of the region.

Iran, to take another part of this tripartite alliance, has a fairly big population, but it's a mixture since half of it is not Persian. It's being armed to the teeth by the U.S. and it will be a major force in the region both militarily and economically. Iran is closely allied with Israel. Iran supplies Israel with oil and Israel is involved in training Iranian military and administrators. There are Iranian students here at MIT who studied in Israel. They don't make a fuss about it, but that's the case.

The logic of this policy is that the U.S. wants to guarantee the "stability" of the major oil producers by posing a strong military threat, particularly against Saudi Arabia. The Saudis are not causing any problems now, but given the instability of the Arab world, it's possible that there might be a Qadaffist coup or something similar, which has come close to happening. If Saudi Arabia ever got out of hand, the U.S. would want to be in a strong position to threaten them. Even more important, they want the Saudi Arabians to recognize that their position is extremely precarious: it is in the interest of the Saudi Arabian ruling class, seeking to maintain their own autonomy, to play the American game. Saudi Arabia is where more of the oil is, and in another 20 or 30 years that's going to be where almost all the oil is.

The Saudi refusal in December 1976 to join the OPEC countries in a price rise was generally regarded as a move to induce the United States to move towards a political settlement of the Arab-Israeli conflict. But here, too, complications abound. This policy would be meaningful if Saudi Arabia were to expand its production significantly, thus driving other producers out of the international market. Early indications raise questions about Saudi intentions. Production did in fact rise rapidly in early January, but was significantly reduced in the latter part of the month. Average daily production for January was lower than it was in December, before the new prices went into effect.[13]

The reduction was attributed in the press to inclement weather, but Foreign Minister Prince Saud al-Feisal stated in late January that Saudi Arabia "still has not taken any decision about increasing our oil production," while the Iranian foreign minister said a few days later that he believes "what my colleague Saud has said," and the Iranian press quoted the oil minister of Qatar as saying "as far as I know officially, Saudi Arabia will not increase its production."[14]

The Shah announced in January that overproduction by Saudi Arabia would be considered "an act of aggression against us," and veiled threats have appeared in the official Iranian press.[15] While a war in the Persian Gulf is the last thing that the U.S. government desires, it may nevertheless view with some favor the potential threat posed to the Arab oil producers by the military powers to which it is closely allied. A Senate report on Iran notes that "the possibility of conflict with the Arabs in the future cannot be discounted, especially if there were to be a revolution in Saudi Arabia and the present regime was replaced by more extremist anti-Western elements."[16]

Incidentally, Iran might invade that area anyway. Iran is going to run out of oil in 20 or 30 years, and it doesn't strike me as very likely that it will go back to being a tenth-rate power when they see all that oil sitting right across the Gulf. They have an enormous military establishment and in, say, 10 years, they may be able to run their army without American technicians. What they may decide to do is simply invade and take over Saudi Arabia.

What is Israel's relationship to the U.S.?

Israel is virtually a dependency of the United States. U.S. exports to Israel, amounting to $1.4 billion in 1976, are exceeded only by those to Saudi Arabia and Iran. But because every other aspect of the problem of the Middle East is fitted into the framework of old reserves, American attitudes towards Israel will vary as they bear on the problem of maintaining control of Middle Eastern energy resources.

Consider the U.S. reaction to Israel's conquest of the Sinai in 1956 and in 1967. In 1956, the U.S. strongly opposed that action. Einsenhower and Dulles were quite forthright and outspoken about it a few days before the presidential election, allegedly a time when political considerations are paramount. Political considerations aside, the U.S. openly compelled Israel to withdraw from the Sinai, not caring about its impact in the presidential election. In contrast, the U.S. supported Israel's conquest of the Sinai in 1967 and has been backing it since that time.

What was the difference between 1956 and 1967? In 1956, Israel was allied with France and England who were trying to reestablish some position of significance in the Middle East, believing still they had some role to play in regulating the affairs of the region. Since Israel was collaborating with rivals of the U.S. in the region, the conquest became illegitimate.

In 1967, Israel was closely allied to the U.S. directly. As a result, the conquest was quite legitimate. U.S. government support of Israel is more or less in accord with the American perception of Israel's strength. The stronger Israel becomes, the more it is able to assist the U.S. in maintaining control of the region, so the more the U.S. will support it. Though the pretense has always been that we're supporting Israel because it is in danger, the opposite would be a much more accurate statement. American support for Israel is contingent upon its strength and ability to aid in maintaining American domination of the Middle East.

Would you explain the logic in American policy that sees a strong Israeli military position as being in the interests of the U.S.?

Since 1967 it's been plain that Israel is, by a long shot, the strongest military power in the region. Contrary to what people believe, it's one of the richest countries in the region, in terms of the GNP per capita. Though not as rich as the oil emirates, it is richer than most of the oil-producing nations. Furthermore, it's an advanced technological society. Its wealth and economic strength are not just contingent on some depreciable resource.

American planners have regarded Israel as a barrier to Russian penetration, and have assumed that "the demise of Israel ... likely would see increased Soviet influence"[17] Israeli power protected the "monarchical regimes" of Jordan and Saudi Arabia from "a militarily strong Egypt" in the 1960s, thus securing American interests in the major oil-producing regions.

The Senate's ranking oil expert, Senator Henry Jackson, is only one of those who have emphasized "the strength and Western orientation of Israel on the Mediterranean and Iran on the Persian Gulf, two "reliable friends of the United States," who, along with Saudi Arabia, "have served to inhibit and contain those irresponsible and radical elements in certain Arab states ... who, were they free to do so, would pose a grave threat indeed to our principal sources of petroleum in the Persian Gulf."[18]

For such reasons, the United States has tacitly supported the Israeli occupation of surrounding Arab territories as well as the forceable takeover of Arab islands by Iran in 1971. The Iran-Israeli alliance not only protects reactionary Arab states allied with the United States, but also stands as a constant threat to them, should they make unwelcome moves. More generally, it is argued that "the Israeli-Iranian interrelationship—wittingly or unwittingly—has contributed to" the stability of the Indian Ocean Basin: "the quiet in the eye of a hurricane."[19]

There seems to be a self-contradictory logic within the U.S. policy.

There is. The stronger these countries become, the more likely it is that they'll do something outside the control of the U.S. foreign policy. It is **an extremely hazardous game** and, as we know, it often fails. Hitler was playing a hazardous game and he lost.

Vance has recently condemned Israel's oil exploration in the Sinai. If the U.S. is interested in a strong Israel, why do they inhibit its independent military capacity by denying it an independent source of petroleum, oil and lubricants?

That's a real bone of contention. For one thing, the U.S. would rather not have Israel have its own internal resources. They want it to be dependent on the U.S. Furthermore, Israel is infringing on the interests of major American corporations in the case of the Gulf of Suez.

American oil companies are linked with Egyptian explorations and liftings and Israel is simply taking over part of the area that they regard as theirs. The thing is pretty small at the moment and it doesn't involve any major oil resources, so the U.S. isn't pressing very hard. But they've always described Israeli actions there as illegal and they simply reiterated it at this point. Of course, what "legality" means is what the big powers determine; it's another rhetorical term. To say that it's illegal is another way of saying, "We disapprove of it and if we disapprove enough we'll make you stop it."

What are the consequences for Israeli society of playing the American game?

The effect on Israel will be very corrosive, both economically and psychologically. There's a tremendous economic drain into military expenditures and that's only going to increase. Furthermore, a commitment to military production is becoming a larger and larger element in the Israeli economy, both internally and for export, and the tie with the U.S. is a strong part of that. This drain of resources in the military means that they can't face internal social problems which are very serious, such as the problem of the Sephardic oriental Jewish community. That's never going to be faced as long as there's a militarized economy. It will become an economy sharply split along class lines, with an extremely rich sector connected to advanced technology and commerce, and the rest of the population will be suppressed and very poor.

The psychological effect will be harder to estimate, but it is very significant. As long as the occupation persists, there will be an unconquerable temptation to use cheap Arab labor, which is what is happening. Israel will inevitably move toward a kind of South African situation, in which there's a very cheap labor force which is atomized and can't organize. They'll take over a good part of the productive labor of the country. This is already starting to happen. That can only have the effect of encouraging racism and all the kinds of attitudes that come along with exploiting a cheap labor force which is totally under your control.

In my opinion, in 10 or 20 years the *kibbutzim* will become a collective management using Arab labor, running factories off the premises, and living in the urban suburbs. It will be extremely hard for them to do anything else. They've got to compete in the capitalist market, which means they have to use the cheapest working force available. At every point, the effect of all this on Israeli culture is frightening. I find it very depressing to read the Israeli press; the attitudes expressed are outrageous. You can't avoid these attitudes when you're oppressing other people and using that oppression as the basis for your prosperity. You have to have a moral justification for it, and the justification is racism.

With the weakening position of the PLO after Lebanon, are the bargaining positions in the Middle East strong enough to achieve a political settlement?

I think a political settlement was possible long before Lebanon. The Palestinians are a very weak force and, furthermore, since 1974, before the disintegration of Lebanon, Palestinians had been pretty clear in saying that they would accept something like a separate state. They certainly have made indications that that would be true, and they have no choice. If Israel had come out for two states in 1967, they would have accepted it. They might have spoken about "our historic rights," but nobody cares what governments say about historic rights or their dreams or their long-term goals. What is important is the concrete political situation. Israel can have a declaration on record saying that it has historic rights to Eretz Yisrael—the "historical land of Israel"—but that has no role in policy and we properly disregard it. Well, properly we ought to disregard the comparable things said by the PLO.

Would the State Department prefer to leave the Saudi Arabians and the Syrians to their own devices in pressuring the Palestinians to accept a two-state solution rather than apply pressure to Israel directly?

Well, there is nothing much to put pressure on the Palestinians about. The Palestinians barely survive as an organized group. Taking them to be the barrier to a settlement is already submitting oneself to the propaganda system. Israel's argument that it can't deal with the Palestinians always turns on Palestinian rhetoric, but that rhetoric doesn't mean much. The objective situation is that the Palestinians are and always have been extremely weak except as a disruptive force within the Arab world. Countries like Saudi Arabia would like to have the disruptive force controlled, which is one of the reasons they would like to have a small state. It would undoubtedly be run by conservative elements among the Palestinians, and it would be very much subject to the forces of other Arab states as well as Israel. That would probably terminate the disruptive role that Palestine plays in the Middle East. Sheehan essentially said this.

Where does Jordan figure into the picture?

The two positions I have described have a particular consequence with regard to Hussein. The position in favor of Israeli dominance as an American lever says, "Let's let Hussein be the spokesman for the Palestinians." The position in favor of the political settlement says, "Let's put Hussein out of the picture and make a Palestinian state." It's interesting that the information about the Hussein payments from the CIA was leaked precisely at the time when Vance was visiting Hussein. That looks too neat. My guess is that it was a CIA leak to support the political settlement by underlying Hussein. The payments weren't a big secret, everyone knew about them, but they decided to make a big fuss about them at the time.

What can one do to encourage a rapprochement between Palestinian definitions of the legitimacy of Israeli self-determination and Israeli recognition of Palestinian national right?

I don't think that is the central issue. I think that rapprochement will come about by itself once the U.S. moves toward a political accommodation. The problem first of all will be to get the U.S. to accept the idea of a political settlement and then to get Israel to accept it. If those problems are overcome, rapprochement will take place by itself because there will be no alternative. So, while it is useful to have the Israeli-Palestinian meetings, their major utility is to influence public opinion about the possibility of this rapprochement. The possibility is there with or without those meetings, but they make it clear to the public that there is that possibility.

So far, Israel has been unwilling to accept that solution because it would mean giving up the occupied territory. Since 1967, Israel has been engaged in a very systematic attempt to implement the Allon Plan. The settlement policies have a very systematic character; if you trace them out, you see it is the Allon Plan. Israel wants to incorporate the Gaza Strip, Northeast Sinai, the Golan Heights, some corridor in East Sinai down to Sharm Al-Sheik, the Jordan Valley, and all parts of the West Bank that aren't areas of heavy Arab population concentration. That would make up a much more powerful and rich state.

That so far excludes Nablus.

Well, Israeli opinion is split between a Gush Emunim, or Greater Israel, view which says, "we take everything," and the Allon Plan view, the so-called dovish view, which says, "we exclude the areas of Arab population concentration." I think the Gush Emunim have a more liberal plan than the Allon, in a sense, because under their policy, which is called the extremist right wing, at least Israel would have technical responsibility for the people in the areas that it annexes, whereas under the Allon Plan it would be like Bantustans. Israel would have those areas under local administrations and would have control but no responsibility to them. They wouldn't be able to survive without integrating themselves, as people without any rights, into the Israeli economy.

Those two positions differ only on this issue, as far as I can see, on the issue of how to control the Arab population centers. The "extremists" would accord the Palestinians technical legal rights, which would give rise to the famous demographic problem. The Allon would keep them in a sort of Transkei, which would "avoid" the demographic problem.

The third, the real dovish view, the one that Moked holds, is that they ought to simply abandon the occupied territory and have a peaceful settlement with the Palestinian state. That appeals to a very small sector of opinion, which is not surprising. I can think of no historical example where a country has been willing to abandon territory it conquered. Often that has led to destruction. Over and over in history that has happened, but nobody ever learns from it, and the next time around ...

You have spoken about the independence of the Jewish electorate and its impact on public opinion and policy, which you saw as minimal. Regarding recent Carter administration moves to limit the Arab boycott, has the situation changed?

I still make the same prediction, that the impact of the Jewish electorate will be minimal. No boycott legislation that has any serious effect on American business relations with Saudi Arabia and other oil-producing states will ever be enacted, or if enacted will ever be administered. The whole thing has a tremendous air of hypocrisy about it. The Army Corps of Engineers has enormous projects in Saudi Arabia, and every one of those projects has to meet the Saudi boycott conditions. The big projects are always ratified by an individual act of Congress. That means that while Congress is supporting the boycott step after step, the same people are yelling about the immorality of it. Business interests are one thing and human rights another. I can't think of a single case in history where a concern for human rights or civil rights has influenced business interests in any serious way and I don't expect it to happen here.

How can a citizen affect U.S. policy in the Middle East?

I think there are alternatives. Despite the fact that the American propaganda system (the press, academic scholarship, etc.) is almost uniformly in favor of the option of military confrontation and occupation, nevertheless public opinion is very strongly in favor of the second option, the two-state political settlement, which is quite remarkable. There have been a couple of polls and they almost invariably show something like a two-to-one support for a Palestinian state despite the fact that almost no one speaks of it. There's a very sharp split between public opinion and the propaganda establishment.

William Quandt and Joseph Nye are involved in the State Department and they have spoken for a political settlement.

Yes, but they don't reach public opinion. They are marginal figures. As I said before, there's split in the government. Though public opinion favors a political settlement, the government's policy has been to reject that solution. A striking case was the January 1976 UN Security Council resolution which called for a political settlement, recognizing borders and international guarantees of security for all states in the area. It was vetoed by the U.S. alone. Some other countries abstained, but the U.S. vetoed it. So there is quite an unstable situation in the U.S. internally. There are two lines being pushed in the government, a military and a political solution, and the U.S. is internationally isolated in taking the hazardous position it does. So it seems to me to be quite possible to reach public opinion and to affect government policy.

I don't think you can affect government policy in matters that would really harm the interests of American capitalism, but **you can affect government policy** in cases where there are alternatives, where it's more or less a toss-up. It was possible to affect policy on the war in Vietnam, partly because Vietnam was so marginal to the interests of American capitalism. It didn't look marginal judging by the American commitment to crushing the Vietnamese, but basically whether Vietnam was independent or a colony didn't seriously affect the interests of American capitalism.

In the Middle East the situation is different. Either of the two options is satisfactory to American interests, it appears, and there is even an argument that could be made for a political accommodation. Under those circumstances, the role of public opinion could be significant. Outside the Jewish community opinion is already strongly in favor of a political settlement, so it would possible to build up something like the peace movement. It would be very hard, because you would be subject to savage attacks, but that is irrelevant, really. I think that as soon as anything large-scale gets started, the attacks will cease and a lot of people will join in. Lots of rats will leave the sinking ship as soon as they see it sinking.

Notes

1. U.S. Department of State. Foreign Relations of the United States. 1945, VIII, 45, cited in Joyce and Gabriel Kolko, *The Limits of Power,* Harper & Row, 1972, which provides a comprehensive analysis of the development of U.S. policy at the time.
2. Until 1968, North America led the Middle East in oil production. Cf. John Blair, *The Control of Oil,* Pantheon, 1976.
3. Leonard Silk, the *New York Times,* Oct. 7, 1976.
4. Don Oberdorfer, *Washington Post,* Dec. 12, 1976.
5. Robert Lieber, *Oil and the Middle East,* Harvard, 1976.
6. V. H. Oppenheim, "Why Oil Prices Go UP? The Past—We Pushed Them," *Foreign Policy,* Winter, 1976–77.
7. John Saar, *Washington Post,* April 12, 1976.
8. Emma Rothschild, "Is It Time to End Food for Peace?," the *New York Times* magazine, March 13, 1977.
9. Dan Smith, "Oil—the Growing Power of Saudi Arabia," *Middle East Annual Review,* 1977.
10. "Multinational Oil Corporations and U.S. Foreign Policy," report to the Committee on Foreign Relations, U.S. Senate, Jan. 2, 1975 (henceforth MNOC).
11. Myra Wilkins, "The Oil Companies in Perspective," *Daedalus,* Fall 1975.
12. Blair, op. cit. Blair provides ample evidence of the government concern to secure the profits of the energy corporations. On the international context, see Kolko & Kolko, op. cit. See also Robert Engler, *The Brotherhood of Oil,* Chicago, 1977, and many other sources.
13. Jim Hoagland, *Washington Post,* Feb. 19, 1977.
14. See "U.S. Trade with the Arab World." *MEMO: Middle East Money,* Beirut, Feb. 7, 1977.
15. Ibid.
16. "U.S. Military Sales to Iran." Staff Report to the Committee on Foreign Relations. U.S. Senate, July 1976.
17. Edward A Bayne, Four Ways of Politics, American University's Field Staff, 1965, cited by Robert B. Reppa Sr., *Israel and Iran: Bilateral Relationships and Effect on the Indian Ocean Basin,* Praeger 1974. Reppa was a staff officer in the Defense Intelligence Agency's national intelligence analysis and estimates office, Middle East branch from 1961–66.
18. *MEMO,* op. cit.
19. Reppa, op. cit. He expects the eye of the hurricane to be followed by the ferocity of the second half of the storm.

Editor's Notes to Interview 11

"An Interview with Noam Chomsky," University of Washington (Seattle) Working Papers in Linguistics 4, Supplement (Spring 1978), pp. 1–26 (typescript pages); reprinted in *Linguistic Analysis* 4:4 (Dec 1978), pp. 301–19, with slight emendations. It is the transcript of a radio interview conducted by Sol Saporta at the University of Washington (Seattle) on Oct. 13, 1977. The text reproduced here is the amended one, minus the phrase "rejecting this position" (*LA* 4, p. 305), which, as Saporta has confirmed, does not belong there.

Two points of reference might help to put this interview in the proper perspective: 1) In a fundamental sense the Galilean revolution in the history of ideas would have taken place even if physicists had continued to work within the framework of Aristotelian physics to this day (this would only have shown them to be incapable of understanding the new revolutionary ideas); 2) about 10 years after the discovery of the structure of the deoxyrubonucleic acid (DNA)—the hereditary material—in early 1953, "classical," that is to say, 19th-century, biology was a thing of the past and the era of a new ("molecular") biology was in full swing (a well known biochemist is sometimes quoted as saying "We're all molecular biologists now"). The discovery of generative grammar, certainly not a smaller step in the history of thought than the discovery of the DNA structure, was made at about the same time and became available for study soon afterwards. Compare the end of I28.

In this interview we are introduced to a new conception of generative grammar which was to be developed in **LGB** three years later. This brief outline of the principles-and-parameters theory is one of the earliest signs on Chomsky's record of what was in store, and the remarks on a theory of justice conceived on the generative grammar model are among the most explicit (see also **ChR**, 183ff.—cf. Robert Nozick, *Anarchy, State, and Utopia*, Basic Books, 1974, 149ff.) He returns to both topics in interview 30 and to the first one in interviews 12, 28 and 42.

For more on "Plato's question" (another early appearance of a new angle on a related central topic), see **KL** (1985), written in 1984.

11. Language Theory and the Theory of Justice
(13 October 1977)

You have always tried to be scrupulous in distinguishing those areas in linguistics where you think progress can be made from those where you don't think progress can be made—what you might call mysteries, starting with discovery procedures and carrying on.

My sense is that in the last few years, the area that you think is profitable to explore has become a little narrower, and that, paradoxically, other linguists continue to make what might seem like exaggerated claims in precisely those other areas, ranging from animal languages to "transformational grammar is dead." Maybe you could respond to both halves of that.

Well, my feeling is that in what I've always regarded as the central areas of linguistic theory, there is quite exciting work in progress. I wouldn't want to suggest that nothing is possible in other domains, like sociolinguistics and so on, but it seems to me that currently the really exciting work is right at the core of theoretical linguistics. I think it is now becoming possible, perhaps for the first time, to develop a theory with a certain degree of deductive structure; that is, with fairly abstract principles that serve as unifying principles bringing together a range of general conditions on the structure of the grammar that have been investigated in particular cases in the really extraordinary work of the last ten or fifteen years.

My feeling is that it's now possible to explore unifying ideas, somewhat more abstract ideas that can provide a level of explanatory theory dealing with the central questions of the structure and organization of the formal systems of syntax and their relations to some properties of logical form. In that domain I think there are really new and quite dramatic possibilities. For the first time, in the last few years I think it's been possible to bring empirical conditions to bear on theories of the precise nature of logical form; for example, on alternative theories of how to represent quantificational structures, involving words like "every," and so on. That's really never seemed possible in the past.

So, in a sense, just talking about my work, I think it has, you might say, narrowed. There is a very specific range of constructions and properties of grammars that I've been concentrating on for several years. But in my opinion, they do cover what one might call a fairly rich core of processes on which the full structure of languages is perhaps built. And within this core, I think it's now possible to propose principles with a degree of depth for investigation that go well beyond anything I had imagined several years ago. Furthermore, many new properties of these core processes have come to light in the work of the past years.

About the matter of the scope of linguistic work, to which you refer, I find some of what is commonly written rather misleading. It is as pointless to argue about the scope of linguistics as it is about the scope of biology. At a particular moment, some topics repay intensive study in that discovery of significant explanatory principles and understanding of mechanisms seems possible, while other topics do not. Suppose that I am right in my feeling that we are, perhaps, on the verge of important insights into some of the basic principles and structures of grammar. The intensive investigation of this "narrow" domain does not limit the scope of linguistics, but rather may offer a more solid basis for the investigation of other topics that may now be relatively inaccessible, in the sense that inquiry into them cannot proceed much beyond description and taxonomy. There is no conflict between those who choose to study intensively the "narrow" question of the basic principles of core grammar, and those who hope to be able to gain some understanding of such questions as, say, the use of language in concrete situations. The point should be self-evident—and is indeed regarded as virtually self-evident in much of the best work on pragmatics, for example (the work of Asa Kasher and Jerrold Katz, to mention just two).

Let me characterize two stages: the stage immediately post Syntactic structures, and then, let's say, the last 10 years, in contrast. It seems to me correct to characterize the first stage as what Kuhn would call a period of extraordinary science; that is, a challenging of fundamental assumptions, an establishment of a new paradigm. And, by the same token, the subsequent period is what you might want to call a period of normal science, a kind of refining, redefining, puzzle-solving stage. And that in this last period, to a certain extent, there is a danger of linguistics almost falling between two stools. That is, there is this kind of pseudorevolution, the exaggerated claims. But at the same time, there is a sense of the unfulfilled promise of language as a mirror on the mind, the view that somehow genuine and new insights into mental processes would be revealed through careful analysis of linguistic structure. Presumably you don't share that perception.

No, I wouldn't think of it that way myself. I don't want to suggest that I represent any majority view; I probably represent a small minority view, and people who are listening should understand that. But my own picture is really quite different. It seems to me that if you take the period of, say, the mid-50s, there was what one perhaps might call a paradigm conflict, if one wants to use that terminology. New proposals arose as to how to view the whole project of doing linguistics; that is, new kinds of questions … In fact, in a sense, they really weren't new questions. That is, there is a way of interpreting the structuralist work which I think perhaps would have been rejected by many of the structuralist linguists themselves, but which nevertheless is, in a sense, consistent with what they were doing. There is a way of interpreting it which leads quite directly to the kinds of questions that have been the focus of attention within the work of generative grammar in the years since. In fact, I wouldn't be surprised if that's characteristic of what are called paradigm shifts. It's not so much that totally new questions are asked, as that it becomes possible to see the import of questions that had been peripherally approached in a way that was not clear in earlier periods.

Let me be quite concrete about it. Take the matter of discovery procedures which you mentioned. In American linguistics—in fact, also in European structuralism of the 30s, 40s, and early 50s—there was very intensive work, as you know, in developing procedures that, in principle, one hoped could be applied in a mechanical way to a corpus of data so as to produce, finally, a grammar of that corpus. Well, a crucial question arises at that point; it's essentially the question of realism, you might say. That is the question, What is the nature of these procedures? Are they simply a device for bringing organization to chaos? And, is it the case that one set of procedures is as good as any other set? Or, is there a kind of truth claim involved in those procedures?

Well, if there is a truth claim, then that means that the system that arises by applying the procedures is claimed to be represented in the mind in some fashion. That is, one claims, at least, that the procedures correspond in some fashion to what the child is doing when he acquires language, and that the result of applying the procedures corresponds in some fashion to the mental representation of the language in his brain. And in fact that conclusion had been drawn. For example, it had been drawn by Charles Hockett in a very perceptive, brief paper that appeared in the late 1940s, where he took a very strong realist position and said, in effect, that the grammar that the linguist constructs is a representation of synaptic connections in the brain, and that the procedures of analysis correspond to what the child is doing when he works with the data and develops the grammar.

Hockett is quite unusual, I think, in taking that position. It was very uncharacteristic of the mood of the times, though I think that one can see that this position echoes ideas of Sapir and Jakobson and others. Still, the general picture at the time is quite different; it is a position that was perhaps best represented by people like, say, Twaddell or Martin Joos, or my teacher, Zellig Harris, who held that the procedures were a device for bringing some kind of organization to chaotic material, and that there is no claimed truth, certainly no claimed explanation, no claim to correctness of representing some mental reality. In fact, all such ideas were more or less laughed at as being absurdities. You might say that a crucial question that arose at that point in the development of linguistics was whether one was going to take a realistic attitude towards the procedures of analysis and the results of those procedures; that is, whether one was going to allege that they truly describe some empirical reality and therefore are subject to confirmation or refutation with regard to their truth; or are we simply going to say that they give us convenient fictions … that they help us collect the data on a smaller piece of paper, or something like that?

Well, it seems to me that there was a certain tension in the field at that point. In fact, I'm sure if you took a roll call, the Linguistic Society would have voted overwhelmingly for the anti-realist position. Nevertheless, implicitly, they were all accepting the realist position. And it's easy to prove that, I think. The way you can prove it is by just looking through the sequence of papers that appeared. Characteristically, what would happen, let's say in the 40s, is that someone would suggest a set of procedures for phonemic analysis or morphemic analysis, and someone else would come along and say, "Look, if you apply these procedures, it gives the following absurd result. So therefore you have to change the procedures." Then the procedures would be changed and someone would find something else wrong with them, and so on.

Well, to try to make sense out of that kind of interchange, one has to take the realist position. That is, if the procedures were just ways of organizing data, than in what sense could it be that they're giving an absurd result? Any way of organizing data is as good as any other. But of course everyone knew intuitively that some results were just absurd. For example, if the procedures of morphemic analysis told you that the word men was not broken down into man plus plural, then you just knew that those procedures were no good, because it's obviously true that men is related to man the way boys is related to boy. That is, it was taken to be a matter of fact. We might say that it is a matter of the way the language is in fact represented in our minds. Given the actual history, I think it's easy to demonstrate that people were implicitly taking the realist position almost universally, Hockett being a rare exception.

Well, if you now bring the issue to the fore, and if you explicitly take the position that was implicit in most of the work of the period, and return to a version of Hockett's question, that is: Is the grammar that is produced by the procedures an accurate representation of the mental reality? Does it characterize our knowledge of language? Could one propose that the procedures that were investigated in fact correspond to the way the child is learning language? Then, I think two conclusions immediately come forth.

Conclusion number one is that the grammars that were provided by the procedures do not capture the mental reality. They didn't even account for the most elementary property of language, the fact that it is infinite in scope. Even that wasn't provided for by any explicit procedure.

Secondly, the procedures of analysis that were used couldn't, by the remotest stretch of the imagination, be thought to correspond to the procedures of language learning. We don't know much about language learning but it's perfectly obvious that the child doesn't work out a theory of the detailed phonetics and phonology of his language before he starts learning any words—which is what those procedures would imply.

So, if we take the realist position, which in my view is the only rational position to take towards the enterprise, we conclude first that it was far off the mark. At the same time, there is a positive side to that; namely, taking the realist position towards the procedures does put at the center of linguistic research what ought to be its central question (and does so, I think, for the first time). Namely, it raises what you might say is **Plato's question:** How is it possible that we have the knowledge that we do have? What is the knowledge that we do have and on what basis could we possibly have acquired it? That is the question that is placed at the center of concern once you take the realist attitude towards the procedures of structural linguistics and reject them as factually wrong under this realist interpretation. But it has posed, as far as I know for the first time in the history of the field, what ought to be the central question of the discipline: How do we come to have our knowledge?

Well, what you might call the paradigm shift, though I think the term is misleading, simply arises from taking the essentially realist attitude towards the question which was implicit in the work of the previous period, rejecting the results—I think it was effectively shown in the work of a lot of people that the procedures were wrong and the results were wrong, and so on—and then trying to face directly the question that sort of grows out of the ashes.

In my view, the greatest merit of structural linguistics was to have implicitly brought forth, for the first time in the several-thousand year history of the discipline, what ought to be its central question. And much of the work of the past 20, 25 years has been directed to trying to address that question immediately, directly.

Well, how has it worked out? This will be a little cavalier, but to put it in a few sentences, it seems to me that it's sort of like this: if you go back to the mid-50s, a number of proposals were advanced of a very general nature as to what kind of devices might be involved in the structure of language to take account of its crucial and central properties. For example, the property of having unbounded scope, of having rules that operate on structural phrases to allow formulation of sentences and interpretation of sound and meaning over an infinite scope. That's obviously the central property of language, and devices were proposed that might have those properties.

Now, those devices were extremely rich. Within the framework of those devices, there were a great many possible languages, an enormous range of possible languages and grammars. It seems to me that one might say that the work of the past, say, 20 years has been directed largely to restricting more and more the devices that are available in principle for the description of language.

Again let me emphasize that this is probably a rather idiosyncratic view. I think most of my colleagues would describe what happened quite differently. But it seems to me, at least, that the productive work in the field—and there has been plenty of it—has systematically led to more and more restrictive theories about the nature of the devices that are used in language, the ways they interact, and the ways in which they operate to characterize sound and meaning and their interrelations. And it seems to me that now (to get back to what I said before) we are in a fairly exciting period in which there are several approaches: I have one, others have other approaches, and probably they'll all turn out to be correct. But at least it's possible to compare and investigate approaches which try to impose richer deductive structure on the system of devices that are held to be available in principle for the description of language.

Now, suppose that these approaches, or one of them or several of them partially succeed—you don't expect more than partial success, obviously, in any stage of science, certainly not in this one. But suppose there is some success in developing a theory of devices available for the representation of language, which have some deductive depth and some explanatory scope; that is, which unifies a variety of different kinds of general conditions that have been noticed, and so on.

Well, if that is the case, then let's turn back to the question you raised about language as a mirror of the mind. It seems to me that that would justify in the strongest possible sense, the strongest sense I can imagine, the claim that linguistic research can reveal the nature of mental processes, because in fact these devices exhibit such processes in their clearest and purest form.

What we are talking about is a particular domain of cognitive psychology; namely, the domain which deals with the structure of one particular faculty, the faculty of language. At the moment I know of no other domain of cognitive psychology where one can propose systems of mental representation, or principles operating on mental representation, that even qualitatively compare with the depth of complexity of devices that can now be studied in the case of language. That is exactly why language is, has always been, and remains, in my view at least, such an exciting area for anyone concerned with cognitive psychology. So my feeling would be that the prospects of success, whatever they may be, for work of the kind I've mentioned, add richness and substance to the hope that research into linguistic structures and into mechanisms involved in creating and manipulating mental representations of language—that this work will in fact shed direct light on the nature of mental functioning, perhaps in quite a new way.

Mental functioning beyond the use of language?

That, I think, has always been a hope that one shouldn't have had. There's a question that arises at this point, a crucial one. It is essentially the question of what you might call **modularity**.

To oversharpen it, there are two quite divergent viewpoints about the way the mind works. There is one extreme position which holds that there is a system of general intelligence, some system of principles of problem solving, of induction, of association, or whatever, which is quite general in character and is simply applied in domain after domain. So you apply that system of principles to learning language; you apply it to recognizing your friends, to finding your way around the city, and so on.

A quite different view is that the mind is modular, in the sense that it consists of separate, at least partially separate systems, each with its own intrinsic structure, each designed specifically to handle a particular problem, with the whole system interacting in such a way as to create a very intricate complex of highly special structures.

Now, on the second view, which I believe to be correct, the mind would be more or less analogous to the body. How do we think of the human body? Well, it is basically a system of organs. One doesn't expect to find principles of functioning which are going to involve the heart as a special case, the spleen as a special case, and so on. There is a level at which they all fall together, namely, the level of cellular biology, but if you really want to study the structure of the body, you will ask how specific organs function, what their structure are, what their principles are, how their development is genetically determined, how they interact with one another, and so on. The physical body, the human body, is an intricate and delicate system of interacting subsystems, each of which has very special characteristics and special modes of development.

Well, the modular approach to the mind takes essentially the same view. It assumes that we are going to find in the brain—which is perhaps the most complicated system we know of in the universe, and maybe the most complicated system that exists in it—what we are going to find there, is qualitatively like what we find in any other biological system known to us, namely, a high degree of modularity and specific structure, and that in fact there will be an array of cognitive faculties, call them **mental organs** if you like—one might think of them as analogous to the physical organs—and that each of these cognitive faculties, each of these mental organs, will have its own very specific properties, its specific structural properties, its specific physical representation, specific mode of development. It'll mature along a course that is predetermined. The result of the flowering of all these systems will be mental representations of a high degree of richness and intricacy, but quite different from one another and interacting in ways which are also biologically determined by the basic genetic structure of the system.

Well, if something of the latter sort turns out to be correct, which I suspect it will, then we can anticipate that language will simply be, in effect, one mental organ; that is, the human mind, and it is unique in this respect, develops this mental organ, much as birds develop wings. We don't expect to find general principles of development which are going to include wings and hearts and so on as subcases. Similarly, there's no particular reason to expect that we'll find principles of mental growth and mental structure that include language and identification of personality structure, let's say, as special cases.

To get back to your point, I myself at least would not expect that study of language would tell me anything much about the principles that are involved in other complex cognitive achievements of humans, such as the recognition of personality structure, which undoubtedly is also a complex and creative intellectual achievement. But there is not the slightest reason to believe that it involves similar mental representations; principles of mental computation similar to those that appear in the language faculty. So, if something like the modular approach is correct, that is, if in fact the mind is essentially a system of mental organs, much as the body is a system of physical organs, we should certainly not anticipate that even great progress in the study of one system should illuminate some other system. It's not going to.

Let me try to relate that to what you said about Plato and see if I can maybe juxtapose two notions. If the question is, What do we know and how could we have learned it?, questions like that were asked about concepts other than language. I seem to recall Bertrand Russell someplace saying, "We all know what it is to be just, and furthermore we know that we ought to be just." The position that you've just taken suggests that perhaps one cannot generalize from language to other kinds of innate notions. In what sense are they related; in what sense do you think they are not?

Well, take that question. I don't doubt that we have a natural moral sense, if you like. That is, just as people somehow can construct an extraordinarily rich system of knowledge of language on the basis of rather limited and degenerate experience, similarly, people develop implicit systems of moral evaluation which are more or less uniform from person to person. There are differences, and the differences are interesting, but over quite a substantial range we tend to make comparable judgments, and we do it, it would appear, in quite intricate and delicate ways involving new cases and agreement often about new cases, and so on, and we do this on the basis of a very limited environmental context available to us. The child or the adult doesn't have much information that enables the mature person to construct a moral system that will in fact apply in a rich range of cases, and yet that happens.

Well, whenever we see that, whenever we see a very rich, intricate system developing in a more or less uniform way on the basis of rather restricted stimulus conditions, we have to assume that there is a very powerful, very rich, highly structured innate component that is operating in such a way as to create that highly specific system on the basis of the limited data available to it—exactly as we assume in the case of the growth of the body. Why does everyone take for granted that we don't learn to grow arms, but rather are designed to grow arms? Well, the reason is that the environmental conditions of embryological growth are just not rich enough so that one could plausibly maintain that arms are a copy of the environment. Obviously they are not.

Similarly, we should conclude that in the case of the development of moral systems, there's a biological endowment which in effect requires us to develop a system of moral judgment and a theory of justice, if you like, that in fact has detailed applicability over an enormous range. And to do it in a way which is comparable to the way in which other people do it, we share a culture and come to do so on the basis of fairly limited experiential conditions.

Now the next question is whether this intrinsic, genetically determined system, this biological endowment which leads to the growth of the mental organ of moral evaluation—whether that system has anything to do with the language system. Well, a priori there is no particular reason to suppose it does, any more than, say, the study of the basis for the growth of the heart can be expected to tell you anything much about the basis for the growth of the visual system. I don't see any reason why the same should not be true in the case of the moral system and the system of language, if of course this modular approach turns out to be more or less correct.

You're one of the few linguists who's not embarrassed to use the word science applied to linguistics. It seems to me that other people prefer to say a discipline or an area. You take the word science seriously in applying it to linguistics, and at the same time, in some of the things you've said, you're not charitable towards studies of variability and variation, where even some geneticists would say that variability is just the different side of the coin to universals. Maybe you could sort of relate those two.

Well, first of all, about the matter of science, my own feeling is that linguistics really has yet to undergo something like **a Copernican or Galilean revolution** in very crucial respects. Again, this will be overgeneralizing, but it seems to me that one of the most striking features of the Galilean revolution was that, perhaps for the first time, those responsible for that revolution (that is, Kepler, Galileo, the major figures in what we now regard as that scientific revolution) recognized that depth of explanation could compensate for lack of coverage of data.

Let me be more concrete. If you go back to the time of Galileo and look at the array of phenomena that had to be accounted for, it seemed prima facie obvious that the Galilean theory, the Copernican theory, could not be supported. That is, there were just masses of unexplained, or even apparently refuting, data. Galileo plowed his way through this, putting much of the data aside, redefining what was relevant and what was not relevant, formulating questions in such a way that what appeared to be refuting data were no longer so, and in fact very often just disregarded data that would have refuted the system. This was not done simply with reckless abandon, but out of a recognition that explanatory principles were being discovered that gave insight into at least some of the phenomena. Now, a willingness to move towards explanatory principles that give insight into some of the phenomena at the cost of not being able to handle all of the phenomena: that I think was one of the most striking intellectual achievements of the great scientific revolution.

So, let's return to the matter of the restriction of the domain of the investigation. If you take, say, the Aristotelian world view, the range of the phenomena taken to fall within a theory of motion was vastly greater than what Galileo could consider. For example, the Aristotelian theory of motion included not only what we call mechanics—that is, things bumping into each other, and so on—but also growth, perception, development, change. All sorts of phenomena fell together within this theory of motion. The Galilean theory threw out most of those phenomena, and in fact restricted itself to matter in motion. I think that what was dramatic about the development of physics in that period was that, within the domain on which it concentrated, explanatory principles were emerging which could integrate and connect, and give a kind of rationale for phenomena that could previously only be described. Now, as a descriptive system the Ptolemaic system was no worse than the Galilean system, maybe even a bit better, but it lacked depth of explanation.

This shift of intellectual attitude from concern for coverage of data to concern for insight and depth of explanation, and the related willingness to deal with highly idealized systems in order to obtain depth of explanation—this shift of point of view has taken place very rarely, I think, in the history of thought. In linguistics I don't think it has taken place, really. Most linguistic work, for better or for worse, is concerned with accumulation of data, organization of data, making sure that any generalization isn't apparently refuted by some half-described phenomenon that someone noticed somewhere. In comparison, a concern for depth of explanation that may serve to integrate and unify and give insight into some range of phenomena at the probable cost of just not being able to say anything about all sorts of other questions for the time being—and maybe even apparently being refuted by them for reasons that are not yet understood—such an attitude is not very highly valued; in fact, it is often regarded with scorn or disbelief.

Until a shift in this direction takes place, I think it would be fair to say that linguistics will not have undergone something like the revolution of early modern science. So in this sense I would tend to be quite specific in the use of the word "science" with regard to modern linguistics, or in fact almost any field outside of a few of the natural sciences. Perhaps it's obvious, but I think that this is a change that ought to take place, and that if it does take place, it'll lead to a much more exciting and important discipline.

As for the matter of variability and universals, we have to be careful to distinguish several issues. There is, in the first place, the matter of variability of languages—that kind of variability is, as you say, the opposite side of the coin of a concern for universals. Secondly, there is the quite separate question of possible genetic variation among individuals with regard to the language faculty itself. For the contemporary study of language, it seems quite reasonable to abstract away from any possible genetic variation. That is, it seems reasonable to assume, as a very good first approximation, that the genotype is invariant across the species as far as the language faculty is concerned, and to proceed from there into the investigation of linguistic universals and variability of languages.

At the same time, it would come as no surprise to discover that there is some genetic variation, and if this could be discovered, it might lead to new and possibly revealing ways to study the intrinsic nature of the language faculty. It has occasionally been observed, for example, that unusually late onset of language use seems to run in families, and one might find other aspects of language use or structure that are subject to a degree of variability—a discovery that might be significant for therapy as well as for research into language.

Variability of language within a fixed system of universals—an invariant genotype—is quite a different matter. We should, I think, aim to construct a theory of language that incorporates a system of principles with certain parameters, to be fixed by experience, with the property that once the parameters are fixed, the core grammars of the various possible languages can be deduced. There is some current work that begins to show promise of leading towards such a theory, I believe, though I cannot try to discuss it here. Again, these possibilities now coming into view, I believe, offer exciting prospects for research in linguistic theory and universal grammar.

I recently had a chance to look again at Problems of Knowledge and Freedom. *I don't mean to be facetious, but it seems to me that there is a considerable discussion there of certain problems of knowledge, and considerable discussion of certain problems of freedom, and very little of the relationship between those two.*

I think that's an accurate perception. In fact, I tried to be explicit about that and to make clear that, at present at least, there is very little that we can say, so far as I can see, about major problems of human life, such as the problem of how to achieve a just society, or overcome coercive systems and break out of authoritarian patterns—there is very little that we can conclude about these questions from a study of those few little areas where we've gained some insight into human nature. So in this respect, what achievements there may have been in the investigation of the growth of cognitive structures, for example, and of the nature of human nature, these advances don't tell us very much about the questions we would like to have answers to.

The most that one can do, I think, is to note some very tenuous and possibly suggestive connections without claiming in the least that they're deductive connections. In fact, they're not; they're at most vague and loose suggestions which perhaps are worth a little bit of thought. To take one case, there's historically a quite interesting connection between approaches to human nature which have stressed its alleged malleability, and certain social attitudes as to what would be a proper organization of society. For example, if the mind is extremely plastic, if we take an extreme empiricist view, if we say there is nothing to human nature apart from the sum of historically given conditions and that, at each point in time, human nature is simply the residue of whatever contingent cultural patterns exist, that the mind as it develops is just a reflection of the materials around it; then, if that is the case, there really are no barriers whatsoever as far as I can see, no moral barriers, to manipulation and domination and control. In fact, the moral basis is laid for a coercive and authoritarian society. My own view is—I've tried to argue this a number of times—that one of the reasons why these empty organism theories have such appeal in our intellectual tradition is that they do in a sense eliminate the moral barriers to coercion and control and domination.

In contrast, if we take the view that was characteristic, say, of Wilhelm von Humboldt, who is, I think, quite important in this connection, that at the essential core of human nature there are certain fundamental needs, such as the need to inquire and to create, to do creative, productive work under conditions of voluntary association in solidarity with others, and so on, if we make such assumptions, then the question, "What would be a just society?" takes a very different form. That is, the answer to that question takes quite a different form. Similarly, if we take the view, say, characteristic of Adam Smith, that essential to human nature is the need to truck and barter, then we'll develop a different image of what a just and proper society would be, namely, an early capitalist society of small traders, or something of that sort.

I think this much is clear: Any view that one puts forth as to the direction that social evolution ought to take—social reform or revolution or whatever—any vision that one has as to the nature of a better or utopian society, a society towards which we ought to strive, or (to be more incremental about it) any point of view that one takes towards the next small change in social evolution, is predicated on some kind of assumption about human nature. I think it's crucially important to try to bring those assumptions forth, and to see whether in fact we can find any evidence bearing on them.

Well, to tie all this together, in the few areas where we have any insight, for example, the question of human language, I think there's some reason to accept the view that intrinsic to human nature is the desire to create under conditions of freedom and lack of constraint. Now, that's very vague; perhaps in particular areas we can make it more precise. But if some such characteristics are at the core of human nature, then any design of a just and decent society will have to accommodate to them. Now, I wish it were possible, as it obviously is not, to deduce from our understanding of human nature that the next stage in social evolution ought to be such and such. That we can't do; at most we can draw very loose, tenuous connections that may be more or less suggestive to people.

When you refer to language as creative and stimulus-free, that seems almost a paraphrase for free will.

Well, I think the connection is appropriate. If you go back to the Cartesian period, a very explicit connection was drawn between **the creativity of language and freedom of the will.** In fact, Descartes regarded the free creative use of language as the most striking evidence for the existence of another mind; that is, a mind that could exercise free will and thought and that was not constrained by mechanical principles, and so on. It would be very nice to be able to learn something about the nature and exercise of freedom of the will. That's what I would call a mystery: at the moment, intrinsically beyond the bounds of human inquiry and comprehension.

But what we can perhaps do at least is find some of the mechanisms that are involved in it. Whatever constraints we can discover on the way in which the mind functions in particular areas, these will provide a framework within which free exercise of will takes place. It's not going to solve the problems of freedom of the will, but it will, perhaps, present some of the framework and structure within which that freedom is exercised, and it may tell us something about the way the system in which freedom of the will is exercised develops in the organism, and in fact, even about its basis in our biological endowment. I think that's the most that can be hoped, even by a very long range projection as to what might be discovered through scientific or quasi-scientific study in the coming years.

You haven't written very much about what your views are in relation, say, to the views of people like Marx. Specifically, the one thing that I recall precisely is that you reject the interpretation of Marx, which claims that human nature is somehow a fiction.

Well, I think you can find in Marx very different things. It's not surprising for a person who wrote over a long period and whose ideas changed. If you look at the early manuscripts, which were heavily influenced by French and German romanticism, there is an emphasis on what he calls "species character"; namely, the species character of free, productive activity, out of which he develops his familiar theory of alienation, which in fact echoes very closely ideas that one finds throughout the romantic period, and in particular, which one finds in, say, somebody like Humboldt some years earlier: that Marx is one who is putting forward claims about the unchangeable and essential character of human nature. Maybe those claims are not very specific, but at least that's the thrust of it.

On the other hand, one can certainly find, even from a period shortly after this, formulations which suggest that human nature is nothing but a historical product and that the only common properties of human nature are that it's susceptible to change, and can be modified, and so on. I think the Marxist tradition has tended to emphasize the latter Marx, and I think there's textual justification for giving that interpretation, but I think it's a partial interpretation. In fact, I don't think one can really make sense of the Marxist system on that assumption. For example, I don't think it's possible to give a rational account of the concept of alienated labor on that assumption, nor is it possible to produce something like a moral justification for the commitment to some kind of social change, except on the basis of assumptions about human nature and how modifications in the structure of society will be better able to conform to some of the fundamental needs that are a part of our essential nature. Now, what Marx would have said about this, I think, one can argue; that's a complicated textual question, but that's the was the issue seems to me to develop.

Maybe you could say something about social change, then. You've argued, to my mind, persuasively, that within the context of the university, intellectual curiosity is not an absolute value, that the scholar has to be sensitive to the political and social context, specifically on questions of race and I.Q. But at the same time, during the war, it seems to me that you were not very enthusiastic about proposals that ROTC be moved off campus or that weapons research be moved off campus. You argued the Vietnamese peasants didn't care whether it was done on campus or off, or that that was critical. Do you see any contradiction there? Is there a sense in which you can have it both ways?

Well, I don't think I convinced many people of this, so maybe there's something wrong with my reasoning, but as I see it, at least, these positions are entirely consistent. That is, it seems to me just elementary (in fact, sort of trivial) that the scholar or the scientist is no more exempt from moral considerations than any other human being. That is, any person in any of his acts has the responsibility to consider the likely, or more or less foreseeable human consequences of what he does, and if those consequences are harmful to people, then he has to stop. That's just a general fact. I don't know how to put it any more simply. It sounds to me like a Sunday school lecture. I think everybody understands that basically. It's an easy Sunday school sermon, but it's sometimes hard to apply in practice; in fact, it's often hard to apply in practice.

Let's try to apply it to the case that you mentioned, the question of weapons research on campus. If one's commitment is to the purity of the campus, if that's the highest principle, then, of course, one will say: Take weapons research off campus, because then the campus is more pure. If, on the other hand, one is concerned with the human consequences of what one does, then the question to raise is: What are the human consequences of having weapons research done on campus or off campus? And this issue has often arisen in very concrete terms. Take, say, MIT, because I know it best. There was extensive weapons research on the MIT campus. There were laboratories at MIT that were involved, for example, in the development of the technology that's used for ballistic missiles, and so on. In fact, a good deal of the missile guidance technology was developed right on the MIT campus and in laboratories run by the university. Or, let's say, take the University of California, which is probably one of the largest nuclear weapons developers in the world. Or take the question of counter-insurgency technology or pacification techniques, and so on. A good deal of this work was done right on campus.

A number of questions arise. First, should this work be done at all? Well, there are differences of opinion about that. Let's take some domain where I think it's clear that we can come to an agreement; say, counter-insurgency technology. As far as I can see, it's elementary that that kind of work simply should not be done. Its only consequence is to harm people, to destroy and murder and control. One can argue that, but I'm going to accept it for now. Assuming that the work shouldn't be done, then the concrete and crucial question arises: Shall we get it off campus? Well, yes or no, depending on how that's going to affect the way it's done. Now, my feeling is that if the work is going to be done, I'd rather have it done on campus. That is, I'd rather have it be visible, have it be the center of protest and activism, rather than moving it somewhere else where it can be done silently, freely, the same people doing it, often, in fact, by just changing the name of the connection—they can be called consultants rather than professors. The campus will be insulated and apparently pure, but the work is done effectively and without constraint.

In fact, my proposal, and I meant this quite seriously, was that universities ought to establish **Departments of Death** that should be right in the center of the campus, in which all the work in the university which is committed to destruction and murder and oppression should be centralized. They should have an honest name for it. It shouldn't be called Political Science or Electronics or something like that. It should be called Death Technology or Theory of Oppression or something of that sort, in the interests of truth-in-packaging. Then people would know what it is; it would be impossible to hide. In fact, every effort should be made to make it difficult to hide the political and moral character of the work that's done. I would think in those circumstances it would tend to arouse the strongest possible opposition and the maximal disruptive effect. And if we don't want the work to be done, what we want is disruption: maybe the disruption will be the contempt of one's fellows, or maybe it'll be something else. But if the purpose to be achieved is stopping the work or at least impeding it, then we always have to ask what's the best device for doing that. Ant it's not at all obvious that the best device is removing it from campus. Now, it's arguable; I don't have a doctrine on the subject. It just seems to me that that's the framework in which the issue should have been raised. It's not the highest principle that the campus should be pure.

Perhaps we agree that the university, like most of the institutions, survived the 60s pretty well in the sense that the conservative elements which dominated then dominate now. What went wrong? Why wasn't there more of a fundamental effect?

Well, first of all, it's very important to bear in mind that the faculty and, quite generally, the adult intellectual community was never affected very much by the movement. There have been studies which tried to correlate attitudes towards the war with level of education, and contrary to what many people believe, the general result that has come out of these studies is that the higher the educational level, the greater was the support for the war. That is, the most opposition to the war from the very early stages was from the least-educated people. Of course those results are subject to complex interpretations; that is, it may be that much of the opposition to the war was of the "win or get out" variety. But whatever the interpretation, that general fact is the case.

Now, as far as the organized intelligentsia, including the faculty, scientists, technicians, writers, and so on—by and large, those groups were by no means strongly opposed to the war nor seriously involved in any of the activism of the 60s. Quite the contrary: they tended to take what they themselves called a pragmatic attitude toward the war. They raised the question of whether the war was going to succeed, whether it was too costly or something like that. But fundamental questions about its nature were rarely considered. And, overwhelmingly, I think it's fair to say that the universities persisted throughout this period, despite the disruption and the confusion and the activism and so on, in service to the state, with very minor modifications. So, not only do the same elements control now that controlled before, but in fact, they controlled all the way through.

Well, again, let me just give MIT as an illustration of **the radical difference between student and faculty attitudes**—which has generally been the case, incidentally. Just two years ago, a major question arose on campus about a proposal to turn over a very substantial part of the Nuclear Engineering Department to the government of Iran for the training of nuclear engineers who were going to be sent by the Iranian atomic energy commission. Well, in effect this meant selling something like a third of the Nuclear Engineering Department to the government of Iran: an utterly scandalous act, in my opinion. Anyway, this came up for a referendum among the students and a faculty vote. The referendum among the students was something like four to one against, and the faculty vote was, I think, approximately four to one in favor. Well, the students are the faculty of tomorrow. There's a gap of five or ten years between them. So, one might ask: Why this remarkable shift in attitude over a short period? I think that it's an interesting question. One shouldn't be glib about the answer. Incidentally, I think this is rather characteristic; I suggest this is a characteristic example.

It seems to me that what happens, somehow, is that incorporation into the institution has a tremendous effect on determining attitudes towards such matters and the natural—I give my own value judgments, I can't help that—the natural and instinctive commitment to justice and truth and decency that one finds in a mind that hasn't yet been corrupted by its institutional commitments very rapidly attenuates when those institutional commitments take over. And that's what I think we've seen. The student movement was of course ephemeral. Students come and go every few years. There's not going to be any stability or persistence in something like a youth movement. That can't be the case. And since the movement always was quite isolated from sectors of the society that are more permanent from a social point of view, it was not at all surprising that it would appear to dissipate and lose its impact as soon as the immediate motive for its activism—the Vietnam War, particularly—was more removed from consciousness.

Nevertheless, one should not exaggerate the changes of the past few years. The moral and intellectual climate of the universities is, I think, quite different from what it was in the 50s, before the impact of the civil rights and anti-war movements. The ideological system that reigned virtually unchallenged at that time was at least bruised, if not undermined, and although efforts are being made with some success to restore what we might call the "state religion"—as was predictable and in fact predicted—still the orthodoxy, conformism, and passivity of the earlier period has not been restored, in the universities or elsewhere. And while the universities do not contain islands of activism or independent critical thought to the extent that they did for a brief period in the late 60s, it should be emphasized that such activism and independent thinking has diffused throughout much of the society. I wouldn't be surprised if the number of people engaged actively in what we regarded then as "movement activities" is of about the same order as it was at the height of the more visible and dramatic activism of the late 60s and early 70s. What the long-term impact will be of the activism of that period is very much an open question, it seems to me.

Editor's Notes to Interview 12

"Language and the Human Mind," in Young-Key Kim-Renaud, *Studies in Korean Linguistics*. Followed by an interview with Noam Chomsky. Seoul, Korea: Hanshin Pub. Co., 1986, pp. 183–210. Interview conducted on Sept. 29, 1978, in Professor Chomsky's office at MIT by Kim-Renaud, at the time assistant program director for linguistics at the U.S. National Science Foundation in Washington, D.C., and subsequently professor at George Washington University. The interview was carried out at the request of the chief editor of a literary magazine published in Seoul, Korea, with a title meaning "Literature and Thought," for a special series of interviews with "intellectual leaders of the world today," and it first appeared there in Korean translation (1979, pp. 44–70). Chomsky read and commented on the typescript of the transcription, which was prepared with the assistance of Professor David Woods of Howard University.

In his introduction to the interview Kim-Renaud writes: "Chomsky's *Syntactic Structures*, published in 1957, was concise and brief, but shook the linguistic world in an epoch-making way. His humanistic approach has made linguistics an important part of all intellectual pursuits that concern human beings. By pointing out that studying language is essential and can contribute to understanding human nature, he destroyed the traditional boundary between different disciplines. It is only natural that his influence now reaches various domains such as psychology, philosophy, mathematics and politics." He goes on to conclude that "a modern intellectual may disagree with Chomsky but cannot ignore him."

The interview covers a broad range of topics, including several ones that are characteristically Chomskyan. The principles and parameters approach, introduced in the preceding interview, will come up again in interviews 28, 34 (which also discusses learnability—on the learnability of finite state languages, see the reference to George Miller in interview 2) and 42 (which also discusses language teaching). About the "marriage" of "the technical achievements of the 20th-century in mathematics with the ancient questions" to "create a very natural discipline," see note to interview 4 (and interview 3, which also touches on his intellectual background).

On Chomsky's undergraduate work on generative grammar (*Morphophonemics of Modern Hebrew*, 1949, 1951), see notes to I3.

The critical anthology edited by Thomas A. Sebeok & J. Umiker-Sebeok (*Speaking Apes*. New York: Plenum, 1980) includes Chomsky's 1978 essay "*Human Language and Other Semiotic Systems*," which people interested in linguistics and semiotics might find enlightening.

12. Language and the Human Mind (29 September 1978)

Professor Chomsky, I am very happy to be able to interview you today for Literature and Thought, *which is the leading intellectual magazine in Korea. At three different American universities in 1967, Korean scholars presented dissertations on Korean syntax employing the transformational generative framework. In addition there was another work in general phonetics using the generative framework that was presented by a Korean at yet another university. Since then many more Koreans have come to America to study and write dissertations and articles in various sub-areas of linguistics including syntax, semantics, phonology, phonetics and historical linguistics. A new dissertation or article often meant applying a new American development in linguistic theory to analyzing the Korean language. Significantly, the new theories were defined and explicated almost always in relation to standard Chomskyan theory. As a result, linguistics in Korea is more lively and possibly more respected a field today than ever before. The so-called Chomskyan revolution has penetrated not only linguistic circles in Korea but its influence is also felt in other parts of the intellectual community there.*

People are very much interested in your strong claim concerning the intimate relationship between the structure of language and innate properties of the human mind. Professor Chomsky, what in your opinion is the most appropriate general framework for the study of the problem of language and mind?

I think that we should study the problem of language and mind very much in the way we study any problem in biology. We can take as an example the ways in which we study the characteristics of organs or systems of the body. If we were to study the human visual system, we would first attempt to abstract this system away from its physical context. Although it interacts with the circulatory system and many other systems, the scientist tries to identify and separate the visual system by the process of idealization. And it has always been that way as long as it's been called science.

Having done this, the scientist then attempts to discover the structural principles that determine how the system functions, the functions that the system attempts to achieve, how the system develops in the organism from the initial genetic codes to its mature state, and the physical mechanisms that enter into the system and how they interact with other systems. There are, of course, a variety of other questions.

The method of approach is reasonably straightforward, and even if the framework is not good, the general method is at least clear. You certainly begin by discovering the characteristics in the mature organ, and then working with the harder question of describing the deeper properties, the innate properties that lead to the growth of a mammalian visual system instead of, say, an insect's eye. All of this would be investigated largely by looking into the nature of the environmental conditions that are available to the embryo and the growing organism. We must also ask what we must assume concerning the initial state of the organism that led to a mature eye. On the basis of that inferential, derivative research, we could speculate and hypothesize about the initial state as well as the other questions I mentioned.

I think we should study language in exactly the manner of the physical sciences. I think the scientists have the right approach to the problems. In this case we should be asking ourselves what kind of cognitive systems there are in the human mind, systems of belief and knowledge and computation and so on. In the case of the human body, it is not easy to identify them since the process of idealization and abstraction is involved. But just as we can identify the visual system on the physical side, it would be reasonable to identify language as one such cognitive system.

When we view language as a cognitive, that is, as a mental organ, as an analog to a physical organ, we can ask the very same questions and proceed in the very same way as we would in the case of study of a physical system of the body. In other words, we can ask what are the structural principles by which this mental organ functions? What are the functions of the system? How does it develop in **the ontogenetic development of the individual from embryo to adult**? What kinds of interactions are there with other mental systems and mental organs?

Then we can proceed to the deeper and interesting question that you have pointed out in your comment about the innate properties: just as we would in the case of the visual system, asking how the structural properties and uniformities that can be discovered and discerned in the mature adult system might have arisen on the basis of an interaction of genetic coding with environmental conditions. When we find, as we often do, that the environment is just far too impoverished to have determined the kind of structures that humans develop, we reasonably assume, as we do in a physical case, that these are properties that are in some way inborn.

Ultimately, one would hope to be able to tie in this investigation with general biology, but that's a long way into the future, both in discovering the actual physical mechanisms involved and the related aspects of the genetic code. But we can barely begin to do it in the case of the visual system and we certainly can't do it yet in the case of the language system.

All of this is the way I would approach the problem of language, and for the general problem of mind it seems to me we should simply generalize this approach where there are other identifiable organs we should proceed in the same fashion, and then the mind will be nothing other than the systematic interaction of the various mental organs that constitute it. Ultimately, we will want to relate this to rich enough studies of the physical body in which these abstract systems are realized and substantiated.

Thinking about the so-called structural linguistic framework, didn't the structuralists also start their research by studying the physical facts? What makes your theory different from theirs?

Of course there are many varieties of structuralists, but let's start with American structuralism. American structuralism really set itself a rather different task than others. There are a few exceptions, but by and large it did not view its problem as trying to determine the characteristics of a certain mental organ; rather, its problem was to give an organized account of the data of the language—and that organized account can be given in many different ways. You could have one technique of phonemic analysis or another technique, you could classify things in this way or that way, and these various modes of organizing the data were conceived as meeting various utilitarian purposes; that is, they were not regarded as an effort to find out the truth about mental processes and mental computation.

In fact, they said you shouldn't make such an effort. They said it was superstition.

Well, they said it was mysticism. I must say that there were very few exceptions, but there was one interesting, brief, 2- or 3-page article by Charles Hockett back around 1948, in which he suggested that one should think of the results of linguistic inquiry as being very much as I described it earlier.

How interesting. He certainly does not keep that point of view today.

Now he doesn't, but he was one of the very few people who articulated it, and I believe correctly so. There are other differences with the structural linguistics approach. Both American and European structural linguistics was based crucially on principles of analysis that, whether right or wrong, had a very narrow scope. There was no provision within structural linguistics for what I think we ought to regard as the central and essential property of language, mainly what has often been called the creative aspect of language use.   *DOES IT?*

Language has infinite scope—though obviously only finite means—and therefore some recursive rule system which iterates in some fashion to generate more and more structures indefinitely must lie at the very core of the language. Although you can find discussion in the traditional literature about innovation or about what Jespersen calls free expressions, to my knowledge there was really no approach prior to the mid-50s, except for some classical work. If you go back to the really classical works, centuries ago Panini in the Indian tradition raised the question in a certain sense, but in the modern European tradition you can find at most only bare hints of recognition that the real answer to the problem of language must be some system of rules which interact to generate this infinite range of structures. And you can prove that the methods of structural linguistics could not possibly reach such structures and in fact they were not intended to. So that's another striking difference.

Doesn't it have to do with the notion of science in the structuralist theory? In structuralism you study what is observed and simplify every possible variable into a manageable proportion.

Well, both European and American structuralists felt they were reflecting the scientific method. I myself disagree. I think that they were very much opposed to the method of natural sciences, although they were very similar to a kind of a caricature of the natural sciences that's very standard in the social sciences.

In much of the social sciences, some of the more descriptive parts or the phenomenological aspects of natural science are assumed to be the scientific method. Their goal and procedure is to try to organize and to clarify the facts and to set them out clearly. It's a data-oriented subject, and while that may have been true of the natural sciences in Babylonian times, it certainly hasn't been true for the last several hundred years. In fact, it's crucial to understand that it has not been true since the scientific revolutions of the 17th century, which were not concerned with the organization of data but rather with the discovery of explanatory principles. At least since Newton, nobody has believed that it is possible that there are methods or procedures for finding out scientific truth.

I think one of your most interesting claims concerns innate capability. What evidence does one have to say that human intellectual capacities, especially as reflected in language, are predetermined?

Well, there are three categories, although one is unavailable to us. One category of evidence would be through direct experimentation. For ethical reasons we cannot carry out the relevant experiments but if we wanted to find out, let's say, what properties of a cat's visual system are innate, we could raise a cat under artificial conditions and see what happens. Obviously we can't do that with humans, so the experimental approach is excluded on ethical grounds. We have to be more clever about it, and that leaves us with two categories of evidence, one less important than the other. Although I differ from many of my colleagues on this matter, I think that the less important one is the study of a wide variety of languages. If you find common properties in a wide variety of languages, it is reasonable to suppose that they may have some roots in human nature. Many people regard that as the best approach to the question, but I myself do not. I don't think it tells you very much; there are all sorts of other reasons why things may be held in common. The study of a wide variety of languages is crucial for different reasons, not so much for inference to universal principles from common properties.

It seems to me that the best approach is exactly the approach that any scientist would use when faced with comparable problems. It's clear that the mature state of language, the mature state of the mind in an adult who has achieved the capacity to speak and understand freely, results through an interaction of two factors. One of these factors is environment, and the other is the innate properties of the mind.

I believe that the way to proceed is to search for properties of the mature state which simply do not appear in the environment at all, or in a way sufficient to ground knowledge. Many examples can be found of things that people know about language, things that are standard and simple in their language use and perception, where they have had no relevant experience at all. New structures that they could not possibly have had experience with and the kinds of **errors that children never make** are interesting.

Whenever you can find properties in a language that everyone knows, and apparently without any evidence, and for which there is no dispute or variation among people, then we have very good reason to believe that those properties arise from the structure of the mind itself, since there's no way in these cases in which they could reflect the course of accidental experience.

Let me be concrete. Suppose you wanted to form questions in English and similar languages, not Korean. You pick some phrase in the sentence and you put an appropriate interrogative word there and then you move it to the front of the sentence. So, for example, "I saw the man," "Who did I see?" But as is well-known, you can't always do that. There are some positions from which you simply cannot question. From the sentence "I believe that John saw the man," we can form the question "Who do I believe that John saw?" But from "I believe Bill's claim that John saw the man," we can't form "Who do you believe Bill's claim that John saw?" That's just not a sentence.

The interesting question that arises is, how do we know that it's not a sentence? One possibility is that someone taught us, that we tried to say it and we were told it was not a sentence. Of course, that's nonsense. No one ever told us such things, and in fact nobody ever makes the error so nobody ever could have been told. Or you could say that you simply did not hear it, but that doesn't help because you have never heard about many other sentences that are good, yet you know that they are all right.

There are just too many, vastly too many structures around for us to have heard even a tiny fraction of them. There is no evidence in our environment to tell us that the example I gave is not a sentence. In fact, if you just think of ordinary inductive procedures, we ought to assume that it is a sentence. Since we can select other noun phrases and put in an interrogative word and move it to the front, why don't we just generalize and say okay, we can always do it?

Well, if we always did do it we would be making an awful lot of mistakes, which means that no one is using inductive procedures. Rather, something is informing us that some structures which we have never heard are perfectly all right and other structures which we have never heard are not allowed. But the relationship between what we have and what is allowed is not an inductive relationship; it's another kind of relationship. In such a circumstance, I don't think that a natural scientist would have the slightest hesitation in assuming that the principles that are involved in making these distinctions are simply rooted in the nature of the organism.

Having come that far, the scientist would try to find those principles and at that point, the study of many languages becomes interesting because if these principles really are innate, we would expect them to be operative universally, unless there is reason to believe that there are genetic differences in language capacity.

You seem to be trying to say that there are not only substantive innate properties but that also all languages are innately constrained in a very predictable way.

They're basically cut to the same mold. They may differ in how they realize the principles that are available, but they are basically of the same structural pattern—and they have to be. If that weren't the case, we would never learn any of them. The richness of the structure of any language is so far beyond any experience that we have that no child would ever learn his language unless it was more or less predetermined.

So this cannot be in any way by association or stimulus-response learning?

Well, any specific approach to learning that has ever been suggested can easily be demonstrated to be inadequate. Of course, you can't prove that no conceivable method would do anything; that's just too vague a question. Evidently there is a way to acquire knowledge of language, though I wouldn't call it "learning." If we attribute to the organism very specific properties which can be made quite explicit in many cases, then I think we can account for the fact that the language one comes to know has such and such a form.

The account we should give, I think, is not really as a learning system. It would make more sense to think of it on the model of a growth system. Then what we could be doing is finding the principles to determine how the language faculty "grows" the language in the mind. Frankly, I don't think it's surprising that when we inquire into this question we should find, as we do, that language acquisition is more like the growth of an organism than it is like learning the names of your friends.

So you are bound to grow up like that.

It's a very central part of human capacity, so it isn't too surprising that it shares a good deal with other biological capacities.

There are actually many things in central areas that are disturbing to some linguists, including myself. For instance, it might not be crucial that recent studies in language acquisition seem to suggest that the language spoken to children is not as degenerate

as you might think, since people have a very systematic way of normalizing or chang-
ing sentences when they speak to their kids, and later when they grow up they change
their structures.

One has to be very careful. There is work concerning what is called "motherese," that is, the simplified language spoken to children. That, however, is
almost irrelevant to the question. The first question you have to ask is whether
the material that's available is in any significant way different with regard to the
properties of language that are acquired. The answer is that it is not. For example, motherese doesn't contain relevant information about the examples that I
just gave. Structures that aren't ever used will not appear in motherese, so the
question of acquisition remains as before.

A minor additional point is that this business about motherese is rather cul-
ture-bound. It's probably true of middle-class families in many parts of the
world, but an awful lot of children learn without anyone paying much attention
to them. It's ridiculous to think that children cannot learn language that way,
that if your children were not given very specific and careful attention, they
would never learn the language. Yet we know that's false. There are plenty of children who learn the language in the streets or who learn from other children in
the worst possible conditions.

A third point is that if you look into this motherese business carefully, as
Lila Gleitman did, one of the few psychologists who has really looked at the matter properly, the things that you find in motherese don't happen to relate closely
to the structures that are acquired by the child. That is, the mother or anybody
who speaks to the child tries to simplify of course, but there's no evidence that
the way in which simplification proceeds is related to the way in which language
development proceeds. In fact, they seem to be more or less uncorrelated.

However, even if it turned out that a child wouldn't learn the language
unless he were presented with a very carefully programmed system, that still
wouldn't change anything much because this programmed system would still not
have in it relevant evidence about the properties that are known to the adult.
That is the main point.

In fact, immigrants' children learn the language of the speech community just as well
as those of the native speakers.

Yes, the immigrant case is a very good example.

I was curious how you arrived at this hypothesis. Who were the most influential peo-
ple in your formational period?

It is very hard for me to answer. When I was an undergraduate, I was working on generative grammar pretty much by myself. I did a generative grammar
of modern Hebrew when I was an undergraduate at the University of
Pennsylvania. At that time, I didn't know there had ever been similar work, but

I later discovered that there had been Panini's, for example; in fact, even recent-ly Bloomfield had done it in a limited but interesting way.

You mean the study of Menomini?

Yes, it was sort of similar, though I didn't know that at the time. I suppose that what got me to thinking in those terms was probably just the familiarity with logic and mathematics.

Maybe I should be a little more specific. How did you become interested in linguistics?

Most of these things in anybody's case are largely accidental, and I suppose they were in my case too. There were at least two influences that I can think of. One obvious one is through my father, who is a scholar of medieval Hebrew grammar. And I was familiar with what he was doing.

You studied medieval Hebrew grammar in college?

No, my father did. I did work in semitics, but my father's work was in his-torical grammar. So I knew about that sort of thing.

When did you begin reading his work?

Oh, when I was eleven or twelve years old.

And the grammar actually interested you at that time?

Yes, and then later I sort of lost interest in it. But when I got to college I happened to meet Zellig Harris, though I met him through political contacts, actually. It was not through linguistics at all.

What kind of political issues were involved?

Well, I was interested in socialist-bi-nationalist approaches in Palestine. This was in 1946 and 1947, and I was planning to go to what was then Palestine and live on a *kibbutz* and work for Arab-Jewish cooperation. He was also interested in that, so I happened to meet him through that connection.

Did you actually go?

I did go later. I lived there for a few months.

And did you regret it?

No, a few years later, in the mid-1950s, I did think of staying there. I had already gotten my PhD and had very little expectation of doing professional work in linguistics because the kind of work I was doing was far removed from anything that existed, and I had no real professional qualifications in linguistics as it was then generally understood.

I'm curious. What did Professor Harris think of you and your work?

We were very close friends and I was his student.

I mean, what did he think of your work?

I don't think that **generative grammar** ever interested him very much. While I was a student of his I was doing work on generative grammar more or less on my own. What I was doing with him were other things, things that he was more interested in. I was then working on his projects on discourse analysis. I was working for many years on trying to improve the methods of structural linguistics that he had designed and developed in some of his work. Only later did I come to feel that that was the wrong approach. Of course there was a lot of interaction. In the early stages of my work, I always talked to him about it.

Although it was not exactly the same goal, didn't he have some influence on your early formation, especially involving the notion of transformation?

No question about it. It was a similar notion. There was a very close relationship through the early 50s. In fact, I think perhaps the most important influence on me was his effort to give a very rigorous and precise account of language structures. I thought it was very important. He more than anyone else tried to give a very explicit and rigorous account of these analytic methods and how they might work. I don't think it was the correct approach, but the general idea he was trying to develop in such procedures was a right one.

Well, you often say how the 17th-century intellectual environment was very much similar to that of now. The modern so-called structural linguistics was very much interested in detailed facts, while the more traditional grammar was interested in abstract generalizations.

There are more similarities than that. For example, the 17th century happened to be very intrigued by automata. There were different kinds of automata then, but the model, the idea of mechanical devices that could do extraordinarily complex things was a very powerful image at that time and there was an effort to try to reconstruct what we might call the mental sciences or psychology on the model of physical mechanisms.

Concern with automata, though of quite different kinds, is also a leading idea in contemporary thought. And of course, the scientific revolutions of the 17th century laid the basis for the concept of explanatory science. They did have a direct impact on the study of language and universal grammar, though there are earlier origins as with anything. But it really became a major discipline in the 17th century under Cartesian influence.

Why didn't it continue?

It continued for well over a century or a century and a half, a long time. It reached a sort of limit, where they couldn't do much more. I don't think they had the technique available to either pose or answer the central question.

The central question has to do with recursion, with iterative rules, and those concepts just weren't available. In fact, they weren't available until about 30 or 40 years ago. Given that lack, people could say, as Humboldt did, that language involves the infinite use of finite means, which is a correct, appropriate characterization, but neither he nor anyone else could know what it meant.

They couldn't devise a model to pursue it?

There was no way of making concrete the idea of using finite means for an infinite purpose. It wasn't really until the 1930s that those ideas developed independently in mathematics and in logic, so that my own feeling is that one can bring together the technical achievements of the 20th-century in mathematics with the ancient questions and create a very natural discipline out of that marriage.

Isn't that what is really meant by the Chomskyan revolution?

Well, that's the basic point. And then, of course, you immediately begin to think of its significance for psychology and for mental representation and so on; that flows quite naturally from posing the question. Beyond that, the technical question arises about whether one has the right principles, etc.

So you believe that the transformational generative grammar provides such a framework?

Well, here one has to be careful, because there are a lot of different varieties of transformational generative grammar.

I am thinking about the so-called standard theory.

Well, I think the standard theory is an approximation to the truth, but I think it's wrong in a lot of respects.

In what respects?

Well, in technical respects. For one thing, I think it is wrong in the assumption that deep structure is what determines semantic representation. It was an interesting idea but turns out to be wrong. It was wrong in a lot of specific respects.

What is your current hypothesis about this meaning-sound relationship?

I think there's reasonably good evidence now that the standard theory was in part correct. That is, that one aspect of the meaning is determined by deep structure, namely the aspect that has to do with grammatical relations. They determine what some people call thematic relations and some call case relations;

that is, the relations of agent, instrument, and so on, seem to be represented in a very natural way on the deep structure level.

It seems that virtually every other aspect of semantic representations is determined by surface structure: scope of quantifiers, relations of co-reference, scope of logical particles, presupposition, and so on. In fact, every other aspect of meaning that has been investigated seems to be determined by something closer to surface structure.

Is there a special reason for that? Or is it just the fact across all languages?

After you've found that it's the case, you can think of reasons why a language might be designed this way, but if it turned out the other way, you could also think of reasons for that. Whatever the reason may be, I think it lies too deep for us to answer now. It's like asking why the law of free-falling bodies involves one physical concept rather than another one.

Well, it is easier to relate the deep structure conceptually with meaning because you have the notion that you first have the meaning and you want to express it.

That is a very traditional view. In fact, that was the view of the 17th-century grammars. Actually, it goes back to Aristotle. The natural—in a sense, naive—view of language is that there's a sound and there's meaning and you have the meaning in your mind and produce the sound. And in the 17th-century grammars where they really tried to work it out, they assume something like deep structures in the mind which represent meaning and which are mapped on to surface structures that represent sound. So it's a very natural idea—it just happens to be wrong. Very often in the sciences simple and natural ideas have turned out to be wrong. It also seems obvious that the sun rises but it just isn't true.

In the recent development of the study of syntax and semantics, one notices what look like two opposite directions. One seems to have gone deeper and the other seems to be approaching the surface.

People say that very often, but I think it's quite misleading. That distinction they have in mind would be, for example, between generative semantics, which tries to go deeper, and the so-called "extended standard theory," which is closer to the surface.

Deeper in the sense that it's more abstract.

Yes, but if you really look carefully you discover that the people who try to go to more abstract structures also introduce a new concept, namely the concept of global rule. And global rules related the surface structure with the so-called "deep" part and that's how they were able to capture the fact that really it's the surface that's determining the meaning, so that appearance of looking deeper was really an illusion.

When you take a careful look at the global rules of the abstract syntax they are essentially the same as the interpretive rules of the extended standard theory.

I think this is by now recognized and in fact generative semantics essentially has ceased to exist. But I think it was based on a kind of conceptual fallacy in the first place.

It was probably part of a general tendency, because your argument against autonomous syntax was so convincing that many people wanted to extend the idea to the syntactic-semantic relationship.

Maybe. My feeling is that generative semantics was certainly a possible hypothesis. I think I was the first person to suggest it, by the way. It's suggested in *Aspects of the Theory of Syntax* as a possibility. In retrospect, it is something that should have been explored, because it might have turned out to be true. For a while, it was the overwhelmingly dominant position.

My guess is that the reason for that appeal is that it seemed intuitively natural, just as it has since Aristotle and just as it seems so intuitively obvious that the sun is rising and not that the earth is turning. But intuitive naturalness is a very dubious guide in any kind of scientific work. We don't have any insight into what's the truth. We may have some insight into the way our minds work, but even that's doubtful and we certainly don't have any special insight into the truth about the matter. We have to discover from the outside, as it were, and from the outside there is no more reason to believe that deep structure determines the scope of quantifiers than that surface structure does. It could have turned out either way, and it turned out that surface structure did.

As for the opposite direction in current trends in linguistics, one of the reasons is probably that some linguists felt that transformational grammar is overly powerful. Wasn't there a movement to constrain the theory?

Well, there has been, but actually generative semantics worked in the opposite direction, making it still more powerful.

I am talking about other theories, not generative semantics.

Most of the work that, in my view at least, has proven to have been of lasting importance is work of this kind. That is, it took the approaches of, say, approximately the mid-1950s, and has tried to impose narrower and narrower restrictions on the types of grammars that are conceivable, which simply means trying to make sharper the theory of linguistic universals, innate principles that constrain the type of grammar, and that's probably the most significant work in the field, including current work.

What do you have in mind when you talk about current work?

There is, as always, heated debate about what the truth is. Just to keep to my own point of view for the moment, since about 1970 I have been working on a system of unifying principles that allow the deduction of a series of conditions on rules. These have certain parameters, certain points that can change so that if you change the parameters, then the resulting system comes out differently. I think that system, sometimes called the conditions framework, has been very productive.

But what about the recent claims that you can write a generative grammar without transformations?

Well, first of all, one wants to know exactly what that claim means. There's a trivial sense in which that is true. That is, you could develop interpretive rules which are equivalent to transformations. Then, of course, you could write a grammar without transformations. Take, for example, the matter of Wh-movement I mentioned before. There are two ways of approaching this. One is, as I did, to say that you have a base structure and then you pick out a phrase with an interrogative word and move it to the front of the sentence. Or you could say that you generate a structure with the interrogative phrase at the front of the sentence and then you have a rule which relates it to the position in the sentence from which it was moved, in the alternative theory.

You could say that the second is a grammar without transformations. But, again, it is just an illusion. It is just using the notations of transformations in a different fashion. In fact, those two grammars may well be indistinguishable. The real point is that there are non-local relationships which are of a certain abstract character, whether you choose to think of those relationships as a movement rule or as a rule relating a phrase to a gap specified in some manner. That is not even a metaphysical question, it is just a question of how to choose to interpret the very same theory. I do not know of any approach to language that doesn't have this same kind of richness, and I don't think there can be one because that's just the way language is.

That is true. For instance, the lexicon can be made extremely complex by ...

Putting in transformation relations that in effect we've seen in non-transformational grammar. I am very skeptical about whether those things are non-transformational grammars in any meaningful sense. I think they're probably other notations for transformational grammars.

Similarly, there have been other ideas presented. Hudson in England has proposed daughter-dependency grammars. If you look at them carefully, they involve remote interactions between phrases. If those are made precise, it's just going to be another variety of transformational grammar, as far as I can see.

I do not want to disparage other approaches. I mean, sometimes it turns out that slightly different interpretations of the same system have significantly different empirical properties, which is very interesting. And if one can show that, of course it is worth doing. But if one simply says, "Well, I am going to have an interpretive rule where you have a transformational rule," then it is not worth discussing.

As far as you are concerned, it will be a notational issue.

Well, one has to show that there is something more than notational issues involved. Sometimes there are and sometimes there aren't.

I was wondering what you think about the relationship between what Kiparsky calls transparency, learnability, and psychological reality.

Well, there are several points that I would like to make. The first point I should emphasize is that one shouldn't be misled by the words "surface" and "deep" in the phrases "surface structure" and "deep structure." That is, what I'm calling surface structure is a technical concept, so is deep structure, and surface structures are in fact very abstract objects. They are not transparently available by inspection.

Many linguists confuse surface structure with physical facts.

Right, and that is just not true. Surface structure in the sense of syntactic theory may include abstract null elements which are co-indexed with other elements, and all sorts of other things which are by no means part of physical reality—at least part of over physical reality.

Secondly, concerning the question of the correctness or falseness of some transparency hypothesis, that is strictly an empirical question. If it turns out to be true, okay; if it turns out to be false, okay. But there's no a priori argument that we are given one way or another. The only thing one can say as far as I can see about the learnability of language is that a language for which our mind is well-designed will be easily learned. In fact, it's easy to come up with what appear to be extremely simple languages that are very hard to learn. Finite state languages are the obvious case, producible by left-to-right finite automata which are conceptually very simple but don't happen to be adapted to the structure of our minds. These therefore would undoubtedly be extraordinarily hard for people to learn, whereas what conceptually are far richer and more complicated languages are much easier for humans because that's the way our minds are.

The languages that exist will be those that reflect the structure of our minds whatever that may be. It's quite impossible to say we have some abstract and general concept of simplicity that tells us how a language ought to look. Suppose we came along and said, "I think the number of elementary particles in the universe should be three because three is such a nice, simple number." That is not an argument. The number is whatever it turns out to be.

Now, as far as the matter of psychological reality is concerned, in my view there is a very serious confusion that is very deep-seated in the field and goes far back, back to the first time that the notion was introduced. I believe it was probably first done by Edward Sapir in his paper on the psychological reality of the phoneme.

There is a general point of view which is very common among linguists, psychologists, philosophers and many others, which I think is totally wrong, and it goes more or less like this: It says, "Suppose that someone comes up with a grammar of a language that has interesting principles in it and explains a lot of things with pretty good empirical coverage, and suppose furthermore that that person comes up with a theory of universal grammar with general principles that explain properties of language, etc. Suppose it's the best system you could imagine. Now someone comes along and says, 'That's fine, you have a theory that works and explains things but how do you know it's psychologically real?'"

That's the standard approach. What is thought is that you have to get some other kind of evidence—processing evidence, or evidence from the psychological laboratory, or neurophysiological evidence, or whatever—to find out whether it is psychologically real. Now, I'm all in favor of getting other kinds of evidence, but it seems to me that there's a logical error at the core of this reasoning.

To see that, I'd suggest again transferring the whole discussion back into the physical sphere, which is usually a good device for seeing what makes sense and what doesn't. So let's imagine the following possibility. Imagine a scientist, a solar physicist, who is interested in discovering the structure and the processes of the interior of the sun. You can't get inside the sun any more than you can get inside the mind. So what he does is use the evidence that is available from the periphery just as we use sounds that come from the periphery of the mental system. So he looks at the light emitted by the sun and does all sorts of experimental analyses and so on, and he finally comes up with a theory of fusion, hydrogen turning into helium or whatever—and that's his theory of the sun. Then he presents it and somebody says, "It's a very interesting theory and seems to explain things, and seems to work very nicely, but how do you know it's physically real?"

Well, that question is never raised in science. It's senseless. What would it mean to say that it's physically real other than that it's true? And how do we know that it's true other than on the basis of the ability to explain the evidence available to us? There is no other way. There's no avenue to physical reality other than the way that the scientist used in the first place to discover and establish the theory. And exactly the same is true in the mental sciences. If someone comes up with a grammar or a theory of language on the basis of some evidence, and then you ask him how he knows it's psychologically real, all he can say is, "I already told you why I believe that it's psychologically real; here's the evidence that supports it." If somebody says, "I don't think that's enough evidence," that's fine. You can always look for more evidence, and the evidence may be from other domains or maybe from the same domain.

What kind of evidence is used? You don't really do actual experiments?

You actually do. For example, if I ask you as a speaker of English whether "Who do you believe John's claim that Bill saw?" is a sentence, that's an experiment. Now it happens that most of the relevant evidence for the study of psychological reality—that is, truth—of linguistic theories now comes from experiments of this kind. It would be very nice to have experimental evidence of other types, from a laboratory of neurophysiology or whatever. We don't have much of it. If it would ever come along, it'd be delightful.

But the mistake that's been made is the mistake that goes back to Sapir's classical papers. What did Sapir do? He developed a phonemic system for some American Indian language and he showed that it was a very good phonemic system, and then he asked how do we know that this is psychologically real? He then sat down with his informant and he tried to figure out if he heard things that weren't physically there. He concluded that if he heard them, then it is psychologically real.

Sapir had two types of evidence. One was the original evidence that he used to set up a phonemic analysis. The second was the evidence from these informal experiments. As far as I can see, the first category of evidence is far more persuasive than the second category. Nevertheless he took the second category to establish psychological reality, not the first category. And I think that's just a big mistake.

But don't you still believe that the surface structure is much closer, for instance, in word order or the like to the possible sentence than deep structure?

By definition the surface structure is closer. It's different precisely because it doesn't represent the transformations.

Right. So isn't that the notion that if you have that kind of grammar it's somehow easier to learn? I am specifically thinking about the direction of language change and how you may explain it in your framework.

Let's first talk about the question of simplicity and suppose it turns out to be true as I think it is true, that languages have very abstract surface structures and that these surface structures are related to deep structures. Suppose that turns out to be true. If that is the case, then a hypothetical language which doesn't use transformations and has simpler surface structures will be harder to learn. If we were able to do the relevant experiments, I think we would find that to be the case.

We are not allowed to do the experiment for ethical reasons but I would predict that if we presented a child with a phrase structure language of a conceptually simple kind, he would find it very hard to learn because that's not the way his mind works. Just as if you presented him with a finite state language, which is even simpler, he would find it hard to learn because that's not the way his mind works. I think there are good reasons why the mind works the other way. You can imagine an organization of the mind in terms of short- and long-term memory which would be very much facilitated by abstract deep structure.

This question of trying to describe the competence of the ideal speaker-hearer: you have been really attacked many, many, times especially since the variationists came along. In a way it seems to me a very good way of explaining the linguistic change, admitting that there are variations—and that's really how language changes.

But that's not even an issue. Sociolinguists are muddled about this matter. They accept the very same notion of an ideal speaker-hearer with an idealized competence. Nobody doubts that; a lot of people say that they doubt it, but they all accept it. Just think what would be involved in denying that assumption.

Suppose one denied that there is a competence of an idealized speaker-hearer. Then they would be saying that it would be impossible for a person to learn a language in a homogeneous speech community. Now certainly nobody believes that. It's certainly possible, that means there must be some property of the mind that makes it possible.

That property of the mind that makes it possible to learn a language in a homogeneous speech community is nothing but the innate structure of the ideal speaker-hearer. Suppose someone were to say that this exists, but it doesn't enter into normal language. Notice how curious that view would be. He would be saying yes, there is a property of the mind which makes it possible to learn language in a homogeneous speech community but it is never used. It's just some biological oddity. Now can anybody conceivably believe that?

What you say is true, although I myself am very interested in the notion of variation.

So am I. You see, there's no contradiction at all between being interested in the notion of variation and believing in the validity of the idealization; that is, believing that there is a property of the mind that would make it possible to acquire an idealized competence in a homogeneous speech community, and that is used in normal language acquisition. You know what this argument reminds me of? Again, it never happens in the physical sciences, because they are not that confused, but just imagine that somebody came along to the physical scientist and said, "You're studying ideal systems of gases and frictionless planes and so on, and since we all know that planes have friction, therefore let's throw out physics." It's approximately the same kind of argument.

Yes. The truth is that even in studying variation, having a kind of grammar of an idealized speaker-hearer is helpful, because you can have a point of comparison. You can talk about what a fact is a variation of. What I am very curious about right now is how, in your framework, you explain language change.

In the same way everybody else does. I mean, there are no homogeneous speech communities. They simply do not exist. The whole notion of the speech community is itself an idealization. What actually exists are lots of different people with lots of different languages in their heads. No human being has a single language in his head. Everyone of us has all kinds of complicated systems intermingling which we picked up, reflecting this or that aspect of complex environment, and this material is always in constant flux. The very concept of a language is a very far-reaching idealization. There is no linguistic concept of language. Take the notion "Korean." There is no notion that can be defined linguistically, it's just an amalgam of more or less similar systems that are mixed up in people's minds. That's what every sociolinguist believes and that's what every generative grammarian believes. There's simply no issue.

Usually people say that the traditional grammar was very much a normative, prescriptive grammar. Can transformational generative grammar considered to be so?

First of all, it wasn't true of traditional grammar. If you look back at the traditional grammars, you'll find that there have been prescriptive grammars but there also were traditional descriptive grammars. As far as transformational generative grammar is concerned, there's nothing normative about it at all. In a more general sense, it's nothing but a theory of the actual nature of mind.

This might be a very superficial thing coming from your claim about the idealized speaker-hearer.

If you recall, when I first advanced that claim I didn't put it forth as controversial, I just said that is what every linguist believes. In fact everyone does believe that, including the ones who deny it; to see that they believe it, all they have to do is think through the consequences of denying it.

I don't think that sociolinguists really deny it, although they always start their argument by saying that. But I feel sociolinguists and abstract linguists are more complementary than contradictory.

They happen to be interested in somewhat different questions. If a person happens to be interested in what happens to a ball rolling down a plane with friction, he is not contradicting someone who is studying the theory of frictionless planes. I don't see how anybody could be confused about this.

Language is often claimed to be species-specific. Can our study of animal communication make any contribution to our understanding of human language?

I think it can and it already has. Contrary to a lot of other people, I think what the study of systems of animal communication has shown is how radically different they are from human systems. There is a lot of very good work on animal communication. There's a very good book that just came out about it, by Tom Sebeok, a huge encyclopedic study of animal communication. We both agree that human language isn't just one of those systems. Maybe human gesture is, but not human language; it's a different system. It differs in its fundamental properties from any system that's known in the rest of the animal world, and it also differs radically from the systems that are laboriously imposed upon other primates, as far as I know. In my opinion, people are very confused about this. It's very common to say that chimpanzees have been taught sign language. What we really ought to say is that chimpanzees have been taught some of the signs of sign language. There is a big difference between having been taught signs of sign language and having been taught sign language.

But what about the cases in which chimps were observed putting signs together to create new information?

It is claimed that they put together two symbols. Well, my cat is far more creative than that. The idea that a pair of symbols can be put together ... sure, I think that would be surprising if it were not the case. But that's as if somebody said, "Well, we found that the human eye is really a camera, because they both take in light and do some similar things." It's meaningless, because they have totally different properties, they function in different ways.

I don't know anything about American Sign Language, but ...

Well, the ASL is probably like any human language.

Yes, I think everyone agrees, but I was fascinated by a statement that there was a very similar acquisition order between these two.

You have to be very careful about that. For example, if you looked at a child and a fledgling bird, you might very well find that up to the point that the bird begins to fly there is a very similar development of the preliminary motions: a bird goes like this [gesture] and a human goes like this [gestures]. But, of course, at the point where the bird begins to fly there is a radical difference.

A great deal of the study of child language is concerned with developments that probably have nothing to do with language at all. They have to do with incipient motions in a pre-linguistic stage, and the fact that that's like what chimpanzees do in a pre-linguistic stage is exactly what you'd expect. Child language studies tend to stop at two or three years old, a point where the normal language is really beginning.

Shouldn't we study not only universality but also diversity? Isn't that a very interesting aspect of language, that also explains human culture and everything connected to things human?

These are two sides of the same coin. Suppose we knew the true universal grammar; then we would also know what diversity there could be.

What I am really interested in is finding out whether you still believe that the problem of accounting for the normal use of acquired knowledge at the moment lies beyond the scope of scientific inquiry.

I was trying to make a distinction between questions that are within the scope of normal scientific inquiry and those that apparently are not. One thing perhaps within the scope of scientific inquiry is finding out how we acquire the grammar that we do acquire, how do we acquire the actual knowledge. That is perhaps within the scope of contemporary science. But the question that as far as I can see is not within the scope of contemporary science, or maybe any possible human science, is how we use the systems that we acquire in expression of thought. We haven't the slightest idea how to approach that question. How do we decide to do what you and I are doing now?

Some linguists criticize the fact that some TG grammarians speak only one language, yet it does not hinder them from making claims about universals. You often say that the best evidence as to what is a universal property of language comes from the study of a single language.

Of course, the evidence from a diverse group of languages is very important. But the fundamental evidence is going to be from comparing the state that's achieved with the evidence that's available, and that's a problem that we can study in the case of a particular language. Again, I find this a curious kind of criticism. Almost all of science is based on the study of a very narrow class of cases. Nobody ever says to a physicist, "You didn't do an experiment in Africa." In fact, most of modern genetics is based on a few exotic organisms. The point is, you study the cases that are subject to study and you study them in the deepest way you can. Naturally you want to turn to wider evidence if it's available.

What is the future direction of linguistic theory? What do you think linguists really need to and should study? What do you consider the most important linguistic topics right now?

I think that the most important topics now, ones that are being studied very successfully, are the questions of conditions on rule systems in phonology, syntax, and semantics. And there are some very intriguing ideas.

If you just think in a very rough way about language, it's pretty clear that languages superficially differ from one another quite a lot, yet they're all acquired very rapidly and with little effort. This just has to mean that there is an abstract system of principles with a small number of parameters of variation, so that when we fix the parameters we get very complicated differences because of the way the principles interact.

For the first time there are now a number of theories that have the right kind of property. That is, they have abstract principles which interact and give very complicated results, so that when you change little things here and there in the principles, you get very different results. Now we know qualitatively that's what we need, and I think for the first time there are theories with qualitatively right properties and with some of the right empirical consequences.

It seems to me that working that out is the most exciting area of linguistics today. Do you think we arrived at a fairly reasonable hypothesis about language so that we could apply it, for instance, to education?

I am pretty skeptical about that. I think people who are involved in education ought to be cautious about applying linguistics. They really have to ask what works, and it's not at all clear the kinds of insights that are now obtainable about language are very helpful for, say, **language teaching**. In fact, my own feeling is,

TEACHING

probably not. I used to be a language teacher for children and also for college students. My feeling always was that ninety-nine percent of the problem was doing something interesting and one percent of the problem was how you did it; all the discoveries that may be made about that one percent really aren't going to change anything. You have to somehow make the language learners want to learn and if they do they'll learn no matter how bad your system is. If they don't, they won't learn no matter how good your system is.

You seem to believe that if you leave them as they are, because of their innate capability they will learn it if the conditions are right. I'm just thinking of some Asian philosophy where there are basically two opposing views regarding this capacity. It was not really a question of whether you are born with capacity or not. It was more a question of whether you are born with a good capacity or bad capacity. For example, Mencius's theory of innate goodness ...

I see. Whatever the answer to that, I think those are reasonable questions, especially in the domain of ethics. But at least in this domain, namely language, it doesn't seem to me that there's any reason to believe that there's an interesting variation among individuals. Undoubtedly at some level of detail, people differ genetically but it's so far beyond what we can study that we might as well regard all human beings as indistinguishable in terms of language capacity, apart from serious pathology.

Is there anything in future research where people can aim at this goal?

Yes, for example, I think that at some stage in the future maybe some problems of genetic defects or genetic differences and their effect on language may turn out to be an important area. In fact, there are some biologists who think it could be studied right now.

Can you elaborate?

Let's take schizophrenia. There is some reason to believe that schizophrenia may have a genetic component. Schizophrenic language certainly appears to be quite different from the normal language. Suppose, for example, you could study twins, one of whom is a schizophrenic and the other is normal. You could ask, you could inquire into the language of the normal one. Suppose you could find some differences between that and normal language. That could give a real insight into genetic properties that might be involved in language. I think that's too far for contemporary study, but sometime in the future, things of that sort might be very interesting.

This has been a most interesting and enjoyable interview. Thank you very much.

Editor's Notes to Interview 13

This interview and five more (29, 32, 47, 52 and 53) are due to Hannu Reime, a journalist covering international events for the Finnish Radio who has studied linguistics at the University of Helsinki and is able to cover Chomsky's scientific work. His interviews have been used as material in radio talks broadcast by the Finnish Broadcasting Company (the national radio/TV, a public institution comparable to the BBC). The titles with which they appear here are those suggested by the interviewer or close variations on them.

This first Reime interview took place in Pisa, Italy, on June 7, 1979, towards the end of Chomsky's sabbatical leave there—an extraordinarily fruitful one, which, among other things, led to a new major breakthrough in the history of linguistics. A letter to the present writer handwritten in Pisa on June12, 1979, begins as follows: "We're just about to leave, on the 16th. Has been extremely busy and interesting. The last two months, particularly, have been very busy, as I got involved in a mass of political talks, interviews, etc., around Italy and a bit elsewhere. In March, I was really quite free, and got quite a lot of work done. Have the notes for a book—lectures that I gave at GLOW conference—that I hope to write up this summer." (In early 1979 he had worked literally day and night to be able to complete *The Political Economy of Human Rights* before leaving for Italy.) The reference is to his celebrated "Pisa lectures," the subtitle of *Lectures on Government and Binding* (his second monumental theoretical work on the structure of language—a far more radical departure from the cultural tradition than the first one), which is a greatly expanded version of his Pisa notes. His hope, however, was not to be fulfilled until December 1980.

Interview 13 is one of those Italy interviews (for others, see Bibliographic Note). It is the only Reime interview that has been published as such. It appeared in Finnish translation in a now defunct Finnish cultural monthly published in Helsinki ("*Lännen uusi ase: Nälkä*" [*The New Weapon of the West: Hunger*], Näköpiiri, February 1980, pp. 18–22).

13. Ideological Reconstruction after Vietnam (7 June 1979)

You have written volumes on international politics and the role of the United States therein. How do you see the position of the United States in the world today, four years after the ending of the Vietnam War?

After the Vietnam War there was a necessary period of reconstruction both at the material and objective level and also at the ideological level. The United States had to come to terms with its partial defeat in Vietnam and to try to reconstruct the international world system that had been to some extent modified by events that took place in those years. At the same time, it had to try to reconstruct the interventionist ideology that had largely collapsed under the impact of the Vietnam War. In both of these respects, I think, the United States and Western imperialism in general have made quite considerable progress.

The response to the crisis of the international order is the system that is generally called trilateralism. It means recognizing the fact that the somewhat unusual post-war situation of the United States had changed significantly and that it was necessary to develop a kind of partnership to manage the international economic and political order, a partnership including the United States, Western Europe and Japan. But it is important to recognize that this kind of trilateralism as perceived in the United States at least is subject to the qualification that Henry Kissinger perhaps put most clearly when he said that other countries such as Germany had their regional responsibilities. These regional responsibilities are to be carried out within the overall framework of order to be managed by the United States. Whether other major powers accept that **version of trilateralism** is another question.

Sympathetic Solidarity versus Apathy and Passivity

At the moment, in fact, there is some conflict as to how this matter shall be resolved: Will that mean a return to a more American-dominated capitalist international order or will there be several centers of capitalist industrialism, in which the United States will, no doubt, be the first among equals?

That has been at the objective and material level. At the ideological level, it was extremely important in the United States, and in fact throughout the world of industrial democracy, to try to reverse the currents of sympathy that developed *in order to have unbridled internat'l capitalism* towards the Third World radical nationalism during the period of the Vietnam War. These are dangerous phenomena for the people who try to manage the international order. They hope to be able to continue the exploitation and plun-

243

déring and the suppression of independence with the Third World. The existence of mass popular movements that have sympathetic feelings, feelings of **solidarity** towards Third World movements, raises impediments to carrying out some modern version of imperialist policy. It has been necessary to find ways to change those currents of sympathy to either **apathy and passivity** or, better still, **contempt and hatred** for Third World nationalism. A major propaganda campaign has been conducted in the United States and also in Western Europe in the past several years to try to effect these changes, and it has been extremely successful. I think that one of the most significant developments in the last couple of years has been the unfolding of this immense and quite successful propaganda campaign to change feelings of sympathy and solidarity for poor and oppressed peoples to feelings of contempt and antagonism or simply apathy and passivity.

So you think that a major effect of the victory of the radical, revolutionary nationalist movements in Indochina was ideological?

I don't really think that they won a victory. I think that in a certain sense the United States won a victory in Indochina. We have to be a bit careful in analyzing this.

The United States did not succeed in one of its objectives, namely in literally incorporating Indochina within the American-dominated world system. It failed in that objective. But that was always a secondary, never a major objective. The major concern of the United States, the reason why they invested such tremendous amount of energy and resources in this remote corner of the world, was expressed in the framework of the <u>domino theory</u>.

The domino theory had several versions. There was one version that was offered up to mass consumption which was rather ridiculous. That was the idea that if one of the dominoes, say Indochina, fell, there would be aggression that would gradually conquer other parts of Southeast Asia, Indonesia, Japan, etc. That, of course, was nonsense. Nobody expected that. But there was another version of the domino theory that was not at all unrealistic and unreasonable. It was the major one that we find expressed in internal planning documents. Here the idea is that if there is successful social and economic development within the framework of independent radical nationalism in one part of the world, that will have a demonstration effect. It will offer a model that may appear quite attractive to masses of peasants and others in oppressed countries who will try to find an alternative to the development model that is favored by the privileged in the West, namely the development model which opens the resources of the Third World countries to Western exploitation. That version of the domino theory was very realistic and reasonable.

In this connection I think it is important to bear in mind the fact that the <u>United States really did win the war</u>. The destruction and devastation of Indochina was so severe that the possibilities of successful development are very slight. Even under the most favorable circumstances it is quite possible that there is no way to overcome the problems that were left by the American war, certainly not without massive reparations or aid. Of course, the United States has been very careful since the war to make sure that aid is very limited and from the United States there is none at all. In fact, the United States has refused even trade and rebuffed every effort at normal relations with Vietnam—again, a very rational and ugly policy directed to ensuring that this "horrible" prospect of successful social and economic development is not realized. And in this connection I think that the American war was a great success; it was efficiently destructive so that it delayed for a long period, maybe permanently, the threat of any successful development within these societies.   *a modern Rosa Luxemburg*

Furthermore, there is another aspect of American policy which again is quite typical: the same policy was used with regard to Cuba, with regard to China, and it was even followed after the Bolshevik revolution. The policy is to try to impose the harshest possible conditions on any country that has escaped from the international economic order dominated by the major Western capitalist powers.

The reasons for this are primarily two. The first reason is the one I mentioned, namely to try to restrict the possibilities of successful development and thus to restrict the demonstration effect, which could be dangerous as it spreads. Secondly, there's a certain ideological element in this. Imposing harsh conditions on an impoverished Third World society is certain to enhance and extend the repressive and authoritarian tendencies that already exist, in fact very strongly exist within the radical nationalist groups. One can increase and enhance these tendencies by imposing harsh external conditions, which more or less compel them to resort to draconian measures.

Similarly, one can force these countries into an alliance with the Soviet Union. It is very useful for Western propaganda, because then we can pretend that we were always fighting the Russians. That is much easier to sell to the public than fighting some impoverished Third World people. This policy—followed in the case of Cuba, for example—has also been effectively followed in the case of Indochina, and it has also been successful. The harshness of the conditions that the West, primarily the United States, has imposed, added to the enormous devastation and destruction of the war, has in fact combined to reinforce the repressive and authoritarian tendencies within the Indochinese countries, Vietnam for one, therefore offering a very significant propaganda victory to the West, just as Vietnam was driven into an alliance with the Soviet Union, which it really did not want, as the only alternative after the United States had rebuffed their efforts at normalization of relations—again, a propaganda coup for the West.

In all these ways, I think, the United States has succeeded in coming to terms with the problems posed by the partial defeat that it suffered in Vietnam. These are **extremely ugly policies**. I think that one should be aware of just how ugly they are. For example, throughout Indochina there's massive starvation. At the end of 1978 Cambodia was the only country in Indochina that had succeeded at all in overcoming the agricultural crisis that was left by the American destruction. It was not overcome at all, and maybe worsened, in Laos and Vietnam. In both of these countries there are certainly hundreds of thousands, if not millions of people, who are facing starvation. The United States is very careful to withhold any aid. It has the largest rice reserves in the world but will not release anything more than a tiny trickle to a country like Laos, where hundreds of thousands of peasants face starvation. It's another version of the same policy that was followed in the 1960s when these areas were being bombed to try to prevent the social revolution from succeeding.

Now the areas are not being bombed. But the United States is doing everything it can—and it can do a lot—to make sure that there's starvation and economic disaster. In my view these peasants of Laos, who are starving to death on areas that were destroyed by American bombing, are being killed by the West just as much as the people who were bombed directly, only different means are used. The fact that this has been covered in the West, and the fact that the United States can pretend to be leading a human rights campaign while persisting in these policies, reveals the enormous successes and power of the Western propaganda system, which is surely one of the most awesome and effective, if not **the most awesome propaganda system that has ever existed in world history.**

Do you think that the wars and conflicts between these post-revolutionary states in Indochina have contributed in this Western propaganda campaign?

Absolutely. I mean that there were plenty of causes for conflict, for national conflicts that are indigenous to the region. It would be completely wrong to suggest that all the causes of conflict in that area are the direct result of Western imperialist manipulation. That's not true. There are historical conflicts between the Vietnamese and the Cambodians and between the Vietnamese and the Chinese. These would be likely to show up in some form or another, no matter what governments there were in these areas. However, it's also true that the West has done whatever it could do to try to enhance and exacerbate these conflicts. And it has had an effect. The American alliance with China was surely one factor that led to the Vietnamese fear of encirclement in a Cambodian-Chinese alliance backed by the United States. I believe that this was one factor that convinced the Vietnamese to try to overcome their barrier conflicts with Cambodia by simply trying to conquer the entire country. It raised a local border conflict to a major international issue.

The American refusal to accept Vietnamese efforts at normalization, as I mentioned, drove the Vietnamese into an alliance with the Soviet Union, which again exacerbated their conflict with China, for obvious reasons, and presumably was intended to have this consequence. In these and many other ways the United States has been acting successfully to embitter the already existing conflicts, to raise their level to the point where they lead to serious hostilities. There is no question that as these conflicts develop and grow, they are having their devastating effects on the people of that region. For example, to take just Cambodia, my own feeling is that the effect of the Vietnamese invasion will be serious disaster, if not catastrophe, for Cambodia, which is already suffering enormously. After the current rainy season there may be really massive starvation. It's quite possible that Khmer nationalism will simply disappear from history as a viable national entity as a consequence of this invasion. That is certainly a possibility.

You have recently taken up the question of the Indonesian invasion of East Timor?

The bare facts of the matter—they are not well known, and that's why I describe them—are the following. After the Portuguese decolonization there was an independence movement which in fact took over effective control of East Timor by late 1975. Immediately the Indonesian army began border harassment and bombardment, and in December 1975 Indonesia invaded East Timor, surely with the collusion of the United States. The invasion took place a few hours after President Ford and Henry Kissinger left Jakarta. The Indonesian army was 90 percent armed with American arms. The American arms flow continued in the following period. The United States has been in fact the primary force in both providing the armaments required for the invasion and also providing diplomatic cover and trying to prevent—successfully in this case—any knowledge of the consequences from spreading throughout the world.

That was December 1975. Since that time evidence has been mounting that there have been quite unprecedented massacres, perhaps the greatest massacres, proportionally to the population, since World War II. There is pretty good evidence by now that something like, perhaps, 100,000 people, maybe 200,000, something in that neighborhood, have died, have been killed in the course of the Indonesian invasion, which will be something like one-sixth, perhaps even one-third of the population. The evidence is reasonably good. Most of it comes from sources that are hostile to the independence movement FRETILIN, sources that are pro-Indonesian. Priests, Indonesian and local, have in fact been probably the major source of information. The Australian parliament—Australia has been the only country that's been concerned about this—has concluded, using largely, I think, leaks from Australian intelligence, that this may be a slaughter of quite unprecedented proportions. We, of course, don't know the details since Indonesia has closed off the entire area and has refused even to permit the Red Cross to enter. But there is very good evidence of a substantial slaughter, maybe an unprecedented slaughter, which is still continuing with Western aid and support.

This issue is extremely important in itself. It is also **a very revealing issue**. We can, for example, compare the attention given in the West and the concern shown in the West with regard to the slaughter in Timor to the concern shown for atrocities in Indochina. A probably natural comparison to undertake is Timor and Cambodia. The time frame is exactly the same, 1975 to the present. The level of atrocities is quite similar. The harshest critics of Cambodia, if you really read them carefully, claim that maybe 100,000 or more people were killed by the Khmer Rouge in Cambodia. The evidence is mixed but let's assume it to be accurate; assume that the harshest critics are correct, Barron & Paul, Ponchaud and others, and that something like 100,000, maybe 200,000 were killed in Cambodia by the Khmer Rouge. Of course, one hears far higher numbers than that. But those higher numbers, first of all, are mostly fabricated, but where not, they include many, many hundreds of thousands of people, if not millions who died from starvation and disease. That, however, is largely a legacy of the American war. It's worth remembering that the American government itself predicted at least one million deaths at the end of the war. But in terms of actual killings and massacres the most harsh critics of Cambodia have estimated these to be perhaps 100,000, something in that neighborhood or somewhat more.

In the case of Timor we have in absolute numbers a similar level of massacres. At this time we can conclude that the estimates given are not by hostile sources but by sources that are actually favorable to the Indonesian invasion or at least tolerated it at first. Proportionally to the population, the massacre in Timor is far higher, maybe five to ten times higher. It is also a massacre as a peasant revenge, which undoubtedly was operative to some extent in Cambodia. And, of course, the crucial matter for the West is that the West is a direct and central participant in these massacres. Indonesia has repeatedly exhausted its stores of arms in the effort to suppress the resistance in East Timor, which still continues, and these arms have been replenished by the West regularly because of their relations with Indonesia. It's a rich country—the population is extremely poor and in fact has been even further impoverished—for the West. It has resources which are open to be plundered by the West and the local elite that is placed in power by Western force. As a result, the West is delighted to sell arms to Indonesia. These arms are being used and, in fact, are of central importance in continuing the struggle.

In contrast, in the case of Cambodia, however horrible the situation may have been—take the worst picture you like—there was nothing that the West could do about it. In the case of Timor there is everything the West can do, namely to stop the massacres by withholding the arms. It is extremely interesting to note that whereas there has been an unprecedented international propaganda campaign about Cambodia and there is just no end to the hysteria and outrage that is expressed by the West with regard to Cambodia, one hears virtually nothing about Timor. That far more significant issue has been suppressed, it's barely noted in the Western press, and where the issue is mentioned at all, it is given as some State Department version or Indonesian propaganda.

I think that this reveals with very great clarity the absolutely total hypocrisy of the human rights clamor concerning Indochina. It would be very easy for a Russian human rights activist to become outraged over the American war in Vietnam but much harder for him to become outraged over the Russian invasion of Czechoslovakia, and we would understand perfectly well how to evaluate the pretended outrage of such a person if he didn't talk about the crimes of the Russian state but limited himself to the crimes of the American state. Exactly the same standards apply in the West and reveal with great clarity the extent to which the West shares the most depraved and odious characteristics of the totalitarian states in this regard. It is perfectly happy to talk about the criminal acts carried out by an enemy, but insists on silence with regard to its own crimes.

I think that the issue of Timor is doubly important. Its primary importance, of course, is that a major massacre is continuing, and that massacre can be stopped if the West will withdraw from its participation. Secondly, the incident gives a very revealing insight into the nature of the so-called human rights crusade in the West, which it reveals to be essentially a propaganda exercise directed to the reconstruction of the ideological system that collapsed during the 1960s. It is interesting to note that—as far as I know—only one country in the world has reacted to this major atrocity by withdrawing its arms sales to Indonesia, namely Sweden, where—I've been informed—the Social Democratic opposition succeeded in getting the government to withhold further arms sales to Indonesia. But the main countries that are providing arms, the United States, France and others, continue blithely to take part in this massacre to the extent they can. Of course, there is no end to their pretended outrage over the crimes conducted by the peasant societies that have escaped from Western domination.

Last fall you presented a testimony to the United Nations. Who is now supporting East Timor?

FRETILIN, the East Timor independence movement, is supported by most of the Third World and by the majority of the non-aligned countries. For the Third World, this has been a major issue, the Indonesian aggression in Timor. The Western countries have been trying to keep quiet, obviously because the West benefits enormously from its relations with Indonesia since the coup of 1965. And since the West happens to control the international flow of information, the issue is simply unknown in most of the world. It is known in small Third World countries, and they take it very seriously. And there are occasional exceptions in the West. But it has been extremely difficult against the concentrated opposition of the Western powers, and especially in the face of the almost total refusal of the mass media in the West to provide any information whatsoever, except the State Department propaganda, about these ongoing massacres. In fact, it is one of the most extreme examples that I know of that demonstrates the fundamentally totalitarian character of the Western mass media and their subservience to the power of the major imperialist states.

What about the Russians?

The Russians, they have not taken a direct role in the massacres in East Timor. On the other hand, they certainly have not been giving any kind of obvious support to the resistance movement. My own guess is that the Soviet Union values its potential relationship with a fundamentally rich country like Indonesia, a country that they have not yet plundered sufficiently, so that it doesn't want to endanger these relationships by supporting a movement that is being wiped out by the Indonesian forces.

Your political writings have mainly been analyses of ideology, of the ruling ideology in the West. What are your own political views, your views on how a decent society should be organized?

The True Aim of a Social Revolution

I'm basically a sort of an anarchist and have been all my life. I believe that for advanced industrial countries at least, an organization in the manner that has been developed in anarchosyndicalist theories is exactly correct; it would be the best form of organization for an industrial society and possibly for any society. The developing societies have very severe problems. There is no historical example that I know of, at least, of modernization and industrialization that has taken place without considerable violence and oppression. Surely that's true in the well-known cases like the United States and Germany, and one can't be clear about making proposals for underdeveloped societies that have very small margin of maneuver and very extreme problems to face.

In the case of the advanced industrial societies, however, it seems to be that a very reasonable position to take is that all forms of centralized domination, including the highly concentrated centers of corporate power, which with state power forms the two major functioning, closely related centers of power in Western capitalism. Both of these are, in my view, historical anachronisms, inconsistent with any fundamental commitment to democracy. I think that the true aim of a social revolution in the West should be to dissolve these centers of power, leading to a social organization based on such principles as workers' control of industry, local control of communities, federal interaction, interchange and so on.

How does that relate to your scientific work in linguistics? You have criticized the empiricist ideology and defended a view of human nature that is more closely related to Cartesian ideas. Does that relate to the way you would like to see a decent society organized?

An Instinct for Freedom

I suppose that there are very loose and tenuous relations that one can find. Certainly, I wouldn't want to exaggerate them. It seems to me that basically the questions are independent. The question of what is the proper social order for which we should strive in the present stage of society is one kind of question and the question of what are the facts about human cognitive structure is another question. They could have quite independent answers.

I believe that the study of human cognitive structures and human intellectual achievements reveals a high degree of genetically determined innate structure that lies at the basis of the creative aspect of human intellectual achievement, which is easily perceived in every aspect of normal intellectual development, most strikingly, most easily, perhaps, in the acquisition and free use of the systems of language, which permit the free expression of thought over an unbounded range.

Similarly, I think (we can here only speculate because so little is known) that related aspects of human nature lie at the core of the continuing human search for freedom from authoritarian rule, from external restriction, from repressive structures, what might be called an instinct for freedom. It is conceivable that such an instinct for freedom exists and is deeply rooted in human nature and is related somehow, in ways that we don't know, to the elements that we can already discover in studying some aspects of human nature, such as human cognitive achievements. However, again, I would want to be extremely cautious in drawing any connections between these two areas. We certainly can't draw any clear, explicit connections between them, only some general hints.

In any case, your work does stress the basic similarity and equality between human beings.

It seems to me a matter of fact, as far as current science perceives it, that there are basic and fundamental elements of human nature in its cognitive aspects which are uniform across the species. The areas that are best understood, in particular such matters as language—here we find, as far as we can tell, **a very rich innate endowment** which seems **to be shared across the species**. If there are variations, they are so slight, at least by current measures, that we can barely detect them. This is not to say that there are no individual differences, only that they are extremely slight and marginal as compared with the major principles and structural elements that simply are definitive of human nature in these domains. That much seems to be true.

Editor's Notes to Interview 14

"Activist, Scholar Chomsky: On Human Rights and Ideology," *Forerunner*, Nov.13, 1979. The interview was conducted two weeks before by *Forerunner* staff member Jeff Sellers at Princeton, during Chomsky's visit to that campus to speak about the then recently published *The Political Economy of Human Rights*, which Princeton Politics Professor Richard Falk had termed "of decisive importance in building the foundation of a humane politics," adding that it "should be read and studied as widely as possible." Sellers was particularly interested in the implications of the analysis presented in the first of the two volumes, concerned with "the support for repressive regimes and state terrorism around the world since World War Two," for activist politics. (The quotes are from the preliminary note to the interview.)

On the first main topic, see **RP** (1981/1984/2003), ch. 12; on ideology, **P&I** (1987), **CT** (1988), **DD** (1991), esp. ch. 12, and references.

14. On Human Rights and Ideology (October 1979)

The past decade has witnessed a trend toward what some observers have described as "neo-conservatism" among some self-proclaimed former members of the liberal intelligentsia. How do you analyze this trend?

You're thinking of people like Nathan Glazer and Patrick Moynihan and so on. Well, I think these people were very much frightened by the mass politics of the 1960s, which for a time threatened to really engage substantial parts of the population in the democratic process and to threaten elite domination. And, of course, as in the case of any mass popular movement, there were aspects of it that were ugly and unpleasant. But that's not what bothered them. What bothered them was particularly the democratic aspect of it, the fact that previously repressed and quiet and apathetic groups were finding a voice and searching for and sometimes finding ways to struggle for their rights. I think that there's been a general tendency, not only among the neo-conservatives but among others, to try to find an approach to contemporary society which would eliminate these democratic strivings.

As an intellectual yourself, how do you see your role in relation to the state?

By and large, it is not a point of principle, but I would see myself as quite antagonistic to any form of concentrated power. Concentrated agglomerations of power, whether state or private—and in our society that's hardly a distinction—will tend to use their power for their own perceived benefit and quite often for the harm of others. And since I'm against the existence of such concentrations of power, I also tend to be opposed to the actions they carry out in the exercise of their power. So I would say that my general position would be adversarial. As far as mass popular movements are concerned, if they existed I would like to do something that could be of service to them.

Does the Carter administration's concern for human rights indicate some sort of shift in American foreign policy?

You're begging the question there. I don't agree that the Carter administration has any concern for human rights. I think it has a human rights rhetoric that is perfectly consistent with supplying armaments for some of the world. On the other hand, it was from a propaganda point of view very effective to suddenly raise the human rights banner in 1976, at a period when there had been a great

253

deal of revulsion over the obvious American role in repressing human rights throughout the world.

What's interesting to me is that public relations exercise can succeed. And it certainly has succeeded. That is, there are people who will say that the Carter administration's policy is inconsistent or indefinite or this or that, but in general it is assumed that there is a human rights policy. Now as far as I know, no great power in the world in history has ever followed a human-rights policy—certainly not this administration.

Should a power follow a human rights policy?

I don't think that any power ever will. I think that the only way in which more humane policies can be imposed on the great powers is by mass popular movements of their citizens. So, for example, the peace movement was one of the factors that forced the United States to restrain what would otherwise have been a much more intensive assault against Vietnam. The civil rights movement caused American power to make moves that ameliorated the situation of oppressed minorities. That's the way to press power towards human rights concerns. There's no other way.

How do you explain reports that the administration's "human rights policy" has at least appeared to achieve some progress toward democracy through promoting free elections in several Latin American countries?

Well, first of all, some of the side effects of the human rights rhetoric have in fact been beneficial. In some cases, for example the Dominican Republic, the Carter administration did apply pressures which allowed a conservative landowner, a businessman, to be elected in place of the fascist dictator who we had installed years earlier. And, in fact, the United States would generally prefer what looks like a liberal democratic government; that would be preferable to having, let's say, a murderer or a torturer. The trouble is that to achieve the kinds of aims to which American policy is directed, for example to improve the investment climate, it is repeatedly necessary to introduce doses of terrorism and repression. So of course we'd much prefer to have a democratic facade, but it's very hard to maintain that.

What about the point that the United States has to curry the favor of Third World countries by aiding their military and police if it wants to retain its influence with them?

If the United States wants to maintain a favorable climate for investment and exploitation, it will have to impose a leadership, or back a leadership, which supports those aims. If we allowed independent development to take place in countries, and in fact supported such independent development, it would harm precisely those interests that dominate American foreign policy: business interests. So we're not going to do it.

What do you think of the argument that some repression is necessary to raise standards of living in the Third World?

Well, I think we can say the following, that a lot of repression is necessary to raise the standards of living for the elites in the Third World. And the historical evidence seems to be conclusive on that score. The actual argument that's put forth is that, in the short run, you have to have repression and lowering standards of living, in order that in the long run there can be growth. And the argument, which is a very weak argument, I think, is that that's the way it worked in the industrial West. If you look at the industrialization of the West, it did involve enormous brutality. Even in England, the most privileged country in resources, it did involve quite possibly an actual lowering of the standards of living for a very large part of the population over a long period, maybe 50 or 100 years.

Now, a couple of questions arise: For one thing, is it necessary for development to have that enormous human cost? The other question is: In the Third World countries, which are by no means as privileged as England and the United States were hundreds of years ago, will that model ever work? What reason is there to believe that they can duplicate our experience? In fact, there are very strong reasons why they can't. They're industrializing in a totally different world, and facing much more onerous conditions.

Do you think development in the Third World is possible under an autarchic model which stresses independence of the economy from Western influence?

I wouldn't want to try that for certain. I don't think one can make rash statements about that. It's certainly a possible model of development, and it might very well turn out that that's the right one. However, what I'm saying is that there will be no possibility of exploring this model, because the outside pressures against it will be so harsh—unless we change the behavior of the industrial countries.

Is that possible?

Yes, I think it's possible. Again, just as in the case of the peace movement, by developing forces within the industrial democracies that will assist meaningful development. This happens in small countries. For example, take Sweden. Now Sweden has in fact a very constructive program supporting Third World development. Of course, one can argue that it's much easier in Sweden than in the United States because Sweden is only marginal in the mansion of capitalism, and that no matter what happens there, if it doesn't happen in the United States it doesn't make a great deal of difference. So while those Third World countries integrated into the capitalist system wouldn't care that much about Sweden, they would care about the United States. Of course the opposite side of that argument is that we all care more about what happens in the United States. These are human institutions; we can affect them. They're not laws of nature that we're talking about.

One major focus of your book is the role of the American press (the New York Times, the wire services, and so on) in filtering the information that reaches the American public about repressive regimes. Several times you compare the information reaching Americans with that reaching the Soviet people through a system of strict state censorship. With an uncensored media in the United States, how is this possible?

Well, first of all, notice that we don't say, and it wouldn't be correct to say, that the devices are the same, or even that the impact is quite the same. The American system, however, does have the same effect in many cases as the system of state censorship. It is more diverse, and far wealthier, and operates by entirely different mechanisms. The way it works here is far more subtle: it works by a system of shared interests. The media are major corporations, and they share the ideological commitments of the core capitalist elite that controls most of the economy and most of the state as well. And, in fact, if they ever began to deviate from these commitments, they would probably go out of business. Furthermore, for individuals to work their way up into the media system, with rare exceptions they must share these professional interests or they are not going to make it in this system of indoctrination. And the sort of backing for this is that the intelligentsia as a whole tend to share the doctrines of the state religion so that the pool of people you have to select from are already preselected. They would have never worked through the educational system and made it into positions of academic power or professional power if they hadn't worked pretty much within the framework of these assumptions. Now always there are a few exceptions. But this whole system of conformity is so overwhelming that, simply allowing that it operates by its own dynamism, there's going to be a very narrow spectrum of opinion expressed, and also a very narrow interpretation of current history which will conform to that of the state propaganda system.

Could you give an example of this self-censorship by the media?

Well, maybe the most dramatic example is the case of the U.S.-backed Indonesian invasion of East Timor, which has probably led to the massacre of several hundred thousand people in the past three years. The Indonesian army is 90 percent armed by the United States, and there is a continual flow of arms to make sure that the massacre continues. Right now, the part of the population that's alive is mostly starving to death under conditions that American aid officials privately say are quite comparable to what exists in Cambodia. And the media refuse to publish a word about this. A few of them have published what is for the most part Indonesian government propaganda, but the majority of them haven't said anything at all. Now in this case, the American media are behaving precisely in the manner of a totalitarian state-controlled press. But they're doing it for their own interests.

You have acknowledged that some information about American-backed fascist regimes does get through the media's system of self-censorship. What role does this information play in the formation of American opinion?

Well, the effect on American opinion is very slight. But for individuals— like me, say—the difference is fantastic. For example, living in a so-called total- itarian state, I couldn't begin to do the things I do here. Even if for some reason I wasn't put in jail, it would be too hard to get information. But for individuals who want to act politically and to sort of work their way through the system of indoctrination, it's incomparably easier in a democratic system of state control than in a totalitarian one. On the other hand, this is almost politically meaning- less, because for the mass of the population it has no consequences. They can't take the time or the effort to devote to the fanaticism that's required to find out the truth about these matters.

As American citizens, what can we do about our country's support of repression and state terrorism in the Third World?

Well, I think we know the answer to that. There's a short-range answer and a long-range answer. The short-range answer is to try to develop popular move- ments like the peace movement of the 1960s, which happened completely with- in the framework of American institutions as a challenge from below, but never- theless repeated the terrorism of the American state, and did so significantly. The long-range answer is to change those institutions significantly enough so that they won't use this built-in tendency to support repressions and immiseration in the Third World.

Do we have any special leverage as members of the university community?

As members of the university community we are highly privileged. We're privileged economically, we're privileged in our class background, we're privi- leged in the freedom that we have, we're privileged in the facilities that we have available. So there are all sorts of possibilities that university people have to act— students, faculty, maybe staff—I think, in a way which will be humane and effec- tive, that less privileged people don't have. Consequently, when we don't use these possibilities, there is just no gain from them.

Editor's Notes to Interview 15

"Chomsky, Questions Réponses," *Révolution* 1 (March 13, 1980), pp. 33–36. One of the purposes of the new publication (a rotogravure issued by the French Communist Party with the motto "Nous vivons le temps de révolutions") was "to enrich the knowledge of the panorama of ideas for its readers, especially at the international level." The interview is not signed. The questions (13 of them) were submitted to Chomsky in writing, and he answered in writing on Feb. 3, 1980. The following text reproduces his 13 answers (his answers to questions 6 and 11 are not included in the published French translation) together with a translation of the questions as printed and a rough reconstruction of the two omitted.

After pointing out that Chomsky had participated in the conference on "Nouvel ordre intérior" organized by the University of Vicennes in 1978 (the proceedings had just appeared in Paris), the preliminary note (from which the new title is taken) refers to the fact that Chomsky set only one condition, namely, that his answers should be published as written or not at all, a request that had just been violated, as pointed out in one of the questions, by the Parisian weekly *Nouvel Observateur* (see Editor's Notes to I18). "This is one more reason," the note continues, "to acquaint our readers, without delay, with a point of view very different from that of the French communists on more than one question: Spain, Afghanistan, existing socialism, the nature of the forces confronting each other in the world, etc." How does this compare with the open mindedness exhibited by the champions of the Free World press?

On the first topic, see Chomsky's "The Soviet Union versus Socialism," *Our Generation* 17:2 (1986), pp. 47–52, later included in D. I. Roussopoulos, ed., *The Radical Papers*. Montréal: Black Rose Books, 1987, pp. 47–52. See notes to I40.

The review of Lewy's book appeared in *Inquiry* (March 19, 1979), pp. 23–27.

This is not the first time Chomsky refers to Gramsci's maxim. See **AWA** (1970), pp. 106–107.

15. An American View of the Ideological Confrontation of Our Time (3 February 1980)

In the course of last year, in several French publications, you made contributions which seem important to us for a reflection about the world strategy of the U.S. and more generally the "West." On this occasion, it was suggested, more or less openly, here and there, that you consider only one side of things and play the other side's game. Now you are expressing yourself in a journal published by French communists and their friends with a viewpoint decidedly "Eurocommunist." Could you define your "political position" for our readers?

There are really two questions here: (1) What is my position? (2) What is the game being played by the superpowers?

My views on social and political issues have not changed in essentials since my first independent political thought. These views fall within what is sometimes called "libertarian socialism." I have been much influenced by work of anarchists and non-Bolshevik Marxists (e.g., Rudolf Rocker, Anton Pannekoek). In general, I think that anarcho-syndicalist conceptions—workers' control, voluntary associations, decentralization and federalism, dissolution of hierarchic and authoritarian structures, and so on—are quite appropriate for the next stage of industrial society. I should add that I have never considered myself a "Marxist," and in fact regard such notions as "Marxist" (or "Freudian," etc.) as belonging more to the domain of organized religion than of rational analysis. Marx was a serious person, not a God. He had significant insights, of lasting value. Like anyone, he made mistakes, and much has happened in the past century that escaped his vision.

As for the so-called "Marxist" movements, I think that Bakunin's early critique was quite perceptive. Particularly since 1917, Marxism—or more accurately, **Marxism-Leninism**—has become, as Bakunin predicted, the ideology of a "new class" of revolutionary intelligentsia who exploit popular revolutionary struggles to seize state power. They proceed to impose a harsh and authoritarian rule to destroy socialist institutions, as Lenin and Trotsky destroyed the factory councils and soviets. They will also do what they can to undermine and destroy moves towards **authentic socialism** elsewhere, if only because of the ideological threat. It is natural that the USSR should have committed itself to the violent destruction of the popular revolution in Spain in 1936, just as workers' councils in Hungary or democratic socialist tendencies in Czechoslovakia were intolerable to the "Red bureaucracy."

The appeal of these doctrines to the radical intelligentsia of the Third World is understandable. The doctrines justify their seizure of state power and their use of this centralized power. At best, they may construct a party dictatorship that is more or less benevolent, in that it will bring about a degree of modernization and development and improve health and welfare standards. Such achievements, if they take place, are not to be lightly dismissed, but they are also not to be confused with "socialism" in any sense of this term that is meaningful for the advanced industrial societies.

Similar considerations may explain in part the appeal of Marxist-Leninist doctrines to certain segments of the Western intelligentsia, as well as the ease with which many of the same people switch to the more typical stance of the intelligentsia: service to their own state, either in a managerial or ideological capacity. The doctrine of state worship has not dramatically changed, though it is shaped by a different assessment of how one can gain privilege and a degree of power. Throughout, I am speaking of tendencies, which I think are real, though there are many individual exceptions.

I have devoted a great deal of time and energy, and have been willing to face some personal risk, in attempting to defend radical nationalist movements in the Third World from the subversion and violence of the industrial democracies, but without illusions as to their character. It is easy enough to criticize these movements, but we should also recognize that they are facing problems far more severe than anything in the historical experience of the West in the modern period, and that many of these problems are the result of harsh Western policies and often extreme terror and violence. This will no doubt continue to be true.

Turning to the second question: What is **the "game" being played by the superpowers?** In my view, the Cold War system has been highly functional for the superpowers in providing a framework within which they can mobilize popular support for military intervention and other harsh measures within our domains. When the U.S. overthrows the reformist government of Guatemala, or restores the Shah to power, or invades Vietnam or the Dominican Republic, or subverts the Allende government, or conducts programs of terror and sabotage against Cuba, it pretends that all of this is done to save freedom from the Russian (or earlier, Chinese) threat. This is much more convenient than the truth: that the U.S. is resorting to force to prevent moves towards national independence outside of its control. Similarly, when the USSR invades Hungary or Czechoslovakia or Afghanistan, it pretends that it is defending "socialism" from the threat of Western imperialism, though in fact it is defending or extending the power of the Russian state.

When a Russian dissident criticizes the cruel practices of his state, he is attacked at home for "playing the other side's game" and asked why he does not condemn the atrocities committed by the "other side." When a Western intellectual criticizes Western atrocities he is attacked in the same way. This is not surprising. It is not surprising, then, that I should be criticized in France for (in your words) "considering only one side of things and playing the other side's game."

In France the anti-communist campaign has domestic policy aims which are easy enough to detect. But it rests on foreign policy events: long before Afghanistan, it found reasons on the situation in Vietnam and in Cambodia. Don't you think that this situation in France largely derives from the campaign developed in similar terms in the United States (reeducation camps in Vietnam, boat people, etc.)? Is there in the United States, as there is in France now, a campaign accusing Vietnam of starving Cambodia by confiscating, for its benefit, the food sent to Cambodia? Le Monde, for example, did not hesitate to speak of a "second Cambodian genocide," due this time to the "Vietnamese occupation."

The West suffered a defeat in Indochina in two respects: First, Indochina escaped from the orbit of Western control; Second, in the course of the French and American wars, dangerous feelings of sympathy and support for radical nationalism in the Third World developed in the Western societies. It was perfectly predictable that Western ideologists should seize upon every opportunity to reverse these feelings, to replace them with hatred and contempt, and to rebuild the domestic basis for harsh and exploitative policies, military intervention if necessary and feasible. Indochina was reduced to misery by French imperialism and virtually destroyed by the American attack.

In contemporary U.S. ideology, the Western role is being excised; all problems, all suffering, are attributed to the villainy of the current leadership, as if history began in 1975. Meanwhile the U.S. tries, in every possible way, to impose the maximum of suffering on Indochina. Not only has it offered no reparations for its crimes, but even aid, trade and normal relations are refused. The U.S. has succeeded in preventing the World Bank from carrying out development projects in Vietnam, and has done what it can to block material aid from elsewhere. If the population starves, that is offered as proof of Communist villainy. As the editor of the *Far Eastern Economic Review* (hardly a radical journal) has pointed out several times, these harsh policies contributed to harsh policies of the regime in Vietnam, as was no doubt intended. The leadership in postwar Indochina is responsible for many failures, and guilty of many crimes. The U.S. exults in these, and does what it can to maximize hardship so as to intensify suffering and brutality. Also, there has been a major propaganda campaign in the West exploiting cruel and brutal actions in Indochina—some real, some invented—so as to reconstruct the image of Western righteousness that was so tarnished as the truth about the Indochina war became known. Notably missing is any effort to provide the massive assistance that might serve to alleviate harsh conditions and brutal practices. The past and continuing American role is also conveniently forgotten.

With regard to Vietnamese "genocide" in Cambodia, there is a major effort in the U.S. to demonstrate that Vietnam is "organizing famine" in Cambodia. For example, exactly this charge is leveled by Leo Cherne, chairman of the International Rescue Committee (the *New York Times*, Jan. 28, 1980), citing French sources. This is the same Leo Cherne who revealed his deep humanitarian commitments by explaining in December 1975 that refugees fleeing the massive American bombardment of the Vietnamese countryside were seeking "sanctuary" from the savage Viet Cong. This propaganda campaign is being impeded, however, by the fairly consistent reports from relief workers in Cambodia that contradict the charges.

The consequences of the Vietnamese invasion of Cambodia are a complicated matter, which I will not attempt to discuss here. For a detailed analysis of how the U.S. press dealt with problems of Indochina from 1975–1978, see volume II of Chomsky and E.S. Herman, *The Political Economy of Human Rights*, South End Press, 1979.

You have brought to our attention the massacres in Timor and the odyssey of the "boat people" from Haiti, particularly in your interview in Change *(no. 38, October 1979). The readers of our journal, which just begins publication, would like to have some information on the topic.*

The Indonesia army invaded the former Portuguese colony of East Timor in December 1975, a few hours after the departure of President Gerald Ford and Henry Kissinger from Jakarta. Beginning immediately and continuing until the present day, a huge massacre has been carried out, with tens and perhaps hundreds of thousands of people killed. Virtually all foreign observers were excluded, even the International Red Cross, until quite recently, though there was ample evidence about the horrors from refugees, letters smuggled out, reports from church sources in Timor and Indonesia, and other sources. At the time of the attack, the Indonesia army was 90 percent-armed by the United States. Contrary to false testimony by government witnesses at congressional hearings, the U.S. immediately made new offers of arms. The arms flow increased dramatically under the "Human Rights" administration, enabling Indonesia to undertake new and even more murderous offensives in 1977–78, destroying villages and crop land and driving the remnants of the population to concentration camps, where they continue to starve and die of disease. Now that a few foreigners have been admitted, the facts can no longer be concealed—they were always known to those who chose to know. It is now widely admitted that the situation is comparable to the horrors witnessed on the Thai-Cambodian border.

All of this evoked no protest in the West. The Western powers, primarily the U.S. but also France and others, provided the arms and the diplomatic support to enable Indonesian policies to be carried out to virtually the level of genocide. The press either concealed the facts, or reported State Department lies and Indonesian propaganda, with rare exceptions. When the French foreign minister announced in September 1978 that France would send arms to Indonesia and would protect Indonesia from embarrassment over East Timor in the United Nations, there was little protest in France. On the contrary, when AFP [Agence France Presse] was invited to a press conference on East Timor at the United Nations shortly after, its representative refused to attend on the grounds that people in Paris are not interested in Timor—which is quite true; they were inter-

ested only in atrocities that could be attributed to Communists, not those supported by France. Throughout, there were rare exceptions, but the general pattern reveals **one of the most disgraceful examples of Western support for huge
atrocities in modern history**. It is very revealing to compare the Western reaction with the response to the Communist atrocities in Indochina, during exactly the same period.

The story continues. Indonesia refuses to permit Timorese to escape, except
for a few, mostly ethnic Chinese, who have been able to bribe their way out.
Their reports indicate that starvation and brutal oppression persist, and that the
relief supplies that are finally being admitted are often stolen by the incredibly
corrupt Indonesian military. None of this evokes any protest on the part of the
International Rescue Committee or other similar humanitarians. Indonesia has
been a valued ally ever since the military regime demonstrated its anti-
Communist credentials by presiding over the massacre of many hundreds of
thousands of people in 1965–66, then turning the country into a "paradise for
investors," who are impeded in their plunder of the country's wealth only by the
rapacity and corruption of the leadership. For this reason, the great crusade for
"human rights" must ignore the misery of Timor—or more accurately, must lend
its constant and increasing support to abetting the Indonesian atrocities and vastly extending their scale, while the press searches for evidence of Communist
crimes.

As for Haiti, "boat people" have been fleeing for years from this miserable
and impoverished country that had also been the beneficiary of French and
American attentions for many years. They are fleeing misery and severe repression. Many die in flight. Others reach Florida, where they are often arrested by
government officials and shipped back to Duvalier's tyranny. All of this takes
place, with little mention in the press, at the same time that Vietnam is being
denounced for its role in inciting the flight of the miserable "boat people" and
other refugees. Other refugees have also escaped the notice of American humanitarians: For example, the 200,000 who fled the marauding Burmese army in
April–May 1978, fleeing to Bangladesh; or the 140,000 who fled the Philippines
to Sabah in 1977; or the hundreds of thousands who fled U.S.-supplied Israeli
bombers in Southern Lebanon in 1978 and again in 1979; or the many millions
in Africa. But the victims of Communist tyranny evoke great cries of distress—
though only limited material aid—from Western humanitarians.

*In France the mass media treated with great discretion the short war between China
and Vietnam; the question of so-called aggression was raised, and China was never
clearly denounced as aggressor. It was discretely pointed out that Vietnam perhaps was
being attacked but that it had "asked for it" ... Was there something similar in the
United States and, in your view, why?*

The situation was quite the same in the United States. The reason is simple
enough to discern: China is an ally, "punishing" an enemy.

What was the reaction of the American mass media when the Vietnamese invaded Cambodia? How do you explain the fact that the Pol Pot regime, although accused of genocide, was able to keep its seat in the United Nations principally with the help of the United States?

The U.S. media generally condemned the Vietnamese invasion of Cambodia, but the condemnation was not in general severe, on the grounds that the Pol Pot regime had been so bloody and oppressive. As for the UN, I do not think it is accurate to say that the Pol Pot regime kept its seat "principally with the help of the United States." The ASEAN [Association of Southeast Asian Nations] countries were instrumental in supporting the Pol Pot regime, and many countries that had condemned it bitterly nevertheless opposed the Vietnamese invasion and refused to accept the client regime instituted by Vietnam as a legitimate government.

The Trilateral Commission report on the "crisis of democracy" was discussed in Le Monde Diplomatique. *Was it widely discussed in the United States? What about Guenter Lewy's book?*

The Trilateral Commission report on the "crisis of democracy" and its other reports have been very little discussed in the United States. There was, for example, nothing comparable to the important critical discussion in *Le Monde Diplomatique* that you mention. The report gives a very revealing indication of the attitude of liberal Western elites to "democracy"—namely, that "democracy" is threatened when substantial parts of the population actually involve themselves in defending their rights within the political arena, and that "democracy" can survive only if they are reduced to apathy and passivity so that the natural leaders can rule without impediment. For this reason, it is improper to present the conclusions of the Trilateral Commission to a wide audience.

Guenter Lewy's book did receive substantial publicity, not only in the United States, but also in England (the London *Economist*, for example, described it as a "splendid" work). This is quite understandable. Putting aside the gross distortions of fact and misrepresentation of documents that disfigure this work of "academic scholarship," the book consists of apologetics for American violence and brutality on the grounds that the victims were not "innocent" because they either supported the Vietnamese enemy or failed to dissociate themselves from the "enemy." The book is the counterpart in academic scholarship to such films as *The Deerhunter*. Its importance lies in its contribution to reconstructing the system of beliefs that will be required as the United States attempts to return to its traditional pattern of responses towards radical nationalism in the Third World.

What role does the "cluster Vietnam-Cambodia" play in the ideological reconstruction in the United States? Could you define what you understand for "ideological reconstruction"? What are its historical origins? What place does the ideology of "human rights," the "new morality" preached by President Carter, occupy there? You have spoken in this respect of a "new state religion." Could you state what you understand by that?

Like most other imperial powers, the United States has disguised its depredations as an exercise of benevolence and selfless idealism. For large parts of the population, these illusions were shattered by the war in Indochina. They must be restored. The institutional structure that led to repeated intervention has not changed, so it is only reasonable to suppose that efforts will be made to renew these practices—though objective factors have significantly changed, and will raise barriers that did not exist in earlier years. Any state, whether totalitarian or democratic, must mobilize popular support for its violence and oppression. Therefore, it is necessary to reconstruct the system of beliefs that was severely damaged.

This "reconstruction of ideology" has been proceeding, as was quite predictable, throughout the 1970s. The so-called "Human Rights" campaign has served as a major element in this propaganda campaign. Its significance is revealed clearly in a statement by Arthur Schlesinger, the liberal historian who was "intellectual-in-residence" during the Kennedy administration. He wrote that the human rights campaign was proving a great success: "In effect, human rights is replacing self-determination as the guiding value in American foreign policy." He is, in a sense, correct. To the exact extent that self-determination was the guiding value of American foreign policy in the era of Iran, Guatemala, Cuba, the Dominican Republic, Vietnam, etc., "human rights" is now the guiding policy, as shown, for example, by the vast increase in armaments to Indonesia under the Carter administration, to enable Indonesia to conduct its massacre in Timor. As already noted, suffering and atrocities in Indochina have been exploited to the extent possible in this process of reconstruction of ideology. I would not call this a "new state religion"; rather, it is a new phase in the traditional state religion.

What resonance does this policy find in the American intelligentsia? What is the influence and the real range of a phenomenon such as the "neo-conservatives"? In an article published by the West German weekly, Die Zeit, *on Jan. 1, 1980, George F. Kennan writes concerning this: "Those 'neo-conservatives' were before, in great part, liberals who tended to keep their distance regarding the explosions of American chauvinism. However, after the Middle East War of 1973, and for reasons that escape me, they have become, with respect to the question of American-Soviet relations, fanatic hawks." What do you think of this evaluation?*

The "new conservatism" is a reflection of the liberal imperialist ideology that has dominated for many years, and of its incapacity to offer solutions to the increasingly severe domestic and international problems that have arisen in an era when American dominance of the international system has somewhat declined. The differences between "liberals" and "conservatives" should not be exaggerated; they are slight. All are committed to basically the same state capitalist ideology, and to the free exercise of state power to construct a global system in which U.S.-based corporations can operate freely, and in which human and material resources can be exploited for their benefit. But there are slight differences. Compare, for example, the Eisenhower administration ("conservative") and the Kennedy administration ("liberal"). The "liberals" criticized Einsenhower because they wanted a larger state role in the state-capital complex. Thus, they demanded a much larger military establishment (which they quickly constructed) and also a greater involvement of the state in domestic management, which includes generally some mild domestic reforms. It is not unusual for a "liberal" administration to become more active in international violence, for similar reasons. But the differences, again, are not very substantial.

I have not read Kennan's article in *Die Zeit*, but it is quite true that after the 1973 October war there was an outburst of war fever, with substantial liberal participation. For example, Robert Tucker, who was one of the liberal critics of the American war in Indochina, wrote an article offering an elaborate justification for U.S. military intervention in the Persian Gulf region. This was symptomatic of a general reaction. As always, it was framed within the Cold War context outlined earlier; the general pattern is for a call for military intervention to be offered in response to an alleged "Soviet threat," which adds a note of credibility to policies designed to ensure that the U.S. will dominate the region. **The real fear**, then as now, was not that the Soviet Union would take over Saudi Arabian oil, but that the enormous petroleum reserves of the Middle East would not be as fully controlled by the U.S. as they have been since the 1940s, when Britain and France were displaced in the region by American power (e.g., when France was excluded from the "Red line" region on the sophisticated grounds that the French companies were "enemies" as a result of Hitler's occupation of France, so that the 1928 agreement on sharing oil was abrogated). In the thinking of many "conservatives," Europe is a more dangerous potential "enemy" than the USSR (though, again, every move to increase U.S. dominance will be justified by the "Russian threat"). For example, when Henry Kissinger announced the "Year of Europe" in 1973 he warned against "the prospects of a closed trading system embracing the European Community and a growing number of other nations in Europe, the Mediterranean, and Africa," from which the U.S. might be excluded; his conception of "cooperation" between Europe and the U.S. was based on the principle that the U.S. is concerned "with the overall framework of order" while the European powers are limited to "regional interests." Similar concerns are no doubt being felt with increasing severity today. There are other factor too, for example, the complex relation between "support of Israel" (which mounted dramatically after Israel demonstrated its military power in 1967) and a more militaristic stance internationally. But these matters are too intricate to treat here.

This array of campaigns brings to mind the role of the media. In the interview in Change *you don't hesitate to say that "compared to the American system, the system of the Third Reich was poor and naive in its propaganda." Of course, neither for you nor for us is it a question of identifying the United States' nazism. But could you explain the reasons which, in the domain of manipulation of public opinion, lead you to such a formulation?*

My point was that the system of thought control that has been developed in the U.S. (and to a large degree throughout the world of capitalist democracy) is much more subtle than the propaganda systems of the totalitarian states, but quite possibly more effective. In a totalitarian state, the official propaganda agencies produce official truth blatantly and overtly; one must simply obey, or take the risk, which is often great, of dissenting. In the American system, debate is encouraged within a certain framework of presuppositions, sometimes articulated, sometimes not even expressed. The more intense the debate, the more effectively the presuppositions—which embody the state religion—are insinuated.

For example, the most extreme critics of the American war in Indochina within the media argue that the war began as a "blundering effort to do good," that the bombing of Cambodia, "however sincerely intended," was a disaster (Anthony Lewis of the *New York Times*), etc. Similarly, though the American media correctly refer to the Russian invasion of Afghanistan as "an invasion," and reject with ridicule the pretense that the Soviet Union was simply responding to the call of the legitimate government for support against foreign-based attack, they never referred to the U.S. invasion of Vietnam as "an invasion" and they accepted with virtually no question the claim by the U.S. government that it was responding to the call of the legitimate government for support against foreign-based attack.

I have given a great number of illustrations in various publications which reveal, I believe, a very systematic pattern: debate takes place, indeed is encouraged, within a certain system of assumptions. If one challenges these assumptions, one is simply excluded from the debate as "irresponsible" or "anti-American" or "emotional," etc.; these are the characteristic charges leveled against someone who suggests that U.S. foreign policy, like that of other powers, is dominated by the material interests of groups that control the domestic economy, rather than being a unique exercise in benevolence, occasionally misguided; or against someone who discusses the extensive documentary record of high level planning, always ignored in the media and academic scholarship, which lays bare the real motives for U.S. aggression in Indochina; and so on. Such people are not sent to concentration camps, but they have virtually no access to the public. My own experience is typical. For example, books of mine on international affairs can be reviewed in academic journals or the mass media in Canada or Europe, but this is a virtual impossibility in the United States, since I do not accept the doctrines of the state religion.

Again, in a complex society not subject to state management one can find exceptions, but they are extremely rare, and the system has created **the illusion of free and open debate** while in fact ensuring that only a narrow spectrum of opinion and analysis reaches a broad public. In addition, of course, there is the matter of outright suppression of fact: e.g., the long suppression and deceit concerning Timor, the suppression by the media of the U.S. bombing of the civilian society of northern Laos for a long period, the suppression until today of the quite explicit rejection by Nixon and Kissinger of the "scrap of paper" they signed in Paris in January 1973, and many other examples that I have discussed at considerable length.

You are an exceptional witness for us because you know France also well. Don't you have the impression of witnessing a sort of "Americanization" of the French media? Isn't the misadventure you experienced with your letter to Nouvel Observateur, *among others, a typical symptom of this evolution?*

I don't feel qualified to comment on the possible "Americanization" of the French media. My acquaintance with them is not sufficiently thorough. As for the incident with *Nouvel Observateur* that you cite—namely, the rewriting by the editor of a letter of mine to make my views conform to his ideological needs of the moment, suppressing my criticism of the Pol Pot regime while claiming that I was refusing to criticize it—it would not be fair to refer to that example of petty deceit as "Americanization." I have seen nothing like it in the United States. In the American journal that is perhaps most similar to *Nouvel Observateur*, namely, the *New Republic*, dishonest editorial practices are standard; for example, the editor devoted a column to a vicious personal attack on me for my alleged views on Cambodia, referring to gossip that he claimed to have heard in Paris, and did not permit me to publish a letter in response, even after he was provided with documentation that demonstrated conclusively that his charges were baseless. But again, I do not think that "Americanization" is a fair term for these practices. I have never encountered them, for example, in the conservative press. Those, in my opinion, are the practices of the statist liberals, the same group who move so easily from Leninist apologetics to apologetics for some other favored state, usually their own (though for the *New Republic*, Israel now plays this role more than any other state).

Do you think that the press is a "fourth power" in France?

Again, I do not feel competent to comment on the situation in France. There is no doubt that for many years *Le Monde* has been an extremely distinguished journal, perhaps unparalleled in the world. I do not think, however, that the "independent press" has ever been anything like a "fourth power" anywhere in the world, surely not in the United States.

How did the press, the media and the American intelligentsia react to a phenomenon such as the popular victory in Nicaragua? Is it perceived as a threat? In a recent interview, published in France by L'Humanité-Dimanche, *Gabriel García Márquez appears very confident regarding the prospects of the democratic and revolutionary currents. What do you think of that? What effect can the reinforcement of these currents produce in the United States?*

The American media reacted cautiously to the overthrow of Somoza. They did not, in general, respond with anti-revolutionary hysteria. Nor did the U.S. government. By the end of Somoza's rule, it was obvious that he was opposed by virtually all circles in Nicaragua, including the business circles that are the natural allies of the U.S. and that are typically favored in press reports of foreign affairs. As for the prospects in Nicaragua, a certain degree of optimism seems reasonable today, but if the U.S. business interests are threatened, I would expect the U.S. government and media reaction to be negative. If there are moves towards authentic democratic and libertarian socialism, I would expect that both superpowers would be hostile, for reasons already mentioned.

Mr. Chomsky, in the writings by you that we recently read, you do not appear to us to be pessimistic or in despair, in spite of the seriousness of the phenomena you describe. What does justify that lucid and reasoned optimism? Do you believe, in particular, that the return to the Cold War is inevitable?

I am not particularly optimistic, and am a little surprised that I sound optimistic. As for the Cold War, I think it is a very stable system, the basic reason being the one I already mentioned: it is highly functional for the superpowers, despite its dangers, in offering a framework within which they can employ harsh measures, violence if necessary, within the domains they take to be their own. Moves towards true independence in Europe would be regarded as a serious threat to this system by both superpowers, in my opinion. I think that the risks of a major war in coming years are not slight. There is a real crisis of resources, particularly energy, but not energy alone. Serious conflicts are likely to develop over access to and control of vital resources, with an extraordinarily dangerous potential. It is quite likely that the industrialized powers will try to prevent significant economic development—surely, independent development—in the Third World. Local conflicts, of which there are many, can rapidly escalate because of the awesome power of contemporary weaponry and because they become entangled, so quickly, in the matrix of resource crises and other conflicts over domination and control. It does not seem to me at all obvious that **human civilization** will survive until the 21st century. The maxim that I consciously try to follow is Gramsci's: "pessimism of the intelligence, optimism of the will." I do not find it easy to observe this reasonable principle in the current period.

Editor's Notes to Interview 16

This answer was written on April 8, 1981, for "LTV informational ad program," and was to be included in an advertisement which was "scheduled to appear in nine different business-oriented magazines," according to the information in Chomsky's files. It first appeared without the sentences before "Typically" in several of the magazines, including *Business Week* (Oct. 12, 1981) and *Smithsonian* (Oct. 1981, following p. 142). After the author protested, the original version (except for the omission of the word "solemnly" and the replacement of "and so on and on" for "etc.") was substituted (see, e.g., *Time*, Nov. 30 1981, pp. 4–5).

Each ad is captioned at the top with "LTV. Looking ahead." The title is "What is America's responsibility for the rest of the world? Sadat vs one of America's brilliant educators." The rest is made up of four contributions: Sadat's, titled "Accept Responsibility"; Chomsky's, titled "No Responsibility"; "What the Public Thinks," reported by Kenneth Schwartz, vice president, Opinion Research Corporation; "What LTV Believes," by Paul Thayer, chairman of the board and CEO, who remarks that "defense technology is only one part of LTV's business, but one we take pride in as an instrument through which we help the nation meet its commitments in the continuing struggle for freedom." (The other three parts are steel, energy and ocean shipping.) According to the book quoted below, this was a second advertising campaign by LTV with involvement in political issues. It ran between April 1981 and February 1982, and it cost approximately $2.5 million, with the highest number of inserts appearing in the *Wall Street Journal* (14) and *Barron's* (10). (The first campaign, which had run in 1980, had begun with an ad with statements from ten presidential candidates, including Reagan). "America's defense responsibility for the rest of the world" was the last of the six issues included in the second campaign.

LTV [formerly Ling-Temco-Vought Aerospace] Corp. of Dallas, the result of a December 1978 merger which was then the biggest in U.S. business history, had generated up to $8 billion in annual sales when Thayer, a former fighter pilot ace (during World War II), resigned as CEO in 1983 to serve as second-in-command in the Pentagon (Caspar Weinberger's right-hand man), after serving a one-year term as chairman of the U.S. Chamber of Commerce. He had been at the Pentagon for barely a year when he unexpectedly resigned on Jan. 4, 1984. The next day, the Securities and Exchange Commission, in one of the biggest cases ever pursued to that point, accused Thayer of passing along confidential information about proposed acquisitions by two corporations of which he was director to his stockbroker and seven other friends and associates, who then traded in the stocks. For months the former deputy secretary of defense maintained he was innocent, but he eventually pleaded guilty to obstruction of justice in the stock trading deal and was sentenced to four years in prison and fined $5,000. He was released after serving 19 months, in December 1986 (*Los Angeles Times*, July 5, 1987, IV, p. 5). On May 14, 1987, he agreed to pay the two companies nearly $600,000 as part of a settlement of a two-year-old, $250 million damage suit against him and eight other defendants (the *New York Times*, May 15, 1987, IV, p. 16; see also, in the same issue, "The Presidency: Espousing 'High Morality,' Living with Scandal").

LTV is said to hold "a unique place in that it is the only company that has dared to provide a paid communication format which presents alternative view-points and expert opinions—some opposed by the company, and even contrary to its immediate interests—on issues the company considers important to itself and to the national public policy" (presumably in that order—see Appendix to this selection). This "unique approach" was part of an attempt to change the public image of the corporation after its senior executives realized that they had "rather severe communication problems"; they "needed to achieve a relatively high profile again, but as a responsible, thoughtful company that was one of the leaders in its various industries"—"a forward looking company, interested in public issues." See S. Prakash Sethi, *Handbook of Advocacy Advertising: Concepts, Strategies, and Applications.* Cambridge, MA: Ballinger Publ. Co, a subsidiary of Harper & Row, 1987, p. 115ff.

The Appendix appeared in *Business and Society Review* 25 (Spring 1978), p. 17, under the subheading "Business and Society Review Misses the Point," as one of 17 answers solicited from "a group of leaders and experts" (from Henry Ford II to Karl Hess—Hess proposes the abolition of the corporation). The opening statement by the managing editor includes the following quote from Milton Friedman in the inaugural issue of the review: "There is nothing that would destroy the private enterprise system more than a real acceptance of the social responsibility doctrine." The "symposium" appears to have been a reaction to the scandals of the time; boxes with excerpts on "corporate social cruelty" from the *Wall Street Journal* (March 24, 1978) and "corporate social monstrosity," "corporate social bribery," and "corporate social perjury," from the *New York Times* (Dec, 13, Feb. 27, March 21, 1978), accompany the answers.

On the beneficial role of the state in a capitalist society, see Karl Polanyi, *The Great Transformation: The Political and Economic Origins of Our Time.* Boston: Beacon, 1957 (originally published in 1944).

16. U.S. Defense Responsibility? (8 April 1981)

I am asked "to address the subject of U.S. defense responsibility for the rest of the world and why America need not perpetuate this role." The question is unanswerable; there is no such role. States use their power to defend "the national interest," a mystification devised to conceal the special interests of those with domestic power. Typically, this policy is disguised in high-sounding rhetoric, which we dismiss with contempt when the official enemy "defends freedom and socialism" by sending tanks to Berlin, Budapest, Prague or Kabul, while solemnly reciting it when our own state acts in a similar way.

When the U.S. Air Force began the systematic bombardment of rural South Vietnam in 1962, it was defending those who were concerned over the "domino effect" of a successful nationalist-Communist revolution that might be emulated elsewhere. The aggression was masked as defense against "internal aggression" by Vietnamese—indeed, South Vietnamese. In 1947, Truman announced that the U.S. would "support free people who are resisting attempted subjugation by armed minorities or by outside pressures," specifically, the Greek royalist elites and Nazi collaborators restored to power by the British army, by then unable to repress the rebellion caused largely by British-backed terrorism. The U.S. proceeded to defend the Greeks from "internal aggression" by supervising a program of massive repression, tens of thousands of political prisoners and exiles, political executions, re-education camps, forced population removal, etc., exactly as any rational person reading the Truman doctrine would have predicted. In this case too what was feared was the domino effect. When the U.S. backed an invasion force in Guatemala in 1954, overthrowing a mildly reformist democratic government and installing a regime whose descendants still administer a huge reign of terror, it was defending "the national interest" but nothing else. The same is true of the destruction of the peasant society of northern Laos, the arming of mass murderers in Indonesia and El Salvador, and on and on.

In each case, the propaganda system invokes the threat of the superpower enemy, exactly as the USSR does. The Cold War has been highly functional for the superpowers, providing each with a framework for carrying out its designs within the reach of its power. Hence its persistence, despite the threat of mutual annihilation.

The world, however, is not what it once was. The relative decline of Soviet and American power brings forth new and increasingly assertive rivals. The EEC [European Economic Community] is moving slowly towards a more independent role, which may engage it in conflict with the U.S. in the Middle East and elsewhere. Similarly, Japan: Before long, pursuit of "the national interest" may require new programs, new forms of violence and terror, and new rhetoric.

Appendix: Corporate Social Responsibility? (Spring 1978)

Is corporate social responsibility a dead issue?

I'm afraid that I cannot discuss the question as put, because I do not accept some of its presuppositions, specifically with regard to the legitimacy of corporate power. Suppose, for example, that I were to ask, with regard to some political oligarchy, whether or how such centralized power might be exercised in a more "socially responsible" way. The point is that such concentration of power is illegitimate in the first place; and what is more, whatever doctrine anyone proposes, it will be used for the benefit of those who wield it, primarily. Apart from random exceptions, they will act in a socially responsible way—as benevolent despots—when social strife, disorder, protest, etc., induce them to do so for their own benefit. The situation is not materially different when we turn to the economic domain. I see no more justification for concentration of private power here than in the political domain, or any reason to expect it to be differently employed.

In a true capitalist society, if such an object were to exist, socially responsible behavior would be penalized quickly in that competitors, lacking such social responsibility, would supplant anyone so misguided as to be concerned with something other than private benefit. In a real capitalist society with only limited competition and substantial state control, as is and always has been required to safeguard social existence in the face of the destructive forces of private capitalism, it is possible for those who have concentrated power in their hands to be more or less benevolent in its use. But the central questions seem to me to be the ones that I have just mentioned, which are not addressed, but rather begged in this inquiry.

Editor's Notes to Interview 17

The three questions answered here were submitted by *Commentary* to a number of people as part of a symposium on "Human Rights and American Foreign Policy." Chomsky's answers, which are enlightening to compare with those of the other 17 respondents (William Barrett, Peter L. Berger, Zbigniew Brzezinski, Midge Decter, Richard Falk, Nathan Glazer, Oscar Handlin, Sidney Hook, Jeane Kirkpatrick, Max Lerner, Seymour Martin Lipset, Charles William Maynes, Eugene J. McCarthy, Robert Nisbet, Michael Novak, Martin Peretz and Bayard Rustin), were written on Sept. 21 and appeared in vol. 72, #5 (November 1981), pp. 30–32. Nine letters from readers, four of which reply to Chomsky's answers, appeared in vol. 73, #2 (February 1982), pp. 2–10.

Jeane Kirkpatrick's concepts "authoritarian" and "totalitarian" appear to have been suggested by a distinction first made, in identical terms, by Juan Linz (a member of her doctoral dissertation at Columbia) in a study of the Franco regime (for him merely "authoritarian"); Linz, however, does not endorse Kirkpatrick's use of the distinction (personal communication). See Linz, "Totalitarian and Authoritarian Regimes," in Fred I. Greenstein & Nelson Polsby (eds.), *Handbook of Political Science*, vol. 3 (macropolitical theory). Reading: Addison-Wesley, 1975, pp. 175–411; cf. Juan Martínez Alier, "Notas Sobre el Franquismo," Papers: *Revista de Sociología 8* (1978), pp. 27–51, an integrated revision of two articles which appeared earlier (1975) in *Cuadernos de Ruedo Ibérico*, the important journal published for many years in Paris by the late José Martínez, a truly outstanding anti-fascist publisher and activist.

On Luiz Inacio da Silva ("Lula"), leader of the Brazilian Workers Party (PT) and since October 2002 President of Brazil, see I53, including the Editor's Notes.

17. Human Rights and American Foreign Policy
(21 September 1981)

What role, if any, should a concern for human rights play in American foreign policy? Is there a conflict between this concern and the American national interest?

We take the trouble to consider the question because we believe we can influence American foreign policy. The question then translates into a more realistic one: Should we attempt to influence this policy in the direction of concern for human rights, or should we renounce any such concern, thus abandoning foreign policy to other concerns such as the climate for business operations and control over resources? Properly put, the question reduces to this: Do we care about the human consequences of our actions (or inactions)? violence a social phenomenon

Acting as individuals, most people are not gangsters. Matters are often different when they subordinate themselves to institutional structures of various sorts, such as corporations or the national state. We regard it as wrong, indeed pathological, to steal food from a starving child. But we engage in such behavior on a massive scale without second thought when the act is disguised in terms of high policy. For example, when U.S. power is employed to overthrow a moderate regime in Guatemala that is attempting to improve the lot of miserable peasants, replacing it by a successor devoted to export-oriented agriculture while tens of thousands starve and most of the work force labors under the conditions of semi-slavery (that is, those who survive the death squads run by the regimes placed and maintained in power by the United States). As individuals, we abhor terrorism and torture, but we participate in them—willingly or blindly, depending on our degree of sophistication—insofar as we tolerate the contribution of the United States to the plague of terror and torture that has spread over Latin America (and not there alone) in the past several decades. A substantial part of political discourse is devoted to obscuring such simple facts as these. If we care about the human consequences of what we do or fail to do, if we accept the most elementary moral principles, then we will attempt to influence state policy towards a concern for human rights.

One of the devices used to obscure plain facts is the concept of "national interest," a mystification that serves to conceal the ways in which state policy is formed and executed. Within the nation, there are individuals and groups who have interests, often conflicting ones; furthermore, such groups do not observe national boundaries. Within a particular nation-state, some groups are sufficiently powerful to exert a major, perhaps dominant influence over state policy *neopluralism*

and the ideological system. Their special interests then become, in effect, "the national interest." To take again the case of Guatemala, in 1954 the United Fruit Company had an interest in blocking land reform; I did not. In subsequent years, other corporations and national security managers had an interest in enhancing state terrorism, for example, by contributing to the violent repression of 1966–68; I did not. What was "the national interest"? In practice, it was the special interest of those with power to influence and execute state policy and to shape the basic structure of the ideological system, including the flow of information.

Occasionally, one can discern something that might be called a "national interest," for example, the shared interest in avoiding a nuclear holocaust. In general, however, the concept is invoked as one part of **a system of disguising reality**, an important task since, again, most people are not gangsters and will act to modify abhorrent policies if they come to understand the facts and their real significance.

Discussion at this level of abstraction provides only the most general guidelines for policy. In practice, there is generally a network of conflicting interests, values and interpretations. Suppose that a concern for human rights does come into conflict with some shared interest of most Americans. The questions that then arise are in principle no different from those we face as individuals: How do we act, for example, when the interests of a starving child conflict with our desire for a scrap of food he possesses? Sometimes the questions are not so simple, and a concern for the human consequences of our actions does not dictate a straightforward conclusion. But it is impossible to deal with these real and substantive questions at the level of abstraction at which the question is posed.

Does the distinction between authoritarianism and totalitarianism seem important to you? If so, what follows from it in practice? If not, what distinctions would you make in judging and dealing with non-democratic regimes?

The standard terminology of political discourse is nebulous and pliable, but not useless. This is true of the concepts "authoritarian" and "totalitarian." The authoritarian regime has been defined as one whose "leaders do not rule by terror, but by that mixture of severity and benevolence that characterize the patriarchal family" (Ralf Dahrendorf, whose example is pre-World War I Imperial Germany);[1] while the "decisive characteristic" of the totalitarian regime is "that a police power ... enjoying unlimited discretionary powers could take 'preventive' action also against persons who at most were suspected of possible opposition or infractions," not only "with the external coercive measures of a dictatorship, but with the creation of ideological and racial policing powers that encroach on every aspect of human life" (Karl Dietrich Bracher, referring to Nazi Germany).[2] In its extreme forms, as the Nazi ideologue Robert Ley stated, "There are no more private citizens. The time when anybody could do or not do what he pleased is past."[3]

But the real world fits poorly into such categories. The terror-and-torture states of Latin America, which are merely "authoritarian" according to contemporary theology, satisfy most of the standard criteria for "totalitarianism"—for example, those formulated by Carl Friedrich[4]—though not all: they do not, for example, attempt to develop mass support but rather rely on violence to subjugate the mass of the population. Brazil is "authoritarian," but labor is regulated by decrees that copy Mussolini's fascist legislation,[5] and those who sell their blood for export or who advertise their kidneys and eyes for sale in a desperate effort to survive,[6] like the peasants and slum dwellers of "authoritarian" societies quite generally, are hardly more able to "do what they please" than citizens of totalitarian states. One can only regard with amazement Jeane Kirkpatrick's solemn assurance that "because the miseries of traditional life are familiar, they are bearable to ordinary people ..."[7] Similarly, South Africa is officially registered as "authoritarian," but for the large majority of its population—for example, the millions now being forcibly removed to "native homelands" where they can starve without interference by the state[8]—it is among the most vicious of existing regimes. Furthermore, the claim that totalitarian societies never develop democratizing tendencies (Kirkpatrick) is plainly false, as the history of the Soviet empire clearly shows.

To take the most recent case, the *Economist* notes that in Poland "a totalitarian state has been turned into one that is now more pluralistic than most countries in the world." In contrast, Lech Walesa would be lucky to survive for a day in Guatemala or Argentina; and, we may add, if he were to be treated in the manner of his counterpart Luis Ignacio da Silva ("Lula") in currently more liberal Brazil, there would be an international outcry, notably lacking in the latter case. Democratizing tendencies in the Soviet empire have regularly been aborted by external force. If that proves the Kirkpatrick thesis, then one can similarly "prove" that autocratic regimes of Central America are incapable of evolving democratic tendencies, as shown by the regular U.S. intervention to suppress them.

While the concepts "authoritarian" and "totalitarian" may have some analytic value in their earlier usage, the current revival is merely an attempt to provide a fig leaf for the traditional policy of supporting regimes that offer their human and material resources for foreign exploitation and plunder, as distinct from those that are less "free" in this crucial respect. This distinction is a real and significant one, but it plainly will not do to state it openly and honestly. Hence the need for some pretentious verbiage to obscure the facts.

Whatever validity the analytic categories may have, the **policy implications** are slight. Furthermore, there is no reason to limit ourselves to non-democratic regimes in considering policy implications. In the case of any regime, we should inquire into the consequences of our actions with regard to it. Israel is a democracy, but that fact does not remove the need to determine what the effect of the unprecedented U.S. military and economic support will be for those suffering mounting repression under the military occupation, or for the victims of Israeli attacks in Lebanon in the past years. Suppose that Argentina carries its mimicry of the Nazis to the point of sending Jews to death camps. It will still be "authoritarian," but will it merit our support on these grounds? If support for totalitarian Hungary or Vietnam would reinforce democratic tendencies or reduce human misery (for which we bear overwhelming responsibility, in the latter case), then it is justified. The real policy questions escape the categories "authoritarian" and "totalitarian," and are not restricted to non-democratic regimes.

Does the approach of the Reagan administration, to the extent that it can be inferred from statements of the president and other high officials, compare favorably or unfavorably with the Carter administration's human rights policy?

One should be cautious about speaking of "the Carter administration's human rights policy." As the record amply demonstrates, the Carter administration lent its full support to aggression and massacre (e.g., in Timor), and to brutal tyrants such as the Shah and Somoza even well after the natural allies of the United States (in the latter case, the Nicaraguan business community) turned against them. There are numerous other examples.

The motivation for the human rights rhetoric was transparent: it was necessary to reconstruct a battered ideology, the traditional appeal to "American benevolence" and "Wilsonian ideals of self-determination" having lost its power to delude, apart from well-behaved segments of the intelligentsia. Nevertheless, **this rhetoric had its value.** It helped create a climate in which people concerned for human rights, including Latin American priests, members of Congress and others, could act, sometimes effectively, in support of significant human values. It is therefore natural that the Reagan administration should have been greeted with enthusiasm by Latin American dictators, South African fascists, and the like. They recognized that the limited barriers to state terrorism posed by U.S. policy in the early post-Vietnam period would be lifted as Reagan and his cohorts undertook their programs of alms for the wealthy, development of what is in effect the state sector of the economy under the euphemism of "defense," international confrontation, and in general, the pursuit of the "national interest" as defined by those with power and privilege. Space does not permit elaboration of the likely consequences, but perhaps they are obvious enough.

Notes

1. Ralph Dahrendorf, *Society and Democracy in Germany*, Weidenfeld and Nicolson, 1968, p. 63.
2. Karl Dietrich Bracher, *The German Dictatorship*, Praeger, 1970, p. 355.
3. Cited in David Schoenbaum, *Hitler's Social Revolution*, Doubleday, 1966, p. 113.
4. For discussion, emphasizing the Cold War backgrounds of the development of the theory of totalitarianism, see Pierre Ayçoberry, *The Nazi Question*, Pantheon, 1981.
5. Cf. Jim Brooke, "Dateline Brazil: Southern Superpower," *Foreign Policy*, Fall 1981.
6. Kenneth Freed, "Desperation: Selling Your Eyes, Kidney," *Los Angeles Times*, Sept. 10, 1981.
7. Jeane Kirkpatrick, "Dictatorships and Double Standards," *Commentary*, November 1979.
8. Gary Thatcher, "South Africa's Archipelago: Where They Put 'Surplus' Blacks," *Christian Science Monitor*, Sept. 14, 1981.

Editor's Notes to Interview 18

The questions below were submitted by a French journalist for an interview which was to appear in the Parisian daily *Liberation*. Chomsky's typewritten answers are dated Oct. 26, 1981. Apparently, these answers were not exactly what the interviewer had in mind, and he did not hesitate to prepare answers more to his liking—which departed radically from the ones he had been sent. Naturally enough, Chomsky did not permit the fabricated answers to appear under his name.

Every attempt to get some other periodical in Paris to publish the original questions together with an honest French translation of Chomsky's answers failed. According to Koerner & Tajima (p. 175—see also pp. 135–6, p. 159), a translation (they do not specify into which language) appeared in *Manadsbulletin*—presumably, *Manedsbulletin*—(Copenhagen) #64–65 (March 1982). An excerpt in French appeared in CPCA [*Centre de Propagande et de Culture Anarchiste*] 16, Avril–Mai–June 1982, pp. 17–20—an excerpt which is reprinted in **EP** (1984), pp. 178–82. A complete (and honest) French translation appears in **RI** (April 1984), pp. 31–58, followed by a "Complément à l'interview non publiée" (pp. 59–88).

In this appendix to the interview Chomsky discusses just two more examples from the extensive "record of lies and deceit" about his "alleged views," a record in which "the very basis for discussion—a minimal respect for fact and logic—has been virtually abandoned," as he says in his answer to the eighth question below. The first part of the discussion (pp. 60–65) is adapted from a letter he wrote on Feb. 28, 1982 to the French linguist Jean-Claude Milner, which concluded: "It is plain and obvious that what you wrote is simply based on false factual claims with regard to my views and writings, and on the remarkable assumption that Faurisson's freedom of expression has at no point been menaced. The honest response would be for you to publicly withdraw these slanders." The second part (pp. 66–87) is adapted from a letter Chomsky wrote on Dec. 2, 1981 to Gérard Chaliand, who had sent him a copy of his review of volume I of **PEHR** (1979). The letter concluded: "I could continue with further examples, but surely this is enough, more than enough. I have been writing to you on the assumption that fact and logic matter, recognizing that it is a highly dubious assumption in this case. I hope that you will prove me wrong, but given the record, it would be naive indeed to expect it." To the best of my knowledge, there has been no honest response and Chomsky has not been proven wrong. I should add that in less trying times both Milner and Chaliand had had good things to say about Chomsky, who is quoted on the back cover of Chaliand's *Mythes Révolutionnaires du Tiers Monde* (Seuil, 1976) and on the front cover of its English translation (Penguin 1978).

In addition, **RI** includes Chomsky's unpublished letters to *Matin de Paris* (dated Dec. 27, 1979) in response to an article by Jacques Attali and Bernard-Henri Lévy they published on Dec. 17, 1979; to *Le Monde* (dated Jan. 14, 1981) in response to Paul Thibaud's article of Dec. 31, 1980; and to *Nouvelles Littéraires* (dated Oct. 26, 1982) in response to an article they published on Sept. 16, 1982. It also includes facsimiles of the mutilated version of the Oct. 26, 1982 letter that was published in *Nouvelles Littéraires* (Dec. 2–8 1982) and of the article by Attali and Lévy. See also "Chomsky et l'Intelligentsia Française" (including "Chomsky et les Faussaires") in **EP** (Mars 1984), pp. 174–88. Cf. I32 and the Editor's Notes, I45, and n. 8 of the Introduction.

For an update of **PEHR** (1979) on Cambodia, see **ChR** (1987), 289ff. For a concise and clear presentation in English of his part in the so-called "Faurisson affair," purportedly a reaction to the fact that Chomsky—like hundreds of other people (he was the only one singled out)—signed a petition in favor of Faurisson's "safety and free exercise of his civil rights," see Chomsky's "His Right to Say It," The Nation, Feb. 28, 1981, pp. 231–35 (reprinted in the Australian journal *Social Alternatives 2:3* (1982), with a preliminary note by Greg George and Drew Hutton). An enlightening review of the whole campaign against Chomsky by Christopher Hitchens appeared in *Grand Street 5:1* (1985), pp. 106–31, later reprinted in C.P. Otero, ed., *Noam Chomsky: Critical Assessments*. vol. III, pp. 401–421. The article by Chomsky that triggered the whole exercise (unintendedly serving as a litmus test for the degree of commitment to freedom of a good number of intellectuals, particularly in the "City of Lights") was first published in English in **CD&E** (2003), as an appendix to ch. 6 ("Two Conceptions of Social Organization"). Its title says it all: "Some Elementary Comments on the Rights of Freedom of Expression."

Chomsky was not much surprised at the French reaction to the petition. His reasons were reported by Carl Oglesby in *Boston Magazine* (Dec. 1981, pp. 130 and 132–4): "For one thing, France does not have a civil-libertarian tradition of the Anglo-Saxon variety. For another thing, there simply is a totalitarian strain among large segments of the French intelligentsia. Marxism-Leninism and Stalinism, for example, were much more viable and significant doctrines among the French than in England or the United States. What's called the Left, especially in France, has a large segment that is deeply authoritarian." (Cf. the section "Justice vs Power" in my Introduction, particularly the references to the Jacobins and insurrectionists and to Foucault.) Many "love to march in step." And they do so because of a guilty conscience, "a piercing guilt over the disgraceful attitude of some of them under the Vichy regime, the lack of protest against the French war in Indochina, the permanent impact of Stalinism and Leninist-type doctrines, the peculiar and Dadaist character of certain currents of intellectual life in postwar France which turns rational discourse into a bizarre and incomprehensible pastime." (Compare the quote below.) It perhaps should be added that the Italian resistance to the Nazi army provides an instructive standard for comparison and contrast with what the French accomplished.

The major international campaign orchestrated against Chomsky on completely false pretexts was only part—though perhaps a crucial part—of the ambitious campaign launched in the late 70s with the hope of reconstructing the ideology of power and domination which had been partially exposed during the Indochina war. The magnitude of the insane attack against Chomsky, which aimed at silencing him and robbing him of his moral stature and his prestige and influence, is of course one more tribute to the impact of his writings and his actions—not for nothing he was the only one singled out. In retrospect it is perhaps clear even to the more obtuse among his detractors that it was a serious miscalculation on the part of its perpetrators. It might have even had one beneficial effect: His commitment and productivity have, if anything, multiplied in the 1980s—in less than a decade he has published thousands of pages, many of them among his best, while continuing to give numerous talks and participate in other political actions. Recall his reaction to the advancing line of soldiers during the demonstrations of October 1967: "When that grotesque organism began slowly advancing—more grotesque because its cells were recognizable human beings— it became obvious that one could not permit that thing to dictate what one was going to do" ("On Resistance," reprinted in **AP** (1969)—the quote appears on p. 373).

Assuming that degree of commitment and range of creativity are significant indices, it should also be instructive to compare Chomsky's contribution as a thinker and as an activist to that of his detractors one by one or taken all together. What is particularly ironic in the context of the Faurisson affair is that it was not the self-appointed defenders of the French cultural heritage that came to see the significance of some of France's greatest contributions to civilization—in particular Descartes' "first cognitive revolution," which in part reemerges in the epoch-making libertarian strain in Rousseau's social thought. It was Chomsky, who is also the one who brought the new understanding to the attention of people all over the world; for a few years he even had to compete with the heavy promotion of the "nouveaux philosophes" and the "nouvelle cuisine," presented as the best Paris had to offer at the time. What is more, he unveiled the uniqueness of Cartesianism, which in an important sense had gone unrecognized until then (see C.P. Otero, Review of Fred d'Agostino's *Chomsky's System of Ideas*, in *Mind & Language 3:3*, Autumn 1988, reprinted in *Noam Chomsky: Critical Assessments*, ed. by C.P. Otero, London: Routledge, 1994, vol. 2), in the years in which peculiar currents of intellectual life in postwar France were indulging in the most "bizarre and incomprehensible pastime." As he wrote in a letter dated June 30, 1980 (see also **L&M** (1968/72), chapter 3, text corresponding to notes 7–10):

> "French intellectual life has, in my opinion, been turned into something cheap and meretricious by the 'star' system. It is something like Hollywood. Thus we go from one absurdity to another—Stalinism, existentialism, structuralism, Lacan, Derrida— some of them obscene (Stalinism), some simply infantile and ridiculous (Lacan and Derrida). What is striking, however, is the pomposity and self-importance, at each stage."

See C.P. Otero, "Chomsky vs Foucault: Pursue Justice or Grab Power?," (UCLA ms., 1999), to be included in *Chomsky, The Masters of Mankind*, ed. by Mark Pavlick. Monroe, Maine: Common Courage Press (forthcoming).

The question about being secretary of state comes up again in I23.

For the source of the quote at the end, see **AP** (1969), p. 19; see also, Rocker, *Nationalism and Culture* (written by 1933—see Introduction), I:iv. The final paragraph of the interview brings to mind a paragraph from Rocker's *The London Years* (London: Robert Anscombe, 1956, p. 145): "Freedom is never attained; it must always be striven for. Consequently its claims have no limit, and can neither be enclosed in a program nor prescribed as a definite rule for the future. Each generation must face its own problems, which cannot be forestalled or provided for in advance. The worst tyranny is that of ideas which have been handed down to us, allowing no development in ourselves, and trying to steam-roller everything to one flat universal level."

18. The Treachery of the Intelligentsia: A French Travesty (16 October 1981)

When one reads you, one has the feeling that the image of today's world you have is quite close to Orwell's 1984. On one side, a massive and repressive totalitarianism which doesn't hide its face, or whose face is easy to unmask (the USSR); on the other, a decentralized, subtle and crafty totalitarianism which gives the appearance, but only the appearance, of freedom (the U.S.), and which, in the final analysis, is more dangerous because it succeeds in side-tracking us and making fools of us: liberals of all colors.

I would not use the term "totalitarian" to refer to the American system of **"brainwashing under freedom."** It is, nevertheless, a remarkably effective system, a fact that is rarely recognized, analyzed or understood. Herman and I give many examples. To cite merely one case: In 1962, the U.S. Air Force began large-scale bombardment of rural South Vietnam, proceeding subsequently to full-scale invasion in support of a client regime that Washington knew had no legitimacy. Almost 20 years have passed, and I have never seen a reference in mainstream journalism or scholarship to "U.S. aggression" or the "U.S. invasion of South Vietnam." Rather, the U.S. was "defending" South Vietnam—unwisely, the doves maintain. Perhaps one will be able to say the same about the Soviet press in 20 years, with regard to Afghanistan. This record of subservience to the state propaganda system is particularly noteworthy in that it is achieved without force. The system operates through a complex of inducements, privileges, class interests, etc., relying on the tendency of much of the intelligentsia to conform to power (while proclaiming their courageous independence of mind), and the unwillingness to endure vilification, lies, and denial of the opportunity to work and publish, as punishment for telling the truth.

I imagine that you can easily find analogues in France. How much principled opposition was there to the French attack on Indochina, for example? How much protest has there been over the fact that France is the main supplier of arms to Chile and South Timor, or that, as *Business Week* happily comments, French military forces "help keep West Africa safe for French, American, and other foreign oilmen"? It is much easier to deplore the other fellow's crimes.

Seen from France, your evolution—to the extent that it is perceived this way—is somewhat bothersome, and even a bit old-fashioned. Indeed, in the evolution of ideas in France, people—at least a part of the Leftist intellectuals—are now overcoming the (retrospective) illusion due to the Marxist analysis according to which the so-called formal liberties, those of bourgeois democracy, are not worth anything, and that only those who are naive or members of the ruling class (which are not exclusive terms) can soak in them, while a deep analysis of society, analysis which can only be a Marxist, Marxian or Marxiforme one, reveals, under deceptive appearances, the servitude and at least the alienation generated equally by the hard totalitarianism (without formal freedoms) and by the soft one (with them).

Thus, in a very paradoxical way, your evolution ends up taking a smell of Stalinism completely unforeseen.

The reaction you describe is remarkable. It is obvious that the so-called "libertés formelles" represented an achievement of enormous significance. **The task for the present** is to extend these achievements to new domains, particularly, by placing decision-making over production and distribution in the hands of producers and communities, while dismantling authoritarian structures. The "analyse approfondie" to which you refer is not only extremely superficial, but is also helplessly misguided. The "totalitarisme dure" of the societies that some (not I) call "socialist" does not begin to approach the guarantee of freedom and rights in the industrial democracies, whatever historical reasons one can give for the fact.

Surely this is well-understood among the serious Left in France. Furthermore, in libertarian socialist circles, the true nature of the Soviet regime was obvious from the start, when Lenin and Trotsky destroyed the soviets and factory councils, instituted the "militarization of labor," etc., and indeed was fully expected before. I am often amazed by what I read about this matter in the French literature, not only by ex-Leninists; for example, the ignorant comment of Paul Thibaud that prior to Solzhenitsyn, "toutes les présentations" of "soviétisme" were within a "trotzkysante" framework, or his plea for "un nouvel universalism," a position so elementary that rational people would be embarrassed to express it except, perhaps, in a Sunday school sermon for children.

Contrasting Views of 1968

Continuing in the same vein, this smell of Stalinism is supported by the pessimism which you show, for example, with respect to the role played by American public opinion in bringing the Vietnam War to an end. If public opinion is indefinitely manipulated and manipulatable, as you seem to want to demonstrate, is freedom of expression and, in particular, freedom of the press, worth defending?

My view is entirely different. I believe, and have often written, that the peace movement had an enormous impact on U.S. foreign policy, far more than I ever expected during the early years, when I was being shouted off of platforms and was futilely attempting to organize resistance. The movement was spontaneous, leaderless, courageous, and extremely effective. It had to escape the constraints of the ideological system, and did so. The fact caused great consternation among elite circles over what they saw as a "crisis of democracy" (Michel Crozier,

Samuel Huntington, et al.), in which the public was illegitimately playing a role in public affairs; and also among much of the intelligentsia who were appalled at this display of independence of mind and courageous action, particularly among students. To cite one case, consider Alain Besançon, who describes students in 1968 as "pus" that had to be "squeezed out of the universities," while blacks were "a curse." There is now a major effort to rewrite the history of this period so as to deny the importance of mass political action. If what you describe is a widely-held interpretation of my views, then it is simply a part of this reconstruction of a history more tolerable to elite groups.

This effort at historical reconstruction is notable in France as well. Consider, again, Paul Thibaud, who writes in *Le Monde* that I belonged to that part of the Left that "a confié l'avenir des libertés vietnamiennes à la bonne volontée supposée des dirigeants du Nord" and failed to consider "le fait que la grande majorité de la population du Sud préférait une solution du type 'troisième force', plutôt que de type Vietcong" (a fact unknown to U.S. government specialists, who regarded the NLF [National Liberation Front] as the only mass-based political organization, much to their distress, and dismissed the "third force" as insignificant).

To begin with, this is **sheer fabrication**. I always stressed the obvious fact that U.S. aggression was designed to prevent the development of neutralist options (including those of the "third force"), and warned that the consequences of this aggression would be to "create a situation in which, indeed, North Vietnam will necessarily dominate Indochina, for no other viable society will remain" (1969). More interesting, however, is Thibaud's belief that an opponent of U.S. aggression must have been a supporter of Hanoi. A perfect victim of the U.S. propaganda system, Thibaud repeated this absurd claim, which was, of course, designed to deflect attention from the U.S. attack against the rural society of South Vietnam, where 80 percent of the population lived. Had Thibaud bothered to look at the writings of mine that he discusses, he would know that it was precisely the attack against the South that I most insistently condemned, noting the obvious consequences, which have in fact ensued. He will not find a word to support his false and ignorant charges, but to the true believer it is simply inconceivable that one can oppose U.S. aggression exactly as one opposes Soviet aggression, or reject the official doctrine that the war was a conflict between the U.S. and North Vietnam.

More Widely Read Than in the 60s

Even when I read you, I have the feeling that the pessimism of your analysis raises questions about the usefulness of your book. Supposing that there are minds that are free enough to read you, the implacable mechanisms that you describe will only make impotent and isolated poor souls of them.

Quite the contrary. In fact, our books are more widely read than those I wrote at the height of the Vietnam War. Contrary to what is often assumed,

American public opinion has shifted away from the blind conformism of earlier years. Compare Vietnam and El Salvador. The U.S. intervention in El Salvador is about at the level of Vietnam in 1960. The level of protest, however, is reminiscent of 1966–67, when hundreds of thousands of U.S. troops had invaded South Vietnam. And it has been effective in imposing some barriers to U.S. support for state terrorism in El Salvador.

So I want to ask you: Who is the book addressed to and what effect do you expect?

These books are written for people who want to understand the social reality in which they live. We hope that the effect will be to aid those who are attempting to maintain the "crisis of democracy" and specifically, to bring about fundamental changes in U.S. foreign policy. And there are many of them. I cannot possibly accept a fraction of the invitations I receive to speak about these subjects, although most of the journals are closed.

A Vigorous Defense of "Bourgeois Freedoms"

How do you reconcile your pessimism with the intransigent defense of freedom of expression that you preached elsewhere?

It should be unnecessary to stress that freedom of expression should always be defended with vigor and commitment. In fact, the "bourgeois freedoms" that are often derided by people who regard themselves as "on the left" are precisely what allowed the major mass movements to develop in the U.S., despite the efforts of political and intellectual elites to contain them, and despite a considerable amount of state terrorism, directed particularly against the blacks who were such a "curse," but against many others too.

In this respect, although my opinions as interviewer are without interest or consequences, to fill the distance that separates us (in writing), allow me to interpolate here that I very much liked the article of yours that ended up as a preface to Thion's book on the Faurisson affair and that I approve of it without reservation.

Thank you for your comments. Perhaps I should clarify, once again, that my statement was not written as a preface to the book, which I did not know existed, and that I asked to have it withdrawn, though too late to affect publication a few weeks after I wrote it, a fact that has been subjected to much absurd and malicious comment in the French press that I will not review.

That leads me to ask you whether, afterwards, you have had the curiosity of interesting yourself in the substance of the affair?

My interest in this affair has been quite limited. I was asked to sign a petition calling on authorities to protect Faurisson's civil rights, and did so. I sign innumerable petitions of this nature, and do not recall ever having refused to sign one. I assumed that the matter would end there. It did not, because **a barrage of lies** in France, claiming, among other absurdities, that by defending Faurisson's civil rights I was defending his views. I then wrote the statement mentioned before. This and similar comments of mine evoked a new wave of falsification.

For example, in the *Le Monde* letter I mentioned earlier, Thibaud wrote that I had condemned "toute l'intelligentsia française," without qualifications. In fact, my statement began by emphasizing that I would comment on "certain segments of the French intelligentsia ... Certainly, what I say does not apply to many others, who maintain a firm commitment to intellectual integrity ... I would not want these comments to be misunderstood as applying beyond their specific scope." *Le Monde* refused to print my response to this and similar absurdities. Similarly, *Le Matin* refused to print my response to ludicrous charges by Attali and Lévy, who claimed that I was opposing protest against Pol Pot, their sole grounds being that I had testified at the United Nations about U.S.-backed massacres in Timor (which, incidentally, I described as comparable to the Pol Pot massacres, as indeed they were). It is striking that in France, alone in Europe, the press has regularly refused to grant me the right of response to lies and slander, though I read about a "debate" that is supposedly in progress.

The sheer irrationality of the comments is astounding, as the examples indicate. To cite another, consider a tirade by Pierre Vidal-Naquet, of which a typical example is this: he claims that I quoted, from his private correspondence, an error that he had corrected in his subsequent published article in *Esprit*, when of course he knows that I quoted his published article. One must have considerable faith in the gullibility of the reading public to venture such a blatant falsehood. To mention one last case, *Le Matin* now claims that I regard "l'idée même de génocide" as "un mythe impérialiste," whereas the editor surely knows that I described "the massacre of the Jews" as "the most fantastic outburst of collective insanity in human history," and the book to which he refers is devoted to example after example of genocidal actions throughout the world.

There is no space here to review the record of lies and deceit about my alleged views, of which this is only a tiny example. In certain intellectual circles in France, the very basis for discussion—a minimal respect for facts and logic—has been virtually abandoned.

Returning to my involvement in the Faurisson affair, it consists of signature to a petition, and, after that, response to lies and slander. Period.

I will add one final comment. The French courts have now condemned Faurisson for failure of "responsibilité" as a historian and "de laisser prendre en charge, par autrui [!], son discours dans une intention d'apologie des crimes de guerre ou d'incitation à la haine raciale," among other similar charges. In a display of moral cowardice, the court then claimed that it was not restricting the right of the historian to express himself freely, but only punishing Faurisson for doing so. This shameful judgment accords to the state the right to determine official truth (despite the protestation of the court) and to punish those who show "irresponsibility." If it does not arouse massive protest, it will be **a sad day for France.**

Do you believe that the doubt about the existence of gas chambers is a reasonable doubt? I mean, that their existence or non-existence is, from the viewpoint of historical research, a real problem?

My own view is that there are no reasonable grounds to doubt the existence of gas chambers. Of course, this is a question of fact, not religious faith. Only a religious fanatic would deny that questions of fact are subject to inquiry.

Freedom to Express Horrendous Views

If you haven't had the opportunity to examine the substance of the record, what is the reason?

My reasons are the same as those of the vast majority of others who have also not done so. The claim that there were no gas chambers seems to me highly implausible, and the denial of the Holocaust, completely so. Like virtually everyone else who has written about this affair or who has not, I see no need to investigate further. It has been alleged (e.g., by Vidal-Naquet) that it is "scandalous" to defend Faurisson's right to freedom of expression without denouncing his conclusions—which would, of course, require a careful analysis of his documentation, etc. By these curious standards, I have often been engaged in "scandalous" behavior. I have frequently signed petitions—in fact, gone to far greater lengths—on behalf of East European dissidents whose views I either do not know, or do know and find horrendous: supporters of current American atrocities, for example. I never mention their views in this context, even if I am familiar with them, a fact that no doubt scandalizes the commissars. The demand that defense of civil rights requires an analysis and commentary on the views expressed would simply eliminate the defense of the rights of those who express unpopular or horrendous views, the usual case where a serious issue arises. This is taken for granted without comment by all civil libertarians. In discussing this issue, I have therefore limited myself to stating that Faurisson's views are diametrically opposed to mine, as indicated in the comments I quoted earlier and others like them. In the case of East European dissidents, for example, I do not even go that far, nor is it necessary to do so.

Do you think that the existence or non-existence of gas chambers is a question which has an ideological, political or ethnic value (even if from the viewpoint of reality their existence is not in question according to you)?

If, contrary to my belief, it were shown that there were no gas chambers but that the massacre of millions of Jews was the result of horrifying conditions in slave labor camps, that would not affect my **evaluation of the Nazi genocide**.

If you think that the existence of gas chambers has such a value, say, as something at stake in a battle about the interpretation of Nazism as a historical phenomenon, would you state precisely your ideas in this respect?

This is too complex a question for me to respond adequately here. Nazism was unique in its horror, perhaps without historical precedent, as I have often written. But we must also recognize that **fascist-style institutions** were developing in one or another form in much of the world in that period, and indeed since. One who views Latin America today might well assume that Hitler had won the war, though in fact it is American liberalism that bears a major responsibility for the plague of terror-and-torture regimes that often mimic the Nazis. I might also mention that commentators within the mainstream of opinion, for example, the Nobel Laureate in economics, Paul Samuelson, have expressed their belief that the future of Western state capitalism may be more similar to Brazil and Argentina than, say, Scandinavian social democracy. This is a topic that I cannot discuss without considerable more space, but it is a very important one.

There is the Chomsky who is a scientist and linguist and the Chomsky who engages in political struggles. What do they say to each other when they meet?

There is no connection, apart from some very tenuous relations at an abstract level, for example, with regard to a concept of human freedom that animates both endeavors.

You seem to think that the only interesting and courageous work for an intellectual is to denounce the abuses perpetrated by his own government and not be concerned with the abuses perpetrated by the governments of other countries, which are easier to denounce. Is this correct?

Not quite. I have always held that criticism of any state or society is legitimate, if it is honest. There are, for example, Western scholars who devote themselves to nothing but the crimes of the Soviet state. I do not criticize them. My own writings include considerable discussion of the criminal nature of Marxist-Leninist doctrine and practice.

But when we consider **the moral significance of one's work and actions**, other criteria enter: a rational person will consider the human consequences of what he does. A person who is concerned with these consequences will concentrate finite energies where they will contribute to alleviating human misery and extending human rights. If a Soviet intellectual chooses to denounce American crimes, that is of little significance. What is important is what he says about the USSR, Czechoslovakia, Afghanistan, Eritrea, etc. The reasons are obvious. However valid his criticism may be, its contribution to human welfare is nil, and may even be negative, insofar as it reinforces a repressive, destructive and murderous system. If a Soviet intellectual chooses to concentrate solely on the crimes of his own state, I have only praise for him. Of course, the commissars see things differently, and will denounce him for "selective outrage." A familiar anti-Stalinist joke 40 years ago was that if you criticized Soviet slave labor camps, you were asked: "What about the lynchings in the south?" The dishonesty is obvious.

Note that an institutional critique of this sort is, in contrast, perfectly legitimate. Thus it is entirely fair (though obvious) to criticize the Soviet media for concentrating on Western crimes, ignoring their own; and it is entirely fair and extremely important for us to analyze the behavior of the Western media insofar as they mirror this deplorable practice, as to a significant extent they do.

An honest person will apply the same standard to himself. In fact, I have been harshly and immediately critical of Soviet crimes, but the importance of this is slight. What is important is to expose the crimes of my own state, which are often hidden from view by the propaganda institutions. The reason is that by doing so I can help arouse public opinion which, in a democracy, can contribute to bringing these crimes to an end. The crimes of Pol Pot could be denounced, but no one had any suggestion as to how to stop them. The comparable crimes in Timor at the same time could have been stopped by an aroused public opinion, since the U.S. and its allies bore prime responsibility for them. Correspondingly, it is no surprise to find that there was vast outrage over Cambodia coupled with silence about Timor. This is typical, as we document at length in our 2 volumes, and elsewhere.

Perhaps one can find the equivalent of the Soviet commissar who will accuse me of "selective outrage" for concentrating my energies where I can actually do something to save lives and defend freedom in a meaningful way, though to my knowledge, such blatant dishonesty is rare in the West, apart from some ex-Stalinists or disillusioned lovers of Third World revolutions.

A Deliberate Effacement of the Record

Since American opinion began to be troubled by doubts about the Vietnam War, you speak of an "ideological reconstruction," in process or completed, which leads to a sort of white washing and amnesia. Is it, in your opinion, a matter of a deliberate and wanted evolution by certain people, or rather a sort of secretion of anti-bodies, half unconsciously, of the American population?

Certainly much of the reconstruction of imperial ideology and effacement of the record of American crimes is quite deliberate. It must be remembered that American liberalism was responsible for many of the worst crimes, not only in Indochina, and the articulate intelligentsia largely supported the war in Indochina, turning against it when business circles did and for the same "pragmatic" reasons. The basic principle, one of long standing, is that the "responsible intellectuals" must undertake what is called "the engineering of consent," the shaping of popular attitudes to support the aims of those with objective power. Again, a person who is concerned to help suffering people will concentrate his energies on combating these forces, which, needless to say, dominate the ideological institutions.

Your effort to "deflate" the Cambodian genocide has been interpreted by certain French intellectuals as your being misguided by the following postulate: everything

*that the CIA says (or arranges) is false, therefore the Cambodian genocide, etc., ...
How do you explain this way of perceiving your action?*

There was no such "effort" on my part. It is interesting that what you report
is actually believed by people in France. It reflects, once again, the total ignorance
of my writings on the part of the people who speak most learnedly about them.
In fact, in my writings on Cambodia I assume that the analyses provided by
American intelligence were probably more or less accurate, as indeed appears to
have been the case.

Revealing Efforts to Disguise the Facts

There has been a vast amount of lying about this matter in France.
Consider, for example, François Ponchaud. In the introduction to the American
edition of his book, he cites my praise for it as "serious and worth reading," and
in turn praises me for the "responsible attitude and precision of thought" shown
in my writing on Cambodia, which in fact covered everything I wrote during the
Pol Pot period. In the introduction to the world edition, dated the same day,
these passages are eliminated and replaced by the claim that I had "sharply criticized" his book, deny that there were massacres, reject refugee testimony, and
insist on relying on "deliberately chosen official statements." These were all lies,
as he knew: compare the American preface written the same day. The world edition is not available in the U.S., where the lies would have been quickly exposed;
the U.S. edition is not available elsewhere, where the facts were generally
unknown. Still more revealing are the subsequent efforts to disguise the facts, as,
for example, when Paul Thibaud writes that Ponchaud made an error in that
only the American edition took account "des remarques de Chomsky"—an interesting way of referring to the fact that the simultaneous world edition contained
outright lies about these "remarques." The editor of *Nouvel Observateur* displayed
comparable dishonesty. He printed a letter of mine, deleting my reference to
"draconian measures" of the Pol Pot regime so that he could maintain his claim
that I refused to criticize the regime, among other similar distortions. There are
numerous other examples.

Herman and I begin our chapter on Cambodia observing that "there is no
difficulty in documenting major atrocities and oppression, primarily from the
reports of the refugees" in a society closed to the West, and that "the record of
atrocities in Cambodia is substantial and often gruesome." We continue in the
same vein, reiterating precisely what Ponchaud and American intelligence officials say about refugee reports; in fact, we criticize the U.S. media for failing to
make use of these reports and failing generally to attend to the analyses of U.S.
intelligence. We cite estimates of killings ranging from "possibly thousands"
killed (*Far Eastern Economic Review*, as our book went to press, the *Review* estimated the population at 8.2 million, well above the 1975 figure) to the claim by
Jean Lacouture in February 1977 that the Pol Pot regime had "boasted" of having killed 2 million people (we wrote too early to cite the claims, which apparently derive from Hanoi propaganda, that the regime had reduced the popula-

tion from 7 to 4 million). We concluded finally that "when the facts are in, it may turn out that the more extreme condemnations were in fact correct," though this would obviously—as a matter of elementary logic—not alter our conclusion on the central matter of our study, namely, "how the available facts were select-ed, modified, or sometimes invented to create a certain image offered to the gen-eral population." We documented extensive fabrication of evidence and suppres-sion of relevant history, not only in the case of Cambodia, but throughout Indochina. The general context was a study of the ways in which the propagan-da system suppressed the record of American crimes throughout the world.

The reason for the remarkable campaign of lies about my writings on Cambodia is quite clear. It began after I wrote a personal letter to Lacouture, pointing out to him that he had grossly falsified Ponchaud's book in a review that appeared in *Nouvel Observateur* and the *New York Review of Books*. Lacouture printed partial corrections in the U.S., but, revealing the total contempt that he and his editor feel for the French intelligentsia, he never issued corrections in France, assuming that no one would care whether what he wrote was true or false. It was then that the campaign of lies began. Evidently, my belief that one should keep to the truth outraged many people who feel that they should be free to lie at will about official enemies.

The Factor of Primary Concern

Doesn't the fact that human rights are not more respected by the socialist regimes, including Cuba, immerse you in a state of complete pessimism in which nothing can be expected from one side or from the other?

Not at all, since I expected little else of these regimes. There are many fac-tors that impel Third World revolutions towards totalitarianism and brutality. One of these factors, and the one that should particularly concern us since it is the only one that we can significantly influence, is the Western role. In the case of Cuba, for example, there is no doubt that the terrorist campaign launched by the Kennedy administration after the Bay of Pigs played a role, as it was intend-ed to do, in enhancing repressive tendencies in the Castro regime. The same is true with respect to Indochina. In Laos, for example, where the U.S. virtually destroyed the agricultural system, the U.S. not only denies food to the starving but also even refuses to aid in removing unexploded ordnance that kills many people and makes farming virtually impossible in the most heavily bombed areas. These monstrous policies, which have few analogues in great power cynicism, are subject to virtually no criticism in the U.S. The goal is to maximize suffering in Indochina and to reinforce the most brutal and repressive elements so that "Western humanists" can then deplore the savagery of the post-revolutionary regimes.

Since gross distortion of these remarks is predictable, let me reiterate the obvious: This is not the sole factor leading to repressive and brutal practice in the regimes called "socialist," but it is the one factor we can influence, and therefore will be the factor that will primarily concern those whose concern is to help suffering people rather than to improve their image or to contribute to imperial violence.

"Selective Outrage" Deconstructed

Have you ever asked yourself: What would I do if I were the U.S. secretary of state? Or, in other words, what should be the foreign policy of the U.S.?

I would rather consider a more realistic question: What can I do to modify American foreign policy so that it will contribute to human welfare rather than pursuing the goal of improving the climate for American business operations and guaranteeing the opportunity to exploit human and material resources. In a democratic society, there is a great deal that one can do, though it will naturally be denounced by those who are committed to oppressive systems, or who interpret a principled commitment to human rights as "selective outrage," mimicking their counterparts among the commissars.

You fear that the complete cynicism of American foreign policy will end up corrupting and destroying what remains of American democracy. Could you be specific?

There are powerful forces in the U.S., as elsewhere, that will labor to secure their wealth and power, whatever the human cost. They will succeed, if they are not opposed by an informed and committed public. This can be done. It was done during the Vietnam War, and it is being done today. This is a continuing struggle, and will remain so, at least until there are revolutionary changes in the superpowers. As to the defense and extension of democracy, this too is a continuing struggle. The anarchist thinker Rudolf Rocker once wrote that "Political rights do not originate in parliaments; they are rather forced upon them from without ... They do not exist because they have been legally set down on a piece of paper, but only when they have become the ingrown habit of a people, and when any attempt to impair them will meet with the violent resistance of the populace." There is much truth to this.

In my view, **the struggle against oppression and injustice will never end,** but will continually take new forms and impose new demands. This is not a reason for pessimism, but for honesty, commitment, and forthright efforts in defense of freedom and justice.

Editor's Notes to Interview 19

First published in *CounterSpy* 6:3 (1982), pp. 27–31, it was reprinted in *RESIST,* Newsletter #152 (November 1982), pp. 4–7, with a new introduction by Dave Schaller, who conducted the interview in January 1982. (On *RESIST,* see **RP** (1981/1984/2003), Editor's Notes to ch. 2; its current address is One Summer Street, Somerville, MA 02143.) The full text of the bill was published in *CounterSpy* 6:2. Beginning with vol. 7 (1982), Chomsky's name appears on the board of advisors.

The bill (which is mild in comparison with the (first) USA PATRIOT ACT, Public Law 107–56, of the new millennium) was signed into law on June 23, 1982. The CIA and its allies in Congress had pressed for the bill for several years as a way to stop CIA critics such as former agent Philip Agee and the editors of the *Covert Action Information Bulletin* (*CAIB*) and *CounterSpy* from trying to hamper agency operations by exposing agents. As passed by the Senate, the new legislation amended the National Security Act of 1947 to ban disclosures of U.S. covert intelligence officers, agents, informants and sources. Several constitutional scholars have said that the act is unconstitutional because it violates the First Amendment. See *Congressional Quarterly Almanac,* 97th Congress, 2nd Session 1982, vol. 38, pp. 131ff.

Neither *CounterSpy* (continued since 1985 by *The National Reporter*) nor *CAIB* had to stop publication, but the latter dropped its "Naming Names" section, a main target of the act. A complete list of the names made public and their locations appeared in *CAIB* 14–15 (October 1981), pp. 27–36.

Schaller turned to Chomsky in order "to better understand the historical and political context in which the act appeared (along with a number of other measures like the president's new executive order on classification and the restriction of the Freedom of Information Act)."

On the extent of the deviation of the media from general subservience to the state ideological system during the Vietnam War, see now **MC** (1988). Chomsky's review of Peter Braestrup's *Big Story* (1977) appeared in *Race & Class* 20 (1978) under the title "The U.S. Media and the Tet Offensive" and was excerpted in *MORE* 8:6 (June 1978), pp. 16–23.

On *The Crisis of Democracy* (1975), by Michel Crozier, Samuel Huntington & Joji Watanuki, see **RP** (1981/1984/2003), ch. 12, pp. 160ff. of the first two editions, and the Editor's Notes to ch. 20.

On the "brazilianization" of American society, see **TCNW** (1982), p. 380.

The final paragraph echoes the quote from Rocker at the end of I18. See **NI** (1988), Appendix V.8.

19. The Intelligence Identities Protection Act
(January 1982)

How do you view the Intelligence Identities Protection Act in terms of the current political situation: the new Cold War?

First of all, speaking rather narrowly and to the most specific point, the bill is a direct attack on the First Amendment. I think there can be no question about that. It aims to penalize free expression, the use of public sources. And if such an act is passed in Congress and holds up in the courts, that in itself will be a very significant step toward the gradual destruction of the system of democratic liberties that is based ultimately on the Bill of Rights. I find it hard to believe that this would hold up in the courts, but we'll see.

More generally, I think the act should be regarded as a threat, not only to *CounterSpy*, but to all of the media, and the articulate intelligentsia as a whole. The context to consider is that which developed out of the Vietnam War—the immediate context. During and after the Vietnam War there was a great deal of outrage among mainstream, elite circles over the fact that the media had, to a very slight extent, deviated from their general **subservience to the state ideological system**. One should emphasize that this deviation was extremely small. The media, to the very end, continued to accept the basic framework of government propaganda with complete loyalty. So, for example, I've never found a case where anyone in the media, or for that matter in scholarship, has described the American invasion of Vietnam as what it was: American aggression, an American invasion of South Vietnam. It was certainly that in 1962, when the U.S. Air Force began the bombing of South Vietnam, then extending to a full-scale invasion a couple of years later, finally to the rest of Indochina.

In fact to the very end of the war, the media, both in their news reporting and in their editorial comment, accepted the basic framework of government propaganda. Virtually the only question that was raised was the question of tactics: "Can we win or can't we win?" By early 1968, substantial business circles had turned against the war, and had decided that it probably was no longer worthwhile. Shortly after that, segments of the press also very timidly raised similar questions. That's the extent of the deviation.

On the other hand, there was very good reporting. There are a lot of foreign correspondents who are real professionals, and they just described what they saw happening in Vietnam. That was important and significant—and very threatening to people in power.

By the early 70s, and since, there was a great deal of concern expressed over the fact that the press has a degree of independence, for example, in the Trilateral Commission report on the Crisis of democracy. Their description seems to me almost hysterical in its accuracy. What they say is that the press has emerged as a new force of national power antagonistic to the state, and that unless the press begins to behave responsibly it will be necessary to find some way to control or constrain it. That's the liberal side of the establishment, that point of view.

To take another case, there was quite a remarkable study, published by Freedom House, a two-volume study written by Peter Braestrup, who had been a journalist in Vietnam. The purpose of this book was to demonstrate, in effect, that the press had lost the war. The press, by misreporting the Tet Offensive, had undermined the American war effort. And the question arose, What should we do about this? How should we prevent the press from undermining national policy, and from acting as traitors and so on.

The commentary on the book was itself quite interesting. For example, John Roche, who is the Academic Dean of the Fletcher School at Tufts University, wrote an ecstatic commentary. He described the book as one of the major works of scholarship of the past quarter century, and said that it should spark a congressional investigation into the behavior of the press. Even what might be called "critical" reviews regarded it as a credible exposure and indictment of how the press had misinformed the public, and had contributed to undermining American policy.

Well, actually I wrote a long review of the book. Parts of it appeared in *MORE*, the alternative journalism review, and the whole article appeared in *Race and Class*. I did the obvious thing. There's one volume of analysis with the documents, and the first thing I discovered was that Braestrup had fabricated much of his evidence. He claimed that things were said that weren't said. He seriously misrepresented his own documentary evidence, and omitted much relevant evidence. So it's hardly a work of scholarship.

More interesting, however, is the nature of Braestrup's critique of the press. His critique of the press was that it was too pessimistic. That's what the treachery was. In other words, he never considered the question—in fact it probably didn't occur to him to do so—whether the press did or did not accept the basic premises of government policy. Of course it did. If you read his own documents and relevant documentation that he excluded, what you find is that the press, almost without exception, accepted the assumption of government policy. When American troops were destroying villages in South Vietnam, for example, the press described that as "defense" of South Vietnam. That's the way it went consistently. So the essence of Braestrup's criticism is that it is not enough for the press to accept government propaganda slavishly, they also have to be optimistic and upbeat about it. That's the criticism.

Well, all right, that may be enough in itself, but if we take a step further we ask: By what criteria was the press too pessimistic? The obvious standard is the internal analysis given by the government—and we know about those. A number of them appear in the *Pentagon Papers*, for example. If you look at them you discover that the press was more optimistic than the government was itself. The CIA analyses, intelligence analyses, were considerably more pessimistic than the press. The government was putting on a bold face publicly, and the press, as usual, was repeating anything the government said as gospel truth.

But the government had to be more in touch with the realities of the war?

The press was reacting to the public image presented by the government. They didn't know about the internal image, or, if they did, they suppressed it. So the fact is the Freedom House criticism, which according to Roche should inspire a congressional investigation, amounted to saying that the media, though completely servile in their acceptance of the framework of government propaganda, were not sufficiently optimistic—even though they were more optimistic than the government was itself. That's the nature of the criticism.

The fact that an organization like Freedom House, or the liberal press, can regard that as a criticism of the press, shows how constrained and limited is the press's sense of its own independence. I'm now taking the strongest case for the claim that the press was free and independent, the very example selected by the critics to prove their case. And even this case collapsed when we look at the facts of the matter. We find quite a different story.

Still, the fact is that the very small degree of independence that was shown, minimal though it was, was regarded as too much of a threat to established power. Through the 1970s there have been continuing attempts to try to overcome the minimal, limited degree of independence that appeared to be developing.

This has been true not only with regard to the press. It is just a part of a much more general effort to overcome what people now call the "Vietnam syndrome," that is, the fact that large parts of the population escaped from the control of the ideological system—which is very threatening and dangerous. A parallel threat is the "crisis of democracy"—the fact that large parts of the population became politically mobilized and active—which is again quite unacceptable. The liberal wing of the establishment's concept of democracy is that the population must be passive and obedient, occasionally coming forth to vote.

Much of the propaganda effort of the 1970s—including, for example, the Carter "human rights" campaign—has been an attempt to try to overcome these maladies, the "Vietnam syndrome" and the "crisis of democracy," and in particular to constrain the limited degree of press freedom that did in fact begin to materialize as a result of popular movements in the country.

How does the Intelligence Identities Protection Act fit into that effort?

It is just another step in this process. It simply poses **a very clear and explicit threat to free expression**, which will be understood by the media, by the intelligentsia, as a warning. If they go too far, then the force of the state will be used to crush them. This is very consistent with the entire drift of the Reagan administration policy. It is described as "conservative," but that's a gross falsification. There's little that is conservative about Reagan's policy—not his economic policy or his social policy. His economic policies involve a program of considerable expansion of, in effect, the state sector of the economy, namely, the state-guaranteed market for high technology production, which is the Pentagon system. Also corresponding to that are increasing state controls and interference in the lives of individual citizens. It would be more accurate to describe the Reagan administration's policy as proto-fascist, rather than conservative.

Apart from the vindictiveness of picking on *CounterSpy*, I think that the agent identification act should be understood as a symbolic gesture towards building up the system of state power—which is to coerce, control, and constrain the behavior and expression of private citizens who are not sufficiently obedient to the prevailing system of ideology, or who actually may act through the political system to challenge it, creating a "crisis of democracy."

There are several contradictions in the agent identities bill that I wondered if you would comment on. One is that it defines "covert agent" in such a broad way as to include people in the press, academics, business people, foreigners, etc. So it seems to me that the bill actually formally defines as state operators people who are in, well, it used to be called "civil society." In other words, one of the effective ways that people who work for the CIA—through the New York Times or at MIT—have operated is to say, "I'm just working on my own as a private citizen; I have no connection with them." By establishing this legal connection, the bill seems to formally extend the state in the way that you are talking about.

I think again there's a much more general context. Business and corporations have a love/hate relationship with the state. And there is a real contradiction there. On the one hand, they don't want a state which is so powerful that it acts as a competitor or constrains their freedom of action. On the other hand, they want a state which is powerful enough to repress dissent, to control foreign countries in their interest, and to organize the market. There have always been initiatives within the business community to increase and centralize the powers of the state in their interests, and also to cut down and weaken the state in their interests. There is never any solution to how to deal with this problem, because it is contradictory.

This shows up very clearly among people who call themselves "conservatives." They want a powerful and violent state to use instrumentally. On the other hand, they don't want the state to be engaged in, say, social welfare programs. They don't want the state to interfere with their prerogatives and their wealth—but they do want the state to enhance their power. To try to create a state which will meet both these conditions is not very easy, and I think this is a case in point. In a state capitalist society like ours, there is of course no sharp separation between the "state" and "civil society." Infiltration, provocation, control and coercion have long been a part of the relation of the state to the citizens—increasingly so since World War II. And I think that we are facing another step.

The sections of the bill you mention presuppose that the state has the right to infiltrate, and to work secretly within the civil society, the institutions of civil society. At least as I read the bill, it states that, for example, if I discover, in an organization that I'm part of, that there are government infiltrators, it is illegal for me to expose them. I mean, not only is the state allowed to infiltrate and send agent provocateurs into my organization, but I'm not allowed to expose them. This is no small thing.

During the 60s, a good deal of the violence and provocation that was attributed to the anti-war movement was in fact directly traceable to government agents who were infiltrated into organizations, and ordered to provoke violence. You knew right away that if there was somebody in your organization who was saying, "Let's off the cops," and so on, they were probably going to show up as a government witness in the next trial. And in fact every serious organization learned how to try to separate out people who were encouraging violence and irrational action, because there was a very high probability that they would be the government agents. And of course if they could be discovered, they would be exposed. Well, the current legislation makes it illegal to expose them. So they're permitted to interfere with your organizations, and to put you under surveillance, and to work their way into your defense team if you're in a court case, and so on, and you're not allowed to expose them. Now that's a new step, a significant step, towards increasing the power of the state to interfere with and control political activity. It's another step towards **the general "brazilianization" of American society**, which increases the power of the coercive state in the state capitalist mix.

How much importance should we place on analyzing the contradictions or the struggles between different factions within the ruling class? For instance, often it's talked about in terms of the financial capital of the East versus the Sunbelt new industrial capital. Is this bill itself a weapon to be used by the newly dominant faction against...

The Eastern liberals?

Right.

There may be something to that. I think there have been valuable insights from that kind of work, by Carl Oglesby, Mike Klare, Kirkpatrick Sale, and others. On the other hand, I don't think they would push that kind of analysis too far, and I don't think anybody else should either. The interactions and connections between these groups within the ruling class are rather tight, and while one can maybe identify tendencies, and maybe one can discover conflicts on an analytical level, I'm not convinced how much it means with regard to the real problem.

Given the fact that this bill is likely to pass, and given the fact that the bill is written so very arbitrarily, how is it going to affect your work?

This kind of legislation, and the whole system that it represents, will succeed to the extent that people submit to it. Now take the McCarthy period, I mean the so-called "McCarthy period," a very misleading term because it had its origins in the programs of the liberals of the Truman administration, but let's refer to it by that name. That was very effective in stilling dissenting opinion and creating a subservient population, and leaving the way free to people with power to exercise it in whatever way, however violently they wished. A large part of its success was due simply to the collapse of the opposition, the unwillingness to face up to it.

Bills of this sort, or what they represent, can only be combated by popular movements that are willing to face them directly, to disregard them, to struggle against them, to continue the work of exposure and activism that's necessary. You don't win your rights because somebody writes it down in a law, and you don't lose your rights because somebody writes it down in a law. You win your rights by struggle, and you maintain your rights by struggle.

Editor's Notes to Interview 20

Unpublished, untitled. It was conducted in the Spring of 1982 by Sheldon Frank for *Soho Weekly News* (New York), which disappeared at about that time in its ninth year; it was later submitted to *In These Times*.

Frank is "a writer living in Hoboken, New Jersey, a working class town invaded by money" where he helps tenants defend their rights. The immediate motivation of the interview was the publication of *Towards a New Cold War*, in which two themes interweave, he notes, quoting from Chomsky's introduction: "the evolution of policy, and the ways it is depicted by the media and scholarship over a fairly broad mainstream of articulate opinion." He then explains his specific goals as follows: "The American war in Indochina is discussed at length for two reasons: (1) because a clear understanding of American intervention there will enable us to more accurately assess our current intervention in Central America; (2) because the recent publication of books like Norman Podhoretz's squalid little polemic, *Why We Were in Vietnam*, which attempts to blame the anti-war movement for the immorality of that debacle, is a significant and frightening indication of the 'resurgent America' propaganda machine cranking up its intellectual artillery. Cuba is discussed in detail for similar reasons."

Robert Tucker's influential "The Purposes of American Power" was the lead article in the prestigious journal *Foreign Affairs* of the Council on Foreign Relations in the issue of Winter 1980/81. Chomsky's "Resurgent America," reprinted as chapter 8 in **TCNW** (1982), appeared first in Spanish translation in Madrid (March) and Mexico (May) and then in English in Canada (*Our Generation*, Summer 1981—simultaneously with the edited version published in *Socialist Review*).

The study of the systematic nature of American support of fascist regimes, mentioned in the last paragraph, is a central concern in Chomsky's work, as we will see. Another (related) concern is "terror" and "terrorism," "the plague of the modern age" of I51, where "a clear distinction between the official definition of the concept of 'terrorism' and the 'prevailing definition' within Western intellectual culture," for which "terror" is another name for resistance (I36). The concern can be easily traced by inspecting the titles or subheadings of the interviews (see, e.g., 20, 30, 41, 47, 48, 51, 54, 56)—or the titles or subtitles of his books: *The Culture of Terrorism* (1988), *Power and Terror* (2003); *Pirates and Emperors: International Terrorism in the Real World* (1986, 2002), *Middle East Illusions: Peace, Security, and Terror* (2003). See also the Editor's Notes to I54.

20. The Barbarism of Non-Communist Monsters
(Spring 1982)

What are the range of policy options now under consideration among the foreign policy elite?

First of all, the range is very narrow. The problem is how to restore, to the extent possible, the American domination of the world system, which has been eroding. That is the problem. And what are the range of policies?

Well, they range roughly from a policy of militant projection of force and subversion, which is sometimes called the "resurgent America" policy, to the policy that Robert Tucker called "moderate containment." And I think that he's right in identifying the range of options being considered. The "minimal option" is that in those areas where what we consider our **"needs"** are at stake, we will use force and violence to maintain those needs. For example, and remember I'm using the terminology and ideology of American policy planners, we have the "need" to control the energy reserves of the Middle East. That's the minimal option. The "maximal option" is that we should use force and violence not only to maintain our "needs," as defined by us, but also to maintain our **"wants."** So, for example, if we want a right-wing military dictatorship in El Salvador, where we don't really need it, according to the maximal option we have a right to install it. It's within that range that the foreign policy decisions are made. And that's a very narrow range.

What about El Salvador, to be specific?

To go back a little while, the Carter administration was threatened by the revolution in Nicaragua, and were concerned that something similar would begin to happen elsewhere, in particular in El Salvador. They therefore backed a military coup there in October 1979 which threw out the then military dictator, and installed a junta in which a range of political positions were represented which could conceivably have led the country in a more constructive direction, and thereby avoided the revolution which they feared was coming.

But though Carter's administration backed Somoza to the end, they didn't do publicly in Nicaragua what the Reagan administration immediately did in El Salvador. Is that a non-trivial difference?

It was a matter of timing. And you can see what happened by continuing with what happened in El Salvador under Carter. Within a few months the junta had fallen apart; they had been taken over by the right wing. The Carter administration backed them to the hilt. The massacre of the peasantry in El Salvador began in the spring of 1980, not reported in the press of course, and it intensified. The Carter administration then expanded the military aid that it was sending to the murderers.

The Reagan administration simply continued and accelerated this policy. They accelerated it, but it was the same policy. They did one crucial new thing, namely, they raised the level of the confrontation to an international level of crisis, and I think we've been close to an invasion for over a year.

What you're saying reminds me of what you've written about our intervention in both Vietnam and Cuba as partial victories, not the total defeats commonly described. Since your argument may be an unfamiliar one, perhaps you could elaborate.

Well, you have to understand what the major purpose was of the American war in Vietnam, and that way you can judge to what extent it was a success. Again, the maximal aim was to incorporate all of Indochina within the American-dominated world system. That was the maximal aim, but that wasn't of extreme importance in itself. Vietnam in itself is not a territory of crucial significance to the American world system. What planners were afraid of was the "domino effect," that is, they were very much concerned about the possibility of an independent Vietnam under so-called "Communist leadership" which would carry out successful social and economic development.

This is not the "domino effect" they talk about publicly.

No, it's in the private documents. There are two versions of the domino theory. One version is that Ho Chi Minh is going to invade Hawaii—that's for public consumption. The internal version of the domino theory is, on their terms, really quite sane, quite reasonable. Their fear was that if there were social and economic development within these so-called "Communist countries"—meaning countries which extract themselves from the American system and use their resources for their independent development, that if that were to take place, it could be a model that would be regarded as attractive by peasant movements elsewhere and might inspire and encourage them, and so on. And this "demonstration effect" could start the dominoes toppling.

The maximal goal is to incorporate the area. The minimal goal is to prevent the domino effect, to prevent social and economic development in Indochina which will be successful and could be a model for peasant movements in the surrounding area. Now that minimal goal was met. The minimal goal was met by the destruction of Indochina. The chances for successful social and economic development there are very slight, for a long time to come.

Furthermore, the American war in South Vietnam, which was the major target of the United States, was a success. The United States won that war. They destroyed the National Liberation Front; they destroyed the society; they destroyed the country. It's important to remember that the core of the American war was an attack against South Vietnam, and that's the one phrase which will never be mentioned in American journalism or scholarship and the reason is because it's **too central a truth**, and therefore it has to be obscured. I've been looking for about 20 years—since the Kennedy administration started the intensive bombing of South Vietnam in 1962—to see if anyone within the mainstream will ever refer to the American attack against South Vietnam, which is what it was. It was an attack against the rural society which had perhaps 85 percent of the population. But no one will say that. In that respect we have proven to be an almost totally indoctrinated society.

That war we won. South Vietnam was so totally destroyed that exactly as I predicted a long time ago, North Vietnam now dominates Indochina. The key point is that the country has been so devastated that **the possibility of really successful development** is, at least in the near future, slight, and the chances for survival are not very great. Furthermore, our policy since that time has been to try to maximize the suffering and brutality inside the country, to insure our partial victory sticks.

Another thing that has to be mentioned is that that kind of military attack against any society leaves really only the harshest elements able to survive. So, for example, suppose the Russians pull out of Afghanistan in another ten years. What will survive will be the most brutal and harsh elements which will probably carry out some kind of massacre.

So while Vietnam itself was not conquered, it was certainly severely damaged, very severely damaged, as was the surrounding area, and meanwhile the other countries of Southeast Asia were, to a substantial extent, incorporated within the Japanese-American system.

And, as you have written, the events which have taken place after our savage devastation of the region are analyzed in the popular press as if the United States had never been there to cause the conditions for the current situation.

Of course. For the popular press now, Indochina history begins in 1975.

Coming closer to home, we get our Cuban policy, which you also call a partial success. There we didn't go the route of total devastation. We couldn't, because it was going to lead to nuclear war. We came pretty close in 1962, but the United States backed off under the threat of possible nuclear war. However, the Kennedy administration launched a major war against Cuba—the so-called "secret war." Cuba alone is **the victim of probably more terrorism than the rest of the world combined**. But this is almost never discussed in the United States. And in fact when it is discussed, it's amazing to see the reaction.

For example, the first book on the American war against Cuba, the secret terrorist war, came out about a year ago, a book titled *The Fish is Red*. Well, it's very instructive to look at the review in the *New York Times*. It was reviewed, but the reviewer said, "Oh, not this old boring stuff again." Here's the first book on the subject, a very serious subject, namely, a terrorist war of 20 years against

Cuba carried out in secret, and the response is, "This is old hat; we've heard all this before."

And some of the worst things aren't even mentioned in the book. For example, it appears to be the case that the United States carried out a very extensive and quite successful destruction by poisoning of the crops and livestock in Cuba. In fact, there was an epidemic of swine fever which was regarded by the United States Food and Agricultural Organization as the most alarming even of 1971, which apparently had been caused by CIA infiltrators.

That's pretty serious stuff. If the Cubans had poisoned our crops and live-stock, we would regard it as serious, but when we do it to them, we regard it as a joke, and it isn't even mentioned. It's not a part of recognized history. It's not a part of our national consciousness.

If you really look over the record of American attacks on Cuba, it's quite astonishing. The shelling of hotels, for example, the blowing up of economic installations, the sinking of boats, etc. I mean, if any single one of those acts had occurred in the U.S., we'd be at war and there would no end to the outrage about the barbarism of the Communist monster.

Okay. Let's return to El Salvador. What's going on?

Well, the maximal objective of our policy may require the dispatch of American troops, but I don't think the country will tolerate that. The minimal objective, mainly just conducting a sufficiently destructive attack so that what is left will either be brutalized or incapable of development, well that won't require American troops. That kind of level of destruction in a country like El Salvador is well within our means. So I think the chances of the U.S. meeting its minimal goals, namely just preventing any constructive nationalist revolutionary movement from taking power and being able to do anything, that minimal goal I think the U.S. can and probably will achieve. The maximal goal of installing the kind of government we succeeded in installing in Guatemala in 1954 may not succeed.

Of course that's not the rhetorical goal. The rhetorical goal is democracy, but to see how meaningful that rhetorical goal is, all you have to do is to look at our actual successes in the countries most under our domination, for example in Latin America and the Philippines. We've been the primary influence in the Philippines for over 80 years now, and you look at the Philippines and you know what our real goals are. But if you look at American journalism and scholarship, the range of opinion that is represented goes between these two extremes: one extreme, a sort of hawkish extreme, says we have the right and, in fact, the duty to regulate and organize the world, and so on. The other extreme, the dovish extreme, says it's not within our power to bring democracy and freedom to the world.

Now that's amazing. If you look around at the world, if you look at **our actual impact upon the world**, it's astonishing that sane people can even discuss this question. Our support of fascist regimes has been systematic, very systematic. If we look at Eastern Europe, if we look at the kinds of societies that are there, we therefore draw some conclusions about the nature of the Soviet Union. Well, okay, then if we look at Latin America and the Philippines and South Korea and Southeast Asia and so on, we should draw some conclusions about ourselves.

Editor's Notes to Interview 21

Conducted in October 1982 by Paul Shannon, it originally appeared as "The Legacy of the Vietnam War" in the *Indochina Newsletter*, Special Double Issue #18 (November–December 1982), 1–5. (Current address: 2161 Mass. Av, Cambridge, MA 02140.) The *Newsletter* was then published by Indochina Aid and Friendship Project, a project of the Bach Mai Fund; now it is a project of the Asia Resource Center. It is published bi-monthly. The interview was reprinted with the new title in *RESIST*, Newsletter #156 (April 1983), 1–3 & 7. (See notes to I19.)

The "huge popular uproar" that forced the Reagan administration "to choose a much more indirect way of supporting the collection of gangsters in power" in El Salvador was part of "the popular movements that developed in the 1960s and that have not been tamed, despite major efforts by business, government and the intellectual elites in the post-Vietnam period," an important fact which "will not penetrate official history," as we read in the introduction ("The Public and State Violence") to **CT** (1988). The next sentence can hardly be overemphasized: "It is important, however, for concerned citizens to think through the matter themselves, and to understand just how the public was able to influence state policy" (which is spelled out in the following two pages of that book).

For an update of the last paragraph of the interview, see "Cambodia" in **ChR**, pp. 289–97.

21. The Lessons of the Vietnam War (October 1982)

When the Indochina war ended in 1975 you wrote that our nation's "official" opin-
ion makers would engage in distortion of the lessons to be drawn from the war so that
the same basic foreign policy goals could be pursued after the war. You felt then that
in order to keep the real meaning of the war from penetrating the general public they
faced two major tasks: First, they would have to disguise the fact that the war "was
basically an American attack on South Vietnam—a war of annihilation that spilled
over to the rest of Indochina." And secondly, they would have to obscure the fact that
the military effort in Vietnam "was restrained by a mass movement of protest and
resistance here at home which engaged in effective direct action outside the bounds of
propriety long before established spokesmen proclaimed themselves to be its leaders."
Where do we stand now on these two issues—seven years later?

As far as the opinion makers are concerned, they have been doing exactly
what it was obvious they would do. Every book that comes out, every article that
comes out, talks about how—while it may have been a "mistake" or an "unwise
effort"—the United States was defending South Vietnam from North
Vietnamese aggression. And they portray those who opposed the war as apologists for North Vietnam. That's standard to say.

The purpose is obvious: to obscure the fact that the United States did attack
South Vietnam and the major war was fought against South Vietnam. The real
invasion of South Vietnam, which was directed largely against the rural society,
began directly in 1962 after many years of working through mercenaries and
client groups. And that fact simply does not exist in official American history.
There is no such event in American history as the attack on South Vietnam.
That's gone. Of course, it is part of real history. But it's not a part of official history.

And most of us who were opposed to the war, especially in the early 60s—
the war we were opposed to was the war on South Vietnam which destroyed
South Vietnam's rural society. The South was devastated. But now anyone who
opposed this atrocity is regarded as having defended North Vietnam. And that's
part of the effort to present the war as if it were a war between South Vietnam
and North Vietnam with the United States helping the South. Of course, it's fabrication. But it's official "truth" by now.

This question of who the United States was fighting in Vietnam is pretty basic in terms of coming to any understanding of the war. But why would the U.S. attack South Vietnam, if the problem was not an attack from North Vietnam?

First of all, let's make absolutely certain that was the fact: that the U.S. directed the war against South Vietnam.

There was a political settlement in 1954. But in the late 50s the United States organized an internal repression in South Vietnam, not using its troops, but using the local apparatus it was constructing. This was a very significant and very effective campaign of violence and terrorism against the Vietminh—which was the communist-led nationalist force that fought the French. And the Vietminh at that time was adhering to the Geneva Accords, hoping that the political settlement would work out in South Vietnam.

And so, not only were they not conducting any terrorism, but in fact, they were not even responding to the violence against them. It reached the point where by 1959 the Vietminh leadership—the Communist Party leadership—was being decimated. Cadres were being murdered extensively. Finally, in May of 1959, there was an authorization to use violence in self-defense, after years of murder, with thousands of people killed in this campaign organized by the United States. As soon as they began to use violence in self-defense, the whole Saigon government apparatus fell apart at once because it was an apparatus based on nothing but a monopoly of violence. And once it lost that monopoly of violence it was finished. And that's what led the United States to move in. There were no North Vietnamese around.

Then the National Liberation Front of South Vietnam was formed. And its founding program called for the neutralization of South Vietnam, Laos and Cambodia. And it's very striking that the National Liberation Front was the only group that ever called for the independence of South Vietnam. The so-called South Vietnamese government (GVN) did not but, rather, claimed to be the government of all Vietnam. The National Liberation Front was the only South Vietnamese group that ever talked about South Vietnamese independence. They called for the neutralization of South Vietnam, Laos and Cambodia as a kind of neutral block, working toward some type of integration in the South with North Vietnam ultimately.

Now that proposal in 1962 caused panic in American ruling circles. From 1962 to 1964 the U.S. was dedicated to try to prevent the independence of South Vietnam. The reason was of course that Kennedy and Johnson knew that if any political solution was permitted in the South, the National Liberation Front would effectively come to power, so strong was its political support of the so-called South Vietnamese government.

And in fact Kennedy and later Johnson tried to block every attempt at neutralization, every attempt at political settlement. This is all documented. There's just no doubt about it. I mean, it's wiped out of history, but the documentation is just unquestionable—in the internal government sources and everywhere else.

And so there's just no question that the United States was trying desperately to prevent the independence of South Vietnam and to prevent a political settlement inside South Vietnam. And in fact it went to war precisely to prevent that. It finally bombed the North in 1965 with the purpose of trying to get the North to use its influence to call off the insurgency in the South. There were no North Vietnamese troops in South Vietnam then as far as anybody knew. And they anticipated of course when they began bombing the North from South Vietnamese bases that it would bring North Vietnamese troops into the South. And then it became possible to pretend it was aggression from the North. It was ludicrous, but that's what they claimed.

Well, why did they do it? Why was the United States so afraid of an independent South Vietnam? Well, I think the reason again is pretty clear from the internal government documents. Precisely what they were afraid of was that the "takeover" of South Vietnam by nationalist forces would not be brutal. They feared it would be conciliatory and that there would be successful social and economic development—and that the whole region might work.

This was clearly a nationalist movement—and in fact a radical nationalist movement which would separate Vietnam from the American orbit. It would allow Vietnam to become another Philippines. It would trade with the United States, but it would not be an American semi-colony.

And suppose it worked. Suppose the country could separate itself from the American-dominated global system and carry out a successful social and economic development. Then that is very dangerous because then it could be a model to other movements and groups in neighboring countries. And gradually there could be an erosion from within by indigenous forces of American domination of the region. So this was no small thing. It was assumed that the key to the problem was preventing any successful national movement from carrying out serious social and economic development inside Indochina. So the United States had to destroy it through a process which would become the war against South Vietnam. And, it should be pointed out that on a lower level we were doing the same things in Laos and Cambodia.

So the irony is that the very reason given in the United States for fighting the war—the independence of South Vietnam—is exactly what had to be destroyed. Exactly.

Do you think this distortion of the war is successful?

It's hard to say. People who lived through the period know better. But younger people who are being indoctrinated into the contemporary system of falsification—they really have to do some research to find out what is the truth. In the general population, people forget or don't care that much. And gradually what you hear drilled into your head everyday comes to be believed. People don't understand what you're talking about anymore if you discuss the American war on South Vietnam.

And the role of the anti-war movement?

The main effort has been to show that the opposition to the war was of two types. One was the serious responsible type that involved Eugene McCarthy and some senators—who turned the tide because we realized it wasn't worthwhile, or was too expensive or something. And then there were these sort of violent and irrational groups, teenagers and so on, whose behavior had little to do with the war really, and whose activity was a form of lunacy. Now, anyone who lived through the period would have to laugh.

But my impression is that the effort to portray the peace movement this way is not working very well. For example, at the beginning of his administration, Reagan tried to set the basis for American military intervention in El Salvador—which is about what Kennedy did when he came into office in regard to Vietnam. Well when Kennedy tried it in Vietnam, it just worked like a dream. Virtually nobody opposed American bombing of South Vietnam in 1962. It was not an issue. But when Reagan began to talk on involving American forces in El Salvador there was a huge popular uproar. And he had to choose a much more indirect way of supporting the collection of gangsters in power there. He had to back off.

And what that must indicate is a tremendous shift in public opinion over the past 20 years as a result of the participation in the real opposition to the war in Indochina—which has lasted and was resurrected when a similar circumstance began to arise.

So you see the inability of the government to maneuver as it would like in El Salvador as directly related to the anti-war movement.

Oh yes, They even have a name for it "Vietnam Syndrome." See, they make it sound like some kind of disease, a malady that has to be overcome. And the "malady" in this case is that the population is still unwilling to tolerate aggression and violence. And that's a change that took place as a result of the popular struggle against the war in Vietnam.

So you feel it was the group officially defined as the "riff-raff, lunatic fringe" who really was the peace movement?

Oh, there's no question. You can see what happened. There were very extensive grass-roots efforts beginning in the mid-60s, developing quite gradually against tremendous opposition. So that in Boston it was impossible to have an outdoor public meeting against the war until about the fall of 1966. Until then they would be broken up. And the media more or less applauded the violence and disruption that prevented people from speaking. But gradually that changed. In fact, it reached such a point that by 1967 it was impossible for the president to declare a national mobilization for war. He was restricted and forced to pretend he was conducting a small war. There were constraints. Because of public opinion which by then was considerably aroused by demonstrations and teach-ins and other types of resistance, Johnson had to fight the war with deficit spending. He had to fight a "guns and butter" war to show it was no big war.

And this policy just collapsed. And it collapsed totally with the Tet Offensive in 1968, which led major sectors of American power to realize we could not carry it off at this level. Either we go to war like in the Second World War, or we pull out. And that was a direct effect of the activities of the peace movement. After this decision was made, then politicians like Eugene McCarthy—whom you had never heard of before that time—came to announce themselves as the leaders of the peace movement.

But by then the basic decision to put a limit to direct American troop involvement had been made. You had to fight for a long time to get the U.S. out, but the basic decision had been made at the Tet Offensive. That's when the programs related to Vietnamization were put in place, and we began to fight a more capital intensive war with less direct participation of American ground troops.

Incidentally, another reason for this was that the American army began to deteriorate internally because, after all, the United States was fighting a very unusual type of war. It's very rare for a country to try to fight a colonial war with a conscript army. Usually wars like the Vietnam War are fought with mercenaries—like the French Foreign Legion. The U.S. tried to fight what amounts to a colonial war with a conscript army. And a colonial war is a very dirty kind of war. You're not fighting armed forces. You're fighting mostly unarmed people. And to fight that kind of war requires professional killers, which means mercenaries. The 50,000 Korean mercenaries we had in Vietnam were professional killers and just massacred people outright. And the American army did plenty of that, too, but it couldn't take it after awhile. It's not the kind of job you can give to conscripts who are not trained to be murderers.

And they had also heard of the anti-war movement's ideas against the war back home.

Exactly. It was a citizen's army, not separated from what's happening in American society in general. And the effect was that, very much to its credit, the American army began to crumble and deteriorate. And it became harder and harder to keep an army in the field.

Are you aware of any other time in history when soldiers came home from the war and organized against their government as many Vietnam veterans did through the Vietnam Veterans Against the War organization?

It's rare. For example, it's happening now to a certain extent in Israel with reservists who are also fighting a war against a civilian population in Lebanon. And it's the same kind of phenomenon. If they just kept professional military men involved they could probably carry it off. But reservists are connected with the civilian population. That's why countries like France and England used mercenary forces to carry out these kinds of wars.

Let me make one final point about the peace movement which is often forgotten. When you look back at the internal documents that we have now you can see that when the big decision was made around the Tet Offensive in 1968—about whether or not to send a couple hundred thousand more troops—one of the factors was that the joint chiefs of staff were concerned that they would not have enough troops for internal control of the domestic American population. They feared tremendous protest and disruption at home if they sent more troops to Vietnam. This means that they understood the level of internal resistance to be virtually at the level of civil war. And I think they were probably right about that. That's a good indication from inside as to how seriously they took the peace movement.

There are indications that the huge demonstrations of October and November of 1969 severely limited Nixon's ability to carry out some of the plans for escalating the war that he had. The domestic population was not under control. And any country has to have a passive population if it is going to carry out effectively an aggressive foreign policy. And it was clear by October and November of 1969 just by the scale of opposition that the population was not passive.

So those are all important events to remember. Again, they're sort of written out of history. But the record is there and the documentation is there, and it's clear that that's what happened.

What is the current U.S. foreign policy toward Indochina?

Well, towards Indochina I think the main policy is what's called "bleeding Vietnam." Even conservative business groups outside the United States have been doing this.

We fought the war to prevent Indochina from carrying out successful social and economic development. Well, I think the chances of that happening are very slight because of the devastation, because of the brutality of war. But the U.S. wants to make sure it will continue. And therefore we first of all of course refused any reparations. We refused aid. We try to block aid from other countries. We block aid from international institutions. I mean, sometimes it reaches a point of almost a fanatic effort to make them suffer.

For example, there was one point when the United States prevented the government of India from sending a hundred buffalo to Vietnam. (The buffalo stock in Vietnam had been decimated by American bombing.) We prevented them by threatening to cut off Food for Peace aid.

So in every conceivable way the United States has tried to increase the harsh conditions of life in Indochina. And right now one of the main ways we're doing that is by supporting the Khmer Rouge on the Thai-Cambodia border.

Editor's Notes to Interview 22

"The Disarmament Debate: New Directions," *National Forum* 63:4 (Fall 1983), pp. 38–39 & 47 (The Phi Kappa Phi Journal, Louisiana State University). On Dec. 15, 1982, Chomsky delivered the address "What Direction for the Disarmament Movement?," the 11th lecture in the Bays Blackwell Lectureship Series sponsored by Emory and Henry College in Virginia. This enlightening interview, which includes a very lucid outline of the workings of the economic system, was conducted by Stephen W. White and Elaine Smoot at the Virginian College.

For references to Chomsky's papers on the direction for the disarmament movement, see **RP** (1981/1984/2003), ch. 24, and Koerner & Tajima, pp. 142–5, entries 1982k, 1982t, 1983c, and 1983d.

22. The Disarmament Debate: New Directions
(15 December 1982)

What historical developments do you see that are important in the discussion of disarmament? How in particular has this debate changed in the past few decades? We've heard for many years that we are living in an age of overkill, that we have the capacity to decimate enemy populations many times over, that under those conditions arms rule, and we've heard those arguments for a long time. How do you see the character of the debate about disarmament changing over the past few decades?

I think that the disarmament movement tends to grow more or less in parallel to the government's commitment to increase the strategic weapons systems. For example, when Kennedy came in there was a huge expansion of the strategic weapons systems under McNamara's defense programs and civil defense. And there was a growing disarmament movement that corresponded to it, quite properly. I think that much of the population, certainly the disarmament movement, perceives the American military system as a threat to its existence. And that's a correct perception. The American military system is probably the greatest threat to our existence. Correspondingly, when this system takes a spurt forward, begins to grow and develop, people who are concerned about that threat to their existence also begin to organize in response to it.

Now, I think that the disarmament movement of the early 60s has faded. But the reason was because something more pressing took place, namely, the kinds of people who were correctly concerned about the threat of nuclear weapons by the mid-1960s did not become less concerned about the potential use of atomic weapons, but more concerned about the actual use of conventional weapons. After all, that was the period when the United States invaded Vietnam, and the rest of Indochina, and that was a very serious war. For us it was a limited war; for them it was a total war and it was a war of enormous scale.

A very substantial peace movement developed in the United States opposed to it and in comparison with the actual devastating use of weaponry in the course of American aggression in Indochina, the potential threat of a nuclear war faded into the background.

But don't you think the fear of nuclear war looms in the background?

For many people around the world, probably the large majority, concern over potential nuclear war is considered something of an abstraction. So for tens of millions of people who are dying of starvation every year, the concern over potential nuclear war is considered a little remote. And in fact I would suspect that they are a little bit cynical about it. What they perceive, and perceive accurately, is that we are now concerned that the horrors that we often impose on others might engulf us as well. That's what causes the disarmament movement here.

You often talk about the sheer quantity of firepower and you put it in quantitative terms that make it easier to grasp why this seems to be such a qualitatively greater threat than we've ever faced before. Do you think this helps people grasp the significance of the arms race?

Yes. But what I often point out are elements of our strategic system that are so minor that nobody's even discussing them. For example, on Dec. 16, 1982, according to the *New York Times*, the claim was made that a new era of strategic weaponry is being opened. And what they were referring to was the fact that the first squadron of updated B-52 bombers with Cruise missiles was going on alert. Now, that's such a small element of the strategic weapons system that nobody even talks about it. In fact, it was just a tiny little item in the back pages of the *Times*. Well, then they give the figures. I think it was approximately like this: one squadron has roughly 200 Cruise missiles; each Cruise missile is 15 Hiroshima equivalents or 15 times the Hiroshima bomb; one bomber is approximately the equivalent of one MX missile in its capacity, both in its tonnage and in the number of missiles. This is one squadron of what is ultimately going to be a triad of many squadrons of air and land and sea Cruise missiles. The latest number I saw mentioned was 3,000 Cruise missiles; that would be 45,000 Hiroshima equivalents. And that's an element of the strategic system that is so minor that nobody's even discussing it.

How does this change the character of defense planning of governments around the world?

The reason why the situation is such a great threat to the United States, as well as everyone else, is the new systems are almost forcing the Russians to adopt a launch-on-warning strategy. Strategic analysts in the United States and in Russia have pointed out that they do not leave time for response.

Why is that?

First of all, the MX-missile systems, and the Trident and I would think also the Cruise, have first-strike capability. That's been conceded by the Pentagon. The Pentagon has pointed out that they have been unable to eliminate the first-strike capability from the MX system. The reason is they are too powerful, too precise. This means that the Russians have to assume that this is a potential first-strike weapon. Furthermore, the Pershing II systems that are to be implanted in Western Europe (if they are deployed in Western Europe) have a very short flight time. The Russians say ten minutes or so. And again that's a first-strike weapon.

It means there is no time for response. For this reason the Russians will duplicate these systems. It means that the chances of human intervention to prevent the nuclear strike are reduced. If it looks as if there is a threat of first strike, they are going to have to launch missiles because there is no way of being sure that the threat is not real.

Aren't there controls programmed into our defense systems?

A computerized response system is extraordinarily dangerous. We have a computerized response system and fortunately nobody pays any attention to it. A number of times (we don't know how many, but certainly many times) it's given a warning that there is a Russian missile attack and therefore we should send our missiles off, and human intervention has aborted it. The warnings happened because of radar misidentifications or computer-programming errors or system malfunctions. So far, there has been time for human intervention and we have not had launch-on-warning. It has been possible to stop the programmed response. Now there is no question but that the Russian systems are worse technically than ours and their systems are going to have more errors. The chances of their launching a nuclear strike will be increased because they will be moving towards the launch-on-warning-type system and computerized systems which leave little time for human response. If there is a threat that Pershing II missiles can hit them in five or ten minutes, there is no time to do anything. For reasons such as these, these systems are an extreme danger to the United States.

Do these systems represent more of a threat than those opposed by the disarmament movement of the 60s?

Then, the scale was much less, although a thousand Minuteman missiles constitute a tremendous firepower. It's interesting to remember that the arms buildup at that time was in response to a completely fabricated Russian threat, a so-called missile-gap, which in fact did not exist. Our firepower far outmatched that of Russia, which was alleged to have had four operational missiles at the time. And I think there is an equally fabricated threat today.

As an educator, how can you accurately assess the facts concerning nuclear weaponry since so much of this information is considered state secrets?

The facts made public in Pentagon releases are certainly sufficient for an educator.

Do you feel that there are enough facts and figures available to the public for people to assess the problems and work out a plan for peace?

Even the popular press provides accurate and sufficient information for assessment. For example, you can read in the public press that the Pentagon says that the MX-missile has a first-strike capability, and that it will therefore drive the Russians to launch-on-warning strategy. Or you can read that in *Science,* the journal of the American Association for the Advancement of Science. Information is certainly available publicly through various publications and government officials. It's true that there may be even more horrifying things that we don't know about. But what we do know about is sufficient for an informed reaction and to be able to discern that new systems are being introduced that are a tremendous threat to our existence.

In discussions of disarmament, one question is: Are you for unilateral disarmament? And the other question that gets confused in all of this is: Are you for total disarmament? If in some sense you feel that having the means of war prevents war and yet you are in favor of disarmament, how do you reconcile these two positions?

What I'm in favor of is the immediate reduction in the means of destruction and, secondly, political or diplomatic moves to reduce tensions and conflicts throughout the world. Those are the immediate things. Now, talk about unilateral disarmament is theology. I mean, it's not politically realistic. And if we want to move to that abstract plane which is quite removed from policy, then in my view we shouldn't have unilateral disarmament. I do think that deterrence probably works. And I think that makes life more complicated, but nevertheless it is true.

What about the economic turn that the disarmament argument has taken? You mentioned that between 1980 and 1982 the business sector seems to have changed its mind about disarmament. What are the reasons for that?

It's very interesting that in 1980 the business community was very strongly in favor of Reagan's program of vastly increasing military spending. And by 1982, that shifted. There's lobbying against an increase of the military budget.

Lobbying by whom?

Business Roundtable, for example, which in 1982 is the main business lobbying group. And there was a poll by the *Wall Street Journal* which reported that about 83 percent of Wall Street executives were opposed to increases or sharp increases in the military budget. They wanted to level them off. Now, these are the same people who were calling for a major expansion in the military budget two years earlier. Well, what happened? Was there a reduction in the military threat to the United States in the last two years? I think not.

Why would the business community make a 90-degree turn in the idea of disarmament?

In 1980, I think the business community assumed that Reagan's program for military buildup had some chance of success. It was to use military expenditures basically as a pump priming technique for the economy, a technique of reindustralization. The military system in the United States is basically a government-guaranteed market for high-technology production. It is the technique that we use for industrial policy planning for encouraging growth and development in high-tech industries such as computers and electronics.

So, in 1980 there was the problem of reindustrialization and the classic mechanism was chosen to resolve the problem: increase the state's share in the economy. It is not a conservative program; in fact, quite the contrary. Reagan's program was to increase the state's component of the state capitalistic system by the classic means. This was the same means Kennedy used, the same means that was used in 1950; as a matter of fact, the same means that got us out of the Depression. In effect, this means the government will intervene by increasing demand for arms and high technology production to get things moving again. In 1980, that looked reasonable, and business supported the policy as it's always supported it.

By 1982 it no longer looked reasonable. The reason had nothing to do with the military; the reason was that it was contributing to huge deficits. Government deficits are now out of sight and that has a dangerous economic impact in the long term. Furthermore, Reagan had not succeeded in one crucial element of this system: he failed to get our so-called allies to follow a similar plan. This is a very harmful system economically; it does spur production but in a very wasteful manner. Therefore, we have to make sure that our commercial rivals also harm their economy, roughly to the extent that we harm ours; otherwise we're in trouble. This wasn't a problem for Kennedy because we were so paramount that it didn't much matter what anybody else did. But now we have real rivals.

Japan is a rival. Europe is a rival, too. We can no longer tolerate the wastefulness of this type of economic pump priming and still expect to be competitive in world trade. Carter tried and failed and Reagan tried and also failed to get Germany to increase substantially its military budget. In the case of an impending Russian attack Germany would be on the front lines, but they refused to increase their military budget by half a percent or one percent.

What about Japan?

Japan's situation is more complicated. Japan has a very low military expenditure relative to its gross national product. But Japan is now interestingly thinking of increasing its military spending and when you look at the reasoning it would appear that they do not see some military threat. Rather, the reason is that they feel that they have more or less saturated the American markets that they can take over and they want in turn to try to take over some new markets. Well, one of the big markets in the United States is arms. And Japan thinks that they may be able to penetrate the American arms market, just as they've penetrated the automobile market and the electronics market. Of course, to do that, they have to have economies of scale. They'd have to have big production of their own, which means they would have to have a big military force. This would allow them to create their own turnover demand which, in turn, would enable them to produce high-quality, advanced-technology weaponry. They can then sell this weaponry to the American military, which has a huge and endless demand. That's one reason why they're now planning to build up their armament system to some extent: geared really towards sales rather than military considerations.

Do you see that pattern repeating itself with other economies as they industrialize?

Yes, to some extent.

Getting in on the world market?

France is a striking case. France relies heavily on arms exports, as does Israel.

Let's pursue this economic argument just a bit further. You mentioned one way in which the armaments are harming the economy—the big deficit. Some people would claim that armaments are inflationary; they contribute to inflation since every amount spent on arms is an amount taken from individual consumers and, consequently, dollars are worth less. This is an argument against military spending. What do you think?

I don't think it's that complicated. We're putting resources into military production and those resources are not going into things that can be sold, that meet consumer needs in the market. It's as simple as that. It's first of all true about material resources; it's also true of our intellectual resources. If our engineers are working on the latest technique for making a missile hit 3 mm closer than it did before, and the Japanese engineers are working on better home computers or something, you know what's going to happen.

We have a system in which the state intervenes in industrial policy planning; the Japanese have a system in which the state intervenes in industrial policy planning. The systems are in many ways similar. In both cases, the state intervenes to encourage the most advanced and potentially profitable industries. So, now it is lasers and fiber optics and microelectronics and so on. In the past, it was computers. In the 1950s, the government was almost the sole purchaser of computers and it invested vast sums in the development of that industry. That is the way we got the computer industry going. Japan is doing the same thing. The government sponsors investment in promising-looking industries. So far it's equivalent.

What's different is that the Japanese system is geared for the commercial market. They try to increase competitiveness among participants. They want to have many people producing a commodity and have the most efficient win out. They try to organize and direct their production towards the international market. Our system, on the other hand, works quite differently, since our system is the Pentagon system. It is only by accident that it has any commercial utility. It's really geared for weapons production, waste production from an economic point of view. And it is or it's geared against competitiveness. The Pentagon wants a monopoly. It's geared for cost overruns. You reward people for cost overruns because they always get it. So it rewards poor management practices and it rewards monopoly. It only by the sheerest accident has a commercial side—a sort of spin-off. Well just compare these two systems and you can predict quite well what's going to happen to world trade. And it's happening. And business understands it, and that's part of the reason for their shift in attitude. Again a crucial point is that none of this has anything to do with military threats. Nothing.

The interesting thing about this argument that you have mounted here is that you are using the same premises that the business community is operating on and yet drawing a different set of conclusions than the business community would have come to several years ago.

I think they made a tactical error. I don't accept their premises but, for the sake of argument, if we accept their premises, I think they made a tactical error in supposing that the military with their traditional methods of management and production could work in 1980. They couldn't. And they now see that they didn't.

Editor's Notes to Interview 23

"Cycles in U.S. Foreign Policy: Of Cold War and Constraints," *Harvard International Review* 5:5 (March 1983), pp. 23–24, part of a group of articles (the first two by Arthur Schlesinger and Zbigniew Brzezinski) under the title "America in the World," the theme of the issue. "Professor Chomsky was interviewed in his MIT office by *IR* Senior Editor Joel Goodfader" on Feb. 1, 1983. "A renowned linguist at MIT [who] has published widely on international politics" (including a major "work on the Middle East in the wake of the Lebanese war," i.e. FT, then in press) and "probably the most well-known and lucid critic of American foreign policy, Noam Chomsky provides yet another incisive and unique critique of the United States as an actor in world affairs." (The quotes are from the preliminary note to the published version.)

"NSC 68" is the April 1950 National Security Council report proposing a vast program of militarization of the U.S. economy. See **TCNW** (1982), pp. 21–23.

For another answer to the the last question, see the end of I18.

23. America in the World (1 February 1983)

Since the theme of this issue is "America in the World: Reagan's Foreign Policy at Midterm," I'd like to take as our point of departure your concept of where the Reagan administration, in terms of its foreign policy, falls in the trajectory of past administrations. In your recent book Towards a New Cold War: Essays on the Current Crisis and How We Got There, *you outline what you see as a direct parallel between the first Cold War and what you have dubbed the "New Cold War," which you sense is emerging at present. Could you please elaborate on some of these points?*

There has been a recurrent cycle in American foreign policy since the end of the Second World War. Repeatedly, there have been moments at which a certain collection of policies have been introduced: acceleration of the military system; intensification of confrontation vis-a-vis the Soviet Union; international aggressiveness, sometimes called counterinsurgency; and the corresponding cutbacks in social programs, and so on and so forth. There's a collection of things which go together, and with some variations we see this collection being reinstituted periodically.

One such point was in the late 1940s. NSC 68 is a clear expression of such a program, and in fact was implemented shortly after a proper excuse was found, namely the Korean War, which took place after the program was enunciated. Nevertheless, the war was the occasion for its implementation. Another occasion was the Kennedy administration, which is very similar to the Reagan administration in its policies—remarkably similar—which tells us something about the real spectrum of policy in the United States. But if you think about what the Kennedy administration actually was, after clearing away all the rhetoric about Camelot and so on, its policies in fact amounted to a massive intensification of the military system; a regressive tax cut to spur investment on the domestic side; international aggressiveness, subversion, and intervention on a huge scale, and heightening of the Cold War confrontation with the Soviet Union—which are the essential policies of the Reagan administration.

There are differences. The actions of the two administrations do not take exactly the same form. One difference, for example, is that the Kennedy administration had the intelligence to buy off the intelligentsia. He also realized that they come very cheap, by giving them the sense of some kind of share in power. As a result, the image of the Kennedy administration is very different from that of the Reagan administration. There's no Camelot today because Reagan expresses utter contempt for the people who do the propaganda work—the intelligentsia, the historians, and so on and so forth. But the policies are quite similar. Of course they're quite different in their outcome. Kennedy's policies basically worked, whereas Reagan's reapplication basically fails, and that's just the difference in the objective status of the United States as a world power in 1960 versus 1980.

To what extent do you think Reagan has succeeded in mobilizing the nation by rattling his confrontational, polarized, "Cold War" saber?

Very badly. The first thing he tried to do as soon as he came into office was to stir up sufficient hysteria over international affairs and Central America so that there would be the basis for actual American intervention, I suppose. Well that just collapsed totally.

Take the White Paper, for example, which came out in February 1981. If you look at the details of the reaction they are really rather interesting. The White Paper was accepted virtually without critical analysis at first. Not as much in Europe, but here if you look at the press response, it was quite favorable and it was taken at its face value. And an effort was made, as always, to get the intelligentsia to go along with the government program to stir up chauvinistic hysteria, and lay the basis for a more aggressive confrontationalist program. Well, it didn't work at all. There was a popular reaction on a remarkable scale. It was a spontaneous, unorganized, American-style thing. As a result, the administration began to draw back and dampen its rhetoric, and shortly afterwards, predictably, all the criticisms of the White Paper started to come out. The *Wall Street Journal*, the *Washington Post*, and the *New York Times*, incidentally, did give critical analyses several months afterwards, after the administration had already gone back on its confrontationalist pose in response to the popular reaction. So, this sort of detailed structure of what happened is not uninteresting. It reflects something about the way ideology and interests interact in a country like this.

But, yes, I think Reagan has failed completely to stir up the chauvinistic passions that Kennedy, for example, succeeded very well in stirring up. Compare Reagan's efforts to move to a more interventionist stance, particularly in Central America, with Kennedy's efforts. Kennedy actually invaded South Vietnam in 1962. That's an event that doesn't appear in official party history in the United States, but it took place nevertheless. In 1962, the American Air Force began the systematic bombardment of South Vietnam. That's what we call aggression when somebody else does it. It's basically party history. Just as in Russian party history there's no such event as the Russian invasion of Afghanistan, in American party history there's no such event as the American invasion of South Vietnam. But it took place under Kennedy and there was no reaction to it. In fact, some of the early decisions of the Kennedy administration which are not very well known are extraordinarily important in contemporary world affairs. In fact, it was one of the most important decisions of modern history that was taken by the Kennedy administration in 1961 when they shifted the mission of the Latin American military from hemispheric defense to internal security. This means war against their own populations, and that's what has set off this wave of terror and torture states throughout Latin America. Brutal neo-Nazi regimes being instituted in one country after another, spreading over the continent in a way that has no precedent—it is a bloody and murderous history. That was the result of an early decision of the Kennedy administration to which there was no critical response.

How egalitarian and stable would Latin America have been anyway?

It's hard to say what might have been. But I think that there were many other possibilities that Chile, and Uruguay, and many other countries might have been very different. Guatemala is a clear case. It would have been a very different country if it had not been for the American intervention. What would have happened? There are many imponderables, but you can say the same about the Nazis.

Moving on to a specific area of foreign policy, what do you think the Israeli invasion success in southern Lebanon means for the Middle East in terms of your personal hopes to see a bi-national state somehow establish? Also, would you comment on the Reagan plan? Where do we go from here?

First of all, I should say that in the long run a bi-national state is a very reasonable idea. But ,unfortunately, from 1967 to 1973, Israel did not have the farsightedness and intelligence that could have instituted such a movement. By 1973 any possibility of this was finished, and the only feasible alternative at that point was what became the international consensus, namely, the two-state settlement. The invasion of Lebanon did succeed in aborting the international consensus which was becoming a danger. Israel's main purpose in invading Lebanon was to create the basis for settlement in the occupied territories along the lines it intends. The most frightening thing to Israel in the last year or so was that the PLO strictly observed the cease-fire and that was, as an Israeli analyst put it, a "veritable catastrophe" for the government of Israel because it was becoming more and more difficult to portray the PLO as simply a gang of thugs. It was assumed that by the destruction of the social life and territorial base of the PLO, it might be possible to get them to revert to random terrorism which would be a much more healthy situation from the viewpoint of Israel and the United States.

Israel itself is a peripheral interest of the United States. The main interest in the Middle East is of course the oil, which is obviously true since the end of the Second World War. The question is how to insure that control over oil production and distribution will be largely dominated by the United States. As far as American foreign policy makers are actually concerned, I think that they want to maintain Israel as a powerful Spartan state, increasingly militarized, increasingly bound to the United States. It's not technically part of the base structure for the Rapid Deployment Force, but it belongs to that same picture and it's the base for the projection of American power. They want to preserve that. At the same time they have to offer the elites in the Arab states something which they can use to calm down their own populations and to repress the kinds of nationalist and radical forces that are aroused by the Israeli occupation and what is happening with the Palestinians. So there's a lot of things to pull together. What they would like to do, therefore, is to achieve some kind of settlement which on a rhetorical level would enable people to use words like "self-determination," but on the concrete level would integrate the areas within Israel.

If you were to wake up tomorrow morning, and find yourself at the State Department, not MIT, and you were secretary of state, what initiative would you take?

First of all, I'd move towards a genuine disarmament, because I think the current technical programs that the United States is pursuing are probably a greater danger to the United States than the policies of any of its enemies. Our new nuclear systems, the MX-missile and the Pershing, are probably going to drive the Russians to some kind of launch-on-warning strategy which almost guarantees the destruction of the United States sooner or later. The first thing I'd do is abort these programs and move toward some genuine disarmament. Then I would move at once to put an end to the American policy of supporting various neo-Nazi monsters all over the world, particularly in Central America, which is the most striking case, and in other regions. As far as the Middle East is concerned, I'd move toward the international consensus and so on.

However, though I could add a whole range of other policies, I should add this qualification: I couldn't do any of these things. The fact is that the constraints of parameters within which any policy-maker operates are rather narrow, and they're set from the outside, they're set by real interests. The real interests in society are those of the people that own it. Objective power lies elsewhere. Decision-making power does not lie in the political sphere.

Editor's Notes to Interview 24

Changes, July–August 1983, pp. 5–6 & 28. It was conducted on June 4 in Chicago by the editor, David Finkel, an activist in the Palestinian Human Rights Campaign.

For more on the first question, see *The Deadly Connection: Nuclear War and U.S. Intervention.* Edited by Joseph Gerson, New England Regional Office of the American Friends Service Committee. Foreword by Bishop Thomas J. Gumbleton. Philadelphia: New Society Publishers, 1986, in particular Chomsky's "Patterns of Intervention," the transcript of a talk given in December 1982.

For more on the resolution of the Santa Monica City Council, "regarded as a virtually socialist enclave," see **FT**, 266ff.; for more on Michael Walzer, "the noted social democratic theorist of 'just wars' …much respected in U.S. intellectual circles as a humanitarian and moral thinker," see **FT**, pp. 117, 139, 263, 265 & 274, and Chomsky's "An Exception to the Rule," a review of Walzer's *Just and Unjust Wars: A Moral Argument with Historical Illustrations,* 1977 (*Inquiry,* April 7, 1978, pp. 23–27), to be included in Chomsky's *The Masters of Mankind,* ed. by Mark Pavlick. Monroe, Maine: Common Courage Press (forthcoming). (Walzer had reviewed **PME** in the *New York Times Book Review,* Oct. 6, 1975, p. 21.) Chomsky's critique of Walzer's position on the "just war" and how their differing views reflect their differing values and standards is the topic of Chapter 1, Section 1, of Shaun Harbord's *An Historian's Appraisal of the Political Writings of Noam Chomsky* (M.A. Thesis, University of Kent in Canterbury, November 1987). Harbord argues that Chomsky presents a more convincing picture of the particular incident they discuss (the Israeli attack on Egypt in June 1967). Compare Edward W. Said's "Canaanite reading" of Walzer's *Exodus and Revolution* in Part 3 ("The 'liberal' alternative") of *Blaming the Victims: Spurious Scholarship and the Palestinian Question,* edited by Said & Christopher Hitchens (London: Verso, 1987), pp. 161–78.

The collection edited by Irving Howe (editor of the American Democratic Socialist journal *Dissent*) and Carl Gershman is *Israel, the Arabs, and the Middle East* (Quadrangle Books, 1972).

24. Priorities for the Peace Movement (4 June 1983)

What do you see as the most important priorities for the American peace movement at this time?

There is a range of concerns, all related a lot more closely than many people think. First, to prevent superpower confrontation and nuclear war; second, **the concern with interventionism** in its current manifestation, which is the American attempt to prevent independent nationalist development anywhere in the world; and then the question of the forces internal to American society which maintain that dynamic. Ultimately, unless one can get to the internal dynamics of this society we'll only be putting bandages on the wounds.

I think these three commitments should be integrated a lot more closely. My feeling is that the part of this movement that is overwhelmingly the largest—the anti-nuclear movement—focuses its concerns on the advances in the technology of the arms race. But those people are making a very serious error in not concerning themselves with the issues of intervention.

Let's say our primary concern is just preventing a nuclear war, let's assume that's all that really matters—even though I don't accept that assumption myself. Now, how do we do that? One issue to be concerned with is the technological developments, but another, and I think far more important, is how to prevent a nuclear war from breaking out. So your concern should be with the flash points at which such a war may erupt—and those are all Third World crises.

The chances of nuclear war breaking out in Europe are just about zero. The Israeli invasion of Lebanon in 1982 had a much greater chance of producing that result, and this is even more true of the potential new war there. If Israel attacks Syria again there could be a Russian response, then an American one, and then the possibility of nuclear war.

The American intervention in Nicaragua is, if anything, intended to bring about a superpower confrontation. I think, for once, that the Reagan administration is telling the truth, in their own way, when they say their goal is to confront Cuba and the Soviet Union, not the Sandinistas themselves. This administration desperately needs such an atmosphere, because they cannot sell their domestic program of transferring resources from the poor to the rich without resorting to the classic technique of international confrontation. So the people who concern themselves only with nuclear war should concern themselves with these issues. But I still reject the single focus on nuclear war. In fact, for the Guatemalan peasant, I think the question of nuclear war is rather abstract.

Is your position essentially the same as that of the current in the European disarmament movement represented by E.P. Thompson, or do you see important differences?

We have differences in emphasis, probably because we have different audiences in mind. From the European point of view, the issues of intervention, while important, are not central in quite the same way they are for Americans. The exception to this would be the French interventions in Africa, which are continuing under the French Socialist Party government, but the French are mostly outside the peace movement.

I don't really think there is a French peace movement. They protest what the United States does, but you can't find any protest in the French press when South Africa attacks Namibia with French planes, or over France selling arms to Indonesia.

But leaving this aside, in terms of **the European movement**, E.P. Thompson is talking to people who on the whole are less directly involved in intervention. That movement is part of a long-term trend to separate Europe from the superpower Cold War system of confrontation, and this accounts for Thompson's emphasis.

How far back does your own involvement with anti-war issues go?

As active involvement, my work goes back about 20 years to the Vietnam War.

What has happened to the peace movement since Vietnam?

I don't accept the perception that the peace movement disappeared after Vietnam. True, it stopped being a visible mass movement. But the number of people involved in **movement activity** wasn't noticeably different **in the 1970s** than the 60s.

In fact, look at feminism, which was extremely small in the 60s. It became a mass popular movement in the 1970s, with a dramatic effect on American society and culture. The fact that people ignore this, and think the movement "died" in the 1970s, proves some of the justice of the feminist critique. Or take the anti-nuclear movement. There are lots of people involved in one or another kind of political activism.

There aren't the central issues around which everyone came together in the late 1960s, say for a mass demonstration against the Vietnam War. But look at what happened when Reagan began escalating in Central America in 1981. I am sure they assumed there would be no popular response, because in their own perceptions the movement was dead. But there was a very large response, in February and March '81, and they had to back off from the track they were on.

Focussing in on the Middle East, I find a sense among activists for Palestinian human rights that they have to reach out to the broader peace movement, that their own forces aren't enough to affect policy. The kind of meeting going on right here is an example. But how do you evaluate the progress overall?

My feeling is that people involved with Palestinian rights—I am one of them—have **a dismal record of reaching the American public.** Not nearly enough effort has been put into that. As a result the expansionist-Israeli point of view, which is called the Zionist point of view, has totally taken over American public opinion to an extent I have never seen on any other issue. It's almost like a totalitarian system. Public opinion is so completely dominated by expansionist-Israeli views that even the Israeli peace movement can barely get a hearing. Not to mention the Palestinian viewpoint.

Against this background the solidarity movements can do very little. True, it's scandalous that the many solidarity movements haven't focussed on, for example, the crucial Israeli connection in Central America. But the solidarity movements around Central America have tended to play this down, because they are afraid they would lose not just liberal, but much of their left-liberal, support.

This goes all the way to the Santa Monica City Council. This past summer they passed a resolution defending the Israeli invasion of Lebanon. And at the time George Schultz became secretary of state, they criticized the appointment—because of his so-called "Arab connection." This when Israel was smashing and destroying Palestinians, and all these extreme leftists—extreme racists, actually—of the Santa Monica City Council, who many people thought were practically some kind of Bolshevik cell, could talk about was "this grave danger to Israel," as they called it.

In my experience, pacifists have given practically no support to Palestinian non-violent resistance. There has been enormous resistance such as shopkeepers' strikes in the West Bank. Or, look at the Golan Heights' strikes. This was classic passive resistance, and the Israeli army came in, imposed curfews, blockaded them, wouldn't let them go to their jobs.

I saw nothing about this in the pacifist press. But passive resistance only works if it attracts attention. If pacifists won't even support the non-violent resistance, then violence of course becomes a certainty.

The most disgraceful people on this issue are the so-called Democratic Socialists. For years they have supported every Israeli brutality. Even Michael Walzer, the "humanist" socialist and Zionist, advocated the transfer of Israeli Arabs out of the country. He says, being a humanist, that when there are groups which are "marginal to the nation," sometimes the most human thing is to help them leave. And of course it's the Arabs in Israel who are "marginal" to that nation.

This sounds like some South African lunatic. Here a Democratic Socialist says it and people applaud and call him a humanist. When the Israeli Labor Party, while it was in power, destroyed the West Bank unions, there was no protest from *Dissent*. (You can find this in the collection edited by Irving Howe and Carl Gershman.) But when Daniel Berrigan protested it, Irving Howe went after him using all the old-style vilification techniques he learned during his years in the old sectarian Left.

People like Irving Howe, contrary to what they claim now, were very much in favor of the American war in Vietnam, and they were worried about the challenge to American society from students, from the black movement, and from Third World forces, which they saw as being all part of a barbarian menace at the gates. What they saw was Israel coming along and showing how to really smash these things up—and they loved it.

There are people, of course, who have a perfectly rational reason for supporting Israeli expansionism: those who feel the U.S. should maintain control of the Middle East and suppress all nationalist movements by force. They naturally support an Israeli Sparta to do that kind of work for them. And they are going to want Israel to be a pariah state. For the militarists and neo-conservatives, that is the best thing, because it makes Israel all the more U.S.-dependent. They're quite right, from their own point of view, so why argue with them?

One must reach the general public who are being spoon-fed this propaganda.

Do you see any possibilities for political action by the peace movement in the coming election year?

The elections should be used as they're always used, to raise issues. I don't think the electoral system means much here, except maybe at the lowest local levels.

The election gives a forum in which issues can be raised, but **electoral tactics** have to be premised on a high degree of **popular support**—which isn't there on the issues we've just been discussing. The attitude in this country toward Palestinians is a form of racism so extreme I cannot remember anything like it.

This is much more extreme than anti-Semitism ever was in the U.S. I know something about that, because I grew up in a German-Catholic neighborhood where we were the only Jews. People were openly pro-Nazi, and I knew there were certain blocks I couldn't walk down or I'd get my head beat in, but even so it was nothing like what we see toward the Palestinians today. You have to go back to the Old South to find anything toward blacks the way Palestinians are portrayed in our mass media.

It's the peace movement's fault to have allowed this, and in fact to have participated in creating the racist climate.

Granted, this is a blind spot in American society and even within the peace movement. How does it affect the other domestic and global issues the peace movement is trying to contend with?

In a certain respect the Reagan administration is actually rather similar to the Kennedy administration, which used a fake "missile gap," confrontation and counter-insurgency around the world, and a regressive tax cut to stimulate the economy.

You can't come to the population and say, "Wouldn't it be nice to kill a couple of thousand more Guatemalan peasants?" People don't like to be gangsters. You have to frighten them with the Russian menace.

So you see these factors coming together, particularly in a period of economic crisis. They're not related to any actual threat to America security. Just as Kennedy's "missile gap" was exposed within weeks, Reagan's "window of vulnerability" was officially disavowed—and the very next day they went for the MX.

There are some slight differences between administrations which may make a great difference. This administration, for example, followed the same policy as the Carter administration in El Salvador after May 1980. But the Carter administration regarded it as a local problem, of applying enough force to keep our friends in power, while the Reagan administration posed it as a struggle against Soviet power. Part of their domestic policy is also massive subsidies of high-technology military industries, and there's only one way to get taxpayers to pay for it: frighten them.

The U.S. has been more than pleased to obtain a dependent, yet technologically advanced client state that will undertake U.S. interests in places and situations, like the Guatemalan genocide, where it is not politically convenient for the U.S. to do so.

For Israel itself the consequences are devastating—from the inevitable moral deterioration of the society, which in my opinion is no small matter, because of the values inherent in carrying out these tasks for the U.S., to the fact that it sooner or later ends in disaster whether from the internal situation or the situation of permanent war. This is why many Israeli doves have actually called for an end of aid to Israel.

The consequences are far more devastating to the people immediately at the other end of the club—the Palestinians, the Guatemalan peasantry—but sooner or later the chances are it must engulf all of us, deliberately or by accident, in a Third World conflict that blows out of control.

There is a threat that Israel is at a point where it may be moving beyond even the United States' ability to control it, in the traditional sense. In some of its actions Israel is beginning to act like a so called "crazy state," a term which was actually invented by an Israeli scholar to refer to states like Libya or Iran, but describes more accurately the behavior of Israel itself at this point. They even talk of having missiles that can reach the southern Soviet Union, or the "Samson complex" under which they would destroy the entire Middle East if threatened themselves. That could bring Russia and the United States in. Once they come into **confrontation in the Middle East**, that's it. You can just forget everything else.

Editor's Notes to Interview 25

Untitled, unpublished. The questions, divided in two groups (politics, science), were submitted on June 13, 1983, during her tenure as a visiting scientist at the MIT Center for Cognitive Science by Dr. Celia Jakubowicz, a researcher at the Centre National de la Recherche Scientifique (CNRS), Laboratoire de Psychologie Experimentale, Paris, and former professor in the department of psychology, Universidad Nacional de Buenos Aires. The written answers are dated June 16, 1983. The interview, one of the most comprehensive, was to appear in Spanish translation in *Síntomas* (Buenos Aires). Some of the topics of the second part are taken up again, one and a half years later, in I34.

On the question of generative grammar and psychoanalysis, see the fourth section of the Introduction.

A representative example of an article written in English by "a 'Marxist' who understands little about Marx or about science" is "The Reactionary Idealist Foundations of Noam Chomsky's Linguistics," *Literature and Ideology* 4 (1969), pp. 1–20; for the reference to one in Italian, see Ramaiah & Chandra, p. 72. Cf. I9.

A variation on Bakunin's "instinct for freedom" is found in I13.

25. Politics and Science (16 June 1983)

I. Politics

Most of your political writings are concerned with U.S. foreign policy and the role played by intellectuals in modern industrial societies. Could you spell out the reasons why these two subjects should be given priority in the analysis of political facts.

The main reasons for my concern with U.S. foreign policy are that I find it in general horrifying, and that I think that is possible for me to do something to modify it, at least to mitigate some of its most dangerous and destructive aspects. In the concrete circumstances of my own society, where I live and work, there are various ways to do this: speaking, writing, organizing, demonstrating, resisting, and others. Over the years, I've been engaged in a variety of such activities.

The foreign policy of other states is also in general horrifying—roughly speaking, states are violent to the extent that they have the capacity to act in the interests of those with domestic power—but there is not very much that I can do about it. It is, for example, easy enough for an American intellectual to write critical analyses of the behavior of the Soviet Union in Afghanistan and Eastern Europe (or in supporting the Argentine generals), but such efforts have little if any effect in modifying or reversing the actions of the USSR. Rather, such efforts, which are naturally much welcomed by those who dominate the ideological institutions here, may serve to contribute to the violence of the American state, by reinforcing the images of Soviet brutality (often accurate) that are used to frighten Americans into conformity and obedience. I do not suggest that this is a reason to avoid critical analysis of the USSR; in fact, I have often written on the foreign policy of the Soviet state. Nor would I criticize someone who devotes much, even all his work to this task. But we should understand that the moral value of this work is at best very slight, where the moral value of an action is judged in terms of its human consequences. In fact, rather delicate judgments sometimes arise, for people who are committed to decent moral values. Suppose, for example, that some German intellectual chose in 1943 to write articles on terrible things done by Britain, or the U.S., or Jews. What he wrote might be correct, but we would not be very much impressed.

The same comments hold for a Soviet intellectual who devotes himself to a critical analysis of U.S. atrocities in Southeast Asia or Central America (or to the American support for the Argentine generals). What he says may be correct; its significance, for people being bombed or terrorized or tortured within the domains of American power and influence is negligible, possibly even negative. These are truisms, constantly denied by intellectual servants of state power who, for obvious reasons, pretend not to understand them and typically criticize those who act in accordance with decent moral principles as having a "double standard" or worse.

I try to concentrate my political activities—writing included—in areas where there is some moral significance to these activities, hence primarily in areas where people I can reach may act to change policies that are abhorrent, dangerous and destructive. Of course there are other factors that influence my choices, facts about my personal history, etc., which are of no interest here. One can have many reasons for engaging in political action. If the reasons are to help suffering people, to avert threats or catastrophes, and so on, then the criteria are fairly clear. For an American intellectual, these criteria dictate a prime concern for policies undertaken and pursued here, whether in the international or domestic arenas.

In some intellectual circles, it is considered naive or foolish to try to be guided by moral principles. About this **form of idiocy**, I will have nothing to say.

I should emphasize that I have tried to follow these criteria (qualified by matters of personal interest and personal history) in all of the areas of political action in which I have been engaged. Writing has been only one part of this, and in fact a rather small part. I do a vast amount of speaking, and for many years was extensively engaged in direct action of one or another sort (demonstrations, resistance, etc.).

Here questions of tactical judgment arise. In the current situation here, there are a number of contributions that intellectuals can make to the struggle for peace and justice—and today, the struggle for survival, not a small consideration in an era when the likelihood of global nuclear war is reaching dangerous levels. One is to serve as a "resource," to provide information and analysis. American intellectuals are highly privileged. They have the kind of training, facilities, access to information and opportunity to organize and control their own work that enable them to make a very significant contribution to people who are trying to escape the confines of indoctrination and to understand something about the real world in which they live; in particular, to people who may be willing to act to change this world. For the same reasons, they can be active and effective as organizers. Furthermore, by virtue of their privilege, intellectuals also are often "visible." They can exploit their privilege in valuable and important ways. For example, if actions of civil disobedience are undertaken by people who do not enjoy the privilege that is very unequally distributed in a class society, they are likely to be neglected, or to be crushed by force. If people who enjoy such privilege play a visible role in such actions, the danger of state violence is considerably lessened (in the U.S.; not everywhere), and the effectiveness of the action may also be enhanced.

These are quite substantive issues, which constantly arise in all forms of political action. People make different decisions, based on their tactical judgments and personal preference, as to how to distribute their commitments and actions among the various possibilities that the society allows. Some of my closest friends have chosen to dedicate themselves almost completely to organizing and direct action. I've chosen a somewhat different mixture, and it has varied at different times. In the 1960s, for example, I was much more involved in direct action on both foreign policy and domestic issues than I am today, the reasons being a different judgment as to how I can most effectively use my energy, my talents, and my privilege.

The reason I have devoted most of my writing and direct political action (though not all of it) to **problems of foreign policy** are several. In part it reflects a judgment as to relative importance: the impact of U.S. foreign policy on millions of people throughout the world is enormous, and furthermore these policies substantially increase the probability of superpower conflict and global catastrophe. In part, it reflects my feeling that while many people here do excellent and important work concerning crucial domestic issues, very few concerned themselves in the same way and with the same depth of commitment to foreign policy issues. In part, I suppose, it reflects personal factors which, again, are of little interest here.

In the domain of foreign policy, I have tried to focus my energies in areas that are not only significant, by the criteria just mentioned, but also relatively ignored. Take a concrete example. In the current period, the regions where U.S. foreign policy is having the most devastating impact—both in terms of immediate effects and long-term consequences—are Central America and the Middle East, in my judgment. I have personally chosen to concentrate most of my efforts on the Middle East, in part because of special knowledge and interest, in part because there are many people doing outstanding and important work on Central America, while the Middle East is generally avoided for reasons too complex to enter into here. Critical analysis of U.S. policy in Central America is relatively "well regarded" within the American system of power and ideology, perhaps because of the fact that many of those with real power are deeply concerned with the drift of American policy there, which they see as harmful to their own interests. The same is not true with regard to the Middle East. On the contrary, in this domain there is a "Party Line" that is extraordinarily effective, particularly among the intelligentsia, and that tolerates little deviation. Given this fact, and the obvious significance of the matter, it seems to me important to focus my own activities at this particular moment on U.S. foreign policy concerning the Middle East. Putting it a bit crudely, it is best to tell people that which they least want to hear, to take up the least popular causes, other things being equal. These are, of course, transitory and sometimes personal judgments.

Turning to the second part of the question, the reasons why I have spent a good deal of time and effort on the question of the role of the intellectuals in modern industrial society are basically two: one, again, reflects a judgment of importance, by the criteria already mentioned; another is simply that these are the circles in which I live and work. I am not, and will never be, a labor or peasant organizer, for example. Because of my own limitations, class background, training, place in the society, and so on, I can do certain things and not others. These considerations alone would lead me to concentrate attention on the ways in which the ideological institutions—the schools, the universities, the media and so on—serve to indoctrinate and control.

The importance of the topic seems to me unquestionable. In the modern period, the intelligentsia have become in large measure a kind of "**secular priesthood,**" devoted to service of the state and private institutions of power. Such service takes two typical forms, which in my view are not very different at their root. The Leninist model has had great appeal to the intelligentsia in certain places and periods because, beneath a facade of concern for the welfare of the masses of the population, it offers a justification for the acquisition of state power by the revolutionary intelligentsia, who, as Bakunin perceptively observed a century ago, will exploit mass popular struggles to construct a regime of terror and oppression. As he wrote, they will beat the people with "the people's stick."

Where such possibilities seem remote, the very same intellectuals typically turn to service existing institutions, since it is in association with state power that they can hope to gain influence, prestige, and sometimes even direct authority. It has been a striking feature of modern industrial societies that people have easily switched from one position to the other. In the United States, for example, a substantial segment of the intelligentsia were attracted by Leninist ideology during the 1930s; they sincerely believed that there was a "revolutionary situation," potentially at least, in the United States. A decade or two later, it was obvious that this assessment was incorrect. Many of the same people then turned to "celebration of America," as it was actually called: reinforcing and helping to create the system of Cold War indoctrination. While individuals have their own reasons, tendencies of this sort are easy to perceive, and easy to explain. The same has been true in many other cases.

The intelligentsia, who are the custodians of history and who play a significant role in creating the image of the present as well, have constructed a very different picture. They regard themselves as dissident, iconoclastic, independent, taking an adversary position to the state and private power. I think a more accurate analysis of the historical and contemporary record reveals something quite different, and that these characteristics are true of only a very few, who are furthermore typically maligned, vilified, marginalized, or in the more violent societies, simply removed or eliminated.

Limiting ourselves just to the United States, the intelligentsia—particularly, the dominant "liberal intelligentsia"—have, in my view, tended to be state propagandists. During the First World War, the liberal intelligentsia overwhelmingly offered their services to the state to help whip a generally pacifist population into the proper mood of chauvinism and hysteria; they took pride in the fact (which they exaggerated) that they had actually played the primary role in creating a consensus in support of war. During this period and subsequently, an explicit ideology was constructed justifying what was called "the manufacture of consent" (Walter Lippmann) or "the engineering of consent" (Edward Bernays, founding father of the public relations industry in the United States), a device that was held to be necessary in democratic societies, where the mass of the population could not be controlled directly by force and violence. Propaganda was highly valued as a technique to manufacture consent. In a variety of ways, a system of indoctrination of quite astonishing success was constructed, with the intelligentsia playing a major role—though to be realistic, a subordinate role, since the power they were serving, often unwittingly of course, lay elsewhere. These are factors of great significance in the capitalist industrial societies, in my view; and with variations, elsewhere as well.

One might ask why such enormous efforts should be devoted—as they are—to the engineering of consent. I think that the answer is quite simple (in fact, social and political issues in general seem to me fairly simple; the effort to obfuscate them in esoteric and generally vacuous theory is one of the contributions of the intelligentsia to enhancing their own power and the power of those they serve, as is the mindless "empiricism" conducted in the name of "science" but in fact in sharp contradiction to the methods of the sciences, which often succeeds in concealing major operative factors in policy and history in a maze of unanalyzed facts). Simply put, most people are not gangsters. Few people, for example, would steal food from a starving child, even if they happened to be hungry and knew they would not be caught or punished. Someone who did so would be properly regarded as pathological, and in fact, very few are pathological in this sense.

But in fact, Americans steal food from starving children on a vast scale. In much of Central America, for example, U.S. intervention has led to an increase in agricultural production while nutritional standards decline and millions starve and die, because crop lands have been devoted to export in the interests of agribusiness, not to the needs of the domestic population. One primary reason for the violent antagonism of the U.S. towards Cuba and Nicaragua, for example, is that they threatened to reverse this process. But since Americans are not gangsters, if they come to understand what they are doing (that they are in fact stealing food from starving children, on a vast scale), they would be appalled and would do something to put an end to this atrocity, as they can. Therefore, they must be protected from an understanding of this aspect of the real world.

There are innumerable similar examples. To achieve these ends, a powerful system of manufacture of consent is required, which takes various forms. The intelligentsia play a crucial part in insuring that it is effective and unchallenged, except in the most marginal fashion. Intellectuals who choose to do so can, correspondingly, assist in a kind of "intellectual self-defense," helping people to extricate themselves from the system of indoctrination and thought control, and thus, indirectly, helping to protect the victims of the violence that results from passive acquiescence or direct support for state policies. So, to return to the original question, this should, I think, be a topic of major concern for intellectuals who are really concerned with human welfare.

The Western liberal press often contrasts "democratic" societies such as the U.S. with "totalitarian" systems, the latter referring mainly to the Soviet Union and, occasionally, to some dictatorial regimes in Third World countries. In your writings you claim that the difference is basically a matter of form, namely, that in totalitarian societies the state establishes official truth and forbids the expression of dissident points of view, whereas in capitalist democracies censorship is imposed by more complex mechanisms. Please give some examples of the similarities and differences between these two forms of state control and answer the two following questions:

(1) If the system of indoctrination is so powerful even in the so-called democratic societies, is there any hope to overcome it or, at least, limit it?

(2) Is there any way the people of the Third World countries suffering from U.S. intervention (e.g. Central America) can do anything to help break U.S. mechanisms of aggression? (I have in mind your observations in class concerning Vietnamese actions with respect to public opinion in the United States.)

There are striking and important differences between the democratic and totalitarian societies, in many dimensions. In particular, the technique of manufacture of consent is entirely different. In a totalitarian society, the state declares official Truth, and individuals must conform—at least overtly—or they will suffer various punishments; how severe these punishments will be varies with the violence of the state. In the capitalist democracies this is generally untrue, at least for those who have relative privilege. One should mention here that the capitalist democracies do on occasion resort to direct violence to enforce consent, though this is not the typical mode. The FBI, throughout its history in the U.S., has been in large measure a national political police, and it has not hesitated to organize or directly employ violence to crush dissent, a fact that I and others have documented. But the typical function of the doctrinal system is quite different. It is also complex, and much more interesting to study and to understand than the totalitarian system for two very good reasons: first, from an intellectual point of view, precisely because the method is not transparent; and second, because that is the system to which we are subjected, and which we can change, if we commit ourselves to the task.

Let's consider just the U.S., though the situation is not markedly different elsewhere. It is too obvious to merit discussion that real power over crucial decision-making lies in the hands of those who own and manage the domestic economy and who, thereby, largely control the state apparatus.

One reflection of this power lies in their control over the media, which are, after all, major corporations and thus share the interests and concerns of other elements of **the corporate system**. If the media were to veer from these interests, pressures (rarely needed) could quickly be applied to control any such deviation, for example, advertising pressures, pressures on stock values, take-over, etc. Furthermore, the top managerial positions in these institutions are held by people whose class interest, associations and aspirations tend in the same direction, overwhelmingly. At a lower level, reporters and columnists will quickly learn that their future is dim unless they conform: those who refuse to do so are generally weeded out; others learn, acquiesce and end up internalizing the values and attitudes that they express.

Very much the same is true of the universities and schools, which are in large measure parasitic institutions, determined in character by outside forces, ultimately by the owners and managers of the domestic society. Again, shared class interest, association and aspiration also play a significant role. Dissidents are removed by a variety of techniques, from the earliest stages of the educational system. Those who are willing to conform ultimately internalize the values that support the institutional structures. The process is often transparent, in concrete cases. Young graduate students who choose to study, say, the topics I have just been discussing, will be made to understand, very quickly, that there is no future in this course. If they persist, they will either be removed in some fashion (irresponsible, lacking in collegiality, etc.), or will find that opportunities for education and employment are limited or nonexistent. Those who choose to concentrate on more acceptable topics, on the other hand, have relatively bright prospects: they can aspire to privilege and even a degree of power, prestige, and so on. It is hardly surprising, then, to find that, as a recent study showed, the question of corporate influences on American foreign policy is literally unmentioned in about 95 percent of standard works on international affairs and U.S. foreign policy (in contrast with such cosmic matters as the influence of scientists and clergymen), and receives "passing mention" in the remainder. A vast number of similar phenomena have been well-documented.

One of the most effective devices used by the properly disciplined (hence successful) intelligentsia is the mechanism of feigned dissent. In a totalitarian state, as noted, official Truth is proclaimed, and one must outwardly conform. In a democratic system of thought control, a more subtle device is used: controversy is encouraged, but within the framework of certain presuppositions, which are never expressed in a properly designed propaganda system, but which define the limits of "responsible" opinion. During and since the Vietnam War, for example, a great debate raged between "doves" and "hawks": the "doves" held that however the U.S. might try, it could not win at acceptable cost; the "hawks" denied this and held that victory was possible. Those who took the stand that the U.S. should not win, that it had no right of aggression and massacre, were simply not part of the debate, in the mainstream. As polls showed, more than two-thirds of the population held that the war was not just a failure or mistake, but that it was fundamentally and morally wrong from the start; they had virtually no voice in the official debate. Among the intelligentsia themselves, such principled objection to the war was extremely rare, as is again well-documented. The vigorous debate between the "doves" and the "hawks" thus has the effect of more firmly implanting the crucial doctrinal position: the U.S. has the right to use force and violence to attend its ends. The doctrine is not asserted; rather, it is presupposed. Acceptance of the doctrine is an entry ticket to respectable circles. The example is an interesting one because it illustrates, in this case, how the intelligentsia are not only the proponents but also the most deluded victims of the ideological system, though in the long run their position will win out, since memories will fade and those who did not experience the facts directly will come to accept the official version. This **technique of feigned dissent** thus makes a notable contribution to the manufacture of consent, and often shows spectacular success. Other devices too might be mentioned. The result is the destruction of any culture of dissidence, and the imposition of passive acquiescence and conformity, to an extent that sometimes reaches quite remarkable levels.

How can we counteract this system? Again, there are no secrets here. Within the capitalist democracies, there is considerable freedom, particularly for those with a degree of privilege. Dissidents are not thrown into concentration camps or torture chambers (in the U.S., that is). There are innumerable opportunities for organization, explanation, and often direct action over a wide range—from electoral politics to resistance of one or another sort. During the Vietnam War, for example, popular forces were organized in this way that departed radically from the doctrinal system and acted, with some effectiveness, to modify policy. The same is true with regard to Central America today. The successes are limited when compared to the scale of the problems, but they suffice to show that success is possible. Notice that in these cases the institutional structures themselves were not seriously challenged, which is, of course, why dissent, protest and resistance could be effective. A challenge to the institutional structures themselves (**a truly revolutionary challenge**) is another matter entirely.

As for what the victims of American power can do, there is unfortunately little to say beyond the obvious, which is that they should attempt to present their case in a way that can be effective and can contribute to the work of those in the U.S. who are concerned with their fate. One can, unfortunately, cite many examples where this has not been done, leading to much suffering.

In your writings you argue that, contrary to what the liberal press leads us to believe, the principal present danger does not lie in a direct confrontation between the U.S. and the USSR, but rather in the struggle that each of the superpowers wages against the countries that are in their respective sphere of influence in order to inhibit independent development. Please illustrate this point and answer the following question: Do you think that two of the present major conflicts, those of Central America and the Middle East, may be analyzed from the perspective that you suggest?

Let's consider Central America and the Middle East, which are, I think, the crucial cases today. Keeping now to the post-World War II period, the U.S. has repeatedly intervened in Central America to prevent the development of independent nationalist forces that would perpetrate the ultimate sin: attempting to devote the limited resources of their country to domestic needs instead of the needs of the U.S. It mattered little whether the country in question was democratic (Guatemala under Arbenz) or not. In each case it was necessary to disguise the U.S. intervention to the American population as a defense of freedom, or a *instrumentalizing the "Communist threat"*

security imperative for the U.S. It is impossible to do so on the basis of the facts, so appropriate facts were invented, and repeated loyally within the submissive ideological institutions. In the case of Guatemala, for example, a pretense was constructed that "international Communism" was establishing a base in Central America, so that we must save the people of Guatemala (and ourselves) from this imminent danger. The same has been true in every case of U.S. intervention. The USSR, incidentally, behaves in exactly the same way when it sends tanks to East Berlin, Budapest, Prague or Kabul.

For each of the superpowers, it is very useful to have a *demonizing* "Great Satan" (to borrow the Ayatollah Khomeini's contribution to contemporary political discourse) that it can invoke to terrorize the domestic population into consent and obedience, when it chooses to carry out one or another form of violence: subversion, aggression, destabilization, a war of terror (as in the case of the 20-year American war against Cuba), or whatever. The reason is the one already noted: people are not gangsters, and if they know the truth, they will refuse to obey. Thus each superpower appeals to the (real) violence and brutality of the Great Satan, when it is useful to do so. The same is true, incidentally, when it is regarded as necessary to resort to military Keynesianism to stimulate the domestic economy. The U.S. has repeatedly turned to this device, never because of any security threat but for internal reasons. The fear of the Great Satan was regularly invoked, sometimes on the basis of complete fabrication (the "missile gap," the "window of vulnerability"), sometimes by exploiting some violent act undertaken by the Great Satan or its alleged clients.

The same is true in the Middle East. The primary concern of the U.S. in this area, since the 1940s, has been to establish and maintain control over its unparalleled resources of relatively cheap and accessible energy. It has repeatedly been necessary to defend this control against indigenous threats: the threat of so-called "radical" nationalism, meaning nationalism. But since this is inappropriate for the manufacture of consent, appeal is constantly made to the alleged "Russian threat." Again, the threat is often simply fabricated. A classic case was the U.S. intervention in Greece in 1947, the first major postwar insurgency and one whose proportions and violence are little-known here. A major concern was Middle East oil, which might be threatened by a "domino effect" (which means, when translated into real world terms, the demonstration effect of successful development within an independent nationalist framework). A Russian threat was manufactured, though in fact Stalin was attempting to curb the Greek guerrillas, knowing that this was American territory and also out of fear of a possible Balkan Communist confederation that would be a rival, perhaps under Titoist influence. The fabrication was effective then, and remains so today. The story has been replayed on numerous occasions. Today, the Rapid Deployment Force is poised for intervention in the Gulf area, the excuse being the "Russian threat," the reason being the threat of indigenous nationalist forces.

The U.S. and the USSR are, in my opinion, quite likely to enter into a confrontation as a result of tensions and conflicts in these areas. The U.S. is now attempting to compel the Sandinistas to call for Russian or Cuban aid, at which point it will be possible to impose a blockade or other direct measures of aggression in defense of the Great Satan, and to pursue the program of returning Nicaragua to the civilized world, perhaps under a new Somoza. This policy poses the serious risk of superpower confrontation. A war may easily break out again in the Middle East (say, an Israeli attack on the Syrian air defense system), as a result of the long-standing refusal of the U.S. to accept a political settlement that would limit the control of its major ally and local gendarme over the occupied territories. Again, the dangers of a superpower confrontation are considerable, as they have been in the past, in particular, in the summer of 1982. In contrast, the possibility that either superpower will directly attack the other is negligible.

What are your predictions about U.S. policy with respect to Latin America, taking into account the Central American conflict, the Malvinas (Falkland Islands) war, and the financial crisis that directly affects the international banking system?

The indebtedness crisis is a serious and mounting one, and it is not at all clear how it will be met in the long term. Apart from that, the U.S. will continue its traditional policy: to inhibit or abort any independent development, outside of the framework of the U.S.-dominated economic and political system, insofar as it can. The prospects are grim. To go further it would be necessary to take up the specific cases, which would carry us too far afield here.

II. Science/Linguistics

Generative grammar is considered a revolutionary theory. In which respects do the successive versions of your theory differ from the other approaches to linguistics of the 20th-century?

The major innovation of generative grammar was that it took seriously, for the first time, the insight expressed by Wilhelm von Humboldt in the early 19th century when he observed that language involves "the infinite use of finite means." This is, in fact, the most elementary and most striking property of human language. A person who knows a particular language has the capacity to speak and understand an indefinitely large number of sentences, and uses this ability freely in normal linguistic behavior: in communication, in expression of thought, and so on. The brain is finite, so there must be a finite representation of this capacity. A generative grammar is a system of rules and principles, finite in size, which assigns representations of sound and meaning to an infinite array of possible sentences. Each person who has learned a language has such a grammar represented somehow in the mind/brain. The two central problems of the theory of generative grammar, then, are (1) to discover what are in fact the grammars for particular languages; and (2) to explain how such grammars are acquired. Though the study of human language has a long and rich history, these questions were never really formulated clearly until the mid-1950s, as a result of the convergence of two intellectual traditions: the mathematical study of formal systems, which provided the appropriate means to formulate the questions and provide some answers to them; and the study of human language, which had achieved considerable insight into the character and variety of possible linguistic systems.

Since your first two main works, Logical Structure of Linguistic Theory *and* Syntactic Structures, *in the mid-1950s, almost 30 years of work have been done in the framework of generative grammar. What are the most important shifts in the development of the theory and the principal achievements? Have some of the initial theoretical notions remained invariant?*

Roughly, I think one can say that the general framework has remained essentially invariant along with many of the basic devices proposed to answer the questions that were raised at the outset, but there has been substantial change, particularly in the past few years, in exactly how the problems are conceived and in the specific principles that have been proposed for description and explanation.

There is a certain tension in the study of generative grammar, a kind of "contradiction" (not real, of course) that gives the field much of its intellectual interest. It is necessary, in the first place, to meet a condition of "descriptive adequacy." That is, the theory of language—what is now sometimes called "universal grammar" (UG) must be sufficiently rich and diverse so that for each human language (in fact, each possible human language) UG provides sufficient devices to describe the way in which this language associates form and meaning. On the other hand, the second of the two basic questions posed—namely, how is a language acquired—leads to a second condition of "explanatory adequacy." UG must be, in effect, a language-acquisition system. It must have the property that when presented with a sample of data known to be empirically sufficient for acquisition of knowledge of some language, UG yields as "output" the grammar that constitutes the knowledge of the person who comes to know this language on the basis of the sample of data. To the extent that a theory of UG can meet this condition, it offers a genuine explanation for the individual phenomena of the particular language. The individual phenomena can be deduced from the principles of UG, given the "boundary conditions" established by experience, much in the way that we can explain why a moving object has a certain trajectory by deducing this from the principles of physics, given certain empirical boundary conditions (its initial position and velocity, etc.). The explanation has two steps: first, UG produces a grammar, given the main data; and second, the individual phenomenon (say, the fact that sentence so-and-so means such-and-such) is derived as a consequence of the grammar.

Pursuit of descriptive adequacy leads us to constantly enrich the structure of UG, but pursuit of explanatory adequacy leads us to construct a more impoverished theory of UG, one with fewer options. The reason is that to meet the empirical condition of explanatory adequacy, UG must provide only a single grammar (or very few, at least), given an appropriate sample of data. But this is possible only if the variety of possible grammars is narrowly constrained. Hence the tension that I mentioned earlier.

In the earliest work, the condition of descriptive adequacy was the dominant one, though the problem of explanation was not neglected. Early work attempted to construct devices that would be rich enough to describe the actual variety of natural languages, the actual ways in which sound and meaning are associated. Subsequent work has attempted to show how descriptive adequacy can be maintained, or even enriched, by restricting the variety of devices available, so that we can approach the condition of explanatory adequacy. Earlier grammars had rich rule systems, and the task of explanation was to show how these rule systems, not others, would be selected on the basis of presented data.

As research proceeded, it gradually became clear that the rule systems were of very restricted types, and that they could in fact be determined by quite general principles that admit only a limited amount of variation (parametric variation). What has emerged from this work, only in the past few years, is **a radically different conception of grammar and of UG.** UG is a system of principles that allow a limited degree of parametric variation; a grammar, a system of rules, is determined by fixing these parameters. Thus in English or Spanish, a verb or preposition precedes its object, while in Japanese a verb or postposition follows its object. If we call the verb the "head" of the phrase in which it appears, and the preposition (postposition) the head of the phrase in which it appears, then in Spanish heads come first, while in Japanese heads come last. The same holds for phrases of other types. The choice of head-first or head-last is a parameter in terms of which languages can vary. But the configurations that appear are otherwise largely invariant.

Thus by setting the parameters, as can be done on the basis of very simple data, UG (mimicking the child) can "project" a system of rules that describe the phrase structure of the language. One can think of the parameters as a set of switches attached to a complex mechanism with rich internal structure. When each switch is set in one of its positions, the mechanism is fully operative. UG is the system with the switches not yet set; a grammar results when the switches are set. It must be that quite simple data allows the switches to be set, but if they are set in one of the possible ways, a rich and complex set of consequences are determined, namely, the forms and meanings of the sentences of the language in question. The languages so derived may appear to be very different, but in fact they are of very similar form, at a deeper level. In the past few years, there has been quite considerable progress in constructing a system of this general character, a system that has some hope, I think, of satisfying jointly the conditions of explanatory and descriptive adequacy over a fairly impressive range.

You consider linguistics a branch of cognitive psychology. Please explain why.

A person who knows a language has, plainly, acquired a certain system of knowledge, which he or she can then put to use. A grammar is a representation of this system of knowledge. Consequently, the basic questions of linguistics become central questions of psychology: What is the nature of a system of knowledge and belief, how is it acquired, and how does it enter into behavior and interpretation of the environment? So, linguistics, so-conceived, is simply a branch of cognitive psychology.

Since the beginning of your work, you have claimed that a theory of language has to answer questions concerning the formal structure of language, its ontogenetic development and its use. However, after the early 1960s, most of the psychologists working on language processing or language acquisition ignored linguistic theory. Only recently some small groups of psychologists began to take linguistic theory seriously into account. What do you think are the reasons underlying research strategy in this field?

At first, a number of psychologists tried to find **experimental correlates** of assumptions about grammatical structure, operating on the basis of extremely simple assumptions about processing and behavior. For example, psychologists tried to determine whether, say, reaction time was a function of the number of rules involved in forming a sentence. The tacit assumption was that processing was linear and additive: that is, in forming or interpreting a sentence, the mind applies one rule after another in sequence, with a fixed "increment" of difficulty for each rule application. This is a very dubious theory of processing, though it made sense to try it first, as perhaps the simplest assumption. Some of the results were positive, some negative. The negative results showed either that the grammar was wrong, or that the processing model was wrong (or, more likely, both). At this point, a rather irrational move was made: it was widely assumed that the negative results showed that the grammar, or the general approach to grammar, was wrong, and the study was largely abandoned. A saner approach would have been to turn to a more realistic processing model (perhaps involving parallel processing, for example) while also seeking to remedy apparent defects in the grammar and UG. The same took place in other areas, e.g., language acquisition. Unfortunately, experimental psychology has often departed from the assumptions that are standard in the well-developed sciences, where all of this would have been obvious. It is only in the last few years, I think, that a more reasonable approach to these questions has been pursued by a number of experimental psychologists.

You have been attacked as an "innatist" or "idealist" because of your instantaneous language acquisition model and, in certain circles, as a "reductionist" because of your characterization of language as a "mental organ." Could you spell out the status of these two "idealizations," as you have often called them, and also explain in which sense a "biological approach to the study of language" should be understood?

I can't really imagine what alternative there is to a "biological approach to language," at least if one is interested in the questions discussed above (one may, of course, be interested in different questions). It is simply a fact that humans have some property of the mind/brain which enables them to acquire knowledge of language on the basis of exposure to a limited range of experience—and it is, furthermore, quite easy to show that the explicit knowledge that each human has acquired is of remarkable delicacy and scope, extending vastly beyond any specific exemplars that might have been presented in experience. So there is, really, no alternative to the general picture that assumes that UG is a biologically-given, innate capacity, and that it operates upon data of experience to provide a generative grammar. The only questions are: what is UG; what are the grammars?

This approach is sometimes called "idealist," primarily, I think, by **people who call themselves "Marxists" but understand little about Marx or about science.** This characterization is so irrational that it is virtually impossible to discuss; plainly, there is no reason to doubt that the principles of UG have a physical realization, as do the "instructions" that lead to the growth of arms and legs, and that there is a physical realization of the resulting grammar, somewhere in the neural system. The charge of "idealism" is strange indeed. As for "innatism," it is a term that I do not use, though others do; the approach is "innatist" in the same sense that it is "innatist" to assume that the human embryo develops arms and a human eye, rather than wings and an insect eye, because of an innate endowment that interacts somehow with the external environment. It is difficult to conceive of a coherent alternative. As for the term "reductionist," if this means that we would like to explain mental function in terms of physical mechanisms, I would certainly accept the characterization, though we should recognize, in all honesty, that there are many aspects of mental function (in particular, matters having to do with will and choice) for which we have not the slightest idea of what the relevant mechanisms or structures might be, even in principle. Note that I have specifically excluded these questions in the preceding account (e.g., the question why we decide to say such-and-such on a particular occasion); in fact, in the domain of language, as elsewhere, we have no idea how to formulate coherent questions let alone suggest serious answers.

When they test hypotheses, linguists mainly make use of native speaker linguistic intuitions. Do these empirical data have a special status in the formulation of the theory in contrast with other kinds of data (i.e. developmental or processing data)?

The reason for using such data is that they are, for the moment, the most readily available and the most instructive. If other relevant data can be obtained, any sensible linguist will certainly attempt to make full use of them. We can only hope that this will be the case, though for the moment, perceptual judgments (e.g., the informant's judgment that such-and-such means so-and-so, etc.) are by a vast margin the most useful. Other sorts of data have, at best, only confirmed conclusions arrived at by the study of informal judgments; e.g., the click experiments that showed that a click superimposed on a speech signal tends to be perceptually displaced to a phrase boundary (you hear it as if it were at the boundary, instead of where it is, under a variety of experimental conditions). Developmental studies may and should lead to a better understanding of the parameters of possible variation and their "unmarked values" (i.e., the way the "switches" are set in the absence of data), and perhaps other matters. These are mostly hopes for the future.

In the introduction to the proceedings of the Royaumont conference it is claimed that, although Piaget and you do not agree on a number of things, you are in agreement in your respective rejections of empiricist hypotheses. Is this claim true? Can you differentiate your position from Piaget's?

If I understand him correctly, **Piaget** assumes that cognitive development passes through a series of stages, and that at each stage it is essentially uniform; thus the principles operating in one domain (say, language) are the same as those operating in every other domain (say, problem solving), at any given stage. Two questions arise: (1) Is this true?; (2) How does the child pass from one stage to the next? As for (1), the evidence indicates that the assumptions are probably false. There is no known analogue to, say, the principles of language in other cognitive domains; it is simply dogmatic to insist, in the face of everything that is known, that linguistic development mirrors the development of sensorimotor skills, etc. In fact, I am aware of no substantive proposal that is not quickly refuted by available evidence. In fact, even the idea of successive stages is very much in question. As for (2), it seems to me that even if we accept the belief that there is a series of "cognitive stages," the Geneva school faces a self-imposed dilemma as to how transition takes place. The transition either results from new information (which they deny) or from some intrinsic process of maturation (which they also deny). No one has proposed any other possibility. The problem is masked in terminology that seems to me semi-mystical (assimilation and accommodation, etc.). But this is a problem internal to Geneva school theory.

It seems to me that what is now known indicates that language develops along an intrinsically determined path, involving specific mechanisms of the language system, which is, in this respect, rather analogous to a physical organ. As in the case of the visual system and others, the course of development is influenced by an interaction with the environment. The task is to fill in the details and find the operative principles, and of course, to relate all of this to physical mechanisms of the brain. I am really not sure whether this picture can be made compatible with Geneva school principles; as presently formulated, they seem incompatible with it, though there is sufficient vagueness so that one cannot say this with any conviction.

Some authors specializing in psychoanalysis have tried to apply notions from generative grammar (for example, the notions of "deep structure," "surface structure," and "transformation") in their work. Even in Argentina there have been such examples (Liberman in the early 1970s). Do you think that, at present, this application may be more than metaphorical?

I'm rather skeptical, though perhaps something is possible (there is some discussion of the matter in my book *Rules and Representations*, chapter 6). Maybe some of the ideas of generative grammar will be suggestive for **psychoanalysis**, but I would be (pleasantly) surprised if it goes beyond that.

Is there a relation between your political views and your scientific work? I don't really know your position on this issue. My idea is that a "biological" approach to language, by focusing on the universal principles underlying human languages rather than on the differences, does have political consequences (Jensen, Bernstein, Labov), which may impinge on educational and social issues concerning minority groups. In its present state of development, does the theory allow for technological applications? In which domain(s)?

I suppose there is a loose connection, certainly not a deductive one. Whatever connection there is lies more at the level of hope and aspiration than of firm result. We have good evidence that the human language capacity, which surely enters into thought, reasoning, human interaction, etc., in the most intimate fashion, is based on biologically-determined principles which underlie (though they do not account for) the free creative use of language that is typical of normal speakers. I presume that the same is true in all cognitive domains, though knowledge elsewhere is sparse.

Now, any social or political theory, whether conservative, reformist or revolutionary, is based on some implicit concept of human nature, a biological given. Thus if we are opposed to slavery, it is because we think that in some sense these institutions are an infringement on essential human nature. I'm inclined to believe that any form of authority or domination is such an infringement, and is therefore essentially illegitimate, however one may justify such infringement of fundamental human rights in terms of material conditions, ideological deformity, or whatever. Thus, there should be an unending struggle to discover, understand, and overcome all structures of authority, domination, subordination, and restriction on the freedom to become and live as a full human being, who can fulfill the need for creative self-expression in solidarity with others.

These beliefs are surely not scientifically well-grounded; they are a mixture of intuition, hope, and a certain reading of history. Perhaps they can be made more precise, in which case they will properly be describable as true or false (or, more likely, partially true and partially false) beliefs about human nature; I emphasize again that any position on such issues rests on some assumption about human nature, though the fact is commonly denied. Suppose that they are in some measure true, as I hope, thus offering a biological grounding to the essentially anarchist views that I tend to accept as reasonable. We might then ask whether, in fact, there is some connection between such **"instinct for freedom"** (in Bakunin's phrase) and the cognitive structures that appear to underlie free and creative self-expression in other domains, where we are beginning to obtain some knowledge and understanding. But I emphasize again that these connections are tenuous, more a matter of the spirit than the content of certain conceptions.

It is commonly alleged that ideas about biological nature lend themselves to racism, sexism, and other forms of oppression, whereas the idea of an "empty organism," lacking biological endowment, is somehow "progressive" or "optimistic." There is little merit to this view. In fact, the concept of an empty organism, completely plastic, eliminates any **moral barriers to control and domination,** to the manufacture of consent, to one or another form of servitude (in the present era, the requirement that one rent oneself to others to survive), and so on.

I rather suspect that this may be one reason why such ideas have proven so attractive to many intellectuals, across the ideological spectrum, given the social role that the intellectuals tend to play, or aspire to play. If we find some capacity such as the language capacity, which appears invariant across the species to a very close first approximation, then this obviously provides no basis for any form of discrimination. Furthermore, it is only on racist, sexist, or other similar assumptions that biological differences among humans can be molded into weapons to justify discrimination.

The fact—surely it is a fact—that humans differ markedly in their capacities, their interests, their aspirations, and so on, should be a source of joy, not concern. It is difficult to think of a vision closer to Hell than a society of clones, biologically identical. We can enjoy and appreciate the achievements of others— whether to paint a picture, to prove a theorem, to run a mile in 4 minutes, or whatever—even if we cannot do so ourselves, ultimately for reasons relating to biological endowment, to a not insignificant degree. Such variety among humans, like other kinds of variety, provides no basis for the belief that certain fundamental human rights may be infringed. The little we know about these matters suggests that there are fundamental cognitive—and probably other— properties that are a species endowment, and that there is a range of individual variation within them, a conclusion that appears to be true, and that we should certainly hope will prove to be true.

Editor's Notes to Interview 26

"Noam Chomsky Interview: The Manufacture of Consent," *Open Road* (Vancouver, Canada), Spring 1984, pp. 16–17. The interview was done during the summer of 1983.

The reference to *Radical Priorities* is found in ch. 20 on p. 236 of the first two editions; the description "derivative fellow traveler," on p. 247 of the same book (cf. p. 244). On libertarian theories of education, see now **CD&E** (2003).

The most recent book by Seymour Melman at the time of the interview was *Profits Without Production*. New York: Knopf, 1983; see **RP**, pp. 182, 232, 241.

For more on the "unending task," see notes to I18.

On Chomsky's early contacts with the *kibbutz* movement and anarchism, see the Introduction and references given there. The answer about Marx is echoed and expanded in **LPF** (1987), 176ff.

See Editor's Notes to I5.

26. The Manufacture of Consent (Summer 1983)

Today you are probably best known as a critic of U.S. foreign policy. What sort of audience are you trying to reach? Are you afraid that you may just be preaching to the converted?

I'm aware of the danger, but don't feel that it is real. The major groups of "the converted"—that is, the deeply indoctrinated with naive and immutable quasi-religious beliefs—are the mainstream elite intelligentsia. But they are much too well-disciplined to listen to anything I have to say, and they know of it, if at all, only through the fabrications of various party-liners or their own incomprehension of anything that parts from doctrinal purity. The reaction among various Marxists sects and the like is similar, and for similar reasons.

The audience I try to reach, and to some limited extent do reach, is a different one: partly, activists of a less doctrinaire sort than the mainstream liberal intelligentsia and sectarian Marxists, partly the kind of general interested audience that one finds everywhere: around universities (primarily students), church groups, and so on.

I'm not trying to convert, but to inform. I don't want people to believe me, any more than they should believe the party line I'm criticizing—academic authority, the media, the overt state propagandists, or whatever. In talks and in print, I try to stress what I think is true: that with a little willingness to explore and use one's mind, it is possible to discover a good deal about the social and political world that is generally **hidden**. I feel that I've achieved something if people are encouraged to take up this challenge and learn for themselves.

There are a vast number of people who are uninformed and heavily propagandized, but fundamentally decent. The propaganda that inundates them is effective when unchallenged, but much of it goes only skin deep. If they can be brought to raise questions and apply their decent instincts and basic intelligence, many people quickly escape the confines of the doctrinal system and are willing to do something to help others who are really suffering and oppressed.

This is naturally less true of better-educated and "more sophisticated" (that is, more effectively indoctrinated) groups who are both the agents and often the most deluded victims of the propaganda system.

What position do you think North American anti-authoritarians should take with regard to Third World liberation movements, especially the more authoritarian,

Leninist/Maoist type of movement? Do you think our first priority should be to simply oppose U.S. imperialism?

The U.S. has not been elected God, and has no authority to impose its will by violence in the Third World. Apart from the matter of principle, some familiarity with recent history shows clearly enough the effects of its benevolence, in Central America and the Caribbean for many years, in Southeast Asia, and elsewhere. Any honest person will therefore oppose and attempt to block such intervention, exactly as in the case of subversion or aggression by any other power.

This truism aside, our attitude towards Third World "liberation movements" should be to find out and tell the truth about them. Where we can do something to defend people who are oppressed, to alleviate suffering, or to expand the scope of freedom, we should do so, though the best we can do, quite often, is to keep our bloody hands out of their affairs. We should also try to offer constructive assistance to people attempting to overcome centuries of misery and oppression, in part because it is just and right, in part out of a recognition of what **the plague of European civilization** has created as it spread through the world. Outside intervention regularly tends to enhance the authoritarian and oppressive elements in these movements, and in fact is often designed to achieve this end (Cuba and Nicaragua are two obvious examples).

It is not clear that there exists any way for most of the people of the Third World to overcome the enormous problems they face, which transcend anything in our historical experience. Whatever slight chance there might be for decent prospects are reduced or eliminated by the violence of the great powers, in part motivated by fear that successful development will take place outside of their control, with a "demonstration effect" that will undermine their dominance elsewhere. These are some of the facts of the world that have to be faced. It is easy to preach to the Third World, a little more difficult to offer constructive recommendations.

Has there been a resurgence of left-wing political activity in the U.S. in the past couple of years?

First, the alleged decline of activism in the 1970s was partly mythical. This was, after all, the period of the rise of the feminist and ecological movements, and much else. In fact, there remained from the 1960s a proliferation of activist groups of many sorts, doing valuable work, generally locally oriented, and many new people joined or began afresh. As the state gradually returned to its natural stance of militancy, subversion and aggression after its partial failures in Vietnam, and as the economic crisis deepened, this activism quickly emerged to public view.

Yet in Radical Priorities, *you deny that either feminism or the ecology movement pose a real threat to capitalism—presumably the demands of both movements can be met within the capitalist system. Do you see any revolutionary potential in these move-*

ments, or do you think that the working class remains the most likely agent of revolutionary transformation?

The feminist movement, and to some extent the ecology movement, have, I think, had a significant and lasting effect on social thought and practice. But it should be recognized that capitalism can easily accommodate the idea that individuals are interchangeable tools of production and that the environment should be maintained to be exploited by the masters of the economic and political system. A radical and emancipatory movement is not necessarily anti-capitalist. There are many forms of authority and domination apart from those of the capitalist system; correspondingly, there are many forms of "revolutionary transformation." It doesn't seem to me a matter of "one or the other," as your formulation tends to suggest.

Isn't industrialism itself becoming obsolete?

Industrialism is far from obsolete. The vast majority of the human race has not even entered the industrial era, or has barely entered it, and in the advanced industrial societies the production of useful goods poses real and imminent problems. One major problem of advanced industrial societies—England, and now the U.S.—is that the capacity for useful production is to a certain extent being lost, a fact that has been emphasized for many years by Seymour Melman, among others.

Do you see any prospects for a libertarian social movement emerging in the U.S.?

Quite often, one tends to find libertarian elements in the various activist groups that are continually forming, disappearing, and transmuting into something else. One of the healthy aspects of American society and culture is the relatively low level of deference to privilege and a general skepticism about hierarchy and authority. I emphasize "relatively"; there is a long way to go. The lack of any live socialist tradition or any party structure also serves to make the U.S. different from other capitalist industrial societies in this respect: on the one hand, it leads to a lack of continuity at the intellectual or activist-organizational levels and a generally shifting and evanescent quality to much that happens here; on the other hand, it often leads to openness and innovation, which helps foster libertarian tendencies that often have quite deep roots, I think. I wouldn't hazard a guess as to where it will lead.

Many of your political writings are directed toward the "new mandarins," the intellectual servants of American power and interests. Why do you think it is important to expose the collusion between intellectuals and the state?

It has been recognized for many years that "the manufacture of consent" is a major task in societies where obedience cannot be ensured by violence. Whether they are aware of it or not, a substantial part of the intelligentsia commit themselves to this task. The result is a system of indoctrination that is often remarkable in its effectiveness.

The first step in freeing oneself from its grip is to recognize that it exists, to come to understand that the pretended objectivity and neutrality of social and political commentary, or simply news reporting, masks presuppositions and ideological principles that should be challenged, and that often collapse very quickly when exposed.

Until people free themselves from the system of indoctrination, they will continue to support the violence of existing institutions. If they can free themselves, they can often combat it effectively in countries such as ours, where the level of institutionalized violence is relatively low, for the privileged at least. So I think it is important to continually bring out the ongoing collusion, whether it is tacit and subconscious or quite consciously undertaken.

This is an **unending task**, since the major institutions and their servants naturally never cease to construct the perceived world in the form that suits their needs. It is a great mistake to believe that once the lies of the propaganda system have been exposed about, say, the Vietnam War, then it is pointless to take the topic up again. On the contrary, the intelligentsia will maintain their natural commitment to restoring the shattered faith and do so in the course of time, quite effectively if unchallenged.

As a self-described "statistical error," meaning that people with your sort of political views are generally excluded from prominent positions in the U.S., how do you see yourself as an intellectual teaching at a major American university, in your role as a member of the very intelligentsia you criticize, and in relation to your students?

In fact, I have very little contact with the so-called academic or intellectual community, apart from a few friends and colleagues. With regard to students, the matter is different. They are in a phase of their lives when they are uniquely able to question and explore. They haven't been completely socialized.

It is, in fact, quite striking to see how differently students and faculty respond to issues involving the university or the larger society. Take just one rather typical example. A few years ago MIT in effect arranged to sell about one-third of the nuclear engineering department to the Shah of Iran. When the scandal surfaced, there was much uproar on campus, leading to a student referendum that showed about 80 percent opposed. There was also a series of well-attended faculty meetings (a rare event), which led to a vote in which about 80 percent approved.

The faculty are simply the students of a few years ago, but the difference in reaction, on a matter of simple academic freedom apart from the obvious broader implications, reflects the fact that they are now a functional part of the institutional structure of power. It is that step towards acceptance and obedience that it is important to try to prevent. Once it has been taken, the rest is fairly predictable.

So do you think a large American university is a suitable place for free education and independent thought?

Insofar as the universities provide the opportunities for free inquiry and expression, it would be crazy not to make use of them, while trying to expand these opportunities. This can be done; it was done quite effectively, in fact, by the student movement of the 1960s, one reason why it was so hated and why it is so maligned by the custodians of history, whose privilege and authority were threatened by the student pressure for free inquiry and who now have to mask their real fears by the pretense that the main thrust of the student movement was totalitarian, Stalinist, opposed to academic freedom, and so on. There is a whole literature of falsification on this topic, which is naturally very highly regarded in intellectual circles.

Anarchists, from Godwin to Goodman, have developed libertarian theories of education very critical of conventional, state-controlled education systems. Do you have any thoughts on this libertarian tradition of educational thought?

I think it often effectively expressed crucially important values. Schools function in many ways as instruments of indoctrination, not only in the content of what is taught, but in the style and manner of teaching and organization, from the earliest years.

Students are rewarded for obedience and passivity—one result is that in the elite institutions students are often pre-selected for these traits and are more effectively indoctrinated than elsewhere.

These are not laws of nature. It is possible in principle for schools to foster the creative impulses that are rather natural from childhood on and to encourage a constant willingness to challenge established doctrine and authority. In fact, this comes close to being true in advanced work in the natural sciences, though very rarely elsewhere. For just this reason, training in the natural sciences might not be a bad way to prepare oneself for a life of serious engagement in social and political issues.

A bit of personal good fortune is that up to high school, I was in such a *education* school—one that was Deweyan, not libertarian in our sense, but that did encourage independent thought and self-realization in the best sense. It wasn't until I entered a city high school, for example, that I discovered, to my surprise, that I was a good student. It was assumed in my earlier school experience that everyone was. Insofar as students were "measured," it was not against one another but against what they could accomplish.

Such **schooling** is fundamentally **subversive**, in the best sense, and therefore rarely undertaken, but it is possible even within the institutional constraints of our societies as they now exist, and the effort to create and expand such possibilities merits much effort and struggle. This is most important within the state educational system, where the overwhelming majority of the population is educated, or dis-educated.

You have argued that your linguistic theories have revolutionary implications. Why do you feel that your theoretical work in linguistics is important, and what is the relation between that work, your political views and social liberation in general? In other words, what do innate structures and generative grammar have to do with human emancipation?

A word of caution: I don't argue that my linguistic theories have revolutionary implications. Rather, that they are merely suggestive as to the form that a libertarian social theory might assume.

One shouldn't claim more than can be shown. Surely one cannot simply deduce social and political consequences from any insights into language. Rather, it is perhaps possible to begin to perceive, if only dimly, how innate structures of mind may lead to an extraordinary richness of understanding, and may underlie and enter human action and thought. On this basis one may hope—it is only a hope—to be able to show, some day, that structures of authority and control limit and distort intrinsic human capacities and needs, and to lay a theoretical basis for a social theory that eventuates in practical ideas as to how to overcome them. But there are huge gaps in any such argument, something I've always taken pains to emphasize.

My own hopes and intuitions are that self-fulfilling and creative work is a **fundamental human need**, and that the pleasures of a challenge met, a work well done, the exercise of skill and craftsmanship, are real and significant, and are an essential part of a full and meaningful life. The same is true of the opportunity to understand and enjoy the achievements of others, which often go beyond what we ourselves can do, and to work constructively in cooperation with others.

You have described yourself as a "derivative fellow traveler" of anarchism and as an "anarchist socialist." Just how do you see yourself in relation to anarchism as a philosophy, and anarchism as a movement?

What I think is most important about **anarchism** as a "philosophy" (a term I'm uncomfortable with) is its recognition that there is and will always be a need to discover and overcome structures of hierarchy, authority and domination and constraints on freedom: slavery, wage-slavery, racism, sexism, authoritarian schools, etc., forever. If human society progresses, overcoming some of these forms of oppression, it will uncover others, particularly as we move from confronting animal problems to confronting human problems, in Marx's phrase.

Anarchism does not legislate ultimate solutions to these problems. I see it as a rather practical "philosophy," inspired by a vision of the future that is more free and more conducive to a wide range of human needs, many of which are in no position even to identify under the intellectual and material constraints of our present existence.

We will each commit ourselves to the problems we feel most pressing, but should be ready to learn from others about the limitations of our own conceptions and understanding, which will always be substantial. It is only in this sense that anarchism can be a "movement." It won't be a party with members and a finished doctrine.

How did you come to embrace such ideas? Is it true you were influenced by the kibbutz movement in Israel when you were young?

Yes, I was influenced by the *kibbutz* movement, and in fact lived for a while on a *kibbutz* and almost stayed on. I think there is much of value in the *kibbutz* experience, but we must also not forget (as I have sometimes tended to do) that the historical particularity of the *kibbutz* movement in Israel embodies many serious flaws, sometimes crimes. One should also explore other facets of the experience, for example, the kinds of coercion that arise from the need for acceptance in a closely-knit community, not a small topic, I think.

I can't really say how I came to be influenced by anarchist ideas; I can't remember a time when I was not so influenced.

What, in general, is your opinion of Marx and Marxism?

Marx was a person, not a God. The concept **"Marxism"** belongs to the history of organized religion, and should not be seriously employed by a free and independent person. Marx was a major intellectual figure and it would be foolish not to learn from him or to value his contributions properly. He was, like anyone, limited in his perceptions and understanding. His personal behavior (not to be confused with his thought) often left much to be desired, to put it mildly. There are also very dangerous and destructive elements in his ideas, some of which underlie the worst elements of Leninist thought and practice.

Just one more question: What does the future hold for Noam Chomsky? What are your plans and your hopes?

Let me rephrase the question and ask what the future holds for all of us. I see little reason to believe that the future will be very long. A cold look at the facts suggests that we are moving inexorably towards nuclear war, quite possibly arising from inadvertence, probably in the context of some Third World conflict that engages the superpowers. This eventuality should not, of course, obscure the fact that much of the human race faces regular and unremitting disaster from hunger and disease, not to speak of back-breaking labor, miserable poverty and oppression. These facts, and facts they unfortunately are, yield the answer to the question, I think.

For reasons of personal sanity, and perhaps a measure of self-indulgence, I also expect to spend as much time and energy as I can on intellectual problems that have always intrigued me. It happens that my own professional field is in an extremely exciting stage right now, and may be approaching the first real "scientific revolution" outside of the natural sciences. I sometimes have the mad fantasy that this goal will be reached just at the time that nuclear war puts all such efforts to an end, but perhaps this is further self-indulgence.

Editor's Notes to Interview 27

First published in English in Wiktor Osiatynski, *Contrasts: Soviet and American Thinkers Discuss the Future*. Translated by Ewa Woydyllo. New York: Macmillan Publishing Co, 1984, pp. 95–101. The book, which was conceived as a bridge between the natural sciences and the humanities, contains 11 pairs of interviews (one with a Soviet thinker and one with an American thinker) divided in three parts: 1) On the universe and life, 2) On man and his environment (which includes Chomsky's), 3) On the future of science. Chomsky is paired with Guram Ramishvili (born in 1923), who, like Chomsky, is interested in the linguistic ideas of Wilhelm von Humboldt (the topic of his doctoral dissertation, published in German in 1970). The two interviews are grouped under the title "On Language and Culture." It is enlightening to compare Chomsky's views with those of each of the other interviewees, and not only with Ramishvili's.

The interview, conducted by Osiatynski, took place in 1975; a Polish translation was apparently included in a book he published shortly afterwards. An English transcription he prepared eight years later was edited on or before Sept. 24, 1983, by Chomsky, who "made some changes and corrections for clarity" (letter to Osiatynski). The text reproduced here follows this corrected transcription.

The first sentence of the first question is based on a wrong assumption: Chomsky's approach to language is psychological (ultimately, biological—see Lyle Jenkins, *Biolinguistics: Exploring the Biology of Language*. Cambridge: Cambridge University Press, 2000). Less surprising is Osiatynski's statement (p. 95) that Chomsky's books "offer an insight into Chomsky's radical, though not revolutionary, approach to contemporary politics," since the people who are incapable of recognizing a truly revolutionary approach for what it is are legion—a clear sign of cultural underdevelopment (see Introduction). Compare AP (1969), p. 22; interviews 4, 8, 15, 25, 26, and particularly 40, among others; and in particular "The Soviet Union vs Socialism" (1985), *Our Generation* 17:2 (1986), pp. 47–52 (see notes to interview 40).

On the matter of "learning," see the fourth section of the Introduction, in particular the paper by Piattelli-Palmarini referred to at the end.

On thought without language, see Chomsky's Introduction to Adam Schaff, *Language and cognition*. McGraw-Hill, 1973.

On "communication," see I9.

27. Language as a Key to Human Nature and Society
(24 September 1983)

You represent an anthropological approach to linguistics. Do you think that linguistics can contribute to the understanding of philosophical problems of human nature and culture?

My feeling is that a human being or any complex organism has a system of cognitive structures which develop much in the way the physical organs of the body develop. That is, in their fundamental character they are innate; their basic form is determined by the genetic nature of the organism. Of course, they grow under particular environmental conditions, assuming a specific form that admits of some variation. Much of what is distinctive among human beings is a specific manner in which a variety of shared cognitive structures develop.

Perhaps the most intricate of these structures is language. In studying language we can discover many basic properties of this cognitive structure, its organization, and also the genetic predispositions which provide the foundation for its development.

So in this respect, linguistics, first of all, tries to characterize a major feature of human cognitive organization. And secondly, I think it may provide a suggestive model for the study of other cognitive systems. And the collection of these systems is one aspect of human nature.

Language, then, is a key to human nature?

In Western scientific thought of the last several centuries there has been a tendency to assume that human nature is limited to the immediate observable physical structure of the organism. And that for other aspects of human nature, specifically for behavior, there are no genetically determined structures of comparable complexity to the directly observable physical organization of the body. So human physical structures and intellectual structures are generally studied in different ways. The assumption is that physical structures are genetically inherited and intellectual structures are **learned**.

I think that this assumption is wrong. None of these structures is learned. They all grow, they grow in comparable ways; their ultimate forms are heavily dependent on genetic predispositions. If we understood, as we do not, the physical bases for these structures, I have little doubt that we would find structures in the brain for social interaction, or language, or analysis of personality—a whole variety of systems developed on the basis of specific biological endowment.

Do you mean that all behavior is innate, genetically determined?

No. But the basic structures for our behavior are innate. The specific details of how they grow would depend on interaction with the environment.

Supposing that linguistics could describe one of such structures, would the findings apply to all our intellectual activity? Do we think only in language or do there exist non-linguistic forms of thinking too?

The analysis of linguistic structures could help in understanding other intellectual structures. Now, I don't think that there is any scientific evidence about the question whether we think only in language or not. But introspection indicates pretty clearly that we don't think in language necessarily. We also think in terms of visual images, we think in terms of situations and events, and so on, and many times we can't even begin to express in words what the content of our thinking is. And even if we are able to express it in words, it is a common experience to say something and then to recognize that it is not what we meant, that it is something else.

What does this mean? That there is a kind of **nonlinguistic thought** going on which we then are trying to represent in language. And that we know that sometimes we fail.

I've read several times that we think in language, but "feel" in a nonlinguistic way.

I know that it is false of me, at least if "language" refers (in my case) to English, and I assume that it is false of everyone else. I don't think that you would have any trouble at all in deciding that you are thinking of some event and then visualizing it happening with its consequences, and constructing a rational analysis of it without being able to verbalize adequately anything like its full complexity.

You used the expression "rational analysis." Do you believe that all our thinking is rational and linear?

I don't think that all thinking is a kind of rational structure. But I don't think that it is correct to identify the rational/non-rational dichotomy with the linguistic/non-linguistic dichotomy.

Can language be non-rational?

Yes. So those are two dimensions that do not correlate. It's true that language is in a sense linear but that is as obvious as that perceptual space is three-dimensional.

As I understand it, language has an innate biological basis. Its use, however, is social. What do you think of the social functions of language? Is it primarily an instrument of communication?

I think that a very important aspect of language has to do with the establishment of social relations and interactions. Often, this is described as **communication**. But that is very misleading, I think. There is a narrow class of uses of language where you intend to communicate. Communication refers to an effort to get people to understand what one means. And that, certainly, is one use of language and a social use of it. But I don't think that is the only social use of language. Nor are social uses the only uses of language. For example, language can be used to express or clarify one's thoughts with little regard for the social context, if any.

I think that the use of language is a very important means by which this species, because of its biological nature, creates a kind of a social space, to place itself in interaction with other people. It doesn't have much to do with communication in a narrow sense, that is, it doesn't involve transmission of information. There is much information transmitted but it is not the content of what is said that is transmitted. There is undoubtedly much to learn about the social use of language, for communication or for other purposes that are important. But at present there is not much in the way of a theory of sociolinguistics, of social uses of language, as far as I am aware.

What, then, in the field of linguistics, are the greatest achievements?

I think that the most important work that is going on has to do with the search for very general abstract features of what is sometimes called universal grammar: general properties of language which reflect a kind of biological necessity rather than logical necessity; that is, properties of language which are not logically necessary for such a system but which are essential invariant properties of human language and are known without learning. We know these properties but we don't learn them. We simply use our knowledge of these properties as the basis for learning.

Do we genetically inherit this knowledge?

Yes, we must. In fact, by universal grammar I mean just that system of principles and structures which are the prerequisite for acquisition of language, and to which every language necessarily conforms.

Does it mean that this genetic basis of language is universal?

Yes, that's right. But we are only one species. You can imagine a different world in which a number of species developed with different genetically determined linguistic systems. It hasn't happened in evolution. What has happened is that one species has developed, and the genetic structure of this species happens to involve a variety of intricate abstract principles of linguistic organization which, therefore, necessarily constrain every language, and, in fact, create the basis for learning language as a way of organizing experience rather than constituting something learned from experience.

Would such knowledge also be helpful in understanding human nature?

It would, in two respects. For one thing, it is by itself a part of a study of human intelligence which is, perhaps, the central aspect of human nature. And, secondly, I think, it is a good **model for studying other human properties**, which ought to be studied by psychologists in the same way.

Do you mean that psychology could benefit from linguistics? Could you explain how?

One thing that you and I know is language. Another thing that you and I know is how objects behave in perceptual space. We have a whole mass of complex ways of understanding what is the nature of visual space. A proper part of psychology ought to be, and in recent years has been, an effort to try to discover the principles of how we organize the visual space. I would say that the same is true of every domain of psychology, of human studies. To understand, for example, how people organize social systems we have to discover the principles that we create to make some societies intelligible.

I understand that we could have a kind of "universal grammar" of nonlinguistic forms of human behavior as well. But if, as you say, our behavior and language are heavily guided by universal principles, why, then, do they differ so much all around the world?

I don't think they differ so much. I think that as human beings we quite naturally take for granted what is similar among human beings and then pay attention to what differentiates us. That makes perfect sense for us as human beings. I suppose that frogs pay no attention to being a frog. They take it for granted. What interests a frog are differences among frogs. From our point of view they are all more or less the same, from their point of view they are all radically different.

Similarly with us. For us, we all are very different, our languages are very different, and our societies are very different. But if we could extract ourselves from our point of view and sort of look down at human life the way a biologist looks at other organisms, I think we could see it a different way. Imagine an extrahuman observer looking at us. Such an extrahuman observer would be struck precisely by the uniformity of human languages, by the very slight variation from one language to another, and by the remarkable respects in which all languages are the same. And then he would notice observing us that we do not pay attention to that because for the purpose of human life it is quite natural and appropriate just to take for granted everything that is common. We don't concern ourselves with that, all we worry about are differences.

Would this extrahuman observer think the same way about our symbols, ideas, needs and values?

Absolutely. I think he would be struck with the uniformity of human societies in every aspect. And there is more than that. Let's imagine again an observer looking at us without any preconceptions. I think he would be struck by the fact that although human beings have the capacity to develop scientific knowledge, it must be a very **limited capacity** because it is done only in very narrow and specific domains. There are huge areas where the human mind is apparently incapable of forming sciences or at least has not done so. There are other areas, so far in fact one area only, in which we have demonstrated the capacity for true scientific progress.

Physics?

Physics and those parts of other fields that grow out of physics: chemistry, the structure of big molecules—in those domains there is a lot of progress. In many other domains there is very little progress in developing real scientific understanding.

Isn't this because humans want to exercise control over the physical world?

I don't think so. I think that probably reflects something very special about the nature of our minds. There is no evolutionary pressure to create minds capable of forming sciences; it just has happened. Evolutionary pressure has not led to higher rates of reproduction for people capable of solving scientific problems or creating new scientific ideas. So if, in fact, the science-forming capacities evolved for other reasons, it would not be too surprising if those particular structures that have developed proved to be rather special in their nature, reflecting the contingencies of their evolution or the working of physical law.

Do you mean that we may, by virtue of this accidental origin of science, be capable of development of some disciplines of science and incapable of others, and that we are not conscious of that?

Yes. As human beings we are not too conscious of that because we naturally assume that our mental structures are universal. But I suppose an outside biologist looking at us would see something very different. He would see that, like other organisms, we have a narrow sphere within which we are very good, but that sphere is very limited. And that, in fact, the very achievements that we can have within that sphere are related to lack of achievements in other spheres.

To construct a scientific theory from the data and to be able to recognize that it is a reasonable theory is possible only if there are some very sharp restrictive principles that lead you to go in one direction and not in another direction. Otherwise you wouldn't have science at all, merely randomly chosen hypotheses. Then human genius may have limitless opportunities to develop in one direction, but at the same time this genius will not go in other directions. And those two considerations are related. The very properties of the human mind that provide an enormous scope for human genius in some domains will serve as barriers to progress in other domains, just as the properties that enable each child to acquire a complex and highly articulated human language block the acquisition of other imaginable linguistic systems.

What domains do you consider the most backward and neglected?

I think that we have basically nothing in the field of human behavior. Maybe that is just **a condition of temporary ignorance.** But it may be that we are simply not intellectually equipped to develop such a theory.

Do you mean that not only do we not have tools to develop such a theory but we are not capable of creating the necessary tools?

Yes. Intellectual tools. Our minds are specifically adapted to developing certain theories and we have a science if the theories which are available to our minds happen to be close to true. Well, there is no particular reason to suppose that the intersection of true theories and theories that are accessible to the mind is very large. It may not be very large.

Can we know at least how large it is?

It is a question of biology how large that intersection is. And if humans are organisms like every other organism, which they are, then we would expect precisely that if there are some domains where real scientific progress is possible, then there are others where it is not.

Editor's Notes to Interview 28

"Interview: Noam Chomsky. The Revolutionary Linguist who Believes We Have a 'Language Organ' in Our Brain Also Thinks There Are Some Things No Amount of Learning Can Teach," *Omni* 6:11 (November 1983), pp. 113–4, 116, 118, and 171–4. Psychologist and science journalist John Gliedman, "who studied Chomsky's theories in the late 60s at MIT, discussed ideas about language and mind in the linguist's austere campus office." Reprinted in **CD&E** as ch. 1, within a systematic frame, and, in part (approximately the first two-thirds), in *Language: Introductory Readings*, edited by Virginia P. Clark, Paul A. Eschholz & Alfred F. Rosa. 4th ed. St. Martin's Press, 1985, pp. 366–375, preceded by a brief introductory note by the editors and followed by five questions for discussion and review. It was not included, however, in *The Omni Interviews*, edited by Pamela Weintraub. New York: Ticknor & Fields, 1984, perhaps because what Chomsky has to say in this interview is less plausible or less interesting or less up-to-date than what B. F. Skinner says in his. Or perhaps because Chomsky has nothing to say about such topics as the relative complexity of the brains of dolphins and humans, the nature of "altered states," the future of "cosmic colonies," and so on.

In the preliminary note to the interview it is pointed out that "before Chomsky's breakthrough in the mid-50s, American linguists did not believe that brain structure played any significant role in shaping language," and that his "rise to scientific prominence was meteoric": in scarcely a decade he became "the world-renowned leader of an intellectual revolution in the field of linguistics." "Aside from the originality of his ideas," the note continues, "Chomsky owes his success to his awesome ability as a debater; he's famous for surgically dissecting the logical flaws in rival views ... His widely recognized gifts as a teacher also helped him." (Cf. Rudolf P. Botha, *Challenging Chomsky: The Generative Garden Game*. Oxford, UK; New York, NY, USA : B. Blackwell, 1989; reprint, 1991.) We are also given the following statistics: After achieving national recognition as a critic of the Vietnam War, "he sometimes made eight speeches a day while producing a torrent of documented critiques of American policy, as well as numerous technical books and papers in linguistics and philosophy ... Since 1958 he has written 21 books and about 100 articles on linguistics, philosophy and psychology. He has also found time to author or coauthor an additional 11 books and perhaps 1,000 articles on political and social themes." (And by now, about 90 books and thousands of articles.) Mention is also made of the fact that he "withheld half of his federal income taxes as a protest against the war."

On the "crisis of modernism," see **RL** (1975), 124ff. (Gunther Stent's paper has been reprinted as chapter 9 in his *Paradoxes of Progress*. San Francisco: Freeman, 1978.)

See notes to interviews 11 and 12.

28. Things No Amount of Learning Can Teach (November 1983)

Why do you believe that language behavior critically depends on the existence of a genetically preprogrammed language organ in the brain?

There's a lot of linguistic evidence to support this contention. But even in advance of detailed linguistic research, we should expect heredity to play a major role in language because there is really no other way to account for the fact that children learn to speak in the first place.

What do you mean?

Consider something that everyone agrees to is due to heredity—the fact that humans develop arms rather than wings. Why do we believe this? Well, since nothing in the fetal environments of the human or bird embryo can account for the differences between birds and men, we assume that heredity must be responsible. In fact, if someone came along and said that a bird embryo is somehow "trained" to grow wings, people would just laugh, even though embryologists lack anything like detailed understanding of how genes regulate embryological development.

Is the role of heredity as important for language as it is for embryology?

I think so. You have to laugh at claims that heredity plays no significant role in language learning, because exactly the same kinds of genetic arguments hold for language learning as hold for embryological development.

I'm very much interested in embryology, but I've got just a layman's knowledge of it. I think that recent work, primarily in molecular biology, however, is seeking to discover the ways that genes regulate embryological development. The gene-control problem is conceptually similar to the problem of accounting for language growth. In fact, language development really ought to be called "language growth," because the language organ grows like any other body organ.

Is there a special place in the brain and a particular kind of neurological structure that comprises the language organ?

Little enough is known about cognitive systems and their neurological basis; so caution is necessary in making any direct claims. But it does seem that the representation and use of language involve specific neural structures, though their nature is not well understood.

But clearly, environment plays some role in language development. What's the rela-
tionship between heredity and environment for human language?

The language organ interacts with early experience and matures into the grammar of the language that the child speaks. If a human being with this fixed endowment grows up in Philadelphia, as I did, his brain will encode knowledge of the Philadelphia dialect of English. If that brain had grown up in Tokyo, it would have encoded the Tokyo dialect of Japanese. The brain's different linguistic experience—English versus Japanese—would modify the language organ's structure.

Roughly the same thing goes on in animal experiments, showing that different kinds of early visual experience can modify the part of the brain that processes visual information. As you may know, cats, monkeys, and humans have hierarchically organized brain-cell networks connected to the retina in such a way that certain cells fire only when there is a horizontal line in the visual field; other hierarchies respond only to vertical lines. But early experience can apparently change the relative numbers of horizontal- and vertical-line detectors. MIT psychologists Richard Held and Alan Hein showed some time ago, for example, that a kitten raised in a cage with walls covered by bold, black vertical lines will display good sensitivity to vertical lines as an adult but poor horizontal-line sensitivity. Lack of stimulation apparently causes the horizontal-line detectors to atrophy.

An even closer analogy exists between language growth and the growth that occurs in human beings after birth—for example, the onset of puberty. If someone came along and said, "Kids are trained to undergo puberty because they see other people," once again everybody would laugh. Would we laugh because we know in great detail the gene mechanisms that determine puberty? As far as I can tell, no one knows much of anything about that. Yet we all assume that puberty is genetically determined.

Still, as your own example shows, environmental factors do play a major role in phys-
iological growth.

And it goes without saying that the onset of puberty may well vary over quite a range depending on childhood diet and all kinds of other environmental influences. Nonetheless, everyone takes for granted that the fundamental processes controlling puberty are genetically programmed. This is probably true of death as well. You may be genetically programmed to die at roughly a certain point; it's a reasonable theory.

Look, all through an organism's existence, from birth to death, it passes through a series of genetically programmed changes. Plainly language growth is simply one of these predetermined changes. Language depends upon genetic endowment that's on a par with the ones that specify the structure of our visual or circulatory systems, or determine that we have arms instead of wings.

What about the linguistic evidence? What have you learned from studying human languages to corroborate your biological viewpoint?

The best evidence involves those aspects of a language's grammar that are so obvious, so intuitively self-evident to everyone, that they are quite rightly never mentioned in traditional grammars.

You mean that school grammars fill in the gaps left by heredity? They teach everything about French or Russian, for example, that can't be taken for granted by virtue of the fact that you're human?

That's right. It is precisely what seems self-evident that is most likely to be part of our hereditary baggage. Some of the oddities of English pronoun behavior illustrate what I mean. Take the sentence, "John believes he is intelligent." Okay, we all know that "he" can refer either to John or to someone else; so the sentence is ambiguous. It can mean either that John thinks he, John, is intelligent, or that someone else is intelligent. In contrast, consider the sentence, "John believes him to be intelligent." Here the pronoun "him" can't refer to John; it can refer only to someone else.

Now, did anyone teach us this peculiarity about English pronouns when we were children? It would be hard to even imagine a training procedure that would convey such information to a person. Nevertheless, everybody knows it—knows it without experience, without training, and at quite an early age. There are any number of other examples that show that we humans have explicit and highly articulate linguistic knowledge that simply has no basis in linguistic experience.

There's just no way that children can pick up this kind of information by listening to the grown-ups around them?

Precisely. But let me give you another example. English contains grammatical constructions that are called parasitic gaps. In these constructions, you can drop a pronoun and still understand the sentence in the same way as when the sentence contains a pronoun. Consider the sentence, "Which article did you file without reading it?" Notice that you can drop the pronoun "it" without changing meaning or grammaticality. You can say, "Which article did you file without reading?" But you can't say, "John was killed by a rock falling on," when you mean, "John was killed by a rock falling on him." This time omitting the pronoun destroys both meaning and grammaticality.

Constructions of this type—where you can or cannot drop the pronoun— are very rare. In fact, they are so rare that it is quite likely that during the period a child masters his native language (the first five or six years of life), he never hears any of these constructions, or he hears them very sporadically. Nonetheless, every native speaker of English knows flawlessly when you can and can't drop pronouns in these kinds of sentences.

So we're faced with a mystery. How could anyone possibly learn enough about the English language to possess the rich and exotic grammatical knowledge that we all seem to possess by the time we are five or six years old?

There's an obvious answer to that: The knowledge is built in. You and I can learn English, as well as any other language, with all its richness because we are designed to learn languages based upon a common set of principles, which we may call universal grammar.

What is universal grammar?

It is the sum total of all the immutable principles that heredity builds into the language organ. These principles cover grammar, speech sounds, and meaning. Put differently, universal grammar is the inherited genetic endowment that makes it possible for us to speak and learn human languages.

Suppose that somewhere else in the universe intelligent life has evolved. Could we, with our specialized language organ, learn the aliens' language if we made contact with them?

Not if their language violated the principles of our universal grammar, which, given the myriad ways that languages can be organized, strikes me as highly likely.

Maybe we shouldn't call it universal, then. But please explain what you mean.

The same structures that make it possible to learn a human language make it impossible for us to learn a language that violates the principles of universal grammar. If a Martian landed from outer space and spoke a language that violated universal grammar, we simply would not be able to learn that language the way that we learn a human language like English or Swahili. We should have to approach the alien's language slowly and laboriously—the way that scientists study physics, where it takes generation after generation of labor to gain new understanding and to make significant progress. We're designed by nature for English, Chinese, and every other possible human language, but we're not designed to learn perfectly usable languages that violate universal grammar. These languages would simply not be within our range of abilities.

How would you assess current research about universal grammar?

In the last three or four years there's been a major conceptual change in the underlying theory. We now assume that universal grammar consists of a collection of preprogrammed subsystems that include, for example, one responsible for meaning, another responsible for stringing together phrases in a sentence, a third one that deals, among other things, with the kinds of relationships between nouns and pronouns that I discussed earlier. And there are a number of others.

These subsystems are not genetically preprogrammed down to the last detail. If they were, there would be only one human language. But heredity does set rather narrow limits on the possible ways that the rules governing each sub-system's function can vary. Languages like English and Italian, for example, differ in their choice of genetically permitted variations that exist as options in the universal grammar. You can think of these options as a kind of linguistic menu containing mutually exclusive grammatical possibilities.

For example, languages like Italian have chosen the "null subject" option from the universal-grammar menu: in Italian you can say "left" when you mean "he left" or "she left." English and French have passed up this option and chosen instead the rule that requires explicit mention of the subject.

What are some other grammatical options on the universal-grammar menu?

In English the most important element in every major grammatical category comes first in its phrase. In simple sentences, for example, we say "John hit Bill," not "John Bill hit." With adjectives we say "proud of John" not "John of proud"; with nouns we say "habit of drinking wine," not "drinking wine of habit"; and with prepositions we say "to John," not "John to." Because heads of grammatical categories always come first, English is what is called a head-initial language.

Japanese is a head-final language. In Japanese you say "John Bill hit." And instead of prepositions, there are postpositions that follow nouns: "John to," rather than "to John." So here's another parameter the child's got to learn from experience: Is the language head-initial or head-final?

These grammatical parameters are interconnected. You can't pick them any more freely than, say, a wine fanatic who insists on white wine with fish and red wine with meat is free to choose any main dish once he's decided on his wine. But grammars are even more sensitive than this culinary example might suggest. A slight change in just one of the universal grammar's parameters can have enormous repercussions throughout the language. It can produce an entirely different language.

Again, there's **a close parallel to embryology**, where a slight shift in the gene mechanisms regulating growth may be all that separates a fertilized egg from developing into a lion rather than a whale.

So what exactly would you say is the grammar of English?

The grammar of English is the collection of choices (head-initial rather than head-final, and null subject forbidden, for example) that define one of a limited number of genetically permitted selections from the universal-grammar menu of grammatical options. And of course there are all the lexical facts. You just have to learn your language's vocabulary. The universal grammar doesn't tell you that "tree" means 'tree' in English.

But once you've learned the vocabulary items and fixed the grammatical parameters for English, the whole system is in place. And the general principles

genetically programmed into the language organ just churn away to yield all the
particular facts about English grammar.

*It sounds as if your present research goal is to reach the point where you can define
every human language's grammar simply by specifying its choices from the universal
grammar's menu of options.*

That's the kind of work you would hope would soon be done: to take a theory of universal grammar, fix the parameters one way or another, and then
deduce from these parameters the grammar of a real human language—Japanese,
Swahili, English, or whatnot.

This goal is only on the horizon. But I think that it is within our conceptual grasp. Undoubtedly the principles of universal grammar that we currently
theorize are wrong. It would be a miracle if we were right this early along. But
the principles are of the right type, and we can now begin to test our present system with complex examples to see what is wrong and to make changes that will
improve our theory.

*Judging from what you've said about language and heredity, it sounds as if you must
be sympathetic to the aims of sociobiology. Is that a fair assumption?*

Well, I think that in some respects the sociobiologists are on the right track.
I think it's true that a good deal of our personal behavior, social behavior, reactions, and so on are the reflection of genetic programs, and I think that it's a
worthwhile enterprise to discover what these programs are. But while I think the
general idea behind sociobiology is right, I also think that sociobiologists should
be extremely cautious about the specific conclusions they draw from their
research. Unfortunately, they often draw conclusions that are remote from evidence or theory.

*Many sociobiologists would dispute your note of caution. They claim that science has
already gained enough information about the relationships between genes and behavior to permit some shrewd guesses about some of the ways heredity influences human
social behavior. What do you say to these claims?*

I'm very skeptical. I haven't really studied the newer research in enough
detail to make any informed judgment. But as for the earlier work (for example,
E.O. Wilson's *Sociobiology*), well, about 90 percent of the book was on non-pri-
mates, and that looked interesting. There was a little bit on primates, which was
more questionable. And there was a final chapter on humans that was completely empty. I don't think Wilson understood what he was talking about in that final
chapter. There were real errors in what he did describe in any detail. I don't even
understand why the chapter on humans was tacked on to the book. It didn't seem
to belong.

What do you think about the claim made by Wilson and others that there's an innate incest taboo in human beings?

Sorting out what is and what is not genetically preprogrammed in human behavior is a very difficult task. As I said, I agree with the general approach of sociobiology. I think it's a reasonable approach. But it's important to be very cautious in making any claims about the role of heredity in human affairs—especially claims that would have social consequences if they were true. Science is held in such awe in our culture that every scientist has special responsibility to make clear to the lay audience where his expert knowledge actually yields scientifically verifiable results and where he is guessing, indulging in sheer speculation, or expressing his own personal hopes about the success of his research. This is an important task because they lay audience is in no position to make these distinctions.

Moving on to another controversial area in the behavioral sciences, how do you think your views differ from B.F. Skinner's behaviorist theory of language, learning, and mind?

Skinner used to take a relatively extreme position. At one point he held that, apart from the most rudimentary functions, essentially nothing of importance was genetically programmed in the human brain. Skinner agreed that humans were genetically programmed to see and hear, but that's about all. Accordingly he argued that all human behavior was simply a reflection of training and experience. This view can't possibly be correct. And, in fact, Skinner's approach has led absolutely nowhere in this area. It has yielded no theoretical knowledge, no nontrivial principles as far as I am aware (thus far, at any rate).

Why is that?

Because Skinnerian behaviorism is off the wall. It's as hopeless a project as trying to explain that the onset of puberty results from social training. But I really don't know whether Skinner still maintains this extreme position.

What about the late Jean Piaget? Where do you stand on his theories of the child's mental development?

Piaget's position is different: it's more complex than Skinner's. Piaget held that the child passes through cognitive states. According to my understanding of the Piagetian literature, Piaget and his supporters were never really clear about what produced a new stage of cognitive development. What they could have said—though they seemed to shy away from it—is that cognitive development is a genetically determined maturational process like puberty, for example. That's what the Piagetians ought to say. They don't like this formulation, but it seems right to me.

In other words, Piagetians place much more emphasis on the role of experience in cognitive development than you do. Are there other differences as well?

Yes. Piagetians maintain that the mind develops as a whole rather than as a modular structure with specific capacities developing in their own ways. This is a possible hypothesis, but in fact it seems to be extremely wrong.

How do you mean?

Well, consider the properties that determine the reference of pronouns that we talked about earlier. Once you ferret out these rules for pronouns, they seem to have nothing in common with the logical operations that Piagetians single out as being typical of the early stages of the child's mental development.

In other words, a four-year-old who may not realize that the amount of water stays the same when you pour the contents of a low, wide glass into a tall, thin container nevertheless displays sophisticated logical abilities in his grasp of the complex rules of English grammar?

Yes. And these abilities are independent of the logical capacities measured by tests. There's just no resemblance between what a child does with blocks and the kind of knowledge that he displays of English grammar at the same age. In fact, I think it's sort of quixotic to expect tight interconnections between language development and growth in other mental domains. By and large, body systems develop in their own ways at their own rates. They interact, but the circulatory system doesn't wait until the visual system reaches a certain stage of organization before proceeding to imitate the visual system's organizational complexity. Cognitive growth shouldn't be different in this respect either. As far as we know, it isn't.

What about the problem of free will? If genes play a crucial role in structuring the mind's abilities, is free will an illusion?

Well, that's interesting. Here, I think I would tend to agree with Descartes. Free will is simply an obvious aspect of human experience. I know—as much as I know that you're in front of me right now—that I can take my watch and throw it out the window if I feel like it. I also know that I'm not going to do that, because I want the watch. But I could do it if I felt like it. I just know this.

Now, I don't think that there's any scientific grasp, any hint of an idea, as to how to explain free will. Suppose somebody argues that free will is an illusion. Okay. This could be the case, but I don't believe that it's the case. It could be. You have to be open-minded about the possibility. But you're going to need a very powerful argument to convince me that something as evident as free will is an illusion. Nobody's offered such an argument or even pretended to offer such an argument.

So where does that leave us? We're faced with an overwhelmingly self-evident phenomenon that could be an illusion even though there's no reason to believe that it is an illusion. And we have a body of scientific knowledge that simply doesn't appear to connect with the problem of free will in any way.

Do you think that science will ever solve the problem of free will?

Personally, I don't think so. People have been trying to solve the problem of free will for thousands of years, and they've made zero progress. They don't even have bad ideas about how to answer the question. My hunch—and it's no more than a guess—is that the answer to **the riddle of free will** lies in the domain of potential science that the human mind can never master because of the limitations of its genetic structure.

Can you spell out what you mean?

We can laugh at a rat that always fails a complicated maze. We can say, "The rat is always going to fail because it can't look at the maze in the right way. It's doomed to fail this test forever."

Similarly, some other intelligence, organized along hereditary lines different from our own, could look at the human race and say, "Those humans are always formulating the problem of free will in the wrong way. And the reason they don't understand the problem has something to do with their biological nature."

It could well turn out that free will is one maze that we humans will never solve. We may be like the rat that simply is not designed to solve a certain type of maze and will never do so even if it works on it for ten million years. Look, in principle, there are almost certainly true scientific theories that our genetically determined brain structures will prevent us from ever understanding. Some of these theories may well be ones that we would like to know about.

That's a discouraging prospect.

I don't see it as much of a reason to despair. In fact, I kind of like the conclusion. I'm not sure that I want free will to be understood.

Do you think that any other human abilities fall into the same mysterious category as free will?

In my opinion all of them do.

All of them?

Take, for example, the aesthetic sense. We like and understand Beethoven because we are humans, with a particular, genetically determined mental constitution. But that same human nature also means there are other conceivable forms of aesthetic expression that will be totally meaningless to us. The same thing is as true for art as it is for science: the fact that we can understand and appreciate certain kinds of art has a flip side. There must be all kinds of domains of artistic achievement that are beyond our mind's capacities to understand.

Do you think genetic barriers to further progress are becoming obvious in some areas of art an science?

You could give an argument that something like this has happened in quite a few fields. It was possible in the late 19th century for an intelligent person of much leisure and wealth to be about as much at home as he wanted to be in the arts and sciences. But 40 years later that goal had become hopeless. Much of **the new work in art and science** since then is meaningless to the ordinary person.

Take modern music, post-Schoenbergian music. Many artists say that if you don't understand modern music it's because you just haven't listened enough. But modern music wouldn't be accessible to me if I listened to it forever. Modern music is accessible to professionals and maybe to people with a special bent, but it's not accessible to the ordinary person who doesn't have a particular quirk of mind that enables him to grasp modern music, let alone make him want to deal with it.

And you think that something similar has happened in some scientific fields?

I think it has happened in physics and mathematics, for example. There's this idea, which goes back to the French mathematicians known collectively as Bourbaki, that the development of mathematics was originally the exploration of everyday intuitions of space and number. That is probably somewhat true through the end of the 19th century. But I don't think it's true now. As for physics, in talking to students at MIT, I notice that many of the very brightest ones, who would have gone into physics 20 years ago, are now going into biology. I think part of the reason for this shift is that there are discoveries to be made in biology that are within the range of an intelligent human being. This may not be true in other areas.

You seem to be saying two things. First, that whatever defines our common human nature will turn out to be a shared set of intuitions that owe much of their strength and character to our common genetic heritage—our species genotype. Second, that the exhaustion of these intuitions in many areas is producing a peculiar kind of artistic and scientific specialization. Further progress in music or mathematics, for example, requires a scientist or artist with an unusual heredity.

Well, it's a different mental constitution—something like being a chess freak or a runner who can do a three-and-a-half-minute mile. It's almost a matter of logic that this change is going to occur sooner or later. Has it happened already? That's a matter of judgment. It's a matter of looking at, say, the 20th century and seeing whether there are signs of this change. Is it the case, for example, that contemporary work in the arts and sciences is no longer part of our common aesthetic and intellectual experience? Well, there are signs. But whether the signs are realistic or whether we are just going through a sort of sea change, and something will develop, who knows? Maybe a 1,000 years from now we'll know.

Do these possibilities ever make you feel that you're living in a time of creative stagnation?

I don't really feel that. I think that there are too many possibilities. There's too much human potential that hasn't as yet been realized. And don't forget that the vast majority of the human race hasn't even entered into the world that we're claiming may be finished. Who knows what the Third World will contribute to mankind's store of science and art when it does catch up with the industrialized nations? We are well short of real stagnation or termination, but that doesn't rule out the possibility that one might be able to perceive signs of such a change, or even be able to gain some insight into the ultimate limits to our intelligence by examining these signs.

How do these ideas fit into your choice of linguistics as a career?

My choice of linguistics was like most people's choice of work. It was an accident that depended on whom I met, where I was, and that sort of thing. Linguistics, however, was a fortunate choice for me because I think that linguistics is an area where it is possible to construct a very rich science.

How would you assess your own contributions to linguistics?

They seem sort of pre-Galilean.

Like physics before the scientific revolution in the 17th century?

Yes. In the pre-Galilean period, people were beginning to formulate problems in physics in the right way. The answers weren't there, but the problems were finally being framed in a way that in retrospect we can see was right.

How "pre-" do you mean? Are you saying that linguistics is about where physics was in the 16th century? Or are we going back still further, to Aristotle and to other Greek ideas about physics?

We don't know. It depends, you see, on when the breakthrough comes. But my feeling is that someday someone is going to come along and say, "Look, you guys, you're on the right track, but you went wrong here. It should have been done this way." Well, that will be it. Suddenly things will fall into place.

And then we'll have a scientific revolution in linguistics?

I would think so, although to speak of scientific revolutions occurring outside a small core of the natural sciences is rather misleading. In fact, there was **one major scientific revolution** in the 17th century, and there have been a lot of outgrowths from it since then, including biochemistry and molecular biology. But that's it. Nothing remotely resembling a scientific revolution has ever occurred in the social sciences.

How should a scientist exercise responsibility for the uses of his research?

The same way that any human does in any area of life.

Do you think that there are areas in science so potentially vulnerable to social misuse that they should not be pursued?

I think there are. For example, research on how to build more effective nuclear weapons. I don't think that should be pursued.

What about fundamental research—say, basic research in molecular biology that might conceivably give the weapons makers of the next generation a new set of destructive tools?

There's no simple answer to that question. Human beings are responsible for the predictable consequences of their actions. I would stop doing what I was doing if I discovered that I was engaged in an area of scientific research that I thought, under existing social conditions, would lead to, say, oppression, destruction, and pain.

An anachronistic question then: If you were a physicist in 1929, would you have done basic work in nuclear physics even though there was already speculation about the possibility of someday building an atom bomb?

It's not an easy question. It's tempting to say, "Yes, because we have to understand the world." On the other hand, it could be that basic research in nuclear physics will lead to the extinction of the human race or to something close to that. So I don't think a glib answer is possible. Still, if you ask me specifically, I'm sure that my answer would have been yes. I would have done the work just out of interest and curiosity and with the hope that things would somehow work out. But whether that would have been the morally responsible path is not clear.

Editor's Notes to Interview 29

This is the second of the Reime interviews (see Editor's Notes to Interview 13). It took place in Lexington, MA, on Nov. 13, 1983.

On the distinction between the "Prussians" and the "traders," see **RP** (1981/1984/2003), Editor's Notes to ch. 8.

The objections of Sharon, now prime minister, to Arafat (to "a PLO Arafat-type"), and its consequences, are front page news these days (see 156 and the Editor's Notes to it for an update). Here is an informative quote from a report by Greg Myre from Jerusalem (*New York Times* online, April 28, 2003):

> Israel has shunned Yasir Arafat, the Palestinian leader, saying he has encouraged terrorism. But Mr. Sharon says he is prepared to meet Mr. [Mahmoud] Abbas [the new Palestinian prime minister], commonly known as Abu Mazen ... Mr. Abbas, meanwhile, could meet Mr. Sharon in the near future, and President Bush said last week that Mr. Abbas would be invited to the White House 'one of these days'.
> But meetings abroad could damage Mr. Abbas in the eyes of Palestinians, who may view him as a creation of the United States and Israel. They could also anger Mr. Arafat, who has left Ramallah only once in more than a year and rarely goes beyond the front steps of his rocket-scorched compound.

See also "U.S.-Israel Handpick New Palestinian Leader" (May 12, 2003), http://www.freespeech.org/fsitv/fscm2/contentviewer.php?content_id=323

29. What's New in Reagan's Program? (13 November 1983)

How do you interpret the foreign policy of the Reagan administration as compared with its predecessors?

In fundamental respects it's the same, and in fact all the administrations are basically the same in fundamental respects. They reflect the same dominating interests and the same concern to maintain a global system which will essentially be open to the penetration of American capital and have a favorable investment climate and where resources will be accessible to the United States and its allies. That's the overriding consideration, and there isn't much deviation from it from administration to administration. But there are some slight differences, and I think they partly reflect Reagan's domestic program.

Reagan's domestic program had two major features. One was to transfer substantial resources from the poor to the rich, so they cut back welfare programs and decreased taxes primarily for the wealthy, and so on and so forth. So there's the resource transfer to the rich. The second aspect was an enormous increase in what in effect is the state component of the economy. The way in which the American government intervenes in production is through creation of a guaranteed market for high technology production; in effect that means arms production. That's our industrial policy planning, which has been in existence since the Second World War. Whenever there's a fear of recession or whenever there's a felt need to spur industrialization, there invariably is a war scare to create a climate in which military build-up is possible. So Reagan was moving in that direction. In this respect it's similar to the Kennedy administration, which did exactly the same thing, and so did the Truman administration in 1950–51, at a time of fear of recession.

But, of course, one correlate to this is a more aggressive foreign policy. Whenever the state turns to domestic militarization—usually for internal economic reasons—at the same time it has to seek confrontation internationally so that you can justify it to the one who has to pay for it. The public has to pay for it. The way it can do it, is if it feels itself threatened. So invariably, at the Kennedy period and during the Truman administration the domestic commitment to re-industrialization through militarization has always correlated with search for confrontation and subversion and counterinsurgency and so on. The Reagan administration did that, and in this respect it really is **a replay of the Kennedy administration.**

Kennedy came into the office in 1961 with the slogan "we have to get the country moving again." Eisenhower had let things drift. There had been several recessions. Corresponding with the Kennedy decisions was the claim that Eisenhower had been insufficiently militant in the international sphere.

In fact, the 1960 campaign was very similar to the 1980 campaign. Reagan's foreign policy differs from Carter's in a way rather analogous to the way in which Kennedy's differed from Eisenhower's. In both cases there were large scale counterinsurgency, global intervention, and seeking confrontations with the superpower enemy. This is a kind of system of commitment, on the one hand to domestic policies of militarization, on the other hand to confrontation to justify it, and along with that a more active undermining of regimes that stand in the way to a continuing commitment to a global economy that will be supportive to American needs.

In this respect there is a difference between, say, Reagan and Carter. You can see that, for example, in Central America. The first foreign policy crisis of the Reagan administration was El Salvador. That had also been a crisis for the Carter administration. Carter treated it as a sort of a local problem. I mean the problem was to maintain in power the military regime that had been created there and to enable it to suppress local dissidents. Carter was supporting a large-scale attack on the peasantry, which was, in fact, quite murderous and brutal, all in the guise of progressive measures, land reform and so on. Reagan continued on pretty much the same trajectory. But the difference was that Reagan immediately turned it into an international confrontation with the Russians. There was a rhetorical change between Carter and Reagan.

Take the case of Nicaragua. Carter was following a policy of trying to support elements in the Sandinista coalition that would be favorable to American business interests, so the Sandinista coalition, particularly at the time, was rather pluralistic, and there were business elements in it. If you look at the Carter policy, he did want to give a degree of aid to Nicaragua, but that aid was designated to go to the private sector, to try to build a private sector and increase its influence within the Sandinista governing coalition and to gradually work Nicaragua back into the American system. That was essentially Carter's policy. Reagan's policy, on the other hand, was to stop that at once and to turn to confrontation, to build up mercenary armies which will attack Nicaragua and to try to drive Nicaragua to the point where it will be compelled to ask for either Cuban or Russian aid, at which point the United States will be able to impose a blockade and then have something like the Cuban missile crisis, a confrontation with the Russians.

The same is true, I think, in the Middle East and, in fact, everywhere in the world. There has been a change towards more militancy, towards search for confrontation. And that's completely predictable on the basis of the domestic program. In fact, it's not so original. It's similar to 1960, it's similar to 1950. It basically grows out of the internal needs of the management of the domestic society.

What you said about the parallels between the Reagan administration and the
Kennedy administration seems to go against the conventional view, which is expressed
in newspaper articles and commentaries, the view that the Kennedy administration
was liberal and committed to welfare policies, whereas Reagan is for so-called free
enterprise"

A Difference in American Power

For one thing, there were very few liberal measures taken in the Kennedy
administration. That was mostly rhetoric. The Great Society measures and so on
were Johnson's. It's true that they grew out of rhetorical commitments during the
Kennedy period. What you say is in part true. Kennedy was much more committed to a narrow version of welfare state measures, and of course Reagan is
strongly opposed to that. He wants to dismantle all the systems like food for the
poor. One part of Reagan's program, namely the transfer of resources from the
poor to the rich, that's different from the Kennedy program. But even that is not
entirely different. For example, the one major legislative achievement of the
Kennedy administration was a regressive tax cut, which favored business, to try
to spur business investments—what's now called supply-side economics.

However, there is a difference, and I think the difference reflects primarily
the difference in American power. In 1960 the world was a very different world.
That was a time when the United States really was the hegemonic power. So, for
example, the Kennedy administration was concerned with the viability of the
Japanese economy. They were afraid that it would not be a viable economy. And,
in fact, the United States had a favorable trade balance with Japan in the early
1960s, until 1965, when the costs of the Vietnam War started to be felt. The
United States had a favorable trade balance with Japan and it was concerned
somehow to support and rebuild the Japanese economy and so to work it into
the American world system as a flourishing economy, as it tried to do with
Europe in the early 1950s. Obviously that is not the case today. Now the problem is to try to compete with Japan. And in general there has been a substantial
decline in American power (of course not absolutely, but in relative terms) since
1960. In 1950 the United States was producing about 50 percent of total world
output, in 1980 it was about 25 percent and in 1960 about a third. That's a significant decline.

In 1980 the United States was suffering from stagflation—the inability to
hold back inflation and, at the same time, maintain production. That was not
true in 1960. In 1960 the Keynesian economists felt (and they were right) that
there was enough flexibility in the economy that they could use government
spending (and that meant military spending primarily) to spur economic development and still have plenty leftover to support some kind of domestic welfare
program at a rather limited level (I mean, not at the European scale).

The Reagan administration cannot afford that. Just the rearmament alone
is causing huge budget deficits. If they didn't at the same time cut back social
programs, the deficits would be totally intolerable.

This was already beginning to happen at the end of the Carter administration. In 1978 Carter proposed an increase in the military budget and a decrease in social programs. That was in 1978, but it couldn't get through the Congress at the time. But after the Russian invasion of Afghanistan and after the Iran hostage crisis, they were able to put through these programs, and Reagan just continued and increased them.

So I don't think that there is all that much difference. I don't think these should be viewed as primarily ideological or even political differences. They are to some extent. I mean, Kennedy was drawing a lot of his support from the liberal establishment and, in fact, the working class, and Reagan isn't. That makes some difference. But I think these are minor factors. I think the major factors have to do with the objective circumstances of American capitalism domestically and in the world scene. And this has simply changed. You can see that from the Carter administration, which was already moving in that direction.

So the Kennedy years were, in a sense, a continuation of the 1940s, when, after the Second World War, the United States had an extraordinary power?

The Lesson of Keynesianism

The United States came out of the Second World War as the only functioning power in the world. I don't think there has been any other time in history when one country was responsible for 50 percent of world output. It probably never happened before, as far as I know. But it was true briefly, and it obviously couldn't last. The other countries were going to reconstruct sooner or later. And, in fact, the United States needed them to reconstruct. The fear in the United States at the end of the Second World War was that there would be no market for American exports, and in fact the major motivation behind the Marshall Plan and the effort to rebuild European capitalism was to create markets for American exports. There was a serious fear that if that was not done, the United States would be right back in the recession, which it had gotten out of because of the war. The Roosevelt New Deal measures were very ineffective—there were still 9 million people unemployed in 1939. But the war changed that. The war taught the lesson of Keynesianism. It taught that if the government becomes directly involved in stimulating production—and the easiest way to do it is military production—then that can, in fact, get the economic system moving again, pretty much as Keynes said. And that lesson was learned.

But of course there has to be market. So the post-war American policy was an effort to reconstruct European capitalism but with the insistence that it not be national capitalism. The United States wanted a world capitalism, which would integrate Europe into the American system, would allow for American investment in Europe and also expansion into growing European markets, which would increase as the industrialization proceeded.

That's what happened. There was an enormous American export and huge American investments in Europe—there had been virtually no American investment in Europe prior to that but it became enormous during the 1950s and 1960s. And to some extent that was true in Japan. The United States knew that Japan was going to be the industrial center of Asia—nobody had any doubts about that—and the United States wanted to ensure that it was now going to be incorporated within the American global system. The United States went to war in 1941 to prevent Japan from creating a closed world system, a "New Order" in East Asia, from which the United States would be excluded. The United States was willing to deal with fascist Japan up until the point when they closed the China market to American penetration. In fact, the negotiations between Japan and the United States in 1941 were to a significant extent at least over the question of closing the New Order to Western—meaning American—penetration. The United States didn't want that to happen again. So Japan would have to be incorporated into the American system but also to re-industrialize. Well, that happened too, but much more slowly than the United States had anticipated. As I said, in the early 1960s it was still a problem.

Of course one consequence of contributing to the reconstruction of a capitalist society is to build competitors. You cannot have it both ways. And in fact compared with the system as it began to develop in Europe and Japan and now even in other parts of the world, for instance in East Asia, the world is now a much more diverse and complex place than it was in 1950 and even in 1960. The same is true with the Russians. I think the Soviet Union is relatively less powerful in world affairs than it was in 1960. It's declined in its degree to influence and coerce. Again, like the United States, its absolute power continues to increase but its ability to dominate decreases.

In fact, there has been something of an erosion of the bipolar world system since that period. And that reflects itself in the difference between Reagan's policies and Kennedy's. But I think it's interesting that although Reagan and Kennedy are regarded as being at the opposite extremes of the political spectrum, nevertheless their policies are remarkably similar, rhetoric aside. I think that tells us something about the relative superficiality of political differences, when the main factors that determine policy lie outside of the political system anyway.

Do you think that it would be possible for an independent capitalist system to be born in Western Europe and Japan? Would that require a powerful army, powerful military forces of the Europeans and the Japanese?

The Real Threat: A Truly Independent Europe

No, I don't think so, because I don't think armies have much to do in keeping the capitalist system going. Military expenditures may be significant. That's been a major technique for all industrial economies for 30, 40 years, and also for maintaining just physical control over areas in the world that might go along nationalist ways. That has to be curbed, so you have to have subversion or counterinsurgency and sometimes even direct aggression, like in Indochina. But I think that's secondary. Japan's is a good case. Japan has been remarkably successful economically. It's by no means weak from a military point of view, but its military strength is not at all commensurate with its economic power. In fact, the United States has been trying to get Japan and Europe to re-arm, to increase their armaments, partly because our industrial planning system, which is so militarily oriented, is very inefficient. It means you are producing waste and our competitors are doing the work on different grounds. Japan also has an industrial planning system, but it's not producing waste, it's producing computers and cameras and tape-recorders and so on. That's driving the United States out of world markets, so we want them to create an inefficient system like ours through the armament.

However, to get back to the main point, I think the United States very much does want Europe and Japan to become independent systems, and they might become so. For example, I think that the European disarmament movement should be seen, to a significant extent, as part of a long-term tendency towards creating a relatively independent Europe, which will separate itself from the bipolar system of global domination, and neither the Russians nor the Americans want that. The Americans don't want it, because a truly independent Europe, even a capitalist Europe, would be a major competitor to the United States. Western Europe's economy is approximately on the scale of the United States—maybe, in fact, even larger. It has an educated population, has a high level of technology, a high level of literacy, and so on and so forth. If Europe could overcome its internal divisions and become, say, some sort of federated economy, that would be a real threat to the United States, a major threat. The Soviet Union is not a threat to the United States. It's a barely functioning economy. Its economy is, I think, something like half the size of the United States' economy. Apart from military production, it's inefficient and, of course, it's no competitor. Europe is quite a different story, and Japan also is quite a different story.

It's perfectly possible that 20 years from now, say, the Europe-America conflict would be a rather serious one. In fact, in some areas it already has been, in the Middle East, for instance. The United States has been very much concerned to keep Europe out of Middle East affairs. I think that was one of the reasons why the United States took such a strong stand at the time of the invasion of Egypt in 1956. You recall that the United States compelled France and England and Israel to leave—quickly. I think the United States perceived that as an effort by France and England to re-introduce themselves in Middle Eastern affairs. The United States has taken considerable pains to exclude France and England from the Middle East. There had been agreements in the 1920s (the 1928 Red Line agreement) that partitioned most of the oil producing areas among France and the United States. After the Second World War the United States, in effect, excluded France totally and it was gradually chipping away at British interests and had cut them back quite considerably. In 1956 France and England were reasserting the position from which they had just been expelled, and the United States wasn't having any of that.

This goes through to the 1970s. For example, the United States has been committed to keeping Europe out of Middle Eastern diplomacy, so the so-called Euro-Arab initiatives were strongly condemned by the United States. In fact, Kissinger, in one of his secret memoranda that came out under the Freedom of Information Act, stated explicitly that one major element of his post-1973 diplomacy was to keep Europe and Japan out of the Middle East negotiations. This is to be an American preserve. Nobody is supposed to touch the oil. The United States has had as the main principle in its postwar foreign policy to keep the American control over the oil-producing regions and to prevent competitors (meaning Europe and, now, Japan) from getting in there. Well, they can't do it completely. For example now, I think, Japanese trade with Saudi-Arabia may even be higher than American; their export to Saudi-Arabia is close, maybe even higher. In an international system the strongest power will, in general, be in favor of what's called free trade because it will win. But the trouble is that in the way the international economy works, it is sometimes necessary to use force to maintain control. This happened with the British Empire. Britain was strongly in favor of free trade as long as it knew it was going to win a competition. When it was facing severe competition, say, from Japan in the 1920s, it began to oppose free trade and put barriers to the penetration of the Commonwealth by Japanese goods. The United States would try to do things like that.

So some of the developments which surely have been taking place are an increase in the relative independence of the European-based system and the Japanese-based system, and the United States is not at all happy about that. That's one of the reasons why the United States is so opposed to the European disarmament movement, which, I think, sees itself—to some extent correctly—as kind of neutralist, as moving towards some kind of separation of Europe from the Cold War conflict. In the long run it's a very serious threat to the United States.

This goes way back. In 1952 Stalin made a proposal, an interesting proposal. We don't know whether it was serious, because it was never taken up, but the proposal was interesting. He suggested a neutralization of Germany, a unification of Germany with internationally supervised free elections, which he was sure to lose totally, of course. The only condition he imposed was that a neutralized, unified Germany be excluded from Western military alliance. Well, considering the recent history of Russia that was not such a crazy proposal. The United States refused it totally (we won't have anything to do with that) and much preferred to see a divided Germany in the Western military alliance and no neutralization in Central Europe.

I think that's perfectly consistent. There have been other attempts since, like the Rapacki plan and others, which tended in that direction. We don't know whether these proposals were serious. Maybe they weren't, maybe they were just for propaganda. But the important thing in this connection is to notice that the United States rejected them out of hand. It didn't want to find out whether they were serious, because we don't want that to happen, we don't want a neutralized

Europe. The worst situation for us would be Russian-controlled Europe. The best situation is an American-controlled Europe. A neutralized Europe, we certainly don't want to see develop. But it is developing. There will be at least tendencies in that direction all the time.

If Stalin's proposal was rejected in the case of Germany, in the case of Austria the same kind of treaty was agreed upon. Was it so because compared with Austria, Germany is a very big country and important economically?

Control Over Europe and Japan

Germany is after all the central economic force in Europe. And a unified Germany ... Remember, this was a call for a unification of Germany that would have made it, by a good margin, the dominant economic force in Europe, and that would have drawn Europe into a neutral sector very likely. It would have meant that very likely France and England and other common market countries would have been drawn into the orbit of a neutralized and re-unified Germany, and the Russians, too, might have, in fact, gone back from domination of their Eastern European satellites (at least it's conceivable, if what they perceive as a NATO threat would have been reduced). So this could have set in motion a move towards creation of a rather substantial European system, probably dominated by Germany, but neutralist and demilitarized, and that would be a very serious threat to the United States. We certainly don't want to see anything like that happen.

I think it's interesting that not only did the United States reject it at the time but it has been essentially wiped out of history. Take a look at the history books. Very few even mention this. There was another similar proposal by Khrushchev in 1955 and there were other feelers all along the way. Well, we don't know whether they were serious. One can't be sure. But they were always rejected out of hand.

How do you interpret, in the light of your remarks, the fact that Western Europe and Japan are much more dependent on Middle Eastern Oil than the United States?

That's part of the system. The United States wants to keep control of the Middle Eastern oil, and that's one of the ways by which we maintain control over Europe and Japan. Right after the Second World War the United States encouraged Japanese reindustrialization—with one exception, however: we did not permit them to set up their own petroleum industry. That was blocked, and that had to be maintained completely in American hands.

As far as Europe is concerned, the United States (Gabriel Kolko is one person who has pointed this out) made significant efforts to try to turn Europe away from a coal-based and towards an oil-based economy, and at the same time it excluded France, virtually entirely, from oil production and cut away the British. And I think that's the same. That gave the United States a strong leverage over

Europe and Japan, because the United States basically controlled the energy supplies of the world.

Now, of course, that, too, is eroding. That kind of almost unique unilateral control over the energy supplies, that has itself changed and by now is much more diffuse. But it simply means that no power, not even a power as great as the United States, is able to run the world. It can only influence it.

What is your view of the Reagan administration's Middle East policy right now?

A Commitment to an Israeli Sparta

Reagan's first significant move in the Middle East was in 1981 when he said that the United States did not oppose Israeli settlements in the West Bank. He was the first American president to say that these were legal—that they were not illegal is the way he put it—and he indicated that there would be no American opposition to an increase in Israeli expansion to the West Bank. That set off a huge land grab. They had already been expanding, and the repression had been intensified in the West Bank, but it escalated significantly at that point in response to Reagan's position.

And over the next year or so Israel took over, nobody exactly knows but maybe by now it's up to 60 percent or so of the West Bank land, and the Golan Heights were incorporated, and the Gaza Strip everyone has forgotten about.

So that was part of Reagan's commitment. I mean Reagan's basic commitment, like Kissinger's, has been to an Israeli Sparta, a militarized, technologically advanced state, which will serve American interests. It will be a strategic asset, a base for the projection of American power in the Middle East. It will be a threat to radical, nationalist movements in the Middle East, a kind of gendarme. This also extended Carter's policy. I mean it was not all that dissimilar but it extended, escalated it. Carter also wanted Israel to provide subsidiary services (as it is doing) by supporting American clients, particularly in Latin America and to some extent in Africa, especially Zaire. There are a number of countries where the congressional human rights campaign, which is misleadingly associated with the American presidency (it is really congressional), has posed barriers to direct intervention. So the United States is barred by law from, say, giving arms to Guatemala, or to Argentina under the generals, or to Pinochet, and so on, and Israel can move in and do that task for us, and Reagan wanted that to go on. In fact, it's going on and maybe has been extended.

The next major move was Reagan's complete support for the Israeli invasion of Lebanon. I mean it was clear from 1981 to 1982 that Israel was going to invade Lebanon. They were looking for any pretext to do it, and this was certainly obvious at the time. The Israeli army was trying to provoke the PLO's response and so on. Even the press reported that Israel was preparing for an invasion of Lebanon. The United States professed not to know anything about this, which is absurd. But the arms flow to Israel increased substantially, evidently in preparation for the invasion. The United States vetoed UN resolutions and gave direct support under Haig and Schultz up to the invasion of West Beirut. However, on Sept. 1 Reagan came out with his plan, which was immediately rejected by Israel (if you noticed, Reagan supported Israel's rejection of it). Israel not only rejected the Reagan plan outright; at that time Reagan did call for a freeze on settlements, and Israel's response was to radically increase the number of settlements. So the Israeli response was to say: the plan is stone dead; we refuse to have anything to do with it and we will do exactly the opposite of what you request, namely you requested the freezing of settlements and we will increase the settlements.

What was the American response to that? Well, the American response was that Reagan asked for an increase to the already phenomenal level of aid to Israel, and the Congress was not satisfied with that, so it increased it still further. OK, that was a message to the Israeli government saying: fine, go ahead with the settlements, we'll pay for it; invade Lebanon, we'll pay for it, and so on. In fact, we paid even more for their achievements over the summer, which meant that the Reagan plan was killed right off by Israel and the United States within days after it was announced. So that was clearly not serious.

The next major American initiative was the Schultz plan for Lebanon, which finally reached its conclusion (technically it has never been accepted by the Lebanese government, but it was more or less accepted in May 1983). That was accepted by the Lebanese government under duress, clearly feeling that that was the best they could get. It called for a partial Israeli withdrawal: it would withdraw most of its troops from southern Lebanon. But it created arrangements which would permit Israel to dominate and control southern Lebanon through the territorial militias and by other means. Partly these were not made public, because there were secret agreements, but according to Israeli military sources, in particular, it would have left Israel in a position where it could dominate Lebanon at least south of the Litani River, a substantial domination of southern Lebanon.

The Schultz negotiations, I think, were designed for failure. They specifically excluded the Syrians. After the agreements were made Schultz presented them to Syria as a fait accompli, and it was just absolutely certain that Syria would reject them. Had the Soviet Union presented proposals on Lebanon which would have left Syria in substantial control of eastern Lebanon and then turned to Israel and said: OK, now you get out. Of course, Israel would not have responded favorably. And it was obvious to anybody with half a brain that Syria was going to reject the agreements. That, of course, they did, and people pretended to be surprised, but it was perfectly obvious they were going to. So I can only assume that this was purposeful and that the United States intended to have a Syrian rejection, out of which they then made a lot of political capital: they were able to show that another Russian proxy is undermining peace in the world, so we have to re-arm, to have missiles in Europe, to build up our military system and so on (it's another element of the search for confrontation, which, as I said before, is a predictable feature of Reagan's foreign policy).

It is important to bear in mind that there was an alternative (a very clear alternative) which was rejected. The alternative was, first of all, to bring the Soviet Union into the negotiations, as the Lebanese government had requested—they wanted the Russians to come into them. And secondly, there was a fairly · reasonable framework for negotiations, which Syria might have accepted, very likely would have accepted.

Syria was scheduled to withdraw from Lebanon in the summer of 1982, at the end of their 6-year mandate. We don't know whether they would have done so, because the Israeli invasion aborted that possibility—and may have been timed to abort it, in fact. But there was a negotiation framework. If the United States had been serious about settling the Lebanese affairs, what it would have done is create a negotiation framework in which Israel would have been compelled to withdraw in accordance with the UN Security Council resolutions, which, in fact, the United States had endorsed—technically—which called for immediate and unconditional Israeli withdrawal, no benefits to the aggressor, just withdrawal. And Syria would have also withdrawn as planned in 1982. I mean that would have been a framework for negotiations which the Syrians might have accepted. They said they would have accepted; in fact, they would withdraw if Israel withdrew unconditionally. And if the Soviet Union had been drawn in as a sort of guarantor, which they were eager to do—they wanted peace in the region—that would have very well worked.

But that option was never considered for a moment. They much preferred a framework in which Syria would be compelled to reject the settlement and in which confrontation would continue.

I don't find it surprising. I mean, when Reagan came in ... well, *Towards a New Cold War* came out just as the Reagan administration came in and my feeling, as discussed there, was that the Reagan administration in fact was going to seek international confrontation, that that was going to be their main foreign policy program. In fact, that's what they were doing. I think the Lebanese case is just another case: they preferred the confrontation and the political capital to be gained from it—intensification of the Cold War and so on and so forth. They preferred that to the possibility of a settlement. Well, that's essentially the Reagan program for the Middle East.

Now, in the immediate aftermath of the Lebanon war there was enough popular opposition here (the sight of the massacre on television and so on), substantial opposition to the Israeli aggression, that had never happened in the United States before. So the United States at that point was unable to pursue the close military relations with Israel that are part of the Kissinger program and was now part of the Reagan program. It has been a major propaganda effort of the past year to place the blame for the failure of the Reagan program and the Schultz plan on the Arabs, and that has been successful. At the propaganda level it has been extremely successful. Now it's possible to reconstitute the strategic understanding with Israel that would lead to a closer military and strategic relationship and to rebuild what Reagan really wants, namely a militarized Israel, which will be a kind of Sparta, basically—technologically advanced, dependent on the United States, able to perform missions for the United States. They can now do that again.

Since May of this year there have been new developments, when the United States has concentrated a big naval force in the area. Do you think there is a great risk for an international conflict in the area?

Yes, I think there's a very substantial risk. I mean, the United States has now in the Eastern Mediterranean three aircraft carriers and, in fact, the largest naval squadron that has been assembled since the Vietnam War, as far as I know. After the Israeli invasion, in which Israel used advanced American technology to demolish second-rate Russian technology, and of course the Russians responded, exactly as anybody in his sense knew they would, by bringing in more advanced air defense systems to Syria, which are now manned by Russian troops (American sources say 5,000 Russian troops, maybe that's true). Anyway, there's a substantial Russian troop commitment in Syria, supporting the anti-aircraft missiles; there's a substantial Russian naval force in the Eastern Mediterranean; a couple of American jets crashed a few days ago, apparently after coming under Syrian anti-aircraft fire, so it would appear; the United States might respond to the bombing of the marine barracks. In fact, there are a number of possibilities that might lead to an American-Syrian confrontation, which could quickly escalate into an American-Russian confrontation, so I think it's a very dangerous prospect. Incidentally, this was true in 1982 as well. During the Israeli attack on Lebanon, they bombarded the Russian embassy and, in fact, occupied the Russian embassy for a couple of days. And it's possible the Russians might have reacted to that. Fortunately they didn't.

How do you interpret, in this light, the recent confrontation between Syria and Arafat-led PLO?

In Accord about a PLO of the Arafat-Type

This is very reminiscent of 1976 when Syria entered Lebanon with the support of the United States and in fact at least tacit support of Israel in order to attack the PLO and the Lebanese National Movement, which is complicated but it's basically a movement of the Lebanese poor (that's what it comes down to) and the United States supported that, and I'm sure the United States is at least tacitly supporting the Syrian attack on the PLO today.

Syria has never wanted (in fact, no country in the Arab world has ever wanted, certainly not Syria) to see an independent PLO. In no country of the Arab world do they want to see a popular, nationalist movement, which draws on popular support: that's a threat to the ruling groups in any country in the Arab world. In order to respond to the pressures from their own populations there has been at least some need to give rhetorical support to Palestinian nationalism. But there has never been actual support.

Another case is 1948, when King Abdullah of Transjordan (later Jordan) and Ben-Gurion secretly agreed to partition the Palestinian state, as scheduled for existence in the UN agreements, a partition between Transjordan and Israel. In fact, since that time Palestinian nationalism has certainly never been supported by the Arab states in other than the rhetorical level or in order to further their short-term interests.

So, it's perfectly understandable that Syria (which, in fact, is internally a terrorist regime run by a clique of gangsters and thugs—there's no question about that) wants to be a dominant force in the Arab world, and that means they don't want independent nationalist movements to exist. To the extent that a Palestinian movement exists at all, they want it to be under their control. Israel agrees. I mean Israel would much prefer to see a "radical," terrorist PLO than to see a PLO of the Arafat-type, which was pressing for negotiations and political settlement, since Israel does not want any political settlement and refuses one. It is a threat to them if PLO is pushing towards a political settlement. The United States does the same, since the United States is supporting an expansionist Israel and is opposed to a political settlement along the lines of the international consensus that has been in existence for many years over a two-state settlement.

The United States has opposed that in every way. It vetoed such a proposal at the United Nations. It blocked any initiative in that direction. Therefore it must ensure that there is no moderate PLO, that there is no PLO which is calling for a political settlement, and supports Syria's efforts to destroy the more conciliatory and more diplomatic elements, which, in fact, have dominated the PLO in recent years. So, although they are not necessarily communicating about it, I'm sure that Syria, Israel, and the United States are in accord with regard to Syria's effort to destroy an independent PLO, and in fact, a PLO which will continue to make moves towards a negotiated political settlement.

Do you think that was also one of the reasons for the Israeli invasion of Lebanon last year?

A major reason. In fact, it was widely discussed inside Israel. The main threat to Israel posed by the PLO was the fact that the PLO scrupulously observed the cease-fire for one year. They had completely observed it. In fact, they had not even reacted to Israeli provocations. That's a real threat.

It is crucial for Israel to portray the PLO as a gang of terrorist murderers, and that was becoming very difficult. In Europe that battle had already basically been lost, but Europe doesn't matter, because they've been excluded from the Middle East anyway. The only place that matters is the United States. I mean in the United States, given the control of the information system, people didn't know. In fact, here the PLO still was represented as a simple collection of terrorists who want nothing but to kill all the Jews. However, sooner or later that was going to erode, too. There's a degree to which you can maintain ideological control over the population in a country that isn't totalitarian. After all, the United States is not a totalitarian state. The control here is due basically to the

subservience of the intelligentsia and not to state violence, and that would sooner or later disappear. If the PLO would be understood as it was, as a group that
increasingly had come towards the international consensus, sometimes even joining it, and had been expressing a rather clear willingness to accept the political
two-state settlement, that would have been a great danger for Israel. So that had
to be destroyed, and in fact that was a major motivation for the invasion. And it
succeeded. It did succeed through the intervention of Syria, as well in destroying
the dominant part of the PLO, which had been in favor of a political settlement.

*Turning from the Middle East to Asia, what do you think is now the Reagan admin-
istration's main strategy in Asia?*

Well, like everywhere else, the main strategy is the one that any American
administration would follow, and that is to make sure that East Asia, which is
now a significant industrial center (not just Japan but the peripheral countries,
too, South Korea, Taiwan, Singapore and so on), that they would remain essentially in the American orbit. So any American administration is, of course, going
to do that. The Reagan administration does want to see a re-armament of Japan.
I think every American administration would want that, and I think the major
reason is to try to reduce the competitiveness of the Japanese economy. This
could backfire. The Japanese have in mind another idea. They feel that they have
essentially saturated most of the American markets with the exception of the
arms market, they think that if they develop high-technology military production, they may get another American market that they can enter. And that'll be
a really complicated conflict if it takes place because that's the last area where the
American industry has a real monopoly. That's a huge market. But anyway, the
United States has pressed for years for Japanese militarization and, I suppose, just
to increase the inefficiency of their own economic system.

Other than that the differences between Reagan and other administrations
are, as everywhere, that they are much more eager to seek confrontation. So, for
example, the Korean plane atrocity (and undoubtedly it was an atrocity) was
built up with complete hypocrisy. It was exploited to try to show that the
Russians are simply barbarians and therefore we have to put the missiles in
Europe. There's no doubt that that was totally hypocritical. For example, just last
week UNITA in Angola took credit for shooting down an Angolan civilian air-
line with over a hundred people killed. That was barely reported in the United
States (I saw it in the British press). The reason is, of course, that South Africa
and the United States support them. They support them so that whenever they
shoot down a civilian airliner, that's fine. In 1973 Israel shot down a Libyan airliner. There was no American protest. A few days later Golda Meir came to the
United States, and she left with more arms.

The reaction to the shooting down of the Korean plane was complete
hypocrisy. This is even putting on the side all sorts of questions about what it was
doing and so on. Let's say that the American story is completely correct, 100 percent correct, which is dubious, but let's assume that. Nevertheless, the reaction

was one of total hypocrisy but very successful. Immediately after the shooting down and the big uproar, military stocks shot up on the stock market; Congress voted in favor of the nerve gas; they voted in favor of the MX-missile; the congressmen who had been trying to put some barriers on the way of the war against Nicaragua backed off. And in fact the whole militaristic program, both domestically and internationally, took a great leap forward. So that was very successful. During Reagan's trip to South Koréa it was very natural to talk about the Russian barbarians. Those are the games of the Cold War. What you do is exploit the atrocities carried out by the official enemy in order to justify programs you should carry out anyway. The Korean plane incident worked out like that exactly. Again, any American administration would have done it, but the Reagan administration did it to a greater extent because of its greater need for an international confrontation.

And it was interesting to see how the American press reacted to that. For example the *Boston Globe*, which is a liberal newspaper, maybe the most liberal newspaper in the United States, the day after the Korean plane was shot down its first pages had no other news, and that gradually reduced to five pages or four pages. I don't think that's ever happened before—probably when the Second World War broke out they did do that. But there was an occasion to show your patriotism, to march in a parade, to scream about the great enemy and what barbarians they are and how marvelous we are. The *New York Times* did more or less the same. It's a marvelous example of the kind of subordination to state power that is so characteristic of the American ideological system. And that was very effective. I think Reagan will opt for other similar options. When you are dealing with international affairs and states that are committed to violence there will be atrocities, and they will be exploited for purposes of confrontation.

What do you think about the future of American-Chinese relations?

Incorporation of China in the U.S.-Dominated System

In the 1950s there was a substantial split among the American business and political elite as to how to deal with China. There was one group that felt that we should try to accommodate China inside the Western system and gradually turn it into an American market, just bring it into the system. There was another group that favored confrontation and said: No, we've got to drive them into the arms of the Russians and use it for the purposes of confrontation. Incidentally, that's the reaction to every revolutionary movement. There is always such a split. That was true in connection with Nicaragua, and before in the case of Cuba; in fact, with regard to the Bolshevik revolution there was a split like that.

Well, the confrontationist group won, and China was the official enemy. The ideologues like Kissinger as late as 1969 said (he says this in his memoirs) that he regarded China as the more aggressive of the two Communist powers. Now, you have to be an ignoramus or an imbecile to say that. Whatever you think about China, to regard it as the more aggressive of the two Communist powers reflects again the extent to which ideological passion can overcome even elementary common sense and historical knowledge.

But Nixon did shift. His position was to drop the confrontation with China and to try to move towards incorporating it into the American-dominated system, which the Chinese were quite willing to do; in fact, they had been making overtures in that direction. And they'll work. I think China will gradually become absorbed in some fashion into the U.S.-dominated system. There are problems. There are problems in connection with, say, Taiwan. Reagan's right-wing constituency wants him to support Taiwan against China, and, of course, he can't do that. So other means will have to be found. Incidentally, that brings us back to the Middle East: one of the means is to set up a Taiwan-Israel connection, which can be used to undercut the fact that the United States will not give Taiwan direct military aid.

Israel will act as a substitute for the United States?

Yes, that's already happening.

Finally, a more general question: What is your view on the foreign policy planning in Washington? How much rationality can one ascribe to it, apart from all moral considerations?

People talk about it as a great problem, but it's elementary. I mean virtually every major planner in Washington, they all come from the same social and economic circles. Essentially they come either from business directly or from the half a dozen law firms that take care of the corporate interests or from investment banks—or else they are ideologues of the Kissinger type, who come in just to express the feelings of their masters, basically. That's the group of people who in our system obviously are going to be in the positions of power. Who else would get in a position of power in a country like the United States? All of this is second nature to them.

It is obvious that if you come from these circles, the major goal of American foreign policy is to ensure that there is a favorable climate for business operations in as much of the world as is possible, including the opportunity to exploit, to gain resources so that your allies don't get privileged access to them. That's just like saying: How much planning does there have to be in the board of directors of General Motors to try to increase profits? It's simple. A child can do that.

Then differences come up as to exactly how to do it, for example the differences between what Mike Klare has called the Prussians and the Traders, as to whether you gain your goals by economic power or by violence. That's a tactical decision, and in fact people will shift from one side to the other. So some like, say, Kissinger are primarily Prussians (they do it by violence) but on the other hand in the case of China Kissinger shifted to the Traders' side. These are matters of tactical judgment on particular issues, and there, maybe, personalities come in and minor factors will go into it. But the major planning is perfectly straightforward, and in fact we have a lot of documentary evidence about it. Extensive studies were done during the Second World War, planning the postwar economy. National Security Council memoranda and other documents also reveal the kind of global planning that you'd expect from any leadership group in the world's dominant power.

The only reason that it seems surprising is that it is wiped out of our scholarship. One of the sort of principles of etiquette almost in what's called responsible scholarship is that you don't mention any of this stuff. You suppress this documentary record and you make it appear as if policies are designed on the basis of personality or ideology or something of that sort. But that's just part of the system of thought control. It only takes a minimal exposure to the facts and ordinary common sense to see that it's complete nonsense. It couldn't be true, and it isn't true.

Editor's Notes to Interview 30

"Interview with Noam Chomsky," *American-Arab Affairs* 10 (Fall 1984), pp. 15–27. It was conducted on Oct. 18, 1984, by Anne Joyce, editor of the journal. "American Middle East Policy" is the title of a section in that issue which included one more interview and one article. Compare I10.

George Ball's quote is from "What is an Ally?," *American-Arab Affairs*, Fall 1983, p. 13. As undersecretary of state under Lyndon B. Johnson, he distinguished himself by expressing serious reservations about the Vietnam policies of his administration. See the comment on his book, then recently published, in I36.

On the way terrorism is treated, see **CT**. See also, the Editor's Notes to I20.

The article of Norman Finkelstein referred to is "A Spectacular Fraud," *In These Times*, pp. 5–11 September 1984, a "condensed version" of his exposé of the Joan Peters' *From Time Immemorial* hoax (his essay was "completed and widely circulated in December 1984"), which appears in full, with a December 1986 postscript, in Part 1 ("The Peters affair") of *Blaming the Victims: Spurious Scholarship and the Palestinian Question*, edited by Edward W. Said & Christopher Hitchens (London: Verso, 1987), pp. 33–69. (In note 1 he writes: "My special thanks to Noam Chomsky, who has assisted me in ways too numerous to enumerate.") Finkelstein has since completed his PhD at Princeton with a thesis on the theory of Zionism. A review by him of Simha Flapan's *The Birth of Israel: Myths and Realities* (Pantheon, 1987) has recently been published (Norman G. Finkelstein, "Palestine: The Truth about 1948," *Against the Current* 15, July–August 1988, pp. 47–51). One of its paragraphs is particularly relevant here (see the quote from the letter by Chomsky in the *Guardian* in introduction to **RP** (1981/1984/2003), p. 16 of the first two editions):

> Noam Chomsky has written of the self-described 'supporters of Israel' in the United States that they should more properly be called 'supporters of the moral degeneration and ultimate destruction of Israel.' For these, mostly Jewish, intellectuals, Israel's degeneration and eventual destruction is apparently a tolerable price to pay (assuming, of course, it doesn't culminate in a terminal nuclear war), given the interim rewards of power, prestige and privilege.

See I36; also, I41, including the Editor's Notes.

Orwell's work and its "fortune" comes up again in I35. See also interviews 18, 35, 36, 39,41 and especially 44. See also Editor's Notes to I5.

30. American Middle East Policy (18 October 1984)

It is a widely held view in the United States that it is the fault of the PLO that peace hasn't been achieved between Israel and its neighbors and that talks could begin immediately upon the PLO's recognition of Israel's right to exist. Is this view based on fact?

No, the view is not based on fact. The position of the government of Israel has always been that the Palestinians (not simply the PLO) are not a party to the dispute and that no organization of Palestinians can have any part in political negotiations. The narrow reason is the commitment on the part of both major political groupings to maintain effective control of the occupied territories. A deeper reason is a concern, often expressed, over the legitimacy of the Zionist enterprise if the indigenous population have a claim to national self-determination in the Land of Israel. This position has been stated very explicitly by the Labor Party. Abba Eban back in 1969 stated that the Palestinians "have no role to play" in any peace settlement. Israel's high court, in fact, maintained that they "are not a party" to the dispute. Yitzhak Rabin in a later Labor government in 1975 issued what the Israeli press referred to as his "three no's," one of the no's was no negotiations with any Palestinians on any political issue. That remains essentially unchanged within the Labor Party—and obviously within the Likud. The latest platform of the Labor Party in the recent elections included four no's; in particular, no negotiations with the PLO. Another one was no withdrawal of settlements from the West Bank. In other words, "no" on everything substantive.

When Arafat made his offer last May, which was barely reported in the United States, with respect to negotiations leading to mutual recognition, Israel immediately responded negatively. I was able to find no official statement by the Labor Party, and only a few Israeli commentators who gave some tentative indication this would be worth following up. The government rejected it outright. As far as I know there has been no deviation from this position.

Exclusion of the Palestinians

Regarding negotiations and peace talks, the two sides are simply talking past each other. The Arab states and the PLO for several years now have been willing to enter negotiations if they include the Palestinians as participants. And everyone knows that the Palestinians means the PLO. The PLO has the same kind of legitimacy that the Zionist organization had in 1940s; it's essentially no different. In the 1940s to talk of negotiations with Jews with the thought of excluding the Zionists would have been absurd. The same is true today for the PLO. The framework for negotiations which has been offered by a very broad range of Arab opinion (including, for example, King Hussein just a couple of weeks ago, the Palestinians themselves, Egypt for a long time and most of the other Arab states) has been a framework, probably under UN auspices, which would include all participants: Israel, the regional states and the Palestinians.

Israel, on the other hand, has offered negotiations on totally different grounds. It wants to negotiate with the Arab states, specifically excluding the Palestinians. If you check through every interchange on this issue over the years, that's exactly where it has foundered. This just happened within the last few weeks. In the American press there were big headlines in the newspapers stating that Israel offers peace and the Jordanians reject it. Actually what happened was rather different. The Jordanian statement which was interpreted as a rejection of the peace offer in fact offered peace negotiations on the basis of an arrangement which would include the Palestinians as a participant.

The United States has blocked a peace settlement throughout by supporting the Israeli position that the Palestinians have no role to play. So, for example, again in January of 1984, the secretary-general of the United Nations, at the request of the General Assembly, attempted to organize peace negotiations which would include the members of the Security Council, the regional states, including Israel, Jordan, Syria and the Palestinians. Jeane Kirkpatrick announced at once that the United States would have nothing to do with it, that the United States regarded this and any such proposal as intolerable. What blocked this initiative was the participation of the Palestinians. Secretary-General Pérez de Cuéllar continued his efforts; he went to the Middle East and apparently got a reasonably positive response from most participants. Israel and, of course, the United States refused totally, and as long as the United States refuses, nothing can happen in the Middle East.

There have been quite explicit proposals from the Arab states and the PLO, in particular one very important proposal which was actually vetoed by the United States at the United Nations. There was a proposal in January 1976 for a two-state settlement along the internationally recognized pre-June 1967 borders, using the wording of UN 242 concerning its territorial guarantees and so on. That meeting was initiated by Syria, Jordan and Egypt (the "confrontation states") and the proposal was backed by the PLO. According to Chaim Herzog, who was then Israel's UN ambassador and is now president, it was not only backed by the PLO but was in fact prepared by the PLO. It was backed by just about everyone, including the Soviet Union and the Palestinians. It was vetoed by the United States. That was the occasion on which Yitzhak Rabin announced that there would be no negotiations or dealings with the Palestinians on any political issue.

A few weeks before that, when the UN session was called in late November (it met the following January), Israel's response was to carry out unprovoked bombing in Lebanon killing about 50 people. They didn't even call it retaliation, but rather a preemptive strike. It was plainly a response to the calling of the UN Security Council session. There was great outrage in Israel at the idea that the Palestinians should be a participant in any form of negotiations. It should be recalled that this was the dovish Rabin Cabinet. To my knowledge there has been no change in position, and I think what happened this May with the Arafat proposal is a striking example. It is hard to imagine that the PLO could go further than what he proposed: negotiations which would ultimately lead to mutual recognition.

Why is the United States reluctant to encourage peace talks and to put pressure on Israel to negotiate?

I think the reasons are complex. Since about 1970, the United States has blocked any meaningful peace settlement. It has been committed to a sort of Greater Israel. Although at the rhetorical level the United States is in favor of UN 242, at the policy level at every point the United States has supported a position which grants Israel effective control over substantial parts of the territories occupied in 1967. U.S. policy, although it hasn't been formulated into words, operates almost in parallel with Labor Party policy, which since about 1968 or 1969 has been that Israel should maintain control of the Golan Heights, the Gaza Strip and, under the Allon Plan, something like 40 percent of the West Bank. Labor originally wanted to keep the Eastern Sinai, but that was settled over considerable Labor opposition at Camp David. The current version of the Labor Party policy is essentially the old Allon Plan. The United States has backed it, as shown in two ways. One is by diplomatic measures which bar any attempt to resolve the conflict in a way which would require Israeli withdrawal or recognize Palestinian national rights—for example, blocking Sadat's 1971 peace offer (which ignored the Palestinians), vetoing the 1976 UN resolution, blocking the 1984 UN meeting and totally ignoring Arafat's offer last May.

U.S. (Unconditional) Aid to Israel

The other mode of support for this policy has been economic. American aid to Israel, which everyone knows is phenomenal, also has another property which people don't know much about: it is given unconditionally. U.S. aid to other countries is project-oriented and supervised. For example, U.S. aid to Egypt, which is the next highest recipient of aid, is very closely monitored and controlled. Israel has different and, to my knowledge, unique arrangements. The money is just given, which is a way of saying: Do anything you like with it. Since we know exactly what they like, what we are telling them is, use it for settlements in the West Bank, for invading Lebanon and so on. There couldn't be a more clear way of telling Israel that we want them to go on doing exactly what they are doing. In fact, that is how the Reagan plan collapsed. The Reagan plan was announced on Sept. 1, 1982, and was immediately rejected by Israel. It received varying reactions from the Arab states and the PLO (some interest but not outright rejection or acceptance). Israel flatly rejected it, as did the United States.

The way we did it was this: a few weeks after the Reagan plan was announced, the administration proposed a substantial increase in aid to Israel and Congress raised that increase still further. There couldn't have been a clearer way of telling them, "You did the right thing. We are now praising and rewarding you for invading Lebanon, for bombing Beirut, for the Sabra-Shatila massacre, for rejecting the Reagan plan. This is your reward: We will now increase the payments." As George Ball puts it rather nicely, "I know of no nation in history that ever launched a serious diplomatic initiative to bring about peace among quarreling nations and then paid one of the parties to sabotage it."

The Nixon Doctrine

In effect, the Reagan plan was killed by the United States almost immediately after it was proposed. This is typical; it has been going on since about 1970, when a split among American planners became very clear. Secretary of State William Rogers and the State Department at that time were in favor of a settlement on approximately the pre-June 1967 borders (the kind of settlement that the international consensus supports). Kissinger, on the other hand, was opposed. There was a struggle between Kissinger and the State Department and Kissinger won. It is rather clear from his memoirs that his greatest enemy was not the Soviet Union, but the State Department, and his major battles were against the adversary, although he was playing games with the Russians and others on the side. He did succeed in winning that fundamental battle of his career. He says in his memoirs that he was able to achieve "stalemate," and he was very proud of it—to achieve a stalemate to block the efforts of the State Department to move toward a political settlement on essentially the 1967 borders of Israel.

It is interesting how he explains why he wanted to achieve a stalemate. He says until the Soviet Union was willing to dissociate itself from the maximal Arab program and until some Arab state recognized that the path to peace was through Washington and was willing to separate itself from the Soviets, he felt we must pursue our policy of stalemate. In their geopolitical fantasies and unspeakable ignorance, these statements have almost no parallel that I can think of. First of all, Sadat had made it plain by 1971, which is the period he is talking about, that the path to peace was through Washington. In fact he offered a peace proposal in February 1971 which was rejected by Israel and the United States. How could Kissinger not have seen that Sadat was asking (virtually begging) to turn Egypt into an American client-state?

As far as the Soviet Union is concerned, what it was supporting was what it has always been supporting—a settlement in accordance with the international consensus, which recognized the rights and security of Israel. As far as no Arab state separating itself from the Soviets, technically he's right, but the reason he is right is that it would have been a logical impossibility. Most of the Arab states didn't even have diplomatic relations with the Soviet Union. Saudi Arabia, which is the most important, not only didn't have diplomatic relations, it never had had diplomatic relations with the Soviet Union. Here is a man who is controlling the foreign policy of the most powerful country in the world saying that we have to have a stalemate because Saudi Arabia won't separate itself from the Soviets.

That was the thinking that led to the insistence on the policy of stalemate and to the rejection of Sadat's very important February 1971 offer. This led directly to the 1973 war, which ought be called "Kissinger war." Kissinger was being informed from every source—American ambassadors, oil companies, and Egypt, constantly—that if the United States continued to block every path to a diplomatic settlement, Egypt would have no choice but to go to war. Kissinger couldn't hear it; it just never got through.

After the war American policy shifted, because then Kissinger finally understood (there was a war, and in fact Egypt and Syria did surprisingly well in the initial stages, so then Kissinger shifted to shuttle diplomacy, which was mostly razzle-dazzle, covering up the policy). The policy was to separate Egypt from the conflict. Once Egypt was separated from the conflict, then Israel would be free to continue its integration of the occupied territories and, of course, to attack its northern neighbor without hindrance, since Egypt would be neutralized. That was the obvious significance of Kissinger's interim agreements and, in fact, of the Camp David accords, which removed Egypt from the conflict. There was no longer any deterrent to the policies that Israel was conducting. They were doing it always with our support, whatever the rhetoric may have been; we were paying them to conduct it and that's all that counts.

Even before the Camp David agreements were signed, Israel increased its integration of the occupied territories and attacked Lebanon. The first attack was in 1978; in 1979–80 there was heavy bombing. Another cease-fire was broken by Israeli bombing in the summer of 1981, leading to about 451 Arab casualties, mostly Lebanese civilians, along with six Israelis. The subsequent July 1981 cease-fire in southern Lebanon was scrupulously observed by the PLO, which was one of the reasons why Israel felt it had to attack (the PLO was gaining too much respectability), so Israel attacked again in June 1982, always with American support, despite occasional rhetorical slaps in the face. It was obvious at the time that this was the content of Kissinger's interim agreement and of Camp David and it's an astonishing fact that this could not be perceived by American commentators. Even in retrospect people don't appear to have perceived it, though by now it's transparent. There could have been no other meaning to these negotiations. Throughout, the Palestinians were excluded; they were never a party to the negotiations, in accordance with the long-standing policies of Israel.

This is what has been going on; the question is, why? It seems to me that there has really been a split among American policy-makers as to the role that Israel should play in the Middle East. The fundamental American interest in the Middle East, everyone agrees, is oil. The question is, how do we best guarantee that these resources will remain effectively under our control. There are two paths that could be taken toward that goal: one path is negotiations, diplomacy and trade; the other path is force. From a purely tactical point of view, putting aside all moral considerations, it is not obvious what the right path is. Rational people could disagree. A very substantial group among American planners and corporations and so on has felt that the United States should pursue diplomacy, trade, negotiations and political settlements. Such people are in favor of a diplomatic settlement of the Arab-Israeli dispute along the lines of the international consensus, which has been possible for many years.

On the other hand, there is the view represented by Kissinger, which won out and which we continue to maintain, that we have to control the region by the threat of force. That was the Nixon doctrine, which said that we must have regional surrogate powers which will be guardians of our interests. Now, the rhetorical enemy is the Soviet Union; the actual enemy is the indigenous population. There has never been any reasonable likelihood that the Soviet Union would make any move toward this region because they know that if they did the world would blow up in a matter of minutes. They have never given any indication of being that crazy. Europe is also something of an enemy; one of the major elements in Kissinger's post-1973 diplomacy was, as he stated, to keep Europe and Japan excluded. That's another reason why we always refused UN negotiations and tried to block the Euro-Arab dialogue. The Europeans are very serious competitors for the control of the region. But the main worry is the indigenous population, what is called "radical Arab nationalism." The Kissinger-Nixon doctrine held that since the United States couldn't enforce its military will everywhere at one time, we require surrogate military forces to serve as a base for the projection of American power as needed and as a threat to indigenous radical movements, where "radical" means not obeying U.S. orders. The early plan was for Iran under the Shah and Israel to be the guardians of the Gulf, the policemen on the beat. American aid to Israel increased rapidly during that period. Once the Shah collapsed, Israel became the last guardian of the Gulf.

If you look at the whole relationship between Israel and the United States over the years, it's very closely keyed to the perception of Israel as a military force that can guard American interests. In the 1950s, relations between Israel and the United States were often rather strained; Eisenhower pushed them out of Sinai in 1956. But by 1958 the National Security Council had stated that a logical corollary to opposition to so-called radical Arab nationalism would be support for Israel as the one reliable pro-Western force in the region. In the early 1960s this became a very serious issue, because Nasser and radical Arab nationalism threatened American domination of the oil-producing regions. There were problems in the Gulf and in Saudi Arabia. Nasserite pressures on the American clients there were quite significant, and that mounted through the 60s. Israel's victory in 1967, which the United States supported and may have participated in, was a smashing blow to Arab nationalist forces and hence a great contribution to the concept of Israel as a guardian of American interests. American aid shot up at that point. In 1970, when Israel threatened to intervene to block possible Syrian moves to support the Palestinians during Black September [the Palestinian uprising against King Hussein in Jordan], that was again recognized as a major contribution to American interests, since the United States was really not capable of intervening at that point (it was right after the Cambodian invasion and the country probably would have blown up). There was concern that the Syrian move might threaten the oil-producing monarchies. Israel was capable of blocking any such possibility, and American aid to Israel quadrupled right after that period. Then through the 1970s, under the Nixon doctrine and its successors, this became established as the core of American policy.

Crucial Parallel Developments

Meanwhile, there were several crucial parallel developments. One was the development of a very close relationship between Israel and the American military system. For example, Israel tests American weapons under live battlefield conditions. Israel is a very effective military force. U.S. policy is turning Israel into a kind of Sparta—a highly militarized and technically advanced state. Just today it was announced that high-technology aid will be given to Israel for the production of the Lavi fighter. According to this morning's *New York Times*, the United States is going to give more aid to Israel to develop the fighter than it is to the Northrop company, which is building the American variant. This is one piece of a long, developing story in military relations, where Israel does the fighting with American weapons, tests them out, capturing Soviet weapons and providing valuable intelligence. It's been a very close, evolving relationship.

Another factor that has become increasingly important over the years is that Israel provides subsidiary services to American power elsewhere in the world. For example, in the 1960s Israel was intervening under a very substantial CIA subsidy in black Africa to support American clients—Mobutu in Zaire is the most successful case; there were others that didn't turn out so well, such as Idi Amin and Bokassa. Israel supported Ethiopia under various of its rulers (both Haile Selassie and Mengistu). With regard to white Africa, there was a UN blockade against Ian Smith's Rhodesia. Israel assisted the United States in evading the blockade by serving as a conduit for oil to Rhodesia in violation of the agreement.

Israeli relations with South Africa are more complex. Probably to some extent the United States approves of the military and commercial relations that have developed between Israel and South Africa, both of which serve as local gendarmes. South Africa plays the same kind of role in disrupting black Africa that Israel is supposed to play in the Middle East in American policy planning. The nuclear relations between Israel and South Africa may not be to the taste of the American government (we don't know, there hasn't been anything made public on this) but it has been a relationship under the aegis of American power. The main countries that the United States supports, like South Africa and Israel, cooperate to insure that no nationalist threat to American domination develops in those regions.

Increasingly in the 1970s, the main focus has shifted over to Latin America. Israel was supporting the dictatorships in the Southern Cone at a time when

Congress was invoking certain constraints on the administration with regard to its support for General Pinochet of Chile and the Argentine generals. And in Central America recently, where the U.S. administration has been blocked by Congress and public opinion from intervening too directly, Israel has been able to move in. It provided most of the support for Somoza at the very end, it supported the Guatemalan massacres of 1982 and has supported the government of El Salvador. It has also happened elsewhere in the world; for example, when the Carter administration was trying to figure out a way to help Indonesia complete its brutal subjugation of Timor but couldn't do this directly, they turned to Israel at one point and asked them to send jet planes to Indonesia. There have been other arrangements of this kind. For a world power which is trying to dominate and organize much of the world and to repress nationalist tendencies it doesn't like, it is useful to have a Sparta to turn to for military force that is efficient and versatile.

In my opinion, the United States is happy with Israel's dependence. I looked at a set of international credit ratings recently, ratings established by the international banks, and they were ranking Israel below Mozambique and Bangladesh. Without the American subsidy the nation couldn't exist. Israel has perhaps the highest per capita debt in the world. It is losing an independently functioning economy. I think that is much to the taste of the American planners, because they want it to be a country that is dependent and dependable, highly efficient and technologically advanced, capable of carrying out tasks that not many people would be willing to undertake, such as supporting the near-genocide in Guatemala. They are the guardian of the Middle East region, a base for the projection of American power. I haven't seen the secret agreements but I'm sure the plans of the Central Command (the U.S. Rapid Deployment Force for the Middle East) include basing facilities in Israel and cooperation with the Israeli military.

This is the conception that over the years has dominated American policy, although there has been conflict within elite circles. One of the major problems in the United States in my opinion is that public debate on this conflict has been almost totally stilled. The United States is the only country that I know of where you can't discuss these matters. In Israel there is much more open discussion of that than there is here. Here there has been a very successful campaign of intimidation. It is reminiscent of the situation with the Communist Party in the 1930s, except that the groups that are doing it now have much more effectiveness and power. The kinds of attempts that were made in the 1930s to stifle debate on the Soviet Union, we are seeing used now, but in a much more effective and widespread way, to intimidate critics of Israel into silence. Discussion of the kinds of things that we have been talking about is virtually unknown in the United States. Many essential facts have been eliminated from the record, including, crucially, the actual diplomatic history. The kind of lively, healthy discussion that goes on in Israel itself and in Western Europe, to some extent, doesn't exist here. While there has been a policy debate between those who are interested in pursuing a peaceful diplomatic settlement and those who want to maintain the military conflict and a powerful, militarized Israel as a center for American power, the public has not been able to take part in it. The public doesn't have command of or even access to the relevant facts to know how to participate. The issue has been removed from the arena of democratic politics. It is almost as if we were in a totalitarian state, with a debate going on internal to its own factions from which the public is excluded. That has in the past been a very dangerous thing in other countries, and it's very dangerous in this one, too.

What is the mechanism for keeping U.S. policy options toward Israel out of the public debate?

It's complicated. Sometimes it's simply intimidation: vilification, denunciation, screaming about anti-Semitism. There are groups that are devoted to this. To give you one example of my own, I recently got, by a leak which I don't want to describe, a copy of my file from the New England office of the Anti-Defamation League of B'nai B'rith. It's just like an FBI file—150 pages of material, clips from newspapers and inter-office memos saying I was going to show up at this or that place, surveillance of talks I have given, characterization of what was said in the talks (often falsified, as is the case with FBI files and others). All this material goes into a central source. Then when I give a talk somewhere, my file will be given to the appropriate local group, who will be able to dig through it, come up with statements that I allegedly made at some time during the last 15 years to be publicized in unsigned pamphlets. The file is also sent to people with whom I have public debates so that they can extract fabricated defamatory material from it. This is done, incidentally, under a tax-free grant to a religious and educational organization.

A Whole Barrage of Techniques to Silence Criticism

There is an amazing campaign also in those parts of the media that are controlled by so-called supporters of Israel, who act very much as in the heyday of the Communist Party. Everybody who has been involved has been exposed to this sort of thing, and a lot of people just don't want that kind of bother in their lives—to be subjected to lies and intimidation by accusations and so forth. I don't think the press wants it. The press is put under a lot of pressure. If they ever make a move towards presenting something which the local supporters of Israel don't like, they are subjected to harassment. They don't like it when it comes from their advertisers or the reading public. Politicians are also intimidated. They know that they can't open their mouths on this issue. If they do, they will be subjected to the same thing: accusations of anti-Semitism and forgetting of the Holocaust. A whole barrage of techniques are used which have been highly refined simply to silence criticism, and they are very effective.

Of course, substantial parts of the elite groups really agree with the current policy and automatically are going to go along with it. The media are, contrary to the public image, quite subservient to the state. They rarely expose or critically analyze state policies. This was demonstrated right through the Vietnam War and the Watergate period. The media are major corporations, they share interests and perceptions with other elite groups. They see things the way central power sees them. So, for example, it was an immediate reaction on the part of the national press to suppress Arafat's Spring 1984 offers, because to report them is to admit that the United States is once again blocking peace. Which newspaper in the United States is going to come out with a headline saying that the United States and Israel, for the hundredth time in the last 15 years, are again blocking a peaceful settlement? Not only can't they do it, they can't even perceive things that way. There is too much cognitive dissonance. They have to accept the picture of their own state as capable of making mistakes but fundamentally decent, not as one of the amoral agents that interact to realize national and private interests in world affairs. That is not the way we perceive the United States and if you start with familiar ideological preconceptions, you just can't see what's happening before your eyes.

There are all sorts of factors that lead to this, but the net effect is obvious. The non-reporting of Arafat's offer is a perfect example. It literally was not mentioned in the *Washington Post* or the *New York Times* when it occurred. Several months later the *Post* had a dismissive reference to it. They certainly knew of it. It was on the UPI wires. The *San Francisco Examiner*, which has the reputation of being one of the worst papers in the country, had a big front page headline that day saying, "Arafat to Israel: Let's Talk," followed by a UPI story which was reasonably accurate. Now that's the way the story should have been treated; it is important. What they should have said is that Arafat once again says, Let's talk. There were stories in the second-level press, the quality press that has a local audience, like the *Los Angeles Times* or the *Boston Globe* or the *Philadelphia Inquirer*, which didn't really get at the heart of the matter, but at least they had the facts.

To take one more case, when Sadat was assassinated, it was a big news story and there was a lot of talk about Sadat and what a great man he was. If you read through the commentary you will notice something quite interesting about it. the *New York Times* had a two-page obituary written by Eric Pace, one of their experts, giving the standard story—that Sadat tried to destroy all the Jews and Israel. He tried in 1973, but under the kind tutelage of Kissinger and later Jimmy Carter, he opted for peace, became a great hero and went to Jerusalem in 1977. That is the story that everybody believes. The fact that Sadat had offered peace in February 1971 and been turned down by the United States and Israel and had then for the next couple of years said he would like to make a peaceful settlement, but failing that, he would have to go to war, that was outside of history.

The Israeli equivalent of the *New York Times*, *Ha'aretz*, had an obituary about Sadat, too, except they referred to what they called his "famous" 1971 peace offer. In Israel it is his "famous" peace offer and in the United States it doesn't exist, because we cannot perceive that the United States has been blocking peace and was responsible for war. Just how that works in the editorial offices

I can't tell you, but this happens over and over again. It feeds into itself, creating an image which then provides the basis for interpreting the next thing that happens.

Are you saying that this takes place at the editorial level rather than at the corporate level?

Only the newspapers can really answer that question. But I think that there are many different factors that tend to press in the same direction: shared interest, the natural tendency to trust the state and think the best of it, pressures and intimidation that come from the outside. There is also a lot of admiration for the successful use of military force. When Israel showed in 1967 that it was capable of smashing up its enemies, that aroused a lot of admiration in the United States. It was particularly striking because at that time (1967), the United States was trying to crush the South Vietnamese resistance—what we called blocking North Vietnamese aggression, in fact continuing our aggression against South Vietnam—and we were incapable of doing it. Israel came along and showed us how to deal with Third World upstarts properly. That had a lot of resonance in the United States. At the psychological level that explains in part the support for Israeli power and successful use of violence. So there are many factors that have led to the current situation in which the simple perception of the basic facts is so distorted that the whole issue is removed from the political arena. This has resulted in total victory by those who want to turn Israel into a militarized society, dependent on the United States, having no independent viability and blocked from a political settlement.

Terrorism is treated in the same way. When there is an Arab terrorist act in Israel—say hijacking a bus—it's denounced by everyone as a terrorist act. When Israel captures a boat on the high seas, which is piracy, and kidnaps people, it may be reported, but no once cares. I remember during the last prisoner exchange there was a little note at the end of one of the articles in the *New York Times* that said that 30 or so of their prisoners were people who had been captured by Israel on the high seas. Like hijacking, that's piracy. Israel has been doing it for years, and we say it's their right. Last January when Israel bombed heavily around Balbek, locally reported casualties were about 400 or 500, including a couple hundred children. The school was completely demolished. That was reported but it was not regarded as an act of terrorism. If the Palestinians had carried out a bombing in Tel Aviv with 500 casualties including many children, we would be talking about a holocaust.

Israel's Terrorism and Violence

This is part of a pattern. The *Washington Post*, one of the more balanced papers in this respect (much more so than the *New York Times*) ran an editorial that I will never forget on April 22, 1982. The day before that, Israel had carried out a completely unprovoked bombing of Lebanon, killing many people. The alleged provocation was that an Israeli soldier in Lebanon had hit a mine and been killed. In response, Israel bombed Lebanon and killed several dozen people. The *Post* editorial said that this was not a time for sermons to Israel: this was a moment for respect for "Israel's anguish." We have to consider Israel's anguish when it kills still more Palestinians in Lebanon. When people in the government of Israel read that, they realize they can carry out as much terrorism and violence as they like and American liberal opinion, which is supposed to be that part of public opinion which is even moderately critical, will approve it. Israel went on from there to further bombing in May and the June invasion. It is that kind of public reaction that laid the groundwork for the invasion. Why shouldn't they go on? If they know that any act of violence and terrorism they are going to carry out will be either dismissed or regarded as somehow legitimate because the Arabs are so terrible, why shouldn't they go on? One can't conceive of a comparable reaction where the Arabs are concerned. Suppose Syria had bombed Israel, killing 25 people because a Syrian soldier had been killed by a land mine in northern Israel. Could the *Washington Post* have had an editorial saying that this is the time to respect Syria's anguish? It's unimaginable. But there is case after case of this, and by now it is self-reinforcing. A climate of opinion has been created in which things are perceived a certain way. To break out of it, even just to lay the simple facts on the table for discussion, is already a tremendous emotional as well as intellectual problem.

Moving to another medium, the new book From Time Immemorial *has attracted both praise and scathing criticism. Joan Peters, the author, claims to have found evidence that the Jews have a prior claim on Eretz Israel and that they didn't displace an indigenous population, but rather attracted Arab immigrants to Palestine during the 19th and early 20th-centuries with economic opportunities. What is your opinion of the book and of the reviews it has received in the press?*

This is **an old Zionist propaganda line**, despite the reviewers' claim that it's an amazing new idea. What's more interesting is that this kind of nonsense has been denounced by reputable Israeli scholars for years. Back in 1975 I read a statement in a Hebrew publication by Yehoshua Porath, Israel's leading scholar on the Palestinians and the author of the standard works in the field, in which he pleaded with people to stop creating fake census figures and other falsifications to try to prove what is patently false: that there were no Palestinians in Palestine. This has been picked up again as part of the attempt to resurrect Israel's somewhat battered image after the Lebanon war.

Peters' book contains page after page lifted almost verbatim out of old Zionist propaganda tracts without any reference. The egregious errors that appeared in the original are repeated. For example, Alexander Cockburn has pointed out in the *Nation* that she quotes a 14th-century Arab as an authority on something that happened in the 19th century. That is the amazing research that is supposed to be so impressive. The references to the documents reveal a level of falsification rarely seen anywhere since the Stalinists' rewriting of history. A graduate student at Princeton, Norman Finkelstein, has traced almost every quote back to its source. Virtually every major reference is a gross falsification, one that couldn't have been done by error.

The demographic figures can only be described as a hoax. In an effort to show that the refugees that fled were from the West Bank, she simply eliminated the ones from Western Galilee, where over 100,000 people were missing. She quotes figures from the Turkish census to try to show that the Jews were a majority in the area that became Israel. Her own figures in the footnotes show this to be false; the Palestinians were a big majority. The book is almost totally incoherent; if you go back to the footnotes you often find accurate quotes. But if you look at the thrust of the text there are gross distortions. She refers repeatedly to the Hope Simpson report of 1930, which she claims states that illegal Arab immigration was very unfair to the Jews, but it should be tolerated anyway. What the actual statement said was that illegal immigrants should be immediately expelled and that pseudo-travelers (visitors who had overstayed their time) in cases that weren't flagrant should be allowed to stay, even though this might do some injustice to the Jewish immigrants. And even in this small category, it turns out that these pseudo-travelers were Jews by a large margin! This gets transmuted in the Peters account into an admission by the British that hordes of illegal Arab immigrants were coming in unnoticed, to the detriment of the Jewish immigrants.

It would be interesting to see how people in Israel would react to the Peters book. Although it has been out for a long time now, I have only seen one review in the Hebrew press. That was in *Maariv*, a mass-audience, right-wing publication, and it was written by a government official (they didn't even give it to a serious reviewer). My guess is that it embarrassed them.

What I find interesting is that whoever wrote the book (Joan Peters herself or whoever is behind it) felt that the American intellectual community is so subservient that it would work; that no matter how extensive the lies or the distortions, it would still be successful. That is somebody's evaluation of the nature of American intellectual culture, and it is probably accurate. Finkelstein and Cockburn and others have published enough information about this book already to make anyone recognize that it's at least dubious, and probably sheer fraud. But this has no effect at all. That means that the assessment of American intellectual culture is correct. It says that any amount of lying, any amount of fraud, is going to be tolerated by the American intellectual community, as long as it conforms with established doctrine. Things like this happened in the 1930s, although not to this extent. For example, when George Orwell's *Homage to Catalonia* came out, it wasn't published in the United States because it was critical of the Communists, an unpopular position among the intelligentsia at the time. It was later published as a Cold War document when things had changed. This sort of thing is not unfamiliar, but now it's happening on a scale that really has no counterpart in the past. It's very dangerous, because by removing these issues from public debate and, in the case of the Peters book, by introducing absurd, fraudulent arguments which have nothing to do with the facts in an effort to try to justify Israel's expansionism and aggression, we risk disaster not only for the region but quite probably for the world.

Editor's Notes to Interview 31

"The media as a Mirror of Society" (editor's title) appeared in *Comity* (num. 6, February 1985, pp. 18–20)—"a magazine of international affairs and opinion" published by the Albany Student Press, State University of New York—as one of three interviews conducted by Brian Jacobs and published under the title "Cover Story—Network Television News: Perspectives on the Medium" followed by this note: "Network news is the primary source of information for most Americans. But the limits of the medium prevent viewers from being truly informed. CBS personnel, Edwin Diamond and Noam Chomsky lend their perspective." Chomsky was interviewed on Oct. 21, 1984. A caption under his photograph states that "the subject of the interview was the print media, which is what he felt most comfortable discussing, but as is apparent from what follows, his comments apply to all forms of the establishment media."

For more on Thomas Friedman (twice a Pulitzer Prize winner for balanced and informed coverage), particularly on his racism and megalomania, see I49. See also Chomsky's "Middle East Terrorism and the American Ideological System," in *Blaming the Victims*, 1988 (see notes to interview 27), p. 118.

On David MacMichael's testimony at the World Court Hearings, see **CT** (1988), p. 121.

31. The Media as a Mirror of Society—But Not Quite in the Usual Sense (21 October 1984)

What credence, if any, is there to the proponents of media's view that news is a mirror of society, that if we blame the news media, we are actually blaming the medium for the message?

Well there is a lot of truth, I think, to the idea that the media are a mirror of society, but not quite in that sense. It's not that they accurately portray social reality. Rather I think the truth in the contention lies in the fact that the media tend to present and interpret social reality within a framework that is very largely set by domestic power. That's true in any society, but in our society that means, ultimately, the corporate system and the closely related state executive, the very extensive and elaborate ideology system (which includes large parts of the mainstream intelligentsia, the schools, and so on). That forms a framework that we could properly call a system of indoctrination, which does reflect social power and the media operate very effectively within it, often unconsciously.

Do news organizations lend themselves to any sort of systematic analysis or do individual idiosyncrasies and judgments varying from operation to operation prevent any sort of general logic?

Oh, I think there is a very general logic. There is something that you might call a kind of party line. Well, first of all there are differences. For example, a local reporter, say working on police corruption, is certainly subjected to some kinds of influences, like maybe a city editor knows a local businessman or something, but, basically, he is pretty free to do what he wants, that is, the pressure of indoctrination is not very heavy. *the closer you get to the Core of Power, the more nebulous the "truth" becomes reported*

On the other hand, when you move to issues of more fundamental concern, to what is real power in the country—questions of foreign policy, questions of national military policy and so on, or general questions of national economic policy, policies that really affect people with real power—in that case one finds that the pressure of the system of indoctrination, of the party line, becomes very heavy, and there are very few people who deviate from it or who even perceive it. They think they're being quite objective, but you can easily demonstrate that they are operating within a framework of shared assumptions that is very far from obvious and often very far from true.

Let me give you an example of how subtle this can be. In the Oct. 7 Sunday *Times* magazine there was a rather interesting article by Thomas Friedman, who is a very good reporter, one of the best. It was extremely interesting to read for students of propaganda. This was an article about the danger of extremism in the Middle East. And he said there is this moderate center where the hope lies, but then there are extremist fringes which are slowly taking over. They believe in violence and so on and so forth.

Well, okay. Terms like moderate and extremist are not very well defined; it depends where you stand. Everybody regards themselves as a moderate and everyone else is an extremist. So it's interesting to see how the terms were used. That's what tells you what the implicit assumptions are. Well, the terms were used as you'd expect. The extremists are the Khomeinis, the Shiite terrorists who bombed the Marines, and in Israel, Kahane. The moderates are the Israeli Labor Party, the United States of course. The PLO, incidentally, are extremists. Arafat is an extremist but the moderates are the Israeli Labor Party and the Reagan administration.

Well, now that's interesting because that tells you what the implicit assumptions are. The implicit assumptions are that the people who reject the possibility of a political settlement based on the principle that the two peoples there have the right to national determination, both Israel and the Palestinians, the people who reject that are the moderates, the people who advance that position, like the PLO, are the extremists.

Now, all that makes sense if you accept the deeply **racist assumption** that the Palestinians don't have the human rights we accord the Jews. If you believe that Palestinians and Jews are human beings with the right to national self-determination, and that the indigenous population at least has that right, then it is the PLO position which is the moderate one and American and Labor Party which is the extremist. In fact, even groups in Israel like "Peace Now" don't go as far as the PLO does in advocating a two-state political settlement. So implicit in the discussion was a real racist assumption. Also implicit in the discussion was the even more crucial assumption that facts are totally irrelevant. For example, the fact that the PLO had come forth with a two-state settlement was considered irrelevant, the fact that the United States had rejected it and the Labor Party had rejected it was considered irrelevant.

Also interesting is the use of the term "terrorist" or "extremist" with regard to people carrying out violent acts in Lebanon. From their point of view it's not terrorism, it's resistance. It's very rare that attacks on an occupying army are called terrorism. It's called that only by occupying armies. So, for example, when we call the attack on the Marines in Lebanon "terrorism," that expresses assumptions that can certainly be questioned. I mean, for much of the population, the Marines were there just to consummate the Israeli invasion. The acts taken against them are resistance. But these are all questions that can't even be raised in the American press.

What is interesting about the Friedman article is that it is a very persuasive article and it gives the impression of moderation and it implicitly incorporates principles which are deeply racist, and which assume the crucial irrelevance of any historical fact. That's the way propaganda really works. That's much more effective than beating people over the head with a bludgeon.

Let me give you another example. Turn to Central America. The big news this week is that Duarte made this offer to have negotiations. So there is headline after headline in the paper about Duarte's dramatic offer and so on.

Well, the fact of the matter is slightly different. What actually happened is that Duarte accepted an offer. The offer for negotiations had been a long-standing guerrilla offer, and in fact it had been repeated insistently since last May, and Duarte finally, for whatever reasons, decided to go along with it. Well, that's a rather different picture. And in fact, if you really read carefully, you can sometimes see it—again, not in the *New York Times*, I haven't seen anything about it in the *New York Times*. But in the AP report on Duarte's offer, at least the one that was published in the *Boston Globe*, when you get down to the 23rd paragraph of the report (literally), you find a remark saying that radio Venceremos, the guerrilla radio, announced that Duarte had accepted the guerrillas' offer. Well, okay, if you're really a fanatic reader of the press, you can see that the whole story is being put on its head. But for most people, and for history, it's going to be Duarte's magnificent offer.

Actually that reminds me of another example. The alleged arms flow from Nicaragua to El Salvador was recently dealt a pretty severe blow by a former CIA officer.

Yes, David MacMichael. Even the ambassador said that he was convinced that by early 1981 the arms flow had reduced to a trickle.

But you see, there is even **something deeper** here. Notice the way the question is framed. This shows you something about the press. I mean, look, we have Argentine proxies, Israeli arms, German, we've got sanctuaries in Honduras. I mean all of this is going on openly. In fact, we're fighting a war against Nicaragua. But the only question you're allowed to ask is whether the Nicaraguans are in fact sending some arms to the guerrillas.

Now the fact of the matter is if the Nicaraguans aren't sending arms to the guerrillas it's because they've been intimidated. They should be sending arms to the guerrillas. Everybody should be sending them arms. Just as you should send arms to the Afghan guerrillas. Imagine we were in the Soviet Union and there was a big debate going on about whether there are actually CIA arms coming in through Pakistan to the Afghan guerrillas. Well, the answer is there ought to be. You ought to give people arms to defend themselves against a gang of thugs supported by a foreign power who are trying to massacre them. But you couldn't raise that question in the Soviet Union, and you can't raise this question here. So even the doves are caught in it. Even the doves are trapped into arguing about whether the Nicaraguans are or are not giving them arms. The fact of the matter is that it would be quite proper to give them arms.

There seems to be a pervasive philosophy of hedonism in this country, the desire to be entertained rather than informed. Do you think the media is responsible for creating this hedonism or is it something that developed naturally? /or homo oeconomicus

Well, my feeling is that there has been a major effort, a concentrated major effort, especially directed against the youth, since about 1970, to try to convince people that they're hedonists. And narcissists. There has been a huge effort to try to convince young people that they're narcissists. So there is all sorts of stuff of the cult of narcissism and everybody is "ME first," and so on and so forth.

Well, you know, such tendencies always exist, but opposing tendencies also exist—tendencies for sympathy, solidarity and care and so on. And it's been very important to drive that out of people's consciousness. In fact the net effect of this propaganda campaign has probably been to convince young people that if they are not narcissists, they're weird. So even if they have feelings of concern and sympathy, they had better suppress them because that's not what their generation is. And I think that's been effective.

Undoubtedly people are interested in their own welfare, but human beings are complicated creatures, they have a lot of drives and interests. And these are the ones that have been emphasized. It's interesting the way this campaign has been presented. It's been presented as if it's a descriptive fact. But really what it is is an **attempt at persuasion and inducement**. There were a lot of people who were really quite scared in the 60s when people did begin to show concern and political activism and so on. That's dangerous.

And the media has been effective?

Oh, I think they have been very effective. And I think much of the Left has contributed to this with all its talk of narcissism and so on. There is a story going on that the Left contributes to as well, saying that activism died in the 70s. That isn't true. There was probably more activism in the 70s than there was in the 60s: you have the feminist movement, the ecological movement, and all these things. These are creatures of the 70s, but they're dangerous, so therefore you want to pretend they don't exist.

And this is basically a concerted effort?

Well, I don't mean to suggest it's a conspiratorial effort. It's just that a lot of shared interests lie behind it.

Editor's Notes to Interview 32

This is the third of the Reime interviews (see the Editor's Notes to 13). It took place at MIT on Nov. 14, 1984.

For more on Shimon Ullman's "rigidity principle," see interview 34. The *Introduction to LSLT* (1955/56) is actually an expanded version of the introduction to the Spanish edition of SS (1957), which was written in August 1973, at the request of the Spanish translator, and was first published in Spanish in 1974 (and again in a collection of articles in 1979—Koerner & Tajima, p. 9), and in French in 1977 (in a collection edited by the late Mitsou Ronat that she refers to in I9). The expanded version was completed in September 1973 and it first appeared in English in 1975.

"It is only in the last few years that the terminology has been sort of cleared up" in that "language" in the sense of a set of expressions, i.e. language in extension, is now referred to as "E-language," while the mental language system, the internalized set of principles that generate the expressions, i.e. language in intension, the crucial notion, is referred to as "I-language" or simply "language." This is the gist of "the Chomskyan turn," in contrast with the earlier "Fregean turn." For a recent overview, see C.P. Otero, "Language, Meaning, and Interpretation: Chomsky Against the Philosophers," in *Semantics: Critical Concepts*, ed. by J. G. Rexach, London: Routledge, 2003.

32. Knowledge of Language, Human Nature, and the Role of Intellectuals (2 November 1984)

The study of generative grammar is now about 30 years old. How would you characterize this research program and its general intellectual and cultural interest?

This is a study which is concerned with certain classical questions. It is concerned with the basic concept "knowledge of language" and it asks a series of questions about this. It asks, first of all, what is knowledge of language, what constitutes it, and secondly, how is such knowledge acquired, and thirdly, how is this knowledge put to use in speaking or understanding what you are presented with.

Language as a Computational System: Mental Representations

The rough answers to the three questions that seem appropriate are that knowledge of language is basically a computational system, that is, a system of principles of one sort or another that determine a set of mental representations, principles which determine it in a very precise and explicit and highly articulated fashion and ultimately correlate them with representations of sound and with other conceptual systems that allow them to be part of their interaction with one another and human intercourse. That's what knowledge of language is. It is a kind of computational system.

How is it acquired? It appears to be the case that it is acquired on the basis of a very richly structured innate system that simply constitutes one component of the human mind, ultimately the human brain, and is probably on a par with the systems that determine the specific organization and structure of particular organs of the body. This system simply grows and matures and becomes a mature computational system. Its initial state is that of a partially specified computational system, and it becomes a specific computational system through the interaction with the external world.

As to how language is used, it appears to be a matter of, basically, rule following, that is, we apply the rules and principles of a computational system in speaking and hearing.

What is the general interest of this? The general interest, I think, apart from what it tells us about language—if it is correct—probably has to do with the theory of knowledge, with our conception of knowledge, how it arises, what is it constituted of and so on. It seems to me that this kind of work produces a very strong challenge to classical paradigms of epistemology.

The knowledge that is acquired includes, in fact, entails a paradigm example of knowing that so-and-so. People know that this sentence means such-and-such and they know that this word is pronounced in such-and-such a way and so on and so forth. Here is, in fact, an unbounded range of essentially paradigm cases of fact that we have knowledge of. And it appears overwhelmingly likely, I think the evidence is extremely strong, that this knowledge is not acquired by any reliable procedures, is not justified in any general terms, and is not grounded in any useful general sense of the term "grounded," in fact, violates virtually every condition that has been proposed as a necessary condition for existence or attainment of knowledge. Rather the knowledge grows, because we are so constituted that under the rather limited and defective experience a certain system takes shape in the mind, and that system is a system of knowledge.

I think that in every domain where we know anything and understand anything (I don't mean as humans but as scientists) the same appears to be the case: our systems of knowledge are highly specific and determined by rather precisely articulated properties of the initial structure of the mind. I think there are rather good reasons to believe that that is true across the board. But language is an interesting case, because the evidence is relatively accessible. You can construct theories of considerable sophistication and a fair degree of explanatory power to an extent that is quite unusual, maybe unique, outside the hard sciences. It does yield some very suggestive answers to quite classical questions about human nature, about the nature of the mind, about what knowledge is, about the basis for its acquisition and so on.

Recently you have drawn some parallels between what the theory of grammar seems to suggest of the human language faculty and some of the latest results of cognitive psychology, the results of the work of David Hubel and Torsten Wiesel and the late David Marr. Could you explain this?

Yes. The work you refer to by Hubel and Wiesel and the late David Marr and others roughly indicates that the peripheral aspects of the human visual system—that means the system from the retina to the peripheral parts of the brain, that part of the processing system that doesn't involve beliefs, expectations and plans, that is just a sort of reflex, just processing without any higher level involvement—that part of the visual system is very highly structured and yields a rather rich interpretation of the stimulus. Hubel and Wiesel's work shows that the peripheral aspects of the processing system already give an interpretation roughly speaking in terms of notions like "line" and "angle" and "depth" and so on. Marr's work tries to show—and gives good reasons to believe—that much of our knowledge of structure and form and nature of objects is really a kind of reflex, that is, it is just the result of a very richly structured peripheral processing system. So, for example, we perceive the external world as being constructed of rigid objects, because the visual system, the peripheral parts of it, is so designed that it imposes the requirements of rigidity on whatever stimuli are presented to it. So even if the stimuli that are presented to it are quite consistent with the conclusion that we are seeing a non-rigid object changing shape as it moves in space, what we will perceive is a rigid object.

Now, here we have to be a bit cautious in drawing analogies to the language system for the obvious reason that it is a different system and, for another thing, because vision is really an "input-output" system. It is an input system, which yields a certain internalized output, the output that is, of course, internal to the brain. But looking at it from the point of view of the next stage of processing, vision is an input-output system, which takes stimuli and yields representations of those stimuli. That's not what language is.

One of the many things that language does is that the language system is forced to represent external stimuli in terms of representations handed on by the processing system. But we do much more with language. Language is not a reflex. We don't speak by reflex, and there are a number of disanalogies to the visual system of this nature. Nevertheless, it is suggestive that this work also leads to the conclusion that this aspect of cognition is really of a nature of a computational system with rigidly determined rules yielding representations, all of this predetermined by human biological nature within pretty narrow bounds. Variation is possible, and experience can induce some changes in the system, but the fundamental ways in which it functions are predetermined. And this is very suggestive. Qualitatively speaking, with all the disanalogies put aside, this is similar to that we have discovered in the case of the language system. And as I said before, where anything is known about human cognition, this is what we discover.

When you speak about representations in the case of language and in the case of other cognitive systems, is it only an analogy?

No, it is not an analogy. In fact, most of this work was done before anything was known, relevantly, about the visual system, at least before the basic ideas were established.

A Surprising Finding about the Human Brain

The analogy is really from formal language theory, logic, computer and automata theory and so on. But the source of the analogy is not terribly important. The point is that it is a particular theoretical approach which makes certain assumptions that have empirical consequences that, I think, are pretty well supported. I mean a lot of things about language can be explained under the assumption that there are mental representations of a very specific kind.

When we speak about mental representations, we don't mean something out of the physical world. Talk about mental representations is simply talk about physical systems undertaken at a certain level of abstraction, rather similar to, say, if we talk about valence or properties of elements in the periodic table. We don't say that there is a domain outside of physics which involves things like valence and periodic tables. We say that whatever the more primitive and underlying elements of the particles of matter may be, at this level of abstraction from mechanisms, what we find is properties like valence and so on. Similarly, at this level of abstraction from mechanisms, whatever the mechanisms of the brain may be, what we find is systems that have all the properties of a computational system. That is rather surprising, because you wouldn't have expected a biological organ to work like a precisely constructed computational system with rigid, logical, deductive operations yielding very sharp interpretations going this way or that way depending on the nature of the rules and representations. But that is what we seem to find. It is a surprising finding, interesting in itself quite apart from details.

Recently you have said something that has been a kind of shock to many linguists, namely, that the object of inquiry of linguistics is not language but grammar. Could you explain this?

I have not put it that way myself. I mean, if I have put it that way, I think it has been misleading.

A Really Serious Misunderstanding

You have to remember that there is a terminological confusion here. What linguists and logicians call language has almost no relation to what is called language in normal usage. When a linguist or a logician uses the term "language," he uses a technical concept: "language" means an infinite set of objects, let's say, sentences or, maybe, sentences associated with meanings or something like that. But that has almost no connection with what we call language when we are just talking. When I say you know Finnish, I don't mean you know an infinite number of sentences, because, of course, you don't know an infinite number of sentences. Nor do I mean you know an infinite number of sentence-meaning pairs. What I mean, when I say you know Finnish and I don't know Finnish, is that you know what makes sound and meaning hang together in Finnish: that is Finnish. The language Finnish is whatever it is that makes sound and meaning hang together in a particular way. But that is a rule system. That means that when I say you know Finnish, I mean you know a rule system: Finnish is a rule system, it is not a set of sentences. Now, the technical term for a rule system is "grammar." So we have this odd and very misleading situation, where the technical term "grammar" is very close to the pre-theoretical intuitive term "language," whereas the technical term "language" has no relation at all to the pre-theoretical term "language."

Some people are surprised when you say that linguistics is about grammar and not language. But that just means that linguistics is not about what we mean by "language." The sense of paradox is due to a really serious misunderstanding on the part of many linguists and logicians and philosophers who, I think, have simply been confused by a terminological point. If you could start from the beginning and make up terminology in a non-misleading way, we were to use the term "language" to refer to what we are now calling grammar, namely some system of rules and principles, and what is now called language does not need any term at all, because it is a totally useless concept: the "infinite class of utterances" or "the infinite class of sound-meaning pairs" is a notion that has no status whatsoever. It does not fit into linguistic theory, it has no existence.

In fact, one of the major conceptual shifts of generative grammar about 30 years ago was to shift attention from this totally artificial and useless concept of "infinite set of sentences" or "infinite set of sound-meaning pairs," which, I think, does not exist in the world (there is no such thing in the world) and it has no utility, and it does not correlate with the ordinary notion of "language." Attention was shifted from that to something real. The rule system is something real, it is in your head, it is in my head, it is physically represented in some fashion. It is as real as the valence of oxygen, it is one of the real things in the world described at a certain level of abstraction, and, in fact, it is very close to what we call language. Unfortunately, this real object was called grammar, not language. It should have been called language. There were historical reasons for that, having to do with the philosophy of mathematics and history of formal systems and so on.

These historical reasons have misled people enormously, including professionals in the field. For example, there has been a big debate over the years by philosophers about the concept "knowledge of grammar." It has been argued that this is somehow mysterious and raises deep philosophical problems, whereas "knowledge of language" is more or less straightforward and not complicated. In fact, quite the opposite is true. "Knowledge of grammar" is the ordinary concept, it is the real system in the brain, that is, knowledge of grammar, the rule system. "Knowledge of language" in the technical sense of "language," meaning "knowing an infinite set of sentences," that is a very mysterious notion. I don't think it makes any sense at all, and we have certainly never tried to give an analysis of it. So most of the debate in the philosophical literature has been completely backwards in this issue. It has misplaced the problem, it has misunderstood the problem. To a very large extent, I think, it has been simply misled by a terminological confusion.

In the 1950s and early 1960s, you did some very important research on mathematical linguistics, namely on formal language and the theory of abstract automata, which form a branch of pure mathematics. Would you say that you were under the same terminological confusion, because as late as in the preface to the published version of The Logical Structure of Linguistic Theory *you speak of "language" and "structure" and "grammar" as the three fundamental notions of the theory of generative grammar.*

It is only in the last few years that the terminology has been sort of cleared up. In the preface you are referring to, which was written in 1975, and, in fact, in subsequent work, I continued to use the terms in the traditional way. The traditional way, as I said, is that "language" refers to some infinite set, not a thing in the world, "grammar" refers to the real object, namely the system that is represented in your brain and mine, and "structure" is the characterization of utterances given by the grammar, the real thing.

The Structure Determined by the Grammar

Of these three notions, the first one, "language," is irrelevant, has no reality, and plays no role in the study of language and in the study of mind. The second notion, "grammar," is the central one, and, as I said, is close to the intuitive term "language." The third notion, "structure," is a very important one. The structure is, in fact, what is determined by the grammar. It is a set of representations, including representations of grammatical sentences and ungrammatical sentences and so on and so forth. The grammar, your knowledge and my knowledge, assigns a status to every noise in the world. Some of those noises are well-formed sentences of English or Finnish or whatever. Some of them are possible sentences of some language but not mine. Some of them have a metaphoric interpretation. Some of them have a perfectly precise literal interpretation but deviate from some well-formedness condition. In fact, there are dozens of categories. The structure is the characterization of every noise in terms of all those possibilities as determined by the grammar. People with different grammars, meaning in intuitive terms with different languages, will assign noises a different status in each of these different categories. This is when we are talking about reality. In this entire discussion about reality the term "language" in the linguist's sense or the logician's sense never appears, because it is just an artifact, has no reality, plays no role in the study of mind or behavior or whatever, and is best dismissed. It is only in the last couple of years that I have come to realize how much people are misled by this and have begun to suggest that we simply overthrow the whole terminology and start over afresh, now using the term "language" to refer to the system of rules and principles, what has previously been called grammar, and dismissing entirely what has previously been called language, because it is a concept with no use, corresponding with nothing in the physical world.

One of the most recent developments in the study of generative grammar is a new comparative, or parametric, approach to syntax. In your dialogue with the late French linguist Mitsou Ronat (Language and Responsibility) *you speak about two senses of the word "interesting": linguistic and other phenomena can be interesting in themselves or they may be interesting in that they bear on explanatory theories. Do you think that the new parametric approach in syntax can unify these two notions of "interesting" in the case of language: phenomena which used to be interesting only in the general sense might now become interesting also from the point of view of explanatory theories?*

Humanly Interesting or Intellectually Interesting?

Not really, because it is a general fact that, let's say, in biology flowers are interesting. From a human point of view flowers are interesting, birds are interesting, sunsets are interesting. I go out of my way to look at a pretty sunset, because it is a nice thing. I like it. But that does not mean it has any intellectual interest. Maybe it does, maybe it does not. Whether a flower, a sunset, or a bird has intellectual interest from the point of view of our understanding of the world, that depends on whether those phenomena play a critical role in helping us test, or evaluate, or make more precise, or sharpen, deeper principles that are part of our explanatory scheme connected with the whole of nature. And there is no relationship at all between what is humanly interesting and what is intellectually interesting. In, say, physics, the phenomena that are intellectually interesting, that bear on the correctness of explanatory principles, have no human interest whatsoever. I don't care, as a human being, what happens to a photographic plate in the space shuttle, but that may be of great interest for some physical theory.

The same is true in the study of language. The elements of language are of intrinsic interest to us: differences in one language are this way and in another that way, this word has this curious shape, and so on. That is an interesting topic. They have sections in newspapers devoted to it, because people are amused by it. But most of these phenomena have no intellectual interest at the moment, because they don't bear on principles of explanation. And the phenomena that do bear on principles of explanation may be of very little human interest. That is, very few human beings are interested in the fact that in the sentence "who did the men expect to see each other," "each other" cannot refer to "the men." Humanly that is not an interesting fact. It is a very interesting fact for linguistics, because it happens to relate to the question of how, precisely, to formulate principles that determine associations between elements and so on and so forth. And that distinction remains.

The New Approach of the 1980s

As far as the move toward comparative studies is concerned, of course everybody has been interested in comparative study, but there has been a very substantial move forward in this domain in the last few years, connected with the really significant recasting of the whole framework of linguistic theory that has taken place in the last three or four years. Where earlier approaches—so far we have been talking of earlier approaches—conceived of a language, what was called grammar, as a kind of rule system, in the last couple of years a rather different point of view and some partial solutions have emerged, although there are problems with this approach. The partial solutions sort of fell together about four, five years ago, yielding a quite different conception of the whole system. It now looks as if there are no rules, no rules of grammar in the traditional sense, that these are artifacts. In fact, what there are is something rather different, namely quite general and quite abstract principles that belong to various different so-called modules, subsystems that are integrated in a certain fashion. All of this is part of the initial state of the mind, our biological endowment. This whole system is associated with a certain finite set of possibilities of variation, which are called parameters, and the choice of one language or another is determined by fixing those parameters. It's as if, to use an image, nature provides us with a rather intricately wired system, the language faculty, so constructed that not all the connections are fixed. Many of them are, and the general structure of the system is fixed entirely. But associated with this system, there is a certain, say, switch-box, a certain set of switches, and each of those switches can be set one way or another. Experience has to determine which way to set the switches, and once you have set them, you've got a language. That is a very different approach. It makes it much harder to find explanations. In the old system, to explain a phenomenon you constructed a rule system to derive it. That is hard enough, but now it is much harder. What we have to do is show that in a fixed system of principles common to all languages, we will explain the phenomena in question by just some modification of the choice of parameters. That is much harder to do. What is particularly exciting at the present moment is that it is being done. It is being done in quite an exciting way for quite a wide range of languages. And it is here where the comparative work becomes particularly interesting, because that is now enabling us to begin to understand really for the first time what are the options of parametric difference, how can you set a switch one way or another and change from one language type to a different language type. That is now becoming possible to study really for the first time ever. There is a real sense of excitement and progress in the field that is rather reminiscent of what it was like about 30 years ago, when all of this got started.

The study of generative grammar supports some of the ideas of Cartesian rationalism as opposed to empiricism. Usually rationalism has been associated with reactionary political viewpoints that defend inequalities between human beings, whereas empiricism has been seen to defend progressive, liberal, reformist, even revolutionary ideas in politics and social thought. How would you comment upon this?

The first point I would make is that truth is truth. You don't decide what is true on ideological grounds. What is true is true. You have to determine what is true on the basis of facts and understanding, sound argument, proper evaluation of evidence and so on, and the question of what is progressive or reactionary is totally irrelevant to this search. So these two questions have to be kept quite separate.

A More Optimistic Progressive World View

That having been said, I think that the traditional interpretation is partially false. I mean, it was true in a certain historical moment that empiricism was associated with progressive ideas. But that, I think, is extremely misleading. By and large that has not been the case. And although this is irrelevant to the truth or falsity of the empiricist or the rationalist approach, I think myself that it is rationalist approaches which provide the basis for a progressive world view, if you like. To put it rather differently, the assumption that the rationalist approach is essentially correct is a much more optimistic one, in my view.

The rationalist view assumes that there are certain intrinsic properties of human nature, and we have to find out what those are. Well, we don't know much about what they are. There is a line of development in traditional rationalism that goes from Descartes through the more libertarian Rousseau—Rousseau is a complex figure, but the more libertarian Rousseau, the Rousseau of the *Discourse on Inequality*—through some of the Kantians like Humboldt, for example, all through the 19th-century libertarians, which holds that essential features of human nature involve a kind of creative urge, a need to control one's own productive, creative labor, to be free from authoritarian intrusions, a kind of instinct for liberty and creativity, a real human need to be able to work productively under conditions of one's own choosing and determination in voluntary association with others. One strain of thinking held that that is essentially the human nature. If so, then slavery, wage-slavery, domination, authoritarianism and so on are evils, which violate essential human principles, which are injurious to the essential human nature, and therefore intolerable. This says that our commitment should be to discover and to overcome to the extent possible the forms of authoritarian control, interference with personal dignity, human liberty and so on and so forth.

An Attractive Ideology to the Modern Intelligentsia

The empiricist view, on the other hand, takes a totally different stand towards all of this. It says that human beings are malleable, that they have no intrinsic characteristics, that they can differ in all sorts of fashion, they can be of different colors and totally as different as a dog and a cat. So there is no moral barrier to interference with fundamental human rights, because there are no fundamental human rights: humans are just some collection of properties, they are malleable, they are changeable. If you like, you can hope that there will become a change for the better, but there are no moral issues involved.

In fact, I don't see any way of associating a progressive moral standpoint with empiricist assumptions about humans. In my opinion, this is one of the reasons why empiricism has been such an attractive ideology to the modern intelligentsia. One has to ask why it has been so attractive. Why does it appear over and over again? In Marxism, in conservatism, all over the place we find a deep commitment to empiricist ideas. It is not because they have been proved successful. It is not because there is some intellectual support for them, some evidence for them. In fact, on the contrary, everything we know shows that they are either unintelligible or false. I am now talking about the empiricist conception of human nature and not questions about how you do science. The empiricist concept of human nature has essentially nothing that supports it and much that goes against it. Why then is it accepted as virtually a kind of doctrine or dogma? Well, I think here we might ask the question how it serves the needs of those who accept it. And I think the answer to that is pretty plain.

The contemporary, the modern intelligentsia, the intelligentsia of the last century or so, are basically managers and largely see themselves as either ideological managers or state managers. For them it is very convenient to have an ideology which says that there are no moral barriers to domination, interference and control, because then they just add one or two assumptions such as: I am the obvious controller, I know what is good, and I will manipulate these people for their own benefit, because that is not interference with their essential rights since they have no essential rights, they are just some collection of properties, and I will therefore dominate them for their own good.

Leninism, Fascism and Neoliberalism

Well, I think that this is part of the strain of thinking that is very central to Marxism, and expresses itself in its clearest form in the Leninist variety of Marxism and also in fascism, which is in many respects not a dissimilar position, and also shows up in what is called "liberalism" today [or neoliberalism, which is neither "neo" nor "liberal" in the classical sense, as Chomsky has pointed out—CPO], which is really a state capitalist ideology, in which the intelligentsia play the role of state managers serving external interests, the state and corporations in their societies. That has been the general social role of intellectuals in one or another form for a long time.

For such a position, empiricism is a very convenient doctrine. My guess is that that is a large part of the reason as to why it has been accepted so uncritically and has revealed itself in all sorts of intellectual oddities such as behaviorism and so on. In any event, I think that any simple association of empiricism with progressive attitudes and approach and rationalism with conservatism just does not make any sense at all.

You have associated yourself with a tradition of the libertarian Left, partly connected with Left-Marxism, partly connected with anarchism and anarchosyndicalism. With the important exception of Spain, these currents, by and large, ceased to have any mass following after the First World War. Do you think that social thought, radical social thought, has advanced at all since that time?

Barely. There were some advances during the Spanish revolution in the late 1930s. In my view there has been very little advance since the 1930s. In fact, I cannot remember a general book of political and social thought that I have read since, let's say, Rudolf Rocker's book *Anarchosyndicalism* from 1938 that has been any major contribution to social thought.

The Spanish revolution, it meant both practice and theory?

It was both practice and theory. In that particular book that I mentioned, and in general, Rocker was not just writing on the basis of the Spanish revolution. It is, in my view, a most important exposition of a strain of libertarian thought, anarchosyndicalist thought, that, I think, has very great relevance to contemporary society. That is not the only thing, by any means, but an important one. I don't mean to suggest that nothing of importance has been written during the last few years, but I don't think that anything of fundamental importance has.

Have you ever discussed with libertarian socialists about your view that rationalist philosophy could be associated with progressive viewpoints?

Yes. I have written about it and have discussed it. Well, actually anarchism or libertarian socialism has also been committed, generally, to empiricist ideologies. Bakunin certainly was. I think that is rather mindless, quite mindless for the reasons that I mentioned. I have tried to convince people thereof but not with very much success, I would say.

Do you think that Bakunin was committed to empiricism because he happened to live in the 19th century?

I don't think he thought about what he was saying. Bakunin had a lot of great insights, but he was not really a profound thinker, certainly not a systematic thinker. Bakunin is very interesting for his sharp flashes of insight, which are often quite brilliant, but not for systematic thought and argument, as he would have been the first to say. So, for example, Bakunin, I think, made an enormously important contribution to what we might call a sociology of the intellectuals. His analysis of the emerging role of the intelligentsia in the late 19th century was very, very sharp and very clever. He was, I think, the first person to use the concept of the "new class." His conception of the new class and its likely evolution was prophetic and very accurate. Much of his critique of authoritarian systems and the state and so on was also highly accurate, although he was by no means a systematic thinker. I mean, there's a lot of confusion and self-contradiction that one can also discover in his work. I suppose his empiricism was just a not very thoughtful adherence to the general assumption that this is a progressive ideology.

How about Anton Pannekoek in this century, another libertarian socialist who criticized the role of the intellectuals?

The only place where Pannekoek comes close to discussing this issue, to my knowledge, is his book *Lenin as Philosopher*, which tends to take a generally empiricist line. But it is mostly critical rather than constructive.

Social Implications of the Two Views of Human Nature

This has not been much of an issue in social thought. I think you can find it in social theory, in fact, in a very simple way. Let's not inflate it too much. Suppose you have an opinion about what ought to be done. We think there has to be some change, some reform in the way our lives are organized, in the way our institutions are structured. Or suppose we believe there has to be some revolutionary change. Anyone that advocates that kind of position at the root is basing the advocacy on some assumption about human nature. Maybe the assumption is not explicit, in fact, it almost never is explicit. But the fact is that if there is any moral character to what we advocate, it is because we believe or are hoping that this change we are proposing is better for humans because of the way humans are. There is something about the way humans fundamentally are, about their fundamental nature, which requires that this change we are advocating take place.

So if we are opposed to slavery, it is because we think that slavery is inconsistent with fundamental human rights, which are rooted in the nature of humans, which demand that they be free and not owned by others. Slavery is an interference with the essential human nature, an essential human right to be free and under one's own control. If we don't believe that or something like that, there is no reason to be opposed to slavery. In fact, the apologists for slavery—we don't have to go back very far in history—they were not bad people; if we think of the apologists for the terrible things today, they were not any worse—their belief was also rooted in assumptions which led to the conclusion that slavery is good for people, that, in fact, it is a moral duty of a slave-owner to own slaves, just as it is a moral duty of a parent to take care of the child and not let the child free in a cold and competitive world, in which it cannot cope. It is the duty of the parent to ensure the child's welfare. Similarly, it is the duty of the slave-owner to take care of the slave, to take care of the slave's needs and not allow it to face the enormous dangers that would follow from setting this poor creature free in a world that it cannot handle. That is essentially what underlies the moral rationale for owning slaves.

Now, at the root of this dispute is a dispute about human nature, a fundamental dispute about human nature. The same is true if we are talking about a change in tax laws. Assume that we are not just doing it for some opportunistic reasons, that we really think that there is some moral content to what we are proposing, if we trace that position to its origins, it will have to do with some assumption about human nature, about the central human nature. Otherwise there is no basis for taking a political position or a stand on issues.

Now, this is very hard to make explicit, and so little is understood that the structures of the argument and belief that we develop are very loose. In fact, they are largely structures of hope and conviction rather than arguments with evidence. But nevertheless those are the structures that must be there for there to be any moral content to our advocacy and action.

Almost all of your political writings have contained criticism of the intelligentsia. In the charges leveled against you by establishment intellectuals, have they ever accused you of anti-intellectualism?

If anti-intellectualism is the opposition to intellectual values, then I would not accept the criticism. In fact, I would regard the organized and articulate intelligentsia as very anti-intellectual, because I think their activities and commitments are deeply opposed to intellectual and often moral values.

The Standard Role of the Intelligentsia

But if by anti-intellectual we mean opposition to the standard role of the intelligentsia in modern society, left or right, from Leninist to modern liberal, then I would gladly accept the term anti-intellectual.

There are individuals who are different, of course, but in its social role this has been an extremely corrupt and dangerous group. It is, in fact, the commissars, the secular priesthood, the state ideologists, the people in charge of the system of indoctrination and control. That is the major commitment, in my view, of the organized, articulate intelligentsia. I am not referring to somebody who is studying 14th-century manuscripts, but I am referring to the intellectuals in the sense of those who hold that they have something important to say about society and human life and human action and so on and so forth.

In general, if we look over modern history, I think we find that Bakunin's warnings were very well-founded, and I think with good reasons for that. Intellectuals are not going to gain power by working through the competitive economic system. If fact, if they do that, we don't call them intellectuals any more. Maybe they are doing intellectual work, but we give them other names. We called them managers or something like that. The people we call intellectuals are those who have, by and large, sought prestige and power elsewhere, usually by association with the state, either because they hope to take over the state as a vanguard, using and exploiting popular struggles so that they take state power and manipulate it, essentially the Leninist view, or else by association with state organs as ideologists of the state religion, as commissars in the Western system of indoctrination. That has been a very standard, very common social role, in fact, the general one.

I think yes, I am very critical over that. I think it is an extremely corrupt group. I think this is also the group that is the most subject to effective indoctrination, tends to have the least understanding of what is happening in the world, in fact, tends to have a sort of institutionalized stupidity. Again, that is not too surprising. You would expect the commissars to be the most deeply indoctrinated and, in general, the stupidest group that exists, because they are the ones who are at the center of the system of indoctrination, they are the ones who are affected by the construction, development and belief in it. So, of course, their understanding of the social world is very primitive, very limited. I think that is largely true in the West as well, much more than we usually tend to believe.

Do you think there are any differences between the United States and Western Europe in this respect?

The Most Free and Most Indoctrinated Society

There are some differences, there are a number of differences. The United States is probably the most open and freest society in the world, I think that considerably more so than any Western European society that I know of. On the other hand, it is also one of the most deeply indoctrinated societies in the world and one of the most depoliticized societies in the world, and one of the societies with the most conformist intelligentsia in the world, in this respect more so than in Western Europe. I don't think this is particularly paradoxical, incidentally. I mean, if there is a society that is free and open but has a highly class-conscious dominating elite, ruling group, such a society is going to be forced to have a very effective system of indoctrination, precisely because it cannot rely on force and violence to ensure obedience. It is going to rely on a very sophisticated indoctrination and thought control.

So it is not at all paradoxical that in the most free and open society you should have the most sophisticated, well-grafted and effective system of indoctrination and thought control. That is very natural. In fact, at the opposite extreme in the Soviet Union you don't need a sophisticated system of thought control, because you can ensure obedience by force. Therefore thought control can be a very vulgar and transparent system with a Ministry of Truth producing doctrines such that people believe in them, if they want, or don't believe, if they don't want. Basically you don't care, if they are obedient. In the United States, which is in many ways the opposite extreme—a very free and open society with rather limited resources of state violence, not zero, it is there and it is used, but by comparative standards relatively limited—you would expect such a society to have much more effective indoctrination, and that is the case.

There is a long and very self-conscious ideology about this. This has been discussed within the doctrinal system for many years, certainly since the First World War. In fact, the basic concept of what Walter Lippmann back in 1921 called "manufacture of consent" has always been recognized as the essential feature of an American style democracy. You need manufacture of consent. You cannot force people to obey by violence, you have to manufacture consent. You have systems of indoctrination that ensure that they agree to what ruling groups want to do.

The U.S. System as a One-Party System

I think that this shows itself in the intellectual caste in the United States in their subservience and conformism. It even shows up in the elections. Take, say, the current presidential election. My guess is that it will be like the 1980 election: close to half the population won't bother to vote. And of those who vote, most will vote for Reagan, but very few of those who vote for Reagan also vote for his position. In fact, most of those who vote for Reagan oppose his position. All this is very natural in a depoliticized society, where people are intelligent enough to understand that they are not voting the issues. They are voting for Coca-Cola or Pepsi-Cola. There are no parties even in the limited Western European sense. I don't want to exaggerate the situation in Western Europe, but, in fact, the approximately half the population, maybe 45 percent of the population, that doesn't vote here, its socio-economic constitution is approximately that of those who vote in Europe for one of the labor-based parties, socialist, labor, communist, one of the reformist labor-based parties. That is roughly the composition of the group that largely does not vote in the United States. I suppose the reason they don't vote is that they just consider themselves as unrepresented. There is essentially a one-party system, what sometimes has been called the property party, and the choice about its various factions. There's not a great interest in it. It is as if in a European society you had the vote between one or another faction of the Tories. If that was the only choice, why would you bother voting?

In fact, if that is the only choice, you have to package the candidates to make them look different. You have to have a huge public relations campaign to make people believe that something is happening, to engage them in the political process. It gives people the illusion that they play a role in determining the nature of their own society, its goals and actions.

Hence we need an enormous publicity campaign. The American elections are a public relations campaign. It is like packaging a commercial product. Most people react to it that way. So they have these performances called debates, which have nothing to do with debates. But if you look at the commentary on them by sophisticated commentators, it is very revealing. After the presidential debate or after a vice-presidential debate there will be political commentary in newspapers asking whether Reagan had a nicer smile than Mondale, whether Mondale picked a wrong tie, or whether Geraldine Ferraro looked down too much instead of looking up at the camera, and similar profound issues. And that is right. I mean, if you are packaging a commercial product and trying to sell it, those are the factors that are interesting and significant.

That is why you get these apparent paradoxes that polls, for example, reveal that the population is overwhelmingly pro-Reagan, while when people are asked: Would the country be better-off or worse-off if Reagan's policies were enacted?, about the same proportion say that the country would be worse-off. So you have a huge majority for Reagan and about an equivalent majority opposed to his policies. That is not unreasonable in a depoliticized society, where there is a certain understanding at some level that there is not much relationship between the game of personalities and image that you are supposed to participate in and the policies that have been formulated, which are developed in a different institutional structure altogether.

One of the tasks of the intelligentsia in the United States has been to try to prevent people from understanding all of this. I think they have succeeded in preventing themselves from understanding, and very effectively. As I said, the intelligentsia tend to be the most effectively indoctrinated group. The commissars are usually effectively indoctrinated. On the other hand, I don't think they have succeeded very well with the population as a whole. It is a very sophisticated and effective system, but it has its limitations.

What do you think are the reasons why there is no reformist labor movement in the United States?

Well, there are a lot of reasons. I think it is hard to identify a single one. Partly I think it just grows out of American history. This was basically an immigrant society. Waves of immigrants came in, one after another, and it was an expanding society. Remember that our predecessors cleared the continent. We don't have genocidal attacks on Indians today the way they do in Guatemala. The main reason for that is we had them 150 years ago. There was not anybody left. So after the clearing of the continent, that is, the virtual elimination of the native population and after half of Mexico was stolen in the mid-19th century, there was this huge continent open with enormous resources and essentially empty, when these waves of immigrants came in one after another. There was a lot of capital inflow from England, when it was needed, and then the country became powerful enough to run its own affairs.

Immigration and Depoliticization: The Crushing of Dissent

All of this led to an enormous possibility for economic expansion without historical parallel. And you could take part in it and, in fact, benefit from it. The poor immigrant who came in could become part of this, could benefit from it, when he kept his mouth shut. If you didn't raise a fuss, if you just integrated yourself into the system, maybe you would work in a sweatshop, as my father did, but your son would go to college, as I did. That is a sort of immigrant experience. That itself attaches a certain priority to obedience, because if you try to organize to protect your rights and you face the violence of the state, as you do, you will lose these options, very likely lose these options, which will be the automatic consequence of conformism and obedience.

I should say, incidentally, that this stopped in the 1930s. That is essentially when we stopped having an expanding economy. Of course, it grew, but the growth was not of the kind that would have absorbed poor, unskilled, untrained workers. And we did have another immigration wave. It happened to be internal immigration, the immigration of blacks from the South. That was associated with mechanization of agriculture in the South that led to immigration and turned share-croppers into industrial workers. And there was also the Hispanic immigration from the peripheral dependencies in the Caribbean and Central America. That has been enormous. Those people could not be absorbed, because the economy was no longer of a sort that could bring in waves of unskilled labor and have them work in sweatshops under horrible conditions but producing wealth so that they themselves could even benefit from it to some extent and their children even more so. That did not happen any more. And that is one of the major sources for the urban problem and the race problem in the United States. These people are just penned up in urban ghettos, where they have to be controlled, from which they have basically no escape.

This is one factor. Another factor is this: although I said that the United States does not use much violence, that has to be qualified. Repeatedly the state has resorted to violence to block organizing, the construction of popular organizations, independent unions and so on and so forth. And that has been successful.

There is a certain combination of American power and affluence, the immigrant nature of the society, the regular resort to violence, the extremely sophisticated indoctrination system with far more class-conscious corporate leadership in the United States than exists anywhere in the world, these factors have, in fact, combined to produce a highly depoliticized society. Also a rather anarchic society. The population as a whole is subject to very radical changes in very brief periods. So, for example, in the mid-60s the general mood of the population changed enormously from jingoist fanaticism to anti-interventionism. It happened very quickly. More recently there has been a huge wave of religious fanaticism of an almost Khomeinist variety. Probably close to half of the electorate, maybe about 40 percent of the electorate, are deeply fundamentalist Christians who have undergone personal religious experiences, have been born again and so on and so forth. That is unheard of in any other industrial society. It is a sort of very chaotic population, in a way rather thinly controlled by the ideological system, but also depoliticized, with very few modes of constructive action open to them in the political arena.

But in the 1930s there were very active labor unions, socialist and Communist parties, anarchist groups and so on?

Yes there were. But that essentially was destroyed. It was destroyed, first of all, by the Second World War. Any major war turns a country into a totalitarian state, almost automatically. So that happened during the Second World War, and then by the rather effective post-war repression.

The Cold War system was used, and, in fact, it was one of its major functions, to crush internal dissent. And that was very self-conscious. If you look back at, say, NSC 68, National Security Council 68, which is one of the founding Cold War documents back in 1950, it calls for huge expansion of the military budget and a roll-back strategy against the Soviet Union. One of the things that they emphasize there is that we cannot tolerate the luxury of dissidence and debate, because we are at war, we are at war to preserve our domination of the world.

That was never made public, of course. It was not made public until 1975, when the document was finally released. That represents the mentality of the ruling groups: dissidence and controversy are really unacceptable luxuries, because we have a war to fight. And that war, we pretend that it is against Russia, but, in fact, the war is against people like the Vietnamese and Salvadoran peasants and people in Zaire and so on. Those are the people we are fighting. We pretend that it is the Russians, and of course they play the same game. They control their own population. The people they are fighting are Afghans and Poles and Czechs. But they pretend to their own population that they are fighting us. That is the essence of the Cold War. It is the beauty of the Cold War system, a fantastic technique of ideological control in both superpowers.

Editor's Notes to Interview 33

"Noam Chomsky: Response," in *Tactics and Strategies for the Peace Movement: Where do we go from here?* A.J. Muste [1885–1967] Memorial Institute Discussion Series, Number One. New York: A.J. Muste Memorial Institute [339 Lafayette St., New York, NY 10012], 1985, pp. 17–19, a publication dedicated to the memory of Barbara Deming (d. Aug 2, 1984), a comrade of A.J. Muste ("They edited *Liberation* magazine together, plotted tactics and strategies to end the war in Vietnam together, and committed civil disobedience together—in the American South and in colonial Saigon.").

The project, part of the Muste Centennial commemoration, was conceived and edited by Marty Jezer (the author of *The Dark Ages: Life in the United States 1945–1960*. Boston: South End Press, 1982), who "has been active in the peace movement since the mid-60s as a writer, editor and activist with *WIN*, *Liberation*, The Resistance, Yippie, WRL, CNVA, etc."; at the time of publication he was active in the anti-interventionist movement and the Rainbow Coalition and was writing a book on "the bohemian Left."

Jezer requested answers to his 8 questions (1500 words) plus a biographical sketch (up to 100 words) by Dec. 1, 1984. Over 80 people "expressed interest in the project, many agreeing that the time was ripe for this kind of examination," but the deadline "was short—less than a month from election day—and many had prior commitments." Only 35 responded. The result "does not reflect a movement cross-sample," but it does "encompass a diverse and interesting group of people" (Jezer's introduction).

Chomsky's written answers, which again are instructive to compare with the answers of the other respondents (see also interview 33), are not dated; they are among the most concise and clearest presentations of his understanding of contemporary reality and his approach to changing it. The middle sentence of his biographical sketch was added in the process of publication: "Noam Chomsky has been an active participant in the peace movement for many years, and writes and speaks extensively on international affairs and social and political issues. His latest book is *The Fateful Triangle: Israel, the U.S., and the Palestinians.* He teaches at MIT." (An expanded second edition of *The Fateful Triangle* was published in 1999, followed by an expanded second edition of *Pirates and Emperors* (2002) and by *Middle East Illusions: Peace, Security, and Terror* (2003).)

Since the numbers of the questions were left out, the phrase "Questions 6–8" at the very beginning of Chomsky's last answer was replaced by "Those three questions."

For more on the Soviet-Western fraud about "socialism," see Chomsky's "The Soviet Union vs Socialism" (notes to I15).

For more on electoral politics, see I40.

The last sentence is a shortened version of the last paragraph of **TT** (1985), then about to appear.

33. Tactics and Strategies for the Peace Movement
(November 1984)

If we are headed inextricably towards nuclear war—as movement activists so often insist—shouldn't we de-emphasize other issues and concentrate solely on issues of war and peace? Or, to phrase it differently, is it useful to relate our concern for peace to broader ideological goals and non-military issues?

The threat of nuclear war is real enough, but attempts to reduce it are no more than a holding action, serving to provide some time in which popular forces may develop that will confront the institutional and cultural sources of the drift towards disaster. To concentrate all energies on delaying an imminent catastrophe while ignoring the causal factors that lie behind it is simply to guarantee that sooner or later it will occur. There are reasons why states devote their resources to improving the technology of destruction, why they seek international confrontation and provoke or maintain tensions and conflicts that are sure to engage the superpowers and lead to a terminal conflict. If these reasons are not addressed, such conflict is inevitable; only the timing is in doubt. It is suicidal to concentrate solely on plugging holes in the dike without trying to **stem the flood at its source.** For us, that means changing the structures of power and dominance that impel the state to crush every move towards independence and social justice in our vast domains and that constantly drive it towards expansion of the military system as a device of industrial policy planning. There is no simple formula to determine how limited energies should be distributed among these many tasks, but unless all are undertaken we can at best hope to delay the inevitable disaster.

Should the peace movement continue to emphasize the arms race and nuclear war (by advocating disarmament and protesting specific weapons systems), or should priority be given to foreign policy and national security issues (by redefining national security to make disarmament feasible)?

New weapons systems increase the likelihood of war for familiar reasons, but there is no way to stop them—every effort will be frustrated—as long as they serve necessary functions, and they do. One function is economic. Across the political spectrum, from Kennedy to Reagan, it is understood that stimulating the economy requires massive government intervention, and this can be done, while preserving and indeed enhancing the privileged position of those who own and manage the society (the bottom line, which cannot be challenged by state policy), only by expanding the state-guaranteed market for high technology waste production, generally armaments. It stands to reason, then, that the U.S. will support arms agreements that permit constant technological advances in weaponry, though it may well accept reduction of numbers since U.S. comparative advantage does not lie in production but in high tech.

A second function was described clearly by Carter's Secretary of Defense Harold Brown, when he informed Congress in 1980 that our strategic weapons permit conventional forces to serve as "meaningful instruments of political and military power"; that is, they provide **an umbrella for intervention and aggression**. Deterrence does work, as intended. Given the U.S. commitment to ensure that as much of the world as possible is subordinated to the needs of domestic power, this umbrella must be in place.

A third factor is that Cold War confrontation is highly functional for the superpowers. As the events of the Cold War show clearly, this system permits each superpower to mobilize its own population and recalcitrant allies for brutal and often costly actions in its own domains, under the guise of defense against the "Great Satan" who threatens its survival. Neither superpower will readily abandon this successful system of domination, even though it constantly risks unintended breakdown and nuclear war. And the violence of the enemy will be welcomed with such pleasure by its opponent and tacit partner, and by the commissars on both sides (what we here call "the intellectual community").

How do we explain the Soviet Union to the American people and so diffuse the Cold War? And how do we deal with the Soviet peace movement which is an official organ of the State? How, also, do we relate to dissident peace activists and East-Bloc advocates of reform?

We should explain the USSR by telling the truth, namely, that Lenin and Trotsky, consciously and with clear intent, instituted a brutal and oppressive system that relies on force to control its own internal empire and its satellites. We should also explain that no Russian government, however instituted, would relinquish control over Eastern Europe as long as Germany is part of a hostile Western military alliance, for obvious reasons. **The Soviet system** is brutal but conservative, and it understands its relative economic and even military weakness. The military-bureaucratic elite that runs this dungeon is mainly concerned to maintain its internal power. If the U.S. were interested in supporting Solidarity—a ludicrous idea—it would move towards reduction of tensions in central Europe, a necessary though not sufficient condition for inducing relaxation of the Soviet grip over its client states.

We should also explain that when the world's two greatest propaganda systems agree on something, it is likely to be widely accepted. They do agree that the USSR is "socialist" or "communist," for opposing reasons: the West, so as to undermine socialism by associating it with totalitarian brutality, the USSR so as to exploit the favorable image of socialism. In fact, Lenin and Trotsky proceeded immediately to destroy workers' organizations and to eliminate any possibility that producers could control the means of production, the minimal condition of socialism, and Stalin simply realized the potential of the proto-fascist structures they instituted.

I see little point in dealing with the state authorities in the USSR (or elsewhere) as if they could be allies, including the official "peace movement" in the Soviet bloc. Dissident and reformist elements should be our allies, but there are many difficulties. One of the most severe indictments of the Soviet system is that it has so undermined independent thought that even honest and courageous dissidents often have little conception of social realities, and are often so controlled by their ideological system that their dissidence becomes a kind of reflexive mirror image of it. The best support that we can offer to these groups is to reduce the Western violence that so delights the Soviet rulers, providing them with a most useful device to control their own population much as we do in reverse. And we should of course protest as strongly as we can the brutal internal repression and aggressive violence of the "communist" system, recognizing however that this honest protest will be converted into an instrument of Western aggression just as protest over Western atrocities within the Soviet bloc lends itself to the needs of ruling groups, enhancing their capacity to enforce their own domination and oppression. These are unfortunate facts of life, reflections of the actual distribution of power.

What should the relationship be between the peace movement and electoral politics? To the Democratic Party? To independent or third party politics?

These are tactical questions that have no general answer. Sometimes electoral politics is a useful activity, particularly at lower levels where there is a degree of responsiveness to public opinion; sometimes it is not.

What role should civil disobedience and other forms of direct action play in the movement?

Again, there seems to be no general answer. Direct action is often useful to the participants, encouraging them in their own efforts (not a small point, given the forces they face and the temptations of disillusionment). It also may encourage others to undertake a broader range of conventional action by extending the range of the thinkable. In some circumstances, when there is real popular understanding of the legitimacy of direct action to confront institutional violence, it may serve as **a catalyst to mass popular action**. In this case, it will evoke state violence, a sign that it is becoming truly significant.

Many activists are committed to "alternative" politics, ignoring, when possible, programmatic reforms in favor of a more visionary stance (building a new society in the shell of the old). This was the strategy of the 1960s counterculture. Is it valid today?

Feminist separatism and the existence of an autonomous women's peace movement is a reality. Many blacks also choose separatist or autonomous organizations.

*Under what circumstances are unity and coalition possible? Is it desirable or neces-
sary? How could the peace movement better incorporate sexual and racial politics?*

*The movement has always nurtured its own cultural forms. Our culture express-
es a vision of human solidarity and sustains us through difficult times. But some feel
the movement has evolved into too much of a subculture, and that our style of protest
drives even sympathetic people away. How do we resolve the necessity of creating a dissident culture with reaching out and organizing in mainstream society? Comment.*

Those three questions merit substantial essays in themselves. It is basically a
question of hanging together or hanging separately. Unless the "movement" can
develop and sustain a vision of an attainable future that expresses the felt need of
the overwhelming mass of the population for freedom, justice, decency, solidarity and meaningful democracy, and unless it can begin to construct the "facts" of
this future within existing society, it will not be able to go beyond the attempt to
mitigate the worst atrocities and to delay the final catastrophe. Surely this has not
happened. In fact, the Soviet-Western fraud about "socialism" has had enormous
success in undermining any such endeavor. Western-style capitalist democracy
aims at a condition in which each individual confronts the organized power of
highly self-conscious ruling groups in isolation, flipping a lever every few years
but with no means to join with others to gain information and understanding,
to raise and consider questions about the nature and functioning of economic or
political institutions, to develop concepts and programs of social change, or even
to enter the relatively narrow arena of decision-making in the political system in
a meaningful way.

In our dependencies, such as El Salvador, we use brute force to ensure this
outcome; here, other means have been effectively employed. Separatism, subcul-
tures that are meaningless or offensive to much of the population, lack of an
articulated vision of the future—these are all reflections of the enormous power
of the Western system of fragmentation and ideological control, and of our
inability, so far, to combat it except sporadically. There are **no magic answers**,
just the familiar ones: honest search for understanding, education, organization,
action—and the kind of commitment that will persist despite many failures and
only the most limited successes.

Editor's Notes to Interview 34

"Aspects of a Theory of Mind: An Interview with Noam Chomsky," *New Ideas in Psychology* 4:2 (1986), pp. 187–202. It was conducted in late 1984 by Richard Beckwith and Matthew Rispoli (questions 1–2 and 4–5 are Rispoli's; the rest are Beckwith's), then in the Department of Developmental and Educational Psychology, Teachers College, Columbia University, New York, from which they both have doctorates in developmental psychology. Beckwith is currently doing postdoctoral research on the lexicon with the Cognitive Science Laboratory at Princeton University. Rispoli, who also has a master's degree in linguistics from the University of Pennsylvania, is currently engaged in postdoctoral research on the crosslinguistic comparison of first language acquisition at the University of California, Berkeley.

The interview, a particularly valuable one (see also the second part of I25), was an indirect consequence of a meeting Beckwith and Rispoli had with Pierre Moessinger, a developmentalist trained in Geneva (the seat of Piagetian influence), who is an editor of the journal. The discussion in this meeting centered on the logical problem of language acquisition and its relation to Piagetian theory. Following this meeting, Moessinger mentioned that his journal wanted an interview with Noam Chomsky because his work was at the forefront of much recent work in psychology and asked if Rispoli and Beckwith would like to do it. (I am indebted to Beckwith for this information.)

Luigi Rizzi's paper on the "null subject parameter" has been reprinted as the last chapter of his *Issues in Italian Syntax*. Dordrecht: Foris, 1982. Richard Kayne's most representative book at the time was *Connectedness and Binary Branching*. Foris, 1984.

The works on the study of vision referred to are David Marr, *Vision* (San Francisco: Freeman, 1982) and Shimon Ullman, *The Interpretation of Visual Motion* (The MIT Press, 1979). The work of Spelke and her co-workers is discussed in Rene Baillargeon, Elizabeth S. Spelke, & Stanley Wasserman, "Object Permanence in Five-Month-Old Infants," *Cognition* 20 (1985), pp. 191–208; the references include one to the following unpublished manuscript: E.S. Spelke & R. Kestelbaum, "Spatiotemporal Continuity in Object Persistence in Infancy," University of Pennsylvania, 1984. See now *Visual Cognition and Action: An Invitation to Cognitive Science*, vol. 2, ed. by Dan Osherson, Stephen M. Kosslyn, and John M. Hollerbach. Cambridge, MA: MIT Press, 1990, and Richard Gregory, *Eye and Brain*, 4th edition. Princeton, NJ: Princeton University Press, 1990.

The "subset principle" is discussed in Robert C. Berwick, *The Acquisition of Syntactic Knowledge*, The MIT Press, 1985 (Series in Artificial Intelligence.) The work of Eric R. Kandel that Beckwith refers to is *Behavioral Biology of Aplysia: A Contribution to the Comparative Study of Opisthobranch Molluscs*. San Francisco: W. H. Freeman, 1979.

The title of Yosef Gordzinsky's Brandeis University dissertation (completed in 1985) is "Language Deficits and Linguistic Theory."

The major work by Kenneth Wexler and Peter Culicover is *Formal Principles of Language Acquisition*. The MIT Press, 1980.

On the history of successful science as a reflection of the nature of human intelligence, see I28.

On the innate basis of morality, see I11.

34. Aspects of a Theory of Mind (December 1984)

Could you discuss your ideas about the kind of psychological basis needed for human language and how they have changed from the time your wrote Aspects of a Theory of Syntax *to the current framework of the theory?*

Well, at a very broad level it hasn't changed very much. There are a lot of theory-internal modifications that I think are quite important and, in fact, just in the last three or four years, there have been some rather sharp changes in perspective and point of view. They really don't leave the enterprise looking very different from the outside, but they make it look rather different from the inside.

In the early 60s, the general picture that most people working in the field had was that a grammar is a rule system and that the basic genetic endowment provided a kind of format, a notation almost, in which grammars could be formulated, a format for rules that said you could have rules of this kind, you could have rules of that kind, and they could interact in such-and-such a way, and so on. Then the question was, "Well how does a child learning the language pick one of those grammars?" And the idea was that there's some sort of evaluation metric, which says when the data are such-and-such, so-and-so is the highest valued grammar of the proper format for the rules to fit the data, and that's the one you pick, that's the one you learn. So it's a kind of hypotheses, each of them a grammar, and what the child does is pick the highest valued hypothesis, given some data. That was roughly the picture.

There were a lot of difficulties and inadequacies. For one thing, it was very hard to convert any of those metaphors into anything that could be a realistic algorithm for language acquisition. I mean, it couldn't be that you searched through all possible hypotheses. In fact, to try to realize it in any empirically meaningful way was not easy. The general problem was reflected in particular linguistic studies. So, for example, the descriptions of phenomena that were given involved very rich and complex rules systems.

In fact, the first task, when generative grammar started, and when the effort to give a precise account of the phenomena of language was initiated, we were immediately flooded with an incredible range of mysterious phenomena, some of which were, in a sense, very simple but most of which nobody had ever noticed. The problem was to devise rule systems that would at least be descriptively adequate to account for these. That meant that you were coming up with very rich and complex rule systems and that simply then compounded the problem of how you could ever learn them. How does the person ever come up with these crazy rule systems given the paucity of the data that are available?

One has to remember that a very sharp change took place in outlook at about that time. If you go back to the early 50s, the general picture was that language was overlearned, and the problem that psychologists formulated was, "How do you deal with this problem of overlearning?" As soon as you begin to look at the facts of the matter it is obvious that the problem is just the opposite, that the real problem is what was called "poverty of stimulus." People just don't have evidence for most of the things they know. The view that people are trained, or that there is "overlearning" (or even "learning" in any useful sense of this notion) is one that was based on a failure to pay attention to even the simplest of phenomena. As soon as you pay attention to actual facts of a person's knowledge it is plain that the child had no relevant experience, or minimal relevant experience. So, if the only way that we had to express the results was in terms of complex rule systems and we were faced with the fact that experience was very limited, that posed a real mystery, namely, how do you go from limited experience to a very complex rule system?

Advances in the Psychology of Language

Well, the way that various people attempted to deal with this problem since approximately the early 60s, was to try to factor out of the rule systems general principles which allow the rules to be only of very limited types, and to try to show that the tremendous complexity of rule systems is actually just the realization of a small number of options that are permitted by much more general conditions on rule systems. That work has been going on for 20 years now with various successes and failures, but a couple of years ago a lot of it fell together and it began to yield a rather different picture of what the whole story looks like. It's what's sometimes called a "principles and parameters" picture.

The conception that I would now want to propose of what's called Universal Grammar, the theory of the initial state, the genetically determined system, would not be a format for rule systems with a method of hypothesis testing to choose among them, but rather something quite different. To select a different metaphor, it would be something like a system which has an intricate and complex wiring but with some of the connections not established and with, say, a box of switches that can be in one of several (perhaps just two) positions, thus putting the system in full working order. Now, the switches are what are called "parameters." They have to be set by experience—experience has to tell you now to set each of these switches. Once you set them in one of the permissible ways, you have acquired a particular language. If the system has a sufficient internal complexity, changing the setting of one switch may have quite wild effects on the outcome, unpredictable and complex effects. You also may find that languages that separated relatively recently—say French versus the other Romance languages—will differ in clusters of properties, maybe only because one switch was flipped somewhere along the line and that had a whole complex range of consequences.

Let's take, say, French and Italian. They're historically closely related, but they are structurally quite different. So, for example, in standard Italian you can delete the subject of a sentence, you can say "left" instead of "he left," and it means "he left"; in French you can't do that. And in Italian or Spanish, you can say "arrived John" but in French you can't—you say "John arrived." There are a collection of properties of that sort in which French differs from Italian, and it has been proposed, in particular by a colleague of mine here, Luigi Rizzi, that the divergence in a certain cluster of properties flows from one choice, one parameter. This he calls the "null subject parameter" which, in fact, has to do with the question of whether or not the subject of a sentence can be left physically unexpressed. The theory is so constructed that if you set that parameter one way, you get one set of consequences, while if you set it another way you get another set of consequences. These are, to a considerable extent, the set of consequences that differentiate French from Italian, and also English and French from the other Romance languages and so on.

There are other parameters of this nature. For example, take reflexives in English, like "himself." A reflexive in English can have as its antecedent either the subject or the object, so I can say, "John told Bill about himself." The antecedent of "himself" can either be "John," the subject of "told," or "Bill," the object of "told." In some other languages the corresponding element can only go back to the subject. So that's another parametric difference, and that has various consequences.

Each of these parameters had to have the property that it can be determined by a very small amount of data, because that's all children have. Once the parameters are fixed, the rest of the system then functions. So, for example, it appears that languages have approximately the same kind of phrase structure systems at some abstract level, and the way they differ is whether verbs follow or precede objects. If the verb precedes the object it's very likely that the adjective will precede its complement and the nouns will precede their complements, and so on: the language has the property of what's called "head first"—that the verb, preposition, adjective, and noun will precede the complement that is associated with it. So in English we say "read—the book," "in—the room," "happy—that John is here," "the fact—that John is here." There are languages, on the other hand, that are "head last," where the verb, adjective, preposition, or noun will follow the complements that are associated with them. English is a typical "head first" language; Japanese is a typical "head last" language. If you set that parameter, "head first—head last," then a lot of things follow. With this and a few other options fixed, the phrase structure rules are essentially given; they don't have to be learned and do not constitute an independent part of our knowledge. In fact, we may dispense with the notion of phrase structure rule.

There are other quite general principles of that sort (some of them are a little hard to describe without a blackboard) with parameters—switches, if you like—that can be set on the basis of very simple data. So, for example, to learn whether your language is "head first" or "head last," English or Japanese, it's enough to hear three word sentences like, "John saw Bill" or "John Bill saw." If you hear, "John saw Bill," you have a "head first" language. If you hear, "John Bill saw," you know it's a "head last" language. Those data are sufficient, and those are the kind of data that children have, of course. Those data suffice to set the parameter, and then the consequences flow from it. Things are not always that simple but that is the general idea.

This is a different view of what language learning is like. In this conception, language learning is not a matter of selecting a hypothesis among an infinite array of very intricate hypotheses. It's a matter of setting parameters in a very highly constrained system, where the complexity of the rules has been factored out, and introduced into the initial wiring. Something like that ought to be right. I mean, that has the right feel to it; it has the right sort of qualitative properties. It would then be possible to explain how one could have so much knowledge on the basis of so little evidence and how the languages could appear to be so rich in structure but yet obviously not have such rich rule systems that one couldn't learn them. In some domains this approach has led to quite interesting results.

At the same time, the range of empirical work has extended enormously. That's obviously been very helpful. So, for example, 20 years ago, most of the significant work that you could count on for theory was in English. You really can't work on a language properly unless you have something like native command of it, which is like saying you can't do chemistry unless you understand the data. You can't do work in a field unless you've got control of the data, and to be in control of the data in this field means to be something like a native speaker. The most fantastic linguist can work on some language for which he lacks near-native command and he'll just get superficial information. Things began to change when native speakers and others with near-native knowledge began to work on other languages. This happened first extensively with the Romance languages. There's now a very excellent school of linguists, mostly young linguists—I guess not so young anymore, but they were young in the 60s and 70s. A lot of them were students of Richard Kayne, who got his PhD here and then went to France and trained a lot of people. They began to do extensive work on the Romance languages.

Out of that came a host of new insights. The same thing happened with Dutch, the Scandinavian languages, Japanese, recently Chinese, a number of American Indian and Australian languages, and quite a few others. As a result the range of relevant data has vastly increased—the kind of data you could rely on, not just descriptive data, but data that really had implications for the way Universal Grammar ought to be formulated and understood. That's raised a whole host of new problems. So there is a convergence of theoretical ideas and expansion of the empirical base, which has led to a new phase, a rather exciting phase. I should say, incidentally, that there are a number of different theories being investigated at this point, all of which are roughly within the domain that I've just outlined.

Of "principles and parameters."

Yes, I mean they don't necessarily formulate it that way, but they're of this character. My guess is they're probably more alike than they seem to be. I think if we find the right level of abstraction, we'll probably find out that several approaches now being actively pursued are more or less saying the same things with different notations. At the moment they look sharply in conflict.

Are these "principles," principles of the organism itself?

Well, I assume these principles are just as much a part of our genetic endowment as are the principles which determine that we're going to have arms and not wings or that we're going to have a human eye and not an insect eye. An analogy that is perhaps relevant comes from David Marr's work. He argues that at some level of representation the visual system provides something more or less like stick figures. To the extent that this is true then it is also a principle of our cognitive representation that is undoubtedly part of the genetic endowment. That very likely wouldn't be the case with some other organism; maybe it's not true of the insect eye, say.

Another example: one of Marr's associates, Shimon Ullman, showed persuasively that the human visual system is based on some kind of rigidity assumption. That is, the two-dimensional presentations that flash on the retina are interpreted as if they were the motions of a rigid object. Metaphorically, it's as if the mind says "I'm going to try to figure out what rigid object could have given rise to that strange sequence of two dimensional images," and so we see what's in front of us as real rigid objects in motion. Presumably the initial structure of the visual system is determining the kinds of things we can see and the way we see them. Principles of Universal Grammar are something like that.

Or, to take another domain, there's been very interesting work recently by Elizabeth Spelke on the way infants identify objects, and what properties are salient. She finds that contour and common fate are salient properties for an infant, but things like, say, same colors are not. Again, this is part of the initial endowment, the way in which the child comes to terms with experience, or organizes experience. And I suppose that linguistic principles are like that.

Innate Ideas, Universal Grammar, and Core Grammar

It sounds like there's been a move away from a perhaps mistaken notion that the Universal Grammar should be something like innate ideas, and moving on to something more like neuronal systems that are in place and reinforced. What exactly would characterize the UG today? Is it the set of all unparameterized principles?

Well, to take the second part of your question first, UG would be the system of principles, the associated collection of parameters, and the interactions among them. But, as to the first part of your question, I don't think there's been the kind of change that you describe. In fact, there's a lot of misunderstanding. The connections to theories of innate ideas were developed in the mid-60s and I think they're of considerable historical interest. In many respects, I think that current theories of cognitive development are a kind of a natural revitalization of the tradition of innate ideas that were developed in very rich ways in the 17th and 18th centuries then largely dropped. Of course, it's a very different theory. We don't assume the metaphysics of mind and body of the Cartesians. Also, one has to recall that their concept of "idea" was quite different from ours. For the Cartesians, ideas included percepts and propositions and semantic representations of all sorts. "Idea" was a term that really meant "theoretical construct of the theory of mind." And the theoretical entities in mind were implanted somehow in the nature of the organism. But, for the Cartesians at least, there was no such thing as human mind; there was just mind. There was mind and matter. Humans had mind and everything else was just body. Of course, we don't accept that. We study the animal mind, and expect it to be different from the human mind.

There are all kinds of differences but there are also interesting similarities to consider, for example, 17th century theories of what was called the "cognoscitive power," the power of forming thoughts and images and concepts. These were very rich theories that invoked all sorts of notions of gestalt properties and Kantian-type notions, long before Kant. It was a very rich and complex tradition. But, of course, we can't talk about resurrecting it—the metaphysical and other assumptions were totally different.

I should also, maybe, mention that the rediscovery of the tradition is sort of post hoc. It wasn't that the traditions inspired current work, it was rather the other way around: current work led to a renewed interest in some antecedents where similar ideas were developed. This is also happening with regard to modularity today. So, for example, Franz Josef Gall has had a recent revival. He was, you know, one of the most vilified figures in psychology for the last hundred years or so, but now he's becoming quite a hero. People have been reading his work again and finding out that it wasn't as stupid as it was made out to be. In fact, it was very smart and probably pretty much on the right track. The kinds of faculties that he was identifying, though they're not connected with bumps on the skull, nevertheless are probably pretty much the right faculties. We often find that our predecessors were not as stupid as they were made out to be.

More modern localization hypotheses do receive some support from current neurolinguistic research. Would you suppose that evidence from neurolinguistics and aphasic syndromes would be relevant to your work? In particular, would you expect that different aphasic syndromes might turn out to reflect linguistic principles?

It would be nice if that were the case. Maybe it will be shown some day. What evidence there is, and ethically could be, is the result of natural experiments and they may be too gross to give precise answers but I imagine that something like that ought to be the case. There ought to be some physical networks of some kind that correspond to different aspects or subparts of the structure of these systems. It could be that injury would differentially affect them. At a very gross level, there are positive results of this nature. For example, there are clinical cases of children who apparently have full language competence, in the sense that they understand sentences the way we do, but they just don't know how to use them. They have lost pragmatic competence. They don't know what's appropriate to say under what circumstances, even though they have the same interpretation of sentences that we have. One would presume that this corresponds to some physical change somewhere. I should mention that some of the recent work on aphasia has been quite suggestive, and may yield more specific evidence concerning linguistic structures and their neural basis, for example, some work presented by Yosef Grodzinsky in a Brandeis University dissertation.

After a series of initial parameterizations proceeding to the next step in the child's development of language, we go to a core grammar?

Well, actually what I described a moment ago is what is sometimes called "core grammar." We should bear in mind that it's very unclear what the term "language" refers to, if anything. What's called a language—what we call English, for example—is really a kind of mess, a collection of different dialects and a conglomeration of irregularities and borrowings. But we wouldn't expect any one of these systems that are used in the social world to reflect precisely the principles of universal grammar. In fact, we expect them not to reflect those principles. You'd expect universal grammar to be realized precisely, only if a child grew up in a completely homogeneous speech community, with no internal contradictions in the data—no cases where one person spoke one way and another person another way. In those circumstances of complete homogeneity and abstraction from residues of historical accident, the grammar that emerged would just be a reflection of universal grammar. But, of course, that never happens in the real world. We're always growing up in a mixture of languages, and so what ends up in our head is something much more complex. So, the distinction that's sometimes made is between a kind of core grammar which is that subsystem of our actual systems that is a direct reflection, that just results from the setting of the switches, from fixing of parameters in the universal grammar, and then some peripheral system around it.

The Role of "Parameters" in Language Acquisition

Could you address the frequent misunderstanding that idealization of the input would circumvent problems of paucity of the input? And also, would you expect that, under ideal circumstances, the mistakes of the child would reflect the initial state?

The problem of poverty of stimulus and paucity of input would arise in essentially the same form even under the idealization. You might argue that in the real world the situation is a little more complex than the idealization, because children not only have to learn how to set the switches but also have to deal with the fact that different people around them are setting the switches differently. So they're faced with not just a poverty of stimulus but also contradictory data which makes the acquisition of language even more difficult to explain. Under the idealization, some of those difficulties would be removed, some dramatically.

As to the things about which children make mistakes, it seems to be they fall into two categories, basically. One is the category of exceptions. So, for example, you expect children to assume at some stage that the past tense of "sleep" is "sleeped," and then indeed to learn that it's not, it's "slept." Maybe some of them never learn it. In some dialect maybe it will persist as "sleeped." And maybe ultimately that verb would be regularized in some dialects. So that's one class of mistakes. The other class of mistakes would be cases where the child simply doesn't yet know how a parameter is set. So, for example, it's quite possible, say, that at some stage of language acquisition the child would assume that reflexives only go back to subjects, and would have to learn the fact that they go back to objects, and failure to go back to objects would be a mistake.

Would the unparameterized principle reflect an unmarked case?

You'd assume so. The parameters could have the property that one value is unmarked. They needn't have that property. For example, a "head first/head last" parameter. Probably neither value is marked; either is just as good as the other. But some things, like the "null subject parameter" or the antecedents for reflexives, probably have a marked and an unmarked value, meaning that the child will set the parameter in the unmarked position unless it gets evidence to the contrary.

There's an interesting doctoral dissertation that was done here in the computer science department by Robert Berwick in which he attempted to construct a program for the acquisition of language, a program which would yield knowledge of language in an algorithmic fashion. One of the questions he asked was just this, "How would you decide which is the unmarked value of a parameter?" He took into account that language is learned from positive evidence only; that is, that corrections are irrelevant. What you hear is the extent of your evidence. And he noted that, within the formal theory of learning, a pure mathematical theory that studies how functions could converge on particular grammars or other systems under various conditions, it's a necessary and sufficient condition for learning under the assumption of only positive evidence that every parameter always be set with the minimal value, that is, the value that will give the smallest language. So, if some parameter has one value that will give more sentences than the other value, then you have to take the smaller one. That's what he calls the "subset principle": you always take the sub-language, if you have a choice. So there's some mathematical support for that principle.

He then naturally went to look at some of the empirical evidence for it. But does it turn out that where children make choices, they pick them in a way that gives a smaller language? It's tricky, because the mathematical theory works on the assumption that the parameters are all independent of one another, but in real life they may not be. It may be that if you set one switch, then other switches are set in some fashion, and that raises some other questions. The empirical evidence is not strong. It's hard to get very convincing empirical evidence in real world situations that will bear on formal idealizations that one knows how to handle abstractly. It's an interesting idea and, in fact, you might almost say it's maybe the first principle of learning that's ever been proposed.

A General Theory of Learning

Could you say something about the relationship between theories of learning and the sorts of things that are possible within the theory? For example, some people suggest that Piaget's learning theory, although not parsimonious or well articulated, is adequate for learning a grammar.

Well, I wonder why anyone would say that because I don't think Piaget's learning theory could learn anything, even the things he's talking about. It's too amorphous. I don't think you could take Piaget's theory and turn it into a set of principles to do anything. The kinds of theories that can work have a lot of built-in structure and the reason that learning takes place is because the built-in structure is there. Now that's exactly what Piaget wanted to reject. In fact, Piaget's main point was that you shouldn't have this intrinsic structure that specifies the form of the resulting theory and that is one of the reasons why he has no theory of learning.

In fact, I'm not so convinced that there ever is going to be such a thing as a theory of learning. But I see what we call learning as one kind of growth. You know we don't learn to grow arms. We also don't learn to have language in any very interesting sense. What happens is that systems that are sort of pre-formed in a certain fashion, or pre-adapted to certain consequences, will interact with the environment in such a way as to sharpen them up by filling in blanks, and you develop a system.

Now, people have been working on just this sort of theory. Steve Pinker has been working on the kinds of assumptions that would be necessary to build into a system for him to develop a theory like lexical-functional grammar. Bob Berwick was working on the kinds of assumptions he had to build into a theory in order to wind up with a theory of government-binding. My guess is that they're not very different. But anyway, anybody's theory of learning is going to be really a theory of innate structure. In fact, the only proposal about learning that I've ever seen is Berwick's "subset principle." The other things that are called theories of learning are really just design of the initial system, the kind of choices it can make, and so on and so forth.

So it sounds like learning might reduce to what Eric Kandel found in his work with Aplysia, the snail. Would you expect learning to reduce to local changes in synaptic effectiveness at particular genetically determined sites?

Yes, I expect it would. It may sound paradoxical but what we call learning may not really be learning, in the sense that the properties that we associate with the concept "learning" may not be properties of the processes that we call learning. For example, if learning is something that is based on association and induction then the processes that we call learning are not learning; they don't fall under rubric. We can hardly fail to be struck by the fact that so-called "learning theory" has been pursued for 70 or 80 years, and is so limited in its results—very little has come out of it.

Many learning theorists do seem to be moving in the direction of Kandel.

The more reasonable of them are moving in the direction of asking what internal structures have to be assumed in order to account for the course of development that an organism follows. But, if you think about it, there really have been no principles of learning except for a few observations about the effect of reinforcements on response strength and the like, and these seem to be of rather limited consequence.

What sorts of principles of learning would you like to see?

I don't think there are going to be principles of learning any more than there will be principles of growth. I mean suppose somebody came along and said: "Look, I'd like a theory of principles of growth that will account for why the visual system becomes what it is, why the liver becomes what it is, why the heart becomes what it is, and so on and so forth." There isn't going to be a set of such principles. The only level at which such principles can be formulated is cellular biology, where it all falls together. But the organs become what they do become because of genetic instructions that give them particular directions and because of the way in which the intrinsic structure relates to the environmental context.

You seem to be suggesting that a lot of the problems we have in constructing theories of psychology and development will only be resolved when we know more about the physiology of the brain. The eliminative materialists, for example, Rorty, would say that as our knowledge of physiology increases, our present theories, which are folk theories, will yield to theories that describe physiology. Do you feel an affiliation with the eliminative materialists?

We hope that the study of physiology will reveal the mechanisms that have the properties expressed and developed in our more abstract theories of mind, perhaps something like the way that physics revealed the mechanisms that satisfy the conditions studied in 19th-century chemistry—valence and the like—and explained why these properties hold. As for the theory of learning, I suspect that we'll find that at the level of cellular biology there will be general principles applying to the various systems, and then if we want to know what particular systems develop in the mind or the rest of the physical body, we'll have to look at the specific instructions that our biological endowment determines. The theory of learning would consist of the principles that govern the interactions that take place between complexly constructed systems and the environment in which they can grow, develop and mature.

A theory of learning would reveal a causal chain from input to mental representation?

Right. Now, let me say again that I think the formal theory of learning has some interesting results. It abstracts away from a lot of these complexities and asks: "Under what conditions could convergence to a fixed system take place?" For example, there is some recent work, which is still unpublished, that shows that under rather reasonable conditions a theory of language learning, let's say, could succeed only if the number of possible languages is actually finite, except for trivial respects—if you look at the structural properties, there would only be a finite number of structurally different languages. Under other conditions, if there were an infinite number of possible languages, then we couldn't learn anything. The learning system could never converge.

That's interesting, because it relates to the difference between our earlier conceptions of language and the more recent ones that we were discussing. One of the differences between the early 60s picture and the current picture that I outline is that according to the current picture there are only a finite number of languages, that is, structured types of language. There are a finite number of switches, each with a finite number of settings. For each array of switch settings, there's one possible language (keeping now to structural type, that is, abstracting from choice of lexical elements), whereas the earlier conception held that there's an infinite number of grammars and you pick the simplest one. Now, this recent formal work assumes pretty reasonable conditions about learning, for example, that one can't remember particular things for too long. Under such conditions, convergence is possible only if the set of essentially different languages—languages that are structurally different in a precisely defined sense—is finite. That suggests something about what the structure of universal grammar should be like. It should allow only a finite number of different grammars. And when you want a theory for them. In fact, there's one major work by Wexler and Culicover which tried to relate some of the problems of formal learning theory to substantive questions of language structure. They came up with some principles motivated by the formal learning theory which turned out to have reasonable empirical analogs. That is very interesting work. One could regard all of this as a contribution to learning theory, but I would imagine ultimately it's just going to be another part of the theory of growth.

Human Intelligence and Psychology as Science

What do you think makes a theory of psychology adequate?

Well, I don't think there is ever going to be such a thing as a theory of psychology. I think that there will be theories in psychology that deal with particular topics. What will make them adequate is what makes any kind of theory adequate: that they give some sort of insight into some domain of phenomena, provide some explanation for puzzling things, or come up with principles that are less than obvious that have empirical support. That's what makes a theory satisfactory. It's hard to do these things outside a very small core of natural sciences. I don't know if there will ever be theories like that in psychology. Perhaps there will.

Would you like to speculate about what fields within psychology might be amenable to this?

There are certain areas in psychology where we can formulate the problems and the questions in terms that are very similar to those in the few areas of the natural sciences where there have been results; in particular, those areas where a problem can be formulated in terms of input/output systems, where we can get some sort of characterization of both the input and the output. The output may be some mental representation that we can find evidence about; we can think of the output as, say, the output of a perceptual system. Then it becomes possible to investigate the kinds of processes or principles that relate stimulus and representation. For example, in the study of vision or in the case of language, it has been possible to arrive at theories with some degree of depth. However, there are many questions that we do not know how to approach in a serious way, questions that have to do with will or choice, for example.

As a matter of fact, this is a classical observation. In the 17th and 18th centuries, it was pointed out that the crucial difference—in the terminology of those days—between man and machine was that machines were compelled to act in a particular way but humans are only incited and inclined, not compelled. That distinction touches on a very essential point. When we get to the areas where we're talking about choice of action, or the fact that we're only incited and inclined but not compelled, I don't think there are any candidates for a theory or explanation. Whether we even have the right kind of intelligence to study those questions or whether they're just too difficult to study, or what, I don't know. But, anyway, it seems to me as much of a blank wall as it's been for the last couple of thousand years.

When we take something that we want to characterize in terms of input/output and mental representation, couldn't there be different mental representations that intervene between the input and output?

Well, the interesting theories currently do talk about many levels of representation and processing. An example is David Marr's theory of vision, which I think is a very successful example of a psychological theory that is non-trivial. A representational theory of language introduces a number of different candidates for possible levels of representation and interactions between them. It is, incidentally, misleading simply to call these input/output systems. For example, a lot of the study of language is really the study of the organization of a system of knowledge, and that's not an input/output system. But it enters into input/output operations like parsing. Also, the study of universal grammar deals with the evidence available to the child as input and the systems of knowledge attained as output, and tries to determine the relation that holds between them. It's really insofar as you can formulate problems in those terms that we seem to know how to deal with them in something like the manner of scientific inquiry.

So, then, an adequate psychology wouldn't be a psychology that would try to account for as much as possible but rather a psychology that would try to account for a limited domain that could be addressed by this particular research strategy.

No. I assume that when you talk about an adequate psychology, you mean an adequate science of psychology. Maybe a more adequate psychology would be literature. If you want to learn about people's personalities and intentions, you would probably do better reading novels than reading psychology books. Maybe that's the best way to come to an understanding of human beings and the way they act and feel, but that's not science. Science isn't the only thing in the world, it is what it is. Insofar as we're asking what an adequate scientific psychology would be, it would be like an adequate scientific physics. It would be a theory that has a certain internal rigor and that provides explanations for empirical phenomena and insight into the principles that account for them, principles that are not obvious and that account for puzzling phenomena. But science is not the only way to come to an understanding of things.

Well then, an epistemological science may look very different from what someone may think of as an adequate psychology.

Well, if what we mean by an adequate psychology is a means of understanding what people do, how they feel, and how they choose their action, it may be that the most descriptively adequate psychology is not the science of psychology. In fact, the science of psychology has very little to say about these matters. But there are other domains in which one can give some insight into these questions: literature, for example. Wolfgang Köhler once argued that one of the reasons it's so hard to construct an adequate science of psychology is that people already have so much intuitive knowledge about the topic that the kinds of things that the science of psychology can discover are already obvious, whereas, in the case of physics, you don't have that kind of intuitive knowledge, so even simple results are surprising. He argued that one of the reasons for the constant failure of psychology to say anything very interesting is that it's just reconstructing things that we have known all along, although maybe we were not consciously aware of them in terms of well formulated principles. His point was that to become a science with surprising results, psychology as going to have to go well beyond the depth of the other sciences.

Maybe that's true, although I also think that there are some domains that we seem to be able to enter with the methods of scientific inquiry available to us. I think we're going to have to keep an open mind about this. But current understanding at least suggests that the human intellect is simply not equipped to deal with certain kinds of questions, including, quite possibly, questions about human behavior. That wouldn't be too surprising. If we regard humans as just another organism in the physical world, then we know that, like every other organism, our mental and physical capacities are bounded. Organisms are good at some things, bad at others—these properties go together. An organism couldn't be equally good at everything or it wouldn't be good at anything. It has to be well adapted to certain kinds of tasks and problems if it is to achieve anything non-trivial. That very adaptation is going to exclude other things. If an organism is good at swimming, it won't be good at flying. The same is true in mental life. If you're capable of solving problems in certain domains, it's because of specific adaptations, highly specific genetic instructions which are going to block access to other domains. If humans are part of the physical world, as certainly we can assume, and if humans are very good at certain tasks, as they are in acquiring language or (at another level of inquiry) constructing quantum theory, then the very intellectual structures that permit them to succeed in these domains are going to lead them to fail constantly in domains that don't happen to be ordered or constructed in a way that corresponds to their intelligence. It is reasonable to suppose that the history of successful science somehow reflects the nature of human intelligence. Throughout the whole range of questions that you can imagine asking, there are areas where humans are able to find answers, where they are able to formulate the problems in such a way that they can enquire into them and sometimes come up with answers. I presume that reflects some particularity of the structure of their intelligence. There may very well be some question right nearby that from the point of view of some other organism or some other intelligence would look equally easy, but we just can't deal with.

Would you also think that the history of ideas within a particular science would reflect the nature of our intelligence?

I think it very much does. For example, in any field that has shown some progress, you find that at particular moments things converge. There is a certain level of understanding that is achieved and there's a certain range of problems that are alive and challenging and suddenly many people will get the same idea or similar ideas as to how to change perspective so as to reach a new level of understanding. This is sometimes called a scientific revolution. What's striking about it is that even if everybody is not capable of carrying it out, it's very widely recognized that is was the right move. We know perfectly well that theories are vastly underdetermined by evidence. But what we find is that certain moves from evidence to theory are regarded as sensible while other moves are regarded as ridiculous. This means that we must be designed specifically to map our current problem situations into a certain small sub-class of possible theories. The whole history of science is an indication of this. But, of course, the very same constraint that leads to the choice of certain theories and the rejection of others is an initial constraint on the nature of our intelligence. And it may be that it leads us in the wrong directions. There's no guarantee that the world is designed so that it will conform to the structure of our intelligence. It's sort of a miracle if it ever happens.

Would you say, then, that we're structured so that we'll be able to detect appropriately some features of the environment?

We're capable of perceiving some kinds of structure in possible worlds. If we're lucky, the actual world is like that in some respects. It's just blind luck if the structure of our intelligence and the nature of the world tend to correspond in some domain. Charles Sanders Peirce, about a century ago, proposed a deus ex machina that was going to solve the problem: evolution. He argued that we had evolved in such a way that we were adapted to the real structure of the world. But this argument doesn't work at all. We have the ability to deal with problems of number theory and to discover quantum theory, yet these abilities were not a factor in evolution. We were adapted to deal with problems involving middle-sized objects in normal circumstances. For example, if humans weren't capable of guessing the trajectory of an object that was coming toward them, they would get into trouble. Those kinds of abilities just don't connect with the capacity to solve the problems in the scientific domains before us. So, there's no magical solution in evolution. It's just the case that if some aspect of the world happens to correspond to the structure of our intelligence as it's evolved, then a science will result; if not, then a science won't result.

The Innate Basis of Morality

If we were to hold Peirce's ideas about a one-to-one mapping between the world and our experience of it, we would lose Kant's distinction between the perceived world and the world as it is. It is frequently assumed that Kantian idealism is central to the Kantian conception of moral judgments. I know that you've discussed modularity and preformism as pointing toward a particular notion of morality. Could you discuss that?

First of all, let me say that a lot of what I've just said could be reformulated in Kantian terms. You could say that the structure of our experience and our understanding of experience is a reflection of the nature of our minds, and that we can't get to what the world really is. All we can do is develop constructs, and if they happen to work, more or less, and to provide what we might regard as insight and understanding, then we're satisfied with them.

As far as moral judgments are concerned, I think we're on pretty shaky ground. However, given what indications we have from anthropology and history and intuition and so on, it seems to me that there is reason to believe that there are biologically rooted principles entering into moral judgments. These principles are not obvious to us; we learn about them through experience. Our moral and ethical judgments, to a certain extent, grow out of those principles, although they are obviously heavily conditioned by various doctrinal systems with social and historical roots, and by perceived choices and available interpretations that are socially and historically conditioned. In fact, it's quite difficult to make any sense out of the things we actually do except under such an assumption. I think it's entirely natural for history to progress from a period when slavery is considered legitimate to a period when it isn't. But I think it would be surprising if history went in the other direction over a long term. It seems to me that, throughout history, it is quite common to find things that were regarded as entirely reasonable, ethical, and acceptable in earlier periods regarded with great contempt and disgust in later periods. This is very true of our own traditions. If you read the Bible, say, you find that it is one of the most genocidal texts in our literature. It's God who orders his chosen people to wipe out the Amalekites down to the last man, woman, and child. People wouldn't be enjoined to do that sort of thing today; they wouldn't want to attribute that to their God, today. That's a mark of some sort of moral progress. On the other hand, you can think of Nazism, which is not quite a sign of moral progress, to put it mildly.

Now what would be the relationship between the modularity thesis and moral judgments?

Let me stress again that it's not obvious. The evidence here is very slight and largely intuitive. However, I would tend to assume that there is some component of our intellectual system that involves moral judgments—judgments about what's right and wrong, or the way people should be treated, what's fair, what's just. I would assume or at least hope that there's some sort of what Bakunin once called an "instinct for freedom," that is a commitment to be free of the constraints of external authority except insofar as they're somehow required for survival in the particular stage of history. So, throughout history, there should be continual efforts to overcome authoritarian structures and to expand the domain of freedom. If that's true, and I think to some extent it is, it probably reflects instinctual patterns that are just part of our moral nature. We continue to learn more about them as history proceeds. So, for example, a little over a century ago, slavery was widely regarded as not only not wrong but even as highly ethical. If you read the justifications of slavery, they were often on ethical grounds. The argument was that it would have been improper to allow the slaves to be free. They were much better off if their owners were able to take care of them. The people who put this forth were civilized people, but now from our point of view, they're moral monsters. And, in fact, from the point of view of a natural morality, they were moral monsters, except that moral and cultural evolution had not reached the point where they could perceive that. I'm sure the same is true about us today. If history goes on for another hundred years, which is dubious, I imagine that people will be looking back to practices that we accept and condone and will regard them as morally monstrous. In fact, it is not difficult to point to some of them. For example, we now regard it as a moral monstrosity for one person to enslave another, but we regard it as proper and just for people to be compelled to rent themselves to others to be able to survive—what was once called "wage slavery." Someday we may come to appreciate that this too is an infringement on fundamental human rights—as, in fact, has long been argued in the libertarian socialist tradition. Similarly, the state system is based on principles of control, domination, and coercion that will, I hope, be regarded someday as morally intolerable. The same can be said about many domains of human existence.

Editor's Notes to Interview 35

This interview of Dec. 1, 1984, is the first of five (Interviews 35–36, 40–41 and 46) by David Barsamian, the first four of which were done in Boulder or from Boulder, Colorado. All five were reprinted four years later, in a different form, in Chomsky's *Chronicles of Dissent*, Common Courage Press / AK Press, 1992, pp. 1–161.) Some of the titles have been supplied, in consultation with Barsamian. Recordings of interviews and talks by Chomsky and by other people are made available by Alternative Radio (AR) to radio stations via satellite, some of which broadcast them. Information about linkages and about copies or transcripts is available from AR, P.O. Box 551, Boulder, CO 80306, 1-800-444-1977, www.alternativeradio.org.

Chomsky shares only in part the widespread belief that misuse or control of language is a central feature of what he calls "Orwell's problem" (see the last section of the Introduction and the Editor's Notes to I5).

On the conquest of the Western Hemisphere (which comes up again in interview 41), see the comment on Las Casas in the last section of the Introduction.

Chomsky's remark about National Public Radio is no longer literally true. He was interviewed on NPR's "All Things Considered" on March 30, 1988. See I35.

For the reference of Gregory P. Maximoff's "excellent detailed analyses of Leninist and Stalinist institutionalized terror going back to the Revolution" (published in 1940 and reprinted in 1979) and other references on the topic, see Introduction, n. 8.

KGNU (88.5FM), Boulder County Public Radio, committed to develop and strengthen alternative sources of information, was at the time celebrating "10 years of community radio."

For an important comment on Orwell's suppressed introduction to *Animal Farm*, see **P&P** (1996), ch. 3.

35. Politics and Language (1 December 1984)

Could you discuss the relationship between politics and language?

There is a tenuous relationship, in fact several different kinds. I think myself that they're exaggerated in importance. There is in the first place the question discussed, for example, by Orwell and by a number of others of how language is abused, tortured, distorted, in a way, to enforce ideological goals. A classic example would be the switch in the name of the Pentagon from the War Department to the Defense Department in 1947. As soon as that happened, any rational person should have understood that the United States would no longer be engaged in defense. It would only be engaged in aggressive war. That was essentially the case, and it was part of the reason for the change in terminology: to disguise that fact. One can go on to give innumerable examples of that sort. Perhaps the classic discussion of it is Orwell's "Politics and the English language."

There's also a more subtle and more interesting but even more tenuous connection which has to do with the fact that any stance that one takes with regard to social issues, for example, advocacy of some kind of reform or advocacy of a revolutionary change, an institutional change, or advocacy of stability and maintaining structures as they are—any such position, assuming that it has any moral basis at all and is not simply based on personal self-interest, is ultimately based on some conception of human nature. That is, if you suggest things should be reformed in this or that fashion and there's a moral basis for it, you are in effect saying: "Human beings are so constituted that this change is to their benefit. It somehow relates to their essential human needs." The underlying concept of human nature is rarely articulated. It's more or less passive and implicit and nobody thinks about it very much. But if the study of humans were ever to reach the point of a discipline with significant intellectual content (and we're very far from this), this concept would have to be understood and articulated. If we search our souls we find that we do have a concept, and it's probably based on some ideas about the underlying and essential human need for freedom from external arbitrary constraints and controls, a concept of human dignity which would regard it as an infringement of fundamental human rights to be enslaved, owned by others, in my view even to be rented by others, as in capitalist societies, and so on.

Those views are not established at the level of science. They're just commitments. They could be issues of scientific investigation, that is, humans are what

471

they are just as birds are what they are (you could find out what they are). At this point, the study of language may have some indirect relation, since ultimately it does investigate some fundamental components of human intelligence and their nature and is at least suggestive of what human cognitive faculties are ultimately like; in fact it's more than suggestive about that. One might draw some tenuous speculations about other aspects of human nature of a sort that I mentioned with regard to freedom from external constraints, to subordination to external power, etc. But that's a real long distance, a hope for the future more than any present reality.

Is freedom a linguistic imperative?

Just a superficial and obvious fact about human language is that it has an essentially creative aspect to it. Every normal human, independently of what we call "intelligence," over a huge range, apart from really severe pathology, quickly and with amazing rapidity, acquires a linguistic system which enables them to express and create new thoughts and to interact with others who also are creating and expressing new thoughts and to do it without bounds, though in a highly constrained fashion, in terms of a rule system that's relatively fixed in its character as part of essential human nature, but that does permit and facilitate free creative expression. That's **a fundamental aspect about human intelligence**. It apparently differentiates humans from any other organism that we know about. How much that extends to other domains is an area of speculation, but I think one can make some interesting guesses.

Could you address the notion that words, language, have inherent power, concepts convey meaning beyond their words? What is happening mechanically when certain phrases are used, such as "the free world" or "strategic interests" or "national interests"?

That's the usual topic that's discussed when people talk about politics and language, and I think it's worth discussing, but I think it's almost obvious to the point of banality. Terms like "the free world" and "the national interest" and so on are mere terms of propaganda. One shouldn't take them seriously for a moment. They are designed, often very consciously, in order to try to block thought and understanding. For example, about the 1940s there was a decision, probably a conscious decision, made in public-relations circles, to introduce terms like "free enterprise" and "free world" and so on instead of the conventional descriptive terms like "capitalism." Part of the reason was to insinuate somehow that the systems of control and domination and aggression to which those with power were committed here were in fact a kind of freedom.

That's just vulgar propaganda exercises. We are inundated with this every moment of our lives, and to the extent that many of us internalize it, one has to defend oneself against it, but once one realizes what's going on it's not very hard to do. When we consider that one of the major debates in the United States over the last 20 years has been whether the United States was right or wrong to have engaged in the defense of South Vietnam against North Vietnamese aggression (the doves say it was wrong and the hawks say it was right), anyone looking at this spectacle from the outside with even a little bit of sophistication would regard it as comic, because in fact what the United States was doing was attacking South Vietnam. That's why it's called the "defense" of South Vietnam.

We understand it at once when we look at an adversary, when we're separated from the situation. For example, if we looked at the Soviet Union and we find a discussion about whether the Soviet Union is right or wrong to defend Afghanistan from terrorists supported from without, we would just laugh. It's obvious that that's a way of covering up to themselves and to others the fact that they're attacking Afghanistan. But we're exactly the same in this respect, except probably more controlled by our own propaganda systems. Here, virtually without exception, the discussion is between those who oppose and those who support the defense of South Vietnam. There was no such event. There was simply an American attack against South Vietnam. Here the use of language—really the use of propaganda is what we should call it—which frames the discussion in terms of a conceptual framework which involves our "defense" of someone, that already wins the propaganda debate. It doesn't matter what conclusion one draws between the hawks and the doves. They're all on the same side. These are ways in which our intellects are dulled and our capacity for thought is destroyed and our possibility for meaningful political action is undermined by very effective systems of indoctrination and thought control that involve, as all such systems do, **abuse of language**. One can see this everywhere.

You have written, "Among the many symbols used to frighten and manipulate the populace of democratic states, few have been more important than terror and terrorism." Could you talk about that?

For example, for the last several years, something called "international terrorism" has been right at the front of the agenda. There are conferences about it, books, articles, etc. We were told when the Reagan administration came in that the struggle against international terrorism was going to be the centerpiece of their foreign policy, and it's continued that way. People debate as if they were in the real world. They're not in the real world. There is such a thing as international terrorism, and the United States is one of the main sponsors of it. For example, according to the official doctrine, the one that we discuss and the one that [then Secretary of State] George Schulz talks about, Cuba is one of the main centers of international terrorism.

The propaganda literature on this topic, meaning people like Claire Sterling and Walter Laqueur and others, basically commissars, even argues that the proof that Cuba is one of the centers of world terrorism, as a Soviet client, is that Cuba has never itself been subjected to terrorism. That's the standard line. The proof that the Communists are behind it all is that all the terrorism is in the so-called "free world." The fact of the matter is that Cuba has been subjected to more international terrorism than probably the rest of the world put together.

This began in the early 1960s when the Kennedy administration launched a major terrorist war against Cuba. It went on for many years (for all we know it's still going on). There's very little reporting on it. You have to work hard to find out what's going on from memoirs and participants' reports and so on. What has happened is a level of international terrorism that as far as I know has no counterpart, apart from direct aggression. It's included attacking civilian installations, bombing hotels, sinking fishing vessels, destroying petrochemical installations, poisoning crops and livestock (on quite a significant scale), assassination attempts, actual murders, bombing airplanes, bombing of Cuban missions abroad, etc. It's a massive terrorist attack. But this never appears in the discussions of international terrorism.

Or, for example, take the Middle East. The very symbol of terrorism is the PLO. What could be more an example of terrorism? The PLO has certainly been involved in terrorist acts, but Israel, which is our client, has been involved in far greater, incomparably greater terrorist acts—except that we don't call them terrorist acts. For example, in the spring of this year, four young Palestinians in the Gaza Strip, who live under conditions of extreme oppression, hijacked a bus and tried to drive it out of the Gaza Strip. They apparently didn't have weapons. The bus was stopped by Israeli soldiers and in the fire they killed an Israeli woman on the bus. The soldiers knew that the bus was hijacked because these Palestinians had allowed a pregnant woman to leave the bus, who then informed them, as a humanitarian act on their part. The people who hijacked the bus were captured. Two were killed at once and two were taken away and murdered, apparently after torture by Israeli soldiers. That's all described as an "act of Palestinian terrorism." There was an investigation of the murder of the two Palestinians by the Israeli army in custody but nothing ever came of it; there's been no prosecution. That's called "an act of Palestinian terrorism."

About the same time, Israel bombed an area in Balbek in Lebanon. According to the press reports, including American press reports, there were about 500 casualties, including approximately 200 children who were killed or wounded in an attack which destroyed a schoolhouse. That wasn't regarded as terrorism. Nobody ever referred to that as a terrorist act paid for by the United States, because of course they used American jets. That's just called an "unwise retaliatory strike" or something of that kind. This goes all the way back to the early 1970s, which was the high point of Palestinian terror attacks, and they were terror attacks, as in Maalot, etc. At that point, Israel was carrying out extensive bombardment of civilian targets in southern Lebanon to the extent that they actually drove out several hundred thousand people. That was never called terrorism.

To use the term "double standard" for our approach is to really abuse the term; it goes beyond anything that you could call a double standard. It's almost a kind of fanaticism. It's a reflection of the extreme success of indoctrination in American society. You don't have any other society where the educated classes, at least, are so effectively indoctrinated and controlled by a propaganda system.

Let's talk about that propaganda system. You've referred many times to the "state prop-
aganda apparatus." What role do the media play in promoting and serving state
interests?

One should be clear that in referring to the "state propaganda apparatus" here I do not mean that it comes from the state. Our system differs strikingly from, say, the Soviet Union, where the propaganda system literally is directed and controlled by the state. We're not a society which has a Ministry of Truth which produces doctrine which everyone then must obey at a severe cost if you don't. Our system works much differently and much more effectively. It's a privatized system of propaganda, including the media, the journals of opinion and in general including the broad participation of the articulate intelligentsia, the educated part of the population. The more articulate elements of those groups, the ones who have access to the media, including intellectual journals, and who essentially control the educational apparatus, they should properly be referred to as a class of "commissars." That's their essential function: to design, propagate and create a system of doctrines and beliefs which will undermine independent thought and prevent understanding and analysis of institutional structures and their functions. That's their essential social role.

I don't mean to say they're conscious of it. In fact, they're not. In a really effective system of indoctrination the commissars are quite unaware of it and believe that they themselves are independent, critical minds. If you investigate the actual productions of the media, the journals of opinion, etc., you find exactly that: a very narrow, very tightly constrained and grotesquely inaccurate account of the world in which we live.

The cases I mentioned in point are examples. There has never been more lively and extended debate in the United States, to my knowledge, than occurred over the war in Vietnam. Nevertheless, except for the very margins at the outside, the debate was entirely between those who were called "doves" and "hawks." Both the doves and the hawks began by accepting a lie so astonishing that Orwell couldn't have imagined it, namely, the lie that we were defending South Vietnam when we were in fact attacking South Vietnam. Once you begin with that premise, everything else follows.

Pretty much the same is true right now. Let's take the recent flap about the MIGs in Nicaragua. What was happening? The United States is sending advanced aircraft to El Salvador so that we are able to step up our attack on the population of El Salvador. The army that's carrying out this attack is really an occupying army, just like the Polish army is an occupying army of Poland, supported by a foreign power, except that the one in El Salvador is far more brutal and carrying out vastly more atrocities. We are trying to step up this attack by sending advanced aircraft and American pilots are now directly participating in controlling air strikes, etc. It's perfectly natural (any student of Orwell would expect) that we would accuse the other side of bringing in advanced aircraft. We're also conducting a real war against Nicaragua through a mercenary army.

They're called "guerrillas" in the press, but they're nothing like any guerrilla army that's ever existed. They're armed at the level of a Central American army. They often outgun the Nicaraguan army. They're completely supplied and controlled by a foreign power. They have very limited if any indigenous support, as far as anybody knows. It's a foreign mercenary army attacking Nicaragua, using Nicaraguan soldiers, as is often the case in imperial wars.

In this context, the big discussion is whether the Nicaraguans did or did not bring in aircraft which they could use to defend themselves. The doves say they probably didn't bring them in and therefore it was exaggerated. The doves also say, and here you can quote them (Paul Tsongas, for example, or Christopher Dodd, the most dovish senators in Congress) that if indeed the Nicaraguans did bring in jets, then we should bomb them, because they would be a threat to us.

When one looks at this, one sees something almost indescribable. Fifty years ago we heard Hitler talking about Czechoslovakia as a dagger pointed at the heart of Germany and people were appalled. But Czechoslovakia was a real threat to Germany, as compared with the threat Nicaragua poses to the United States. If we heard a discussion like this in the Soviet Union, where people were asking whether, let's say, Denmark should be bombed because it has jets which could reach the Soviet Union, we would be appalled. In fact, that's an analogy that's unfair to the Russians. They're not attacking Denmark as we're attacking Nicaragua and El Salvador. But here we accept it all. We accept it because the educated classes, the ones who are in a position, through prestige, privilege, education, etc., to present an intelligible understanding of the world, are so subordinated to the doctrinal system that they can't even see that two plus two equals four. They cannot see what's right in front of their eyes: that we are attacking Nicaragua and El Salvador, and that of course the Nicaraguans have every right to defend themselves against our attack. If the Soviet Union had a mercenary army attacking Denmark, carrying out terrorist acts and trying to destroy the country, Denmark would have a right to defend itself. We would agree with that. When a comparable thing happens in our domains, the only thing we ask is, Are they or are they not bringing in planes to defend themselves? If they are, then we have a right to attack them even more. That assumption is essentially across the board. There's virtually no voice in the press which questions our right to take even more violent action against Nicaragua if they're doing something serious to defend themselves. That's an indication of a highly brainwashed society. By our standards Hitler looked rather sane in the 1930s.

Let's talk a bit further about language and politics, specifically in the case of Nicaragua. The United States' ambassador to Costa Rica, Curtin Winsor, was quoted in the New York Times *as saying that "The Nicaraguan government has an extreme left network working for them in Washington. This is the same network that worked against American interests in Vietnam. It's sad to say that many Congressmen are prisoners of their own staffs, who rely on a preponderance of information from the Left." The ambassador then likens Nicaragua to Nazi Germany, and he makes this final statement that I'd particularly like you to address: "Nicaragua has become just like an infected piece of meat attracting these insects from all over," the insects being Libyans, Basque separatists, Cubans, the PLO, etc.*

All of this is very reminiscent of Nazi Germany. The ambassador's remarks are very typical of those produced by the Nazi diplomats at the same point, even in their style (the talk about "insects" and so on). Of course, what he describes is so remote from reality that it's superfluous even to discuss it. The idea of a leftist network in Washington is hilarious. What he would call "leftists" are people like Tsongas and Dodd. Those are precisely the kind of people he's referring to. The people who say that we should bomb Nicaragua if they do something to defend themselves. That's what to the ambassador is a leftist attempting to undermine our policy. This is like a discussion of true Nazi propaganda, which doesn't even make a pretense of being related to reality and regards any deviation from the most direct, extreme, unlimited attack as unacceptable. We have to have total conformity, from his view, to the position that we are permitted and justified in carrying out any act of subversion, aggression, torture, murder, etc., and any deviation from that position is, from his point of view, a leftist conspiracy directed from Moscow.

This is the extreme end of the propaganda system, and in fact it's not the important part, in my view. It's so crazy that anybody can see through it. The important part is the kind that doesn't seem so crazy, the kind that's presented by the doves, who ultimately accept not dissimilar positions. They accept the principle that we do have the right to use force and violence to undermine other societies that threaten our interests, which are the interests of the privileged, not the interests of the population. They accept that position and they discuss everything in those terms. Hence our attack of another country becomes "defense" of that country. Hence an effort by Nicaragua to acquire jets to defend itself becomes an unacceptable act that should evoke further violence on our part. It's that apparently critical position that plays the most significant role in our propaganda system. That's a point that's often not recognized. I think it's clearer if it's something that's a little more remote, so that we're not directly engaged in it now.

Let's take the Vietnam War. The major contribution to the doctrinal system during the Vietnam War period, in my view, is certainly the position of the doves. The doves were saying that we were defending South Vietnam (that's just a given), but that it was unwise, that it was costing too much, that it was beyond our capacity and beyond our power. If we're capable of thinking, we'll see that their position is very much like that of Nazi generals after Stalingrad, who said it was a mistake to get into a two-front war, and we probably won't carry it off, and this is probably an effort that should be modified and changed, though it is of course just and right. We don't consider the Nazi generals doves. We recognize what they are. But in a society in which that position is considered to be the dissenting, critical position, in that society the capacity for thought has been destroyed. It means the entire spectrum of thinkable thoughts is now caught within the propaganda system. It's the critics who make the fundamental contribution to this. They are the ones who foreclose elementary truth, elementary analysis, independent thought by pretending and being regarded as adopting a critical position, whereas in fact they are subordinated to the fundamental principles of the propaganda system. In my view that's a lot more important than the really lunatic comments that you just quoted.

What can people do to cut through this elaborate and ornamented framework of propaganda and get at what is real, get at the truth?

I frankly don't think that anything more is required than ordinary common sense. What one has to do is adopt towards one's own institutions, including the media and the journals and the schools and colleges, the same rational, critical stance that we take towards the institutions of any other power.

For example, when we read the productions of the propaganda system in the Soviet Union or Nazi Germany, we have no problem at all in dissociating lies from truth and recognizing the distortions and perversions that are used to protect the institutions from the truth. There's no reason why we shouldn't be able to take the same stance towards ourselves, despite the fact that we have to recognize that we're inundated with this, constantly, day after day. A willingness to use one's own native intelligence and common sense to analyze and dissect and compare the facts with the way in which they're presented is really sufficient.

If the schools were doing their job, which of course they aren't, but they could be, they would be providing people with **means of intellectual self-defense**. They would be devoting themselves with great energy and application to precisely the kinds of things we're talking about so that people growing up in a democratic society would have the means of intellectual self-defense against the system. That means that individuals have to somehow undertake this task themselves. I don't think it's really very hard. I think once one perceives what is happening and is willing to take the first step of adopting a stance that is simply one of critical intelligence towards everything you read (in this morning's newspaper or tomorrow's newspaper or whatever) and discover the assumptions that underlie it, analyze those assumptions, restate the account of the facts in terms that really are true to the facts, not simply reflections of the distorting prism of the propaganda system. Once one does that I think the world becomes rather clear. Then one can become a free individual, not merely a slave of some system of indoctrination and control.

Could you talk about the 20th-century nation-state? I know you've written extensively about it. What is it in its makeup that permits first genocide, and now what Edward Said called in an article in Harper's *the "phenomenon of refugees." Are these phenomena of the 20th-century nation-state? Would you accept those assumptions?*

I don't entirely. I think there's some truth to it, simply because the modern nation-state and the European model, that is, including the United States, happened to be by historical standards enormously powerful. The degree of power in the hands of a modern nation-state is something with no historical parallel. Also, this power is centrally controlled to a very high extent with a very limited degree of popular participation in how that power is exercised. Also, we have an awesome increase in the level of power and balance in the hands of the state, and as a result we have an enormous amount of violence. However, it's very misleading to think of, say, genocide as being a 20th-century phenomenon.

Let's just take our own history, the history of **the conquest of the Western Hemisphere**. At least in Massachusetts, we have a holiday called "Columbus Day," which we celebrate every year, and very few people are aware that they're celebrating one of the first genocidal monsters of the modern era. That's exactly what Columbus was. It's as if in Germany they would celebrate "Hitler Day." When the colonists from Spain and England and Holland and so on came to the Western Hemisphere, they found rich societies. Current anthropological work indicates that the number of native people in the Western Hemisphere may have approached something like 100 million (maybe about 80 million south of the Rio Grande and 12 million or so north of the Rio Grande). Within about a century, that population had been destroyed. Take just north of the Rio Grande, where there were maybe 10 or 12 million Native Americans. By 1900 there were about 200,000, and most of them were killed off very quickly. In the Andean region and Central America there were very extensive Indian societies, maybe something like 80 million people throughout the southern part of the continent south of the Rio Grande, and they're mostly gone. Many of them were just totally murdered or wiped out, others succumbed to European-brought diseases. This is massive genocide, and that's long before the emergence of the 20th-century nation-state. It may be one of the most, if not the most extreme example from history, but far from the only one. These are facts that we don't recognize. And the ways in which we protect ourselves from these facts are often quite astonishing.

Let me give you a personal example. This past Thanksgiving, last week, my family was here. We went for a walk in a national park not far from here. We came across a gravestone which had on it the following inscription, placed by the National Parks as a testimonial, in fact as a gesture, no doubt conceived as a liberal gesture toward the Indians in the past: "Here lies an Indian woman, a Wampanoic. She and her family gave of themselves and their land so that this great nation might be born and could grow." That is so appalling that one doesn't even know how to discuss it. She and her family didn't "give of themselves and their land," rather they were murdered by our forefathers and driven out of their land. It's as if 200 years from now you came to Auschwitz and found a gravestone saying, "Here lies a Jewish woman. She and her family gave of themselves and their possessions so that this great nation might grow and prosper." These things are so appalling one doesn't even know how to describe them. But these are reflections of what is regarded here as a liberal, accommodating, forthcoming attitude. That's what's appalling and frightening. For example, the very fact that we celebrate Columbus Day is appalling. All of these aspects of our historical experience, of the foundations of our own society, we are protected from seeing. Sometimes when they are described they are described in these unimaginable appalling ways. Again, these are all aspects of the system of indoctrination to which we are subjected. Looking at that gravestone, any person of even minimal common sense and just the most elementary knowledge of history should be totally appalled. But person after person passes it by and thinks it's fine. It's again an indication of a level of indoctrination which is quite frightening.

This raises the question of who controls history in our society.

History is owned by the educated classes. They are the people who are the custodians of history. They are the ones who are in universities and throughout the whole system of constructing, shaping and presenting to us the past as they want it to be seen. These are groups that are closely associated with power. They themselves have a high degree of privilege and access to power. They share class interests with those who control and in fact own the economic system. They are the cultural commissars of the system of domination and control that's very pervasive.

I'm avoiding nuances. There are important exceptions. There are people who write honest history. But the point I'm describing is something that is overwhelmingly dominant, to the extent that only specialists would be likely to know things that fall outside it. For the ordinary citizen, one that doesn't have the resources or the time or the training or the education to really dig into things deeply on their own, the position they're presented with is the one I've described. For example, you can have a gravestone like that. That's why we can talk about genocide as a 20th-century phenomenon, failing to recognize what happened not too far back in our own past.

Could you talk about what is called "the first genocide of the 20th-century," which occurred in 1915 in Ottoman Turkey to the Armenians. Why is that a virtually unknown event? Why is that relegated to the periphery of our awareness?

Essentially because people had very little interest in it at the time. What happened is that something between several hundred thousand, maybe over a million people, were massacred in a quite short time. It was in Turkey, remote, no direct interest to Westerners, and hence they paid very little attention to it.

I think much more dramatic and striking is the fact that **comparable genocidal acts** which are much closer to us, and in fact in which we have been directly involved, are suppressed. For example, I would wager that more people are aware of the Armenian genocide during the First World War than are aware of the Indonesian genocide in 1965 when 700,000 people were massacred within a couple of months, with direct participation of the United States. People were aware of it at the time and it was greeted with polite applause in the United States because it "returned Indonesia to the free world," as we described it at the time.

That genocide was used, including by American liberals, I should say, as justification for our war in Indochina. It was described as having provided a "shield" behind which these delightful events could take place. That's a much more striking fact than our casual attitude towards a genocidal attack on the Armenians 70 years ago.

That connects directly with a two-volume set that you co-authored with Edward Herman, The Washington Connection and Third World Fascism *and* After the Cataclysm. *You talk extensively about the events in 1965 in Indonesia and then the events in 1975, in East Timor [a former Portuguese colony in Indonesia, now, at long last, an independent country (since 1999)] …*

Which are still going on [in late 1984], incidentally. There's a case of genocide that's going on right today and is continuing precisely because the United States supports it. That's what blocks any possible termination of that genocidal attack. There's one right in front of our eyes for which we're directly responsible and there's virtually no awareness of it. I doubt if one person in 100 in the United States ever even heard of Timor.

Why is that? Does it serve some ideological interest that there's no information?

Sure. It's quite improper for people in the United States to know that their own government is involved in a genocidal massacre which is quite comparable to Pol Pot. Therefore they better not know about it, and they don't. This is particularly striking because it began, as you say, in 1975, just at the time that the Pol Pot massacres began. They're rather comparable in many ways, except that the Timorese massacre was carried out by an invading army rather than by a peasant revolutionary army taking revenge and controlled by a gang of fanatics who were carrying out huge massacres in their own society. These two are rather comparable in scale. Relative to the population, in fact, the Timorese massacre is maybe five times as great, once all the propaganda is filtered away and we look at the actual facts.

The treatment of them was quite different. The Pol Pot massacres received enormous attention, tremendous protest, this was compared to the Nazis. The Timorese massacre that we were responsible for was suppressed. People went way out of their way to try to find Cambodian refugees on the Thai-Cambodian border so that they could tell horror stories. They didn't go to Lisbon, which is much easier to reach than the Thai-Cambodian border, to talk to Timorese refugees who would tell them what the United States was backing in Timor.

That whole near-genocidal attack (the term is not exaggerated in this case) was almost entirely suppressed for over four years. Even today it's barely discussed, and when it is discussed, the American role is suppressed. For example, the *New York Times* finally began to talk about it and ran editorials. One was called "The Shaming of Indonesia." Sure, it's the shaming of Indonesia, but it's the shaming of the United States. We're the ones who blocked every diplomatic effort to stop it. The Carter administration, which was supposedly committed to human rights, vastly increased the flow of arms to Indonesia with the certain knowledge that they were going to be used to extend the massacre in East Timor (there was nothing else that they could be used for). None of this is the shaming of the United States. Nor is it the shaming of the *New York Times* that they didn't report it for four years (even today aren't reporting what's going on).

These are again ways of protecting ourselves from understanding of the world in which we live and function as agents. The population has to be protected from any understanding of that. That's one of the main purposes of the indoctrination system: to prevent the population from understanding what they are participating in indirectly through the institutions that they support.

And one sees, for example, in the case of the massacre and ongoing killings in East Timor, a certain sense of bipartisanship. It started under the Ford administration in 1975, it continued during the Carter years ...

It escalated during the Carter years. The worst period was the Carter period, and it's still continuing now. Last year there was another major Indonesian offensive. Once again the Red Cross has been withdrawn, so there's virtually no international observation. About the only information we're getting from it is refugees and the Catholic church. The church has been reporting these atrocities, but that virtually never reaches an American audience.

We should ask ourselves, why are our institutions so concerned to prevent us from knowing what we're doing? I think the reason for that is that the people in power are simply afraid of the population. What they're afraid of is if the general population has any awareness and understanding of what the state is up to, they'll protest and they'll stop it. That's why we have these extremely elaborate and very effective systems of thought control. Why don't they just tell us the truth? They don't tell us the truth because they're afraid of us. They're afraid that if we know we're going to stop them. Hence the lies. Hence the educational system. Hence the media. And so on.

Let's talk about what I reluctantly call "censorship." Perhaps you can find a better word for it here in the United States. Earlier I mentioned the two-volume set that you have co-authored with Edward Herman, The Washington Connection *and* After the Cataclysm. *Correct me if I'm mistaken, but I believe that neither of those books received any prominent media coverage or book reviews, and now you have a new book with the title* The Fateful Triangle, *which has only received two reviews. One can draw two conclusions: Either the books are indeed terrible and not worth writing about, or perhaps a more cynical point of view would be that there's some kind of censorship being exercised here.*

As to whether they're worth writing about, obviously I think so or I wouldn't have written them. We can make a kind of objective test of that. For example, we can ask how the same books are received in other societies similar to ours.

Take, say, Canada. Canada is a country very similar to the United States and has essentially the same values, institutions, social organizations, etc. Kind of like an adjunct to the United States. But as soon as we cross the border, we find that the treatment of these books and their authors is radically different than it is here.

For example, *The Fateful Triangle*, which came out about a year ago, is primarily concerned with American policy. It's peripheral to the interests of Canadians, but central to the interests of Americans. It was barely mentioned in the press here, and is very hard to find. You have to really work to dig it out somewhere. It's probably not in the libraries. But in Canada it was radically different. It was reviewed in every major journal. It was reviewed in most minor journals, even in the *Financial Post*, which is sort of like the *Wall Street Journal*. It was reviewed in the news weeklies, the equivalent of *Time* and *Newsweek*. Every time I go to Canada I'm immediately on Canadian radio and television. I was there last week for a day, and I had three interviews on national CBC.

In the United States, it's radically different. People with similar views, not just me, are marginalized, excluded, no reviews, no purchases of books, individuals can do it, but you rarely find such books in the libraries, media almost totally closed off. If we look at other countries similar to the United States, the same is true. In England and Australia, again countries very much like us, these books are widely reviewed, discussed, etc. Not in the United States, however. If the judgment is one of quality, then it's striking that the judgment is so different across the border. Incidentally, many of the reviews are quite critical, but that's fair enough. People say what they think.

Could you speculate why, for example, you're not on occasionally Dan Rather's "CBS Evening News" or National Public Radio's "All Things Considered." Has Noam Chomsky been marginalized, to use the very term that you've coined?

That's always been the case. For example, during the Vietnam War, when I was very visible in opposition to the war on the international scene, and here too, I live in Boston and I was constantly in the radio and television studios here. But always for foreign interviews. I think I was once on public radio in the Boston area during the Vietnam War. I had just returned from a trip to Indochina and I was on for about five minutes.

But I was constantly on Australian, Canadian, British, continental European television. That's constantly the case. Just in the last few weeks I've been on national Italian television, on Canadian television, on Irish radio, all over the place. In another couple of weeks I'm going to England for a day for a big television program discussing politics. This is constant and common. In the United States it's virtually unknown.

In fact it's very striking that I'm now talking over a Colorado radio station. When you get out of the main centers in the United States, out of New York, Boston and Washington, then the controls ease. For example, if I go to Denver or Boulder or Des Moines or Minneapolis or San Diego, then it's not at all unlikely that I'll be asked to talk on political topics on radio and sometimes television. But in the main ideological centers it's unimaginable. Again, that's not just me, it's other people who are essentially dissenting critics.

This reflects the sophistication of our ideological system. What happens in areas that are marginal with respect to the exercise of power doesn't matter so much. What happens in the centers of power matters a great deal. Therefore the controls are tighter to the extent that you get closer to the center. As soon as you cross the border to Canada, nobody really cares much what happens, so therefore it's much freer.

So essentially if, as you did last year, you come to Boulder and give many public lectures and appear on KGNU and now doing a phone interview on KGNU, that's OK since we're out here in the boondocks, as it were.

It's not totally OK, but it's better. It could never happen on National Public Radio.

One final question, about George Orwell. I sense from your writing and from some of the comments you've made in this interview that you feel a certain kinship with Orwell. Have you been influenced by him at all?

It's a little complicated. I think Orwell wrote one really great book which did influence me a lot. That was *Homage to Catalonia*. This is the book that he wrote about his experiences during the Spanish Civil War in the late 1930s.

Pro-Communist and "Pro-Israel" Intellectuals

The history of that book is itself interesting and revealing. It appeared in 1937. It was not published in the United States. It was published in England, and it sold a couple of hundred copies. The reason that the book was suppressed was because it was critical of Communists. That was a period when pro-Communist intellectuals had a great deal of power in the intellectual establishment. It's similar to the kind of control that many people called "pro-Israel" (although I think it's a bad term) have over media and expression today (they're similar in many respects). They succeeded in preventing Orwell's book from appearing. It did appear about 15 years later [in 1952], and it appeared as a Cold War tract because it was anti-Russian and fashions had changed. That was a really important book. I think there were things wrong with it, but I think it was a book of real great significance and importance. It's probably the least known of Orwell's major political books.

His better-known books in my view are not very significant. For example, *1984*, which is very popular here—in fact it's a major bestseller—because it can be easily construed as anti-Russian propaganda. But it's a very shallow book, basically. Orwell was giving a satirical analysis based upon existing Soviet society. Existing Soviet society and its terror have been very well described by factual analyses not very well known here, but they existed. People like Maximov, for example, the anarchist historian, had given excellent detailed analyses of Leninist and Stalinist institutionalized terror going back to the Revolution. You didn't have to go to Orwell and fantasy to find this out. Orwell's fictionalized account was in my view no contribution and also not very well done. I think it's a really tenth-rate novel. We also tend to suppress some of the aspects of it. He was actually talking about England, not Russia. He was talking about what he expected to happen in the industrial democracies, and as a prediction that was very bad, that hasn't happened.

I also think he missed the main techniques of thought control and indoctrination in the democracies. For example, in England and the United States we do not use for control the devices he described, crude vicious use of highly visible power. That's not the way thought control works here. It works by much more subtle and much more effective devices, the kinds we've been talking about. Orwell completely missed this. He didn't understand anything about it. So I think that *1984* is very much overrated.

On the other hand, he was an honest man. He did try to, and often succeeded in extricating himself from the systems of thought control, and in that respect he was very unusual and very praiseworthy. But the one great book that he wrote, in my view, is the one that I mentioned, *Homage to Catalonia*.

Bernard Crick, who is a British biographer of Orwell, seems to corroborate what you say. He suggests that it is in Orwell's essays, where "the dirty work of imperialism is illuminated," such as "A Hanging" and "Shooting an Elephant," that Orwell would be best remembered and the earlier mentioned "Politics and the English Language."

I agree with that. The famous works are the least significant.

Editor's Notes to Interview 36

This is the second Barsamian interview (see Editor's Notes to I35). It was recorded in March of 1985.

The book by Chomsky where the whole diplomatic record of Arab proposals is reviewed is of course the first edition of FT, mentioned in a subsequent question. The U.S. rejectionist stand (adopted by Israel) is a stumbling block to genuine peace Chomsky repeatedly refers to (interviews 38, 41, 49, 51, 55). See Editor's Notes to I55.

On Joan Peters' *From Time Immemorial* (1984) and on George Ball's position, see notes to interview 30. The book by Ball (see notes to interviews 30 and 39) referred to is *Error and Betrayal in Lebanon: An Analysis of Israel's Invasion of Lebanon and the Implications for U.S.-Israeli Relations*. Washington, D.C.: Foundation for Middle East Peace, 1984.

For an update on Sharon and its impact, see I56 and the Editor's Notes to it.

On Orwell, see Editor's Notes to I30.

36. Israel: The Strategic Asset (23 March 1985)

One of the most interesting aspects of the relationship between the United States and Israel is the fact that in this country there is virtually unanimous agreement on U.S. support for Israeli policies. To just cite one example, in the March 4, 1985, New York Times, Senator Daniel Inouye said, "[He] doesn't understand why administration after administration, Republican and Democrat, puts the squeeze on Israel. I am convinced that it is in our best national interest to make sure a strong, viable Israel continues to exert its influence in that part of the world." He continues, in asking for more aid for Israel, that "we have received more than our money's worth." I'd like you to discuss some of the factual and moral premises inherent in Inouye's comments about Israel and that it is in our best national interest.

I'd also like to comment about how we "put the squeeze on Israel." Since 1978 they've gotten something ranging between a third to a half of total American military and economic aid in the world. That's a country of 4 million people, so the concept of the "squeeze" is interesting.

A "Strategic Asset": A Kind of an Attack Dog

I think it's clear what Inouye means, and there's some logic to it. Israel has served certain kinds of American interests, and the aid to Israel is closely correlated to the American conception of how they can serve American interests. What the United States wants from Israel is that it become a technologically advanced, highly militarized society without any independent or viable economy of its own so that it's totally dependent on the United States and therefore dependable. We maintain it in a position, our policy is designed to create a system of dependence with a capacity for organized violence so that we can use it as what we call a "strategic asset," which means a kind of an attack dog. It's what was called under the Nixon doctrine a "guardian of the Gulf," a force which can be used either as a base for projection of American military force or its own military force in the case of any conceived threat to quite narrowly perceived American interests in the region, the main interest being to ensure that there's no development of what we call "radical nationalism," where radical nationalism is a technical term which means nationalist forces that don't obey American orders. It's counterposed to "moderate nationalism," which means nationalism that does follow American orders.

The Largest and Cheapest Energy Resources in the World

The major American interest in the region is of course not Israel but the energy resources which, it's been known for 40 or 50 years, are the largest and cheapest in the world, and we want to make sure that there's no indigenous threat to our domination of that system.

In the early years we assumed that our own power could achieve that result, but increasingly over the years, as the world has become more complex and the American capacity to intervene directly has been reduced, the United States has turned to surrogates. This became more or less formalized in the Nixon-Kissinger doctrine, which quite explicitly explained that while the United States would be committed to maintaining what Kissinger called the "overall framework of order," regional powers would pursue particular goals within this system. That meant it was a matter of designating the "local cop on the beat" to control the neighborhood, while police headquarters remains in Washington. That's in effect the Nixon-Kissinger doctrine.

With regard to the extremely crucial Middle East region (primarily the Gulf and the Arabian Peninsula, where most of the oil is), the conception was that Israel and Iran under the Shah would be what was then called "guardians of the Gulf." That's the primary basis for this enormous military support, which has the predictable consequence of turning Israel into a kind of Sparta, essentially eliminating its status as a viable society other than as a military force. It's a kind of Spartan military force designed to serve American interests in the region. Correspondingly, Israel is also expected to provide subsidiary services. That's part of the quid pro quo.

This began in the 1960s as Israel began to be framed in the American geopolitical conception as a strategic asset in this sense. In the 1960s, under a large CIA subsidy, Israel penetrated black Africa, in the interests of American power. They were, for example, the main force that succeeded in establishing the Mobutu dictatorship in Zaire. They supported Idi Amin in Uganda in the early days, Haile Selasse in Ethiopia, Emperor Bokassa in the Central Africa Republic, and various others who the United States was trying to cultivate and use for its Latin Americanization of Africa, the establishment of dependable client regimes, generally military-based, which would be assured to control the local societies.

Increasingly, these secondary services have moved elsewhere, however, primarily Latin America. During the 1970s, under popular pressure, Congress legislated human rights constraints which restricted the American executive in its attempts to support the worst murderers and monsters in Latin America. Therefore they had to move, under the Carter administration, and since under the Reagan administration, to do it indirectly using surrogates. Israel was able to establish close relations with the neo-Nazi regimes in the Southern Cone, Argentina and Chile, and that's in the American interest, since the United States had to sidestep direct support for them. In Central America the United States relied primarily on Argentine Nazis, but increasingly, and by now primarily, on

Israeli forces to support, for example, genocidal attacks on the Indian population in Guatemala or to send arms to El Salvador and Honduras to support the Contras. This is a long and very ugly story, and that's a secondary aspect to the services that Israel is expected to provide for us. All of this is in the public record.

A Barrier to "Nationalist Pressure"

If we speculate about what's in the secret record, the United States has major conventional military forces aimed at the Persian Gulf. It's called the Central Command; it used to be called the Rapid Deployment Force. The idea is that if any unwanted nationalist developments take place in that region, we'll invade. But we need a basing system for that, and we have by now a very elaborate basing system stretching from Turkey all the way around the region to the Indian Ocean. Though there is no public document on this, it's a fair guess, a near certainty, that Israel is regarded as a central part of that basing system.

Much of what I have just said is not only obvious from the way history has evolved but it's expressed in the declassified record. For example, you can see how the American relation to Israel has changed over the years. In the early 1950s it was rather cool and conflicted. In 1956 we ordered Israel out of the Sinai after it had attacked Egypt, the reason being that it had attacked Egypt jointly with France and England (we were then referring to France and England as essentially our enemies). They were attempting to reassert a position from which we had expelled them because we wanted to control that region ourselves. Israel, in its attack on Egypt jointly with them, was essentially conspiring with the enemy, so we threw them out.

In the early 1950s, at least, it wasn't clear who the United States was going to use as the basis for its regional power. There was some support for using Nasser's Egypt for this purpose. Nasser had some CIA backing at the time and other support. By the mid-1950s it became pretty clear that Nasser was going to be a radical nationalist, that is, he wasn't going to follow American orders, and Nasserite influence began to spread throughout the region. By 1958 a National Security Council memorandum on the Middle East concluded that "a logical corollary to our opposition to radical Arab nationalism would be support for Israel as the only reliable pro-Western force in the region." Through the 1960s this increased. American intelligence through the 1960s regarded Israel as a barrier to "nationalist pressure" (Nasserite pressure) in the Arabian Peninsula, and there was a kind of proxy war going on in the southern part of the Peninsula between Egypt and Saudi Arabia. Israel was regarded as a shield protecting the monarchies which controlled the oil and very much subordinated to the United States.

Israel's 1967 victory, which really showed that it was the overwhelmingly dominant military force in the region, confirmed its value as a strategic asset. The United States certainly supported Israel in that attack and may actually have participated in it. There's evidence to that effect. It certainly supported it. At that point American aid to Israel increased enormously and it seemed like Senator

Inouye and others of that type recognized that this could be a valuable military force.

In 1970, American aid to Israel quadrupled, the reason being that Israel had succeeded in doing something that we desperately needed at that time. There was concern that Syria might intervene in Jordan to protect Palestinians, who were at that point being massacred by the Jordanian army. The United States was very much concerned about that and regarded it as a potential threat to the oil-producing region. Israel was able to use its overwhelming military force to block any possible Syrian support for the Palestinians and American aid shot up. It was at that point that the Nixon doctrine was explicitly formulated and Israel's role was more or less formalized regarding the Gulf. When the Shah fell in 1979, Iran lost that role, plainly, and Israel was left the sole reliable militarized base for the United States. Again, aid to Israel shot up enormously at that point.

The "Peace Process": A Strictly Orwellian Term

At that time we also carried through what is called here the "peace process," which is kind of an Orwellian term, referring to the fact that we instituted a system whereby Egypt was totally excluded from the conflict, the Camp David agreements, and the intent and consequences of that policy were to leave Israel free to extend and intensify its occupation of the occupied territories and also to attack its northern neighbor without any concern for a deterrent force. That's exactly what happened from 1978. The first invasion of Lebanon was in 1978. The repression and expansion of settlement in the occupied territories increased rapidly. Israel continued to attack Lebanon, and in 1982 it invaded directly, and we know the consequences since. All of this flowed quite predictably and directly from the Camp David process, which just played this role which we here called the "peace process," a strictly Orwellian term. That again is part of the whole system of turning Israel into a militarized state. That's exactly what's happened.

By now it's probably the most militarized society in the world. It has probably the highest per capita debt in the world. Its status as an economic entity, for example, is reflected in its credit ratings with international banks, which is below that of Mozambique or Bangladesh, and that's even with the huge American subsidies. Increasingly it's undergoing the kind of internal changes, cultural changes and others, which follow from this debt. This is related to the reason why the United States has consistently blocked any possibility of a diplomatic settlement. There have been many possibilities, at least since 1971, for a peaceful political settlement. The United States has consistently blocked all of them because they would require that Israel be a peaceful member of a region in which relations are conducted by diplomacy rather than violence, and we won't accept that. That won't be the role that we want Israel to play.

Virtually all of this has been very easily documented. I've written about it, there's plenty of material, but it's almost totally suppressed and distorted in the official versions. We talk about the "peace process" and "Israel's search for peace," etc. That's the real story. How much Senator Inouye actually understands of what he's saying, I don't know. But the people who do the actual planning surely understand this, and it's this evolving conception of Israel's strategic role in the region which accounts for its enormous and rather special kind of subsidy that we provide for it, one that's guaranteed to maintain it as a military force and to maintain a situation of military confrontation in the region, which is part of this whole thing.

Indeed, the Camp David process has kind of entered the popular mythology. It has a Nobel Peace Prize mystique about it and we celebrate it as a model, as the proper vehicle for settlement of the Arab-Israeli dispute. Senator John Kerry, in Denver, on March 16, 1985, said that he favored "a return to the Camp David process." Why is Camp David so firmly established as the model?

That's an indication of the marvelous effectiveness of the American indoctrination system. Let's recall what Camp David was. Camp David was an agreement whereby Israel left the Sinai and foreign forces, including American, were placed in the Sinai to ensure that that's not an area of military confrontation. That, in effect, excluded Egypt from the conflict. That's the only thing that was done in Camp David, to exclude Egypt from the conflict. Egypt is the major Arab military force. If Egypt is excluded from the conflict, as in fact they wanted to be, that means that there is no deterrent to Israel's doing whatever it feels like doing. What it felt like doing was obvious: it felt like moving towards taking over and integrating the occupied territories and harassing the northern border, expanding towards the north. It has continued to do that until it suffered its first military defeat in the last couple of months at the hands of the Lebanese resistance. They are well aware of that. Up until that point it was just regular expansion towards the north. In order to ensure that they would do this effectively, we massively increased military aid to Israel at the same time, 1978–79. The fall of the Shah was a side element in this that left Israel the sole reliable guardian of the Gulf.

Apart from that, this American aid reached enormous proportions. In 1979 it was something like 50 percent of total American aid overseas. It was completely obvious what this was going to mean. What was in Jimmy Carter's mind I have no idea, but it was obvious to any rational person that if you free Israel from any deterrent force by eliminating the only substantial Arab military force in the region, and if you then provide it with enormous subsidies, which incidentally are unspecified. In the case of every other aid program in the world, it's project-oriented: we require specific indications of what the aid is going to be used for. Usually it has to be used for purchase of American exports or something like that, but it's closely supervised. For example, in Egypt, which is the next largest aid recipient, we have something like 125 technicians supervising the aid down to the last detail and making sure it's used for exactly the project we want it used for. Israel, uniquely, with the aid which is unbelievable in scale per capita, off the chart, also happens to be unsupervised. It's just a cash grant. We're telling them, "Do whatever you like with it." That's a not too subtle way of telling them, "Use it for settlement of the occupied territories, use it for military attacks against Lebanon, etc."

"Terror": Resistance by Another Name

That was perfectly predictable, and furthermore it's exactly what happened. Even people who couldn't see it at the time can look back now and see that that's what happened. The expansion into the occupied territories, which had been going on for ten years at that point, then increased very rapidly, it just shot up. Also, the repression in the occupied territories increased. The military occupation, which had always been harsh, became much more brutal, especially in 1981 and 1982. And Israel attacked Lebanon. It invaded Lebanon in 1978. Through 1979 there was heavy bombardment against Lebanon, with hundreds, maybe thousands of people killed. Israel repeatedly broke cease-fires to initiate attacks against Lebanon. In July 1981, in one important case, Israeli planes broke a cease-fire, attacked Lebanon. There was at that point a light rocket response, at which time Israel stepped up the attacked and bombed Beirut, killing several hundred people. After that there was a heavier rocket response against the northern Galilee, and even heavier Israeli bombings. These were finally stopped by an American-imposed cease-fire in late July. At the time it was stopped, about 450 Arabs and 6 Israelis had been killed, which are normal proportions reflecting the power balance.

The only thing that's remembered from all that today is that rockets were fired at northern Galilee. That's in the news reports; that's always cited now as a justification for Israel's attack on Lebanon. Yes, rockets were fired on northern Galilee in response to heavy Israeli bombing which killed hundreds of civilians. After this point, the PLO did adhere to the cease-fire scrupulously, there were no attacks across the Lebanese border for 11 months or so. Israel, on the other hand, attempted throughout that period, 1981–82, to elicit some kind of PLO action which could be used as an alleged provocation, a pretext for the further attack on Lebanon, which they began planning in July 1981.

Again, this was completely predictable. The American press either couldn't or pretended not to be able to see it, but it was obvious at the time. Throughout 1981 and 1982 that's exactly what happened. There were repeated Israeli provocations, including bombing of Lebanese towns, in an effort to elicit some kind of action, maybe shelling of the north or something, which could be used as a pretext for the invasion that they had been planning. When no pretext could be found, they simply concocted one and invaded in June 1982, with full American support, incidentally. That was the Lebanese war. After that they attempted to consolidate their position in Southern Lebanon and in fact would have done so had it not been for the Southern Lebanese resistance, what is here called "terror." All of that is the Camp David "peace process."

A Consistent Attempt at a Real Peace Process

It's an interesting fact about our own propaganda system that these elementary facts can't be perceived, just as in the Soviet Union, I suppose, the propaganda system pretends or just can't see that the Soviet Union is engaged in severe repression in Eastern Europe and an invasion of Afghanistan. They just can't see it, or at least can't say it. Comparably, we don't see or can't say these things here. I should mention that one might ask, or any reporter who's even moderately serious would ask, What is the attitude of the indigenous population in the occupied territories? We know that. For example, there are Israeli-run polls concerning the Camp David peace process. It turns out that the population overwhelmingly, over 90 percent, regards the Camp David peace process as detrimental to their interests. It's obvious why. The peace process is just a way of unleashing Israel to extend its repression and take over the occupied territories as well as the attacks on Lebanon. Again, American reporters either can't or pretend not to be able to see that, and that includes commentators here.

A final comment that should be made about this is that on the part of this "peace process" there has been a consistent attempt, which the United States has blocked, on the part of the Arab states and the Europeans to initiate a real peace process. That began clearly in February 1971, when President Sadat of Egypt offered Israel a full peace settlement. In his proposal there was nothing offered to the Palestinians at all, they were simply ignored. The full peace settlement was to be on the internationally recognized borders, the pre-1967 borders, with recognized borders, guaranteed security, etc. Israel refused it because they wanted to take over the territories. This was the dovish Labor government at the time. The United States backed them in that refusal. That's remained constant until today.

For example, just about a year ago Arafat offered Israel negotiations leading to mutual recognition. Of course, Israel immediately rejected it. The United States didn't even bother to respond. This was virtually blacked out of the American media. Today it's as if it didn't exist. In between that period are numerous similar cases where the United States has vetoed peace offers at the UN that came from Syria, Jordan, Egypt and the PLO and called for a two-state settlement, which everyone recognizes is the only peaceful settlement, which guaranteed recognized borders, etc. Repeatedly over the years the United States has refused to accept any genuine peace offer. So there is something that we might call the "peace process" except that it's been aborted by the United States and of course rejected by Israel consistently. It's out of history, it just doesn't exist. For example, when the *New York Times* runs a news story reporting on the history of peace efforts, as it did a couple of days ago by Thomas Friedman, their reporter in Jerusalem, none of this is mentioned, it's just down the memory hole. The only thing that exists is the American-run system, the Camp David system, which we call the peace process, which in fact is just a war process.

You've said that the United States and Israel have stood in the way of an international settlement, basically on racist grounds. Although they accept the right of Israel to be a national state, primarily for Jews, they do not accept that the indigenous population has a parallel right. Could you talk about that?

I think the American position is strictly racist, there's no question about it. There are two national groups which claim the right of national self-determination in what was once Palestine: there is an indigenous population, the Palestinians, and there are the settlers who partially replaced them, namely the Jewish immigrants. We accept without any question the right of the Jewish immigrants to national self-determination in Palestine and therefore we unequivocally support Israel as an expression of that national right. However, we deny a comparable right to the indigenous population. Our current position, for example, is that we will only agree even to talk to Palestinians, the indigenous population, if they're not associated with the PLO. The PLO is plainly the organization which they recognize as the expression of their national rights. There's no doubt about this.

More Support than the Zionist Organization Had

Returning to these Israeli-run polls, something like 98 percent of the population in the occupied territories calls for an independent Palestinian state, that's what they want. Something like 86 percent of them in the latest Israeli-run poll want it to be run solely by the PLO. The rest want to see it run largely by the PLO. The same is true in Palestinian diaspora. That's more support than the Zionist organization had among Jews in the 1940s. If in the 1940s the United States government had said, Yes, we'll be willing to talk to Jews about Palestine, but only if they're not connected with the Zionist organization, and of course not permitting any Jewish state, that would have been regarded as racist, and correctly, to say, We'll talk to the Jews but not to the Zionists, to say, We'll talk to the Jews but we don't allow you your own choice of national expression. I should say that the Jewish world was divided over this issue. To refuse to talk to the PLO today is to take the same stand. Again, it's kind of remarkable that American commentary cannot perceive the extraordinary racism of this position.

I should mention that this racism shows up elsewhere as well. Take the way in which we react to what's happening today in southern Lebanon. The American commentary regards it as quite legitimate for the Israeli occupying army to use violence to suppress resistance. In fact, here it's sometimes even called "terror against terror," which is a term that's chilling. That's the name of an organization set up by Klaus Barbie in France to attack the French resistance. We use it without any qualms to refer to what's going on in southern Lebanon, except we support it. Even when it reaches the point of Israel murdering CBS reporters, as happened a couple of days ago, the president gets on television and says, This is perfectly fine, they were just doing it in self-defense, etc. There's no comment on this in the press as yet.

Again, take the commentary on Israel's forced withdrawal from the south (it is being forced to withdraw because of local resistance). There are anguished stories in the media about the traumatic consequences for the people of northern Galilee, who will once again be under rocket fire from Lebanon. The border was completely peaceful for a year before Israel attacked, and the rocket fire, as I mentioned, was in retaliation to Israeli bombing. Murder of Arabs is considered a perfectly legitimate occupation. Israel killed dozens, maybe hundreds of local people, Lebanese, in its so-called "iron fist" operations in the last months, including real terrorist acts like breaking into hospitals, taking people away who are trying to give blood to people wounded in Israeli attacks, beating up a hospital director, real barbarism. That's considered legitimate. It's their right to use military force in another country to suppress the local population.

This is just another aspect of the same racism. It shows up quite dramatically in our diplomatic stance, our refusal to recognize that the indigenous population has the rights that we naturally accord to the Jewish settlers who immigrated to the country. It's even reached the point that in the United States there's a pretense that the indigenous population didn't exist. There's a rather comical incident in the last year that involves a completely fraudulent book by Joan Peters which became a bestseller in the United States, virtually every review of it here was extremely laudatory. The book claims that the Palestinians didn't exist. It's a concoction of lies and distortions. As soon as the publishers made a tactical error and allowed it to appear in England where the intelligentsia are not so totally controlled on this issue, it was immediately blasted out of the water. Every review pointed out grotesque errors and ridiculous fabrications. But here it was accepted as Gospel truth because it says what we want to hear. If the Palestinians didn't exist, that justifies our racist attitudes towards them.

June 1985 is the third anniversary of the "Peace for Galilee," the Israeli invasion of Lebanon. What has Israel accomplished in Lebanon?

It accomplished quite a bit. We can look at their own statements.

Not a Military but a Political Danger

For example, Prime Minister Shamir pointed out that Israel faced a real danger in Lebanon before 1982. He then went on to explain that it was not a military but a political danger, that the PLO had scrupulously adhered to the cease fire and had increased its attempts to lay the basis for a political settlement, and that's a danger, because if there is to be a political settlement and the Palestinians are to be recognized as participants, then Israel will not be able to maintain its control over the occupied territories and will have to settle for peace and peaceful integration into the region, which it does not want to do. So there was a political danger, as Shamir pointed out. One of the best Israeli journalists, a well-known Israeli satirist, B. Michael, had an article right after Shamir's statement in which he stated, "Thank God there's no one to talk to." Israel did succeed in eliminating this political threat. The attack on the Palestinians, which meant the destruction of organized Palestinian society (the purpose of the war), that was successful. Organized Palestinian society was destroyed, the PLO was somewhat marginalized, and the danger of a political settlement was reduced.

Israel had further goals, larger goals beyond that, namely to essentially take over Lebanon and install there what they called a "new order," which would mean a client regime based on right-wing Christians and selected privileged Muslim elites. This is sometimes called Sharon's plan, and now people denounce it because Sharon was so terrible. But it should be remembered when it looked as though that plan was going to be successful, in late August 1982, after the bombing of Beirut, the popular support for it in Israel was enormous, support for Likud, Begin and Sharon reached about 80 percent, which was totally unprecedented in Israel. After the savage bombings of Beirut and after the destruction of southern Lebanon, it was only when the plan began to fall apart that opposition developed. That was the large plan, namely the establishment of a client state based on those Christian and selected Muslim elements. That failed. They were unable to do that, for a number of reasons, one of them being the intense resistance in the south.

In fact, in the south Israel has suffered its first military defeat ever. It has been compelled by local resistance to partially withdraw from southern Lebanon. I don't believe it really intends to withdraw, what they're intending to do is to hold on to as much of southern Lebanon as they can, and that will take violence, because the local population does resist. But they'll do that. There may be moves towards trying to depopulate southern Lebanon if that's necessary, as they did along the Jordan Valley in the late 1960s. They'll maintain a foothold there, I would imagine, at least if the United States supports them.

Can you talk about the problems discussing Israeli policies in the United States without being labeled "anti-Semitic." You, for example, speak out frequently, and you've written many books. Have you personally encountered any difficulties?

I can't be called "anti-Semitic," because I'm Jewish, so there's another label that's used. There are two labels that are used by people who call themselves "supporters of Israel." Actually they are **the real enemies of Israel**. They're supporting the development of what I have described, the development of a militarized, unviable society geared towards war and subservient to American interests, that's not support for Israel in any meaningful sense. People who call themselves "supporters of Israel" have two categories with which they try to silence criticism. One is "anti-Semite," the other is "self-hating Jew." That takes care of everyone. You're either an anti-Semite or a self-hating Jew if you don't follow the party line strictly.

I should say that these tactics run across the board, so it's not just right-wing extremist Israeli circles, or supporters of Israel here that adopt that position, but also people like Abba Eban, a Labor dove, who have explicitly stated that the task of Israeli agitprop is to make it clear that any criticism of Israel is either anti-Semitism or the position of self-hating Jews, some comment like that. In the

United States a rather effective system of intimidation has been developed to silence critique.

Let me just give you one example. Take the Anti-Defamation League of the B'nai Brith, which is reputed to be a civil rights organization. It's rather comical. It's actually an organization devoted to trying to defame and intimidate and silence people who criticize current Israeli policies, whatever they may be. I myself, through a leak in the New England office of the Anti-Defamation League, was able to obtain a copy of my file there. It's 150 pages, just like an FBI file, interoffice memos warning that I'm going to show up here and there, surveillance of talks that I give, comments and alleged transcripts of talks, of the sort that you'd expect mostly fabricated because people don't hear or can't understand, this material has been circulated, if I'm going to give a talk somewhere, if I came out to Boulder to give a talk, this material would be sent to some local group which would use it to extract defamatory material which would then be circulated, usually in unsigned pamphlets outside the place where I'd be speaking. I happened to get this material when it was being sent to a Harvard law professor named Alan Dershowitz in preparation for a debate that we were to have a few days later, so that he would be able to extract from it defamatory material concocted by the Anti-Defamation League surveillance system, which is in fact exactly what he did.

This is typical of the way they act. If there's any comment in the press which they regard as insufficiently subservient to the party line, there'll be a flood of letters, delegations, protests, threats to withdraw advertising, etc. The politicians of course are directly subjected to this, and they are also subjected to substantial financial penalties if they don't go along. The Israeli press is very open about this. For example, after the last election, there was an article in one of the major Israeli journals by a very good journalist named Yaof Karney. The headline of the article was actually a pun. It reads in Hebrew "Jewish Money Buys the Vote," but it could also be read as "Jewish Money Buys Everything." That was the headline. Then came a report of a speech by Thomas Dine, head of the Israeli lobbying group in Washington, AIPAC [American Israel Public Affairs Committee], in which he just gloated over the successes of the Jewish political lobby, the Israeli political lobby here, in controlling the American congressional elections. He said that their major achievement was to eliminate Senator Charles Percy, who was too critical of Israel. He went on to say that they felt that now they had, by judicious election wins and victories, Congress in their pocket until the year 2000. If this appeared somewhere in the United States it would be regarded as some kind of fanatic, anti-Semitic publication, sort of like the Protocols of the Elders of Zion. But this is a Hebrew article in the Hebrew press.

I should mention that the journalist was appalled by all of this. He said it was a real threat to American democracy. But here the Israeli lobbying groups regard it as a great success and they are quite proud of it, though, of course, they don't publicly say the things that they say privately. This is a very effective system, particularly since there's no counterweight to it. There's no pressure on the other side.

There is a very broad international consensus, and there has been for many years, over a political settlement to the dispute. It's essentially a two-state settlement which would recognize the national rights of both Jews and Palestinians. It's supported by most of the world. It's blocked by the United States, which leads the rejectionist camp. But the point is that there's no articulate voice here expressing anything like the international consensus, or there's no articulate voice here opposing repression and atrocities conducted quite freely by Israel, which encourages them to go on and do more of it. That's one of the reasons why they're capable of such really barbaric actions in south Lebanon. They've never been criticized in the past, why should it begin now? There's occasional criticism when things really get out of hand, like the Sabra-Shatila massacres, but that's quickly silenced and things return to their norm. This totally one-sided pressure and this, by now, very effective system of vilification, lying, defamation, and judicious use of funds in the political system, that has created a highly biased approach to the whole matter, which is why the United States can continue to block a political settlement, to maintain a system of military confrontation, a very dangerous one, one which repeatedly threatens global war, and do it with complete impunity. There's no internal criticism here.

What about genuine Israeli fears? You're quite familiar with the level of lexical violence from Arabs and others talking about Israel as a "cancer in the Middle East" that needs to be "exterminated" and "eliminated."

First of all, I'm not familiar with those, because they're mostly fabricated. They did exist, primarily in the 1960s, but since early 1970, most of the Arab world has been quite willing to reach an accommodation with Israel. This was explicit in the case of Egypt in 1971, also Jordan in 1971 made a similar proposal. I don't want to bother going through the whole diplomatic record here, I reviewed it in a book not too long ago. Through the 1970s there were repeated Arab offers, Egypt, Syria, the PLO, Saudi Arabia and others, to arrange for a political settlement in accord with the international consensus. There is talk about a "cancer," and so on, but that typically comes from Israeli sources. Israel typically refers to the PLO as a "cancer" which is "metastasizing" and a "disease which has to be stamped out," etc.

Gideon Hausner said that.

Yes, who was the prosecutor in the Eichmann trial, the person who used this terminology which is in fact rather reminiscent of Eichmann himself. However, I wouldn't downplay the threat to Israel, I think it's real. As long as military confrontation persists, Israel is in real danger of destruction, there's no doubt about that. My own feeling is that they're heading for destruction. They happen to be the dominant military force in the region now, but there's no guarantee that that will persist. In a system of continued and unending military confrontation, sooner or later they're going to lose. Military intelligence is a very low-credibility operation. It rarely knows what it's talking about. Modern history shows that quite well. They may think that they're in a position of military dominance, and they may find that they're wrong. Unexpected things do happen in the case of war. They came close to being destroyed in 1973 after two years of rejecting Sadat's peace offers. However, they have not learned the lesson from that. The lesson plainly is that if they want to maintain control of the occupied territories and they want to keep harassing the northern border, then they're going to be in a situation of permanent military confrontation. That's going to mean repeated chance of war and sooner or later destruction. So the threats are very real, except that I think that by now a lot of these threats are self-generated.

A central thesis of your book The Fateful Triangle, *is that although the United States claims to be the friend of Israel, the policy it's pursuing will ultimately destroy it.*

I think that's true. I think it's even more dramatically true of the people who call themselves supporters of Israel. I should say that this view is shared very widely by the small group of Israeli doves. They put things in terms much more extreme and harsh than I would use. For example, take Meir Pail, who's a real member of the Israeli establishment. He's a retired colonel, a well-known military historian, formerly a leading military strategist in the army. He was head of the officer's training school in the Israeli army, so straight out of the establishment. He had an article about a year ago in which he was attacking the American Jewish community. I think he was targeting it too narrowly, but what he said was that, the title of the article was "Zionism and the Danger of Cancer." He said that the danger was coming from the American Jewish community, that what they want is an Israel which is a "war god similar to Mars." They get their psychological thrills from seeing Israel, a superman, stomping on people's faces.

He went on to say that the attitude of the American Jewish community and their monolithic support for these tendencies in Israel and their intolerance of any discussion and debate of them are going to create an Israel which "will be a new development in political history, a combination of the worst features of South Africa and Northern Ireland." He virtually pleaded with the American Jewish community to stop what they call support for Israel, which is, in fact, driving it in this direction. As I say, those are terms much more extreme than I would use, and they come from a mainstream Israeli establishment figure who happens to be a dove. I think he's much too narrowly focused when he talks about the American Jewish community. That's what they tend to see. In fact, the support for that kind of policy in the United States is only very partially based on the American Jewish community. It's far broader than that.

There seems to be much more pluralism and political diversity in Israel on some of these issues than in the United States itself.

There's no doubt of that. For the Jewish population of Israel, let's put aside the Arab citizens, it achieves a level of democracy that's well beyond that of the United States. These issues in particular are commonly debated in Israel. In the United States they're so marginalized as to be non-existent. Again, to take a personal case, I can virtually not publish in the United States on these topics, but I've been asked by mainstream Israeli journals to write regular articles for them.

You read Hebrew and you closely follow Israeli press and politics. Do you see any signs in Israel today that point toward a two-state settlement?

There can be no signs in Israel, for a very simple reason. Israel is so utterly dependent on the United States at this point that no group can attain any degree of credibility in Israel unless it has substantial American support. That's one of the reasons that people like Meir Pail and others like him are so upset by the monolithic and chauvinistic and rather hysterical tendencies in the United States on this issue. They know that unless some American support develops for a political settlement, then those groups within Israel, and they certainly exist, that regard current developments as dangerous and intolerable, those groups will have no domestic support. In fact, that's correct.

Let's take a look at the current Knesset, the Parliament. I'd suppose maybe 10 percent of its members would tend to support some sort of political settlement of the kind that corresponds to the international consensus. That's a rather optimistic appraisal. It may be much less than that. Explicitly committed to that are a smaller group. If American support, however, developed for a political settlement, then such tendencies would develop in Israel in this direction too.

Can you make some suggestions as to what people can do to become aware of this issue and effect some movement in United States foreign policy vis-a-vis Israel?

This is one of the easier questions. To change American policy with regard to, say, Central America, would be extremely difficult because the United States has a long-time historic interest in violence and repression in Central America and we're not going to give it up easily. But in the case of the Middle East I think it would be quite an easy thing to do. Even though there's virtually no articulate voice in the United States in support of the international consensus on a political settlement, nevertheless polls indicate that a large percentage of the population, in many polls up to two-thirds or three-quarters of the population, support a Palestinian state, that is, they believe that the indigenous population should have the right of national self-determination alongside of Israel. That means that there's a potential popular support. Within elite planning groups there's a real sharp division on this topic.

There are people who feel that we should maintain Israel as a strategic asset and a base for projection of American power and a source of violence and threat to intimidate the region. There are many other people, including people who represent quite powerful economic and political interests in the United States, who believe to the contrary that we should go along with the international consensus and try to reach an authentic political settlement, people like George Ball, a good example of a spokesman for this point of view. A recent book of his, which I'm sure will never be reviewed here, is a good, clear, lucid and I think quite persuasive exposition of this point of view. This is not an open political issue in the United States, and I think this is one of the rare cases where virtual domination, total domination of articulate expression of the media, the books, schools, the whole ideological system, the domination of that by one extremist position has in fact shifted the political balance very radically.

The potential split among dominant American elites has even not emerged into policy, because the ones who support the hawkish, extremist, violent policy have almost total support in articulate opinion. That can be changed if people are willing to face the intimidation apparatus, which will be unpleasant. It's unpleasant to have mud thrown at you and be denounced, etc. But if you're willing to face that and to do some self-education, and the facts are available, and then some real education of others, organizing and so on, I think that political pressures can be developed to make it possible for congressional representatives and for the press, this means pressure on the press, too, to take a stance which at least recognizes reality, which isn't such a grotesque distortion of reality as I've been describing, what you see in the papers every day. And also to effect political decisions and to move the United States towards joining what is a very broad international consensus on this issue. That could happen. It's easily within range. It would have large-scale support even among powerful American interests. In this respect it's quite different, an easier task, than what faces people who are trying to change the American policy of organized violence in Central America.

Editor's Notes to Interview 37

Included in *Before the Point of No Return. An Exchange of Views on the Cold War, the Reagan Doctrine, and What Is to Come.* Edited by Leon Wofsy. New York: Monthly Review Press, 1986, pp. 87–92, and in its predecessor, *The Cold War: Can There be a Peaceful Ending?* Edited by Leon Wofsy. Berkeley: Department of Microbiology and Immunology, University of California, 1986 (a booklet used as a supplementary reader in Peace and Conflict Studies courses), pp. 1–7. The MRP volume is divided in two parts. Part 1 ("The Cold War World") consists of 11 selected talks transcribed from tapes and excerpted for publication. Part 2 ("The Future of the Cold War") includes the answers to the same two questions by 13 respondents: Stanley Hoffmann, Strobe Talbott, Hans A. Bethe, Noam Chomsky, Paul M. Sweezy, Flora Lewis, Rev. Theodore M. Hesburgh, Barbara Epstein, Michael McGuire, Gil Green, Manning Marable, Malcolm W. Gordon and Marcus G. Raskin.

Chomsky's answer, which is instructive to compare with each of the others, particularly with the one across the page by Nobel Laureate Hans Bethe, was written on Oct. 5, 1985. It is singled out by the editor of the volume in this remarkable statement (p. 140):

"For me the most distressing response to our question on the possibility for ending the Cold War came from Noam Chomsky—not only because it is so absolute in its pessimism, but also because I have great respect for the author and a case he argues is never easily dismissed."

The careful reader of the following pages (the key phrase is "without significant institutional changes, no serious alternative is in sight") will have little difficulty in judging the perceptiveness of this assessment.

37. Alternatives to the Cold War (5 October 1985)

Do you think peaceful termination of the Cold War is a real possibility in the foreseeable future? If so, under what circumstances?

I see no possibility that Cold War tensions can be significantly reduced in the foreseeable future. The reasons are basically two. First, each superpower is, in fact, an impediment to the ambitions of the other. Second, despite the fundamental conflict, each has come to rely on the other's existence, and its brutality, for its own purposes.

The first point is relatively transparent. The primary goal of the military-bureaucratic elite who rule the USSR is to run their dungeon without interference, including the East European satellites, while seeking targets of opportunity elsewhere. It should further be noted that no Russian government will abandon control over Eastern Europe so long as a rearmed Germany remains part of a hostile Western alliance, for obvious historical and security reasons. Given this posture, the USSR has generally favored detente, meaning: a system of joint global management by the two superpowers, in which each concedes to the other an area of domination in which it may act without serious interference. The U.S. has generally rejected this arrangement, and thus stands as a barrier to Soviet policy.

U.S. goals have been more expansive. The U.S. emerged from World War II in a position of global dominance with few if any historical parallels, and U.S. planners were determined to ensure that the U.S. would remain "the hegemonic power in a system of world order," in the words of a 1975 Trilateral Commission study, deploring the decline of this system. Planners sought to construct what they called a "Grand Area," a region subordinated to the needs of the U.S. economy, including at a minimum the Western Hemisphere, the Far East, and the former British Empire, as well as the Middle East and Western Europe. Early goals were to assure access to Eurasian resources quite generally. As George Kennan explained the matter in Policy Planning Study 23 (February 1948), the U.S. had 50 percent of the world's wealth but only 6 percent of its population, a fact that led to "envy and resentment": "Our real task in the coming period is to devise a pattern of relationships which will permit us to maintain this disparity ... To do so, harsh measures will be necessary, and we must put aside such 'vague' and unreal objectives as human rights, the raising of the living standards, and democratization...The less we are then hampered by idealistic slogans, the better." The prescription was specifically for the Far East, but the U.S. is a global power, and in both planning and actual practice the doctrine extended worldwide, despite the regular resort to "idealistic slogans" for public consumption.

The primary U.S. objective was to ensure that within the Grand Area there would be no serious challenge to its dominance, no form of independent development. This is why the U.S. turned at once to a systematic program of destruction of the anti-fascist collaborators; one facet of this program was the use of Nazi war criminals of the Klaus Barbie variety, dispatched to Latin America when the trail got too hot, where they could continue their work in a manner that establishes a direct connection, via the U.S., from the Nazis to the killing fields in Central America today. With regard to the USSR, though the U.S. did toy with a "rollback" strategy in the early years (cf. NSC 68, 1950), and one hears echoes of this among more fanatic jingoist elements today, clearer minds understood that it was beyond the bounds of feasibility. The USSR poses barriers to U.S. goals in two respects: by its existence, dominating a bloc that is not open to U.S. economic exploitation and political control, and by offering a measure of support to forces within U.S. domains that seek to pursue a path unacceptable to the United States.

Each superpower would undoubtedly prefer to see the other disappear, but each has come to understand that this is impossible short of mutual annihilation. The conflict has therefore settled into a system of hostility combined with mutual accommodation. This brings us to the second and more subtle point: the exploitation of the brutality of the enemy for the implementation of policy goals.

While on both sides, the rhetoric of the Cold War focuses on the superpower enemy, the actual events of the Cold War yield a different picture. The substance of the Cold War system consists primarily of intervention and subversion by the two superpowers within their own domains: East Berlin, Hungary, Czechoslovakia, Poland, Afghanistan (the sole large-scale example of the use of Soviet forces beyond the borders conquered by the Red Army during World War II)—Greece, Iran, Guatemala, Cuba, Indochina, the Dominican Republic, Chile, El Salvador and Nicaragua, and all too many others.

Any power, whether democratic or totalitarian, must find a way to mobilize public support, at home and among allies, for costly and brutal actions. Throughout history, the primary means for accomplishing this end has been the appeal to the threat of some "Great Satan." Soviet interventions have been presented at home as defensive: the USSR must defend itself from the threat posed by aggressive forces dominated by the global enemy. There is no such event as the "invasion of Afghanistan" in Soviet theology; rather, a "defense of Afghanistan" against terrorists supported by the CIA and other warmongers. Our doctrinal system is similar. Thus, the U.S. attack against South Vietnam—beginning with bombing and defoliation in 1962 as part of an effort to drive millions of people into concentration camps after seven years of state terror, followed by direct invasion and expansion of the aggression to all of Indochina—literally does not exists in U.S. history; rather, there is a "defense of South Vietnam" against terrorists unleashed by the USSR (in other variants, by China) and its client, North Vietnam—a "defense" which as unwise or excessively brutal, the doves contend. Throughout the history of the real Cold War, the same has been true.

The utility of the Great Satan extends further. The Soviet system is held under control by violence, so that its leader naturally require a militarized society. The costs are severe, and the populace must agree to bear them. To some extent, terror suffices, but a better method is acquiescence out of a perceived need to defend the society against the great enemy. As for the U.S., it has been clearly recognized by government and business leaders that the state must intervene in the economy to stimulate production, and for a variety of reasons, the Pentagon system developed as the optimal means to achieve this result. This system funnels public subsidies to advanced sectors of industry, not merely the arms industry, covering the costly phase of research and development while assigning profits to the private sector during this phase and when commercial applications become possible. It is an elegant system of public subsidy, private profit. A state-guaranteed market for rapidly obsolescing high-technology waste production (armaments) is optimally designed to benefit existing private power and privilege while offering minimal interference with the businessman's prerogatives. The long-term costs may be severe, but planning is not undertaken in this framework in a competitive society, and once the system is established, powerful vested interests ensure its maintenance. Again, the population must be willing to bear the costs. It is a rare political leader who might approach the public with the news that it is necessary for the poor to subsidize the wealthy, who control investment, for the ultimate health of the economy. It is much simpler to appeal to what the president called the "monolithic and ruthless conspiracy" that aims to thwart our benevolence throughout the world; President Kennedy, in this case, as he initiated the vast military build-up that set off the current phase of the arms race under the pretext of a fraudulent "missile gap." His Keynesian successor Ronald Reagan behaves in much the same way, and indeed the same has been true throughout.

It is for this reason that the U.S. rejects any arms control agreement that would limit development of more advanced weapons systems, and concocts such fantasies as "Star Wars," a system designed to maintain the arms race and provide subsidies for the most advanced sectors of high-technology industry, which will be pursued regardless of the evident risks to national security that it entails. For the same reason, a nuclear freeze is not a policy option, despite support for it by some three-fourth of the population and its clear feasibility, given Soviet advocacy of this position and endorsement by a large majority of the United Nations. For the same reason, the U.S. cannot accept a ban on nuclear weapons or missile tests, though this would reduce the threat of the first strike that the "Star Wars" program theoretically aims to deter at far less cost and risk, and no serious problem of verifiability. Neither public opinion, nor feasibility, nor security is a major concern; there are more important considerations. The U.S. will agree to limitation of weapons; our comparative advantage is not in production, but in advanced technology. But the system of state industrial management through the Pentagon can hardly face a challenge.

In short, the Cold War has evolved into a system of tacit cooperation, in which the leadership of each superpower exploits the violence and brutality of the enemy—real enough, in both cases—to achieve quite different purposes: intervention and militarization of the domestic society; in our case, as a technique for compelling the public to invest in advance sectors of the economy without sharing in the profits or interfering with management.

There is no space here to explore further complexities, which exist, or to document this history, but the essentials should be plain enough to those who choose to penetrate the rhetoric that clouds it.

The system is both costly and unstable. The major costs are borne by the victims of superpower intervention, but the domestic societies also bear a serious burden: material, cultural and moral. Sooner or later, the system is bound to collapse. The two greatest threats are technical advances in weaponry which lead to increased reliance on automated rapid response systems, which raise the probability of war by error, inadvertence, or misjudgment in times of crises; and the even more serious threat that tensions and conflicts in the Third World may engage the superpowers and rapidly escalate, as has repeatedly come close in the past and will again, the Middle East being the primary "tinder box."

The Cold War system, then, is one of potential mutual suicide, and vast suffering, massacre, torture, starvation, semi-slave labor, and so on, throughout the dependent areas. There are indigenous causes too, but the contribution of the superpowers is not slight. Nevertheless, the Cold War system has a short-term rationality from the point of view of dominant groups in the two societies, and without significant institutional changes, no serious alternative is in sight.

The bipolar world of the early postwar period has slowly eroded, as new centers of power developed in a more complex global system. The capacity of each superpower to coerce has steadily declined, while their absolute power to destroy continually increases. Serious conflicts are arising within the U.S.-dominated system and are sure to increase, and there is a bare possibility that Europe and Japan might come to pursue a more independent course, with consequences that cannot be pursued here. But for the foreseeable future, the Cold War system of global conflict and global management appears fairly stable, with the prospect of a terminal war, one of the ever-present elements of this system, an increasing likelihood.

Editor's Notes to Interview 38

"Noam Chomsky on the Middle East and Central America," *Athabasca University Magazine* 9:5 (Nov–Dec 1985), pp. 46–52. It took place in Edmonton, Alberta, Canada, and it was conducted by Richard Titus, an audio-teleconferencing technician at Athabasca University; typically, "what was supposed to be a 25-minute interview quickly turned into a full-hour discussion." Titus presents Chomsky as a committed leading commentator who "cuts through the myths to tackle the most basic questions," including the following: "Why did the U.S. invade Grenada? Was that invasion a dry run to sound the depth of public apathy before embarking on more major incursions in Nicaragua and elsewhere? Will the conflicts in the Middle East lead to Armageddon? Is there a complicity between Western media and liberal intelligentsia to help governments suppress facts detrimental to their cause?"

The address referred to by Titus is "The United States: From Greece to El Salvador," in N. Chomsky, J. Steele & J. Gittings, *Superpowers in Collision: The Cold War Now.* New [expanded] ed. Penguin, 1984, pp. 24–58, which is based on a talk given at a seminar on "The superpowers and the Cold War" held in London in March 1981; updated March 14, 1984.

For an update on Sharon and its impact, see I56 and the Editor's Notes to it; on U.S.-Israeli rejectionism, see Editor's Notes to I36.

38. The Question for Canadians—and Not Only Canadians (November 1985)

The most recent publication of yours to reach us in Canada is The Fateful Triangle: Israel, The United States and the Palestinians. *Perhaps we could look at recent developments in the Middle East. Western media largely portrays the withdrawal of Israeli forces from Lebanon as an Israeli army attempting a peaceful retreat while their path home is plagued by continuing attacks from so-called terrorists, neglecting to mention that Israel is bulldozing homes of suspected terrorists or collaborators. Is this part of laying the ground-work for future incursions by Israel into Lebanon?*

It's important to recognize that Israel suffered a military defeat in southern Lebanon. What the Western media call terrorists are ordinarily called a resistance. Resistance to military occupation is not terrorism, it's resistance. The resistance has been significant enough so that Israel has been compelled to abandon their original plan of maintaining literal control of large areas of Lebanon. What they originally hoped was that they could install a client military force, the South Lebanon army, which was an extension of their earlier force, the Haddad army. They hoped that that force could essentially run southern Lebanon and give them free access to it and its resources, particularly the waters of the Litani River. The resistance has been so strong that the so-called South Lebanon army has just deteriorated under the resistance attacks, which have also carried over to the Israeli army.

What I suspect they'll now do is take a fall-back position and try to restore the situation that existed prior to their invasion of Lebanon—control over a piece of southern Lebanon. But I don't know if they'll be able to because they've aroused a lot of resistance through their own terrorism in the last couple of years. Israeli attacks on Lebanon go back about 15 years to when, in the early 1970s, Israel carried out extensive attacks with heavy bombardment, the killing of thousands of people, and the drawing of hundreds of thousands out of southern Lebanon. Whether they'll be able to continue that pattern is not now clear because they have evoked a very substantial resistance.

Do you think domestic opposition within Israel will contribute to a failure of further incursions into Lebanon?

Israeli public opinion was strongly in favor of the Lebanese war. In fact, the peak of support for the war, and for Begin and Sharon, was in late August 1982, after the bombing of Beirut, which was savage and brutal and quite visibly portrayed. Then it began to tail off when the costs of the war started to come in. As far as the economic consequences are concerned, the assumption is that the United States is always going to pay the costs. Israel has the highest per capita debt in the world. No small state is really independent, but they've given up independence to a very substantial degree by essentially relying on the expectation of constant American payoffs. This will lead to sufficient support for further violence as long as there are no other costs and not too many Israeli soldiers die.

Once again Egypt has made overtures to initiate peace talks or negotiations with other Arab nations vis-a-vis Israel and the Palestinian question. Will U.S. interests object to this? After all, for Egypt to follow through on such an initiative could imply that it desires to remove itself from the U.S. client-state status to which it was assigned after the Camp David accords.

That's not really clear. Egypt is extremely dependent on the United States. While Egypt would like to reassert an independent position in the Arab world, I think it's unlikely to act in serious opposition to American demands. The new Egyptian and Jordanian and PLO initiatives are really not so new. They are just a continuation of long-standing initiatives. The two sides are irreconcilably divided on **one crucial issue**, and that issue is national self-determination for the Palestinians. Israel is opposed to it totally. They don't want any form of **meaningful self-determination** for the indigenous population, and the United States so far has backed them on that 100 percent. The minimal position for the Arab states is that there be some form of national self-determination, some real autonomy in the occupied territories. The minimal negotiating position that any Palestinian group could conceivably accept is that they don't commit national suicide. Israel would never accept that because they'd have to give up control of certain regions, which they don't want to do. They want those regions for good solid reasons not having much to do with security—because these regions provide them with a cheap unorganized labor force which now does much of the dirty work in Israeli society. It also provides them with a market worth something close to $1 billion a year, and it provides them a third of their water. The United States has backed them so far in this rejection of Palestinian national rights. Now that's where everything founders all the time, and again there's nothing particularly new about these Egyptian offers.

The crucial issue is whether the Palestinians, that is the indigenous population, will have the same right of national self-determination that we automatically accord to the settlers who largely replaced them. The issue of Israeli self-determination does not arise, but the issue of self-determination for the indigenous population very much does arise. Israel is strongly opposed to it. The United States backs them. The Arab world cannot yield on that issue.

I don't know if this was reported in Canada (it was well suppressed in the United States), but last April and May (1984) Arafat made a series of proposals in Europe and Asia which were widely reported in the major European press, in which he called for negotiations with Israel leading to mutual recognition. There's nothing more conciliatory than that other than saying you'll commit suicide. That was immediately rejected by Israel and was simply ignored by the United States. The U.S. media didn't even cover it. the *New York Times* didn't even report it.

Sadat's initiatives in early 1971 seemed to set off the opposite reaction in Israel—to aggravate the situation and, as you mention, set off a kind of panic in the Israeli parliament.

That phrase "evoking panic" I actually quoted from a liberal Israeli intellectual, Amos Elon, who wrote an article after one of the other later Arab peace initiatives. He pointed out that that peace initiative had evoked panic in Israel just as Sadat's 1971 offer evoked panic because the fear always is that somehow they'll be driven to negotiations. To be driven to negotiations can only mean something like a settlement on the international borders and giving up the occupied territories. Now it's interesting that Sadat's offer, as Elon put it, evoked panic in Israel. That didn't even involve Palestinian national rights. Sadat made what we ought to call a rejectionist offer. His offer was to restore the status prior to the '67 war in which the Palestinians had no rights. Nevertheless, Israel and the United States rejected it.

In your book Towards a New Cold War *and again in* The Fateful Triangle, *you used the word "Armageddon" to describe the possible end of the conflicts in the Middle East. In terms of the global nature of the Cold War, do you see the Middle East as the most dangerous element in the present and foreseeable makeup of the Cold War jigsaw?*

Yes. There was a Pentagon study called "Airforce 2000" that was leaked a little over a year ago. It was reported in the Toronto *Globe and Mail.* It was pretty well blanked out of the American press. The Pentagon studied the prospects for global peace up until the year 2000, and it concluded that the major dangers were in the Third World. The dangers of a war breaking out in Europe are remote and always have been, but in the Third World, they are very real. They concluded that **the major danger** was in the Middle East.

Repeatedly, the superpowers have come close to confrontation as a result of the regional conflict in the Middle East. There was a threat in 1956 and 1958, but it became serious in 1967. In 1967, for example, Israel attacked Syria after the cease-fire and conquered the Syrian Golan Heights. Syria was a Soviet ally. When that happened, the Soviets became quite outraged. According to Secretary of Defense McNamara, Kosygin used the hot line and virtually threatened war at that point if the United States did not call off the Israeli attack. They didn't know how far it was going to go then; they thought it might go all the way to Damascus. The Russian and American fleets were in confrontation positions in the eastern Mediterranean. According to McNamara, the American fleet actually turned around some Russian naval vessels and MacNamara said, and I'm quoting, "We damned near had war." The threat of accidental superpower confrontation is very real and will stay that way.

In the address you contributed to the book Superpowers in Collision, *you outline a method by which the United States sought to reinstill in the domestic population of the U.S. the appropriate support and acquiescence to "Grand Area" corporate-global strategies after World War II. The events that followed in Greece in 1947 seemed to be a kind of market test or model for future propaganda techniques used to legitimate violent regimes friendly to U.S. business interests. The invasion of Grenada, although in no way as deeply violent or subversive as events in Greece, bear some similarities to that model. Is it legitimate to infer that Grenada was a dry run to sound the depth of public apathy or antipathy before embarking on major incursions into Nicaragua or elsewhere?*

To understand the Grenada invasion we'd have to go back a couple of years to the time when the new Bishop regime came into power in Grenada in 1979. The United States was immediately very hostile for the same reason we're hostile to any government that begins to move towards **using resources for domestic purposes**. Some of the first policies of the Sandinistas in Nicaragua were land reform, a tripling of the health budget, a cut-back in infant mortality which was so dramatic that they won a World Health Organization award for it, and other policies of that nature. That automatically made them enemies because they were using resources for domestic purposes instead of allowing themselves to be integrated into the "Grand Area" of American control and penetration.

Even Grenada, where we have no interest in their domestic resources, is a threat. Just as in Greece, the threat falls under "the domino theory." What has always been feared is that there will be a demonstration effect of successful development. If a speck in the Caribbean could begin to do something constructive then why not us? As the American planners put it: "the rot will spread," the rot being independent social and economic development. Gradually the fabric of the American-controlled system will erode. So that's why the United States responds, often with much savagery, to attempts at constructive development even in a tiny and remote place where we have no immediate interest.

In Grenada there were the beginnings of some use of resources for domestic purposes, and that's intolerable. The Carter administration at once began to destabilize Grenada. Aid was cut off. Soon the U.S. began running threatening naval exercises nearby. Enough pressure was put on Grenada to cause a weak government and a small movement to fall apart under internal pressure. At that point, the United States moved in to deliver the coup de grace. It was probably a test-case to see if we could get away with it.

The Reagan administration has been trying to intervene directly with American military force in Central America and hasn't been able to. The situation is very similar to Southeast Asia in the late 50s and early 60s. In the late 1950s, the United States installed the terrorist regime in South Vietnam, which immediately subverted the proposed Geneva Agreement. More crucially, it turned to a direct attack against the population, in particular against the former anti-French resistance, what we call the Viet Cong. It was pretty brutal. They probably killed 70 or 80 thousand people during the late 50s. When Kennedy came in, he simply responded by bombing South Vietnam. He began the bombing in 1962 as part of a major project of trying to drive millions of people into camps where we could control them under armed guard. No opposition existed when Kennedy bombed South Vietnam.

The situation in Central America is similar. Under Carter, a terrorist regime was installed in El Salvador which carried out a major war against the population. About 30,000 people were killed from 1980–1981, creating 600,000 refugees, according to church sources. Those figures have approximately doubled since. When Carter started this war against the popular organizations and against the peasantry, there were a couple of thousand guerrillas, and by the end of another year there were many thousands of them.

In Central America, as in Vietnam, the next step was to intervene directly with military force. Reagan was moving in that direction, but there was much too much popular opposition. The United States has changed quite dramatically over the past 20 years. Now there is substantial opposition to intervention and aggression. The government has had to use more indirect pressure both against El Salvador and Nicaragua.

Grenada was an attempt to see if direct aggression would work. It was an ambiguous lesson. It evoked a real jingoist response in the United States which was very frightening. It was short-lived, and it was recognized as something of a joke. Six thousand American elite troops succeeded in overcoming the resistance of maybe a couple of dozen armed Cubans and some Grenada military men. These 6,000 troops won 8,000 medals for their valor and that was noticed. What was noticed was that this was a joke, and much of the subsequent commentary has been about the incompetence of the American military forces. This was the response to a cheap, quick victory and not an indication that the population was willing to accept a substantial intervention. Popular activities of one sort or another are continuing to demonstrate that large parts of the population strenuously oppose American intervention. The government is aware of that, and that's holding them back.

You don't think that the U.S. government can completely disregard popular domestic opinion?

It can, but at great risk. That's what happened in the late 1960s, and it caused a severe crisis in the United States. The American army fell apart in Indochina, very much to its credit, I should say. Part of the reason it had to be withdrawn was because it was no longer an effective fighting force. There was too much internal dissension. After all, this was a citizen's army, not the French Foreign Legion. As a citizen's army it reflected closely what happened in the domestic society. It fell apart, as a reflection of domestic processes. Furthermore, opposition to the war compelled the government to fight the war on deficit spending. As they put it, they had to have both guns and butter.

That had a serious effect on the American economy and set off the later wave of stagnation and inflation. It also **weakened the American position** vis-a-vis its real rivals, Europe and Japan. That's the main reason the American business community turned against the war in about 1968—because it was getting too costly. To fight a war against the opposition of large parts of the population is difficult. People who basically own and manage the country want an apathetic, passive, obedient citizenry. They don't want dissent. They don't want political organization. They don't want activism. They don't want attempts to participate in the political arena, either through the political process or through more indirect means like civil disobedience. This is true in any country, even in a totalitarian state, but it's certainly true in a democratic one.

In Nazi Germany, if you read Albert Speer's memoirs, he complains that the Nazis were never able to impose the full range of totalitarian controls that the democratic societies were able to impose because they had to essentially buy off the population. They didn't have the kind of domestic support that the Western democracies had so that they could move to the full level of totalitarian control necessary for a real national mobilization and a major war. The same is true in the Soviet Union or elsewhere. Any country is going to have to make sure that its domestic population is passive and obedient. Some states do it by terror. The United States does not. It's not organized that way. The U.S. doesn't use terror to impose domestic apathy. The same is true of Canada. Canadians could impede American aggression if they wanted to because Canada is essentially regarded as a colony of the United States, and the colonies also have to be kept in line. If they're not in line, and they're disobedient and troublesome, that's a cost that planners have to take into account.

Earlier this year, our respective heads of state met in Quebec City for the so-called "Shamrock Summit" and ratified accords regarding defense and fisheries, an odd combination. Prime Minister Mulroney, to the open delight of your president, made some rather rash resurgent Canada-type promises to his electorate in terms of our domestic economy and the blessing that First World accommodation will bestow upon us. These promises come to us from a former American, branch-plant mining executive who seems to be carrying that mentality into office. Reagan can now rant comfortably in Canada as compared to his relative restraint when Trudeau was in power. This demonstrates the degree to which Mulroney has committed us to First World accommodation with the U.S. in its stance in the Cold War. What real significance can a resurgent Canada hold for the American administration beyond a propaganda victory?

The United States wants to have what it regards as its colonies to be subordinated to its policy line, its economic and political international planning. So it's a net gain for American power. I would rather change the focus. Compared to various societies of the world, Canada and the United States are countries where the state does not use excessive violence against its own population to secure obedience. A large range of action is open to people who aren't outright heroes, and the question for Canadians is whether they feel comfortable being accomplices to mass murder. In the past, the answer has been yes, Canadians do feel comfortable. During the Vietnam War there was a lot of Canadian opposition to the war. There was a lot of rhetorical condemnation. Nevertheless, Canada became **the largest per capita military exporter in the world**, supplying arms and enriching itself through the destruction of Indochina. As long as Canadians feel comfortable playing that role, they will continue to play it. If they look at the consequences of that, they'll see that they are playing a role parallel to that of the people we condemn as the "good Germans" under the Nazis. They just sit back quietly and make what profit they can out of the suffering and misery of other people.

Do you think this will have any effect on current American-Soviet attitudes in the arms negotiation?

No. These negotiations aren't going anywhere, and can't really. The United States was forced into the **arms negotiations** by the public uproar over the early hysteria of the Reagan administration. It looked as though they were just going to try to destroy the world quickly, and that raised a lot of popular opposition. It led them to accept some form of negotiations. There's now more interest in negotiations but not on security grounds. One has to recognize that questions of security, international security or American security, are secondary in the arms race.

The arms race has two fundamental domestic factors driving it. One is that for years it has been perceived to have been necessary to create a protected area within which the United States could intervene directly with conventional forces without any concern that anyone was going to deter us. That's one thing strategic nuclear weapons do. They provide a region, and for us that means a good part of the world, in which the direct use of conventional forces is possible for intervention without concern that there'll be any real inhibition from any other power. That has been stated quite openly back to the early 1950s. Look at National Security Council Memorandum 141 written by Paul Nitze back in January 1953. He points out that the danger posed to us by Russian strategic nuclear forces is dual. First, the Russian strategic forces may impede us if we decide to carry out a first strike against the Soviet Union. The second is that they will, as he puts it, impose caution on us in our use of conventional forces elsewhere in the world. That is, we will not be free to carry out our Cold War policies, policies of intervention without concern and caution. We can't tolerate that. So one major factor is this conception that we must preserve an umbrella for the free use, without caution, of American conventional forces. That's one major factor in the arms race.

The second major factor has been that **the military system** is basically our **system of industrial management**. Every modern industrial state has to have substantial state intervention in the economy, and the way we do it is through the military system. The military system, in effect, amounts to a taxpayer subsidy to the most advanced sectors of the industrial system. The way we work it is that the state provides a guaranteed market for high-technology production, high-technology waste production, that is, armaments. For example, when the United States wants the next major advance in computer technology, the way we do it is by financing weapons. Financing for research development is carried out under military auspices, and the primary users will be the weapons systems, at least in the first instance, and then other areas of consumer-oriented technology will pick up what they can. Every time it's necessary for the state to stimulate the economy, we have a rise in militarism, including military rhetoric.

These two factors, the domestic need for the state to intervene dramatically in the economy to support advanced industry and the need to preserve a very large area of the world where we can carry out our military and subversive actions without caution, drive the arms race; and they make it impossible for any meaningful negotiations to take place.

Take the nuclear freeze. The nuclear freeze campaign received the support of about 75 percent of the population, which is enormous. It's official Russian policy. It's been endorsed overwhelmingly by the United Nations. But basically it's not a political option because it would interfere with these fundamental institutional structures which really can't be modified without a substantial change in the society. So you could have 90 percent of the population supporting a nuclear freeze, but it wouldn't have any effect on decision making.

Now, what does that mean for arms negotiations? At the very most, any arms negotiations have to satisfy certain conditions. One condition is that they permit indefinite expansion of the armament system, the military system, and continual support for research and development of new technology. That's the real significance of the so-called Star Wars story. People are debating whether it's going to work or not. That's beside the point. It doesn't matter whether it works or not. Star Wars has been devised to allow the government to funnel enormous subsidies to advanced sectors of industry to permit the development of high technology over a broad range, and that's why we need Star Wars. If not Star Wars, it would be something equivalent.

One of the reasons it's always a military choice, is that that's one of the few things you can get the population to pay for willingly; after all, somebody's got to pay for all of this, and people will pay if they feel threatened. So these moves toward what is sometimes called military Keynesianism are invariably accompanied with a lot of hysterical rhetoric about how the Russians are coming, the Russians are advancing from strength to strength: missile gaps, windows of vulnerability, all fabricated but necessary in order to beat the population into submission.

There are real contradictions in this policy. For example, this military Keynesianism is an extremely wasteful and expensive form of industrial management, and it carries severe costs: a huge deficit, for example, or deterioration of

American industry and a mounting trade deficit. Those costs sooner or later have to be faced. You can predict quite precisely what position the administration is going to take toward international affairs by looking at these domestic factors. So when the Reagan administration came in, their domestic program was what they called reindustrialization, rebuilding industrial capacity, and that meant huge military spending because that's our system for doing it, and that means confrontation all over the world and screaming about the Russians. But now they've got to start facing the costs of all of that. The major financial institutions, for example, are concerned about the deficit, and something has to be done to pay the cost. So as a result, predictably, the United States has a more conciliatory posture—**the Russians aren't quite as evil** as they were a couple of years ago, they've been tamed, they're sort of human, and therefore we can enter into negotiations with them. Actually, the Russians haven't changed a bit. What has changed are the needs of the domestic economy, and if you trace the arms race since the beginning, this is what you find.

People who are debating the arms race are simply caught in a trap. They're trapped as usual in an effective ideological system. They're trapped into debate over things which are irrelevant. For example, is Star Wars going to work? The doves say no, let's not do it, and the hawks say yes, let's try. That's not what the system is for. It's not there in order to work, it's there in order to provide a method for the state to maintain its substantial subsidy and support for advanced industry and, secondarily, it's there to keep an intimidating posture so we can use our forces freely in the Third World. I'm sure the Russians have their own reasons for maintaining a similar system so there's tacit cooperation in this area. The arms negotiations can't significantly change this. At best, they can lead to an orderly procedure in which the two superpowers combine in an orderly approach to arms development.

Editor's Notes to Interview 39

"Interview: Noam Chomsky. 'The First Prime-Time Bombing in History'," *Middle East Report*, May–June 1986, pp. 12–14. Joan Mandell and Zachary spoke with Chomsky in Cambridge, MA, in late April 1986.

For more on terrorism against Cuba (and on Robert Tucker's position), see interviews 20 and 48..

COINTELPRO was the code-name of a covert and illegal FBI COunterINTELligence PROgram of "harassment and disruption of legitimate political activity" (the *New York Times*). See Nelson Blackstock, *COINTELPRO: The FBI's Secret War on Political Freedom*. With an Introduction by Noam Chomsky. Vintage, 1976 (first published in 1975). Chomsky's introduction (written in July 1975, revised and enlarged in Feb. 1976) was to be reprinted in **TCNW** (1982), but was left out (with the reluctant approval of the author) to reduce (ever so lightly) the size of the book.

For other references to George Ball's advocacy of the Rogers line, see interviews 30 and 35 (also the comment on Jackson's campaign in the notes to interview 50); on the Israeli connection (and on the terms "conservative"/"liberal"), interview 40.

There is extensive discussion of some of the topics of this interview in **P&E** (1986) and **CT** (1987).

On Orwell, see Editor's Notes to I30.

39. The First Prime-Time Bombing in History
(Late April 1986)

Why Libya and why right now?

Public relations. This is the first bombing in history that was scheduled for prime-time television, to be picked up on the evening news as it was happening. It was also timed right before the crucial House vote on aid to the Contras. In case anybody didn't get the point, Reagan made a speech the same day in which he said that this "mad dog" Qaddafi was bringing the war home to the United States by sending arms to Nicaragua. One pro-Contra lobbying group has been distributing pamphlets with pictures of Qaddafi and Nicaragua's Daniel Ortega on the cover.

The earlier Gulf of Sidra shoot-out was also timed right before a crucial Senate Contra-aid vote. Each of four or five previous incidents involving Libya were similarly timed. In February 1983, there was a sharp right-wing attack on the Reagan administration, particularly George Schultz, as being insufficiently militant. So it was necessary to strike some heroic poses. The administration concocted a ludicrous fable about a Libyan coup attempt in Sudan, a good excuse to send the Navy into the Gulf of Sidra. Then George Schultz could get up on television and talk about "putting Qaddafi back in his box." The one American reporter who actually went to the Sudan, James Dorsey of the *Christian Science Monitor*, discovered the plot was so subtle that Sudanese and Egyptian intelligence had never even heard of it. "We're getting our information from the Americans," they said. About a year before that, there was another fable about a Libyan invasion of Sudan. And another show of force. Before that there was the tale about the Libyan hit-men wandering the streets of Washington to assassinate Reagan.

The point of all these incidents is that they are a way of keeping the country in a fever of militancy. For that you need confrontations with the Evil Empire. Qaddafi is such a cheap target. He's easy to hate. There's no danger. The U.S. can beat him up at will. Iran and Syria can defend themselves, and you've got the Russians around and so on. But Libya is a pariah state, and weak. So if you want to bomb a city and kill a hundred people, the best place to do it is Tripoli.

It has nothing to do with terrorism. They're hoping to incite terrorism, and they've done so. The disco bombing—whoever was responsible, and the administration story is shot full of internal contradictions even if Libya was involved—

that was plainly a reaction to the Gulf of Sidra incident. Prior to that, Libyan terrorism had been overwhelmingly directed against Libyans. We know about it in detail. Amnesty International, for example, lists 14 Libyans killed, several overseas, and gives the precise circumstances. That's terrorism. But in the same years in which Qaddafi was killing 14 Libyans, José Napoleón Duarte was presiding over the slaughter of tens of thousands of Salvadorans with U.S. assistance. Qaddafi is not in our league. Even the "terrorologists" acknowledge that Libya is a marginal player in this game.

But this focus on terrorism is an important political tool.

That was clear in the first days of the Reagan administration, when Haig announced that international terrorism was going to be the core of their foreign policy instead of human rights. In fact, U.S. foreign policy today is about as concerned with terrorism as Carter's was with human rights. It's related to Reagan's domestic agenda, which is essentially three things: a substantial transfer of resources from the poor to the wealthy; support for military intervention, subversion and aggression; and a forced public subsidy of high-technology, military-based industry. Knowing that agenda, you have to have a mobilized population. You've got to stir up militarist sentiments. Libya was a natural target.

Why is "terrorism" such a useful ideological construct?

First, their concept of terrorism is highly selective. There's a wonderful story in St. Augustine's *City of God*, where Alexander the Great captures a pirate and says, "How dare you molest the seas!" And the pirate turns to him and says, "How dare you molest the world! I have a small ship, so I'm a pirate, a thief. But you have a big navy, so you're an emperor." If the emperor disturbs the world, that's not terrorism, but if a thief disturbs the seas, that is terrorism.

Our thieves are not terrorists. When they started this hype in 1981, the great insight was that the Russians were behind it—the proof being that communist states are never targeted. In fact, Cuba has probably been subjected to more terrorism than the rest of the world combined. The U.S. had a major terrorist operation against Cuba in the early 1960s. Nobody denies that. In 1970–71 the U.S. destroyed crops and poisoned livestock in Cuba. Former CIA operative Orlando Bosch is probably the world's deadliest terrorist. He was involved in blowing up a Cuban airliner in which 73 people were killed. His group bombs Cuban missions abroad. None of that counts as terrorism; it's the emperor's side.

Just take a look at how it works. Random attacks against Americans—even if it's only five a year—strike terror into the hearts of Americans. They're afraid to go to Greece. That means something. But if the U.S. carries out massive terrorism in the Third World, that doesn't hurt anybody here. When Israel bombed Tunis and killed 20 Tunisians and 55 Palestinians, everybody thought that was wonderful. Israel has been hijacking ships going from Cyprus to Lebanon for at least 10 years. When Israel carries out "iron fist" operations in southern Lebanon, that doesn't bother anybody here. But if somebody occasionally blows up an airplane, that hurts people here. When people talk about terrorism, they're talking about acts against Americans, not acts carried out by the American government, which are vastly greater in scale, but are directed against people who don't count.

What is the Reagan administration's larger agenda?

Reagan himself probably doesn't understand the words he's reading from his cue-cards, but the people around him do. You can't approach people and say, "Look fellas, the poor are going to have to subsidize the rich, and you're going to have to cut down on your consumption, so as to provide a forced subsidy to IBM, and we're going to start overthrowing governments around the world." You have to frighten people with the Evil Empire conquering the world, and with international terrorism, the scourge of the modern age. Planners and propaganda specialists can figure this out in a minute. It's Reagan's agenda, and the Democrats went along with it.

The use of terrorism today is analogous to the use of communism in the 1950s to support counterrevolution abroad. Anti-communism also had domestic political uses—to destroy the Left. Do you see terrorism being used in that way?

They would like to use it for that purpose, but it's not going to work. Government force was no greater in the early 1950s than in the late 1960s. But the student movement and the other connected movements didn't just collapse; they resisted. There was nothing like COINTELPRO in the early 1950s. There was vilification, which is a pain, but it's not death. I don't want to understate what happened—people did lose their jobs—but it was mainly a kind of moral collapse of the old Left. In the 1960s, people were stronger. The government did do some serious things in the late 1960s, mainly against the black movement. But the efforts to undermine the white movement didn't have a major effect. The one good thing about American democracy is that the state is relatively limited in its capacity to use violence against the more privileged sectors of the population. That means there's a lot of space for people's movements without very serious consequences: you're not going to end up in psychiatric prison or a death camp.

The U.S. seems to have adopted the Israeli approach to terrorism.

Israel, like the United States, chooses its targets by weakness, not relevance. Tunis was completely undefended—a cheap target. In late March, the Lebanese resistance attacked the South Lebanon army, an Israeli mercenary force, which then shelled the marketplace in Nabatiyeh, killing several people. Then a Katyusha rocket was fired at Kiryat Shmona [Israel]; and Israel bombed refugee camps near Sidon [Lebanon], killing 10. The Israeli military commander said they did not know who shot the rocket. That's not retaliation.

Hasn't the U.S. put itself in the position of having to repeat its bombing of Libya?

They may have trapped themselves into a very dangerous situation. Most of the so-called terrorism is actually coming out of Lebanon, the consequence of the 1982 Israeli invasion. When Washington accuses Syria and Iran, they mean Lebanese groups who they claim are connected to Syria and Iran. Attacking Syrian positions means getting involved with the Soviet Union. There may be a joint Israel-American attack on Syria, maybe this summer. It's possible they'll set up an American retaliation for some terrorist act allegedly supported by Syria, which could be combined with an Israeli "preemptive strike," another rationale that has been established.

Why have U.S. peace and anti-intervention movements been so reluctant to get involved in the Middle East?

I think a combination of racism and fear. Racism reflecting an assumption that Arabs are something less than human beings. For most of the peace movement, there's no conception that the indigenous population in what was Palestine has rights even equivalent to the rights of the settlers who largely displaced them. No one questions whether Israel should be a party to negotiations, but we're supposed to debate whether the PLO should be.

A second element is fear. There's a marvelous defamation apparatus. Naturally, in the age of Orwell, it's run by organizations with names like the Anti-Defamation League. If anybody is even mildly critical of Israel, they'll be subjected to discredit, lies and abuse. They don't send death squads, but they can make life rather unpleasant. And there's no way of responding to all the lies.

The attitude towards Israel is entirely reminiscent of Stalinism: if you criticized Russia, you were objectively against the revolution, therefore, you had to defend it no matter what. That's essentially the attitude towards Israel.

How can we confront this?

Talk about it openly. The facts are pretty clear. The public at large has a much better position on this than the Left. Polls generally show that two-thirds of the people here even favor a Palestinian state. It's not a matter of the Left leading. They've got a long way to go to catch up with the general public.

Some people explain U.S. support for Israel in terms of the influence of the Zionist lobby. It could also be explained in terms of what American planning strategies see as the defense of American hegemony in the region.

It's both. The lobby can be effective only insofar as what it's advocating coincides with major forces inside the American establishment—which is not uniform. The ruling class has different strategies as to how to protect American interests in the region. The different conceptions showed up quite clearly in the Rogers-Kissinger contest 15 years ago. They each had a point—forgetting any question of morality or legality and considering only the problem of how to ensure U.S. domination in oil-producing regions. One way is the Nixon Doctrine: having a range of gendarmes, powerful regional states which can suppress any incipient nationalist developments—that's the Kissinger line. The other approach, the Rogers line, was to encourage a diplomatic settlement with the countries in the region and assume that the oil-producers thereby would be in the pocket of the U.S., as things quieted down and they weren't threatened too much by their own populations. Each is a plausible conception. George Ball eloquently advocates the Rogers line, among whose proponents are many ex-ambassadors. This is another instance which shows how meaningless terms like conservative and liberal are. Among "conservatives," substantial groups support a political/diplomatic settlement. The "liberals" overwhelmingly support the Kissinger approach: use force, support a militant Israel, block any political settlement.

The Jewish lobby pushes the extreme hawk position, which happens to coincide with powerful interests, well-represented in corporate circles and the Pentagon. But it is opposed by powerful groups like the oil companies. The lobby may have a swing effect, where the debate within the circles of power could have gone the other way if it hadn't been for the lobby's influence.

Under Reagan the practice has been virtually to write off Arab client regimes in favor of "strategic understanding" with Israel. Is there any room for a future change of course?

Sure, any time. One of the beauties of ruling the world is you can decide what to do at each point. At the moment you can essentially disregard the oil producers. When there's pressure on the energy markets, the decision could be what people like Robert Tucker suggest: unleash Israel. Or it could be the Rogers/Ball/oil company approach. For the moment the issue can simply be disregarded.

How do you see the Israel-Central America-South Africa connection?

That's very important. It's not just Israel as a regional power. Long before the Nixon Doctrine was established, Israel was already performing very useful services for the U.S., particularly in Africa. The services Israel could provide as kind of a mercenary state were becoming apparent and became quite significant in the 1970s. Israel provided a way for the UN embargo against Rhodesia, for example. Undoubtedly Israel served that purpose with regard to South Africa. And in Latin America, Carter couldn't deal with the dictators of the Southern Cone directly because of the human rights constraints, but Israel was perfectly able to do so. Central America is a still more important example.

It's very useful to the U.S. for Israel to be a pariah state, highly militarized, no economy, totally dependent, completely dependable and available to carry out missions as needed: a kind of a Sparta you can send out whenever you need to. And for that, you have to ensure that military conflict keeps going. If there were a political settlement, Israel would probably become another Luxembourg, of no use to the United States. It's of much greater advantage to have the conflict go on. I suspect that's the of the major reasons, quite apart from the Zionist lobby, why the hawks always win.

Editor's Notes to Interview 40

In this "interview" the questions come from the audience after a talk Chomsky gave on Oct. 22, 1984, in Boulder, CO, under the title "*The Right Turn in U.S. International and Security Policy*" (a title shortened here). The recording is due to David Barsamian.

"Star Wars," now re-christened "National Missile Defense," is of course another respect in which the Bush 2 administration can be accurately described as a resurrection and revitalization (with crucial unintended help from the 9-11 criminals) of the Reagan administration.

The answer to the third question is a sort of preview of **MC** (1988), which was to be published four years later. See I43, including the Editor's Notes.

The books referred to are Cheryl Rubenberg's *Israel and the American National Interest: A Critical Examination*. Urbana: University of Illinois Press, 1986; and Benjamin Beit-Hallahmi, *The Israeli Connection: Who Israel Arms and Why*. Pantheon, 1987. On **TT** (1985), see in particular ch. 1, n. 80, especially Israel Shahak, Israel's Global Role, Belmont: Association of Arab-American University Graduates, 1982.

Chomsky's article "The Soviet Union vs Socialism," written on Sept. 2, 1985, was commissioned by the Canadian journal *New Internationalist*, which, revealingly, failed to publish it. It appeared in *Our Generation* 17:2 (1986), pp. 47–52, and was later (December) included in *The Radical Papers*, edited by Dimitrios I. Roussopoulos. Montréal: Black Rose Books, 1987, pp. 47–52.

40. The "Right Turn" in U.S. Policy (22 October 1986)

I guess what I want to ask about is activism, what can be done. Do elections matter? What do you think?

Elections matter to the extent that the population creates a crisis of democracy. If elections are just something in which some portion of the population goes and pushes a button every couple of years, elections don't matter. In fact, they're irrelevant. On the other hand, if the public organizes to press its position, elections do matter. If citizens are constantly pressing their representatives, they can make a difference. The way our system works, it's the amount of organization and the amount of pressure that counts. What that means is kind of obvious, and everybody who thinks about it knows it. Your congressional representatives can be influenced much more easily than your senator, and the senator can be influenced somewhat more easily than the president, who is usually immune. When you get to the level of the executive, policy answers almost totally to elite groups. Basically, those who own the society and manage it. At the level of congressional representatives, popular opinion makes a difference because you can organize at a scale which will influence your representative. You can get your representative to come to your home, for example, and get a group of neighbors and yell at him, or have people sit in his office or whatever works considering the circumstances. It can make a difference. Often it can make an important difference. Take, say, Contra aid. That came close. A little more political activism could have swung that vote, which would have made a tremendous difference in the amount of torture and murder and destruction in Central America. We didn't do it, we failed, and it could have been done at the congressional level.

Scale of Protest and Significant Change

When you're trying to reverse things like the arms race it's harder because there you're talking about real institutional structures which are very hard to change. Nevertheless, things can be done. For example, it might be possible to put enough pressure on Congress to essentially compel the government to join the comprehensive test ban, to extend it to a comprehensive ban on both nuclear weapons tests and missiles. Every arms analyst will tell you what that means: that the threat of a first strike erodes. It's a costless, verifiable protection against a first strike.

Frankly, I think a first strike is a total fantasy. Anyone who believes this stuff knows that to carry out a first strike—let's get into the world of illusion in which

527

people talk about these things—to carry out a first strike requires very high confidence in your weapons. A test ban, including a missile ban, will over time erode confidence. Therefore, it's a literally costless and certainly verifiable way of achieving what SDI [Strategic Defense Initiative], "Star Wars," is theoretically supposed to achieve. It might be possible to get the United States to join that. That would have long-term effects. It wouldn't change the system right off. But it would have the effect of beginning to modify the system of industrial management which uses the Pentagon as the way of forcing the public to subsidize high-tech industry and, if it was combined with another parallel citizens' effort to block intervention and hence undermine the necessity for a nuclear umbrella to permit it to continue, you can imagine very significant changes in the country. But that takes a scale of protest that's well beyond a group of people sitting in here and there at their congressman's office or inviting their representatives to their house.

Sure, elections can matter, if they are just the forward edge of a citizenry that's really insisting on participating and determining policy at every stage of the game from planning through implementation. If elections are just something you just show up for every once in a while, you're just playing a game that's being run by elites.

As you may know, there's been a lot of activity here on the University of Colorado campus with regard to the Central Intelligence Agency. There's also been relatively a lot in the mainstream media about the role of the CIA in Central America recently because of Hasenfus and a few other things. I'm wondering if you can comment a little bit on the role of the CIA in Central America and maybe relate that to the fact that there was a congressional study that said that the CIA needed more money as they weren't carrying out their intelligence role.

The CIA in Central America, what they're doing in secret, one doesn't know, and nobody should be surprised that **an administration committed to lawlessness** will find complex ways to evade congressional restrictions just as it snubs its nose at international law and the World Court. Obviously. So nobody should be surprised at the discovery that the Reagan administration had established a complex network to provide arms for what it itself calls its "proxy army" in violation of congressional restrictions. However, it's harder than if it's open, and now it's open.

The worst feature of the recent congressional vote was not so much the $100 million. A lawless administration will find a way to fund its terrorist army one way or another. The worst feature of it was the involvement of the CIA, which is now open and legitimate. Sources have already leaked that that means right off about $400 million in CIA funds, but the point is that it's essentially endless. The CIA does what it wants. Theoretically there's senatorial control, but since it's secret it doesn't exist. That means that now the CIA can escalate the war as it chooses with limitless funds. The United States is a very rich and powerful and also very violent and murderous state. No small country can possibly resist

democratic loophole

this kind of attack. We could buy up the whole country and turn it into merce-naries, given the relative scale. We can carry out massive terror. There's almost no limit to what the United States can do. Just look at the comparison between the United States and Nicaragua. It's ridiculous. So once the CIA is let loose the bars are let down.

Apart from what that means to Nicaragua and maybe the rest of the region, we might bear in mind that it has other possible consequences.

The CIA in Central American and the Rest of the World

For example, one thing that the CIA might try to do, if the CIA's terrorist army cannot succeed in its aims … But notice that it's already succeeded: The United States has already won the war; we have forced the Sandinistas to divert resources away from social reforms, exactly as the government states, and that opens the way for every hypocrite in the United States, as I said, to point to that fact as their failure, and therefore to argue that we're going to attack them more—just as any commissar would say under comparable circumstances in the Soviet Union. So that's already won. The only question is can we pursue it to the point where we do, say, what the liberal editors of the *Washington Post* tell us ought to be done: "To restore Nicaragua to the Central American mode." Can we turn it into a state based on terror and torture like El Salvador and Guatemala, or can we return it to a state like Honduras, where half the population is starving to death? Can we do that?—It's what they're asking. Well, maybe we can. If the terrorist army can't succeed in that itself, the CIA, once it's involved, will do other things. For example, they may begin to do what they began to do before the congressional restrictions were imposed: to use high-technology resources, where we of course dominate, to impose a blockade on Nicaragua. You can do that with high-speed boats, the same piranha speedboats that were used to bomb the ports and attack the oil installations in some of the many activities which were condemned by the World Court as "aggression." (Remember that aggression is the crime that people were hanged for after World War II.) So you can continue with those operations. Nicaragua plainly doesn't have the technology to stop them.

But those operations, if they move towards a blockade, will be directed par-ticularly against Cuban and Soviet shipping. Cuba and the Soviet Union have the means to respond. If they choose to carry out those means, if they choose to defend their shipping against an American attack, you can be quite certain that the American media and American liberal congressmen will express incredible outrage against this new expression of Communist aggression and a desire to conquer the world, as illustrated by the fact that they're defending their ships against our attack. That's what will happen, and we will then respond by esca-lating the violence. It doesn't take long for that to go to a global war, not long at all. In fact, in that respect, the United States is once again playing with fire. So quite apart from what all of this means for the region, it also means a not incon-siderable threat of global war. That's the CIA in Central America.

Of course, that's not the only place where they're active. You can tell other stories in the rest of the world, and it's not just the CIA. We have many resources of violence. For example, we use client states. You'll have noticed in the current Hasenfus story that it has surfaced that the United States is using Saudi Arabia as a way of funneling arms to the terrorist army. If you think it through, notice how intricate this planning is, just as in the cases I've mentioned. The planners are not stupid. Look at the fine print of what's coming out in the *New York Times* and the *Wall Street Journal* today, and you'll notice the following: "In 1981 the Reagan administration supported sending AWACS [airborne warning and control system] aircraft (super high-tech surveillance aircraft) to Saudi Arabia over the opposition of the Israeli lobby." That's kind of unusual. They rarely are ready to run that kind of political risk. But this time they did it, which means they had a real reason. Notice, incidentally, that when state policy is involved, the Israeli lobby is not very significant. They're only significant when they conform to state policy. So in this case the government overrode the Israeli lobby, which is a powerful political force, and sent AWACS to Saudi Arabia.

Iran Contra

It wasn't so obvious then what was the big stake. Now we know. The stake was lining up Saudi Arabia in the United States' crusade for international terrorism in Central America. We use Israel for the same purpose, incidentally. As I mentioned, contrary to many falsehoods, under the Carter administration American arms to the murderous regime of Guatemala continued at virtually the norm, even publicly, that's what Panama official figures say, what was going on by other means was another story, more certainly. But it wasn't enough, because *democratic* there was a rather significant war going on and Congress was preventing the *loopholes* American executive from participating directly. So we used proxies. We used Argentine neo-Nazis who in the words of Brian Jenkins, the Rand Corporation's specialist on terrorism, were "proxies for the United States." We used Taiwan. But primarily we used Israel. Just as we're using Saudi Arabia to support terrorists attacking Nicaragua, we were using Israeli specialists to support state terrorism in Guatemala. It was effective. The numbers killed during those years is estimated at roughly 75,000, which is not inconsiderable. Again, brutal murder and torture all the way through. We do the same in our efforts to destabilize southern Africa, what's called "constructive engagement." That requires supporting South Africa, as it required supporting Rhodesia and undermining the international boycott against Rhodesia. We use Israel for that purpose and probably Saudi Arabia too. The United States is a very powerful state. There hasn't been such a powerful state in history, and it has many mechanisms that it can use for its purposes of, in this case, international terrorism. The CIA is one, an important one, but it's not the only one.

You spoke briefly about mass media a while ago, and I'd like you to expand on that. In your opinion, how do they control the mass media and who does it?

The mass media are, in the first place, major corporations. They are some of the biggest corporations in the country. They are closely interlocked with other corporations. They are part of the small network of individuals and interests which effectively own the private economy and staff the state executive. If you look at the people who hold the high planning positions in the state executive under any administration, they come from corporate boardrooms, investment banks, a half a dozen law firms that cater to corporate interests, and so on. There are a number of studies of this, if you're interested. That's the same group of people, the same interests, who own the media. So naturally they share a perception of the world and general interests. That's at the top level.

Now suppose you're down to the editorial level, or the reporter's level. At that point, you find pressures to conform. A young journalist will quickly learn that certain things are reportable and other things aren't. You can say things in a certain way and you can't say things in other ways. And you learn it from your editors, the people right above you, and they've learned it from the people above them.

Keep in mind that corporations are the private equivalent of what we call fascism in the political realm. The decision-making structure in a corporation is top down. You give orders and they are executed down below, etc., and the orders ultimately come from the owners. Furthermore, the media have a market. That market is other corporations. The market for the media is advertisers. Remember that the media do not make their money on sales to you and me. In fact, every purchase of a newspaper or journal usually costs them money. That's the way **the political economy of the media** work. Their market is advertisers, which imposes yet another constraint. They want to maintain a relationship to the state, which is their friend. There's a kind of interpenetration up and back. Even individuals flow up and back: Bernard Kalb, Leslie Gelb, etc. Of course they flow up and back because they represent the same interests. There's a constant flow between corporate boardrooms, state managers, media executives and top-level media people, university elites who play the game by the rules, etc. They all belong to the same privileged elite. They all benefit the same way. They perceive the world the same way. If any of them get out of line, they're excluded. That can happen even at a very high level. For example, a couple of years ago the top editorial staff of the *New York Times* was essentially thrown out (John Oakes and others) because they were beginning to deviate a little bit.

If you look at the mechanisms it's very clear. In the mid-70s there began to be reports in the business press (the *Wall Street Journal, Business Week*) pointing out subtly that the *New York Times'* stock was declining on the stock market. They pointed out: if the *New York Times* doesn't realize that it's a business, soon it won't be in business any more. In fact, they did replace a good part of the top editorial board at that time.

What was the great crime that the *New York Times* was committing at that point? If you look back, it turns out that they were editorially supporting some very mild fiscal reform measures that business didn't happen to like. That was enough to set in motion the technique of control.

You'll notice that the state is under exactly the same technique of control in a capitalist democracy. Suppose that the state is staffed by those who have resources, but suppose it tried to deviate. Suppose it tried to pursue policies that didn't conform to the interests of those who make the investment decisions, who essentially own the place. What would happen—in fact, does happen? A decline in investment, the beginning of capital flight, just a little bit, enough to tell them that the country's going to go down the tubes unless they go back to the main course. What that means is that when true decision-making power is in private hands, the political system is marginal and the ideological institutions are limited. These conditions almost never arise, because they're all staffed by people with the same background and interests and perceptions anyway.

Getting back again to the reporter: they just shape up or else they're out. This happens in universities, too. Those of you who are going into the ideological professions, the social sciences, etc., will learn this. You'll learn that you've got to conform. It's not 100 percent; the system is willing to tolerate statistical error. But it's got to be enough so that there isn't any significant deviation. You do come under pressures to conform, all sorts of pressures. You'll find out what they are, if you don't know already. Those pressures are effective. What they do is weed out independent people. But there's also something very interesting that you might as well be aware of if you haven't faced it yet, because it'll happen. What happens is that if you decide, well, I'll conform a little, I'll do what they say but I'll keep my independence of mind, if you begin to do that, you're lost unless you're a very rare individual. What happens is you begin to conform, you begin to get the privilege of conformity, you soon come to believe what you're saying because it's useful to believe it, and then you've internalized the system of indoctrination and distortion and deception and then you're a willing member of the privileged elites that control thought and indoctrination. That happens all the time, all the way to the top. It's a very rare person, almost to the point of non-existence, who can tolerate what's called "cognitive dissonance"—saying one thing and believing another. You start saying certain things because it's necessary to say them and pretty soon you believe them because you just have to.

There is no atrocity, in my view, that has been carried out in the world that wasn't justified by its perpetrators as highly moral. That includes the Nazi genocide. If you read Himmler's diaries, to go to the extreme, they're full of how noble this is and how much strength it requires, etc. Slavery was justified by the slave owners with moral arguments. If we had records from Attila the Hun, we'd probably find out that what he was doing was highly moral. Same with Stalin and every mass murderer in history.

It happens at a much lower level for individuals. You're all familiar with this from your personal lives, and it's worth bearing in mind. I doubt if there's anyone here who hasn't done pretty rotten things in their life at some time. I also am willing to bet that every one of you has figured out a way to make that exactly the right and morally correct thing to do.

That's what happens when you become parts of institutions, too. That's the way the indoctrination works on the participants. And it ends up being a very effective system, ultimately rooted in control of the resources, exactly as you'd expect. It's not very mysterious. People talk about it as a conspiracy theory. That's really idiotic. It's not a conspiracy. If the board of managers of General Motors decides to maximize profit, that's not a conspiracy. If they didn't do it, they'd be thrown out. It's the institutional role they have to play. The ideological institutions also have a role that they have to play within a nexus of institutions, and if they don't play that role, or if individuals within them don't play that role, they'll be replaced by others who do, because these are institutional facts, like the arms race.

On the way in here a number of us were given material about Israel and Zionism. I'm wondering if you can give us some brief examples of the connection between Israel and, let's say, Guatemala, El Salvador and Somoza's Nicaragua.

I'm afraid, given the time, that I can't answer, but let me refer you to some sources. The general fact is that, as in many other parts of the world, Israel did serve as the agent of the Carter and Reagan administrations to circumvent the fact that the congressional human rights campaign had put certain constraints on their ability to participate in genocide. So we did it through Israel. Not only Israel: Taiwan, Argentina, Saudi Arabia. There's a network of pariah states that we use for that purpose. Israel is the best because they're the most dependable since they're totally dependent. That's one of the reasons we maintain the military confrontation in the Middle East and block peace. We want to keep them dependent. They're technologically advanced. It's highly militarized. It's a Sparta. The United States wants to keep them that way. They were very good at it.

For example, they provided the computer systems which enabled the Guatemalan government to monitor electricity and water flow in apartments in Guatemala City so that if some apartments seemed to have too many people in them they could send in the death squads to get rid of them and various things like that worked pretty well. The so-called model villages (which are a system for controlling the rural population in a vicious fashion, I should say), they also organized that. That's Guatemala. The same is true in a lot of other places.

If you want some details on it, there's some stuff in my book *Turning the Tide* and a lot of references. You'll find a lot of material in a journal called *Israeli Foreign Affairs*, if your library has it (they may not). There's a new book by Cheryl Rubenberg, who is a professor at Florida State University. There's a book coming out by an Israeli scholar named Benjamin Beit-Hallahmi, a professor at Haifa University; he goes through this and other similar things in great detail. These are some sources you can look at for details. This isn't the time to go into it.

With respect to disinformation and political and social rhetoric, would you comment on the uses of humor historically and their relative impact to other methods of straight education and editorial in dealing with shifting political awareness?

Let me suggest that I not answer. It's an interesting question, but I think that it's enough off track so that, given the hour, if you don't mind, I won't answer it.

I'm interested in hearing you speak on the terms "liberal" and "conservative," since you obviously use "conservative" in a much more narrow sense.

In its dictionary sense.

It's rather ambiguous in terms of what is to be conserved.

The terms of political discourse are at best not models of clarity. In fact, liberal and conservative are interesting in that they've just shifted around totally. What is now called **"conservative" in the dictionary sense** was called "liberal" in the late 19th century. There's a whole set of ideas called **"classical liberalism"** represented by a lot of Enlightenment figures. Some of the most important are von Humboldt, who inspired John Stuart Mill, and Mill himself, and it goes back to Locke and that tradition of classical liberalism. Nowadays that's called conservatism. That's what should be called conservatism, when the term is used properly. It's opposition to state power. This is part of what the underlying conception of the United States government was before it became a state capitalist system in the 19th century. But when we go back to the 18th century, the conception was basically this: Imagine a society of essentially equal people—in fact, if you look, it was equal white male property owners, but if you put that aside, a society of equal people, roughly equal. And what barriers are there to liberty? Slavery, the church and the state. So therefore we've got to weaken state power, weaken church power and end slavery. Ideas of that sort are basically classical liberalism developed with a good deal of sophistication. A modern conservative, like Taft, wants to cut back state power, cut back state intervention in the economy—the same as someone like Mark Hatfield—to preserve the Enlightenment ideals of freedom of expression, freedom from state violence, of law-abiding states, etc. That's roughly modern conservatism. There's almost no conservatives these days. Hatfield's one, I'm another, you can find a couple of others. The way the term "conservative" is now used, it's used for people like Reagan, people who want to expand the power of the state, to increase state intervention in the economy, to protect the state from public surveillance, to destroy civil liberties, to tear whatever there is of law to shreds, etc. That has nothing to do with conservatism.

What about liberalism? Liberalism, as I said, used to mean what I just described. The **modern** term **"liberalism,"** however, means something quite different. Certainly since the 1930s, "liberalism" has meant a commitment to the use of state power for welfare purposes, New Deal-type measures, etc. That's very different from classical liberalism. It sort of sheds off towards modern **social democracy**. You can make some sense out of these terms, they all have some sort of vague meaning. The new meaning of the term **"conservative"** as applied to the Reaganites, that has no meaning at all. These guys are the opposite of conservative in any sense, on any issue you can think of. They are fanatic statists. They believe in state power and state violence and expansion of state power. They believe in lawlessness. It has nothing to do with conservatism. The fact that you can even use the word "conservative" to refer to this is astonishing. If Robert Taft heard this, he would turn over in his grave. These are all the things he and any conservative fought against.

Could you speculate briefly on the impact that the dismissal of the diplomats from the United States and the U.S.S.R will have on our future?

The impact will be to somewhat harshen relations between the two powers. I don't think it will have a major impact, frankly. The reason is, I think, that both sides want to keep talking. The Russians want to keep talking because they're in trouble. Soviet society is in fact a dungeon, a totalitarian dungeon. But the fact of the matter is that the Gorbachev government wants to devote resources towards domestic needs and to turn away from the arms race, for all kinds of reasons. For one thing they're scared; for another thing they're trying to be a more benevolent dictatorship, etc. That means they need negotiations.

That's why **Gorbachev** has made this **incredible series of offers**. It's unbelievable, when you think about it. Much of it isn't even reported here. Just think of what they've offered lately: for over a year they've had a unilateral test ban. The last offer, they offered to withdraw all of their intermediate-range missiles and to permit Britain and France not only to maintain their missile force but even to improve it. I don't even think that was mentioned here. I mean we somehow pretend that the British and French missiles don't hurt when they hit. They do, they're just like anybody else's missiles. It doesn't matter whose name is on them. But they were willing to withdraw their missiles and let the British and French missiles remain. They have proposed elimination of the pact system, just eliminating it. I don't know if they mean it, since the United States was terrified and immediately backed down and we never pursued it. Gorbachev proposed dismantling NATO and the Warsaw Pact. If Americans cared even minimally about Poland or Hungary, we'd jump at that opportunity. We don't need NATO to control Germany or France, but they do need the Warsaw Pact to control Poland. So if we, I mean, if the U.S. government and U.S. elites even had a marginal interest in the welfare of the Poles, which of course they don't, they would at once leap at this opportunity and see if you could pursue it. No Soviet government in the world, even if it's run by liberal democrats, is ever going to withdraw its control over Eastern Europe if Germany is part of a hostile military alliance.

That's transparent. Germany alone almost destroyed Russia not long ago. Germany as part of a hostile military alliance is part of a real threat. They happen to have real threats. We don't, but they do. They're surrounded by powerful enemies in Western Europe, Turkey and elsewhere. We're not. They proposed a dismantling of the pacts. We fled from that one. It was not even mentioned here. They proposed withdrawing all Russian and American fleets from the Mediterranean. That's extremely important. The Russian and American fleets have repeatedly come into confrontation in the Mediterranean. Every time there's an Arab-Israeli war, the Russian and American fleets come into confrontation. In fact, in 1967, we almost went to war, McNamara testified about it. The two fleets came into confrontation, and it's happened over and over. That's the way a nuclear war is likely to start. They're offering to withdraw the two fleets. For us, the Mediterranean is much less significant than it is to them. For them the Mediterranean is kind of like the Caribbean is for us: that's their only warm-water exit. But they're willing to withdraw their fleet, they say. We won't pursue it. And on and on. They've made a number of really astounding proposals which the United States does not want to accept. So I think from their point of view they're going to try to play down this conflict.

What about from the Reagan point of view? I don't think the Reagan administration wants any kind of a settlement. They would like to have a reduction of the number of missiles, for the reason I mentioned, because it's totally insignificant and irrelevant and our comparable advantage is not in production anyway. In fact, our missiles are now using Japanese components. That's true. We're increasingly relying on Japan and even South Korea for the most sophisticated parts in our missiles because this Pentagon system of public subsidy is so inefficient that we can't compete with our industrial rivals. So production of missiles is not a big business for us. Our comparative advantage is in new technology. We've got to keep that going, and we have no other method other than the Pentagon system. It's very hard to think of another. They're going to keep the confrontation going. They need a shield for intervention. They need, of course, the public to subsidize high technology. They might accept, in fact welcome, a reduction in actual level of armaments, but they're always going to keep insisting on continual improvement for these reasons. That's why we're ahead and that's the way we keep our industrial system going. But nevertheless the Reagan administration does want to talk, and the reason is, again, they're afraid of their major enemy, the domestic population, both here and in Europe. You've got to shut them up. You don't want too much turmoil in Europe, you don't want too much turmoil here, so the way you do it is to continue to show a forthcoming willingness to participate in negotiations.

You want to look at disinformation, look at the way they handled that Reykjavik summit. Magnificent. They came out of the Reykjavik summit with George Schultz with a long face, everybody with a long face, all on television, saying, oh God, it was a catastrophe, a disaster. Then they realized that's not going to play in Peoria. So they switched 180 degrees and all of a sudden George Schultz comes on beaming and Reagan comes on beaming. It was a fantastic success, and the whole press switched around like parrots: yes, it was a fantastic success, everybody loved it, like trained parrots. And they've got to keep doing that because you've got to keep worrying about your primary enemy, the domestic population; to keep them quiet.

So to get back to your comment, I don't think that this is going to have a big effect, because each side, for different reasons, wants to keep the discussions going.

There's a segment of the industrial portion of the United States that makes a tremendous amount of money off the arms race, but in the Soviet Union they don't apparently have that, they don't have a system where people get rich off the arms race. That's one reason to believe they're sincere in offering to stop testing and to dismantle their portion of the arms race. Are there any other reasons to believe that they're insincere? Are there ways in which they really may gain or profit from the arms race?

Your point is very important. They don't have exactly the same motives we do to keep the military system going. Nevertheless, you'll notice that they also have been dedicated to building up their military system way beyond any conceivable need of defense. They have actual security problems that we don't, but nevertheless, their arms buildup has been well in advance of any reasonable defensive needs. So why do they do it? This is a command economy. People just follow orders. So you don't have to get the public to subsidize industry through devious means.But it is a state based on force and violence. First of all, the Soviet Union itself is an empire internally. The thing that is colored red on the map, that's an empire run by a Russian minority with complex ethnic groupings which are not small, like 40 million Muslims and I don't know how many Ukrainians. There's a whole pile of people within that internal empire who are controlled by force. Furthermore, they control their own population by force.

I talked about some of the techniques of use of terminology to delude. One of the most extreme such cases is the use of the term "socialism" to refer to the Soviet Union. The Leninist coup, the Bolshevik coup in 1917 (and that's what it was) was not a revolution. There was a popular revolution that was taken over by a managerial elite who immediately dismantled all the socialist institutions. They dismantled the workers' councils, they dismantled the "soviets" [democratic councils] and they placed the state in the hands of a revolutionary vanguard of managerial intellectuals (rather like the statist intellectuals in the West, I should say), who took power on the backs of a popular revolution, dismantled the popular institutions and turned the country into what they themselves called a labor army (that's what Trotsky was calling it in 1918), a labor army which will be subordinated to the needs of a leader who will drive them on to utopia, etc.

That's a dream of the intellectuals way back (it's almost **a disease of the intelligentsia**) to use state power, which you can attain on the basis of popular struggles, so that you can then create a properly managed society, run by smart intellectuals, where everybody does his job and does what he's told and it'll all work fine. That's Leninism. That's **the exact opposite of socialism**. If socialism means anything, it means workers' control of production and then on from there. That's the first thing they destroyed. So why do we call it socialism?—and, incidentally, if you're running that kind of society, you need violence.

That's the answer to your question. That's why they build up their system: first the internal empire, and then, because they need violence to run that managerial state—which is just kind of an extreme form of what Western so-called liberals want, one of the reasons they shift so easily from being Communists to celebrating America. And, furthermore, they've got Eastern Europe to contend with. As long as we keep Germany in a hostile military alliance, they're certainly going to control Eastern Europe, and they're going to do it by force, because there's no other way.

So a last comment, which does not exactly answer your question, is, why is this stuff called socialism? Here you have one of the rare cases where the two major propaganda systems in the world agree on something, agree on a certain form of deception, and when that happens it's very hard to extricate yourself from it. Why do they agree? The United States propaganda system wants to call that socialism so as to defame socialism, to destroy the idea that there could really be popular democratic control over the basic institutions of the society. That's hated by American elites, so if you can associate it with a Soviet dungeon, great. That's why we call it socialism on this side.

What about their propaganda system? They are trying to get the maximal mileage that they can out of the moral force (which is quite real and quite justified) that's associated with the socialist ideals. And in fact libertarian socialism, in my view, is the true inheritor of classical conservatism and liberalism—when you really think through what the classical liberals were saying, in a society in which it's not just the state and the church that are powerful institutions that dominate, but the state, the church and corporations. They didn't think of that. That's something later. But the same ideals under these new circumstances lead you right on to libertarian socialist ideals. A lot of people understand that outside of the United States. The United States is intellectually and culturally a very backward area where these topics can't be discussed. But in other parts of the world that are less controlled they can be, and there's a certain proper moral prestige or aura associated with these libertarian ideals. The Soviet leadership would like to gain for themselves whatever they can by association with them, so they call their system "socialist." We call that system "socialist" in order to defame it by associating it with them, so everybody calls it "socialist." That's one of the most useful techniques for destroying socialism that exists. If you want more stuff on this, I have an article that just came out called "The Soviet Union vs Socialism," which was in fact sent to a Marxist journal which wouldn't publish it, although they commissioned it and it later came out in an anarchist journal.

Editor's Notes to Interview 41

This is the third Barsamian interview (see Editor's Notes to I35). The first four questions and answers appeared in an undated issue of *Nerve* (an innovative periodical published in Denver), pp. 3 & 13.

Chomsky might very well be the only one still trying to make sure we never forget about the assassination of Fred Hampton, a very dedicated and very effective activist. See his 1976 introduction to *COINTELPRO* (notes to I39), p. 12ff.; Derek S. B. Davis, "The Academic Renegade," *Pennsylvania Gazette* 79:1, October 1980, p. 26; and I43. It should be added here that when the black community in Chicago wanted a white representative to appear at Hampton's mass funeral, they asked Chomsky, perhaps because he was one of those who was involved with the more serious elements of the Panthers during the period when they were under severe police attack. (As noted in Introduction, n. 39, the verb "to mace," first used in 1968 (not exactly by sheer chance), means "to attack with the liquid Mace (a trademark)", ("a temporarily disabling liquid that when sprayed in the face of a person ... causes tears, dizziness, immobilization, and sometimes nausea.") See Editor's Notes to I20.

On the sacrilege of using the Holocaust as a justification for oppressing others, see interviews 18, 30, and 49; also, Norman G. Finkelstein's *The Holocaust Industry: Reflection on the Exploitation of Jewish Suffering* (London; New York: VERSO, 2000), a best-seller in England and most of the Continent, and the topic of an enormous amount of public discussion in the European media. On U.S.-Israeli rejectionism, see Editor's Notes to I36.

On Orwell, see Editor's Notes to I30.

41. Political Discourse and the Propaganda System (24 October 1986)

To what extent does the control of language shape and form our perceptions and understanding of reality?

There are obvious examples. One important fact to bear in mind when one listens to or is subjected to political discourse is that most terms are used in a kind of a technical meaning that's really very much divorced from their actual meaning, sometimes even the opposite of it. For example, take a term like "national interest." The term "national interest" is commonly used as if it's something good for us, and the people of the country are supposed to understand that. So if a political leader says that "I'm doing this in the national interest," you're supposed to feel good because that's for me. However, if you look closely, it turns out that the national interest is not defined as what's defined in the interest of the entire population; it's what's in the interests of small, dominant elites who happen to be able to command the resources that enable them to control the state—basically, corporate-based elites. That's what's called the "national interest." And, correspondingly, the term "special interests" is used in a very interesting related way to refer to the population. The population are called the "special interest" and the corporation elite are called the "national interests"; so you're supposed to be in favor of the national interests and against the special interests.

This became very clear in the last few presidential campaigns. The Reagan administration is largely a figment of the public relations industry, and the public relations aspects of it, including control over language, are very striking—it's a professional public relations outfit. It was interesting to see how every choice of terms they use is carefully crafted. In both the 1980 and 1984 elections, they identified the Democrats as the "party of special interests," and that's supposed to be bad, because we're all against the special interests. But if you look closely and ask who were the special interests, they listed them: women, poor people, workers, young people, old people, ethnic minorities—in fact, the entire population. There was only one group that was not listed among the special interests: corporations. If you'll notice the campaign rhetoric, that was never a special interest, and that's right, because in their terms that's the national interest. So if you think through it, the population are the special interests and the corporations are the national interests, and since everyone's in favor of the national interests and against the special interests, you vote for and support someone who's

541

against the population and is working for the corporations. This is a typical case of the way the framework of thought is consciously manipulated by an effective choice and reshaping of terminology so as to make it difficult to understand what's happening in the world. A very important function of the ideological institutions—the media, the schools, and so on—is to prevent people from perceiving reality, because if they perceived it they might not like it and might act to change it, and that would harm privileged people who control these things.

Perhaps it's like George Orwell said in his essay "Politics and the English Language," that in our time political speech and writing is largely the "defense of the indefensible."

Yes, he gave interesting examples which are now classic, like the term "pacification." It is used for mass murder; thus we carried out "pacification" in Vietnam. If you look at what the pacification programs were, they were literally programs of mass murder to try to suppress and destroy a resisting civilization population. Orwell wrote long before Vietnam, but he already noted that pacification was being used that way, by now it's an industry. Orwell had pointed out early examples of this kind of usage. A standard example is "defense." In the United States up until 1947 we used to have something called the "War Department." Since 1947 we haven't had a War Department; we've had a "Defense Department." Anyone who had his head screwed on realized in 1947 that we were not going to be involved in defense any more, we were only going to be involved in war, and that's why the War Department has to be renamed the Defense Department, because "defense" means "aggression." By now this is a sophisticated operation.

It's the same with every term you can think of. Take the term "conservative." Conservative is supposed to be a good thing, and this is supposed to be a conservative administration. A true conservative, like, say, Robert Taft, would turn over in his grave to see what's being called conservative. Everything the conservatives have always fought against is being advanced by this administration. This administration is in favor of extending the power of the state and increasing the intervention of the state in the economy, which has increased faster under this administration than under any since the Second World War. It's also interested in protecting the state against its citizens, cutting down access to the state, controlling thought, controlling expression, attacking civil liberties, attacking individual rights—total lawlessness. It's the most lawless administration we've ever had. All of these things are an anathema to conservatives. Conservatives want the opposite in every respect, so naturally they call the administration conservative, and if you like it you're supposed to be conservative. These are all **ways of undermining the possibility of independent thought** by eliminating even the tools that you can use to engage in it.

Could you talk a little bit about the power of naming? That seems to be crucial in this whole process.

These are all examples of it. Language is, after all, a tool for thought. If you debase the language, you debase the thought. I don't want to exaggerate this element of it, but it is one element, and one that's certainly consciously manipulated in order to introduce confusion and lack of perception.

It seems in recent years, certainly starting in the 70s and through the 80s and for the foreseeable future, the term "terrorism" has become a dominant issue, a theme and focus for the media and politicians. I wonder if you could talk about the word itself. It seems to have undergone a curious transformation in the last couple of centuries.

It definitely has, it's a very interesting case. The word "terrorism" came into general use at the end of the 18th century, and it was then used to refer to acts of violent states that suppressed their own populations by violence. Terror was the action of a state against its own citizens. That concept is of no use whatsoever to people in power so, predictably, the term has come to be changed. Now it's the actions of citizens against states; in fact, the term "terrorism" is now almost entirely used for what you might call "**retail terrorism**": the terrorism of small, marginal groups, and not the terrorism of powerful states. We have one exception to this: if our enemies are involved in terrorism, then you can talk about "state terrorism." So there are really two things that define terrorism. First, it's done against states, not by states against their citizens, and it's done by them, not us. So, for example, take Libya. Qaddafi is certainly a terrorist. The latest edition of the Amnesty International publication *Political Killings by Governments* lists Qaddafi as a terrorist; he killed 14 people, Libyans, mostly in Libya, in the 1980s. There may be a handful of others, but even taking the most extreme estimate it couldn't be more than several dozen, probably less. That's terrorism, and he's therefore the "Mad Dog of the Middle East" and the "King of International Terrorism." That's because he meets our criteria: he's them, not us, and the terrorism that one talks about is carried out generally by small groups, not by one of our major states.

Let's compare it with El Salvador. In the same years in which Libya killed maybe 14, maybe 20 people, mostly Libyans, the government of El Salvador slaughtered about 50,000 people. Now that's not just terrorism, that's international terrorism, because it was done by us. We instituted the government as much as the Russians instituted the government in Afghanistan; we created the army, a terrorist army; we supplied, organized and directed it. The worst atrocities were carried out by American-trained elite battalions fresh from their training; the U.S. Air Force participated directly in coordinating bombing strikes— the terror was not ordinary killing. Libyan terror is bad enough, they kill people. But our terrorists first mutilate, torture, rape, cut them to pieces—it's hideous torture, Pol Pot-style. That's not called terrorism. El Salvador is not called a terrorist state. José Napoleón Duarte, who has presided over all this, who has perceived his role from the beginning as ensuring that the murderers are supplied with weapons, and that nothing will interfere with the massacre which he knew was coming when he joined the military junta—he's called a great liberal hero, and El Salvador is considered a kind of magnificent triumph of democracy. Here's a major terrorist state—Libya is a very, very minor terrorist state—but we see it the other way around, and the reason is because "terrorism" is used for them, not us, and because in the case of El Salvador it's plainly being done by a major state against its own citizens—in fact a state that we established, a client state of the United States. Therefore it can't be terrorism, by definition. This is true in case after case. My book about it, *Pirates and Emperors*, takes its title from a rather nice story by St. Augustine in his *City of God*. St. Augustine describes a confrontation between Alexander the Great and a pirate whom he caught. Alexander the Great asks the pirate, "How dare you molest the sea?" The pirate turns to Alexander the Great and says, "How dare you molest the whole world? I have a small boat, so I am called a thief and a pirate. You have a navy, so you're called an emperor." St. Augustine concludes that the pirate's answer was elegant and excellent and that essentially tells the story. **Retail terrorism** directed against our interests is terrorism; **wholesale terrorism** carried out for our interests isn't terrorism.

The same is true in the Middle East region. In case after case this is the way the term is used, and very effectively. In fact it was very predictable that the Reagan administration would take international terrorism to be the core of its foreign policy, as it announced right off. The reason was that the administration made it very clear that it was going to be engaged in international terrorism on a massive scale, and since it's going to be engaged in international terrorism, naturally, in a good public relations-directed world, you start off by saying that you're opposed to international terrorism. That shifts attention away from the crucial issue: that you're going to maximize international terrorism.

Why the tremendous fascination with terrorism—the TV specials, the articles, the documentaries, the symposia, the conferences, and on and on—is there something deeper that's being touched by this?

Oh, yes, very deep. It's very close to the Reagan administration's domestic policies. It's important to remember that the Reagan administration's policies are extremely unpopular, and for obvious reasons. The polls show this very clearly; on just about every major issue the public is strongly opposed to the Reagan programs. Take, say, social spending versus military spending. When the question is asked in polls: Would you prefer to have a decrease in welfare payments or in military spending? the overwhelming majority of the population supports social spending and opposes military spending. In fact, much of the population is quite willing to see taxes raised to improve social spending. The same is true on just about every issue. On intervention abroad (in other words, international terrorism, if we were to be honest), the population is strongly against it, by large majorities. The Reagan administration is for it. On the nuclear freeze, the public is overwhelmingly in favor of it; the figure is something like three to one. The administration is against it. And so on. As you go down the line, every major policy program is unpopular. This is a problem, of course; you've got to control the population. There is a classic answer to this problem: you frighten them.

Let me just go back to another step of the Reagan program which is even more obvious. An essential part of the Reagan program was to try to transfer resources from the poor to the rich. Now, that's going to be unpopular, and the attack on social spending is a part of it. Much of the Reagan program is turning an increasingly powerful state into a welfare state for the rich. The military program is very largely for that purpose. That's a forced public subsidy to advance industry, again unpopular, and you can't present it in these terms. What do you do? You have to get the public lined up. They oppose your policies. There's only one way to deal with this; every leader throughout history has understood it. You've got to frighten them, make them think their lives are at stake, that they've got to defend themselves, and then they'll accept these programs that they despise or dislike as an unfortunate necessity. How do you terrify people? Again, there's a classic answer: you find some "Evil Empire" that's threatening to destroy them. In our case, it's now the Soviet Union; it used to be the Huns, before that the British, and so on. But since the Bolshevik revolution, it's been the Soviet Union that's threatening to destroy us. So that's the Evil Empire.But here you run into a problem. Confrontations with the Evil Empire are dangerous. That's a big, powerful state; it can fight back, and you don't want to get involved with them because you might get hurt. So what you have to do is have confrontations, but not with the Evil Empire—too dangerous. The best way out is to have confrontations with groups that you designate as "proxies" of the Evil Empire. What you do is to try to find essentially defenseless countries or groups that can be attacked at will and designate them to be proxies of the Evil Empire, and then you can defend yourself against them by attacking them.

Libya, for example, is perfect for this purpose. It has loose associations with the Soviet Union. It's a minor actor in the world of international terrorism. Against the background of anti-Arab racism, which is rampant in the United States—it's the last legitimate form of racism—you can easily talk about the mad dog and how he ought to get down from the trees and all this kind of stuff, and that works, that scares people. Furthermore, if you can manage to elicit terrorism, which some of our acts have done, that will really frighten people, since that strikes at home. In fact, actual terrorism is very slight; you're much more likely to be hit by lightning. But people can get scared, and a confrontation with Libya is cheap. You can kill Libyans at will; they can't fight back, it's a tiny, defenseless country, we can beat them up every time we feel like it. It will make people here feel that somehow our courageous cowboy leader is defending us from these monsters who are going to destroy us, most of which is a public relations concoction. In fact, throughout the history of the Reagan administration there has been a sequence, half a dozen or so, of carefully concocted fraudulent incidents created in order to give us an opportunity to attack and kill Libyans, always for some specific political purpose at home, like building up support for the rapid deployment force, an intervention force in the Middle East or gaining support for Contra aid or one thing or another. They're very carefully timed, as I said; this is a public relations administration. Their genius is manipulation of the public; that's what they're good at, and Libya is a perfect proxy of the Evil Empire, as I say: you can kill them, you can attack them, you can bomb them, people here can be frightened enough to think that they're somehow being defended by these terrorist attacks, and that way, if people feel sufficiently embattled, they'll support these programs that they oppose. And they do. The spring of 1986, for example, was a brilliant exercise in public relations …

The bombing of Libya …

And the impact. The pretext for it was completely fabricated. It was covered up by the media, which know the true story but will not report it. It terrified the domestic population—people wouldn't even go to Europe, they were so scared, which is ludicrous, you're a hundred times as safe in any European city as in any American city—but people were so terrified they stayed at home. That's wonderful, because if you can terrify the domestic population then they'll support things like Star Wars or whatever lunacy comes along with the feeling that you have to defend yourself. Crucially, you can't have confrontations with the Russians; they can fight back. So you've got to find somebody you can beat up at will: Grenada, Libya, Nicaragua, anybody who can't fight back, that's what you need. I should say, incidentally, that this is understood very well abroad. When you read the foreign press, they regularly comment on the thugishness and the cowardice of this administration, the sort of "bully on the block mentality": you find somebody little enough to beat up and you go send your goon squads to beat him up. That's essentially their style. But here somehow people can't see it.

This retail minor-actor terrorism you've been talking about—when it's presented in the media it occurs ahistorically: it has no context, it's totally irrational, so it seems that the logical response would be one of loathing and fear, and it's very effective.

That's right. And most of the retail terrorism—what is called "terrorism" in the United States—comes out of Lebanon, and that started in 1982. It was a very marginal phenomenon before that, a major phenomenon, mainly in Europe, after 1982; so plainly something must have happened in 1982 to cause terrorism to start coming out of Lebanon. Well, yes, something happened in 1982: with enthusiastic American support, Israel attacked Lebanon. The purpose of the Israeli attack was to demolish the civilian society of the Palestinians so as to ensure Israeli control over the West Bank, and in the process it also destroyed what was left of Lebanon. Lebanon was left in ruins, the Palestinian community was destroyed, and Lebanon, already in bad shape, got the final blow. The United States supported it all the way. We vetoed UN resolutions trying to stop the aggression, we supplied them with arms, diplomatic support, the whole business, and naturally it was perfectly predictable that that was going to evoke international terrorism. You cut off every political option for people and they are going to turn to terrorism. And I should say that this was well understood in Israel. Here you can't talk about it, because we're a much more indoctrinated country, but in Israel, which is a more democratic society—at least for the Jewish majority—this was openly discussed.

For example, the current Prime Minister, Yitzhak Shamir, pointed out that there was a threat to Israel from the Palestinians, but said it was a political, not a military threat. The threat was that they would compel Israel to enter into a political settlement, which it didn't want, and that had to be stopped. Israel's and perhaps the world's leading specialist on the Palestinians, a professor at Hebrew University named Yehoshua Porath, wrote an analysis shortly after the invasion, a long, detailed article in *Ha'aretz*, Israel's major newspaper (kind of like Israel's *New York Times*), in which he explained what he thought, very plausibly, the invasion was about. He said, and I'm paraphrasing: Look, here's the situation. For the last year, the PLO has not engaged in any cross-border terrorism. Israel has tried to get them to do it, we have continually bombed them and murdered them and so on to try to evoke some response across the border, but they haven't done it. They've kept discipline despite the fact that we've bombed them, killing dozens of people and so forth. This is a veritable catastrophe for the Israeli leadership, since if the PLO continues to maintain this posture of not engaging in cross-border terrorism and demanding a diplomatic settlement, Israel might be driven to a political settlement, which it does not want because in a political settlement it would have to give up control of the occupied territories. What the Israeli leadership wants is to return the PLO to much earlier days when it engaged in random terrorism, a PLO that will hijack airplanes, kill many Jews and be a source of loathing and horror throughout the world. They don't want a peaceful PLO that refuses to respond to Israeli terrorist attacks and insists on negotiation. That's what the invasion will achieve.

Others also commented in the same way, and that's a very plausible analysis. I presume that's what the planners in the Reagan administration wanted, too. From their point of view, terrorism coming out of Lebanon is very beneficial. It frightens the American population; terrorist acts are indeed loathsome, and if you cut people off from every possible option, you can predict pretty well that that's what they're going to do. So let's take, for example, the Karachi hijacking. It appears—we don't know for sure—as if the hijackers were victims of the Sabra-Shatila massacre. Everybody knows what that was. That's what happens—you send killers into a defenseless civilian area for the purpose of slaughtering and torturing people, and those who survive are very likely to turn to terrorism, and that's in effect what happened. People pretend they don't understand, but anyone who can look at dates can figure it out. The Lebanese-based terrorism, mainly in Europe, since 1982 is a direct, predictable and probably desired effect of the U.S.-backed Israeli aggression in Lebanon, which eliminated the hope of a political settlement, demolished the civilian society and the PLO—brutally, I should say—and smashed what was left of Lebanon to pieces; so that's what happens. And every time we look there's a context.

There's an interesting reaction here when this is brought up: "You're justifying terrorism." We're not justifying terrorism; justification and explanation are two different things. What you're pointing out is that there's an explanation for terrorism, and if you want to stop it you look at the explanation. When you look at the explanation you quite often find that violent, powerful states try to evoke terrorism because it's in their interest. That's no justification; it's an explanation. Terrorist acts are indeed loathsome. It was loathsome when Leon Klinghoffer was thrown off a boat in a wheelchair and killed on Oct. 7, 1985. It was also loathsome when, a week earlier, Israeli bombed Tunis and killed about 75 people using smart bombs that the United States probably supplied them. That's loathsome too. We regard one, but not the other, as terrorism, because one was wholesale terrorism on our side and the other was retail terrorism on their side.

That particular attack, the Tunis bombing, is, of course, always framed in the concept of retaliation; it was a response, not initiated.

Every terrorist act is always called retaliation. The sequence is as follows: first came a PLO attack in Larnaca, Cyprus, where three Israelis were killed. The killers were immediately caught and placed on trial; they're now in jail. About a week later came the Israeli bombing of Tunis in which, according to Israeli correspondents, about 75 people were killed, 20 Tunisians and 55 Palestinians, mostly civilians. Then, a week after that came the Achille Lauro hijacking with the Klinghoffer assassination. All three of these things were called retaliations by the people who did them. The Larnaca, Cyprus operation was called a retaliation for a fact which is suppressed here, namely that the Israeli navy, apparently using agents based on Cyprus, has been hijacking boats for over ten years—that's called terrorism when the other guy does it—boats in transit between Cyprus and various parts of northern Lebanon. In fact, they have often taken Palestinians off those boats and handed them over to their own Maronite allies in Lebanon, who then killed them. The PLO claimed that the Larnaca was in retaliation for the many years of hijacking, which certainly happened, there's no doubt. We didn't call that retaliation, we just called it terrorism.

Then came the Israeli bombing, which they called retaliation, except with one slight problem: it was not directed against the people who carried out the terrorist attack. In fact, Israel had conceded that the people they were bombing in Tunis apparently had nothing to do with the attack. But it was a cheap target. The people who had to do with the attack probably came from Syria, but that's not a cheap target; they can fight back. Tunis, on the other hand, is a defenseless target, so you attack that. That's the way it's always done. It was done, incidentally, with the complicity of the United States, the U.S. Sixth Fleet in the Mediterranean certainly had the Israeli bombers under surveillance. They claimed they couldn't see them, which was ridiculous. They had to fly all the way across the Mediterranean; they were refueled in flight, they passed by the most sophisticated radar and surveillance systems that the U.S. government and military can establish, and somehow we claimed that they were invisible. That's nonsensical; they obviously knew they were coming, and they didn't warn Tunis. Tunis is a loyal American ally, but we didn't warn them that the killers were on the way. Anyhow, they called that a retaliation, but of course it wasn't. It had nothing to do with the attack. Then came the Achille Lauro hijacking. They called that a retaliation, namely for the Tunis bombing, and you can trace it back as far as you like, go back to the first interaction, and every step is called by the terrorists a retaliation for what came before, and in a certain sense it is. That's the cycle: repression, violence, retaliation, more retaliation, preemption, etc. In our ideological system, we have a very simple way to handle it. When the guys we don't like do it, it's terror. When the guys we do like do it, it's retaliation.

You've talked extensively about the politics of language and semantics, and you've said, "We have to peel away veil after veil of distortion to see the truth." My question is, in the age of Orwell, and given the U.S. educational system, what intellectual tools is that system providing to students to decode, decipher and translate those Orwellian terms?

Let me first comment that, although we always, I too, call this the age of Orwell, the fact is that Orwell was a latecomer on the scene. The American public relations industry, which is a very sophisticated industry, already in the early 1920s was developing these tools, writing about them, and so on. In fact, even earlier, during the First World War, American historians offered themselves to President Woodrow Wilson to carry out a task that they called "historical engineering," meaning designing the facts of history so that they would serve state policy. That's Orwell, long before Orwell was writing. Shortly after that, American journalists like Walter Lippmann, the famous American journalist, said in 1921 that the art of democracy requires what he called "manufacture of consent," what the public relations industry calls "engineering of consent," another Orwellism meaning "thought control." The idea was that in a state in which the government can't control the people by force it had better control what they think. So well before Orwell this was understood, the techniques were designed and had been implemented extensively.

As to what the schools teach to defend people against this, the answer is simple: zero. In fact, the schools are quite on the opposite side: they are part of the disinformation apparatus. In fact, this is well understood, too. It's even well understood by liberal intellectuals, democratic theorists, and so on. For example, in the important study called *Crisis of Democracy*, another Orwellism meaning "beginnings of democracy," published by the Trilateral Commission, a group of international essentially liberal elites, people of whom Carter was a kind of representative, the ones who staffed his administration, international liberalism, they refer to the schools as "institutions responsible for the indoctrination of the young." Of course, they're talking to one another there, that's not what you say in public. But that's the way they're understood. They are **institutions for indoctrination**, for imposing obedience, for blocking the possibility of independent thought, and they play an institutional role in a system of control and coercion.

Real schools ought to provide people with techniques of self-defense, but that would mean teaching the truth about the world and about the society, and schools couldn't survive very long if they did that.

C.P. Otero, who has edited a collection of your essays titled Radical Priorities, *notes in his introduction as he outlines your social theory that "The totalitarian system of thought-control is far less effective than the democratic one, since the official doctrine parroted by the intellectuals at the service of the state is readily identifiable as pure propaganda, and this helps free the mind. In contrast, the democratic system seeks to determine and limit the entire spectrum of thought by leaving the fundamental assumptions unexpressed. They are presupposed but not asserted."*

That's quite accurate; I've also written about that many times. Just think about it. Take, say, a country which is at the opposite end of the spectrum from us domestically, the Soviet Union. That's a country run by the bludgeon, essentially. It's a command state, the state controls, everybody basically follows orders. It's more complicated than that, but essentially that's the way it works. There, it's very easy to determine what propaganda is: what the state produces is propaganda. That's the kind of thing that Orwell described in *1984*—not a very good book, incidentally, a very bad book. One of the reasons it's so popular it because it's kind of trivial, and another reason is that it's talking about our enemies, so that makes it popular. If he was dealing with a serious problem, ourselves, then it wouldn't have been popular, in fact, it probably wouldn't have been published. In a country like that, where there's a kind of Ministry of Truth, propaganda is very easily identifiable. Everybody knows what it is, and you can choose to repeat it if you like, but basically it's not really trying to control your thought very much; it's giving you the party line. It's saying, "Here's the official doctrine; as long as you don't disobey you won't get in trouble. What you think is not of great importance to anyone. If you get out of line we'll do something to you because we have force." Democratic societies can't really work like that, because the state can't control behavior by force. It can to some extent, but it's much more limited in its capacity to control by force. It therefore has to control what you think. And again, democratic theorists have understood this for 50 or 60 years and have been very articulate about it. If the voice the people is heard, you'd better control what that voice says, meaning you have to control what they think. The method Otero mentions there is one of the major methods. One of the ways you control what people think is by creating a debate so it looks like there's a debate going on, but making sure that that debate stays within very narrow margins, namely you have to make sure that both sides in the debate accept certain assumptions, and those assumptions turn out to be the propaganda system. As long as everyone accepts the propaganda system, then you can have a debate.

The Vietnam War is a classic example. In the official media, in the major media, the *New York Times* or CBS or whatever, in fact, all across the spectrum except at the very far-out periphery which reaches almost no one, in the major media which reach the overwhelming majority of the population, there was a lively debate. It was between people called "doves" and people called "hawks." The people called hawks said, "If we keep at it we can win." The people called doves said, "Even if we keep at it we probably can't win, and besides, it would probably be too costly for us, and besides maybe we're killing too many people," something like that. Both sides, the doves and the hawks, agreed on something: we have a right to carry out aggression against South Vietnam. In fact, they didn't even admit that that was taking place. They called it the "defense" of South Vietnam, using "defense" for "aggression" in the standard Orwellian manner. We were in fact attacking South Vietnam, just as much as the Russians are attacking Afghanistan, and in fact very similar. Like them, we first established a government that invited us in, and until we found one we had to overturn government after government. Finally we got one that invited us in, after we'd been there for years, and we then attacked the countryside and the population. That's an aggression. Nobody thought that was wrong, or rather, anyone who thought that was wrong was not admitted to the discussion. If you're a dove, you're in favor of aggression, if you're a hawk you're in favor of aggression. The debate between the hawks and the doves, then, is purely tactical: can we get away with it? Moderately on grounds of "is it too bloody or too costly?" which is kind of irrelevant. The real point is that aggression is wrong, like when the Russians invaded Czechoslovakia. They got away with it, they didn't kill anybody, but it was wrong because aggression is wrong.

We all understand that. But we can't allow that understanding to be expressed when it relates to the violent actions of our state, obviously. If this were a totalitarian state, the Ministry of Truth would simply have said, "It's right for us to go into Vietnam," period. Don't argue with it. People would have known that that's the propaganda system and they could have thought what they wanted. They could have seen that we were attacking Vietnam just like we can see that the Russians are attacking Afghanistan. You couldn't permit that understanding of reality in this country, it's too dangerous. People are much more free, they can express themselves, they can do things. Therefore it was necessary to try to control thought to try to make it appear as if the only issue was a tactical one: Can we get away with it? There's no issue of right or wrong. That worked partially, but not entirely. Among the educated part of the population it worked almost totally. There are good studies of this that show, with only the most marginal statistical error, that among the more educated parts of the population the government propaganda system was accepted unquestioningly. On the other hand, after a long period of popular spontaneous opposition, dissent and organization, the general population got out of control As recently as 1982, according to the latest polls I've seen, over 70 percent of the population still was saying that the war was, quoting the wording of the Gallup poll, "fundamentally wrong and immoral, not a mistake." That is, the overwhelming majority of the population is neither hawks nor doves, but opposed to aggression. On the other hand, the educated part of the population, they're in line. For them, it's just the tactical question of hawk versus dove.

This is, incidentally, not untypical. Propaganda very often works better for the educated than it does for the uneducated. This is true on many issues. There are a lot of reasons for this, one being that the educated receive more of the propaganda because they read more. Another thing is that they are the agents of propaganda. After all, their job is commissars, they're supposed to be the agents of the propaganda system so they believe it. It's very hard to say something unless you believe it. Other reasons are that by and large they are just part of the privileged elite so they share their interests and perceptions, whereas the population is more marginalized. It by and large doesn't participate in the democratic system, which is an elite game overwhelmingly, and people learn from their own lives to be skeptical, and in fact most of them are. There's a lot of skepticism and dissent and so on. But this is a typical example. Here's a case which is an interesting one because while the technique of thought control worked very effectively, in fact to virtually 100 percent effectiveness, among the educated part of the population, after many years of atrocities and massacres and hundreds of thousands of people killed and so on, it began to erode among the general population. There's even a name for that: it's called the "Vietnam Syndrome," a grave disease: people understand too much. But it's very striking, very illuminating to see how well it worked among the educated. If you pick up a book on American history and look at the Vietnam War, there is no such event as the American attack against South Vietnam. It's as if in the Soviet Union, say, in the early part of the 21st century, nobody will have ever said there was a Russian invasion of Afghanistan. Everyone says it's a Russian defense of Afghanistan. That's not going to happen. In fact, already people talk about the Russian invasion of Afghanistan, maybe they defend it, maybe not, but they admit that it exists. But in the United States, where the indoctrination system is vastly more effective, the educated part of the population can't even see that it exists. We cannot see that there was an American invasion of South Vietnam, and it's out of history, down Orwell's memory hole.

Who engineers this, who pulls this off, who are the mandarins, perhaps as in Gramsci's term the "experts in legitimation"? Who are these people?

The **experts in legitimation**, the ones who labor to make what people in power do legitimate, are mainly the privileged educated elites. The journalists, the academics, the teachers, the public relations specialists, this whole category of people have a kind of an institutional task, and that is to create the system of beliefs which will ensure the effective engineering of consent. And again, the more sophisticated of them say that. In the academic social sciences, for example, there's quite a tradition, explaining the necessity for the engineering of democratic consent. There are very few critics of this position. There are a few; there's a well known social scientist named Robert Dahl who has criticized this, and he pointed out—as is obviously true—that if you have a political system in which you plug in the options from a privileged position, and that's democracy, it's indistinguishable from totalitarianism. It's very rare that people point that out.

In the public relations industry, which is a major industry in the United States and has been for a long time, 60 years or more, this is very well understood, and in fact that's their purpose. That's one of the reasons this is such a heavily polled society, so that business can keep its finger on the popular pulse and recognize that if attitudes have to be changed we'd better work on it. That's what public relations are for, very conscious, very well understood. When you get to what these guys call the "institutions responsible for the indoctrination of the young," the schools and the universities, at that point it becomes somewhat more subtle. By and large, in the schools and universities people believe they're telling the truth. The way that works, with rare exceptions, you cannot make it through these institutions unless you've accepted the indoctrination. You're kind of weeded out along the way. Independent thinking is encouraged in the sciences but discouraged in these areas, and if people do it they're weeded out as radical or there's something wrong with them. It doesn't have to work 100 percent, in fact, it's even better for the system if there are a few exceptions here and there, it gives the illusion of debate or freedom. But overwhelmingly, this works.

In the media it's still more obvious. The media, after all, are corporations, major corporations. Some of the major corporations in the country. The people who own and manage them belong to the same narrow elite of owners and managers who control the private economy and who control the state, so it's a very narrow nexus of corporate media and state managers and owners. They share the same perceptions, the same understanding, and so on. That's one major point. So naturally they're going to perceive issues, suppress, control and shape in the interest of the groups that they represent, ultimately the interests of private ownership of the economy, that's where it's really based. Furthermore, the media also have a market   advertisers, not the public. People have to buy newspapers, but the reason is that otherwise advertisers won't advertise there. The newspapers are designed that the public will buy them so that they can raise their advertising rates. But the newspapers are essentially being sold to advertisers via the public, which is part of the medium for selling newspapers to advertisers. Since the corporation is selling it and its market is corporations, that's another respect in which the corporate system or the business system generally is going to be able to control the content of the media, in other words, if by some unimaginable accident they began to get out of line, advertising would fall, and that's a constraint. State power has the same effect. The media want to maintain their intimate relation to state power. They want to get leaks, they want to get invited to the press conferences. They want to rub shoulders with the Secretary of State, all this kind of business. To do that you've got to play the game, and playing the game means telling their lies, serving as their disinformation apparatus. Quite apart from the fact that they're going to do it anyway out of their own interest and their own status in the society, there are these kinds of pressures that force them into it. It's a very narrow system of control ultimately.

Then comes the question of the individual journalist, you know, the young kid who decides to become an honest journalist. Well, you try. You pretty soon are informed by your editor that you're a little off base, you're a little too emotional, you're too involved in the story, you've got to be more objective, there's a whole pile of code words for this, and what those code words mean is "Get in line, buddy, or you're out." Get in line means follow the party line. One thing that happens then is that people drop out. But those who decide to conform usually just begin to believe what they're saying. In order to progress you have to say certain things, what the copy editor wants, what the top editor is giving back to you. You can try saying it and not believing it, but that's not going to work, people just aren't that dishonest, you can't live with that, it's a very rare person who can do that. So you start saying it and pretty soon you're believing it because you're saying it, and pretty soon you're inside the system. Furthermore, there are plenty of rewards if you stay inside. For people who play the game by the rules in a rich society like this there are ample rewards. You're well off, you're privileged, you're rich, you have prestige, you have a share of power if you want, if you like this kind of stuff you can go off and become the State Department spokesman on something or other, you're right near the center of at least privilege, sometimes power, in the richest, most powerful country in the world, and you can go far, as long as you're very obedient and subservient and disciplined. So there are many factors, and people who are more independent are just going to drop off or be kicked out. In this case there are almost no exceptions. The degree of control on this is astonishing.

Let me just give you one example. In March 1986, came the major vote on Contra aid. For the three months prior to that the administration was heating up the atmosphere to try to reverse the congressional restrictions on aid to the terrorist army that's attacking Nicaragua, what they internally call a "proxy army," a proxy terrorist army attacking Nicaragua, which is of course what it is.

Also called "freedom fighters."

To the public they call them freedom fighters. If you look at the internal documents they're a proxy army which the Pentagon described a couple of years ago as a terrorist army, but that's internal, so I'll call them by the accurate internal terms: proxy terrorist army. So the question is: Could we reverse the congressional restrictions on this? That was the government's problem. The first three months of that year were very interesting in that respect: How were the media going to respond to the government campaign to try to reverse the congressional vote on Contra aid? I was interested, so I took the two national newspapers, the *Washington Post* and the *New York Times*, and I went through all their opinion pieces, every column written by one of their own columnists, every authored submitted opinion piece and so on for January, February and March.

There were 85. Of the 85, 85 were anti-Sandinista. On that issue, no discussion was even tolerable. So 85 out of 85 followed the party line: Sandinistas are bad guys. It's incidentally interesting that there is one person of those 85 who has written elsewhere, in a more nuanced fashion, but not here, he knows that he could never have gotten in unless he took that position. So on the major issue:

Are we against the Sandinistas?: 100 percent control. Not a whisper of debate discussed. Now comes the next point. There are two very striking facts about the Sandinista government as compared with our allies in Central America: Honduras, Guatemala, El Salvador, and so on. These facts are undeniable, whatever you think about them. One is that the Sandinistas, among these Central American countries, are unique in that the government doesn't slaughter its population. That's just not open to discussion. That's a fact. Second, it's the only one of those countries in which the government has tried to direct services to the poor, has in fact diverted resources to social reform. Again, that's not under discussion. You can read that in the Inter-American Development Bank reports or anywhere you like. So these are two rather striking facts that differentiate Nicaragua from Guatemala, El Salvador and in fact even Honduras, where about half the population is starving to death. Those three countries, especially Guatemala and El Salvador, are among the world's worst terrorist states. In the 1980s they have slaughtered maybe over 150,000 of their own citizens with ample U.S. support and great enthusiasm. They are simply violent terrorist states. They don't do anything for their population except kill them. Honduras is more like a government where the rich rob the poor, that's the government. They do some killing but not on the scale of their major allies, but maybe half the population is starving. In contrast, the Sandinista government, whatever you think about them, has not slaughtered the population and has diverted resources to them. That's a big difference.

So the next thing I looked at was: How often were those two facts mentioned in these 85 editorials? The fact that the Sandinistas are radically different from our allies in that they don't slaughter their population was not mentioned once. No reference to that fact. The fact that they have carried out social services for the poor was referred to in two phrases in 85 columns, both sort of buried. One was an oblique reference which said that because of the Contra war they can't do it any more, it didn't say what they were doing, the other was a passionate attack against the Sandinistas as totalitarian monsters and so forth and so on which said, "Well, of course, they did divert resources to the poor." So two phrases in 85 columns on that crucial issue, zero phrases in 85 columns on the not-insignificant fact that as distinct from our allies they haven't slaughtered their population, they haven't killed 150,000 people. That's again really remarkable discipline.

After that I went through all the editorials in the *New York Times* from 1980 to the present, just editorials, on El Salvador and Nicaragua, and it's essentially the same story. For example, in Nicaragua on Oct. 15, 1985, the government instituted a state of siege. This is a country under attack by the regional superpower, and they did what we did in the Second World War in Hawaii, instituted a state of siege. Not too surprising. There was a huge uproar, editorials, denunciations, it shows that they're totalitarian Stalinist monsters, and so on. Two days after that, on Oct. 17, El Salvador renewed its state of siege. This is a state of siege that had been instituted in March 1980 and has been renewed monthly since, and it's far more harsh than the Nicaraguan state of siege. It blocks freedom of expression, freedom of movement, virtually all civil rights, it's the framework for mass slaughter within which the army we organized has carried out massive torture, slaughter; still doing it in fact, all you have to do is look at the latest Amnesty International report or whatever, so here, within two days, Nicaragua instituted a state of siege, and El Salvador renewed its monthly renewal of a state of siege under which they had carried out a major mass slaughter and torture campaign. The Nicaragua state of siege was a great atrocity, the El Salvador state of siege, which was far harsher in its measures and its application, literally was not mentioned. Furthermore, it has never been mentioned. There is not one word in about 180 editorials which mentions it, because that's our guys, so we can't talk about it, they're a budding democracy, so they can't be having a state of siege. In fact the editorial comment and the news reporting on El Salvador is that this is somehow a moderate centrist government which is under attack by terrorists of the Left and terrorists of the Right, which is complete nonsense. Every human rights investigation, the church in El Salvador, even the government itself in its own secret documents, concedes that the terrorism is by the centrist government, they are the terrorists. The death squads are simply the security squads. Duarte is simply a front for terrorists, as he knows. But you can't say that publicly, because it gives the wrong image.

You can go on and on, but these are very dramatic examples of **the utter servility of the media** right at the top. They will not even permit opinion pieces, not only editorials, even opinion pieces won't be permitted that stray from the party line, because it's just too dangerous. Similarly, throughout the whole Vietnam War there was never an opinion piece in the *New York Times* or any other newspaper that I know of that said that the United States was wrong to attack South Vietnam. Here's a research project for someone: If you can find one word in any opinion piece in any American newspaper or in the media, I'd be very surprised. I haven't read everything, of course, but I've been following it pretty closely for years, and I've never seen it.

Is the control of capital the source, the bedrock of power in the American state?

Certainly, there's no doubt of it. The first chief justice of the Supreme Court and the president of the Constitutional Convention, John Jay, expressed it very accurately. He said: "The people who own the country ought to govern it." And that's the way it works. There are all sorts of mechanisms. For one thing, they have the resources to participate in politics. They can get information, they can put pressure, they can lobby, they can build platforms, they in fact are the real market for the political parties, they allow the parties to survive. They staff the executive, by and large, they staff Congress even. Furthermore, if any government ever got out of line, even in the slightest way, they could stop it, simply by disinvestment, by cutting back investment, by capital flight, and so on. Here this isn't a problem, because the corporations so totally own the government that it never gets out of line. But in other countries, especially Third World countries, that problem sometimes arises, and then very quickly, if the government tries to carry out social reform, it's stopped. Why? Just a little bit of capital flight is enough to do it, and it means the country grinds to a halt. So an effective control over the basic decisions in the society is in private hands, narrowly concentrated. That's going to control the state.

The rewards for playing ball with the system in this society and this culture are very clear. The financial rewards are obvious. We've talked about the prestige and class rewards as well. What about the other side of the coin? What about the punishments?

Here again, societies differ. For example, in the Soviet Union the punishments for honest dissidence are that you may very well end up in a psychiatric prison or in exile under ugly conditions. If you're a dissident in a typical American satellite like El Salvador, you're likely to find yourself in a ditch tortured after hideous mutilation. In the United States those are not the punishments. Here again we still have to make distinctions. If you're a black organizer in the ghetto you can be assassinated by the national political police or at least with their complicity, as happened with Fred Hampton in Chicago in 1969, a straight Gestapo-style assassination of a sleeping man, probably drugged, in a 4:00 a.m. attack by the police, coordinated with the FBI. In fact the black movement was decimated by government terrorism, a lot of that's pretty well documented. If you're essentially defenseless you can be subjected to a fair amount of violence, nothing like El Salvador, of course, but not so trivial either.

Or there's the example in your home town of Philadelphia, the first domestic air raid in American history.

Yes, that's another one. It can happen, but it's not on the scale of a state that really terrorizes its own citizens. If you come from the more privileged classes, if you're a white middle-class person, then the chances that you are going to be subjected to literal state terror are very slight. It could happen, but it's slight. What will happen is that you'll be marginalized, excluded. Instead of becoming part of the privileged elite, you'll be driving a taxi cab. It's not torture, but very few people are going to select that option, if they have a choice. And the ones who do select it will never be heard from again. Therefore they are not part of the indoctrination system. They don't make it. It could be worse, but it's enough to discipline people.

Generally speaking your books are ignored. They're not reviewed. You're not invited on "Face the Nation" or the evening news with Dan Rather, nor are you interviewed on National Public Radio, and the few times that Noam Chomsky's books are reviewed—I'll just mention two examples here, one is a New York Times *review of* Turning the Tide *written by Alan Tomlinson, who is the associate editor of* Foreign Policy *magazine. He begins the review by calling you a "New Left stalwart" and then he says that the evidence that you present in your book is a "clip job drawn from secondary sources, source histories, from news articles and reports from the usual assort-*

ment of liberal and left-leaning, Latin American human rights groups." Is that typical? •

It's surprising it was reviewed at all, but that's a typical sort of putdown. All you have to do is to look at the footnotes to see how false it is. First of all, the "left-leaning human rights groups" are the standard human rights groups. There's nothing "left-leaning" about Americas Watch. From his point of view they are "left-leaning" because they criticize Western as well as Eastern atrocities. And that, of course, is "left-leaning." As for it being a "clip job," like every scholarly work, I deal with original sources, which are press reports of ongoing events. Exactly the same is true in the most honored works of scholarship. Furthermore, there is plenty of use of unused primary sources, suppressed primary sources, for example, government documents that would never be used in the mainstream because they tell the wrong story.

It's not because it's me. Any critic of the party line must meet very high standards. If you're following the party line you don't have to document anything; you can say anything you feel like. There are major books, well reviewed, highly regarded, which are just an expression of opinion—there is nothing in them that you can even trace to its source—but that doesn't matter as long as you're producing the party line. That's one of the privileges you get for obedience. On the other hand, if you're critical of received opinion, you have to document every phrase. He also later in the review calls my writing "turgid." That's right, and part of the reason it's turgid is because every three words I have to have a footnote with big documentation explaining it. On the other hand, if you're on the other side you can just pay attention to style, because it doesn't matter what you say. I should say, incidentally, that I benefit from that privilege too, so that when I write critically of the Soviet Union I don't have to document anything, nobody ever cares. They think it's fine. Since you're attacking the enemy, why do you have to document anything? And if you're always within the party line you never have to document anything.

But the main point of interest about the review is his total incapacity to perceive the words. In fact, if you read through the review he never takes issue with any thing I say, this looks correct, and so on, but he says I'm missing the point because I don't explain how the United States should defend the national interest. He says something like, "Since he doesn't offer an alternative to defending the national interest, there's something missing, missing the point." In fact I discussed that matter at great length. I pointed out that the phrase "national interest" is an Orwellism used to refer to the interests of corporate elites, if I had more space there I'd give a lot of documentation of it, and I said that of course in that sense of national interest the citizens of the country shouldn't want to defend it. It's often opposed to their interests. But he cannot understand that—a deeply indoctrinated person. A real sign of deep indoctrination is that you can't understand elementary thoughts that any 10-year-old can understand. That's real indoctrination. So for him it's kind of like a theological truth, a truth of received religion, that the national interest is what we should defend. If somebody says "everyone like you is using the term 'national interest' in a very deceitful way, it's not in the interest of the nation. It's the interest of a powerful privileged group, maybe this is the right way to defend their interests, but I'm not interested in defending their interests. I'm interested in defending the interests of the population of the United States, in fact the world, so I don't have to answer to your question. I don't have to provide a better way to serve the interests of the corporate elite. I'm just not interested in that question." He cannot understand that. It's not that he has an answer. He cannot understand the point. It's too far out of the way of thinking.

In this respect there's been **a very sharp decline since the Middle Ages.** In the Middle Ages, when you read Thomas Aquinas, he felt that he had to deal with heresy. He wanted to defend the doctrines of the faith against heresy, but he felt he had to understand it. Medieval theology was an honest intellectual atmosphere: if people had heretical arguments you had to pay attention to them, think about them, find answers to them. We've degenerated far below that in modern culture. Here you don't have to understand heresy, you just point to it, you just say, "Look, this guy's involved in heresy," and that's the end of that discussion. Now we go on. That wouldn't have been tolerated in more honest and intellectually advanced societies such as medieval theology. And this is another sign of the dramatic decline of the intelligentsia as they become the commissars for external power, state or private, and this is a fine example of it.

Perhaps still another example was in another New York Times *book review in 1982 of your book* Towards a New Cold War, *written by Michael Mandelbaum. This book, for those who haven't read it, is one of the most heavily and carefully documented books I've ever read. Mandelbaum really doesn't deal with any of the substantive issues you raise, but he accuses you of—"if the book has a consistent theme at all—it's one of anger." So you're an angry person, and we know how to deal with angry people, just dismiss them.*

That's, incidentally, true. I don't pretend not to be angry. When I'm talking about torture, mass murder and slaughter and so on, I am angry. If I have to express it, fine. I'm not trying to deceive anyone. But the point you make is quite accurate: somehow you have to get rid of the stuff. You can't deal with the arguments, that's plain, for one thing you have to know something, and most of these people don't know anything. Secondly, you wouldn't be able to answer the arguments because they're correct. Therefore what you have to do is somehow dismiss it. So that's one technique: "It's just emotional, it's irresponsible, it's angry."

In fact, it's a very striking fact that books that really are emotional, that don't try to document, get a much better press. Those are honest and important books, but if somebody comes out with a sermon, saying "I hate the war in El Salvador, it drives me up the wall, I don't want to see any more people tortured," that book will get a good review, because it's very unthreatening.

Joan Didion's book Salvador *was precisely like that.*

Yes, that gets good reviews because it's unthreatening. It doesn't direct attention to the reality of what's happening. It's something over there, you know, some atrocities going on over there. Oh, it's horrible. It makes me feel awful. But that atrocity is not going on over there, it's going on in Washington, in New York and Chicago, just as the atrocities in Afghanistan are going on in Moscow, not in Kabul. As long as you don't get people to understand that, you're all right, but as soon as you point out that those atrocities are systematic, they have happened over and over again, they've happened in the same ways, we have a lot of documentation to explain why American planners want those atrocities to go on in that way—as soon as you put it in the framework of consistent systematic history and institutional structure that leads to it, especially when you give them the documentation to prove it, then you've got to be eliminated, because that might get people to understand something. On the other hand, it's interesting, they especially do this with women, like Joan Didion. If a woman writes a book which has an emotional character to it, that's terrific, like "Oh well, look at this, we understand about women, so emotional, so they get upset about these things, but that's because they don't understand the harsh realities, and so on, so that's fine."

Could we talk a little bit about the peace and student movements of the 60s, because you've made a number of statements about them and I'd like you to further explain them. You say that the peace and student movements of the 60s "changed consciousness and raised the cultural and moral level of the country. It changed the character of the country, probably permanently." In what ways?

There was a very striking increase in the intellectual, cultural and moral climate of the country. You can see this in all kinds of ways, it wasn't just the student movement. There were also all the popular movements that developed in that period—the women's movement, the environmental movement, this whole complex of groups of which the students and the youth were a central and early component. For one thing, we are now able to face, at least, certain forms of repression and coercion and atrocities that we couldn't face before. In fact, the women's movement is a perfect example of that. Sexist oppression existed before 1970, but it wasn't an issue. Now it still exists but it's an issue, and undoubtedly consciousness has been changed on that.

Take something more remote, the treatment of Native Americans. Here's an interesting fact if you think about it. The United States is founded on the destruction of the native population. Before Columbus the population north of the Rio Grande was maybe 12–15 million. At the turn of the century it was 200,000. The whole history of the conquest of the continent from the time that the saintly Pilgrims landed is destruction of the native population by various means, sometimes just plain mass slaughter, like the Pequot Massacre by the Puritans or George Washington's destruction of the Iroquois civilization right in the middle of the War of Independence, and many later events running through the conquest of the national territory. Sometimes it was criminal expulsion like Jackson's expulsion of the Cherokees, really hard-line things. Anyway, that's the history. That was not under discussion, it's hard to remember now, but it was discussed in the context of cowboy and Indian movies. The Indians were the bad guys, the cowboys were the good guys. That's 200 years, 300 years in fact, that we couldn't come to terms with it. Even scholarship couldn't. Incidentally, this changed in the 1970s. For the first time it has become possible to give a relatively honest account of the interaction between the European conquerors and the native population whom they destroyed. There is still a long way to go, but it's beginning. While you can find occasional examples over the past few centuries, a book here and there, the mythology was intact in the scholarly world and popular consciousness until the rise in cultural level.

Sometimes this is true in an astonishing fashion, for example, the Declaration of Independence, which we print on a full page every July 4 and everyone reads in elementary school and so on. We went 200 years, as far as I know, before anyone, at least anyone I can find, noticed a rather astonishing fact about that document. In the Bill of Indictment against King George of England, he is accused of "unleashing the merciless Indian savages against us with their known methods of warfare," which are extermination and so on. That's a statement of astonishing cowardice and fantastic deceit, because in fact what had happened, as the framers of the Constitution well knew, was that it was **the merciless European savages**, and their ancestors and descendants, with their methods of warfare—destruction of men, women and children—that was unleashed against the native population. This astonishing inversion went on—I don't know anything in the American literary or historical tradition that even commented on it. Probably there's something somewhere, but I can't find it.

In the 1970s people finally noticed that for 200 years we had been living a violent, cowardly lie, not a marginal one. It's not marginal that the native population was wiped out in the course of the conquest of the national territory. The same is true of other things. It became possible to have a more honest look at the Philippine war, which was a war of slaughter, hundreds of thousands killed, not a great victory. It became possible for the first time to begin to look at Woodrow Wilson's war in Haiti and the Dominican Republic, brutal murderous counterinsurgency wars. The counterinsurgency war in Greece in the late 1940s, with tens of thousands of people killed and 60,000 sent to what were then called re-education camps where they were tortured or executed, and the political system destroyed and the labor unions destroyed. That was a hidden story until late 1970s. We could go on in case after case. There was an awakening, a willingness to face some of the realities of the world.

What do you attribute that to?

I attribute it to the rise in the cultural level caused by the student movement and other associated movements, it just broke down a lot of barriers and made it possible for people to think.

Has not the American state attempted to reconstruct the past and destroy that memory?

Very definitely, absolutely. There has been a major campaign on every issue to try to restore order and obedience. Among the educated elites it has basically worked, but of course they have never deviated very much either, so there wasn't far to go. Among much of the population it's worked partially but not too much. For example, they have finally succeeded in reconstituting a kind of jingoist consensus, an atmosphere of fear and terror in which people say, "Let's go out and kill the bastards." They have succeeded in instituting that. But they haven't overcome the understanding or even the sympathy for oppressed people or even the opposition to atrocities. The population is just a lot more sophisticated. I can see that myself in the talks that I give, I've been doing this for a long time. During the 1960s and early 70s, at the peak activity of the peace movement, if I was talking to selected peace movement audiences, radicals, I could not say the things that I say to general audiences today. The kind of things I'm saying now, for example, I could never have said to a public audience or even for that matter to most peace movement audiences, even at the peak of the peace movement. What's happened is that there's been a general change; you can approach people much more honestly, especially those who are not part of the tiny educated, privileged elite who are immune, they are the commissars, you can't talk to them. But apart from that, much of the population has changed significantly, and I think and I hope that that's a permanent thing.

After the Vietnam War ended you wrote a number of essays predicting the attempts of the American state to reconstruct what had happened in Indochina. Have those attempts been successful, Rambo *aside?*

I think they have been successful among the educated elite. In the general population, I think much less so, but they don't matter much. It's important to bear in mind that most of the population is marginal; they're not part of the system, they just watch. The politically active parts of the population are the ones who are really dangerous. As long as the population is unorganized, apathetic, marginalized, doesn't do anything, nobody really cares what they think; they're just not part of the system. It's the articulate, educated elites, the groups that are politically active, that can make a difference, those are the ones you have to watch. Among them, the reconstruction of history has been very successful, but then, it didn't have far to go.

In an op-ed article in the Aug. 10, 1986, New York Times, *George McGovern, very much associated with opposition to the Vietnam War, wrote, "I am anguished over our disastrous involvement in Vietnam. Only history and Providence will know finally who was right or wrong on that tragic issue." What do you think of that?*

That's rather consistent throughout. McGovern was not an early opponent of the Vietnam War. In the hard, early years of opposition, before it became a popular issue, before even much of the business community turned against it on grounds of cost, he wasn't particularly visible. He was in fact marginal in the hard years. Later he came along, I'm sure honestly, but I think that his position probably expresses his feeling quite accurately. For him it's a question of, who was right? Notice, if you had asked him about the Russian invasion of Afghanistan, he wouldn't say, "History and Providence will decide," because there it's obvious. But suppose you were to ask him who is right about the American invasion of South Vietnam. You'll get a blank stare, he won't know what you are talking about. And the same is true about just about any other educated person, because that didn't even happen. We defended South Vietnam, and then only history and Providence will tell whether we were right. If you go to the Faculty Club at Moscow University and ask them who is right about the Russian invasion of Afghanistan, you'll also get a blank stare, probably less blank because they understand more, they're less indoctrinated, but still, they'll tell you, "No, we defend Afghanistan, you've got it wrong." The comment that you're making reflects mainstream liberal opinion. We can't know whether the United States was right to defend South Vietnam; the fact that we attacked them you can't even discuss.

And if it's left for history, given what we've been talking about, the engineering of history …

They'll take care of it.

Don't you find it odd that there's little expression of anguish for the peoples of Vietnam, Laos and Cambodia, whose countries were turned into free-fire zones?

That's true of all the discussion. There's a big fuss about American veterans who have suffered under Agent Orange, and there should be a fuss. However, there's a slight observation that might be made, and that is that the people of Vietnam suffered a thousand times as much, and we're certainly not trying to help them, in fact we want to increase their suffering.

What did you think of the PBS series on Vietnam?

I thought it was cheap propaganda and vulgar and nonsense. On the early parts of the war, the French parts, it was pretty accurate. They were able to deal with a French war. That's safe. As soon as it got to the American war, it shifted over into the mainstream propaganda system. Some talk about atrocities, individual atrocities, which is not terribly important. Individual soldiers in the field who are fighting under horrible conditions are almost certain to conduct atrocities in every war. It's easy to blame them; we sit here in comfort and the grunts in the field kill somebody and we get all upset.

The real atrocities were carried on in Washington, and they were basically two: first was a war crime, the crime for which people were hanged at Nuremberg, mainly aggression; second was crimes against humanity, that is, planned attacks, organized in Washington, with the purpose of mass murder and slaughter. Crimes for which people were hanged at Nuremberg. Those weren't discussed, and there was no political context for it.

Actually, I wrote a long review of the book that was the companion for it, by Stanley Karnow, and that's the way it works: it was a noble cause, failed effort, only history will tell, etc. The whole thing is falsified. In fact, incident by incident, even the particular incidents are falsified, case after case, it doesn't matter. And also there's no documentation, no support, no nothing. The arguments are often ridiculous.

If a book of that caliber were written critical of the United States, it would be demolished across the board as Communist propaganda of the most absurd sort. But here it's considered a sober, careful analysis somewhat on the liberal side. In fact the whole thing had to be attacked from the Right because it was too liberal. It's very interesting that that series and the book were subjected to two attacks: one from the Right and one from the Left. The one from the Right was real nonsense, even worse that the original series. ["Accuracy in Media"— C.P.O.]. It was childish, in fact, it was embarrassing. I've gone through the transcript and will write about it some day. But it was really infantile and embarrassing. Nevertheless it had to be aired. The critique on the other side, what is called the Left, although I don't like the word, said, "Look, this thing is biased toward government propaganda." That one was honest, accurate, very well documented, but didn't have to be answered. There was a reason for that. Power lies on the right. That's where the takeover bids are. That's where the control over capital is. So that argument you've got to deal with. The argument on the other side has no power behind it, and since truth and honesty are total irrelevancies, you can forget about it.

You just mentioned the Left and being a bit uncomfortable using that term; in a lecture at Oberlin in 1969 you quoted Orwell as saying, "Political thought, especially on the left, is a sort of masturbation fantasy in which the world hardly matters." You added, "That's true, unfortunately, and it's part of the reason that our society lacks a genuine left-wing movement." Do you still feel that way?

I don't like terms like "right" and "left"; especially in the United States, I don't think they mean very much. But if we mean by **the Left** what it historically meant, that is, that component of the body politic which is concerned with defending human rights, increasing democracy, increasing public control over the major decisions in the society, including democratization of the private economy, placing it under public, democratic control, workers' control of production, community control over their affairs—if we are talking about left in that sense, that is, an extension of the movement towards popular democracy and popular control to new and other spheres, overcoming authority and repression and autocratic structures and so on, if that's what we mean by the Left, there isn't much of it in the United States. And the part of it that there is doesn't have a well-established intellectual tradition and has no institutions to speak of.

But there's a good reason for that: they have no power. They have no control over resources. They essentially have no wealth, and therefore they cannot develop institutions of a sustaining nature. They can't develop a literature. They can't learn, they can't improve over time. Everything starts from the beginning all the time. That's the genius of a society in which power is overwhelmingly in the hands of the owners of the private economy and all the institutions, including the political parties, are subservient to them. The comment that Orwell made remains true to a certain extent, perhaps not as strong as those words indicate, and that again is a reflection of the nature of power. You can have brilliant works produced on the left, and there have been some, but they're kind of irrelevant, they're down the memory hole, too. They can't reach people, people can't use them, people can't understand them. They're just too far off the received doctrinal position that's associated with real power.

One of your books, The Fateful Triangle, *focuses specifically on the Middle East, and I was wondering if you could talk about your position on a possible two-state solution to the Palestinian question.*

I don't think that's the optimal solution, but it has been the realistic political settlement for some time. We have to begin with some fundamentals here. The real question is: there are plainly **two national groups that claim the right of self-determination** in what used to be Palestine, roughly the area now occupied by Israel minus the Golan Heights, which is part of Syria. So there are two national groups which claim national self-determination. One group is the indigenous population, or what's left of it—a lot of it's been expelled or driven out or fled. The other group is the Jewish settlers who came in, originally from Europe, later from other parts of the Middle East and some other places. So there are two groups, the indigenous population and the immigrants and their descendants. Both claim the right of national self-determination. Here we have to make a crucial decision: Are we racists or aren't we? If we're not racists, then the indigenous population has the same rights of self-determination as the settlers who replaced them. Some might claim more, but let's say at least as much right. Hence if we are not racist, we will try to press for a solution which accords them—we'll say they are human beings with equal rights, therefore they both merit the claim to national self-determination. I'm granting that the settlers have the same rights as the indigenous population; many do not find that obvious but let's grant it.

Then there are a number of possibilities. One possibility is a democratic secular society. Virtually nobody is in favor of that. Some people say they are, but if you look closely they're not really. There are various models for multi-ethnic societies, say Switzerland or whatever. And maybe in the long run these might be the best idea, but they're unrealistic. The only realistic political settlement, for the time being, in the past 10 or 12 years, that would satisfy the right of self-determination for both national groups is a two-state settlement. Everybody knows what it would have to be: Israel within approximately the pre-June 1967 borders and a Palestinian state in the West Bank and the Gaza Strip, and a return of the Golan Heights to Syria, or maybe some other arrangement. This would be associated with maybe demilitarized zones and international guarantees of some sort or another, but that's the framework of a possible political settlement.

As I say, I don't think it's the best one, but that's the realistic one, very realistic. It's supported by most of the world. It's supported by Europe, by the Soviet Union, has been for a long time, by almost all the non-aligned countries, it's supported by all the major Arab states and has been for a long time, supported by the mainstream of the PLO and again has been for a long time, it's supported even by the American population, by about two to one according to the polls. But there are also people who oppose it. It's opposed by the rejection front in the Arab world, the minority elements of the PLO, Libya, a few others, minority rejectionist elements, but crucially it's opposed by the leaders of the rejection front, namely the United States and Israel. The United States and Israel adamantly oppose it. The United States will not consider it. Both political groupings in Israel reject it totally. They reject any right of national self-determination for the indigenous population in the former Palestine. They can have Jordan if they want, or the former Syria, or something, but not the area that they now hold under military occupation. In fact they're explicit about it. There are carefully fostered illusions here that the Labor Party is interested in compromise over the issue. But if you look closely, there's no meaningful compromise. The position of the Labor Party remains what was expressed by their representative, who is now president, Chaim Herzog, who said that "no one can be a partner with us in a land that has been holy to our people for 2,000 years."

That's the position. They're willing to make minor adjustments. They don't want to take care of the population in the West Bank, because there are too many Arabs; they don't want a lot of Arabs around, so what they would like to do is take the areas and the water and the resources they want from the West Bank but leave the population, either stateless or under Jordanian control. That's what's called a "compromise solution." It's a very cynical proposal, even worse in many respects than annexation. But that's called here compromise and the reason is that we are again educated elites in the United States and national discussion takes a strictly racist view of this. The Palestinians are not human, they do not deserve the rights that we accord automatically to the settlers who displaced them. That's the basis of articulate American discussion: pure, unadulterated racism. Again, that's not true of the population, as usual, but it is of the politically active and articulate parts of it and certainly the government. As long as the United States and Israel reject the political settlement, there can't be one.

There certainly have been very plausible opportunities for a political settlement over many years, in fact, just to mention a few which have disappeared from history because they're too inconvenient: in February 1971 President Sadat of Egypt offered a full peace treaty to Israel on the pre-June 1967 borders. In accordance with official American policy, incidentally, but not operative policy, offering nothing to the Palestinians, he didn't even offer them a Palestinian state, nothing. Nevertheless Israel rejected it, and the United States backed them in that rejection. In January 1976 Syria, Jordan and Egypt, the so-called "confrontation states," made a proposal in the UN Security Council for a two-state settlement with international guarantees and territorial rights secured and so on. That was backed and even prepared by the PLO, supported by the Soviet Union and most of the world. It was vigorously opposed by Israel, which even boycotted the session, in fact, it bombed Lebanon in retaliation against the United Nations, killing about 50 people, no excuse at all, just a fit of anger, "We're going to kill anybody who gets in our way if you push this," and the United States vetoed it.

There have been a series of such things ever since. The United States has always blocked them and Israel has always refused them, and that means there's no political settlement. Rather there is a state of permanent military confrontation. That's aside from what it means to the Palestinians, which is obvious and terrible; it's very bad for Israel. It's leading to their own destruction, in my view, certainly to their economic collapse and moral degeneration and probably sooner or later their physical destruction, because you can't have a state of military confrontation without a defeat sooner or later. It's leading the world very close to nuclear war, repeatedly. Every time we have an Arab-Israeli conflict—and there will be more of them, as long as we maintain a military confrontation—the Soviet Union and the United States come into confrontation. Both are involved. The Soviet Union is close by, it's not like Central America, it's a strategic region right near their border, they're involved; it's very far from us but it's a strategic region for us because of the oil nearby, primarily. So we're involved, the fleets come into confrontation, it's very close. In 1967 it came very close to nuclear war and it will again. So it's very dangerous, it's the most likely spot where a nuclear war would develop, but we are pursuing it, because we don't want a political settlement. The United States is intent on maintaining a military confrontation.

You've mentioned racism vis-a-vis the Palestinians. To what extent, if any, have Israelis of Ashkenazic origin absorbed German racial attitudes toward not just Arabs but even to the Oriental Jews, the Sephardim, is there anything in that?

I wouldn't call it particularly German.

European?

Yes. It's part of European culture to have **racist attitudes toward the Third World**, including us, we're part of Europe in that respect. Naturally the Jewish community shared the attitudes of the rest of Europe, not surprising. There certainly are such things inside Israel. My feeling is they could be overcome in time under a situation of peace. I think they're real, but I don't think they're lethal, through slow integration they could probably be overcome. The one that probably can't be overcome is the anti-Arab racism, because that requires subjugation of a defeated and conquered people and that leads to racism. If you're sitting with your boot on somebody's neck, you're going to hate him, because that's the only way that you can justify what you're doing, so subjugation automatically yields racism, and you can't overcome that. Furthermore, anti-Arab racism is rampant in the United States and much of the West, there's no question about that. The only kind of racism that can be openly expressed with outrage is anti-Arab racism. You don't put caricatures of blacks in the newspapers any more; you do put caricatures of Arabs.

But isn't it curious that they're using the old Jewish stereotypes, the money coming out the pockets, the beards, the hooked nose?

I've often noticed that the cartoons and caricatures are very similar to the ones you'd find in the Nazi press about the Jews, very similar.

What dimension does the Holocaust play in this equation? Is it manipulated by the Israeli state to promote its own interests?

It's very consciously manipulated. I mean, it's quite certainly real, there's no question about that, but it is also undoubted that they manipulate it, in fact they say so. For example, in the *Jerusalem Post*, in English so you can read it, their Washington correspondent Wolf Blitzer, I don't recall the exact date, but after one of the big Holocaust memorial meetings in Washington he wrote an article in the *Jerusalem Post* in which he said it was a great success. He said, "Nobody mentioned arms sales to the Arabs but all the congressmen understood that that was the hidden message. So we got it across." In fact, one very conservative and very honest Zionist leader, Nachem Goldman, who was the president of the World Zionist Organization and who was detested towards the end because he was much too honest—they even refused to send a delegation to his burial, I believe, or a message. He's one of the founders of the Jewish state and the Zionist movement and one of the elder statesmen, a very honest man—he, just before his death in 1982 or so, made a rather eloquent and unusual statement in which he said that it's (he used the Hebrew word for "sacrilege"), he said it's sacrilege to use **the Holocaust as a justification for oppressing others**. He was referring to something very real, exploitation of probably the world's most horrifying atrocity in order to justify oppression of others. That kind of manipulation is really sick.

That disturbs you and …

Really sick. Many people find it deeply immoral but most people are afraid to say anything about it. Nachem Goldman is one of the few who was able to say anything about it and it was one of the reasons he was hated. Anyone who tries to say anything about it is going to be subjected to a very efficient defamation campaign of the sort that would have made the old Communist Party open-mouthed in awe, people don't talk about it.

I ask you this question because I know that you have been plagued and hounded around the United States specifically on this issue of the Holocaust. It's been said that Noam Chomsky is somehow agnostic on the issue of whether the Holocaust occurred or not.

My agnosticism is in print. I described the Holocaust years ago as the most fantastic outburst of insanity in human history, so much so that if we even agree to discuss the matter we demean ourselves. Those statements and numerous others like them are in print, but they're basically irrelevant because you have to understand that this is part of a Stalinist-style technique to silence critics of the holy state and therefore the truth is entirely irrelevant, you just tell as many lies as you can and hope that some of the mud will stick. It's a standard technique used by the Stalinist parties, by the Nazis and by these guys.

There's tremendous support for Israel in the United States at least in elite groups. There's also on another level a very steady, virulent anti-Semitism that goes on. Can you talk about that?

Anti-Semitism has changed, during my lifetime at least. Where I grew up we were virtually the only Jewish family, I think there was one other. Of course being the only Jewish family in a largely Irish-Catholic and German-Catholic community …

In Philadelphia?

In Philadelphia. And the anti-Semitism was very real. There were certain paths I could take to walk to the store without getting beaten up. It was the late 1930s and the area was openly pro-Nazi. I remember beer parties when Paris fell and things like that. It's not like living under Hitler, but it's a very unpleasant thing, there was a really rabid anti-Semitism in that neighborhood where I grew up as a kid and it continued. By the time I got to Harvard in the early 1950s there was still very detectable anti-Semitism. It wasn't that they beat you up on the way to school or something, but other ways, kind of Waspish anti-Semitism. There were very few Jewish professors on the faculty at that time. There was beginning to be a scattering of them, but still very few. This was the tail-end of a long time of Waspish anti-Semitism at the elite institutions. Over the last 30 years that's changed very radically. Anti-Semitism undoubtedly exists, but it's now on a par, in my view, with other kinds of prejudice of all sorts. I don't think it's more than anti-Italianism or anti-Irishism, and that's been a very significant change in the last generation, one that I've experienced myself in my own life, and it's very visible throughout the society.

How would you account for that?

How would I account for it? I think partly that the Holocaust did have an effect. It brought out the horrifying consequences of anti-Semitism in a way that certainly is striking. I presume, I can't prove this, but there must be, at least I hope there is, a kind of guilt feeling involved, because the role of the United States during the Holocaust was awful, before and during. They didn't act to save Jews, and they could have in many respects. The role of the Zionist organization is not very pretty either. In the late 1940s there were plenty of displaced persons in the Jewish DP [displaced persons] camps, some survived. It remained awful, they stayed in the DP camps, in fact for a while they were dying at almost the same rate they were under the Nazis. Many of those people, if they had been given a chance, surely would have wanted to come to the United States. There are debates about how many, but it's just unimaginable that if they'd been given a chance they wouldn't have wanted to come here. They didn't. A tiny scattering came. There was an immigration bill, the Stratton Bill, which I think admitted about 400,000 people, if I remember, to the United States, very few Jews among them. Plenty of Nazis, incidentally, straight out of their SS uniforms.

The reason that bill passed, I think it was 1947, was that it was the beginning of the Cold War and priority was being given to basically the Nazis, because we were resurrecting them all over the world, a lot of them were brought in, a lot of Nazi war criminals, and others, but very few Jews. That's not a very pretty sight. You say, during the war you could have given some argument, not an acceptable argument, but you could have given at least a not-ridiculous argument that you had to fight the war and not worry about the people being sent to the gas chambers, but after the war you couldn't give any argument. It was a matter of saving the survivors, and we didn't do it. I should say the Zionist organization didn't support it either, they didn't even lobby for the bill. The only Jewish organizations that lobbied for the admission of Jewish refugees to the United States were the non-Zionist or the anti-Zionist organizations. The reason was that they wanted to send them off to Palestine. Whether they wanted to go there or not is another story, the same matter being relived today, incidentally, with the Russian emigres. The Zionist organization wants to force them to go to Israel. Most of them, especially from the European parts of Russia, want to come to the United States, and all sorts of pressures are being brought to bear to prevent that. It's kind of a reenactment at a less hideous level of the same story. I suppose there's some element of guilt, certainly over the Holocaust and maybe over the post-war matter.

Besides that, the Jewish community has changed socially and economically. It's now become substantial, not huge in numbers, but given its numbers it's a substantial part of the dominant, privileged elite groups in every part of the society—professional, economic, political, etc. It's not like the anti-Semitic stereotype, they don't own the corporations, but relative to the numbers they're very influential, particularly in the ideological system, lots of writers, editors, etc., and that has an effect. Furthermore, I think it's changed because of what's happened since 1967. In 1967 Israel won a dramatic military victory, demonstrated its military power, in fact smashed up the entire Arab world, and that won great respect. A lot of Americans, especially privileged Americans, love violence and want to be on the side of the guy with the gun, and here was a powerful, violent state that smashed up its enemies and demonstrated that it was the dominant military power in the Middle East, put those Third World upstarts in their place.

This was particularly dramatic because that was 1967, a time when the United States was having only minimal success in carrying out its invasion of by then all of Indochina, and it's well worth remembering that elite opinion, including liberal opinion, overwhelmingly supported the war in Vietnam and was quite disturbed by the incapacity of the United States to win it, at least at the level they wanted. Israel came along and showed them how to do it, and that had a symbolic effect. Since then it has been presenting itself, with some justice, as the Sparta of the Middle East, a militarily advanced, technologically competent, powerful society. That's the kind of thing we like. It also became a strategic asset of the United States; one of the reasons why the United States maintains the military confrontation is to assure that it's a dependable, reliable ally that will do what we want, like, say, support genocide in Guatemala or whatever, and that also increases the respect for Israel and with it tends to diminish anti-Semitism. I suppose that's a factor.

But you've pointed out that as long as U.S. state interests are being served and preserved, Israel will be favored, but the moment that those interests ...

That's right, it'll be finished, in fact, anti-Semitism will shoot up. Apart from the moral level, it's a very fragile alliance on tactical grounds.

So what happens to the moral commitment, the concern for justice in the Jewish state and all that—out the window?

On the part of whom?

The United States.

There's no concern for justice and there never was. States don't have a concern for justice. States don't act on moral grounds.

Except on a rhetorical level.

On a rhetorical level they all do, even Nazi Germany. On the actual level they never do. They are instruments of power and violence, that's true of all states; they act in the interests of the groups that dominate them, they spout the nice rhetorical line, but these are just givens of the international system.

You've been very critical of the American liberal community and in fact you've said that they're contributing to Israel's destruction. Please talk a little bit about that.

The American liberal community since 1967 has been mobilized at an almost fanatic level in support of an expansionist Israel, and they have been consistently opposed to any political settlement. They have been in favor of the aggrandizement of Israeli power. They have used their position of quite considerable influence in the media in the political system to defeat and overcome any

challenge to the system of military confrontation using all the standard techniques of vilification, defamation, closing off control over expression, etc., and
it's certainly had an effect. I don't know if it was a decisive effect, but it had some
noticeable effect on bringing about U.S. government support for the persistent
military confrontation and U.S. government opposition to political settlement.
For Israel that's destructive. In fact, Israeli doves constantly deplore it. They constantly refer to it as Stalinism. They refer to the Stalinist character of the support
for Israel on the part of what they call the "Jewish community," but that's because
they don't understand enough about the United States. It's not just the Jewish
community, which is what they see; it's basically the intellectual community at
large.

*Edward Said, for example, has pointed out that there is much more pluralism in
terms of the discussion, the debate, in Israel itself than inside the United States.*

There's no question about that. For example, the editor of the *Labor Party
Journal*, the main newspaper of the Labor Party, has asked me to write regular
columns. I won't do it because I'm concerned with things here, but that's totally
inconceivable in the United States, you can't even imagine it, you can't even
imagine an occasional op-ed. That's quite typical. Positions that I maintain,
which are essentially in terms of the international consensus, they're not a majority position in Israel, but they're part of the political spectrum, they're respectable
positions. Here it's considered outlandish.

*In the time we have remaining, I'd like to ask you two questions. The first one is, in
what ways, if any, has your work in linguistics and grammar informed your political analyses and perspectives?*

I suspect very little. Maybe, I don't know, I'm probably not the person to
ask, but I think working in a science is useful because you somehow learn, you
get to understand what evidence and argument and rationality are and you come
to be able to apply these to other domains where they're very much lacking and
very much opposed, so there's probably some help in that respect. There's probably at some very deep and abstract level some sort of common-core conception
of human nature and the human drive for freedom and the right to be free of
external coercion and control, that kind of picture animates my own social and
political concerns, my own anarchist interests, which go way back to early childhood, and on the other hand, they enter here in a clear and relatively precise way
into my work on language and thought and so on, but it's a pretty loose connection, not a kind of connection where you can deduce one connection from
another or anything like that.

*You have an international reputation for your work in linguistics and philosophy and
obviously you weren't content with that, you wanted to go out into the social and
political world.*

Quite the contrary. It's one of the many examples that show that people often do things that they don't want to do because they have to. I made a very conscious decision about this. Actually, my political views haven't changed much since I was about 12 or 13. I've learned more—I suppose they're more sophisticated—but fundamentally they haven't changed. However, I was not an activist. I was, until the early 1960s, working in my own garden, basically, doing the kind of work I liked, intellectually exciting, rewarding, satisfying, you make progress. I would have been very happy to stick to it. It would have been from a narrow personal point of view much better for me in every imaginable respect. I remember I knew as soon as I got involved in political activism that there was going to be no end, the demands would increase forever, there would be unpleasant personal consequences—and they are unpleasant. I mean there are less unpleasant things than being maced, for example, or spending a day in a Washington jail cell or being up for a five-year jail sentence or being subjected to the endless lies of the Anti-Defamation League and its friends, etc. There are more pleasant things. I didn't know in detail, but I knew it was going to be much less pleasant than just working in the fields where I felt I was good and I could make progress and so on. And I knew I had to cut back on things I really wanted to do and that I enjoyed doing, many things in personal life, and I knew personal life was going to contract enormously—something has to give—and in many ways there would be negative consequences. And I really thought about it pretty hard and I finally took the plunge, but not with any great joy, I must say.

I think a lot of people are grateful that you did.

Thanks.

Editor's Notes to Interview 42

"Interview with Noam Chomsky," *The Reading Instruction Journal* (A publication of the New Jersey Reading Association) 31:3 (Spring 1988), pp. 2–7 (placed there "as a prologue" to the special issue—a thematic one on "New Directions in Reading Instruction"). Lillian Putnam, Professor and Director of the Reading Clinic, Kean College, Union, New Jersey, spoke with Chomsky in November 1987, while she was a Visiting Scholar at the Harvard Graduate School of Education, eliciting one of the clearest expositions of Chomsky's conception of language.

The answer to the last question deserves to be pondered by people with different positions on the controversial issue, which has numerous ramifications. See, for example, "'English-only' Breeding Bigotry in the U.S.," *RESIST* Newsletter #208 (Aug–Sep 1988),pp. 3–5, by Edward M. Chen, staff counsel for the American Civil Liberties Union of Northern California. (Information about groups working against English-only initiatives is provided by the ACLU, 1663 Mission St., Suite 460, San Francisco, CA 94103; EPIC, 227 Mass. Av., N.E., Suite 120, Washington, D.C. 20002; or MALDEFF, Martha Jimenez, 1430 K St., N.W., Suite 700, Washington, D.C., 20005. For information on *RESIST*, see notes to interview 17). As many people are aware, it is no more difficult for a child to learn several languages than to learn one—under appropriate conditions. See **CD&E** (2003), II.ii; also, J. R. Strozer, *Language Acquisition after Puberty*, Washington, D.C.: Georgetown University Press, 1994.

42. A Really New Way of Looking at Language
(November 1987)

Dr. Chomsky, many of our teachers are unfamiliar with your work, because the study of linguistics is not required in their professional training. It would be helpful and would arouse some interest in this field, if you answered the following questions.

Your 1957 publication, entitled, Syntactic Structures, *presented a completely new way of looking at language. What was it that started you on this exploration?*

One may be interested in language for many different reasons, and from many different points of new. My own interest has been dominated by several central questions: (1) What is it that we know, when we know a language? (2) How is this knowledge acquired? (3) How is this knowledge put to use? (4) What is the physical basis, in neural mechanisms, for systems of knowledge and use of language? The fourth question remains on the horizons of research. Let us keep, then, to the first three.

In the early 1950s, typical answers to these questions would have been something like this. (1) A language is a certain system of habits and skills; to know a language is to have mastered these skills. (2) Knowledge of language is acquired by such mechanisms as conditioning, association, practice in exercising skills, etc. (3) Use of language is exercise of the skills that have been mastered. Within psychology, the dominant framework of thinking was one or another variety of behaviorism. Within linguistics, the dominant assumptions were structuralist. As a theoretical discipline, linguistics was devoted to devising principles of analysis that could be used to provide an organized and systematic account of the elements of a language, their relations, the orders in which they appear, the way they are grouped into larger elements, and so on.

It seemed to me clear that these approaches were entirely inadequate, in fact, that the entire conception was completely wrong. Normal use of language is not an exercise of any "habit" or "skill." Typically, use of language is **"creative,"** in the sense that it constantly involves the production and interpretation of new forms, new in the experience of the language user or even in the history of language. This is not an exotic phenomenon, but rather the norm. Thus readers of these sentences may not have seen any of them before, or anything like them, yet they have no difficulty recognizing them as sentences of their language and assigning to them a specific meaning. They do this in the same way as other speakers of (similar varieties of) English. If these sentences were modified in some arbitrary way—say, in reverse order—they would be equally novel for the

575

reader, but they would be gibberish. It is easy to show that speakers of a language, even young children, assign specific and precise meanings to very simple sentences that are entirely new in their experience.

Consider, for example, the following sentences, to illustrate what is in fact the norm in language use:

(1) we expect to like each other
(2) John wonders who [we expect to like each other]
(3) John is too clever to catch Bill
(4) John is too clever to expect anyone to catch Bill
(5) John is too clever to catch
(6) John is too clever to expect anyone to catch
(7) John is too clever to meet anyone who caught

In case (1), we know that the sentence means, roughly, that each of us expects that we will like the others of us. In case (2), the very same sentence is embedded in the context: "John wonders who___," yet we interpret it quite differently. The reciprocal phrase "each other" does not relate to "we," but rather to the more remote phrase "who." The meaning is something like: "John wonders which people are such that we expect that each of those people will like the others of those people." In example (3), we understand that John is to do the catching; in (4), John is to do the expecting. But in (5) and (6), which differ from (3) and (4) only by the deletion of the final noun, the meaning is quite different: it is not John who is to do the catching and expecting, but someone else, maybe us; John is the person to be caught. (To understand sentence (6) often takes a moment's reflection, whatever that means exactly.) Sentence (7) appears to be of the same complexity and roughly the same form as (6), but it is complete gibberish, unless we understand "catch" quite differently, as in "he catches for the Yankees."

These are very short and simple sentences. We understand them in a precise and explicit way, even though they may be novel in our experience, and unlike others that we have heard (in fact, we typically have no idea what sentences we have heard, apart from conventional greetings and the like). Children are not instructed to interpret these sentences in the ways they do, nor are foreigners learning English. Examples such as these do not appear in grammar books or teaching texts, and would only confuse people if they did appear; in fact, the properties of these sentences were not even noticed until recently. The sentences seem "familiar," but that is not because we have come across others resembling them. In fact, inspection of actual texts would show that such constructions are quite rare. Plainly, we cannot be carrying out these accomplishments by "habit," and there is no mere "skill" involved. Our inability to associate "each other" with "we" in (2) is not a lack of ability; it is not that we haven't practiced enough, or that we are too weak, or that we should try harder. Furthermore, such examples show that no notion of "analogy" or "similarity" will be of any help at all in explaining the core properties of language. Thus the phrase given within brackets in (2) is identical with (1), and thus is surely analogous to it in any reasonable sense of analogy, but it is interpreted quite differently. Such examples also show that the entire framework of behaviorist psychology is simply irrelevant to normal linguistic behavior, though to demonstrate this point, much simpler observations suffice, as they suffice to demonstrate **the irrelevance of behaviorist doctrine** to behavior generally, apart from its peripheral aspects.

Attention to the facts shows that the answers to the three questions posed must be entirely different from those that were conventional at the time. Recognition of such facts as these in various domains, and ideas as to how to account for them, led to the "cognitive turn" in psychology in the mid-1950s, and to the development of generative grammar within linguistics, one primary factor in this "cognitive revolution," as it is sometimes called. It seems that the right answers to the three questions are something like this: (1) to know a language is to have mastered a system of rules and principles; (2) the child acquires this knowledge on the basis of a very rich biological endowment that determines, quite precisely, the kinds of systems that can develop in language growth; (3) use of language is rule-governed behavior. At the heart of language, and much of human action and thought, is a system of mental representations and computations. The goal of linguistics, then, is to discover these systems, and more deeply, to discover the fixed, invariant biological endowment that enables each child to develop a very rich and highly articulated system of knowledge on the basis of quite fragmentary and limited evidence.

These ideas were by no means entirely novel. In fact, they recall a rich tradition that had long been forgotten by the mid-1950s, and is still little known.

For those of us who are not linguists, how would you state the basic idea of your generative transformational theory?

The basic idea is that knowledge of language involves a system of rules and representations, of **mental computation**, linked to the motor and perceptual apparatus; and that much of this system is fixed and invariant, just as the essential form and organization of the human body is fixed and invariant, determined by our biological endowment. To develop these ideas further would lead us to the principles that determine the form and meaning of sentences. Phenomena such as those illustrated above are common to the languages of the world, so far as we know. Notice that in all of these examples certain elements are "missing" in the physical form, but understood. Thus in (1) and (2) the subject of like is not expressed, but is understood; it is understood differently in the two cases. The same is true in the other examples. The principles of language determine where these missing elements must appear, and how they must be understood. They are "missing" only in the sense that they are not pronounced: the mind "sees" them and uses them in its mental computations, and they are just as real as the elements "John," "we," etc., which happen to be lined to the vocal apparatus in the system of mental computation.

Languages of course differ; English is not Japanese. But it seems that languages differ only in their lexical choices and in selection of certain options that are not fully determined by the fixed principles of our biological endowment. Thus in every language, verbs take objects; but the object may follow the verb, as in English, or precede it, as in Japanese. This option holds not only for verb phrases, but for all phrases. Thus English has prepositions, while Japanese has postpositions. Japanese in many ways seems a "mirror image" of English, and seems superficially to differ in many other respects as well. But the systems are cast to the same mold. The same is true of other languages, so far as we know, however different they may seem superficially. Indeed, we know that this must be the case, or children would never be able to learn any of these languages. A language can be acquired, in all of its richness and complexity, because the child basically already "knows it," as part of its biological endowment. The same is true much more broadly, in every domain of human achievement.

You have written that a major contribution of the study of language is understanding of the character of mental processes, i.e. "language is a mirror of the mind." At the present point in your work, what important reflections are in this mirror?

The idea that "language is a mirror of mind" is a traditional one, which has received expression in various ways over the centuries. I have never felt that this metaphor should be taken too literally. Rather, it seems that language is one essential component of the human mind. The human brain is **the most complex and intricate biological system** we know. When we study its properties and manifestations, we are studying what we call "mind." The human mind appears to consist of different systems, each intricate and highly specialized, with interactions of a kind that are largely fixed by our biological endowment; in these respects it is like all other known biological systems, the physical organs of the body below the neck, for example. One of these systems is the human language faculty. It is particularly interesting because it is a common property of humans, with little if any variation apart from quite serious impairment, and it appears to be unique to the human species; contrary to much mythology, other organisms appear to lack even the most rudimentary features of the human language faculty, a fact that has been shown quite dramatically in recent studies of apes. Thus human language appears to be a true "species property," and one that enters in a central way into thought and understanding. But it is not, in my view, a "mirror of mind"; rather, an essential component of the human mind, a crucial element of the human essence.

In Language and Mind, *you wrote in essence that as research in grammar continues, we may expect boundaries that seem clear today to shift for a new basis for organization of grammar. Now in 1987, which, if any, have shifted?*

There have been many changes in our conception of the nature of language over the past 30 years. Early work in generative grammar, as in syntactic structures, was in some respects similar to traditional grammar. Specifically, it involved rules that were specific to particular constructions and to particular languages. Thus the rule for forming questions in English, or passives in English, was language-particular and construction-particular, just as in a traditional grammar there will be a chapter on passives, one on questions, and so on. The so-called "rules" of traditional grammars are really only hints, understandable to an intelligent reader who already knows the language, just as the rules in a teaching grammar presuppose that the learner already knows the basic structure of language. Generative grammar, in contrast, attempted to make explicit what is presupposed—indeed, what was not even recognized to exist—in traditional and pedagogic grammar. But apart from this crucial distinction, the rule systems of early generative grammar had a rather familiar look to them.

More recent work has led to the conclusion that the rules of traditional and early generative grammar are an artifact, not real elements of the mind/brain. There appear to be no construction-particular rules, but rather very general principles, such as the principles for interpreting missing elements, that are common to all languages and all constructions. Languages differ in the manner indicated earlier, but not by selection of different rules. There is thus, in recent work, a **very radical departure from the tradition of study of language** over the past several thousand years.

Reading teachers are concerned with language acquisition since oral language provides a basis for reading. In your writings, you state that at birth, children are genetically programmed to acquire language and that it is innate. Is then the heavy emphasis placed on "language development" by nursery schools and kindergartens justified?

There is little doubt that the basic structure of language and the principles that determine the form and interpretation of sentences in any human language are in large part innate. But it does not follow that emphasis on language development is misplaced. If a child is placed in an impoverished environment, innate abilities simply will not develop, mature, and flourish. To take an extreme case, a child who wears a cast on its legs for too long will never learn to walk, and a child deprived of appropriate nutrition may undergo puberty only after a long delay, or never, though there is no doubt that walking and sexual maturation are innately-determined biological properties. Similarly, a child brought up in an institution may have ample experience and nutrition, but still may not develop normally, either physically or mentally, if normal human interaction is lacking.

It is a traditional insight that teaching is not like filling a cup with water, but more like enabling a flower to grow in its own way; but it will not grow and flourish without proper care. Language development, like all human development, will be heavily determined by **the nature of the environment**, and may be severely limited unless the environment is appropriate. A stimulating environment is required to enable natural curiosity, intelligence and creativity to develop, and to enable our biological capacities to unfold. The fact that the course of development is largely internally determined does not mean that it will proceed without care, stimulation, and opportunity.

We realize that linguistics is the scientific study of language, and not a recipe for language instruction. But if teachers in primary grades were familiar with your work, what kind of changes or even emphasis might they make in reading instruction? What general suggestions would help them?

I'm hesitant even to suggest an answer to this question. Practitioners have to decide for themselves what is useful in the sciences, and what is not. As a linguist, I have no particular qualifications or knowledge that enables or entitles me to prescribe methods of language instruction. As a person, I have my own ideas on the topic, based on my own experience (in part, as a teacher of language to children), introspection, and personal judgment, but these should not be confused with some kind of professional expertise, presented from on high. My own feeling, for what it is worth, is that at any level, from the nursery to graduate school, teaching is largely a matter of encouraging natural development. The best "method" of teaching is to make it clear that the subject is worth learning, and to allow the child's—or adult's—natural curiosity and interest in truth and understanding to mature and develop. That is about 90 percent of the problem, if not more. Methods of instruction may influence the residue.

Many of the early beliefs concerning the nature of language of "disadvantaged children" have been disproved by research, i.e. that "Black English" is deficient or inferior; that it fails to provide an adequate basis for abstract thinking. Yet speakers of Black English want their children to learn standard English. Is this best done by direct instruction or by "osmosis"?

Anyone who was familiar with language took for granted, or should have taken for granted, that so-called Black English is simply a language, on a par with my urban Philadelphia dialect of English, the English of High Table at Oxford, Japanese, Greek, etc. If race, class and other power relations were to change, Black English might emerge as the standard language and what I speak would be regarded as "defective." None of this has anything to do with the nature of the languages. The idea that Black English, or my urban dialect, or any other language fails to provide an adequate basis for abstract thinking is utterly implausible, and I think one should be extremely skeptical about claims to the contrary. Typically, they are based on gross misunderstanding.

Questions nevertheless arise about **what should be taught in the schools**. If speakers of Black English came to dominate and control American society, so that my speech would be regarded as nonstandard and "defective," then it might be argued that my children should be taught the language of the dominant culture, not the particular variety of English that I speak. The decision would not be based on characteristics of the language, or on some ludicrous beliefs about how certain languages stand in the way of abstract thought, but rather on other considerations. Thus one would have to ask whether my children would suffer in the real world of power, authority, inequality and coercion if they were not to acquire relevant features of the dominant culture. Surely this consideration would have to be given weight, if the welfare of my children were to be taken into account. On the other hand, if my children were to be instructed in what amounts to a foreign language, their intellectual development might be inhibited; there is little doubt, for example, that it would be harder for them to learn to read if the language of instruction were Black English, which is not the language that they acquired in their pre-school environment. The same questions would arise if I had moved to Italy when my children were young. Exactly how these factors should be balanced is not a simple question and there is no reason to believe that there is any uniform answer to them: too many factors vary.

My own personal judgment, for what it is worth, is that speakers of a language that is not that of groups that dominate some society should probably be taught in their own languages at least at very early stages, until basic skills are acquired, and should be taught in the dominant language at later stages, so that they can enter the society without suffering disadvantages that are rooted in prevailing power, privilege and domination. One might hope to modify these features of the dominant society, but that is another question. Children have to be helped to function in the world that exists, which does not mean, of course, that they—or others—should not try to change it to a better world.

I am not presuming to express any firm judgments or to offer general proposals. There are a great many factors to consider, and the answers will surely not be the same for every person or every circumstance. We have to do here not with the problems of language, but of the society at large, and they have to be confronted in these terms.

Editor's Notes to Interview 43

This is the fourth Barsamian interview (see Editor's Notes to I35).

The book just finished, also mentioned in the next interview, is **MC** (1988), then still called *The Political Economy of the Mass Media* (earlier title, now subtitle).

43. Techniques of Marginalization (24 January 1988)

In your 1978 book Human Rights and American Foreign Policy *you write: "If we hope to understand anything about the foreign policy of any state, it is a good idea to begin by investigating the domestic social structure." Would you talk about that?*

Foreign policy, like all state policy, flows from domestic institutions. It reflects the interests and concerns of those who have the capacity to organize the resources to either control the state directly or to influence what the state does. In the case of foreign policy, it's those segments of the domestic society that are particularly concerned with international affairs who will naturally have the major voice. So if you want to understand foreign policy you begin by looking at domestic structures. In the case of our society, the answers to those questions are rather straightforward. Domestic power is highly concentrated in the corporate system, and those segments of the corporate system that are particularly concerned with international affairs typically exert an overwhelming influence on the design and execution of foreign policy.

You can see that simply enough by just who staffs the executive and the top decision-making positions. They're overwhelmingly drawn from major corporations with international interests, investment firms, half a dozen law firms that cater primarily to corporate interests and therefore have a kind of overarching conception of the needs of the corporate sector rather than a parochial concern for one or another segment of it. Occasionally you are allowed into the crowd if you are an "expert" in the sense in which Henry Kissinger explained the concept. Pretty frankly, he pointed out that an "expert" is someone who is able to articulate the consensus of people with power, and if you have that capacity, which in fact he had, then you can come in as an expert and be a state manager in the interests of external power. That's the core of it. Beyond that there are other influences, there are domestic lobbies and so on, but I think that's the essential core.

This analysis is characterized as a "radical critique."

I think it's **a very conservative critique**, in fact, it's just plain common sense and there's nothing there that would have been surprising to 18th-century figures of the kind who founded this country. It's merely an extension of conventional doctrine of the kind they articulated to the specific structure of our own society. It's called "radical," but you have to recall that "radical" is just one of several terms of abuse which have no meaning, like "Marxist." There's a whole array of terms of abuse which are used to protect ourselves from understanding of the world in which we live.

In The Culture of Terrorism *you discuss two trends, the "right turn" and the "crisis of democracy." What are they, and are they connected?*

They are very closely connected. The "**crisis of democracy**," which is not my term, happens to be the title of an important book published by the Trilateral Commission in 1975, their one major book-length publication. The Trilateral Commission was established by David Rockefeller. It includes more or less liberal elite elements from the three major centers of industrial capitalism, the United States, Japan and Western Europe, hence Trilateral Commission. This book reflects the results of an extensive study they did of the phenomenon that they referred to as the crisis of democracy. The crisis of democracy, as they outline it, has to do with the fact that during the 1960s and the early 70s substantial sectors of the population which are usually apathetic and passive became organized and began to enter the political arena and began to press for their own interests and concerns and that created a crisis, because that's not the way democracy is supposed to work. As the chief American contributor, Samuel Huntington, professor at Harvard, put it, back in the days of Truman, before there was a crisis of democracy, policy could be executed simply by a handful of Wall Street lawyers and financiers. That's a bit of an exaggeration, but it expresses the conception of the commission as to the way democracy ought to function.

That was threatened in the 1960s as minorities, youth, women, aged people, all sorts of groups began to be organized and enter into the political system. That crisis, the participants agreed, which was world-wide, had to be overcome, and the population had to be returned to its proper state of apathy and ignorance, returned to its task, which is ratifying decisions made by elites. Various mechanisms were proposed for doing this. One of the mechanisms, in fact, constitutes the "**right turn**," which is a phenomenon among elites. It hasn't taken place among the general population. But among elites there has been a very notable right turn, meaning a turn towards a kind of reactionary jingoism, mislabeled conservatism very often. It has nothing to do with conservatism. That reflects the recognition that something has to be done to restore the earlier order of privilege and overcome threats to privilege. That has a domestic aspect and an international aspect. The international aspect is the Reagan doctrine, which is just a phrase referring to international terrorism, the use of violence, subversion, and other methods to overcome the crisis of democracy that was beginning to arise elsewhere in the world. For example, in Central America there was a serious threat of meaningful democracy, meaning real rather than nominal democracy, actual participation of usually dispossessed segments of the population. There was also a rising threat of social reform that had to be countered, and the Reagan doctrine is an effort to counter that by the usual methods of violence and repression. At home, you can't just call out the death squads, so other, more subtle methods are necessary. So there have been major efforts at indoctrination. At an extreme level we find such interesting institutions as the Office of Public Diplomacy at the State Department, which is dedicated to controlling what they quite openly called "enemy territory," the domestic population. Since this right turn represents a general elite consensus, it also includes the doves, the establishment liberals. The goal, only partially achieved, was to create a reactionary consensus which will support the right of U.S. power to exercise violence in the world for domestic interests and will also at home weaken the labor movement, break up the growing popular movements, restore the population to apathy, bring them to accept the policies of domestic austerity required for large parts of the population if American business is to recover its competitive advantages in the world, and so on. All of that constitutes the elite right turn.

You contend that elite groups view the domestic population as an enemy.

Typically, yes. It's true of all states and all elites. Usually the enemy can be disregarded because it's sufficiently passive and apathetic. But if the domestic enemy begins to make unpleasant noises, then something has to be done about it. As I say, the methods are different abroad and at home. The conception of the population as an enemy is often rather clearly articulated. For example, on the right wing it's articulated when high administration officials use the phrase. When the Office of Public Diplomacy was first exposed by Alfonso Chardy of the *Miami Herald* in July 1987, he inquired among administration officials as to what it was up to, and they described it as the most spectacular achievement of the Reagan administration and one high administration official, whom he quoted, referred to it as the kind of program that you would carry out in "enemy territory," which is exactly right. At the liberal end, you have the viewpoint expressed in the Trilateral Commission study, which is concerned quite explicitly with restoring apathy, passivity and obedience so that democracy in the preferred sense can survive, and that again reflects a conception of the population as an enemy which has to be controlled or suppressed or somehow marginalized. I might mention in this connection that the rise of clandestine operations is a reflection of the strength of the domestic enemy. If the enemy, the population, can't be controlled by force, can't be indoctrinated and can't be marginalized, it will in fact drive the state underground. The government will have to carry out its actions in secret because the domestic enemy won't tolerate them. The scale of clandestine operations is often a very good measure of domestic dissidence.

I'd like you to clarify your views about elite groups, and let me make a point of argument here. Can you completely discount their necessity? For example, the mechanic who repairs the brakes on your car, you want him to be a member of an elite group, don't you?

You want people to have specialized skills. The question is whether those specialized skills should confer power. Should the ability of a mechanic to fix your car lead to a system in which he can determine what car you buy? The answer is no. Let's say—I'm not sure that this is true—but suppose that there are skills required for management. That's a dubious assumption, but let's assume it. Then we might want people who have those alleged skills to be able to exercise them. In a real democracy they would exercise them under public control, just as a doctor would or a mechanic or anyone else. No sane person would want a society without skilled people. The question is how power is distributed. Does power reside in the population or does it reside in elite elements, in our society, elements that gain their effective decision-making power ultimately by their ownership of the central parts of the society, the domestic economy, typically?

You frequently mention the fact that in 1962 the Kennedy administration attacked South Vietnam and that this information is not known, not discussed, "down the memory hole." Why is that?

It's not quite true that the information was not discussed. In fact it was on the front page of the *New York Times*. It's just that in a well-indoctrinated society the information doesn't have any meaning. So the *New York Times* can report, as it did, I think it was October 1962, that the Kennedy administration has committed U.S. planes and U.S. pilots to undertake direct participation, not just control, in the bombing and defoliation operations in South Vietnam directed against the rural population, which was the large majority, about 80 percent of the population. Now that's aggression, but it wasn't understood as that. As the facts became filtered through our very effective indoctrination system, it became defense. It became defense against what Adlai Stevenson, our UN ambassador at the time, referred to as "internal aggression," namely the aggression of the Vietnamese, and particularly the Vietnamese peasants, against the United States in South Vietnam. A society that can use phrases such as "internal aggression" and can perceive the bombing of peasant villages as a defense of either us or our clients, that society has gone a long way towards a kind of operative totalitarianism.

Using the example of the Indochina war, can you talk about how dissident groups in the United States affected U.S. public policy?

They certainly did affect it. It was an indirect kind of effect. Plainly it was not through the electoral system. In 1964, the population voted two-to-one in favor of Lyndon Johnson, who put himself forth as the "peace candidate," and to a large measure that vote was because Johnson stated openly and repeatedly that "we do not want a wider war." That was a vote against expansion of the war. As we now know, at that very moment Lyndon Johnson's advisers were planning the escalation of the war, the escalation of the attack against South Vietnam, the expansion of the war to North Vietnam, which took place as soon as they had won the election. Plainly, the effect was not through the electoral system. However, over a long period, a difficult period of education, organization, demonstration, protest and so on, the population became sufficiently disaffected by the war that the Johnson administration was unable to declare a national mobilization. As the war became a really serious, major war, that raised serious domestic problems. It was necessary to fight the war on deficit financing, to fight a "guns and butter" war, as it was called, The reason was that the population was simply too disaffected to go along. It wasn't like World War II, when people were quite willing to accept domestic austerity because of a commitment to the war. That was not true during the Vietnam War, in part, as a result of the continual activities of the peace movement. There were other factors too, but it was a large part of it. The effects of that were quite significant. By the time of the Tet Offensive, in 1968, when it became evident that this was going to be a long, protracted war for the United States to attain its objectives of subjugating and controlling at least South Vietnam, at that point elite elements began to become disaffected, and the reason was, very explicitly, that the war was becoming too costly.

In economic terms.

Yes, in terms of relations between the United States and its major rivals, Europe and Japan. The effects of fighting a guns and butter war were harming the U.S. economy. While stagflation was setting in, in contrast, our rivals were enriching themselves through the destruction of Indochina. For example, Canada became the largest per capita war exporter in the world—to us. That was its participation in the destruction of Indochina. The war gave a huge shot in the arm to Japan. Japan was not a serious rival to the United States in the early 1960s, but in 1965 the balance of trade shifted and after that Japan became a very serious rival. The industrial takeoff of South Korea dates from the same time, largely as an off-shore producer for the American war and from the remittances of ultimately about 300,000 mercenaries that they sent to fight the war with us in South Vietnam. All of this was beneficial to our rivals but harmful to the United States. Since it was impossible to create a national mobilization here, the war had to be fought in a way which was quite harmful to the U.S. economy. That became evident by early 1968. It led elite groups to urge, in fact, demand and require, significant change in policy. That's an indirect **effect of the domestic dissidence**, powerful but indirect, a large part of which can be traced to the activism of people associated in one way or another with the peace movement. It was actually more than that. The secret records tell us more. They tell us that by about May 1967 or earlier, the Pentagon was beginning to be concerned about domestic dissidence. Robert McNamara warned the president in a memo in May 1967 that things could get out of hand in the United States. After the Tet Offensive, the joint chiefs were concerned about the danger of a real uprising. They wanted to make sure they had enough troops for "civil disorder control," as they put it. They were particularly concerned about massive civil disobedience involving many sectors of the population, including particularly women, youth, segments of the intelligentsia. The ethnic minorities were beginning to blow up, the armies were beginning to collapse, a reflection of the youth culture at home. It was a citizens' army, not a mercenary army, so it's not dissociated from developments at home. All of these factors were beginning to create a serious internal crisis, and in these respects, too, the state managers, who were carrying out what was a simple war of aggression, were compelled to face costs that they ultimately decided they could not tolerate. In all of these indirect ways, domestic dissidence played a very significant, I think a decisive role in slowly, very, very slowly, with agonizing slowness, forcing the United States to abandon its effort to literally conquer South Vietnam.

Thus provoking a "crisis of democracy."

That was the crisis of democracy which then had to be faced. The crisis was rather broad. It was not only the crisis of democracy, the fact that segments of the population that are usually apathetic were beginning to participate in the political system or to demand that the state respond to their interests. There was also a serious threat to the profitability of American business as a result of the consequences of the war and the way it was fought. Stagflation was the fundamental phenomenon, and that required an attack on unions, lowering of real wages, breakup of the unions and, in general, dismantling of the popular structures in the United States that would enable ordinary citizens to fight for their rights in opposition to those of the owners and managers of the society, and we've seen that strikingly during the Reagan period with an elite consensus behind it. The attack on the social welfare system, the transfer of resources from the poor to the rich, which was a very notable feature of the 1980s, all of these are part of the same effort of the dominant social groups in the United States, the owners and managers of the corporate system, to ensure their own privilege and to defend themselves against the rising domestic enemy.

You were very active in those years in the resistance against the war in Indochina, and that's why I want to explore this with you, because you are a historical source and record as well. There has been a lot of "historical engineering" that has occurred since that period. Two things come to mind: one is the popular notion that somehow it was the media in the 1960s that galvanized popular dissent against the war in Vietnam. You take exception to that.

That's totally false, every study of the media completely refutes that really quite absurd view. I've just finished with Edward Herman, a colleague of mine, a book on the mass media, a large segment of which, about half, is devoted to **the media coverage of the Indochina war**, beginning around 1950 and up to today. There's simply no question that the media were very, very supportive of the war. Up until the late 60s there isn't even any debate over this. Everyone agrees on all sides that through about 1966 or 1967 the media were highly supportive of the war, very hawkish. A number of studies have shown that the effect of television in particular was to make the population more hawkish.

It's easy to demonstrate that on every major issue the media simply went along with state policy. The only respect in which this was not true is that sometimes journalists on the scene had a different perception. They were basically seeing the war from the point of view of the American military command on the scene. They never reported the war from the point of view of the Vietnamese resistance, as they do, say, in Afghanistan. Rather, the war was seen by correspondents from the point of view of American military commanders in the field, often junior officers, and they did to some extent reflect the perception on the part of officers and soldiers on the scene that things were different from the way they were being portrayed in Washington. So for example at the time of the formation of the strategic hamlets everyone on the ground could see that this method of trying to control the population, by violence, was simply not working. Washington was claiming that it was, the military on the scene knew much better, and the correspondents, reflecting the officers and sometimes men who they were with, did, to some extent, reflect their attitudes.

Only in this very narrow and limited respect did the media diverge from state policy. By January 1968, when the Tet Offensive took place, there was one significant change. For the first time the journalists were able to see the war not under the control of the U.S. military. They weren't simply flown somewhere in a military helicopter and shown what the military wanted them to see. They could look out their window and see the war going on. As a result, there was some very graphic reporting, but within the framework of U.S. government propaganda, contrary to what is claimed. For example, the media described the destruction of cities in the Mekong Delta south of Saigon graphically and vividly and they knew, as everyone knew, including the American command, that the cities were being destroyed to "rescue" them, as it was being put, from their own populations. It was understood that there were virtually no North Vietnamese there. The people who were doing the fighting were South Vietnamese, who we called Viet Cong, the National Liberation Front troops. The only foreign force in the Delta was the United States and the Thai and Korean and other mercenaries that the United States brought in. Nevertheless, the media described all of this as defense. We were "rescuing" Ben Tre when we conquered it from its own population. One famous phrase was we had to "destroy the town in order to save it," and that was the conception of the media: the United States was engaged in defense when it was destroying and murdering and attacking South Vietnamese. There was no departure from that. Again, contrary to many claims, the media portrayed the Tet Offensive as essentially an American military victory. If you compare the media portrayal with the internal record of U.S. intelligence, the media were considerably more optimistic about U.S. successes than U.S. intelligence was. The reason was that the media were largely reflecting public statements. They didn't know what was being reported by the CIA. If you make that comparison, it's dramatically the case.

After that, the media simply continued to portray the war largely as perceived by Washington. So as Washington began its attempt at a negotiated settlement that would leave it in control of South Vietnam, the media shifted attention away from the fighting in the south to the negotiations. This is particularly striking because this was the period of the greatest mass murder operations carried out by the U.S. military in South Vietnam, what was called the "post-Tet accelerated pacification campaign," which completely devastated the South Vietnamese resistance and prepared the way for the ultimate North Vietnamese takeover. That was sometimes described. There were some reporters on the scene who wrote about it, and there were even some very good analyses of it, in particular by Kevin Buckley of *Newsweek*. He investigated one of these mass murder operations in depth, although his report was delayed for several years before it was published, and then only in part. But by and large the media shifted public attention away, television almost completely, and these mass murder operations proceeded with minimal coverage and virtually no understanding. And that continued. At the time of the Paris peace treaty, for example, the media went along totally with the immediate U.S. efforts to unravel and undermine them, which succeeded, and to this day that's barely known. There's simply no point at which the media diverged from this framework, apart from very limited exceptions.

There's another little anecdote which involved you and Tip O'Neill. In 1987 he wrote his autobiography (Man of the House). *It was reviewed by John Kenneth Galbraith. Can you talk about that?*

Tip O'Neill was described by Galbraith, and describes himself, as one of the early leaders of the anti-war movement in Congress. The facts are a little bit different. The personal anecdote you have in mind, I suppose, was April 8 or 9, 1965, the day after a major speech by Johnson, when a group of New England professors, of whom I was one, Howard Zinn was another, and there were a few others, went to Washington to lobby, to try to talk to Tip O'Neill, who was the representative from Cambridge, where I teach and others of us lived and worked. We went to see the Massachusetts delegation just to talk to them about the war. The position we were taking was extremely narrow, embarrassingly narrow. You have to remember that this was 1965. It was impossible then to talk about the American war in South Vietnam, nobody could even hear the words when you talked about that. So we limited ourselves pretty much to the bombing of North Vietnam. The reactions were different among different people. Tip O'Neill's reaction was extreme. He didn't even let us into his office. He wasn't even going to listen to constituents who opposed the bombing of North Vietnam. Others were willing to let us into their offices. Some of the Republican congressmen from Massachusetts were more or less sympathetic, but that was about it. Tip O'Neill was the most extreme example. This went on through about 1967. There was virtually no congressional opposition to the war. As elite groups, as the U.S. corporate elite began to become disaffected with the war, segments of Congress went along, in particular by early 1968, when there was real, very extensive corporate disaffection. A famous meeting took place of a group of "wise men," as they were called—Dean Acheson, McGeorge Bundy, John McCloy, I believe, the usual people who staff the executive and represent the corporate and the military systems. They actually went to Washington to give an evaluation of the war and told the president that he had to change course.

In fact, that's when Johnson gave up and the process called "Vietnamization" began taking place. It was then that you began to get some very limited congressional opposition. It's very similar to current congressional opposition to Contra aid. Violence is not succeeding, so we had better turn to something else to achieve our objectives. At that point you began to get the people who are the famous "anti-war leaders" appearing, for example, Gene McCarthy. He was invisible during the hard period of opposition to the war. Opposition to the war was extremely unpopular in 1966–67, and then you heard nothing from Gene McCarthy. McCarthy is a particularly interesting example. Galbraith has identified him as the "real hero" of the anti-war movement. You get an understanding of a liberal elite political culture thinking that through. There was some early congressional opposition to the war: Wayne Morse and Ernst Gruening were the only people to vote against the Tonkin Gulf resolution, and there were a handful of others who spoke up, but not Gene McCarthy. He joined the opposition to the war in an extremely vague way. If you look back at his speeches it's completely unclear what he was saying. But he was willing to put himself forth as the leader at the point when he thought that he could exploit the mass popular movement that he had done nothing to help organize. He thought that he could exploit it for personal political power. When he saw that he couldn't, he dropped from sight. That's extremely clear in McCarthy's case. He appeared, briefly. For a few months until the Democratic Convention of August 1968 he was willing to let himself be represented as an anti-war leader, because he needed the troops. When he didn't win the nomination, he effectively disappeared.

We can tell exactly how seriously he took the war issue by looking at what he did at that point. He had a lot of completely undeserved prestige, he was a public figure. He could have used that if he had cared a bit about ending the attack against Indochina, or the war—however he would have conceived of it, the defense of South Vietnam or whatever phrase he would have used. If he'd even cared minimally about it, he could have used the prestige he had obtained without any right, but he had obtained it, to act as a public spokesman against the war. All we have to do is check and find out what he did. Answer: Virtually nothing. He disappeared. He had lost his **bid for political power**, he therefore disappeared, and he is now constituted among the highest-ranking liberal pantheon of anti-war heroes. That tells you something about the political culture.

Talking about American political culture, you've often pointed out that the U.S. lacks political parties, lacks an opposition press and is essentially depoliticized. Might that be an explanation for the fact that tens of millions of Americans don't vote, don't participate in the political process?

I think there's very little doubt of that. There have been a number of studies of non-voters. Walter Dean Burnham, a political scientist, is one of those who's done some of the best work on this, and the facts are pretty clear. If you do a socio-economic analysis, **a profile of the non-voters**, it turns out that they're very similar to the groups that in some European industrial democracies vote for one of the labor-based parties. Almost every other industrial democracy has some political party with roots in the working class, the poor, the dispossessed, and so on. The party has various names. It's called sometimes labor or Communist or socialist or one thing or another, but such a political formation has in the past existed. They're now beginning to decline elsewhere, but they have in the past existed in the other industrial democracies. The one major exception is Japan, and even there it exists to a limited extent, and of course we created the Japanese political system. But the glaring exception is the United States, where the only two parties are the business-based parties. If you look at the non-voters, they are the people who would vote labor, communist, socialist, one of those groupings in the other industrial democracies. Voting in the United States is heavily class-based. It's skewed towards skilled rather than unskilled workers, towards white-collar rather than blue-collar, employed rather than unemployed, the rich rather than the poor, the professionals rather than the homeless, and so on. That reflects the same fact. Large parts of the population, half roughly in presidential elections, two-thirds roughly in congressional elections, simply don't participate. There are a number of reasons for that, some technical reasons like difficulty of registering, but the main reason appears to be that they don't feel part of the political system.

That also shows up in other ways. There were some very striking polls taken after the last two elections, which were very revealing. After the 1984 election, voters were asked whether they hoped that Reagan's legislative agenda would be enacted, and voters, by three to two, hoped that it would not. That is, the people who voted for Reagan hoped that his legislative program would not be enacted. That means they were voting against interest, and that indicates a complete cynicism with regard to the political system. They were voting for some other reason, not because they thought they were influencing policy. Other polls help explain what those reasons were. At the same time, about half the population, when asked, "Who runs the government?" answered "yes" to the question "Is the government run by a few big interests looking out for themselves?" That was the opinion of about half the population, and presumably that's correlated with the half that didn't vote, or the segments who voted for Reagan while hoping that his legislative program will not be enacted. That does reflect in my view a kind of understanding of the political system, or to put it more neutrally, a kind of cynicism about the political system, that's very widespread, particularly among the less educated, who typically tend to be more sophisticated and perceptive about these matters, the reason being that education is a form of indoctrination, and the less educated are less indoctrinated. Furthermore, the educated tend to be the privileged and they tend to have a stake in the doctrinal system, so they naturally tend to internalize and believe it. As a result, not uncommonly and not only in the United States, you find a good deal more sophistication among people who learn about the world from their experience rather than those who learn about the world from the doctrinal framework that they are exposed to and that they are expected as part of their professional obligation to propagate.

In the 1980s one hears much talk on a social level of "co- dependency relationships." You've suggested that there is such a relationship between the United States and the USSR

There is an interesting relationship that's developed since the late 1940s. Without going into the details of how the Cold War got started, the fact is that the Cold War has had a kind of functional utility for both superpowers. I'm convinced that that's one of the reasons why it persists. It's in a way in their interests, the interests of the elite groups that run the two superpowers. This is true in spite of the enormous cost that it entails and the great dangers that it poses, including the danger of terminal disaster. You can see this very clearly if you look over the actual events of the Cold War. On the Russian side, what are the events of the Cold War? The events are such actions as the sending of tanks to East Berlin in 1953, or the invasion of Hungary in 1956, the invasion of Czechoslovakia, now the invasion of Afghanistan, and so on. Those are the events of the Cold War. In every one of those cases, the Soviet Union was attacking someone in its domains, actually in the area conquered by the Red Army, or in the case of Afghanistan, in an area in which it had already attained substantial, in fact dominant influence. It was effectively attacking a client state and it had to mobilize its own population. Because you have to do that; any state, whether it's a democracy or totalitarian or whatever, has to organize and mobilize its own population for costly and violent actions. And it did it by appealing to the threat of the Great Satan. All of these actions were defensive. They were taken in defense against the threat posed by the United States, which threatens to attack and overwhelm and destroy the Soviet Union. That's the way you mobilize people, by convincing them that they have to defend their homes against some great enemy. For popular mobilization, the Cold War was very functional for Soviet elites.

Exactly the same has been true here. On our side, the events of the Cold War have been regular interventions, subversion and aggression. When we overthrew the democratic capitalist government of Guatemala in 1954, for example, we were defending ourselves from Soviet attack. When we invaded South Vietnam, we were defending ourselves from an agent of the Russians or the Chinese. And so on up till today. When we attack Nicaragua today we're defending ourselves from Soviet expansionism. That's the way you mobilize a domestic population, and it must be done. There's essentially no other method. It can be done up to levels of extraordinary absurdity. For example, the conquest of Grenada was actually presented in the United States as a defense of the United States against a threat. This speck in the Caribbean, which you could barely find on a map, which has 100,000 people, was a threat to the existence of the United States. They could never convince the American population of that. But if you could pretend that somehow it was an outpost of the Soviet Union, a dangerous power with an ample record of brutality and bristling with missiles and so forth, then it becomes more plausible. So we defended ourselves by conquering this invisible speck in the Caribbean. That kind of functional utility is required for imposing domestic controls.

That's the main method. Typically, any state will try to defend itself against its domestic enemy by inducing fear to get the domestic enemy, the population, to accept policies to which they are opposed, policies under which they suffer. There is only one way that has ever been thought of to do that, and that is to **induce fear**. To induce fear, you need an enemy. If you look back at our history there have been a number of enemies. In the 19th century we were defending ourselves from the British and the Spanish. During the First World War, when Woodrow Wilson sent his troops to Haiti and the Dominican Republic, where they carried out brutal and murderous counterinsurgency operations, destroyed the constitutional system, reinstated slavery, and so on, there were no Russians then, it was before the Bolshevik revolution, so we were defending ourselves against the Huns. After the Bolshevik revolution, we've been defending ourselves against them. We need an enemy to defend ourselves against. There's an interesting little twist to this during the Reagan period. During the Reagan years the population was strongly opposed to the major thrust of the Reagan program, the polls show that very dramatically, so we had a lot of "evil empire" rhetoric, we have to defend ourselves against the Russian, and so on.

However, a confrontation with the Russians is a little bit too dangerous, so it was necessary to find an enemy which is weak enough so that we can attack them and destroy them and kill them without any cost to ourselves but yet strong enough so that you can use it to frighten the domestic population. The public relations agents of the Reagan administration very quickly found the solution to this dilemma: international terrorism. They concocted an array of "little Satans"—Qaddafi, the PLO, the Sandinistas, Grenada, and so on—countries and even individuals who are sufficiently weak so that we can attack them without any cost to ourselves. We can bomb Tripoli and Benghazi and kill a hundred people at no cost to us. But nevertheless they are threatening because they are identified as agents of the evil empire. That was a brilliant public relations coup. It's now becoming difficult because of the enormous costs of the Reaganite follies, which have seriously damaged the domestic economy. It's becoming extremely difficult to conduct this aggressive foreign policy. As a result we discover that the Russians are less threatening, international terrorism is declining, now there's a need for statesmanlike poses, and so on. Nothing much has changed in the world, but something has changed at home. A general point throughout this whole period is that the Soviet Union and its alleged clients have been a very convenient device to induce fear to mobilize the domestic population. Something of the same sort has been true on their side. That's the functional utility of the Cold War.

How do you view Gorbachev's glasnost and perestroika policies and might they be unwelcome in certain U.S. circles given what you said about the need to maintain fear?

I think they're very frightening in elite circles in the United States. That's why there's been a continual effort to downgrade and downplay them. It's already been harmful to the United States in Europe. A lot of **Gorbachev's policies** are quite welcome in Europe, not to the European elites, who are just as frightened of them as U.S. elites are. But there's undoubtedly a general popular major mass movement which would prefer to see a reduction in tensions, a reduction of the dungeon-like character of the Soviet Union and Eastern Europe, and who therefore welcome these policies. Gorbachev is a very popular figure in Western Europe, as indeed he's even becoming here. After the Reykjavik summit, the U.S. Information Agency carried out a secret study of the reaction in Europe to the summit. It was leaked and published in Europe. As far as I know, it was never published in any American newspaper. It was mentioned in columns occasionally but never published as news, to my knowledge. It was published as news in Europe, and what it showed was that the European population in every country outside of France was overwhelmingly supportive of Gorbachev against Reagan by figures of four to one and seven to one and so on, and of course that's frightening. The United States has to ensure control over its clients, Western Europe in particular, that's the most important one, and the threat of detente has to be taken quite seriously. At the same time there's conflict here. It's important to recognize how seriously Reaganite policies have harmed the American economy. It's extremely serious, and there's going to be a real cost to pay. As a result, the United States is not going to be able to throw its weight around in world affairs to the extent that the right wing would like, and hence it's necessary for the United States to move towards a less confrontational stance. In this respect there are factors here driving the country towards a kind of detente. At the same time, the loss of this mode of control over the domestic population and control over the client states and the allies, that's serious. It'll be interesting to see how these conflicting needs play themselves out in the coming years.

You have advanced the notion that the managers of the U.S. security state are not really interested in national security.

I think it's not only true in the United States, it's generally true. Here you have to be a little cautious. If you look at the public, or for that matter even secret, documents, public proclamations and secret documents of just about any state, any I know of, quite typically, although not always, they describe what they are doing in terms of security. I say not always because often there's frank discussion in secret documents, occasionally even publicly. But in general, state managers see themselves as defending **security**. But you have to do a little bit of decoding here—security of what? For example, is the United States protecting itself from attack? Let's say in 1950, when we carried out the first major military buildup, approximately quadrupled the Pentagon system, were we defending ourselves against the threat of attack? That's ludicrous. The United States was in a position of security that had never been attained by any country in history. We had no enemies nearby. We controlled both oceans. We controlled the opposite sides of both oceans. There was no conceivable threat of attack. We were overwhelmingly the most powerful state in the world, far more powerful than the Soviet Union. In fact, even Western Europe was roughly comparable to the Soviet Union economically, and that means militarily if it had wanted to be, and it was much more advanced in its institutional structure and the cohesion of its population. So it was plain we weren't defending ourselves against attack.

The conventional explanation was that this was a reaction to the Korean War, which was perceived as Soviet expansionism. Two problems with that. There wasn't a particle of evidence that the Russians had anything to do with the North Korean attack, nor is there today. More significantly, we know perfectly well that the decision to increase the military budget preceded the Korean War. The crucial planning document is National Security Council Memorandum 68, declassified in 1975. It's a very interesting document. It was two months before the Korean War when it called for a huge expansion in the military budget because of the threat of destruction at the hands of the Soviet Union. If you look carefully at the document, you'll discover that it estimated that the United States was vastly more powerful than the Soviet Union, even excluding Europe and Canada. Nevertheless, we were faced with destruction. They even have an explanation. Their explanation was that the Soviet Union was so backward that they can do "more with less," so their weakness is their strength, and therefore we have to defend ourselves from them. There was also a breath of reality in it. NSC 68 pointed out that the United States might be heading into a depression, that there was an economic decline. It pointed out that military spending would be a stimulus to the economy, as it had been during the Second World War. Furthermore, there was a need to protect the very far-flung domains of the United States, which requires a deterrent posture. We have to deter any resistance to U.S. intervention, an idea very clearly articulated in the secret record. As a result, we had to build up U.S. military power, both for domestic and international reasons, but defense was not among them.

The same thing is true if you look at the other periods of big military buildup, say the Kennedy period. In the early Kennedy years there was a big military buildup, in fact, that set off the current stage of the arms race. The excuse at that time was the missile gap, but we know that the missile gap was a fraud, and the Kennedy people and managers knew that it was a fraud. They probably knew even before they came into office, but when they came into office they certainly knew. The internal documents are interesting. McGeorge Bundy, for example, recommended that the administration keep the phrase "missile gap" even though there was none because, he said, it's a "useful shorthand to express our basic military posture," or words to that effect. To be precise, there was a missile gap at that time—vastly in our favor, about ten to one. The Russians had four operational missiles which were exposed somewhere on some airstrip, but it was necessary to carry out a big military spending program for the usual reasons: for stimulation of the domestic economy and for carrying out an aggressive interventionist foreign policy. There was nothing here about security. Exactly the same is true in the Reagan period. In the Reagan period, you recall, the pretext for the big military spending was the "window of vulnerability" so that the Russians could rampage all over the world. We don't have to debate this because the president's own Scowcroft commission pointed out that there was not and never had been a window of vulnerability. By now it's conceded across the board that it was certainly false, in fact just a fraud. The military buildup went on nevertheless.

Whenever you find that the pretext is not the reason, you know that something else is going on. If you look at the details of U.S. security policy, you will see that security in the sense of defense of the country or defense of client states or defense of others, is almost never a concern. The concerns are quite different. The concerns are using the power of the state to organize a public subsidy for advanced technology to the military system, or creating an international system in which we can intimidate others sufficiently so that we can intervene directly without threat or simply conduct direct intervention. A huge part of the military budget is simply for intervention costs. Nevertheless, all this is perceived as security. The reason is very simple. I don't say that they're lying. The more intelligent people are just lying, but the less intelligent believe it, and they believe it by a very simple and very **familiar psychological mechanism.** Everybody knows it from their personal life, and it also works in political life. In your personal life, you want to do something. You know it's not the right thing to do, but you want it because it's in your interest, so you do it, and you find a system of justification that explains exactly why it was the right and proper thing to do. Anyone who is sufficiently honest knows that they do this all the time. It's a very typical phenomenon of political life. You decide that you're going to overthrow the government of Guatemala because we can't tolerate social reform and democracy, but you can't put it that way, so therefore you create a threat. If you look carefully at the secret documents you can see just what the threat was. The secret documents, which are now declassified, are full of all sorts of raving about "Guatemalan aggression," in fact the operative policy was a National Security document called something like "Actions in the Event of Guatemalan Aggression in the Hemisphere." Guatemalan aggression in the hemisphere is about like Grenadan or Nicaraguan aggression, but they believed it and they even gave examples. The example they gave was a strike in Honduras where they said there might have been some support from Guatemala. That's the kind of aggression they were concerned about. Guatemalan reformist, capitalist democracy might have an effect elsewhere in inspiring things like strikes against American corporations, and of course that's aggression, so therefore we have to defend ourselves against it by military action that overthrows the regime. That's very typical, when you look closely. It's in this sense that while security managers may perfectly well believe that they are defending the security of the nation, the facts very clearly are that they're defending something totally different. They're defending domestic privilege and power.

Just to mention one other example where it's less contentious and perfectly obvious: there are repeatedly surveys of businessmen in which corporate managers are asked to explain what they're doing. Typically, what they say is that they are deeply committed humanitarians who are dedicated to bringing people the best possible goods at the cheapest price out of their overflowing human kindness. The fact of the matter is that they're maximizing profit and market share, and they're doing that not because they're either good or bad, but because that's the way the institutions work. If they didn't do it, they wouldn't be managers of the board any more. Insofar as maximizing profit and market share can be rationalized, justified in terms of these lofty objectives, they'll believe the lofty objectives. But if the lofty objectives ever happen to conflict with maximizing profit and market share, they're going to do the latter. We all understand this, and nobody is or should be deluded. Very much the same is true of political life, where people sometimes are deluded, even people who should know better.

There's a paradox here that bewilders me, and I'd like you to cast some light on it, if you will. You're talking about the state managers, whose function is to preserve power and privilege. If that indeed is the case, how could they create this apparatus of extinction?

The reason is that in a competitive system you do **short-term planning only**. Exactly the same is true in the business world. Let's take corporate managers, where there's no real confusion about what they're doing. They are maximizing profit and market share in the short term. In fact, if they were not to do that, they would no longer exist. Let's be concrete. Suppose that some automobile company, say General Motors, decides to devote their resources to planning for something that will be profitable ten years from now. Suppose that's where they divert their resources: they want to think in some long-term conception of market dominance. Their rivals are going to be maximizing profit and power in the short term, and they're going to take over the markets, and General Motors won't be in business. That's true for the owners and also for the managers. The managers want to stay managers. They can fight off hostile takeover bids, they can keep from being replaced, as long as they contribute to short-term profitability. As a result, long-term considerations are rarely considered in competitive systems. Exactly the same attitudes take over when the same managers move over into the state planning system. Which is also, to an extent, a competitive system. What you find specifically is short-term maximization of gain and very little concern for the longer term. This shows up all over the place.

Let's take another example, one which is more remote than nuclear destruction, say, depletion of American energy resources. Back in the 1940s and early 50s, it was pretty well known where the world's energy reserves were; there haven't been many surprises. It was known that U.S. reserves would be depleted if they were extensively used, and that the major reserves in the world would remain in the Middle East. If anybody was concerned with long-term U.S. security, what they would have done would be to protect Northern Hemisphere reserves, the Gulf of Mexico and so on, save those and exploit Middle Eastern reserves. They did the exact opposite. They depleted American reserves, for reasons of short-term profitability. We're now in a situation where Louisiana and Texas are producing very little oil. We've got to import oil from abroad to fill holes in the ground as a strategic reserve. This was all completely predictable. It's just that basically nobody cared. They're making calculations in terms of short-term profitability. If in the long term it means that you destroy your own corporation, or you destroy the world, that's somebody else's business. We saw it in the Reagan administration. It was transparent that Reaganomics was going to lead to massive debt and a massive trade deficit, it was going to really harm the country very seriously. But they were interested in short-term gain for the privileged. The longer term would somehow take care of itself. Or it's somebody else's business. That is absolutely typical of corporate capitalism, state capitalism, to the extent that it's competitive, and it's very typical of state managers.

You occasionally appear on radio interviews, talk shows, call-ins and the like. Do you have any observations about the time constraints within which you are allowed to express your views?

That depends on where it is. Let me just compare it with others. In Europe, Canada, Latin America, in fact just about everywhere I know **outside the United States**, the situation's dramatically different from what it is here in essentially two respects. For one thing, there's fairly easy access to the media for dissident opinion. Just to keep it personal—but others have the same experience—when I go to Canada or Europe or virtually anywhere, I spend a lot of time on major media, national television, national radio and so on, whereas here it's listener-supported radio, particularly, and virtually nothing else. That's one difference.

The second difference is an interesting structural one. Outside the United States, it is typically the case that discussion of issues can be the way we're doing it, long, extended discussion. In the United States there's a different system. The only other country I know that works like this is Japan. In the United States, if you do get on commercial radio or television, you're allowed a minute or two, you can have a few words between commercials—that's what it comes down to—or you're asked to express an opinion. Pretty much the same is true of op-eds. It's not too difficult—in the national press it's almost impossible, but in the local quality press it's possible—for dissidents to write an op-ed of seven hundred words, short. To get into one of the major journals of opinion, however, is extremely difficult. There's a logic to this. In two minutes, between two com-

600   Noam Chomsky

mercials, or in a few hundred words, you can say some conventional things. For example, if I'm given two minutes on the radio and I want to condemn the Russians for invading Afghanistan, that's easy. I don't need any evidence, I don't need any facts, I can make any claim that I want, anything goes because that's conventional thought, that's what everybody believes anyway, so if I say it it's not surprising, and I don't have to back it up. On the other hand, suppose I were to try in two minutes to condemn the U.S. invasion of South Vietnam, or the U.S. attack against Nicaragua. That sounds crazy. The U.S. isn't attacking people! So within two minutes between two commercials it sounds absurd, in fact any unconventional opinion sounds absurd. The reason is that if you say anything in the least way unconventional you naturally, and rightly, are expected to give a reason, to give evidence, to build up an argument, to say why you believe that unconventional thing. The very structure of the media in the United States prevents that, makes it impossible. The result is that what's expressible are conventional thoughts and conventional doctrine. That's a very effective technique for blocking thought and criticism. Of course life is always much easier when you just express conventional doctrine. You don't have to do any work. But you're not allowed to do the work, even those who are willing to do it. They're not given the opportunity to back up their unconventional ideas, even on the rare occasions when they do get access to the media. That's a brilliant feature of the American mass media system.

In an interview in The Chomsky Reader, *you comment that sometimes when you're driving you listen to radio talk shows on sports and you're struck by the enormous detail and concentration of analysis that callers bring to sports issues, but they can't bring it to social and political issues, which indeed have a greater impact on their lives.*

I don't follow sports, but apparently you can find out quite a lot about the details of the New England Patriots, the Red Sox or whoever's around. What's very striking is that the people who call in not only seem to know an awful lot, and judging by the reaction of the experts on the radio, they seem to talk like equals, but also they are perfectly free to give advice. They tell what the coach did wrong yesterday and what he ought to do tomorrow. The people who are running the talk show, the experts that they have, interact with the callers at a reasonable intellectual level.

On the other hand, people do not feel that they have the capacity to talk about affairs that affect their lives in international and domestic policy, and so on, and they don't. They don't have the information, they can't get the information. They are taught from childhood that they're not allowed to know about those things and that they're too stupid to think about them, and that they have to be put into the hands of experts. And unless you're pretty much of a fanatic, that's true. It takes real fanaticism to get enough information. There is in the public domain enough information to gain an understanding of what's happening in the world, but it takes an almost fanatic level of devotion to do so, whereas apparently it doesn't take that much effort to find out about the local sports team.

I don't think that **international affairs** are harder. I don't think that national security policy is intellectually more challenging. In fact, that's a pretense of the social sciences—that they're dealing with deeply complex issues that are beyond the level of the ordinary person. That's mostly fraud. Outside the natural sciences and mathematics, there are very few things that ordinary people can't understand if they put their minds to it. They're simply not given an opportunity. You want to find out what's happening in Central America, you're really going to have to work. You're going to have to read exotic newspapers, you're going to have to compare today's lies with yesterday's lies and see if you can construct some rational story out of them. It's a major effort, and normal people, quite naturally, can't dedicate that effort to it. It's one of the techniques of marginalization. What you mentioned before about the encapsulation of expression, that's another technique. You never hear anything except conventional views. If you do hear them, they sound lunatic, rightly, because there's no opportunity to back them up.

I'd like you to talk about something I call "rotten apples vs rotten barrels." It seems to be one of the techniques of the state managers to focus, let's say, during the Watergate or the Iran-Contra scandals, on individuals, to personalize the evil and to deflect attention from institutions.

You're exactly correct. When something goes wrong and can't be suppressed any longer, when some **scandal** breaks out into the open, it's necessary somehow to prevent people from understanding what's really going on. In the Iran/Contra hearings, for example, it's very interesting to look at what was investigated. What was investigated were the alleged wrongdoings of particular individuals. Let's take sending arms to Iran. That's supposed to be the wrong thing to do, there seems to be an agreement about that. What was the focus of attention? It was on the so-called "transaction"—with Ollie North and William Casey and so on—that took place from mid-1985 until it was exposed by the courageous press in the fall of 1986.

An obvious question comes up: What was the U.S. government doing before 1985 with regard to arms to Iran? The answer is very simple: it was sending arms to Iran via Israel, exactly what it was doing during the "transaction." That has been public knowledge since 1980. The first notice I saw of it was in *Business Week*, I think it was in December 1980. In the early 1980s, it was reported widely. In February 1982 it was completely public. In March or April 1982, Leslie Gelb of the *New York Times* had a front-page story in which he described the arms flow to Iran. He said that about 50 percent of it is coming from Israel with much of the rest from private arms merchants with Israeli connections. Arms from Israel means arms from the United States. Israel is a client state. They don't send arms to anyone unless we agree; in fact, it's mainly American arms. And that continued, publicly. Furthermore, absolutely in public, the Israeli officials involved explained why they were doing it. On the BBC, for example, in February 1982, the very same Israeli officials who came up in the Iran/Contra hearings were interviewed, and they explained that they were selling arms to Iran with the intent of finding military officers who would be sufficiently murderous that they would carry out a military coup. On the same program were high American officials, Richard Helms, former CIA director, who is also a former ambassador to Iran, and Robert Komer of the Defense Department. They said, yes, that was a good idea, they thought that's probably what we ought to do. The Israeli ambassador to the United States said openly in 1982 that Israel was supplying arms to Iran in coordination with the U.S. government at "almost the highest of levels," his words, and the purpose again was to try to carry out a military coup. That's the way you do it. You send arms in order to establish relations with elements in the military.

None of this was discussed in the hearings. Certainly what was not discussed is that this was typical U.S. policy, typical systematic policy. For example, when we were trying to overthrow the Allende government of Chile in the early 1970s, it's no secret that the United States was doing everything to overthrow that government, we were also sending arms, and we were rewarded, namely with the Pinochet coup. The way you find internal elements to overthrow a government is to arm the military. We did exactly the same thing in Indonesia in the early 1960s. We were very hostile to the government. We sent arms to the military and we were rewarded with a coup and a huge massacre of 700,000 or 800,000 people killed and the destruction of the only mass-based party. The coup was very warmly welcomed in the West. And there are many other cases.

To look into these issues would focus on institutional facts. Therefore they are out. You can talk about "juntas" and "rogue elements out of control," "loose cannons," "patriots who have gone berserk," or something like that. All of that's safe because it doesn't lead to any understanding of the way the institutions work. I should say that dissidents also contribute to this. This talk about "secret teams" and all that kind of business is highly misleading. The secret teams and the clandestine operations are normal government policy when the state is driven underground by its own population. When the population will not tolerate certain actions the state will be driven underground and will carry out clandestine actions. That's what happened in the 1980s. It's happened often before. There's very little indication in my view that there are any "loose cannons" around. Maybe occasionally somebody gets out of control briefly, but it's a very marginal phenomenon. What happens is systematic behavior, very well intelligible in terms of the fundamental institutions, but you can't look at that. The Iran/Contra hearings were just a cover-up.

Let's take the fact that the United States was illegally supplying arms to the Contras during the period of the Boland Amendment. The claim that that was a secret is ludicrous. I discussed it in *Turning the Tide*, which came out in 1985. I don't have any secret records. I was using the public record. In fact, I even identified Oliver North as the person involved, because it was all public. Again, I was writing about the U.S. arms sales to Iran through Israel in 1983. I discussed it in *The Fateful Triangle*, which came out in 1983. It was all public. But to deal with the public record and to show what's continually happening, that's going to lead you to institutional critique, and that's no good. What you have to do is personalize it.

The same was true during Watergate—it was very dramatic—during the Watergate hearings. In fact, just think what Watergate was about. What was the big crime of Watergate? The crime was that the Republican Party had hired a bunch of kind of Keystone Cops to break into the Democratic Party headquarters for reasons which remain obscure to this day. That was the crime—there were some ancillary things—terrible crime.

At exactly the time of the Watergate hearings it was exposed in court cases and through the Freedom of Information Act that the FBI, at that point for 12 or 13 years, had been regularly carrying out burglaries of the Socialist Workers Party, which is a legal political party, for the purpose of disrupting their activities, stealing their membership lists, using the membership lists to intimidate people who joined the party, get them to lose their jobs, etc. That's vastly more serious than Watergate. This isn't a bunch of petty crooks. This is the national political police. It wasn't being done by some loose cannon, it was being done systematically by every administration. It was seriously disrupting a legal political party, whereas Watergate did nothing to the Democratic Party. Did that come up at the Watergate hearings? Not a mention. What's the difference? The difference is that the Democratic Party represents domestic power, the Socialist Workers Party doesn't. So what the Watergate hearings showed, the great principle that was being defended, was "people with power are going to defend themselves." That's what it is. But you can't say that. If you were to say that, you begin to understand how the legal system works, how the state repression system works, therefore it's out. Watergate was framed and designed so that it could focus on the misdeeds of a particular individual, Richard Nixon, who made the serious tactical error of attacking people with power.

Just to take another example, Nixon's "enemies list" was a great scandal.

People like Tom Watson of IBM were on the list.

Yes, actually, I was on the enemies list, too. I know perfectly well from my own experience that absolutely nothing happened to anybody on the enemies list. They didn't even audit our income tax returns, and that was particularly striking in my case because I was publicly organizing tax resistance. Nothing happened to anybody on the enemies list. Nevertheless it was a scandal. Why? Not because I was on it, but because people like Tom Watson were on it, and McGeorge Bundy and James Reston. In other words, it's a scandal to call powerful people bad names in private. But at the very same time that the enemies list came out, it was revealed in court hearings that the FBI had been involved in **an outright political assassination** of a Black Panther organizer, Fred Hampton. Did that show up in the Watergate hearings? No, although it happened during the Nixon administration. Why? Because if the state is involved in a Gestapo-style assassination of a Black Panther organizer, that's OK. He has no power, and he's an enemy anyway. On the other hand, calling powerful people bad names in private, that shakes the foundations of the republic. Again, powerful people are going to defend themselves, and that's all that Watergate amounted to. The whole thing was crafted to focus on a particular individual, who incidentally was very unpopular in elite circles and who had been since he more or less tore apart the international economic system during the Nixon shock a couple of years earlier, and they were going to get rid of him. Of course, once that one bad apple was thrown out of the body politic, we were right back to our traditional purity. The institutional crimes just continue. Even the bombing of Cambodia was not part of the indictment. It entered into the hearings. This was not a small thing: a bombing of another country in which several hundred thousand people were killed, a neutral country, a country that was supposed to be a friendly country—pretty serious business. It entered the hearings, but only in one respect—they didn't inform Congress—and that was considered so insignificant it didn't even enter the bill of indictment. Again, it means it's OK to attack another country, aggression is fine, but just notify powerful people about it. Don't encroach upon their prerogatives. To bring out any of these things would be to give some light as to how the system functions, and that's intolerable. Obviously, any powerful system is going to defend itself against understanding on the part of others. It's not obscure why.

Editor's Notes to Interview 44

In interviews 44 and 45, the questions were asked by students in my UCLA Honors Collegium course "The Cognitive Revolution: Mind and Language, Culture and Ideology, Freedom and Creativity." The recording is due to David Barsamian.

Chomsky, "widely considered to be the prime mover of the 30-year-old 'cognitive revolution,' which is now beginning to be the object of general attention" (from the description of the course in the Honors Collegium brochure), was one of a number of guest lecturers in the course in the winter of 1988, and instead of lecturing he gave the students the opportunity of asking questions during two entire two-hour classes (those of January 26 and 28, 1988). Since the questions were often barely audible on the recording, they had to be reconstructed, sometimes in a shortened form; some of the questions and corresponding answers, particularly the most technical ones (beginning with the very first one, on "parsing," to which the later incidental remark "the parser turns off at that point," refers) are not (or at least not yet) part of the available transcription.

On Reinhold Niebuhr, see Chomsky's review-article in *Grand Street* 6:2 (Winter 1987), pp. 197–212 (to be reprinted in his book *The Masters of Mankind*. Ed. by Mark Pavlick, Monroe, Maine: Common Courage Press, forthcoming). See also **NI** (1988).

On Orwell, see Editor's Notes to I30.

The study of the systematic destruction of the anti-fascist resistance in the aftermath of War World II is a much neglected topic that is of great interest to Chomsky. See, e.g., **TT** (1985), 4.4.4; **P&I** (1987) , chs. 1–2.

On the potential base for fascism, see **AP** (1969), 17ff.

The references to the documents quoted in the first chapter of **P&I** (1987) are given on page 137.

44. The Cognitive Revolution, I (26 January 1988)

When we talk about Descartes as having carried out the first cognitive revolution, it brings to mind that he said, "I think, therefore I am." I've heard that sentence before in arguments not about linguistics but about idealism and materialism.

That's a different aspect of Cartesian thought. It's related but it's different.

To me, Descartes was an idealist. He says, "I think, therefore I am." In other words, if you don't think you are, you aren't.

I don't understand those terms. He certainly was a materialist. He thought there was a physical world. He not only was a materialist, he thought he could prove there was a physical world, literally prove, like mathematics, the truths of physics. He wrote a long book called *Principles of Philosophy*. You have to remember that in those days **philosophy** meant what we call **science**, so we nowadays would have called it "Principles of Physics." In this book he started with what he took to be indubitable principles, axioms, things that just couldn't be false, like 2+2=4, and then he went on through this long book and at the end he was allegedly proving things about why things have certain colors and why things fall at a certain rate, etc. He certainly believed in the physical world; he thought he could prove things about it.

The business about "I think, therefore I am" does relate to what I'm talking about, but it does it in the following way: what I was talking about it what is sometimes called the "theory of other minds." I think I mentioned that in yesterday's lecture. How do we determine whether somebody else has a mind like ours? How do we determine whether a computer or an ape can think? Here the typical Cartesian answer, as is the modern answer, would be to try to do experiments and try to exhibit characteristic aspects of human action, like the creative aspect of language use, that's the way you decide whether something else has a mind, like yours.

But how do you find out whether you yourself have a mind? That we assume you just know. The only thing that's definitely true, he said, that we can't question, is "I think." According to Descartes, you can't question "I think" because to doubt that I think is already to think. Therefore the argument—and maybe the argument is no good—but the argument is: that's an indubitable truth, like 2 = 2. It couldn't be wrong, because if you doubt it you're already proving it. So here's an indubitable truth, a foundation of all knowledge: I think; but since I think, therefore I must exist, otherwise who's doing the thinking? Thus "I think, therefore I am." And once I exist, then I start doing some other things.

Now, in order to get the argument off the ground, you have to prove that God is not a deceiver. You have to prove that God is not deceiving you. Because once you say "I think," then you say, well, look, I see this, that and the other thing, and therefore it's really there. But how do I know it's really there? Because God's not deceiving me. And he tries to prove that God couldn't be a deceiver, by looking at the definition of God, and here the argument starts to get haywire. That's where he goes from there. This has to do with how you determine that you yourself have a mind.

I wasn't looking at that problem, because it doesn't go anywhere, really. I was looking at the parts of Descartes that do go somewhere. How do you figure out whether somebody else has an intelligence like your own?

Incidentally, I should say that I think that the way people read traditional philosophy today is extremely misleading. We read traditional philosophers like Descartes from the point of view of contemporary interests, which crucially distorts the way they looked at what they were doing. For example, for Descartes all the stuff that you study in your philosophy courses was kind of on the margins, not what he was really interested in. What he was was a scientist; he was what we would call a scientist. He was interested in figuring out things like physics, perception, language, and so on. In his more speculative moments he asked foundational questions about what he was up to. All we study is the foundational questions; we don't look at what he was interested in. I'm sure they don't have a course around here in which you study Descartes' theory of vision, but you do study Descartes' philosophy. That's as if a couple of hundred years from now people would be studying Einstein and they don't look at the theory of relativity because that's all been surpassed and shown to be false and some other thing was true. What they do is look at Einstein's letters to his friends where he sort of makes some comments about what science is about. You'd get a very distorted picture of what Einstein thought he was doing that way.

That's pretty much the way philosophy is studied. It wasn't until the 19th century that there was any systematic difference made between science and philosophy. In fact the word "science" doesn't have its current usage until about the middle of the 19th century. There was no real divorce between science and philosophy. You could find people who were more on one or the other side of what we take to be a divide, but they didn't particularly see it as a divide. You can even see it in the terms. I suppose even today at Oxford if you're studying physics they call it "natural philosophy" or something like that, or they did until pretty recently.

Would you discuss Orwell's Newspeak?

You don't have to go to Orwell to find it, all you have to do it look in the newspaper. Take this morning's *Los Angeles Times*, if you happened to look at it. There's a big front-page article: George Schultz flying to Latin America to try to implement the peace process, or something like that. The first part says that Schultz is going to try to make the peace process work, the next paragraph says he's going to try to build up support for Contra aid. Now, Contra aid destroys the peace process, because the peace process says that the indispensable element for peace in the region is termination of all aid to irregular forces—that's the core of the peace agreement. So it's logically impossible to both be implementing the peace process and trying to build up Contra aid. It's impossible.

How can the reporter in the *Los Angeles Times* write it? Because by "peace process" they don't mean the peace accords in Guatemala, they mean what's invented in Washington. And what's invented in Washington is some other version which says that we have the right to attack any country we want, that's the peace process. And the way you implement that peace process is of course by building up congressional support for attacking another country. That's **Newspeak**. Now, the reporter who's writing those words probably doesn't think about it, maybe the reporter's a total cynic, that's conceivable but very unlikely. They are just totally brainwashed. They have come to use the term "peace process" to mean the process by which the United States attacks another country, that's the peace process. Hence the reporter can write those first two paragraphs and everybody can read it and nobody goes screaming and smashing down the doors of the *Los Angeles Times* because they're such fanatic liars because nobody notices it. Well, that's Newspeak. Everything you've been fed since kindergarten is a piece of it. The whole system of indoctrination is based on this.

Sometimes it's contrived. That's what we call the **public relations industry**, for example. The public relations industry was designed, consciously, as they put it, back around 1910, to "control the public mind." That was its purpose. The concern was very conscious in this case that the main enemy of the corporations is the population, which is also the main enemy of the state. That's true of any country that's conscious. In our country the elites happen to be very self-conscious. The United States is very advanced in this respect. Other countries don't have things like the public relations industry, it's a U.S. invention. We're a more advanced society—more advanced towards a kind of an Orwellian system. Here the public relations industry is very consciously constructed in order to control the public mind. That meant you had to design concepts and principles and frameworks and modes of approaching people and subliminal advertising and all those things. There's a huge industry devoted to this, trying to figure out how to properly indoctrinate people so that they become passive and apathetic and hedonistic and that their normal human impulses are eliminated and they just fit into the needs of the people who are running the system, basically the corporations.

That part is conscious. Among the intelligentsia it's also pretty conscious. There's a big tradition in American social science about how you have to control the public mind because people are too stupid to understand what's in their interest. Only their leaders can understand what's in their interest. For people's own safety, you don't let a three-year-old cross the street, because it's just too dangerous, so you take care of him. Similarly, you don't let an ordinary person think for themselves, they'll get confused and get crazy ideas and so on. Therefore we, who are somehow immune from this, the privileged smart guys, as the revered moralist Reinhold Niebuhr put it, we have to construct "necessary illusions because of the stupidity of the average man." That's the task of the intelligentsia. And that's conscious indoctrination. The understanding always was that it's particularly important in a country like the United States because the trouble with this country is that you can't control people by violence. If it was a fascist or military-run society, then if people did the wrong thing you'd just send the death squads after them like you do in El Salvador. But here you can't get away with that. The problem here is that technically the voice of the people is heard and you can't stop them, you can't just send in the cops to kill them. That's a bad situation. And it was understood to be a bad situation. So what you have to do is make sure the voice of the people says the right thing. That means you have to have thought control. Therefore you have to have much more sophisticated thought control in a country where the state lacks proper methods of coercion.

In a normal totalitarian state, or in what is a special phenomenon in the world that the United States has invented (it has no name, we ought to call it a "terror state"), like El Salvador. It's a terror state, not a totalitarian state. It's a state in which the terrorist forces, called the army and the police, just kill anybody or cut them up with a machete or whatever. They do their own thing. That's the kind of country that we try to establish, that's called a "democracy" in Newspeak. In a terror state you don't care too much what people think. You can be a behaviorist: you only care what they do. They can think anything they like. Because if they do the wrong thing, you're just going to kill them. In a totalitarian state, they will be put in prison. But in a country where you don't have means of control over the population, you have to have indoctrination. That's long been understood, very consciously. I'll give you references if you like. It's way back in the literature of the sophisticated intellectuals, social science literature and so on. That requires conscious construction of Newspeak. But in fact that's unusual. The more usual thing is like the first paragraph in the lead story in the *Los Angeles Times*, where people have already been so effectively socialized and so indoctrinated they don't even understand what they're saying.

I'll give you one last example. There's been a big blast in the media over the last month claiming that Nicaragua is planning to get MIGs. You've all read about this. This is a terrible scandal. They're planning to get MIGs and if they do, of course, we'll have to blast them into the sea. Everybody agrees on that, incidentally, the doves, the hawks, the liberals, everyone, they can't be allowed to get MIGs. Well, what does that mean? What are the MIGs for? Of course everyone knows what they're for. Why do they want MIGs? Why don't they want French Mirages? In fact they do want French Mirages, but we won't let them get them. We want them to have MIGs because once they have MIGs they become a Soviet threat. If they just get French Mirages, what are you going to say? Therefore the United States stops them from getting Mirages. Nobody in the press will ever report this. Are they lying? Not really, no. They've already been sufficiently socialized and they suppress it.

So when Steven Kinzer of the *New York Times* has an interview with some comandante and the guy says, look, we'd be glad to get Mirages, the words don't penetrate his mind. The parser turns off at that point. It doesn't go through. (That's the other parser—the perception system I was talking about.) He's not lying outright, he just doesn't hear it because it doesn't fit the ideological structure. So first of all they've got to get MIGs. What do they need MIGs for? They need MIGs because they have to protect their air space. The CIA is flying two or three supply flights a day in there in order to maintain a foreign-run army. It's as if Russia had an army up there in the hills around Los Angeles and since they don't have any popular support you have to keep flying arms in every day, food, uniforms, etc., and it's as if the United States under such circumstances tried to get the means to defend itself and the Soviet Union said, "You're not allowed to do that. It's our right to attack you. You're not allowed to get the means to defend yourselves." We would consider that a version of Nazism, or something. But that's us. We are saying in effect that Nicaragua does not have a right to defend itself. That's the only thing the MIGs are for. They have to be MIGs because we insist on it, and secondly they're not allowed to get them, and everyone will agree on this, Alan Cranston, your favorite liberal in Congress. They all agree. I doubt if you could find one columnist in the entire United States who responded to this by saying that they had a right to defend themselves. The response to this, if you look at the doves, was, well, it's just a contingency plan, the story wasn't true. The assumption across the board was, of course, that no country has a right to defend itself, because the United States has the right to kill and attack anybody it likes.

That's beyond Newspeak. I don't think you can find a country in history that has reached this level of indoctrination. Let's take Nazi Germany, which was pretty extreme. Hitler accused the Poles of aggression, but I don't believe he ever accused the Poles of getting arms to defend themselves against attack. That's a level of fanatic indoctrination that's unique in history. But we're all part of it. Nobody bats an eyelash when you read about it because you're all so totally indoctrinated. I suppose a few people notice it, but most people don't even notice it, because this is a level of indoctrination that goes far beyond anything that Orwell ever conceived of. He was very unimaginative in this respect. The U.S. public relations industry had already gone far beyond Orwell when he wrote *1984*. In fact, you might ask yourself why Orwell's *1984* is a popular book. Why does anybody bother reading it? One reason is because it's obviously modeled on an enemy. It's about the Soviet Union, a very thinly disguised account of the Soviet Union, and anything bad that you say about an official enemy is fine.

Suppose that Orwell had written a more interesting book. It's kind of trivial to write about the Soviet Union, with its obvious forms of indoctrination. Suppose he'd written an interesting book, namely about us. That's much more interesting than about somebody else. Suppose he had exposed the kind of indoctrination that goes on here, like that I've just mentioned. You bet your life that wouldn't be a bestseller. Nobody would have heard of Orwell. Nobody would have published it and it would have gone right down the "memory hole"—his "memory hole." The very fact that you even think of Orwell is already a sign of how indoctrinated you are. Not that it's your fault. From kindergarten you just get deluged with this stuff until you just don't know how to think any more. How many of you noticed in all this talk about MIGs that what it amounts to is reinforcing the assumption that the United States has a right to kill anybody it wants, that they don't have a right to defend themselves? [A number of the students raise their hands.] That's pretty good. It's because you're not totally indoctrinated yet. Try it in 10 years.

But you are here right now. Is something like this going on on a large scale around the country?

The fact that I'm here has to do with this defect in American society that troubles the liberals so much. They can't stop you. That's their problem. They can't stop you with force, and that's a defect. So you've got to overcome it in all sorts of ways. It's overcome by institutional structures, what you're involved in now. It's a matter of shaping you so that you fit into the institutional structures. There may be some people who resist. This starts way down in elementary school, there were kids who were **behavior problems.** Who are the behavior problems? They're the kids who have enough **independence of mind** that they're not going to accept the structure of authority. Most of us, including me, you and other people who got to elite colleges, how did we do it? We did it because we were willing to be obedient. We were willing to do every stupid thing that some idiot told us to do. No matter how crazy we thought it was, we were willing to do it. That's a form of subservience. There's a preselection for obedience and subservience which is required in order to get you into the elites in the first place. If you're unwilling to do it, if you're too independent, and you say, this is crazy, I don't see any point in it, you're thrown out, you become a drug pusher, or something like that. This begins right at the beginning. By the time you get into the elite institutions, first of all you're already preselected for obedience and you sort of learned your way around, and then you begin to internalize the values. It's very hard to believe one thing and do something else, so you start believing what you're saying. It's a lot easier. You stop thinking, you cut off your mind. You do what you're supposed to do. Being students, you're still more or less free because you don't have a commitment yet to a functioning institution. You're just in a stage of indoctrination, not controlling and decision-making, etc. Get out and you get a job and it becomes different. When you're a faculty member or a journalist or a manager, then you better believe the stuff. You're not free to doubt any more. If you start doubting, you won't be able to make the decisions that are required by the institutional structure. If people do doubt, they're usually kicked out. If they don't, so you have more selection and you end up with people who quite honestly believe everything they're saying.

They don't want to think about it.

And we know how it's done. Take a look at this morning's *New York Times* (I had fifty cents to kill, so I bought a copy). There's a story about Israel, John Kifner, a pretty good reporter, is reporting about attitudes in Israel, breaking people's bones and this sort of thing. And he quotes a lot of people. He quotes one guy there who says, look it's just too unpleasant, an Israeli business administration student or something, I'm not looking at it any more. I don't want to hear about it. I just can't face it. It's ugly, it's horrible. I don't want to hear about it, I don't want to know about it. Go away. Leave me alone. That's a normal human reaction. That's what we all do in connection with Central America. The United States in the last seven or eight years has been responsible for the slaughter of maybe 200,000 people in Central America. And not just killing: mutilation, Pol-Pot-style torture, rape ... Nobody wants to think about it. It's just too unpleasant, so we think about something else. That's why there were gas chambers, because people just want to think about something else. But it's not hard to understand. We're right in the middle of it all the time. John Kifner could write an article about it in Israel, but no *Times* reporter could write an article about it in New York City. You could ask the same question. You could ask a question in New York City: What do you think about the army in El Salvador going out and torturing and murdering people and blowing up the press, etc.? And if anybody's even heard of it, which they probably wouldn't have, they would say, I don't want to think about it. But you couldn't write that article, because that would tell you something about yourselves and we are only allowed to dump on other people.

It's like Orwell again. You can criticize the Soviet Union but you can't apply the same lessons here. That's why there's no field that studies the United States. Suppose you take a political science course. You may do sort of technical things, like how Congress works or something, but mostly you study other things. Like if you study foreign policy, you study other countries. And the peace movement falls for this too. I've been in 10,000 teach-ins in my life, I don't know how many. Every one of them is about something happening somewhere else. I go to a teach-in on Central America, a teach-in on the Middle East, a teach-in on Vietnam. That's all nonsense. Everything's happening in Washington. It's just the same things in Washington just playing themselves out in different parts of the world. But you don't have a teach-in on Washington. In fact, people wouldn't understand that. You have to have a teach-in on El Salvador where you talk about all the details of what's going on there.

You said that propaganda goes back to 1910.

That was just the public relations industry. The propaganda goes back to Adam.

What was the idea behind the Marshall Plan? Wasn't it set up to help the world?

The Marshall Plan was directed at Europe, not the world. One major component of the Marshall Plan was an export promotion operation for U.S. industry. U.S. industry had built up enormous capacity during the Second World War. At the end of the war there was real concern that it wasn't going to be able to sell. What you do is to force the public to pay for what industry produces. One way we do that is the military system—that's in fact the standard way. You want to make high-technology industry profitable what you have to do is let them sell their stuff. What they're selling is waste production, so what you have to do is convince the public to buy it. And that's what we all do, we pay taxes so that they can buy high-technology waste production and then throw it away, or do something else with it. That's one method.

Another method, the one that was used at the end of the Second World War, having to do with the special contingencies of the times, was foreign aid. You give other countries money so that they can buy American exports. There is a political science mythology in which they talk about things like the United States and the national interest. That's of course nonsense. There's no such thing as "the nation," there's just different groups. The Marshall Plan was a system in which the American public paid American corporations to send their surplus exports to Europe. That's what is basically was. In fact, almost all of the Marshall Plan aid went to U.S. corporations. It was funneled through Europe technically, but if you look at what happened to the dollars, they went to American corporations. Out of the $13 billion Marshall Plan dollars, $2 billion went straight to the oil companies. That's $2 billion right off to the American oil companies who sent oil to Europe, meaning the American taxpayer was paying American oil companies to give oil to Europe.

Why didn't they just toss it in the ocean? Why did they give it to Europe? First of all it would be hard to convince the taxpayer to do that. Secondly, there was a problem in Europe. The problem was one of preventing democracy. It was necessary to prevent democracy after the Second World War. Here I mean democracy in the real sense of the word, not the Orwellian sense that we use. You have to look at what was happening in Europe at the end of the Second World War.

The Second World War was mainly a war in which the traditional conservative elites who were everywhere associated with the fascists were defeated, discredited. In Japan, Germany, and so on. In the course of this there was a tremendous revival of a kind of radical democracy in the resistance movements. Look at the resistance against Germany or the resistance in the occupied countries or in the Third World. It ranged from social democratic to very revolutionary, but it was interested in changing the society radically so that it would be truly democratic in a much deeper sense. For example, in Europe right after the war, with the conservative elites discredited, there was a tremendous revival of efforts to establish worker control of factories, workers councils in factories that could put the economy under the control of the people who worked there, an so on. The same was true in Japan right after the war. As the old traditional autocratic order collapsed with the defeat of fascism, a lot of populist sentiment emerged. That the United States couldn't tolerate, obviously, because we don't want that kind of democracy. We want the kind of democracy in the Orwellian sense, the kind we have, in which certain segments of business run the state and the rest of the population is allowed to ratify their decisions every couple of years, that's all. That's what we want. We had to do something to stop that in Germany and France and Italy and Japan, and the Marshall Plan was one component of that.

There were other components. For example, if you look, you'll discover that in just about every country in the world, from Korea to the Philippines to Indochina, Japan, southern Greece, Italy, France, Germany, and so on, in every single one of those countries **the United States destroyed the anti-fascist resistance and restored the fascist collaborators to power.** This is the most systematic fact about the early post-war period. If there existed such a field of history, of political science, that would be chapter one. It happened everywhere, very systematically. It's never studied, there isn't a single book about it. If you look into the technical monographic literature, like the monographs on Korea, you'll find they'll say it happened, but it was kind of a mistake because the United States didn't understand the local situation and in their naivete they were confused, etc. How did they make the same mistake everywhere? Systematically, without exception? You go to the planning documents and you understand exactly what they're doing. We've got to prevent this kind of radical democracy from taking place. You've got to eliminate the resistance, break up the unions, restore the old order, but now under American control, not under the domestic fascists who are our enemies.

The Marshall Plan was part of that. It was the soft side. There was a hard side, but that was the soft side. Other aspects of it were the CIA in one of its earliest efforts, controlling food supplies, controlling the police in Italy so as to buy the 1948 election and prevent the Left from winning it, probably the major CIA operation since 1948 for preventing democracy in Italy in terms of actual money. In France, it meant rebuilding the drug racket, which had been knocked off by the fascists. The fascists run a very tight ship; they don't like any competition. The fascist states, Germany and Japan, had pretty well destroyed the mob. The mafia had been wiped out, since they don't like competitors. As the United States liberated Italy from the South, it reconstructed the mafia. It was after all necessary to break up the unions, because the unions were a threat. You can't allow people to be independent and free. In order to break up the unions, it was necessary to hire goons, guys who will go and break up strikes, beat people up and so on, and the natural place to look was the mob. So one of the first CIA operations was to reconstruct the Corsican Mafia in early 1946–47 and use them as strikebreakers and goon squads. But of course they don't do it for nothing. They don't do it just because they like to break peoples' bones. You've got to offer them something. They offered them the drug racket. That's where the famous French connection comes from. Up until the early 1970s Marseille was the center of the international heroin racket. The reason was that it was reconstructed by the U.S.

and the CIA as part of the effort to destroy the democratic forces in the post-war world and to reconstruct the old order.

The Marshall Plan was just a piece of that. That's how you just sort of pay them off to do the kinds of things you want. The Marshall Plan is talked about as a "noble gift." Winston Churchill called it **the "greatest moral act in history."** It wasn't a moral act from the point of view of the people who were designing the policies. They were profiting from it. The corporate executives in Washington who were carrying out this "gift"—they were profiting, because the gift was going back to their corporations for export. That's an easy kind of a gift. The people who were carrying out the "moral act" were the American taxpayers, who were never asked—who didn't understand what was happening anyway.

Even though the U.S. economy has major problems and poverty is increasing, we are still sending money to the Contras.

First of all, it's not "we." Who's sending the money?

Washington.

No, it's the American taxpayers, the American taxpayers—like poor people who don't have enough to eat and are homeless, they're sending it because we have to do exactly what we did after the Second World War. We have to prevent the possibility of democracy and social reform because the people who plan American policy have other … you look at these secret documents, they say they have to fulfill their function, countries like in Central America have to fulfill their function, and their function is to provide resources and raw materials for U.S. corporations. It's not to build health clinics and carry out literacy programs. That's not their function. If they try to do that, you've got to destroy them, and therefore you have to get the American taxpayer to pay for it and to destroy them.

In fact, what you said is quite right. By now, elite opinion, what they call "leaders," businessmen, that sort of thing, is about 80 percent opposed to Contra aid, strongly opposed. The reason is that they think it's not cost-effective anymore. There are other ways to achieve it. That's called the liberal position. Take Senator Alan Cranston. He testified before Congress that this is just not working, the Contra thing, and therefore what we have to do, he said, is to take this "reprehensible regime in Managua" and let them "fester in their own juices." We don't have to do that to the regime in El Salvador. They slaughtered 60,000 people. They wiped out the press. They destroyed all the popular organizations, but we don't have to let them "fester in their own juices," because they're doing the job that we want them to do. On the other hand, from the point of view of the liberals like Cranston, it's the reprehensible regime in Managua that has to be left to fester in their own juices. And now that we've pretty well destroyed the economy there—after all the United States is a powerful state and that's a tiny, nothing country, it doesn't take much; we've basically destroyed the economy—there's going to be mass starvation, the social fabric will break up, and so on. Fine, let's let them fester in their own juices. If we heard this coming from the Soviet Union, we'd say, the guy's a Nazi. When it comes from your liberal congressman, you say he's a liberal, a humanitarian.

How did Washington ever allow the Sandinistas to overthrow Somoza?

Here's what happened: First of all, the United States backed Somoza, put him in power and backed him forever—the Carter administration backed him up until the end. The problem is because the thugs that we put in power to run various parts of the empire, they tend to cause trouble after a while. Typically, Marcos, Somoza, Duvalier, Trujillo, all do the same thing: they start robbing their own people. Instead of just robbing the poor, which is their job, they start robbing us. They start interfering with U.S. corporations, or they interfere with other sectors of the business community, or whatever. At that point, you obviously have to get rid of them. They're just robbing the wrong people. There comes a point, and this always happens, where you've got to get rid of them. It happened with Marcos in 1986. He began robbing the wrong people and elite groups didn't like it any more. They had this revolt and finally the U.S. backed it. In the case of Trujillo, one of the worst of these monsters we ever created, the CIA actually tried to assassinate him finally. He had bought up three-quarters of the Dominican Republic, which meant that he was getting in the way of U.S. corporations, who were supposed to own the Dominican Republic. So you've got to get rid of him, and they actually tried an assassination campaign. He was assassinated. It's not known whether it was the CIA or somebody else, but we know they did try to assassinate him.

In the case of Somoza, about late 1978 or early 1979, Washington began to understand that he was making the regular transition to robbing the wrong people and therefore even the elites, the business community, the landowners, our friends, were beginning to get disruptive and join the revolution because he was robbing them. That's the Contra leadership, the people we call the democrats, like Calero and so on. These are guys who turned against Somoza. You constantly read that these people were anti-Somoza. It's perfectly true. At the time when Somoza began robbing them, they became anti-Somoza, but not before, when he was just robbing the poor. You never heard a peep out of them. They were just making money. But by 1978–79 he was turning against them, and that meant that the United States was in an odd situation. The United States tried to maintain Somoza. By mid-1978 it was clear that that was impossible.

At that point the Carter administration tried a compromise. They tried to get rid of Somoza but to retain the system. Crucially that meant to retain the national guard. The national guard was the mercenary force run by the United States, trained and armed by the United States, which was essentially terrorizing the population. They had killed 40–50,000 people. Carter, the human rights administration, wanted to keep them in power and get rid of Somoza because Somoza was a nuisance at that point. So you get rid of Somoza, retain the system, but with other names, and crucially retain the guard, and they tried. In fact, the Carter administration tried to get the Organization of American States to intervene to prevent the guard from being destroyed and to block the Sandinista revolution. That didn't work. The timing was wrong, they couldn't carry it off. The next thing they did was to try to rescue the guard. They rescued them. They took them out of the country as much as possible. The Carter administration, for example, sent American planes with Red Cross markings to pick up national guard leaders in Managua and carry them out of the country.

That's incidentally a war crime under international law. We're doing it right now, too. Since the United States regards itself as a completely lawless state, you can see this in the front pages of the newspapers. Take a look some time at the pictures of the Contra planes. Notice they have Red Cross markings on them. The Red Cross has bitterly complained about this, because this is a violation of the laws of war, a war crime, the kind of thing you hang people for. But here we don't even try to conceal it. I've seen it in *Newsweek*, *U.S. News*, *Christian Science Monitor*, all over the place. You see pictures of CIA supply flights disguised with Red Cross markings. We take it for granted, just like we take it for granted that we can attack other countries, that the laws don't apply to us, so we don't have to hide it. **Carter** did that to rescue the guard. This is sort of at the end of the Carter administration. They actually offered a loan to Nicaragua, but that's always described as an example of our willingness to assist the Sandinistas until you look at the fine print and you discover that the loan was directed to the business community. It was like **the Marshall Plan**. It was an effort to support those elements of the coalition that would support U.S. corporate interests and try to reconstruct the old order. And undermine the ones that were trying to do crazy things like improve agricultural production and build health clinics and all of that intolerable stuff. That didn't work. At that point you had the transition to Reagan, we just attacked them. Just organized an army to attack them. That's what's been going on ever since.

Why didn't they send troops down?

They can't because the U.S. population wouldn't tolerate it. The American population is very dissident. It's a disorganized population, but it's extremely dissident.

As soon as the Reagan administration got in, they quite vocally began to build up a lot of rhetoric to support an attack actually on El Salvador, which was what they were more worried about then. They came out with a White Paper in February 1981 which was a prelude to an invasion of El Salvador. There was an unexpected reaction. The country started to blow up. There were demonstrations, churches started screaming, people started yelling at Washington, etc. There's a tremendous amount of dissidence in the country. It's not in elite circles, and it's never articulated, but it's all over the place. They didn't estimate it right. When they saw it coming they backed off. Because they were afraid it was going to threaten more central elements of the policy, like the big military buildup and they didn't want that threatened. So the rhetoric toned down and they backed off and they turned to clandestine warfare. What's been going on since 1981 is basically clandestine, that's what the Iran/Contra hearings are about. Just ask yourself, why does any government ever undertake clandestine warfare? Why do they have covert operations? Who are covert operations a secret from? Ask yourself that question. They're obviously not a secret from the victims, they know all about it. Take the stuff in the Iran/Contra hearings. They weren't a secret from all the mercenary states, from Israel and Iran, everybody knew about them.

In fact, they weren't even a secret from the press, if you want to know the truth. It was perfectly public. I was writing about it in 1984 and 1985. It was just suppressible. The point is that it was a secret from the American population, that's all. Typically, clandestine operations are undertaken when **the government is driven underground by its own population.** If you can't control the population by force and you can't indoctrinate them, what you do is go underground. That's secret operations. It's just standard executive policy, the policy of domestic population management. The answer to your question, I think, is an interesting one. It is that the American population is too dissident, despite all the brainwashing and indoctrination and so on, the less educated, non-elite part of the population just won't go along. The educated elites, they go along, because they're effectively indoctrinated and they're part of the system of privilege and power anyway. They don't raise any fuss. There's a lot of ferment out there, people in power don't want it. They don't like to see it. There's all kinds of reasons, who knows what their reasons are, but the point is that direct, overt aggression became very hard. The state was driven underground, and that's exactly what the Iran/Contra hearings were about, this enormously intricate international terror network that the Reagan administration was forced to construct because they couldn't do what John F. Kennedy did. Kennedy and Johnson, they just invaded South Vietnam, there was nothing secret. They could do that because nobody cared. But by the 1980s the country was a lot different, and they couldn't do it.

Is access to information better now than in the 1960s?

It's way better now than it was then. I think we're much more sensitized. Compare the early 1960s with the early 1980s. In 1962 in Indochina things were getting out of hand. If you know the history of this period, after the Geneva agreements of 1954, which technically settled it, the United States instituted a typical Latin-American style terror state in South Vietnam and organized it to attack its own population in typical fashion, like El Salvador. By 1960 they had killed off maybe 70,000 or 80,000 people, kind of like El Salvador. Nobody batted an eyelash here. Literally. You couldn't get two people to talk about it. By 1959–60, they were beginning to get some internal resistance. When the resistance came the thing fell apart because it had no popular support. At that point Kennedy had to escalate. Part of the escalation was that they sent the U.S. Air Force, not surrogates, the U.S. Air Force was sent to start bombing South Vietnam. They carried out extensive bombing attacks against rural South

Vietnam, which is where about 80 percent of the population lives. They also carried out massive defoliation. There were no North Vietnamese, no Russians, no nothing, just South Vietnamese. The purpose of this was to drive approximately 7 million people, almost half the population, into concentration camps so that we could undermine the guerrillas who were living and working in the rural areas. That's outright aggression. That's like the Russians invading Afghanistan. Nobody batted an eyelash. It wasn't secret. It was on the front page of the *New York Times*, but nobody cared. It just went on. In 1965 the United States actually sent an invading army to attack South Vietnam. That army built up to over half a million men, four times as many as the Russians have in Afghanistan. There was no protest. Protest only began at a serious level by about 1966 or 1967 when we had hundreds of thousands of troops there and we had practically wiped the place out. To this day, nobody ever talks about an invasion of South Vietnam. Nobody ever talks about U.S. aggression in South Vietnam. The reason is that in those days the country was so totally brainwashed that we couldn't see that an attack against another country was an attack. It was a "defense." When we attacked South Vietnam we were "defending" it. Every book you look at, every television program you see, everything refers to the U.S. "defense" of South Vietnam, which according to the doves was not wise or was too bloody or something. That's like saying that Hitler was defending Poland, or the Russians are defending Afghanistan. It was just direct invasion. We can't see it, nobody could see it then.

Now let's compare that with the early 1980s. Nowadays the state can't do that any more. They could not send B-52s to bomb Nicaragua. They couldn't send an invading army. They had to go directly to clandestine operations, and the reason is because the public has become much more sensitized. So the level of opposition and dissent is far higher than it was in the 1960s. For example, what I'm talking about now, at the peak of the peace movement, of student opposition, I couldn't talk like this anywhere. I couldn't have talked to the most radical peace movement group, I couldn't have talked like this. They wouldn't have understood what I was talking about. The level of sophistication of the general public is far higher than it was then. And that's affected the media. Reporting is far better than it was. It's still horrible, but it was much worse then, much worse. I have just finished a book—a couple of hundred pages—reviewing the American media through the Indochina war. I lived through it, but when you look at it again it's just mind-boggling. There wasn't a particle of dissent. Nothing. All this business about Dan Rather and so on, all total lies. It was completely supportive all the way along, never raised the most minimal question. It never even reported on the war except as it was seen by the U.S. military. This went on right to the end. A totalitarian country could barely have asked for more.

Do we look at ourselves and our actions a little more?

A little more. There's been a change for the better in the last 20 years, which is exactly why the Reagan administration was forced underground. Clandestine operations are a pretty good measure of domestic dissidence. Clandestine operations are pretty inefficient. The overt use of terror is much more efficient. So a state will turn to clandestine operations only when it's forced to, and typically it's forced to by its own population. Take a look at the scale of clandestine operations and that gives you a pretty good measure of what domestic dissidence is like. Now the Reagan administration has broken all records. There has never been anything like the international terrorist network that they constructed, little bits of which were exposed in the hearings. There's just nothing like it in history. That's a measure of domestic dissidence. It was not secret to anybody except the U.S. population. They were the only ones who didn't know about it, which means it was carried out against them. What's more, the more sophisticated people in the Reagan administration are quite aware of it. I don't know if this was reported here, but over last summer, in the middle of the Iran/Contra hearings, there were two or three reporters in the country who were actually reporting on the Iran/Contra hearings, I mean like journalists, not just taking the latest public relations release for the Committee. One of them was a man named Alfonso Chardy of the *Miami Herald*, who actually was doing some work, like when the hearings would release documents; virtually nobody did that, it was too much work. He did, and he kept exposing all sorts of things that never made it to the mainstream press.

One of the things he exposed was this Office of Public Diplomacy. There's real Orwell for you. The State Department in 1971 set up an Office of Public Diplomacy which was supposed to carry out things like what they called "Operation Truth," literally, that was the phrase, and the idea was to try to control the discussion over Central America. The documents came out in the middle of the hearing. Chardy went through them. In a way they were very comical. It's like a parody of *1984*. He went and interviewed people in the administration, and they described it as the "most spectacular success" of all the Reagan programs. Notice who this is aimed at: this is aimed at the American population. They described that as—their phrase was—the "most spectacular success." And it was, in fact: it controlled the entire debate and discussion in the media. One of these guys he quoted said that "this was the kind of operation that you would carry out in enemy territory." That's exactly right. The population is enemy territory from the point of view of the state. If you can't control the enemy by indoctrination or force, you turn to clandestine operations because you've got to marginalize them. In fact, the country is way more dissident than it was, and the dissidence today is in completely different sectors of the population. Back in the 1960s it was a youth movement, students, youth, etc. Now in the 1980s it's all over the place. It's middle America, Kansas, Arizona. Take for example the sanctuary movement. That's very courageous stuff. These people are facing long years in jail. Those are sectors of the population that had nothing to do with the peace movement for the most part, in fact they were even hostile to it in the 1960s.

Would you discuss the Rather-Bush confrontation on the CBS evening news? Also, we had four congresspeople who went to Managua and participated in a demonstration of support for the Contras. It was front-page news. Two days after that, House Speaker Jim Wright met with Ortega and everyone was blasting Wright for interfering in foreign affairs. But no one even questioned what the four congresspeople did.

Take a look at the four congresspeople and ask yourself the following question: Suppose that in 1943 a group of Japanese fascist legislators landed in Washington and organized a demonstration to overthrow the United States and to support the Japanese fascists and then went home to Japan to try to organize more support to liberate the world from American imperialism. What would have happened? For one thing, the whole thing is lunatic; if they had ever come near the place, they would have been either dead or in jail forever. Remember that the United States was not under threat at that time. There was no threat whatsoever to the national territory of the United States. In fact, there hasn't been a threat to the territory of the United States since the War of 1812.

Nicaragua, on the contrary, is under serious threat from a major terrorist superpower. Nevertheless, we take it for granted that they should allow in hostile legislators to take part in demonstrations to try to overthrow the government. Notice that we take it for granted that, say, correspondents for the *Los Angeles Times* should be allowed into Nicaragua. That's astonishing, if you think about it. We didn't allow Japanese journalists to wander around the United States in 1943. England didn't allow Nazi journalists from Germany to walk around London. Israel won't allow journalists from Libya to wander around the place. But Nicaragua is under much more threat. Nevertheless we take it for granted that they have to do it. That's part of the same thing as our believing we have a right to attack any other country. Nobody bats an eyelash. In fact, they are totalitarians. That's a more open society than we are, way more open. But we don't see that because we take it for granted that we have a right to overthrow everybody else and to attack anybody else, etc. If they try to defend themselves, either with airplanes or by the normal mode of ideological control that we use and Israel uses and that every democracy uses, that's just not allowed. They're not allowed to defend themselves. The real story in my view about the four congressmen is that people weren't astonished that they allowed them in their country. They ought to be astonished that any American journalist is allowed into the country. As far as the Bush-Rather thing is concerned, any time there's a big flap about something, you know that it's totally insignificant. What difference does it make whether Bush advised Reagan or not? Does it make the slightest bit of difference, any difference whatsoever? It didn't have to do with anything, it has nothing to do with anything. It doesn't merit a line in the society columns. It's less important than what's happening on the sports page. So therefore you can make a big flap about it and people can start screaming, the press is too antagonistic, etc. As long as the press gets antagonistic about things that have absolutely no significance whatsoever, that's fine. You can have a big debate about whether freedom of the press going too far, etc. But simply ask yourself what difference does it make whether George Bush was sleeping during those meetings or listening during those meetings, which is essentially what's at stake. The answer is, There isn't any difference whatsoever. Nothing follows from it—nothing at all, except whether he was asleep, like Reagan probably was.

You have this indoctrination system which says people are not supposed to care what Bush says.

They don't. They're right. Who cares what Bush says?

The problem is that Bush may be the next president.

But, you see, Bush's attitude towards attacking other countries isn't coming up here. What's coming up is a totally trivial question about whether he happened to be listening when somebody said we're sending arms to Iran. That doesn't matter.

Right. So how do you go about starting to change the indoctrination system?

The first thing you have to do is to worry about your own mind. The second thing you've got to do is to extricate yourself from the whole system. It's got to get the point where it's like a reflex to read the first page of the *Los Angeles Times* and to count the lies and distortions and to put it into some sort of rational framework. The first thing you have to do is recognize that you're regarded as the enemy and to defend yourselves. If there were a real educational system, there would be courses in intellectual self-defense where people would have the experience of going through this kind of thing and learning how to defend themselves from the attack by the people who regard you as the enemy, namely the privileged groups in general—the state, the corporations, the press, etc. Since there aren't such courses, and obviously universities can't do it, being part of the indoctrination system, you have to find other ways to do it. The beginning is to learn how to defend yourself, and it's extremely hard to do alone. So what you have to do is to organize people to defend themselves. People working together can do an awful lot of things they can't do alone. They have to think things out, interact, etc. There's a combination of education and organization. Ultimately it has to reach the point where it can affect policies and even change institutions.

Do you think that indoctrination is promoted by the general prosperity of the country? Would a financial crisis trigger changes?

That's hard to say. One thing you have to give Reagan credit for: he has to a certain extent broken down the distinction between the United States and the Third World. He's a real egalitarian. You now have Third World conditions in Kansas and so on for the first time. For the first time in American history you're getting real malnutrition. There are more homeless in the streets of the United States than in Managua, per capita, so he did succeed in bringing parts of the

United States down to the level of the Third World, which is quite an achievement in a country that is as rich and well-endowed as this one. And that's a conscious policy—part of the destruction of the social net and transfer of resources to the wealthy—a very conscious policy, with an elite consensus—the Democrats went along.

What's the effect of all of that? The trouble is that when you bring people down to the level of utter destitution, they sink below despair, they don't get politicized. They try to survive. If this happens to substantial parts of the population it becomes **a potential mass base for a fascist movement**. People say, look, we live in this fantastically wealthy society, how come we're suffering? It must be the Jews or the blacks or the communists or the Catholics or somebody. In this kind of society, in which people are basically depoliticized—they don't have the option of participating in the political system in any meaningful way, and they know it—where there's no independent press—everything's run by a narrow business-based consensus—people are aware of it. You look at polls and people feel very alienated. Typically large parts of the population say everything's run by a few big interests looking out for themselves. That's the kind of situation where, if some charismatic figure comes along and says, look, I'm going to take care of the blacks or the homosexuals, or whoever's doing all this to you, the communists or whatever, that's exactly the way fascist movements get started. They feed on despair.

The United States is ripe for that. One element of the United States that's very frightening from a historical point of view is the level of religious fanaticism. If you look at countries of the world, the only country that's like the United States really is Iran in the proportion of the population that's involved in really fanatic religious movements, I don't mean they go to church, I mean born-again experiences, Armageddon is coming, all this kind of thing. That kind of religious fanaticism is typically found in non-industrialized societies. There's a study of the relation between religious fanaticism and other things and it correlates pretty well with industrialization. As countries become more industrialized and more urbanized, the level of religious fanaticism, belief in witches, etc., tends to decline. The only major exception to this is the United States, which is the most industrialized and the most fanatic, it's at the level of Bangladesh in these analyses. Or maybe where Iran is now. That's a very frightening phenomenon. Because in such a system, if a charismatic religious figure comes along, you really have a mass base for dangerous fascism. We're really lucky here that every one of these television evangelists is such a crook. We should be happy when guys like Jim Bakker want gold Rolls Royces. As long as all they want is wealth and sex and that kind of business, then it's not a big problem. They're just robbing the people who are paying them. But if any of them ever want power, you know, if you get someone who's really serious, a Hitler type, if somebody wants power, not just personal wealth, there is a basis for building a mass fascist movement here. And that's part of the problem with a depoliticized society—people who are cynical, who distrust everything, who think somebody's screwing them but don't exactly know who. Poverty doesn't lead to insight, typically. A lot of support for Hitler came from people who were really dispossessed and, you know, they were going to get back at whoever was after them, the Jews or something.

You're an expert on linguistics and you also do so much political work. How do you do it?

I work like a maniac. I mean, you can really learn a lot if you're fanatic enough. They don't make it easy for you, you have to really work hard.

I'd like to find out some of your sources. How would you suggest I go about it?

First you have to decide to become a fanatic. It's not easy. You have to work, because nobody's going to make it easy for you. No society is going to make is easy to figure out what's going on inside it. Just like no corporation is going to help you understand what their strategy is. Why should they? They don't want you to know. Institutional structures are going to protect themselves from understanding. It doesn't have to be conscious. It works out that way in the normal course of things, like I've been describing. There are all kinds of methods to prevent you from understanding things.

Major documents dealing with U.S. planning happen to be publicly available because this is an unusually free society. We have a fantastic documentary record of all of it. You won't find them in the books on international affairs, foreign policy or any of that. Take my book *On Power and Ideology*. The first chapter quotes extensively from top-level planning documents on U.S. policy for Latin America. They're fantastically revealing. As far as I know those documents have never appeared in the professional literature. Never been mentioned in professional literature by Latin Americanists or political scientists. They've been declassified for years. But they just say the wrong things. You can find that stuff, but it's work.

That's why you need organization. The more organizational structure you have, the less fanatic you can be. The more you have to work on things alone, the harder it is. For one thing, you can lose your sanity. If you're alone and totally different from everybody in the world, you begin to think you must be crazy or something. It takes a big ego to withstand the fact that you're saying something different from everyone else.

On the other hand, if you're part of a community, you can think things through, get some reinforcement, help one another, etc. That's exactly why the genius of American democracy has been to break up all communities. That's why you don't have unions or political parties or political clubs, community organizations, nothing. That's very important. As long as people are isolated, they can't do very much. The way to learn something is first to go and commit yourself, but it's much easier if you can join a community where there's some solidarity and support. Then you can criticize each other and each other's ideas. That's why things like listener-supported radio, the kind of thing David Barsamian does out in Colorado, are very important, like Pacifica here, has that effect. In the communities that have listener-supported radio there's **another view of the world** that can be presented systematically, continuously, with interaction, people call in and yell at the newscaster, the community gets involved, etc. It has a very noticeable effect on the communities. I travel around the country a lot, and you can really see it. In communities that have listener-supported radio, there's a method of intellectual self-defense. You hear something different and you can think about things other than what you hear in the mainstream indoctrination system. Maybe what's coming across the community-supported radio is wrong, but at least it's different, a different kind of wrong. You can think a little better. The same is true of all kinds of community structures.

Editor's Notes to Interview 45

See Editor's Notes to I44.

The *Daily Bruin* is the UCLA student newspaper, which the day before (Jan. 27,1988) had published a "Viewpoint" article (p. 17) under the title "Noam Chomsky: A Man of Questionable Integrity," by N. Christopher Phillips, identified at the bottom of the article as "a visiting assistant professor of mathematics." In the article, Phillips repeats the two charges re. Cambodia and Faurisson discussed in I18, and falsely states that Chomsky "admits to lying on behalf of regimes such as those of Cuba and Vietnam," citing the three sentences "Honest people ... oppression" at the bottom of page 27 of **ChR** (1987) from the "review" of this book in the *Los Angeles Times* referred to in my Introduction (see I46). The last sentence of his article reads: "It is an outrage that the graduate students are paying for an apologist for the most barbaric regimes in history." On page 14 of the same issue there is an article titled "Israelis Fire on Protesters," filed by Nicolas Tatro (Associated Press) from Jerusalem, which Phillips could not have had in mind when he wrote. What is likely to have been uppermost in his mind is the talk Chomsky was scheduled to give that very evening at UCLA on the topic "U.S. Policies in the Middle East"—which was to attract a crowd that filled the Royce Hall Auditorium, the largest at UCLA (see Introduction).

Thirteen pages before Tatro's article, that is, on the front page of that issue, there was another item from AP, unsigned: "Anti-Semitic Violence up 121 Percent," which begins: "A 121-percent jump in anti-Semitic violence in California in 1987 helped reverse a 5-year downward trend nationally, the Anti-Defamation League of B'nai B'rith said Tuesday. The nationwide total of incidents was up 17 percent." But the main feature (illustrated with a photograph) is a companion front page story about a talk that the local head of the Jewish Defense Organization had given at UCLA the day before to an audience of "nearly 50 students." The story notes that the speaker "was challenged by several students in the audience who asserted that he was only perpetuating violence with his militant attitude." "I don't think that violence is a good thing," the speaker is said to have retorted; "I think it is a necessary thing." The following day the *Bruin* published a paid advertisement (white letters against a black background), "sponsored by Hillel Student Center and Jewish Student Council: A Forum of Jewish Organizations," in which the name of this advocate of violence and Chomsky's appeared above the following text: "What do these people have in common? Both propose extreme, simplistic solutions to a complicated problem: the Middle East. A peaceful solution depends on dialogue and tolerance not violence and hatred. It requires moderation and compromise, not extremism and closed minds." See the second section of the Introduction.

Two "Counterpoint" responses to Phillips' article appeared subsequently in the *Bruin*: One by Colin Starger (a student in "The Cognitive Revolution" course), which was given the title "Chomsky's Arguments Are Better When They're Quoted in Context" (Feb. 2,1988, p. 14), and one (published in full after some delay) by the present writer, which was titled "The Recent Attack on Noam Chomsky Was Baseless" (Feb. 25, 1988, pp. 20–21).

On the matters relating to the *Bruin* article, see interview 18 and the references given in the Editor's Notes, in particular **ChR**, 289ff.

On the importance of a stimulating, complex, supportive, nurturing environment, see interview 42.

On the rise in the carbon dioxide level, see **RP** (1981/1984/2003), introduction, n. 52. (See also Editor's Notes to I5.) A recent update in the popular press is "'Greenhouse effect': Stratosphere Becoming a Hot Topic," by Maura Dolan & Mark Lawrence, *Los Angeles Times*, Sept. 1, 1988, pp. 1 & 30. The main point of the article is that "nearly 100 years after the first scientific paper on the greenhouse effect was published, the nation is taking notice. Interest in global warming has exploded in Congress, the news media and among world organizations, rapidly taking the topic from the laboratory to the living room." (Wishful thinking?) A letter mailed out in August 1988 by a member of Congress states that some scientists believe that the unprecedented high temperatures and drought conditions of 1988 ("nearly 40 percent of the counties in this country have been declared disaster areas, and experts have predicted that food shortages resulting from the droughts will cause large increase in food prices") are the result of a "greenhouse effect"; the first five months in 1988 were the hottest on record. A scientist with the World Resources Institute recently told Congress that "a 9 degree increase in the Earth's temperature would exceed any climatic change which has occurred in the last 10 million years."

Needless to say, this is not the only pressing ecological issue. Many people are becoming aware of problems such as ozone depletion and deforestation. These problems are often linked (thus forests contribute to decrease the greenhouse effect when they grow and to increase it when they die, since when they grow, they absorb, and when they die, they emit, carbon dioxide). They are also global problems.

See Editor's Notes to I5.

45. The Cognitive Revolution, II (28 January 1988)

Has there ever been a government or a very powerful nation that you think has used its power well?

It's almost a logical impossibility. First of all, governments aren't moral agents. Governments are serving certain interests, whatever the interest of some domestic power is. It would be just the merest accident if that happened to have a morally favorable quality to it. Why should it? Maybe by accident sometimes it just happens that what serves the interests of domestic power helps other people too, but if so, it would just be an accident, and it's rarely true.

Are governments inherently bad?

No, concentration of power is. If you had diffusion of power, then some administrative authority could respond to the needs of a diffuse power and it would be much less destructive.

Have there ever been any examples of that?

There are small-scale examples. If you have ever lived in a small town in the United States that has a town meeting that runs the school system, the sewers and so on; it's a fairly democratic system. And there are other, broader cases, surely. A lot of voluntary associations are democratically run. But when you move to state power it's very unlikely that they will be because when you move to state power you get organized systems of violence and coercion and the people who have real power are going to take them over because they need them and want them. It's like asking to have an "honest media." There's absolutely no reason why media that are a corporate monopoly should be honest. Why should they? It would be crazy. It would be absurd for a corporation to want people to know the truth about how the world works. Why should they? It's like expecting a corporation to sell its commodities so low that it would go broke. There's no reason to expect that. Expecting the *New York Times* to tell the truth is approximately the same. It doesn't make sense. They have interests to serve. And you want the world to be perceived from the point of view of the interests that you represent.

What are your views on the state? Are you an isolationist? How would you characterize yourself politically?

629

I don't think most political terms mean much, to tell you the truth. If you wanted a term, I'm some kind of anarchist. But the terms don't mean much. Reasonably, you're presupposing that there have to be states. But that's a **transitory historical phase.** The state system is like saying, what kind of feudal system should we have that would be the best one? What form of slavery would be the best kind? There might have been a period in history when it would have been sensible to ask, what's the best form of slavery, the least awful form of slavery? Then you could discuss different forms of slavery and which ones would be best. But there is something wrong with that question because it assumes that some system of coercion and control is necessary. And it isn't.

The state system is a very artificial system. In its modern form it developed in Europe, and you can see how artificial it is by just looking at European history for the last hundreds of years, a history of massacre, violence, terror, destruction, most of which has to do with trying to impose a state system on a society to which it has very little relation. As Europe expanded over the rest of the world, pretty much the same thing happened—you look at Africa, India, Asia, any place you go, they've got these boundaries which are the result of coloring different colors on the map that usually have to do with European colonization. They cut across all kinds of communities and interests and they bring people together who have nothing to do with each other. The result is constant warfare and struggle and oppression and so on. Furthermore, within each of these artificial systems, imposed usually by force, you have some kind of usually very sharply skewed distribution of power internally. The concentration of power inside usually takes over the state for its own good. It suppresses other people, suppresses people outside, etc. So we're stuck with this state system, for a while, at least. This is the way the world was stuck with slavery for a while. But we shouldn't expect it to be permanent. In fact, if it is a permanent condition, it isn't going to last very long because it's a lethal system. It's a miracle that it has survived as long as it did. In Europe, for example, the wars went from the beginnings of the modern period up until 1945, when a stable system was established. The only reason why stability was established was because the next step was going to destroy everything, given the level of weaponry. That's the nature of the state system. It's going to lead to more and more destruction. Maybe there will be a way to abort it now, because the next step is to kill everything, but maybe not, in which case we will kill everything. From every point of view the state system looks artificial in the sense that it's unrelated to human needs and imposed by certain interests and power distribution.

Within the state system—let's forget the long-term thing—what would a reasonable U.S. policy be? A reasonable policy, for example, would be to follow the U.S. Constitution. That's a good start. According to the U.S. Constitution, treaties that are duly entered into are the supreme law of the land. And there's a number of treaties that are not unreasonable, like the United Nations Charter, which among other things prevents the use or threat of force in international affairs. That's a good principle. I'd like to see some U.S. government start to abide by domestic U.S. law. That would be a good start. That position is considered very radical, so when I say the U.S. government ought to observe U.S. law, that's considered radical. The reason is because we intuitively take it for granted that it's a lawless state and we're a lawless and violent people, so we do anything we feel like. The law is only something that you apply to other people if they get in the way. But if we had the honesty to say that we also ought to follow our own laws, then I think there would be improvement.

For example, much of what the United States does is flatly illegal by U.S. law, and sometimes it's even condemned. Just a couple of years ago it was condemned by the World Court. You can't get a higher authority than that. So just to take a start, if we began by abiding by the laws that we orate about, that would be a start. Is that isolationist? That's a scare word. If the only alternatives are aggression or isolation, I'd rather be an isolationist. But those aren't the alternatives. It's possible to have a constructive relation with other parts of the world. That alternative, either aggression or isolationism, assumes that the only way we can interact with the rest of the world is to murder them. That's not an obvious assumption. There are other forms of interaction. For example, the U.S. is an extraordinarily rich country. You can imagine giving aid that would be helpful instead of harmful. You can imagine, it would take some enormous internal changes in the United States, because aid is after all given for purposes. It's given for export promotion or to control other societies, or whatever. It would take a big change in the United States before different motives for giving aid were expressed through the political system, but those would all be possibilities without breaking down the state system.

Can we be in an institution like UCLA [University of California at Los Angeles] that shapes and informs our thought but in which we can still maintain an aspect of creativity?

Sure, a lot of people do. It's a struggle. But after all, there are people in the media—I mean, I have friends in the media—who understand perfectly well what's going on. They shape what they write. They make a guess as to what the editors will allow through at a particular stage. After the Iran/Contra hearings, sophisticated reporters understood that things were going to open up a little bit because of the ferment. So they began to write and publish things they knew they couldn't have gotten through a couple of months before, things they knew all along but weren't able to say. You kind of make an estimate. Some people do it very consciously, they really craft their articles to the expectations of what higher authorities are going to accept. It's a difficult position to be in, but quite apart from that, take academic institutions. If you ever make it into an academic institution, there's very little anybody can do to you. They're set up in such a way that there isn't much available in the way of coercion. It's hard to get through those cracks, but if you ever do, you've got a lot of potential freedom. It's different in journalism, you can be thrown out at any time. The same is true in other institutions. You've got all sorts of leeway. What I was saying were kind of generalizations. There would naturally be **a general tendency to conform**, it's a lot easier, and people tend to do what's easier, and the people who try to do what's harder usually get weeded out. You look at the process, it's going to end up with a conformist, disciplined society, but not necessarily every individual, and individuals will vary in all sorts of ways.

So we don't have to feel bad about becoming part of an institution?

I don't think so. Why deny yourself the possibilities of whatever institutions offer? Why give a gift to the enemy? For example, for various reasons, mainly because it's a business-run society, the state doesn't have the power to coerce. Civil liberties just happen to be preserved in the United States because business doesn't want a powerful state that will interfere with it. Should we therefore not make use of the civil liberties? It doesn't make sense. That would be like saying, well, we'll give in to the enemy.

You say you're an anarchist. Maybe you shouldn't take any benefits from the state?

That view is published repeatedly. For example, I remember a book by Norman Podhoretz, some right-wing columnist, in which he accused academics in the peace movement of being ingrates because we were working against the government but we were getting grants from the government. That reflects an extremely interesting conception of the state, in fact a fascist conception of the state. It says the state is your master, and if the state does something for you you have to be nice to them. That's the underlying principle. So the state runs you, you're its slave, and if they happen to do something nice for you, like giving you a grant, you have to be nice to them, otherwise it's ungrateful. Notice how exactly opposite that is to democratic theory. According to democratic theory you're the master, the state is your servant. The state doesn't give you a grant, the population is giving you a grant. The state's just an instrument. But the concept of democracy is so remote from our conception that we very often tend to fall into straight fascist ideas like that, that the state is some kind of benevolent uncle, external thing up there, it's not your representative, and of course it's true, but it's not supposed to be, and therefore if your benevolent uncle happens to give you a piece of candy, it's not nice not to be nice to him back. But it's a strictly fascist conception. That's one of the reasons why fascism would be so easy to institute in the United States. It's deeply rooted in everybody's mind already.

Why shouldn't you want to overthrow the state? The state is not, according to democratic theory at least, some institution outside society that society has some relation to. It's a form of organization of the society. Why shouldn't you want a different form of organization for your society?

Is it your view that the U.S. is blocking a Mideast peace settlement and wants to keep Israel as a confrontational state and subservient to U.S. power?

That's part of it. As I said [in yesterday's evening public talk], there's been a real split over this among U.S. elites, but the position that's won out has had that kind of thrust to it.

Would you comment on the op-ed piece in the Bruin?

Sure. There was a kind of moral point and a lot of factual points, but the moral point is the most interesting one. The moral point, which I think was in the first paragraph somewhere, had to do with a statement of mine, which was accurately quoted, in which I said that people had to be responsible for the human consequences of their actions. If you are a moral agent, if you're not a moral imbecile, you'll ask the question of what the consequences are of what you're going to do, what's it going to mean to people. In particular, suppose, say, you're a journalist, and you want to write a critical article about some enemy or whatever, you'll ask yourself what the consequences will be. Do we believe in that or not? Let's try it out. Suppose, for example, that you're a journalist in Germany in 1943. You discover that there's a Jewish child hiding in a house somewhere, and you know that if you write an article about him he'll be killed or sent to an extermination camp. Is it your duty to write an article about it and put it in the Nazi press? According to the author of that article, it is your duty.

Let's take the example of Afghanistan. Suppose you're a Russian journalist and you live in Moscow and you discover something about the terrorism of the Afghan resistance and their being involved in drugs—all of this happens to be true. You know perfectly well that if you publish that article in *Pravda*, it's going to be used to intensify the attack against Afghanistan, to murder more people, etc. Is it your duty to publish that article in *Pravda?* Well, according to those assumptions, it is. As far as I can see, that's monstrous. In fact, I'm sure the author of the article would understand that it's monstrous too, if you talked to him about other cases. It's just that we can't apply the same principles to ourselves. But the moral issue is trivial. Either you're a **moral monster** or you'll ask the question, What are the consequences of what I do? In fact, I didn't draw any conclusions there about what you should do, I just said to think about it. But for the author of the article—he probably didn't write it; there's a central source from which all those articles come, they are all over the place, probably the Anti-Defamation League office in New York, because you see the same stuff everywhere—but whoever's writing that stuff, either they can't think this through or they don't care. That's the moral issue.

Then come the factual issues. Whoever wrote the article interprets my statement that you have to think about the consequences of what you do as saying that I admitted that I lied for the Khmer Rouge or something, I don't know how you make that logical leap exactly. What I said was think about what you're doing when you do things. Conclusion: I conceded that I lied about the Khmer Rouge. Well, big leap. In fact, nothing was said there on what you should do.

As far as the other issues are concerned, it's just total fraud. Take a look at the Cambodia scholarship. Actually I've written two articles on Cambodia.

Nobody's ever found even the most minimal error in either of them. Not even anything mildly misleading. There is a scholarly literature on Cambodia and that's pointed out; it's pointed out years later, after all the information is in, that the basic data—mostly speculations, because there wasn't much data—are essentially correct.

For example, one of the things he says there is that I deny the figure of 3 million dead. Actually I don't deny it. These are jointly co-authored articles. In the two co-authored articles we pointed out that there is a range of opinion and guesses on the matter. At the low end of the range are the people who knew anything, like State Department intelligence, the Cambodia-watchers in Bangkok, who had actual information on Cambodia—the only people who had any actual information—they were at the low end. Then at the high end you had people like, for example, Jean Lacouture, who wrote this review which was extremely influential, who wrote that the Khmer Rouge has boasted of having killed 2 million people. He was basing that on a book by a French priest [François Ponchaud] which was only in French. The review appeared in the United States and it was quoted everywhere that these monsters are killing 2 million people.

I was kind of curious. The book wasn't around, nobody had read it. They were just quoting Lacouture. I wrote to some friends in France and asked them to send me the book. It turns out that there wasn't anything even remotely like that in the book. What he did was this: According to the book, which might or might not have been right, 800,000 people were killed during the American war. The U.S. was responsible for killing 800,000 people. Then he claimed that according to the American Embassy in Bangkok, the Khmer Rouge were responsible for the deaths—not killings—of 1.2 million people. So he took those two figures, including the 800,000 killed by the United States, added them up, added a boost—changed deaths to killings—and ended up with the Khmer Rouge boasting of having killed 2 million people.

I checked further. The American Embassy in Bangkok denied that it ever made any such estimate or statement. It was way higher than what the Cambodia-watchers were presenting. There's a lot of things like this. He also had quotes, horrifying quotes, the Khmer Rouge says so-and-so. You look at the book and it turns out that it's not the Khmer Rouge, it's some Thai newspaper being mistranslated. I wrote him [Lacouture] a letter saying, I don't know what's going on, but you're not quoting the book accurately, you might as well quote the book accurately. He then wrote corrections in the *New York Review*, where the review appeared, in which he essentially withdrew everything he said: Well, maybe it wasn't 2 million, maybe it was only thousands, etc. But he said, Does it really matter?—that there's no difference between boasting of killing 2 million people and boasting of killing thousands of people. I think there's a difference. For example, if somebody came along and said, At My Lai the United States killed 2 million people, and they said, Look, it's not 2 million, it's a couple of hundred, and they said, Well, what's the difference, 2 million, a couple hundred?, would we take that seriously? That's about the story.

In fact, the context of all of this is that my co-author, Ed Herman, and I were comparing the way comparable atrocities are treated in the media. We went through a whole lot of cases and look at, as close as you could get, comparable atrocities. In this case we compared Timor and Cambodia. Timor is the same time frame, 1975–1978, same part of the world, same scale—by all the evidence around it's about the same scale. In the case of Timor it's much higher proportional to the population, much higher, but they're roughly the same scale and the same kind of atrocities. But there's a couple of differences. One difference is that nobody ever heard of Timor while everybody knows about Pol Pot. The second difference, which is not uncorrelated with that, is that we were responsible for the atrocities in Timor, while some official enemy was responsible for the Pol Pot atrocities. And the third difference is that with regard to Pol Pot there was vast lying and fabrication at this time—I mean, unbelievable: Stalin would not have believed the amount of fabrication there was—and the people who knew something were suppressed, like the State Department intelligence wasn't quoted. We were about the only people who quoted State Department intelligence. We didn't say it was right; we just said, look, this is one of the things that ought to be considered, namely the only people who know anything. We ended up the chapter saying, we don't know what the facts are, but here's the evidence and here's the way it's filtering through the system. If it's an enemy atrocity, the worst conceivable interpretation is given, with fabrication of evidence, invention of numbers, screaming and yelling and so on, and that's all that comes through; when it's our comparable atrocity, nothing. Nobody interviews a refugee, nobody listens to the church sources, you can bring a priest to the office of the *New York Times*, as I did in fact. They wouldn't interview him. That's the difference. And we went through case after case like this. In fact, the book was about U.S. ideology. We never drew any specific conclusions about what the facts were in Timor or Cambodia or other cases. We said, here's the evidence, here's the way it's being treated. Incidentally, one of the reasons why nobody's ever found any errors in it is that it was mostly a logical exercise, we made virtually no factual claims.

That gets transmuted in the ideological system into a defense of the Khmer Rouge. How do you figure that? I remember he quotes there a statement in which we said something like refugee statements must be treated with care. First of all, that's a truism. Secondly, we were quoting Charles Twining, who was a Cambodia-watcher in the American Embassy, a State Department intelligence specialist, who pointed out, as everybody knows, in congressional testimony, that you've got to be really cautious with refugee testimony because the refugees are scared.

I've actually taken refugee testimony in Laos. When you talk to refugees, it's a very difficult situation. These were from U.S. bombings. The refugees are trying to figure out who you are and what you want them to say. As far as they know, you're some foreign power figure. You may be the guy who's been bombing them. They're in a very desperate situation. They have nothing. They're living in some miserable camp somewhere. There's this powerful figure coming in from the outside. They have to be extremely cautious.

When I was taking refugee testimony in Laos, it was a time when the press wouldn't cover it because it was an American atrocity. I could see that there were people—there were very few young people around, most of them were the relatives, the women and children, and so on, brought in by the CIA after they swept through the area—there were a couple, a few people, I could see they were telling everybody to shut up and not to tell me anything. The only time I really got real testimony was when one of the people who was with me drew some of these guys aside. I'm sure they were Pathet Lao guerrilla cadres, who were trying to get people not to tell anything to whitey, because you don't know who he is. He could be an American soldier or a CIA agent.

It's natural, you just think about it for a second. Suppose you were in a refugee camp. You would try to figure out what those guys want, and that's what you would tell them. Everybody who's ever dealt with refugees knows this. We happened to be quoting the guy who did all the refugee interviewing for the U.S. government. He was pointing out that the State Department, the Congress would have to evaluate refugee testimony. And, in fact, this is a truism. The striking thing was that in the case of Timor they never took refugee testimony. In the case of Cambodia, all bars were down. I remember Henry Kamm of the *New York Times* interviewed refugees who were literally inside police cages in Thai jails and just quoted everything they said. What do you think those guys are going to say? What's a guy going to say who's in a cage in a jail in a terror state? He's not going to say anything that's going to do him any harm. Any journalist who has a piece of a brain in his head knows that. In fact, one thing that we pointed out extensively is that refugee testimony was being ignored by the press. We went through a lot of refugee testimony that was simply ignored because it wasn't telling the right story. This included the most careful analyses of refugees done by the few Cambodia scholars around who did take extensive refugee testimony and it just turned out to be a more nuanced and complex story, so it's of no use. They left it out. It's exactly the opposite. The media, the whole propaganda system was denying refugee testimony. They wanted a message, they didn't want the facts.

As for the story of 3 million killed, you know where that comes from? That's Hanoi propaganda. The first time in history that anyone has assumed that Communist war-time propaganda has got to be true. Vietnam was at war with Cambodia and in the context of that war they invented this 3 million figure as part of their war-time propaganda. That became orthodox in the United States. All of a sudden we have to follow Hanoi propaganda, even though there's no basis for it—even if the State Department intelligence says it's off by a factor of ten.

Is the anti-apartheid movement a safety valve for people who have liberal guilt feelings and who can't change anything at home?

I wouldn't quite put it that way, but I understand what you're saying. There's a respect in which joining **the anti-apartheid movement** is easy. Woody Allen had an idiotic op-ed today in the *New York Times* about the first three-quarters of which were patting himself on the back for what a marvelous guy he is and then at the end he said that he does things too, like he's against apartheid. That's the kind of thing Woody Allen could be against because it's cheap. Everybody's against apartheid. In that respect it's true. I think it's extremely important and one should be part of it, but you have to understand why it's so easy. When you have an anti-apartheid demonstration, you don't get broken up by attacks and sent to jail, typically. Mayors get arrested and civil disobedients get their pictures in the papers and everybody applauds. It's very unusual. Usually any kind of demonstration about anything gets repressed. So how come this one's not getting repressed?

The answer is the usual one: the corporations are anti-apartheid. South Africa's going through a transition from a slave society to an industrial society. A generation back, South Africa was a society based on extraction of minerals, so they'd send black slaves into the mines, and they'd die after a couple of years, and they'd move in new ones. For that, apartheid is perfect. Now South Africa is becoming more industrialized. In an industrial society you need a trained, docile work force. You don't want slaves any more. The same reason why you had a civil war here: the North was becoming industrialized. They wanted what's called "free labor," rented labor, not owned labor. Owned labor is no good for an industrial society. You can't get rid of it when there's a recession. What you wanted was rented labor, people you could throw out when you don't need them. You also needed people who were trained and educated, because you need a little bit of training to work in a factory, not like picking cotton. There was opposition to slavery in the industrial North. And you're seeing that now in South Africa. For most of the corporations, especially the U.S. corporations who are investing there, mostly advanced technology—for them slavery is not a good system. Apartheid is not a good system. They need a docile work force. They need low-level managers from the working class. They need people who are going to organize things and quiet it down. For that, apartheid is not a good idea. So they're quite honestly anti-apartheid now, and that helps make it an easy thing to be involved in—not to say one shouldn't be involved in it, but one should understand why they're not throwing you in jail.

But the corporations are not pulling out of South Africa. There's a movement on campus for UC [University of California] to divest but they haven't.

Because you'd lower profits that way. I mean, the corporations in the United States would like to see apartheid changed, but the University of California doesn't want to get less return on its investment.

In terms of the cognitive revolution, I'm interested in your philosophical views and how you look at what your contribution has been, for example, your showing how the mind is actually an abstraction.

I don't take any credit for that—that was shown by Descartes.

On a philosophical level, what are the consequences of your cognitive revolution?

I think philosophy is a somewhat artificial discipline. It didn't really exist until fairly recently. Until about the 19th century, there was no real difference between **science and philosophy**. So when you read Hume, for example, say his *Treatise on Human Nature*, he describes himself as carrying out a scientific enterprise, somewhat speculative, but essentially a scientific enterprise. In fact, he compares it to Newton's. He says he's going to try to find springs and the origins of human nature in the same way in which Newton figured out the things that make the physical world work. To a large extent, that's what philosophy was. This was a part of it that had to do with science. Other parts of it had to do with the way the social order ought to be organized; it was kind of a social inquiry into the way things are, the way they ought to be, and so on. As science advanced, you could even be a physicist, you're going to continue asking the kinds of questions that philosophy asked. More and more philosophy sought a task. It turned more and more to foundational and conceptual questions. When you read Descartes or Hume, there's no distinction. Descartes did straight science, and he also did what we call straight philosophy, but he didn't see any difference, I'm sure: it was just more foundational, more speculative, more experimental. It's not clear that that distinction makes much sense. I don't have any philosophical view, and I don't think there are such views. I think we ought to try to understand the world, understand ourselves, society, and do it by whatever methods there are. The sciences do it one way, and so on.

To phrase it differently, in terms of your scientific views in this cognitive revolution, it seems that Descartes was trying to capture something of what human nature was about, and focussed correctly on the fact that the dividing line between us and the other animals is in the brain. But then he didn't understand it fully in the way that we do now.

Descartes' logic is intelligible. He started with a certain conception of physics, a conception of mechanics, things pushing and pulling each other, a common-sense mechanics. Take a common-sense view of how things work in the world, something moves if something pushes it, if you knock something against the wall it bounces back: that's Cartesian mechanics. He tried to see what you could explain in those terms. He convinced himself, wrongly, of course, that he could explain almost everything. If you look at his actual work, it's an attempt to explain how everything, just about, can be accounted for in those terms: motion of falling bodies, any sensation, the actions of animals, just about anything you can think of. But he discovered, he thought, that there were certain things that didn't fall into this conception: things like the creative aspect of language use, indeterminate human action, etc. So therefore, he said, these are the limits of mechanism: it doesn't include some of the things in the world. These other things are mind. The reasons why he had to set up mind as a second substance have to do with his particular metaphysical assumptions, but let's put that aside.

What happened with Newton, like 30 years later? Newton showed that the theory of body didn't work. He showed that the motions of the heavenly bodies could not be accounted for in terms of Cartesian mechanics. That's Newton's first major contribution. The second major contribution was to show that you could account for the motion of heavenly bodies and other forms of motion and so on if you invented what he considered a kind of occult force, a mysterious force—attraction at a distance—which doesn't make any sense. How can anything out here affect anything over here? But Newton recognized that you needed that and somehow if you postulated it, it explained things.

Well, at that point the theory of body was finished. There was no more any conception of what is a body. In Cartesian science you had a conception of body and therefore you could talk about the things that were outside the domain of body. By the time Newton had shown that that theory of body didn't work, you had no theory of body. In fact, from the time of Newton until today, nobody talks about the theory of body any more. It just means anything you understand about the world. Scientists come along and say: there's electromagnetic forces. OK, that's a theory of body. They say: there's massless particles. Fine, that's a theory of body. Whatever crazy thing they invent, if it turns out to work, that's going to be the theory of body. In fact, everything that's understood is the theory of body. There isn't any more mind. We can't even formulate the mind/body problem in Descartes' sense. In order to be able to formulate it you have to have a theory of body, and we don't have a theory of body. We really haven't had one since Newton, and therefore we can't formulate the mind/body problem. Without a theory of body, you can't ask the question, What lies outside it? So all we can say is, look, there are these phenomena in the world which we don't understand, and we want to understand them; to the extent we understand them, we'll incorporate them into what we call the theory of body. That's all there is to say.

The phenomena that Descartes described, which he called mind, those phenomena are real. They're puzzling and you try to understand them, and to the extent that we understand them, we incorporate them into a theory of physics. You may have to change physics as you do this. That's often been the case. Physics has been changing to accommodate new phenomena. But either you succeed or you fail. If you fail you've got problems. If you succeed, it's part of physics. I don't see any other question.

What is the relationship between the brain and its need for freedom and your theory of freedom?

First of all, nobody knows anything about the brain, including me. When we talk about a theory of freedom, we're talking about guesses, hopes, expectations. The word "theory" is a little bit inflated. I think some things we do know. It's pretty well known that a stimulating, complex, supportive, nurturing environment in fact enables people to flourish. There's a difference between children who grow up in an orphanage and those who grow up in a supportive environment where they're free to explore. You can see all that. It's a dramatic difference. And it probably reflects things about human nature. I suppose that, at least I would like to believe that people have **an instinct for freedom**, that they really want to control their own affairs. They don't want to be pushed around, ordered, oppressed, etc., and they want a chance to do things that make sense, like constructive work in a way that they control, or maybe control together with others. I don't know any way to prove this. It's really a hope about what human beings are like—a hope that if social structures change sufficiently, those aspects of human nature will be realized.

It seems humanity doesn't have the fundamental bases to deal with major problems.

If you look at the Earth from an angel's point of view, you would probably describe human beings as **an evolutionary error**. That's what it looks like. I mean, a species developed which has a fantastic capacity to destroy and very little capacity to overcome those aspects of its existence. From a biological point of view human beings have been extraordinarily destructive. The number of species that have been destroyed, the effects on the ecology, and so on, is devastating. In the long run, maybe termites are more destructive because they're producing all this carbon monoxide, but if you look at it kind of like a biologist, humans would look like a kind of blind alley.

The question is whether we can do something to change that in time. It's not obvious. Quite apart from nuclear war and so on and so forth, which is always likely, there are tendencies in human society and technological development toward ecological catastrophe, and they're not so far off. Maybe the most striking is the rise in the carbon dioxide level, which results from combustion—any kind of combustion increases it. Nobody doubts that it's going to warm the earth's surface. There are doubts about the rate, but it's probably detectable in the not-too-far future, and that will raise the ocean level and will probably inundate agricultural areas and probably wipe out human civilization. Well, we're not equipped socially to deal with that problem, apparently. I mean, our social organizations and our intellectual culture just tell us, don't worry, it'll get taken care of. But there isn't any reason to believe that. The assumption is that there's going to be a technological fix. Maybe. But it's by no means obvious.

Are there things that can be done?

I think there are ways to turn away from it right now. If we had, say, conservation, for example, or tried to look for alternative energy sources that didn't involve combustion. If a tenth of the money that's going into Star Wars were going into solar energy, we'd probably get an answer to the problem. But it just doesn't fit the structure of power and domination in our society. That's **a kind of social pathology** which could very well lead to biological destruction.

What do you think would be the contribution of molecular biology, which has had some major advances in the last ten years, to the study of cognitive science?

I've got my fingers crossed. Molecular biology is looking at extremely simple and rudimentary systems. But that looks like a point where you could hope some day to get a relationship between **molecular biology and neural structure**. I think one of the things that may come out of molecular biology is a realization that a lot of this loose talk about evolutionary adaptation is hogwash and that the way things change through time has an awful lot to do with our physical nature, just the way molecules work, and so on, and that may help understand something about the special structures of the brain. You'd hoped that molecular biology would reach the point where it could deal with complex organisms. The brain is a long way off—a fantastically complex organism. Molecular biology is still worrying about proteins and amino acids and E. coli, and so on. But, sure, we hope that there will be a point of contact some day.

Is it really possible?

Fifty years ago it would have seemed impossible to decode the human genetic endowment. Now it's possible. There's just no way of knowing. As understanding advances, a lot of things that looked extremely complex turn out to have simple factors that determine them. If that happens, the answer could be yes. If it's just a huge big mess of neurons and all kinds of connections, then no, you never understand it.

One of the big movements nationwide is the CIA-on-campus issue. It seems that there's two sides to the issue, one is freedom, one is justice, with the university administration taking the stand that there's a demand, that the students want the CIA on campus. Then there's the other side on the left that says it's ridiculous, the CIA doesn't abide by any laws or anything.

Suppose the students decided they were going to have the Mafia or the KGB on campus?

That's exactly what we brought up with the UCLA administration. We said, What if the KKK wants to come and there are people who want to join? What's your feeling on this freedom vs justice?

The questions about freedom, and they're serious questions, are posed in a totally fake context. If you had equality of power, you could talk about freedom, but when all the power is concentrated in one place, then freedom's a joke. People talk about a "free market." Sure. You and I are perfectly free to set up an automobile company and compete with General Motors. Nobody's stopping us. That freedom is meaningless. Or let's say you and I are free to open up a newspaper and publish things that the *Los Angeles Times* isn't publishing. Nobody's going to stop you. It's just that power happens to be organized so that only certain options are available. Within that limited range of options, those who have the power say, "Let's have freedom." That's a very skewed form of freedom. The principle is right. How the freedom works depends on what the social structures are. If the freedoms are such that the only choices that you have objectively are to conform to one or another system of power, there's no freedom. The university could tell you, "The KGB can recruit on campus, we are not going to stop them." But there's no possibility for that. The Mafia can recruit on campus, the only trouble is that the cops are going to come in and arrest them. The CIA is just as crooked as the Mafia and the cops aren't going to come in and arrest them because they happen to be the cops. But that's not an exercise in freedom, that's just adaptation to power. How one ought to relate to this situation, that's another question. That raises further questions, but I don't think one should be deluded about the ideal of freedom being pursued by anybody. It's not.

Do you believe the Constitution has any role in preserving freedom?

Sure it does. Take the First Amendment.

How about freedom of speech for the KKK or the KGB?

I think they ought to have freedom of speech.

What if the government decided that the KKK should not be allowed on campus?

I'd be opposed to that, personally. I'd be opposed to it because I wouldn't like the government to have the power to decide what you can hear. Actually, that's related to another piece of that *Daily Bruin* article which I didn't discuss and I'd like to mention.

The issue there, which was concealed, was that a guy in France was thrown out of his job teaching French literature, brought to court, tried for falsification of history, and condemned. Now that means that the state has the right to decide what is historical truth, and if it decides "this is historical truth" and you say something else, you're a criminal. In my view, that's a fantastic scandal. I don't care whether what the guy said is true, false, indifferent; I don't even give a damn what he said. The idea of giving the state the right to decide what's true, that's just straight, flat-out fascism. Now, this guy [the author of the *Bruin* article] and the people he's quoting really think we should have fascism. In fact they say, "Yes, you should allow the state to have the right to decide what's true, and if somebody says something and the state decides it's false, you put them in jail." That's essentially the issue. I don't want the state to have that right. If Henry Kissinger comes to campus, I'm sure he's going to lie through his teeth, but I don't want the state to have the right to stop him.

Do you want people to have the opportunity to make their own choice?

As I said, this is a little bit abstract, because in fact you're not getting the opportunity because this is not a free society. It's a society which has formal freedom but concentration of power, and that allows only certain options. But you are only going to make it worse if you assign one of those power groups the right to impose their conception of truth. That will only make it worse.

Editor's Notes to Interview 46

This is the fifth Barsamian interview (see Editor's Notes to I35).
On the European conquest of most of the world, see **Y501**.

46. Helping People Persuade Themselves (15 February 1988)

You frequently use the term "elite." I think a working definition would be useful.

There are various segments of the groups that we ought to call "**elites.**" In the first place, there are those who are in the position to make decisions which affect crucially what happens in the general society. That would include political decisions, decisions over investment, production, distribution, and so on. Then there are the groups that are in managerial positions with regard to the political and economic institutions, the state managers, the corporate managers, and so on, and also with regard to the ideological institutions, the top editorial positions and other positions of control within the media, the journals, etc. These groups, which are not only closely interconnected and interlocked, but also share a common set of values, associations, belong to the highly privileged class, are generally quite wealthy. They determine the basic framework of what happens in the society based on their power, which ultimately is rooted in economic power, in simple ownership of the basic facilities out of which the society is constituted.

And what of the role of the control of information and the decision-making processes?

As far as control of information is concerned, it's largely dominated by a fairly small number of major sources of information. There are a number of good studies of this, but without going into the details, it's pretty narrow. This essentially is a set of major corporations, news or information corporations, including the major television networks, which themselves are part of broader industrial and financial conglomerates, the major newspapers, half a dozen or so of which are also substantial corporations, the wire services which are interconnected with them, etc. These are major corporations which sell a product to other businesses. The product that they sell is audiences and readers. Newspapers and journals typically don't finance themselves through sales. They often lose money through subscribers, and obviously if you watch a television set you are not paying the channel. But the product that is sold is readers, and what's more, elite readers. Your advertising profile rises with the audience that you can offer to the advertiser. If it's a high-quality audience in terms of privilege and buying capacity your advertising rates go up. The information system, from an economic point of view at least, is fundamentally a system of major corporations trying to sell their product, namely relatively privileged and influential elite audiences, to other corporations. Hence it's all deeply embedded within the same system of domination and control that organizes the economy and largely runs the state.

Is there a collective unspoken understanding of shared interests? Or are there back-room meetings with men smoking cigars and deciding what's going to happen?

Of course that happens. There's nothing particularly conspiratorial about it. The same goes on in the business world, so it's not surprising to find the head of a corporation taking a business associate out to some fancy country club where they can have drinks and play golf and make business deals in the back-room. In fact we all know that there's no sharp break between the personal and cultural interactions in business practices. There's nothing in the least conspiratorial. These are very small groups relative to the population that are very narrowly concentrated in high privilege. The values are shared, often articulated, often unspoken, and the interactions apply at every level, from Washington dinner parties to meetings of the Council on Foreign Relations to delegations from corporate law firms to state officials, or simply the staffing of top executive positions in the government by representatives of the major investment firms, corporations, information corporations, a lot of flow between the top levels of media and the government. There's a natural interpenetration due to shared interests, shared privilege, and simply the desire to wield power effectively in the interest of the institutions one represents.

In this "procedural democracy," as you've termed it in the past, do the elite view the role of the public as essentially one of ratification at the polls?

That's a very conscious view. It's consciously regarded to be the duty of the public. I think it was Maxwell Taylor, Kennedy's eminence grise, grey eminence, who once said that the role of the public is to know just enough to be able to do their duty, which is to ratify decisions at the polls. They don't have to know any more than that. The general attitude of any system of authority towards the public is as of an enemy, because they've got to be kept under control. If they get out of control they might do all sorts of dangerous things, and typically a state regards its **domestic population as a potential enemy**. That's been notoriously true in the United States for a long time. One high Reagan official recently compared the public to "enemy territory." This was in the context of the exposures of the State Department Office of Public Diplomacy, which is a state propaganda agency designed to control discussion and debate over Central America, which it succeeded in doing spectacularly, this same administration official said quite accurately, and in the context he pointed out that these spectacular achievements were the kinds of operations that one carries out in "enemy territory," which is exactly right, the public is enemy territory.

This shows up in all sorts of ways. This happens to be the right wing, but at the more liberal end, consider the Trilateral Commission Report on the problems of the democracies in 1975, the group around Carter, in fact the group that invented Carter. They looked back nostalgically to the period when Truman had been able to govern the country with the aid of a small group of Wall Street lawyers and financiers, in words approximately to that effect, an exaggeration, but an exaggeration of something that's true. And that fortunate situation, they said, is now declining because of the annoying efforts of the public to become engaged in the public arena, which have to be beaten back because that's not the role of the public, that causes a "crisis of democracy."

You can trace this all the way back to the origins of the republic. John Jay's favorite maxim, according to his biographer, was that "the people who own the country ought to govern it." That's in fact exactly the way the constitutional system was established. It was a system in which propertied white males, who were regarded as more or less equal, inaccurately but not absurdly, they were to govern the country. They had the franchise. As things have changed over the years with the rise of corporate power on the one hand, which restricted the possibilities of democracy, and the extension of the franchise, which theoretically extended it, this struggle between narrowly concentrated power and the enemy public has of course continued.

Is your societal vision outside the current state paradigm?

I think the state paradigm is a **very unnatural** one. If you look at history, you can see that easily. To establish the **state system** in Europe required hundreds of years of murderous and brutal warfare and the only reason it stopped is that when it reached its latest stage in the early 1940s it was plain that the next stage would be total annihilation of human civilization. At that point the internal conflicts in Europe terminated, at least for a time. It was centuries of brutal warfare, murder, destruction, and that reflects the unnaturalness of the system. Everywhere Europe has spread throughout the world we find what we would call, if we were honest, the "plague of European civilization." Everywhere it spread over the world it has led to exactly the same thing. In the colonial areas, where the European invasion imposed a version of the state system, it has also led to interminable and brutal conflict. The problems are that this system has very little to do with people's perceived interests and needs and that it therefore has to be imposed by violence and force. It happens to be the governing world system at the moment, thanks to the European conquest of most of the world. But in the long term I would think it ought to be replaced by forms of association more related to actual human needs and concerns. That's a long term, however.

In the United States, what kind of ingredients, what kind of conditions would be necessary for the development of an alternative or, for want of a better term, a "progressive" culture?

Talk about erosion of the state system is so far off that I don't think it's useful to even think about what would be needed. What's needed in the shorter term is exactly what elite groups fear. Anything they fear is probably good, and what they fear is what they call the "crisis of democracy," that is simply the engage-ment of the population in the political arena. The political arena is not enough, but even the engagement of the population in the political arena would be use-ful progress towards democracy in the United States, meaning not just watching the candidates on television and clapping for them, but actual participation, real participation in formation of programs, in meaningful selection and recall of rep-resentatives, etc. That, which virtually doesn't exist in the United States, would be a large step towards functioning democracy. But then, even if it were to be achieved in some measure, it would still be limited. The fact is that what can happen in the political system altogether, the range of decisions open in the political system, is very sharply constrained by private power. This is not a prob-lem that arises in the United States because the political system is so narrow and so much under business control that there are virtually never any major policy options offered. But in countries that function in a more democratic fashion, where there really are policy options, say in Latin America, you see it all the time. If a reform candidate comes into office with real policy alternatives, there may be a military coup, but if not there will be a capital strike, capital flight, other pres-sures by the owners of the society to ensure that these policies can't be pursued. That doesn't really arise in the United States because there are basically no major policy issues in the public domain. But it would happen if the political system ever opened up. What that reflects is the fact that in a system of private enter-prise, with private control over the means of production and distribution and decisions over investment and so on, the range of political choices is restricted. It's heavily influenced by the resources available to those who own the basic insti-tutions of the society, but it's also restricted simply by their capacity to control whether the society survives, how it survives, how people live, etc. That means that meaningful democracy will involve actual popular takeover of decision-mak-ing in the essential institutions, and that includes crucially the economic institu-tions. They are what determine basically what our lives are.

What do you mean by "fascism"? I'm particularly intrigued by a comment you made: "Fascism is deeply rooted in everyone's mind in the United States."

When we talk about fascism, first of all, we're talking about a system of political, economic, social and cultural organization. If we want to talk about it reasonably, we have to dissociate it from concentration camps and gas chambers. There was fascism before there were extermination camps, and it was bad enough then. Fascism meant, from a socio-cultural point of view, **an attack on the ideals of the Enlightenment**, an attack on the conceptions of what was in those days called "brotherhood of man" (we would now put it in a perhaps more civilized form), but an attack on the idea that people had natural rights, that they were fundamentally equal, that it was an infringement of essential human rights if sys-tems of authority subordinated some to others, the insistence that there were real bonds of unity and solidarity among people across cultures, etc.

All of that was under attack. The ideas of solidarity were under attack under the principle of "purity of race and blood," typically in the Nazi version of fascism. The economic system was to be one of class collaboration between owners and workers, all working for the common cause, the cause of the nation and the state, under the control of a powerful state which would coordinate and intervene significantly in economic life to maintain authority, structures of power, etc. This is connected with control by the coordinated state-private monopolies over information, extensive censorship, permission for the state to determine what's true, historical truth, to enforce those decisions, etc. That whole range of ideas, loosely interconnected, revealed itself in various fascist movements which spread over much of the industrial world in the 1920s and 1930s. They took various forms in different societies, but elements of them could be perceived virtually everywhere.

A lot of these principles unfortunately are very deeply rooted. For example, there's a very far-reaching willingness to allow the state, in coordination with private power, to control very substantial aspects of life. There's very little objection to this, whether it's cultural life, information flow, political organizations, etc. At the grass roots level in the United States there's a lot of opposition to it. You find a lot of independence and fierce individualism among the population, but it doesn't show up much in the dominant culture, that is, the culture that actually makes decisions and controls.

We've touched upon the question that I'm about to ask you: You've said that the non-educated classes in American society are not as indoctrinated with the state ideology as are the educated classes. Isn't that a bit romantic, and what kind of evidence do you have to substantiate that?

It's not only not romantic, but it's pretty close to tautological. Education is a form of indoctrination, therefore we typically find in any society that the educated classes are more indoctrinated. They're the one's who are subjected to the constant flow of propaganda which is largely directed to them because they're more important, so they have to be more controlled. Furthermore, the educated classes become the instruments of propaganda. Their function in the society is to promulgate and develop the ideological principles. As a result they inculcate them, if they don't they're usually weeded out and are no longer part of the privileged elite. It's not at all unusual to discover the basic principles of the ideological system in any society most deeply entrenched and least critically accepted by the educated classes.

It would be romantic to suppose that the lesser level of indoctrination on the part of the less educated part of the population leads to some sort of revolutionary spirit or progressive impulse or whatever. It doesn't at all. It can lead to almost anything. For example, this can help create the mass base for a fascist movement.

In many respects, fascist ideals are inconsistent with the demands of the elite culture and system of power and privilege. That's why in the United States you typically find the attack on real fascist tendencies led by business interests. The American Civil Liberties Union, for example, is basically a very conservative organization. It's a very valuable organization, I'm glad to be part of it, but we shouldn't delude ourselves as to what it's about. It's basically defending rights which are demanded by the wealthy and the privileged. They don't want a state which is able to infringe with their privilege, and as a result these rights are defended.

You could see it in the summer of 1987 in the Ollie North phenomenon. There was a kind of brief whiff of fascism there. It was detected, and you could see it in the editorials in the *New York Times*. Even the *Wall Street Journal* ran a column by its Washington correspondent, lecturing to North et al. about the dangers of fascism. The business classes are quick to pick up the scent of fascism and they don't like it. They might turn to it in a time of crisis, but typically they want the state to be powerful enough to work for their interests, but not powerful enough to infringe upon their privileges. We find right at the roots of power some of the defenses against fascism. But among the general population, the less educated, less articulate part of the population, which also is typically the most depressed part of the population, there you can find at times appeal by charismatic figures who promise to lead them out of their problems and to attack either the powerful or some other bogeyman, the Jews or the homosexuals, or the communists, or whoever is identified as responsible for their troubles.

That kind of appeal is often vivid and powerful. We've seen it plenty of times in modern times. In the United States, which is a highly depoliticized society, it's a very dangerous possibility. In particular **the growth of religious fanaticism** is a very **threatening** phenomenon. Fortunately the leading figures in this movement have been extremely corrupt, which is a very good thing. Every time I find that one of them wants nothing but gold Cadillacs or free sex, etc., I applaud. As long as they're corrupt they're not very dangerous. They'll just rip off their partisans. But if one of them wants power, they could be very dangerous. If someone comes along out of those movements who can combine religious fanaticism with the lust for power, not privilege and corruption, then it could be extremely dangerous in a country like this, particularly in a period in which much of the population may be compelled to accept a degree of austerity. Right now, to pay off the lunacies of Reaganite economic management, but more generally, or in periods in which the relative decline in power of the state, its decline in capacity to control the world, leads to all sorts of paranoid concerns about knives in the back and enemies outside and within. That kind of combination does make it possible for the less indoctrinated segments of the population to deviate from the official ideology but off towards fascism. At the same time, these same groups have been and continue to be the basis for a very impressive resistance to state and corporate power and its violence.

Take Central America. The sources of the substantial public opposition to U.S. atrocities in Central America are not in elite circles, by any means. They're out in the general population, in the churches, in the Middle West, in sectors of the population that were not engaged much, may even have been hostile towards the movements of the 1960s. So it's a complex affair, lesser indoctrination is not necessarily a hopeful phenomenon. It may be the basis for more hopeful developments, but it doesn't provide them.

In your essay, "The Responsibility of Intellectuals," originally published in American Power and the New Mandarins *and reprinted in* The Chomsky Reader, *you discuss the role of intellectuals and the need to speak the truth. Steve Wasserman, in an August 1987* Los Angeles Times *book review of the* Reader, *accuses you of not following your own advice in relation to Nicaragua. Have you muted your criticisms of the Sandinistas?*

Have I muted my criticism of the Sandinistas? No, I don't think so. What exactly did you have in mind? I read the review, but I don't remember that comment.

He suggested that you were very reluctant to criticize revolutionary liberation movements in the Third World.

Actually, that was one of the innumerable misquotations in the review. There was a section to which he took exception, as many people do, in which I pointed out that an intellectual, like any human being, has the moral responsibility to consider the human consequences of what they do. That's just a truism. If you write, you have a moral responsibility to consider the consequences of what you write, what are the consequences going to be for human beings. Then I gave a number of examples, which he excluded because they didn't help with his political aims. So I said, for example, imagine a Russian intellectual now. Should that person write accurate criticism of the terror and atrocities of the Afghan resistance in the Soviet press, knowing that that accurate criticism will enable the Soviet Union to mobilize its own population for further atrocities and aggression? Would that be a morally responsible thing to do? I didn't answer that question, but if you want my answer I would say no, it's not a morally responsible thing to do. That example was not mentioned in his review.

But I also pointed out that we face exactly the same problem. We have to ask whether we want to act in such a way as to enhance the atrocities and violence of our own state. To take another example, suppose that I was a German citizen in 1938. Would it have been morally responsible for me to write an article in the Nazi press about the atrocities carried out by Jewish terrorists in Palestine, or about the crimes of Jewish businessmen, even if it was all accurate? Would it have been morally responsible for me to write those truths in the Nazi press? Well, again, I didn't answer the question there, but my own answer would be no, it would not. These are just truisms. If we are capable of recognizing truisms about others, then we're just cowardly and dishonest if we refuse to apply the truisms to ourselves. This leads to **moral dilemmas**. It leads to moral dilemmas in the case of the Russian intellectual and Afghanistan and it leads to the same moral dilemmas in the case of the American intellectuals in the United States. How one resolves moral dilemmas is a problem that individuals have to face.

In the United States today there is a good deal of awareness of and interest in Central America. There are solidarity groups, sister cities projects, delegations travel to the region. There are conferences, symposia, lectures and a plethora of books and articles. Alexander Cockburn has called it a "very sophisticated and mature movement." But it seems that that sophistication and maturity does not extend to the Israeli/Palestinian issue. Why not?

First of all, this sophistication and maturity extends to virtually nothing. The typical phenomenon is exactly contrary to what is always claimed. What history shows is that even the peace movement is very much controlled by the official agenda. It has definite illusions and moral blind spots, namely about atrocities for which the United States is responsible. That's the typical phenomenon. Now that's not what you read, because the purpose of what you read is to undermine and destroy the peace movement and anyone else, so there's a flood of propaganda, most of it fabricated, about how the peace movement has illusions and blind spots with respect to our enemies and the Third World dictators.

Exactly the opposite is very easily demonstrable. Simply to take one striking case: Timor is a perfect example. During the entire Timor atrocity, which still continues and which was comparable to Pol Pot and, relative to the population, greater, there's been almost total peace movement silence. The reason is, this simply does not conform to the state agenda, since the U.S. is responsible for it. There are numerous other examples. With regard to Central America things have been different, and it's very striking. To take an indicator, like letters to the editor: you look around the country and it's dramatic that letters to the editor are more sophisticated, more knowledgeable, more penetrating, more balanced and far more accurate than the material that appears in the opinion columns, op-eds, news reports, etc. I assume that the newspapers are not specifically picking letters that undermine their own position. They are obviously flooded by them. That does reflect a difference of consciousness.

But that happens to be focused on this issue, for particular reasons. The Israeli/Arab conflict, like most issues, is just outside this. There are special reasons for that. They have to do largely with what happened in 1967. In 1967 or about that time Israel succeeded in establishing itself as what's called a "strategic asset." There had been a debate and Israel had already been regarded as a kind of strategic asset, as useful for American power, as a barrier to what was called "radical Arab nationalism," meaning nationalist forces that are out of U.S. control, and 1967 established this position rather forcefully as Israel succeeded in destroying particularly the role of Gamel Abdel Nasser in Egypt, who was the leading figure in so-called "radical Arab nationalism."

This tremendous Israeli victory established a considerably closer relation between Israel and U.S. elite circles, since it was doing their job for them. This becomes complex and I don't want to oversimplify it, but the strategic asset principle was established in many circles. At the same time there was a very interesting reaction to the Israeli victory among the intellectual elites that control the information system, liberal to right-wing, in this case. There was tremendous euphoria over the Israeli victory, and Israel really endeared itself to liberal and other intellectuals at that time because of its success in using the mailed fist. That's a phenomenon that has to be explained. It's obvious why it should be true with the ultra right, but it's particularly interesting with regard to left-liberal American intellectuals.

I think there you have to look back at American society to understand the phenomenon. It was at that point that Israel became the object of awe and love. You find that until that time, even among the New York Jewish intellectuals, Israel and Zionism were pretty minor phenomena. You check back over journals like *Dissent* in earlier years and there's nothing about the topic, and the editors regarded themselves as non-Zionists at the time. All this changed in 1967. I think the reason it changed largely had to do with domestic events. You have to understand what was happening in the United States at that time. In the first place, this was 1967. The United States was not succeeding in destroying the indigenous resistance in Indochina. We weren't able to "defend South Vietnam," as it was put, namely destroy and attack South Vietnam.

It's important to bear in mind that liberal opinion was very strongly in favor of the war. There was a lot of concern that the United States wasn't winning. Here Israel came along and showed how to use violence against Third World upstarts, and that was impressive. Furthermore, the failure to win the war in Vietnam was combined with a growing threat to privilege at home. This came from many sectors of the society, the student movement the students were not obeying authority, they were asking the wrong questions, there were signs of intellectual independence, independent moral judgment, etc. All of that is obviously going to be intolerable in the faculty club. You could see the women's movement coming, the ethnic minorities were pressing for their rights, in fact a "crisis of democracy" was beginning to develop. There was a kind of a general sense of a threat to privilege coming from the Viet Cong, the Black Panthers, the students, the bearded Cuban revolutionaries, the Maoists, all sorts of partially paranoid fantasies, but partial recognition of the reality of popular ferment threatening authority and privilege.

Again, Israel came along and showed how to use violence effectively in restoring order, and that was an impressive demonstration. It was particularly important for liberal humanists, because Israel was capable, with its very effective propaganda system, of portraying itself as being the victim, while it very efficiently used force and violence to crush its enemies. This combination is absolutely irresistible. The liberal humanist is supposed to be in favor of the victim, and in this case he could shed tears for the alleged victim while secretly applauding the victim's successes in the effective use of violence. That's an irresistible combination. It stayed that way. That has swung debate in the United

States to the point where sane discussion of this issue has become extremely difficult in educated circles, and in the organs of communication and information that they control.

There are other factors. For example, there were people, Irving Howe is the most notorious, who quite cynically exploited the passionate enthusiasm for Israel that developed in order to undermine and attack activist elements of the peace movement and the student movement. He wrote vicious articles in the *New York Times* and elsewhere claiming that unidentified elements of the peace movement wouldn't be satisfied until Israel was destroyed by bloodthirsty Arab terrorists and wanted fascism in Israel, etc., and that was an effective device at the time. I wouldn't call it McCarthyist, because it goes **far beyond McCarthy**, but that kind of device to try to undermine the organized and activist peace movement and dissident elements was a very popular position among elites. That's why he could write these things in the *New York Times*. That also entered in.

This was a period in which there was a general elite effort to try to beat back and control the crisis of democracy, to try to undermine the popular movements that had begun to develop. The use of Israel turned out to be one effective device. That again strengthened the natural association between the liberal intellectuals, who were the commissars who were supposed to carry this out, and Israel. For all these reasons, some of them quite objective, namely the role of Israel as an actual strategic asset for the United States, some of them more complex, having to do with American culture and internal society, the issues were simply driven off the agenda. Here the difference between the general population and the elites is very dramatic. Polls—and polls have to be regarded a bit cautiously, but they tell you something—have indicated regularly that about two-thirds of the population is in favor of a Palestinian state. That's just not part of American politics. You can't find an American politician who will call for it. It's not part of discussion and debate. What's striking is that even without virtually any articulate presentation, it's still the position held by a majority of the American public, conforming to the international consensus that's been blocked by the United States for at least 17 years.

One question about the American Left, and I know you're not terribly comfortable using that term: you've spoken about its marginalization, its lack of resources, lack of continuity. What about this phenomenon on the left of internecine warfare and what I call left-left-bashing? Is that a product of this marginalization?

It's partly that, and it's partly, to an extent that we don't like to recognize, that external power and privilege set the agenda for the Left. For example, take *New England Peacework*, which is a Quaker-based journal and a very good journal for the local peace movement. Right now it's devoting page after page to a debate which is essentially determined by the Office of Public Diplomacy and they don't recognize it. There's a debate going on every issue, with half the issue devoted to it, about whether the Left, so-called, took exactly the right position with regard to Cambodia in the late 1970s. The fact of the matter is that the Left, such as it is, barely existing, took approximately the position that was taken by virtually all competent authorities, State Department intelligence, Cambodia scholarship, etc., while at the same time the Left and the peace movement were avoiding major atrocities elsewhere. Nevertheless, there's no debate going about about, let's say, the failure to respond to East Timor, or the failure of the Left to respond to the U.S. bombing of Cambodia in the early 1970s, which probably killed tens if not hundreds of thousands of people, or the failure of the Left to respond to the growing and already quite horrifying crisis in Central America. There's no discussion about that. There's discussion about the alleged failure of the peace movement to respond to Pol Pot. In the course of that what you find on the one side is lies, fabrication and deceit requiring no evidence because they are the position of established power, which never requires any evidence, and on the other side, apologies or responses that are largely a waste of time.

In fact, any effort to respond to the lies is self-destructive because the response to the lies and exposure of the lies simply proves you're an apologist for atrocities, within the framework of official doctrine, which also controls dissident thought to a notable extent. It's a no-win situation, since the agenda is determined by established power. I give this example to illustrate that even the most sophisticated elements of the peace movement are trapped by the indoctrination system and to a large extent follow its dictates, and that is another factor that leads to recrimination. In addition to that, there are just all sorts of power plays, personal, group, etc. Everybody who's been involved in the popular movements for years knows perfectly well that one or another sect has got their technique for trying to take control of any popular development that takes place. They're parasitic on it, and try to bring people in and mobilize them and bring them into their own organization or their own particular cult or whatever. This is all going to go on, and as long as there are no stable and healthy popular institutions, you can anticipate that it will continue.

I remember you talking about the June 1982 peace demonstration in New York, where you were initially involved and then you chose not to participate.

That was a different story. It's true, I didn't participate in that. That was the demonstration that brought hundreds of thousands, maybe a million people to New York at the time of the UN disarmament sessions. This happened to have taken place about a week after the Israeli invasion of Lebanon. The Israeli invasion of Lebanon, apart from tearing the country up and destroying it, also happened, at that very point, to be bringing the world very close to global war. There were hot-line communications, Israel had attacked Syria. Syria had not expected that attack, even after the war began they thought Israel was going after Palestinians. Israel attacked Syria, which was a Soviet ally, Russians were killed, the Russian fleet was in the eastern Mediterranean, there was a real danger of global war, the United States was supporting the attack. You couldn't imagine a more urgent issue. The organizers of the demonstration decided to exclude it. That's part of the way in which the movements on the left protect Israel. They, as I saw it, thereby expressed their position that nuclear war is less important than protecting Israel from criticism. That was so outrageous that I personally decided not to even show up. That's a special thing, again, it's a case in which the agenda established by external power determines to a very large extent what is thought and what is done even in the dissident movements. This is a very different question on the nature of evil.

You're a scientist working with objective material. You've discussed U.S. atrocities in Indochina in the 1960s and 1970s and atrocities in Central America in the 1980s. For example, you've written about soldiers who throw babies up in the air and then bayonet them. The question arises: Many of these soldiers are fathers and brothers who have held babies in their arms; How could they be reduced to that? Also, as an addendum, you've said that individuals are not evil but that institutions are. Isn't that a cop-out?

First of all, I've very rarely talked about atrocities committed by soldiers. I've explained why. The reason is that soldiers, in a situation of conflict, are frightened. The options open to them are very few. They can be enraged. These are situations in which people can't use their normal human instincts. You can find a few sentences in which I've quoted things of this sort from human rights groups, but I don't harp on it and I almost never discuss it.

To take one case, I was asked by the *New York Review* to write an article about the My Lai incident when it broke, and I did write such an article. But I had about three sentences on My Lai in which I pointed out exactly these things—that the actions carried out by half-crazed GI's in the field don't tell you very much.

The much more serious question, I think, is how people who are subject to no threat, who are comfortable, educated and if they don't know what's going on it's because of a conscious decision not to know what's going on, how such people can, in the quiet of their living rooms, tolerate and support and back horrifying atrocities, and plan them in their well-appointed offices. That's the real evil, far worse than what's done by soldiers in the field. As to how soldiers can do it: apart from the conditions of combat, which are never very pretty and are in fact life-threatening, apart from that, you're talking about young kids, teenagers, who in fact are easily indoctrinated and can be turned into killers. Take this example you mentioned. It happened to be the Salvadoran army. This is an army which is press-ganged. It's not a drafted army. They're press-ganged from poor areas. You take kids from poor areas, give them guns, give them training, give them indoctrination, and you can turn them into professional killers. Imperial powers have been doing this for centuries, and we're doing it too.

As regards the question of evil, we don't have to think of exotic examples. We can look at ourselves and ask the question about ourselves. You ask, Is it a cop-out to say that it's **a matter of institutions, not individuals**? I don't think so. Individuals are certainly capable of evil. We don't have to look very far to see that. But individuals are capable of all sorts of things. Human nature has lots of ways of realizing itself. Humans have lots of capacities and options. Which ones reveal themselves depends to a large extent on the institutional structures. If we had institutions which permitted pathological killers free rein, they'd be running the place. The only way to survive would be to let those elements of your nature manifest themselves. If we have institutions which make greed the sole property of human beings and encourage pure greed at the expense of other human emotions and commitments, we're going to have a society based on greed, with all that follows. A different society might be organized in such a way that human feelings and emotions of other sorts (say, solidarity, support, sympathy) become dominant. Then you'll have different aspects of human nature and personality revealing themselves.

Who has inspired and influenced you intellectually?

There are too many people to mention. I could mention personal examples, but that would mean going back into personal history. The thing that inspires me most is exactly what inspired Rousseau, namely the sight of (I wish I could quote his words exactly) half-naked savages, and other ordinary people, fighting for their liberty and independence with courage and integrity. That's more inspiring than the writings of the sages.

Do you recognize or acknowledge the spiritual life, and is it a factor in who you are?

By the spiritual life, do you mean the life of thought and reflection and literature, or the life of religion? It's a different question.

The spiritual dimension in terms of religion. Is that at all a factor?

For me, it's not. I am a **child of the Enlightenment**. I think irrational belief is a dangerous phenomenon, and I try consciously to avoid irrational belief. On the other hand, I certainly recognize that it's a major phenomenon for people in general, and you can understand why it would be. It does, apparently, provide personal sustenance, but also bonds of association and solidarity and a means for expressing elements of one's personality that are often very valuable elements. To many people it does that. In my view, there's nothing wrong with that. My view could be wrong, of course, but my position is that we should not succumb to irrational belief.

Do you derive any strength from the Jewish tradition?

I'm obviously very much part of it. I grew up deeply immersed in it and still feel that, but whether it's a source of strength, I'd find it hard to say. I couldn't identify any way in which that's true.

Who are some people today that you admire and that you learn from?

There are too many such people. I can't say. Take my friend Rubén Zamora, for example, who is now, with tremendous courage, expressing his willingness to go back to the terror state that the United States has established in El Salvador (facing a high likelihood of assassination) and trying to exploit some political opening for his basically left-Christian Democrat commitment. I find that pretty inspiring. And I could think of numerous other examples. I know that's not the question you're asking, but I'm purposely evading it. I know there are people who have said smart things, which is fine. It's not hard to say smart things.

You're in great demand as a public speaker, you're booked into the 1990s. I traveled with you in Colorado and California during the last week of January 1988, and everywhere you went you drew appreciative and capacity audiences, standing ovations were de rigueur. What do you attribute that to?

As you know from having heard me speak, I'm not a particularly charismatic speaker, and if I had the capacity to do so I wouldn't use it. I'm really not interested in persuading people. I don't want to and I try to make this point obvious. What I'd like to do is **help people persuade themselves**. I tell them what I think, and obviously I hope they'll persuade themselves that that's true. But I'd rather have them persuade themselves of what they think is true. I think there are a lot of analytic perspectives, just straight information, that people are not presented with. The only thing I would like to be able to contribute is that. I think by and large audiences recognize that. I think the reason people come is because that's what they want to hear. There are many people around the country, all sorts of people, who feel that they simply do not have access to an awful lot of information, analysis, interpretation, that is relevant to understanding the world, and I think it's a very healthy reaction to try to gain such access.

I noticed a very different Noam Chomsky when you were speaking about linguistics and philosophy. You were much more relaxed, you were given to humor. Clearly when you were talking about political and social issues in the other talks it affects you.

You can't talk about the tremendous suffering that we're inflicting upon people without having a good deal of emotion, either under control or actually expressed. I try to keep it under control, but it's certainly there.

You have a singular position in the intellectual life of the country today. Whether you like it or not, it's there. You're a "life preserver" for many people, organizations, bookstores, and community radio stations. People depend upon you for information and analysis. You're a kind of intellectual "axis mundi." Is that a burden?

First of all, let me say that to the extent that that's true, it's not a particular comment about me. It's a comment about the intellectual class in general, which has simply abandoned this responsibility of honest inquiry and some degree of public service in favor of the pursuit of privilege and power and subordination to external power. To an overwhelming extent that's true. To put it as simple as possible, there just aren't enough speakers available. If a group around the country wants a speaker on such-and-such a topic, there are very few people they can turn to. The few people who do this are under incredible demands. That's a comment about the intellectual classes, including the Left, which does not provide this kind of service to ordinary people, or only to a very limited extent. Any group around the country who tries to get speakers is aware of this.

Is it a burden? It's both a burden and a kind of privilege. A burden in the sense that there are 24 hours in a day and only so many things you can do, so obviously it's a burden. But it's certainly one that I would choose and do choose.

In response to questions about your prodigious work productivity, you say you are a "fanatic"? Do you like that about yourself?

I neither like it nor dislike it. I recognize it. It does require a degree of fanaticism even to be able to break out of the constant drumbeat of ideology and indoctrination and to gain the relevant information and organize it. Even that limited commitment requires a degree of fanaticism, and to pursue it beyond that (the constant travel, speaking, etc.), sure, that's another form of fanaticism.

Where do you see yourself and your work?

In these areas, as far as I'm aware, I know what I'm trying to do. Others can judge how well it's done. What I'm trying to do is simply provide the kind of service to popular dissident movements and scattered individuals that any person who has the resources, the privilege, the training, etc. should perform. Nothing beyond that.

Editor's Notes to Interview 47

This is the fourth of the Reime interviews (see the Editor's Notes to I13). It was done by phone from Finland on March 16, 1988.

For more from the 1986 report of the U.S. Department of Commerce mentioned in this interview, see CT (1988), p. 54. For more on the Jackson campaign, see I50.

It is no wonder that Chomsky's analysis of the policies of the Reagan administration is directly applicable to the Bush II administration: most of the top decision makers are the same. The difference in degree, a not unimportant one, derives of course directly from the timely cover provided by the 9-11 monstrosity. This ascendancy and prevalence of what Chomsky calls here quasi-fascism should not be much of a surprise for those with some awareness of a trend recognized even by the mainstream, as this minimal sample shows:

> "From the 1960s to the present the Right has been striking for its expansion and differentiation ... The lines have been blurred between [the part of the Right that never accepted the New Deal] and what is now often called the Republican center ... Thus, ... President George Bush [I] and Senator Robert Dole are often term centrist ... Yet in substantive terms these figures are centrist mainly because the overall political spectrum has moved even further to the right. What was once called liberal or centrist Republicanism (Rockefeller) has dwindled and in some regions disappeared altogether." (David Plotke, Introduction to the third edition of *The Radical Right*, ed. by Daniel Bell, New Brunswick (U.S.A) and London (U.K.): Transaction Publishers, 2002 [originally published in 1955], pp. xxxv–xxxvi.)

Plotke places G. W. Bush with Reagan under far right "Reaganism," which he, in sharp contrast with Chomsky, characterizes as "a dynamic combination of antistatism and cultural conservatism" (p. xxxiv–xxxv).

47. A Historic Shift in American Politics (16 March 1988)

The Reagan period in the U.S. is now approaching its end, at least as far as Reagan himself is concerned. How would you assess this transition?

Well, we have to consider the domestic and the international front, because they are of course interrelated.

Quasi-fascism, International Terrorism and Military Keynesianism

Domestically, the Reagan administration came into office with several specific goals, which it largely achieved. One goal was to transfer resources from the poor to the rich. That was achieved by dismantling elements of the welfare system, by regressive fiscal measures and so on. And the effect is a considerable shift in the distribution of income, so wealth has shifted towards the wealthy and away from the poor, as was intended.

A second major component of the Reagan program was to vastly increase the power of the state in its ability to interfere in personal and economic life, and to protect it from the scrutiny of the citizens. It's called a conservative program. That's just a reflection of the corruption of our language. It's the exact opposite of a conservative program. In fact, if you want a technical term, it can be called quasi-fascism. The major change was a substantial increase of the role of the state in controlling the economy. The way that this was done is the traditional way: by building up the state-protected system for high-technology industry and organizing a massive public subsidy for advanced technology. That's done traditionally in the United States through the Pentagon system, and this meant the fastest peace-time growth of the military system in history. In fact, the ratio of state expenditures to the gross national product increased more rapidly under Reagan than, I think, at any time in peace-time American history.

Yet we have to bear in mind that, with all the talk about free trade, the United States has always been a highly protectionist country. The economy developed in the 19th century with protectionist measures, and the sectors of the economy that function and are more or less competitive are very highly protected. At the moment these are two major sectors: one is capital intensive agriculture, which is protected and subsidized substantially by the state, and the other is high-technology industry, which is provided with a guaranteed market for waste production by the state (that's the Pentagon system), and in fact is granted very substantial subsidy again through the Pentagon system.

This was associated with efforts to impose a heavier censorship, to prevent people from being able to obtain information about the state, and so on and so forth. In fact, one major component of this was simply to resort to clandestine, covert actions such as the kind that were partially exposed in the Iran-contra hearings. These actions are essentially directed against the domestic population. Everyone else in the world knows about them. These are a means for protecting the state from public scrutiny. The immediate and very substantial resort of the Reagan administration to clandestine measures is just another reflection of this highly anti-democratic, statist reactionary threat. So that's the second major component.

And the third major component of their policy was what usually goes along with these things, namely an increase in global intervention, what they call an activist foreign policy, just a fancy word for international terrorism. They constructed an extraordinary international terrorist network of really quite remarkable scale (nothing remotely comparable in history), and used it to initiate and organize terror and violence in Central America, in connection with Libya, in support of South Africa in its regional disruption, in the Middle East, and elsewhere, the most striking case being Central America. That's essentially the Reagan program, and it was largely carried out.

Now we get to the transition. The effects of it were, of course, devastating for the victims of the massive international terror. But domestically the Reagan economic management succeeded in administering an extremely severe blow to the American economy. These policies of military Keynesianism, which are traditional, happened to have been carried out in an extraordinarily stupid fashion. Keynesian methods leading to deficit spending, in other words, can be constructive—if the deficit, the borrowing, is used for productive investment either in infrastructure, in industry, or whatever—the effects can be beneficial. But here they were not. There were very little in the way of productive investments. What there was was a substantial increase in luxury consumption, which was one consequence of the transfer of resources to the wealthy. That was part of what made the enormous trade imbalance with imports of luxury goods. A second consequence was financial speculation and manipulation, which of course are completely unproductive, probably negative with regard to production. And the third was waste production, production of high-technology waste—the military system. So the net effect of all of this, which was completely predictable, and was, in fact, predicted eight years ego, was an enormous trade deficit and a huge budget deficit.

A Shameful Period

Just to give one measure: when the Reagan administration came into office, the United States was the largest creditor in the world. It had taken about 70 years to build up to this position. Its credits were approximately, I think, $150 billion with regard to the rest of the world. By 1985 the United States became a debtor nation; by 1986, the world's largest debtor. And time projections of the

Commerce Department are that by 1990 or so the debt may be on the order of $800 billion to $1 trillion. If something like that is true, it would mean, roughly, a transfer of a trillion dollars in a decade from the world's richest and most powerful country. There's nothing comparable to that in history. I mean, this is a form of destructive economic management at a level of stupidity and incompetence that has no parallel. And what it means is that the poor sectors of the population will be called upon to accept a degree of austerity in the coming years to try to pay off the costs of these policies. In fact, that's a part of what was intended. That's another way in which social policy of the Reaganites intended to compel the poor to subsidize the wealthy. So that's the net effect.

Internationally, what it has led to is lawlessness, violence, terror; hundreds of thousands of people slaughtered; possibilities of successful development, of some form of independent development, in Central America, gone; terror and warfare in South Africa, they've been continuing blocking of peaceful settlement in the Middle East, supporting Israeli aggression in Lebanon, supporting Pol Pot in Cambodia … I mean, it's just a shameful period.

How would you assess the leading contenders for the Republican and Democratic candidacies at the moment?

First of all, this is not to be taken too seriously. In the American political system, the question is which group of investors, which segment of the business community, do they represent? That's the basic question one should ask about any American election.

An Extreme of Lawlessness, Violence and Blind Greed

In the United States there's basically only one party, one political party, the business party, and it has various factions, and groups of investors coalesce behind one or another element of the business party—that's what we call an election. So, in this one, I suppose Bush, who may already have won the Republican nomination, is balked by groups that are not very different from the Reaganites except that they draw more, I suppose, from the eastern liberal Republicans. The group around Reagan was, within the American political spectrum, at an extreme of lawlessness, violence and blind greed. Bush, I suppose, will be less of that extreme. As a former CIA director, he also has roots in the intelligence and military communities and at the same kind of high-technology waste system that was also part of the Reagan balking. I'd expect, with the Bush presidency, a general continuation of the Reaganite policies but at a less extreme and violent level.

As far as the Democrats are concerned, it's hard to say. I mean, they tend to be somewhat more—mildly more—reformist, they can be more fiscally conservative. There's been a kind of historic shift. The Democrats used to be the party of Keynesian growth, and the Republicans were a party of fiscal conservatism. To a certain extent, that has shifted. For example, in the 1984 election Walter Mondale was supported by banks and others who were concerned with the trade deficit, the deterioration of the financial system and so on, and he called for fiscal conservatism, the traditional Republican policy. Reagan, the people about Reagan, the people who write his speeches for him, called for a Keynesian growth, you know, "bull times are ahead," the traditional democratic slogan. And there'll be something of that in the next election.

But crucially, I think, every candidate (whoever he is, whoever will be elected) is going to be compelled to live with certain realities. One of these realities is that the costs of the Reaganite program are going to have to be paid. And in fact you can already see that. The same people who eight years ago talked about the Evil Empire conquering the world have now discovered that the Russians aren't bad after all, and you can deal with them and you can have arms negotiations, and a statesman like Reagan can have summits with them and "international terrorism" isn't as bad as it was, and so on and so forth. The fact of the matter is that the outside world has not changed very much. What's changed is the domestic scene. It's no longer as possible to appeal to international terrorism and the Soviet threat in order to mobilize the population, to reach deep into their pockets to pay subsidies to waste production. You just can't do that under current circumstances. So now one suddenly recognizes that the statesmanlike thing is to enter into negotiations and to constrain or reorganize the arms race and so on. And they're going to have to figure out some way to impose the lowering of the standard of living, lowering the consumption level, increasing austerity and production so as to simply pay the costs of these Reaganite follies.

I suspect that means that the United States will not be able to throw its weight around quite so much in world affairs. During the Reagan years the United States was becoming extremely isolated. You can see this, for example, in the United Nations or in other international forums, in its refusal of a World Court decision, and so on. And I presume that any subsequent administration will try to overcome this. Even a country like the United States, as powerful as it is, cannot become simply a pariah state as the Reaganite people essentially were driving it to be.

What is the significance, in your view, of the Jackson campaign?

Well, there is no chance that Jackson can be nominated. But it's an interesting phenomenon. It does create the bare possibility of **a revival of some kind of populist politics**, which would appeal to sectors of the population that are essentially disenfranchised in the United States: the poor, the working people, you know, the less privileged, less educated in general, the large mass of the population in fact, who are pretty much excluded from American politics—after all, they don't even bother voting. Jesse Jackson does present a kind of an appeal to those groups. Now the problem is that those groups are torn by racist and ethnic hatred, and Jackson's program, if it were expressed by someone with a white face, would appeal to the ethnic working classes, but when it's proposed by Jackson, it probably won't be. So, in fact, yesterday in Illinois, which is really his constituency, I think, he got about 10 percent of the white vote. If the Jackson campaign leaves some organizational structure behind it, instead of just being an

American political campaign (meaning you shoot for power and then you go on and do something else), if it leaves a real organization behind, a real political structure, then in the long run it could be the first political party in the United States. But I don't think it's going to do that, to tell you the truth.

You have very often stressed that the extent of the right turn during the Reagan years has been exaggerated. So would you say that among the general population there has all the time been a relatively strong opposition against an interventionist foreign policy, against military spending, and so on?

Well, it's not just that the "right turn" has been exaggerated; it just didn't happen. I mean, it happened among elite groups, but among the general population the tendency was exactly in the other direction.

Polls show this very clearly. Throughout the Reagan years, with a few little blips here and there, there was essentially a continuation of the long, slow drift towards a New Deal-style welfare state, reformist capitalist programs of the European social-democratic type. That continued right through the Reagan years, except for a very brief period (a few months in 1980–81). Except for that period, the population was very strongly in favor of social over military spending, and it opposed military intervention. In fact, it opposed every component of the Reagan program.

But since the general public is largely irrelevant in a system of elite decision and public ratification, this had no effect on policy. So the Democrats and the Republicans cheerfully move to dismantle the welfare state, while the public was strongly opposed, by an overwhelming margin. Now they have to turn back towards public concerns, towards cutting back military spending, cutting back intervention. And the reason they do it is that these programs are simply no longer feasible in the situation that the Reaganites have left, severely weakening the domestic economy.

Editor's Notes to Interview 48

"All Things Considered," National Public Radio, March 30, 1988, pp. 5–7PM. In the first question, "Noam Chomsky's" in the first sentence and "his" in the fourth one were replaced by "Your," and the third sentence ("Professor Chomsky is a world renowned scholar of linguistics") was omitted; in the other questions, a couple of "widow words" were edited out. Also omitted were the two closing sentences: "Noam Chomsky's most recent book is about U.S. policy toward Central America and Iran, and about the Iran-Contra affair. It's called *The Culture of Terrorism.*" See Editor's Notes to I20.

The expression *Hizbollah* or *Hezbollah* ("Hizb Allah"), the name of a well-known Shiite Muslim movement, means 'party of God'. The Scud missiles are made in the Soviet Union.

This was the first (and so far the only) time that Chomsky was interviewed on current issues by NPR (see interview 43). An earlier interview, scheduled for Thursday, March 24, 1988, was pulled off the air ("something that rarely, if ever, happens," according to an informed source) after it was announced at the top of the program under the headline "Chomsky on Noriega, Panama, and the U.S." as something that was coming up. When questioned about it, the executive producer of "All Things Considered" replied that Chomsky has "a very provocative thesis" (the United States supports terrorism) "and our interviewer did not challenge him."

But if not as a student of domestic and foreign policy, Chomsky was actually first interviewed by NPR, at his home in Lexington, Mass, in June 1979, for a program ("Noam Chomsky: A Portrait in Sound," narrated by Robert Prosky) presumably broadcast in December 1980 (a transcript of the broadcast in Chomsky's files is dated Dec. 15, 1980). This program was part of the series "A Question of Place: Sound Portraits of 20th-century Humanists" (technical director: John Whitoff; principal consultant: Jonathan Culler of Cornell University; producer: Mary Lou Finnegan), which, I am told, included also Freud, Russell, Joyce, Brecht, Foucault, and others. Parts of Chomsky's answers of June 1979 and parts of those he gave on May 10, 1972, when he testified before the Senate Foreign Relations Committee, were interlaced with those of other "interlocutors": Narrator (who uses quotes from Chomsky's writings on language and other materials), Speaker, Teacher, Child, Bernstein (from his 1973 Charles Elliot Norton lectures at Harvard University), and Senator Javits. Here is a sample (see last chapter of **AWA**, 1970):

"CHOMSKY: This is a case where the system really failed. I mean, clearly the Justice Department will protect the inheritors of policies rather than try to prosecute possible criminal acts that were conducted by them. Here I think another forum is needed— a forum to investigate, for example, the question whether the American intervention in Vietnam, at least since 1960, certainly since 1965, and particularly now, is not, strictly speaking, criminal.

JAVITS: Professor Chomsky, I don't want to take your wonderful mind off our alternatives, but if you'll allow me to just add something to what you've said about the Pentagon Papers. *Isn't it a fact, in sustaining our system, that the Department of Justice is not the last word? Sure, you can indict, you can sue, but so long as there are courts who will redress it, you can't say the system has broken down and failed.*

CHOMSKY: No, I'm sorry, I would say the system has broken down and failed at this point, and I don't really see the remedy. The system has broken down because of the selective prosecution. You see, the government may lose the case, as it failed in its efforts at prior restraint of the Times, but it is not prosecuting or even investigating, let alone indicting, those who may very well be guilty of the crimes revealed in the Pentagon Papers. *Now that's ...*

JAVITS: There's going to be an election this fall, and if the people want another attorney general and another approach, they'll have the opportunity to do that.

CHOMSKY: That is not the way that crimes are supposed to be treated.

NARRATOR: Noam Chomsky, the world's most eminent professor of linguistics; Chomsky, the political activist. What's the connection between these two roles?"

At this point, Chomsky gives yet another answer, perhaps one of the best ones, to the (often asked) question of the narrator—to be added to all the others he has given, including about ten in this collection of interviews, not surprisingly given its title.

48. The Only State Officially Committed to Terrorism
(30 March 1988)

Your newest book is called The Culture of Terrorism. *The title doesn't refer to Palestinian groups or the KGB. It refers to U.S. foreign policy, to the Contras, and to the Israeli defense forces ... Your political critique of the U.S. role in the world is a radical one in which U.S. intervention abroad is described as state terrorism.*

There are many terrorist states in the world but, as far as I'm aware, the United States is the only one that's officially committed to terrorism as we define it. So, for example, if you take the State Department definition of terrorism and you compare it with the doctrine of what's called "low intensity conflict," as outlined in Pentagon studies, you discover that the definitions are virtually identical. In fact, the commitment goes to fine detail. The State Department has explicitly authorized attacks on agricultural collectives as legitimate by the U.S.-sponsored proxy forces. That's exactly as if someone, say Libya, endorsed attacks against Israeli *kibbutzim* by Abu Nidal. And, in fact, in scale of international terrorism, as the term is defined by the State Department or U.S. law, the United States is certainly one of the leaders—arguably the leader—in international terrorism.

Might one not argue that what you're referring to is an American mania for saying and putting in print what others might do without bothering to ever rationalize?

Yes, that's possible. As I said, the United States is, to my knowledge, the only country that officially endorses terrorism. There are other terrorist states. Iran is certainly a terrorist state, although, as far as I know, they don't have an official endorsement of it. And if we ask ourselves what is the most extreme involvement of Iran in international terrorism, as far as I'm aware the most extreme involvement of Iran would be the fact that they helped supply the Contras, which is a major international terrorist force, and their international terrorism, to my knowledge, exceeds anything remotely attributable to Iran. So we could then say, if we were to be honest with ourselves, that the real scandal of the Iran/Contra hearings was that Iran was found dealing with Washington—terrorist commanders in Washington—its major terrorist act.

But some people listening would say "now you're playing games with words," and that actually Iranian sponsorship of Hizbollah in southern Lebanon, and the kidnapping of people who were probably doing nothing more than either trying to report or even working at American University in Beirut, that indeed that was a more conscious act of terrorism on the part of Iran.

It was certainly more conscious than their support for the Contras, which, as far as we know, was unconscious. Our support for the Contras was, of course, extremely conscious, and, as I say, it's Iran's unwitting involvement in our major terrorist actions that is arguably their most extreme such involvement. Of course the support for *Hizbollah*, the kidnappings and so on, those are real terrorist acts which should be punished, but we're not talking about scale.

Let me take some examples now of possible intervention or state terrorism, however you want to call it, and ask about whether you can see exceptions being made. A few years ago the Israelis knocked out an Iraqi nuclear reactor. Over the past couple of weeks when the Iraqis have attacked Teheran with modified Scud missiles, and when they've been accused, it seems fairly convincingly, of dropping poison gas on a Kurdish town inside Iraq and possibly killing thousands, have you had any second thoughts that perhaps knocking out that power plant is a case of justified, but plainly lawless, international, as you would say, state terrorism?

Well, if we believe that preventing proliferation by bombing nuclear power plants is legitimate, then we should at once bomb the Dimona power plant in Israel, which is apparently being used to produce probably hundreds of nuclear weapons, possibly even hydrogen bombs. As far as the Iraqi use of chemical warfare, most recently against Iraqi cities (Kurdish towns), that is, of course, a major crime. Use of chemical warfare is a major crime. But if we believe that that kind of crime requires punishment, then we should also be consistent. For example, we might bear in mind that, at a much lower level to be sure, Israel is in effect using chemical warfare with our support right now. They're using very powerful tear gas provided by the United States, with canisters dated as recently as February, which are clearly marked as "not to be used in closed areas." They're being used in closed areas—tossed into houses and refugee camps—where the people are left in there with a substantial number of abortions, infant deaths, and so on.

But if I could somehow make you accept the hypothetical case, that is, that by now a modified Soviet short, intermediate-range missile would have delivered a nuclear weapon at Teheran, that the Iraqis would have done this by now had they not been deprived by force of their reactor plant, would you still say that taking out that plant was utterly unjustified and wrong?

I would, and so would anyone who believes that the United States should not bomb Dimona, because it's quite possible that in the next war (as the Israel command regularly calls it), especially if they're under duress, they might—as they say, they will—resort to any weapon, and that could include the nuclear weapons that they have. Now I don't believe that the United States should bomb Dimona, but we have to find other means, not violent means and not aggression, to prevent proliferation.

Editor's Notes to Interview 49

"Interview: Noam Chomsky," by Burton Levine, *Shmate: A Journal of Progressive Jewish Thought* 20 (Summer 1988), pp. 24–32. In his preliminary note, Levine writes:

> "For exposing the unspeakable secrets of the American foreign policy elite, Chomsky has been a constant target of attacks. Although he has criticized the Soviet invasion of Afghanistan, he is called a Soviet apologist. Like Freud before him, Chomsky upsets nice people because, in his devotion to a rational search for the truth, he does not stop at the boundaries of social propriety. The genius of both is to follow their thoughts beyond the point where the internal censors in most of us say 'Don't think this. This is not a nice thought.'
> I spoke with Chomsky in early May in his office at MIT. Although his work in linguistics, his academic specialty, is recognized throughout the world as having permanently changed the field, he carries his authority lightly. He has the manners of the egalitarian anarchists he admires. His soft, gentle voice is in sometimes jarring contrast to his tough, pointed phrases."

The comparison with Freud, even in this narrow sense (for a broader one, see the Introduction), may still be less helpful than it might appear, particularly for those familiar with Jeffrey Moussaieff Masson's book (*The Assault on Truth: Freud's Suppression of the Seduction Theory*. With a new preface. Penguin Books, 1985.)

This interview (see also I41, including the Editor's Notes, and I36, again including the Editor's Notes, where Meir Peled is first mentioned) should perhaps be read as a companion piece to Chomsky's "Scenes from the Uprising," completed a month later and published in *Z* magazine 1:7–8 (July 1988), pp. 9–20; for background, see **FT** (1983, 1999)—on Dov Yirmiah, for example, pp. 237ff. Both the interview and the article bring out a little-known aspect of Chomsky's activism, already reflected in **AWA** (1970). (Contributions can be sent to Friends of YESH GVUL [resisters], 1636 Martin Luther King Rd., #G, Berkeley CA 94709, and DOWN WITH THE OCCUPATION [Dai l'kibbush], PO Box 3742, Jerusalem, Israel.)

From more on Thomas Friedman, see I31.

Simha Flapan's "interesting book" is *The Birth of Israel: Myths and Realities* (Pantheon, 1987), recently reviewed by Norman Finkelstein (see I30).

The denunciation of the "real double standard" at the end of the interview brings to mind a letter, expressing "general agreement" with Chomsky, from a reader (Richard Hoffman) of Kathleen Hendrix's article-interview: "Noam Chomsky Is A Voice Crying in the Wilderness, But Nobody Listens" (*Los Angeles Times*, March 2 1988, V). See the Introduction.

The Appendix is from the Indianapolis weekly the *Jewish Post and Opinion* 47:25 (March 6, 1981), upper half of front page, where it appeared under the title "Reagan's Election Devastating Setback for Poor: Chomsky Sees Pressure for Israel Harmful." The interview was conducted by Jo-Ann Pinkowitz, perhaps with the epigraph of the weekly in mind: "If you let the people know, they can act intelligently." The words "for speech imposition" were replaced by "[from teaching]" to restore what seems to be the basic sense of the sentence.

49. A Candid View of Israel and the Occupied Territories
(Early May 1988)

You just returned from the Middle East?

From Israel and the occupied territories.

Are we getting an accurate account of events in the American press. How, for instance, does the New York Times *compare with* Ha'aretz?

It has typically been the case that you get much better coverage in the Hebrew press in Israel. That's is no longer true. *Ha'aretz* is one of the worst. *Ha'aretz* has caved in completely. It does not give honest reporting. It has a tremendous amount of self-censorship. There are other journals like *Hadashot* that are much more honest. I do not know exactly what happened internally in *Ha'aretz*. I don't want to say that there is nothing good in *Ha'aretz*, but the general character of its reporting has deteriorated radically during the uprising. I read the Hebrew press pretty carefully and for the first time in my experience the coverage in the American press has been as good, if not better. Israeli television has been particularly bad. They are even complaining about it there because of the censorship, self censorship and denial. What's remarkable about Israel is how much they are able to avoid attention to what's going on.

Neither the American press nor the Israeli press adequately cover the background. It is covered better in the Hebrew press. So, for example, in *Ha'aretz* they did report in mid-April that Arafat once again called for a partition. He said that we have to accept the basic concept of partition, and by that he did not mean the lines of the UN recommendation but, rather, the current lines. That would never be reported in the United States. The *New York Times* has a principle of never reporting conciliatory statements from Arab sources. They usually don't even print any letters referring to it. Interestingly, they broke that rule just a few weeks ago with a letter by Norman Finkelstein reviewing some of the documentary evidence they have been suppressing for years, and I mean suppressing. I don't mean failing to report. They won't permit letters to appear referring to it. There are even letters by the *New York Times'* editors saying they will not permit the material to appear.

Is there a reason why American reporting has improved? Does it reflect a change in attitudes either among the American public or elite?

I think it's a mixture. For one thing there are couple of good reporters there. I was very pleased to see that the *New York Times* withdrew Thomas Friedman. That made it possible for some good reporting. They sent John Kifner, who is a very good professional journalist. When they send John Kifner somewhere it's because they want the story to come out, not because they want it to be covered up. Friedman's job is to cover it up. Similarly, in the *Post* there was good reporting. The *Boston Globe* had, perhaps, the best reporting of all.

In part there is, I expect, a reaction to the way journalists themselves are being treated. The foreign press corps in Israel has already reported somewhere between 100 and 150 attacks on journalists, some including physical violence. In the West Bank whenever I was stopped by soldiers, the first question was, Are you a journalist? That's what they are really worried about. They want the journalists out of there.

On the other hand the newspapers continue to suppress the background. The background facts are that for years the Arab states and the PLO have been calling for a political settlement, and for years Israel, both political parties in the United States, and the American media have been opposing them. And that truth is still inexpressible.

I expect Jewish leaders will also complain that the American media are not giving the background. Well, that is true, but the background is the opposite of what they believe it to be. There still continues to be an extraordinary double standard in favor of Israel in that regard.

Is there protest in Israel against the current policies?

One good thing that has happened in Israel is that for the first time, **a significant, authentic peace movement** has developed. I don't mean **Peace Now**, which is largely there in order to convince American liberals that they should continue to support Israel. In part this is around Yesh Gvul, which has been around for a couple of years. But there are a couple of new groups: Dy L'Kvush, Shomrei Esrim v'Echad, Kav Adom. I don't know what appeal they have in the population. Polls would indicate maybe 10 percent or 15 percent. I went on a demonstration with some of them, down to Dhahrieh, a prison camp, one of the worst by reputation. The demonstration had not a lot, maybe 70 or 80, people. Of course that's a long trek. It's way down in the Negev.

Does the Peace Movement grow out of an older tradition?

Partly. Yesh Gvul has been around since 1982. A lot of the people have been involved in things for years. For example, one of the activists of Kav Adom is Dov Yirmiah, who is an old activist. In fact he was thrown out of the army in 1982. He goes way back in Haganah. He was the oldest soldier in the Israeli army during the 1982 war. He volunteered for the war and was put in charge of dealing with the civilian population, but was so appalled by the sadistic treatment of the civilian population in Lebanon, that he wrote an article in the Hebrew press denouncing it. I don't remember the exact timing. He was then removed from his military position. He then published a war diary in Hebrew violating censorship. The book was actually translated into English, but I don't think anybody ever heard of it or referred to it. It's a definite no-no in the United States. For several years he has been active. He went to Dheisheh refugee camp a couple of years ago and wrote a very bitter article about treatment of people there. He is a guy with a long record, going back many years, of honest committed dissidence. But I met with a number of activists in Tel Aviv from Dy L'Kvush, Shomrei Esrim v'Echad, End the Occupation and Yesh Gvul. They were mostly young, very committed and very serious. There are some who are older—Peretz Kidron, who reports here for National Public Radio. But most of them are younger people, some of them were students of mine.

What do they want?

They are calling for an end to the occupation, a real end to the occupation. They don't have any far-reaching positions. I pressed them on that for a long time. Each group has its own political position but, as organizations, they are basically concerned with an end to the occupation. They have a kind of New Leftish flair to them. They are concerned with taking actions to show regularly and constantly that they are not accepting the occupation policies. They want it to become a part of Israeli culture to recognize that ending the occupation is an option.

Now that is extremely important in Israel, because there has been no political group in Israel, including Peace Now, that has called for an end to the occupation. There's a lot of deceit about that in the U.S. Here in the U.S. Shimon Peres and others are called doves and the claim is that they differ materially from the Likud in calling for an end to the occupation. That's absolutely not true. They just have a different tactical approach. Yitzhak Rabin just had an interview in England a few days ago. He said that the Labor proposal is that they will keep the Gaza Strip and 40 percent of the West Bank, meaning that is what they want on the West Bank. That's been their position since the 1960s. That's in many ways worse than the Likud position as far as the Arabs are concerned.

As far as Peace Now goes, I met with their activists while I was there, and I read their literature. They refuse to take a position. They are extremely evasive. They say things vaguely like "Palestinians have rights." But I have been pressing them for years to show me something on paper where they have taken a position that begins to approach the **PLO** and their proposal for a political settlement. They have never come out with anything like the degree of commitment to a diplomatic settlement and mutual recognition that the PLO mainstream has. In fact the PLO is more of a peace movement than Peace Now. Peace Now condemns the PLO and rightly, I think, for its evasiveness. They say something, and then they retract it. But Peace Now does much worse. Their statements are much more evasive.

Even the new peace groups do not come out with very clear political statements. Part of the reason is that in Israel the idea of a political settlement is so remote from consciousness that, if a group does come out with it, they think they will lose political credibility.

They are not exactly popular now. How much credibility can they lose?

I agree with you. We had discussions on that and we disagreed. My feeling is that they should come out with a clear, forthright political statement. At times they do. In Peace Now you never find it. Peace Now is a very establishment group. They say in private that they see their role as ensuring that American liberals and liberals in the American Jewish community don't give up on Israel. I consider them very damaging. They are very harmful for the cause of peace. I have told them that many times.

How are they harmful?

I don't know what their impact is in Israel. But in the United States people like Amos Oz come here presenting himself as the beautiful Israeli—a *kibbutznik*, good-looking, honest and an honest toiler. Then he deplores all the bad things that are happening. But the bottom line is: If only there was an Arab as beautiful as me, then everything would be all right; unfortunately, we are the only beautiful ones; they are all monsters, terrorists and gangsters, so what can you do? There is a phrase in Hebrew, "yorim v'vochim," you cry and you shoot. If you are a beautiful Israeli, you cry when you shoot. If you are not a beautiful Israeli, you just shoot. Now that's extremely deceitful. It is essentially a way of ensuring that the confrontation continues and that the occupation continues. The truth of the matter is that Amos Oz is no more an advocate for peace than the mainstream of the PLO, maybe less so.

There is a whole cult in Israel of deception of the West. There are people who specialize in it. Abba Eban has made an entire career out of presenting undemocratic, harsh, and often rather brutal policies in a framework in which they appear to be peace-loving and democratic. You have to read his work carefully to see what he is really saying. He is widely regarded as a dove. He signs Peace Now statements. On the other hand, if you look at what he actually says, it's straight Labor Party rejectionism. His position is that Israel should give up the heavily occupied population centers in the West Bank, but take everything it wants on the West Bank. It should take all of the resources, the land that it needs, water, the Jordan valley. And it should just leave the population stateless in little Bantustans in which they can continue to be a cheap labor force for the Israeli government. Now it's only when you get to the small print that you see that that's what he is saying. But he has learned over the years to put those things in a way that makes it seem that it's the beautiful Israeli speaking.

There are people in Israel whom I almost believe have been invented by the hasbarah system, the propaganda system, for the purpose of talking to American journalists. No article by a serious reporter in an American journal is complete if it does not quote the "philosopher" David Hartman. Now as far as I know the "philosopher" David Hartman is some marginal character who runs a weird religious school on private money and has never had an idea in his head. But he is there in order for Thomas Friedman to quote the "philosopher" David Hartman, saying some statements of mock profundity, which make it clear that there is a beautiful Israel. If he has any other role in the world, I don't know what it is.

Israel is an embattled country. They rely very heavily on U.S. support. So they have developed a very sophisticated system of propaganda. They don't call it propaganda. They call it hasbarah. It is the only country I know of in the world that refers to **propaganda as explanation**. The Ministry of Propaganda is the Ministry of Explanation. The idea being that our position on everything is so obviously correct that if we only explain it to people, they will see that it is right. And they do it well. People like Abba Eban, Amos Oz, David Hartman and others know how to do the job. American reporters, either out of naivete or, in the case of Thomas Friedman, just cynicism, play the game for them.

Thomas Friedman, I should say, has by now revealed himself, in the Israeli press, as the astonishing racist and megalomaniac that he is.

Which is why he won the Pulitzer prize?

He won two Pulitzer prizes. He won for balanced and informed coverage. You may have noticed that it was announced on April Fools' Day, which was not by accident. For years the guy has been covering up for Israel, falsifying facts. When the Israeli press comes out with headlines saying "Arafat Calls for Negotiations, Peres Refuses," as they did in December of 1986, Tom Friedman will choose that occasion to write one of his many articles saying that Peace Now is losing credibility because there is no counterpart in the Arab World. Now he has left the *New York Times* and, while I was in Israel, he had a couple of long interviews in the Hebrew press, which are very revealing. First of all, they are revealing about his megalomania. The headline of one was "The Man Who Predicted the Uprising," and then it goes on with his self-adulation for having been the one reporter who predicted the uprising. Well you read his columns and you won't find a hint that the uprising was coming.

I don't remember anything.

Nothing. But now he is the man who predicted the uprising. Then he goes on to say that he is the only journalist who really understands anything, because he is a really deep thinker. It's all nonsense. But what's particularly interesting is that they asked him in one interview, Now that you are leaving after four years, what is your recommendation about the West Bank? And he says, You should treat the West Bank like southern Lebanon—meaning put it under the control of a terrorist mercenary army, set up torture chambers if you need them and so forth. That is his recommendation. He knows what southern Lebanon is. And then he says, Don't ask for too much; if Achmed gets his seat in the bus, he will lower his demands. Well, you know you can imagine a racist Southern sheriff 30 years ago saying, If you give Sambo a seat in the bus, maybe he will shut up. I don't think anybody in the United States would say that today. But Thomas Friedman says it without batting an eyelash and, in fact, Israel is so **racist** that nobody even notices it. That's Thomas Friedman, the great journalist.

And that kind of statement is not criticized in Israel?

Well I talked about it with friends of mine. But as far as I know, nobody even noticed it. The country is extremely racist. You sort of know it from reading. But when you see it, it's pretty traumatic. What's happening there is absolutely standard historically in systems of colonial oppression. The oppressors, whether they are slave owners or foreign military occupiers or elites, in order to defend themselves psychologically from understanding what they're doing, have to become racists. They have to assume that these are not real people. Because if you regard them as people, you cannot accept what you are doing. One consequence of oppression is racism. It depends on what the nature of the conflict is. It can be color of skin, or religion, or something else. One or another form of **racism**, in the generic sense, is an automatic consequence of **oppressive** relationships. I am sure you find it in bureaucrats dealing with slums. But the consequence of racism is **ignorance**. Since these people are just donkeys, they're not real people; you don't have to pay attention to what they are doing or thinking. Then you don't know what's going on. And the result of that is that there will be an uprising and you won't understand it. And you have to react with more violence, because that is the only thing you understand.

This is a typical phenomenon. It has been going on for years. And it is also typical of many other situations. Take a recent case, the United States in Honduras. The United States must have Honduras penetrated with every CIA agent imaginable. But they did not know that there was so much hatred of America that the Hondurans were going to burn up the American Embassy, while the Honduran army sat by applauding. They are all shocked in the intelligence apparatus. Part of the reason is either they don't read the newspapers, where it was perfectly obvious, or they don't notice because, after all, these are just "spics." Who cares what they say? We give them some money, so they shut up.

This happens over and over again. In fact in Israel it is the third time it has happened with a major event. In the early 1970s, when Israel was in a really triumphalist mood, the generals were talking about conquering everything from Baghdad to Khartoum in a week or a month. During this period, when Sadat's army mobilized in the Sinai, they didn't pay any attention. How can these "gooks" do anything to us? In fact military intelligence was saying things like "War is not the Arabs' game." Well, they paid for that attitude. They were practically destroyed. It was a very big psychological blow to Israel when it happened. The second major time it happened was in 1982 and '83 when they went into Lebanon. They had big plans. First of all, they were going to kick the Syrians out. Well, it turned out that they couldn't. Although they won the technological war with the Syrians, the war on the ground they did not win. They did not displace the Syrians from fixed defensive positions, and there is plenty of internal critique in the Israeli technical military press. Unfortunately, the Arabs know which end of the gun to hold and that is dangerous.

They were going to conquer Lebanon and put their puppet in charge, take the waters of the Litani River probably, and everything was going to be beautiful. The only trouble is that they were kicked out of Lebanon, driven out by the Lebanese resistance. And that was another shock. Well, they sort of accounted for that on the assumption that we are just civilized and won't accept the level of casualties and they are a bunch of Shiite crazies who think they are going to heaven and we cannot deal with them like a civilized people. But on the West Bank, we can control everything. They are just peasants and businessmen and not serious.

Well, now comes another explosion. Each time they are suffering the consequences of the racism that results from their oppressiveness, and it will continue. It will continue until there is a political settlement. One of the remarkable things about this current uprising is how nonviolent it is. The Arabs have not responded with lethal force. And that's astonishing.

Is that a disappointment to the Israelis?

I think so.

Were the expulsions from the West Bank and the assassination in Tunisia an attempt to goad the Palestinians into violence?

I would assume so. They would much rather have real violent resistance. You could see it when the girl, Tirza Porat, was killed in Beita. The country went insane. They were ready to kill every Arab. You know the army was upset about that, because they knew right away that she had been killed by a Jewish settler. They were worried about the settlers' reaction. They don't want to have to control a gang of lunatics inside their own country. They tried to calm it down. But you could see what was happening inside the country—mass hysteria.

The response to the attack actually illustrates the extraordinary racism in the society. Here was a case which was a clear provocation by settlers. They came into a closed military area and village lands. A madman, who was technically not allowed to carry a gun, killed an Arab in the fields. They were then brought into the village. Another Arab was killed. The mother of one of the Arabs who was killed threw a stone at this lunatic, who then started firing around wildly, killing a Jewish girl. The net effect of all this is 30 houses either totally demolished or virtually destroyed. I was there with a few Arab lawyers. I got in through back roads and climbed over hills avoiding military curfew. They really wrecked the place pretty badly. They say 14 houses destroyed, but that's a joke. You have to look at the houses 50 feet away which are half smashed. So about 30 houses either destroyed or unlivable, which is serious business. This means old people cooking in the rain in the rubble. It's not pretty. Six people deported. The police just announced two days ago in Israel that they are planning to carry out criminal prosecutions against the mother of the murdered Arab man who threw the stones. They are going to charge her with complicity in the murder of the Jewish girl.

Meanwhile what about any punishment for the settlers? Has anybody blown up houses in Eilon Moreh?, the head of the military command was asked by the *New York Times*. He said, No, there would be no punishment of this Roman Aldubi, the guy who did all of the killing, because the tragic incidents were already penalty enough. The Arabs, in contrast to the Jews, you have to smash in the face. Nobody reacts to this. The only reaction even in the liberal Israeli press is, well, they overdid it because they blew up the houses of some people who may not have been involved in the confrontation.

One way in which the peace groups in Israel could respond is just go to Beita and rebuild the damn houses. Why wait? In fact, while I was in Beita, we asked, How would you feel if Israelis came to rebuild? These are peasants, very stolid, very quiet, very dispassionate. It is amazing when you see peasants throughout the world. They just assume that the world is a place of violence and terrorism, that the guys on the outside are going to smash them in the face; that's their role.

They thought about it. They talked about it and they said it would have to be a political decision. Their conclusion was that if the Jews came out of real sense of political solidarity, because they want to help them, they would be happy to work with them to rebuild the village. But if they were just coming to make Israel look good or to salve their conscience, then they don't want them.

That's pretty sophisticated reaction.

I thought it was a very sophisticated reaction. In fact, I must say I was extremely impressed by the people on the ground, whether it was in villages under curfew or refugee camps under curfew—those we could get into—or towns that had just been swept through by the army or the hospitals in the old city of Nablus. The people are just **extremely dedicated and determined**. There is even a sense of exaltation, as if they had stars in their eyes, but in a quiet way.

I was at the hospital in Ramallah right after the demonstrations, with people smashed up. There were no doctors, because the doctors all flee after the demonstrations. They are afraid they are going to be picked up. There were a few nurses. We talked to a 13-year-old kid with a bullet wound in his leg. According to his story, he was just running away from a demonstration and he was shot. Anyway, the Arab friend of ours, who was taking us around, asked him at the end, How do you feel about it all? And you could see his face light up and he said, My spirit is higher than the wind. Or a guy lying in a bed with tubes coming out of him, paralyzed from the waist down, who describes how he got his bullet wounds, but then he ends up saying, If this is what you have to do for a homeland, then we are going to pay the price.

Others have seen this too. The Israeli reporter, Joel Greenberg, who writes for the *Jerusalem Post*—he is quite good, incidentally—went into Kabatiya. It is a town that was under, well, it was a concentration camp for about 40 days. No one was allowed in or out. Water was cut off. Electricity was cut off. Telephones were cut off. Everything. He said when they finally went in there, he found the people were exhilarated. They said if they had to go back to eating grass they would. And that's the same sense I got.

The moods in Israel and in the occupied territories were quite different. In Israel most people probably do not know what is happening, they know about as much as we do. But the more thoughtful people have a sense of foreboding. They are asking, Are we going to be here in 20 years? Whereas, on the other side, where people are getting smashed up, beaten and tortured, put in prison, deported, they feel that they are going to win. It's very dramatic when you see it.

What is their relationship to the PLO? Some reports here, even in the New York Times, give the impression that they are unhappy with the PLO. Some say their devotion to the PLO is partly lip service.

Well, it is more than lip service. It is partly true, but not quite. I pressed this very hard. I had good Arab contacts, so I was able to meet people in the old village of Nablus, who were among the local organizers of the popular committees. These are not particularly educated people. One is a taxi driver. Another is a municipal clerk. They are very sensible people. No rhetoric. It is not like talking to the PLO. I have talked to top PLO people, who are full of revolutionary rhetoric. There is none of that stuff. These are very down-to-earth people, very serious about what they hope and plan to do. I asked them what they thought about the PLO. They give the same kind of responses that I would give and do give, and that irritated the Arab intellectuals when I said it to them in East Jerusalem. They spoke about the corruption, the incompetence, the failure to send money and the crazy things, like playing for the international press gallery with ships, and living in five star hotels. They had no illusions about the PLO.

But they have their own organizational structure. At the level of this unified leadership, the party structures emerge. So you get the Communist Party, which is much more influential in my opinion than people make it out to be; it is illegal of course. Also the Popular Front, Fatah (which is the largest group), and the Democratic Front. In the Gaza Strip, but not so much on the West Bank, there is Islamic Jihad. That is the grouping at the level of leadership. The leadership send directives, but the directives are rather vague, like they will say, today should be subsistence day. That was the day I happened to be in Nablus, and people were clearing fields of rocks and planting subsistence crops. They were supposed to carry out the vague directive themselves.

On the other hand, if you ask questions about politics and what they want, they will say, well, independence of the West Bank and Gaza, but if you want to talk about that go to the PLO. So with all the reservations about the PLO and their lack of illusion about it, they still see the PLO as the symbol of Palestinian nationality. I asked them, Why go to the PLO, if they are so incompetent? They said, Look, it's a national problem and that is our national leadership. If you want to talk about settlements, go talk with them. Again I think it is a sophisticated, realistic reaction. It is a realistic assessment of the facts and a plausible response to them.

It sounds a little like labor union members who support leaders who they know are corrupt.

Exactly. Those guys are crooks, but that's what we are stuck with. We would like a different world, but this is the world. If you want to bargain, go bargain with them. But it's worse here because they recognize it as a general national problem. My own guess, frankly, is that if Israel ever does agree to a political settlement, there could be a very sharp conflict between the local people on the ground and the PLO bureaucrats and mucky-mucks from outside.

What about the Palestinian intellectuals we hear so much about, people like Hanna Siniora and Mubarak Awad?

I asked about them. They are the people the press and Peace Now go to. The people I talked to were contemptuous of them. That includes Mubarak Awad, who does not have any relation to what is going on, who is just splitting things. One of them said about Siniora that he is the one the PLO sends to try to undercut local leadership. These are the people the Israelis go to to find out what is going on. I don't think they know what's going on. Now some of these people they do have respect for—for example, Feisal Husseini, a Fatah person who has been in administrative detention off and on and is now back in again. Him, I noted, they respected.

The section of your book The Fateful Triangle *that really struck me was on the secret agreement between King Abdullah and Ben Gurion to partition the Palestinian lands between them.*

More material has come out on that since. Simha Flapan's interesting book has more on it. Nobody yet has a document which says it. But the evidence is accumulating pretty strongly. And Flapan has more evidence. The evidence is circumstantial, but pretty strong. If you look at the actual military history you will see that both sides essentially kept to the positions in the bargain. At the end of the war Israel sent all of its forces down to the south to surround the Egyptian forces in the one place where the Egyptian army reached to Israeli territory. Israel had a very narrow waist. The Arab Legion was the only serious military force, but they did not do a thing in reaction. They could have cut Israel in half and saved the Egyptian army. In fact, they never moved into Israeli controlled territory. People say they went into Jerusalem, and that's true, but Jerusalem was to be international territory.

On the Israeli side, Yigal Allon, who was commanding the southern front, knew that they had the force to conquer the West Bank. But apparently Ben Gurion held him back. The only plausible reason is that they had an arrangement.

Flapan takes a much stronger position. He claims that the Arab armies intervened on May 15 primarily to frustrate Abdullah. In his new book he gives more evidence. It is a very strong possibility that Flapan is right. Remember, Egypt was under British occupation. Their main problem was England. Abdullah was just a British stooge. If Abdullah conquered, say, the Negev, that would have been just a big British base in the Middle East. That was the last thing the Egyptians wanted. They were trying to expel Britain. That was their struggle. We look at it from our point of view. That's just racist and colonialist.

Also, it is a fact that Abdullah did have a plan to attack Syria. He thought he had a deal with Haganah. Haganah was going to attack Syria and Abdullah was going to go in and save Syria and then keep it. It did not work out, but it was an actual plan.

Was this post-1948?

It was either 1948 or 1949. Right in that period. This is discussed with some documentation in Flapan's book. In general, I think the idea is extremely plausible. Syria in 1949 offered a full peace treaty to Israel, which Israel rejected. There are good indications that the Arab states did not want to go to war in May 1948. Nahum Goldmann was opposed to declaring the state, and his reason was not that he was against a Jewish state. You see, the state was actually declared prior to the time when the Partition Recommendation proposed it. It was advanced. Goldmann's proposal was that they should hold off, and he always held throughout his entire life that, had he done that, they would have avoided war. Flapan tries to explore that in his book. His own conception is that Goldmann knew that the Arab states would accept a proposal if it was worked out properly, and he thought they should have explored that path. But Ben Gurion and other leaders were pretty confident. They thought they would be able to grab some land. There was a period of about 10 days from about May 14 to May 24 when it was touch and go; it wasn't at all clear how it was going to work out. But aside from that 10-day period, there was no doubt who was going to win.

Syria was willing to settle in 1949. How about Egypt?

By the time Nasser consolidated power in 1953, he was already moving toward a peace settlement with Israel. In fact, that is almost certainly one major reason for the Israeli terrorist acts in Egypt in 1954, when they blew up American installations. Part of the reason was, probably, to exacerbate relations between the United States and Egypt. Part, probably, was to undermine the negotiations then going on between Moshe Sharett and Nasser, which it succeeded in doing. Also, when Ben Gurion got back into power in early 1955, pushing out Sharett, the first thing he did was carry out a major military attack in Gaza, killing lots of Egyptians, which killed any possibility of negotiations. In fact, you know, there is very interesting documentation in Hebrew, *Pentagon Papers*-style. Years ago they published, in Hebrew, the captured Egyptian documents from the 1956 war. As far as I know, no scholars in America have touched them. What they tell is that Egypt was trying very hard to keep their word by arresting Palestinians and keeping Palestinians out of the army. Israel was sending in letter bombs to try to kill the Egyptian commanders who were trying to quiet down the Palestinians. There is every indication that they were trying to inspire Palestinian terrorism.

Did Sharett represent a real difference from Ben Gurion?

You can find hawkish statements in his stuff. But he did think that they were following the wrong course, that they ought to follow the course of diplomacy. He was a contrast to Ben Gurion. People always quote Ben Gurion in the 1960s. But as long as he was in, he was very forthright. He said no foreign factor can set Zionist aspirations, they will be set by the Jewish people alone. As far as borders are concerned, there are no limits. We should never settle on borders. We should always go on. Every political agreement we make is **a temporary expedient**, and we will go on to get more.

He had the same position that people criticize the PLO for its Covenant.

Exactly. I've pointed that out before. I do not think that was reason not to negotiate with Ben-Gurion. A substantial part of the Zionist movement never accepted the partition. Just three or four weeks ago the Herut program committee—Herut is the main group in Likud—which writes the platform, once again stated that they have not yet given up on their aims in Jordan, though they said they are not going to march on Amman. About two years ago the head of the Likud parliamentary delegation, Ronnie Milo, stated in parliament that they have not abandoned their claims in east Jordan. They might give up some of them in the course of negotiations. That's east Jordan.

Achdut Haavodah was the mainstream of the *kibbutz* movement for years and of the Labor coalition. They do not exist any longer, but as long as they existed they held that they did not accept the 1922 partition, let alone the 1947 partition. These are major components of the Israeli system. Even today they have never stated what borders they accept, and they never will.

What about Lebanon? There has been a lot of reaction in America to the uprising in Gaza and the West Bank. Yet Israeli air and ground raids in Lebanon have killed many more civilians than the repression on the West Bank.

Take the last few days. They invaded, but nobody knows what they really did, because they do not allow any reporters. But they obviously totally destroyed one village and they were shelling very heavily. But nobody cares. Even when it's reported here, nobody cares. Some of the things that are reported are mind boggling. For example, in January 1984, Israel carried out bombing in the Bekaa valley. There were 400 casualties, including 150 children. Some of the bombings are front page news, but nobody cared. Part of the reason is just normal anti-Arab racism, which is extreme in the United States. But partly the point is that Israel is a U.S. client state. It inherits the right of terrorism and aggression from us.

You remember the big furor over the alleged Nicaraguan invasion of Honduras. The Nicaraguan troops swept maybe a couple of kilometers across the border in hot pursuit, driving a terrorist force out of the country. That same week Israel carried out several bombings in Lebanon, north of the area of occupation, for a military action. The ability to maintain control over the cognitive dissonance is astonishing. All of this was on the same page. All of these liberal senators were screaming about communist totalitarians who dare to drive terrorists out of their country. On the other hand, this other stuff is going on and nobody bats an eyelash. It's **a real double standard**. It is extreme.

Take the treatment of the press. If Nicaragua were to treat the press the way Israel does, we would have blown the place away. Israel has 18 journalists in jail. They have been closing newspapers for years. The week *La Prensa* was suspended, they permanently closed two newspapers. When *La Prensa* was opened, they closed another newspaper. For the first time a couple of weeks ago they closed a Hebrew newspaper. The editor, Michal Schwartz, is in jail. She is not permitted to see her lawyer, because the lawyer might reveal what the investigation is about. I don't even know if it's been reported in the United States. Suppose Nicaragua were to do something like that?

It would be on the front page of the New York Times.

Oh my God! We would be bombing. All of these pretended advocates of free speech are just frauds. Maybe there are half a dozen people in the U.S. who believe in freedom of the press, if that many.

Speaking of censorship, what about your relations to American Jews? Your Fateful Triangle *was an important book about the Middle East. American Jewish journals consciously avoided it. They would not even print negative reviews, hatchet jobs.*

It is interesting. Take a look at England. In England that book was reviewed in the *Jewish Quarterly* by Noah Lucas, who is a well-known historian. It was a very favorable review. He later picked it as one of the most important books of the last decade. That is England.

Here you must have total censorship. The Jewish community here is deeply totalitarian. They do not want democracy, they do not want freedom. Israeli doves like Meir Pail and Matti Peled have been saying for years that the American Jewish community is their worst enemy, that it is a totalitarian community, that it does not want democracy in Israel, that it does not believe in democracy in

Israel, that it does not believe in democracy here. These guys say things I would never say. Pail is no big dove, but his critique of the American Jewish community is that what they want is for Israel to be a war god similar to Mars. But they certainly do not want discussion. In fact they have a whole vilification apparatus which is pretty impressive. The Anti-Defamation League office in Boston is a pretty leaky place. Many of the people who work there are appalled, so I have received stuff from them. For example, I got my file, a 150-page file.

They keep a file on you?

It reads kind of like an FBI file—half-truth, half-lies. People go to talks and send in what they claim I said, often an inversion of what they heard. Also clippings, inter-office memos, correspondence that they picked up. I got it because I was going to have a debate with Alan Dershowitz. This stuff was being sent to Dershowitz, so that he could cull defamatory material from it—as he did—for the debate. Somebody in the office who was appalled sent me a copy. People like Dershowitz, who is just an Israeli hack, a strict party liner, go to the ADL to get defamatory material. People like me, I don't care. But if you are in politics or journalism, you cannot live with this.

A temporary secretary at the ADL office told me that after the 1982 war there have been correspondence between the ADL and the *Partisan Review* in which the editors, William Phillips and Eith Kurzweil, offered the *Review* to the ADL as a way of defaming critics of Israel, me in particular. I believe that story is true. At the same time these people were inviting me to their cocktail parties. But that is typical of the intellectual community. It's basically Communist Party style.

This vilification apparatus is really effective in shutting people up. It scares a lot of people off, especially people in exposed positions. There is just no way to respond. If you are denounced as being an anti-Semite, what are you going to say, I'm not an anti-Semite? Or if you are denounced as being in favor of the Holocaust, what are you going to say, I'm not in favor of the Holocaust? I mean, you cannot win. Stalinist types of the ADL understand the beauty of throwing mud is that nobody can follow the details. You write it. Somebody else quotes it. Then somebody else says something.

Some people are really extreme. Dershowitz has actually written articles in the ADL journals in which he says I told him that I was "an agnostic about the Holocaust." First of all, I would not have a conversation with Alan Dershowitz if I met him in the street. But this is pure fabrication.

It is actually a quote that comes up a lot attached to your name now

Sure. Why not. Why not say I am in favor of the Holocaust. I think all Jews should be killed. That is the next thing to say. The point is that they can say anything they want. It is a kind of status that the Communist Party had aspired to but never achieved. And they have achieved it. They are totalitarians. They are plenty of others like them. Take, say, Elie Wiesel. His position is that one must maintain silence in the face of atrocities carried out by one's favorite state. That is his position, reiterated over and over again in the clearest possible terms. At the time of the last big uprising on the West Bank (there were real atrocities, 15 people were killed in early 1982—it was even making the papers at that time), he was asked to comment on it in the Jewish press, not even the public press, and he responded that only people in power are in a position to know, and I am not in a position of power, and therefore I cannot comment. He finally wrote an article in the Hebrew press in which he simply reiterated his position that you must maintain silence. That is your job. I must say that he is hated in Israel. When he won the Nobel prize, the vituperation in the Israeli press was just explosive. They absolutely despise him. What is an interesting fact about American culture is that a man who puts forth this position can be regarded as a moral hero.

Appendix: Harmful Pressure for Israel (6 March 1981)

Do you think the election of President Reagan was a setback for programs to adjust the economy to give more opportunities to the poor?

I think it was a devastating setback. The Reagan programs are a vicious attack on the poor and the major drift of his programs is to transfer resources from the poor to the wealthy.

Do you feel that the insistence of the American Jewish community on the United States backing of Israel's positions is harmful to the position of the Jewish community in America?

I don't think it's harmful to the Jewish community in America, although it could be in the long run. However, it's harmful to Israel. The chauvinist hysteria in Jewish communities has narrowed the options for the state of Israel, and has been a factor impelling them into policies which are self-destructive. In this respect the Jewish community is working towards the destruction of Israel.

Do you see a trend towards conservatism in the American Jewish community, and what does this portend for the former Jewish allegiance to liberal views?

I think there's a notable trend toward conservatism and this is a complicated issue with many factors involved. A few generations ago the Jewish community was an immigrant community working its way up into the system and quite successfully. Now it's a middle-class, upper-middle class community trying to protect positions already attained against others who are trying to work their way up. The destructive support for Israeli expansionism has also colored the attitudes of American Jews on certain issues. If American Jews want to keep pressing Israel toward such policies and want to identify with them afterwards, then this is a factor which is creating, I wouldn't say conservative, but reactionary positions.

What would you recommend to bring about peace between Israel and the Arabs?

In the short range I think the only reasonable step is for Israel to accept what is in fact the international consensus that there should be a state settlement more or less along the 1967 borders with various kinds of adjustments and arrangements about demilitarization. That will mean that the West Bank will probably be a state organized by the PLO. Longer-term prospects would be moves toward some kind of federation in the area of the former Palestine, but that would have to come from the wishes of the people themselves.

How do you view the future of the Jewish community in the United States?

I think it will be subject to a substantial amount of assimilation and erosion, but that it will remain a more or less organized community of people with some kind of ethnic or occasionally religious commitment.

What has been the reaction to the forward you wrote on civil liberties to the book by the French historian Robert Faurisson on the thesis that Nazi gas chambers never existed?

The reaction has been hysterical, and it's one of the major issues in Europe. Here's a case of someone whose views are almost universally condemned who has been suspended [from teaching] simply because of falsification of history. This is a shocking attack on civil liberties and a particularly important one to take up because Faurisson's views are so universally condemned.

Editor's Notes to Interview 50

"No Stone Left Unturned: Noam Chomsky Talks to the Amandla Press about Student Activism, U.S. Foreign Policy, the Jackson campaign and the Legacy of Ronald Reagan," *Amandla Press* 1 (June 10, 1988), pp. 5–6. The interview took place on May 23.

The *Amandla Press* "is published by students, staff and faculty of the UC [University of California] Riverside community" (The Women's Resource Center, UC Riverside, Riverside, CA 92521). The opening of the statement of purpose by Hugh Smith states that "amandla is the word black South Africans use to refer to empowerment" and goes on to say that "as citizens of the United States we have to start realizing that no act of injustice or exploitation is an island, and that we are as responsible for what occurs in Pretoria as for what occurs in Riverside … Why are blacks and Latinos so expendable? The Red Threat has been a justification for an international campaign of torture and mass murder on the part of the Reagan administration for the past eight years. We must question this justification when it is used against countries whose only crime is to seek independence from our domination … It requires an act of imagination to picture the daily reality of those on whom we impose such hardship. But that is the first and final step toward peace—imagining what it is like to be someone else."

The significance of the Jackson campaign comes up also in interview 42, done on March 16, 1988. A question from the floor after Chomsky's lecture on "Thought Control" at the University of Minnesota on April 6, 1988 elicited a somewhat more comprehensive answer, including the following remarks (see also interview 33):

"I suspect there's another position [in addition to "we can butter this guy up and get him on our side—he is salvageable" (reaction of some right-wing journalists) and "OK, let's try to go after him—this Third Worldism is no good" (another position of the media)], which isn't appearing. One question one would like to ask is why he picked Burt Lance as his major adviser. As far as I'm aware, Burt Lance is mainly a conduit to the oil companies, and I wouldn't be in the least surprised if the oil corporations are quite happy about Jackson's bringing into the debate some kind of concern over the Palestinian issue, believe it or not. Because for a long time the oil corporations have been favoring a political settlement in the Middle East—they've been opposed to the main drift of American policy. And—here I know of no evidence, I'm just guessing—my guess is that they don't mind at all all of this populist rhetoric because they know that if by some miracle he ever got elected he couldn't do anything anyway, because he couldn't. But the idea of a slight shift in international policy, which is not out of the question—the United States could join a very broad international consensus on the political settlement and Jackson is pushing the discussion in that direction, you know, he's opening that up in a way that other candidates aren't—they probably like that. So I suspect it's that element too. And there are other things.

I think that he has obviously been a shot in the arm for the underclass in the United States, which is itself a good thing. It makes people realize they've got more power than they thought. So it's a mixed story. The media obviously are trying to contain and control it and make it useful. But I think there hasn't been anything surprising about it."

A recent editorial in *Business Week* (Sept. 12, 1988, p. 138), titled "The UN Needs Two Sides to Tango," includes the following: "If Israel and the Palestinians eventually move, as they must, to end their conflict, a UN role in any settlement seems likely ... the administration has reaffirmed a basic rule of peace keeping. To settle conflicts, the UN and its members must deal with both sides and try to resolve the issues rather than ignore them."

50. No Stone Left Unturned (23 May 1988)

Dr. Chomsky, you've been involved in academia for 30 years either as a professor or a student. You've witnessed the change in political climate during the 60s, through the Vietnam War and the civil rights movement up to the present. It seems that at UC Riverside and other universities nationwide the level of student activism and political consciousness is remarkably low compared to what it was. If anything, students seem to reflect the prevailing conservatism that is present in the United States today. I'd like to ask you what you feel the role of universities is in either promoting or discouraging this prevailing conservatism.

First of all, I think we should be careful about the assumption: Is there a prevailing conservatism in the United States?

There are two problems with this. One problem is that what is called conservatism these days is about as remote from anything that deserves that relatively honorable name as you can imagine. For example, Reaganite conservatism as so called is in fact a commitment of a very powerful state which intervenes massively in the economy, creates a vast state-guaranteed market for high technology production, and organizes a vast public subsidy to advance technology. It's a state which is violent and aggressive overseas, and is protective to the extent it can be, given public scrutiny. It is in every respect very different from conservatism. That's one problem.

The second problem is that this so-called conservatism, which ought to be called some variety of reactionary jingoism, is by no means prevalent. It might be prevalent among the elite groups, but that's not too surprising because it is an ideology that favors transfer of the resources from the poor to the rich, power for the privileged and so on. Among the general public it has never been particularly popular. In fact, Reagan's popularity has been by no means unusually high, judging from the polls. Furthermore, the public has been strongly opposed to every major element of the Reaganite program with very rare exception. Throughout the 1980s, for example, the polls have shown the public has been strongly in favor of social rather than military spending. In general, the public has continued in **a long slow drift towards a New Deal-style, welfare kind of social democracy.**

So on the one hand, there is not the case that among the general public this so-called conservatism is prevalent, and secondly this is not conservatism. There are very few people in the U.S. political system that could be called conservative; maybe Mark Hatfield and a few others, but very few.

Now as far as students are concerned, the matter is very complex. Among the more elite sectors, there is a tendency to share in elite attitudes. On the other hand, I don't know of any reason to believe student activism in general is lower or student concern for social and political issues is lower than in the past. There is one kind of blip in the curve. From about 1968 through the early 1970s there was quite an extensive student involvement in the anti-war movement. In general there was interest and involvement in the late 60s among large sectors of the student body in changing universities, changing social life and so on. That is less evident now than it was then. In part this is because that kind of activism has spread over wider sectors of the population. For example, the Central American solidarity groups are not particularly rooted in the student movement the way the anti-war movement was in the late 60s, that makes the student movement look relatively less significant. So I think there, one has to be a bit cautious about assessing the changes.

You mention in The Chomsky Reader, *a collection of some of your work that was recently published, the need for "mass popular organization." Do you see universities playing a role in this?*

I wouldn't expect the universities as such to do it. I think **students** could very well do it. Students happen to be at a stage in their lives when they are really quite free. They're not part of the system of management and control; they're not part of dominant institutions as yet. They are therefore somewhat freer to think, act, explore, inquire, and that offers them opportunities. It is the stage in one's life where one should be exploring alternatives, thinking through problems, setting the structure of one's future life. Students are a transitional population. They are never going to be a stable center of any ongoing movement, but they can certainly contribute to it with their energy and enthusiasm and the use that they can make of the relative degree of freedom that they have. If there is to be a significant form of democratization in this country; that is, if there is to be an organization structure that really allows ordinary people to play a significant role in running their own affairs, it will have to be based on the stable adult community that works, produces and so on. Students should certainly be a part of this.

The reason I'm stressing this in reference to UCR [University of California at Riverside], which is only one university, is that here the only student organization with any sort of political validity is the College Republicans. They sponsored a pro-Contra rally last year and more recently talks by RENAMO and UNITA which, as you know, are essentially terrorist proxies for South Africa. This is the main kind of organization that is seen on this campus, and there is very little in the way of alternative organization seen among the students here.

I don't know UCR, but if I were you I wouldn't generalize from that. I travel a lot across the country and what you describe is very unusual. I've been giving talks and having visits from the elite universities to state universities and city colleges and so on, and what you describe is very far from what I've discovered. I don't know what the university draws from, whether it reflects the local political and economic climate or whether it is just the failure of others to organize. I would really be surprised if that is the only form that student activism or concern could take there.

I'm glad to hear that it doesn't seem to be the norm to you. We are speaking about the universities as centers of learning or purveyors of national opinion. An obvious counterpart to the universities are the media, i.e. the national press and television. What role do you see the media playing in influencing the assessments people make of the actions of the U.S. government overseas and at home?

We have to ask ourselves what the media are, first of all. The national media are major corporations, which are owned by or linked to even larger corporations. They have a product and a market. The market is other businesses, namely advertisers. That's what supports the media. And the product they produce is audiences. For the national and elite media, they generally are the privileged audiences. That is what raises advertising rates. So just from a strictly economic point of view, the media are major corporations selling privileged audiences to other businesses. Furthermore, there are many management positions in the media. Editors and so on are themselves part of a narrow privileged sector that basically owns and runs the society. They share those perspectives, associations, and interests. There is a constant interflow of it back between top managerial positions in the media and governmental and corporations that tend to keep the media in line if there were any possibility they would get out of it. So it is entirely natural to expect and in fact we discover that the media tends to present an overwhelming picture of the world that conforms to the interest and needs of the sectors of the population it serves and represents. Basically that is the state corporate nexus that constitutes the ownership and management group for the economy and social life. The media are simply the ideological institutions of that nexus. Hence they do tend to support a spectrum of opinion ranging from so-called liberal to conservative. I don't believe in either of those terms, which reflects essentially the spectrum of alternatives that are considered serious tactical issues from among the elite groups that constitute the corporate state ideological management groups. It's a pretty narrow spectrum.

What suggestions would you give to people starting an alternative paper, which we hope will be free of the constraints of marketability.

The only advice I can offer is the obvious thing—telling people the truth. Bring them the news that they aren't getting. Give them the kinds of analyses they are not receiving. I think some people will be surprised, if my experience is any guide. I think people can be reached with critical analyses and **truths** that are generally **hidden** from them.

I'd like to ask you a little about the Jackson campaign. The Reverend Jackson has stepped forward as a man who has not been afraid to identify himself with causes that are out of the mainstream. What do you feel the Jackson campaign has accomplished so far, and looking ahead, what do you feel its long-term effects will be?

What **the Jackson campaign** has primarily done is bring into the mainstream of American political concerns interests and large sectors of the population that are typically quite marginalized. The liberal or progressive content to the Jackson campaign undoubtedly reflects the feelings and concerns of very large sectors of the population. This has given those people who are generally isolated and marginalized a sense of their own potential power if they organize and sustain themselves. Now as far as the significance of the Jackson campaign is concerned, the long-term significance, I think that can be measured straightforwardly. If the campaign is understood as a mechanism to try and gain political power for a certain individual or set of individuals, if it is understood as a device to make them power brokers, then it is not very important. On the other hand, if the campaign becomes a device to build long-term, lasting, self-sustaining organizations that will bring people together to construct for themselves political programs, to advance those programs, if it constructs groups that become a form of pressure on any candidate, whether the name is Jesse Jackson or George Bush, then it could have a long-term effect. Now I don't think that is going to come out of the campaign itself. It depends on how people react to the campaign and the opportunities it provides.

We have roughly seven more months of Ronald Reagan, and then there will be some kind of a changing of the guard in the White House. Whether it will be a significant change or not we don't know. How do you think this shift in leadership may affect the prospects for peace in Central America?

Politics in the United States generally falls in a pretty narrow spectrum. It falls within the spectrum of debate among the elites as to the proper tactics to achieve shared goals. Those we call the "hawks" are those who think you should obtain shared objectives by violence. The "doves" argue that you should try to obtain the shared objectives by diplomatic pressures, and so on. The Reaganites have been at the hawkish extreme.

In the last couple of years they have been compelled to move away from that extreme. They have to react to objective realities. One of the objective realities is that the Reagan administration has dealt **a very serious and probably long lasting blow to the American economy**. The Reagan administration is the very opposite of conservatism. It was a strictly Keynesian economy, a kind of mad dog Keynesian economy that made use of very extensive government deficit spending. That can be done in constructive ways, if it is done to build a productive economy that can be useful and significant. But they did not carry it out for that purpose. Their extreme Keynesianism supported non-productive investment, overwhelmingly military investment. That is, waste production.

The fiscal and other measures which led to a transfer of resources to the rich also led to luxury consumption and financial manipulations. Well, the very visible effects of that have been a huge trade deficit, budget deficit, a trade imbalance and so on. When the Reagan administration came in, the U.S. was the largest creditor nation, and within a few years it became the world's greatest debtor nation.

These are all facts that have to be dealt with. They probably mean that for a substantial sector of the population, largely the poor sectors, there will be a degree of austerity facing them in the future. It is also going to be much harder to mobilize the population to subsidize high-technology industry through the military system to act aggressively in the world.

Any administration, whether it's the Reaganites or anyone else, is going to have to react to this. We can see this in the shift in the last few years from the fanatic "Evil Empire" rhetoric and the hysteria over international terrorism. Suddenly the Russians aren't as dangerous as they were before, and the international terrorists aren't about to destroy us as they were a couple of years ago. In fact, in the outside world not very much has changed, but things have changed domestically and people and power have to react to it. So I wouldn't underestimate the extent to which the radical economic mismanagement of the Reagan administration and the harm it has caused to the economy will affect policy.

In regards to Central America, this group happens to be at an extreme level of fanaticism. The commitment of people like Elliot Abrams and George Schultz and others to destroy the cancer of Nicaragua just reached a level of true fanaticism. I think that almost any administration that replaces this one is likely to shift towards a less extremist course. I think they will continue the general policy of trying to undermine Nicaragua and to support the murderous terrorist client states in El Salvador and Guatemala, but on that there is a general elite consensus.

That's based on a real understanding that traditionally the United States has refused to accept the possibility of social reform and meaningful democracy; meaning democracy with participation of the majority of the population. We have refused to accept those options on the assumption that they would harm American dominance on our client regions. Those principles have not been changed because they are rooted in institutional factors. They will lead any administration to seek ways of maintaining privilege, blocking social reform, of preventing democratic structures that could bring the large majority of the population into participation in political life. They will therefore lead us to support terrorist states and support governments that attempt to shift their resources away from the needs of the poor majority. The general population of the United States can modify that, but only by imposing severe pressures on whatever administration is in power.

In reference to terrorist states, the Reagan administration has refused, except in word, to distance itself from South Africa or to impose any measures that would cause South Africa to end the apartheid system. How would you describe the importance of South Africa to the Reagan administration, and what changes would you like to see in the next administration as far as dealing with South Africa?

South Africa is important to American industrial capitalism as a whole. It's a major producer of raw materials and the major industrial sector of Africa. It will obviously be the dominant part of the economy of Africa for a long time to come.

As far as policy towards South Africa is concerned, there are really two issues that we have to consider. One is the South African subversion and direct aggression in Angola, Mozambique, Zimbabwe and so on. This is a policy some have called "beggaring your neighbors." Secondly, there is the internal structure of South Africa, that is the apartheid system—the system by which 90 percent of the population are kept at the level of semi-slavery.

Now as far as our policy should be concerned, we should be able to terminate our support of the South African disruption of the surrounding region, and to act much more constructively, more realistically to try to undermine the apartheid system. On the second of those two goals, I think among a very substantial part of American industry, American capitalism, there is little support of the apartheid system. It does not serve the needs of American industry or the American state. It did when South Africa was a partially extractive economy. South Africa at that point needed a chief pliable work force that you could send into the mines, where they would work a couple of years, drop dead and then be replaced.

South Africa has been moving towards an industrial economy, and we are seeing the same kinds of changes that were taking place in the United States in the 19th century. An industrial economy needs a trained docile labor force with skilled workers and low-level managers. That is not consistent with the apartheid system. So I think American business would be happy to see an end to apartheid as long as the economy remains open to United States economic penetration and the system remains subject to a sufficient degree of U.S. political control. That means delicate maneuvering. As far as American business is concerned, it means trying to overcome the apartheid system without introducing any significant social change. My own view in contrast is that we should try to pressure South Africa to overcome the apartheid system along with significant social change. Over that, such a proposal would again require substantial pressure on the government to be made a real policy option.

Editor's Notes to Interview 51

The following questions were selected among those submitted by telefax by Hannes Hofbauer for *Moz*, an Austrian "alternative monthly for politics, economy and culture." The original set is divided in three parts: 1) The term and idea of terrorism (1–12); 2) relations between terrorism and imperialism (13–24); 3) relations between mass-media, public opinion and terrorism (25–34). Only two questions of the first part were skipped and only two of the second part were answered (none from the third); the first three original questions are consolidated into one because they were answered as a single unit. The answers were transmitted by telefax from MIT-Communications on May 25, 1988. A shortened and edited version in German translation of the text reproduced here appeared in *Moz*, Jul/Aug 1988, pp. 48–50.

For an extended treatment of the topics discussed and related topics, see **CT** (1988). See also the Editor's Notes to I20.

On U.S.-Israeli rejectionism, see Editor's Notes to I36.

51. The Plague of the Modern Age (25 May 1988)

If you ask the Western European common run of men and women about the concept and idea of terrorism, they will spontaneously think of the PLO, other Palestinian organizations, radical Shiites, Muammar Qaddafi, IRA, the Basque ETA, the Red Brigades in Italy, the Red Army faction in Western Germany. In recent years terrorist attacks of these groups killed 300 to 400 people in one year. Every case of a single person being killed is tragic and brutal, but compared to violence on a worldwide scale it is a very small amount of people who are murdered this way. In every big U.S. city there are more people murdered in a year than those killed by attacks of the above-mentioned groups. What is the prevailing definition of terrorism and what makes this kind of terrorism so important? You always refer to the problem that the prevailing definition is far too narrow. Could you please work out the complexity of it? The instrumentalization of terrorism starts with the manipulation of the term. What do you think of the statement that terrorist is always the other?

We have to make a clear distinction between **the official definition of the concept of "terrorism"** and the "prevailing definition" within Western intellectual culture. The official definitions are, in my view, quite appropriate. A typical example appears in a U.S. Army manual on countering terrorism, which defines "terrorism" as "the calculated use of violence or threat of violence to attain goals that are political, religious, or ideological in nature. This is done through intimidation, coercion, or instilling fear." Other characterizations are similar, including those in the official U.S. code and international conventions.

Terrorism comes in several varieties. There is "wholesale terrorism" targeted against large populations, or "retail terrorism" targeted against individuals. There is state terrorism, individual terrorism, or state-supported terrorism, depending on the agency and initiators of the terrorist actions. International terrorism is the subcategory that extends beyond state boundaries in the planning, initiation and conduct of the acts. The most serious issue, of course, is wholesale terrorism, generally state-conducted or state-supported.

The "prevailing definition" differs from the official definition in that it restricts the concept of terrorism to terrorist acts carried out by them, not us, and to retail terrorism (allegedly directed by states that are official enemies), not wholesale terrorism, for which we are commonly responsible. It is entirely natural for a propaganda system to focus on acts of the enemy, real or fabricated, and we therefore should not be surprised that Western state propaganda adopts this standard practice. What is more interesting is the readiness of respectable circles to adopt the framework of state propaganda, **a remarkable example of servility to power**. This is merely one example of the functioning of Western propaganda systems, which are particularly interesting for the student of propaganda in that they are not centrally controlled and do not rely on force to ensure obedience. They therefore provide substantial light on the nature and functioning of social societies in which the population cannot be controlled by threat or force, so that they must be marginalized by other means, a matter clearly understood and articulated in the literature of the business community and also among more sophisticated segments of the commissar class.

The issue of state-supported international terrorism was raised to the primary focus of concern by the Reagan administration in the early 1980s, referring to the alleged Soviet role in inspiring or supporting terrorism in an effort to undermine Western democracy. This propaganda campaign led to a vast literature, many conferences, even a new breed of "terrorologists" devoted to those examples of terrorism admitted into the official canon under the "prevailing definition": Claire Sterling, Walter Laqueur, and others. More serious work that does not obey state dictates on the matter (e.g., Edward Herman's 1982 study *The Real Terror Network*) exists only on the remote margins of discussion, exactly as one would expect within a well-functioning propaganda system.

How can it be possible to make fighters for freedom out of the Contras in Nicaragua and to make political and military actions (for defending the system) out of terrorist attacks of the CIA, the Mossad, the French secret services?

Again, this is just the normal and familiar way in which an effective propaganda system functions. Our terrorists are heroes, defending freedom, justice and all good things; their terrorists are monsters who have to be destroyed. Recent practice in the West simply follows the conventional norms. To illustrate with the most extreme example of criminality, recall the Nazi slogan "Terror gegen Terror." The Nazis alleged that they were defending Germany, and civilized values, against the terror of the Czechs and Poles, and carrying out "defensive action against the Jewish world-criminals." And they were compelled—reluctantly of course—to resort to terror in self-defense. "Terror against terror" was also the name of a segment of the Jewish terrorist underground in Israel's occupied territories that was responsible for the killing and maiming of Arabs (West Bank mayor Bassam Shak'a, among others). The front cover of *Der Spiegel* featured this slogan in its lengthy report on the U.S. terrorist bombing of Libya in April 1986, an appropriate choice of phraseology, if we recall the origins of the term and its significance.

Could you please give some examples of what you call state terrorism: a) examples of recent history: Cuba, Vietnam; b) examples of the present: Central America, Middle East, Libya?

International terrorism is not a discovery of the 1980s. In the preceding two decades, the major targets of international terrorism were probably Cuba and Lebanon. Cuba was the victim of extensive terrorist operations since the Kennedy administration adopted international terrorism (sometimes called "counterinsurgency," among other euphemisms) as a central device of U.S. foreign policy. Lebanon was subjected to devastating Israeli attacks from the early 1970s with thousands killed and hundreds of thousands driven from their homes while the entire population was held hostage to enforce their acceptance of U.S.-Israeli arrangements for the region. U.S. terrorism in Cuba included sinking of civilian vessels, bombardment of hotels, destruction of industrial installations, repeated attempts to assassinate the political leadership, poisoning of crops and livestock, and so on, in terrorist operations running weekly at certain times. There is one example that might well have sparked a nuclear war. It has recently been revealed that at a moment of peak tension during the Cuban missile crisis in 1962, a CIA-run "Mongoose" terror team blew up a factory; the effects could have been catastrophic, but fortunately, the USSR and Cuba did not react. This revelation was considered so significant that it merited mention within a footnote in an article in the Harvard University journal *International Security*, but no notice elsewhere, to my knowledge. This is another example of the ease with which we dismiss Western international terrorism, an example that is particularly dramatic because of the circumstances and possible consequences.

As for Israeli terrorism in southern Lebanon in the early 1970s, its purpose was explained lucidly by the noted Israeli dove Abba Eban in response to his adversary Menachem Begin, who had cited a series of actions in Lebanon under the Labor government which, Eban agreed, are **"reminiscent of regimes which neither Mr. Begin nor I would dare to mention by name,"** in Eban's words. But Eban went on to justify Israeli violence in Lebanon under the labor government in which he served on the grounds that "there was a rational prospect, ultimately fulfilled, that affected populations would exert pressure for the cessation of hostilities," thus accommodating to Israeli policy, namely, the unremitting rejectionist policy of refusing a political settlement that takes into account even the minimal rights of the indigenous population. This was a serious matter during the period in question, the early 1970s, particularly after Israel's rejection, with U.S. backing, of President Sadat's 1971 offer of a full-scale peace treaty (one framed in accord with official though not operative U.S. policy), an event that has passed from history in the West.

The policy of holding the population of southern Lebanon hostage persists until today. Uri Lubrani, who is in charge of Israeli operations in southern Lebanon, explains that the 150,000 Lebanese in the Israeli-controlled southern zone of Lebanon realize that Israel is willing to use force, "and that's the reason we have a manageable situation." If they resist, Israel will resort again to a "scorched earth" policy, he warns. The resort to methods to "intimidate or coerce a civilian population"—to use the terms in which terrorism is defined by the

U.S. State Department—comes naturally to a powerful state that operates under few internal or international constraints.

As for U.S. actions in Vietnam, they fall under the category of international terrorism in the 1950s and early 1960s, when tens of thousands were slaughtered by U.S. mercenary forces. But from the time that John F. Kennedy committed the U.S. Air Force directly to the attack against South Vietnam (1961–1962), and surely when Lyndon Johnson sent an expeditionary force to invade South Vietnam, the acts fall under the category of aggression, a war crime, analogous to the aggression of the fascist states, the Soviet invasion of Afghanistan, and so on.

Turning to the present, the U.S. attack against Nicaragua is a particularly clear case of international terrorism—unless it is considered an instance of the more serious crime of aggression, as suggested by the World Court ruling condemning the U.S. for "the unlawful use of force" and violation of treaties in its attack against Nicaragua. That this attack is "state-supported terrorism" on a huge scale, has been noted, for example, by former CIA director Admiral Stansfield Turner, in congressional testimony. Though the fact is not commonly recognized, the even greater state terror in El Salvador also qualifies as international terrorism, conducted by a mercenary army organized, trained, armed and directed by the U.S. government, with the direct participation of the U.S. military (the U.S. Air Force assists in coordinating air strikes, a move that substantially improved the "kill rate" among fleeing peasants and defenseless villagers). U.S. support for the even greater state terror in Guatemala—enthusiastic support, under the Reagan administration—might also be considered state-supported international terrorism, if we were willing to apply our own concepts and rhetoric to ourselves—an idea too ludicrous to merit further comment.

The principles of U.S. propaganda dictate that we focus our concern on the Middle East/Mediterranean region when we consider this plague of the modern age. Let us turn then to this region, focusing now on the 1980s, as state propaganda demands. Even under these conditions, we discover that the major examples of international terrorism are traceable to the U.S., including the bombing of Libya in 1986 and the CIA-directed car bombing in 1985 in Beirut aimed at Sheikh Fadlallah that killed 80 people, the worst single terrorist acts in the region in these two years, when concern over the plague of international terrorism reached its peak. Other examples include the Israeli bombing of Tunis (though this, like the U.S. bombing of Libya, might be assigned to the category of aggression) and the Israeli "Iron Fist" operations in southern Lebanon, designed to hold the civilian population of the region hostage, the major sustained campaign of international terrorism (if not aggression) during this period. In these cases **the U.S. again shares responsibility**, for obvious reasons. Other examples include Israeli hijacking and piracy on the high seas for many years, also U.S.-supported, or the car-bomb blast of November 1981 in Damascus that took 110 lives, carried out by French intelligence in retaliation for the murder of France's ambassador to Lebanon.

Without extending the record, which is substantial, the conclusion appears obvious enough. Let us agree with George Schultz that international terrorism is a plague spread by "depraved opponents of civilization itself" in "a return to barbarism in the modern age." During the period when Reagan administration officials succeeded in placing this plague in the focus of international concern, they were among the leading agents of the crime, arguably its most effective and skilled practitioners. In Central America, the death toll may reach 200,000 during this period. As one would expect in terrorist campaigns, the acts surpass mere slaughter and assassination, including large-scale torture, mutilation, rape, disappearance (again, a device borrowed from the Gestapo) and other means to "intimidate and coerce a civilian population." This is Pol Pot-style terrorism, in style and even in scale, as we would discover if we were willing to accept the conditions of honest inquiry.

If we see it like this, isn't terrorism only another word for making war on a lower level, low-intensity warfare?

To answer this question, let us once again turn to official U.S. sources. Consider a Pentagon-sponsored study on "low-intensity conflict" (LIC) by the noted terrorologist Robert Kupperman. He defines LIC as the threat or use of force "to achieve political objectives without the full-scale commitment of resources," that is, "the unlawful use of force" designed to fall just short of the war crime of direct aggression. LIC is, of course, the policy to which the United States is officially committed, for example, in Nicaragua and El Salvador. Note that LIC is simply international terrorism, as a simple matter of logic, here adopting throughout the concepts and definitions provided by the U.S. government.

There are many terrorist states, but the U.S. is unusual, possibly unique, in that it is officially committed to international terrorism. The commitment reaches fine details. Thus the U.S. "proxy force" (as its lobbyists term it in international documents circulated in the White House) attacking Nicaragua from foreign bases is directed by its U.S. commanders to avoid combat and attack "soft targets," according to NATO Commander General John Galvin, when he testified before Congress as head of the U.S. Southern Command in Panama. The State Department has officially endorsed this policy. State Department spokesman Charles Redman explained that agricultural cooperatives in Nicaragua are legitimate targets because they are defended by people bearing arms. By the same logic, Libya could justify attacks by Abu Nidal against Israeli cooperatives, which are far more heavily defended. All of this passes without notice in **an intellectual culture dedicated to terrorist values and policies.**

What is the aim of this low-intensity warfare, of this state-terrorism? Is it the liquidation of peoples' organizations, the destruction of revolutionary and democratic infrastructure?

Shortly before his assassination by elements of the U.S.-supported security services, Archbishop Oscar Romero of El Salvador wrote a letter to President Carter pleading with him to refrain from offering any aid to the military junta, because such aid would be used "to destroy the peoples' organizations fighting to defend their fundamental human rights." The archbishop, a conservative who came to be dedicated to defense of the poor and suffering people of El Salvador after such atrocities as the murder of Father Rutilio Grande, among thousands of others, understood very well the purpose of U.S. international terrorism in the region: to destroy popular organizations that might lay the basis for social reform and for meaningful democracy in which the poor majority might begin to participate in the political system. There is no space here to elaborate the rich documentary and historical record that supports this conclusion; I have reviewed it elsewhere, and I think it leaves little doubt of this conclusion. The U.S. is willing to tolerate formal democratic procedures, but only if the structure of power guarantees that the system will be dominated by business elements favorable to the interest of U.S. elites and free from what secret documents call **the sin of "ultranationalism,"** that is, efforts to carry out independent development in ways responsive to popular pressures and concerns.

In their own curious way, even the doves tacitly concede the point. Within the American political system in the past several generations, it would be difficult to find anyone who is more liberal, more opposed to state violence, than Robert Pastor, the Latin American specialist of the National Security Council under President Carter. In a recent book, he takes issue with those who believe that the U.S. has aimed to control Latin American countries. "The United States did not want to control Nicaragua or the other nations of the region," he writes, "but it also did not want to allow developments to get out of control. It wanted Nicaraguans to act independently, except when doing so would affect U.S. interests adversely." In short, Latin Americans should be free to choose their own way, as long as this "free choice" conforms to U.S. demands—what we call "democracy." And if they abuse their freedom by making the wrong choices, then we must plainly administer discipline, as with an errant child. Perhaps we must even resort to what our friends in the Salvadoran military call "the pedagogy of terror," with enthusiasm if we are hawks, with pain in our hearts if we are liberal humanitarians.

How would you, Professor Chomsky, estimate the last spectacular state-terrorist attacks, the killing of the ANC woman Dulcie September in the middle of Paris—obviously by the South African secret service—and the commando-attack of Israeli soldiers to kill Abu Jihad in Tunis?

These are two examples of retail rather than wholesale international terrorism. South African state terror is universally condemned, at least at the rhetorical level, but in the United States Israeli state terror is generally regarded as legitimate. The argument, in the case of Abu Jihad, is that he directed terrorist attacks against Israel and therefore merited his fate. By the same argument, it would be entirely legitimate for Palestinians and Lebanese to assassinate the Israeli political leadership, and for Nicaraguans (and many others) to assassinate Ronald Reagan, George Schultz, Elliot Abrams, and their colleagues. Naturally, the logical conclusion is not drawn, and would be regarded as a reversion to Nazism, among well-behaved intellectual elites.

Back to the term "state terrorism." Does state-terrorism show itself only in open or subversive military aggression or do diplomatic and economic threats belong to it as well, for example how the U.S. acts against Nicaragua? Is there a relation between diplomatic and economic threats and extortions on the one side and physical terrorist attacks on the other.

The terminology of political discourse is hardly precise, but I think we should make efforts to avoid the standard practice of propagandists who distort it for their own purposes. We should, I think, restrict the term "terrorism" to the standard usage illustrated earlier, from U.S. official documents. U.S. economic warfare against Nicaragua is criminal in my view, but it is not, strictly speaking, terrorism. Its goal, however, is much the same. Nicaragua under the Sandinistas was "out of control," in Robert Pastor's sense. The Sandinistas were diverting the scarce resources of the country to the needs of the poor majority, an intolerable abuse of freedom, according to U.S. doctrine. The major U.S. planning documents that have so far been declassified identify the primary threat to U.S. interests in Latin America as "nationalistic regimes" responsive to "popular demands for improvement in the low living standards of the masses" and diversification of production for domestic needs; such developments are inconsistent with U.S. policy, which is committed to "a political and economic climate conducive to private investment of both domestic and foreign capital," including guarantees for the "opportunity to earn and in the case of foreign capital to repatriate a reasonable return" (NSC 5432, August 1954). As State Department dove George Kennan had earlier explained, a prime concern of U.S. foreign policy in Latin America is "the protection of our raw materials," and more generally, the human and material resources in our domains. The primary enemy against whom these resources must be protected is the indigenous population, which often succumbs to curious ideas about using "our resources" in their lands for their own ends. We must therefore support police states, Kennan went on, in preference to "a liberal government if it is indulgent and relaxed and penetrated by Communists," where the term "Communist" is used, as is conventional in U.S. political rhetoric, to refer to those whose actions "affect U.S. interests adversely," in Robert Pastor's phrase, whatever their political commitments may be: priests organizing Bible-study groups that become peasant self-help organizations in El Salvador, for example.

U.S. economic warfare has succeeded in destroying the economy of Nicaragua, with effects that are probably more lethal and long-lasting than the terrorist attack. Similarly, on the diplomatic front the U.S. has sought to overcome the threat of a peaceful negotiated settlement. All of this is shameful, arguably criminal (as held, in fact, by the International Court of Justice), but it is not terrorism; great powers have **many means of criminal action** at their disposal.

Aren't there scenarios of extortion which are growing more and more serious? Take, for example, Nicaragua: one gets the impression that the U.S. administration gives "lessons of good political conduct" to the Nicaraguan government, to hold parliamentary elections, to accept the Contadora initiative, to negotiate with the leaders of the Contra troops. The U.S. administration launches such lessons and is never content with the results, even if Nicaragua is willing.

There is an elite consensus in the United States that Nicaragua must be returned to "the Central American mode" and must be compelled to observe "regional standards," in the words of the liberal doves (the *Washington Post* editors, in this case). There is no such problem in the case of El Salvador and Guatemala, which adhere to the Central American mode of mass slaughter, terror, exploitation, starvation, semi-slave labor, and subordination to the needs of "domestic and foreign capital."

The U.S. was furious over the election in Nicaragua in 1984 and sought in every way to disrupt it. According to U.S. doctrine, the election did not take place; the media regularly contrast the "fledgling democracies" of El Salvador, Guatemala and Honduras, which have "elected presidents," with Nicaragua, ruled by the dictator Ortega. To protect this doctrine, the media grossly falsified the circumstances and conditions of the election, exactly as they did, though in the opposite direction, in the case of the elections in El Salvador; the facts in this regard have been documented at length (see a forthcoming book by Edward Herman and Noam Chomsky, *Manufacturing Consent: The Political Economy of the Mass Media*, for a detailed review). The media barred the reports of the many international observers, including the careful official study of the Nicaraguan elections conducted by the Latin American Studies Association (the professional association of Latin American scholars), which concluded, as did observers generally, that the elections were quite respectable by Latin American standards, surely more so than the elections in El Salvador at the same time. These **conclusions** being **unacceptable**, they were simply excluded, along with other similar reports.

The elections in El Salvador took place after years of terror and slaughter, with the political opposition murdered and the independent media physically destroyed by the security forces, and the population traumatized. These elections were conducted in an atmosphere of "terror and despair, macabre rumor and grim reality," in the words of Lord Chitnis, who observed them as a representative of the British parliamentary human rights group. They were, naturally, lauded by the U.S. media, much as *Pravda* lauds elections in Poland—though the comparison, in this case, is unfair to the Soviet Union.

Similarly, the U.S. has sought in every way to undermine any diplomatic effort, including the Contadora negotiations and the Central American peace plan of August 1987. And it succeeded in these efforts, contrary to many illusions, a fact easily documented. The U.S. has also sought to undermine negotiations with its proxy army leading to a cease-fire and political settlement.

During the Vietnam War, studies by U.S. government scholars and captured Viet Cong documents agreed that the U.S. was politically weak but militarily strong. The same has been true in Central America, as generally elsewhere in the Third World. The fact is recognized in secret planning documents, which quite explicitly draw the obvious conclusion: since the programs to which the U.S. is dedicated will obviously gain little public support, it is necessary for the U.S. to take control of the military, described as the least anti-American of the "political groups" in Latin America. The military can then fulfill its function, overthrowing civilian governments if necessary and controlling civilian elements under the guise of "internal security." Since the U.S. is politically weak though militarily strong, it naturally seeks to remove conflict from the political to the military arena, where it can hope to prevail. This is the general pattern, and there is every expectation that it will persist.

Professor Chomsky, in your book Turning the Tide, *you speak about the enforcement of the so-called fifth freedom in connection with state terrorism. What do you mean by this fifth freedom? Which four freedoms does it complete and how important is its enforcement?*

President Roosevelt defined U.S. war aims as freedom of speech, freedom of worship, freedom from want, and freedom from fear. This appealing rhetoric helped maintain cohesion in the war against fascist powers, but it had as much reality as most state propaganda. In reality, as the documentary and historical record show with great clarity, U.S. policy has been guided by what we may call **"the fifth freedom,"** the freedom to rob, to exploit, and to control. If this freedom can be secured under parliamentary democratic forms, then the latter are tolerable—even preferable, since they are useful for ideological management at home and among the allies. Otherwise, democratic forms must be eliminated in the service of the fifth freedom, the one that really counts. Guatemala, Chile, the Dominican Republic and other examples where the U.S. has supported or organized the destruction of democratic structures illustrate the operative principles. There is no space to review the record here; again, I have done so elsewhere, and the conclusions seem as well established as any that can be reached in the study of state policy and international affairs.

There is or was the argument of the Moscow Connection that says that every terrorist attack has something to do with the Soviet Union. Does this argument have any importance today, after the meeting of Reagan and Gorbachev?

Reagan administration propaganda identified the Soviet Union as the source of international terrorism throughout the world, and this theme was adopted with great enthusiasm by the new breed of terrorologists, who offered as proof of this thesis the alleged fact that terrorism occurs "almost exclusively in democratic or relatively democratic countries" (Walter Laqueur). As already noted, the conclusion is manifestly false, if by the term "terrorism" we mean terrorism. But of course, within the propaganda system this is not the meaning of the term "terrorism." Rather, their term refers to terrorist acts against us, so that Laqueur's conclusion is true by definition, whatever the facts may be; and the thesis it allegedly supports can therefore be assumed to be true within the propaganda system, whatever the facts. Again, this is the normal practice of state propaganda, though admittedly the practice in this case reaches unusual levels of vulgarity and childish absurdity.

The reasons for this propaganda campaign were evident from the first days of the Reagan administration. The administration was dedicated to three basic programs: transfer of resources from the poor to the wealthy; expansion of state power, in particular, state intervention in the economic system by compelling the public to subsidize high-technology industry and provide a state-guaranteed market for the production of high technology waste (so-called "military Keynesianism"); and an "activist" foreign policy, i.e., subversion, aggression, international terrorism, violent measures to bar social reform and meaningful democracy, etc., the essential content of the Reagan doctrine. Under the Reagan administration, the power of the state was substantially enhanced (state expenditures grew faster relative to GNP than ever before in peacetime), terrorist operations organized or supported by the United States exacted a fearful toll, and the state was converted, even more than before, into a welfare state for the privileged.

These policies plainly lack popular appeal; in fact, they have been opposed by the public by large margins throughout the Reagan years, as the polls show quite conclusively. There is a classic means to compel the public to accept policies to which it is opposed: induce fear of some Great Satan bent on our destruction—then the policies may be supported, however distasteful they may be, as necessary for our survival. Hence the hysterical rhetoric of the early Reagan years about the "Evil Empire" that is the source of all problems in the world, the "window of vulnerability" that leaves the U.S. defenseless before overwhelming Soviet power, etc. But propagandists were compelled to face a second problem: confrontations with the Evil Empire itself are far too dangerous, and must be avoided. The solution is obvious: the propaganda system must construct an array of "little Satans," states or groups that are weak enough so that we can attack them with impunity, but that can be stigmatized as tentacles of the Evil Empire, who seek to destroy us: Grenada, the Sandinistas, Qaddafi, the PLO, etc. We thus derive, predictably, the thesis of Soviet-sponsored international terrorism, the plague of the modern age.

The Keynesian programs of Reaganite state economic management were conducted in a particularly foolish way. These devices were not used to stimulate useful production, but to yield luxury consumption by the rich, financial speculation, and waste production (largely military). All of this carried inevitable costs, which must now be faced, specifically, the huge budget and trade deficits. It is no longer possible to mobilize the population to subsidize the rich and powerful and to devote resources to their needs through the Pentagon system. Predictably, then, the Soviet Union is less threatening and international terrorism has been reduced from a threat to our existence to a problem that must be controlled. A more statesmanlike stance is mandatory: summitry and negotiations, not confrontation and hysterical rhetoric. There have also been some changes in the outside world, but the major ones flow from domestic needs.

Editor's Notes to Interview 52

This is the fifth of the Reime interviews (see Editor's Notes to I13). It was done on the phone (a call from Helsinki to Lexington, Massachusetts), on Oct. 29, 1990.

Does the following sound like something said almost thirteen years ago?:

> "So we have a situation in which the United States is sitting there with a huge army suffering. The U.S. economy is heading into a more severe slump. There's turbulence in the Third World and in the Arab world which is basically anti-American ... the United States will find itself at war with Iraq, which Israel very much wants. They want the United States to be at war with Iraq, and they want Iraq destroyed. [Done. Next?—CPO] Second thing that will happen is that the alliance with the Arab world will break up, and the United States will be virtually at war with the Arab world, which is what they also want. So that's the outcome that they would prefer."

Plus ça change ... Not quite. One big difference is that Germany and Japan were "barely contributing" in October 1990, but shortly afterwards they contributed plenty of money (at least $70 billion, we are told), thus making mercenaries out of the American troops—ultimately for the benefit of the richest and most powerful of their fellow Americans. Having the victim pay for having been destroyed is something else.

52. Building Up for Military Attack (29 October 1990)

You have often written that it has virtually been an Axiom Number One in international politics since the Second World War that the oil resources in the Arabian peninsula must be kept in the hands of friendly forces to the United States. Do you think that recent events in the area after the Iraqi aggression against Kuwait can be deduced from this postulate?

I think they derive quite directly from it. This is a straight forward illustration of that principle. Saddam Hussein was a murderous gangster prior to August 2nd [1990], and the United States regarded him as an amiable friend and a favored trading partner. On August 2nd he violated this axiom, and therefore he turned into a reincarnation of Genghis Khan, and he has to be destroyed, following Nasser, and Khomeini, and others who have become independent indigenous forces that are trying to get substantial control over the Middle East energy resources. That is not tolerable to the United States.

The Issue? Not Access to Oil but a Lever of World Control

Why precisely so, because in any case Saddam Hussein must sell his oil to somebody?

Remember that U.S. policy was exactly the same as far back as the 1940s, when the United States was virtually not using Middle East oil. In fact, even in the oil crisis of the early 70s, the United States was importing very little oil. In fact, until 1968 the Western Hemisphere, which is overwhelmingly dominated by the United States, was the largest oil producer in the world. So the issue is plainly not access to oil. Nor in fact is the issue simply the cost of oil. I mean it's commonly said that the United States wants to lower the cost, ensure low cost. However, that's not true either. The United States has been quite supportive of OPEC [Organization of Petroleum Exporting Countries] agreements that raised the cost. In the early 1970s, the United States was not at all opposed to the very sharp rise in the price of oil, which benefited U.S. oil companies, even benefited indirectly the U.S. economy, because it led to huge exports to Saudi Arabia and recycling of petrodollars here and so on. So it's much more complex.

It's perfectly true that the oil has to be sold. And it's perfectly true that the price can't go too high, or else you drive consumers to other sources. But there's a range. There's a range within which the production level and the price can be administered. And the United States wants to make sure that it has its hands on that lever and nobody else does. And the reason is because that's a lever of world control. Whoever has their hand on that lever can exert quite considerable influence throughout the world. And in the case of the United States, this goes back to the 1940s. The primary concern has been Japan and Europe, which it was always recognized would be ultimately the major rivals, and have to be kept under control. Control over energy is one way to do it.

Do you think this anti-Saddam united front comprising the United States and the Western powers will last for a long time?

First of all, there is no united front. That's mostly propaganda. The European Community has made it very clear that they want to have nothing to do with the U.S. forces in Saudi Arabia. It's obvious enough, if you look at it. Aside from England (and marginally France), which has its own policies, the troops in Saudi Arabia are American. In fact, the European Community stated in its official response back in August (and it hasn't really changed) that the troops in Saudi Arabia are bilateral arrangements primarily between the United States and Saudi Arabia and that the European Community has nothing to do with it. Germany, in particular, stated that it won't do anything. Same with Japan. Same with most of the rest of the world. There are some exceptions but the reliance on military force is primarily [on the part of] the United States. Just yesterday the Italian prime minister, Andreotti, stated again that use of military force has to be the absolute last resort. He said anyone with any sense understands that the use of military force is an absolute last resort.

A United Front on Sanctions

There is a united front on another issue, namely on sanctions. The united front is in fact expressed quite accurately in the UN Security Council resolutions which call for an embargo and sanctions. They're very evasive about how you enforce them. In fact, they don't authorize really enforcing them. The United States tried to get the wording "minimal use of force" introduced but the Security Council wouldn't agree to that. They're not clear as to whether the sanctions include food and medicine, which is, incidentally, something quite unprecedented, even in much more severe cases of human rights abuses and aggression than this. The consensus is narrow, and it holds that sanctions should be used to try to compel Iraq to withdraw from Kuwait, and the United States joins that consensus.

But it also goes much further. The United States is plainly building up for military attack. Forces in Saudi Arabia are far beyond any defensive need. The major issue, the crucial issue, is: Will there be an effort to pursue a diplomatic track and negotiated settlement of some kind, as in every other case? Or, alternatively, will there be war? And on this, I think the United States is quite isolated. The United States has said over and over again that it will not consider any possible diplomatic settlement. There must be complete capitulation, after which maybe—and I stress maybe—the United States will permit some other issues to be discussed. That's not diplomacy. That's the opposite of diplomacy. And on this, I think the U.S. position is quite isolated.

What is, according to your view, the so-called cost-benefit analysis in the United States on the prospects for war?

Well, I think there's clearly **an internal split in the United States**. First of all, as far as the general population is concerned, it's quite strongly opposed to war. Polls reveal that very clearly. As far as the elite opinion is concerned, there's a split. I mean there are people (Henry Kissinger's a good example) who say, Well, we just have to go to war. And there are others, not of different political position than his, basically (like, say, Brzezinski), who says, No, it's too costly for us to go to war. I'm sure there's a split over that.

However, the trouble is, in my opinion, that I think the United States is trapping itself into a position in which it will have no choice but to go to war. The reason is pretty simple, I think. The logic of the situation has been quite clear since early August. There is an agreement, and I think it's the right agreement, that Saddam Hussein ought to be forced out of Kuwait. That's right. Now, there are three ways in which that could happen: it could happen through an embargo and sanctions; it could happen through war; and it could happen through diplomacy. There are no other ways. The chances are very high that the first path, embargo, will not have that effect within a reasonable amount of time, and by reasonable I mean an amount of time in which the United States will be able to sustain a massive military force in Saudi Arabia. That's very costly.

For one thing, it's extremely hard on the military forces: morale is going to erode; the equipment is not going to work; and so on and so forth. Although it just plainly costs a lot of money, it furthermore is politically costly. It's doubtlessly increasing discontent and turbulence throughout the Arab world, and in fact much of the Third World, where this international consensus is not shared. These are all very severe costs and they are increased by the fact that major rivals of the United States, namely basically Germany and Japan, are not paying the costs; in fact, are probably benefiting from the situation. Despite a lot of threats, and pleading, and cajoling, they are barely contributing.

So we have a situation in which the United States is sitting there with a huge army suffering. The U.S. economy is heading into a more severe slump. There's turbulence in the Third World and in the Arab world which is basically anti-American. Europe and Japan are doing just fine, going on to exploit Eastern Europe and all the things they want to do. That's not a situation the United States can tolerate for very long. That's what I mean by a reasonable time. Within a reasonable time, the time in which the United States can tolerate this, the embargo is not going to work. And that means the choices are quite stark: either war or diplomacy. Of course, there's the possibility of withdrawal but that's virtually ruled out. There's a lot of cynical posturing here about defense of high principle. So every time George Bush or anyone else makes a speech, there's a lot of talk about how aggressors cannot be rewarded, and we have to stand up for the principle that you can't acquire territory by force and on and on. And there's also a lot of rhetoric; you could easily collect a hundred articles saying that there's a new world order, post-Cold War new world order.

The United Nations for the first time in its history is acting the way it's supposed to do. It's no longer impeded by the Russians, and we don't have to worry about the Third World psychotics any longer, and now we can go on marching towards peace and justice with the United States in the lead. Now, if you take a position like that, you're trapped. In defense of high principle, you really don't compromise. And in fact, the United States has barred any diplomatic option, of which there are several on the grounds that the principles are so high and we are so noble that we can't consider them. Now this is very dangerous. For one thing the picture is so fraudulent that it's an astonishing commentary on Western intellectual culture and its ideological fanaticism that this doesn't just elicit ridicule. I mean, it takes five minutes of research to discover that the reason why the United Nations has not been able to carry out its peace-keeping missions is overwhelmingly that the United States has blocked them.

The United States is far in the lead (right up to the present, way back for 20 or 25 years) in vetoing Security Council resolutions and voting alone or with client states against General Assembly resolutions on every relevant issue: aggression, annexation, terrorism, human rights abuses, observance of international law, all of those issues. I mean, the only country that is even in the competition is England, because it has vetoed a number of Security Council resolutions on South Africa. There are exceptions but the overwhelming pattern is that the Soviet Union has voted with a large majority, and the Third World has largely been calling for observance of international order, international law, because that's the only thing that protects them against the depredations of the powerful. Again there are exceptions, but this is the overwhelming pattern.

The Pretense of High Principle

It's just the point of logic that you cannot defend principles selectively. If you defend principles, you defend them even when you don't like their application. Even Hitler and Stalin could defend, say, freedom of speech in the United States. So the U.S. is not defending any principle, nor is any other state. The UN can function in the present case because for once the United States happens to be opposed to the aggression, instead of either carrying it out or supporting it. That makes Saddam Hussein's aggression different from, say, the Turkish invasion and annexation of northern Cyprus, or the Israeli invasion of Lebanon, or Israel's annexation of the Golan Heights, or Morocco's aggression in the Sahara, or Indonesian aggression in East Timor, or U.S. invasion of Panama, and on and on.

Saddam Hussein's atrocities are horrifying, and they were horrifying before August 2nd, but they are not worse than other cases. So, for example, they don't even compare to the Indonesian aggression in East Timor, which was near genocidal, with U.S. aid. Or take, say, Namibia. The UN declared the South African occupation of Namibia illegal back in the 60s. The World Court declared it illegal in 1970 or 1971. Nobody called for going to war with South Africa. In fact, the United States insisted on "quiet diplomacy" and "constructive engagement" for decades, while South Africa robbed the place blind, terrorized it, and used it as a base for attacking its neighbors with plenty of violence, with outright aggression. All of that was fine. We just carried out "quiet diplomacy."

The point is, there is no principle involved here. Maybe there ought to be, but the fact of the matter is that no state, certainly not the United States, is acting on the basis of principle. And this is never pointed out. I mean literally. If you look at the massive discussion of this here, there is no critical analysis of the pretense of high principle. And that is extremely dangerous, because if that pretext is accepted, as it is by the educated sectors of the population, the articulate sectors, if that premise is accepted, then, of course, you have to go to war. You can't have negotiations. It is in this sense that I think the fanaticism of the political culture in the United States, and in the West generally in fact, is driving us towards war, whereas in fact there are other options that should be explored. The critical question is: Are there real diplomatic options?

I think it's been pretty clear since August what the possible shape of a negotiated settlement would be. It would involve Iraqi withdrawal from Kuwait, some form of guaranteed access to the Gulf, maybe leasing of the Bubiyana and Warba islands in the Gulf, and some arrangement about the Rumaila oil field, 95 percent of which is in Iraq, over a disputed border. Those are all negotiable issues.

Would Iraq accept negotiation on those issues? Well, actually Iraq has proposed this settlement back in late August. It was rejected by the United States. We don't know, however, whether that proposal was serious. There's only one way to determine whether a diplomatic track can be successful, and that is to pursue it, to explore it. If you block it at every turn, of course it won't work. That's obvious. The U.S. position (and here it's not just the administration but articulate opinion generally) is that we've got to block it at every turn, because we are so noble and standing up for such high principles. In fact, you might almost argue, for cultural reasons (for reasons having to do with the cultural fanaticism, the political fanaticism of Western culture) that we've been driven towards a war which could be absolutely catastrophic.

How do you see the role of the Soviet Union in all of this? Because it might have been very dangerous if they had responded the way they used to before the Gorbachev period.

It's dangerous if they respond; it's dangerous if they don't respond. One of the features of this new world order is that there's only one military superpower. Up until now the Soviet Union provided a kind of a deterrent to the use of U.S. force, a real deterrent. In fact, U.S. strategic analysts and, you know, right-wing interventionists of the Elliot Abrams variety, are very pleased now and say so. They are pleased that there no longer is a deterrent to the use of U.S. military force. Elliot Abrams pointed out after the invasion of Panama with great glee that the United States didn't have to worry for once that it might become entangled with the Soviet Union. We are much freer to use military force than before.

That's an extremely dangerous situation for the world. It's perfectly true that the United States feels quite free to use military force. No one is going to sustain the targets of U.S. aggression, as the Soviet Union sometimes did in the past, and there no longer is any fear that the use of force might turn into a major super-power conflict. That always has been a deterrent. I mean, the West, again in its own cultural fanaticism, likes to talk about the modern world as one in which the United States contained and deterred the Soviet Union. The other half of the story, a very significant part, is that the Soviet Union contained and deterred the United States. And that deterrent has gone. That's not to say that the Soviet Union was pretty. It was horrifying, but it was a deterrent.

How do you see the role of Israel in this conflict?

Well, within Israel the mood is, I think, rather ominous. There's a lot of commentary in Israel now. There's deep concern in Israel that the United States is forging close alliances with the Arab states, and that is a nightmare for Israel. Frankly, I think they're exaggerating in this interpretation of what's happening. But what matters here is their subjective interpretation. Their interpretation is that Bush and Baker are very anti-Israel and pro-Arab, and that they are now forging alliances with the Arab states, with Saudi Arabia, Syria, Egypt, and that Israel is losing its value as a strategic ally, which is (they understand very well) the basis for U.S. support for it. And they are deeply concerned about this.

The Shamir government and, in fact, larger sectors, are likely to try to do what they can to break this perceived growing relationship. How could they do that? Well, unfortunately, there are some pretty unpleasant ways in which it might be occurring to them. I don't think this is a high probability, but I think there is a small probability (big enough to be worried about, but small) that it could occur to, say, people around Shamir, that one way they can achieve this with the result they want is to get involved in a war with Iraq themselves. That's not very difficult. It's easy to take something that's happening and attribute it to Iraq and then to retaliate, so-called. That's easy. Any half-decent propaganda agency can work that out. They might do something which would in fact involve them in a conflict with Iraq.

The consequences of that will be immediate. For one thing, the United States will find itself at war with Iraq, which Israel very much wants. They want the United States to be at war with Iraq, and they want Iraq destroyed. Second thing that will happen is that the alliance with the Arab world will break up, and the United States will be virtually at war with the Arab world, which is what they also want. So that's the outcome that they would prefer. I'm beyond having any evidence, but I would be extremely surprised if such thoughts were not occur-ring, and also I strongly suspect that the United States is warning them not to do that. However, whether they hear those warnings, I don't know.

In the 1970s, before the Iranian revolution, the U.S. strategy in the area was based on a triangle comprising Israel, the Iran of the Shah, and Saudi Arabia.

It still is. It pretty much is. In the early 1980s, when the United States was sending arms to Iran via Israel (this is long before the hostages; it had nothing to do with hostage exchange), the purpose was very openly stated by high Israeli officials and participants. The purpose was basically to lay the basis for a military coup in Iran that would restore the triangular relationship, and I'm convinced that they must be trying to do the same thing right now. We'll find out about it in 20 years [ca 2010]. But the relationship between Israel and Saudi Arabia remains. Saudi Arabia is important because they control the oil (under U.S. control, of course) and Israel is still the major military force in the region. If the United States does go to war with Iraq, there's no doubt that Israel will be a base, and maybe a participant.

But Iran is still under the leadership that came to power in the Islamic revolution.

Right. And that's exactly what they've said for the last ten years. There have been continuous efforts to try to restore Iran to this alliance. That's what the arms sales were about. Here in the West there's a pretense that they were an arms-for-hostages deal. That cannot be the case, as we know very simply from the fact that this was going on before the hostages.

What is the role of public opinion in the United States? Do you think it is one possible factor in the calculations of Washington in its decisions?

Yes, that's a factor. Popular opinion is pretty strongly against going to war. Depending on what poll you read, a substantial majority of the population does not want war, and surprisingly, about half the population doesn't even want an attack against Iraq if U.S. forces are attacked. When people are asked: If Iraq attacks the United States, should we respond with an attack against Iraq?, I think about 47 percent said yes in the last poll. There's a strong opposition to going to war. It has all sorts of reason. There's a resurgence of old-fashioned Midwest right-wing isolationism, for example. Some of it is racist: they don't merit our involvement. Some of it is anti-interventionist. It has all sorts of sources, but it's strong. There certainly is no strong public support for war, in fact, quite to the contrary.

The question is how important that is. By and large, the public has little influence on policy unless it becomes articulate and disruptive and so on. At the moment, the critical elements, I think, are elite opinion, and I think that's split. It's split not on any principled grounds. All sides are equally unprincipled, but there just are different cost-benefit analyses, as you put it.

Editor's Notes to Interview 53

This is the sixth of the Reime interviews (see Editor's Notes to I13). It took place at MIT on Nov. 22, 1991.

It might be helpful to keep in mind the following quote from **Y501** (1992), 3.1: "Avid U.S. support for Mussolini from his 1922 March on Rome, later support for Hitler, was based on the doctrine that Fascism and Nazism were understandable, if sometimes extreme, reactions to the far more deadly Bolshevik threat—a threat that was internal, of course; no one thought the Red Army was on the march." On the related post-revisionist synthesis and its "leading figure, by common consent"(**CD&E** (2003), ch. 19, p.324), John Lewis Gaddis, see **NI** (1989), App. II; **DD** (1991), ch. 1 and 3.6; **Y501** (1992), 3.1; **WOON** (1994, 1996), 1.4–5.

On the imperial European conquest of the world, "what we call the North-South-conflict," "the fundamental conflicts … in a sense for 500 years," see in particular **Y501**.

The parallelism of the ideologies of state "socialism" and state "capitalism" ("ideas that go right back to the response to the earliest modern democratic revolution in 17th-century England") is lucidly discussed in (**CD&E** (2003), ch. 7.

The most perceptive discussion of the Spanish revolution of 1936–1937 known to me is found in **APNM** (1967), I.ii. The new era of hegemony is the subject matter of Chomsky's book , *Hegemony or Survival* (see also I58 and the Editor's Notes).

For an updated view on international solidarity, see interviews 56 and 57 and the Editor's Notes to them. About the "huge working-class movement in Brazil," where "there is something [important] going on," at least one thing is now clear: the candidate of the Workers Party (PT), Luis Ignacio da Silva ("Lula"), stopped just short of a first-round victory in Brazil's presidential election of 2002, which then he won by a landslide on Oct. 27, a victory that could "mark a juncture in history that could be described as almost revolutionary," not just "a turning point for the whole region," since "in becoming Brazil's first ever working-class president, Lula will break a tradition of rule by a small southern elite, the military and local political chieftains dating back to Portugal's discovery of the country in 1500" (*NYT*, Oct. 25, 2002). See I17, **Y501** (1992), 7.9, and *The Common Good* (1998), pp. 80ff., esp. pp. 86–87.

On the biology of language, see Lyle Jenkins, *Biolinguistics* (Cambridge University Press, Cambridge, 2000). ; also, Marc D. Hauser, N. Chomsky & W. Tecumseh Fitch. 2002. "The Faculty of Language: What Is It, Who Has It, and How Did It Evolve?," *Science*, vol. 128 (Nov. 22, 2002), pp. 1569–1579. On the meanings of words, the interpretation of constructions, see **NHSLM** (2000); also, C.P. Otero, "Language, Meaning and Interpretation: Chomsky Against the Philosophers," in *Semantics: Critical Concepts*, ed. J. G. Rexach. London: Routledge, 2003, and references there.

53. After the Fall (22 November 1991)

There have been quite a number of changes in the world during the last couple of years. If we start from the changes in Eastern Europe, the collapse of Bolshevism, how do you interpret this phenomenon?

Well, I have (as you know) always regarded the Cold War as basically a North-South conflict, as it's called. That is, the major or, to put it into a broader perspective, **the main theme of modern history** has been the European conquest of the world. That's the main theme of the last 500 years. And Europe is by now rather the concept which includes Japan and the former European colonies, basically G7 [the Group of 7] and their periphery, the rich industrial states. That's what used to be Europe. They have a conception of world organization that's now mainly run by the United States. Their conception is that what we call the South, the Third World, the former colonial domains, they have a function: their service role. Their role is to be a source of resources, raw materials, markets, cheap labor, opportunities to invest and export pollution, and so on. That's essentially their role.

If any of them move towards what's called nationalism, or ultra-nationalism (in the internal documents, the planning record, that's what it's called), that's a crime. That has to be stopped, because that interferes with their service role. If any of them fall under the plague of democracy, that's also a danger, and that has to be overcome, because popular pressures will interfere with this service function. Their role is to support, to create a proper investment climate, provide cheap labor and make resources available, etc. Independent nationalism in these countries becomes particularly dangerous if it has a kind of spreading effect, if it incites similar things elsewhere. If it inspires others to try to do the same thing, it's particularly dangerous. That's sometimes called a virus that might infect the region, or a rotten apple that might infect the barrel. For the public, that's called the domino theory, you know, they're gonna conquer other people. But the real problem is the threat that there might be an influence: others might try to do the same thing.

So when the U.S. was overthrowing Guatemalan democracy, it described the Guatemalan regime (in internal documents, of course, in secret documents), as a threat to the stability of the region, because its successful agrarian reform and its acts in support of the rights of peasants and workers were stimulating others in other countries, who had the same problems, to do likewise, and that undermines the security of the wealthy classes and foreign investors. That's what's meant by stability. Stability means security for the wealthy classes and foreign investors.

That's, of course, in internal documents. What the public faces is somewhat different. Independent nationalism has to be destroyed, and if it has the kind of a demonstration effect, if it stimulates others to do likewise, if it's regarded as successful, then even more so. It must be destroyed, because then it could be a virus. And that's a good deal of modern history. The reasoning is the same whether you're dealing with a little speck in the Caribbean like Grenada, or you're dealing with a huge country like Russia, the same reasoning.

Now, pre-Bolshevism Russia was essentially part of what we now call the Third World. It was a quasi-colonial dependency of Western Europe in pre-Iron Curtain days. The same was true of substantial parts, not all but substantial parts of Eastern Europe, say, Bulgaria, was no different. It was developing, but the same is true of the Third World. The sectors that were developing and industrializing were mostly under Western control. They were Western investments, largely. And in fact, it was falling behind the Western powers at that point. It was very poor, very impoverished. Sectors that were developed were mostly foreign related and falling behind the industrial capitalist countries, which is typical of the Third World. It was different from other parts of the Third World because they had a big military force, but that had always been true. I mean, centuries before, under the czar, it was a deeply impoverished region but with a military force sufficient to frighten people in Europe and to penetrate large parts of Europe, and so on.

"Ultranationalism" and "Regime Change": A Problem and A Solution

It doesn't matter whether these nationalist regimes are, it doesn't matter what their politics are. I mean, they can be run by Mother Teresa, and the reaction would be the same. The problem is independent nationalism. As long as they're dependent and regarded as dependable, they can be any kind of murderous thug you like. Saddam Hussein is the most recent example. The U.S. strongly supported Mussolini, for example, as long as it thought that he was subordinated to Western interests. He was "that admirable Italian gentleman," as Franklin Delano Roosevelt put it. Even Hitler was supported on the same grounds. It can be Hitler, it can be Mussolini, Saddam Hussein, Guatemalan generals, Suharto. Any amount of atrocities or gruesome massacres or whatever is just fine as long as you play a subordinate role. But if you move towards independence, you have to be wiped out. And as I said, it's the same with something like Grenada or something like the Soviet Union.

As soon as the Soviet Union succumbed to "nationalism," that is, started an independent role, in 1917, the West, by reflex, took the obvious action, the usual one. You've got to intervene, to stop it. That intervention was described at the time as defensive, and it is described to this day as defensive, if you read contemporary diplomatic history. Perhaps the leading diplomatic historian in the

West is John Lewis Gaddis in the United States, a rather liberal and very good diplomatic historian who is now president of the Association of Diplomatic Historians. He has a recent book on the Cold War (*The Long Peace*, it's called), in which he discusses this. He says that Western intervention in the Soviet Union after the revolution was a defensive action undertaken in response, in justifiable response, to a challenge that the Bolsheviks had issued against the very survival of the capitalist order in the West.

In other words, they had carried out programs of social reform, and they had announced revolutionary intentions, and they were going to run in an independent way. They had separated that area out of the domains of Western control, and furthermore, others might be tempted to follow them. And that is aggression. Announcement of revolutionary intentions and change of the social order is aggression, and therefore we have a right to defend ourselves, of course, against aggression, and we have a right to invade them in defense.

That's been the picture all along. It's the same when you invade Grenada, or you overthrow the government of Guatemala, or you carry out ten years of terror against Nicaragua, or whatever it may be. Always the same. And the logic is the same. You've got to stop the virus before it spreads. You have to ensure "stability" in the sense of security for the upper classes and the wealthy investors, the foreign enterprises. Nothing very much changes.

A Typical Third World Pattern

That's why I really don't agree that there have been big changes in the international order. Grenada and the Soviet Union are rather different. Grenada you can overthrow in a weekend; the Soviet Union took 70 years. But it happened,. And it was pretty predictable. I mean, it always had a big military force, but it was always a partially developed country, never with anything like the industrial capacity or the industrial infrastructure of Western Europe. It could not sustain itself against the foreign pressures. Nor could it sustain the internal tyranny against domestic pressures to free up the country.

By the mid-70s, it was already pretty clear that the Soviet Union was having problems. The economy was stagnating. The military spending leveled off in the mid-70s. Western propaganda was quite different: the Russians are on the march and so on. But it was clear that that was happening (the CIA already was reporting the leveling of military expenditures). They couldn't move to further stages of industrialization: too tyrannical, too backward, and so on. By the early 1980s, it was clear that the game was over.

The United States, particularly, has been dragging its feet on this to this day. I mean, right now the Unites States is trying very hard to preserve central authority there and to retard movements towards independence of the particular republics. Through the 1980s the U.S. was almost alone in trying to cut back trade and interchange, which would have accelerated the liberalization and the opening of the economy. The reason for that is kind of obvious. The U.S. is not gaining very much from this. Its rivals are gaining much more, especially

Germany. This part of the Third World is a European domain, and Germany and its periphery, the other industrial countries of Europe, will be the prime beneficiaries of the Latin Americanization of this part of the world, its return to its more or less traditional Third World status. Hence the U.S. has no special interest in this, and it is trying to retard it. But it's happening. By the late 80s the Soviet Union had disappeared from the world scene. It's precisely because it has disappeared that Gorbachev is now allowed to show up at Madrid. If he represented any power interest, he would not be permitted to interfere with unilateral U.S. settlement of the Middle East conflict. But being a totally powerless representative of a country that doesn't exist, he's allowed to be there for show.

There are changes. One change is that this region of the world will undergo a kind of process like Latin Americanization (not all of it). There were parts of that region that were, in fact, part of the industrial West or close to becoming so, and they may proceed in that direction, like, say, Czechoslovakia, the Czech part of Czechoslovakia, maybe the Baltic countries, and so on. But large parts of it are very likely to become what we now see them becoming, similar to Third World countries. A typical Third World country has sectors, a small sector of quite wealthy, privileged people, who live by the wealthiest Western European or American standards, and then a vast part of the population...

Like Brazil.

Yes. Take, say, Brazil, where maybe five percent, 10 percent, live like, say, London and Paris or even richer, maybe 75 percent live like Central Africa, and the rest are sort of in between. And that's a typical Third World pattern. One can expect that to be the case in much of that region, too. The wealthy sectors are those that are linked to foreign enterprises, by and large: somebody's got to run the local franchises and that kind of thing. And that will happen in the Soviet Union, too, and it's likely to be the ex-nomenklatura, the old Communist Party hierarchy. They're the ones who know the ropes, and they're the ones the Western banks would prefer to deal with and so on. And in fact, it's already happening. You can see they are becoming the managers of the Western branches. They're running the local branch offices and becoming the enterprising capitalists, and so on and so forth. Ultimately this will be beneficial to, especially, Europe, which will be able to exploit this region and reconstruct the tradition of trade and exploitation patterns, which were broken by the Russian revolution.

No More Deterrence

A second effect is that there is no more deterrence. There was a deterrent to the use of force by the United States in the past, namely, the Soviet Union did have a big military force. It wasn't much of an economic power, but it had a big military force. And that had a very definite deterrent effect. The way it's put in the United States is: "We had to fight wars with one hand tied behind our back, we couldn't go all out," meaning if you go all out, you might run into the Russians, and you're not gonna fight anybody who can shoot back. That's a stupid error. You may only attack defenseless people. So therefore there always were restraints on U.S. power. Now the restraints are gone, and by the late 80s (1987, 1988), American strategic analysts were already quite enthusiastic (openly, quite publicly), about the new prospects for the use of military force now that the deterrent had disappeared.

That's another effect. We saw that in the Gulf. Ten years ago the U.S. and Britain, which is more or less its lieutenant in these operations, would not have dared to put half a million troops in the desert. It would simply have been too dangerous. But now all constraints are gone. You're not gonna fight with one hand behind your back. Unlimited destruction is possible. This is well understood in the Third World. There's a great deal of fear and trepidation throughout the Third World, because they can see this. Europe and the United States are much too deeply indoctrinated to be able to see such obvious facts, but in the more civilized parts of the world, in the South, they see it very well. That's another effect.

Rhetorical Change in the Framework of Propaganda

Another effect still internal to the United States, is that there's need for a kind of rhetorical change in the framework of propaganda. So for the last 70 years, every Third World intervention has been justified as defense against the Russians, and one obviously can't play that game any longer. There's been a kind of problem of the vanishing pretext all throughout the 1980s. So you had to conjure up new chimeras (Hispanic narco-traffickers, or crazed Arabs, Libyan terrorists, one thing or another), who are plotting to overthrow us. It's striking, and it takes some discipline not to notice this after the Berlin Wall fell in November 1989. I mean, that ended any pretense that the Cold War was still on. A couple of weeks later George Bush invaded Panama, restoring the rule of the 10 percent white minority (bankers and drug pushers and money launderers and so on), retaking control over the military forces, which had been lost, ensuring U.S. domination of the canal, the usual sort of thing. It was like a footnote to history, barely worth mentioning, it's so standard. But there was one difference: for the first time in 70 years, they couldn't present it as defense against the Russians.

So we're back to the days of Woodrow Wilson doing exactly the same thing a year before the Bolshevik revolution. We're defending ourselves from somebody else. In those days it was the Huns, or the British. Now it's the drug peddlers led by the arch-maniac Noriega who's gonna conquer the world unless we stopped him on time. So there's a new rhetorical framework needed. And this is clear, incidentally, in internal documents as well.

But apart from that, I don't think the world order has changed very much. The fundamental conflicts remain what they've been in a sense for 500 years, the imperial conquests, what we call the North-South conflict.

Would you say that at some periods of time during these past 70 years the Western powers were contemplating co-opting the Bolsheviks, because, objectively, inside the Russian Revolution, they were playing a counter-revolutionary role?

There's always been a split in the West over this: the German Ostpolitik, for example. And it goes all the way back to the 1920s. Shall we integrate them into our system, or shall we try to overthrow them by force? The same has been true, say, of China. So, for example, in the 1950s, there was a significant internal policy debate in the United States between those who thought we should overthrow them by force, and those who thought we should integrate them into our system with trade relations and so on. The hardliners won for a while, but in the 1970s it was reversed, and there was a move to integrate them into the capitalist West, basically, the state capitalist West. And there were always such questions with the Soviet Union, too. There was not much of a chance of co-optation. They were too big, militarily too powerful.

This kind of North-South element of the Cold War was interrupted for a while by what happened in Europe: the rise of Hitler. At first the U.S. tended to support Hitler. As late as 1937, the U.S. Embassy in Berlin was reporting back that Hitler is a moderate, who's holding a line against the extremists in the Nazi Party, and we should therefore support him, and also describing the Nazi terror as, as they put it, excessive but understandable reaction to the real atrocities, namely, those of the working class, and the Bolsheviks, and so on. Ultimately, I'm convinced, that will be the interpretation that's given to this period in the West, just as it's the interpretation by the kind of ultra-right historians in Germany today. In my view, it's bound to take over. It's just too convenient not to be accepted. But that was certainly the internal thinking in major, probably dominant, State Department circles at least as late as 1937. It was only when it became very clear that Hitler was going to turn against the West and become one of those unacceptable nationalists (like Saddam Hussein on August 2nd, 1990) that Hitler became the enemy, and then there was a break. You know, we had to work with Uncle Joe for a while, and there was a certain period of love of the Russians, really nice guys. But that changed very quickly.

So you would say that there was no kind of insoluble contradiction between Western capitalism and the Bolshevik system, as some Trotskyists say?

I don't think so. I don't agree with most of that. Stalin himself, as far as I could understand Russian policy, was rather conservative. I mean, he was a monster internally, but quite conservative internationally. And his position seemed to be that he would have liked to see Russia become a kind of a junior partner in the U.S. dominated system.

Managing the world.

Yes. Whether they would have opened up Russia to Western penetration, I doubt. And that was the problem. As long as they don't open it up to Western penetration and exploitation, it's an enemy that has to be destroyed. And as I said, that's true whether it's Grenada setting up a fishing cooperative for 10 people, or Russia pulling a huge area of the Third World out of Western domains.

You never saw a great difference between original Leninism and Stalinism.

There was a difference, but…It depends…In my view, Leninism was the most extreme form of totalitarianism that had yet existed. It's true that Stalin made it a lot worse, a lot more vicious. But the basic structure was established by Lenin and Trotsky, in my view, and I've always thought this. When they took over, it looks to me like **a coup more than a revolution** in **October 1917**. It's not that there weren't popular forces. They were there. But when [the Leninists] took over in this coup, almost their first act was to destroy the working-class organizations. They moved very quickly to eliminate factory councils, to reduce soviets to more or less meaningless organizations, of course to eliminate Constituent Assembly, and to break down both the democratic and the popular structures, including the working-class structures. It's not just that they were worried about the social revolutionaries. Factory councils had to go as well.

And the logic was explained very clearly. Trotsky put it clearly in 1918, that is, before the intervention even: we have to turn the country into a labor army under the command of the optimal leader, who will simply drive the ignorant and stupid Russian masses on to industrialization. That's the essence of Leninist theory. Not very different from the conceptions of [present-day] liberal democracy, in my view: the masses of the population are too stupid and ignorant to be able to manage their own affairs. They shouldn't be permitted to meddle. If you can control them by force, OK; if you can't, you have to control them by other means. And these are ideas that go right back to the response to the earliest modern democratic revolution in the 17th-century England, including people regarded as libertarians like, say, John Locke. The Leninist system very quickly established the structures that were turned by Stalin into organizations of mass slaughter. I mean, I'm not suggesting that Lenin and Trotsky would have, say, slaughtered kulaks in anything like that level, or set up the GULAG, and so on. Probably they wouldn't. But the totalitarian structures were there right away.

The system was there.

The system was there. The institutions were there. The ideology was there. They happened to fall into the hands of an extraordinarily brutal fanatic, but I don't think it could have been much different with those institutions.

The same was repeated in Spain in 1937.

Well, Spain was a little different. The Communist Party in Spain was the party of the police officers and the petty bourgeoisie and so on, and its main task was to destroy the popular revolution. It was only after the revolution was destroyed (you know, Communist armies swept through Aragon and destroyed the collectives and smashed up collectivization in Barcelona, and so on), after that was done, there was some kind of a war against the Fascists. But that was a secondary process.

Incidentally, in this there was more or less unity throughout the world. The Western powers, the Fascist states, and Stalin agreed that the popular revolution had to be smashed. One of the reasons why Roosevelt and Britain tended actually to support the Fascists in the early stages was the fear of the popular rebellion. After that was crushed, then they could start fighting one another. That was a dramatic case, but it's pretty much the same always.

Do you regard it as an important fact that some Third World countries have been industrializing, and there's a new working class (like in Brazil and in some parts of East Asia), so that a new kind of working class movement might develop, creating new forms of international solidarity?

Well, international solidarity would be hard to say.

Fascism as an Efficient Technique of Development

East Asia is an interesting case. The former Japanese colonies like Taiwan and South Korea and so on (mostly those two and the two city states, Singapore and Hong Kong, which are much in the Japanese orbit) have undergone an economic development, industrial development, from a purely economic point of view pretty impressive, in the last 20 years. That got a very strong stimulus from the Vietnam War, in fact, probably a crucial stimulus, just as Japan's industrial development got a huge stimulus, probably the decisive one, from the Korean War, as did much of Europe, incidentally. But then they've taken off under what we, if we're accurate, would call semi-fascist structures. And fascism is a pretty efficient technique of development. I mean, actually Hitler showed that, too. And it succeeded. There certainly are working class struggles and organizations, and probably at least the hope there'll be moves towards democratization and liberalization.

But that's one special thing. Latin America, so far, is rather different. There is a huge working-class movement in Brazil, but Brazil is an absolute catastrophe. I mean, the West likes to talk about the collapse of Communism, but the collapse of capitalism in the same years is much more dramatic. The domains of the capitalist powers, the countries that could be more or less compared to Eastern Europe in terms of development and resources and so on, they just were smashed in the 1980s. Brazil, in particular, is an absolutely catastrophic area, although a very rich country potentially. There's a big working-class movement, but the whole social system and economy is devastated. It's not clear what could happen. The last time they tried to do something, the generals took over with Western backing. That was considered the greatest triumph for freedom in the mid-20th-century, the State Department called it, and we know what the result was then, and it still remains. However, there is something going on. That's important.

Here's a real change in the world order, in my view, much more important than the ones we've been talking about. In the early 70s, there was a qualitative change in the internationalization of capital. Corporations had always been international, of course; General Motors and Du Pont and so on and I.G. Farben always were based to an extent internationally. But by the early 70s, it was beginning to change in a qualitative manner. Banks were becoming international institutions with hardly any national base or control. The same was happening with major corporations. That means an internationalization of capital. That does lead to the development of productive industry in much of the Third World (although under the control of the transnationals), and that has a very serious effect on the national economies of the industrial states.

The U.S. is a striking case. Capital can move; humans can't. So American corporations, (say, an American automobile company) can set up a plant in northern Mexico or, for that matter, in Papua New Guinea, which can get super-cheap labor and be a very advanced plant, has no pollution control as well as no environmental problems. American workers with a different standard can't possibly compete. So they are just basically thrown out.

With these changes plus the internationalization of money, you know, with the one level (if you think like Eurodollars, which are not state-determined, but also much more broadly), just the amount of capital in the hands of essentially uncontrolled international banks and international institutions is huge. And those are big changes in the world system, as is the diffusion of power in Western domains to the three major centers, the German-based Europe, Japan, and the United States. All this was pretty evident in the early 1970s, and plays a major role in what's been happening since, I think.

I would like to ask a couple of questions on linguistics. For the first, it seems to be the case that the development of generative grammar shows that some parts of the human mind are closer to inorganic matter than organic, biological systems. What does it lead up to?

I don't like to say it, but I've always noticed it. I mean, it's perfectly true that the kinds of work that's been done on the structure of language seems constantly to reveal features that are in a way more typical of what you'd expect in the inorganic world than what we find in the organic world.

Language, Like Other Organs, Is Not Well-Designed for Use

Now, it's conceivable that this is an artifact due to the way in which we're investigating it. But it doesn't look likely. It looks real. So, for example, the research that follows guiding ideas such as search for symmetry and simple principles and non-redundancy and so on, these seem to be useful over and over again. They seem very successful. For some reason, which nobody understands, that's what you seem to find in the study of the inorganic world, if you understand things well enough. And it has also been a useful research strategy there. But in the organic world, you typically don't expected to find it. Biological systems are messy. They tend to be highly redundant. Redundancy is, in fact, a virtue: it means that if you hit a head with a crowbar, some other system will take over and do the same things. They develop over time in ways that aren't at all understood. François Jacob once described evolution as a tinkerer. It does the best out of whatever material is at hand, and usually does a sort of bad job of it. And you wouldn't expect these kinds of properties to emerge.

This is kind of impressionistic. One can't really nail it down. But it looks to me as though there's something paradoxical turning up.

You have said in your recent writings that in a way language is unusable or at least not very functional. On the other hand, you have stressed that the language faculty is a kind of mental organ. Is there some kind of, not inconsistency or contradiction, but some kind of tension between these two views?

No. I think most organs are non-functional in the same sense. That was meant to be deliberately provocative. When I say that it's not functional and not usable, I don't mean you can't use it. It just means that it's not well-designed for use. But in that respect it's like most organs.

Take one that I'm concerned with, that happened to strike me recently, namely the spine. The spine is very poorly designed, and apparently this poor design goes all the way back to the origins of vertebrate history. We live, but if an engineer was designing a vertebrate, he would not do it this way. So in that sense it's not functional. Of course, that's not surprising. I mean, evolutionary pressures simply say that if something is so dysfunctional that you can't reproduce, you're not gonna exist. But it doesn't say that the organs that are around are gonna be well-adapted to use. That doesn't mean anything. There isn't any measure of how well-adapted things are to use. And in this respect it seems to me that language is like other organs. There are aspects of it that are usable; they carry a selectional advantage, in fact. But there are fundamental features of language that render large parts of it completely unusable. The unusable parts are those that we don't use.

Where is the boundary in language between what is culturally determined and what is biologically given?

Well, culture is biologically given, too, so that's a little hard to answer. But there is variation among languages, like Finnish isn't English. If you were to talk Finnish, I wouldn't understand a word of what you're saying. But nevertheless, the more we understand languages, the more we discover that they're really cast pretty much to the same mold, that the differences among them are pretty narrowly circumscribed. Now, narrowly circumscribed and minor differences in quite intricate systems can lead to an output that looks very different. You make small changes in the internal workings of an intricate system, and what comes out may look like a radical difference. But the more we understand, the more it does appear to turn out that those differences are small. And, in fact, we know that this must be the case. I mean, it's by something almost close to logic, with very few facts.

There are some facts that are not controversial. One fact is that humans across the species are about the same with regard to their capacity to acquire language. So if I had moved to Finland, my children would speak Finnish perfectly. Everybody knows that's true. There's no special adaptation to learning Finnish, or English, or Japanese, or something like that. That's not controversial. Another thing that's not controversial is that children learn a language on the basis of extremely limited evidence. They don't have anything like enough evidence to determine the particular conclusions they draw about the meaning of lexical items, or about the phonetic structures, or about syntactic forms, or anything else. And from those two facts it follows that either everything's a miracle, or else what children are coming to know is coming from inside of them, basically. It's the internal structure of the language organ that's simply manifesting itself and yielding the meanings of words, the interpretation of constructions, the array of sounds, and so on, on the basis of very small stimulation from experience, which is sort of setting things one way or another and fixing options, and so on.

This is a conclusion based on extremely weak and not controversial evidence, and it leads us to conclude that languages must be very much alike. If we don't see it, it's because we don't understand enough, and the more we understand, the more we see it. So the effect of what people call culture, environment, is just to select among the few options that are available. And those selections may yield outputs which look very different. But that doesn't tell you a lot. That just tells you that it's an intricate structure.

How do you see in this connection elements like Case and Agreement and so on?

Take Case. Finnish has a very rich Case system morphologically: you see the Cases; English has a very poor Case system: you don't see them at all, virtually. But the more we understand, it seems to be that English has probably the same Case system as Finnish. It just shows up in mental computation and doesn't come up the mouth. And the reason we see it is that, when you understand Case systems, if you look at the effect of Case systems in Finnish, you seem to get those same effects in English. It's just that they show up in more indirect ways. So whereas languages like, say, English and Chinese and some others, have extremely meager physical representation of Case systems, nevertheless it seems that the Case systems are all there. They're just not coming up the mouth. And similarly, in languages like, say, English and French, questions are formed by taking the question word and putting it at the beginning of the sentence; in Chinese and Japanese, it sits there. But by now, there's very strong reason to believe that Chinese and Japanese are doing exactly the same thing. It's just that it happens in mental computation without any overt expression. One of the ways in which languages differ is what comes up the mouth, what parts of the mental computation actually are manifested. But the mental computations themselves seem remarkably identical. I mean, not remarkably, because they have to be. If they weren't near identical, we couldn't learn language in the first place.

If you have some rather well-established principles of grammar, like the principles of the well-formedness of chains or something like that, and then you have some language that seems to break these principles, would you say that this a kind of exciting situation?

Well, not really, because anywhere in the natural sciences it's easy to come up with what looks like counter-examples. I mean, the world is so little understood that a lot of things that are happening, seem to refute what we know.

Take the simplest thing. Take a ball rolling down an inclined plane. Suppose a high-school teacher predicts that it's gonna get to the bottom in such-and-such an amount of time. And let's say one of the students says: "No, I don't believe you." And the teacher says: "Fine, we'll run an experiment." And he puts a ball on the top of the inclined plane, and it starts going down. The student reaches over and picks it up and throws it out of the window. OK, it didn't get down to the bottom. He says he refuted the experiment. What does the teacher say, if he doesn't throw him out of the class? Does he say: "OK, you refuted the experiment; physics is false"? No, what he says is: "Look, this only works in a closed system, and a system in which you're not a part; your voluntary acts aren't part of that closed system. That's where it works." Suppose the student's pretty clever and he says: "Well, you said it works or not-works. Why am I not part of the system? I'm a physical object. So why am I not part of the system? I mean, of course, anything works or not-works. So therefore physics is tautological. There's nothing to it. You can do this, if you like."

In fact, the student's quite right. The student is part of the physical world. It's just that the physicist has no way of explaining what the student is doing. So therefore we rule it out as irrelevant. And in fact in every aspect of the natural sciences you can find tons of what appears to be counter evidence, often very close to what you call actual evidence. That's one reason why the advanced physical sciences don't even really study the natural world as it appears to us. I mean, physicists don't take moving pictures of what's happening out the window. They study the natural world under the highly artificial and contrived conditions of very complex experiments. That's what they study, because that's really where you find things that teach you something. But most of what's going on outside the window nobody knows how to explain, although it's the physical world.

And in the case of language, which is not physics, of course, there's an awful lot of material around that nobody knows how to explain. So when you find something when you're studying, not necessarily an exotic language, that appears to contradict some principle, you simply put it aside, until you understand things better. Maybe it really does contradict the principle. So you don't forget about it. You sort of shelve it and leave it there. There seems to be a problem. I tried to understand what I can understand. Maybe you'll be able to show later that it wasn't a contradiction, if you understand it properly. You have to interpret things differently. Those are the normal situations of research in the empirical sciences.

You've noted the similarity between language and the number system, the human ability to compute discrete infinities. Are they both results of some more basic aspect of human mind?

Nobody knows. The number system is based on a system of digital infinity, discrete infinity, which is unusual. The biological world doesn't have many systems of discrete infinity. It has finite systems, it has continuous systems, but not many things like, you know, one, two, three, four, but not three, six. The number system has now been expanded by human ingenuity to yield continuous systems, but at the core it's a system of discrete infinity. And language is like that, too. I mean, a language has a one-word sentence, a two-word sentence, a three-word sentence but not a three, six-word-sentence, or a n-word sentence, or something like that. And that's true of every aspect of language.

We know that the capacity for the number system has got to be in the genes somewhere. If we didn't have it there, we wouldn't be able to learn it. You can't teach an ape the number system, or a bird, or something else. It just apparently doesn't have the genetic endowment for it. And that means that throughout the entire history of human evolution, the capacity wasn't used, though it was there. And there still are cultures in which it hasn't been elicited.

Well, those things suggest (they don't prove) that the number system is, in a way, abstracted from the language system, that for some reason, unexplained, the language faculty developed with principles of discrete infinity (nobody knows why and how). And that capacity was used. In fact, it's been used for maybe a couple of hundred thousand years in some form or other. And maybe the core of the number system is some kind of abstraction from it, just waiting around to be stimulated by appropriate external events. If you like fairy tales about evolution, that one's as good as any other. And most of what we say about evolution is fairy tales.

So would you say that language was born as a kind confluence of a conceptual system and a computational one?

Maybe. It looks as though other organisms (at least, say, primates) may have conceptual systems that are in some respects similar to ours. Maybe they pick out objects the way we do and so on. I'm not sure, of course, but they might. They don't have the capacity of discrete infinity, it appears. If you put these two capacities together, the conceptual system and the system of discrete infinity, at least, you have the rudiments of language. It's as if the system of discrete infinity provides a mechanism for formulating and expressing thoughts, using materials that were already available, possibly. And this is such wild speculation that you can say anything else, too, if you like. I mean, the study of evolution makes sense when you're talking about amino acids or maybe different kinds of snails, and so on, but when you get to things like complex organisms, there's essentially nothing much to say.

What do you think is at the moment the most promising line of research in linguistics?

Right now there's very exciting work going on, I think, in both the formal structure of natural language, and things like lexical semantics, and semantic interpretation, and phonetic interpretation, the core areas of linguistics. There's a lot of progress, and it's very exciting and changing rapidly, and lots of new discoveries.

Editor's Notes to Interview 54

This is one of the online interviews made available on ZNet (as a ZNet commentary), a by now well-known online resource, on Feb. 21, 2002. (The interviewer is not identified.) It is reprinted here with permission from Z Communications: www.zmag.org.

The Cato Institute journal for which Chomsky used to write when few outlets were available to him in the U.S. is *Inquiry*. For example, the 1979 review referred to in I15 was published in the March 19, 1979, of *Inquiry*, and the original version of his outstanding review of Kissinger's *The White House Years*, in the issue of April 7, 1980, and later reprinted as ch. 6 of **TCNW** (1982), as noted on p. 59.

In the 1950s and subsequent decades until the fall of the Soviet Union, the term "communism" was essentially used to support counterrevolution abroad, and the term "terrorism" is used in pretty much the same way today. "International Terrorism in the Real World" is something else (as shown in I56, **NI** (1989) and **P&E** (2002)—see also Edward Herman, *The Real Terror Network* (South End, 1982) and, with Gerry O'Sullivan, *The 'Terrorism' Industry*, Pantheon, 1989), and so is its domestic counterpart. See Editor's Notes to I20.

The "largely fraudulent 'drug war' " ("a leading device to imprison the unwanted population") plays a role similar to communism or terrorism. As Chomsky observes, "people huddle beneath the umbrella of authority for protection from the menace." Thus, "the drug war not only gets rid of the superfluous population, it frightens everybody else." "If most people are dissatisfied and others are useless, you want to get rid of the useless and frighten the dissatisfied." No wonder that "As drug czar under the Reagan administration, George Bush ["canceled the small Federal program aimed at banks engaged in laundering drug money"] and thus was instrumental in terminating the main thrust of the real 'war on drugs'. Officials in the enforcement section of the Treasury Department monitored the sharp increase in cash inflow to Florida (later Los Angeles) banks as the cocaine trade boomed in the 1970s, and 'connected it to the large-scale laundering of drug receipts' (Treasury Department brief)." See **DD** (1991), esp. 4.2 and ch. 5 (the bracketed quote is on p. 155); **Y501** (1992), 2.5, 3.4; **WOON** (1993), ch. 1; **P&P** (1996), ch. 5; "The Drug War, Colombia and U.S. policy," talk given at MIT on March 13, 1995, available from www.alternativeradio.org; and "Noam Chomsky on the Drug-Terror Link," *The Week Online* (DRCNet.org), Feb. 14, 2002, among many other interviews, talks and writings by Chomsky. See also I44.

54. From "Communism" to "Terrorism" and the "Drug War" (21 February 2002)

During Sunday's Super Bowl, the drug czar's office ran a series of paid ads attempting to link drug use and the "war on terrorism." If you use drugs, the ads said, you support terrorism. What is your take on this?

Terrorism is now being used and has been used pretty much the same way communism was used. If you want to press some agenda, you play the terrorism card. If you don't follow me on this, you're supporting terrorism. That is absolutely infantile, especially when you consider that much of the history of the drug trade trails right behind the CIA and other U.S. intervention programs.

Going back to the end of the Second World War, you see (and this is not controversial, it is well-documented) the U.S. allying itself with the French mafia, resulting in the French connection, which dominated the heroin trade through the 1960s. The same thing took place with opium in the Golden Triangle during the Vietnam War, and again in Afghanistan during the war against the Russians.

The cocaine trade is the primary given reason for U.S. intervention in Colombia's civil war. In your opinion, to what degree is the drug angle a pretext? And a pretext for what?

Colombia has had the worst human rights record in the hemisphere in the last decade while it has been the leading recipient of U.S. arms and training for the Western Hemisphere and now ranks behind only Israel and Egypt worldwide.

Human Rights Violations and U.S. Military Aid and Training: A Close Correlation

There exists a very close correlation that holds over a long period of time between human rights violations and U.S. military aid and training. It's not that the U.S. likes to torture people; it's that it basically doesn't care. For the U.S. government, human rights violations are a secondary consequence.

In Colombia, as elsewhere, human rights violations tend to increase as the state tries to violently repress opposition to inequality, oppression, corruption, and other state crimes for which there is no political outlet. The state turns to terror. That's what's been happening in Colombia for a long time, since before there was a Colombian drug trade.

Counterinsurgency has been going on there for 40 years (President Kennedy sent a special forces mission to Colombia in the early 1960s). Their proposal to the Colombian government was recently declassified, and it called for "paramilitary terror" (those are their words) against what it called known Communist proponents. In Colombia, that meant labor leaders, priests, human rights activists, and so on. Colombian military manuals in the 1960s began to reflect this advice. In the last 15 years, as the U.S. has become more deeply involved, human rights violations are up considerably.

On a more serious point: suppose that the drug pretext were legitimate. Suppose that the U.S. really is trying to get rid of drugs in Colombia. Does Colombia then have the right to fumigate tobacco farms in Kentucky? They are producing a lethal substance far more dangerous than cocaine (more Colombians die from tobacco-related illnesses than Americans die from cocaine). Of course, Colombia has no right to do that.

Domestically, state, local, and federal governments have spent tens of billions of dollars on the "war on drugs," yet illicit drugs remain as available, as pure, and as cheap as ever. If this policy is not accomplishing its stated goal, what is it accomplishing? Is there some sort of latent agenda being served?

They have known all along that it won't work. They have good evidence from their own research studies showing that if you want to deal with substance abuse, criminalization is the worst method. The RAND report did a cost-effectiveness analysis of various drug strategies and it found that the most effective approach by far is prevention and treatment.

Police action was well below that, and below police action was interdiction, and at the bottom in terms of cost-effectiveness were out-of-country efforts, such as what the U.S. is doing in Colombia. President Nixon, by contrast, had a significant component for prevention and treatment that was effective.

Drug Criminalization as a Technique of Social Control

U.S. domestic drug policy does not carry out its stated goals, and policy makers are well aware of that. If it isn't about reducing substance abuse, what is it about? It is reasonably clear, both from current actions and the historical record, that substances tend to be criminalized when they are associated with the so-called dangerous classes, that the criminalization of certain substances is a technique of social control.

The economic policies of the last 20 years are a rich man's version of structural adjustment. You create a superfluous population, which in the U.S. context is largely poor, black, and Hispanic, and a much wider population that is economically dissatisfied.

You read all the headlines about the great economy, but the facts are quite different. For the vast majority, these neoliberal policies have had a negative effect. With regard to wages, we have only now regained the wage levels of 30 years ago. Incomes are maintained only by working longer and harder, or with both adults in a family working. Even the rate of growth in the economy has not been that high, and what growth there is has been highly concentrated in certain sectors.

If most people are dissatisfied and others are useless, you want to get rid of the useless and frighten the dissatisfied. The drug war does this. The U.S. incarceration rate has risen dramatically, largely because of victimless crimes, such as drug offenses, and the sentences are extremely punitive. The drug war not only gets rid of the superfluous population, it frightens everybody else.

Drugs play a role similar to communism or terrorism, people huddle beneath the umbrella of authority for protection from the menace. It is hard to believe that these consequences aren't understood. They are there for anyone to see. Back when the current era of the drug war began, Senator Moynihan paid attention to the social science, and he said if we pass this law we are deciding to create a crime wave among minorities.

For the educated sectors, all substance abuse was declining in the 90s, whether we're talking about cocaine or cigarette smoking or eating red meat. This was a period in which cultural and educational changes were taking place that led the more educated sectors to reduce consumption of all sorts of harmful substances.

For the poorer sectors, on the other hand, substance abuse remained relatively stable. Looking at these curves, we see what will happen: it is obvious you will be going after poor sectors. Some legal historians have predicted that tobacco would be criminalized because it is associated with poorer and less-educated people.

If you go to McDonald's, you see kids smoking cigarettes. But I haven't seen a graduate student who smoked cigarettes for years. We are now beginning to see punitive consequences related to smoking, and of course the industry has seen this coming for years. Philip Morris and the rest have begun to diversify and to shift operations abroad.

Many ardent drug reformers are self-identified "libertarians." As an anarchist (I assume it is fair to call you that) what is your take on libertarianism?

The term "libertarian" as used in the U.S. means something quite different from what it meant historically and still means in the rest of the world. Historically, the libertarian movement has been the anti-statist wing of the socialist movement. Socialist anarchism was libertarian socialism.

In the U.S., which is a society much more dominated by business, the term has a different meaning. It means eliminating or reducing state controls, mainly controls over private tyrannies. Libertarians in the U.S. don't say, Let's get rid of corporations. It is a sort of ultra-rightism.

From Criminalization to Prevention

Having said that, frankly, I agree with them on a lot of things. On the drug issue, they tend to oppose state involvement in the drug war, which they correctly regard as a form of coercion and deprivation of liberty. You may be surprised to know that some years ago, before there were any independent left journals, I used to write mainly for the Cato Institute journal.

What should be done about drug use and the drug trade?

I agree with RAND. It is a problem. Cocaine is not good for you. If you want to deal with substance abuse, the approach should be education, prevention, rehabilitation and so forth. That is what we have successfully done with other substances. We did not have to outlaw tobacco to see a reduction in use; that is the result of cultural and educational changes.

One must always be cautious in recommending social policy because we can't know what will happen, but we should be exploring steps toward decriminalization. Let's undertake this seriously and see what happens. An obvious place to begin is with marijuana. Decriminalization of marijuana would be a very sensible move. And we need to begin shifting from criminalization to prevention. Prevention and treatment are how we should be addressing hard drugs such as cocaine and heroin.

Editor's Notes to Interview 55

This is the first of two interviews (the second in two parts) by Michael Albert, reprinted here with permission from Z Communications: www.zmag.org. (See Editor's Notes to I57.) It was completed on April 2, 2002, and made immediately available on ZNet.

As is to be expected, most of the "material posted regularly on ZNet, reviewing developments as they proceeded" comes from Chomsky.

On the Orwellian use of the technical term "rejectionism" see **FT** (1983, 1999), esp. ch. 10; **P&E** (1986, 2002), ch. 1 and passim, esp. p. 169f.; **MEI** (2003), chs. 6–9, and the editors notes to 30. See also I56.

For more on Sharon and its impact, see I56 and the Editor's Notes to it.

Zeev Sternhell (author of a recent study on the origins of Israel, *The Founding Myths of Israel: Nationalism, Socialism, and the Making of the Jewish State*, 1998), like Ilan Pappé of Haifa University and other Israeli scholars, is called a "new historian" (perhaps echoing the use of the term in the U.S. beginning in the 1960s) for a not obscure reason. After Israel's invasion of the refugee camps in 2001 he wrote that "In colonial Israel ... human life is cheap" and that the leadership is "no longer ashamed to speak of war when what they are really engaged in is colonial policing, which recalls the takeover by the white police of the poor neighborhoods of the blacks in South Africa during the apartheid era." Like his Hebrew University colleague sociologist Baruch of Kimmerling (who a couple of years ago observed that "what we feared has come true, " since Jews and Palestinians are "regressing to superstitious tribalism ..." and an "evil colonial" war "appears an unavoidable fate"), Sternhell, as Chomsky writes (**MEI** (2003), ch. 9, p. 227), "stress[es] the obvious: there is no symmetry between the 'ethno-national groups' regressing to tribalism. The conflict is centered in territories that have been under harsh military occupation for 35 years." See *Propaganda and the Public Mind*, Cambridge, MA: South End Press, 2001, p193f.

55. The Fateful Triangle: A Fearful Asymmetry
(2 April 2002)

Is there a qualitative change in what's happening now?

I think there is a qualitative change.

From a Potential Bantustan to a Demolition of the Palestinian Authority

The goal of the Oslo process was accurately described in 1998 by Israeli academic Shlomo Ben-Ami just before he joined the Barak government, going on to become Barak's chief negotiator at Camp David in summer 2000. Ben-Ami observed that "in practice, the Oslo agreements were founded on a neo-colonialist basis, on a life of dependence of one on the other forever." With these goals, the Clinton-Rabin-Peres agreements were designed to impose on the Palestinians "almost total dependence on Israel," creating "an extended colonial situation," which is expected to be the "permanent basis" for "a situation of dependence." The function of the Palestinian Authority (PA) was to control the domestic population of the Israeli-run neo-colonial dependency. That is the way the process unfolded, step by step, including the Camp David suggestions. The Clinton-Barak stand (left vague and unambiguous) was hailed here as "remarkable" and "magnanimous," but a look at the facts made it clear that it was (as commonly described in Israel) a Bantustan proposal; that is presumably the reason why maps were carefully avoided in the U.S. mainstream.

It is true that Clinton-Barak advanced a few steps towards a Bantustan-style settlement of the kind that South Africa instituted in the darkest days of Apartheid. Just prior to Camp David, West Bank Palestinians were confined to over 200 scattered areas, and Clinton-Barak did propose an improvement: consolidation to three cantons, under Israeli control, virtually separated from one another and from the fourth canton, a small area of East Jerusalem, the center of Palestinian life and of communications in the region. And of course separated from Gaza, where the outcome was left unclear.

But now that plan has apparently been shelved in favor of demolition of the PA. That means destruction of the institutions of the potential Bantustan that was planned by Clinton and his Israeli partners; in the last few days, even a human rights center. The Palestinian figures who were designated to be the counterpart of the black leaders of the Bantustans are also under attack, though not killed, presumably because of the international consequences. The prominent

Israeli scholar Ze'ev Sternhell writes that the government "is no longer ashamed to speak of war when what they are really engaged in is colonial policing, which recalls the takeover by the white police of the poor neighborhoods of the blacks in South Africa during the apartheid era." This new policy is a regression below the Bantustan model of South Africa 40 years ago to which Clinton-Rabin-Peres-Barak and their associates aspired in the Oslo "peace process."

None of this will come as a surprise to those who have been reading critical analyses for the past 10 years, including plenty of material posted regularly on ZNet, reviewing developments as they proceeded.

Exactly how the Israeli leadership intends to implement these programs is unclear (to them too, I presume).

It is convenient in the U.S., and the West, to blame Israel and particularly Sharon, but that is unfair and hardly honest. Many of Sharon's worst atrocities were carried out under Labor governments. Peres comes close to Sharon as a war criminal. Furthermore, the prime responsibility lies in Washington, and has for 30 years. That is true of the general diplomatic framework, and also of particular actions. Israel can act within the limits established by the master in Washington, rarely beyond.

What's the meaning of Friday's Security Council Resolution?

The primary issue was whether there would be a demand for immediate Israeli withdrawal from Ramallah and other Palestinian areas that the Israeli army had entered in the current offensive, or at least a deadline for such withdrawal. The U.S. position evidently prevailed: there is only a vague call for "withdrawal of Israeli troops from Palestinian cities," no time frame specified. The resolution therefore accords with the official U.S. stand, largely reiterated in the press: Israel is under attack and has the right of self-defense, but shouldn't go too far in punishing Palestinians, at least too visibly.

Evasion of the Central Immediate Issues

The facts (hardly controversial) are quite different. Palestinians have been trying to survive under Israeli military occupation, now in its 35th year. It has been harsh and brutal throughout, thanks to decisive U.S. military and economic support, and diplomatic protection, including the barring of the long-standing international consensus on a peaceful political settlement. There is no symmetry in this confrontation, not the slightest, and to frame it in terms of Israeli self-defense goes beyond even standard forms of distortion in the interests of power. The harshest condemnations of Palestinian terror, which are proper and have been for over 30 years, leave these basic facts unchanged.

In scrupulously evading the central immediate issues, the Friday Resolution is similar to the Security Council Resolution of March 12, which elicited much surprise and favorable notice because it not only was not vetoed by the U.S., in the usual pattern, but was actually initiated by Washington. The Resolution called for a "vision" of a Palestinian state. It therefore did not rise to the level of

South Africa 40 years ago when the apartheid regime did not merely announce a "vision" but actually established black-run states that were at least as viable and legitimate as what the U.S. and Israel had been planning for the occupied territories.

Trying to Destroy the Main Forces of Secular Arab Nationalism

What is the U.S. up to now? What U.S. interests are at stake at this juncture?

The U.S. is a global power. What happens in Israel-Palestine is a sidelight. There are many factors entering into U.S. policies. Chief among them in this region of the world is control over the world's major energy resources. The U.S.-Israel alliance took shape in that context. By 1958, the National Security Council concluded that a "logical corollary" of opposition to growing Arab nationalism "would be to support Israel as the only strong pro-Western power left in the Middle East." That is an exaggeration, but an affirmation of the general strategic analysis, which identified indigenous nationalism as the primary threat (as elsewhere in the Third World); typically called "Communist," though it is commonly recognized in the internal record that this is a term of propaganda and that Cold War issues were often marginal, as in the crucial year of 1958. The alliance became firm in 1967, when Israel performed an important service for U.S. power by destroying the main forces of secular Arab nationalism, considered a very serious threat to U.S. domination of the Gulf region. So matters continued, after the collapse of the USSR as well. By now the U.S.-Israel-Turkey alliance is a centerpiece of U.S. strategy, and Israel is virtually a U.S. military base, also closely integrated with the militarized U.S. high-tech economy.

Within that persistent framework, the U.S. naturally supports Israeli repression of the Palestinians and integration of the occupied territories, including the neo-colonial project outlined by Ben-Ami, though specific policy choices have to be made depending on circumstances. Right now, Bush planners continue to block steps towards diplomatic settlement, or even reduction of violence; that is the meaning, for example, of their veto of the Dec. 15, 2001, Security Council resolution calling for steps towards implementing the U.S. Mitchell Plan and introduction of international monitors to supervise the reduction of violence.

For similar reasons, the U.S. boycotted the Dec. 5 international meetings in Geneva (including the EU [European Union], even Britain) which reaffirmed that the Fourth Geneva Convention applies to the occupied territories, so that critically important U.S.-Israeli actions are "grave breaches" of the convention (war crimes, in simple terms, as the Geneva declaration elaborated). That merely reaffirmed the Security Council Resolution of October 2000 (U.S. abstaining), which held once again that the convention applied to the occupied territories. That had been the official U.S. position as well, stated formally, for example, by George Bush I when he was UN ambassador. The U.S. regularly abstains or boycotts in such cases, not wanting to take a public stand in opposition to core principles of international law, particularly in the light of the circumstances under which the conventions were enacted: to criminalize formally the atrocities of the Nazis, including their actions in the territories they occupied. The media and intellectual culture generally cooperate by their own "boycott" of these unwelcome facts: in particular, the fact that as a High Contracting Party, the U.S. government is legally obligated by solemn treaty to punish violators of the conventions, including its own political leadership.

That's only a small sample. Meanwhile the flow of arms and economic support for maintaining the occupation by force and terror and extending settlements continues without any pause.

What's your opinion of the Arab summit?

The Arab summit led to general acceptance of the Saudi Arabian plan, which reiterated the basic principles of the long-standing international consensus: Israel should withdraw from the occupied territories in the context of a general peace agreement that would guarantee the right of every state in the region, including Israel and a new Palestinian state, to peace and security within recognized borders (the basic wording of UN 242, amplified to include a Palestinian state).

The Plan for the Palestinians: "You Shall Continue to Live Like Dogs"

There is nothing new about this. These are the basic terms of the Security Council Resolution of January 1976 backed by virtually the entire world, including the leading Arab states, the PLO, Europe, the Soviet bloc, the non-aligned countries (in fact, everyone who mattered). It was opposed by Israel and vetoed by the U.S., thereby vetoed from history. Subsequent and similar initiatives from the Arab states, the PLO, and Western Europe were blocked by the U.S., continuing to the present. That includes the 1981 Fahd plan. That record too has been effectively vetoed from history, for the usual reasons.

U.S. rejectionism in fact goes back 5 years earlier, to February 1971, when President Sadat of Egypt offered Israel a full peace treaty in return for Israeli withdrawal from Egyptian territory, not even bringing up Palestinian national rights or the fate of the other occupied territories. Israel's Labor government recognized this as a genuine peace offer, but decided to reject it, intending to extend its settlements to northeastern Sinai. That it soon did, with extreme brutality, the immediate cause for the 1973 war.

The plan for the Palestinians under military occupation was described frankly to his Cabinet colleagues by Moshe Dayan, one of the Labor leaders more sympathetic to the Palestinian plight. Israel should make it clear that "we have no solution, you shall continue to live like dogs, and whoever wishes may leave, and we will see where this process leads." Following that recommendation, the guiding principle of the occupation has been incessant and degrading humiliation, along with torture, terror, destruction of property, displacement and settlement, and takeover of basic resources, crucially water.

Sadat's 1971 offer conformed to official U.S. policy, but Kissinger succeeded in instituting his preference for what he called "stalemate": no negotiations, only force. Jordanian peace offers were also dismissed. Since that time, official U.S. policy has kept to the international consensus on withdrawal (until Clinton, who effectively rescinded UN resolutions and considerations of international law). But in practice, policy has followed the Kissinger guidelines, accepting negotiations only when compelled to do so (as Kissinger was after the near-debacle of the 1973 war, for which he shares major responsibility), and under the conditions that Ben-Ami articulated.

A "Hysterical" Israeli Reaction Backed by the U.S.

Official doctrine instructs us to focus attention on the Arab summit, as if the Arab states and the PLO are the problem; in particular, their intention to drive Israel into the sea. Coverage presents the basic problem as vacillation, reservations, and qualifications in the Arab world. There is little that one can say in favor of the Arab states and the PLO, but these claims are simply untrue, as a look at the record quickly reveals.

The more serious press recognized that the Saudi plan largely reiterated the Saudi Fahd Plan of 1981, claiming that that initiative was undermined by Arab refusal to accept the existence of Israel. The facts are again quite different. The 1981 plan was undermined by an Israeli reaction (that even its mainstream press condemned as "hysterical") backed by the U.S.. That includes Shimon Peres and other alleged doves, who warned that acceptance of the Fahd plan would "threaten Israel's very existence."

An indication of the hysteria is the reaction of Israel's president Chaim Herzog, also considered a dove. He charged that the "real author" of the Fahd plan was the PLO, and that it was even more extreme than the January 1976 Security Council resolution that was "prepared by" the PLO, at the time when he was Israel's UN ambassador. These claims can hardly be true, but they are an indication of the desperate fear of a political settlement on the part of Israeli doves, backed throughout by the U.S.. The basic problem then, as now, traces back to Washington, which has persistently backed Israel's rejection of a political settlement in terms of the broad international consensus, reiterated in essentials in the current Saudi proposals.

Until such elementary facts as these are permitted to enter into discussion, displacing the standard misrepresentation and deceit, discussion is mostly beside the point. And we should not be drawn into it—for example, by implicitly accepting the assumption that developments at the Arab summit are a critical problem. They have significance, of course, but it is secondary. The primary problems are right here, and it is our responsibility to face them and deal with them, not to displace them to others.

Editor's Notes to Interview 56

This interview, conducted by Dimitriadis Epaminondas, was made available online by ZNet on July 3, 2002, and is reprinted here with permission from Z Communications: www.zmag.org.

For more on the possibility of scattering al-Qaeda and spawning new terrorist networks, see **9-11** (2001), Chomsky's first best-seller, and **P&T** (2003). See also I57.

On Chomsky's visit to Turkey, see ch. 30 of the third edition of **RP** (2003), including the editor's notes.

The great praise for Sharon (one of the leading terrorist commanders in the world for the last half century), now considered a great statesman in the United States, is not without interest, even granting that his ultra-right 1992 proposals scarcely differ from those of Labor. For a review of the various Israeli peace proposals over the years, see **WOON** (1993, 1996), ch. 3 and Epilogue. See also **P&P** (1996), ch. 6. For more on Sharon and its impact, see interviews 55, 38, 36 and 29, and the Editor's Notes to I29 and to I20.

The "no magic keys" theme is a recurrent one in Chomsky's work. A particularly memorable passage is the paragraph that closes **TT** (1985).

On the World Social Forum, see the reference to **RP** above.

56. The Enormous Impact of State-Directed International Terrorism (3 July 2002)

How far do you believe will the U.S. sacrifice its basic civil liberties for a greater sense of security?

American Reactionary Jingoism and Popular Commitment to the Rights Won

It is doubtful that the current attack on civil liberties has much to do with security. In general, one can expect the state to use any pretext to extend its power and to impose obedience on the population. Rights are won, not granted, and power will seek any opportunity to reduce them.

The current incumbents in Washington are at an extreme of reactionary jingoism and contempt for democracy. The question we should ask, I think, is how far citizens will allow them to pursue their agendas. So far, they have been careful to target vulnerable populations, like immigrants, though the laws they have passed have much broader implications. My feeling is that popular commitment to the rights that have been won in hard struggle is too deep to allow the attack to proceed very far.

How can we keep the balance between protecting safety, protecting civil liberties and protecting privacy?

Proposed Measures that Probably Harm Safety

It is impossible to answer in the abstract. It is necessary to consider proposals case by case. As I mentioned, the measures proposed and sometimes implemented generally have only a limited relation to "protecting safety." Many of them probably harm safety.

Take the bombing of Afghanistan, for example. Whatever one thinks about it, did it increase security? U.S. intelligence doesn't think so. They recently reported that by scattering al-Qaeda and spawning new terrorist networks, the bombing may have increased the threat of terror.

Does that matter? Not really, as far as state planners are concerned. When Prince Abdullah of Saudi Arabia came to the U.S. recently to urge the administration to pay more attention to the effect of his policies in the Arab world, he was told by high officials that "if he thought we were strong in Desert Storm, we're 10 times as strong today." This was to give him some idea what Afghanistan demonstrated about our capabilities. In brief: Follow orders, or you'll be pulverized. That's what the bombing of Afghanistan was about.

The war against terrorism will have a lot more casualties, a lot more innocent casualties. Can this be justified?

Rejection of the Most Elementary Moral Principles

Again, the question cannot be answered in the abstract. But there are some criteria for answering it. One simple criterion is that if some action is legitimate for us, then it is legitimate for others. To take an example: if it is legitimate for the U.S. to bomb Afghanistan because Washington suspects that the plot to carry out the 9-11 atrocities was hatched there (the FBI has recently conceded they still have only suspicions, no firm evidence), then *a fortiori*, it would have been legitimate for Nicaraguans (Cubans, Lebanese, and a long list of others) to bomb Washington, because they know, not suspect, that it is the source of terrorist atrocities that far exceed even 9-11. Those who do not accept the latter conclusion (that is, every sane person) cannot accept the former one, unless they reject the most elementary moral principles, and thereby abandon any claim to speak of right and wrong, good and evil.

The same criterion applies universally. It does not answer all questions, but does answer a great many of them. It is true that elementary moral principles such as this cannot be considered by the rich and powerful, because of the consequences that follow very quickly. Nevertheless, honest people should be willing to entertain them.

What is the impact of terrorism on the world and especially in the U.S.?

The Impact of Terrorism is Enormous.

To take just some recent examples: Central America was devastated by state-directed international terrorism in the 1980s, as was Haiti in the early 1990s. I've just returned from Colombia, the scene of the worst terrorist atrocities in the Western hemisphere in the past 10 years, now getting even worse. Even the State Department concedes that the overwhelming majority are attributable to the military and paramilitaries, which are so closely linked that Human Rights Watch, which has done some of the most detailed studies, calls the paramilitaries the "sixth division" of the Colombian army, in addition to the five official divisions. Political murders are running now at maybe 20 a day, more than 300,000 people are added every year to those displaced (mostly by terror). Colombia holds the world record for murder of trade unionists and journalists, though of course the victims as usual are mostly peasants. And so on.

Shortly before, I visited Turkey, where some of the worst state terrorist atrocities of the 1990s took place in the Kurdish southeast, and the population now lives in a virtual dungeon. All of this is international terrorism, because of its crucial reliance throughout on massive U.S. support, not only military but also ideological support: silence and apologetics. Because of the agent, it is not counted in the annals of terrorism. It is easy to continue.

Healthy Reactions to the Restricted Use of the Term "Terrorism"

The term "terrorism" is used, standardly, to refer to the terrorism that they carry out against U.S., whoever "we" happen to be. Even the worst mass murderers (the Nazis, for example) adopted this practice. I imagine the fascist generals in Greece must have done the same.

Since the rich and powerful set the terms for discussion, the term "terrorism" is restricted, in practice, to the terror that affects the U.S. and its clients and allies. Keeping to that very narrow category of terrorism, the atrocities of 9-11 had an enormous impact on the West. Not because of the scale (regrettably, that was not unusual) but because of the choice of innocent victims. For hundreds of years, it has been the prerogative of Europe and its offshoots to carry out such acts against others, with virtual impunity. It had been understood for some time that with new technology, the industrial societies were likely to lose their virtual monopoly of violence, maintaining only an enormous preponderance. On 9-11, that expectation was realized, though in a way that was completely unanticipated. Of course, it is a great shock.

The reaction was complex. Among intellectuals, it was mostly jingoist hysteria, but that is quite normal. Among the general population, reactions varied. For many people, it was a "wake-up call," which has led to considerable openness, concern, skepticism, and dissidence. These are healthy reactions, and though it is difficult to measure their scale, it is surely substantial.

What is your opinion about the U.S. long-awaited policy statement on how to end the Middle East conflict?

The U.S. Planners' "Vision" of an Eventual Palestinian State

George Bush's planners constructed a series of demands that they know the Palestinians cannot conceivably meet. They demanded that under harsh and brutal military occupation, Palestine should become Sweden, learning the ways of democracy from Saudi Arabia and Egypt (that is what the words the president spoke imply). They should have free elections, in which they choose a candidate the U.S. selects for them. If they fail these conditions, the U.S. will continue to provide massive support for the terror conducted by the official "man of peace," Ariel Sharon, and the U.S. will continue to bar the international consensus on a political settlement, as it has been doing for 25 years. If Palestinians were to meet U.S. conditions, then they would be permitted to contemplate George Bush's "vision" of an eventual Palestinian state, somewhere: maybe in the Arabian desert, as House Majority Speaker Dick Armey recently proposed. By staring soulfully into the future with this noble vision, Bush approaches (from below) the moral level of the more extreme partisans of apartheid 40 years ago. They not only had a "vision" of black-run states, but actually implemented their vision, even providing them with some economic support.

For Israel, Bush calls for a "freeze" on settlements—with a wink of the eye. Everyone familiar with the topic knows that settlements can be "frozen" but nevertheless expand without any disruption, by virtue of a device called "natural growth."

In short, the U.S. will continue to carry forward the goal of the Oslo process: to establish a "permanent neo-colonial dependency" for Palestinians (in the words of Prime Minister Barak's chief negotiator at Camp David two years ago, representing the position of the doves). The Middle East conflict is to be resolved by force, not diplomacy, in accord with this long-standing conception.

What is the impact of globalization on the world?

Two Opposed Views of "Globalization": Worldwide Solidarity versus Investor-Rights

The term "globalization" is used by power centers to refer to the specific form of international economic integration that has been instituted within the "neoliberal" framework of the past several decades. The impact of this investor-rights version of globalization is reasonably clear. Virtually all macroeconomic indicators have declined worldwide: rate of growth of the economy, of productivity, of capital investment, even trade. There are exceptions, namely, the countries that did not follow the rules, like China. In general, the regions that followed the rules more religiously, like Latin America, had the worst records. In the U.S., contrary to many claims, the period was one of slow growth, as compared to the preceding decades, furthermore highly skewed towards the most wealthy sectors of the population. The majority suffered stagnation or decline. Social indicators also declined fairly steadily in contrast to earlier years, when they tracked growth.

In general, the impact was about as presumably intended. The process has been highly successful for those who designed it, not surprisingly (for those sectors called "the masters of the world" by the international business press, with only a touch of irony). For others, the impact has been mixed, often gloomy. But what happens to them is incidental: policies are not designed for their benefit.

Do you have any advice on how to institute an effective anti-globalization program without the assistance of violence?

The World Social Forum: Towards the First Genuine International?

"Anti-globalization" is a propaganda term devised by the advocates of a particular investor-rights version of international integration. No sane person is opposed to globalization, surely not the Left or the workers movements, which were founded on the commitment to international solidarity, that is, a form of globalization that is concerned with the rights and needs of people, not private capital. As for the role of violence, official "globalization" relies very heavily on it: that should be obvious without comment. But I see no reason why people-oriented globalization movements (called "anti-globalization" in the propaganda system) should do so; on the contrary, such tactics lack justification and undermine the goals of the movements.

The right ways to proceed are those that have been used for centuries in popular struggles for peace, justice, and human rights. We all know what they are. There are no magic keys. They require patient education, organization, when possible and appropriate direct action (as, for example, in the actions of the Landless Workers Movement in Brazil, one of the most important components of the international peoples-globalization movements). There are no general rules, only specific proposals depending on circumstances and goals. One highly promising expression of the mass popular movements supporting a human-oriented form of globalization is the World Social Forum that has met twice in Porto Alegre, Brazil, perhaps sowing the seeds of the first genuine International, one might hope.

What do you think the political impact of U.S. corporate, accounting scandals will be? Are you concerned about it?

They will presumably lead to some retraction of the lunatic version of markets that have been imposed by extreme reactionaries in recent years. There is a serious impact for workers who have lost their jobs and pensions, and for many others. But wealth and power will mostly escape unscathed, even enriched, as has already happened for many of those in charge. I doubt that there will be a long-term impact beyond a return to some of the regulatory apparatus that has been dismantled, predictably leading to disaster, as in the past.

What do you think about the formation of the Euro-army?

Europe is under no serious military threat, so a Euro-army is unlikely to be involved in defense (though whatever the military does is called "defense," typically). We should ask, then, what tasks will be assigned to it. In a world that is far less than perfect, one can think of some legitimate tasks. But those who have an eye on history will expect something different, and not very pleasant to contemplate.

These consequences are, however, in the domain of choice, and given the at least partially democratic character of Western societies, the choices can lie in the hands of a concerned public to no slight extent.

Editor's Notes to Interview 57

In the summer of 2002 a number of questions were circulating among people worried about a seemingly imminent U.S. attack against Iraq. On Aug. 29, Michael Albert put some of them to Chomsky, via email (Part I). On April 12, 2003, he asked him a few more questions about the aftermath of the attack and its ramifications (Part II). Questions and answers were immediately made available on ZNet, and are reprinted here with permission from Z Communications: www.zmag.org. (See Editor's Notes to I55.)

The (dissident) literature on the Middle East "one could read about … in Z magazine at the time, maybe nowhere else" is of course mostly due to Chomsky.

Regarding major atrocities as insignificant in the light of higher "reasons of state" is of course nothing new or rare. See **FRS** (1973).

On the U.S.-supported Israeli invasion of Lebanon, see the updated edition of **FT** (1999), in particular the last two chapters; also, the new edition of **P&E** (2002), ch. 7, and Part II of **MEI** (2003).

Scott Ritter was the UN's top weapons inspector in Iraq until he resigned in 1998 and since then he has been a vocal opponent of U.S. policies towards Iraq.

The Strategic Command is the highest military agency that's concerned with nuclear strategy and use of nuclear weapons. See **WOON** (1993), 1.4, esp. p. 73, his "Hegemony or Survival" (Part One), ZNet Commentary, July 3, 2001, and his Hegemony and Survival (2003). Here is a related quote from his "A World Without War," featured opening address at the second World Social Forum on January 31, 2002, in Porto Alegre (Brazil), reprinted in the third edition of **RP** (2003) as ch. 30:

"We cannot say much about human affairs with any confidence, but sometimes it is possible. We can, for example, be fairly confident that either there will be a world without war or there won't be a world—at least, a world inhabited by creatures other than bacteria and beetles, with some scattering of others. The reason is familiar: humans have developed means of destroying themselves, and much else, and have come dangerously close to using them for half a century. Furthermore, the leaders of the civilized world are now dedicated to enhancing these dangers to survival, in full awareness of what they are doing, at least if they read the reports of their own intelligence agencies and respected strategic analysts, including many who strongly favor the race to destruction. Still more ominous, the plans are developed and implemented on grounds that are rational within the dominant framework of ideology and values, which ranks survival well below hegemony, the goal pursued by advocates of these programs, as they frankly insist."

57. The Iraq Operation, Before and After (29 August 2002, 12 April 2003)

I

Has Saddam Hussein been as evil as mainstream media says? Domestically? Internationally?

He is as evil as they come, ranking with Suharto and other monsters of the modern era. No one would want to be within his reach. But fortunately, his reach does not extend very far.

Evil Monsters and Their Terrible Crimes—and Accomplices

Internationally, Saddam invaded Iran (with Western support), and when that war was going badly turned to chemical weapons (also with Western support). He invaded Kuwait and was quickly driven out.

A major concern in Washington right after the invasion was that Saddam would quickly withdraw, putting "his puppet in [and] everyone in the Arab world will be happy" (Colin Powell, then chief of staff). President Bush was concerned that Saudi Arabia might "bug out at the last minute and accept a puppet regime in Kuwait" unless the U.S. prevented Iraqi withdrawal. The concern, in brief, was that Saddam would pretty much duplicate what the U.S. had just done in Panama (except that Latin Americans were anything but happy). From the first moment the U.S. sought to avert this "nightmare scenario," a story that should be looked at with some care.

Saddam's worst crimes, by far, have been domestic, including the use of chemical weapons against Kurds and a huge slaughter of Kurds in the late 80s, barbaric torture, and every other ugly crime you can imagine. These are at the top of the list of terrible crimes for which he is now condemned, rightly. It's useful to ask how frequently the impassioned denunciations and eloquent expressions of outrage are accompanied by three little words: "with our help."

The crimes were well known at once, but of no particular concern to the West. Saddam received some mild reprimands; harsh congressional condemnation was considered too extreme by prominent commentators. The Reaganites and Bush 1 continued to welcome the monster as an ally and valued trading partner right through his worst atrocities and well beyond. Bush authorized loan guarantees and sale of advanced technology with clear applications for weapons of mass destruction (WMD) right up to the day of the Kuwait invasion, sometimes overriding congressional efforts to prevent what he was doing. Britain was

755

still authorizing export of military equipment and radioactive materials a few days after the invasion.

When ABC correspondent and now ZNet commentator Charles Glass discovered biological weapons facilities (using commercial satellites and defector testimony), his revelations were immediately denied by the Pentagon and the story disappeared. It was resurrected when Saddam committed his first real crime, disobeying U.S. orders (or perhaps misinterpreting them) by invading Kuwait, and switched instantly from friend to reincarnation of Attila the Hun. The same facilities were then used to demonstrate his innately evil nature. When Bush 1 announced new gifts to his friend in December 1989 (also gifts to U.S. agribusiness and industry), it was considered too insignificant even to report, though one could read about it in *Z* magazine at the time, maybe nowhere else. A few months later, shortly before he invaded Kuwait, a high-level Senate delegation, headed by (later) Republican presidential candidate Bob Dole, visited Saddam, conveying the president's greetings and assuring the brutal mass murderer that he should disregard the criticism he hears from maverick reporters here.

Saddam had even been able to get away with attacking a U.S. naval vessel, the USS Stark, killing several dozen crewmen. That is a mark of real esteem. The only other country to have been granted that privilege was Israel, in 1967. In deference to Saddam, the State Department banned all contacts with the Iraqi democratic opposition, maintaining this policy even after the Gulf War, while Washington effectively authorized Saddam to crush a Shiite rebellion that might well have overthrown him—in the interest of preserving "stability," the press explained, nodding sagely.

That he's a major criminal is not in doubt. That's not changed by the fact that the U.S. and Britain regarded his major atrocities as insignificant in the light of higher "reasons of state," before the Gulf War and even after—facts best forgotten.

Looking into the future, is Saddam Hussein as dangerous as mainstream media says?

The world would be better off if he weren't there, no doubt about that. Surely Iraqis would. But he can't be anywhere near as dangerous as he was when the U.S. and Britain were supporting him, even providing him with dual-use technology that he could use for nuclear and chemical weapons development, as he presumably did. Ten years ago the Senate Banking Committee hearings revealed that the Bush administration was granting licenses for dual-use technology and "materials which were later utilized by the Iraq regime for nuclear missile and chemical purposes." Later hearings added more, and there are press reports and a mainstream scholarly literature on the topic (as well as dissident literature).

A Country Devastated by a Decade of Sanctions

The 1991 war was extremely destructive, and since then Iraq has been devastated by a decade of sanctions, which probably strengthened Saddam himself (by weakening possible resistance in a shattered society), but surely reduced very significantly his capacity for war-making or support for terror. Furthermore, since 1991 his regime has been constrained by "no fly zones," regular overflights and bombing, and very tight surveillance. Chances are that the events of Sept. 11 weakened him still further. If there are any links between Saddam and al-Qaeda, they would be far more difficult to maintain now because of the sharply intensified surveillance and controls. That aside, links are not very likely. Despite enormous efforts to tie Saddam to the 9-11 attacks, nothing has been found, which is not too surprising. Saddam and bin Laden were bitter enemies, and there's no particular reason to suppose that there have been any changes in that regard.

The rational conclusion is that Saddam is probably less of a danger now than before 9-11, and far less of a threat than when he was enjoying substantial support from the U.S.-UK (and many others). That raises a few questions. If Saddam is such a threat to the survival of civilization today that the global enforcer has to resort to war, why wasn't that true a year ago? And much more dramatically, in early 1990?

How should the problem of the existence and use of weapons of mass destruction in the world today be dealt with?

They should be eliminated. The non-proliferation treaty commits countries with nuclear weapons to take steps towards eliminating them. The biological and chemical weapons treaties have the same goals. The main Security Council resolution concerning Iraq (687, 1991) calls for eliminating weapons of mass destruction and delivery systems from the Middle East, and working towards a global ban on chemical weapons. Good advice.

Israel: Virtually an Offshore U.S. Military Base

Iraq is nowhere near the lead in this regard. We might recall the warning of General Lee Butler, head of Clinton's Strategic Command in the early 90s, that "it is dangerous in the extreme that in the cauldron of animosities that we call the Middle East, one nation has armed itself, ostensibly, with stockpiles of nuclear weapons, perhaps numbering in the hundreds, and that inspires other nations to do so." He's talking about Israel of course. The Israeli military authorities claim to have air and armored forces that are larger and more advanced than those of any European NATO power (Yitzhak ben Israel, *Ha'aretz*, April 16, 2002, Hebrew). They also announce that 12 percent of their bombers and fighter aircraft are permanently stationed in Eastern Turkey, along with comparable naval and submarine forces in Turkish bases, and armored forces as well, in case it becomes necessary to resort to extreme violence once again to subdue Turkey's Kurdish population, as in the Clinton years. Israeli aircraft based in Turkey are reported to be flying reconnaissance flights along Iran's borders, part of a general U.S.-Israel-Turkey policy of threatening Iran with attack and perhaps forceful partitioning. Israeli analysts also report that joint U.S.-Israel-Turkey air exercises are intended as a threat and warning to Iran. And of course to Iraq (Robert Olson, *Middle East Policy*, June 2002). Israel is doubtless using the huge U.S. air bases in Eastern Turkey, where the U.S. bombers are presumably nuclear-armed. By now Israel is virtually an offshore U.S. military base.

And the rest of the area is armed to the teeth as well. If Iraq were governed by the most Gandhi-like of foreseeable leaders, it would be developing weapons systems if it could, probably well beyond what it can today. That would very likely continue, perhaps even accelerate, if the U.S. takes control of Iraq. India and Pakistan are U.S. allies, but are marching forward with the development of WMD and repeatedly have come agonizingly close to using nuclear weapons. The same is true of other U.S. allies and clients.

That is likely to continue unless there is a general reduction of armaments in the area.

Suppressing the Facts: An Important Service to State Violence

Would Saddam agree to that? Actually, we don't know. In early January 1991, Iraq apparently offered to withdraw from Kuwait in the context of regional negotiations on reduction of armaments, an offer that State Department officials described as serious and negotiable. But we know no more about it, because the U.S. rejected it without response and the press reported virtually nothing. It is, however, of some interest that at that time—right before the bombing—polls revealed that by two to one the U.S. public supported the proposal that Saddam had apparently made, preferring it to bombing. Had people been allowed to know any of this, the majority would surely have been far greater. Suppressing the facts was an important service to the cause of state violence. Could such negotiations have gotten anywhere? Only fanatical ideologues can be confident. Could such ideas be revived? Same answer. One way to find out is to try.

Some argue that there is ample justification for treating Iraq's potential for weapons of mass destruction differently from those of other countries because, under the terms of Security Council Resolution 687, agreed to by Saddam Hussein, Iraq is to be disarmed, in part as punishment for its flagrant violation of international law in invading Kuwait. Is the international community justified in trying to restrict Iraq's weapons of mass destruction? If one accepts this argument, as put, what would be the international ramifications? Is there a different version of this argument with better logic and methodology, and what would be its implications?

As noted, 687 has other provisions, rather significant ones.

The invasion of Kuwait is one of Saddam's lesser crimes. It is not very different from one of the footnotes to U.S. crimes in its own traditional domains: the invasion of Panama a few months earlier, which didn't have even a marginally credible pretext. The main difference is that the U.S. could veto Security

Council resolutions condemning the invasion, disregard the harsh condemnations from the Latin American democracies (barely reported), and basically do what it liked. It's all removed from sanitized history for the same reasons. As I mentioned, Washington feared that Saddam would emulate the Panama invasion and worked hard to prevent it. In the region itself, the invasion of Kuwait, criminal as it was, doesn't compare with the U.S.-supported Israeli invasion of Lebanon, which left some 20,000 dead. And it's embarrassingly easy to continue with much worse cases that we all know.

A Crucial Requirement: U.S. Acquiescence

That aside, these arguments are somewhat beside the point. Those who believe that the Security Council resolutions of a decade ago (which said nothing about use of force) indirectly authorize an invasion have a very easy way to prove that they are serious in that claim: they can urge the U.S. to approach the Security Council for Chapter VII authorization to use force. That will settle the matter. Authorization could probably be obtained: a veto is unlikely. But the U.S. does not want such authorization, at least now, just as it refused it when it chose to bomb Afghanistan, though authorization would surely have been given. For such reasons alone, these discussions are irrelevant.

As for the "international community," in practice, it means the U.S. and whoever will go along with it.

More generally, it would make good sense to try to implement the non-proliferation treaty, the chemical and biological weapons treaties, and the relevant provisions of 687. And to proceed with more serious efforts at disarmament across the board. But any such steps would require U.S. acquiescence, a remote contingency unless there are significant changes here.

Hasn't the history of previous weapons inspections shown that weapons inspectors can be fooled, delayed, and otherwise prevented from actually accomplishing their task? Is there a viable inspections method or related policy, and could it be applied universally?

Sure they can be fooled. However, the weapons inspections were vastly more effective than bombing in destroying Iraq's military capacities, and appear to have been largely successful. Going a step beyond, when was the last time there was a meaningful (or any) international inspection of Israel's nuclear and (probably) chemical weapons facilities? Or those of the U.S.? Inspection regimes should be established, and universalized, but that again requires U.S. acquiescence.

During the recent congressional hearings on Iraq, one witness stated that for inspections to be truly effective, a rapid-reaction military force would be needed, so that Saddam Hussein could not prevent the inspectors from making a surprise visit to some site where improper activity was going on. The witness said there's no way Iraq would agree to this, but by demanding such a force the U.S. would seize the high moral ground. Is such a force a necessary component of an effective inspection regime? Would the U.S. be on high moral ground? What reciprocal demands might others reasonably make of us?

Is the goal propaganda ("seizing the high moral ground")? Or reducing the threat of weapons of mass destruction (WMD)? If the former, we can dismiss the matter. If the latter, some obvious questions arise. Weapons inspection appears to have been highly effective, even if imperfect. Scott Ritter's testimony on the topic is compelling, and I know of no serious refutation of it. Those who want to reduce the threat of WMD will, therefore, try to create the conditions for meaningful inspection, as required by Resolution 687 and earlier ones, and supported by the actual international community. For some years, the U.S. has sought in every way to block such eventualities. The inspections were used as a cover for spying on Iraq, with the open intent of overthrowing the regime and probably assassinating the leadership. Apart from the violation of elementary norms, these practices were sure to undermine the inspections regime, and to sharply reduce the likelihood that Iraq would accept inspections. Would Israel agree to inspection of its military facilities by spies for Hamas?

A Particularly Stunning Hypocrisy

In 1998, Clinton withdrew the inspectors in preparation for bombing—acts that have been reconstructed in propaganda as Iraqi expulsion of the inspectors. The U.S.-UK bombing was carefully timed to coincide with an emergency meeting of the Security Council on inspections, hence to demonstrate the utter contempt of the enforcers for the UN. And the bombing was another blow to the renewal of inspections. Since then, Washington has been insisting that even if Iraq accepts the most intrusive inspections by American spies seeking to prepare the ground for invasion, it will not make any difference. In Cheney's recent version, "A return of inspectors would provide no assurance whatsoever of [Saddam's] compliance with UN resolutions." This stance amounts to pleading with Iraq not to accept inspectors.

It has been reported, not implausibly, that one reason why Washington forced out the highly respected director of the UN Organization for the Prohibition of Chemical Weapons, Jose Bustani, was that he was seeking to arrange inspections of chemical weapons in Iraq, thus interfering with Washington's efforts to prevent WMD inspections. The hypocrisy was particularly stunning, mainstream commentators pointed out, after the Bush administration undermined the chemical and biological weapons conventions by refusing at the last minute to ratify enforcement protocols, in part because of its opposition to arms agreements, in part to protect commercial secrets of U.S. corporations, and possibly in part to keep its own violations of the conventions from too much exposure (though some has already leaked).

So back to the first question: Is the goal to block inspections, or to expedite them? The witness, as quoted, evidently seeks to block them, and therefore need not be taken seriously. If, in contrast, the goal is to expedite inspections, then it's necessary to address the U.S. government as well as Iraq.

Just to summarize quickly, WMD programs make the world a more dangerous place, Saddam's in particular. And the problem should be addressed in such a way as to make the world safer. The best approach would be global: treaties with meaningful provisions, and universal inspections to verify adherence to them. The next best approach would be something similar at a regional level. Both approaches would require U.S. acquiescence, but that's a remote contingency, at least right now. Sensible people should try to change that. The next best approach is to return inspectors to Iraq, alone. Every effort should be made to achieve that result—at least by those who hope to reduce serious threats, not just to find a pretext for war. The worst approach would be to try to prevent the return of inspectors along the lines just discussed. That continues to be U.S. policy, in an effort to set the stage for an invasion. The planned invasion will strike another blow at the structure of international law and treaties that has been laboriously constructed over the years, in an effort to reduce the use of violence in the world, which has had such horrifying consequences. Apart from other consequences, an invasion is likely to encourage other countries to develop WMD, including a successor Iraqi government, and to lower the barriers against resort to force by others to achieve their objectives, including Russia, India, and China.

It is sometimes said that Saddam Hussein wouldn't be crazy enough to launch a nuclear weapon at the U.S. or (more realistically) Israel, knowing the inevitable consequences. But wouldn't a nuclear-armed Iraq be able to conventionally attack weaker neighboring states, knowing that his victims could not successfully call on the U.S. (or even the UN) for assistance, because Washington would fear a nuclear strike on Tel Aviv?

All sorts of outlandish possibilities can be imagined. That's kept many people employed at RAND and other think-tanks ever since WMD became available. This is hardly one of the more credible examples. One reason is that the situation will almost certainly not arise. The scenario assumes that Saddam has provided credible evidence that he has WMD available and is capable of using them. Otherwise, such weapons are not a threat or a deterrent at all. But if there ever is any indication that he does have significant WMD capacity, he'll be wiped out before he can threaten anyone with invasion.

The "Samson Complex": An Element of Israeli Planning

Suppose, however, just to play the game, we accept the absurd assumption that the U.S. and Israel will just sit there quietly while Saddam brandishes WMD as a potential deterrent, in advance of the invasion of some other country. Then the U.S. and Israel would instantly respond to the invasion, expelling him (and probably destroying Iraq). His WMD would be no deterrent at all. A sufficient reason is that to allow his invasion to succeed would leave him as a far greater threat. Furthermore, it would be assumed that he would not use whatever WMD capacity he has because that would mean instant suicide, and if he was bent on suicide he would have used his WMD against Israel (or someone else) even before invading another country. The scenario has such slight plausibility that it is hardly worth considering in comparison with real problems that do not have to be conjured up by fevered imaginations.

If one wants to play such games, why not take some more plausible scenarios. Here's one: suppose that the U.S. shifts policy and joins the international consensus on a two-state Israel-Palestine settlement. Suppose, for example, the U.S. endorses the recent Saudi plan adopted by the Arab League. Suppose Israel reacts by threatening the U.S.—not threatening to bomb it, but in other ways. For example, suppose Israel sends bombers over the Saudi oil fields (maybe nuclear armed, but that's unnecessary), just to indicate what it can do to the world if the U.S. doesn't get on board again. It would be too late to react, because Israel could then carry out its warnings. That scenario has a certain plausibility because apparently it actually happened, 20 years ago, when the Saudi government floated a similar plan, violently opposed by Israel.

According to the Israeli press, Israel reacted by sending bombers over the oil fields, as a warning to the U.S., but one that was unnecessary because the Reagan administration joined Israel in rejecting that possibility for a political settlement, as it has consistently done. True, Israel might have been facing destruction, but one might argue that Israel's strategy allows that possibility. As far back as the 1950s, leaders of the then-ruling Labor Party advised that Israel should "go crazy" if the U.S. wouldn't go along with its demands, and the "Samson complex" has been an element of planning—how seriously, we don't know—ever since. So we should bomb Israel right away, before it has a chance to carry out these evil plots.

Do I believe any of this? Of course not. It's nonsensical. However, it doesn't compare too badly with the scenario about Iraq.

It should be added that there are circumstances under which Saddam might use WMD, assuming he has the capacity. If Iraq is invaded with the clear intention of capturing or more likely killing him, he would have every incentive to go for broke, since he'd have nothing to lose. But it is hard to imagine other circumstances.

How will the Iraqi people react to a U.S. attack on Iraq? What are the likely humanitarian consequences of a U.S. war?

No one has a clue. Not Donald Rumsfeld, not me, no one. One can imagine a delightful scenario: a few bombs fall, the Republican Guards rebel and overthrow Saddam, crowds cheer as U.S. soldiers march in while the band plays "God Bless America," the people of the region hail the liberator who proceeds to turn Iraq into an image of American democracy and a modernizing center for the entire region—and one that produces just enough oil to keep the price within the range that the U.S. prefers, breaking the OPEC stranglehold. And Santa Claus smiles benignly from his sleigh. One can easily imagine rather more grim outcomes. That's a normal concomitant of the decision to resort to massive violence, and one of the many reasons why those who advocate that course have a very heavy burden of proof to bear. Needless to say, neither Rumsfeld nor Cheney nor any of the intellectuals urging war against Iraq have remotely begun to meet this burden.

Longstanding Background Reasons and Immediate Domestic Needs

What in your view are the true motives propelling a possible war?

There are longstanding background reasons, which are well known. Iraq has the second largest oil reserves in the world. It has always been likely that sooner or later, the U.S. would try to restore this enormous prize to Western control, meaning now U.S. control, denying privileged access to others. But those considerations have held for years; 9-11 offered new opportunities to pursue these goals under the pretext of a "war on terror"—thin pretexts, but probably sufficient for propaganda purposes. The planned war can serve immediate domestic needs as well. It's hardly a secret that the Bush administration is carrying out an assault against the general population and future generations in the interest of narrow sectors of wealth and power that it serves with loyalty that exceeds even the usual norms. Under those circumstances, it is surely advisable to divert attention away from health care, social security, deficits, destruction of the environment, development of new weapons systems that may literally threaten survival, and a long list of other unwelcome topics. The traditional, and reasonable, device is to terrify the population. "The whole aim of practical politics," the great American satirist H. L. Mencken once said, is "to keep the public alarmed (and hence clamorous to be led to safety) by menacing it with an endless series of hobgoblins, all of them imaginary." In fact the menaces invoked are rarely imaginary, though they are typically inflated beyond all reason. That's a good part of the history of "practical politics," not only here of course. It doesn't take much skill to evoke an image of Saddam Hussein as the ultimate force of evil about to destroy the world, maybe the universe. And with the population huddling in fear as our gallant forces miraculously overcome this awesome foe, perhaps they won't pay attention to what is being done to them, and may even join the chorus of distinguished intellectuals chanting praises for Our Leaders. The U.S. preponderance of power is so extraordinary that there will be plenty in reserve if things seem to be going wrong. And if that happens down the road, it can all be shoveled deep into the memory hole, or blamed on someone else, or maybe on our naive faith that others are as benign as we are. It's pretty easy: there's a treasure trove of experience to draw from.

Some advocates of war have suggested that if the economic sanctions on Iraq are as horrible as the Left claims, then a war, even a war that killed 100,000 civilians, would be a humanitarian blessing, since, presumably, after a U.S. victory there would be no more sanctions. How do you answer this argument?

I've heard some zany arguments in the past, but this must break some new records. I suspect it was offered tongue-in-cheek. Note first the conception of "the Left": the UN's humanitarian coordinators (Denis Halliday, Hans van Sponeck) who know more about the country than anyone else, UNICEF, etc. It's a bit like saying that the Left is concerned about global warming—and tells us something about where those who question "the claim" place themselves on the political spectrum.

But that aside, the argument does have appeal. For example, we could offer Iran assistance in conquering Israel and carrying out appropriate "regime change," so that suicide bombings would stop. Since the war advocates doubtless regard suicide bombing as atrocious, they should be calling for that. Or, we could help Russia grind Chechnya to dust, so that Chechens would no longer have to suffer Russian terror and atrocities. The possibilities are endless.

What will the implications of war be in the Mideast, and also other parts of the world? Do U.S. elites care?

Elites of course care, though the small group that holds the reins of power currently may not care very much. They evidently believe that they have such overwhelming force at their command that it doesn't really matter much what others think: if they don't go along, they'll be dismissed, or if they are in the way, pulverized. The thinking in high places was made pretty clear when Prince Abdullah of Saudi Arabia visited the U.S. in April to urge the administration to pay some attention to the reaction in the Arab world to its strong support for Israeli terror and repression. He was told, in effect, that the U.S. did not care what he or other Arabs think. A high official explained that "if he thought we were strong in Desert Storm, we're 10 times as strong today. This was to give him some idea what Afghanistan demonstrated about our capabilities." A senior defense analyst gave a simple gloss: others will "respect us for our toughness and won't mess with us." That stand has precedents that need not be mentioned. But in the post-9/11 world it gains new force. Are they right? Could be. Or maybe the world will blow up in their face, perhaps after a "decent interval," as it's called in diplomacy. Again, resort to large-scale violence has highly unpredictable consequences, as history reveals and common sense should tell us anyway. That's why sane people avoid it, in personal relations or international affairs, unless a very powerful argument is offered to overcome "the sickly inhibitions against the use of military force" (to borrow the phrase of Reaganite intellectual Norman Podhoretz, paraphrasing Goebbels).

Christopher Hitchens makes the point that while Saudi Arabia, Scowcroft, and Kissinger oppose war with Iraq because of its potential destabilizing effect in the region, the Left should not care about the stability of the reactionary and corrupt regimes of the Middle East. Does this refute a commonly-heard objection to war?

It is hard to imagine what the point is supposed to be. The Left has always been strenuously opposed to U.S. support for "the reactionary and corrupt regimes of the Middle East," and would of course welcome their "destabilization" in favor of something better. On the other hand, if "destabilization" brought to power something even worse—say, what Hitchens calls "Islamic fascism"—then the Left would oppose it, and I presume he would too. So what is the point?

I don't see how these considerations bear on any "objection to war," commonly heard or not, at least from the Left. What Scowcroft and Kissinger may have in mind is another matter.

II

Why did the U.S. invade Iraq, in your view?

These are naturally speculations, and policy-makers may have varying motives. But we can have a high degree of confidence about the answers given by Bush-Powell and the rest: these cannot possibly be taken seriously. They have gone out of their way to make sure we understand that by a steady dose of self-contradiction ever since last September, when the war drums began to beat. One day the "single question" is whether Iraq will disarm; in today's version (April 12): "We have high confidence that they have weapons of mass destruction—that is what this war was about and is about."

That was the pretext throughout the whole UN-disarmament farce, though it was never easy to take seriously; UNMOVIC was doing a good job in virtually disarming Iraq, and could have continued, if that were the goal. But there is no need to discuss it, because after stating solemnly that this is the "single question," they went on the next day to announce that it wasn't the goal at all: even if there isn't a pocket knife anywhere in Iraq, the U.S. will invade anyway, because it is committed to "regime change." The next day we hear that there's nothing to that either; thus at the Azores summit, where Bush-Blair issued their ultimatum to the UN, they made it clear that they would invade even if Saddam and his gang left the country. So "regime change" is not enough. The next day we hear that the goal is "democracy" in the world. Pretexts range over the lot, depending on audience and circumstances, which means that no sane person can take the charade seriously.

The Prime Issue of Contention

The one constant is that the U.S. must end up in control of Iraq. Saddam Hussein was authorized to suppress, brutally, a 1991 uprising that might have overthrown him because "the best of all worlds" for Washington would be "an iron-fisted Iraqi junta without Saddam Hussein" (by then an embarrassment), which would rule the country with an "iron fist" as Saddam had done with U.S. support and approval (*New York Times* chief diplomatic correspondent Thomas Friedman). The uprising would have left the country in the hands of Iraqis who might not have subordinated themselves sufficiently to Washington. The mur-

derous sanctions regime of the following years devastated the society, strengthened the tyrant, and compelled the population to rely for survival on his (highly efficient) system for distributing basic goods. The sanctions thus undercut the
possibility of the kind of popular revolt that had overthrown an impressive series
of other monsters who had been strongly supported by the current incumbents
in Washington up to the very end of their bloody rule: Marcos, Duvalier,
Ceausescu, Mobutu, Suharto, and a long list of others, some of them easily as
tyrannical and barbaric as Saddam. Had it not been for the sanctions, Saddam
probably would have gone the same way, as has been pointed out for years by the
Westerners who know Iraq best, Denis Halliday and Hans van Sponeck (though
one has to go to Canada, England, or elsewhere to find their writings). But overthrow of the regime from within would not be acceptable either, because it
would leave Iraqis in charge. The Azores summit merely reiterated that stand.

The question of who rules Iraq remains the prime issue of contention. The
U.S.-backed opposition demands that the UN play a vital role in post-war Iraq
and rejects U.S. control of reconstruction or government (Leith Kubba, one of
the most respected secular voices in the West, connected with the National
Endowment of Democracy). One of the leading Shiite opposition figures, Sayed
Muhamed Baqer al-Hakim, who heads the Supreme Council for Islamic
Revolution in Iraq (SCIRI), just informed the press that "we understand this war
to be about imposing U.S. hegemony over Iraq," and perceive the U.S. as "an
occupying rather than a liberating force." He stressed that the UN must supervise elections, and called on "foreign troops to withdraw from Iraq" and leave
Iraqis in charge.

U.S. policy-makers have a radically different conception. They must impose
a client regime in Iraq, following the practice elsewhere in the region, and most
significantly, in the regions that have been under U.S. domination for a century,
Central America and the Caribbean. That too is well-understood. Brent
Scowcroft, national security adviser to Bush I, just repeated the obvious: "What's
going to happen the first time we hold an election in Iraq and it turns out the
radicals win? What do you do? We're surely not going to let them take over."

The same holds throughout the region. Recent studies reveal that from
Morocco to Lebanon to the Gulf, about 95 percent of the population want a
greater role in government for Islamic religious figures, and the same percentage
believe that the sole U.S. interest in the region is to control its oil and strength-
en Israel. Antagonism to Washington has reached unprecedented heights, and
the idea that Washington would institute a radical change in policy and tolerate
truly democratic elections, respecting the outcome, seems rather fanciful, to say
the least.

Turning to the question, one reason for the invasion, surely, is to gain control over the world's second largest oil reserves, which will place the U.S. in an
even more powerful position of global domination, maintaining "a stranglehold
on the global economy," as Michael Klare describes the long-term objective,

which he regards as the primary motive for war. However, this cannot explain the timing. Why now?

The drumbeat for war began in September 2002, and the government-media propaganda campaign achieved a spectacular success. Very quickly, the majority of the population came to believe that Iraq posed an imminent threat to U.S. security, even that Iraq was involved in 9-11 (up from 3 percent after 9-11) and was planning new attacks. Not surprisingly, these beliefs correlated closely with support for the planned war. The beliefs are unique to the U.S.. Even in Kuwait and Iran, which were invaded by Saddam Hussein, he was not feared, though he was despised. They know perfectly well that Iraq was the weakest state in the region, and for years they had joined others in trying to reintegrate Iraq into the regional system, over strong U.S. objections. But a highly effective propaganda assault drove the American population far off the spectrum of world opinion, a remarkable achievement.

The September propaganda assault coincided with two important events:

One was the opening of the mid-term election campaign. Karl Rove, the administration's campaign manager, had already pointed out that Republicans have to "go to the country" on the issue of national security, because voters "trust the Republican Party to do a better job of … protecting America." One didn't have to be a political genius to realize that if social and economic issues dominated the election, the Bush administration did not have a chance. Accordingly, it was necessary to concoct a huge threat to our survival, which the powerful leader will manage to overcome, miraculously. For the elections, the strategy barely worked. Polls reveal that voters maintained their preferences, but suppressed concerns over jobs, pensions, benefits, etc., in favor of security. Something similar will be needed for the presidential campaign. All of this is second nature for the current incumbents. They are mostly recycled from the more reactionary sectors of the Reagan-Bush administrations, and know that they were able to run the country for 12 years, carrying out domestic programs that the public largely opposed, by pushing the panic button regularly: Libyan attempting to "expel us from the world" (Reagan), an air base in Grenada from which the Russians would bomb us, Nicaragua only "two-days driving time from Harlingen Texas," waving their copies of *Mein Kampf* as they planned to take over the hemisphere, black criminals about to rape your sister (Willie Horton, the 1988 presidential campaign), Hispanic narcotraffickers about to destroy us, and on and on.

To maintain political power is an extremely important matter if the narrow sectors of power represented by the Bush administration hope to carry out their reactionary domestic program over strong popular opposition, if possible even to institutionalize them, so it will be hard to reconstruct what is being dismantled.

A Colossal "Exemplary" Action: Neither "Pre-emptive" nor "Preventive"

[2] Something else happened in September 2002: the administration released its National Security Strategy, sending many shudders around the world,

including the U.S. foreign policy elite. The strategy has many precedents [total-itarianism], but does break new ground: for the first time in the post-war world, a powerful state announced, loud and clear, that it intends to rule the world by force, forever, crushing any potential challenge it might perceive. This is often called in the press a doctrine of "pre-emptive war." That is crucially wrong; it goes vastly beyond pre-emption. Sometimes it is called more accurately a doctrine of "preventive war." That too understates the doctrine. No military threat, however remote, need be "prevented"; challenges can be concocted at will, and may not involve any threat other than "defiance"; those who pay attention to history know that "successful defiance" has often been taken to be justification for resort to force in the past.

When a doctrine is announced, some action must be taken to demonstrate that it is seriously intended, so that it can become a new "norm in international relations," as commentators will soberly explain. What is needed is a war with an "exemplary quality," Harvard Middle East historian Roger Owen pointed out, discussing the reasons for the attack on Iraq. The exemplary action teaches a lesson that others must heed, or else.

Why Iraq? The experimental subject must have several important qualities. It must be defenseless, and it must be important; there's no point illustrating the doctrine by invading Burundi. Iraq qualified perfectly in both respects. The importance is obvious, and so is the required weakness. Iraq was not much of a military force to begin with, and had been largely disarmed through the 1990s while much of the society was driven to the edge of survival. Its military expenditures and economy were about one-third those of Kuwait, with 10 percent of its population, far below others in the region, and of course the regional superpower, Israel, by now virtually an offshore military base of the U.S.. The invading force not only had utterly overwhelming military power, but also extensive information to guide its actions from satellite observation and overflights for many years, and more recently U-2 flights on the pretext of disarmament, surely sending data directly back to Washington.

Iraq was therefore a perfect choice for an "exemplary action" to establish the new doctrine of global rule by force as a "norm of international relations." A high official involved in drafting the National Security Strategy informed the press that its publication "was the signal that Iraq would be the first test, but not the last." "Iraq became the petri dish in which this experiment in pre-emptive policy grew," the *New York Times* reported—misstating the policy in the usual way, but otherwise accurate.

All of these factors gave good reasons for war. And they also help explain why the planned war was so overwhelmingly opposed by the public worldwide (including the U.S., particularly when we extract the factor of fear, unique to the U.S.). And also strongly opposed by a substantial part of economic and foreign policy elites, a very unusual development. They rightly fear that the adventurist posture may prove very costly to their own interests, even to survival. It is well-understood that these policies are driving others to develop a deterrent, which could be weapons of mass destruction, or credible threats of serious terror, or even conventional weapons, as in the case of North Korea, with artillery massed to destroy Seoul. With any remnants of some functioning system of world order torn to shreds, the Bush administration is instructing the world that nothing matters but force—and they hold the mailed fist, though others are not likely to tolerate that for long. Including, one hopes, the American people, who are in by far the best position to counter and reverse these extremely ominous trends.

There is some cheering in the streets of Iraqi cities. Does this retrospectively undercut the logic of anti-war opposition?

I'm surprised that it was so limited and so long delayed. Every sensible person should welcome the overthrow of the tyrant, and the ending of the devastating sanctions, most certainly Iraqis. But the anti-war opposition, at least the part of it I know anything about, was always in favor of these ends. That's why it opposed the sanctions that were destroying the country and undermining the possibility of an internal revolt that would send Saddam the way of the other brutal killers supported by the present incumbents in Washington. The anti-war movement insisted that Iraqis, not the U.S. government, must run the country. And it still does—or should; it can have a substantial impact in this regard. Opponents of the war were also rightly appalled by the utter lack of concern for the possible humanitarian consequences of the attack, and by the ominous strategy for which it was the "test case." The basic issues remain:

(1) Who will run Iraq, Iraqis or a clique in Crawford, Texas?
(2) Will the American people permit the narrow reactionary sectors that barely hold on to political power to implement their domestic and international agendas?

There have been no WMD found. Does this retrospectively undercut Bush's rationale for war?

Only if one takes the rationale seriously. The leadership still pretends to, as Fleischer's current remarks illustrate. If they can find something, which is not unlikely, that will be trumpeted as justification for the war. If they can't, the whole issue will be "disappeared" in the usual fashion.

If WMD are now found, and verified, would that retrospectively undercut anti-war opposition?

That's a logical impossibility. Policies and opinions about them are determined by what is known or plausibly believed, not by what is discovered afterwards. That should be elementary.

Will there be democracy in Iraq, as a result of this invasion?

Depends on what one means by "democracy." I presume the Bush PR team will want to put into place some kind of formal democracy, as long as it has no substance. But it's hard to imagine that they would allow a real voice to the Shiite majority, which is likely to join the rest of the region in trying to establish closer relations with Iran, the last thing the Bushites want. Or that they would allow a real voice to the next largest component of the population, the Kurds, who are likely to seek some kind of autonomy within a federal structure that would be anathema to Turkey, a major base for U.S. power in the region. One should not be misled by the recent hysterical reaction to the crime of the Turkish government in adopting the position of 95 percent of its population, another indication of the passionate hatred of democracy in elite circles here, and another reason why no sensible person can take the rhetoric seriously. Same throughout the region. Functioning democracy would have outcomes that are inconsistent with the goal of U.S. hegemony, just as in our own "backyard" over a century.

What message has been received by governments around the world, with what likely broad implications?

The message is that the Bush administration intends its National Security Strategy to be taken seriously, as the "test case" illustrates. It intends to dominate the world by force, the one dimension in which it rules supreme, and to do so permanently. A more specific message, illustrated dramatically by the Iraq-North Korea case, is that if you want to fend off a U.S. attack, you had better have a credible deterrent. It's widely assumed in elite circles that the likely consequence is proliferation of WMD and terror, in various forms, based on fear and loathing for the U.S. administration, which was regarded as the greatest threat to world peace even before the invasion. That's no small matter these days. Questions of peace shade quickly into questions of survival for the species, given the case of means of violence.

What was the role of the American media establishment in paving the way for this war, and then rationalizing it, narrowing the terms of discussion, etc.?

The media uncritically relayed government propaganda about the threat to U.S. security posed by Iraq, its involvement in 9-11 and other terror, etc. Some amplified the message on their own. Others simply relayed it. The effects in the polls were striking, as often before. Discussion was, as usual, restricted to "pragmatic grounds": Will the U.S. government get away with its plans at a cost acceptable at home? Once the war began it became a shameful exercise of cheering for the home team, appalling much of the world.

What is next on the agenda, broadly, for Bush and Co., if they are able to pursue their preferred agendas?

They have publicly announced that the next targets could be Syria and Iran—which would require a strong military base in Iraq, presumably; another reason why any meaningful democracy is unlikely. It has been reliably reported for some time that the U.S. and its allies (Turkey, Israel, and some others) have been taking steps towards dismemberment of Iran. But there are other possible targets too. The Andean region qualifies. It has very substantial resources, including oil. It is in turmoil, with dangerous independent popular movements that are not under control. It is by now surrounded by U.S. military bases with U.S. forces already on the ground. And one can think of others.

What obstacles now stand in the way of Bush and Co.'s doing as they prefer, and what obstacles might arise?

The Prime Responsibility of the American People

The prime obstacle is domestic. But that's up to us.

What has been your impression of anti-war opposition and what ought to be its agenda now?

Anti-war opposition here has been completely without precedent in scale and commitment, something we've discussed before, and that is certainly obvious to anyone who has had any experience in these matters here for the past 40 years. Its agenda right now, I think, should be to work to ensure that Iraq is run by Iraqis, that the U.S. provide massive reparations for what it has done to Iraq for 20 years (by supporting Saddam Hussein, by wars, by brutal sanctions which probably caused a great deal more damage and deaths than the wars); and if that is too much honesty to expect, then at least massive aid, to be used by Iraqis, as they decide, which well be something other than U.S. taxpayer subsidies to Halliburton and Bechtel. Also high on the agenda should be putting a brake on the extremely dangerous policies announced in the security strategy, and carried out in the "petri dish." And related to that, there should be serious efforts to block the bonanza of arms sales that is happily anticipated as a consequence of the war, which will also contribute to making the world a more awful and dangerous place. But that's only the beginning. The anti-war movement is indissolubly linked to the global justice movements, which have much more far-reaching goals, properly.

What do you think is the relationship between the invasion of Iraq and corporate globalization, and what should be the relation between the anti-corporate globalization movement, and the peace movement?

The invasion of Iraq was strongly opposed by the main centers of corporate globalization. At the World Economic Forum in Davos in January [2003], opposition was so strong that Powell was practically shouted down when he tried to present a case for the war—announcing, pretty clearly, that the U.S. would "lead" even if no one followed, except for the pathetic Blair. The global justice and peace movements are so closely linked in their objectives that there is nothing much to say. We should, however, recall that the planners do draw these links, as we should too, in our own different way. They predict that their version of "globalization" will proceed on course, leading to "chronic financial volatility" (meaning still slower growth, harming mostly the poor) "and a widening economic divide" (meaning less globalization in the technical sense of convergence). They predict further that "deepening economic stagnation, political instability, and cultural alienation will foster ethnic, ideological and religious extremism, along with violence," much of it directed against the U.S.—that is, more terror. Military planners make the same assumptions. That is a good part of the rationale for rapidly increasing military spending, including the plans for militarization of space that the entire world is trying to block, without much hope as long as the matter is kept from the sight of Americans, who have the prime responsibility to stop it. I presume that is why some of the major events of last October [2002] were not even reported, among them the U.S. vote at the UN, alone (with Israel), against a resolution calling for reaffirmation of a 1925 Geneva convention banning biological weapons and another resolution strengthening the 1967 Outer Space Treaty to ban use of space for military purposes, including offensive weapons that may well do us all in.

The agenda, as always, begins with trying to find out what is happening in the world, and then doing something about it, as we can, better than anyone else. Few share our privilege, power, and freedom—hence responsibility. That should be another truism.

Editor's Notes to Interview 58

The following interview, conducted in May 1995 by Kevin Doyle, appeared in *Red & Black Revolution: A Magazine of libertarian Communism*, num. 2 (1995–1996), under the title "Noam Chomsky on Anarchism, Marxism & Hope for the Future."

R&BR, "an anarchist theory and history magazine produced in Ireland," is published by the Workers Solidarity Movement (WSM), Irish anarchist organization affiliated to International Libertarian Solidarity, whose motto is Bakunin's "Freedom without socialism is privilege and injustice. Socialism without freedom is slavery and brutality." The WSM "was founded in Dublin, Ireland, in 1984 following discussions by a number of local anarchist groups on the need for a national anarchist organization." Some back issues may be available at the WSM bookservice (WSM Books, P.O. Box 1528, Dublin 8, Ireland), where it's possible to write for a catalogue. The six issues published so far (1994 through Spring 2002) are available on the website (http://struggle.ws/rbr.html) as PDF files that can be downloaded and printed out.

As indicated in the Editor's Preliminary Note to this edition, this last interview offers a particularly lucid exposition of Chomsky's encouraging views on the prospects of human endeavor, given the range of social organizations humans appear to be able to create (from this perspective, it can be seen as a sort of supplement to "Two Conceptions of Social Organization" (1970), ch. 7 of Chomsky on democracy and education). So it seems particularly apt to close the collection.

For a more extensive discussion of David Hume's *First Principles of Government*, see **DD** (1991), ch. 12.

The introduction to Guérin's book ("Notes on Anarchism") is ch. 8 in **FRS**. On the Spanish revolution of 1936—1937 (discussed at length in **APNM** (1967), I.ii)., and on the new era of hegemony (the subject of Chomsky's book, *Hegemony or Survival*), see also I53.

For an important discussion of the Cartesian conception of human nature, including a fresh and insightful interpretation of Rousseau's thought, see "Language and Freedom," reprinted as ch. 9 in **FRS** (the quote below appears on p. 392).

58. Marxism, Anarchism, and Alternative Futures
(May 1995)

First off, Noam, for quite a time now you've been an advocate for the anarchist idea. Many people are familiar with the introduction you wrote in 1970 to Daniel Guérin's Anarchism, _but more recently, for instance in the film_ Manufacturing Consent, _you took the opportunity to highlight again the potential of anarchism and the anarchist idea. What is it that attracts you to anarchism?_

Anarchism: Placing the Burden of Proof on Authority

I was attracted to anarchism as a young teenager, as soon as I began to think about the world beyond a pretty narrow range, and haven't seen much reason to revise those early attitudes since. I think it only makes sense to seek out and identify structures of authority, hierarchy, and domination in every aspect of life, and to challenge them; unless a justification for them can be given, they are illegitimate, and should be dismantled, to increase the scope of human freedom. That includes political power, ownership and management, relations among men and women, parents and children, our control over the fate of future generations (the basic moral imperative behind the environmental movement, in my view), and much else. Naturally this means a challenge to the huge institutions of coercion and control: the state, the unaccountable private tyrannies that control most of the domestic and international economy, and so on. But not only these.

That is what I have always understood to be the essence of anarchism: the conviction that the burden of proof has to be placed on authority, and that it should be dismantled if that burden cannot be met. Sometimes the burden can be met. If I'm taking a walk with my grandchildren and they dart out into a busy street, I will use not only authority but also physical coercion to stop them. The act should be challenged, but I think it can readily meet the challenge. And there are other cases; life is a complex affair, we understand very little about humans and society, and grand pronouncements are generally more a source of harm than of benefit. But the perspective is a valid one, I think, and can lead us quite a long way.

Beyond such generalities, we begin to look at cases, which is where the questions of human interest and concern arise.

It's true to say that your ideas and critique are now more widely known than ever before. It should also be said that your views are widely respected. How do you think your support for anarchism is received in this context? In particular, I'm interested in *the response you receive from people who are getting interested in politics for the first time and who may, perhaps, have come across your views. Are such people surprised by your support for anarchism? Are they interested?*

The general intellectual culture, as you know, associates "anarchism" with chaos, violence, bombs, disruption, and so on. So people are often surprised when I speak positively of anarchism and identify myself with leading traditions within it. But my impression is that among the general public, the basic ideas seem reasonable when the clouds are cleared away. Of course, when we turn to specific matters (say, the nature of families, or how an economy would work in a society that is more free and just), questions and controversy arise. But that is as it should be. Physics can't really explain how water flows from the tap in your sink. When we turn to vastly more complex questions of human significance, understanding is very thin, and there is plenty of room for disagreement, experimentation, both intellectual and real-life exploration of possibilities, to help us learn more.

Perhaps, more than any other idea, anarchism has suffered from the problem of misrepresentation. Anarchism can mean many things to many people. Do you often find yourself having to explain what it is that you mean by anarchism? Does the misrepresentation of anarchism bother you?

All misrepresentation is a nuisance. Much of it can be traced back to structures of power that have an interest in preventing understanding, for pretty obvious reasons. It's well to recall David Hume's *First Principles of Government*. He expressed surprise that people ever submitted to their rulers. He concluded that since "Force is always on the side of the governed, the governors have nothing to support them but opinion. 'Tis therefore, on opinion only that government is founded; and this maxim extends to the most despotic and most military governments, as well as to the most free and most popular." Hume was very astute (and incidentally, hardly a libertarian by the standards of the day). He surely underestimates the efficacy of force, but his observation seems to me basically correct, and important, particularly in the more free societies, where the art of controlling opinion is therefore far more refined. Misrepresentation and other forms of befuddlement are a natural concomitant.

So does misrepresentation bother me? Sure, but so does rotten weather. It will exist as long as concentrations of power engender a kind of commissar class to defend them. Since they are usually not very bright, or are bright enough to know that they'd better avoid the arena of fact and argument, they'll turn to misrepresentation, vilification, and other devices that are available to those who know that they'll be protected by the various means available to the powerful. We should understand why all this occurs, and unravel it as best we can. That's part of the project of liberation—of ourselves and others, or more reasonably, of people working together to achieve these aims.

Sounds...

Sounds simple-minded, and it is. But I have yet to find much commentary on human life and society that is not simple-minded, when absurdity and self-serving posturing are cleared away.

How about in more established left-wing circles, where one might expect to find greater familiarity with what anarchism actually stands for? Do you encounter any surprise here at your views and support for anarchism?

If I understand what you mean by "established left-wing circles," there is not too much surprise about my views on anarchism, because very little is known about my views on anything. These are not the circles I deal with. You'll rarely find a reference to anything I say or write. That's not completely true of course. Thus in the U.S. (but less commonly in the UK or elsewhere), you'd find some familiarity with what I do in certain of the more critical and independent sectors of what might be called "established left-wing circles," and I have personal friends and associates scattered here and there. But have a look at the books and journals, and you'll see what I mean. I don't expect what I write and say to be any more welcome in these circles than in the faculty club or editorial board room—again, with exceptions.

The question arises only marginally, so much so that it's hard to answer.

A number of people have noted that you use the term "libertarian socialist" in the same context as you use the word "anarchism." Do you see these terms as essentially similar? Is anarchism a type of socialism to you? The description has been used before that anarchism is equivalent to socialism with freedom. Would you agree with this basic equation?

The introduction to Guérin's book that you mentioned opens with a quote from an anarchist sympathizer a century ago, who says that "anarchism has a broad back," and "endures anything." One major element has been what has traditionally been called "libertarian socialism." I've tried to explain there and elsewhere what I mean by that, stressing that it's hardly original; I'm taking the ideas from leading figures in the anarchist movement whom I quote, and who rather consistently describe themselves as socialists, while harshly condemning the "new class" of radical intellectuals who seek to attain state power in the course of popular struggle and to become the vicious "red bureaucracy" of which Bakunin warned; what's often called "socialism." I rather agree with Rudolf Rocker's perception that these (quite central) tendencies in anarchism draw from the best of Enlightenment and classical liberal thought, well beyond what he described. In fact, as I've tried to show they contrast sharply with Marxist-Leninist doctrine and practice, the "libertarian" doctrines that are fashionable in the U.S. and UK particularly, and other contemporary ideologies, all of which seem to me to reduce to advocacy of one or another form of illegitimate authority, quite often real tyranny.

In the past, when you have spoken about anarchism, you have often emphasized the example of the Spanish Revolution. For you there would seem to be two aspects to this example. On the one hand, the experience of the Spanish Revolution is, you say, a good example of "anarchism in action." On the other, you have also stressed that the Spanish Revolution is a good example of what workers can achieve through their own efforts using participatory democracy. Are these two aspects—anarchism in action and participatory democracy—one and the same thing for you? Is anarchism a philosophy for people's power?

Grassroots Democracy versus Parliamentary Democracy

I'm reluctant to use fancy polysyllables like "philosophy" to refer to what seems ordinary common sense. And I'm also uncomfortable with slogans. The achievements of Spanish workers and peasants, before the revolution was crushed, were impressive in many ways. The term "participatory democracy" is a more recent one, which developed in a different context, but there surely are points of similarity. I'm sorry if this seems evasive. It is. But that's because I don't think either the concept of anarchism or of participatory democracy is clear enough to be able to answer the question whether they are the same.

One of the main achievements of the Spanish Revolution was the degree of grassroots democracy established. In terms of people, it is estimated that over 3 million were involved. Rural and urban production was managed by workers themselves. Is it a coincidence to your mind that anarchists, known for their advocacy of individual freedom, succeeded in this area of collective administration?

No coincidence at all. The tendencies in anarchism that I've always found most persuasive seek a highly organized society, integrating many different kinds of structures (workplace, community, and manifold other forms of voluntary association), but controlled by participants, not by those in a position to give orders (except, again, when authority can be justified, as is sometimes the case, in specific contingencies).

Anarchists often expend a great deal of effort at building up grassroots democracy. Indeed they are often accused of taking democracy to extremes. Yet, despite this, many anarchists would not readily identify democracy as a central component of anarchist philosophy. Anarchists often describe their politics as being about "socialism" or being about "the individual"—they are less likely to say that anarchism is about democracy. Would you agree that democratic ideas are a central feature of anarchism?

Criticism of "democracy" among anarchists has often been criticism of parliamentary democracy, as it has arisen within societies with deeply repressive features. Take the U.S., which has been as free as any, since its origins. American democracy was founded on the principle, stressed by James Madison in the Constitutional Convention in 1787, that the primary function of government is "to protect the minority of the opulent from the majority." Thus he warned that in England, the only quasi-democratic model of the day, if the general population were allowed a say in public affairs, they would implement agrarian reform or other atrocities, and that the American system must be carefully crafted to avoid such crimes against "the rights of property," which must be defended (in fact, must prevail). Parliamentary democracy within this framework does merit sharp criticism by genuine libertarians, and I've left out many other features that are hardly subtle—slavery, to mention just one, or the wage slavery that was bitterly condemned by working people who had never heard of anarchism or communism right through the 19th century, and beyond.

The importance of grassroots democracy to any meaningful change in society would seem to be self evident. Yet the Left has been ambiguous about this in the past. I'm speaking generally, of social democracy, but also of Bolshevism—traditions on the left that would seem to have more in common with elitist thinking than with strict democratic practice. Lenin, to use a well-known example, was skeptical that workers could develop anything more than trade union consciousness (by which, I assume, he meant that workers could not see far beyond their immediate predicament). Similarly, the Fabian socialist, Beatrice Webb, who was very influential in the Labor Party in England, had the view that workers were only interested in horse racing odds! Where does this elitism originate and what is it doing on the left?

The Spanish Revolution versus the Bolshevik Coup

I'm afraid it's hard for me to answer this. If the Left is understood to include "Bolshevism," then I would flatly dissociate myself from the Left. Lenin was one of the greatest enemies of socialism, in my opinion, for reasons I've discussed. The idea that workers are only interested in horse-racing is an absurdity that cannot withstand even a superficial look at labor history or the lively and independent working-class press that flourished in many places, including the manufacturing towns of New England not many miles from where I'm writing—not to speak of the inspiring record of the courageous struggles of persecuted and oppressed people throughout history, until this very moment. Take the most miserable corner of this hemisphere, Haiti, regarded by the European conquerors as a paradise and the source of no small part of Europe's wealth, now devastated, perhaps beyond recovery. In the past few years, under conditions so miserable that few people in the rich countries can imagine them, peasants and slum-dwellers constructed a popular democratic movement based on grassroots organizations that surpasses just about anything I know of elsewhere; only deeply committed commissars could fail to collapse with ridicule when they hear the solemn pronouncements of American intellectuals and political leaders about how the U.S. has to teach Haitians the lessons of democracy. Their achievements were so substantial and frightening to the powerful that they had to be subjected to yet another dose of vicious terror, with considerably more U.S. support than is publicly acknowledged, and they still have not surrendered. Are they interested only in horse-racing?

I'd suggest some lines I've occasionally quoted from Rousseau:"when I see multitudes of entirely naked savages scorn European voluptuousness and endure hunger, fire, the sword, and death to preserve only their independence, I feel that it does not behoove slaves to reason about freedom."

Speaking generally again, your own work (Deterring Democracy, Necessary Illusions, *etc.) has dealt consistently with the role and prevalence of elitist ideas in societies such as our own. You have argued that within "Western" (or parliamentary) democracy there is a deep antagonism to any real role or input from the mass of people, lest it threaten the uneven distribution in wealth which favors the rich. Your work is quite convincing here, but, this aside, some have been shocked by your assertions. For instance, you compare the politics of President John F. Kennedy with Lenin, more or less equating the two. This, I might add, has shocked supporters of both camps! Can you elaborate a little on the validity of the comparison?*

The "New Class": Totalitarian to Neoliberal

I haven't actually "equated" the doctrines of the liberal intellectuals of the Kennedy administration with Leninists, but I have noted striking points of similarity—rather as predicted by Bakunin a century earlier in his perceptive commentary on the "new class." For example, I quoted passages from McNamara on the need to enhance managerial control if we are to be truly "free," and about how the "undermanagement" that is "the real threat to democracy" is an assault against reason itself. Change a few words in these passages, and we have standard Leninist doctrine. I've argued that the roots are rather deep, in both cases. Without further clarification about what people find "shocking," I can't comment further. The comparisons are specific, and I think both proper and properly qualified. If not, that's an error, and I'd be interested to be enlightened about it.

Specifically, Leninism refers to a form of Marxism that developed with V.I. Lenin. Are you implicitly distinguishing the works of Marx from the particular criticism you have of Lenin when you use the term "Leninism"? Do you see a continuity between Marx's views and Lenin's later practices?

Bakunin's warnings about the "Red bureaucracy" that would institute "the worst of all despotic governments" were long before Lenin, and were directed against the followers of Mr. Marx. There were, in fact, followers of many different kinds; Pannekoek, Luxemburg, Mattick and others are very far from Lenin, and their views often converge with elements of anarcho-syndicalism. Korsch and others wrote sympathetically of the anarchist revolution in Spain, in fact. There are continuities from Marx to Lenin, but there are also continuities to Marxists who were harshly critical of Lenin and Bolshevism. Teodor Shanin's work in the past years on Marx's later attitudes towards peasant revolution is also relevant here. I'm far from being a Marx scholar, and wouldn't venture any serious judgement on which of these continuities reflects the "real Marx," if there even can be an answer to that question.

Recently, we obtained a copy of your own "Notes on Anarchism" (re-published last year by Discussion Bulletin *in the U.S.). In this you mention the views of the early Marx, in particular his development of the idea of alienation under capitalism. Do you generally agree with this division in Marx's life and work—a young, more libertarian socialist but, in later years, a firm authoritarian?*

The Early Marx as a Figure of the Late Enlightenment

The early Marx draws extensively from the milieu in which he lived, and one finds many similarities to the thinking that animated classical liberalism, aspects of the Enlightenment and French and German Romanticism. Again, I'm not enough of a Marx scholar to pretend to an authoritative judgement. My impression, for what it is worth, is that the early Marx was very much a figure of the late Enlightenment, and the later Marx was a highly authoritarian activist, and a critical analyst of capitalism, who had little to say about socialist alternatives. But those are impressions.

From my understanding, the core part of your overall view is informed by your concept of human nature. In the past the idea of human nature was seen, perhaps, as something regressive, even limiting. For instance, the unchanging aspect of human nature is often used as an argument for why things can't be changed fundamentally in the direction of anarchism. You take a different view? Why?

Moral Agents with Some Conception of Human Nature

The core part of anyone's point of view is some concept of human nature, however it may be remote from awareness or lack articulation. At least, that is true of people who consider themselves moral agents, not monsters. Monsters aside, whether a person who advocates reform or revolution, or stability or return to earlier stages, or simply cultivating one's own garden, takes stand on the grounds that it is "good for people." But that judgement is based on some conception of human nature, which a reasonable person will try to make as clear as possible, if only so that it can be evaluated. So in this respect I'm no different from anyone else.

You're right that human nature has been seen as something "regressive," but that must be the result of profound confusion. Is my granddaughter no different from a rock, a salamander, a chicken, a monkey? A person who dismisses this absurdity as absurd recognizes that there is a distinctive human nature. We are left only with the question of what it is—a highly non-trivial and fascinating question, with enormous scientific interest and human significance. We know a fair amount about certain aspects of it—not those of major human significance. Beyond that, we are left with our hopes and wishes, intuitions and speculations.

There is nothing "regressive" about the fact that a human embryo is so constrained that it does not grow wings, or that its visual system cannot function in the manner of [the visual system of] an insect, or that it lacks the homing instinct of pigeons. The same factors that constrain the organism's development also enable it to attain a rich, complex, and highly articulated structure, similar in fundamental ways to conspecifics, with rich and remarkable capacities. An organism that lacked such determinative intrinsic structure, which of course radically limits the paths of development, would be some kind of amoeboid creature, to be pitied (even if it could survive somehow). The scope and limits of development are logically related.

Take language, one of the few distinctive human capacities about which much is known. We have very strong reasons to believe that all possible human languages are very similar; a Martian scientist observing humans might conclude that there is just a single language, with minor variants. The reason is that the particular aspect of human nature that underlies the growth of language allows very restricted options. Is this limiting? Of course. Is it liberating? Also of course. It is these very restrictions that make it possible for a rich and intricate system of expression of thought to develop in similar ways on the basis of very rudimentary, scattered, and varied experience.

What about the matter of biologically-determined human differences? That these exist is surely true, and a cause for joy, not fear or regret. Life among clones would not be worth living, and a sane person will only rejoice that others have abilities that they do not share. That should be elementary. What is commonly believed about these matters is strange indeed, in my opinion.

Is human nature, whatever it is, conducive to the development of anarchist forms of life or a barrier to them? We do not know enough to answer, one way or the other. These are matters for experimentation and discovery, not empty pronouncements.

To begin finishing off, I'd like to ask you briefly about some current issues on the left. I don't know if the situation is similar in the U.S. but here, with the fall of the Soviet Union, a certain demoralization has set in on the left. It isn't so much that people were dear supporters of what existed in the Soviet Union, but rather it's a general feeling that with the demise of the Soviet Union the idea of socialism has also been dragged down. Have you come across this type of demoralization? What's your response to it?

My response to the end of Soviet tyranny was similar to my reaction to the defeat of Hitler and Mussolini. In all cases, it is a victory for the human spirit. It should have been particularly welcome to socialists, since a great enemy of socialism had at last collapsed. Like you, I was intrigued to see how people—including people who had considered themselves anti-Stalinist and anti-Leninist—were demoralized by the collapse of the tyranny. What it reveals is that they were more deeply committed to Leninism than they believed.

From Two Superpowers to One: Reasons to Be Concerned

There are, however, other reasons to be concerned about the elimination of this brutal and tyrannical system, which was as much "socialist" as it was "democratic" (recall that it claimed to be both, and that the latter claim was ridiculed in the West, while the former was eagerly accepted, as a weapon against socialism—one of the many examples of the service of Western intellectuals to power).

One reason has to do with the nature of the Cold War. In my view, it was in significant measure a special case of the "North-South conflict," to use the current euphemism for Europe's conquest of much of the world. Eastern Europe had been the original "Third World," and the Cold War from 1917 had no slight resemblance to the reaction of attempts by other parts of the Third World to pursue an independent course, though in this case differences of scale gave the conflict a life of its own. For this reason, it was only reasonable to expect the region to return pretty much to its earlier status: parts of the West, like the Czech Republic or Western Poland, could be expected to rejoin it, while others revert to the traditional service role, the ex-Nomenklatura becoming the standard Third World elite (with the approval of Western state-corporate power, which generally prefers them to alternatives). That was not a pretty prospect, and it has led to immense suffering.

Another reason for concern has to do with the matter of deterrence and non-alignment. Grotesque as the Soviet empire was, its very existence offered a certain space for non-alignment, and for perfectly cynical reasons, it sometimes provided assistance to victims of Western attack. Those options are gone, and the South is suffering the consequences.

A third reason has to do with what the business press calls "the pampered Western workers" with their "luxurious lifestyles." With much of Eastern Europe returning to the fold, owners and managers have powerful new weapons against the working-classes and the poor at home. GM and VW can not only transfer production to Mexico and Brazil (or at least threaten to, which often amounts to the same thing), but also to Poland and Hungary, where they can find skilled and trained workers at a fraction of the cost. They are gloating about it, understandably, given the guiding values.

We can learn a lot about what the Cold War (or any other conflict) was about by looking at who is cheering and who is unhappy after it ends. By that criterion, the victors in the Cold War include Western elites and the ex-Nomenklatura, now rich beyond their wildest dreams, and the losers include a substantial part of the population of the East along with working people and the poor in the West, as well as popular sectors in the South that have sought an independent path.

Such ideas tend to arouse near hysteria among Western intellectuals, when they can even perceive them, which is rare. That's easy to show. It's also understandable. The observations are correct, and subversive of power and privilege; hence hysteria.

In general, the reactions of an honest person to the end of the Cold War will be more complex than just pleasure over the collapse of a brutal tyranny, and prevailing reactions are suffused with extreme hypocrisy, in my opinion.

In many ways the Left today finds itself back at its original starting point in the last century. Like then, it now faces a form of capitalism that is in the ascendancy. There would seem to be greater "consensus" today, more than at any other time in history, that capitalism is the only valid form of economic organization possible, this despite the fact that wealth inequality is widening. Against this backdrop, one could argue that the Left is unsure of how to go forward. How do you look at the current period? Is it a question of "back to basics"? Should the effort now be towards bringing out the libertarian tradition in socialism and towards stressing democratic ideas?

Corporate Mercantilism ("Capitalism"): Unaccountable Private Tyrannies

This is mostly propaganda, in my opinion. What is called "capitalism" is basically a system of corporate mercantilism, with huge and largely unaccountable private tyrannies exercising vast control over the economy, political systems, and social and cultural life, operating in close cooperation with powerful states that intervene massively in the domestic economy and international society. That is dramatically true of the United States, contrary to much illusion. The rich and privileged are no more willing to face market discipline than they have been in the past, though they consider it just fine for the general population.

Merely to cite a few illustrations: the Reagan administration, which reveled in free market rhetoric, also boasted to the business community that it was the most protectionist in post-war U.S. history—actually, more than all others combined. Newt Gingrich, who leads the current crusade, represents a super-rich district that receives more federal subsidies than any other suburban region in the country, outside of the federal system itself. The "conservatives" who are calling for an end to school lunches for hungry children are also demanding an increase in the budget for the Pentagon, which was established in the late 1940s in its current form because (as the business press was kind enough to tell us) high-tech industry cannot survive in a "pure, competitive, unsubsidized, 'free enterprise' economy," and the government must be its "savior." Without the "savior," Gingrich's constituents would be poor working people (if they were lucky). There would be no computers (electronics, generally), aviation industry, metallurgy, automation, etc., etc., right down the list. Anarchists, of all people, should not be taken in by these traditional frauds.

Ominous Portent—and Signs of Great Hope

More than ever, libertarian socialist ideas are relevant, and the population is very much open to them. Despite a huge mass of corporate propaganda, outside of educated circles, people still maintain pretty much their traditional attitudes. In the U.S., for example, more than 80 percent of the population regard the economic system as "inherently unfair" and the political system as a fraud, which serves the "special interests," not "the people." Overwhelming majorities think working people have too little voice in public affairs (the same is true in England), that the government has the responsibility of assisting people in need, that spending for education and health should take precedence over budget-cutting and tax cuts, that the current Republican proposals that are sailing through Congress benefit the rich and harm the general population, and so on.

Intellectuals may tell a different story, but it's not all that difficult to find out the facts.

To a point anarchist ideas have been vindicated by the collapse of the Soviet Union (the predictions of Bakunin have proven to be correct). Do you think that anarchists should take heart from this general development and from the perceptiveness of Bakunin's analysis? Should anarchists look to the period ahead with greater confidence in their ideas and history?

I think (at least hope) that the answer is implicit in the above. I think the current era has ominous portent—and signs of great hope. Which result ensues depends on what we make of the opportunities.

Lastly, Noam, a different sort of question. We have a pint of Guinness on order for you here. When are you going to come and drink it?

Keep the Guinness ready. I hope it won't be too long.

Less jocularly, I'd be there tomorrow, if we could. We (my wife came along with me, unusual for these constant trips) had a marvelous time in Ireland, and would love to come back. Why don't we? Won't bore you with the sordid details, but demands are extraordinary, and mounting—a reflection of the conditions I've been trying to describe.

Bibliographical Note

In the last half century Noam Chomsky has spent many hours answering questions and participating in discussions. During the Vietnam War, he "was constantly in the radio and television studios" in Boston—"always for foreign interviews ... Australian, Canadian, British, continental European television." That's still "constantly the case." In the span of a few weeks he can be on national Italian television, on Canadian television, and on Irish television (see interviews 35 and 43, and for an exceptional trace, the Editor's Notes to I13). In half a century this adds up to a sizable number—all over the world. Two of his books, *Language and Responsibility* (1977/79) and *The Generative Enterprise* (1982), are transcriptions of extended interviews (an expanded edition of the second one is now in progress); others—*Modular Approaches to the Study of the Mind* (1984), *Language and Problems of Knowledge* (1987)—include some of his answers to questions from the audiences. Collections of interviews that appeared after the first edition of *Language and Politics* are *Chronicles of Dissent* (1992), *The Prosperous Few and the Restless Many* (1993), *Keeping the Rabble in Line* (1994), *Secrets, Lies and Democracy* (1994), *Class Warfare* (1996), *The Common Good* (1998), and *Propaganda and the Public Mind* (2001), all David Barsamian. An edited and reorganized combination of the transcription of dozens of question-and-answer sessions since 1989 published in 2002 by Peter R. Mitchell and John Shoeffel under the title *Understanding Power: The Indispensable Chomsky* (explanatory footnotes available at www.understanding power.com).

The present collection is fairly comprehensive, but far from exhaustive, up to 1989. Needless to say, it does not include all the interviews known to the editor—not even all the items listed in Part III ("Interviews and Discussions with Noam Chomsky") of Koerner & Tajima 1986 (pp. 165–77; see also, pp. 135–6 & 141—1981t).

Among the categories systematically excluded are the following: interviews in which the English original is unavailable to the editor or available in recorded form but not in transcription; those that are long and readily accessible in book form; those in which Chomsky's answers are intertwined with those of other interviewees; interview-articles which reproduce only parts of Chomsky's answers (usually not explicitly related to particular questions).

The same criteria apply also in the case of interviews not included in Koerner & Tajima's list. Here is a suggestive sample:

Anonymous ("Education" section), "Academic disciplines: The Scholarly Dispute Over the Meaning of Linguistics," Time, Feb. 16, 1968, pp. 69–70. (The caption under a picture of Chomsky at the typewriter and one of Charles Hockett of Cornell at his desk reads "Goals Far Grander than Grammar.")

Anonymous ("Education" section), "Who Believes in Ghosts?," *Newsweek*, Aug. 26, 1968, pp. 55–56. (With a picture of B.F. Skinner of Harvard and one of Chomsky. The captions read: "Skinner: Short Shrift for Critics"; "Chomsky: A Role to Relish.") [ADD from Preface to NC:CA]

Robert Sklar, "Chomsky's Revolution in Linguistics," the *Nation*, Sept. 9, 1968, pp. 213–217.

Israel Shenker, "A Linguistics Expert Believes that Academicians Should Also Be Activists," the *New York Times*, Sunday, Oct. 27, 1968.

John Leo, "Radical Agitation among Scholars Grows: It Plays Large Role at Meetings in the Academic Field," the *New York Times*, Sunday, Dec. 29, 1968. (The caption under picture reads: "Noam Chomsky, a Leader in Seeking Academic Changes.")

Daniel Yergin, "The Chomskyan Revolution," the *New York Times* magazine, December 3, 1972, pp. 42–43 & 112,127.

Richard M. Restak, *The Brain: The Last Frontier. An Exploration of the Human Brain and Our Future*. Garden City, NY: Doubleday, 1979.

National Public Radio, "A Question of Place: Noam Chomsky, a Portrait in Sound," narrated by Robert Prosky (the transcript of the broadcast is dated Dec, 15, 1980, in Washington D.C. by Mazen Alwaer; Chomsky was interviewed for this program at his home in Lexington, Mass, in June 1979), part of the NPR series "A Question of Place: Sound Portraits of Twentieth Century Humanists," which includes Freud, Russell, Joyce, Brecht, Foucault, and other figures. See notes to I48.

Review of **PEHR**, the *Valley Advocate* (Northampton, Mass), Feb. 13, 1980.

Derek S. B. Davis, "The Academic Renegade. Noam Chomsky Learned His Linguistics at Penn, But He Soon Created His Own Brand of the Science of Language, As Well As His Own Brand of Politics," the *Pennsylvania Gazette* 79:1 (October 1980), pp. 22–27.

Frank Green, "Biologically speaking, we're born to talk: At first, language is not learned per se. The basic structure of language is already there in the human biological endowments. It is similar to the digestive system, which is enhanced by experience (Noam Chomsky)," the *San Diego Union* (San Diego, CA), Nov. 18, 1980. Cf. **MASM**, a lecture delivered in San Diego at that time.

Television interview, channel 15, Los Angeles, Jan. 22, 1981, 7PM; repeated on Jan. 23, 11PM.

"Chomsky back on the warpath," interview conducted by Jonathan Mirsky on March 25, 1981 for *London Observer Service*, no. 41241.

"Noam Chomsky's Two Worlds: El Salvador and Syntax. Paul Barker Talks to Chomsky about His Politics and His Linguistics," *New Society*, April 2, 1981, pp. 7–10.

Carl Oglesby, "New Ideas: Denying the Holocaust," *Boston* magazine, December 1981, pp. 128–137. (The letter Chomsky wrote to the editor on December 5, 1981 about the misleading caption under his picture was published in a subsequent issue.)

Anonymous, "Mark These Linguists," the *English Magazine*, Summer 1981, pp. 4–6. (Reprinted in **CD&E** as ch. 24.)

"Chomski [sic]: 'Il est raisonnable d'espérer', propos recueillis par Andrée Ferretti," *Le Devoir* (Montréal), June 12, 1982, pp. 23–4.

Isabel Raventós, "Noam Chomsky: 'La Política Exterior de Reagan Es Idéntica a la de Kennedy.' Lingüista y Filósofo, Es el más Significado Representante de los Intelectuales Radicales Norteamericanos," *El País* (Madrid, Spain), July 11, 1982, pp. 8–9.

Mary Arias, "Rebelde con Causa: Noam Chomsky—Opiniones en Libertad del Disidente Número Uno de los Estados Unidos," *Cambio* 16 [Madrid], Sept. 10, 1984, pp. 70–73.

Phil Donahue, *The Human Animal. Who Are We? Why Do We Behave the Way We Do? Can We Change?* Simon and Schuster, 1985, 319ff.

Heinz Dieterich, "Nicaragua: La Construcción de la Sociedad sin Clases. Entrevista con Noam Chomsky." México: Unomásuno, 1986 (August), pp. 195–205. (This interview was conducted on May 3, 1986 at the Johann Wolfgang Goethe University (Frankfurt am Main), and was first published, also in Spanish, in the Mexican periodical *Uno más Uno*, pp. 21–24 May 1986.)

"International Terrorism is a Political Term," interview by Afif Safieh and Christ'l Safieh on Nov. 28, 1986, *Al-Fajr*, 1986, pp. 9 & 15.

"Interview with Noam Chomsky," in Bernard J. Baars, *The Cognitive Revolution in Psychology*. New York/London: The Guilford Press, 1986, pp. 341–51.

Interview by Jim Peck in **ChR** (1987), excerpted in *The Progressive*, July 1987 (cited and quoted in the Introduction).

"Noam Chomsky's Unraveled Ironies" by Ellie Kirzner in *NOW: Toronto's Alternative Weekly*, Oct. 22–28, 1987, p. 21. Excerpted in *Utne Reader*, 29 (September–October 1988), p. 82, under the title "Still Chomsky after All These Years: The Life of America's Leading Dissident."

Kathleen Hendrix's interview-article in the *Los Angeles Times*, Feb. 1, 1988 (cited and quoted in the Introduction).

Pat McDonnell, "U.S. Use of Israel as Strategic Ally Offers Little Hope for Mideast," *Sada Alwatan*, Feb. 20–26, 1988, pp. 1 & 10.

Erik Asard, "Noam Chomsky: Folket deltar inte," *Expressen* (Sweden), Aug. 14, 1988, p. 4.

Richard Higgins, "Academia.- A Critic with Targets Galore: Chomsky Pays a Price for Independent Thinking," *Boston Globe* magazine, Sept. 4, 1988, pp. 73–74.

Monika Bauerlein, "An Interview with Noam Chomsky," *Hungry Mind Review* (A Midwestern Book Review) 8, Summer 1988, pp. 16–17. (Conducted in May at the University of Minnesota—where Bauerlein was doing graduate work as a Fulbright Fellow from Germany—while Chomsky was there to lecture on "Ideological Bias in the Media.")

Jay Parini, "Noam is an Island: Why is One of America's Most Brilliant Men Treated like a Kook?," *Mother Jones*, October 1988, pp. 36–41. (This carefully prepared interview-article was irresponsibly edited by *Mother Jones* to conform to widespread prejudices. For a glimpse of the actual procedure, see *Zeta* magazine, December 1988, pp. 3–4.)

Alison Bass, "Nobels Are Distorting Science, Critics Say," *Boston Globe*, Oct. 17, 1988, p. 1. (The interview took place at MIT on Sept. 27, 1988)

"A World of Ideas, with Bill Moyers. Guest: Linguist/Philosopher Noam Chomsky," PBS Television, Nov. 3–4, 1988. (Taped on Sept. 26,1988 in Boston.) Transcripts of the two programs are available for $3 each from *A World of Ideas, Journal of Graphics*, 267 Broadway, New York NY 10007. Included in *Bill Moyers, A World of Ideas. Conversations with Thoughtful Men and Women about American Life Today and the Ideas Shaping our Future*. Ed. by Betty Sue Flowers. New York: Doubleday, 1989, PP. 38–58.

Television interview on **MC** taped on Nov. 21, 1988 in New York for "Kwitny Report."

"Deliver Us from Evil. Martin Woollacott on Noam Chomsky's Cynical and Unforgiving Analysis of Power Politics," the *Guardian*, Saturday Jan. 14, 1989. (Picture with caption: "Noam Chomsky: The Essence of His Message is that Power is Evil.")

"Society, the University and Language: An Interview with Noam Chomsky," conducted by Sol Saporta on Jan. 24–25, 1989 in Seattle, a version of which was published in *Crítica: a Journal of Critical Essays* 2:2 (1990), pp. 19–42.

"Profile: Enduring Champion of Ordinary People. Andrew Goreing Talks to Noam Chomsky, Activist and Outcast," the *Times Higher Education Supplement*, Feb. 3, 1989.

Invaluable nuggets can be found in other sources, e.g. in Stephen J. Whitfield's *A Critical American: The Politics of Dwight Macdonald*. Hamden, Conn.: Archon Books, 1984, 113ff.— in this case from a partially used interview. From this it is a short step to valuable sources of quotes from letters. (It is likely that the volume of Chomsky's correspondence exceeds that of the letters written by any other single individual—and it includes some long letters that discuss matters of great intellectual interest, e.g. the three included in Marcus G. Raskin & H.J. Bernstein, *New Ways of Knowing*. Lanham, MD: Rowman & Littlefield, 1987, pp. 104–12, 130–7, 146–52, written on Oct. 1, 1983, and on Jan. 4 and April 8, 1984). The most recent item in this category of sources that comes to mind is Trevor Pateman's *Language in Mind and Language in Society: Studies in Linguistic Reproduction*. Oxford: Clarendon Press, 1987; see Index, s.v. Chomsky. Other examples are

Charles F. Hockett, *The State of the Art*. The Hague, Mouton, 1968, pp. 38–43. (Chomsky's responses were written in 1965—see Sgroi, pp. 130–1.)

John Lyons, *Noam Chomsky*. Viking, 1970 (Modern Masters, 8); rev. ed., Penguin, 1978.

George Steiner, *Extraterritorial: Papers on Literature and Language Revolution*. London: Faber & Faber, 1971, pp. 102–125. (See Koerner & Tajima, p. 166).

Index

A

Abdullah, King: 401, 682, 683
Abrams, M. H.: 102
Abrams, Elliot: 56, 697, 707, 717
Abu Jihad: 706
Achdut Haavodah: 684
Acheson, Dean: 106, 591
Achille Lauro: 548, 549
Adams, Hazard: 52
Adler, Sandy: 6
Affix movement: 88
Afghanistan: 258, 260, 261, 267, 287,
    293, 309, 473, 493, 504, 543,
    551, 560, 589, 620, 633, 651,
    671, 737, 749, 750, 759, 764
    Russian invasion of Afghanistan:
        330, 392, 552, 563, 704
    Soviet Union in Afghanistan: 341
Agee, Philip: 298
Agnew, Spiro: 136
al-Hakim, Sayed Muhamed Baqer: 766
al-Qaeda: 748, 749, 757
Albert, Michael: 51, 742, 754
Aldubi, Roman: 680
Alexander the Great: 520, 544
Allon, Yigal: 683
American Civil Liberties Union: 162,
    650
Amin, Idi: 488
Amnesty International: 520, 543, 556
Anarchism: 34, 56, 139, 142–144,
    149, 153, 364, 777, 779
    anarchist critique of Communism:
        155
    anarcho-communism: 149
    anarcho-syndicalism: 149, 153
    anarcho-syndicalist conceptions:
        259
    communism-anarchism: 153
anarchists: 9, 45, 259, 778, 784, 785
    anarchist thought: 23
    Spanish anarchists: 9
    Angel Pestaña (1886–1937): 48
    *Setenta Días en Rusia: Lo que Yo
        Vi*: 48
Andreotti, Giulio: 714
Angola: 402, 698
    UNITA: 402, 694
Anti-Defamation League: 415, 497,
    627, 633, 686
    of B'nai B'rith: 415
anti-Semitism: 168, 169, 338, 415,
    496, 569, 571
    Waspish anti-Semitism: 569
Aoki, Minoru: 50

apartheid: 637, 698, 742, 743–745,
    751
    anti-apartheid movement: 636,
        637
    apartheid press: 179
Appalachia: 61
Arab League: 762
Arab Legion: 682
Arabic: 9
Arafat, Yasir: 388, 407, 409, 493, 510,
    673, 677. See also Palestine
    non-reporting of Arafat's offer:
        416
    Spring 1984 offers: 416
ARAMCO: 186
Argentina: 171, 279, 280, 293, 355,
    397, 488, 533
    Junta to ban Chomskyan linguis-
        tics as materialist: 171
Arias, Mary: 788
Aristotle: 37, 231, 232, 385
    Aristotelian: 40, 202, 211
    Aristotelian doctrines: 39
Armey, Dick: 751
Arnold, Matthew: 129
Asard, Erik: 788
ASEAN: 264
Asia Resource Center: 312
Asner, Ed: 51
Atik, Leslie: 6
Atlantic: 24, 106, 187
Attali, Jacques: 283, 291
Australia: 247, 483
    Australian languages: 456
auto-da-fe: 17
Awad, Mubarek: 682
Aycoberry, Pierre : 281

B

Baars, Bernard J. : 788
Bach Mai Fund: 312
Baillargeon, Rene: 451
Bakker, Jim: 624
Bakunin, Mikhail: 15, 117, 120, 144,
    181, 259, 340, 344, 356, 439,
    441, 468, 774, 777, 780, 785
    Bakunin's conception of anar-
        chism: 15
Ball, George: 406, 410, 486, 501, 518,
    523
Baltzell, E. Digby: 48
    *Puritan Boston and Quaker
        Philadelphia: Two Protestant
        Ethics and the Spirit of Class
        Authority and Leadership*: 48
Bangladesh: 263, 414, 490, 624

Barak, Prime Minister Ehud: 752. See
    also Israel
Barbie, Klaus: 494
Barcelona: 2, 9, 18, 39, 48, 99, 103,
    728
Barker, Paul: 48, 787
Barnard, Philip: 102
Barrett, William: 276
Barsamian, David: 6, 470, 486, 526,
    540, 582, 606, 625, 644, 786
Bass, Alison: 789
Bauerlein, Monika: 788
Bay of Pigs: 296
Bayne, Edward A.: 201
Bechtel: 771
Beckwith, Richard: 451
Beethoven, Ludwig von: 44, 47, 383
Begin, Menachem: 496, 509, 703
behavioral sciences: 28, 92, 173, 381
    behaviorism: 44, 66, 67, 70, 91,
        93, 95, 131, 381, 438, 575
    behaviorist: 28, 31, 32–34, 70, 93,
        113, 114, 127, 130, 131, 164,
        165, 381, 577, 610
Beit-Hallahmi, Benjamin: 526, 533
Beita: 680. See also Israel
Bell, Daniel: 117, 120, 660
Ben-Ami, Shlomo: 743, 745, 747
Ben-Gurion, David: 16, 401, 682–684
Berger, Peter L.: 276
Berlin: 273, 349, 504
    Berlin Wall: 725
    East Berlin in 1953. See also Cold
        War
    U.S. Embassy in Berlin: 726
Berlin, Isaiah: 49
    Personal Impressions: 49
Bernal, J.D.: 49
    Science in History: 49
Bernays, Edward: 345
Bernstein, H.J.: 52, 789
Berrigan, Daniel: 338
Berwick, Robert C.: 451, 460
Besancon, Alain: 289
Bethe, Hans A. : 502
Bible: 13, 17, 37, 55, 468, 707
bin Laden, Osama: 757
Black Panthers: 110, 540, 604, 653
Black Rose Collective: 142
Black September: 412
Blackburn, Robin: 102
Blair, John: 201
Blair, Tony: 771
Blatt, Morris: 50
Blitzer, Wolf: 568
Blitzstein, Marc: 48
Bloomfield, Leonard: 91

Ordering Information

AK Press
674-A 23rd Street,
Oakland, CA 94612-1163,
USA

Phone: (510) 208-1700
E-mail: akpress@akpress.org
URL: www.akpress.org
Please send all payments (checks, money orders, or cash at your own risk) in U.S. dollars. Alternatively, we take VISA and MC.

AK Press
PO Box 12766,
Edinburgh, EH8 9YE,
Scotland

Phone: (0131) 555-5165
E-mail: ak@akedin.demon.uk
URL: www.akuk.com
Please send all payments (cheques, money orders, or cash at your own risk) in U.K. pounds. Alternatively, we take credit cards.

For a dollar, a pound or a few IRC's, the same addresses would be delighted to provide you with the latest complete AK catalog, featuring several thousand books, pamphlets, zines, audio products and stylish apparel published & distributed by AK Press. Alternatively, check out our websites for the complete catalog, latest news and updates, events, and secure ordering.

Also available from AK Press

What is Anarchism? by Alexander Berkman
$13.95. ISBN 1 902593 70 7
A reprint of perhaps the first and best exposition of Anarchism by one of its greatest propagandists (by both word and deed) and thinkers. In a clear conversation with the reader Berkman discusses society as it now exists, the need for Anarchism and the methods for bringing it about. Combines the oft-reprinted texts of *What is Communist Anarchism?* and the *ABC of Anarchism* back into its original format. Forewords by his comrade and lover Emma Goldman and Barry Pateman.

Addicted to War by Joel Andreas
$8.00. ISBN 1 902593 57 X
Addicted to War takes on the most active, powerful and destructive military in the world. Hard-hitting, carefully documented, and heavily illustrated, it reveals why the United States has been involved in more wars in recent years than any other country. Read Addicted to War to find out who benefits from these military adventures, who pays—and who dies.
"A witty and devastating portrait of U.S. military policy."—Howard Zinn

The Politics of Anti-Semitism ed. by Alexander Cockburn and Jeffrey St. Clair
$11.95. ISBN 1 902593 77 4
How did a term, once used accurately to describe the most virulent evil, become a charge flung at the mildest critic of Israel, particularly concerning its atrocious treatment of Palestinians? Edited by Cockburn and St. Clair of the print and online journal *Counterpunch* and includes contributors Cynthia Mckinney, Robert Fisk, Michael Neumann, Norman Finklestein, Yuri Avneri and Yigal Bronner.

Workers Councils by Anton Pannekoek
$15.00. ISBN 1 902593 56 1
"Good, solid, working-class literature."—Noam Chomsky
In this timeless text, Anton Pannekoek provides his analysis of how we can create and sustain this practical model for social equality. Includes introductory interview with Noam Chomsky.

Facing the Enemy by Alexandre Skirda
$17.95. ISBN 1 902593 19 7
The finest single volume history of European Anarchism is finally available in English. Drawing on decades of research, Alexandre Skirda traces anarchism as a major political movement and ideology across the 19th and 20th centuries illuminating the Bakuninist secret societies, the clash with Marx, the mass trade unions, illegalists, bombers, assassins and the revolutionary heroism of the Russian and Spanish revolutions.

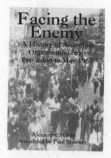

No Gods No Masters (2 vols.) by Daniel Guerin
Vol. I $18.95. ISBN 1 873176 64 3
Vol II $16.95. ISBN 1 873176 69 4
This is the first English translation of Guerin's monumental anthology of Anarchism. It details, through a vast array of hitherto unpublished documents, writings, letters and reports, the history, organization and practice of the anarchist movement—its theorists, advocates and activists.
Book I includes the writings of Max Stirner, Pierre-Joseph Proudhon, Mikhail Bakunin, James Guillaume, Max Nettlau, Peter Kropotkin, Emma Goldman and Cesar de Paepe amongst others
Book II includes work from the likes of Malatesta, Emile Henry, Emile Pouget, Augustin Souchy, Gaston Leval, Voline, Nestor Makhno, the Kronstadt sailors, Luigi Fabbri, and Buenaventura Durruti.

Moving Forward by Michael Albert
$11.95. ISBN 1 902593 41 3
If not capitalism, then what? In *Moving Forward* Albert argues that we have to change how we conceive of work and wages, rewarding effort and sacrifice rather than output, and moving from heirarchical workplace structures to worker self-management. From here he moves to a proposal for how we might organize the larger functions of the economy in workers' councils and a general discussion of how our society might look with a participatory economy.

The Spanish Anarchists: The Heroic Years 1868–1936 by Murray Bookchin
$19.95. ISBN 1 873176 04 X
A long-awaited new edition of the seminal history of Spanish Anarchism. Hailed as a masterpiece, it includes a new prefatory essay by the author. Murray Bookchin has written widely on politics, history and ecology. His books *To Remember Spain: The Anarchist And Syndicalist Revolution Of 1936*, *Anarchism, Marxism and the Future of the Left* and *Social Anarchism Or Lifestyle Anarchism: An Unbridgeable Chasm* are all published by AK Press.

Quiet Rumors: An Anarcha-Feminist Reader ed. Dark Star Collective
$15.00. ISBN 1 902593 40 5
From consciousness-raising groups to hair-razing punk rockers, here's a fascinating window into the development of the women's movement, in the words of the women who moved it. These classic essays span the century, providing welcome context for feminism as part of a larger politics of liberation and equality. Includes Emma Goldman, Peggy Kornegger, Voltairine DeCleyre, Alice Nutter and others.

Noam Chomsky Books/CDs/DVDs available from AK Press

Radical Priorities by Noam Chomsky edited by C.P. Otero
$18.95. ISBN 1 902593 69 3
In *Radical Priorities*, C.P. Otero sets out to "provide relatively easy access to Chomsky's libertarian philosophy and political analysis". Taken from a wide variety of sources, many never widely published--some never in a book at all and spanning four decades, the reader is furnished with a truly comprehensive window into Chomsky's anarchist convictions. Convictions which, while ever-present in his analysis are left largely misunderstood or worse-ignored. In seeking to combat the great challenges facing humanity, Chomsky's analysis and the traditions that bore it must not be left in obscurity.

Distorted Morality DVD by Noam Chomsky
$25.00 ISBN 1 905293 76 6
Here Chomsky offers a devastating critique of America's current War on Terror—arguing that it is a logical impossibility for such a war to be taking place. Chomsky presents his reasoning with refreshing clarity, drawing from a wealth of historic knowledge and analysis. The DVD includes a shorter; more recent talk on the danger, cruelty, and stupidity of the U.S. and Israel's policy of Pre-emptive War and a lively Q&A session all in an easily searchable user friendly format.

The Emerging Framework of World Power: Everlasting War CD by Noam Chomsky
$14.98. ISBN 1 902593 75 8
Chomsky's state-of-the-world address. America's leading foreign policy critic surveys the role of the U.S. in a post-911 world—and finds nothing has changed.

The New War on Terrorism: Fact and Fiction CD by Noam Chomsky
$14.98. ISBN 1 902593 62 6
"We certainly want to reduce the level of terror... There is one easy way to do that... stop partici-pating in it."—Noam Chomsky, from the CD
What is terrorism? And how can we reduce the likelihood of such crimes, whether they are against us, or against someone else? With his vintage flair, penetrating analysis, and ironic wit, Chomsky, in perhaps his most anticipated lecture ever—delivered a month after 9/11, and his first public statement—makes sense of a world apparently gone mad.

Free Market Fantasies: Capitalism in the Real World CD by Noam Chomsky
$13.98. ISBN 1 873176 79 1
There is endless talk about the free market and its virtues. Entrepreneurs compete on level playing fields and the public benefits. The chasm between such fantasies and reality is acute and growing wider. Megamergers and monopolies are limiting competition. Fewer than 10 corporations control most of the global media. The existing free market depends heavily on taxpayer subsidies and bailouts. Corporate welfare far exceeds that which goes to the poor. Economic policy is based on the dictum: take from the needy, and give to the greedy. The captains of industry of today make the robber barons of the 19th century look like underachievers. The gap between CEO and work-er salaries has never been sharper. One union leader put it this way, "Workers are getting the absolute crap kicked out of them."

An American Addiction: Drugs, Guerillas, Counterinsurgency—U.S. Intervention in Colombia CD by Noam Chomsky
$13.98. ISBN 1 902593 44 8
"Colombia has been the leading recipient of US arms and training in the Western Hemisphere through the 1990s. It has also had the worst human rights record by far in the Western Hemisphere

during these years. That correlation is one of the best correlations in contemporary history....It's a very important correlation that should be known and understood by the people who are paying for it. That's us. And it will get worse." (From the CD)

Propaganda and Control of the Public Mind 2XCD by Noam Chomsky
$20.00. ISBN 1 873176 68 6
"The war against working people should be understood to be a real war. It's not a new war. It's an old war. Furthermore it's a perfectly conscious war everywhere, but specifically in the U.S... which happens to have a highly class-conscious business class... And they have long seen themselves as fighting a bitter class war, except they don't want anybody else to know about it." [Noam Chomsky, from the CD]

Case Studies In Hypocrisy: U.S. Human Rights Policy 2XCD by Noam Chomsky
$20.00. ISBN 1 902593 27 8
With the recent celebration of the fiftieth anniversary of the Universal Declaration Of Human Rights, and America's undisputed position as the world's only superpower, the contrast between the rhetoric and the reality of U.S. foreign policy has never been more stark. With his inimitable penetrating analysis and dry wit, Chomsky leads us through the murky blood-soaked reality of America's New World Order.

For A Free Humanity: For Anarchy 2XCD by Noam Chomsky/Chumbawamba
$18.00 ISBN 1 873176 74 0
A Double CD with Noam Chomsky and Chumbawamba. Disc One comprises the Noam Chomsky lecture 'Capital Rules' - another articulate, and immediately accessible description of Corporate America's unrelenting attack on poor and working class people. Disc Two is Chumbawamba's best collection of live sounds - Showbusiness!, previously only available as an expensive import. Recorded live in 94. The double CD is accompanied by a 24 page booklet, with extensive interviews with both Noam Chomsky - discussing corporate structure as private tyranny, domestic surveillance of activists, and visions for a new society - and Chumbawamba discussing their past, politics, and anarchism.

Prospects For Democracy CD by Noam Chomsky
$14.98 ISBN 1 873176 38 4
Beginning with a broad review of democratic theory and political history, he argues that classical democrats such as Thomas Jefferson would be shocked at the current disrepair of American democracy. The enormous growth of corporate capitalism has already devastated democratic culture and government by concentrating power in the hands of the wealthy. And the future looks no brighter. In spite of this dark assessment, Chomsky maintains that any hope for democracy rests ultimately with you and me - on whether we can shake off our political malaise and build a democratic future.

Also available from AK Audio

Come September CD by Arundhati Roy
$14.98. ISBN 1 92593 80 4
In this acclaimed Lannan Foundation lecture, Arundhati Roy speaks poetically to power on the U.S. government's "War on Terror", globalization, and the misuses of nationalism. With lyricism and passion, Roy combines her literary talents and encyclopedic knowledge to expose injustice and provide hope for a future world. Includes question and answer with Howard Zinn.

Arists in a Time of War CD by Howard Zinn
$14.98. ISBN 1 902593 65 0
In this brand new lecture, recorded a month after 9/11, America's finest social historian examines the role, and response, of artists in society, and particularly, during wartime and crisis.

Life in Occupied America CD by Ward Churchill
$14.98. ISBN 1 902593 72 3
The systematic elimination of the American Indians didn't end with Columbus, smallpox laden blankets or the scalp bounty. Here, pre-eminent Native activist/scholar Ward Churchill passionately unveils the 500-year conquest and demonstrates its continuation today.

Mob Action Against the State 2XCD Various
$20.00 ISBN 1 902593 51 0
The Bay Area is rich in local radicals, and most of them have taken a turn at the microphone of the Bay Area Anarchist Bookfair. Here's an all-star collection from the speakers' corner of the bookfair: Jello Biafra, Lawrence Ferlinghetti, Roxanne Dunbar-Ortiz, Christian Parenti, Craig O'Hara, Ruth Wilson Gilmore, Cindy Milstein, Lorenzo Komboa Ervin, and Barry Pateman.

Pacifism and Pathology in the American Left CD by Ward Churchill
$14.98 ISBN 1 902593 58 8

Taking Liberties: Policing, Prisons and Surveliance in an Age of Crisis CD by Christian Parenti
$14.98 ISBN 1 902593 63 4

Stories Hollywood Never Tells CD by Howard Zinn
$13.98. ISBN 1 902593 36 7

In a Pig's Eye 2XCD by Ward Churchill
$20.00 ISBN 1 902593 50 2

Beating the Devil CD by Alexander Cockburn
$14.98 ISBN 1 902593 49 9
In this collection of recent talks, maverick commentator Alexander Cockburn defiles subjects ranging from Colombia to the American presidency to the Missile Defense System. Whether he's skewering the fallacies of the war on drugs or illuminating the dark crevices of secret government, his erudite and extemporaneous style warms the hearts of even the stodgiest cynics of the left.

A People's History of the United States: A Lecture at Reed College 2XCD by Howard Zinn
$20.00 ISBN 1 873176 95 3
Here Zinn explains with great humor and passion how his teaching, his history and his activism are parts of the same project. The stories of social movements—labor, civil rights, feminists, antiwar—are usually left out or grossly distorted in mainstream history writing. The efforts of Zinn and others to recover and pass on those stories offers to their students, to their readers and to us, models, ideas, inspirations for how and why we might go about challenging and changing the structures of power.

Prisons on Fire: George Jackson, Attica & Black Liberation CD produced by the Freedom Archives
$14.98 ISBN 1 902593 52 9

Monkeywrenching The New World Order 2XCD Various
$20.00 ISBN 1 902593 35 9

175 Progress Drive CD by Mumia Abu-Jamal
$14.98 ISBN 1 902593 45 6

The Prison Industrial Complex CD by Angela Davis
$14.98 ISBN 1 902593 22 7

Heroes and Martyrs: Emma Goldman, Sacco & Vanzetti and the Revolutionary Struggle 2XCD by Howard Zinn
$20.00 ISBN 1 902593 26 X

All Things Censored CD by Mumia Abu-Jamal
$14.98 ISBN 1 902593 06 5

Other Titles from AK Press

Books

MARTHA **ACKELSBERG**—*Free Women of Spain*

KATHY **ACKER**—*Pussycat Fever*

MICHAEL **ALBERT**—*Moving Forward: Program for a Participatory Economy*

JOEL **ANDREAS**—*Addicted to War: Why the U.S. Can't Kick Militarism*

ALEXANDER **BERKMAN**—*What is Anarchism?*

HAKIM **BEY**—*Immediatism*

JANET **BIEHL** & PETER **STAUDENMAIER**—*Ecofascism: Lessons From The German Experience*

BIOTIC BAKING BRIGADE—*Pie Any Means Necessary: The Biotic Baking Brigade Cookbook*

JACK **BLACK**—*You Can't Win*

MURRAY **BOOKCHIN**—*Anarchism, Marxism, and the Future of the Left*

MURRAY **BOOKCHIN**—*Social Anarchism or Lifestyle Anarchism: An Unbridgeable Chasm*

MURRAY **BOOKCHIN**—*Spanish Anarchists: The Heroic Years 1868–1936, The*

MURRAY **BOOKCHIN**—*To Remember Spain: The Anarchist and Syndicalist Revolution of 1936*

MURRAY **BOOKCHIN**—*Which Way for the Ecology Movement?*

DANNY **BURNS**—*Poll Tax Rebellion*

CHRIS **CARLSSON**—*Critical Mass: Bicycling's Defiant Celebration*

JAMES **CARR**–*Bad*

NOAM **CHOMSKY**—*At War With Asia*

NOAM **CHOMSKY**—*Language and Politics*

NOAM **CHOMSKY**—*Radical Priorities*

WARD **CHURCHILL**—*On the Justice of Roosting Chickens: Reflections on the Consequences of U.S. Imperial Arrogance and Criminality*

HARRY **CLEAVER**—*Reading Capital Politically*

ALEXANDER **COCKBURN** & JEFFREY **ST. CLAIR** (ed.)—*Politics of Anti-Semitism, The*

ALEXANDER **COCKBURN** & JEFFREY **ST. CLAIR** (ed.)—*Serpents in the Garden*

DANIEL & GABRIEL **COHN-BENDIT**—*Obsolete Communism: The Left-Wing Alternative*

EG SMITH COLLECTIVE—*Animal Ingredients A–Z (3rd edition)*

VOLTAIRINE **de CLEYRE**—*Voltairine de Cleyre Reader*

HOWARD **EHRLICH**—*Reinventing Anarchy, Again*

SIMON **FORD**—*Realization and Suppression of the Situationist International: An Annotated Bibliography 1972–1992, The*

YVES **FREMION** & **VOLNY**—*Orgasms of History: 3000 Years of Spontaneous Revolt*

DANIEL **GUERIN**—*No Gods No Masters*

AGUSTIN **GUILLAMON**—*Friends Of Durruti Group, 1937–1939, The*

ANN **HANSEN**—*Direct Action: Memoirs Of An Urban Guerilla*

WILLIAM **HERRICK**—*Jumping the Line: The Adventures and Misadventures of an American Radical*

FRED **HO**—*Legacy to Liberation: Politics & Culture of Revolutionary Asian/Pacific America*

STEWART **HOME**—*Assault on Culture*

STEWART **HOME**—*Neoism, Plagiarism & Praxis*

STEWART **HOME**—*Neoist Manifestos / The Art Strike Papers*

STEWART **HOME**—*No Pity*

STEWART **HOME**—*Red London*

STEWART **HOME**—*What Is Situationism? A Reader*

JAMES **KELMAN**—*Some Recent Attacks: Essays Cultural And Political*

KEN **KNABB**—*Complete Cinematic Works of Guy Debord*

KATYA **KOMISARUK**—*Beat the Heat: How to Handle Encounters With Law Enforcement*

NESTOR **MAKHNO**—*Struggle Against The State & Other Essays, The*

G.A. **MATIASZ**—*End Time*

CHERIE **MATRIX**—*Tales From the Clit*

ALBERT **MELTZER**—*Anarchism: Arguments For & Against*

ALBERT **MELTZER**—*I Couldn't Paint Golden Angels*

RAY **MURPHY**—*Siege Of Gresham*

NORMAN **NAWROCKI**—*Rebel Moon*

HENRY **NORMAL**—*Map of Heaven, A*

HENRY **NORMAL**—*Dream Ticket*

HENRY **NORMAL**—*Fifteenth of February*

HENRY **NORMAL**—*Third Person*

FIONBARRA **O'DOCHARTAIGH**—*Ulster's White Negroes: From Civil Rights To Insurrection*

DAN **O'MAHONY**—*Four Letter World*

CRAIG **O'HARA**—*Philosophy Of Punk, The*

ANTON **PANNEKOEK**—*Workers' Councils*

BEN **REITMAN**—*Sister of the Road: the Autobiography of Boxcar Bertha*

PENNY **RIMBAUD**—*Diamond Signature, The*

PENNY **RIMBAUD**—*Shibboleth: My Revolting Life*

RUDOLF **ROCKER**—*Anarcho-Syndicalism*

RON **SAKOLSKY** & STEPHEN **DUNIFER**—*Seizing the Airwaves: A Free Radio Handbook*

ROY **SAN FILIPPO**—*New World In Our Hearts: 8 Years of Writings from the Love and Rage Revolutionary Anarchist Federation, A*